THE
WISDEN
BOOK OF TEST CRICKET
2014–2019

THE
WISDEN
BOOK OF TEST CRICKET
2014–2019

Sixth edition, Volume 5

Edited by
STEVEN LYNCH

WISDEN
LONDON • OXFORD • NEW YORK • NEW DELHI • SYDNEY

WISDEN
Bloomsbury Publishing Plc
50 Bedford Square, London, WC1B 3DP, UK

BLOOMSBURY, WISDEN and the Wisden wood-engraving device are trademarks of
Bloomsbury Publishing Plc

First published in Great Britain 2020

Copyright © Steven Lynch, 2020

For legal purposes the Acknowledgments on p. vi
constitute an extension of this copyright page

All rights reserved. No part of this publication may be reproduced or transmitted in any
form or by any means, electronic or mechanical, including photocopying, recording,
or any information storage or retrieval system, without prior permission in
writing from the publishers

Bloomsbury Publishing Plc does not have any control over, or responsibility for, any
third-party websites referred to or in this book. All internet addresses given in this book
were correct at the time of going to press. The author and publisher regret any
inconvenience caused if addresses have changed or sites have ceased to exist,
but can accept no responsibility for any such changes

www.wisdenalmanack.com
www.wisdenrecords.com
Follow Wisden on Twitter @WisdenAlmanack
and on Facebook at Wisden Sports

A catalogue record for this book is available from the British Library

ISBN: HB: 978-1-4729-6548-6; eBook: 978-1-4729-6546-2

2 4 6 8 10 9 7 5 3 1

Typeset in Times New Roman by Deanta Global Publishing Services, Chennai, India
Printed and bound in Great Britain by CPI Group (UK) Ltd, Croydon CR0 4YY

To find out more about our authors and books visit www.wisdenalmanack.com
and sign up for our newsletters

Contents

Preface and Acknowledgments	vi
Test Match Scorecards	1
Individual Test Career Records	225
Index of Player Names	317

Preface and Acknowledgments

This book follows on from the previous four volumes of *The Wisden Book of Test Cricket*, the most recent of which was published in 2015. Since then, over 220 Test matches have been played around the world, taking the total number well over 2,350. This volume fills the gap, with scorecards of all the Tests played since September 2014, up to the end of the English season of 2019.

The scorecards are taken directly from *Wisden Cricketers' Almanack*. The match reports are usually edited versions of *Wisden*'s own accounts, and include the Almanack's traditional mix of informative comment, facts and figures – and, occasionally, fun. The information given includes close-of-play scores, changes of batting and bowling order in the second innings, details of substitute catchers, the identity of umpires (including the TV official) and referees – and the number of matches in which they have stood – plus the winners of Man of the Match awards, while the fall-of-wicket information includes the identity of the outgoing batsman. For the first time, this volume also includes the identity of players performing run-outs (one name means a direct hit, while two or more indicate a return to a player near the stumps or a relayed throw), and also identifies wicketkeeping dismissals made by someone other than the designated keeper in the match. These are signified by a dagger (†) next to the player's name.

Test career records are given at the back of the book, as well as an Index showing in which matches a particular player appeared. A range of other records, regularly updated, can be found on the wisden.com website.

Each match has a reference number to show its overall position, and its place in that particular series. For example this volume – as the cover shows – includes the first Test match ever played with a pink ball under floodlights: Australia v New Zealand at Adelaide in November 2015. Its full reference number here is "Test No. 2187/55 (A783, NZ404)". This indicates that it was the 2,187th Test match overall, and the 55th played between Australia and New Zealand; furthermore, it was Australia's 783rd Test, and New Zealand's 404th. The overall numbers are arranged chronologically by series – so all the Tests of a particular series appear together and in numerical sequence, even if a match started in another country before the end of the series in question.

Many people gave invaluable assistance in compiling this latest volume. Christopher Lane at Wisden had the original idea for an update, while my colleagues Lawrence Booth, Hugh Chevallier, Harriet Monkhouse and Richard Whitehead were always helpful, and didn't seem to mind that I was occasionally diverted from helping to produce next year's Almanack by having my nose stuck in previous editions. Charlotte Croft, Katy McAdam and Zoë Blanc at Bloomsbury saw the project through, while the typesetters Deanta Global Publishing Services dealt capably with the demanding layout. Philip Bailey produced the Test Career Records and the Index with his customary accuracy and speed, while Charles Barr assisted with the proofreading. And at home, my wife Inese was a great help, while my sons Daniel and Mark showed welcome signs of being captivated by cricket: they sat spellbound through the closing stages of Headingley 2019, as their father had been by Headingley '81.

Finally, a great many people contributed to the accuracy of the original facts and figures in *Wisden*, and they are acknowledged in appropriate annual editions of the Almanack.

STEVEN LYNCH
October 2019

Test No. 2140/58 (P383, A768)

PAKISTAN v AUSTRALIA 2014–15 (1st Test)

At Dubai International Cricket Stadium on 22, 23, 24, 25, 26 October 2014.
Toss: Pakistan.   Result: PAKISTAN WON BY 221 RUNS.
Debuts: Pakistan – Imran Khan, Yasir Shah. Australia – M. R. Marsh, S. N. J. O'Keefe.
Man of the Match: Younis Khan.

Younis Khan was the key in an unexpected Pakistan triumph. Twin hundreds took him past Inzamam-ul-Haq (25) as their leading century-maker. He became the seventh Pakistani to score a century in each innings, the first from anywhere to do so against Australia since New Zealand's Glenn Turner in 1973–74, and the first Pakistani to make hundreds against all nine Test nations. Younis had entered at seven for two, but steadied the innings with Azhar Ali and Misbah-ul-Haq. Then Sarfraz Ahmed's second-day hundred came straight out of the Adam Gilchrist manual, ripping the game away from the opposition just when they had a sniff. He reached three figures from 80 balls; among wicketkeepers, only Gilchrist had got there faster. Pakistan's four frontline bowlers had only eight caps between them; Saeed Ajmal had been suspended for an illegal bowling action, while Junaid Khan and Wahab Riaz were injured. But once Rogers played on, an end was opened up, and the bowlers could expose Australia's weakness against spin in Asian conditions. Warner made his third century in successive Test innings, before he was finally beaten by a ripping leg-break from the debutant Yasir Shah. Once Pakistan had secured a substantial lead, the game was up. Younis made his second hundred, and helped Ahmed Shehzad to another. The end came seven overs after tea on the final day, mainly thanks to Yasir and slow left-armer Zulfiqar Babar, who wrapped up victory – and his maiden Test five-for – a few weeks short of his 36th birthday.

Pakistan

Ahmed Shehzad b Siddle	3	– lbw b O'Keefe	131
Mohammad Hafeez lbw b Johnson	0		
Azhar Ali c Doolan b Johnson	53	– (2) c Haddin b O'Keefe	30
Younis Khan lbw b Johnson	106	– (3) not out	103
*Misbah-ul-Haq c Johnson b Smith	69		
Asad Shafiq c Marsh b O'Keefe	89		
†Sarfraz Ahmed st Haddin b Lyon	109	– (4) not out	15
Yasir Shah c Rogers b O'Keefe	2		
Zulfiqar Babar retired hurt	7		
Rahat Ali c Rogers b Lyon	0		
Imran Khan not out	0		
B 2, l-b 14	16	B 2, l-b 3, w 2	7
(145 overs)	454	(2 wkts dec, 78 overs)	286

1/1 (2) 2/7 (1) 3/115 (3) 4/198 (4)   1/71 (2)
5/291 (5) 6/415 (6) 7/442 (8) 8/454 (7) 9/454 (10)   2/239 (1)
In the first innings Zulfiqar Babar retired hurt at 454-8.

Johnson 31–18–39–3; Siddle 24–11–50–1; O'Keefe 30–3–107–2; Marsh 17–4–44–0; Lyon 37–4–148–2; Smith 6–0–50–1.
Second innings—Johnson 12–2–34–0; Siddle 14–5–44–0; Lyon 18–0–72–0; O'Keefe 27–3–112–2; Marsh 7–1–19–0.

Australia

C. J. L. Rogers b Rahat Ali	38	– b Imran Khan	43
D. A. Warner b Yasir Shah	133	– st Sarfraz Ahmed b Zulfiqar Babar	29
A. J. Doolan run out (Rahat Ali)	5	– lbw b Zulfiqar Babar	0
*M. J. Clarke c Azhar Ali b Zulfiqar Babar	2	– lbw b Yasir Shah	3
S. P. D. Smith c Mohammad Hafeez b Yasir Shah	22	– (6) c Asad Shafiq b Yasir Shah	55
M. R. Marsh lbw b Zulfiqar Babar	27	– (7) c Azhar Ali b Zulfiqar Babar	3
†B. J. Haddin b Imran Khan	22	– (8) b Zulfiqar Babar	0
M. G. Johnson c sub (Shan Masood) b Rahat Ali	37	– (9) st Sarfraz Ahmed b Yasir Shah	61
P. M. Siddle lbw b Mohammad Hafeez	0	– (10) c Azhar Ali b Zulfiqar Babar	15
S. N. J. O'Keefe c Misbah-ul-Haq b Yasir Shah	6	– (11) not out	0
N. M. Lyon not out	4	– (5) lbw b Yasir Shah	0
B 4, l-b 2, n-b 1	7	B 4, l-b 1, n-b 2	7
(103.1 overs)	303	(91.1 overs)	216

1/128 (1) 2/151 (3) 3/158 (4) 4/206 (5) 5/207 (2)   1/44 (2) 2/44 (3) 3/49 (4) 4/49 (5) 5/92 (1)
6/249 (7) 7/262 (6) 8/267 (9) 9/299 (8) 10/303 (10)   6/101 (7) 7/105 (8) 8/170 (6) 9/213 (9) 10/216 (10)

Rahat Ali 19–0–55–2; Mohammad Hafeez 25.4–5–54–1; Imran Khan 15–3–41–1; Zulfiqar Babar 27–2–81–2; Yasir Shah 16.3–1–66–3. *Second innings*—Imran Khan 7–2–22–1; Rahat Ali 13–4–36–0; Mohammad Hafeez 15–4–29–0; Zulfiqar Babar 31.1–7–74–5; Yasir Shah 25–6–50–4.

Umpires: M. Erasmus *(South Africa)* (27) and R. A. Kettleborough *(England)* (23).
Third umpire: N. J. Llong *(England)*.   Referee: R. S. Madugalle *(Sri Lanka)* (151).

Close of play: first day, Pakistan 219–4 (Misbah-ul-Haq 34, Asad Shafiq 9); second day, Australia 113–0 (Rogers 31, Warner 75); third day, Pakistan 38–0 (Ahmed Shehzad 22, Azhar Ali 16); fourth day, Australia 59–4 (Rogers 23, Smith 3).

PAKISTAN v AUSTRALIA 2014-15 (2nd Test)

At Sheikh Zayed Stadium, Abu Dhabi, on 30, 31 October, 1, 2, 3 November, 2014.
Toss: Pakistan.　　Result: PAKISTAN WON BY 356 RUNS.
Debuts: none.
Man of the Match: Misbah-ul-Haq.　　Man of the Series: Younis Khan.

Pakistan completed their first series victory over Australia since 1994-95 in emphatic fashion. It put Misbah-ul-Haq level with his country's most successful Test captains, Imran Khan and Javed Miandad, on 14 wins. And he could now boast the joint-fastest Test century, alongside Viv Richards: after a 166-ball hundred in the first innings, he reached three figures in the second in just 56, with 11 fours and five sixes, four of them off Smith. Misbah overshadowed Younis Khan's double-century, and Azhar Ali's own twin tons. It was only the second time two batsmen from one team had scored two hundreds in a Test, after the Chappell brothers against New Zealand at Wellington in 1973–74. That series also contained the most recent instance of anyone scoring two in a match against Australia; now three Pakistanis had done it in a fortnight (and Virat Kohli would follow suit for India in December). Australia's batsmen struggled on a slow, low pitch, and their bowlers managed just nine wickets. Where Pakistan coaxed both spin and reverse swing, Australia managed little of either, although Lyon bowled well in patches. Clarke admitted sombrely that his team had not improved in these conditions from their 4–0 defeat in India in 2012–13. The only bright spots for his side came during Smith's 97, their most assured innings against spin, while Mitchell Marsh's 87 in his second Test bulged with promise. But neither was anywhere near enough to avert Pakistan's biggest Test victory by runs – and a 2–0 whitewash.

Pakistan

Ahmed Shehzad lbw b Lyon	35	– b Johnson	14
Mohammad Hafeez c Haddin b Johnson	45	– c Starc b Johnson	3
Azhar Ali c † Warner b Starc	109	– not out	100
Younis Khan b Siddle	213	– lbw b Smith	46
*Misbah-ul-Haq c and b Smith	101	– not out	101
Asad Shafiq b Starc	21		
†Sarfraz Ahmed not out	19		
Yasir Shah not out	1		
B 10, l-b 11, w 1, n-b 4	26	B 23, l-b 4, w 1, n-b 1	29
(6 wkts dec, 164 overs)	570	(3 wkts dec, 60.4 overs)	293

1/57 (1) 2/96 (2) 3/332 (3) 4/513 (5)　　1/14 (1)
5/537 (4) 6/561 (6)　　2/21 (2) 3/152 (4)

Zulfiqar Babar, Rahat Ali and Imran Khan did not bat.

Johnson 25–7–59–1; Starc 27–3–86–2; Siddle 31–8–75–1; Lyon 37–1–154–1; Marsh 12–2–32–0; Maxwell 16–2–78–0; Clarke 6–0–24–0; Smith 10–0–41–1. *Second innings*—Johnson 7–1–45–2; Lyon 18–3–48–0; Starc 11.4–2–56–0; Siddle 14–4–48–0; Smith 6–0–54–1; Marsh 4–1–15–0.

Australia

D. A. Warner c Yasir Shah b Rahat Ali	19	– (2) c Yasir Shah b Mohammad Hafeez	58
C. J. L. Rogers c Sarfraz Ahmed b Imran Khan	5	– (1) c Asad Shafiq b Zulfiqar Babar	2
N. M. Lyon b Rahat Ali	15	– (11) c Azhar Ali b Zulfiqar Babar	0
G. J. Maxwell b Zulfiqar Babar	37	– (3) lbw b Zulfiqar Babar	4
*M. J. Clarke b Imran Khan	47	– (4) b Zulfiqar Babar	5
S. P. D. Smith lbw b Zulfiqar Babar	0	– (5) lbw b Yasir Shah	97
M. R. Marsh c Rahat Ali b Imran Khan	87	– (6) c Asad Shafiq b Mohammad Hafeez	47
†B. J. Haddin b Yasir Shah	10	– (7) b Zulfiqar Babar	13
M. G. Johnson c Mohammad Hafeez b Yasir Shah	0	– (8) b Yasir Shah	0
P. M. Siddle c Yasir Shah b Mohammad Hafeez	28	– (9) not out	4
M. A. Starc not out	0	– (10) b Yasir Shah	2
L-b 6, n-b 7	13	B 5, l-b 1, n-b 3, p 5	14
(67.2 overs)	261	(88.3 overs)	246

1/21 (2) 2/34 (1) 3/75 (4) 4/97 (3) 5/100 (6) 6/164 (5)　　1/19 (1) 2/31 (3) 3/43 (4) 4/101 (2) 5/208 (6)
7/193 (8) 8/199 (9) 9/261 (7) 10/261 (10)　　6/238 (5) 7/238 (7) 8/238 (8) 9/245 (10) 10/246 (11)

Imran Khan 14–1–60–3; Mohammad Hafeez 5.2–0–13–1; Zulfiqar Babar 25–5–94–2; Rahat Ali 9–0–41–2; Yasir Shah 14–2–47–2. *Second innings*—Rahat Ali 8–6–3–0; Imran Khan 8–1–29–0; Mohammad Hafeez 17–4–38–2; Zulfiqar Babar 32.3–2–120–5; Yasir Shah 22–4–44–3; Azhar Ali 1–0–1–0.

Umpires: R. A. Kettleborough *(England)* (24) and N. J. Llong *(England)* (26).
Third umpire: M. Erasmus *(South Africa)*.　　Referee: R. S. Madugalle *(Sri Lanka)* (152).

Close of play: first day, Pakistan 304-2 (Azhar Ali 101, Younis Khan 111); second day, Australia 22-1 (Warner 16, Lyon 1); third day, Pakistan 61-2 (Azhar Ali 21, Younis Khan 16); fourth day, Australia 143-4 (Smith 38, Marsh 26).

BANGLADESH v ZIMBABWE 2014–15 (1st Test)

At Shere Bangla National Stadium, Mirpur, Dhaka, on 25, 26, 27 October, 2014.
Toss: Zimbabwe.   Result: BANGLADESH WON BY THREE WICKETS.
Debuts: Bangladesh – Jubair Hossain. Zimbabwe – T. Kamungozi.
Man of the Match: Taijul Islam.

After two days this match was intriguingly poised. But 17 wickets tumbled for 210 on a crazy third day, which ended with Bangladesh stumbling over the line to complete their fifth Test victory. Zimbabwe lost seven wickets before lunch on that third day: Taijul Islam, in only his third Test, took eight for 39, Bangladesh's best figures, beating Shakib Al Hasan's seven for 36 against New Zealand at Chittagong in 2008–09. Only two left-armers had recorded better figures: Rangana Herath for Sri Lanka against Pakistan just two months earlier, and Johnny Briggs for England in South Africa in 1888–89. Needing just 101, Bangladesh nosedived to nought for three, only the fifth such scoreline in Test history. It could have been worse: Mahmudullah and Shakib were both dropped by Nyumbu in the gully before the total passed five. After taking two early wickets, Chigumbura returned after tea with a double-wicket maiden; Bangladesh were soon 82 for seven. But Taijul collected 15 of the 19 required, including a pulled four to win the match. The excitement of the third day was a far cry from the sober cricket that had preceded it. Sikandar Raza lasted more than three hours for 51, but the rest of Zimbabwe's batting was disappointing. Their total looked rather better when Bangladesh could improve it by only 14. Mominul Haque made 53, and Mahmudullah 63 in three and a half hours – but otherwise only Mushfiqur Rahim lasted for long as seamer Panyangara picked up a maiden Test five-for.

Zimbabwe

V. Sibanda c Mushfiqur Rahim b Shahadat Hossain	6 – c Mushfiqur Rahim b Taijul Islam	14
Sikandar Raza c Mahmudullah b Jubair Hossain	51 – (4) c Shakib Al Hasan b Taijul Islam	25
H. Masakadza c Jubair Hossain b Shakib Al Hasan	13 – b Shahadat Hossain	5
*B. R. M. Taylor c Taijul Islam b Jubair Hossain	28 – (5) not out	45
E. Chigumbura c Mominul Haque b Shakib Al Hasan	29 – (6) c Shuvagata Hom b Taijul Islam	0
C. R. Ervine c Mominul Haque b Taijul Islam	34 – (7) lbw b Taijul Islam	10
†R. W. Chakabva c Shamsur Rahman b Shakib Al Hasan	25 – (2) c Shamsur Rahman b Taijul Islam	10
J. C. Nyumbu lbw b Shakib Al Hasan	14 – c Mushfiqur Rahim b Shakib Al Hasan	1
T. Panyangara c sub (Marshall Ayub) b Shakib Al Hasan	8 – c Shamsur Rahman b Taijul Islam	0
T. L. Chatara not out	14 – lbw b Taijul Islam	4
T. Kamungozi c Shamsur Rahman b Shakib Al Hasan	5 – c Mushfiqur Rahim b Taijul Islam	0
B 12, n-b 1	13	
(75.5 overs)	240	
	(35.5 overs)	114

1/6 (1) 2/31 (3) 3/83 (4) 4/128 (2) 5/142 (5) 6/192 (6)   1/19 (1) 2/24 (3) 3/53 (4) 4/58 (2) 5/58 (6) 6/92 (7)
7/200 (7) 8/221 (8) 9/230 (9) 10/240 (11)   7/93 (8) 8/104 (9) 9/114 (10) 10/114 (11)

Shahadat Hossain 14–1–45–1; Al-Amin Hossain 8–2–22–0; Shakib Al Hasan 24.5–5–59–6; Taijul Islam 13–3–42–1; Jubair Hossain 15–1–58–2; Mahmudullah 1–0–2–0. *Second innings*—Shahadat Hossain 8–2–25–1; Shakib Al Hasan 10–2–44–1; Taijul Islam 16.5–7–39–8; Jubair Hossain 1–0–6–0.

Bangladesh

Tamim Iqbal c Masakadza b Panyangara	5 – c Taylor b Chigumbura	0
Shamsur Rahman c Chigumbura b Panyangara	8 – b Panyangara	0
Mominul Haque run out (Sikandar Raza)	53 – c and b Chigumbura	0
Mahmudullah lbw b Sikandar Raza	63 – b Chigumbura	28
Shakib Al Hasan run out (Chigumbura/Chatara)	5 – c Nyumbu b Chatara	15
*†Mushfiqur Rahim c Ervine b Panyangara	64 – not out	23
Shuvagata Hom c Chigumbura b Kamungozi	14 – c Chakabva b Chigumbura	0
Taijul Islam b Panyangara	19 – (9) not out	15
Shahadat Hossain run out (Ervine)	0 – (8) c Taylor b Panyangara	11
Jubair Hossain not out	7	
Al-Amin Hossain b Panyangara	9	
L-b 6, w 1	7	B 4, w 5 9
(98 overs)	254	(7 wkts, 33.3 overs) 101

1/10 (1) 2/29 (2) 3/92 (3) 4/114 (5) 5/178 (4)   1/0 (1) 2/0 (2) 3/0 (3) 4/46 (5)
6/209 (7) 7/226 (6) 8/226 (9) 9/244 (8) 10/254 (11)   5/62 (4) 6/62 (7) 7/82 (8)

Panyangara 23–5–59–5; Chatara 22–11–27–0; Chigumbura 14–6–34–0; Nyumbu 15–1–65–0; Kamungozi 21–5–51–1; Sikandar Raza 3–0–12–1. *Second innings*—Chigumbura 10.3–4–21–4; Panyangara 8–2–30–2; Chatara 8–2–34–1; Kamungozi 5–1–7–0; Sikandar Raza 1–0–1–0; Nyumbu 1–0–4–0.

Umpires: H. D. P. K. Dharmasena *(Sri Lanka)* (27) and S. Ravi *(India)* (4).
Third umpire: B. F. Bowden (New Zealand).   Referee: B. C. Broad (England) (63).

Close of play: first day, Bangladesh 27–1 (Shamsur Rahman 8, Mominul Haque 14); second day, Zimbabwe 5–0 (Sibanda 5, Chakabva 0).

BANGLADESH v ZIMBABWE 2014–15 (2nd Test)

At Sheikh Abu Naser Stadium, Khulna, on 3, 4, 5, 6, 7 November, 2014.
Toss: Bangladesh.   Result: BANGLADESH WON BY 162 RUNS.
Debuts: Zimbabwe – B. B. Chari, N. Mushangwe.
Man of the Match: Shakib Al Hasan.

Shakib Al Hasan marked Khulna's second Test with 137, then took five wickets in each innings, a Test double previously achieved only by Ian Botham and Imran Khan. A positive result had looked unlikely when Bangladesh batted almost 20 overs into the final day, before leaving a target of 314 in 68 overs. But Zimbabwe were soon 15 for three, and all out shortly after tea. Slow left-armers Shakib and Taijul Islam took the new ball, and shared eight wickets. Ervine fell to the last ball before tea, and Masakadza soon afterwards: the final four wickets could add only nine. It was hard on Masakadza, who had survived seven hours in the first innings for his fourth Test century, and a further 144 minutes in the second. Determined batting had been a theme of the first four days. Bangladesh's big total was set up by contrasting centuries from Tamim Iqbal (whose 312-ball ton was their slowest in Tests) and a friskier one from Shakib. Zimbabwe also had two century-makers: Masakadza added 147 for the sixth wicket with wicketkeeper Chakabva, who made his maiden Test hundred. At 336 for five Zimbabwe looked set for a lead, but the rest tumbled for 32. With Bangladesh showing little urgency on the fourth day, a draw looked the likeliest result until Shakib took a hand. It was only the second time Bangladesh had won successive Tests, after the 2009 West Indian tour. Zimbabwe off-spinner Waller was reported – and later banned – for a suspect action.

Bangladesh

Tamim Iqbal c Ervine b Masakadza	109	– c and b Panyangara	20
Shamsur Rahman lbw b Chigumbura	2	– c Taylor b Waller	23
Mominul Haque c and b Panyangara	35	– c Chakabva b Waller	54
Mahmudullah lbw b Panyangara	56	– c Masakadza b Mushangwe	71
Shakib Al Hasan b Waller	137	– lbw b Waller	6
*†Mushfiqur Rahim run out (Sikandar Raza)	11	– c Chakabva b Waller	0
Shuvagata Hom c Chari b Waller	15	– c Masakadza b Mushangwe	50
Taijul Islam c Masakadza b Chatara	32	– c Panyangara b Mushangwe	1
Shahadat Hossain c Mushangwe b Chatara	18	– c Masakadza b Mushangwe	3
Jubair Hossain lbw b Mushangwe	1		
Rubel Hossain not out	0	– (10) not out	8
B 6, l-b 6, w 2, n-b 3	17	B 4, l-b 4, w 3, n-b 1	12
(158.5 overs)	433	(9 wkts dec, 83.5 overs)	248

1/6 (2) 2/78 (3) 3/173 (4) 4/305 (1) 5/322 (6)   1/28 (1) 2/75 (2) 3/131 (3) 4/145 (5)
6/376 (5) 7/383 (7) 8/426 (8) 9/433 (9) 10/433 (10)   5/145 (6) 6/220 (4) 7/222 (8) 8/236 (9) 9/248 (7)

Panyangara 29–10–49–2; Chigumbura 22–5–60–1; Chatara 27–7–61–2; Mushangwe 40.5–7–127–1; Waller 23–4–65–2; Sikandar Raza 11–2–31–0; Masakadza 6–1–28–1. *Second innings*—Chigumbura 6–2–13–0; Panyangara 12–3–45–1; Chatara 7–3–19–0; Waller 27–4–59–4; Sikandar Raza 6–0–22–0; Mushangwe 25.5–2–82–4.

Zimbabwe

Sikandar Raza lbw b Taijul Islam	11	– c Mominul Haque b Shakib Al Hasan	9
B. B. Chari c Tamim Iqbal b Taijul Islam	25	– c and b Taijul Islam	4
H. Masakadza b Shakib Al Hasan	158	– c Mominul Haque b Shakib Al Hasan	61
*B. R. M. Taylor c Mominul Haque b Shakib Al Hasan	37	– c Shuvagata Hom b Shakib Al Hasan	0
C. R. Ervine c Mushfiqur Rahim b Shakib Al Hasan	17	– (6) st Mushfiqur Rahim b Jubair Hossain	21
E. Chigumbura c Mominul Haque b Shakib Al Hasan	1	– (7) c Mahmudullah b Shakib Al Hasan	12
†R. W. Chakabva lbw b Taijul Islam	101	– (5) c Mahmudullah b Jubair Hossain	27
M. N. Waller c Mushfiqur Rahim b Shakib Al Hasan	6	– b Taijul Islam	4
T. L. Chatara c and b Rubel Hossain	0	– (11) lbw b Taijul Islam	1
N. Mushangwe c Mushfiqur Rahim b Rubel Hossain	0	– c Mushfiqur Rahim b Shakib Al Hasan	0
T. Panyangara not out	1	– (9) not out	8
B 2, l-b 7, w 1, n-b 1	11	B 4	4
(135.1 overs)	368	(51.1 overs)	151

1/17 (1) 2/84 (2) 3/151 (4) 4/181 (5) 5/189 (6) 6/336 (3)   1/11 (2) 2/13 (1) 3/15 (4) 4/85 (5) 5/117 (6)
7/350 (8) 8/351 (9) 9/351 (10) 10/368 (7)   6/137 (3) 7/142 (8) 8/142 (7) 9/142 (10) 10/151 (11)

Shahadat Hossain 11–2–24–0; Taijul Islam 32.1–6–96–3; Shakib Al Hasan 41–11–80–5; Jubair Hossain 19–2–64–0; Rubel Hossain 22–6–55–2; Shuvagata Hom 7–0–27–0; Mominul Haque 1–1–0–0; Mahmudullah 2–0–13–0. *Second innings*—Taijul Islam 15.1–3–44–3; Shakib Al Hasan 18–5–44–5; Shuvagata Hom 4–2–9–0; Rubel Hossain 4–2–8–0; Jubair Hossain 10–0–42–2.

Umpires: Aleem Dar *(Pakistan)* (91) and B. F. Bowden *(New Zealand)* (80).
Third umpire: S. Ravi *(India)*.   Referee: B. C. Broad *(England)* (64).

Close of play: first day, Bangladesh 193–3 (Tamim Iqbal 74, Shakib Al Hasan 13); second day, Zimbabwe 53–1 (Chari 21, Masakadza 15); third day, Zimbabwe 331–5 (Masakadza 154, Chakabva 75); fourth day, Bangladesh 201–5 (Mahmudullah 63, Shuvagata Hom 23).

Test No. 2144/14 (B88, Z97)

BANGLADESH v ZIMBABWE 2014–15 (3rd Test)

At Zohur Ahmed Chowdhury Stadium, Chittagong, on 12, 13, 14, 15, 16 November, 2014.
Toss: Bangladesh.   Result: BANGLADESH WON BY 186 RUNS.
Debuts: none.
Man of the Match: Mominul Haque.   Man of the Series: Shakib Al Hasan.

Bangladesh completed their first 3–0 whitewash with a confident performance after taking first use of a perfect track: the openers responded with a stand of 224. Tamim Iqbal and the recalled Imrul Kayes reached their hundreds just before tea: it was the first time Bangladesh's openers had survived the first two sessions of a Test. Tamim's sixth Test century equalled Mohammad Ashraful's national record. Zimbabwe had more success next day, but a fluent 71 from Shakib and a late blast from Rubel Hossain helped Bangladesh pass 500 for only the fourth time. Although Chari fell to Rubel for a duck, Sikandar Raza and Hamilton Masakadza put on 160, before a clatter of wickets made it 209 for five. Chakabva (relieved of the wicketkeeping gloves) then added 113 with Chigumbura, whose 88 was a Test-best, and the follow-on was avoided – but the tail again failed to make much headway. Teenage leg-spinner Jubair Hossain took his maiden five-for in his third Test. Bangladesh rattled along as the lead mounted, with Mominul Haque cantering to his fourth hundred in only his 12th Test, the ninth in succession in which he had scored at least a half-century. A target of 449 predictably proved well beyond Zimbabwe. The unfortunate Chari completed a pair and, after some resistance from Raza and Masakadza, only Chakabva hung around. He was still there at the end, after 208 minutes – but no one else lasted an hour. Bangladesh now had seven Test victories (five against Zimbabwe) to offset 70 defeats.

Bangladesh

Tamim Iqbal c H. Masakadza b Sikandar Raza	109	– b Mushangwe		65
Imrul Kayes c sub (V. Sibanda) b H. Masakadza	130	– c Mutumbami b Panyangara		15
Mominul Haque c Taylor b Panyangara	48	– not out		131
Mahmudullah lbw b S. W. Masakadza	16	– c Mutumbami b Panyangara		30
Shakib Al Hasan c Ervine b Sikandar Raza	71	– c Ervine b Mushangwe		17
*†Mushfiqur Rahim b H. Masakadza	15	– c Mushangwe b Sikandar Raza		46
Shuvagata Hom run out (S. W. Masakadza/Mutumbami)	35	– not out		3
Taijul Islam c Mutumbami b S. W. Masakadza	1			
Shafiul Islam c Ervine b Sikandar Raza	10			
Rubel Hossain not out	45			
Jubair Hossain b Panyangara	5			
B 2, l-b 10, w 6	18	B 8, l-b 3, w 1		12
(153.4 overs)	503	(5 wkts dec, 78 overs)		319

1/224 (1) 2/272 (2) 3/312 (3) 4/339 (4) 5/378 (6)   1/36 (2) 2/149 (1) 3/204 (4)
6/428 (5) 7/429 (8) 8/451 (9) 9/452 (7) 10/503 (11)   4/237 (5) 5/308 (6)

Panyangara 20.4–2–70–2; Chigumbura 14–4–40–0; S. W. Masakadza 25–5–77–2; Mushangwe 47–5–149–0; Sikandar Raza 36–2–123–3; Chari 2–0–9–0; H. Masakadza 9–1–23–2. *Second innings*—S. W. Masakadza 7–0–28–0; Panyangara 12–3–31–2; Sikandar Raza 25–0–114–1; Mushangwe 18–2–77–2; Chigumbura 9–2–19–0; H. Masakadza 7–1–39–0.

Zimbabwe

Sikandar Raza c Mahmudullah b Jubair Hossain	82	– c Taijul Islam b Shuvagata Hom		65
B. B. Chari c Mushfiqur Rahim b Rubel Hossain	0	– lbw b Rubel Hossain		0
H. Masakadza lbw b Shafiul Islam	81	– c Mushfiqur Rahim b Shuvagata Hom		38
*B. R. M. Taylor c Taijul Islam b Jubair Hossain	1	– c Shakib Al Hasan b Jubair Hossain		24
R. W. Chakabva lbw b Shafiul Islam	65	– not out		89
C. R. Ervine b Jubair Hossain	14	– (7) lbw b Mahmudullah		16
E. Chigumbura c Imrul Kayes b Jubair Hossain	88	– (6) c Imrul Kayes b Jubair Hossain		5
†R. Mutumbami lbw b Shakib Al Hasan	20	– lbw b Taijul Islam		2
S. W. Masakadza c Mahmudullah b Taijul Islam	0	– (10) b Shafiul Islam		0
T. Panyangara not out	6	– (9) lbw b Rubel Hossain		2
N. Mushangwe c Mahmudullah b Jubair Hossain	8	– lbw b Shafiul Islam		0
B 6, l-b 1, n-b 2	9	B 14, l-b 6, w 1		21
(106 overs)	374	(85 overs)		262

1/9 (2) 2/169 (3) 3/172 (4) 4/172 (1) 5/209 (6)   1/4 (2) 2/97 (3) 3/116 (1) 4/165 (4) 5/179 (6)
6/322 (5) 7/356 (8) 8/357 (9) 9/360 (7) 10/374 (11)   6/228 (7) 7/237 (8) 8/261 (9) 9/262 (10) 10/262 (11)

Shafiul Islam 18–5–50–2; Rubel Hossain 9–1–46–1; Taijul Islam 30–2–100–1; Shakib Al Hasan 25–4–67–1; Jubair Hossain 20–1–96–5; Shuvagata Hom 1–0–1–0; Mahmudullah 3–0–7–0. *Second innings*—Shafiul Islam 9–1–17–2; Rubel Hossain 4–2–16–2; Taijul Islam 22–4–48–1; Jubair Hossain 19–3–56–2; Shakib Al Hasan 11–2–35–0; Shuvagata Hom 16–1–66–2; Mahmudullah 4–1–4–1.

Umpires: Aleem Dar *(Pakistan)* (92) and C. B. Gaffaney *(New Zealand)* (2).
Third umpire: H. D. P. K. Dharmasena *(Sri Lanka)*.   Referee: B. C. Broad *(England)* (65).

Close of play: first day, Bangladesh 303–2 (Mominul Haque 46, Mahmudullah 5); second day, Zimbabwe 113–1 (Sikandar Raza 54, H. Masakadza 51); third day, Bangladesh 23–0 (Tamim Iqbal 8, Imrul Kayes 11); fourth day, Zimbabwe 71–1 (Sikandar Raza 43, H. Masakadza 26).

PAKISTAN v NEW ZEALAND 2014–15 (1st Test)

At Sheikh Zayed Stadium, Abu Dhabi, on 9, 10, 11, 12, 13 November, 2014.
Toss: Pakistan.   Result: PAKISTAN WON BY 248 RUNS.
Debuts: none.
Man of the Match: Rahat Ali.

Misbah-ul-Haq won the toss, said "We'll bat", and galloped to the shade of the dressing-room, sentencing New Zealand to almost two days of desert sun; the only respite during Pakistan's 566 for three was a westerly wind to wick away sweat. The openers started by putting on 178, and the rest joined in: for the first time in a Test, the top five all passed 80. New Zealand's bowlers stuck at it, although the fielding suffered. Ahmed Shehzad motored to 176 – his third century in eight Tests – before his bat fell on to the stumps after he was clonked on the helmet by Anderson. He had a minor skull fracture, and sat out the rest of the series. Misbah cruised to another hundred, after two in his previous Test, also on this ground, against Australia. Apart from Latham – and No. 10 Sodhi in the second innings – the visitors floundered against spin and reverse swing, while the cacophony of chirping around the bat must have felt like being in an aviary. Latham's maiden century made him and Rod the third New Zealand father and son to score Test hundreds, after Walter and Richard Hadlee and Ken and Hamish Rutherford. There was a brief interlude as Pakistan topped up their lead, taking their match aggregate to 741 for five. When Mohammad Hafeez (who would miss the next match for tests after his bowling action was reported again) reached his hundred, Misbah declared for the fifth successive innings, and soon had a national-record 15th Test win as captain.

Pakistan

Mohammad Hafeez c and b Anderson	96	– not out	101
Ahmed Shehzad hit wkt b Anderson	176		
Azhar Ali b Sodhi	87	– (2) lbw b Sodhi	23
Younis Khan not out	100	– (3) lbw b Sodhi	28
*Misbah-ul-Haq not out	102		
†Sarfraz Ahmed (did not bat)		– (4) not out	13
B 2, l-b 2, n-b 1	5	B 6, l-b 2, w 2	10
(3 wkts dec, 170.5 overs)	566	(2 wkts dec, 39.2 overs)	175

1/178 (1) 2/347 (2) 3/373 (3)   1/69 (2) 2/139 (3)

Asad Shafiq, Yasir Shah, Zulfiqar Babar, Rahat Ali and Imran Khan did not bat.

Boult 26–7–62–0; Southee 23–5–62–0; Craig 33–1–126–0; Sodhi 43–6–162–1; Anderson 19–3–68–2; Neesham 16–0–50–0; McCullum 10.5–1–32–0. *Second innings*—Boult 7–2–25–0; Southee 9–0–33–0; Sodhi 13–1–66–2; Anderson 5–1–11–0; Craig 5–0–29–0; McCullum 0.2–0–3–0.

New Zealand

T. W. M. Latham lbw b Rahat Ali	103	– c Yasir Shah b Zulfiqar Babar	20
*B. B. McCullum c Younis Khan b Zulfiqar Babar	18	– lbw b Yasir Shah	39
K. S. Williamson b Rahat Ali	3	– st Sarfraz Ahmed b Mohammad Hafeez	23
L. R. P. L. Taylor c Asad Shafiq b Zulfiqar Babar	0	– lbw b Yasir Shah	8
C. J. Anderson b Rahat Ali	48	– lbw b Imran Khan	23
J. D. S. Neesham st Sarfraz Ahmed b Mohammad Hafeez	11	– c Sarfraz Ahmed b Rahat Ali	0
†B-J. Watling lbw b Zulfiqar Babar	42	– b Rahat Ali	0
M. D. Craig run out (Rahat Ali/ Sarfraz Ahmed/Yasir Shah)	1	– b Yasir Shah	28
T. G. Southee c Sarfraz Ahmed b Rahat Ali	0	– b Zulfiqar Babar	5
I. S. Sodhi b Yasir Shah	25	– lbw b Imran Khan	63
T. A. Boult not out	0	– not out	19
L-b 7, n-b 4	11	B 1, l-b 2	3
(87.3 overs)	262	(70.3 overs)	231

1/33 (2) 2/38 (3) 3/47 (4) 4/130 (5) 5/150 (6) 6/215 (1)   1/57 (1) 2/61 (2) 3/69 (4) 4/111 (3) 5/112 (6)
7/219 (8) 8/219 (9) 9/262 (10) 10/262 (7)   6/112 (7) 7/121 (5) 8/138 (9) 9/177 (8) 10/231 (10)

Rahat Ali 17–10–22–4; Imran Khan 11–2–29–0; Zulfiqar Babar 27.3–5–79–3; Mohammad Hafeez 15–1–60–1; Yasir Shah 17–1–65–1. *Second innings*—Rahat Ali 11–1–48–2; Imran Khan 10.3–1–37–2; Zulfiqar Babar 24–6–48–2; Yasir Shah 18–1–74–3; Mohammad Hafeez 7–0–21–1.

Umpires: R. E. J. Martinesz *(Sri Lanka)* (5) and R. J. Tucker *(Australia)* (34).
Third umpire: P. R. Reiffel *(Australia)*.   Referee: A. J. Pycroft *(Zimbabwe)* (31).

Close of play: first day, Pakistan 269–1 (Ahmed Shehzad 126, Azhar Ali 46); second day, New Zealand 15–0 (Latham 5, McCullum 9); third day, Pakistan 15–0 (Mohammad Hafeez 5, Azhar Ali 9); fourth day, New Zealand 174–8 (Craig 27, Sodhi 27).

Test No. 2146/52 (P386, NZ396)

PAKISTAN v NEW ZEALAND 2014–15 (2nd Test)

At Dubai International Cricket Stadium on 17, 18, 19, 20, 21 November, 2014.
Toss: New Zealand.   Result: DRAWN.
Debuts: none.
Man of the Match: L. R. P. L. Taylor.

New Zealand emerged with respect after their Abu Dhabi trouncing. McCullum set Pakistan 261 in 72 overs, and they finished 65 short of victory, with New Zealand five wickets away. Off-spinner Craig dismissed Azhar Ali and Younis Khan, but he and Sodhi did not use the footmarks as effectively as Pakistan's slow men; in New Zealand's second innings, Zulfiqar Babar and Yasir Shah took all nine wickets before the declaration. Taylor negotiated them well for his 12th Test century before Yasir had him stumped – for the first time in a Test – but his seventh-wicket partnership of 60 with Craig extricated New Zealand from a perilous position with a day remaining. They had claimed the early honours, with Latham making 137 on the first day to become the second New Zealander, after John F. Reid in 1984–85, to score centuries in consecutive Tests against Pakistan, before Watling and Craig lifted them towards 400. Pakistan had fielded the same side in winning their last three Tests, but were forced to change both openers, with disappointing results. Azhar Ali and Younis Khan fought back, but the rest looked out of touch, which was unsurprising: Pakistan had not needed to call on anyone beneath No. 5 in four of their previous seven innings. At 312 for nine they were facing a potentially terminal deficit, but Sarfraz Ahmed and Rahat Ali put on 81, a tenth-wicket record against New Zealand. Sarfraz finally slapped a return catch, McCullum's first wicket in any form of top-level cricket.

New Zealand

T. W. M. Latham c Sarfraz Ahmed b Rahat Ali	137	– c Asad Shafiq b Yasir Shah	9
*B. B. McCullum c Shan Masood b Ehsan Adil	43	– lbw b Zulfiqar Babar	45
K. S. Williamson b Zulfiqar Babar	32	– c Taufeeq Umar b Zulfiqar Babar	11
L. R. P. L. Taylor c Shan Masood b Yasir Shah	23	– st Sarfraz Ahmed b Yasir Shah	104
C. J. Anderson c Azhar Ali b Ehsan Adil	9	– b Yasir Shah	0
J. D. S. Neesham c Misbah-ul-Haq b Yasir Shah	17	– b Zulfiqar Babar	11
†B-J. Watling c sub (Haris Sohail) b Azhar Ali	39	– c Asad Shafiq b Yasir Shah	11
M. D. Craig lbw b Zulfiqar Babar	43	– c Rahat Ali b Yasir Shah	34
T. G. Southee b Zulfiqar Babar	17	– c Azhar Ali b Zulfiqar Babar	20
I. S. Sodhi not out	32	– not out	2
T. A. Boult c Rahat Ali b Zulfiqar Babar	2		
L-b 9	9	L-b 3	3
(156 overs)	403	(9 wkts dec, 64.5 overs)	250

1/77 (2) 2/153 (3) 3/226 (4) 4/245 (5) 5/245 (1)   1/42 (1) 2/63 (3) 3/78 (2) 4/79 (5) 5/125 (6)
6/278 (6) 7/346 (7) 8/348 (8) 9/387 (9) 10/403 (11)   6/166 (7) 7/226 (8) 8/228 (4) 9/250 (9)

Rahat Ali 32–8–69–1; Ehsan Adil 29–9–73–2; Zulfiqar Babar 45–8–137–4; Yasir Shah 41–7–92–2; Azhar Ali 9–1–23–1. *Second innings*—Rahat Ali 8–0–39–0; Ehsan Adil 8–1–33–0; Zulfiqar Babar 27.5–5–96–4; Yasir Shah 21–1–79–5.

Pakistan

Shan Masood b Sodhi	13	– lbw b Boult	40
Taufeeq Umar st Watling b Craig	16	– c Watling b Southee	4
Azhar Ali b Sodhi	75	– c Neesham b Craig	24
Younis Khan c Craig b Neesham	72	– c Taylor b Craig	44
*Misbah-ul-Haq c Taylor b Boult	28	– c Watling b Boult	0
Asad Shafiq c Taylor b Southee	44	– not out	41
†Sarfraz Ahmed c and b McCullum	112	– not out	24
Yasir Shah c Watling b Southee	2		
Ehsan Adil lbw b Southee	0		
Zulfiqar Babar c Watling b Boult	5		
Rahat Ali not out	16		
B 7, l-b 2, n-b 1	10	B 15, l-b 2, w 1, n-b 1	19
(147 overs)	393	(5 wkts, 67 overs)	196

1/28 (1) 2/32 (2) 3/145 (4) 4/195 (5) 5/220 (3)   1/8 (2) 2/70 (3) 3/73 (1)
6/279 (6) 7/285 (8) 8/287 (9) 9/312 (10) 10/393 (7)   4/75 (5) 5/149 (4)

Boult 30–8–69–2; Southee 30–5–67–3; Craig 28–5–117–1; Sodhi 39–9–92–2; Anderson 7–0–26–0; Neesham 11–2–12–1; McCullum 2–1–1–1. *Second innings*—Boult 10–6–12–2; Southee 11–3–21–1; Craig 17–3–66–2; Sodhi 21–5–63–0; Anderson 3–1–4–0; Neesham 2–1–1–0; McCullum 3–0–12–0.

Umpires: R. E. J. Martinesz *(Sri Lanka)* (6) and P. R. Reiffel *(Australia)* (12).
Third umpire: R. J. Tucker *(Australia)*.   Referee: A. J. Pycroft *(Zimbabwe)* (32).

Close of play: first day, New Zealand 243-3 (Latham 137, Anderson 7); second day, Pakistan 34-2 (Azhar Ali 4, Younis Khan 1); third day, Pakistan 281-6 (Sarfraz Ahmed 28, Yasir Shah 1); fourth day, New Zealand 167-6 (Taylor 77, Craig 0).

Test No. 2147/53 (P387, NZ397)

PAKISTAN v NEW ZEALAND 2014–15 (3rd Test)

At Sharjah C. A. Stadium on 26, 27 *(no play)*, 28, 29, 30 November, 2014.
Toss: Pakistan.   Result: NEW ZEALAND WON BY AN INNINGS AND 80 RUNS.
Debuts: none.
Man of the Match: M. D. Craig.   Man of the Series: Mohammad Hafeez.

The death in Sydney on November 27 of the Australian batsman Phillip Hughes cast a pall over this match; the scheduled second day was abandoned, and another added. But after losing the toss on a pitch of shiny batting-friendly clay, New Zealand regrouped to square the series. Vettori, whistled up for a 112th and final cap 28 months after his 111th, claimed two wickets, but Craig led the way, becoming only the third New Zealand spinner, after Vettori himself (three times) and John Bracewell, to take ten in a Test – and the first from anywhere to do so at Sharjah, eclipsing Shane Warne's two hauls of eight in October 2002. On what became the second morning, the absence of exultation when Southee had Misbah-ul-Haq caught behind reflected the change of mood; as Pakistan lost seven wickets for 70, it was as if the mute button had been pressed. Misbah admitted his side lost their focus. Records tumbled when New Zealand batted: 690 was their highest total, and the second-biggest conceded by Pakistan, while 22 sixes was the most (by five) in any Test innings. McCullum's 78-ball hundred was his country's fastest, and he joined Don Bradman (1930), Ricky Ponting (2003) and Michael Clarke (2012) in scoring three or more double-centuries in a year. Leading by 339, New Zealand were thankful for a breeze which helped Southee and Boult bend the ball around. Pakistan limped to 24 for three on the fourth morning, and fell short despite Asad Shafiq's stylish 137.

Pakistan

Mohammad Hafeez c Boult b Sodhi	197	– c and b Craig	24
Shan Masood b Craig	12	– c Southee b Boult	4
Azhar Ali c Taylor b Craig	39	– b Boult	6
Younis Khan lbw b Vettori	5	– lbw b Boult	0
*Misbah-ul-Haq c Watling b Southee	38	– c Watling b Craig	12
Asad Shafiq c Sodhi b Craig	11	– c Craig b Boult	137
†Sarfraz Ahmed c Watling b Craig	15	– c Taylor b Sodhi	37
Yasir Shah c Taylor b Craig	25	– lbw b Sodhi	10
Mohammad Talha c Latham b Craig	0	– lbw b Vettori	19
Rahat Ali c Taylor b Craig	0	– c McCullum b Craig	6
Zulfiqar Babar not out	0	– not out	0
L-b 4, w 4, n-b 1	9	L-b 2, w 1, n-b 1	4
(125.4 overs)	351	(63.3 overs)	259

1/44 (2) 2/131 (3) 3/160 (4) 4/285 (5) 5/311 (1)   1/13 (2) 2/20 (3) 3/24 (4) 4/36 (1) 5/63 (5)
6/313 (6) 7/336 (7) 8/336 (9) 9/346 (10) 10/351 (8)   6/136 (7) 7/146 (8) 8/180 (9) 9/258 (6) 10/259 (10)

Boult 21–6–54–0; Southee 24–4–54–1; Vettori 19–5–41–1; Anderson 12–4–28–0; Craig 27.4–5–94–7; Sodhi 22–3–76–1. *Second innings*—Boult 15–6–38–4; Southee 11–3–20–0; Craig 20.3–2–109–3; Vettori 5–2–8–1; Sodhi 12–0–82–2.

New Zealand

T. W. M. Latham c Sarfraz Ahmed b Rahat Ali	13
*B. B. McCullum b Yasir Shah	202
K. S. Williamson c Younis Khan b Rahat Ali	192
L. R. P. L. Taylor c Younis Khan b Yasir Shah	50
C. J. Anderson c Yasir Shah b Rahat Ali	50
D. L. Vettori lbw b Rahat Ali	15
†B-J. Watling lbw b Mohammad Hafeez	8
M. D. Craig c and b Mohammad Hafeez	65
T. G. Southee c Mohammad Talha b Yasir Shah	50
I. S. Sodhi c Younis Khan b Yasir Shah	22
T. A. Boult not out	0
B 2, l-b 7, w 8, n-b 6	23
(143.1 overs)	690

1/51 (1) 2/348 (2) 3/464 (4) 4/488 (3) 5/528 (6)
6/537 (5) 7/546 (7) 8/637 (9) 9/682 (8) 10/690 (10)

Mohammad Talha 22–2–136–0; Rahat Ali 29–2–99–4; Zulfiqar Babar 23–1–135–0; Yasir Shah 44.1–4–193–4; Mohammad Hafeez 23–2–110–2; Azhar Ali 2–0–8–0.

Umpires: P. R. Reiffel *(Australia)* (13) and R. J. Tucker *(Australia)* (35).
Third umpire: R. E. J. Martinesz *(Sri Lanka)*.   Referee: A. J. Pycroft *(Zimbabwe)* (33).

Close of play: first day, Pakistan 281–3 (Mohammad Hafeez 178, Misbah-ul-Haq 38); second day, no play; third day, New Zealand 249–1 (McCullum 153, Williamson 76); fourth day, New Zealand 637–8 (Craig 34).

Test No. 2148/87 (A770, I484)

AUSTRALIA v INDIA 2014–15 (1st Test)

At Adelaide Oval on 9, 10, 11, 12, 13 December, 2014.
Toss: Australia.   Result: AUSTRALIA WON BY 48 RUNS.
Debuts: India – K. V. Sharma.
Man of the Match: N. M. Lyon.

This series was delayed after the death of Phillip Hughes on November 27, but Adelaide Oval provided the perfect setting for an event marinated in emotion. Warner started by channelling the grief of the loss of his "little mate" to make a sizzling 145. Clarke retired hurt after aggravating back and hamstring problems, but was back next day to reach a record seventh century here, and helped Smith put on 163. Then Kohli, captaining for the first time as Dhoni was injured, made a sumptuous hundred, although Lyon mopped up to give Australia a lead of 73. Warner rode his luck to complete his second hundred of the game, to reprise his feat at Cape Town in March, and an overnight declaration left India 364 in 98 overs. At tea they needed 159 with Kohli purring along and eight wickets left, but Lyon trapped Vijay in front for 99, and Rahane went five balls later, caught – off pad only – at short leg. The tide was turning, but Kohli was more like Cnut. His second century reduced the requirement below 100 – but finally he picked out Marsh on the midwicket fence. More than 16 overs remained: India might still have managed a draw, but the tail hit out. Lyon, who at one point had one for 116, finished with seven for 152, and was the first Australian off-spinner to take 12 wickets in a home Test. He was lauded by team-mates and the largest fifth-day crowd at Adelaide (24,836) since Bodyline.

Australia

C. J. L. Rogers c Dhawan b I. Sharma	9	– c R. G. Sharma b K. V. Sharma	21
D. A. Warner c I. Sharma b K. V. Sharma	145	– b K. V. Sharma	102
S. R. Watson c Dhawan b Aaron	14	– b Mohammed Shami	33
*M. J. Clarke c Pujara b K. V. Sharma	128	– c Saha b Aaron	7
S. P. D. Smith not out	162	– not out	52
M. R. Marsh c Kohli b Aaron	41	– c Vijay b R. G. Sharma	40
N. M. Lyon b Mohammed Shami	3		
†B. J. Haddin c Saha b Mohammed Shami	0	– (7) not out	14
M. G. Johnson not out	0		
L-b 4, w 9, n-b 2	15	B 1, l-b 6, w 5, n-b 9	21
(7 wkts dec, 120 overs)	517	(5 wkts dec, 69 overs)	290

1/50 (1) 2/88 (3) 3/258 (2) 4/345 (6)   1/38 (1) 2/140 (3) 3/168 (4)
5/352 (7) 6/354 (8) 7/517 (4)   4/213 (2) 5/266 (6)

R. J. Harris and P. M. Siddle did not bat.

In the first innings Clarke, when 60, retired hurt at 206-2 and resumed at 354-6.

Mohammed Shami 24–2–120–2; Aaron 23–1–136–2; I. Sharma 27–5–85–1; K. V. Sharma 33–1–143–2; Vijay 13–3–29–0. *Second innings*—Mohammed Shami 11–2–42–1; I. Sharma 14–3–41–0; K. V. Sharma 16–2–95–2; Vijay 6–0–27–0; R. G. Sharma 12–2–35–1; Aaron 10–0–43–1.

India

M. Vijay c Haddin b Johnson	53	– lbw b Lyon	99
S. Dhawan b Harris	25	– c Haddin b Johnson	9
C. A. Pujara b Lyon	73	– c Haddin b Lyon	21
*V. Kohli c Harris b Johnson	115	– c Marsh b Lyon	141
A. M. Rahane c Watson b Lyon	62	– c Rogers b Lyon	0
R. G. Sharma c and b Lyon	43	– c Warner b Lyon	6
†W. P. Saha c Watson b Lyon	25	– b Lyon	13
K. V. Sharma b Siddle	4	– not out	4
Mohammed Shami c Watson b Siddle	34	– c Johnson b Harris	5
I. Sharma c Smith b Lyon	0	– (11) st Haddin b Lyon	1
V. R. Aaron not out	3	– (10) lbw b Johnson	1
L-b 4, w 1, n-b 2	7	B 5, l-b 8, w 2	15
(116.4 overs)	444	(87.1 overs)	315

1/30 (2) 2/111 (1) 3/192 (3) 4/293 (5) 5/367 (4)   1/16 (2) 2/57 (3) 3/242 (1) 4/242 (5) 5/277 (6)
6/399 (6) 7/406 (8) 8/422 (7) 9/422 (10) 10/444 (9)   6/299 (7) 7/304 (4) 8/309 (9) 9/314 (10) 10/315 (11)

Johnson 22–6–102–2; Harris 21–6–55–1; Lyon 36–4–134–5; Siddle 18.4–2–88–2; Marsh 11–4–29–0; Watson 5–1–13–0; Smith 3–0–19–0. *Second innings*—Johnson 16–2–45–2; Harris 19–6–49–1; Lyon 34.1–5–152–7; Siddle 9–3–21–0; Watson 2–0–6–0; Smith 3–0–18–0; Marsh 4–1–11–0.

Umpires: M. Erasmus *(South Africa)* (28) and I. J. Gould *(England)* (42).
Third umpire: M. D. Martell *(Australia).*   Referee: J. J. Crowe *(New Zealand)* (68).

Close of play: first day, Australia 354–6 (Smith 72); second day, Australia 517–7 (Smith 162, Johnson 0); third day, India 369–5 (R. G. Sharma 33, Saha 1); fourth day, Australia 290–5 (Smith 52, Haddin 14).

AUSTRALIA v INDIA 2014–15 (2nd Test)

At Wolloongabba, Brisbane, on 17, 18, 19, 20 December, 2014.
Toss: India.   Result: AUSTRALIA WON BY FOUR WICKETS.
Debuts: Australia – J. R. Hazlewood.
Man of the Match: S. P. D. Smith.

Inconspicuous in the First Test, Johnson now made two devastating interventions. Australia were drifting when he surged to 88; next day he splintered India's middle order like matchwood with three for ten in 11 balls. He was batting when the winning runs were scored, extending Australia's undefeated streak at the Gabba to 26 Tests, only seven of them drawn. It was India's sixth successive defeat in Australia. Smith, in his first Test in charge – Clarke was injured, and vice-captain Haddin bypassed – remained unruffled after losing the toss and watching India amass 311 for four on a boiling day. Vijay compiled a polished 144, although he was dropped twice by Shaun Marsh, playing his first Test alongside his brother. Josh Hazlewood, on debut, forced his way through on the second morning, and Haddin finished with six catches. Smith then took breezy command, collecting the first century by a new Australian captain since Graham Yallop against England in 1978–79, before a riotous partnership of 148 with Johnson; the last four wickets eventually added 258 in just 48.3 overs. Before the start of the fourth day, Dhawan – struck on the wrist in the warm-up – decided he could not resume; instead, Kohli entered, and soon dragged Johnson on. India had been almost level, but now lost four for 11. Dhawan soon returned, and showed no ill-effects while progressing to 81. Left 128, Australia were grateful to Rogers's second 55 of the match. The overall run-rate of 4.12 was the highest in Australian Test history.

India

M. Vijay c Haddin b Lyon	144	– b Starc 27
S. Dhawan c Haddin b M. R. Marsh	24	– lbw b Lyon 81
C. A. Pujara c Haddin b Hazlewood	18	– c Lyon b Hazlewood 43
V. Kohli c Haddin b Hazlewood	19	– b Johnson 1
A. M. Rahane c Haddin b Hazlewood	81	– c Lyon b Johnson 10
R. G. Sharma c Smith b Watson	32	– c Haddin b Johnson 0
*†M. S. Dhoni c Haddin b Hazlewood	33	– lbw b Hazlewood 0
R. Ashwin c Watson b Hazlewood	35	– c Haddin b Starc 19
U. T. Yadav c Rogers b Lyon	9	– c Haddin b Johnson 30
V. R. Aaron c sub (M. Labuschagne) b Lyon	4	– c Hazlewood b Lyon 3
I. Sharma not out	1	– not out 1
B 4, l-b 1, w 2, n-b 1	8	L-b 2, w 5, n-b 2 9
(109.4 overs)	408	(64.3 overs) 224

1/56 (2) 2/100 (3) 3/137 (4) 4/261 (1) 5/321 (5)   1/41 (1) 2/76 (4) 3/86 (5) 4/86 (6) 5/87 (7)
6/328 (6) 7/385 (8) 8/394 (7) 9/407 (10) 10/408 (9)   6/117 (8) 7/143 (3) 8/203 (2) 9/211 (10) 10/224 (9)

In the second innings Dhawan, when 26, retired hurt at 71-1 and resumed at 117-6.

Johnson 21–4–81–0; Hazlewood 23.2–6–68–5; Starc 17–1–83–0; M. R. Marsh 6–1–14–1; Lyon 25.4–2–105–3; Watson 14.4–6–39–1; Warner 1–0–9–0; Smith 1–0–4–0. *Second innings*—Johnson 17.3–4–61–4; Hazlewood 16–0–74–2; Starc 8–1–27–2; Watson 13–6–27–0; Lyon 10–1–33–2.

Australia

C. J. L. Rogers c Dhoni b Yadav	55	– c Dhawan b I. Sharma 55
D. A. Warner c Ashwin b Yadav	29	– c Dhoni b I. Sharma 6
S. R. Watson c Dhawan b Ashwin	25	– c Dhoni b I. Sharma 0
*S. P. D. Smith b I. Sharma	133	– run out (Yadav/Dhoni) 28
S. E. Marsh c Ashwin b Yadav	32	– c Dhoni b Yadav 17
M. R. Marsh b I. Sharma	11	– (7) not out 6
†B. J. Haddin c Pujara b Aaron	6	– (6) c Kohli b Yadav 1
M. G. Johnson c Dhoni b I. Sharma	88	– not out 2
M. A. Starc b Ashwin	52	
N. M. Lyon c R. G. Sharma b Aaron	23	
J. R. Hazlewood not out	32	
L-b 4, w 5, n-b 10	19	B 4, l-b 4, w 1, n-b 6 15
(1) (109.4 overs)	505	(6 wkts, 23.1 overs) 130

1/47 (2) 2/98 (3) 3/121 4/208 (5) 5/232 (6)   1/18 (2) 2/22 (3) 3/85 (1)
6/247 (7) 7/395 (8) 8/398 (4) 9/454 (10) 10/505 (9)   4/114 (5) 5/122 (4) 6/122 (6)

I. Sharma 23–2–117–3; Aaron 26–1–145–2; Yadav 25–4–101–3; Ashwin 33.4–4–128–2; R. G. Sharma 2–0–10–0. *Second innings*—I. Sharma 9–2–38–3; Yadav 9–0–46–2; Aaron 5.1–0–38–0.

Umpires: M. Erasmus *(South Africa)* (29) and I. J. Gould *(England)* (43).
Third umpire: S. D. Fry *(Australia)*.   Referee: J. J. Crowe *(New Zealand)* (69).

Close of play: first day, India 311-4 (Rahane 75, R. G. Sharma 26); second day, Australia 221-4 (Smith 65, M. R. Marsh 7); third day, India 71-1 (Dhawan 26, Pujara 15).

AUSTRALIA v INDIA 2014–15 (3rd Test)

At Melbourne Cricket Ground on 26, 27, 28, 29, 30 December, 2014.
Toss: Australia.   Result: DRAWN.
Debuts: Australia – J. A. Burns. India – K. L. Rahul.
Man of the Match: R. J. Harris.

Australia regained the Border–Gavaskar Trophy after Smith set India 384 in two sessions on a blameless pitch. He might have wished for more time when they promptly slumped to 19 for three, but rested content with the first draw at Melbourne for 17 years. Shortly afterwards, Dhoni's retirement from Test cricket was announced after a match in which he made an Indian-record nine dismissals. After Rogers and Watson shared a steady second-wicket partnership of 115, Smith became the first to score centuries in his first two Tests as Australia's captain. Having given away at least 486 for the eighth time in 2014, India began their reply under pressure, but it didn't show: the fourth-wicket pair played with authority, eventually adding 262. Kohli took 11 of his 18 fours off an increasingly disgruntled Johnson, but Rahane arguably played even better, outscoring his glamorous partner. He eventually fell to Lyon, the first of seven wickets in 21 overs as India conceded an advantage of 65, and Australia were back in charge. Midway through the fourth afternoon, they were nearly 200 ahead and only two down – but tight bowling in the last 32-over session brought three wickets and only 87 runs. Rain shortened the final day, and Smith eventually settled for the draw. Shaun Marsh looked set for a century before he pushed to Kohli at mid-off and ran – and became the third Australian to be run out for 99 in a home Test, after Bill Brown (1947–48) and Arthur Morris (1952–53).

Australia

C. J. L. Rogers c Dhoni b Mohammed Shami	57	– (2) b Ashwin	69
D. A. Warner c Dhawan b Yadav	0	– (1) lbw b Ashwin	40
S. R. Watson lbw b Ashwin	52	– c Dhoni b Sharma	17
*S. P. D. Smith b Yadav	192	– c Rahane b Yadav	14
S. E. Marsh c Dhoni b Mohammed Shami	32	– run out (Kohli)	99
J. A. Burns c Dhoni b Yadav	13	– c Dhoni b Sharma	9
†B. J. Haddin c Dhoni b Mohammed Shami	55	– c Dhoni b Yadav	13
M. G. Johnson st Dhoni b Ashwin	28	– c Rahane b Mohammed Shami	15
R. J. Harris lbw b Ashwin	74	– c Dhoni b Mohammed Shami	21
N. M. Lyon b Mohammed Shami	11	– not out	1
J. R. Hazlewood not out	0	– not out	0
B 1, l-b 9, w 1, n-b 5	16	L-b 13, w 2, n-b 5	20
(142.3 overs)	530	(9 wkts dec, 98 overs)	318

1/0 (2) 2/115 (1) 3/115 (3) 4/184 (5) 5/216 (6) 6/326 (7)   1/57 (2) 2/98 (3) 3/131 (4) 4/164 (2) 5/176 (6)
7/376 (8) 8/482 (9) 9/530 (10) 10/530 (4)   6/202 (7) 7/234 (8) 8/303 (9) 9/317 (5)

Sharma 32–7–104–0; Yadav 32.3–3–130–3; Mohammed Shami 29–4–138–4; Ashwin 44–9–134–3; Vijay 5–0–14–0. *Second innings*—Yadav 22–3–89–2; Mohammed Shami 28–4–92–2; Sharma 20–5–49–2; Ashwin 28–4–75–2.

India

M. Vijay c Marsh b Watson	68	– lbw b Hazlewood	11
S. Dhawan c Smith b Harris	28	– lbw b Harris	0
C. A. Pujara c Haddin b Harris	25	– (6) b Johnson	21
V. Kohli c Haddin b Johnson	169	– c Burns b Harris	54
A. M. Rahane lbw b Lyon	147	– c Marsh b Hazlewood	48
K. L. Rahul c Hazlewood b Lyon	3	– (3) c Watson b Johnson	1
*†M. S. Dhoni c Haddin b Harris	11	– not out	24
R. Ashwin c and b Harris	0	– not out	8
Mohammed Shami c Smith b Johnson	12		
U. T. Yadav c Haddin b Johnson	0		
I. Sharma not out	0		
L-b 1, w 1	2	L-b 6, n-b 1	7
(128.5 overs)	465	(6 wkts, 66 overs)	174

1/55 (2) 2/108 (3) 3/147 (1) 4/409 (5) 5/415 (6)   1/2 (2) 2/5 (3) 3/19 (1) 4/104 (4)
6/430 (7) 7/434 (8) 8/462 (4) 9/465 (10) 10/465 (9)   5/141 (6) 6/142 (5)

Johnson 30.5–6–135–3; Harris 26–7–70–4; Hazlewood 25–6–75–0; Watson 16–3–65–1; Lyon 29–3–108–2; Smith 2–0–11–0. *Second innings*—Johnson 15–3–38–2; Harris 16–8–30–2; Hazlewood 15–3–40–2; Lyon 12–0–36–0; Watson 6–1–14–0; Smith 2–0–10–0.

Umpires: H. D. P. K. Dharmasena *(Sri Lanka)* (28) and R. A. Kettleborough *(England)* (25).
Third umpire: J. D. Ward *(Australia).*   Referee: R. S. Mahanama *(Sri Lanka)* (55).

Close of play: first day, Australia 259–5 (Smith 72, Haddin 23); second day, India 108–1 (Vijay 55, Pujara 25); third day, India 462–8 (Mohammed Shami 9); fourth day, Australia 261–7 (Marsh 62, Harris 8).

AUSTRALIA v INDIA 2014–15 (4th Test)

At Sydney Cricket Ground on 6, 7, 8, 9, 10 January, 2015.
Toss: Australia.   Result: DRAWN.
Debuts: none.
Man of the Match: S. P. D. Smith.   Man of the Series: S. P. D. Smith.

The highest-scoring four-Test series of all ended with 5,870 runs (219 more than these sides shared in 2003-04), a fourth hundred for each captain, and only the second draw at the SCG in 20 years. Smith set a target of 349 on the last day, but any hopes of an Indian win ended when Kohli was caught at slip just after tea, the first of four wickets for 16. That included Raina, who completed a pair with his fifth duck in seven innings. The Australians were back at the ground where five of them had witnessed Phillip Hughes's fatal injury. It weighed heavily on them; when Warner reached another power-packed hundred, he gave a long look skywards. At the other end, Rogers – in his last home Test – helped him put on 200 in under 45 overs, and the score was then almost doubled by Watson and Smith, who joined South Africa's Jacques Kallis (at home to West Indies in 2003–04) in scoring a century in all four Tests of a series. It was the first time Australia's top six had all reached 50 in the same innings. Rahul enjoyed two let-offs – one when Smith was distracted by the Spidercam – and went on to a studious 110, while Kohli became the first to make hundreds in his first three innings as captain. India's last five wickets added 183, but Smith's 71 gave Australia impetus, before Burns biffed 66 in 39 balls. He added 86 with Haddin, and left Yadav with Test cricket's costliest three-over analysis.

Australia

C. J. L. Rogers b Mohammed Shami	95	– c Raina b Bhuvneshwar Kumar	56
D. A. Warner c Vijay b Ashwin	101	– c Vijay b Ashwin	4
S. R. Watson c Ashwin b Mohammed Shami	81	– b Ashwin	16
*S. P. D. Smith c Saha b Yadav	117	– lbw b Mohammed Shami	71
S. E. Marsh c Saha b Mohammed Shami	73	– c Vijay b Ashwin	1
J. A. Burns c Rahul b Mohammed Shami	58	– c Yadav b Ashwin	66
†B. J. Haddin not out	9	– not out	31
R. J. Harris c Ashwin b Mohammed Shami	25	– not out	0
L-b 6, w 7	13	B 2, l-b 2, n-b 2	6
(7 wkts dec, 152.3 overs)	572	(6 wkts dec, 40 overs)	251

1/200 (2) 2/204 (1) 3/400 (3) 4/415 (4)
5/529 (5) 6/546 (6) 7/572 (8)

1/6 (2) 2/46 (3) 3/126 (1)
4/139 (5) 5/165 (4) 6/251 (6)

M. A. Starc, N. M. Lyon and J. R. Hazlewood did not bat.

Bhuvneshwar Kumar 34–5–122–0; Yadav 27–5–137–1; Mohammed Shami 28.3–3–112–5; Ashwin 47–8–142–1; Raina 16–3–53–0. *Second innings*—Bhuvneshwar Kumar 8–0–46–1; Ashwin 19–2–105–4; Mohammed Shami 6–0–33–1; Yadav 3–0–45–0; Raina 4–0–18–0.

India

M. Vijay c Haddin b Starc	0	– c Haddin b Hazlewood	80
K. L. Rahul c and b Starc	110	– c Warner b Lyon	16
R. G. Sharma b Lyon	53	– c Smith b Watson	39
*V. Kohli c Rogers b Harris	147	– c Watson b Starc	46
A. M. Rahane lbw b Watson	13	– not out	38
S. K. Raina c Haddin b Watson	0	– lbw b Starc	0
†W. P. Saha c Smith b Hazlewood	35	– lbw b Lyon	0
R. Ashwin c Haddin b Starc	50	– lbw b Hazlewood	1
Bhuvneshwar Kumar c Watson b Lyon	30	– not out	20
Mohammed Shami not out	16		
U. T. Yadav c Haddin b Harris	4		
B 4, l-b 7, w 1, n-b 5	17	B 4, l-b 8	12
(162 overs)	475	(7 wkts, 89.5 overs)	252

1/0 (1) 2/97 (3) 3/238 (2) 4/292 (5) 5/292 (6)
6/352 (4) 7/383 (7) 8/448 (9) 9/456 (8) 10/475 (11)

1/48 (2) 2/104 (3) 3/178 (1)
4/201 (4) 5/203 (6) 6/208 (7) 7/217 (8)

Starc 32–7–106–3; Harris 31–7–96–2; Hazlewood 29–8–64–1; Lyon 46–11–123–2; Watson 20–4–58–2; Smith 4–0–17–0. *Second innings*—Starc 19–7–36–3; Harris 13–3–34–0; Lyon 30.5–5–110–2; Hazlewood 17–7–31–2; Smith 2–0–7–0; Watson 8–2–22–1.

Umpires: H. D. P. K. Dharmasena *(Sri Lanka)* (29) and R. A. Kettleborough *(England)* (26).
Third umpire: S. D. Fry *(Australia)*.   Referee: R. S. Mahanama *(Sri Lanka)* (56).

Close of play: first day, Australia 348–2 (Watson 61, Smith 82); second day, India 71–1 (Rahul 31, Sharma 40); third day, India 342–5 (Kohli 140, Saha 14); fourth day, Australia 251–6 (Haddin 31, Harris 0).

SOUTH AFRICA v WEST INDIES 2014–15 (1st Test)

At Centurion Park, Pretoria, on 17, 18, 19, 20 December, 2014.
Toss: West Indies.　　Result: SOUTH AFRICA WON BY AN INNINGS AND 220 RUNS.
Debuts: South Africa – S. van Zyl.
Man of the Match: H. M. Amla.

Dale Steyn grabbed six for 34 to seal victory with more than five sessions unused. After going wicketless in the first innings, he tried to articulate his love for Test cricket: "I want to take all ten, all 20." Ramdin had won the toss under cloudy skies, and made what might have been the bullish decision to field. But his side lost their best chance on the first evening when Roach, who had rattled Amla's off stump on 25 without dislodging a bail, went off with an ankle injury (he played no further part in the series). Roach had taken two of the three wickets that fell in 15 deliveries with the score 57. Amla took full advantage with 208, in eight hours of understated batting. South Africa rolled into the next afternoon before declaring at 552. De Villiers's 152 – his 20th Test century – shimmered with inventive flamboyance, and his stand of 308 with Amla was a national fourth-wicket record. Finally left-hander Stiaan van Zyl made a sturdy debut century, only South Africa's fifth in Tests. A thunderstorm prevented an immediate resumption after the declaration, and South Africa began the third day with neither du Plessis (virus) nor de Kock (injured ankle); after tea, Steyn and Philander also went off. Even so, West Indies were soon following on, 351 behind; Philander and Morkel had taken seven wickets between them. Two more went down before stumps, and Steyn took six of the seven to fall for 44 on the fourth morning.

South Africa

A. N. Petersen c Smith b Roach	27
D. Elgar c Samuels b Cottrell	28
F. du Plessis c Ramdin b Roach	0
*H. M. Amla c Taylor b Benn	208
A. B. de Villiers c Blackwood b Benn	152
S. van Zyl not out	101
†Q. de Kock not out	18
B 8, l-b 6, w 2, n-b 2	18
(5 wkts dec, 140.3 overs)	552

1/57 (1) 2/57 (2) 3/57 (3) 4/365 (5) 5/520 (4)

V. D. Philander, K. J. Abbott, D. W. Steyn and M. Morkel did not bat.

Taylor 26.1–5–108–0; Cottrell 28–1–124–1; Roach 15.5–4–52–2; Benn 46–7–148–2; Samuels 20–0–89–0; Brathwaite 1–0–2–0; Blackwood 3.3–0–15–0. 68th over Roach injured ankle after 5 balls, completed by Taylor.

West Indies

K. C. Brathwaite c Amla b Philander	34	– c Petersen b Morkel	20
D. S. Smith c †de Villiers b Philander	35	– c sub (T. Bavuma) b Philander	5
L. R. Johnson c sub (R. J. Peterson) b Abbott	31	– c †de Villiers b Steyn	39
M. N. Samuels b Morkel	33	– c Elgar b Steyn	17
S. Chanderpaul c Petersen b Philander	21	– c †de Villiers b Steyn	4
J. Blackwood c Petersen b Philander	12	– c sub (T. Bavuma) b Morkel	15
*†D. Ramdin c van Zyl b Elgar	14	– c †de Villiers b Steyn	4
J. E. Taylor c and b Morkel	4	– c Amla b Steyn	9
S. J. Benn not out	6	– not out	6
S. S. Cottrell b Morkel	2	– c Abbott b Steyn	4
K. A. J. Roach absent hurt		– absent hurt	
L-b 6, w 3	9	L-b 3, w 4, n-b 1	8
(60.2 overs)	201	(42.3 overs)	131

1/72 (2) 2/73 (1) 3/117 (3) 4/162 (4) 5/169 (5) 6/184 (6)　　1/8 (2) 2/52 (1) 3/87 (3) 4/91 (5) 5/101 (4)
7/193 (7) 8/193 (8) 9/201 (10)　　　　　　　　　　　　　　6/105 (7) 7/117 (6) 8/121 (8) 9/131 (10)

Steyn 14–3–53–0; Philander 15–6–29–4; Abbott 14–3–50–1; Morkel 15.2–4–55–3; Elgar 2–0–8–1. *Second innings—* Steyn 8.2–2–34–6; Morkel 11.1–1–43–2; Philander 7–4–6–1; Abbott 3–0–11–0; van Zyl 10–2–22–0; Elgar 3–0–12–0.

Umpires: Aleem Dar *(Pakistan)* (93) and B. F. Bowden *(New Zealand)* (81).
Third umpire: P. R. Reiffel *(Australia)*.　　Referee: R. S. Madugalle *(Sri Lanka)* (153).

Close of play: first day, South Africa 340–3 (Amla 133, de Villiers 141); second day, South Africa 552–5 dec; third day, West Indies 76–2 (Johnson 33, Samuels 13).

SOUTH AFRICA v WEST INDIES 2014–15 (2nd Test)

At St George's Park, Port Elizabeth, on 26, 27, 28, 29, 30 *(no play)* December, 2014.
Toss: West Indies.   Result: DRAWN.
Debuts: South Africa – T. Bavuma. West Indies – K. K. Peters.
Man of the Match: K. C. Brathwaite.

With almost three days' play lost to rain, including the whole of the fifth, it would have taken an epic meltdown, even by West Indian standards, to produce anything other than a draw. But South Africans could still rejoice in the fact that their 320th Test cap – the 85th since readmission in 1991-92 – was Temba Bavuma, only the sixth black African on the list, and the first batsman. A diminutive 24-year-old from Cape Town, he batted for an hour, making ten before edging the pacy Gabriel. Despite better bowling by West Indies, whose attack included Kenroy Peters, a wiry left-arm seamer from St Vincent playing his only Test at 32, South Africa were rarely tested before declaring at 417 for eight. Elgar and du Plessis both scored centuries in their partnership of 179. Even so, du Plessis said he found conditions a struggle. Steyn didn't seem to worry, hammering five sixes in his 28-ball 58. There were also two hundreds for the tourists – Brathwaite's third and Samuels's sixth, as they built their stand of 176, a West Indian record for any wicket in Tests in South Africa. But they were dismissed four balls apart and, an hour's play later, West Indies had slipped to 275 for nine, the last five wickets going down for 15. Three of them, including Ramdin and Chanderpaul, fell to the leg-spin of Imran Tahir, who had been whistled up late after Robin Peterson injured a finger. But the last-day washout spared West Indies further misery.

South Africa

D. Elgar c Ramdin b Peters	121
A. N. Petersen c Johnson b Gabriel	17
F. du Plessis c Ramdin b Taylor	103
*H. M. Amla lbw b Holder	33
†A. B. de Villiers b Taylor	10
T. Bavuma c Ramdin b Gabriel	10
S. van Zyl c Ramdin b Peters	29
V. D. Philander not out	13
D. W. Steyn c Holder b Benn	58
B 4, l-b 5, w 6, n-b 8	23
(8 wkts dec, 122 overs)	417

1/47 (2) 2/226 (1) 3/274 (3) 4/300 (4)
5/304 (5) 6/325 (6) 7/348 (7) 8/417 (9)

M. Morkel and Imran Tahir did not bat.

Taylor 30–7–114–2; Peters 20–7–69–2; Holder 22–7–43–1; Gabriel 21–0–80–2; Benn 28–4–102–1; Samuels 1–1–0–0.

West Indies

K. C. Brathwaite c Petersen b Morkel	106
D. S. Smith c Amla b Morkel	22
L. R. Johnson c du Plessis b Morkel	0
M. N. Samuels lbw b Philander	101
S. Chanderpaul b Imran Tahir	7
*†D. Ramdin lbw b Imran Tahir	20
J. O. Holder c de Villiers b Morkel	1
J. E. Taylor not out	10
S. J. Benn c Petersen b Imran Tahir	4
K. K. Peters run out (Steyn/de Villiers)	0
L-b 4	4
(9 wkts, 79 overs)	275

1/55 (2) 2/55 (3) 3/231 (4) 4/233 (1) 5/260 (6)
6/261 (5) 7/265 (7) 8/270 (9) 9/275 (10)

S. T. Gabriel did not bat.

Steyn 14–3–48–0; Philander 18–4–41–1; Morkel 20–2–69–4; Imran Tahir 26–2–108–3; Elgar 1–0–5–0.

Umpires: B. F. Bowden *(New Zealand)* (82) and P. R. Reiffel *(Australia)* (14).
Third umpire: Aleem Dar *(Pakistan)*.   Referee: R. S. Madugalle *(Sri Lanka)* (154).

Close of play: first day, South Africa 270–2 (du Plessis 99, Amla 17); second day, South Africa 289–3 (Amla 23, de Villiers 9); third day, West Indies 147–2 (Brathwaite 65, Samuels 60); fourth day, West Indies 275–9 (Taylor 10).

SOUTH AFRICA v WEST INDIES 2014–15 (3rd Test)

At Newlands, Cape Town, on 2, 3, 4, 5, 6 January, 2015.
Toss: West Indies.   Result: SOUTH AFRICA WON BY EIGHT WICKETS.
Debuts: South Africa – S. R. Harmer.
Man of the Match: A. B. de Villiers.   Man of the Series: H. M. Amla.

For a change, West Indies decided to bat first. For another change, they made a fist of things. For yet another, they limited South Africa to a lead of less than 100. But the Windies of change blew themselves out: South Africa won shortly before lunch on the fifth day. Johnson, Blackwood and Ramdin steadied the tourists on the opening day, but none of them reached 60. Still, taking South Africa's bowlers into the second day represented progress. One of those bowlers, off-spinner Simon Harmer, had received an unexpected call from the selectors while out shopping, and took three of the six wickets South Africa captured on the first day. The jewel in his crown was Chanderpaul, the teetering victim of a leg-side stumping. Steyn and Morkel dismissed West Indies on the second morning. De Villiers led the response with a disciplined 148, the major reason South Africa earned a lead of 92 – though 30 extras helped. For two hours on a fourth day that started at 3pm because of rain, Samuels and Chanderpaul played very responsibly – but then Samuels, who had survived a fearsome battle with Steyn, lost his head, playing the stroke of a juvenile delinquent to Harmer, and holed out for 74. The last five contributed just four runs and, when Chanderpaul was finally run out for 50, West Indies had lost seven for 33. Steyn and Harmer finished with identical match figures of seven for 153, and South Africa were left a modest target of 124.

West Indies

K. C. Brathwaite c Elgar b Steyn	7	– b Harmer	16
D. S. Smith b Harmer	47	– c de Villiers b Morkel	7
L. R. Johnson lbw b Harmer	54	– c Amla b Morkel	44
M. N. Samuels c du Plessis b van Zyl	43	– c Elgar b Harmer	74
S. Chanderpaul st de Villiers b Harmer	9	– run out (Bavuma)	50
J. Blackwood lbw b Steyn	56	– b Steyn	13
*†D. Ramdin c and b Steyn	53	– c Harmer b Steyn	0
J. O. Holder c van Zyl b Steyn	23	– c Amla b Harmer	2
J. E. Taylor c Steyn b Morkel	13	– c Elgar b Harmer	0
S. J. Benn c Bavuma b Morkel	5	– c de Villiers b Steyn	0
S. T. Gabriel not out	4	– not out	2
L-b 5, w 8, n-b 2	15	B 4, l-b 3	7
(99.5 overs)	329	(79.5 overs)	215

1/30 (1) 2/80 (2) 3/131 (3) 4/162 (4) 5/172 (5)   1/23 (2) 2/27 (1) 3/95 (3) 4/182 (4) 5/202 (6)
6/266 (7) 7/299 (6) 8/316 (8) 9/319 (9) 10/329 (10)   6/204 (7) 7/213 (8) 8/213 (9) 9/213 (10) 10/215 (5)

Steyn 25–6–78–4; Philander 19–2–73–0; Morkel 19.5–1–83–2; Harmer 26–5–71–3; van Zyl 8–2–13–1; Elgar 2–0–6–0. *Second innings*—Steyn 23.5–3–75–3; Philander 16–4–27–0; Morkel 14–7–18–2; Harmer 24–7–82–4; van Zyl 2–0–6–0.

South Africa

A. N. Petersen run out (Blackwood)	42	– (2) b Benn	0
D. Elgar lbw b Holder	8	– (1) not out	60
F. du Plessis st Ramdin b Benn	68	– c Blackwood b Benn	14
*H. M. Amla c Ramdin b Holder	63	– not out	38
†A. B. de Villiers c Gabriel b Samuels	148		
T. Bavuma b Gabriel	15		
S. van Zyl lbw b Samuels	33		
V. D. Philander run out (Holder/Benn)	0		
S. R. Harmer lbw b Taylor	10		
D. W. Steyn run out (Johnson)	0		
M. Morkel not out	4		
L-b 7, w 13, n-b 10	30	B 8, l-b 2, n-b 2	12
(122.4 overs)	421	(2 wkts, 37.4 overs)	124

1/48 (2) 2/104 (1) 3/157 (3) 4/254 (4) 5/288 (6)   1/9 (2) 2/51 (3)
6/384 (7) 7/385 (8) 8/404 (9) 9/408 (10) 10/421 (5)

Taylor 20–2–80–1; Gabriel 17–2–64–1; Holder 24–4–87–2; Samuels 16.4–0–68–2; Benn 45–9–115–1. *Second innings*—Taylor 7–3–20–0; Samuels 3.4–0–24–0; Benn 17–8–24–2; Holder 5–0–19–0; Gabriel 5–1–27–0.

Umpires: Aleem Dar *(Pakistan)* (94) and P. R. Reiffel *(Australia)* (15).
Third umpire: B. F. Bowden *(New Zealand)*.   Referee: R. S. Madugalle *(Sri Lanka)* (155).

Close of play: first day, West Indies 276–6 (Blackwood 45, Holder 5); second day, South Africa 227–3 (Amla 55, de Villiers 32); third day, West Indies 88–2 (Johnson 37, Samuels 26); fourth day, South Africa 9–1 (Elgar 5).

NEW ZEALAND v SRI LANKA 2014–15 (1st Test)

At Hagley Oval, Christchurch, on 26, 27, 28, 29 December, 2014.
Toss: Sri Lanka.   Result: NEW ZEALAND WON BY EIGHT WICKETS.
Debuts: Sri Lanka – P. H. T. Kaushal.
Man of the Match: B. B. McCullum.

On its first day of Test cricket, after succeeding earthquake-ruined Lancaster Park, leafy Hagley Park resembled a battle zone. Balls cracked off bats as if in a shooting range, and spectators ducked for cover as 429 runs cascaded. New Zealand won soon after tea on the fourth day – pedestrian, perhaps, after that rapid start. Sent in on a hard, grassy surface, they raced along at better than five an over, and peaked at 7.84 during the fifth-wicket stand of 153 between McCullum and Neesham. McCullum's first ovation came when he lofted Mathews over long-off for the first of 11 sixes; his fifty needed just 29 deliveries, and a 74-ball hundred was four quicker than his own national record, set a month earlier in Sharjah. The 55th over, bowled by Lakmal, went for 26. McCullum's luck ran out when he found long-off after making 195 off 134 balls, and extending Adam Gilchrist's record of 22 sixes in a year by 50% to 33. Sri Lanka's reply was shorter than a one-day innings: Boult and Southee, who would send down 99 overs between them in the match, were too hot to handle. Sangakkara had scored a fifty in 14 of his last 15 Tests, but now Boult dismissed him twice for a combined total of seven. Sri Lanka did knuckle down in the follow-on, surviving for 154 overs, with Karunaratne lasting more than eight hours. New Zealand were left to knock off 105 for a national-record fifth Test win in a year.

New Zealand

T. W. M. Latham c Kaushal b Eranga	27	– c Mathews b Kaushal	17
H. D. Rutherford b Lakmal	18	– c Dickwella b Eranga	10
K. S. Williamson b Prasad	54	– not out	31
L. R. P. L. Taylor run out (Silva)	7	– not out	39
*B. B. McCullum c Karunaratne b Kaushal	195		
J. D. S. Neesham c Sangakkara b Mathews	85		
†B-J. Watling lbw b Mathews	26		
M. D. Craig not out	12		
T. G. Southee c Thirimanne b Mathews	0		
N. Wagner c Kaushal b Lakmal	4		
T. A. Boult c Jayawardene b Lakmal	0		
L-b 4, w 2, n-b 7	13	L-b 6, w 2, n-b 2	10
(85.5 overs)	441	(2 wkts, 30.4 overs)	107

1/37 (2) 2/60 (1) 3/88 (4) 4/214 (3) 5/367 (5)   1/23 (1) 2/43 (2)
6/420 (6) 7/429 (7) 8/431 (9) 9/440 (10) 10/441 (11)

Lakmal 19.5–3–90–3; Eranga 18–1–82–1; Mathews 12–2–39–3; Prasad 12–2–62–1; Kaushal 22–0–159–1; Thirimanne 2–0–5–0. *Second innings*—Lakmal 6–2–16–0; Kaushal 13–0–48–1; Eranga 7–2–20–1; Prasad 4.4–1–17–0.

Sri Lanka

F. D. M. Karunaratne lbw b Boult	0	– b Boult	152
J. K. Silva lbw b Boult	4	– c Watling b Southee	33
K. C. Sangakkara c Southee b Boult	6	– c Watling b Boult	1
H. D. R. L. Thirimanne c Craig b Southee	24	– c Watling b Neesham	25
*A. D. Mathews c Latham b Wagner	50	– c Watling b Southee	66
D. P. D. N. Dickwella c McCullum b Southee	2	– c Neesham b Boult	4
†H. A. P. W. Jayawardene c Williamson b Wagner	10	– (8) c Southee b Craig	23
K. T. G. D. Prasad c McCullum b Neesham	18	– (9) c Taylor b Southee	4
P. H. T. Kaushal c Williamson b Wagner	6	– (7) c Craig b Southee	12
R. M. S. Eranga not out	10	– not out	45
R. A. S. Lakmal c McCullum b Neesham	2	– c Southee b Boult	16
L-b 3, w 2, n-b 1	6	B 4, l-b 20, w 1, n-b 1	26
(42.4 overs)	138	(154 overs)	407

1/0 (1) 2/8 (2) 3/15 (3) 4/58 (4) 5/60 (6) 6/88 (7)   1/85 (2) 2/94 (3) 3/181 (4) 4/277 (1) 5/287 (6)
7/105 (5) 8/118 (9) 9/128 (8) 10/138 (11)   6/307 (7) 7/320 (5) 8/325 (9) 9/348 (8) 10/407 (11)

Boult 11–4–25–3; Southee 12–4–17–2; Neesham 6.4–1–28–2; Wagner 11–0–60–3; Craig 2–0–5–0. *Second innings*— Boult 39–8–100–4; Southee 37–8–91–4; Wagner 30–6–76–0; Craig 38–10–83–1; Neesham 8–2–29–1; McCullum 1–0–3–0; Williamson 1–0–1–0.

Umpires: R. K. Illingworth *(England)* (14) and B. N. J. Oxenford *(Australia)* (21).
Third umpire: S. J. Davis *(Australia)*.   Referee: B. C. Broad *(England)* (66).

Close of play: first day, New Zealand 429–7 (Craig 5); second day, Sri Lanka 84–0 (Karunaratne 49, Silva 33); third day, Sri Lanka 293–5 (Mathews 53, Kaushal 5).

NEW ZEALAND v SRI LANKA 2014–15 (2nd Test)

At Basin Reserve, Wellington, on 3, 4, 5, 6, 7 January, 2015.
Toss: Sri Lanka.   Result: NEW ZEALAND WON BY 193 RUNS.
Debuts: none.
Man of the Match: K. S. Williamson.

Although the Basin is usually regarded as New Zealand's best pitch, of late it had held terrors for touring sides. An emerald-green strip barely discernible from the outfield left Sri Lanka fearing the worst, but although it did seam around on day one, it then flattened out. Mathews was relieved to bowl first, and his pacemen knocked New Zealand over for 221, the last eight falling for 80. That wasn't the end of the fun: by stumps, 15 wickets had tumbled as Sri Lanka slumped to 78 for five, three of them to the recalled Bracewell. But conditions grew easier, and Sangakkara gave a masterful display, joining Don Bradman, Wally Hammond and Brian Lara by making a fifth Test double-century away from home. Chandimal helped add 130 before Neesham removed both, Sangakkara to a stunning one-handed grab by Boult at cover. Sri Lanka took their lead to 135, then Pradeep Fernando helped reduce the hosts to 159 for five, only 24 in front. Williamson changed the momentum of an absorbing match: dropped three times, he raised his first Test double-century, while Watling made his fourth hundred. They forged an unbroken stand of 365 to erase the sixth-wicket record of Watling and McCullum against India here 11 months earlier, for which a plaque had just been unveiled; another was hastily commissioned. McCullum gave his bowlers 107 overs to wrap up a 2–0 win. After Sangakkara was controversially dismissed on review it was a quick slide, as Craig's off-breaks started biting.

New Zealand

T. W. M. Latham c Jayawardene b Lakmal	6	– c Jayawardene b Fernando		35
H. D. Rutherford c Jayawardene b Fernando	37	– c Chandimal b Fernando		40
K. S. Williamson b Prasad	69	– not out		242
L. R. P. L. Taylor b Fernando	35	– b Herath		0
*B. B. McCullum b Lakmal	0	– lbw b Prasad		22
J. D. S. Neesham c Jayawardene b Fernando	15	– lbw b Fernando		19
†B-J. Watling c Chandimal b Mathews	11	– not out		142
M. D. Craig c Mathews b Lakmal	7			
D. A. J. Bracewell b Prasad	16			
T. G. Southee c Sangakkara b Fernando	0			
T. A. Boult not out	16			
L-b 1, w 3, n-b 5	9	B 7, l-b 7, w 4, n-b 6		24
(55.1 overs)	221	(5 wkts dec, 172 overs)		524

1/31 (1) 2/62 (2) 3/141 (4) 4/142 (5) 5/162 (6)   1/75 (2) 2/78 (1) 3/79 (4)
6/181 (7) 7/182 (3) 8/194 (8) 9/195 (10) 10/221 (9)   4/122 (5) 5/159 (6)

Lakmal 17–2–71–3; Fernando 16–0–63–4; Prasad 11.1–1–50–2; Mathews 9–3–29–1; Herath 2–0–7–0. *Second innings*—Lakmal 32–4–89–0; Fernando 37–4–117–3; Herath 56–8–154–1; Prasad 28–1–102–1; Mathews 11–3–29–0; Thirimanne 8–1–19–0.

Sri Lanka

F. D. M. Karunaratne c Neesham b Boult	16	– c Rutherford b Craig		17
J. K. Silva b Bracewell	5	– c Craig b Bracewell		50
K. C. Sangakkara c Boult b Neesham	203	– (4) c Watling b Boult		5
H. D. R. L. Thirimanne c McCullum b Bracewell	0	– (5) not out		62
*A. D. Mathews c Watling b Southee	15	– (6) c Williamson b Bracewell		8
†H. A. P. W. Jayawardene c Neesham b Bracewell	6	– (7) c Williamson b Craig		10
L. D. Chandimal c Watling b Neesham	67	– (8) c Watling b Craig		13
K. T. G. D. Prasad c Watling b Neesham	11	– (3) c Neesham b Boult		6
H. M. R. K. B. Herath c Watling b Boult	15	– lbw b Craig		0
R. A. S. Lakmal st Watling b Craig	5	– run out (Bracewell/Watling)		6
A. N. P. R. Fernando not out	0	– b Southee		1
L-b 4, w 6, n-b 3	13	B 12, l-b 2, w 3, n-b 1		18
(102.1 overs)	356	(72.4 overs)		196

1/18 (1) 2/25 (2) 3/29 (4) 4/58 (5) 5/78 (6) 6/208 (7)   1/42 (1) 2/51 (3) 3/61 (4) 4/94 (2) 5/110 (6)
7/242 (8) 8/289 (9) 9/356 (3) 10/356 (10)   6/133 (7) 7/156 (8) 8/156 (9) 9/189 (10) 10/196 (11)

Boult 24–3–75–2; Southee 26–3–87–1; Bracewell 24–2–93–3; Neesham 11–0–42–3; Craig 17.1–3–55–1. *Second innings*—Boult 21–2–55–2; Southee 17.4–6–41–1; Bracewell 13–3–25–2; Craig 18–8–53–4; Rutherford 1–0–2–0; Williamson 2–0–6–0.

Umpires: S. J. Davis *(Australia)* (55) and R. K. Illingworth *(England)* (15).
Third umpire: B. N. J. Oxenford *(Australia)*.   Referee: B. C. Broad *(England)* (67).

Close of play: first day, Sri Lanka 78–5 (Sangakkara 33); second day, New Zealand 22–0 (Latham 9, Rutherford 12); third day, New Zealand 253–5 (Williamson 80, Watling 48); fourth day, Sri Lanka 45–1 (Silva 20, Prasad 1).

Test No. 2157/149 (WI504, E953)

WEST INDIES v ENGLAND 2014–15 (1st Test)

At Sir Vivian Richards Stadium, North Sound, Antigua, on 13, 14, 15, 16, 17 April, 2015.
Toss: West Indies.   Result: DRAWN.
Debuts: none.
Man of the Match: J. O. Holder.

Anderson's pair of two-wicket hauls would normally have been a footnote to a nailbiting draw. But they took him, in his 100th Test, past Ian Botham's national record. Wicket No. 384 arrived on the final afternoon when Ramdin fended to slip, ending a seventh-wicket stand of 105. It gave England renewed hope on a benign pitch – but Holder, in only his fourth Test, scored a belligerent maiden hundred to earn a draw after West Indies were left 130 overs to score 438. In their first Test for eight months – and after a disappointing group-stage exit at the World Cup – England started slowly. Trott, restored in the unaccustomed position of opener, edged the fifth ball to first slip, but Bell put on 177 with Root and 130 with Stokes; his 22nd Test century put him level with Wally Hammond, Colin Cowdrey and Geoff Boycott. West Indies' reply was dominated by Blackwood's maiden century. He rode his luck: Stokes had him caught off a no-ball when 21 and dropped at gully when 43. The next-best score was Chanderpaul's 46, and England led by 104. They started poorly again, but regained control thanks to Ballance's fourth century in nine Tests. When West Indies dipped to 155 for five at lunch on the final day an England victory looked certain – until Holder dug in. Only once before, in making 408 for five in 164.3 overs against England during a timeless Test in Jamaica in 1929-30, had West Indies batted longer to save a game.

England

*A. N. Cook b Roach	11	– c Benn b Taylor	13
I. J. L. Trott c Bravo b Taylor	0	– c Ramdin b Taylor	4
G. S. Ballance c Bravo b Holder	10	– c Blackwood b Benn	122
I. R. Bell c Ramdin b Roach	143	– run out (sub [D. Bishoo]/Ramdin)	11
J. E. Root b Taylor	83	– b Holder	59
B. A. Stokes c Holder b Taylor	79	– st Ramdin b Benn	35
J. C. Tredwell c Bravo b Holder	8		
†J. C. Buttler c Ramdin b Roach	0	– (7) not out	59
C. J. Jordan not out	21	– (8) c Bravo b Roach	13
S. C. J. Broad c Blackwood b Roach	0		
J. M. Anderson c Holder b Samuels	20		
B 7, l-b 3, w 8, n-b 6	24	B 1, l-b 6, w 5, n-b 5	17
(110.4 overs)	399	(7 wkts dec, 86 overs)	333

1/1 (2) 2/22 (1) 3/34 (3) 4/211 (5) 5/341 (4)   1/15 (2) 2/20 (1) 3/52 (4)
6/357 (6) 7/357 (7) 8/361 (8) 9/361 (10) 10/399 (11)   4/166 (5) 5/226 (6) 6/281 (3) 7/333 (8)

Taylor 20–4–90–3; Roach 29–6–94–4; Holder 25–11–69–2; Benn 26–3–85–0; Samuels 10.4–0–51–1. *Second innings*— Taylor 14–5–42–2; Roach 14–1–53–1; Holder 17–5–63–1; Benn 26–3–115–2; Samuels 15–0–53–0.

West Indies

K. C. Brathwaite c Jordan b Tredwell	39	– c Root b Broad	5
D. S. Smith c Buttler b Anderson	11	– c Ballance b Tredwell	65
D. M. Bravo c Buttler b Jordan	10	– c Jordan b Root	32
M. N. Samuels c Buttler b Broad	33	– c Tredwell b Anderson	23
S. Chanderpaul c Stokes b Tredwell	46	– lbw b Root	13
J. Blackwood not out	112	– c Buttler b Jordan	31
*†D. Ramdin c Buttler b Broad	9	– c Cook b Anderson	57
J. O. Holder c Ballance b Tredwell	16	– not out	103
K. A. J. Roach c Buttler b Jordan	5	– not out	15
J. E. Taylor run out (Broad/Buttler)	0		
S. J. Benn c Root b Anderson	2		
L-b 4, w 6, n-b 2	12	B 2, l-b 2, n-b 2	6
(113 overs)	295	(7 wkts, 129.4 overs)	350

1/19 (2) 2/42 (3) 3/89 (4) 4/99 (1) 5/192 (5)   1/7 (1) 2/90 (3) 3/119 (2)
6/227 (7) 7/276 (8) 8/292 (9) 9/292 (10) 10/295 (11)   4/127 (4) 5/155 (5) 6/189 (6) 7/294 (7)

Anderson 23–9–67–2; Broad 22–2–67–2; Jordan 23–8–46–1; Stokes 19–3–64–0; Tredwell 26–12–47–4. *Second innings*—Anderson 24.4–3–72–2; Broad 21–5–61–1; Tredwell 40–14–93–1; Jordan 18–6–48–1; Stokes 13–0–50–0; Root 13–6–22–2.

Umpires: B. F. Bowden *(New Zealand)* (83) and S. J. Davis *(Australia)* (56).
Third umpire: B. N. J. Oxenford *(Australia)*.   Referee: A. J. Pycroft *(Zimbabwe)* (34).

Close of play: first day, England 341–5 (Stokes 71, Tredwell 0); second day, West Indies 155–4 (Chanderpaul 29, Blackwood 30); third day, England 116–3 (Ballance 44, Root 32); fourth day, West Indies 98–2 (Smith 59, Samuels 2).

Test No. 2158/150 (WI505, E954)

WEST INDIES v ENGLAND 2014–15 (2nd Test)

At Queen's Park, St George's, Grenada, on 21, 22, 23, 24, 25 April, 2015.
Toss: England.   Result: ENGLAND WON BY NINE WICKETS.
Debuts: none.
Man of the Match: J. E. Root.

On an island famed for nutmeg, this Test was proceeding with a distinct lack of spice. But suddenly a slow burner exploded into life: in a manner reminiscent of the 2013 Trent Bridge Ashes Test, Anderson sewed things up almost single-handed. He was involved in all six wickets to fall on the last morning, with three for one in 23 balls, two catches and a run-out. England needed only 143; almost from nowhere, they led 1–0. Samuels had been the central character early on. Dropped by Cook at slip on 32, he made half his side's runs on a rain-shortened first day then, commenting on England's fruitless bouncers and fruity sledging, said: "Let's see what they say when I'm 150." He did reach three figures next morning, but then fell to a delighted Anderson for 103. Cue one of Broad's trademark bursts: suddenly threatening 90mph, he took three wickets in 20 balls, before a last-wicket stand lifted the total to 299. Cook and Trott put on 125, and then Root piloted his side to a decisive lead of 165. He equalled the England record of six successive scores of 50-plus, and would surely have reached his second double-century if Anderson had not carelessly run himself out. But he was soon forgiven, as West Indies lost their last eight for 83. Ballance completed 1,000 runs in only his tenth match, as England wrapped up their first win abroad for 11 Tests, stretching back to December 2012, to retain the Wisden Trophy.

West Indies

K. C. Brathwaite b Anderson	1	– c Root b Anderson	116
D. S. Smith c Buttler b Jordan	15	– b Anderson	2
D. M. Bravo c Cook b Broad	35	– c Buttler b Broad	69
M. N. Samuels c Bell b Anderson	103	– c Buttler b Anderson	37
S. Chanderpaul c Ali b Stokes	1	– c Cook b Anderson	7
J. Blackwood lbw b Jordan	26	– c Anderson b Jordan	10
*†D. Ramdin c Buttler b Broad	31	– lbw b Ali	28
J. O. Holder c Buttler b Broad	22	– run out (Anderson)	2
K. A. J. Roach c Root b Broad	1	– c Anderson b Ali	10
D. Bishoo lbw b Ali	30	– not out	15
S. T. Gabriel not out	20	– lbw b Ali	0
B 5, l-b 6, w 1, n-b 2	14	B 8, l-b 2, n-b 1	11
(104.4 overs)	299	(112 overs)	307

1/2 (1) 2/28 (2) 3/65 (3) 4/74 (5) 5/129 (6) 6/223 (4)   1/3 (2) 2/145 (3) 3/224 (1) 4/238 (5) 5/239 (4)
7/233 (7) 8/246 (8) 9/247 (9) 10/299 (10)   6/257 (6) 7/260 (8) 8/282 (9) 9/307 (7) 10/307 (11)

Anderson 24–10–47–2; Broad 24–9–61–4; Jordan 25–4–65–2; Ali 13.4–1–47–1; Stokes 17–7–66–1; Trott 1–0–2–0. *Second innings*—Anderson 22–7–43–4; Broad 21–2–71–1; Ali 24–9–51–3; Jordan 21–6–69–1; Stokes 8–0–34–0; Root 16–7–29–0.

England

*A. N. Cook b Gabriel	76	– not out	59
I. J. L. Trott c Blackwood b Bishoo	59	– b Gabriel	0
G. S. Ballance b Samuels	77	– not out	81
I. R. Bell b Gabriel	1		
J. E. Root not out	182		
M. M. Ali run out (Blackwood/Ramdin)	0		
B. A. Stokes c Blackwood b Bishoo	8		
†J. C. Buttler st Ramdin b Bishoo	13		
C. J. Jordan run out (Holder/Ramdin)	16		
S. C. J. Broad c Smith b Bishoo	0		
J. M. Anderson run out (Gabriel/Holder)	2		
B 9, l-b 2, w 1, n-b 18	30	W 1, n-b 3	4
(144.1 overs)	464	(1 wkt, 41.1 overs)	144

1/125 (2) 2/159 (1) 3/164 (4) 4/329 (3) 5/335 (6)   1/2 (2)
6/364 (7) 7/387 (8) 8/426 (9) 9/431 (10) 10/464 (11)

Roach 28–4–100–0; Gabriel 22–3–67–2; Holder 21.1–6–57–0; Bishoo 51–10–177–4; Samuels 21–4–38–1; Blackwood 1–0–14–0. *Second innings*—Roach 7–1–18–0; Gabriel 7–3–20–1; Holder 1.4–0–11–0; Samuels 12.3–1–54–0; Bishoo 8–0–32–0; Brathwaite 5–1–9–0.

Umpires: S. J. Davis *(Australia)* (57) and B. N. J. Oxenford *(Australia)* (22).
Third umpire: B. F. Bowden *(New Zealand)*.   Referee: A. J. Pycroft *(Zimbabwe)* (35).

Close of play: first day, West Indies 188–5 (Samuels 94, Ramdin 6); second day, England 74–0 (Cook 37, Trott 32); third day, England 373–6 (Root 118, Buttler 4); fourth day, West Indies 202–2 (Brathwaite 101, Samuels 22).

Test No. 2159/151 (WI506, E955)

WEST INDIES v ENGLAND 2014–15 (3rd Test)

At Kensington Oval, Bridgetown, Barbados, on 1, 2, 3 May, 2015.
Toss: England.　　Result: WEST INDIES WON BY FIVE WICKETS.
Debuts: West Indies – S. D. Hope.
Man of the Match: J. Blackwood.　　Man of the Series: J. M. Anderson.

West Indies pulled off a joyous three-day victory to share the series, the first they hadn't lost to a side other than New Zealand, Bangladesh or Zimbabwe since drawing at home with Pakistan in 2010–11. It was their first win over England in 12 attempts, since February 2009, and only their second in 29 since June 2000. England squandered a first-innings lead of 68. Cook did have something to celebrate, completing his 26th century on the first evening, 704 days, 20 Tests and 36 innings after the 25th. Batting first had seemed an advantage, yet Trott soon became the first England opener to collect three ducks in a three-match series. He confirmed his international retirement after another failure in the second innings. England's overnight 240 for seven seemed underwhelming, but it looked rather better next day: 18 wickets fell, the most on any day in 231 Tests played in the West Indies. By stumps, England had staggered to 39 for five, a precarious lead of 107. Bell completed his first pair since the 2005 Ashes finale, and England ground to a halt, losing five for 28 in 15 overs. Needing 192, West Indies struggled at first: Chanderpaul, in what turned out to be his final Test, and only 45 short of Brian Lara's West Indian record of 11,912 runs, made nought. At 87 for four, Blackwood attempted to heave Root over long-on, and misjudged the line. Unfortunately for England, so did Buttler, who fluffed the stumping. It proved the turning point.

England

*A. N. Cook c Ramdin b Samuels	105	– c Brathwaite b Gabriel	4
I. J. L. Trott c Permaul b Gabriel	0	– lbw b Taylor	9
G. S. Ballance b Holder	18	– c Bravo b Permaul	23
I. R. Bell c and b Holder	0	– lbw b Taylor	0
J. E. Root c Ramdin b Permaul	33	– c Bravo b Holder	1
M. M. Ali run out (Hope/Ramdin)	58	– b Permaul	8
B. A. Stokes c Hope b Gabriel	22	– c Chanderpaul b Permaul	32
†J. C. Buttler not out	3	– not out	35
C. J. Jordan c Ramdin b Taylor	3	– lbw b Holder	2
S. C. J. Broad b Taylor	10	– b Holder	0
J. M. Anderson b Taylor	0	– lbw b Taylor	2
L-b 1, w 1, n-b 3	5	B 4, l-b 2, n-b 1	7
(96.3 overs)	257	(42.1 overs)	123

1/0 (2) 2/38 (3) 3/38 (4) 4/91 (5) 5/189 (6)　　1/11 (2) 2/13 (1) 3/18 (4) 4/28 (5) 5/39 (6)
6/233 (7) 7/240 (1) 8/247 (9) 9/257 (10) 10/257 (11)　　6/62 (3) 7/95 (7) 8/98 (9) 9/98 (10) 10/123 (11)

Taylor 18.3–8–36–3; Gabriel 15–3–47–2; Holder 16–4–34–2; Samuels 27–5–53–1; Permaul 20–1–86–1. *Second innings*—Taylor 11.1–1–33–3; Gabriel 7–4–16–1; Holder 9–3–15–3; Permaul 11–3–43–3; Samuels 4–1–10–0.

West Indies

K. C. Brathwaite c Jordan b Anderson	0	– c Jordan b Ali	25
S. D. Hope c Cook b Anderson	5	– lbw b Jordan	9
D. M. Bravo c Jordan b Ali	9	– c Broad b Stokes	82
M. N. Samuels lbw b Anderson	9	– b Broad	20
S. Chanderpaul c Jordan b Root	25	– b Anderson	0
J. Blackwood c Ali b Anderson	85	– not out	47
*†D. Ramdin c Buttler b Broad	13	– not out	0
J. O. Holder c Buttler b Stokes	5		
V. Permaul c sub (A. Lyth) b Anderson	18		
J. E. Taylor b Anderson	15		
S. T. Gabriel not out	0		
B 4, l-b 1	5	B 5, l-b 6	11
(49.4 overs)	189	(5 wkts, 62.4 overs)	194

1/0 (1) 2/5 (2) 3/21 (4) 4/37 (3) 5/82 (5) 6/107 (7)　　1/35 (2) 2/35 (1) 3/70 (4)
7/124 (8) 8/162 (9) 9/178 (10) 10/189 (6)　　4/80 (5) 5/188 (3)

Anderson 12.4–5–42–6; Broad 10–3–31–1; Ali 10–2–56–1; Root 9–1–34–1; Jordan 6–3–4–0; Stokes 2–0–17–1. *Second innings*—Anderson 13–4–35–1; Broad 13–5–29–1; Jordan 11–5–24–1; Ali 12.4–1–54–1; Root 8–4–16–0; Stokes 5–0–25–1.

Umpires: B. F. Bowden *(New Zealand)* (84) and B. N. J. Oxenford *(Australia)* (23).
Third umpire: S. J. Davis *(Australia)*.　　Referee: A. J. Pycroft *(Zimbabwe)* (36).

Close of play: first day, England 240–7 (Buttler 0); second day, England 39–5 (Ballance 12, Stokes 0).

BANGLADESH v PAKISTAN 2014–15 (1st Test)

At Sheikh Abu Naser Stadium, Khulna, on 28, 29, 30 April, 1, 2 May, 2015.
Toss: Bangladesh.   Result: DRAWN.
Debuts: Bangladesh – Mohammad Shahid, Soumya Sarkar. Pakistan – Sami Aslam.
Man of the Match: Tamim Iqbal.

This match started three days after a devastating earthquake in nearby Nepal, which caused 9,000 deaths. Despite being 400 miles from the epicentre, the teams felt aftershocks while practising the following day. When play started, Pakistan restricted Bangladesh on a docile pitch, then ran up a big lead. Mohammad Hafeez converted his eighth Test century into his first double, five months after making 197 against New Zealand; he put on 227 with Azhar Ali, then Asad Shafiq and Sarfraz Ahmed added 126 for the sixth wicket. The loss of the last five for 34 on the fourth morning kept the lead under 300 – just. The last of slow left-armer Taijul Islam's six expensive wickets was a stumping by Mahmudullah, keeping as Mushfiqur Rahim had injured a finger, and Imrul Kayes, his original stand-in, needed a rest. Seasoned Bangladesh-watchers feared a collapse in the face of a deficit of 296 with five sessions to survive, but they could hardly have been more wrong. Tamim Iqbal and Imrul scorched past their own national first-wicket record (224 against Zimbabwe at Chittagong in November 2014). They eventually put on 312, a Bangladesh record for any wicket, and the highest opening partnership in any Test team's second innings, beating 290 by England's Colin Cowdrey and Geoff Pullar against South Africa at The Oval in 1960. Zulfiqar Babar finally removed Imrul for a career-best 150, but Tamim sailed on to 206, with seven sixes, and eclipsed Mushfiqur's 200 at Galle in 2012-13 as Bangladesh's highest Test score.

Bangladesh

Tamim Iqbal c Azhar Ali b Yasir Shah	25	– st Sarfraz Ahmed b Mohammad Hafeez	206
Imrul Kayes c and b Mohammad Hafeez	51	– c sub (Babar Azam) b Zulfiqar Babar	150
Mominul Haque lbw b Zulfiqar Babar	80	– b Junaid Khan	21
Mahmudullah c Sarfraz Ahmed b Wahab Riaz	49	– lbw b Junaid Khan	40
Shakib Al Hasan c Asad Shafiq b Zulfiqar Babar	25	– not out	76
*†Mushfiqur Rahim c Misbah-ul-Haq b Yasir Shah	32	– lbw b Mohammad Hafeez	0
Soumya Sarkar c Asad Shafiq b Mohammad Hafeez	33	– c Mohammad Hafeez b Asad Shafiq	33
Shuvagata Hom not out	12	– not out	20
Taijul Islam b Yasir Shah	1		
Mohammad Shahid c Misbah-ul-Haq b Wahab Riaz	10		
Rubel Hossain c Sarfraz Ahmed b Wahab Riaz	2		
L-b 5, n-b 7	12	L-b 4, w 2, n-b 3	9
(120 overs)	332	(6 wkts, 136 overs)	555

1/52 (1) 2/92 (2) 3/187 (4) 4/236 (3) 5/243 (5)   1/312 (2) 2/345 (3) 3/399 (1)
6/305 (7) 7/310 (6) 8/312 (9) 9/329 (10) 10/332 (11)   4/463 (4) 5/464 (6) 6/524 (7)

Junaid Khan 16–2–40–0; Wahab Riaz 26–7–55–3; Mohammad Hafeez 18–5–47–2; Zulfiqar Babar 32–3–99–2; Yasir Shah 28–4–86–3. *Second innings*—Junaid Khan 21–5–88–2; Zulfiqar Babar 32–1–125–1; Mohammad Hafeez 20–0–82–2; Wahab Riaz 20–3–75–0; Yasir Shah 30–2–123–0; Azhar Ali 6–1–26–0; Asad Shafiq 7–0–32–1.

Pakistan

Mohammad Hafeez c Mahmudullah b Shuvagata Hom	224
Sami Aslam c Mushfiqur Rahim b Taijul Islam	20
Azhar Ali b Shuvagata Hom	83
Younis Khan b Taijul Islam	33
*Misbah-ul-Haq c Rubel Hossain b Taijul Islam	59
Asad Shafiq c and b Shakib Al Hasan	83
†Sarfraz Ahmed c sub (Liton Das) b Mohammad Shahid	82
Wahab Riaz b Taijul Islam	0
Yasir Shah lbw b Taijul Islam	13
Zulfiqar Babar st †Mahmudullah b Taijul Islam	11
Junaid Khan not out	0
B 5, l-b 8, w 3, n-b 4	20
(168.4 overs)	628

1/50 (2) 2/277 (3) 3/339 (4) 4/402 (1) 5/468 (5)
6/594 (7) 7/595 (8) 8/617 (6) 9/617 (9) 10/628 (10)

Rubel Hossain 22–3–82–0; Mohammad Shahid 19–4–59–1; Taijul Islam 46.4–4–163–6; Shuvagata Hom 34–1–120–2; Shakib Al Hasan 37–4–146–1; Mahmudullah 4–0–30–0; Soumya Sarkar 1–0–2–0; Mominul Haque 5–0–13–0.

Umpires: N. J. Llong *(England)* (27) and R. E. J. Martinesz *(Sri Lanka)* (7).
Third umpire: P. R. Reiffel *(Australia)*.   Referee: J. J. Crowe *(New Zealand)* (70).

Close of play: first day, Bangladesh 236–4 (Shakib Al Hasan 19); second day, Pakistan 227–1 (Mohammad Hafeez 137, Azhar Ali 65); third day, Pakistan 537–5 (Asad Shafiq 51, Sarfraz Ahmed 51); fourth day, Bangladesh 273–0 (Tamim Iqbal 138, Imrul Kayes 132).

BANGLADESH v PAKISTAN 2014-15 (2nd Test)

At Shere Bangla National Stadium, Mirpur, Dhaka, on 6, 7, 8, 9 May, 2015.
Toss: Bangladesh. Result: PAKISTAN WON BY 328 RUNS.
Debuts: none.
Man of the Match: Azhar Ali. Man of the Series: Azhar Ali.

Normal service was resumed after the defiance of Khulna, with Pakistan easing to their ninth victory in ten Tests against Bangladesh, whose decision to choose only two seamers looked suspect when Mushfiqur Rahim opted to bowl – and even more so when Shahadat Hossain limped off after tripping while delivering the first ball. Azhar Ali made hay against the lopsided attack, extending his eighth Test century to his first double, and putting on 250 with Younis Khan, who reached his 29th Test hundred. Both survived being caught off what replays showed were no-balls. Azhar, who also added 207 with Asad Shafiq, batted for 562 minutes and faced 428 balls. Misbah-ul-Haq eventually declared at tea on the second day, and watched his own bowlers make the most of the pitch. Junaid Khan removed Tamim Iqbal fourth ball and, after Imrul Kayes cracked four boundaries in an over, had Mominul Haque caught behind. Yasir Shah's third delivery knocked back Imrul's leg stump. It was a surprise when Misbah waived the follow-on, despite a lead of 354; he led the way himself with 82 from 72 deliveries before finally declaring. Bangladesh were left to score 550 in more than two days, but there was no repeat of the openers' Khulna heroics. Tamim, having become the second Bangladeshi, after Habibul Bashar, to pass 3,000 Test runs, departed quickly on the fourth morning. He swished at Imran Khan, who had earlier become the first man not to face a single ball in his first four Tests.

Pakistan

Mohammad Hafeez c Mushfiqur Rahim b Mohammad Shahid	8	– c Mushfiqur Rahim b Mohammad Shahid	0
Sami Aslam c Shahadat Hossain b Taijul Islam	19	– c Mahmudullah b Mohammad Shahid	8
Azhar Ali c Mahmudullah b Shuvagata Hom	226	– c Shuvagata Hom b Soumya Sarkar	25
Younis Khan c Shuvagata Hom b Mohammad Shahid	148	– c and b Taijul Islam	39
*Misbah-ul-Haq b Shakib Al Hasan	9	– c sub (Abul Hasan) b Mahmudullah	82
Asad Shafiq c Mahmudullah b Shuvagata Hom	107	– b Shuvagata Hom	15
†Sarfraz Ahmed not out	21	– not out	18
Wahab Riaz c Imrul Kayes b Taijul Islam	4		
Yasir Shah lbw b Taijul Islam	0		
L-b 8, w 2, n-b 5	15	L-b 2, w 6	8
(8 wkts dec, 152 overs)	557	(6 wkts dec, 41.1 overs)	195

1/9 (1) 2/58 (2) 3/308 (4) 4/323 (5)
5/530 (3) 6/545 (6) 7/552 (8) 8/557 (9)

1/0 (1) 2/25 (2) 3/49 (3)
4/107 (4) 5/140 (6) 6/195 (5)

Junaid Khan and Imran Khan, sen. did not bat.

Shahadat Hossain 0.2–0–4–0; Soumya Sarkar 17.4–1–57–0; Mohammad Shahid 31–10–72–2; Taijul Islam 51–3–179–3; Shuvagata Hom 16–0–76–2; Shakib Al Hasan 30–3–136–1; Mominul Haque 3–0–12–0; Mahmudullah 2–0–12–0; Imrul Kayes 1–0–1–0. *Second innings*—Mohammad Shahid 10–4–23–2; Taijul Islam 10–0–56–1; Soumya Sarkar 9–0–45–1; Shakib Al Hasan 8–0–43–0; Shuvagata Hom 2–0–18–1; Mahmudullah 2.1–0–8–1.

Bangladesh

Tamim Iqbal lbw b Junaid Khan	4	– c Sarfraz Ahmed b Imran Khan	42
Imrul Kayes b Yasir Shah	32	– b Yasir Shah	16
Mominul Haque c Sarfraz Ahmed b Junaid Khan	13	– c Asad Shafiq b Yasir Shah	68
Mahmudullah c Azhar Ali b Wahab Riaz	28	– c Younis Khan b Imran Khan	2
Shakib Al Hasan not out	89	– c Wahab Riaz b Mohammad Hafeez	13
*†Mushfiqur Rahim b Yasir Shah	12	– b Yasir Shah	0
Soumya Sarkar c Azhar Ali b Wahab Riaz	3	– c Sarfraz Ahmed b Wahab Riaz	1
Shuvagata Hom c Asad Shafiq b Wahab Riaz	0	– b Junaid Khan	39
Taijul Islam b Mohammad Hafeez	15	– c Sami Aslam b Yasir Shah	10
Mohammad Shahid c Azhar Ali b Yasir Shah	1	– not out	14
Shahadat Hossain absent hurt		– absent hurt	
L-b 2, w 2, n-b 2	6	B 4, l-b 4, n-b 8	16
(47.3 overs)	203	(56.5 overs)	221

1/4 (1) 2/38 (3) 3/69 (2) 4/85 (4) 5/107 (6)
6/113 (7) 7/119 (8) 8/140 (9) 9/203 (10)

1/48 (2) 2/86 (1) 3/95 (4) 4/121 (5) 5/126 (6)
6/139 (7) 7/143 (3) 8/177 (9) 9/221 (8)

Junaid Khan 6–2–26–2; Imran Khan 7–0–31–0; Wahab Riaz 15–2–73–3; Yasir Shah 15.3–4–58–3; Mohammad Hafeez 4–1–13–1. *Second innings*—Junaid Khan 10.5–1–45–1; Imran Khan 11–1–56–2; Yasir Shah 21–3–73–4; Wahab Riaz 11–1–36–1; Mohammad Hafeez 3–0–3–1.

Umpires: N. J. Llong *(England)* (28) and P. R. Reiffel *(Australia)* (16).
Third umpire: R. E. J. Martinesz *(Sri Lanka)*. Referee: J. J. Crowe *(New Zealand)* (71).

Close of play: first day, Pakistan 323–3 (Azhar Ali 127, Misbah-ul-Haq 9); second day, Bangladesh 107–5 (Shakib Al Hasan 14); third day, Bangladesh 63–1 (Tamim Iqbal 32, Mominul Haque 15).

Test No. 2162/100 (E956, NZ400)

ENGLAND v NEW ZEALAND 2015 (1st Test)

At Lord's, London, on 21, 22, 23, 24, 25 May, 2015.
Toss: New Zealand.   Result: ENGLAND WON BY 124 RUNS.
Debuts: England – A. Lyth, M. A. Wood. New Zealand – M. J. Henry.
Man of the Match: B. A. Stokes.

A classic match – the 100th between England and New Zealand – was enjoyed by large crowds, including 21,052 on the final day. In the 17 days since defeat in Barbados – England's shortest gap between home and away Tests – the ECB's new director of cricket, Andrew Strauss, had sacked coach Peter Moores and batsman Kevin Pietersen. When England dipped to 30 for four, you could sense KP's cheerleaders flexing their Twitter fingers. But Root and Stokes piled on 161, Buttler kept the momentum going, and Ali chipped in. New Zealand's openers replied with 148, although Guptill was caught at slip when 24 – but replays showed a marginal no-ball. Wood had to wait nearly a day for his first Test wicket. Williamson and Watling put on 189. New Zealand's 523 included 67 extras, the most in any Test innings in England; only nine higher totals had led to defeat. Trailing by 134, England stuttered again, but Cook – with his 27th Test century – and Root took them in front. Stokes stormed to the fastest hundred in a Lord's Test, from 85 balls, beating Mohammad Azharuddin's 1990 cameo by two. New Zealand needed 345 in 77 overs, but both openers departed for ducks, then Stokes removed Williamson and McCullum with successive deliveries. At tea (168 for five) a draw seemed the likeliest result, but England chipped away and, with 9.3 overs left, Boult uppercut Broad to third man. The match produced 1,610 runs, the most for a time-limited Test in which 40 wickets fell, beating 1,553 between England and Pakistan at Headingley in 2006.

England

A. Lyth c Watling b Southee	7	– c Southee b Boult	12
*A. N. Cook c Watling b Henry	16	– c †Latham b Boult	162
G. S. Ballance c Southee b Boult	1	– b Southee	0
I. R. Bell b Henry	1	– c †Latham b Southee	29
J. E. Root †Latham b Henry	98	– c Boult b Henry	84
B. A. Stokes b Craig	92	– c Taylor b Craig	101
†J. C. Buttler lbw b Boult	67	– c †Latham b Henry	14
M. M. Ali c †Latham b Boult	58	– lbw b Boult	43
S. C. J. Broad c †Latham b Boult	3	– b Boult	10
M. A. Wood not out	8	– not out	4
J. M. Anderson c and b Henry	11	– b Boult	0
B 16, l-b 6, w 2, n-b 3	27	B 2, l-b 12, w 5	19
(100.5 overs)	389	(129 overs)	478

1/17 (1) 2/25 (3) 3/25 (2) 4/30 (4) 5/191 (6)
6/251 (5) 7/354 (7) 8/363 (8) 9/368 (9) 10/389 (11)

1/14 (1) 2/25 (3) 3/74 (4) 4/232 (5) 5/364 (6)
6/389 (7) 7/455 (2) 8/467 (9) 9/478 (8) 10/478 (11)

Boult 29–6–79–4; Southee 24–1–104–1; Henry 24.5–3–93–4; Craig 18–2–77–1; Anderson 5–1–14–0. *Second innings*—Boult 34–8–85–5; Southee 34–4–162–2; Henry 29–3–106–2; Craig 28–3–96–1; Anderson 3–0–13–0; Williamson 1–0–2–0.

New Zealand

M. J. Guptill c Ballance b Broad	70	– c Ballance b Anderson	0
T. W. M. Latham lbw b Ali	59	– lbw b Broad	0
K. S. Williamson c Ballance b Ali	132	– c Root b Stokes	27
L. R. P. L. Taylor c Buttler b Broad	62	– lbw b Broad	8
*B. B. McCullum c Root b Wood	42	– (6) b Stokes	0
C. J. Anderson c Buttler b Wood	9	– (7) lbw b Root	67
†B-J. Watling not out	61	– (5) c Buttler b Wood	59
M. D. Craig lbw b Ali	0	– b Stokes	4
T. G. Southee c Wood b Anderson	11	– c and b Ali	20
M. J. Henry c Root b Wood	10	– not out	10
T. A. Boult c Anderson b Broad	0	– c Ali b Broad	10
B 26, l-b 34, w 6, n-b 1	67	B 5, l-b 7, w 2, n-b 1	15
(131.2 overs)	523	(67.3 overs)	220

1/148 (2) 2/148 (1) 3/337 (4) 4/403 (5) 5/420 (6) 6/470 (3)
7/470 (8) 8/493 (9) 9/515 (10) 10/523 (11)

1/0 (1) 2/0 (2) 3/12 (4) 4/61 (3) 5/61 (6) 6/168 (5)
7/174 (7) 8/198 (8) 9/198 (9) 10/220 (11)

Anderson 29–7–88–1; Broad 26.2–4–77–3; Wood 27–2–93–3; Stokes 21–2–105–0; Ali 26–4–94–3; Root 2–0–6–0. *Second innings*—Anderson 14–5–31–1; Broad 16.3–3–50–3; Wood 13–3–47–1; Stokes 11–3–38–3; Ali 8–3–35–1; Root 5–3–7–1.

Umpires: M. Erasmus *(South Africa)* (30) and S. Ravi *(India)* (5).
Third umpire: R. J. Tucker *(Australia)*.   Referee: D. C. Boon *(Australia)* (25).

Close of play: first day, England 354–7 (Ali 49); second day, New Zealand 303–2 (Williamson 92, Taylor 47); third day, England 74–2 (Cook 32, Bell 29); fourth day, England 429–6 (Cook 153, Ali 19).

ENGLAND v NEW ZEALAND 2015 (2nd Test)

At Headingley, Leeds, on 29, 30, 31 May, 1, 2 June, 2015.
Toss: England.   Result: NEW ZEALAND WON BY 199 RUNS.
Debuts: New Zealand – L. Ronchi.
Man of the Match: B-J. Watling.   Men of the Series: A. N. Cook and T. A. Boult.

New Zealand halved the series with their fifth and most emphatic win in England, going flat-out throughout; their run-rate of 4.93 was the quickest in any Test by a side receiving 150 overs. And they did so after losing two quick wickets in both innings, attacking almost incessantly. But not all McCullum's tactics were so revolutionary. His seamers swung the ball on a good length, and the catching was superb. Guptill soon became Anderson's 400th Test wicket, but eighties from Latham and Ronchi – making his Test debut at 34 after 64 white-ball internationals, seven of them for Australia – lifted New Zealand towards 350. Broad's five-for was the least economical in Tests by run-rate. England exactly matched that – only the eighth such instance in Tests – thanks to a maiden century from local boy Lyth, although they would have expected more after an opening stand of 177. Cook, when 29, passed Graham Gooch's national-record haul of 8,900 runs; for the first time since Jack Hobbs and Sydney Barnes in 1913–14, England had both their leading run-scorer and wicket-taker in the same side. New Zealand had often struggled in the third innings, but now hurtled to 454, which included 120 from the normally sedate Watling. When McCullum finally declared, eight different batsmen had hit sixes, another record. Rain set in soon after lunch on the fourth day, but England couldn't survive the fifth, with Williamson's part-time off-spin breaking three important partnerships. Just before 5pm, England lost their fourth Test out of six at Headingley.

New Zealand

M. J. Guptill c Bell b Anderson	0	– (2) c Root b Wood	70
T. W. M. Latham c Root b Broad	84	– (1) c Buttler b Broad	3
K. S. Williamson c Buttler b Anderson	0	– c Buttler b Broad	6
L. R. P. L. Taylor lbw b Broad	20	– c Stokes b Wood	48
*B. B. McCullum c Wood b Stokes	41	– lbw b Wood	55
B-J. Watling b Wood	14	– c Root b Anderson	120
†L. Ronchi c Anderson b Broad	88	– c Buttler b Anderson	31
M. D. Craig not out	41	– not out	58
T. G. Southee c Lyth b Wood	1	– c Anderson b Ali	40
M. J. Henry c Buttler b Broad	27	– not out	12
T. A. Boult c Lyth b Broad	15		
B 4, l-b 14, n-b 1	19	B 4, l-b 6, w 1	11
(72.1 overs)	350	(8 wkts dec, 91 overs)	454

1/2 (1) 2/2 (3) 3/68 (4) 4/123 (5) 5/144 (6) 6/264 (2)   1/15 (1) 2/23 (3) 3/122 (4) 4/141 (2) 5/262 (5)
7/265 (7) 8/281 (9) 9/310 (10) 10/350 (11)   6/315 (7) 7/368 (6) 8/435 (9)

Anderson 13–3–43–2; Broad 17.1–0–109–5; Wood 14–4–62–2; Stokes 17–4–70–1; Ali 11–3–48–0. *Second innings*—Anderson 23–4–96–2; Broad 16–1–94–2; Wood 19–2–97–3; Stokes 12–1–61–0; Ali 16–0–73–1; Root 5–0–23–0.

England

A. Lyth run out (Boult/Ronchi)	107	– c Ronchi b Boult	24
*A. N. Cook lbw b Craig	75	– lbw b Williamson	56
G. S. Ballance b Boult	29	– b Boult	6
I. R. Bell c Craig b Southee	12	– c Williamson b Craig	1
J. E. Root c Ronchi b Southee	1	– c Latham b Craig	0
B. A. Stokes c Craig b Boult	6	– c Ronchi b Williamson	29
†J. C. Buttler c Taylor b Southee	10	– lbw b Craig	73
M. M. Ali c Guptill b Southee	1	– b Henry	2
S. C. J. Broad b Henry	46	– b Williamson	23
M. A. Wood c Ronchi b Craig	19	– c Craig b Southee	17
J. M. Anderson not out	10	– not out	8
B 19, l-b 5, w 5, n-b 5	34	B 12, l-b 2, w 2	16
(108.2 overs)	350	(91.5 overs)	255

1/177 (2) 2/215 (1) 3/238 (3) 4/239 (5) 5/247 (6) 6/257 (4)   1/47 (1) 2/61 (3) 3/62 (4) 4/62 (5) 5/102 (6)
7/266 (7) 8/267 (8) 9/318 (10) 10/350 (9)   6/141 (2) 7/153 (8) 8/188 (9) 9/230 (10) 10/255 (7)

Boult 30–7–98–2; Southee 30–5–83–4; Henry 20.2–4–92–1; Craig 26–12–48–2; Williamson 2–1–5–0. *Second innings*—Boult 23–4–61–2; Southee 18–7–43–1; Craig 31.5–12–73–3; Henry 12–2–49–1; Williamson 7–1–15–3.

Umpires: S. Ravi *(India)* (6) and R. J. Tucker *(Australia)* (36).
Third umpire: M. Erasmus *(South Africa)*.   Referee: D. C. Boon *(Australia)* (26).

Close of play: first day, New Zealand 297–8 (Craig 16, Henry 14); second day, England 253–5 (Bell 12, Buttler 6); third day, New Zealand 338–6 (Watling 100, Craig 15); fourth day, England 44–0 (Lyth 24, Cook 18).

Test No. 2164/112 (WI507, A774)

WEST INDIES v AUSTRALIA 2015 (1st Test)

At Windsor Park, Roseau, Dominica, on 3, 4, 5 June, 2015.
Toss: West Indies.   Result: AUSTRALIA WON BY NINE WICKETS.
Debuts: West Indies – S. O. Dowrich. Australia – A. C. Voges.
Man of the Match: A. C. Voges.

For a time on the second day it appeared as though West Indies would make it difficult for Australia to win, and perhaps even emerge as winners themselves. Bishoo's sharp spin, which brought him the best Test figures by a West Indies leg-spinner, had confounded several: Smith was stumped, and a statuesque Haddin bowled by one that pitched outside leg before screwing back to hit off, which made it 126 for six. But Adam Voges produced an innings of rare quality, and found willing allies down the order, notably last man Hazlewood, who joined him when he had 77. He completed an unbeaten 130 to become, at 35 years and 243 days, the oldest Test-debut centurion, beating Zimbabwe's Dave Houghton (also 35, in 1992–93). Voges ensured that Australia made the most of blowing West Indies away in the first two sessions for 148, largely a combination of sharp fielding and poor batting. No one reached 40: the ballast often provided by Shivnarine Chanderpaul over his 164-Test career was badly missed (he had been jettisoned after the preceding England series). Facing an unexpected deficit of 170, West Indies were soon in trouble at 37 for three. A determined stand of 144 between Samuels and the game's other debutant, Shane Dowrich, raised hopes – but their dismissals signalled the start of a familiar slide; six men fell in single figures. Australia were able to dash off their target of 47 before the light worsened, and had retained the Frank Worrell Trophy inside three days.

West Indies

K. C. Brathwaite c Haddin b Hazlewood	10	– b Starc	15
S. D. Hope c Marsh b Johnson	36	– c Clarke b Johnson	2
D. M. Bravo c Clarke b Lyon	19	– c Warner b Hazlewood	5
S. O. Dowrich b Hazlewood	15	– c Watson b Hazlewood	70
M. N. Samuels c Hazlewood b Starc	7	– c Starc b Johnson	74
J. Blackwood c Clarke b Hazlewood	2	– st Haddin b Lyon	12
*†D. Ramdin b Johnson	19	– b Lyon	3
J. O. Holder c Marsh b Starc	21	– not out	12
J. E. Taylor c Voges b Smith	6	– lbw b Starc	0
D. Bishoo not out	9	– b Starc	1
S. T. Gabriel c Clarke b Johnson	2	– b Starc	0
W 1, n-b 1	2	B 11, l-b 10, w 1	22
(53.5 overs)	148	(86 overs)	216

1/23 (1) 2/63 (3) 3/75 (2) 4/85 (4) 5/87 (6)   1/21 (2) 2/21 (1) 3/37 (3) 4/181 (4) 5/198 (6)
6/91 (5) 7/121 (7) 8/133 (8) 9/144 (9) 10/148 (11)   6/198 (5) 7/206 (7) 8/206 (9) 9/216 (10) 10/216 (11)

Johnson 13.5–2–34–3; Hazlewood 15–7–33–3; Starc 15–5–48–2; Lyon 6–1–20–1; Watson 3–1–11–0; Smith 1–0–2–1. *Second innings*—Johnson 15–3–38–2; Starc 18–7–28–4; Hazlewood 16–7–17–2; Lyon 24–7–67–2; Smith 2–0–16–0; Watson 7–3–6–0; Voges 2–0–15–0; Clarke 2–0–8–0.

Australia

D. A. Warner c Blackwood b Taylor	8	– (2) c Bravo b Taylor	28
S. E. Marsh c Bravo b Holder	19	– (1) not out	13
S. P. D. Smith st Ramdin b Bishoo	25	– not out	5
*M. J. Clarke c Ramdin b Bishoo	18		
A. C. Voges not out	130		
S. R. Watson c Holder b Bishoo	11		
†B. J. Haddin b Bishoo	8		
M. G. Johnson c Samuels b Bishoo	20		
M. A. Starc b Bishoo	0		
N. M. Lyon lbw b Gabriel	22		
J. R. Hazlewood b Samuels	39		
B 9, l-b 3, w 1, n-b 5	18	N-b 1	1
(107 overs)	318	(1 wkt, 5 overs)	47

1/13 (1) 2/38 (2) 3/61 (4) 4/97 (3) 5/112 (6)   1/42 (2)
6/126 (7) 7/178 (8) 8/178 (9) 9/221 (10) 10/318 (11)

Taylor 20–0–72–1; Gabriel 15–3–38–1; Holder 14–3–30–1; Bishoo 33–10–80–6; Samuels 22–2–71–1; Blackwood 3–0–15–0. *Second innings*—Taylor 3–0–22–1; Gabriel 2–0–25–0.

Umpires: Aleem Dar *(Pakistan)* (95) and R. A. Kettleborough *(England)* (27).
Third umpire: I. J. Gould *(England)*.   Referee: R. S. Mahanama *(Sri Lanka)* (57).

Close of play: first day, Australia 85–3 (Smith 17, Voges 20); second day, West Indies 25–2 (Bravo 3, Dowrich 1).

Test No. 2165/113 (WI508, A775)

WEST INDIES v AUSTRALIA 2015 (2nd Test)

At Sabina Park, Kingston, Jamaica, on 11, 12, 13, 14 June, 2015.
Toss: West Indies.   Result: AUSTRALIA WON BY 277 RUNS.
Debuts: West Indies – R. Chandrika.
Man of the Match: S. P. D. Smith.   Man of the Series: J. R. Hazlewood.

Australia swept the series against a lacklustre West Indian side without Bishoo, Gabriel and Samuels through injury. The pitch had pace and bounce, and Taylor's opening spell of 5–5–0–2 took full advantage. But he did not bowl again until the penultimate over of the session, another maiden; in between, Smith and Clarke established a bridgehead. Clarke was sketchy – Roach held a return catch when he had three, only to be no-balled – but he got the scoreboard going. No one else reached 50, but useful stands down the order took the total close to 400. Taylor, who finished with career-best figures, yorked Smith one short of a maiden double-century; for the second time in four matches, he was out in the 190s. It was his fifth hundred in six Tests, the first from No. 3. The worrying state of Caribbean batsmanship was illustrated when Guyana's Rajendra Chandrika, with a first-class average of 25 and no hundreds, walked out to face Starc – and walked back inside three overs. Lyon removed Brathwaite to surpass Hugh Trumble (141 wickets) as Australia's most prolific off-spinner. Holder's defiance avoided a follow-on Clarke would have been unlikely to enforce anyway. Eventually he set West Indies 392 in more than two days: they lasted only 42 overs. Chandrika's pair was the first by a West Indian debutant since Alf Valentine in 1950, and only the fourth for any opener in his maiden Test, after New Zealand's Ken Rutherford, Saeed Anwar of Pakistan and Zimbabwe's Dirk Viljoen.

Australia

D. A. Warner c Hope b Taylor	0	– (2) c Ramdin b Roach	62
S. E. Marsh lbw b Taylor	11	– (1) c Holder b Permaul	69
S. P. D. Smith lbw b Taylor	199	– not out	54
*M. J. Clarke c Ramdin b Holder	47	– not out	14
A. C. Voges c Ramdin b Taylor	37		
S. R. Watson b Taylor	25		
†B. J. Haddin b Taylor	22		
M. G. Johnson c Bravo b Roach	5		
M. A. Starc b Holder	6		
J. R. Hazlewood c Blackwood b Permaul	24		
N. M. Lyon not out	5		
B 5, l-b 7, n-b 6	18	B 9, l-b 4	13
(126.5 overs)	399	(2 wkts dec, 65 overs)	212

1/0 (1) 2/16 (2) 3/134 (4) 4/210 (5) 5/264 (6)   1/117 (2) 2/163 (1)
6/296 (7) 7/306 (8) 8/330 (9) 9/393 (3) 10/399 (10)

Taylor 25–10–47–6; Roach 25–2–113–1; Holder 22–3–64–2; Permaul 34.5–7–124–1; Brathwaite 19–2–39–0; Blackwood 1–1–0–0. *Second innings*—Taylor 10–2–24–0; Roach 9–2–26–1; Permaul 21–3–83–1; Holder 10–2–24–0; Brathwaite 11–3–23–0; Blackwood 4–1–19–0.

West Indies

K. C. Brathwaite b Lyon	4	– b Starc	0
R. Chandrika c Haddin b Starc	0	– c Marsh b Starc	0
D. M. Bravo lbw b Lyon	14	– c Marsh b Hazlewood	11
S. O. Dowrich c Haddin b Hazlewood	13	– b Starc	4
S. D. Hope c Haddin b Lyon	26	– b Johnson	16
J. Blackwood c Warner b Hazlewood	51	– b Hazlewood	0
*†D. Ramdin lbw b Hazlewood	8	– c Clarke b Johnson	29
J. O. Holder not out	82	– c Starc b Watson	1
V. Permaul c Haddin b Johnson	0	– not out	23
K. A. J. Roach c Haddin b Hazlewood	7	– c Smith b Lyon	3
J. E. Taylor lbw b Hazlewood	0	– b Lyon	0
B 6, l-b 2, w 1, n-b 1, p 5	15	B 13, l-b 11, w 2, n-b 1	27
(59.5 overs)	220	(42 overs)	114

1/1 (2) 2/9 (1) 3/25 (4) 4/44 (3) 5/77 (5) 6/119 (7)   1/0 (1) 2/1 (2) 3/20 (4) 4/27 (3) 5/33 (6) 6/55 (5)
7/142 (6) 8/143 (9) 9/220 (10) 10/220 (11)   7/62 (8) 8/111 (7) 9/114 (10) 10/114 (11)

Starc 14–2–50–1; Hazlewood 15.5–8–38–5; Lyon 14–4–55–3; Johnson 14–2–54–1; Watson 2–0–10–0. *Second innings*—Starc 13–5–34–3; Hazlewood 10–5–18–2; Lyon 7–3–12–2; Johnson 8–1–23–2; Watson 4–2–3–1.

Umpires: I. J. Gould *(England)* (44) and R. A. Kettleborough *(England)* (28).
Third umpire: Aleem Dar *(Pakistan)*.   Referee: R. S. Mahanama *(Sri Lanka)* (58).

Close of play: first day, Australia 258–4 (Smith 135, Watson 20); second day, West Indies 143–8 (Holder 13); third day, West Indies 16–2 (Bravo 8, Dowrich 1).

BANGLADESH v INDIA 2015 (Only Test)

At Narayanganj Osmani Stadium, Fatullah, on 10, 11 *(no play)*, 12, 13, 14 June, 2015.
Toss: India.   Result: DRAWN.
Debuts: Bangladesh – Liton Das.
Man of the Match: S. Dhawan.

There had never previously been a Test in Bangladesh in June, and it soon became apparent why: heavy rain was rarely far away, with at least one session washed out every day, and all three on the second. A draw was inevitable – only the second time in eight meetings that Bangladesh had escaped defeat by India, following a similarly soggy encounter at Chittagong in May 2007. Kohli had promised attacking cricket, and Vijay and Dhawan responded with 283, India's fourth-highest opening stand, and their best for any wicket against Bangladesh. They rattled along at more than four an over against an unbalanced attack with four frontline spinners but only one regular seamer. Dhawan scorched to 150 on the truncated first day, while Vijay was more sedate, lasting 401 minutes for 150, his sixth Test century. Later Rahane hit an attractive 98 before attempting a third successive four off Shakib Al Hasan, and gifting him a fourth wicket. Only one session was possible on the fourth day, when Tamim Iqbal overtook Habibul Bashar (3,026) as Bangladesh's leading Test run-scorer. Liton Das – making his debut as wicketkeeper to spare Mushfiqur Rahim, who had an injured finger – cracked 44 from 45 balls, but fell just when it seemed the follow-on might be averted. With Ashwin collecting his best figures outside India, and three wickets for Harbhajan Singh in his first Test for more than two years, Bangladesh did have to bat again. But, with time for only 15 more overs, there was no danger of defeat.

India

M. Vijay lbw b Shakib Al Hasan	150
S. Dhawan c and b Shakib Al Hasan	173
R. G. Sharma b Shakib Al Hasan	6
*V. Kohli b Jubair Hossain	14
A. M. Rahane b Shakib Al Hasan	98
†W. P. Saha b Jubair Hossain	6
R. Ashwin not out	2
Harbhajan Singh not out	7
B 4, l-b 1, n-b 1	6
(6 wkts dec, 103.3 overs)	462

1/283 (2) 2/291 (3) 3/310 (4)
4/424 (1) 5/445 (6) 6/453 (5)

U. T. Yadav, V. R. Aaron and I. Sharma did not bat.

Mohammad Shahid 22–2–88–0; Soumya Sarkar 3–0–11–0; Shuvagata Hom 14–0–52–0; Shakib Al Hasan 24.3–1–105–4; Taijul Islam 20–0–85–0; Jubair Hossain 19–1–113–2; Imrul Kayes 1–0–3–0.

Bangladesh

Tamim Iqbal st Saha b Ashwin	19	– not out	16
Imrul Kayes st Saha b Harbhajan Singh	72	– not out	7
Mominul Haque c Yadav b Harbhajan Singh	30		
*Mushfiqur Rahim c R. G. Sharma b Ashwin	2		
Shakib Al Hasan c Saha b Ashwin	9		
Soumya Sarkar b Aaron	37		
†Liton Das c R. G. Sharma b Ashwin	44		
Shuvagata Hom c R. G. Sharma b Ashwin	9		
Taijul Islam not out	16		
Mohammad Shahid c Dhawan b Harbhajan Singh	6		
Jubair Hossain run out (Ashwin/Saha)	0		
L-b 9, n-b 3	12		
(65.5 overs)	256	(no wkt, 15 overs)	23

1/27 (1) 2/108 (3) 3/110 (4) 4/121 (5) 5/172 (2) 6/176 (6)
7/219 (8) 8/232 (7) 9/246 (10) 10/256 (11)

I. Sharma 7–0–24–0; Ashwin 25–6–87–5; Yadav 7–0–45–0; Aaron 9–0–27–1; Harbhajan Singh 17.5–2–64–3. *Second innings*—Yadav 2–1–4–0; Ashwin 6–2–8–0; Harbhajan Singh 5–2–11–0; Vijay 1–1–0–0; Dhawan 1–1–0–0.

Umpires: H. D. P. K. Dharmasena *(Sri Lanka)* (30) and N. J. Llong *(England)* (29).
Third umpire: Sharfuddoula *(Bangladesh)*.   Referee: A. J. Pycroft *(Zimbabwe)* (37).

Close of play: first day, India 239–0 (Vijay 89, Dhawan 150); second day, no play; third day, India 462–6 (Ashwin 2, Harbhajan Singh 7); fourth day, Bangladesh 111–3 (Imrul Kayes 59, Shakib Al Hasan 0).

Test No. 2167/49 (SL236, P390)

SRI LANKA v PAKISTAN 2015 (1st Test)

At Galle International Stadium on 17 *(no play)*, 18, 19, 20, 21 June, 2015.
Toss: Pakistan.   Result: PAKISTAN WON BY TEN WICKETS.
Debuts: none.
Man of the Match: Sarfraz Ahmed.

When Pakistan were 96 for five in response to a serviceable 300, Sri Lanka's worst-case scenario appeared to be a draw, especially as the first day had been washed out. But after Sarfraz Ahmed cut loose, they slid to their first home defeat by Pakistan in nine Tests since April 2006. After reaching 1,000 Test runs in his 28th innings, a record for a Pakistan wicketkeeper, Sarfraz hurried to 96 from 86 balls. Pakistan were still 65 adrift, but Asad Shafiq held firm for 376 minutes: his most memorable moment was a lofted drive to reach his seventh Test hundred, one of only five boundaries. The lead was swelled by his ninth-wicket stand of 101 with Zulfiqar Babar, who had managed only 50 runs in eight previous Tests, but now reached a maiden half-century with his second six. Earlier, Silva had struck a patient second Test hundred after being dropped when six. Sri Lanka's second innings began on the fourth evening and, as so often at Galle, a spinner sent the match hurtling to a conclusion. Yasir was aggressive, uncommonly accurate and, on the final day, irresistible. Three batsmen were stumped – the most in a Sri Lankan Test innings – and two more slogged to leg. Seven for 76 were the best figures for a visiting bowler in Sri Lanka, beating Shane Warne's seven for 94 for Australia against Pakistan at the Sara Oval in 2002–03. Pakistan had a session to score 90, which the openers knocked off in 11.2 overs.

Sri Lanka

F. D. M. Karunaratne c Sarfraz Ahmed b Wahab Riaz	21	– (2) st Sarfraz Ahmed b Yasir Shah	79
J. K. Silva c Sarfraz Ahmed b Zulfiqar Babar	125	– (1) c Azhar Ali b Wahab Riaz	5
K. C. Sangakkara c Younis Khan b Wahab Riaz	50	– c Azhar Ali b Yasir Shah	18
H. D. R. L. Thirimanne c Zulfiqar Babar b Mohammad Hafeez	8	– (5) c Younis Khan b Wahab Riaz	44
*A. D. Mathews b Wahab Riaz	19	– (6) c Azhar Ali b Yasir Shah	5
†L. D. Chandimal b Zulfiqar Babar	23	– (7) st Sarfraz Ahmed b Yasir Shah	38
K. D. K. Vithanage c and b Mohammad Hafeez	18	– (8) c Zulfiqar Babar b Yasir Shah	1
M. D. K. Perera c Sarfraz Ahmed b Yasir Shah	15	– (4) b Yasir Shah	0
K. T. G. D. Prasad lbw b Zulfiqar Babar	0	– st Sarfraz Ahmed b Zulfiqar Babar	2
H. M. R. K. B. Herath not out	6	– c Mohammad Hafeez b Yasir Shah	1
A. N. P. R. Fernando c and b Yasir Shah	4	– not out	0
L-b 5, w 2, n-b 4	11	B 5, l-b 1, w 6, n-b 1	13
(109.3 overs)	300	(77.1 overs)	206

1/30 (1) 2/142 (3) 3/154 (4) 4/189 (5) 5/226 (6) 6/261 (7) 7/277 (8) 8/288 (9) 9/291 (2) 10/300 (11)
1/18 (1) 2/63 (3) 3/63 (4) 4/132 (5) 5/144 (6) 6/167 (2) 7/175 (8) 8/200 (9) 9/203 (10) 10/206 (7)

Junaid Khan 16–5–38–0; Wahab Riaz 26–3–74–3; Zulfiqar Babar 27–8–64–3; Yasir Shah 30.3–6–79–2; Mohammad Hafeez 10–0–40–2. *Second innings*—Wahab Riaz 16–4–46–2; Junaid Khan 7–1–23–0; Yasir Shah 30.1–6–76–7; Mohammad Hafeez 10–3–24–0; Zulfiqar Babar 14–4–31–1.

Pakistan

Mohammad Hafeez c Karunaratne b Prasad	2	– not out	46
Ahmed Shehzad lbw b Prasad	9	– not out	43
Azhar Ali lbw b Herath	8		
Younis Khan b Perera	47		
*Misbah-ul-Haq c Sangakkara b Fernando	20		
Asad Shafiq st Chandimal b Perera	131		
†Sarfraz Ahmed b Prasad	96		
Wahab Riaz b Perera	14		
Yasir Shah c Chandimal b Fernando	23		
Zulfiqar Babar c Vithanage b Perera	56		
Junaid Khan not out	6		
L-b 1, w 1, n-b 3	5	B 3	3
(113.1 overs)	417	(no wkt, 11.2 overs)	92

1/2 (1) 2/11 (2) 3/35 (3) 4/86 (4) 5/96 (5) 6/235 (7) 7/273 (8) 8/302 (9) 9/403 (10) 10/417 (6)

Prasad 24–4–91–3; Fernando 19–1–71–2; Herath 30–4–99–1; Perera 31.1–3–122–4; Mathews 6–1–12–0; Vithanage 3–0–21–0. *Second innings*—Herath 4.2–0–30–0; Prasad 2–1–10–0; Fernando 2–0–18–0; Perera 3–0–31–0.

Umpires: R. K. Illingworth *(England)* (16) and P. R. Reiffel *(Australia)* (17).
Third umpire: C. B. Gaffaney *(New Zealand)*.   Referee: B. C. Broad *(England)* (68).

Close of play: first day, no play; second day, Sri Lanka 178–3 (Silva 80, Mathews 10); third day, Pakistan 118–5 (Asad Shafiq 14, Sarfraz Ahmed 15); fourth day, Sri Lanka 63–2 (Karunaratne 36, Perera 0).

Test No. 2168/50 (SL237, P391)

SRI LANKA v PAKISTAN 2015 (2nd Test)

At P. Sara Oval, Colombo, on 25, 26, 27, 28, 29 June, 2015.
Toss: Pakistan. Result: SRI LANKA WON BY SEVEN WICKETS.
Debuts: Sri Lanka – P. V. D. Chameera.
Man of the Match: K. T. G. D. Prasad.

Sri Lanka shook up their side, and two vibrant young bowlers set up a series-squaring win. In the first innings, 22-year-old off-spinner Tharindu Kaushal claimed a maiden five-for; in the second, 23-year-old Dushmantha Chameera rattled the batsmen with his pace. After Pakistan were skittled for 138, Sri Lanka's response was slow but steady: Silva made 80 in almost five and a half hours, though he was lucky to survive a review for a slip catch off Zulfiqar Babar when 13 (it wasn't caught, but the TV umpire omitted to check for lbw). Mathews compiled 77 in 153 balls as the lead stretched to 177. Yasir Shah took six wickets, but lacked support; Wahab Riaz's hand had been broken by Chameera. Azhar Ali then lasted 511 minutes for 117, his fifth Test century against Sri Lanka, and ninth in all. He put on 120 with Ahmed Shehzad, and 73 with Younis Khan, who was winning his 100th cap, but the last six fell for 55. Chandimal made six dismissals, equalling Amal Silva's national record, set against India in 1985-86. Sri Lanka needed 153 for their 50th Test win on home soil, but could not start until the fifth morning because of rain. With more forecast for the afternoon, they looked to collect the runs quickly. Although Sangakkara was out for a golden duck in his final innings against long-suffering Pakistan – he finished with 2,911 runs at 74 against them – Mathews and Thirimanne settled matters before the weather could make a difference.

Pakistan

Mohammad Hafeez b Kaushal	42	– c Sangakkara b Mathews	8
Ahmed Shehzad c Sangakkara b Prasad	1	– c Chandimal b Prasad	69
Azhar Ali c Chandimal b Prasad	26	– st Chandimal b Herath	117
Younis Khan c Chandimal b Prasad	6	– c Chandimal b Mathews	40
*Misbah-ul-Haq run out (Mathews/Chandimal)	7	– lbw b Prasad	22
Asad Shafiq lbw b Kaushal	2	– c Chandimal b Chameera	27
†Sarfraz Ahmed c Mathews b Kaushal	14	– c Chandimal b Prasad	16
Wahab Riaz lbw b Kaushal	4	– (11) lbw b Chameera	6
Yasir Shah c Sangakkara b Kaushal	15	– (8) b Prasad	0
Zulfiqar Babar b Chameera	5	– (9) not out	7
Junaid Khan not out	2	– (10) c Chandimal b Chameera	3
L-b 4, w 3, n-b 7	14	B 2, l-b 2, w 5, n-b 5	14
(42.5 overs)	138	(118.2 overs)	329

1/5 (2) 2/51 (3) 3/74 (4) 4/89 (1) 5/95 (6) 6/96 (5)   1/9 (1) 2/129 (2) 3/202 (4) 4/234 (5) 5/274 (6)
7/113 (7) 8/117 (8) 9/124 (10) 10/138 (9)   6/301 (7) 7/303 (8) 8/313 (3) 9/323 (10) 10/329 (11)

Prasad 13–2–43–3; Mathews 9–4–16–0; Chameera 10–0–33–1; Kaushal 10.5–0–42–5. *Second innings*—Prasad 29.3–3–92–4; Mathews 11–5–15–2; Herath 34–7–89–1; Chameera 18.5–1–53–3; Kaushal 25–3–76–0.

Sri Lanka

F. D. M. Karunaratne c Sarfraz Ahmed b Junaid Khan	28	– lbw b Yasir Shah	50
J. K. Silva run out (Yasir Shah/Sarfraz Ahmed)	80		
K. C. Sangakkara c Asad Shafiq b Zulfiqar Babar	34	– c Azhar Ali b Yasir Shah	0
H. D. R. L. Thirimanne c Azhar Ali b Yasir Shah	7	– (5) not out	20
*A. D. Mathews lbw b Yasir Shah	77	– (4) not out	43
†L. D. Chandimal b Yasir Shah	1		
K. D. K. Vithanage b Yasir Shah	3	– (2) c Mohammad Hafeez b Zulfiqar Babar	34
K. T. G. D. Prasad lbw b Mohammad Hafeez	35		
H. M. R. K. B. Herath not out	18		
P. H. T. Kaushal c Misbah-ul-Haq b Yasir Shah	18		
P. V. D. Chameera c Younis Khan b Yasir Shah	2		
B 6, l-b 4, w 1, n-b 1	12	L-b 6	6
(121.3 overs)	315	(3 wkts, 26.3 overs)	153

1/47 (1) 2/98 (3) 3/119 (4) 4/191 (2) 5/194 (6)   1/49 (2) 2/49 (3) 3/121 (1)
6/202 (7) 7/275 (8) 8/275 (5) 9/303 (10) 10/315 (11)

Wahab Riaz 9–2–19–0; Junaid Khan 29–5–89–1; Zulfiqar Babar 32–8–82–1; Yasir Shah 41.3–5–96–6; Mohammad Hafeez 10–2–19–1. *Second innings*—Junaid Khan 4–0–30–0; Mohammad Hafeez 4–0–20–0; Zulfiqar Babar 8–0–42–1; Yasir Shah 10.3–0–55–2.

Umpires: R. K. Illingworth *(England)* (17) and S. Ravi *(India)* (7).
Third umpire: P. R. Reiffel *(Australia)*.   Referee: B. C. Broad *(England)* (69).

Close of play: first day, Sri Lanka 70–1 (Silva 21, Sangakkara 18); second day, Sri Lanka 304–9 (Herath 10, Chameera 0); third day, Pakistan 171–2 (Azhar Ali 64, Younis Khan 23); fourth day, Pakistan 329.

SRI LANKA v PAKISTAN 2015 (3rd Test)

At Muttiah Muralitharan Stadium, Pallekele, on 3, 4, 5, 6, 7 July, 2015.
Toss: Pakistan.   Result: PAKISTAN WON BY SEVEN WICKETS.
Debuts: none.
Man of the Match: Younis Khan.   Man of the Series: Yasir Shah.

The odds were against Pakistan when they started their chase of 377 to snatch the series. They had never made so many to win a Test – only five higher targets had ever been reached – and were soon 13 for two. But, with Younis Khan making a superb unbeaten 171, they skated home, losing just one more wicket. Shan Masood, playing only because Mohammad Hafeez was undergoing tests on his bowling action, made his maiden century in his fifth Test, while Younis purred to his 30th, a record fifth in the fourth innings. When Masood fell after a stand of 242, Younis found an equally resolute partner in Misbah-ul-Haq. It was remarkably smooth sailing: they attacked Kaushal and milked the seamers, and whisked Pakistan home without further loss. Mathews clearly missed the control usually offered by Rangana Herath, left out when the pitch looked green at the start. Misbah had bowled first, but Karunaratne held firm for his second Test century; the best of the rest was 25 from 34-year-old Jehan Mubarak, who had been recalled after seven years. Pakistan were rescued by Sarfraz Ahmed's forthright unbeaten 78, but Imran Khan – batting for the first time, in his fifth Test – made an eight-ball duck, and a total of 215 looked insufficient. Sri Lanka again started poorly, before being rescued by Mathews, last out after 397 minutes. The last five tumbled for 35, all to Imran, who hustled to his maiden five-for in 33 balls, which seemed immaterial – until Younis booked in.

Sri Lanka

F. D. M. Karunaratne st Sarfraz Ahmed b Azhar Ali	130	– b Rahat Ali	10
J. K. Silva c Sarfraz Ahmed b Rahat Ali	9	– c Misbah-ul-Haq b Ehsan Adil	3
W. U. Tharanga c Younis Khan b Yasir Shah	46	– c Azhar Ali b Yasir Shah	48
H. D. R. L. Thirimanne c sub (Babar Azam) b Yasir Shah..	11	– b Rahat Ali	0
*A. D. Mathews c sub (Babar Azam) b Yasir Shah	3	– c Sarfraz Ahmed b Imran Khan	122
J. Mubarak st Sarfraz Ahmed b Yasir Shah	25	– c Azhar Ali b Yasir Shah	35
†L. D. Chandimal lbw b Rahat Ali	24	– lbw b Imran Khan	67
K. T. G. D. Prasad c Yasir Shah b Azhar Ali	0	– c Sarfraz Ahmed b Imran Khan	0
P. H. T. Kaushal lbw b Rahat Ali	18	– c Sarfraz Ahmed b Imran Khan	8
R. A. S. Lakmal not out	6	– c Sarfraz Ahmed b Imran Khan	0
A. N. P. R. Fernando lbw b Yasir Shah	0	– not out	4
L-b 3, w 3	6	B 4, l-b 9, w 3	16
(89.5 overs)	278	(95.4 overs)	313

1/15 (2) 2/106 (3) 3/133 (4) 4/137 (5) 5/204 (6)
6/248 (1) 7/248 (8) 8/264 (9) 9/277 (9) 10/278 (11)

1/12 (1) 2/22 (2) 3/35 (4) 4/80 (3) 5/161 (6)
6/278 (7) 7/278 (8) 8/290 (9) 9/306 (10) 10/313 (5)

Rahat Ali 21–4–74–3; Ehsan Adil 14–3–37–0; Imran Khan 16–3–51–0; Yasir Shah 31.5–4–78–5; Azhar Ali 7–0–35–2. *Second innings*—Rahat Ali 21–3–82–2; Ehsan Adil 17–4–66–1; Imran Khan 20.4–3–58–5; Yasir Shah 32–7–80–2; Azhar Ali 5–1–14–0.

Pakistan

Shan Masood lbw b Prasad	13	– st Chandimal b Kaushal	125
Ahmed Shehzad c Chandimal b Fernando	21	– b Lakmal	0
Azhar Ali c Karunaratne b Fernando	52	– c Chandimal b Prasad	5
Younis Khan run out (Silva)	3	– not out	171
Asad Shafiq lbw b Prasad	15		
†Sarfraz Ahmed not out	78		
*Misbah-ul-Haq lbw b Fernando	6	– (5) not out	59
Ehsan Adil lbw b Kaushal	0		
Yasir Shah c Chandimal b Prasad	18		
Rahat Ali lbw b Kaushal	2		
Imran Khan b Kaushal	0		
L-b 4, w 1, n-b 2	7	B 5, l-b 10, w 2, n-b 5	22
(66 overs)	215	(3 wkts, 103.1 overs)	382

1/32 (1) 2/40 (2) 3/45 (4) 4/91 (5) 5/135 (3)
6/151 (7) 7/152 (8) 8/197 (9) 9/202 (10) 10/215 (11)

1/0 (2) 2/13 (3) 3/255 (1)

Prasad 19–1–78–3; Lakmal 14–1–64–0; Fernando 15–5–29–3; Mathews 4–1–3–0; Kaushal 14–1–37–3. *Second innings*—Prasad 20–2–65–1; Lakmal 19–5–48–1; Fernando 17–3–51–0; Mathews 13–2–34–0; Kaushal 31–1–153–1; Mubarak 3.1–0–16–0.

Umpires: I. J. Gould *(England)* (45) and P. R. Reiffel *(Australia)* (18).
Third umpire: S. Ravi *(India)*.   Referee: B. C. Broad *(England)* (70).

Close of play: first day, Sri Lanka 272–8 (Kaushal 17, Lakmal 1); second day, Pakistan 209–9 (Sarfraz Ahmed 72, Imran Khan 0); third day, Sri Lanka 228–5 (Mathews 77, Chandimal 39); fourth day, Pakistan 230–2 (Shan Masood 114, Younis Khan 101).

ENGLAND v AUSTRALIA 2015 (1st Test)

At Sophia Gardens, Cardiff, on 8, 9, 10, 11 July, 2015.
Toss: England.   Result: ENGLAND WON BY 169 RUNS.
Debuts: none.
Man of the Match: J. E. Root.

The 2015 Ashes started like a rerun of the previous series in Australia: England lost three quick wickets to the seamers, then Root edged Starc. Haddin saw the ball late, went for it with one hand – and dropped the catch. England never looked back: Root purred to 134. By the end of the summer, he was top of the ICC's batting rankings, and Haddin had been dropped. Ballance survived for 223 minutes and, with Stokes and Ali making perkier half-centuries, England reached 430. Australia made a solid start, with Rogers unusually outscoring Warner, and equalling the Test record of seven successive 50-plus scores. However, no one else could reach 40, as England's seamers set up a lead of 122. While Bell and Root were putting on 97, it looked as if the advantage would stretch over the horizon – but both fell for 60 and, with Lyon extracting four wickets, Australia's eventual target was 411. Either side of lunch on the fourth day came the passage of play that decided the match: Australia lost four for nine in 36 balls, including Smith for his second 33 of the game, and Clarke to Broad, for the tenth time in a Test. Later Watson reviewed an lbw in desperation, but walked off anyway (and, as it turned out, out of Test cricket). Johnson and Starc crashed 72 for the eighth wicket, but just as it seemed they might extend the match into the rain-threatened fifth day, Root winkled out both, and Ali sealed the win.

England

A. Lyth c Warner b Hazlewood	6	– c Clarke b Lyon		37
*A. N. Cook c Haddin b Lyon	20	– c Lyon b Starc		12
G. S. Ballance lbw b Hazlewood	61	– c Haddin b Hazlewood		0
I. R. Bell lbw b Starc	1	– b Johnson		60
J. E. Root c Watson b Starc	134	– b Hazlewood		60
B. A. Stokes b Starc	52	– b Starc		42
†J. C. Buttler c Johnson b Hazlewood	27	– c Haddin b Lyon		7
M. M. Ali c Watson b Starc	77	– c Haddin b Johnson		15
S. C. J. Broad c Haddin b Lyon	18	– c Hazlewood b Lyon		4
M. A. Wood not out	7	– not out		32
J. M. Anderson b Starc	1	– b Lyon		1
B 17, l-b 3, w 5, n-b 1	26	B 7, l-b 6, w 6		19
(102.1 overs)	430	(70.1 overs)		289

1/7 (1) 2/42 (2) 3/43 (4) 4/196 (3) 5/280 (5) 6/293 (6)   1/17 (2) 2/22 (3) 3/73 (1) 4/170 (4) 5/207 (5)
7/343 (7) 8/395 (9) 9/419 (8) 10/430 (11)   6/236 (7) 7/240 (6) 8/245 (9) 9/288 (8) 10/289 (11)

Starc 24.1–4–114–5; Hazlewood 23–8–83–3; Johnson 25–3–111–0; Lyon 20–4–69–2; Watson 8–0–24–0; Warner 2–0–9–0. *Second innings*—Johnson 16–2–69–2; Hazlewood 13–2–49–2; Starc 16–4–60–2; Lyon 20.1–4–75–4; Watson 5–0–23–0.

Australia

C. J. L. Rogers c Buttler b Wood	95	– c Bell b Broad		10
D. A. Warner c Cook b Anderson	17	– lbw b Ali		52
S. P. D. Smith c Cook b Ali	33	– c Bell b Broad		33
*M. J. Clarke c and b Ali	38	– c Stokes b Broad		4
A. C. Voges c Anderson b Stokes	31	– c Buttler b Wood		1
S. R. Watson lbw b Broad	30	– lbw b Wood		19
N. M. Lyon lbw b Wood	6	– (11) not out		0
†B. J. Haddin c Buttler b Anderson	22	– (7) c Cook b Ali		7
M. G. Johnson c Ballance b Broad	14	– (8) c Lyth b Root		77
M. A. Starc c Root b Anderson	0	– (9) c Lyth b Root		17
J. R. Hazlewood not out	2	– (10) c Root b Ali		14
B 6, l-b 11, w 3	20	B 4, l-b 3, n-b 1		8
(84.5 overs)	308	(70.3 overs)		242

1/52 (2) 2/129 (3) 3/180 (1) 4/207 (4) 5/258 (5)   1/19 (1) 2/97 (2) 3/101 (3) 4/106 (4) 5/106 (5)
6/265 (6) 7/265 (7) 8/304 (8) 9/306 (9) 10/308 (10)   6/122 (7) 7/151 (6) 8/223 (9) 9/242 (8) 10/242 (10)

Anderson 18.5–6–43–3; Broad 17–4–60–2; Wood 20–5–66–2; Ali 15–1–71–2; Stokes 14–5–51–1. *Second innings*—Anderson 12–3–33–0; Broad 14–3–39–3; Ali 16.3–4–59–3; Stokes 8–2–23–0; Wood 14–4–53–2; Root 6–1–28–2.

Umpires: H. D. P. K. Dharmasena *(Sri Lanka)* (31) and M. Erasmus *(South Africa)* (31).
Third umpire: C. B. Gaffaney *(New Zealand)*.   Referee: R. S. Madugalle *(Sri Lanka)* (156).

Close of play: first day, England 343–7 (Ali 26, Broad 0); second day, Australia 264–5 (Watson 29, Lyon 6); third day, England 289.

ENGLAND v AUSTRALIA 2015 (2nd Test)

At Lord's, London, on 16, 17, 18, 19 July, 2015.
Toss: Australia.   Result: AUSTRALIA WON BY 405 RUNS.
Debuts: Australia – P. M. Nevill.
Man of the Match: S. P. D. Smith.

Australia bounced back to level the series with a massive victory at Lord's, their third-biggest by runs in the Ashes after 562 at The Oval in 1934, and 409 here in 1948. Their 15th win at Lord's (to England's seven) was set up by a magisterial innings from Smith, whose 215 was Australia's third double-century at Lord's. He shared a second-wicket partnership of 284 with Rogers, playing on the ground where he had done well for Middlesex. Since his maiden century – at The Oval in 2013 – Smith had hit ten hundreds, all in the first innings, none in defeats, and averaged 80. Faced with a huge total of 566, England lost Lyth second ball, a catch for the debutant wicketkeeper Peter Nevill (Haddin had withdrawn when his daughter fell ill; he stayed with the tour but did not feature again in a Test). Stokes biffed 87 while Cook grafted to 96, before both inside-edged Marsh into their stumps, and England trailed by 254. With two days left, Clarke ignored the follow-on, and his side doubled the lead at five an over. One worrying incident came when Rogers, who had been hit on the head two days previously by Anderson, suffered a dizzy spell and retired. England had five sessions (plus three overs) to survive, but lasted less than three hours: Johnson and Starc shook up the top order with pace, and later Stokes was run out when he failed to ground his bat ahead of Johnson's scudding throw from wide mid-on.

Australia

C. J. L. Rogers b Broad	173	– retired hurt	49
D. A. Warner c Anderson b Ali	38	– c Cook b Ali	83
S. P. D. Smith lbw b Root	215	– b Ali	58
*M. J. Clarke c Ballance b Wood	7	– not out	32
A. C. Voges c Buttler b Broad	25		
M. R. Marsh b Broad	12	– (5) not out	27
†P. M. Nevill c Ali b Root	45		
M. G. Johnson c Anderson b Broad	15		
M. A. Starc not out	12		
B 8, l-b 14, w 1, n-b 1	24	L-b 5	5
(8 wkts dec, 149 overs)	566	(2 wkts dec, 49 overs)	254

1/78 (2) 2/362 (1) 3/383 (4) 4/426 (5)   1/165 (2) 2/210 (3)
5/442 (6) 6/533 (3) 7/536 (7) 8/566 (8)

J. R. Hazlewood and N. M. Lyon did not bat.

In the second innings Rogers retired hurt at 114-0.

Anderson 26–4–99–0; Broad 27–5–83–4; Wood 28–7–92–1; Ali 36–4–138–1; Stokes 19–2–77–0; Root 12–0–55–2; Lyth 1–1–0–0. *Second innings*—Anderson 7–0–38–0; Broad 8–2–42–0; Ali 16–0–78–2; Wood 10–3–39–0; Stokes 3–0–20–0; Root 5–0–32–0.

England

A. Lyth c Nevill b Starc	0	– c Nevill b Starc	7
*A. N. Cook b Marsh	96	– c Nevill b Johnson	11
G. S. Ballance b Johnson	23	– c Nevill b Marsh	14
I. R. Bell b Hazlewood	1	– c sub (S. E. Marsh) b Lyon	11
J. E. Root c Nevill b Johnson	1	– b Hazlewood	17
B. A. Stokes b Marsh	87	– run out (Johnson)	0
†J. C. Buttler c Nevill b Lyon	13	– c Nevill b Johnson	11
M. M. Ali lbw b Hazlewood	39	– c sub (S. E. Marsh) b Johnson	0
S. C. J. Broad c sub (S. E. Marsh) b Johnson	21	– c Voges b Lyon	25
M. A. Wood b Hazlewood	4	– not out	2
J. M. Anderson not out	6	– b Hazlewood	0
B 12, l-b 8, n-b 1	21	B 4, l-b 1	5
(90.1 overs)	312	(37 overs)	103

1/0 (1) 2/28 (3) 3/29 (4) 4/30 (5) 5/175 (6) 6/210 (7)   1/12 (1) 2/23 (2) 3/42 (3) 4/48 (4) 5/52 (6) 6/64 (7)
7/266 (2) 8/294 (8) 9/306 (10) 10/312 (9)   7/64 (8) 8/101 (9) 9/101 (5) 10/103 (11)

Starc 22–1–86–1; Hazlewood 22–2–68–3; Johnson 20.1–8–53–3; Lyon 16–1–53–1; Marsh 8–3–23–2; Smith 2–0–9–0. *Second innings*—Starc 7–3–16–1; Hazlewood 8–2–20–2; Johnson 10–3–27–3; Marsh 3–2–8–1; Lyon 9–3–27–2.

Umpires: H. D. P. K. Dharmasena *(Sri Lanka)* (32) and M. Erasmus *(South Africa)* (32).
Third umpire: C. B. Gaffaney *(New Zealand)*.   Referee: R. S. Madugalle *(Sri Lanka)* (157).

Close of play: first day, Australia 337–1 (Rogers 158, Smith 129); second day, England 85–4 (Cook 21, Stokes 38); third day, Australia 108–0 (Rogers 44, Warner 60).

Test No. 2172/339 (E960, A778)

ENGLAND v AUSTRALIA 2015 (3rd Test)

At Edgbaston, Birmingham, on 29, 30, 31 July, 2015.
Toss: Australia.   Result: ENGLAND WON BY EIGHT WICKETS.
Debuts: none.
Man of the Match: S. T. Finn.

Early on the third afternoon, there was a fateful lapse. England had made most of the running in a frenetic match, largely thanks to outstanding bowling from Anderson and the returning Finn, but had been left with a potentially ticklish chase of 121. With the score 35, and a wicket already gone, Bell guided the ball straight to second slip. Clarke shelled it, continuing a wretched tour for Australia's captain. Bell went on to his second half-century of the game, and was still there when Root hit the winning boundary. It not only restored England's series lead, but extended their unprecedented sequence since the Grenada Test in April – win, lose, win, lose, win, lose, win. After Lord's, it was England's turn to bounce back on their favourite ground. They did, in style: probably only a side injury to Anderson – which put him out of the series – prevented the first two-day Ashes Test since 1921. Anderson had finished with none for 137 at Lord's, but improved on that with his eighth delivery here, his first Test wicket for 278 balls. In a twinkling he had six for 47 as Australia were demolished for 136, only Rogers making it to 20. England's patchy reply was given late impetus by Ali and Broad, and a lead of 145 looked more than enough when Australia nosedived to 111 for six, which included an attacking 77 from Warner. In Anderson's absence, Nevill prolonged the match into the third day, when Starc clouted a rapid 58.

Australia

C. J. L. Rogers lbw b Broad	52	– lbw b Broad		6
D. A. Warner lbw b Anderson	2	– c Lyth b Anderson		77
S. P. D. Smith c Cook b Finn	7	– c Buttler b Finn		8
*M. J. Clarke b Finn	10	– c Lyth b Finn		3
A. C. Voges c Buttler b Anderson	16	– c Bell b Finn		0
M. R. Marsh c Buttler b Anderson	0	– b Finn		6
†P. M. Nevill b Anderson	2	– c Buttler b Finn		59
M. G. Johnson c Stokes b Anderson	3	– c Stokes b Finn		14
M. A. Starc c Buttler b Broad	11	– c sub (J. E. Poysden) b Ali		58
J. R. Hazlewood not out	14	– c Root b Stokes		11
N. M. Lyon b Anderson	11	– not out		12
L-b 7, n-b 1	8	B 2, l-b 9		11
(36.4 overs)	136	(79.1 overs)		265

1/7 (2) 2/18 (3) 3/34 (4) 4/77 (5) 5/82 (6)   1/17 (1) 2/62 (3) 3/76 (4) 4/76 (5) 5/92 (6) 6/111 (2)
6/86 (7) 7/94 (8) 8/110 (1) 9/119 (9) 10/136 (11)   7/153 (8) 8/217 (7) 9/245 (10) 10/265 (9)

Anderson 14.4–2–47–6; Broad 12–2–44–2; Finn 10–1–38–2. *Second innings*—Anderson 8.3–5–15–1; Broad 20–4–61–1; Finn 21–3–79–6; Ali 16.1–3–64–1; Stokes 11–3–28–1; Root 2.3–0–7–0.

England

A. Lyth c Voges b Hazlewood	10	– lbw b Hazlewood		12
*A. N. Cook c Voges b Lyon	34	– b Starc		7
I. R. Bell c Warner b Lyon	53	– not out		65
J. E. Root c Voges b Starc	63	– not out		38
J. M. Bairstow c Nevill b Johnson	5			
B. A. Stokes c Nevill b Johnson	0			
†J. C. Buttler lbw b Lyon	9			
M. M. Ali c Warner b Hazlewood	59			
S. C. J. Broad c Marsh b Hazlewood	31			
S. T. Finn not out	0			
J. M. Anderson c Nevill b Starc	3			
B 6, l-b 4, w 4	14	W 2		2
(67.1 overs)	281	(2 wkts, 32.1 overs)		124

1/19 (1) 2/76 (2) 3/132 (3) 4/142 (5) 5/142 (6)   1/11 (2) 2/51 (1)
6/182 (4) 7/190 (7) 8/277 (9) 9/278 (8) 10/281 (11)

Starc 16.1–1–71–2; Hazlewood 15–0–74–3; Johnson 16–2–66–2; Marsh 7–2–24–0; Lyon 13–2–36–3. *Second innings*—Starc 6–1–33–1; Hazlewood 7–0–21–1; Lyon 11–1–52–0; Johnson 7–3–10–0; Marsh 1.1–0–8–0.

Umpires: Aleem Dar *(Pakistan)* (96) and C. B. Gaffaney *(New Zealand)* (3).
Third umpire: M. Erasmus *(South Africa)*.   Referee: R. S. Madugalle *(Sri Lanka)* (158).

Close of play: first day, England 133–3 (Root 30, Bairstow 1); second day, Australia 168–7 (Nevill 37, Starc 7).

ENGLAND v AUSTRALIA 2015 (4th Test)

At Trent Bridge, Nottingham, on 6, 7, 8 August, 2015.
Toss: England.   Result: ENGLAND WON BY AN INNINGS AND 78 RUNS.
Debuts: none.
Man of the Match: S. C. J. Broad.

The run of tit-for-tat results was emphatically ended, as England reclaimed the Ashes in another match that barely made it into the third day. It was effectively over on the first morning, when Australia were blitzed for 60 in 18.3 overs, the shortest opening innings in any Test. Broad was irresistible: his eight for 15, the best Test figures at Trent Bridge, included Rogers (for his first duck) and Smith in a frenetic first over. The batsmen were nonplussed by the swinging ball: nine were caught in the cordon, including Voges to a stupendous grab by Stokes in the gully. Extras top-scored, for the first time in the Ashes. England were batting before lunch on the first day, only the fourth such instance, and led by 214 by the close. Root became the first to score a century on the first day of an Ashes Test for the side batting second, and put on 173 with Bairstow. Cook declared before lunch on the second day, 331 ahead, but Australia's openers soon scooted past their puny first-innings total, eventually putting on 113. But then Stokes, who had not even bowled on the first day, made his presence felt, and the middle order caved in. Voges ensured the match would spill into the third day, but only just. Stokes finished with six for 36, the fourth successive innings in which a different England bowler had taken six or more. After the match, a disconsolate Clarke announced he would retire after the Oval Test.

Australia

C. J. L. Rogers c Cook b Broad	0	– c Root b Stokes	52
D. A. Warner c Buttler b Wood	0	– c Broad b Stokes	64
S. P. D. Smith c Root b Broad	6	– c Stokes b Broad	5
S. E. Marsh c Bell b Broad	0	– c Root b Stokes	2
*M. J. Clarke c Cook b Broad	10	– c Bell b Wood	13
A. C. Voges c Stokes b Broad	1	– not out	51
†P. M. Nevill b Finn	2	– lbw b Stokes	17
M. G. Johnson c Root b Broad	13	– c Cook b Stokes	5
M. A. Starc c Root b Broad	1	– c Bell b Stokes	0
J. R. Hazlewood not out	4	– b Wood	0
N. M. Lyon c Stokes b Broad	9	– b Wood	4
L-b 11, n-b 3	14	B 20, l-b 16, w 1, n-b 3	40
(18.3 overs)	60	(72.4 overs)	253

1/4 (1) 2/10 (2) 3/10 (3) 4/15 (4) 5/21 (6)
6/29 (5) 7/33 (7) 8/46 (9) 9/47 (8) 10/60 (11)

1/113 (1) 2/130 (2) 3/136 (3) 4/136 (3) 5/174 (5)
6/224 (7) 7/236 (8) 8/242 (9) 9/243 (10) 10/253 (11)

Broad 9.3–5–15–8; Wood 3–0–13–1; Finn 6–0–21–1. *Second innings*—Broad 16–5–36–1; Wood 17.4–3–69–3; Finn 12–4–42–0; Stokes 21–8–36–6; Ali 6–0–34–0.

England

A. Lyth c Nevill b Starc	14
*A. N. Cook lbw b Starc	43
I. R. Bell lbw b Starc	1
J. E. Root c Nevill b Starc	130
J. M. Bairstow c Rogers b Hazlewood	74
M. A. Wood b Starc	28
B. A. Stokes c Nevill b Hazlewood	5
†J. C. Buttler b Starc	12
M. M. Ali c Smith b Johnson	38
S. C. J. Broad not out	24
S. T. Finn not out	0
B 14, l-b 2, w 2, n-b 4	22
(9 wkts dec, 85.2 overs)	391

1/32 (1) 2/34 (3) 3/96 (2) 4/269 (5) 5/297 (4)
6/306 (6) 7/320 (8) 8/332 (7) 9/390 (9)

Starc 27–2–111–6; Hazlewood 24–4–97–2; Johnson 21.2–2–102–1; Lyon 10–1–47–0; Warner 3–0–18–0.

Umpires: Aleem Dar *(Pakistan)* (97) and S. Ravi *(India)* (8).
Third umpire: M. Erasmus *(South Africa)*.   Referee: R. S. Madugalle *(Sri Lanka)* (159).

Close of play: first day, England 274–4 (Root 124, Wood 2); second day, Australia 241–7 (Voges 48, Starc 0).

ENGLAND v AUSTRALIA 2015 (5th Test)

At Kennington Oval, London, on 20, 21, 22, 23 August, 2015.
Toss: England.   Result: AUSTRALIA WON BY AN INNINGS AND 46 RUNS.
Debuts: none.
Man of the Match: S. P. D. Smith.   Men of the Series: J. E. Root and C. J. L. Rogers.

This unpredictable series had one final twist. Australia, who had surrendered the Ashes with two feeble batting displays, were put in again on what looked a bowler-friendly surface – and won easily. England's attack lacked sparkle, perhaps because the urn was already won: Smith cashed in with 143, Warner made his fifth half-century of the series, and Voges made 76. Clarke, in what turned out to be his final innings, was applauded to the crease but soon left, after a futile review, for 15. Then it was the England batsmen's turn to misfire: only Ali, at No. 8, reached 30 against a disciplined attack, bolstered by the inclusion of Siddle, apparently against the captain's wishes. He took four more wickets in the follow-on, finishing with match figures of six for 67, which suggested he had been missed in the previous two games. Cook at least battled well in the second innings, although his search for a maiden Test century against Australia at home (in his 15th match) foundered at 85, when he prodded the sixth ball of Smith's exploratory over of leg-breaks to short leg. Buttler found a semblance of form to prolong the match into the fourth day, but Australia were soon celebrating their second huge win in London – and ruing their form outside the capital. The only other time these two sides had traded innings defeats in successive matches was in 1965–66, and there had been only one previous Ashes series in England with five definite results, in 2001.

Australia

C. J. L. Rogers c Cook b Wood	43
D. A. Warner c Lyth b Ali	85
S. P. D. Smith b Finn	143
*M. J. Clarke c Buttler b Stokes	15
A. C. Voges lbw b Stokes	76
M. R. Marsh c Bell b Finn	3
†P. M. Nevill c Buttler b Ali	18
M. G. Johnson b Ali	0
M. A. Starc lbw b Stokes	58
P. M. Siddle c Lyth b Finn	1
N. M. Lyon not out	5
B 1, l-b 24, w 6, n-b 3	34
(125.1 overs)	481

1/110 (1) 2/161 (2) 3/186 (4) 4/332 (5) 5/343 (6)
6/376 (7) 7/376 (8) 8/467 (3) 9/475 (9) 10/481 (10)

Broad 20–4–59–0; Wood 26–9–59–1; Stokes 29–6–133–3; Finn 29.1–7–90–3; Ali 18–1–102–3; Root 3–0–13–0.

England

A. Lyth c Starc b Siddle	19	– c Clarke b Siddle	10
*A. N. Cook b Lyon	22	– c Voges b Smith	85
I. R. Bell b Siddle	10	– c Clarke b Marsh	13
J. E. Root c Nevill b Marsh	6	– c Starc b Johnson	11
J. M. Bairstow c Lyon b Johnson	13	– c Voges b Lyon	26
B. A. Stokes c Nevill b Marsh	15	– c Clarke b Lyon	0
†J. C. Buttler b Lyon	1	– c Starc b Marsh	42
M. M. Ali c Nevill b Johnson	30	– (9) c Nevill b Siddle	35
S. C. J. Broad c Voges b Marsh	0	– (10) b Siddle	11
M. A. Wood c Starc b Johnson	24	– (8) lbw b Siddle	6
S. T. Finn not out	0	– not out	9
B 1, l-b 7, n-b 1	9	B 12, l-b 18, w 7, n-b 1	38
(48.4 overs)	149	(101.4 overs)	286

1/30 (2) 2/46 (1) 3/60 (3) 4/64 (4) 5/83 (5)   1/19 (1) 2/62 (3) 3/99 (4) 4/140 (5) 5/140 (6)
6/84 (7) 7/92 (6) 8/92 (9) 9/149 (10) 10/149 (8)   6/199 (2) 7/221 (8) 8/223 (7) 9/263 (10) 10/286 (9)

Starc 8–3–18–0; Johnson 8.4–4–21–3; Lyon 10–2–40–2; Siddle 13–5–32–2; Marsh 9–2–30–3. *Second innings—* Johnson 16–2–65–1; Starc 16–4–40–0; Lyon 28–7–53–2; Siddle 24.4–12–35–4; Marsh 16–4–56–2; Smith 1–0–7–1.

Umpires: Aleem Dar *(Pakistan)* (98) and H. D. P. K. Dharmasena *(Sri Lanka)* (33).
Third umpire: S. Ravi *(India)*.   Referee: J. J. Crowe *(New Zealand)* (72).

Close of play: first day, Australia 287–3 (Smith 78, Voges 47); second day, England 107–8 (Ali 8, Wood 8); third day, England 203–6 (Buttler 33, Wood 0).

BANGLADESH v SOUTH AFRICA 2015 (1st Test)

At Zohur Ahmed Chowdhury Stadium, Chittagong, on 21, 22, 23, 24 *(no play)*, 25 *(no play)* July, 2015.
Toss: South Africa.   Result: DRAWN.
Debuts: Bangladesh – Mustafizur Rahman.
Man of the Match: Mustafizur Rahman.

South Africa's first Test for six months was intriguingly poised after three days, only for the monsoon to wipe out the last two. The world's No. 1-ranked team had started rustily, before fighting back. A draw at least allowed Bangladesh to end their 100% losing record against South Africa, but they might have hoped for better. At 104 for one at lunch on the first day, Amla's decision to bat looked a good one. However, Bangladesh changed their approach, and tried to dry up the runs: Mohammad Shahid sent down seven consecutive maidens, five of them in one spell. Mustafizur Rahman, a 19-year-old left-arm swinger and cutter, tore out the middle order with three wickets in four balls: Amla became his maiden Test wicket when he edged a drive. Bavuma made 54, but South Africa were bowled out for a modest 248. Bangladesh went on to a lead of 78, their biggest in a Test in which they batted second – but it could have been more. Tamim Iqbal missed a full-toss from Elgar on 57, and Shakib Al Hasan's slog high to midwicket off Harmer was grim. Tamim had an altercation with de Kock, who was fined 75% of his match fee. When Bangladesh reached 179 for four by the second-day close, South Africa were under real pressure, but Steyn finally discovered some rhythm next morning, and the last six fell for 131. The new opening pair of van Zyl and Elgar narrowed the deficit before the weather closed in.

South Africa

D. Elgar c Liton Das b Taijul Islam	47	– (2) not out		28
S. van Zyl c Liton Das b Mahmudullah	34	– (1) not out		33
F. du Plessis lbw b Shakib Al Hasan	48			
*H. M. Amla c Liton Das b Mustafizur Rahman	13			
T. Bavuma c Jubair Hossain b Mustafizur Rahman	54			
J-P. Duminy lbw b Mustafizur Rahman	0			
†Q. de Kock b Mustafizur Rahman	0			
V. D. Philander c Shakib Al Hasan b Jubair Hossain	24			
S. R. Harmer c Mominul Haque b Jubair Hossain	9			
D. W. Steyn c Tamim Iqbal b Jubair Hossain	2			
M. Morkel not out	3			
B 8, l-b 5, n-b 1	14			
(83.4 overs)	248	(no wkt, 21.1 overs)		61

1/58 (2) 2/136 (1) 3/136 (3) 4/173 (4) 5/173 (6)
6/173 (7) 7/208 (8) 8/237 (9) 9/239 (10) 10/248 (5)

Mohammad Shahid 17–9–34–0; Mustafizur Rahman 17.4–6–37–4; Shakib Al Hasan 14–2–45–1; Mahmudullah 3–0–9–1; Taijul Islam 18–3–57–1; Jubair Hossain 14–1–53–3. *Second innings*—Mustafizur Rahman 5–0–21–0; Taijul Islam 2–0–4–0; Mahmudullah 1–1–0–0; Shakib Al Hasan 5–0–19–0; Mohammad Shahid 6–1–12–0; Jubair Hossain 2.1–1–5–0.

Bangladesh

Tamim Iqbal b Elgar	57
Imrul Kayes st de Kock b van Zyl	26
Mominul Haque b Harmer	6
Mahmudullah lbw b Philander	67
*Mushfiqur Rahim lbw b Steyn	28
Shakib Al Hasan c Duminy b Harmer	47
†Liton Das c de Kock b Harmer	50
Mohammad Shahid c van Zyl b Philander	25
Taijul Islam c Elgar b Steyn	9
Mustafizur Rahman c Duminy b Steyn	3
Jubair Hossain not out	0
L-b 7, n-b 1	8
(116.1 overs)	326

1/46 (2) 2/55 (3) 3/144 (1) 4/178 (4) 5/195 (5)
6/277 (6) 7/311 (8) 8/319 (7) 9/325 (9) 10/326 (10)

Steyn 22.1–5–78–3; Philander 20–2–40–2; Morkel 19–2–52–0; Harmer 35–8–105–3; van Zyl 13–4–23–1; Elgar 3–0–6–1; Duminy 4–0–15–0.

Umpires: R. A. Kettleborough *(England)* (29) and J. S. Wilson *(West Indies)* (1).
Third umpire: P. R. Reiffel *(Australia)*.   Referee: B. C. Broad *(England)* (71).

Close of play: first day, Bangladesh 7–0 (Tamim Iqbal 1, Imrul Kayes 5); second day, Bangladesh 179–4 (Mushfiqur Rahim 16, Shakib Al Hasan 1); third day, South Africa 61–0 (van Zyl 33, Elgar 28); fourth day, no play.

BANGLADESH v SOUTH AFRICA 2015 (2nd Test)

At Shere Bangla National Stadium, Mirpur, Dhaka, on 30, 31 *(no play)* July, 1 *(no play)*, 2 *(no play)*, 3 *(no play)* August, 2015.
Toss: Bangladesh.   Result: DRAWN.
Debuts: South Africa – D. J. Vilas.
Man of the Match: Mushfiqur Rahim.   Man of the Series: D. W. Steyn.

Dale Steyn became the 13th bowler to reach 400 Test wickets on the first – and only – day's play, as Bangladesh made 246 for eight on a bone-dry surface. That was a better score than it looked but, once again, everyone was left frustrated by the weather. Tamim Iqbal was the man to oblige Steyn, flashing at a wide, cross-seam delivery to provide Amla with a regulation head-high catch at first slip. Steyn was sporting a white headband to keep his long locks in place, making him appear more like Bjorn Borg, until he whipped it off to oblige the photographers. He got to 400 in just 16,634 deliveries, around 4,000 quicker than the next man, New Zealand's Richard Hadlee (Jimmy Anderson, who also reached 400 in 2015, needed 23,096 balls). Rain meant the pitch had been under covers 48 hours before the start, which was too late to water it or prepare it adequately. Bangladesh's batsmen made a familiar glut of thirties and forties, though Mushfiqur Rahim was rewarded for his application. Asked why this series was scheduled during the monsoon season – only four days' cricket was possible out of ten over the two Tests – both boards lamented the absence of suitable fixture windows, while locals pointed out that the previous two monsoon times had been unusually dry. The South Africans were particularly irked, as their lead at the top of the ICC Test rankings was cut by five points after a series drawn through little fault of their own.

Bangladesh

Tamim Iqbal c Amla b Steyn	6
Imrul Kayes lbw b Duminy	30
Mominul Haque c Vilas b Duminy	40
Mahmudullah c Bavuma b Steyn	35
*Mushfiqur Rahim c Vilas b Elgar	65
Shakib Al Hasan c Elgar b Morkel	35
†Liton Das c Elgar b Duminy	3
Nasir Hossain not out	13
Mohammad Shahid b Steyn	1
B 5, l-b 11, n-b 2	18
(8 wkts, 88.1 overs)	246

1/12 (1) 2/81 (3) 3/86 (2) 4/180 (4) 5/215 (5)
6/220 (7) 7/245 (6) 8/246 (9)

Mustafizur Rahman and Jubair Hossain did not bat.

Steyn 16.1–4–30–3; Philander 11–2–25–0; Morkel 14–2–45–1; Harmer 23–3–76–0; van Zyl 2–1–5–0; Elgar 7–0–22–1; Duminy 15–4–27–3.

South Africa

D. Elgar, S. van Zyl, F. du Plessis, *H. M. Amla, T. Bavuma, J-P. Duminy, †D. J. Vilas, V. D. Philander, S. R. Harmer, D. W. Steyn, M. Morkel.

Umpires: R. A. Kettleborough *(England)* (30) and P. R. Reiffel *(Australia)* (19).
Third umpire: J. S. Wilson *(West Indies)*.   Referee: B. C. Broad *(England)* (72).

Close of play: first day, Bangladesh 246–8 (Nasir Hossain 13); second day, no play; third day, no play; fourth day, no play.

SRI LANKA v INDIA 2015–16 (1st Test)

At Galle International Stadium on 12, 13, 14, 15 August, 2015.
Toss: Sri Lanka.   Result: SRI LANKA WON BY 63 RUNS.
Debuts: none.
Man of the Match: L. D. Chandimal.

The numbers spoke of Indian dominance. They skittled Sri Lanka for 183, and boasted two of the game's three centurions, a ten-wicket bowler, and a record-breaking fielder. And yet they were soundly beaten with nearly a day and a half to spare. Sri Lanka had been sent into a tailspin by Ashwin, and bundled out inside 50 overs. Sri Lanka's spinners couldn't find the same purchase. India did lose two quick wickets, but Dhawan and Kohli – who made his fourth hundred in four Tests as captain – put on 227. Dhawan batted despite having broken his right hand when he dropped Silva (he missed the rest of the series). India stretched their lead to 192. Only six larger deficits had been overturned in Tests – and when Sri Lanka's openers both bagged ducks in the four overs before stumps, a three-day finish loomed. They lurched to 95 for five next morning, but then the game turned on its head. Chandimal added 125 with Thirimanne, both benefiting from early umpiring errors, then 82 with Mubarak. Rahane held eight catches – six at slip off the spinners, and two at gully off the quicks – to break a record shared by five others. India were left 176 on a track which had slowed considerably. Only once, at Bridgetown in 1996-97, had they lost when chasing under 200. But they went on the defensive, which suited Herath: he collected seven for 48, figures bettered at Galle only by Muttiah Muralitharan, with seven for 46 against England in 2003–04.

Sri Lanka

F. D. M. Karunaratne c Rahane b I. Sharma	9	– b Ashwin	0
J. K. Silva c Dhawan b Aaron	5	– b Mishra	0
H. D. R. L. Thirimanne c Rahane b Ashwin	13	– (7) c Rahane b Ashwin	44
K. C. Sangakkara c Rahul b Ashwin	5	– c Rahane b Ashwin	40
*A. D. Mathews c R. G. Sharma b Ashwin	64	– c Rahul b Mishra	39
J. Mubarak c Rahul b Ashwin	0	– (8) c Rahane b Harbhajan Singh	49
†L. D. Chandimal c Rahane b Mishra	59	– (6) not out	162
K. T. G. D. Prasad lbw b Ashwin	0	– (3) c Rahane b Aaron	3
H. M. R. K. B. Herath b Ashwin	23	– c Rahane b Mishra	1
P. H. T. Kaushal c R. G. Sharma b Mishra	0	– c Saha b I. Sharma	7
A. N. P. R. Fernando not out	0	– b Ashwin	3
B 1, l-b 1, n-b 3	5	B 3, w 8, n-b 8	19
(49.4 overs)	183	(82.2 overs)	367

1/15 (1) 2/15 (2) 3/27 (4) 4/54 (3) 5/60 (6)
6/139 (5) 7/155 (8) 8/179 (7) 9/179 (10) 10/183 (9)

1/0 (1) 2/1 (2) 3/5 (3) 4/92 (4) 5/95 (5) 6/220 (6)
7/302 (8) 8/319 (9) 9/360 (10) 10/367 (11)

I. Sharma 11–3–30–1; Aaron 11–0–68–1; Ashwin 13.4–2–46–6; Mishra 6–1–20–2; Harbhajan Singh 8–1–17–0. *Second innings*—Ashwin 28.2–6–114–4; Mishra 17–2–61–3; Harbhajan Singh 17–0–73–1; Aaron 7–0–39–1; I. Sharma 13–0–77–1.

India

K. L. Rahul lbw b Prasad	7	– lbw b Herath	5
S. Dhawan b Fernando	134	– c and b Kaushal	28
R. G. Sharma lbw b Mathews	9	– (4) b Herath	4
*V. Kohli lbw b Kaushal	103	– (5) c Silva b Kaushal	3
A. M. Rahane lbw b Kaushal	0	– (6) c Mathews b Herath	36
†W. P. Saha c Chandimal b Fernando	60	– (7) st Chandimal b Herath	2
R. Ashwin b Fernando	7	– (9) c Prasad b Herath	3
Harbhajan Singh b Kaushal	14	– c Silva b Herath	1
A. Mishra b Kaushal	10	– (10) c Karunaratne b Kaushal	15
I. Sharma not out	3	– (3) lbw b Herath	10
V. R. Aaron c Mathews b Kaushal	4	– not out	1
L-b 10, w 3, n-b 11	24	L-b 2, w 1, n-b 1	4
(117.4 overs)	375	(49.5 overs)	112

1/14 (1) 2/28 (3) 3/255 (4) 4/257 (5) 5/294 (2) 6/302 (7)
7/330 (8) 8/344 (9) 9/366 (6) 10/375 (11)

1/12 (1) 2/30 (3) 3/34 (4) 4/45 (5) 5/60 (2) 6/65 (7)
7/67 (8) 8/81 (9) 9/102 (6) 10/112 (10)

Prasad 22–4–54–1; Fernando 26–2–98–3; Mathews 4–1–12–1; Kaushal 32.4–2–134–5; Herath 33–4–67–0. *Second innings*—Prasad 4–2–4–0; Herath 21–6–48–7; Kaushal 17.5–1–47–3; Fernando 6–3–8–0; Mathews 1–0–3–0.

Umpires: N. J. Llong *(England)* (30) and B. N. J. Oxenford *(Australia)* (24).
Third umpire: R. E. J. Martinesz *(Sri Lanka)*.   Referee: A. J. Pycroft *(Zimbabwe)* (38).

Close of play: first day, India 128–2 (Dhawan 53, Kohli 45); second day, Sri Lanka 5–2 (Prasad 3, Sangakkara 1); third day, India 23–1 (Dhawan 13, I. Sharma 5).

Test No. 2178/37 (SL240, I490)

SRI LANKA v INDIA 2015–16 (2nd Test)

At P. Sara Oval, Colombo, on 20, 21, 22, 23, 24 August, 2015.
Toss: India.   Result: INDIA WON BY 278 RUNS.
Debuts: none.
Man of the Match: K. L. Rahul.

Kumar Sangakkara's final international appearance confirmed that sport and fairytale finishes rarely coincide. His 134th Test delivered neither personal glory nor collective success, as India roared back to square the series. At Galle, he had struggled against Ashwin, who now dismissed him in both innings with turning, bouncing deliveries he could only prod to slip. India celebrated Kohli's first win as captain, and their first in ten Tests since shocking England at Lord's a year earlier. From 12 for two, Kohli had joined Rahul in a stand of 164 that tipped the balance India's way. Rahul made his second century in his fourth Test. Sri Lanka countered Ashwin's threat on a surface providing little assistance to the spinners: the real thrust came from a wonderful hundred by Mathews, who added 127 for the fourth wicket with Thirimanne before becoming a prize maiden Test wicket for Stuart Binny, who had toiled without reward in three matches in England in 2014. Sri Lanka lost their last seven for just 65. India built on their lead of 87 thanks to Rahane's polished 126 and his second-wicket stand of 140 with Vijay. By the time Kohli declared, 412 ahead, Sri Lanka needed to score more than ever before in a fourth innings to win. Recent history suggested it would be beyond them, and they were rolled for 134. Ashwin did the early damage, and Mishra's googly bamboozled the tail. Rahul stood in as wicketkeeper in the second innings, as Saha had an injured hamstring.

India

M. Vijay lbw b Prasad	0	– lbw b Kaushal	82
K. L. Rahul c Chandimal b Chameera	108	– b Prasad	2
A. M. Rahane c Karunaratne b Prasad	4	– c Chandimal b Kaushal	126
*V. Kohli c Mathews b Herath	78	– lbw b Kaushal	10
R. G. Sharma lbw b Mathews	79	– c Mubarak b Kaushal	34
S. T. R. Binny c Chameera b Herath	10	– c Thirimanne b Prasad	17
†W. P. Saha lbw b Herath	56	– not out	13
R. Ashwin c Silva b Mathews	2	– c Chandimal b Prasad	19
A. Mishra c Chandimal b Chameera	24	– c Mubarak b Prasad	10
I. Sharma lbw b Herath	2		
U. T. Yadav not out	2	– (10) not out	4
B 8, l-b 13, w 4, n-b 3	28	L-b 4, w 3, n-b 1	8
(114 overs)	393	(8 wkts dec, 91 overs)	325

1/4 (1) 2/12 (3) 3/176 (4) 4/231 (2) 5/267 (6)   1/3 (2) 2/143 (1) 3/171 (4) 4/256 (5)
6/319 (5) 7/321 (8) 8/367 (9) 9/386 (7) 10/393 (10)   5/262 (3) 6/283 (6) 7/311 (8) 8/318 (9)

In the second innings Saha, when 5, retired hurt at 267-5 and resumed at 311-7.

Prasad 24–7–84–2; Mathews 15–7–24–2; Chameera 20–2–72–2; Herath 25–3–81–4; Kaushal 30–2–111–0. *Second innings*—Prasad 15–0–43–4; Herath 29–4–96–0; Chameera 14–0–63–0; Mathews 2–1–1–0; Kaushal 31–1–118–4.

Sri Lanka

F. D. M. Karunaratne lbw b Yadav	1	– (2) b Ashwin	46
J. K. Silva c Ashwin b Mishra	51	– (1) c Binny b Ashwin	1
K. C. Sangakkara c Rahane b Ashwin	32	– c Vijay b Ashwin	18
H. D. R. L. Thirimanne c Saha b I. Sharma	62	– (6) c sub (C. A. Pujara) b Ashwin	11
*A. D. Mathews c Vijay b Binny	102	– (4) c †Rahul b Yadav	23
†L. D. Chandimal c Rahul b I. Sharma	11	– (5) b Mishra	15
J. Mubarak b Mishra	22	– c Kohli b I. Sharma	0
K. T. G. D. Prasad c Rahane b Mishra	5	– c Mishra b Ashwin	0
H. M. R. K. B. Herath lbw b Ashwin	1	– not out	4
P. H. T. Kaushal st Saha b Mishra	6	– lbw b Mishra	5
P. V. D. Chameera not out	0	– lbw b Mishra	4
B 2, l-b 6, n-b 5	13	L-b 4, w 1, n-b 2	7
(108 overs)	306	(43.4 overs)	134

1/1 (1) 2/75 (3) 3/114 (2) 4/241 (4) 5/259 (6)   1/8 (1) 2/33 (3) 3/72 (4) 4/91 (5) 5/106 (6) 6/111 (7)
6/284 (5) 7/289 (8) 8/300 (7) 9/306 (9) 10/306 (10)   7/114 (8) 8/123 (2) 9/128 (10) 10/134 (11)

I. Sharma 21–3–68–2; Yadav 19–5–67–1; Binny 18–4–44–1; Ashwin 29–3–76–2; Mishra 21–3–43–4. *Second innings*—Ashwin 16–6–42–5; Yadav 7–1–18–1; I. Sharma 11–2–41–1; Mishra 9.4–3–29–3.

Umpires: B. N. J. Oxenford *(Australia)* (25) and R. J. Tucker *(Australia)* (37).
Third umpire: R.S. A. Palliyaguruge *(Sri Lanka).*   Referee: A. J. Pycroft *(Zimbabwe)* (39).

Close of play: first day, India 319–6 (Saha 19); second day, Sri Lanka 140–3 (Thirimanne 28, Mathews 19); third day, India 70–1 (Vijay 39, Rahane 28); fourth day, Sri Lanka 72–2 (Karunaratne 25, Mathews 23).

Test No. 2179/38 (SL241, I491)

SRI LANKA v INDIA 2015–16 (3rd Test)

At Sinhalese Sports Club, Colombo, on 28, 29, 30, 31 August, 1 September, 2015.
Toss: Sri Lanka.   Result: INDIA WON BY 117 RUNS.
Debuts: Sri Lanka – M. D. K. J. Perera. India – N. V. Ojha.
Man of the Match: C. A. Pujara.   Man of the Series: R. Ashwin.

One of the golden rules in the subcontinent is to bat first. But, carried away by a rare covering of grass on a relaid pitch at a ground notorious for high-scoring draws, Mathews gambled. It helped India secure their first overseas series in more than four years, and their first in Sri Lanka in five attempts since 1993–94. It was also Sri Lanka's first defeat at the SSC for 15 Tests. With Sangakkara retired, only Mathews, with a battling hundred, and Kusal Perera, who became the third wicketkeeper to make two half-centuries on Test debut – after Chandimal in 2011–12 and India's Dilawar Hussain in 1933–34 – offered any resistance. Otherwise, the Sri Lankans were blown away by the pace of Ishant Sharma. Recalled after injuries to Dhawan and Vijay, India's batting hero was Pujara, only the fourth Indian to carry his bat, with a classy unbeaten 145. He put on 104 for the eighth wicket with Mishra to steer India to an extremely good total in the conditions. It was boosted by five penalty runs when Perera dropped a nick off Kohli, and the ball hit the helmet behind him. Sri Lanka were reeling at 47 for six before Perera rallied them, but India still led by 111. They then slipped to seven for three, but the lower order set up a stiff target of 386. Sharma and Yadav made early inroads, before Mathews dropped anchor – but once Perera reverse-swept Ashwin to point, after a stand of 135, the end arrived swiftly.

India

K. L. Rahul b Prasad	2	– (2) b Fernando	2
C. A. Pujara not out	145	– (1) b Prasad	0
A. M. Rahane lbw b Fernando	8	– lbw b Fernando	4
*V. Kohli c Perera b Mathews	18	– c Tharanga b Fernando	21
R. G. Sharma c Tharanga b Prasad	26	– c Fernando b Prasad	50
S. T. R. Binny lbw b Prasad	0	– c Tharanga b Prasad	49
†N. V. Ojha c Tharanga b Kaushal	21	– c Karunaratne b Herath	35
R. Ashwin c Perera b Prasad	5	– (9) c Perera b Prasad	58
A. Mishra st Perera b Herath	59	– (8) run out (Silva)	39
I. Sharma b Herath	6	– (11) not out	2
U. T. Yadav b Herath	4	– (10) c Herath b Fernando	4
L-b 2, w 4, n-b 7, p 5	18	B 1, l-b 1, w 3, n-b 5	10
(100.1 overs)	312	(76 overs)	274

1/2 (1) 2/14 (3) 3/64 (4) 4/119 (5) 5/119 (6)
6/173 (7) 7/180 (8) 8/284 (9) 9/298 (10) 10/312 (11)

1/0 (1) 2/2 (2) 3/7 (3) 4/64 (4) 5/118 (5) 6/160 (6)
7/179 (7) 8/234 (8) 9/269 (10) 10/274 (9)

Prasad 26–4–100–4; Fernando 22–6–52–1; Mathews 13–6–24–1; Herath 27.1–3–84–3; Kaushal 12–2–45–1. *Second innings*—Prasad 19–3–69–4; Fernando 17–2–62–4; Herath 22–0–89–1; Mathews 6–3–11–0; Kaushal 12–2–41–0.

Sri Lanka

W. U. Tharanga c Rahul b I. Sharma	4	– c Ojha b I. Sharma	0
J. K. Silva b Yadav	3	– c Pujara b Yadav	27
F. D. M. Karunaratne c Rahul b Binny	11	– c Ojha b Yadav	0
L. D. Chandimal lbw b Binny	23	– c Kohli b I. Sharma	18
*A. D. Mathews c Ojha b I. Sharma	1	– lbw b I. Sharma	110
H. D. R. L. Thirimanne c Rahul b I. Sharma	0	– c Rahul b Ashwin	12
†M. D. K. J. Perera c Kohli b I. Sharma	55	– c R. G. Sharma b Ashwin	70
K. T. G. D. Prasad st Ojha b Mishra	27	– (10) c Binny b Ashwin	6
H. M. R. K. B. Herath c Ojha b I. Sharma	49	– (8) lbw b Ashwin	11
P. H. T. Kaushal lbw b Mishra	16	– (9) not out	1
A. N. P. R. Fernando not out	2	– lbw b Mishra	0
L-b 1, w 2, n-b 7	10	B 4, l-b 2, n-b 7	13
(52.2 overs)	201	(85 overs)	268

1/11 (1) 2/11 (2) 3/40 (4) 4/45 (5) 5/47 (3)
6/47 (6) 7/127 (7) 8/156 (10) 9/183 (9) 10/201 (8)

1/1 (1) 2/2 (3) 3/21 (4) 4/74 (2) 5/107 (6) 6/242 (7)
7/249 (5) 8/257 (8) 9/263 (10) 10/268 (11)

In the first innings Prasad, when 1, retired hurt at 48-6 and resumed at 156-8.

I. Sharma 15–2–54–5; Yadav 13–2–64–1; Binny 9–3–24–2; Ashwin 8–1–33–0; Mishra 7.2–1–25–2. *Second innings*—
I. Sharma 19–5–32–3; Yadav 15–3–65–2; Binny 13–3–49–0; Mishra 18–1–47–1; Ashwin 20–2–69–4.

Umpires: N. J. Llong *(England)* (31) and R. J. Tucker *(Australia)* (38).
Third umpire: R. R. Wimalasiri *(Sri Lanka)*.   Referee: A. J. Pycroft *(Zimbabwe)* (40).

Close of play: first day, India 50–2 (Pujara 19, Kohli 14); second day, India 292–8 (Pujara 135, I. Sharma 2); third day, India 21–3 (Kohli 1, R. G. Sharma 14); fourth day, Sri Lanka 67–3 (Silva 24, Mathews 22).

PAKISTAN v ENGLAND 2015–16 (1st Test)

At Sheikh Zayed Stadium, Abu Dhabi, on 13, 14, 15, 16, 17 October, 2015.
Toss: Pakistan.   Result: DRAWN.
Debuts: England – A. U. Rashid.
Man of the Match: A. N. Cook.

A largely turgid battle that was flattered by the final afternoon. As the light faded, England's dash for runs resembled a blitz finish to a cagey game of chess. Two monumental innings dominated the scorecard. Shoaib Malik, in his first Test for more than five years, hit 245 in 639 minutes, and was put on a drip to rehydrate. He was trumped by Cook, who played the longest Test innings by an England batsman, and the third-longest by anyone. For 836 minutes – four short of 14 hours – he grafted calmly to 263, like Shoaib's an unprecedented Test score (of lower ones, only 229, 238 and 252 remained unclaimed). Cook's 528 balls produced just 18 fours, but almost set up the most unlikely success. Anderson produced an exacting new-ball spell, before Stokes ran out the dilly-dallying Mohammad Hafeez. Only 16 wickets had fallen on the first four days but, after tea, Pakistan lost their last seven for 60. Rashid, having suffered the most expensive wicketless figures by any debutant, now claimed the first five-for by an England wrist-spinner since Tommy Greenhough against India at Lord's in 1959. Suddenly England needed 99 from a theoretical 19 overs – though they knew the light would not last. Buttler, Ali and Stokes departed to aggressive shots in the first six overs, from which England made 35. The floodlights came on around 5.20, but made only a brief impact before the umpires called a halt at 5.46. Pakistan had bowled 11 overs in 58 minutes, and England were 25 short.

Pakistan

Mohammad Hafeez lbw b Stokes	98	– run out (Stokes)	34
Shan Masood b Anderson	2	– b Anderson	1
Shoaib Malik c Bell b Stokes	245	– c Bairstow b Anderson	0
Younis Khan c Cook b Broad	38	– c Stokes b Rashid	45
*Misbah-ul-Haq c Buttler b Anderson	3	– b Ali	51
Asad Shafiq lbw b Wood	107	– c Buttler b Rashid	6
†Sarfraz Ahmed c Bell b Stokes	2	– c Anderson b Rashid	27
Wahab Riaz not out	2	– c Bairstow b Ali	1
Zulfiqar Babar c Anderson b Stokes	0	– c Anderson b Rashid	1
Rahat Ali (did not bat)		– not out	0
Imran Khan, sen. (did not bat)		– c Anderson b Rashid	0
B 4, l-b 21, n-b 1	26	B 3, l-b 2, n-b 2	7
(8 wkts dec, 151.1 overs)	523	(57.5 overs)	173

1/5 (2) 2/173 (1) 3/247 (4) 4/251 (5)   1/3 (2) 2/3 (3) 3/47 (1) 4/113 (4) 5/139 (6)
5/499 (6) 6/514 (7) 7/521 (3) 8/523 (9)   6/159 (5) 7/165 (8) 8/168 (9) 9/173 (7) 10/173 (11)

Anderson 22–7–42–2; Broad 21–8–44–1; Stokes 17.1–3–57–4; Wood 22–5–58–1; Rashid 34–0–163–0; Ali 30–2–121–0; Root 5–1–13–0. *Second innings*—Anderson 10–3–30–2; Broad 8–5–8–0; Wood 7–2–29–0; Rashid 18.5–3–64–5; Stokes 7–4–9–0; Ali 7–0–28–2.

England

*A. N. Cook c Shan Masood b Shoaib Malik	263		
M. M. Ali c Sarfraz Ahmed b Imran Khan	35	– (1) c Shoaib Malik b Zulfiqar Babar	11
I. R. Bell c Mohammad Hafeez b Wahab Riaz	63	– (6) not out	5
M. A. Wood b Wahab Riaz	4		
J. E. Root c Sarfraz Ahmed b Rahat Ali	85	– (3) not out	33
J. M. Bairstow lbw b Wahab Riaz	8	– (5) st Sarfraz Ahmed b Zulfiqar Babar	15
B. A. Stokes b Shoaib Malik	57	– (4) c Mohammad Hafeez b Shoaib Malik	2
†J. C. Buttler c Asad Shafiq b Zulfiqar Babar	23	– (2) lbw b Shoaib Malik	4
A. U. Rashid b Imran Khan	12		
S. C. J. Broad not out	17		
J. M. Anderson not out	3		
B 7, l-b 7, w 3, n-b 11	28	L-b 2, w 2	4
(9 wkts dec, 206 overs)	598	(4 wkts, 11 overs)	74

1/116 (2) 2/281 (3) 3/285 (4) 4/426 (5)   1/13 (2) 2/29 (1)
5/443 (6) 6/534 (7) 7/549 (1) 8/563 (8) 9/590 (9)   3/35 (4) 4/66 (5)

Rahat Ali 28–1–86–1; Imran Khan 27–7–74–2; Zulfiqar Babar 72–17–183–1; Wahab Riaz 37–3–125–3; Asad Shafiq 7–0–19–0; Shoaib Malik 35–4–97–2. *Second innings*—Zulfiqar Babar 5–0–27–2; Shoaib Malik 4–0–25–2; Wahab Riaz 2–0–20–0.

Umpires: B. N. J. Oxenford *(Australia)* (26) and P. R. Reiffel *(Australia)* (20).
Third umpire: S. Ravi *(India)*.   Referee: A. J. Pycroft *(Zimbabwe)* (41).

Close of play: first day, Pakistan 286–4 (Shoaib Malik 124, Asad Shafiq 11); second day, England 56–0 (Cook 39, Ali 15); third day, England 290–3 (Cook 168, Root 3); fourth day, England 569–8 (Rashid 6, Broad 0).

PAKISTAN v ENGLAND 2015–16 (2nd Test)

At Dubai International Stadium on 22, 23, 24, 25, 26 October, 2015.
Toss: Pakistan.   Result: PAKISTAN WON BY 178 RUNS.
Debuts: none.
Man of the Match: Wahab Riaz.

England's tail almost pulled off an unlikely draw, but in the end a collapse of seven for 36 on the third morning, set up by a fiery burst from Wahab Riaz, proved too costly. England had looked likely to match Pakistan's patient first innings of 378. That included 102 from their captain, Misbah-ul-Haq, at 41 the oldest Test centurion since Australia's Bob Simpson in 1977–78. Cook and Root shared a century stand, but the predatory Yasir Shah worked his way through the rest. Pakistan built calmly on their lead of 136. This time it was Younis Khan's turn for a century, his 31st in all and his tenth in 24 matches in the UAE. Misbah, who helped Younis put on 141, fell just short, but joined Andrew Flintoff (in the 2005 Edgbaston Ashes Test) in hitting at least four sixes in both innings. England were left 491 in almost five sessions, and were soon 19 for two, with Cook unable to repeat his Abu Dhabi heroics. Twice on the final day a Pakistan victory looked a formality: first when Root departed after another accomplished fifty (his 12th of 2015, beating Keith Fletcher's 1973 national record for a calendar year), and then when Broad's dismissal made it 253 for eight, with 41 overs left. But Rashid hung on heroically, putting on 55 with Wood, before suddenly holing out with last man Anderson for company and the sun setting. Only 39 balls remained: England's last four had faced 322, another Test record.

Pakistan

Mohammad Hafeez c Bairstow b Ali	19	– c Root b Wood	51
Shan Masood c Buttler b Anderson	54	– c Buttler b Anderson	1
Shoaib Malik c Bairstow b Stokes	2	– b Wood	7
Younis Khan c Buttler b Wood	56	– c Ali b Rashid	118
*Misbah-ul-Haq lbw b Broad	102	– c Cook b Anderson	87
Asad Shafiq c Root b Wood	83	– lbw b Ali	79
†Sarfraz Ahmed c Anderson b Ali	32	– not out	3
Wahab Riaz c Anderson b Ali	6		
Yasir Shah c Stokes b Rashid	16		
Zulfiqar Babar lbw b Wood	3		
Imran Khan, sen. not out	0		
L-b 4, w 1	5	B 6, l-b 1, n-b 1	8
(118.5 overs)	378	(6 wkts dec, 95 overs)	354

1/51 (1) 2/58 (3) 3/85 (2) 4/178 (4) 5/282 (5)
6/334 (7) 7/342 (8) 8/370 (9) 9/377 (10) 10/378 (6)

1/1 (2) 2/16 (3) 3/83 (1)
4/224 (5) 5/337 (4) 6/354 (6)

Anderson 20–5–40–1; Broad 17–4–48–1; Ali 25–3–108–3; Wood 19.5–7–39–3; Stokes 17–3–55–1; Rashid 20–1–84–1. *Second innings*—Anderson 15–7–22–2; Broad 10–1–34–0; Wood 14–3–44–2; Ali 11–0–60–1; Stokes 17–3–54–0; Rashid 25–1–107–1; Root 3–0–26–0.

England

*A. N. Cook c sub (Ahmed Shehzad) b Yasir Shah	65	– c Wahab Riaz b Yasir Shah	10
M. M. Ali c Shan Masood b Wahab Riaz	1	– c Younis Khan b Imran Khan	1
I. R. Bell c Sarfraz Ahmed b Imran Khan	4	– c Younis Khan b Zulfiqar Babar	46
J. E. Root c Sarfraz Ahmed b Wahab Riaz	88	– c Younis Khan b Zulfiqar Babar	71
J. M. Bairstow lbw b Yasir Shah	46	– b Yasir Shah	22
B. A. Stokes c Sarfraz Ahmed b Wahab Riaz	4	– c Misbah-ul-Haq b Imran Khan	13
†J. C. Buttler c Sarfraz Ahmed b Wahab Riaz	0	– c Younis Khan b Yasir Shah	7
A. U. Rashid c Mohammad Hafeez b Yasir Shah	0	– c Zulfiqar Babar b Yasir Shah	61
S. C. J. Broad not out	15	– b Wahab Riaz	30
M. A. Wood c Younis Khan b Yasir Shah	1	– c Mohammad Hafeez b Zulfiqar Babar	29
J. M. Anderson c Sarfraz Ahmed b Imran Khan	4	– not out	0
B 4, l-b 1, w 5, n-b 4	14	B 12, l-b 4, w 1, n-b 5	22
(75.2 overs)	242	(137.3 overs)	312

1/5 (2) 2/14 (3) 3/127 (1) 4/206 (4) 5/212 (6) 6/216 (7)
7/218 (8) 8/223 (5) 9/233 (10) 10/242 (11)

1/9 (2) 2/19 (1) 3/121 (3) 4/157 (4) 5/163 (5)
6/178 (7) 7/193 (6) 8/253 (9) 9/308 (10) 10/312 (8)

Imran Khan 13.2–4–33–2; Wahab Riaz 19–5–66–4; Zulfiqar Babar 10–2–35–0; Yasir Shah 29–4–93–4; Shoaib Malik 4–1–10–0. *Second innings*—Imran Khan 14–4–41–2; Wahab Riaz 25–4–78–1; Yasir Shah 41.3–15–87–4; Shoaib Malik 10–2–37–0; Zulfiqar Babar 47–23–53–3.

Umpires: B. N. J. Oxenford *(Australia)* (27) and P. R. Reiffel *(Australia)* (21).
Third umpire: C. B. Gaffaney *(New Zealand)*.   Referee: A. J. Pycroft *(Zimbabwe)* (42).

Close of play: first day, Pakistan 282–4 (Misbah-ul-Haq 102, Asad Shafiq 46); second day, England 182–3 (Root 76, Bairstow 27); third day, Pakistan 222–3 (Younis Khan 71, Misbah-ul-Haq 87); fourth day, England 130–3 (Root 59, Bairstow 6).

Test No. 2182/77 (P395, E965)

PAKISTAN v ENGLAND 2015–16 (3rd Test)

At Sharjah C. A. Stadium on 1, 2, 3, 4, 5 November, 2015.
Toss: Pakistan. Result: PAKISTAN WON BY 127 RUNS.
Debuts: none.
Man of the Match: Mohammad Hafeez. Man of the Series: Yasir Shah.

In their first Test at Sharjah, England were in touch until the fourth afternoon, but disintegrated as if in homage to their previous series in the UAE, in 2011-12, when their batsmen could scarcely leave their hotel rooms without wondering whether the corridors would take spin. Pakistan celebrated a 2–0 triumph, and briefly went second in the rankings. The turning-point came early in their second innings, when Mohammad Hafeez was given out caught behind off Anderson for two, only to be saved on review despite the absence of Hot Spot and the Snickometer. He continued to an accomplished 151, which meant England had to chase 284 – 75 more than they had ever made to win a Test in Asia – even though Taylor's Test-best 76 had set up a first-innings lead of 72. They fell well short, not helped by an injury to Stokes, who had hurt his shoulder on day one attempting a catch. The eight runs from Nos 3–7 equalled England's worst effort, at Sydney in 1886–87 (a match they still won). The spinners made the difference: Pakistan's claimed 17 wickets for 313, with Yasir Shah finishing things off, England's seven for 423. Shoaib Malik, who took seven himself, announced his Test retirement afterwards. In the first innings, Anderson passed Shaun Pollock (421) to go eighth on the Test-wickets list, while Broad sent down 48 successive dot balls during a miserly 13-over spell of two for 13. England's players wore black armbands on the fourth day after the death of Tom Graveney.

Pakistan

Mohammad Hafeez c Broad b Ali	27	– c Bell b Ali	151
Azhar Ali c Bairstow b Anderson	0	– run out (Bell/Rashid)	34
Shoaib Malik c Bairstow b Broad	38	– lbw b Anderson	0
Younis Khan lbw b Anderson	31	– lbw b Broad	14
*Misbah-ul-Haq c Root b Anderson	71	– (6) lbw b Broad	38
Asad Shafiq c Bairstow b Patel	5	– (7) b Broad	46
†Sarfraz Ahmed c Root b Ali	39	– (8) b Patel	36
Wahab Riaz b Patel	0	– (10) run out (Bell/Bairstow)	21
Yasir Shah c Patel b Broad	7	– c Broad b Rashid	4
Zulfiqar Babar not out	6	– (11) not out	0
Rahat Ali c Ali b Anderson	4	– (5) b Anderson	0
B 1, l-b 5	6	B 6, l-b 5	11
(85.1 overs)	234	(118.2 overs)	355

1/5 (2) 2/49 (1) 3/88 (3) 4/103 (4) 5/116 (6) 1/101 (2) 2/105 (3) 3/146 (4) 4/152 (5) 5/245 (6)
6/196 (7) 7/196 (8) 8/224 (9) 9/224 (5) 10/234 (11) 6/257 (1) 7/312 (8) 8/319 (9) 9/354 (7) 10/355 (10)

Anderson 15.1–7–17–4; Broad 13–8–13–2; Stokes 11–4–23–0; Patel 23–3–85–2; Ali 13–3–49–2; Rashid 10–1–41–0. *Second innings*—Anderson 26–8–52–2; Broad 23–6–44–3; Patel 19–1–79–1; Ali 21.2–1–72–1; Rashid 29–3–97–1.

England

*A. N. Cook c Azhar Ali b Yasir Shah	49	– (2) st Sarfraz Ahmed b Shoaib Malik	63
M. M. Ali c Younis Khan b Shoaib Malik	14	– (1) lbw b Shoaib Malik	22
I. R. Bell st Sarfraz Ahmed b Yasir Shah	40	– b Shoaib Malik	0
J. E. Root c Sarfraz Ahmed b Rahat Ali	4	– lbw b Yasir Shah	6
J. W. A. Taylor c Sarfraz Ahmed b Rahat Ali	76	– c Younis Khan b Zulfiqar Babar	2
†J. M. Bairstow b Zulfiqar Babar	43	– lbw b Yasir Shah	0
S. R. Patel b Yasir Shah	42	– lbw b Zulfiqar Babar	0
A. U. Rashid c Azhar Ali b Shoaib Malik	8	– b Rahat Ali	22
S. C. J. Broad not out	13	– c Shoaib Malik b Yasir Shah	20
J. M. Anderson b Shoaib Malik	7	– (11) not out	0
B. A. Stokes b Shoaib Malik	0	– (10) st Sarfraz Ahmed b Yasir Shah	12
L-b 6, n-b 4	10	B 7, w 1, n-b 1	9
(126.5 overs)	306	(60.3 overs)	156

1/19 (2) 2/90 (1) 3/97 (4) 4/139 (3) 5/228 (5) 1/34 (1) 2/34 (3) 3/48 (4) 4/57 (5) 5/58 (6)
6/245 (6) 7/285 (8) 8/287 (7) 9/296 (10) 10/306 (11) 6/59 (7) 7/108 (8) 8/138 (9) 9/150 (2) 10/156 (10)

Rahat Ali 22–12–48–2; Yasir Shah 36–3–99–3; Wahab Riaz 20–5–33–0; Zulfiqar Babar 37–6–80–1; Shoaib Malik 9.5–3–33–4; Azhar Ali 2–0–7–0. *Second innings*—Rahat Ali 5–1–23–1; Wahab Riaz 5–0–25–0; Zulfiqar Babar 18–5–31–2; Shoaib Malik 15–4–26–3; Yasir Shah 17.3–2–44–4.

Umpires: C. B. Gaffaney *(New Zealand)* (4) and B. N. J. Oxenford *(Australia)* (28).
Third umpire: P. R. Reiffel *(Australia)*. Referee: A. J. Pycroft *(Zimbabwe)* (43).

Close of play: first day, England 4–0 (Cook 0, Ali 4); second day, England 222–4 (Taylor 74, Bairstow 37); third day, Pakistan 146–3 (Mohammad Hafeez 97, Rahat Ali 0); fourth day, England 46–2 (Cook 17, Root 6).

SRI LANKA v WEST INDIES 2015–16 (1st Test)

At Galle International Stadium on 14, 15, 16, 17 October, 2015.
Toss: Sri Lanka.   Result: SRI LANKA WON BY AN INNINGS AND SIX RUNS.
Debuts: Sri Lanka – T. A. M. Siriwardene.
Man of the Match: H. M. R. K. B. Herath.

Sri Lanka were easy winners in the end, running up a huge total and then letting their spinners loose on the ever-helpful Galle pitch. But it might have been different had West Indies not dropped five catches – two of them from Chandimal, who went on to make 151. After a careful start on a sluggish surface, he and Karunaratne had opened out to complete the first 200 partnership by either side in this fixture. Karunaratne, who reached three figures with a six off Bishoo, went on to a chanceless career-best 186, before the last seven wickets tumbled for 59. Sri Lanka's spinners soon got stuck in: Herath, on for the sixth over, soon had three wickets. Bravo made a studied 50, but no one else could make much headway, although Ramdin lasted 99 minutes and Roach 108. Herath finished with his eighth five-for at Galle. West Indies had prolonged their first innings past tea on the third day, but Mathews still enforced the follow-on. This time it was the other slow left-armer, the debutant Milinda Siriwardene, who made the breakthrough. Samuels failed again – a miserable match got worse when his bowling action was reported for the third time – and, when Bravo was caught behind, West Indies were sinking fast at 88 for five. Blackwood counter-attacked, hitting three sixes, but only delayed the inevitable. He was last out, midway through the fourth day, as Sri Lanka completed the ninth win in their last 14 Tests at Galle, dating back to July 2009.

Sri Lanka

F. D. M. Karunaratne c and b Samuels	186
J. K. Silva c Ramdin b Roach	17
H. D. R. L. Thirimanne c sub (R. Chandrika) b Bishoo	16
L. D. Chandimal c Blackwood b Taylor	151
*A. D. Mathews c and b Holder	48
T. A. M. Siriwardene c Ramdin b Taylor	1
†M. D. K. J. Perera b Gabriel	23
K. T. G. D. Prasad c Holder b Bishoo	13
H. M. R. K. B. Herath lbw b Bishoo	0
P. H. T. Kaushal not out	9
A. N. P. R. Fernando c Gabriel b Bishoo	0
B 4, l-b 5, w 5, n-b 6	20
(152.3 overs)	484

1/56 (2) 2/101 (3) 3/339 (1) 4/425 (4) 5/427 (6) 6/448 (5) 7/467 (8) 8/467 (9) 9/475 (7) 10/484 (11)

Taylor 20–4–65–2; Roach 19–3–57–1; Holder 21–4–36–1; Gabriel 20–2–76–1; Samuels 27–4–84–1; Bishoo 40.3–2–143–4; Brathwaite 5–0–14–0.

West Indies

K. C. Brathwaite lbw b Herath	19	– lbw b Herath	34
S. D. Hope b Herath	23	– b Siriwardene	6
D. M. Bravo c Chandimal b Herath	50	– c Perera b Fernando	31
M. N. Samuels b Herath	11	– (5) lbw b Herath	0
J. Blackwood c Siriwardene b Prasad	11	– (6) c Silva b Prasad	92
†D. Ramdin c Perera b Fernando	23	– (7) c Silva b Siriwardene	11
*J. O. Holder c Perera b Prasad	19	– (8) run out (Mathews)	18
K. A. J. Roach st Perera b Herath	22	– (9) st Perera b Herath	5
J. E. Taylor c Mathews b Kaushal	31	– (10) lbw b Prasad	5
D. Bishoo not out	23	– (4) c Mathews b Herath	10
S. T. Gabriel b Herath	0	– not out	7
B 5, l-b 6, w 1, n-b 7	19	L-b 3, w 2, n-b 3	8
(82 overs)	251	(68.3 overs)	227

1/33 (1) 2/49 (2) 3/70 (4) 4/111 (5) 5/132 (3) 6/165 (7) 7/171 (6) 8/217 (9) 9/251 (8) 10/251 (11)

1/18 (2) 2/60 (1) 3/74 (4) 4/74 (5) 5/88 (3) 6/136 (7) 7/172 (8) 8/178 (9) 9/189 (10) 10/227 (6)

Prasad 15–6–38–2; Fernando 15–4–56–1; Herath 33–9–68–6; Kaushal 14–4–65–1; Siriwardene 5–2–13–0. *Second innings*—Prasad 9.3–3–28–2; Herath 22–5–79–4; Fernando 14–1–28–1; Siriwardene 12–1–60–2; Kaushal 11–3–29–0.

Umpires: M. Erasmus *(South Africa)* (33) and R. K. Illingworth *(England)* (18).
Third umpire: S. D. Fry *(Australia)*.   Referee: D. C. Boon *(Australia)* (27).

Close of play: first day, Sri Lanka 250–2 (Karunaratne 135, Chandimal 72); second day, West Indies 66–2 (Bravo 15, Samuels 7); third day, West Indies 67–2 (Bravo 20, Bishoo 6).

Test No. 2184/17 (SL243, WI510)

SRI LANKA v WEST INDIES 2015–16 (2nd Test)

At P. Sara Oval, Colombo, on 22, 23, 24, 25 *(no play)*, 26 October, 2015.
Toss: Sri Lanka.   Result: SRI LANKA WON BY 72 RUNS.
Debuts: Sri Lanka – B. K. G. Mendis. West Indies – J. A. Warrican.
Man of the Match: T. A. M. Siriwardene.   Man of the Series: H. M. R. K. B. Herath.

In front of Sir Garfield Sobers, and hordes of schoolchildren admitted free, West Indies twice threatened to square the series, only for their batsmen to fall short again. They owed the chance of a first Test win in 11 attempts in Sri Lanka to two unheralded bowlers: Jomel Warrican, the debutant slow left-armer from Barbados, took four wickets as Sri Lanka were bowled out for 200, then Kraigg Brathwaite, whose off-breaks had claimed a solitary wicket in 23 previous Tests, polished off the second innings with six. But West Indies' batting would have made Sobers wince: all out for 163 to concede a lead of 37, then – needing a modest 244 on a track that was turning a little – rolled for 171. It was a team effort: Sri Lanka's spinners shared 14 wickets, while paceman Prasad took five. Siriwardene also made the highest score of the match on the first afternoon – a maiden Test half-century – after Sri Lanka had slipped to 90 for five. After rain wiped out the fourth day, Herath – who had just one wicket in 32 previous overs in the match – virtually decided the issue in his 33rd, when Ramdin and Bravo (after battling 155 minutes for 61) both edged to slip. Herath finally sealed a 2–0 win with the 11th successive positive result in a Test at the Sara Oval, though only Sri Lanka's second victory in the last six. Blackwood took five catches in the second innings, equalling the Test record for an outfielder.

Sri Lanka

F. D. M. Karunaratne lbw b Holder	13	– c Bishoo b Taylor	0
J. K. Silva c Ramdin b Taylor	0	– c Blackwood b Warrican	32
B. K. G. Mendis c Ramdin b Roach	13	– c Ramdin b Warrican	39
L. D. Chandimal b Taylor	25	– c Ramdin b Taylor	12
*A. D. Mathews c Brathwaite b Holder	14	– c Blackwood b Brathwaite	46
T. A. M. Siriwardene c Taylor b Warrican	68	– c Blackwood b Brathwaite	42
†M. D. K. J. Perera c and b Warrican	16	– c Ramdin b Brathwaite	5
M. D. K. Perera st Ramdin b Bishoo	5	– (9) c Roach b Brathwaite	7
H. M. R. K. B. Herath not out	26	– (8) c Blackwood b Brathwaite	18
K. T. G. D. Prasad c Ramdin b Warrican	7	– not out	1
A. N. P. R. Fernando lbw b Warrican	0	– c Blackwood b Brathwaite	0
B 10, l-b 3	13	B 2, l-b 2	4
(66 overs)	200	(75.3 overs)	206

1/1 (2) 2/34 (1) 3/34 (3) 4/59 (5) 5/90 (4) 6/127 (7)   1/0 (1) 2/55 (3) 3/84 (2) 4/84 (4) 5/151 (6)
7/149 (8) 8/173 (6) 9/200 (10) 10/200 (11)   6/165 (7) 7/195 (8) 8/203 (9) 9/206 (5) 10/206 (11)

Taylor 15–2–50–2; Roach 12–4–30–1; Holder 11–1–22–2; Warrican 20–2–67–4; Bishoo 8–0–18–1. *Second innings*—
Taylor 8–3–26–2; Roach 6–1–15–0; Holder 5–1–9–0; Warrican 25–2–62–2; Bishoo 20–3–61–0; Brathwaite 11.3–4–29–6.

West Indies

K. C. Brathwaite c M. D. K. J. Perera b Siriwardene	47	– lbw b Prasad	3
S. D. Hope lbw b Prasad	4	– st M. D. K. J. Perera b Siriwardene	35
D. Bishoo c M. D. K. J. Perera b Prasad	13	– (10) run out (Mathews/M. D. K. J. Perera)	0
D. M. Bravo b Prasad	2	– (3) c Mathews b Herath	61
M. N. Samuels c Mathews b Siriwardene	13	– (4) c Mathews b M. D. K. Perera	6
J. Blackwood c M. D. K. J. Perera b Prasad	16	– (5) lbw b Siriwardene	4
†D. Ramdin b Herath	14	– (6) c Mathews b Herath	10
*J. O. Holder c Mathews b M. D. K. Perera	21	– (7) lbw b Siriwardene	7
K. A. J. Roach not out	17	– (8) lbw b Herath	13
J. E. Taylor lbw b M. D. K. Perera	1	– (9) c Siriwardene b Herath	1
J. A. Warrican c and b M. D. K. Perera	1	– not out	20
B 9, l-b 3, w 1, n-b 1	14	B 3, l-b 1, w 1, n-b 6	11
(64.2 overs)	163	(65.5 overs)	171

1/7 (2) 2/33 (3) 3/37 (4) 4/76 (5) 5/89 (1)   1/20 (1) 2/80 (2) 3/97 (4) 4/102 (5) 5/124 (6)
6/105 (6) 7/137 (7) 8/149 (8) 9/151 (10) 10/163 (11)   6/125 (3) 7/133 (7) 8/136 (9) 9/138 (10) 10/171 (8)

Prasad 12–3–34–4; Fernando 11–3–24–0; Herath 20–5–39–1; M. D. K. Perera 11.2–3–28–3; Siriwardene 10–2–26–2.
Second innings—Prasad 10–2–38–1; Fernando 3–0–11–0; Herath 19.5–3–56–4; M. D. K. Perera 20–4–37–1;
Siriwardene 13–1–25–3.

Umpires: S. D. Fry *(Australia)* (1) and R. J. Tucker *(Australia)* (39).
Third umpire: M. Erasmus *(South Africa)*.   Referee: D. C. Boon *(Australia)* (28).

Close of play: first day, West Indies 17–1 (Brathwaite 4, Bishoo 5); second day, Sri Lanka 76–2 (Silva 31, Chandimal 5); third day, West Indies 20–1 (Hope 17); fourth day, no play.

Test No. 2185/53 (A781, NZ402)

AUSTRALIA v NEW ZEALAND 2015–16 (1st Test)

At Woolloongabba, Brisbane, on 5, 6, 7, 8, 9 November, 2015.
Toss: Australia.   Result: AUSTRALIA WON BY 208 RUNS.
Debuts: none.
Man of the Match: D. A. Warner.

Australia made a belated start to their international season, after declining to go to Bangladesh in October for security reasons. There were concerns a rejigged side might struggle against the seamers, yet after some early encouragement for Southee the pattern of so many Gabba Tests was re-imposed, as Australia chugged relentlessly to 556 for four. For the third home season in a row, Warner hit a century in Australia's opening match. And, for the second year running, he did it in both innings, joining Ricky Ponting and Sunil Gavaskar in making twin tons three times. He put on 163 with Burns, then 150 with Khawaja, who reached his maiden Test hundred just before the first-day close. Next day Khawaja and Voges added 157, before Smith – in his first Test since succeeding Michael Clarke as captain – called a halt. Williamson provided New Zealand's only resistance, with a superb 140 – but the three below him mustered just nine between them. Burns and Warner became the first Australian openers to put on 100 in both innings; Warner had now uniquely been involved in four successive century opening stands, following 113 at Trent Bridge and 110 at The Oval with Chris Rogers. The only other pair to share two 150-plus stands in a Test were Paul Gibb and Eddie Paynter, for England's second wicket against South Africa at Johannesburg in 1938–39. Burns reached his own maiden century with two sixes in three balls off Craig. Set 504, New Zealand hoped for rain, but there wasn't enough. Latham and Guptill stonewalled, Williamson batted fluidly again before being adjudged lbw, and McCullum entertained with a run-a-ball 80.

Australia

J. A. Burns c Watling b Southee	71	– c Taylor b Craig	129
D. A. Warner c Taylor b Neesham	163	– c Boult b Craig	116
U. T. Khawaja c Guptill b Williamson	174	– not out	9
*S. P. D. Smith b Boult	48	– c Williamson b Boult	1
A. C. Voges not out	83	– (6) not out	1
M. R. Marsh (did not bat)		– (5) c McCullum b Craig	2
L-b 7, w 4, n-b 6	17	L-b 1, w 1, n-b 4	6
(4 wkts dec, 130.2 overs)	556	(4 wkts dec, 42 overs)	264

1/161 (1) 2/311 (2)   1/237 (2) 2/254 (1)
3/399 (4) 4/556 (3)   3/258 (4) 4/263 (5)

†P. M. Nevill, M. G. Johnson, M. A. Starc, J. R. Hazlewood and N. M. Lyon did not bat.

Southee 24–8–70–1; Boult 29–3–127–1; Bracewell 27–3–107–0; Craig 31–3–156–0; Neesham 11–1–50–1; Williamson 8.2–0–39–1. *Second innings*—Boult 8–0–61–1; Bracewell 11–1–63–0; Neesham 9–0–61–0; Craig 14–0–78–3.

New Zealand

M. J. Guptill c Warner b Hazlewood	23	– (2) c Smith b Lyon	23
T. W. M. Latham c Lyon b Starc	47	– (1) lbw b Starc	29
K. S. Williamson c Nevill b Starc	140	– lbw b Lyon	59
L. R. P. L. Taylor c Smith b Johnson	0	– c Smith b Hazlewood	26
*B. B. McCullum c Voges b Johnson	6	– c Smith b Marsh	80
J. D. S. Neesham b Starc	3	– c Burns b Johnson	3
†B-J. Watling c Nevill b Johnson	32	– lbw b Lyon	14
M. D. Craig c Marsh b Lyon	24	– not out	26
D. A. J. Bracewell b Marsh	16	– lbw b Marsh	0
T. G. Southee b Starc	14	– c Nevill b Hazlewood	5
T. A. Boult not out	0	– c Nevill b Starc	15
L-b 4, w 1, n-b 7	12	B 7, l-b 5, w 2, n-b 1	15
(82.2 overs)	317	(88.3 overs)	295

1/56 (1) 2/102 (2) 3/105 (4) 4/114 (5) 5/118 (6)   1/44 (1) 2/98 (2) 3/136 (3) 4/165 (4) 5/205 (6)
6/185 (7) 7/231 (8) 8/273 (9) 9/310 (10) 10/317 (3)   6/242 (7) 7/243 (5) 8/243 (9) 9/249 (10) 10/295 (11)

Starc 17.2–4–57–4; Johnson 21–3–105–3; Hazlewood 21–5–70–1; Lyon 17–3–46–1; Marsh 5–0–32–1; Voges 1–0–3–0. *Second innings*—Starc 20.3–5–69–2; Johnson 19–6–58–1; Hazlewood 18–3–68–2; Marsh 10–3–25–2; Lyon 21–3–63–3.

Umpires: R. K. Illingworth *(England)* (19) and N. J. Llong *(England)* (32).
Third umpire: S. Ravi *(India)*.   Referee: R. S. Mahanama *(Sri Lanka)* (59).

Close of play: first day, Australia 389–2 (Khawaja 102, Smith 41); second day, New Zealand 157–5 (Williamson 55, Watling 14); third day, Australia 264–4 (Khawaja 9, Voges 1); fourth day, New Zealand 142–3 (Taylor 20, McCullum 4).

AUSTRALIA v NEW ZEALAND 2015–16 (2nd Test)

At W. A. C. A. Ground, Perth, on 13, 14, 15, 16, 17 November, 2015.
Toss: Australia.   Result: DRAWN.
Debuts: none.
Man of the Match: L. R. P. L. Taylor.

The WACA promised a return to its famed ferociously fast pitches – but this one was more sponge than trampoline. Nicks didn't carry; runs were plonked at will; the bowlers couldn't work on swing because the ball kept going out of shape. Even the sightscreen broke down for 17 minutes. The match always seemed destined for a draw once New Zealand made a decent start in reply to Australia's 559, which included another masterclass from Warner. He hit 244 on the first day alone – more than anyone in a Test bar Don Bradman, who made 309 at Leeds in 1930 (and 244 himself at The Oval in 1934). Warner, who had never lasted 200 balls in an innings before his 163 at Brisbane, now faced 286; his innings was measured and controlled. It was Perth's second-highest Test score, after Matthew Hayden's then-record 380 against Zimbabwe in 2003–04 – at least until Taylor trumped it with 290 for New Zealand, soon after receiving treatment for an eye complaint following a miserable match in Brisbane. He and Williamson shared a third-wicket stand of 265, during which Mitchell Johnson found himself wondering about the futility of it all. On the final day he announced his Test retirement, finishing with 313 wickets (and 2,065 runs). Centuries from Smith and Voges had preceded a conservative declaration which left New Zealand 321 in two sessions. A draw was assured once Williamson and Taylor bedded in again, following Johnson's fiery farewell burst, in which he bounced out both openers.

Australia

J. A. Burns b Henry	40	– c Taylor b Southee	0
D. A. Warner c Craig b Boult	253	– c Latham b Boult	24
U. T. Khawaja c Latham b Bracewell	121		
*S. P. D. Smith c Watling b Henry	27	– (3) c Watling b Boult	138
A. C. Voges c Watling b Boult	41	– (4) lbw b Southee	119
M. R. Marsh c and b Bracewell	34	– (5) lbw b Bracewell	1
†P. M. Nevill st Watling b Craig	19	– (6) c Watling b Southee	35
M. G. Johnson st Watling b Craig	2	– (7) c Watling b Southee	29
M. A. Starc c Latham b Craig	0	– (8) not out	28
J. R. Hazlewood not out	8	– (9) not out	2
N. M. Lyon not out	4		
B 4, l-b 1, w 1, n-b 4	10	B 4, l-b 3, w 1, n-b 1	9
(9 wkts dec, 133 overs)	559	(7 wkts dec, 103 overs)	385

1/101 (1) 2/403 (3) 3/427 (2) 4/462 (4) 5/512 (5)
6/539 (6) 7/547 (7) 8/547 (9) 9/547 (8)

1/8 (1) 2/46 (2) 3/270 (3)
4/277 (5) 5/294 (4) 6/355 (7) 7/366 (6)

Southee 29–6–88–0; Boult 26–2–123–2; Henry 22–2–105–2; Bracewell 25–1–81–2; Craig 23–0–123–3; Williamson 3–0–11–0; Guptill 3–0–7–0; McCullum 2–0–16–0. *Second innings*—Southee 25–4–97–4; Boult 19–2–77–2; Bracewell 20–5–62–1; Henry 20–7–53–0; Craig 18–1–81–0; Williamson 1–0–8–0.

New Zealand

M. J. Guptill lbw b Starc	1	– (2) c Burns b Johnson	17
T. W. M. Latham c Smith b Lyon	36	– (1) c Hazlewood b Johnson	15
K. S. Williamson c Johnson b Hazlewood	166	– not out	32
L. R. P. L. Taylor c sub (J. W. Wells) b Lyon	290	– not out	36
*B. B. McCullum b Marsh	27		
†B-J. Watling c Lyon b Starc	1		
D. A. J. Bracewell c Nevill b Johnson	12		
M. D. Craig c Johnson b Lyon	15		
M. J. Henry b Starc	6		
T. G. Southee c and b Starc	21		
T. A. Boult not out	23		
B 7, l-b 11, w 5, n-b 3	26	B 4	4
(153.5 overs)	624	(2 wkts, 28 overs)	104

1/6 (1) 2/87 (2) 3/352 (3) 4/432 (5) 5/447 (6)
6/485 (7) 7/525 (8) 8/554 (9) 9/587 (10) 10/624 (4)

1/34 (1) 2/44 (2)

Starc 37–7–119–4; Hazlewood 32–2–134–1; Johnson 28–2–157–1; Lyon 37.5–6–107–3; Marsh 15–1–73–1; Smith 4–0–16–0. *Second innings*—Starc 6–1–33–0; Hazlewood 6–3–3–0; Johnson 6–2–20–2; Lyon 7–0–35–0; Marsh 3–0–9–0.

Umpires: N. J. Llong *(England)* (33) and S. Ravi *(India)* (9).
Third umpire: R. K. Illingworth *(England)*.   Referee: R. S. Mahanama *(Sri Lanka)* (60).

Close of play: first day, Australia 416-2 (Warner 244, Smith 5); second day, New Zealand 140-2 (Williamson 70, Taylor 26); third day, New Zealand 510-6 (Taylor 235, Craig 7); fourth day, Australia 258-2 (Smith 131, Voges 101).

AUSTRALIA v NEW ZEALAND 2015–16 (3rd Test)

At Adelaide Oval on 27, 28, 29 November, 2015 (day/night).
Toss: New Zealand.   Result: AUSTRALIA WON BY THREE WICKETS.
Debuts: New Zealand – M. J. Santner.
Man of the Match: J. R. Hazlewood.   Man of the Series: D. A. Warner.

The first floodlit Test was an unqualified success, drawing 123,736 spectators over the three days, a record for an Adelaide Test not involving England. Starc sent down Test cricket's first delivery with a pink ball at 2pm. Guptill was the first victim, lbw to Hazlewood in the fourth over. Afternoon gave way to a spectacular sunset, and a new problem for Tests: no one wanted to bat under the lights. Latham notched a fine fifty, but all out for 202 soon after the dinner (second) break looked insufficient. Warner and Burns did fall in the evening, but actually things unravelled in the bright light next day. Australia should have been 118 for nine when Lyon swept Santner; the ball clipped the back of his bat, and was caught by Williamson at second slip via Lyon's shoulder. Third umpire Nigel Llong examined TV footage for five minutes, said a Hot Spot mark "could have come from anywhere", watched a ball-tracking prediction of the wrong delivery, and said not out. Lyon, standing by the boundary with a pink mark on his bat, was more surprised than anyone. He and Nevill slogged 74 – the highest partnership of the match – which sentenced New Zealand's batsmen to a session under lights; they lost five wickets, and inched to 208 on the third day. With Starc nursing an ankle problem, Hazlewood finished with a Test-best six for 70. Needing 187, Australia made an uncertain start, but the edgy Shaun Marsh hung on for 49, and his side squeaked home under the lights.

New Zealand

M. J. Guptill lbw b Hazlewood	1	– (2) c M. R. Marsh b Hazlewood	17
T. W. M. Latham c Nevill b Lyon	50	– (1) c Nevill b Hazlewood	10
K. S. Williamson lbw b Starc	22	– c Nevill b M. R. Marsh	9
L. R. P. L. Taylor c Nevill b Siddle	21	– lbw b Hazlewood	32
*B. B. McCullum c Nevill b Starc	4	– lbw b M. R. Marsh	20
M. J. Santner b Starc	31	– st Nevill b Lyon	45
†B-J. Watling c Smith b Hazlewood	29	– c Smith b Hazlewood	7
M. D. Craig b Lyon	11	– c Nevill b Hazlewood	15
D. A. J. Bracewell c Burns b Siddle	11	– not out	27
T. G. Southee c Warner b Hazlewood	16	– c Lyon b M. R. Marsh	13
T. A. Boult not out	2	– b Hazlewood	5
L-b 1, w 2, n-b 1	4	B 6, l-b 2	8
(65.2 overs)	202	(62.5 overs)	208

1/7 (1) 2/59 (3) 3/94 (2) 4/98 (4) 5/98 (5) 6/142 (6)   1/29 (2) 2/32 (1) 3/52 (3) 4/84 (5) 5/98 (4) 6/116 (7)
7/164 (8) 8/184 (7) 9/194 (9) 10/202 (10)   7/140 (8) 8/175 (6) 9/192 (10) 10/208 (11)

Starc 9–3–24–3; Hazlewood 17.2–2–66–3; Siddle 17–5–54–2; Lyon 15–1–42–2; M. R. Marsh 5–1–12–0; Smith 2–0–3–0. *Second innings*—Hazlewood 24.5–5–70–6; Siddle 14–6–35–0; M. R. Marsh 14–2–59–3; Lyon 10–1–36–1.

Australia

J. A. Burns b Bracewell	14	– (2) lbw b Boult	11
D. A. Warner c Southee b Boult	1	– (1) c Southee b Bracewell	35
*S. P. D. Smith c Watling b Craig	53	– lbw b Boult	14
A. C. Voges c Guptill b Southee	13	– c Southee b Boult	28
S. E. Marsh run out (McCullum)	2	– c Taylor b Boult	49
M. R. Marsh c Watling b Bracewell	4	– c Williamson b Santner	28
†P. M. Nevill c Santner b Bracewell	66	– c Watling b Boult	10
P. M. Siddle c Latham b Craig	0	– not out	9
J. R. Hazlewood b Santner	4		
N. M. Lyon c Williamson b Boult	34		
M. A. Starc not out	24	– (9) not out	0
B 5, l-b 3, w 1	9	L-b 2, w 1	3
(72.1 overs)	224	(7 wkts, 51 overs)	187

1/6 (2) 2/34 (1) 3/63 (4) 4/67 (5) 5/80 (6) 6/109 (3)   1/34 (2) 2/62 (1) 3/66 (3)
7/109 (8) 8/116 (9) 9/190 (10) 10/224 (7)   4/115 (4) 5/161 (6) 6/176 (5) 7/185 (7)

Southee 17–1–50–1; Boult 17–5–41–2; Bracewell 12.1–3–18–3; Santner 16–1–54–1; Craig 10–1–53–2. *Second innings*—Southee 16–1–58–0; Boult 16–3–60–5; Bracewell 11–2–37–1; Craig 6–0–22–0; Santner 2–0–8–1.

Umpires: R. K. Illingworth *(England)* (20) and S. Ravi *(India)* (10).
Third umpire: N. J. Llong *(England)*.   Referee: R. S. Mahanama *(Sri Lanka)* (61).

Close of play: first day, Australia 54–2 (Smith 24, Voges 9); second day, New Zealand 116–5 (Santner 13, Watling 7).

INDIA v SOUTH AFRICA 2015–16 (1st Test)

At Punjab C. A. Stadium, Mohali, Chandigarh, on 5, 6, 7 November, 2015.
Toss: India.   Result: INDIA WON BY 108 RUNS.
Debuts: South Africa – K. Rabada.
Man of the Match: R. A. Jadeja.

India won through a masterful display of spin by Ashwin, who opened the bowling in both innings. It was a confident start for Kohli, whose first home Test as captain began when he won the toss on his 27th birthday. Du Plessis had admitted: "We are expecting the ball to spin on day one." It did. This was not a dangerous pitch, although it did largely nullify the seamers – but Amla and du Plessis, South Africa's most careful batsmen, offered no stroke to deliveries that did not venture far off the straight. Vijay's flinty 75 was the highlight of India's modest first innings, in which Elgar – whose crabby slow left-armers had produced only six wickets in 17 previous Tests – took four for 22. Before tea next day, South Africa had been bowled out, 17 behind. Elgar, Amla and de Villiers dug in for nearly seven hours between them, but no one else made it into double figures. Next day India lost their last eight for 39 inside 20 overs as, with Steyn sidelined with a groin strain, South Africa's spinners boosted their match haul to 15 wickets, their most in a Test since 1952–53. Still, a target of 218 looked beyond them: among visiting sides only West Indies, at Delhi in 1987–88, had chased more to win a Test in India. Philander opened, but soon became the first of a maiden five-for for Jadeja's left-arm spin. South Africa's second defeat in 22 away Tests was confirmed an hour after tea.

India

M. Vijay lbw b Harmer	75	– c sub (T. Bavuma) b Imran Tahir	47
S. Dhawan c Amla b Philander	0	– c de Villiers b Philander	0
C. A. Pujara lbw b Elgar	31	– c Amla b Imran Tahir	77
*V. Kohli c Elgar b Rabada	1	– c Vilas b van Zyl	29
A. M. Rahane c Amla b Elgar	15	– c sub (T. Bavuma) b Harmer	2
†W. P. Saha c Amla b Elgar	0	– c Vilas b Imran Tahir	20
R. A. Jadeja lbw b Philander	38	– lbw b Harmer	8
A. Mishra c Steyn b Elgar	6	– c du Plessis b Harmer	2
R. Ashwin not out	20	– c Amla b Imran Tahir	3
U. T. Yadav b Imran Tahir	5	– b Harmer	1
V. R. Aaron b Imran Tahir	0	– not out	1
B 6, l-b 1, n-b 3	10	B 9, l-b 1	10
(68 overs)	201	(75.3 overs)	200

1/0 (2) 2/63 (3) 3/65 (4) 4/102 (5) 5/102 (6)
6/140 (1) 7/154 (8) 8/196 (7) 9/201 (10) 10/201 (11)

1/9 (2) 2/95 (1) 3/161 (4) 4/164 (3) 5/164 (5)
6/178 (7) 7/182 (8) 8/185 (9) 9/188 (10) 10/200 (6)

Steyn 11–3–30–0; Philander 15–5–38–2; Harmer 14–1–51–1; Rabada 10–0–30–1; Elgar 8–1–22–4; Imran Tahir 10–3–23–2. *Second innings*—Philander 12–3–23–1; Harmer 24–5–61–4; Elgar 7–1–34–0; Imran Tahir 16.3–1–48–4; Rabada 12–7–19–0; van Zyl 4–1–5–1.

South Africa

D. Elgar c Jadeja b Ashwin	37	– c Kohli b Aaron	16
S. van Zyl lbw b Ashwin	5	– (6) c Rahane b Ashwin	36
F. du Plessis b Jadeja	0	– c Rahane b Ashwin	1
*H. M. Amla st Saha b Ashwin	43	– b Jadeja	0
A. B. de Villiers b Mishra	63	– b Mishra	16
†D. J. Vilas c Jadeja b Ashwin	1	– (7) b Jadeja	7
V. D. Philander c Rahane b Jadeja	3	– (2) lbw b Jadeja	1
S. R. Harmer lbw b Mishra	7	– c Rahane b Jadeja	11
D. W. Steyn st Saha b Jadeja	6	– c Vijay b Ashwin	2
K. Rabada not out	1	– not out	1
Imran Tahir c Pujara b Ashwin	4	– lbw b Jadeja	4
B 6, l-b 7, n-b 1	14	B 8, l-b 5, w 1	14
(68 overs)	184	(39.5 overs)	109

1/9 (2) 2/9 (3) 3/85 (1) 4/105 (4) 5/107 (6)
6/136 (7) 7/170 (8) 8/179 (9) 9/179 (5) 10/184 (11)

1/8 (2) 2/9 (3) 3/10 (4) 4/32 (5) 5/45 (1) 6/60 (7)
7/102 (8) 8/102 (6) 9/105 (9) 10/109 (11)

Ashwin 24–5–51–5; Yadav 6–1–12–0; Aaron 8–1–18–0; Jadeja 18–0–55–3; Mishra 12–3–35–2. *Second innings*—Ashwin 14–5–39–3; Jadeja 11.5–4–21–5; Mishra 8–0–26–1; Aaron 3–0–3–1; Yadav 3–0–7–0.

Umpires: H. D. P. K. Dharmasena *(Sri Lanka)* (34) and R. A. Kettleborough *(England)* (31).
Third umpire: V. A. Kulkarni *(India)*.   Referee: J. J. Crowe *(New Zealand)* (73).

Close of play: first day, South Africa 28–2 (Elgar 13, Amla 9); second day, India 125–2 (Pujara 63, Kohli 11).

INDIA v SOUTH AFRICA 2015-16 (2nd Test)

At M. Chinnaswamy Stadium, Bangalore, on 14, 15 *(no play)*, 16 *(no play)*, 17 *(no play)*, 18 *(no play)* November, 2015.
Toss: India.   Result: DRAWN.
Debuts: none.
Man of the Match: no award.

Only one day's play was possible before a depressing, grey drizzle descended – and refused to abate. Wet weather hampered the groundsman, even though a marquee was erected over the square to keep it as dry as possible. Kohli had expected more seam movement, and South Africa found themselves on a trustworthy pitch not dissimilar, in pace and bounce, to many of their own. But, de Villiers apart, they made a mess of things, and were bowled out for 214. Ashwin and Jadeja took four wickets apiece. Van Zyl left a straight one, and du Plessis was smartly caught at short leg. Amla was cleaned up by a beauty from Aaron – a rare wicket for an Indian seamer – then Elgar tried an aggressive sweep in the first over after lunch, after battling through the morning. In a peculiar twist of fate, de Villiers was playing his 100th Test in the city and stadium where his IPL exploits for the Royal Challengers had made him a household name, as revered and cheered as any Indian. He was in glorious touch, and might well have celebrated the occasion with a century had he received any meaningful support. Instead he was left with the tail, and finally fell for 85, via the faintest of touches off the glove, after a solo effort to rescue an embarrassing total. The ease with which Dhawan and Vijay cruised to 80 was equally embarrassing for South Africa – but happy confirmation for India that they were in control of the series.

South Africa

S. van Zyl lbw b Ashwin	10
D. Elgar b Jadeja	38
F. du Plessis c Pujara b Ashwin	0
*H. M. Amla b Aaron	7
A. B. de Villiers c Saha b Jadeja	85
J-P. Duminy c Rahane b Ashwin	15
†D. J. Vilas c and b Jadeja	15
K. J. Abbott run out (Dhawan/Saha)	14
K. Rabada c Pujara b Jadeja	0
M. Morkel c Binny b Ashwin	22
Imran Tahir not out	0
L-b 2, n-b 6	8
(59 overs)	214

1/15 (1) 2/15 (3) 3/45 (4) 4/78 (2) 5/120 (6)
6/159 (7) 7/177 (5) 8/177 (9) 9/214 (10) 10/214 (8)

Sharma 13–3–40–0; Binny 3–2–1–0; Ashwin 18–2–70–4; Aaron 9–0–51–1; Jadeja 16–2–50–4.

India

M. Vijay not out	28
S. Dhawan not out	45
B 4, n-b 3	7
(no wkt, 22 overs)	80

C. A. Pujara, *V. Kohli, A. M. Rahane, †W. P. Saha, R. A. Jadeja, S. T. R. Binny, R. Ashwin, V. R. Aaron and I. Sharma did not bat.

Morkel 7–1–23–0; Abbott 6–1–18–0; Rabada 5–1–17–0; Duminy 2–0–9–0; Imran Tahir 2–0–9–0.

Umpires: I. J. Gould *(England)* (46) and R. A. Kettleborough *(England)* (32).
Third umpire: C. Shamsuddin *(India).*   Referee: J. J. Crowe *(New Zealand)* (74).

Close of play: first day, India 80–0 (Vijay 28, Dhawan 45); second day, no play; third day, no play; fourth day, no play.

INDIA v SOUTH AFRICA 2015–16 (3rd Test)

At Vidarbha C. A. Stadium, Jamtha, Nagpur, on 25, 26, 27 November, 2015.
Toss: India.   Result: INDIA WON BY 124 RUNS.
Debuts: none.
Man of the Match: R. Ashwin.

A pitch which looked as though it had already hosted a week's play was a spinners' jackpot: India's slow men shared all 20 wickets for the first time in a Test, breaking their record of 19, set three weeks earlier in Mohali. Scores of 20 or 30 seemed to be worth double, and it was India who produced most of those: when South Africa cascaded to 12 for five early on day two, the contest was virtually over. Duminy's 35 from 65 balls was one of his most skilled efforts, but even that swelled the total only to 79 – South Africa's lowest since 1956–57, when they made 72 against England at both Johannesburg and Cape Town. Imran Tahir celebrated his second-innings five-for in typically ebullient style, but it was relatively meaningless, as India's advantage had stretched past 300; it was 218 even before he came on. South Africa's first innings had lasted only 33.1 overs, but they made a mess of the argument that the pitch was unplayable by surviving almost 90 in their second. Amla batted with a suitable grimness, but his captaincy betrayed the pressure. He twice sent the hapless Tahir out as nightwatchman in his stead, and both times had to come out anyway. Ashwin finished with a career-best seven for 66, the best by an Indian against South Africa. Kohli's annoyance that a thumping victory and famous series win were put down to the pitch – which was later censured by the ICC – was understandable, but naive.

India

M. Vijay lbw b Morkel	40	– c Amla b Morkel 5
S. Dhawan c and b Elgar	12	– c Vilas b Imran Tahir 39
C. A. Pujara lbw b Harmer	21	– b Duminy 31
*V. Kohli c Vilas b Morkel	22	– c du Plessis b Imran Tahir 16
A. M. Rahane b Morkel	13	– c Duminy b Imran Tahir 9
R. G. Sharma c de Villiers b Harmer	2	– c Elgar b Morkel 23
†W. P. Saha c Duminy b Harmer	32	– c Amla b Imran Tahir 7
R. A. Jadeja b Rabada	34	– b Harmer 5
R. Ashwin b Imran Tahir	15	– lbw b Morkel 7
A. Mishra lbw b Harmer	3	– b Imran Tahir 14
I. Sharma not out	0	– not out 1
B 15, l-b 3, w 2, n-b 1	21	B 8, l-b 5, n-b 3 16
(78.2 overs)	215	(46.3 overs) 173

1/50 (2) 2/69 (1) 3/94 (3) 4/115 (5) 5/116 (4)   1/8 (1) 2/52 (3) 3/97 (2) 4/102 (4) 5/108 (5)
6/125 (6) 7/173 (8) 8/201 (7) 9/215 (9) 10/215 (10)   6/122 (7) 7/128 (8) 8/150 (9) 9/171 (6) 10/173 (10)

Morkel 16.1–7–35–3; Rabada 17–8–30–1; Harmer 27.2–2–78–4; Elgar 4–0–7–1; Imran Tahir 12.5–1–41–1; Duminy 1–0–6–0. *Second innings*—Morkel 10–5–19–3; Harmer 18–3–64–1; Rabada 5–1–15–0; Duminy 2–0–24–1; Imran Tahir 11.3–2–38–5.

South Africa

D. Elgar b Ashwin	7	– lbw b Ashwin 18
S. van Zyl c Rahane b Ashwin	0	– c R. G. Sharma b Ashwin 5
Imran Tahir b Jadeja	4	– lbw b Mishra 8
*H. M. Amla c Rahane b Ashwin	1	– c Kohli b Mishra 39
A. B. de Villiers c and b Jadeja	0	– lbw b Ashwin 9
F. du Plessis b Jadeja	10	– b Mishra 39
J-P. Duminy lbw b Mishra	35	– lbw b Ashwin 19
†D. J. Vilas b Jadeja	1	– c Saha b Ashwin 12
S. R. Harmer b Ashwin	13	– not out 8
K. Rabada not out	6	– c Kohli b Ashwin 6
M. Morkel c and b Ashwin	1	– b Ashwin 4
L-b 1	1	B 9, l-b 5, n-b 4 18
(33.1 overs)	79	(89.5 overs) 185

1/4 (2) 2/9 (3) 3/11 (1) 4/12 (4) 5/12 (5) 6/35 (6)   1/17 (2) 2/29 (3) 3/40 (1) 4/58 (5) 5/130 (4)
7/47 (8) 8/66 (9) 9/76 (7) 10/79 (11)   6/135 (6) 7/164 (7) 8/167 (8) 9/177 (10) 10/185 (11)

I. Sharma 2–1–4–0; Ashwin 16.1–6–32–5; Jadeja 12–3–33–4; Mishra 3–0–9–1. *Second innings*—I. Sharma 15–6–20–0; Ashwin 29.5–7–66–7; Jadeja 25–12–34–0; Mishra 20–2–51–3.

Umpires: I. J. Gould *(England)* (47) and B. N. J. Oxenford *(Australia)* (29).
Third umpire: A. K. Chaudhary *(India)*.   Referee: J. J. Crowe *(New Zealand)* (75).

Close of play: first day, South Africa 11–2 (Elgar 7, Amla 0); second day, South Africa 32–2 (Elgar 10, Amla 3).

INDIA v SOUTH AFRICA 2015–16 (4th Test)

At Feroz Shah Kotla, Delhi, on 3, 4, 5, 6, 7 December, 2015.
Toss: India. Result: INDIA WON BY 337 RUNS.
Debuts: none.
Man of the Match: A. M. Rahane. Man of the Series: R. Ashwin.

South Africa briefly took the upper hand when off-spinner Piedt grabbed four wickets on the first day. Later they staged an epic rearguard – but India still took the series 3–0. India dipped to 139 for six, but Rahane made a delightful century – the first of the series – and put on 136 with Ashwin. The eventual 334 looked well above par on a track which, while less spiteful than Mohali and Nagpur, still helped the spinners. Jadeja winkled out five, only de Villiers making more than 22. Kohli waived the follow-on and made 88, surviving being given out caught behind after replays showed Imran Tahir had overstepped. Rahane became the fifth Indian to make twin centuries in a Test, before South Africa were set 481 in around 160 overs. They took bloody-mindedness to another level, with the three slowest Test partnerships of over 200 balls. First Bavuma put on 44 with Amla in 38 overs. Then Amla and de Villiers dropped a gear, adding 27 in 42. Amla fell on the final morning, after making 25 from 244 balls in 289 minutes. De Villiers stayed put, adding 35 at a run per over with du Plessis. Seven balls after tea Ashwin finally removed de Villiers: he made 43 in 354 minutes, scoring off only 21 of his 297 balls in the longest-known Test innings under 50. The 143.1 overs South Africa faced for their 143 runs was a fourth-innings record by any team in Asia. But it wasn't quite enough.

India

M. Vijay c Amla b Piedt	12	– c Vilas b Morkel	3
S. Dhawan lbw b Piedt	33	– b Morkel	21
C. A. Pujara b Abbott	14	– (4) b Imran Tahir	28
*V. Kohli c Vilas b Piedt	44	– (5) lbw b Abbott	88
A. M. Rahane c de Villiers b Imran Tahir	127	– (6) not out	100
R. G. Sharma c Imran Tahir b Piedt	1	– (3) b Morkel	0
†W. P. Saha b Abbott	1	– not out	23
R. A. Jadeja c Elgar b Abbott	24		
R. Ashwin c de Villiers b Abbott	56		
U. T. Yadav not out	10		
I. Sharma lbw b Abbott	0		
B 8, w 1, n-b 3	12	L-b 2, n-b 2	4
(117.5 overs)	334	(5 wkts dec, 100.1 overs)	267

1/30 (1) 2/62 (2) 3/66 (3) 4/136 (4) 5/138 (6)
6/139 (7) 7/198 (8) 8/296 (5) 9/334 (9) 10/334 (11)
1/4 (1) 2/8 (3) 3/53 (2)
4/57 (4) 5/211 (5)

Morkel 24–5–58–0; Abbott 24.5–7–40–5; Piedt 38–6–117–4; Imran Tahir 16–2–66–1; Elgar 11–0–33–0; Duminy 4–0–12–0. *Second innings*—Morkel 21–6–51–3; Abbott 22–9–47–1; Piedt 18–1–53–0; Imran Tahir 26.1–4–74–1; Elgar 13–1–40–0.

South Africa

D. Elgar c Saha b Yadav	17	– c Rahane b Ashwin	4
T. Bavuma b Jadeja	22	– b Ashwin	34
*H. M. Amla c Saha b Jadeja	3	– b Jadeja	25
A. B. de Villiers c I. Sharma b Jadeja	42	– c Jadeja b Ashwin	43
F. du Plessis c Rahane b Jadeja	0	– lbw b Jadeja	10
J-P. Duminy b Yadav	1	– lbw b Ashwin	0
†D. J. Vilas b I. Sharma	11	– b Yadav	13
K. J. Abbott lbw b Ashwin	4	– b Yadav	0
D. L. Piedt c Rahane b Jadeja	5	– c Saha b Yadav	1
M. Morkel not out	9	– b Ashwin	2
Imran Tahir c sub (K. L. Rahul) b Ashwin	1	– not out	0
B 5, n-b 1	6	B 8, l-b 3	11
(49.3 overs)	121	(143.1 overs)	143

1/36 (1) 2/40 (2) 3/56 (3) 4/62 (5) 5/65 (6)
6/79 (7) 7/84 (8) 8/103 (9) 9/118 (4) 10/121 (11)
1/5 (1) 2/49 (2) 3/76 (3) 4/111 (5) 5/112 (6)
6/136 (7) 7/136 (4) 8/140 (8) 9/143 (9) 10/143 (10)

I. Sharma 12–5–28–1; Yadav 12–3–32–2; Ashwin 13.3–5–26–2; Jadeja 12–2–30–5. *Second innings*—I. Sharma 20–12–23–0; Ashwin 49.1–26–61–5; Jadeja 46–33–26–2; Yadav 21–16–9–3; Dhawan 3–1–9–0; Vijay 2–0–2–0; Kohli 1–1–0–0; Pujara 1–0–2–0.

Umpires: H. D. P. K. Dharmasena *(Sri Lanka)* (35) and B. N. J. Oxenford *(Australia)* (30).
Third umpire: C. K. Nandan *(India)*. Referee: J. J. Crowe *(New Zealand)* (76).

Close of play: first day, India 231–7 (Rahane 89, Ashwin 6); second day, South Africa 121; third day, India 190–4 (Kohli 83, Rahane 52); fourth day, South Africa 72–2 (Amla 23, de Villiers 11).

Test No. 2192/31 (NZ405, SL244)

NEW ZEALAND v SRI LANKA 2015–16 (1st Test)

At University Oval, Dunedin, on 10, 11, 12, 13, 14 December, 2015.
Toss: Sri Lanka.   Result: NEW ZEALAND WON BY 122 RUNS.
Debuts: Sri Lanka – M. D. U. S. Jayasundera.
Man of the Match: M. J. Guptill.

Put in on a chilly morning at the world's southernmost venue, New Zealand's batsmen seized control, then their bowlers clinched victory on the final afternoon. A thick covering of grass didn't automatically mean a seamer's haven; after a quiet start, Guptill drove well in his first home Test appearance since March 2012, reaching his third Test century – the first for 41 innings – during a stand of 173 with Williamson; McCullum then biffed 75 from 57 balls. By stumps New Zealand already had 409. They had chosen four pacemen, who all had to work hard as Sri Lanka survived 212 overs in total. Karunaratne dug in for more than four hours, and Chandimal for nearly five. Sri Lanka trailed by 137, even though they received 21 more overs. Latham extended the lead with his third Test century, before a declaration set 405 in around 140 overs. McCullum's brief innings occupied only six balls, but included two sixes, the second his 100th in Tests, equalling Adam Gilchrist's record. The weather looked the likely winner when hailstones cascaded on the final day, but the seamers worked their way through. Mathews's odd dismissal was the beginning of the end. Casually pushing the pad forward to let a full delivery sail down leg, he was mortified as it cannoned into his stumps. Watling took nine catches, to equal the national record he already shared with McCullum; he was only the third keeper to take nine in a Test twice, after Mark Boucher and Brad Haddin.

New Zealand

M. J. Guptill c Chandimal b Mathews	156	– (2) b Herath	46
T. W. M. Latham c and b Lakmal	22	– (1) not out	109
K. S. Williamson c Karunaratne b Fernando	88	– b Chameera	71
L. R. P. L. Taylor lbw b Fernando	8	– b Herath	15
*B. B. McCullum c Vithanage b Siriwardene	75	– not out	17
M. J. Santner c Chandimal b Chameera	12		
†B-J. Watling c Vithanage b Chameera	5		
D. A. J. Bracewell lbw b Fernando	47		
T. G. Southee c Siriwardene b Lakmal	2		
N. Wagner c Jayasundera b Fernando	7		
T. A. Boult not out	0		
B 4, l-b 3, w 1, n-b 1	9	B 4, n-b 5	9
(96.1 overs)	431	(3 wkts dec, 65.4 overs)	267

1/56 (2) 2/229 (3) 3/245 (4) 4/334 (5) 5/359 (6)   1/79 (2) 2/220 (3) 3/247 (4)
6/365 (7) 7/394 (1) 8/399 (9) 9/426 (10) 10/431 (8)

Lakmal 16–1–69–2; Fernando 23.1–2–112–4; Mathews 9–2–28–1; Chameera 20–2–112–2; Herath 19–1–46–0; Jayasundera 5–0–33–0; Siriwardene 4–0–24–1. *Second innings*—Lakmal 13–0–40–0; Mathews 4–1–4–0; Chameera 14–0–61–1; Fernando 13–1–52–0; Herath 11.4–1–62–2; Siriwardene 8–0–32–0; Jayasundera 2–0–12–0.

Sri Lanka

F. D. M. Karunaratne c Watling b Santner	84	– c Watling b Southee	29
B. K. G. Mendis c Watling b Boult	8	– c Watling b Southee	46
M. D. U. S. Jayasundera c Watling b Wagner	1	– c Watling b Wagner	3
†L. D. Chandimal c Guptill b Southee	83	– lbw b Santner	58
*A. D. Mathews c Watling b Southee	2	– b Wagner	25
K. D. K. Vithanage c Watling b Southee	22	– lbw b Southee	38
T. A. M. Siriwardene c Taylor b Wagner	35	– c McCullum b Boult	29
H. M. R. K. B. Herath c Boult b Wagner	15	– c Guptill b Boult	6
P. V. D. Chameera c Taylor b Boult	14	– b Wagner	14
R. A. S. Lakmal not out	18	– c and b Bracewell	23
A. N. P. R. Fernando c Watling b Santner	3	– not out	4
B 1, l-b 4, n-b 2	9	B 2, l-b 4, w 1	7
(117.1 overs)	294	(95.2 overs)	282

1/19 (2) 2/29 (3) 3/151 (1) 4/156 (5) 5/198 (4)   1/54 (1) 2/64 (3) 3/109 (2) 4/165 (5) 5/165 (4)
6/209 (6) 7/252 (7) 8/273 (8) 9/287 (9) 10/294 (11)   6/213 (6) 7/236 (8) 8/249 (7) 9/268 (9) 10/282 (10)

Boult 22–7–52–2; Southee 27–4–71–3; Bracewell 21–6–42–0; Wagner 25–5–87–3; Santner 21.1–8–37–2; Williamson 1–1–0–0. *Second innings*—Boult 15–2–58–2; Southee 21–6–52–3; Bracewell 19.2–5–46–1; Santner 22–6–53–2; Wagner 17–5–56–2; Williamson 1–0–11–0.

Umpires: R. A. Kettleborough *(England)* (33) and N. J. Llong *(England)* (34).
Third umpire: P. R. Reiffel *(Australia)*.   Referee: D. C. Boon *(Australia)* (29).

Close of play: first day, New Zealand 409–8 (Bracewell 32, Wagner 0); second day, Sri Lanka 197–4 (Chandimal 83, Vithanage 10); third day, New Zealand 171–1 (Latham 72, Williamson 48); fourth day, Sri Lanka 109–3 (Chandimal 31).

NEW ZEALAND v SRI LANKA 2015–16 (2nd Test)

At Seddon Park, Hamilton, on 18, 19, 20, 21 December, 2015.
Toss: New Zealand.   Result: NEW ZEALAND WON BY FIVE WICKETS.
Debuts: none.
Man of the Match: K. S. Williamson.

The Seddon Park pitch was a verdant green carpet, and almost inevitably this became the 16th successive Test in New Zealand in which the captain winning the toss bowled first. Although there was not as much movement as expected, batting was still difficult. Williamson's class told, despite a fine display from the speedy Chameera. The home bowlers tried too hard at first: Mathews and Siriwardene tucked in, both hitting three sixes during a stand of 138 in 30 overs, and 292 looked like a competitive total. Guptill and Latham put on 81, helped by Mathews's mysterious reluctance to try Chameera. He eventually came on as third change, and induced a collapse of four for eight. In his 99th Test – all consecutive from debut, breaking A. B. de Villiers's record – McCullum lasted 80 minutes for 18, but Chameera took five to ensure a lead of 55. Sri Lanka's openers put on 71 but, after that, facing a short-pitched barrage, all ten tumbled for 62 in 14 overs. A fascinating Test had been turned on its head, and New Zealand had to chase 189. Chameera removed both openers, but Williamson calmly reached his 13th Test century to ensure a 2–0 win. It took him to 1,172 Test runs in 2015, eight more than McCullum's national record set the year before. New Zealand had now gone 13 home Tests without defeat, equalling their longest such run, between 1986–87 and 1990–91. This was their fourth successive win at home, all against Sri Lanka.

Sri Lanka

F. D. M. Karunaratne c Watling b Southee	12	– c Southee b Bracewell	27
B. K. G. Mendis c Watling b Southee	31	– c Santner b Southee	46
M. D. U. S. Jayasundera run out (Santner/Watling)	26	– c Watling b Bracewell	0
†L. D. Chandimal c Watling b Bracewell	47	– c Guptill b Wagner	4
*A. D. Mathews c Latham b Southee	77	– c Watling b Southee	2
T. A. M. Siriwardene c Taylor b Boult	62	– c Boult b Wagner	26
K. D. K. Vithanage c McCullum b Boult	0	– c Bracewell b Wagner	9
H. M. R. K. B. Herath run out (Williamson)	4	– b Southee	0
P. V. D. Chameera c McCullum b Bracewell	4	– run out (Boult/Wagner)	2
R. A. S. Lakmal c Williamson b Wagner	4	– not out	1
A. N. P. R. Fernando not out	2	– c Watling b Southee	0
L-b 11, w 12	23	B 4, l-b 2, w 7, n-b 3	16
(80.1 overs)	292	(36.3 overs)	133

1/39 (1) 2/44 (2) 3/115 (3) 4/121 (4) 5/259 (6)
6/259 (7) 7/264 (8) 8/284 (5) 9/288 (10) 10/292 (9)

1/71 (1) 2/71 (3) 3/77 (4) 4/87 (2) 5/110 (5)
6/123 (6) 7/123 (8) 8/131 (7) 9/133 (9) 10/133 (11)

Boult 20–2–51–2; Southee 21–5–63–3; Bracewell 22.1–4–81–2; Wagner 9–1–51–1; Santner 7–0–34–0; Williamson 1–0–1–0. *Second innings*—Boult 7–1–30–0; Southee 12.3–2–26–4; Bracewell 8–1–31–2; Wagner 9–2–40–3.

New Zealand

M. J. Guptill c Mathews b Herath	50	– (2) c Karunaratne b Chameera	1
T. W. M. Latham c Karunaratne b Chameera	28	– (1) c Fernando b Chameera	4
K. S. Williamson c Lakmal b Chameera	1	– not out	108
L. R. P. L. Taylor c Chandimal b Chameera	0	– c sub (J. D. F. Vandersay) b Chameera	35
*B. B. McCullum c Mendis b Herath	18	– c Mathews b Chameera	18
M. J. Santner c Chandimal b Fernando	38	– c Chandimal b Lakmal	4
†B-J. Watling c Vithanage b Lakmal	28	– not out	13
D. A. J. Bracewell not out	35		
T. G. Southee c Jayasundera b Chameera	4		
N. Wagner c Vithanage b Chameera	17		
T. A. Boult c Herath b Fernando	0		
L-b 3, w 8, n-b 7	18	L-b 1, n-b 5	6
(79.4 overs)	237	(5 wkts, 54.3 overs)	189

1/81 (2) 2/83 (3) 3/86 (1) 4/89 (4) 5/128 (5)
6/168 (6) 7/196 (7) 8/201 (9) 9/232 (10) 10/237 (11)

1/4 (1) 2/11 (2) 3/78 (4)
4/130 (5) 5/142 (6)

Lakmal 16–4–48–1; Mathews 11–7–25–0; Fernando 17.4–4–39–2; Herath 22–1–75–2; Chameera 13–3–47–5. *Second innings*—Chameera 17–1–68–4; Lakmal 12–4–20–1; Herath 11–0–48–0; Fernando 12–1–43–0; Mathews 1–0–4–0; Siriwardene 1.3–0–5–0.

Umpires: N. J. Llong *(England)* (35) and P. R. Reiffel *(Australia)* (22).
Third umpire: R. A. Kettleborough *(England)*.   Referee: D. C. Boon *(Australia)* (30).

Close of play: first day, Sri Lanka 264–7 (Mathews 63, Chameera 0); second day, New Zealand 232–9 (Bracewell 30); third day, New Zealand 142–5 (Williamson 78, Watling 0).

AUSTRALIA v WEST INDIES 2015–16 (1st Test)

At Bellerive Oval, Hobart, on 10, 11, 12 December, 2015.
Toss: Australia.   Result: AUSTRALIA WON BY AN INNINGS AND 212 RUNS.
Debuts: none.
Man of the Match: A. C. Voges.

There was snow on Hobart's Mount Wellington as the match ended. It felt appropriate, given the latest cold snap in Caribbean cricket's endless winter. Taylor and Roach both began with no-balls, and Australia's openers rattled up 75 in 11 overs. Warner and Smith both fell to slow left-armer Warrican, playing only his second Test, but that brought together Voges and Shaun Marsh, team-mates for Western Australia. Voges broke free with four boundaries in a Warrican over. His third Test century came at a run a ball – Hobart's fastest Test hundred – and next day he glided to 269 by the lunchtime declaration; he faced 285 balls and hit 33 fours. By the time Marsh slog-swept Warrican to deep midwicket they had put on 449 – the highest fourth-wicket stand in Tests (previously 437 by Mahela Jayawardene and Thilan Samaraweera for Sri Lanka v Pakistan at Karachi in 2008-09), the highest for any wicket in Australia (405 by Sid Barnes and Don Bradman for the fifth, v England at Sydney in 1946–47), and the highest against West Indies (411 by Peter May and Colin Cowdrey at Edgbaston in 1957). Only five Test partnerships had yielded more. Bravo made a defiant century, with 20 fours, but West Indies were batting again early on day three. Pattinson, returning after 21 injury-blighted months, claimed four wickets in his first four overs. Brathwaite threatened Charles Bannerman's 1876–77 record for the highest percentage of a Test innings (67.34%), but Hazlewood bowled him just before tea on the third day, completing West Indies' heaviest defeat by Australia for almost 85 years.

Australia

J. A. Burns b Gabriel		33
D. A. Warner c Ramdin b Warrican		64
*S. P. D. Smith c Blackwood b Warrican		10
A. C. Voges not out		269
S. E. Marsh c Bravo b Warrican		182
M. R. Marsh not out		1
B 4, l-b 3, w 3, n-b 14		24
(4 wkts dec, 114 overs)		583

1/75 (1) 2/104 (3) 3/121 (2)
4/570 (5)

†P. M. Nevill, P. M. Siddle, J. L. Pattinson, J. R. Hazlewood and N. M. Lyon did not bat.

Taylor 17–0–108–0; Roach 16–1–99–0; Gabriel 10–1–59–1; Holder 24–3–75–0; Warrican 28–1–158–3; Brathwaite 13–0–52–0; Blackwood 6–0–25–0.

West Indies

K. C. Brathwaite lbw b Hazlewood	2	– b Hazlewood	94
R. Chandrika c Smith b Lyon	25	– c Smith b Pattinson	0
D. M. Bravo c Lyon b Siddle	108	– b Pattinson	4
M. N. Samuels c and b Lyon	9	– c Warner b Pattinson	3
J. Blackwood c Burns b Lyon	0	– b Pattinson	0
†D. Ramdin b Hazlewood	8	– c Warner b M. R. Marsh	4
*J. O. Holder lbw b Siddle	15	– c Nevill b Pattinson	17
K. A. J. Roach c Nevill b Hazlewood	31	– c Nevill b Hazlewood	3
J. E. Taylor b Hazlewood	0	– c Pattinson b Hazlewood	12
J. A. Warrican not out	2	– not out	6
S. T. Gabriel absent hurt		– absent hurt	
B 7, l-b 10, w 1, n-b 5	23	L-b 1, w 1, n-b 3	5
(70 overs)	223	(36.3 overs)	148

1/17 (1) 2/58 (2) 3/78 (4) 4/78 (5) 5/89 (6)   1/2 (2) 2/20 (3) 3/24 (4) 4/24 (5) 5/30 (6)
6/116 (7) 7/215 (8) 8/215 (9) 9/223 (3)   6/60 (7) 7/91 (8) 8/117 (9) 9/148 (1)

Hazlewood 18–5–45–4; Pattinson 15–5–36–2; Lyon 19–6–43–3; M. R. Marsh 3–1–14–0. *Second innings*—Hazlewood 10.3–3–33–3; Pattinson 8–2–27–5; Siddle 7–1–34–0; M. R. Marsh 7–0–36–1; Lyon 4–0–17–0.

Umpires: M. Erasmus *(South Africa)* (34) and I. J. Gould *(England)* (48).
Third umpire: C. B. Gaffaney *(New Zealand)*.   Referee: B. C. Broad *(England)* (73).

Close of play: first day, Australia 438-3 (Voges 174, S. E. Marsh 139); second day, West Indies 207-6 (Bravo 94, Roach 31).

AUSTRALIA v WEST INDIES 2015–16 (2nd Test)

At Melbourne Cricket Ground on 26, 27, 28, 29 December, 2015.
Toss: West Indies.   Result: AUSTRALIA WON BY 177 RUNS.
Debuts: West Indies – C. R. Brathwaite.
Man of the Match: N. M. Lyon.

All the talk beforehand was about how long it would take Australia to go 2–0 up. So when West Indies stretched the match deep into the fourth day, it felt as if they had exceeded expectations. On a damp first morning, the pitch was green enough to persuade Holder to bowl – but Warner struck five of his first eight balls for four. The second-wicket pair added 258: Burns made his second Test century, while Khawaja's third in successive Tests was the 1,000th for Australia in all internationals (England had 964, and India 688). Next day Smith joined in, after missing out at Hobart, and Voges made the innings' fourth century, which took his average against West Indies to 542, the highest against a single team, beating Jacques Rudolph's 293 for South Africa v Bangladesh. Lyon started another batting slide: West Indies were soon 83 for six. Bravo stood alone, before finally receiving some help from the debutant Carlos Brathwaite, who survived two dismissals to Pattinson no-balls to make 59. Khawaja and Smith laid about them before Australia declared for the third innings running: West Indies needed 460, or to bat for two days. Chandrika embodied a more committed effort, but his side slipped to 150 for five before a spirited stand of 100 between Holder and Ramdin. But the pacy Mitchell Marsh dismissed both en route to a Test-best, as the tail fell in a flurry. For the 11th time in a row, the Frank Worrell Trophy was Australia's.

Australia

J. A. Burns st Ramdin b K. C. Brathwaite	128	– c K. C. Brathwaite b Holder	5
D. A. Warner c Samuels b Taylor	23	– c Holder b C. R. Brathwaite	17
U. T. Khawaja c Ramdin b Taylor	144	– c Ramdin b Holder	56
*S. P. D. Smith not out	134	– not out	70
A. C. Voges not out	106		
M. R. Marsh (did not bat)		– (5) not out	18
L-b 10, w 4, n-b 2	16	L-b 6, w 2, n-b 5	13
(3 wkts dec, 135 overs)	551	(3 wkts dec, 32 overs)	179

1/29 (2) 2/287 (1) 3/328 (3)   1/7 (1) 2/46 (2) 3/123 (3)

†P. M. Nevill, P. M. Siddle, J. L. Pattinson, J. R. Hazlewood and N. M. Lyon did not bat.

Taylor 22–2–97–2; Roach 17–1–97–0; Holder 22–7–47–0; C. R. Brathwaite 30–3–109–0; Warrican 26–2–113–0; K. C. Brathwaite 18–1–78–1. *Second innings*—Taylor 3–0–25–0; Holder 11–1–49–2; C. R. Brathwaite 6–1–30–1; Roach 4–0–22–0; Warrican 8–0–47–0.

West Indies

K. C. Brathwaite c Burns b Lyon	17	– c Smith b Lyon	31
R. Chandrika lbw b Pattinson	25	– lbw b Pattinson	37
D. M. Bravo c Smith b Pattinson	81	– c Nevill b Siddle	21
M. N. Samuels lbw b Pattinson	0	– c Nevill b Marsh	19
J. Blackwood c and b Lyon	28	– lbw b Lyon	20
†D. Ramdin c Burns b Siddle	0	– c Nevill b Marsh	59
*J. O. Holder b Siddle	0	– c Hazlewood b Marsh	68
C. R. Brathwaite c and b Lyon	59	– b Lyon	2
K. A. J. Roach lbw b Pattinson	22	– c Warner b Pattinson	11
J. E. Taylor c Nevill b Lyon	15	– c Pattinson b Marsh	0
J. A. Warrican not out	11	– not out	4
B 5, l-b 3, n-b 5	13	L-b 7, w 1, n-b 2	10
(100.3 overs)	271	(88.3 overs)	282

1/35 (1) 2/50 (2) 3/50 (4) 4/82 (5) 5/83 (6)   1/35 (1) 2/83 (3) 3/91 (2) 4/118 (4) 5/150 (5)
6/83 (7) 7/173 (8) 8/215 (9) 9/239 (10) 10/271 (3)   6/250 (6) 7/253 (8) 8/274 (7) 9/278 (9) 10/282 (10)

Hazlewood 21–6–49–0; Pattinson 22.3–1–72–4; Lyon 29–8–66–4; Siddle 18–3–40–2; Marsh 7–4–15–0; Smith 3–0–21–0. *Second innings*—Hazlewood 20–6–40–0; Pattinson 17–4–49–2; Lyon 23–7–85–3; Siddle 9–2–35–1; Marsh 17.3–2–61–4; Smith 2–1–5–0.

Umpires: M. Erasmus *(South Africa)* (35) and C. B. Gaffaney *(New Zealand)* (5).
Third umpire: I. J. Gould *(England)*.   Referee: B. C. Broad *(England)* (74).

Close of play: first day, Australia 345–3 (Smith 32, Voges 10); second day, West Indies 91–6 (Bravo 13, C. R. Brathwaite 3); third day, Australia 179–3 (Smith 70, Marsh 18).

AUSTRALIA v WEST INDIES 2015–16 (3rd Test)

At Sydney Cricket Ground on 3, 4, 5 *(no play)*, 6 *(no play)*, 7 January, 2016.
Toss: West Indies. Result: DRAWN.
Debuts: none.
Man of the Match: D. A. Warner. Man of the Series: A. C. Voges.

Torrents of rain not seen at a Sydney Test for a quarter of a century denied Australia the chance of a 3–0 victory. The West Indian batsmen showed some improvement, but too often wickets were lost just as a partnership was blossoming. Kraigg Brathwaite dropped anchor for 85, but the comical run-out of Samuels, stranded after Brathwaite dropped his bat mid-pitch, encapsulated West Indies' struggles. The pitch suited the twirlers from the first day: Lyon's hard-spun delivery to bowl Blackwood pitched so far outside off that he offered no shot. The Australian selectors got it right in picking O'Keefe, the slow left-armer playing his second Test. He removed Holder, caught one-handed by Burns at short leg as West Indies finished the day on 207 for six. Then came the rain. Only 11.2 overs were possible on the second day, although there was time for Carlos Brathwaite to smash Pattinson over the fence twice. After the third and fourth days were washed out, Smith suggested a mix of forfeited innings and declaration bowling, but Holder was keen for his side to pass 300 for the first time in the series. And so they did, guided by Ramdin's 62, an innings that spanned all five days. Three wickets apiece for Australia's spin twins was just reward. Warner had been the only member of Australia's top five yet to notch a century in the series, but he made amends with a hundred from 82 balls, the fastest in Tests at the SCG.

West Indies

K. C. Brathwaite c Smith b Lyon	85
S. D. Hope c Nevill b Hazlewood	9
D. M. Bravo c Khawaja b Pattinson	33
M. N. Samuels run out (Hazlewood/Nevill)	4
J. Blackwood b Lyon	10
†D. Ramdin c Smith b O'Keefe	62
*J. O. Holder c Burns b O'Keefe	1
C. R. Brathwaite b Pattinson	69
K. A. J. Roach c Burns b Lyon	15
J. E. Taylor c Lyon b O'Keefe	13
J. A. Warrican not out	21
B 5, l-b 2, n-b 1	8
(112.1 overs)	330

1/13 (2) 2/104 (3) 3/115 (4) 4/131 (5) 5/158 (1)
6/159 (7) 7/246 (8) 8/296 (6) 9/300 (9) 10/330 (10)

Hazlewood 18–5–49–1; Pattinson 18–3–76–2; Lyon 46–12–120–3; Marsh 4–1–15–0; O'Keefe 26.1–7–63–3.

Australia

D. A. Warner not out	122
J. A. Burns c Roach b Warrican	26
M. R. Marsh c Blackwood b Warrican	21
†P. M. Nevill not out	7
(2 wkts dec, 38 overs)	176

1/100 (2) 2/154 (3)

U. T. Khawaja, *S. P. D. Smith, A. C. Voges, S. N. J. O'Keefe, J. L. Pattinson, J. R. Hazlewood and N. M. Lyon did not bat.

Taylor 4–0–27–0; Holder 4–1–15–0; Roach 4–0–29–0; Warrican 15–1–62–2; C. R. Brathwaite 7–0–23–0; K. C. Brathwaite 4–0–20–0.

Umpires: C. B. Gaffaney *(New Zealand)* (6) and I. J. Gould *(England)* (49).
Third umpire: M. Erasmus *(South Africa)*. Referee: B. C. Broad *(England)* (75).

Close of play: first day, West Indies 207–6 (Ramdin 23, C. R. Brathwaite 35); second day, West Indies 248–7 (Ramdin 30, Roach 0); third day, no play; fourth day, no play.

Test No. 2197/142 (SA397, E966)

SOUTH AFRICA v ENGLAND 2015–16 (1st Test)

At Kingsmead, Durban, on 26, 27, 28, 29, 30 December, 2015.
Toss: South Africa.   Result: ENGLAND WON BY 241 RUNS.
Debuts: England – A. D. Hales.
Man of the Match: M. M. Ali.

Both sides had lost their most recent series, but it was England who bounced back better, even though Anderson was missing with a calf problem. Finn stepped up with six wickets, while Broad collected five. For South Africa, Steyn was restricted by a shoulder niggle. Put in, England made 303, Compton top-scoring in the city of his birth in his first Test since May 2013 with 85 in 383 minutes, while Taylor made a tidy 70. The reply owed much to Elgar, who became only the sixth South African to carry his bat in a Test: of the rest, only de Villiers made more than 17. England built carefully on their lead of 89: Root's 73 took him to 1,385 runs in 2015, exceeded for England in a calendar year only by Michael Vaughan, with 1,481 in 2002; Cook's failure left him with 1,364 in the year (fourth for England, behind Dennis Amiss's 1,379 in 1974). Boosted by Bairstow's purposeful 79, England left a target of 416. South Africa rushed to 53 in the 11th over, but then hit trouble: Elgar, third out, edged to second slip after spending the previous 1,406 minutes of play on the field. Ali trapped de Villiers with the final day's third ball, and the rest soon followed: Ali's three wickets gave him seven for the match, and included England's first Test stumping for three years. It was their sixth win in 16 Tests at Durban, to go with a sole defeat, back in 1927–28.

England

*A. N. Cook c Elgar b Steyn	0	– lbw b Piedt	7
A. D. Hales c de Villiers b Steyn	10	– c Abbott b Piedt	26
N. R. D. Compton c de Villiers b Morkel	85	– c de Villiers b Morkel	49
J. E. Root lbw b Piedt	24	– c van Zyl b Abbott	73
J. W. A. Taylor c de Villiers b Steyn	70	– st de Villiers b Piedt	42
B. A. Stokes c Duminy b Morkel	21	– c Elgar b Piedt	5
†J. M. Bairstow c Elgar b Abbott	41	– c Duminy b van Zyl	79
M. M. Ali c de Villiers b Morkel	0	– lbw b Piedt	16
C. R. Woakes lbw b Morkel	0	– c Duminy b van Zyl	23
S. C. J. Broad not out	32	– c de Villiers b van Zyl	0
S. T. Finn lbw b Steyn	12	– not out	0
B 1, l-b 3, w 1, n-b 3	8	B 3, l-b 3	6
(100.1 overs)	303	(102.1 overs)	326

1/3 (1) 2/12 (2) 3/49 (4) 4/174 (5) 5/196 (6) 6/247 (3)   1/13 (1) 2/48 (2) 3/119 (3) 4/192 (4) 5/197 (6)
7/253 (8) 8/253 (9) 9/267 (7) 10/303 (11)   6/224 (5) 7/272 (8) 8/315 (9) 9/315 (10) 10/326 (7)

Steyn 25.1–5–70–4; Abbott 24–4–66–1; Morkel 26–5–76–4; Piedt 16–2–63–1; van Zyl 2–1–2–0; Elgar 7–2–22–0. *Second innings*—Steyn 3.5–0–10–0; Morkel 20.3–5–38–1; Abbott 21.4–3–62–1; Piedt 36–4–153–5; Elgar 9–0–32–0; van Zyl 10.1–3–20–3; Duminy 1–0–5–0.

South Africa

S. van Zyl b Broad	0	– (2) b Stokes	33
D. Elgar not out	118	– (1) c Root b Finn	40
*H. M. Amla c Bairstow b Broad	7	– c Bairstow b Finn	12
†A. B. de Villiers c Bairstow b Broad	49	– lbw b Ali	37
F. du Plessis b Ali	2	– c Cook b Finn	9
T. Bavuma b Broad	10	– (7) st Bairstow b Ali	0
J-P. Duminy c Stokes b Ali	2	– (8) not out	26
K. J. Abbott c Taylor b Ali	0	– (9) lbw b Ali	2
D. W. Steyn c Woakes b Ali	17	– (6) b Finn	2
D. L. Piedt c Bairstow b Finn	1	– c Taylor b Woakes	0
M. Morkel c Root b Finn	0	– lbw b Broad	8
B 4, l-b 3, w 1	8	B 2, l-b 3	5
(81.4 overs)	214	(71 overs)	174

1/0 (1) 2/14 (3) 3/100 (4) 4/113 (5) 5/137 (6)   1/53 (2) 2/85 (3) 3/88 (1) 4/136 (5) 5/136 (4)
6/150 (7) 7/156 (8) 8/210 (9) 9/214 (10) 10/214 (11)   6/136 (7) 7/138 (6) 8/143 (9) 9/155 (10) 10/174 (11)

Broad 15–6–25–4; Woakes 14–1–28–0; Ali 25–3–69–4; Finn 15.4–1–49–2; Stokes 9–1–25–0; Root 3–1–11–0. *Second innings*—Broad 13–5–29–1; Woakes 10–5–25–1; Finn 15–6–42–4; Stokes 7–1–26–1; Ali 26–9–47–3.

Umpires: Aleem Dar *(Pakistan)* (99) and R. J. Tucker *(Australia)* (40).
Third umpire: B. N. J. Oxenford *(Australia)*.   Referee: R. S. Madugalle *(Sri Lanka)* (160).

Close of play: first day, England 179–4 (Compton 63, Stokes 5); second day, South Africa 137–4 (Elgar 67, Bavuma 10); third day, England 172–3 (Root 60, Taylor 24); fourth day, South Africa 136–4 (de Villiers 37, Steyn 0).

Test No. 2198/143 (SA398, E967)

SOUTH AFRICA v ENGLAND 2015–16 (2nd Test)

At Newlands, Cape Town, on 2, 3, 4, 5, 6 January, 2016.
Toss: England.   Result: DRAWN.
Debuts: South Africa – C. H. Morris.
Man of the Match: B. A. Stokes.

There were only a few periods when an outright result looked even remotely likely – mainly on the final day, when England stumbled as they sought to bat out time. But this match will still be fondly remembered, thanks mainly to an astonishing 258 from Stokes, the highest Test score by a No. 6 batsman, beating Doug Walters's 250 for Australia against New Zealand at Christchurch in 1976–77. Stokes reached his double-century in just 163 balls, the second-fastest known in Tests, and in all faced only 198, hitting 30 fours and 11 sixes. He put on 399 with Bairstow – including 196 on the second morning alone – a sixth-wicket record in Tests, beating the unbroken 365 by Kane Williamson and B-J Watling for New Zealand against Sri Lanka at Wellington in 2014–15. Bairstow's hundred was his first in Tests, and was marked by a gaze skywards in memory of his later father, David, also an England wicketkeeper. South Africa replied by passing 600 themselves, their total including a double-hundred for Amla (who ceded the captaincy to de Villiers after the match; this was his first score over 43 in 12 Test innings), and a landmark century for Bavuma, the first by a member of the majority black African population. De Villiers passed 8,000 runs in his 104th Test during his 88, which occupied 69 overs. England dipped to 19 for two on the final morning, but the middle order prevented an unlikely collapse, helped by rain which ended proceedings 31 overs early.

England

*A. N. Cook c Morris b Rabada	27	– c de Kock b Rabada	8
A. D. Hales c de Villiers b Morkel	60	– c Morris b Morkel	5
N. R. D. Compton c Bavuma b Rabada	45	– c du Plessis b Piedt	15
J. E. Root c de Kock b Morris	50	– b Morris	29
J. W. A. Taylor c de Kock b Rabada	0	– c Bavuma b Piedt	27
B. A. Stokes run out (de Villiers)	258	– c Morkel b Piedt	26
†J. M. Bairstow not out	150	– not out	30
M. M. Ali not out	0	– not out	10
B 12, l-b 6, w 13, n-b 8	39	L-b 4, n-b 5	9
(6 wkts dec, 125.5 overs)	629	(6 wkts, 65 overs)	159

1/55 (1) 2/129 (2) 3/167 (3)   1/17 (1) 2/19 (2) 3/55 (4)
4/167 (5) 5/223 (4) 6/622 (6)   4/85 (3) 5/115 (6) 6/116 (5)

S. C. J. Broad, S. T. Finn and J. M. Anderson did not bat.

Morkel 29–5–114–1; Morris 28–3–150–1; Rabada 29.5–2–175–3; Piedt 25–5–112–0; van Zyl 10–0–43–0; Elgar 4–0–17–0. *Second innings*—Morkel 16–7–26–1; Rabada 13–2–57–1; Morris 12–4–24–1; Piedt 18–8–38–3; Elgar 6–2–10–0.

South Africa

D. Elgar c Compton b Stokes	44
S. van Zyl run out (Compton/Bairstow)	4
*H. M. Amla b Broad	201
A. B. de Villiers c Anderson b Finn	88
F. du Plessis c Stokes b Anderson	86
T. Bavuma not out	102
†Q. de Kock c Anderson b Broad	5
C. H. Morris c Root b Finn	69
K. Rabada not out	2
B 4, l-b 9, w 13	26
(7 wkts dec, 211 overs)	627

1/7 (2) 2/85 (1) 3/268 (4) 4/439 (3)
5/439 (5) 6/449 (7) 7/616 (8)

D. L. Piedt and M. Morkel did not bat.

Anderson 35–12–77–1; Broad 34–8–94–2; Ali 52–14–155–0; Finn 39–5–132–2; Root 20–4–54–0; Stokes 28–4–100–1; Hales 3–1–2–0.

Umpires: Aleem Dar *(Pakistan)* (100) and B. N. J. Oxenford *(Australia)* (31).
Third umpire: R. J. Tucker *(Australia)*.   Referee: R. S. Madugalle *(Sri Lanka)* (161).

Close of play: first day, England 317–5 (Stokes 74, Bairstow 39); second day, South Africa 141–2 (Amla 64, de Villiers 25); third day, South Africa 353–3 (Amla 157, du Plessis 51); fourth day, England 16–0 (Cook 8, Hales 5).

SOUTH AFRICA v ENGLAND 2015–16 (3rd Test)

At New Wanderers, Johannesburg, on 14, 15, 16 January, 2016.
Toss: South Africa.   Result: ENGLAND WON BY SEVEN WICKETS.
Debuts: South Africa – G. C. Viljoen.
Man of the Match: S. C. J. Broad.

On a riotous third afternoon, South Africa were torn apart in front of a crowd that turned from raucous to stunned across 33 overs of mayhem. The passage sealed England's first overseas series win since beating India in 2012–13. Broad flicked the switch, claiming five or more wickets in a single Test spell for the seventh time, and passing Bob Willis's tally of 325 to become England's third-highest wicket-taker. But this was a team effort: Broad's brilliance was buttressed by insistent fast bowling at the other end, and inspired close catching, especially from Taylor. All South Africa's batsmen reached double figures in their first innings, the 13th such instance in Tests – but, with no-one reaching 50, the total of 313 was the smallest of those. England inched past, thanks largely to Root's stand of 111 with Stokes. And then came Broad, as South Africa imploded on the third afternoon: 23 for none became 71 for eight by tea. At one point Broad had figures of 3.4–1–13–0, but he then ripped out six for four in 51 deliveries, including South Africa's new captain de Villiers and Bavuma for ducks. England mopped up their target with two days to spare. Vilas, whistled up when de Kock injured his knee while walking his dogs the day before the match, arrived halfway through the opening session. Hardus Viljoen, in his only Test, took a wicket (Cook) with his first ball, not long after hitting the first delivery he faced for four.

South Africa

D. Elgar c Bairstow b Ali	46	– c Bairstow b Broad	15
S. van Zyl c Bairstow b Stokes	21	– c Stokes b Broad	11
H. M. Amla c Bairstow b Finn	40	– c Taylor b Broad	5
*A. B. de Villiers c Bairstow b Stokes	36	– c Bairstow b Broad	0
F. du Plessis c Hales b Finn	16	– c and b Broad	14
T. Bavuma run out (sub [C. R. Woakes]/Bairstow)	23	– b Broad	0
†D. J. Vilas c Ali b Broad	26	– c Taylor b Finn	8
C. H. Morris c Bairstow b Broad	28	– b Stokes	1
K. Rabada c Bairstow b Anderson	24	– c Bairstow b Stokes	16
G. C. Viljoen not out	20	– lbw b Anderson	6
M. Morkel c Cook b Stokes	12	– not out	4
B 9, l-b 9, w 1, n-b 2	21	L-b 2, n-b 1	3
(99.3 overs)	313	(33.1 overs)	83

1/44 (2) 2/117 (1) 3/127 (3) 4/161 (4) 5/185 (5)   1/23 (1) 2/28 (2) 3/30 (4) 4/31 (3) 5/35 (6) 6/45 (7)
6/212 (6) 7/225 (7) 8/281 (8) 9/281 (9) 10/313 (11)   7/46 (8) 8/67 (9) 9/77 (10) 10/83 (5)

Anderson 25.2–5–60–1; Broad 22–5–82–2; Finn 18–4–50–2; Ali 16–4–50–1; Stokes 18.1–1–53–3. *Second innings*— Anderson 10–1–26–1; Broad 12.1–6–17–6; Stokes 8–1–24–2; Finn 3–0–14–1.

England

*A. N. Cook c Vilas b Viljoen	18	– c Vilas b Morris	43
A. D. Hales c de Villiers b Rabada	1	– lbw b Elgar	18
N. R. D. Compton c Elgar b Rabada	26	– c Morkel b Elgar	0
J. E. Root c Vilas b Rabada	110	– not out	4
J. W. A. Taylor c Bavuma b Morkel	7	– not out	2
B. A. Stokes c and b Morkel	58		
†J. M. Bairstow c van Zyl b Rabada	45		
M. M. Ali c Vilas b Morris	19		
S. C. J. Broad b Rabada	12		
S. T. Finn c Vilas b Morkel	0		
J. M. Anderson not out	0		
B 1, l-b 14, w 9, n-b 3	27	B 4, l-b 2, w 17	7
(76.1 overs)	323	(3 wkts, 22.4 overs)	74

1/10 (2) 2/22 (1) 3/74 (3) 4/91 (5) 5/202 (6)   1/64 (2) 2/68 (3) 3/71 (1)
6/242 (4) 7/279 (8) 8/309 (9) 9/311 (10) 10/323 (7)

Morris 15–1–71–1; Rabada 23.1–5–78–5; Morkel 20–1–76–3; Viljoen 15–0–79–1; van Zyl 3–0–4–0. *Second innings*— Morkel 5–2–7–0; Rabada 4–0–28–0; Viljoen 4–2–15–0; Morris 6–2–8–1; Elgar 3.4–1–10–2.

Umpires: Aleem Dar *(Pakistan)* (101) and R. J. Tucker *(Australia)* (41).
Third umpire: C. B. Gaffaney *(New Zealand)*.   Referee: R. S. Madugalle *(Sri Lanka)* (162).

Close of play: first day, South Africa 267–7 (Morris 26, Rabada 20); second day, England 238–5 (Root 106, Bairstow 4).

SOUTH AFRICA v ENGLAND 2015–16 (4th Test)

At Centurion Park, Pretoria, on 22, 23, 24, 25, 26 January, 2016.
Toss: South Africa.   Result: SOUTH AFRICA WON BY 280 RUNS.
Debuts: South Africa – S. C. Cook.
Man of the Match: K. Rabada.   Man of the Series: B. A. Stokes.

Kagiso Rabada placed a much-needed smile on the face of South African cricket with a match haul of 13 for 144 to gloss over their series defeat, and set up their first victory in ten Tests. England were made to pay for a dreadful bowling performance in the first two sessions, and an embarrassing capitulation on the final morning, when they lost seven for 43 in 65 balls. Just as England had done throughout the first three Tests, South Africa won the decisive moments, capitalising on the tourists' poor start, adding 139 for their final three wickets, then dismissing Cook and Root for 76 apiece when they looked set to minimise the lead. A first-innings advantage of 133 was always likely to be crucial on a testing, cracking surface. Amla narrowly missed twin tons, with 109 – his 25th Test century – and 96. The 33-year-old Stephen Cook, son of the former opener Jimmy, became South Africa's sixth Test-debut centurion; there was also an attacking maiden hundred for the recovered de Kock. As Rabada began his rampage, England were looking at a huge deficit before Ali narrowed it, but Amla and Bavuma set up a distant target of 382, although de Villiers bagged a four-ball pair. Three wickets went down on the fourth evening, and the rest in a hurry next morning. Rabada, 20, was the youngest bowler to take 13 wickets in a Test since 19-year-old Narendra Hirwani extracted 16 on his 1987–88 debut for India against West Indies at Madras.

South Africa

S. C. Cook b Woakes	115	– c Bairstow b Anderson	25
D. Elgar c Taylor b Ali	20	– c Bairstow b Anderson	1
H. M. Amla b Stokes	109	– c Bairstow b Broad	96
*A. B. de Villiers c Root b Broad	0	– lbw b Anderson	0
J-P. Duminy lbw b Ali	16	– c Bairstow b Stokes	29
T. Bavuma c Bairstow b Broad	35	– not out	78
†Q. de Kock not out	129	– not out	9
K. Rabada lbw b Anderson	0		
K. J. Abbott lbw b Stokes	16		
D. L. Piedt c Bairstow b Stokes	19		
M. Morkel lbw b Stokes	0		
L-b 12, w 4	16	B 2, l-b 5, w 3	10
(132 overs)	475	(5 wkts dec, 83.2 overs)	248

1/35 (2) 2/237 (3) 3/238 (4) 4/271 (1) 5/273 (5)   1/5 (2) 2/49 (1) 3/49 (4)
6/335 (6) 7/336 (8) 8/386 (9) 9/468 (10) 10/475 (11)   4/106 (5) 5/223 (3)

Anderson 30–6–91–1; Broad 28–4–91–2; Ali 25–5–104–2; Woakes 22–3–91–1; Stokes 27–3–86–4. *Second innings*—Anderson 18–5–47–3; Broad 15–4–33–1; Stokes 16–4–36–1; Woakes 13.2–0–53–0; Ali 17–3–60–0; Root 4–0–12–0.

England

*A. N. Cook c de Kock b Morkel	76	– c and b Morkel	5
A. D. Hales c Piedt b Rabada	15	– lbw b Rabada	1
N. R. D. Compton lbw b Rabada	19	– c de Kock b Rabada	6
J. E. Root c de Kock b Rabada	76	– c Elgar b Piedt	20
J. W. A. Taylor c de Kock b Rabada	14	– c de Kock b Morkel	24
B. A. Stokes c Amla b Rabada	33	– c Cook b Morkel	10
†J. M. Bairstow c de Kock b Rabada	0	– c de Kock b Rabada	14
M. M. Ali c Piedt b Morkel	61	– not out	10
C. R. Woakes c Elgar b Duminy	26	– c de Kock b Rabada	5
S. C. J. Broad c Cook b Rabada	5	– c de Villiers b Rabada	2
J. M. Anderson not out	5	– lbw b Rabada	0
B 2, l-b 7, w 3	12	L-b 2, w 1, n-b 1	4
(104.2 overs)	342	(34.4 overs)	101

1/22 (2) 2/78 (3) 3/177 (1) 4/208 (4) 5/211 (5)   1/2 (2) 2/8 (1) 3/18 (3) 4/58 (5) 5/58 (4) 6/83 (7)
6/211 (7) 7/252 (6) 8/295 (9) 9/320 (10) 10/342 (8)   7/83 (6) 8/91 (9) 9/101 (10) 10/101 (11)

Abbott 19–9–36–0; Rabada 29–6–112–7; Piedt 24–4–78–0; Morkel 23.2–4–73–2; Elgar 4–0–13–0; Duminy 5–0–21–1. *Second innings*—Morkel 12–5–36–3; Rabada 10.4–2–32–6; Abbott 2–0–10–0; Piedt 7–2–11–1; Elgar 2–1–8–0; Duminy 1–0–2–0.

Umpires: H. D. P. K. Dharmasena *(Sri Lanka)* (36) and C. B. Gaffaney *(New Zealand)* (7).
Third umpire: R. J. Tucker *(Australia)*.   Referee: R. S. Madugalle *(Sri Lanka)* (163).

Close of play: first day, South Africa 329–5 (Bavuma 32, de Kock 25); second day, England 138–2 (Cook 67, Root 31); third day, South Africa 42–1 (Cook 23, Amla 16); fourth day, England 52–3 (Root 19, Taylor 19).

NEW ZEALAND v AUSTRALIA 2015–16 (1st Test)

At Basin Reserve, Wellington, on 12, 13, 14, 15 February, 2016.
Toss: Australia.   Result: AUSTRALIA WON BY AN INNINGS AND 52 RUNS.
Debuts: New Zealand – H. M. Nicholls.
Man of the Match: A. C. Voges.

Australia took charge from the start: Hazlewood removed both openers, before McCullum was caught at slip for a duck in his 100th Test. Siddle collected Williamson from an inside edge, brilliantly caught by Nevill, then Test debutant Henry Nicholls on the drive; 34 for five after nine overs left New Zealand nowhere to go. They were briefly back in it when Southee claimed both openers cheaply, but Craig at second slip dropped Smith on 18, and he added 126 with Khawaja. In the first day's final over Voges left an inswinger, which plucked out his off stump – but Richard Illingworth called no-ball. Replays showed Bracewell's entire heel behind the line, but there was no way to unscramble the omelette. Voges returned next day like an old Soviet soldier in Eastern Europe: he shouldn't have been there, but his occupation was undeniable. By stumps he had taken his career average above Bradman's 99.94; he said he was relieved to drop back to a mortal 97.46 after he was finally dislodged for 239, though by then he had the record for most Test runs between dismissals – 614, beating Sachin Tendulkar's 497. In their previous two Tests at Wellington, New Zealand had recovered from deficits of 135 (to beat Sri Lanka) and 246 (to draw with India). But there would be no third escape. McCullum was nailed in the final over of the third day, and next day they slipped to their first innings defeat at home since England won here in 1996–97.

New Zealand

M. J. Guptill c Smith b Hazlewood	18	– (2) c Marsh b Lyon	45
T. W. M. Latham c Nevill b Hazlewood	6	– (1) c Khawaja b Lyon	63
K. S. Williamson c Nevill b Siddle	16	– c Nevill b Hazlewood	22
H. M. Nicholls c Nevill b Siddle	8	– b Bird	59
*B. B. McCullum c Warner b Hazlewood	0	– lbw b Marsh	10
C. J. Anderson c Khawaja b Lyon	38	– lbw b Marsh	0
†B-J. Watling c Nevill b Hazlewood	17	– b Lyon	10
D. A. J. Bracewell c Voges b Siddle	5	– lbw b Hazlewood	14
M. D. Craig not out	41	– not out	33
T. G. Southee c Hazlewood b Lyon	0	– c Khawaja b Lyon	48
T. A. Boult c Khawaja b Lyon	24	– b Marsh	12
B 4, lb 1, nb 5	10	B 2, lb 5, nb 4	11
(48 overs)	183	(104.3 overs)	327

1/17 (2) 2/38 (1) 3/44 (3) 4/47 (5) 5/51 (4)   1/81 (2) 2/121 (3) 3/157 (1) 4/178 (5) 5/185 (6)
6/88 (7) 7/97 (8) 8/137 (6) 9/137 (10) 10/183 (11)   6/214 (7) 7/218 (4) 8/242 (8) 9/301 (10) 10/327 (11)

Hazlewood 14–2–42–4; Bird 10–1–52–0; Siddle 12–5–37–3; Marsh 6–1–15–0; Lyon 6–0–32–3. *Second innings—* Hazlewood 29–7–75–2; Bird 19–4–51–1; Siddle 8–0–30–0; Marsh 17.3–2–73–3; Lyon 31–10–91–4.

Australia

J. A. Burns c Watling b Southee	0
D. A. Warner c Watling b Southee	5
U. T. Khawaja lbw b Boult	140
*S. P. D. Smith c and b Craig	71
A. C. Voges c and b Craig	239
M. R. Marsh c and b Boult	0
†P. M. Nevill c Watling b Anderson	32
P. M. Siddle c Anderson b Bracewell	49
J. R. Hazlewood c Southee b Bracewell	8
N. M. Lyon c and b Anderson	3
J. M. Bird not out	3
B 4, lb 3, w 2, nb 3	12
(154.2 overs)	562

1/0 (1) 2/5 (2) 3/131 (4) 4/299 (3) 5/299 (6)
6/395 (7) 7/494 (8) 8/508 (9) 9/532 (10) 10/562 (5)

Southee 31–5–87–2; Boult 33–6–101–2; Bracewell 33–4–127–2; Anderson 18–0–79–2; Craig 35.2–2–153–2; Williamson 4–0–8–0.

Umpires: R. K. Illingworth *(England)* (21) and R. A. Kettleborough *(England)* (34).
Third umpire: R. E. J. Martinesz *(Sri Lanka)*.   Referee: B. C. Broad *(England)* (76).

Close of play: first day, Australia 147–3 (Khawaja 57, Voges 7); second day, Australia 463–6 (Voges 176, Siddle 29); third day, New Zealand 178–4 (Nicholls 31).

Test No. 2202/57 (NZ408, A788)

NEW ZEALAND v AUSTRALIA 2015–16 (2nd Test)

At Hagley Oval, Christchurch, on 20, 21, 22, 23, 24 February, 2016.
Toss: Australia.   Result: AUSTRALIA WON BY SEVEN WICKETS.
Debuts: none.
Man of the Match: J. A. Burns.

Hagley Oval stages Tests only because the 2011 Christchurch earthquake damaged Lancaster Park, and remains one of the few places in the city where the ravages of the disaster are not evident. This was the idyllic setting for Brendon McCullum's last hurrah for New Zealand. His only other Test innings here, against Sri Lanka in 2014–15, was 195 off 134 balls – and now he marched out at 32 for three, on the first morning, on a lively pitch, against fired-up bowlers… and smashed the fastest Test century of all. His fifth delivery was lofted straight for his 101st Test six, one clear of Adam Gilchrist's record; Marsh's over cost 21. He was caught off a Pattinson no-ball when 39, and roared to three figures in just 54 balls, breaking the old record – shared by Viv Richards and Misbah-ul-Haq – by two. McCullum and Anderson piled on 179 at 9.76 an over, the highest in Tests for any stand over 150. Between lunch and tea alone, New Zealand added 199. But the magic ended there. Wagner's bouncers brought him a career-best, but it took him a day and a half, with Burns and Smith sharing a third-wicket stand of 289, before Voges made an average-lowering 60. New Zealand were in again before tea on the third day; Williamson compiled 97 and Henry a maiden Test fifty – and McCullum's 25 included one final six – but Australia chased down 201 with ease. Still, New Zealand's eventual defeat felt almost immaterial after McCullum's fiery farewell.

New Zealand

M. J. Guptill c Burns b Pattinson	18	– (2) c Nevill b Pattinson	0
T. W. M. Latham c Smith b Bird	4	– (1) c Nevill b Pattinson	39
K. S. Williamson c Smith b Marsh	7	– b Bird	97
H. M. Nicholls lbw b Hazlewood	7	– c Smith b Pattinson	2
*B. B. McCullum c Lyon b Pattinson	145	– c Warner b Hazlewood	25
C. J. Anderson c Voges b Lyon	72	– b Bird	40
†B-J. Watling c Burns b Bird	58	– c Burns b Pattinson	46
T. G. Southee c Hazlewood b Lyon	5	– c Smith b Bird	0
M. J. Henry c Khawaja b Lyon	21	– b Bird	66
N. Wagner c Nevill b Hazlewood	10	– not out	3
T. A. Boult not out	14	– c Pattinson b Bird	0
Lb 2, w 5, nb 2	9	B 2, lb 14, nb 1	17
(65.4 overs)	370	(111.1 overs)	335

1/21 (1) 2/23 (2) 3/32 (4) 4/74 (3) 5/253 (5)   1/8 (2) 2/66 (1) 3/72 (4) 4/105 (5) 5/207 (6)
6/266 (6) 7/273 (8) 8/297 (9) 9/333 (10) 10/370 (7) 6/210 (3) 7/210 (8) 8/328 (7) 9/335 (9) 10/335 (11)

Hazlewood 18–5–98–2; Pattinson 15–2–81–2; Bird 14.4–4–66–2; Marsh 8–1–62–1; Lyon 10–0–61–3. *Second innings*— Hazlewood 34–11–92–1; Pattinson 26–8–77–4; Bird 17.1–5–59–5; Lyon 17–3–42–0; Marsh 17–4–49–0.

Australia

D. A. Warner c Guptill b Boult	12	– (2) c Watling b Wagner	22
J. A. Burns c Guptill b Wagner	170	– (1) b Boult	65
U. T. Khawaja c McCullum b Boult	24	– c McCullum b Southee	45
*S. P. D. Smith c Guptill b Wagner	138	– not out	53
A. C. Voges c Latham b Wagner	60	– not out	10
N. M. Lyon c McCullum b Williamson	33		
M. R. Marsh c Nicholls b Wagner	18		
†P. M. Nevill c Watling b Wagner	13		
J. L. Pattinson c Boult b Anderson	1		
J. R. Hazlewood c McCullum b Wagner	13		
J. M. Bird not out	4		
B 9, lb 10	19	Lb 4, nb 2	6
(153.1 overs)	505	(3 wkts, 54 overs)	201

1/25 (1) 2/67 (3) 3/356 (2) 4/357 (4) 5/438 (6)   1/49 (2) 2/113 (3) 3/179 (1)
6/464 (5) 7/483 (7) 8/484 (9) 9/496 (8) 10/505 (10)

Southee 25–4–85–0; Boult 31–5–108–2; Henry 32–8–101–0; Anderson 22–2–66–1; Wagner 32.1–6–106–6; Williamson 7–0–17–1; McCullum 4–2–3–0. *Second innings*—Boult 17–1–60–1; Southee 7–2–30–1; Henry 9–1–33–0; Wagner 18–4–60–1; Anderson 3–0–14–0.

Umpires: R. A. Kettleborough *(England)* (35) and R. E. J. Martinesz *(Sri Lanka)* (8).
Third umpire: R. K. Illingworth *(England).*   Referee: B. C. Broad *(England)* (77).

Close of play: first day, Australia 57–1 (Burns 27, Khawaja 18); second day, Australia 363–4 (Voges 2, Lyon 4); third day, New Zealand 121–4 (Williamson 45, Anderson 9); fourth day, Australia 70–1 (Burns 27, Khawaja 19).

ENGLAND v SRI LANKA 2016 (1st Test)

At Headingley, Leeds, on 19, 20, 21 May, 2016.
Toss: Sri Lanka.   Result: ENGLAND WON BY AN INNINGS AND 88 RUNS.
Debuts: England – J. M. Vince. Sri Lanka – M. D. Shanaka.
Man of the Match: J. M. Bairstow.

Test cricket resumed after a three-month hiatus caused by the World Twenty20 in India, where England had the trophy dashed from their grasp by West Indies' Carlos Brathwaite. But England responded with a thumping victory over Sri Lanka, who had upset them in a similar early-season series two years previously thanks to a penultimate-ball victory here. But this side lacked the retired Kumar Sangakkara and Mahela Jayawardene, and succumbed for 91 and 119; Sri Lanka's match aggregate was the lowest in any Test in which they lost 20 wickets. Had it not been for rain, the match would have been all over inside two days. The architect of defeat was the peerless Anderson, with the sixth-cheapest ten-for in Test history, which took him past Kapil Dev (434) on the wicket-takers' list; the last England seamer to take ten at Headingley was Fred Trueman, against Australia in 1961. Broad chipped in with five scalps, including Karunaratne and Mendis for first-innings ducks. Anderson had taken only 19 previous wickets at Leeds, and explained: "It's taken us nine years to realise we're bowling at the wrong ends." Ahead of Sri Lanka's two collapses, Bairstow rescued England from a rickety 83 for five – medium-pacer Dasun Shanaka started his Test career with wickets from his seventh, tenth and 14th balls – putting on 141 with Hales, before celebrating his first Test century on home turf; of Yorkshire players, only Geoff Boycott (twice) and The Hon. Stanley Jackson (in 1905) had made higher Test scores at Headingley.

England

*A. N. Cook c Chandimal b Shanaka	16
A. D. Hales c Chameera b Herath	86
N. R. D. Compton c Thirimanne b Shanaka	0
J. E. Root c Mendis b Shanaka	0
J. M. Vince c Mendis b Eranga	9
B. A. Stokes c Mathews b Fernando	12
†J. M. Bairstow c Fernando b Chameera	140
M. M. Ali c Mendis b Chameera	0
S. C. J. Broad b Chameera	2
S. T. Finn st Chandimal b Herath	17
J. M. Anderson not out	1
Lb 8, w 4, nb 3	15
(90.3 overs)	298

1/49 (1) 2/49 (3) 3/51 (4) 4/70 (5) 5/83 (6)
6/224 (2) 7/231 (8) 8/233 (9) 9/289 (7) 10/298 (10)

Eranga 19–4–68–1; Fernando 19–7–56–1; Mathews 11–2–31–0; Chameera 17–0–64–3; Shanaka 13–3–46–3; Herath 11.3–1–25–2.

Sri Lanka

F. D. M. Karunaratne c Bairstow b Broad	0	– c Bairstow b Anderson	7
J. K. Silva c Bairstow b Anderson	11	– c Bairstow b Anderson	14
B. K. G. Mendis c Bairstow b Broad	0	– b Anderson	53
†L. D. Chandimal c Vince b Stokes	15	– b Ali	8
*A. D. Mathews lbw b Anderson	34	– c Bairstow b Broad	5
H. D. R. L. Thirimanne c Finn b Broad	22	– c Root b Finn	16
M. D. Shanaka c Bairstow b Anderson	0	– c Bairstow b Anderson	4
H. M. R. K. B. Herath c Stokes b Anderson	1	– c Broad b Finn	4
P. V. D. Chameera c Finn b Broad	2	– c Compton b Finn	0
R. M. S. Eranga c Bairstow b Anderson	1	– not out	2
A. N. P. R. Fernando not out	0	– b Anderson	0
Nb 2	5	Lb 5, nb 1	6
(36.4 overs)	91	(35.3 overs)	119

1/10 (1) 2/12 (2) 3/12 (3) 4/43 (4) 5/77 (5)   1/10 (1) 2/35 (2) 3/79 (4) 4/93 (5) 5/93 (3) 6/101 (7)
6/81 (7) 7/83 (8) 8/90 (9) 9/91 (6) 10/91 (10)   7/111 (8) 8/117 (9) 9/118 (6) 10/119 (11)

Anderson 11.4–6–16–5; Broad 10–1–21–4; Stokes 7–2–25–1; Vince 1–0–10–0; Finn 7–0–19–0. *Second innings—* Anderson 13.3–5–29–5; Broad 13–0–57–1; Finn 8–0–26–3; Ali 1–0–2–1.

Umpires: Aleem Dar *(Pakistan)* (102) and R. J. Tucker *(Australia)* (42).
Third umpire: S. Ravi *(India)*.   Referee: A. J. Pycroft *(Zimbabwe)* (44).

Close of play: first day, England 171-5 (Hales 71, Bairstow 54); second day, Sri Lanka (second innings) 1–0 (Karunaratne 0, Silva 0).

Test No. 2204/30 (E971, SL247)

ENGLAND v SRI LANKA 2016 (2nd Test)

At Riverside Ground, Chester-le-Street, on 27, 28, 29, 30 May, 2016.
Toss: England.   Result: ENGLAND WON BY NINE WICKETS.
Debuts: none.
Man of the Match: J. M. Anderson.

After taking four outstanding catches on the first day, Sri Lanka returned next morning full of pep. Then, like an untied balloon, they deflated at an alarming rate. The pitch was fair, but the match lasted only four days. On three of those, Sri Lanka competed; on the second, their cricket was abysmal, enough to define their series. On the first morning Cook was well taken at second slip, leaving him with 9,995 Test runs; only Brian Lara (out twice on 9,993 against England in 2004), and Mahela Jayawardene (run out on 9,999 at Centurion in 2011–12) had previously succumbed in the nervous 9,990s. Hales and Root both reached 80, but Ali turned the match; dropped by Karunaratne at slip off Pradeep Fernando when 36, he skeetered to a career-best undefeated 155 as England surged to 498. Herath took his 300th Test wicket, a return catch from Finn. But then Sri Lanka were bundled out for 101, with Anderson, Broad and Woakes sharing all the wickets. There was sterner resistance in the follow-on: Chandimal made an adhesive century – his sixth in Tests but the first outside Asia – while Mathews knuckled down for 80. Overall, the innings lasted longer than Sri Lanka's previous three put together. Anderson claimed five more wickets, giving him 18 for 139 in the series, but Ali's off-spin looked worryingly toothless. England needed just 79, and Cook finally reached 10,000 – at 31, the youngest to get there, beating Sachin Tendulkar by 169 days – as his side clinched the series.

England

*A. N. Cook c Karunaratne b Lakmal	15	– not out	47
A. D. Hales c Mathews b Siriwardene	83	– b Siriwardene	11
N. R. D. Compton c Lakmal b Fernando	9	– not out	22
J. E. Root c Silva b Fernando	80		
J. M. Vince c Thirimanne b Siriwardene	35		
†J. M. Bairstow c Chandimal b Fernando	48		
M. M. Ali not out	155		
C. R. Woakes c †Mendis b Lakmal	39		
S. C. J. Broad c †Mendis b Fernando	7		
S. T. Finn c and b Herath	10		
J. M. Anderson not out	8		
B 1, lb 8	9		
(9 wkts dec, 132 overs)	498	(1 wkt, 23.2 overs)	80

1/39 (1) 2/64 (3) 3/160 (2) 4/219 (4) 5/227 (5)   1/35 (2)
6/297 (6) 7/389 (8) 8/400 (9) 9/472 (10)

Eranga 27–3–100–0; Lakmal 29–4–115–2; Fernando 33–5–107–4; Herath 29–1–116–1; Mathews 6–2–16–0; Siriwardene 8–0–35–2. *Second innings*—Herath 10–3–18–0; Fernando 2–0–12–0; Siriwardene 7.2–0–37–1; Lakmal 3–0–9–0; Eranga 1–0–4–0.

Sri Lanka

F. D. M. Karunaratne b Anderson	9	– c Root b Woakes	26
J. K. Silva c Bairstow b Broad	13	– c Bairstow b Finn	60
B. K. G. Mendis c Anderson b Woakes	35	– c Bairstow b Anderson	26
†L. D. Chandimal c Cook b Anderson	4	– (6) b Broad	126
*A. D. Mathews c Bairstow b Woakes	3	– c Bairstow b Anderson	80
H. D. R. L. Thirimanne c Compton b Anderson	19	– (4) b Ali	13
T. A. M. Siriwardene c Bairstow b Woakes	0	– c Hales b Anderson	35
H. M. R. K. B. Herath c Anderson b Broad	12	– lbw b Anderson	61
R. M. S. Eranga c Root b Broad	2	– b Anderson	1
R. A. S. Lakmal c Bairstow b Broad	0	– c Broad b Woakes	11
A. N. P. R. Fernando not out	2	– not out	13
Lb 1, nb 1	2	B 5, lb 11, w 1, nb 6	23
(43.3 overs)	101	(128.2 overs)	475

1/10 (1) 2/44 (2) 3/53 (4) 4/58 (5) 5/67 (3)   1/38 (1) 2/79 (3) 3/100 (4) 4/182 (2) 5/222 (5)
6/67 (7) 7/88 (8) 8/90 (9) 9/93 (10) 10/101 (6)   6/314 (7) 7/430 (8) 8/442 (9) 9/453 (6) 10/475 (10)

Anderson 12.3–2–36–3; Broad 13–2–40–4; Woakes 7–4–9–3; Finn 7–3–15–0; Ali 4–4–0–0. *Second innings*—Anderson 27–9–58–5; Broad 24–6–71–1; Woakes 27.2–8–103–2; Finn 19–0–78–1; Ali 28–5–136–1; Vince 1–1–0–0; Root 2–0–13–0.

Umpires: Aleem Dar *(Pakistan)* (103), S. Ravi *(India)* (11) and R. J. Tucker *(Australia)* (43).
Third umpire: R. J. Tucker *(Australia)* and D. J. Millns *(England)*.   Referee: A. J. Pycroft *(Zimbabwe)* (45).
Tucker replaced Dar (ill) during the fourth day, and Millns took over as third umpire.

Close of play: first day, England 310–6 (Ali 28, Woakes 8); second day, Sri Lanka 91–8 (Thirimanne 12, Lakmal 0); third day, Sri Lanka 309–5 (Chandimal 54, Siriwardene 35).

Test No. 2205/31 (E972, SL248)

ENGLAND v SRI LANKA 2016 (3rd Test)

At Lord's, London, on 9, 10, 11, 12, 13 June, 2016.
Toss: England.   Result: DRAWN.
Debuts: none.
Man of the Match: J. M. Bairstow.   Men of the Series: J. M. Bairstow and J. K. Silva.

England's hopes of a clean sweep were washed away: there were only 45 overs on the fourth day, and 12.2 on the fifth. Sri Lanka escaped with their first draw in 17 Tests, but their fifth in a row at Lord's. It was also the first draw in 14 in England. After Cook and Hales shared England's first half-century opening partnership for 14 innings at home, they hit trouble: if Eranga at midwicket had caught Bairstow – 11 at the time – it would have been 102 for five. It was a surprise Eranga was playing at all, as his action had been reported at Chester-le-Street. Bairstow capitalised on his reprieve, hitting an unbeaten 167, one behind the highest by a wicketkeeper in England (by the West Indian Clyde Walcott, also at Lord's, in 1950), as the total passed 400. Sri Lanka made a decent start, Karunaratne and the recalled Silva putting on 101, but subsided against the seamers to trail by 128; with Hales biffing a Test-best 94, that was soon extended to 361. Compton's double failure cost him his Test career, but Cook came in at No. 7 after being hit on the knee while fielding, clonked a six and even tried a reverse-sweep. Sri Lanka had 110 overs to survive – but the weather played spoilsport. Bairstow finished with 19 dismissals, an England record for a three-match series, beating Geraint Jones's 17 – also against Sri Lanka – in 2006. Only Sri Lanka's Amal Silva, with 22 against India in 1985–86, had taken more.

England

*A. N. Cook lbw b Fernando	85	– (7) not out		49
A. D. Hales c Mathews b Herath	18	– lbw b Mathews		94
N. R. D. Compton c Chandimal b Lakmal	1	– (1) c Chandimal b Eranga		19
J. E. Root lbw b Lakmal	3	– (3) b Fernando		4
J. M. Vince b Fernando	10	– (4) b Fernando		0
†J. M. Bairstow not out	167	– (5) b Fernando		32
M. M. Ali c Mathews b Herath	25	– (8) c Herath b Eranga		9
C. R. Woakes c and b Herath	66	– (9) not out		0
S. C. J. Broad c Mendis b Lakmal	14			
S. T. Finn c Lakmal b Herath	7	– (6) lbw b Eranga		7
J. M. Anderson c Chandimal b Eranga	4			
Lb 16	16	B 6, lb 4, w 1, nb 8		19
(128.4 overs)	416	(7 wkts dec, 71 overs)		233

1/56 (2) 2/67 (3) 3/71 (4) 4/84 (5) 5/164 (1)
6/227 (7) 7/371 (8) 8/396 (9) 9/411 (10) 10/416 (11)

1/45 (1) 2/50 (3) 3/50 (4) 4/101 (5)
5/120 (6) 6/202 (2) 7/224 (8)

Eranga 25.4–2–94–1; Lakmal 27–2–90–3; Fernando 27–4–104–2; Mathews 13–5–31–0; Herath 36–8–81–4. *Second innings*—Lakmal 13–2–45–0; Eranga 14–1–58–3; Fernando 15–5–37–3; Herath 20–2–63–0; Mathews 9–3–20–1.

Sri Lanka

F. D. M. Karunaratne c Bairstow b Finn	50	– not out		37
J. K. Silva c Bairstow b Broad	79	– lbw b Anderson		16
B. K. G. Mendis lbw b Woakes	25	– not out		17
H. D. R. L. Thirimanne c Root b Finn	17			
*A. D. Mathews c Root b Woakes	3			
†L. D. Chandimal lbw b Finn	19			
M. D. K. J. Perera c Bairstow b Anderson	42			
H. M. R. K. B. Herath b Broad	31			
R. M. S. Eranga c Vince b Woakes	1			
R. A. S. Lakmal c Root b Anderson	0			
A. N. P. R. Fernando not out	0			
B 4, lb 16, w 1	21	B 1, lb 6, nb 1		8
(95.1 overs)	288	(1 wkt, 24.2 overs)		78

1/108 (1) 2/162 (3) 3/166 (2) 4/169 (5) 5/202 (6)
6/205 (4) 7/276 (8) 8/288 (7) 9/288 (10) 10/288 (9)

1/45 (2)

Anderson 23–6–61–2; Broad 23–7–79–2; Finn 18–1–59–3; Woakes 17.1–5–31–3; Ali 14–2–38–0. *Second innings*—Broad 11–4–27–0; Anderson 9–2–27–1; Woakes 2–1–7–0; Ali 2–1–4–0; Root 0.2–0–6–0.

Umpires: S. Ravi *(India)* (12) and R. J. Tucker *(Australia)* (44).
Third umpire: Aleem Dar *(Pakistan)*.   Referee: A. J. Pycroft *(Zimbabwe)* (46).

Close of play: first day, England 279–6 (Bairstow 107, Woakes 23); second day, Sri Lanka 162–1 (Silva 79, Mendis 25); third day, England 109–4 (Hales 41, Finn 6); fourth day, Sri Lanka 32–0 (Karunaratne 19, Silva 12).

ENGLAND v PAKISTAN 2016 (1st Test)

At Lord's, London, on 14, 15, 16, 17 July, 2016.
Toss: Pakistan.   Result: PAKISTAN WON BY 75 RUNS.
Debuts: England – J. T. Ball.
Man of the Match: Yasir Shah.

A genuinely competitive Test was turned Pakistan's way by the mesmeric leg-breaks of Yasir Shah, who returned the best match figures by a spinner at Lord's since Derek Underwood's 13 for 71 *against* Pakistan in 1974. Not far behind was Misbah-ul-Haq, the tourists' 42-year-old captain, who became the oldest Test centurion for 82 years (since England's Patsy Hendren, 45 in 1934). On reaching three figures, Misbah performed some press-ups, a nod to the Pakistan army, which had helped his side prepare. His stand of 148 with Asad Shafiq – which more than doubled the score – made them the first fifth-wicket pair with seven century stands in Tests. Woakes made up for the absence of the injured Anderson with six wickets (and five more in the second innings); the debutant Jake Ball received his cap from his uncle, the former Test wicketkeeper Bruce French, before taking the new ball with his county colleague Broad. Yasir also took six as England foundered after reaching 118 for one; only Cook managed a half-century, before falling to Mohammad Amir, in his first Test for almost six years, after serving a ban (and a jail term) for bowling deliberate no-balls on this ground in 2010. Broad and Woakes ensured Pakistan did not disappear over the horizon: Misbah now made an 11-minute duck, and the eventual target was 283. Vince, Ballance and Bairstow all made it into the forties, but not beyond – then Yasir and Amir gobbled up the rest, the last four wickets adding only 12.

Pakistan

Mohammad Hafeez c Bairstow b Woakes	40	– c Root b Broad	0
Shan Masood c Bairstow b Woakes	7	– c Cook b Woakes	24
Azhar Ali lbw b Ball	7	– lbw b Woakes	23
Younis Khan c Ali b Broad	33	– b Ali	25
*Misbah-ul-Haq b Broad	114	– c Hales b Ali	0
Asad Shafiq c Bairstow b Woakes	73	– b Woakes	49
Rahat Ali b Woakes	0	– (11) not out	0
†Sarfraz Ahmed c Vince b Woakes	25	– (7) c Bairstow b Woakes	45
Wahab Riaz b Woakes	0	– c Bairstow b Woakes	0
Mohammad Amir c Root b Broad	12	– c Bairstow b Broad	1
Yasir Shah not out	11	– (8) c Bairstow b Broad	30
B 4, lb 10, w 2, nb 1	17	B 6, lb 11, nb 1	18
(99.2 overs)	339	(79.1 overs)	215

1/38 (2) 2/51 (1) 3/77 (3) 4/134 (4) 5/282 (6) 6/282 (7)
7/310 (8) 8/310 (9) 9/316 (5) 10/339 (10)

1/2 (1) 2/44 (2) 3/59 (3) 4/60 (5) 5/129 (4) 6/168 (6)
7/208 (7) 8/214 (9) 9/214 (8) 10/215 (10)

Broad 27.2–9–71–3; Ball 19–5–51–1; Woakes 24–7–70–6; Finn 21–2–86–0; Ali 7–0–46–0; Vince 1–0–1–0. *Second innings*—Broad 19.1–7–38–3; Ball 16–7–37–0; Finn 13–4–42–0; Woakes 18–6–32–5; Ali 13–3–49–2.

England

*A. N. Cook b Mohammad Amir	81	– c Sarfraz Ahmed b Rahat Ali	8
A. D. Hales c Azhar Ali b Rahat Ali	6	– c Mohammad Hafeez b Rahat Ali	16
J. E. Root c Mohammad Hafeez b Yasir Shah	48	– c Yasir Shah b Rahat Ali	9
J. M. Vince lbw b Yasir Shah	16	– c Younis Khan b Wahab Riaz	42
G. S. Ballance lbw b Yasir Shah	6	– b Yasir Shah	43
†J. M. Bairstow b Yasir Shah	29	– b Yasir Shah	48
M. M. Ali lbw b Yasir Shah	23	– b Yasir Shah	2
C. R. Woakes not out	35	– c Younis Khan b Yasir Shah	23
S. C. J. Broad b Wahab Riaz	17	– b Mohammad Amir	1
S. T. Finn lbw b Yasir Shah	5	– not out	4
J. T. Ball run out (Shan Masood/Wahab Riaz)	4	– b Mohammad Amir	3
Nb 2	2	B 1, lb 5, w 1, nb 1	8
(79.1 overs)	272	(75.5 overs)	207

1/8 (2) 2/118 (3) 3/139 (4) 4/147 (5) 5/173 (1) 6/193 (6)
7/232 (7) 8/260 (9) 9/267 (10) 10/272 (11)

1/19 (1) 2/32 (2) 3/47 (3) 4/96 (4) 5/135 (5)
6/139 (7) 7/195 (6) 8/196 (9) 9/204 (8) 10/207 (11)

Mohammad Amir 18–2–65–1; Rahat Ali 14–1–68–1; Wahab Riaz 18.1–0–67–1; Yasir Shah 29–6–72–6. *Second innings*—Mohammad Amir 17.5–4–39–2; Rahat Ali 14–0–47–3; Yasir Shah 31–9–69–4; Wahab Riaz 13–1–46–1.

Umpires: H. D. P. K. Dharmasena *(Sri Lanka)* (37) and J. S. Wilson *(West Indies)* (2).
Third umpire: R. J. Tucker *(Australia)*.   Referee: R. B. Richardson *(West Indies)* (1).

Close of play: first day, Pakistan 282–6 (Misbah-ul-Haq 110); second day, England 253–7 (Woakes 31, Broad 11); third day, Pakistan 214–8 (Yasir Shah 30, Mohammad Amir 0).

ENGLAND v PAKISTAN 2016 (2nd Test)

At Old Trafford, Manchester, on 22, 23, 24, 25 July, 2016.
Toss: England.   Result: ENGLAND WON BY 330 RUNS.
Debuts: none.
Man of the Match: J. E. Root.

After the Lord's misadventure, the northern triumph. Led by Root's superb double-century, England gambolled to victory inside four days. Uncharacteristically careless the week before, Root was classically magnificent here, putting on 185 with Cook (who made his 29th Test century, the first for 20 innings), then going on to his highest score. Finally, after 614 minutes, 406 balls and 27 fours, Root misread Wahab Riaz's slower ball and was out for 254, the third-highest by an England No. 3, behind Wally Hammond's 336 not out at Auckland in 1932-33 and Tom Graveney's 258 v West Indies at Trent Bridge in 1957. With Woakes and Bairstow contributing punchy 58s, England declared in sight of 600; Yasir Shah, irresistible at Lord's, finished with one for 213. Pakistan lost four wickets on the second evening, and lurched to 119 for eight next day before Misbah-ul-Haq and Wahab Riaz added 60. The only PR hiccup for England came on the third afternoon, when Cook cautiously chose not to enforce the follow-on, with Pakistan 391 behind. Never before in a time-restricted Test had England led by so many without asking the opposition to bat again. The lead was quickly extended to 565 and, with the threatened rain staying away, England were soon among the wickets again, Woakes taking his two-Test haul to 18. No one reached 50 as the innings fizzled out: the only bad news for England was a calf injury to Stokes, which ruled him out of the rest of the series.

England

*A. N. Cook b Mohammad Amir	105	– not out		76
A. D. Hales b Mohammad Amir	10	– c Sarfraz Ahmed b Mohammad Amir		24
J. E. Root c Mohammad Hafeez b Wahab Riaz	254	– not out		71
J. M. Vince c Sarfraz Ahmed b Rahat Ali	18			
G. S. Ballance b Rahat Ali	23			
C. R. Woakes c and b Yasir Shah	58			
B. A. Stokes c Sarfraz Ahmed b Wahab Riaz	34			
†J. M. Bairstow c Misbah-ul-Haq b Wahab Riaz	58			
M. M. Ali not out	2			
Lb 9, w 8, nb 10	27	Lb 2		2
(8 wkts dec, 152.2 overs)	589	(1 wkt dec, 30 overs)		173

1/25 (2) 2/210 (1) 3/238 (4) 4/311 (5)   1/68 (2)
5/414 (6) 6/471 (7) 7/577 (3) 8/589 (8)

S. C. J. Broad and J. M. Anderson did not bat.

Mohammad Amir 29–6–89–2; Rahat Ali 29–4–101–2; Wahab Riaz 26.2–1–106–3; Yasir Shah 54–6–213–1; Azhar Ali 11–0–52–0; Shan Masood 3–0–19–0. *Second innings*—Mohammad Amir 11–2–43–1; Rahat Ali 8–0–54–0; Yasir Shah 9–0–53–0; Azhar Ali 2–0–21–0.

Pakistan

Mohammad Hafeez c Root b Woakes	18	– c Ballance b Ali		42
Shan Masood c Root b Anderson	39	– c Cook b Anderson		1
Azhar Ali c and b Woakes	1	– lbw b Anderson		8
Younis Khan c Bairstow b Stokes	1	– c Hales b Ali		28
Rahat Ali c Ballance b Woakes	4	– (11) not out		8
*Misbah-ul-Haq c Cook b Ali	52	– (5) b Woakes		35
Asad Shafiq c Hales b Broad	4	– (6) lbw b Anderson		39
†Sarfraz Ahmed c Root b Stokes	26	– (7) c Bairstow b Woakes		7
Yasir Shah c Root b Woakes	1	– (8) lbw b Ali		10
Wahab Riaz c Hales b Ali	39	– (9) c Cook b Root		19
Mohammad Amir not out	9	– (10) c Broad b Woakes		29
Lb 2, nb 2	4	B 2, lb 4, w 1, nb 1		8
(63.4 overs)	198	(70.3 overs)		234

1/27 (1) 2/43 (3) 3/48 (4) 4/53 (5) 5/71 (2)   1/7 (2) 2/25 (3) 3/83 (1) 4/102 (4) 5/145 (5)
6/76 (7) 7/112 (8) 8/119 (9) 9/179 (6) 10/198 (10)   6/163 (7) 7/167 (6) 8/190 (8) 9/208 (9) 10/234 (10)

Anderson 13–5–27–1; Broad 12–5–20–1; Ali 7.4–0–43–2; Woakes 16–1–67–4; Stokes 15–1–39–2. *Second innings*—Anderson 16–2–41–2; Broad 14–3–37–0; Stokes 5.2–0–21–0; Ali 18.4–1–88–3; Woakes 15.3–2–41–3; Root 1–1–0–1.

Umpires: H. D. P. K. Dharmasena *(Sri Lanka)* (38) and R. J. Tucker *(Australia)* (45).
Third umpire: J. S. Wilson *(West Indies)*.   Referee: R. B. Richardson *(West Indies)* (2).

Close of play: first day, England 314-4 (Root 141, Woakes 2); second day, Pakistan 57-4 (Shan Masood 30, Misbah-ul-Haq 1); third day, England 98-1 (Cook 49, Root 23).

Test No. 2208/80 (E975, P398)

ENGLAND v PAKISTAN 2016 (3rd Test)

At Edgbaston, Birmingham, on 3, 4, 5, 6, 7 August, 2016.
Toss: Pakistan.   Result: ENGLAND WON BY 141 RUNS.
Debuts: none.
Man of the Match: M. M. Ali.

After trailing by 103 in their 500th home Test, England completed a stunning comeback at 5.24 on the final afternoon, only the sixth time they had overcome a first-innings deficit of 100-plus to win. The turnaround in this slow-burning classic started with the second day's last ball, which Azhar Ali edged to slip after a patient 139, his tenth Test century but first outside Asia (in 2010 he had made a 32-ball duck here). Next day England's seamers hustled out the last five for 42, then the batsmen – who had misfired after being put in, apart from Ballance and Ali – all performed well in the second innings. Cook became England's leading scorer in all formats, passing Kevin Pietersen's 13,779, while Hales reached his only fifty of the series; it was their first century opening stand, at the 18th attempt. Ballance's 28 was the lowest of the top seven, and Ali added another sprightly half-century during a rattling partnership of 152 with Bairstow. Chasing 343 in 84 overs, Pakistan were done in by their own invention – reverse-swing: Woakes and Finn – restored for the injured Stokes – ripped out four for one in 23 balls before tea. By next morning, as a Pakistan TV channel insinuated ball-tampering, the irony had come full circle. No one could accuse anyone of conforming to stereotype. Anderson's dismissal of Mohammad Hafeez with the fourth ball of the second day gave him 50 Test wickets against everyone bar Bangladesh and Zimbabwe (only Muttiah Muralitharan could boast all nine).

England

*A. N. Cook lbw b Rahat Ali	45	– c Yasir Shah b Sohail Khan	66
A. D. Hales c Sarfraz Ahmed b Sohail Khan	17	– c Younis Khan b Mohammad Amir	54
J. E. Root c Mohammad Hafeez b Sohail Khan	3	– c Mohammad Hafeez b Yasir Shah	62
J. M. Vince c Younis Khan b Sohail Khan	39	– c Younis Khan b Mohammad Amir	42
G. S. Ballance c Sarfraz Ahmed b Yasir Shah	70	– c Asad Shafiq b Yasir Shah	28
†J. M. Bairstow c Sarfraz Ahmed b Sohail Khan	12	– lbw b Sohail Khan	83
M. M. Ali c Sarfraz Ahmed b Mohammad Amir	63	– not out	86
C. R. Woakes c Sarfraz Ahmed b Rahat Ali	9	– not out	3
S. C. J. Broad c Azhar Ali b Mohammad Amir	13		
S. T. Finn not out	15		
J. M. Anderson lbw b Sohail Khan	5		
Lb 1, w 1, nb 4	6	B 4, lb 7, w 2, nb 8	21
(86 overs)	297	(6 wkts dec, 129 overs)	445

1/36 (2) 2/48 (3) 3/75 (1) 4/144 (4) 5/158 (6)
6/224 (5) 7/244 (8) 8/276 (9) 9/278 (7) 10/297 (11)

1/126 (1) 2/126 (2) 3/221 (3)
4/257 (4) 5/282 (5) 6/434 (6)

Mohammad Amir 16–3–53–2; Sohail Khan 23–3–96–5; Rahat Ali 20–4–83–2; Yasir Shah 27–3–64–1. *Second innings*—Mohammad Amir 31–8–75–2; Sohail Khan 29–3–111–2; Rahat Ali 21–8–54–0; Yasir Shah 43–4–172–2; Azhar Ali 5–0–22–0.

Pakistan

Mohammad Hafeez c Ballance b Anderson	0	– c Woakes b Broad	2
Sami Aslam run out (Vince)	82	– b Finn	70
Azhar Ali c Cook b Woakes	139	– c Cook b Ali	38
Younis Khan c Bairstow b Woakes	31	– c Bairstow b Anderson	4
*Misbah-ul-Haq b Anderson	56	– c Bairstow b Finn	10
Asad Shafiq b Broad	0	– lbw b Woakes	0
†Sarfraz Ahmed not out	46	– c Root b Woakes	0
Yasir Shah run out (Woakes/Bairstow)	7	– c Hales b Anderson	7
Mohammad Amir lbw b Woakes	1	– c Woakes b Broad	16
Sohail Khan lbw b Broad	7	– c and b Ali	36
Rahat Ali c Root b Broad	4	– not out	15
B 5, lb 21, nb 1	27	Lb 2, nb 1	3
(136 overs)	400	(70.5 overs)	201

1/0 (1) 2/181 (2) 3/257 (3) 4/274 (4) 5/296 (6)
6/358 (5) 7/367 (8) 8/368 (9) 9/386 (10) 10/400 (11)

1/6 (1) 2/79 (3) 3/92 (4) 4/124 (5) 5/125 (6)
6/125 (7) 7/125 (2) 8/149 (8) 9/151 (9) 10/201 (10)

Anderson 29.1–7–54–2; Broad 30–4–83–3; Finn 27.5–7–76–0; Woakes 30–7–79–3; Ali 17–2–79–0; Vince 1–0–2–0; Root 1–0–1–0. *Second innings*—Anderson 13–3–31–2; Broad 15–7–24–2; Woakes 11–2–53–2; Finn 13–5–38–2; Ali 17.5–4–49–2; Root 1–0–4–0.

Umpires: B. N. J. Oxenford *(Australia)* (32) and J. S. Wilson *(West Indies)* (3).
Third umpire: H. D. P. K. Dharmasena *(Sri Lanka)*.   Referee: R. B. Richardson *(West Indies)* (3).

Close of play: first day, England 297; second day, Pakistan 257–3 (Younis Khan 21); third day, England 120–0 (Cook 64, Hales 50); fourth day, England 414–5 (Bairstow 82, Ali 60).

Test No. 2209/81 (E976, P399)

ENGLAND v PAKISTAN 2016 (4th Test)

At Kennington Oval, London, on 11, 12, 13, 14 August, 2016.
Toss: England.   Result: PAKISTAN WON BY TEN WICKETS.
Debuts: Pakistan – Iftikhar Ahmed.
Man of the Match: Younis Khan.   Men of the Series: C. R. Woakes and Misbah-ul-Haq.

A majestic innings by 38-year-old Younis Khan lifted his side to a series-squaring total: as against Australia the previous year, England lost both Tests in London by wide margins. Younis had failed in the first three matches, but now stood taller at the crease and dictated, all the way to 218, his 32nd Test hundred to set against 30 fifties (and only one dismissal in the nineties). He put on 150 with Asad Shafiq, who had been pushed up to No. 4, and then dragged Pakistan 214 in front. England had been rescued from 110 for five by Ali, who shook off a fearsome blow on the helmet from Wahab Riaz to fashion another attractive century, and shared stands of 93 and 79 with Bairstow and Woakes. The hard-working seamer Sohail Khan took a five-for for the second match running. Pakistan's total put England's in perspective, and another poor start – Vince added a duck to his first-innings single – left the later order with too much to do. Bairstow's 81 helped stave off an innings defeat, but Yasir Shah fizzed and zipped to five wickets (after none in the first innings), and Pakistan needed only 40 to win. Azhar Ali clinched victory with a six on the 69th anniversary of his country's founding, lifting spirits back home after a terrorist attack in Quetta. The result also came as a tribute to Pakistan's first great batsman, Hanif Mohammad – on the winning side at The Oval in 1954 – who died during this Test.

England

*A. N. Cook b Sohail Khan	35	– c Iftikhar Ahmed b Wahab Riaz	7
A. D. Hales c Yasir Shah b Mohammad Amir	6	– lbw b Yasir Shah	12
J. E. Root c Sarfraz Ahmed b Wahab Riaz	26	– lbw b Yasir Shah	39
J. M. Vince c Sarfraz Ahmed b Wahab Riaz	1	– c Misbah-ul-Haq b Yasir Shah	0
G. S. Ballance c Azhar Ali b Wahab Riaz	8	– c Sarfraz Ahmed b Sohail Khan	17
†J. M. Bairstow c Sarfraz Ahmed b Mohammad Amir	55	– c Azhar Ali b Wahab Riaz	81
M. M. Ali c Yasir Shah b Sohail Khan	108	– c Sarfraz Ahmed b Yasir Shah	32
C. R. Woakes c Sarfraz Ahmed b Sohail Khan	45	– run out (Wahab Riaz)	4
S. C. J. Broad lbw b Sohail Khan	0	– c Younis Khan b Yasir Shah	5
S. T. Finn b Sohail Khan	8	– not out	16
J. M. Anderson not out	6	– lbw b Iftikhar Ahmed	17
B 8, lb 7, w 7, nb 8	30	B 8, lb 10, nb 5	23
(76.4 overs)	328	(79.2 overs)	253

1/23 (2) 2/69 (1) 3/73 (4) 4/74 (4) 5/110 (5)
6/203 (6) 7/282 (8) 8/282 (9) 9/296 (10) 10/328 (7)

1/14 (1) 2/49 (2) 3/55 (4) 4/74 (3) 5/128 (5)
6/193 (7) 7/209 (8) 8/209 (6) 9/221 (9) 10/253 (11)

Mohammad Amir 18–1–80–2; Sohail Khan 20.4–1–68–5; Wahab Riaz 20–0–93–3; Yasir Shah 16–2–60–0; Iftikhar Ahmed 2–0–12–0. *Second innings*—Mohammad Amir 21.4–7–65–0; Sohail Khan 15–2–50–1; Wahab Riaz 11.2–1–48–2; Yasir Shah 29–4–71–5; Iftikhar Ahmed 2.2–1–1–1.

Pakistan

Sami Aslam lbw b Broad	3	– not out	12
Azhar Ali c Bairstow b Ali	49	– not out	30
Yasir Shah c Root b Finn	26		
Asad Shafiq c Broad b Finn	109		
Younis Khan lbw b Anderson	218		
*Misbah-ul-Haq c Hales b Woakes	15		
Iftikhar Ahmed c Ali b Woakes	4		
†Sarfraz Ahmed c Bairstow b Woakes	44		
Wahab Riaz st Bairstow b Ali	4		
Mohammad Amir not out	39		
Sohail Khan c Broad b Finn	2		
B 18, lb 6, w 3, nb 2	29		
(146 overs)	542	(no wkt, 13.1 overs)	42

1/3 (1) 2/52 (3) 3/127 (2) 4/277 (4) 5/316 (6)
6/320 (7) 7/397 (8) 8/434 (9) 9/531 (5) 10/542 (11)

Anderson 29–10–78–1; Broad 29–5–99–1; Finn 30–1–110–3; Woakes 30–8–82–3; Ali 23–1–128–2; Root 5–0–21–0. *Second innings*—Woakes 4–0–11–0; Finn 0.2–0–0–0; Ali 5.5–0–30–0; Root 3–2–1–0.

Umpires: M. Erasmus *(South Africa)* (36) and B. N. J. Oxenford *(Australia)* (33).
Third umpire: J. S. Wilson *(West Indies)*.   Referee: R. B. Richardson *(West Indies)* (4).

Close of play: first day, Pakistan 3–1 (Azhar Ali 0, Yasir Shah 0); second day, Pakistan 340–6 (Younis Khan 101, Sarfraz Ahmed 17); third day, England 88–4 (Ballance 4, Bairstow 14).

Test No. 2210/91 (WI514, I496)

WEST INDIES v INDIA 2016 (1st Test)

At Sir Vivian Richards Stadium, North Sound, Antigua, on 21, 22, 23, 24 July, 2016.
Toss: India.   Result: INDIA WON BY AN INNINGS AND 92 RUNS.
Debuts: West Indies – R. L. Chase.
Man of the Match: R. Ashwin.

Often slow starters, India hit the ground running this time, and coasted to a thumping victory. After Kohli won a crucial toss, Dhawan weathered a sharp early burst from Gabriel, then feasted on an otherwise insipid attack. He missed out on a hundred, missing a sweep at Bishoo, and the other batsmen were tied down. But Kohli had no such problems: he toyed with the bowling after reaching his 12th Test hundred, mixing confident straight-drives with assured hits through cover. Next day he motored to his maiden first-class double-century, before chopping Gabriel into his stumps. Promoted to No. 6, Ashwin helped Kohli add 168, and went on to his third Test hundred, all against West Indies, before the declaration. Kraigg Brathwaite showed it was possible to occupy the crease, even if runs did not come at a fast clip, but few of his colleagues displayed the determination, technique or appetite required to resist a disciplined attack. Mohammed Shami, returning to Test cricket after a knee injury had kept him out for a year, picked up four wickets as West Indies stumbled to 243; they got that far only thanks to a maiden fifty from Dowrich (playing his third Test but keeping for the first time). West Indies followed on at home for the first time in ten years, and had no answer to Ashwin, who finished with his fourth seven-for in Tests as India eased to their first innings-victory in the Caribbean, and their biggest win anywhere outside Asia.

India

M. Vijay c K. C. Brathwaite b Gabriel	7
S. Dhawan lbw b Bishoo	84
C. A. Pujara c K. C. Brathwaite b Bishoo	16
*V. Kohli b Gabriel	200
A. M. Rahane c Bravo b Bishoo	22
R. Ashwin c Gabriel b K. C. Brathwaite	113
†W. P. Saha st Dowrich b K. C. Brathwaite	40
A. Mishra c Holder b K. C. Brathwaite	53
Mohammed Shami not out	17
B 6, lb 2, nb 6	14
(8 wkts dec, 161.5 overs)	566

1/14 (1) 2/74 (3) 3/179 (2) 4/236 (5)
5/404 (4) 6/475 (7) 7/526 (6) 8/566 (8)

U. T. Yadav and I. Sharma did not bat.

Gabriel 21–5–65–2; Holder 24–4–83–0; C. R. Brathwaite 25–5–80–0; Chase 34–3–102–0; Bishoo 43–1–163–3; K. C. Brathwaite 14.5–1–65–3.

West Indies

K. C. Brathwaite c Saha b Yadav	74	– lbw b Sharma	2
R. Chandrika c Saha b Mohammed Shami	16	– c Saha b Ashwin	31
D. Bishoo st Saha b Mishra	12	– (10) c Pujara b Ashwin	45
D. M. Bravo c Saha b Mohammed Shami	11	– (3) c Rahane b Yadav	10
M. N. Samuels c Saha b Mohammed Shami	1	– (4) b Ashwin	50
J. Blackwood c Rahane b Mohammed Shami	0	– (5) c Kohli b Ashwin	0
R. L. Chase c Kohli b Yadav	23	– (6) c sub (K. L. Rahul) b Ashwin	8
†S. O. Dowrich not out	57	– (7) lbw b Mishra	9
*J. O. Holder c Saha b Yadav	36	– (8) b Ashwin	16
C. R. Brathwaite b Yadav	0	– (9) not out	51
S. T. Gabriel b Mishra	2	– b Ashwin	4
B 4, lb 2, w 2, nb 3	11	Nb 5	5
(90.2 overs)	243	(78 overs)	231

1/30 (2) 2/68 (3) 3/90 (4) 4/92 (5) 5/92 (6)   1/2 (1) 2/21 (3) 3/88 (2) 4/92 (5) 5/101 (4) 6/106 (6)
6/139 (7) 7/144 (1) 8/213 (9) 9/213 (10) 10/243 (11)   7/120 (7) 8/132 (8) 9/227 (10) 10/231 (11)

Sharma 20–7–44–0; Yadav 18–8–41–4; Mohammed Shami 20–4–66–4; Ashwin 17–5–43–0; Mishra 15.2–4–43–2.
Second innings—Sharma 11–2–27–1; Mohammed Shami 10–3–26–0; Yadav 13–4–34–1; Ashwin 25–8–83–7; Mishra 19–3–61–1.

Umpires: Aleem Dar *(Pakistan)* (104) and I. J. Gould *(England)* (50).
Third umpire: G. O. Brathwaite *(West Indies)*.   Referee: R. S. Madugalle *(Sri Lanka)* (164).

Close of play: first day, India 302–4 (Kohli 143, Ashwin 22); second day, West Indies 31–1 (K. C. Brathwaite 11, Bishoo 0); third day, West Indies 21–1 (Chandrika 9, Bravo 10).

WEST INDIES v INDIA 2016 (2nd Test)

At Sabina Park, Kingston, Jamaica, on 30, 31 July, 1, 2, 3 August, 2016.
Toss: West Indies. Result: DRAWN.
Debuts: West Indies – M. L. Cummins.
Man of the Match: R. L. Chase.

Tropical Storm Earl intervened after India claimed a lead of 304, but once it blew through, India were hit by a different sort of whirlwind. Led by Roston Chase, in only his second Test, West Indies saved the game with panache, scoring 340 runs on the final day. Things had looked grim at the start, when Holder won the toss and inexplicably decided to bat on a damp surface. West Indies were soon seven for three and, although Samuels and Blackwood added 81 in 20 overs, the innings was over before tea for 196. India were only 70 behind by the end of a hectic first day. They stretched their legs on the second, with Rahul and Rahane making sparkling centuries, and Kohli declared at 500 after lunch on the third day. Chase's off-breaks produced a maiden Test five-for, and he also ran out Pujara with a direct hit from square leg. Now the weather took a hand. West Indies could not start their second innings that day, and faced only 15.5 overs on the fourth, although they did lose four wickets. The final day dawned bright, and most expected India to wrap things up – but they reckoned without Chase, who batted for almost six hours and became the first West Indian since Garry Sobers 50 years earlier to score a hundred and take a five-for in the same Test. Chase shared stands of 93 with Blackwood, 144 with Dowrich and 103 with Holder to confirm Sabina Park's first draw in 16 Tests.

West Indies

K. C. Brathwaite c Pujara b Sharma		1 – c Rahul b Mishra	23
R. Chandrika c Rahul b Mohammed Shami		5 – b Sharma	1
D. M. Bravo c Kohli b Sharma		0 – c Rahul b Mohammed Shami	20
M. N. Samuels c Rahul b Ashwin		37 – b Mohammed Shami	0
J. Blackwood lbw b Ashwin		62 – c Pujara b Ashwin	63
R. L. Chase c Dhawan b Mohammed Shami		10 – not out	137
†S. O. Dowrich c Saha b Ashwin		5 – lbw b Mishra	74
*J. O. Holder c Rahul b Ashwin		13 – not out	64
D. Bishoo c Dhawan b Ashwin		12	
M. L. Cummins not out		24	
S. T. Gabriel c Kohli b Mishra		15	
W 2, nb 10		12	Lb 2, w 1, nb 3 ... 6
(52.3 overs)		196	(6 wkts, 104 overs) ... 388

1/4 (1) 2/4 (3) 3/7 (2) 4/88 (5) 5/115 (4) 6/127 (7)
7/131 (6) 8/151 (9) 9/158 (8) 10/196 (11)

1/5 (2) 2/41 (1) 3/41 (4)
4/48 (3) 5/141 (5) 6/285 (7)

Sharma 10–1–53–2; Mohammed Shami 10–3–23–2; Ashwin 16–2–52–5; Yadav 6–1–30–0; Mishra 10.3–3–38–1. *Second innings*—Sharma 18–3–56–1; Mohammed Shami 19–3–82–2; Mishra 25–6–90–2; Yadav 12–2–44–0; Ashwin 30–4–114–1.

India

K. L. Rahul c Dowrich b Gabriel	158
S. Dhawan c Bravo b Chase	27
C. A. Pujara run out (Chase)	46
*V. Kohli c Chandrika b Chase	44
A. M. Rahane not out	108
R. Ashwin lbw b Bishoo	3
†W. P. Saha lbw b Holder	47
A. Mishra c Chandrika b Chase	21
Mohammed Shami b Chase	0
U. T. Yadav c Holder b Chase	19
B 8, lb 3, w 6, nb 10	27
(9 wkts dec, 171.1 overs)	500

1/87 (2) 2/208 (3) 3/277 (1) 4/310 (4) 5/327 (6)
6/425 (7) 7/458 (8) 8/458 (9) 9/500 (10)

I. Sharma did not bat.

Gabriel 28–8–62–1; Cummins 26.4–4–87–0; Holder 34.2–12–72–1; Chase 36.1–4–121–5; Bishoo 35–5–107–1; Brathwaite 11–0–40–0.

Umpires: Aleem Dar *(Pakistan)* (105) and I. J. Gould *(England)* (51).
Third umpire: N. Duguid *(West Indies)*. Referee: R. S. Madugalle *(Sri Lanka)* (165).

Close of play: first day, India 126–1 (Rahul 75, Pujara 18); second day, India 358–5 (Rahane 42, Saha 17); third day, India 500–9 dec; fourth day, West Indies 48–4 (Blackwood 3).

Test No. 2212/93 (WI516, I498)

WEST INDIES v INDIA 2016 (3rd Test)

At Darren Sammy Stadium, Gros Islet, St Lucia, on 9, 10, 11 *(no play)*, 12, 13 August, 2016.
Toss: West Indies.   Result: INDIA WON BY 237 RUNS.
Debuts: West Indies – A. S. Joseph.
Man of the Match: R. Ashwin.

After West Indies' rearguard in Jamaica, things returned to script in St Lucia, where another big first innings set up a series-clinching triumph, the first time India had won two Tests in the Caribbean. Their start was less certain: the lively 19-year-old debutant Alzarri Joseph struck quickly. Rahul made a defiant 50 but, when Rahane fell for 35, West Indies were on top at 126 for five. Ashwin and Saha changed all that, eventually adding 213, India's best for the sixth wicket against West Indies. It was Ashwin's fourth Test century – all against West Indies – but Saha's first, in 14 matches spread over six years. The last five wickets tumbled for 14, and West Indies began well enough, reaching 107 for one by the end of the second day, before rain obliterated the third. When play resumed, Ashwin removed Brathwaite after more than four hours, but at 202 for three a draw looked likely – before West Indies outdid India's collapse. Bhuvneshwar Kumar, in his first Test for 19 months, got the ball swinging after lunch, and seven wickets tumbled for 23. From nowhere, India had a lead of 128, and more than doubled that by stumps. After 60 runs in nine overs on the final morning – Cummins ended with six of the seven wickets to fall – Kohli declared for the third Test in a row, setting 346 in 79 overs. West Indies never got close: although Bravo resisted for three hours, they were bundled out in less than 48 overs.

India

K. L. Rahul c Brathwaite b Chase	50	– c Brathwaite b Cummins	28
S. Dhawan c Dowrich b Gabriel	1	– lbw b Chase	26
*V. Kohli c Bravo b Joseph	3	– lbw b Cummins	4
A. M. Rahane b Chase	35	– not out	78
R. G. Sharma c Dowrich b Joseph	9	– lbw b Cummins	41
R. Ashwin c Blackwood b Cummins	118	– (8) c Brathwaite b Cummins	1
†W. P. Saha c Dowrich b Joseph	104	– (6) c Dowrich b Cummins	14
R. A. Jadeja c Dowrich b Cummins	6	– (7) c Samuels b Cummins	16
Bhuvneshwar Kumar c Johnson b Gabriel	0		
Mohammed Shami not out	0		
I. Sharma c Johnson b Cummins	0		
B 7, lb 8, w 2, nb 10	27	B 1, lb 2, nb 6	9
(129.4 overs)	353	(7 wkts dec, 48 overs)	217

1/9 (2) 2/19 (3) 3/77 (1) 4/87 (5) 5/126 (4)   1/49 (1) 2/58 (3) 3/72 (2)
6/339 (7) 7/351 (8) 8/353 (9) 9/353 (6) 10/353 (11)   4/157 (5) 5/181 (6) 6/213 (7) 7/217 (8)

Gabriel 23–4–84–2; Joseph 24–6–69–3; Cummins 21.4–8–54–3; Holder 19–7–34–0; Chase 33–9–70–2; Brathwaite 9–1–27–0. *Second innings*—Gabriel 3–0–19–0; Joseph 4–0–23–0; Cummins 11–1–48–6; Holder 9–1–50–0; Chase 11–1–41–1; Brathwaite 10–1–33–0.

West Indies

K. C. Brathwaite c Saha b Ashwin	64	– lbw b Bhuvneshwar Kumar	4
L. R. Johnson run out (Rahul)	23	– c R. G. Sharma b Mohammed Shami	0
D. M. Bravo c Jadeja b I. Sharma	29	– c R. G. Sharma b Mohammed Shami	59
M. N. Samuels b Bhuvneshwar Kumar	48	– b I. Sharma	12
J. Blackwood c Kohli b Bhuvneshwar Kumar	20	– (6) st Saha b Jadeja	1
R. L. Chase c Rahane b Jadeja	2	– (5) b I. Sharma	10
†S. O. Dowrich c Dhawan b Bhuvneshwar Kumar	18	– c Kohli b Mohammed Shami	5
*J. O. Holder lbw b Bhuvneshwar Kumar	2	– run out (Ashwin)	1
A. S. Joseph c Rahul b Bhuvneshwar Kumar	0	– c Mohammed Shami b Ashwin	0
M. L. Cummins c Saha b Ashwin	0	– not out	2
S. T. Gabriel not out	0	– c Bhuvneshwar Kumar b Jadeja	11
B 13, lb 2, w 2, nb 2	19	Lb 2, nb 1	3
(103.4 overs)	225	(47.3 overs)	108

1/59 (2) 2/129 (3) 3/135 (1) 4/202 (5) 5/203 (4)   1/4 (2) 2/4 (1) 3/35 (4) 4/64 (5) 5/68 (6)
6/205 (6) 7/212 (8) 8/212 (9) 9/221 (10) 10/225 (7)   6/84 (7) 7/88 (8) 8/95 (3) 9/95 (9) 10/108 (11)

Bhuvneshwar Kumar 23.4–10–33–5; Mohammed Shami 17–3–58–0; Ashwin 26–7–52–2; I. Sharma 13–2–40–1; Jadeja 24–9–27–1. *Second innings*—Bhuvneshwar Kumar 12–6–13–1; Mohammed Shami 11–2–15–3; I. Sharma 7–0–30–2; Ashwin 12–2–28–1; Jadeja 5.3–1–20–2.

Umpires: N. J. Llong *(England)* (36) and R. J. Tucker *(Australia)* (46).
Third umpire: G. O. Brathwaite *(West Indies)*.   Referee: R. S. Madugalle *(Sri Lanka)* (166).

Close of play: first day, India 234–5 (Ashwin 75, Saha 46); second day, West Indies 107–1 (Brathwaite 53, Bravo 18); third day, no play; fourth day, India 157–3 (Rahane 51, R. G. Sharma 41).

WEST INDIES v INDIA 2016 (4th Test)

At Queen's Park Oval, Port-of-Spain, Trinidad, on August 18, 19 *(no play)*, 20 *(no play)*, 21 *(no play)*, 22 *(no play)* August, 2016.
Toss: West Indies.   Result: DRAWN.
Debuts: none.
Man of the Match: no award.   Man of the Series: R. Ashwin.

A match supposed to celebrate 125 years of the Queen's Park Cricket Club descended into embarrassment for both them and the West Indian board when only 22 overs were possible, all on the first day. A sharp shower had sent the players off and – with the groundstaff slow bringing on the covers – parts of the outfield were soaked. Then a clogged drain prevented water from seeping away, even after a day of bright sunshine. To make matters worse, no super-sopper was available. Although it was the rainy season in Trinidad – a time when no Test had been attempted before – it should have been possible to get some play. Instead, the second day was called off, after which the Indians did not even bother turning up; the umpires finally put everyone out of their misery at 9.30 on the fifth morning. Referee Ranjan Madugalle rated the ground management "poor", and the ICC later issued an official warning (jointly with Durban, which staged a similarly soggy Test at almost the same time). India had to settle for a series win – their sixth in succession over West Indies – but were unhappy at not being able to push for another victory, which would have taken them top of the Test rankings. Instead, Pakistan grabbed the No. 1 spot, before India overhauled them by beating New Zealand at home. Ashwin was deprived of the chance of equalling the Australian leg-spinner Clarrie Grimmett's record of reaching 200 wickets in 36 Tests, ending this match with 193.

West Indies

K. C. Brathwaite not out	32
L. R. Johnson c R. G. Sharma b I. Sharma	9
D. M. Bravo b Ashwin	10
M. N. Samuels not out	4
Lb 6, nb 1	7
(2 wkts, 22 overs)	62

1/31 (2) 2/48 (3)

J. Blackwood, R. L. Chase, †S. O. Dowrich, *J. O. Holder, D. Bishoo, M. L. Cummins and S. T. Gabriel did not bat.

Bhuvneshwar Kumar 6–1–13–0; Mohammed Shami 6–2–14–0; I. Sharma 5–3–7–1; Ashwin 5–1–22–1.

India

M. Vijay, K. L. Rahul, C. A. Pujara, *V. Kohli, A. M. Rahane, R. G. Sharma, R. Ashwin, †W. P. Saha, Bhuvneshwar Kumar, Mohammed Shami, I. Sharma.

Umpires: N. J. Llong *(England)* (37) and R. J. Tucker *(Australia)* (47).
Third umpire: N. Duguid *(West Indies)*.   Referee: R. S. Madugalle *(Sri Lanka)* (167).

Close of play: first day, West Indies 62–2 (Brathwaite 32, Samuels 4); second day, no play; third day, no play; fourth day, no play.

Test No. 2214/27 (SL249, A789)

SRI LANKA v AUSTRALIA 2016 (1st Test)

At Muttiah Muralitharan Stadium, Pallekele, on 26, 27, 28, 29, 30 July, 2016.
Toss: Sri Lanka.   Result: SRI LANKA WON BY 106 RUNS.
Debuts: Sri Lanka – D. M. de Silva, P. A. D. L. R. Sandakan.
Man of the Match: B. K. G. Mendis.

Australia's failure to take a decisive first-innings lead left the door ajar, and Kusal Mendis barged through. To start with the home batsmen struggled as Hazlewood, Lyon and O'Keefe delivered exacting spells. Sri Lanka were bundled out for 117 soon after lunch and, although Australia's openers played around straight balls, Khawaja and Smith took them halfway to parity. But a moment of arrogance changed the tone: Smith was stumped aiming an unsightly heave at Herath's second ball of the second day. Left-arm wrist-spinner Lakshan Sandakan claimed his first Test wicket (Marsh) with a lovely wrong'un, and flummoxed the tail: Australia led by only 86. Four wickets went down before Sri Lanka got their noses in front, but Mendis reaching his maiden century with a six off Lyon, and motored to a superb 176, a ground record. He put on 117 with Chandimal, then some late-order biffing inflated the target to 268. Australia were quickly in difficulty, and looked done for when four wickets tumbled for 18. But an extraordinary period of defiance followed. After O'Keefe – hobbling from a hamstring injury while fielding – hit a four in the 63rd over to make it 161 for eight, there were 154 successive dot balls, including Nevill's wicket, beating England's 92 against West Indies at Lord's in 1950. They blocked in the hope of late-afternoon rain, but it never came. Herath eventually dismissed O'Keefe – for a 98-ball four – to seal Sri Lanka's second Test win over Australia (after Kandy in 1999–2000), and Smith's first defeat as captain.

Sri Lanka

F. D. M. Karunaratne lbw b Starc	5 – (3) lbw b Starc	0
J. K. Silva c Voges b Hazlewood	4 – lbw b O'Keefe	7
B. K. G. Mendis lbw b Hazlewood	8 – (4) c Nevill b Starc	176
†L. D. Chandimal c Nevill b Hazlewood	15 – (6) lbw b Marsh	42
*A. D. Mathews c Smith b O'Keefe	15 – c Burns b Lyon	9
D. M. de Silva c Burns b Lyon	24 – (7) c Khawaja b Lyon	36
M. D. K. J. Perera b Lyon	20 – (1) lbw b Starc	4
M. D. K. Perera lbw b Lyon	0 – lbw b Hazlewood	12
H. M. R. K. B. Herath lbw b Starc	6 – c sub (M. C. Henriques) b Hazlewood	35
P. A. D. L. R. Sandakan not out	19 – b Starc	9
A. N. P. R. Fernando c Smith b O'Keefe	0 – not out	10
Lb 1	1 B 1, lb 12	13
(34.2 overs) 117	(93.4 overs)	353

1/6 (1) 2/15 (3) 3/18 (2) 4/43 (5) 5/67 (4)
6/87 (6) 7/87 (8) 8/94 (7) 9/100 (9) 10/117 (11)

1/6 (1) 2/6 (3) 3/45 (2) 4/86 (5) 5/203 (6) 6/274 (7)
7/290 (4) 8/314 (8) 9/323 (10) 10/353 (9)

Starc 11–1–51–2; Hazlewood 10–4–21–3; O'Keefe 10.2–3–32–2; Lyon 3–0–12–3. *Second innings*—Starc 19–4–84–4; Hazlewood 18.4–3–59–2; O'Keefe 16.2–3–42–1; Lyon 27–2–108–2; Warner 1–0–10–0; Voges 1.4–0–3–0; Marsh 9–1–33–1; Smith 1–0–1–0.

Australia

J. A. Burns b Herath	3 – b Sandakan	29
D. A. Warner b Fernando	0 – b Herath	1
U. T. Khawaja lbw b Herath	26 – lbw b M. D. K. Perera	18
*S. P. D. Smith st Chandimal b Herath	30 – lbw b Herath	55
A. C. Voges c Mendis b Fernando	47 – c and b Herath	12
M. R. Marsh b Sandakan	31 – lbw b Herath	25
†P. M. Nevill c M. D. K. J. Perera b Herath	2 – c Chandimal b de Silva	9
S. N. J. O'Keefe c Mendis b Sandakan	23 – (10) b Herath	4
M. A. Starc c †M. D. K. J. Perera b Sandakan	11 – (8) c and b Sandakan	0
N. M. Lyon lbw b Sandakan	17 – (9) lbw b Sandakan	8
J. R. Hazlewood not out	2 – not out	0
B 4, lb 7	11	
(79.2 overs) 203	(88.3 overs)	161

1/3 (2) 2/7 (1) 3/69 (4) 4/70 (3) 5/130 (6)
6/137 (7) 7/160 (5) 8/179 (9) 9/190 (8) 10/203 (10)

1/2 (2) 2/33 (3) 3/63 (1) 4/96 (5) 5/139 (6) 6/140 (4)
7/141 (8) 8/157 (9) 9/161 (7) 10/161 (10)

Fernando 16–6–36–2; Herath 25–8–49–4; M. D. K. Perera 14–1–43–0; Sandakan 21.2–3–58–4; Mathews 3–1–6–0. *Second innings*—Fernando 6–3–16–0; Herath 33.3–16–54–5; M. D. K. Perera 13–3–30–1; Sandakan 25–8–49–3; de Silva 11–7–12–1.

Umpires: R. A. Kettleborough *(England)* (36) and S. Ravi *(India)* (13).
Third umpire: C. B. Gaffaney *(New Zealand).*   Referee: B. C. Broad *(England)* (78).

Close of play: first day, Australia 66–2 (Khawaja 25, Smith 28); second day, Sri Lanka 6–1 (Silva 2, Karunaratne 0); third day, Sri Lanka 282–6 (Mendis 169, M. D. K. Perera 5); fourth day, Australia 83–3 (Smith 26, Voges 9).

SRI LANKA v AUSTRALIA 2016 (2nd Test)

At Galle International Stadium on 4, 5, 6 August, 2016.
Toss: Sri Lanka.   Result: SRI LANKA WON BY 229 RUNS.
Debuts: Sri Lanka – M. V. T. Fernando. Australia – J. M. Holland.
Man of the Match: M. D. K. Perera.

A sign outside the stadium read "Breakfast in Kandy, Lunch in Galle, Dinner in Colombo". And Sri Lanka's spinners showed their appetite again, chewing Australia up inside three days: only Starc's 11 wickets were worth plucking from a wreckage in which no Australian passed 42. Sri Lanka's batsmen did just enough: the middle order provided the bulk of their first-innings 281. They went after the spinners – Lyon and the debutant left-armer Jon Holland – allowing neither to settle, nor exploit a turning surface; between them, they leaked 142 from 33 overs. In reply, Burns pulled left-arm seamer Vishwa Fernando's second ball in Test cricket to square leg, while Warner was positive until he edged an off-break just before stumps. The second morning was pure chaos, as Australia lost eight for 47; Khawaja was late on a straight one, and Smith missed a cut. Herath completed a hat-trick (only Sri Lanka's second, after Nuwan Zoysa's at Harare in 1999-2000) when he trapped Starc lbw on review, while Dilruwan Perera shared the spoils. Sri Lanka's second innings mirrored the first: brittle against Starc, but the spinners struggled again in helpful conditions. Perera punched 64 from No. 8, and Sri Lanka led by 412. Having lasted 33.2 overs in the first innings, Australia decided to attack, but were all out in 50.1, all delivered by spinners. Perera's ten-for included a straight one that Khawaja courteously allowed to flatten his off stump, and halfway through the third day Sri Lanka were celebrating a series win.

Sri Lanka

F. D. M. Karunaratne c Burns b Starc	0	– (2) c Marsh b Starc	7
J. K. Silva c Nevill b Starc	5	– (1) c Smith b Hazlewood	2
M. D. K. J. Perera c Smith b Lyon	49	– b Lyon	35
B. K. G. Mendis c Nevill b Starc	86	– c Nevill b Starc	7
*A. D. Mathews c Nevill b Marsh	54	– b Lyon	47
†L. D. Chandimal c Khawaja b Hazlewood	5	– c Nevill b Starc	13
D. M. de Silva lbw b Holland	37	– c Nevill b Starc	34
M. D. K. Perera lbw b Lyon	16	– b Starc	64
H. M. R. K. B. Herath b Starc	14	– b Holland	26
P. A. D. L. R. Sandakan b Starc	1	– not out	0
M. V. T. Fernando not out	0	– c Voges b Starc	0
B 4, lb 10	14	Lb 1, w 1	2
(73.1 overs)	281	(59.3 overs)	237

1/0 (1) 2/9 (2) 3/117 (3) 4/184 (4) 5/199 (6)   1/5 (1) 2/9 (2) 3/31 (4) 4/79 (5) 5/98 (6) 6/121 (5)
6/224 (5) 7/259 (8) 8/265 (7) 9/274 (10) 10/281 (9)   7/172 (7) 8/233 (9) 9/237 (8) 10/237 (11)

Starc 16.1–7–44–5; Hazlewood 15–3–51–1; Lyon 18–1–78–2; Marsh 9–0–30–1; Holland 15–0–64–1. *Second innings*—Starc 12.3–1–50–6; Hazlewood 9–3–13–1; Lyon 19–2–80–2; Holland 10–1–69–1; Voges 1–0–4–0; Marsh 4–1–7–0; Smith 4–0–13–0.

Australia

J. A. Burns c M. D. K. J. Perera b Fernando	0	– (2) c de Silva b Herath	2
D. A. Warner c Mathews b M. D. K. Perera	42	– (1) lbw b M. D. K. Perera	41
U. T. Khawaja b M. D. K. Perera	11	– (4) b M. D. K. Perera	0
*S. P. D. Smith b Herath	5	– (5) c Silva b M. D. K. Perera	30
A. C. Voges c Karunaratne b Herath	8	– (6) b M. D. K. Perera	28
M. R. Marsh c Karunaratne b Sandakan	27	– (7) lbw b Sandakan	18
†P. M. Nevill lbw b Herath	0	– (8) run out (Mendis)	24
M. A. Starc lbw b Herath	0	– (3) b Herath	26
N. M. Lyon c Mendis b M. D. K. Perera	4	– (3) c Silva b M. D. K. Perera	0
J. R. Hazlewood c Mathews b M. D. K. Perera	3	– c and b M. D. K. Perera	7
J. M. Holland not out	0	– not out	0
B 5, lb 1	6	Lb 7	7
(33.2 overs)	106	(50.1 overs)	183

1/0 (1) 2/54 (2) 3/59 (3) 4/59 (4) 5/80 (5)   1/3 (2) 2/10 (3) 3/10 (4) 4/61 (1) 5/80 (5) 6/119 (7)
6/80 (7) 7/80 (8) 8/85 (9) 9/89 (10) 10/106 (6)   7/123 (6) 8/164 (9) 9/181 (10) 10/183 (8)

Fernando 2–0–16–1; Herath 11–2–35–4; M. D. K. Perera 15–4–29–4; Mathews 3–1–13–0; de Silva 2–1–7–0; Sandakan 0.2–0–0–1. *Second innings*—Herath 19.1–1–74–2; M. D. K. Perera 23–5–70–6; Sandakan 6–1–30–1; de Silva 2–0–2–0.

Umpires: C. B. Gaffaney *(New Zealand)* (8) and R. A. Kettleborough *(England)* (37).
Third umpire: S. Ravi *(India)*.   Referee: B. C. Broad *(England)* (79).

Close of play: first day, Australia 54-2 (Khawaja 11); second day, Australia 25-3 (Warner 22, Smith 1).

Test No. 2216/29 (SL251, A791)

SRI LANKA v AUSTRALIA 2016 (3rd Test)

At Sinhalese Sports Club, Colombo, on 13, 14, 15, 16, 17 August, 2016.
Toss: Sri Lanka.   Result: SRI LANKA WON BY 163 RUNS.
Debuts: none.
Man of the Match: H. M. R. K. B. Herath.   Man of the Series: H. M. R. K. B. Herath.

Australia were more competitive, but still surrendered dramatically on the final day. Sri Lanka won 3–0, with more laurels for Herath, who finished with 28 wickets: only Richard Hadlee (33 in 1985–86) and Harbhajan Singh (32 in 2000–01) had taken more in a three-Test series against Australia. Mathews batted first on a pitch predicted to crumble. There was a rickety start as Starc and Lyon reduced Sri Lanka to 26 for five, but the sixth-wicket pair put on 211 – and when de Silva's beautifully crafted maiden Test hundred ended, Chandimal coaxed another 118 out of the last four. Marsh and Smith both hit centuries in a stand of 246, easily Australia's best of the series. But after Marsh dragged Lakmal on, Herath got to work. Smith was the first of his six victims in a decline of nine for 112, stumped by Kusal Perera, keeping in place of the tired Chandimal. Despite their start, Australia led by only 24. Kaushal Silva emphatically ended a run of five single-figure scores with a handsome hundred, and Mathews had the luxury of a final-morning declaration, 323 ahead. Warner made a sprightly start, but a collapse seemed inevitable – and 77 for none duly became 160 all out. The crowd were chanting Herath's name when he sealed victory with his 13th wicket – Sri Lanka's best haul against Australia, beating Muttiah Muralitharan's 11 for 212 at Galle in 2003–04. Herath now had more fourth-innings five-fors (eight) than anyone; Murali and Shane Warne both had seven.

Sri Lanka

J. K. Silva c Smith b Starc	0	– (3) c Smith b Holland	115
F. D. M. Karunaratne b Starc	7	– st Nevill b Lyon	22
M. D. K. J. Perera c Smith b Lyon	16	– (4) c Nevill b Holland	24
B. K. G. Mendis c Smith b Starc	1	– (5) lbw b Starc	18
*A. D. Mathews c Starc b Lyon	1	– (6) c Smith b Lyon	26
†L. D. Chandimal c Nevill b Starc	132	– (7) lbw b Lyon	43
D. M. de Silva c S. E. Marsh b Lyon	129	– (8) not out	65
M. D. K. Perera c Lyon b Holland	16	– (1) lbw b Starc	8
H. M. R. K. B. Herath retired hurt	33	– c Smith b Lyon	5
R. A. S. Lakmal c M. R. Marsh b Starc	5	– not out	4
P. A. D. L. R. Sandakan not out	4		
B 4, lb 7	11	B 8, lb 3, w 1, nb 5	17
(141.1 overs)	355	(8 wkts dec, 99.3 overs)	347

1/2 (1) 2/21 (3) 3/23 (2) 4/24 (5) 5/26 (4)   1/8 (1) 2/44 (2) 3/69 (4) 4/98 (5)
6/237 (7) 7/267 (8) 8/348 (6) 9/355 (10)   5/156 (6) 6/246 (7) 7/276 (3) 8/297 (9)

In the first innings Herath retired hurt at 340-7.

Starc 25.1–11–63–5; Hazlewood 18–4–52–0; Lyon 50–11–110–3; Holland 37–8–69–1; M. R. Marsh 10–1–45–0; Smith 1–0–5–0. *Second innings*—Starc 19.3–4–72–2; Lyon 37–7–123–4; Holland 20–4–72–2; Hazlewood 14–2–33–0; Smith 2–0–13–0; M. R. Marsh 3–1–3–0; Henriques 2–0–9–0; Voges 2–0–11–0.

Australia

D. A. Warner c †M. D. K. J. Perera b de Silva	11	– (2) b M. D. K. Perera	68
S. E. Marsh b Lakmal	130	– (1) c Mendis b M. D. K. Perera	23
*S. P. D. Smith st †M. D. K. J. Perera b Herath	119	– b Herath	8
A. C. Voges lbw b Herath	22	– lbw b Herath	1
M. C. Henriques st †M. D. K. J. Perera b Herath	4	– run out (Mathews)	4
M. R. Marsh c Mendis b Herath	53	– c †M. D. K. J. Perera b Herath	9
†P. M. Nevill lbw b M. D. K. Perera	14	– c Mathews b Herath	2
M. A. Starc not out	9	– c †M. D. K. J. Perera b Herath	23
N. M. Lyon c Mendis b M. D. K. Perera	3	– lbw b Herath	12
J. R. Hazlewood b Herath	0	– st †M. D. K. J. Perera b Herath	0
J. M. Holland c Mathews b Herath	1	– not out	0
B 4, lb 9	13	B 4, lb 6	10
(125.1 overs)	379	(44.1 overs)	160

1/21 (1) 2/267 (2) 3/275 (3) 4/283 (5) 5/316 (4) 6/353 (7)   1/77 (1) 2/100 (3) 3/102 (4) 4/114 (2) 5/115 (5)
7/367 (6) 8/376 (9) 9/377 (10) 10/379 (11)   6/123 (6) 7/140 (7) 8/157 (8) 9/159 (10) 10/160 (9)

M. D. K. Perera 44–4–129–2; de Silva 7–0–27–1; Herath 38.1–11–81–6; Sandakan 19–0–70–0; Lakmal 13–0–54–1; Mathews 4–1–5–0. *Second innings*—Herath 18.1–3–64–7; M. D. K. Perera 22–3–71–2; de Silva 4–0–15–0.

Umpires: C. B. Gaffaney *(New Zealand)* (9) and S. Ravi *(India)* (14).
Third umpire: R. A. Kettleborough *(England)*.   Referee: B. C. Broad *(England)* (80).

Close of play: first day, Sri Lanka 214–5 (Chandimal 64, de Silva 116); second day, Australia 141–1 (S. E. Marsh 64, Smith 61); third day, Sri Lanka 22–1 (Karunaratne 8, Silva 6); fourth day, Sri Lanka 312–8 (de Silva 44, Lakmal 0).

Test No. 2217/16 (Z98, NZ409)

ZIMBABWE v NEW ZEALAND 2016 (1st Test)

At Queens Club, Bulawayo, on 28, 29, 30, 31 July, 2016.
Toss: Zimbabwe.   Result: NEW ZEALAND WON BY AN INNINGS AND 117 RUNS.
Debuts: Zimbabwe – C. J. Chibhabha, M. T. Chinouya, P. S. Masvaure.
Man of the Match: L. R. P. L. Taylor.

Two days before the match, an already heavy roller was loaded with concrete railway sleepers to deaden the pitch. But Wagner rose above those challenges as surely as his deliveries steepled towards ribs and heads, and took a career-best six for 41. An hour before the close, Zimbabwe were all out for 164. It could have been worse: four wickets fell at 72, before the debutant Prince Masvaure and No. 10 Donald Tiripano put on 85. By stumps next evening, New Zealand were 151 ahead with six wickets in hand; Tom Latham's fourth Test century – in the city where his father, Rod, made his only one almost 24 years previously – was in the bank and Taylor's 14th in the making. Watling's sixth followed on the third day, before a declaration, 412 ahead, soon after tea. Williams (flu) and wicketkeeper Chakabva (tonsillitis) were not at the ground on the second day; Chari took the gloves and held three catches. But, as Zimbabwe shambled to 17 for four, both were urgently summoned. Ervine and Sikandar Raza ensured Williams didn't have to go in after all, and he returned home to look after his wife, who had caught his bug. She fainted, and he got to sleep only at 5am; not long afterwards he was batting, and stroked 20 fours in a maiden Test century – Zimbabwe's fastest, at 106 balls, one quicker than Neil Johnson's against Pakistan at Peshawar in 1998-99. He was ninth out as New Zealand wrapped the game up by tea.

Zimbabwe

B. B. Chari c Guptill b Southee	4	– (3) b Boult	5
C. J. Chibhabha c Latham b Wagner	15	– (1) c Taylor b Boult	7
H. Masakadza c and b Santner	15	– (2) c Taylor b Southee	4
C. R. Ervine st Watling b Santner	13	– c Watling b Boult	50
S. C. Williams c Sodhi b Wagner	1	– (8) c Williamson b Santner	119
Sikandar Raza c Latham b Wagner	22	– c †Latham b Wagner	37
P. S. Masvaure lbw b Southee	42	– (5) lbw b Boult	0
†R. W. Chakabva c Watling b Wagner	0	– (9) b Southee	11
*A. G. Cremer c Nicholls b Wagner	0	– (7) lbw b Sodhi	33
D. T. Tiripano not out	49	– c Watling b Wagner	14
M. T. Chinouya b Wagner	1	– not out	0
Lb 2	2	B 6, lb 9	15
(77.5 overs)	164	(79 overs)	295

1/4 (1) 2/35 (2) 3/35 (3) 4/36 (5) 5/72 (4)   1/7 (2) 2/12 (3) 3/17 (1) 4/17 (5) 5/86 (6) 6/124 (4)
6/72 (6) 7/72 (8) 8/72 (9) 9/157 (7) 10/164 (11)   7/242 (7) 8/277 (9) 9/285 (8) 10/295 (10)

Southee 17–8–28–2; Boult 11–5–23–0; Santner 14–5–16–2; Wagner 20.5–8–41–6; Sodhi 15–3–54–0. *Second innings*—Southee 15–3–68–2; Boult 17–3–52–4; Wagner 17–1–62–2; Santner 17–6–32–1; Sodhi 12–1–66–1; Williamson 1–1–0–0.

New Zealand

M. J. Guptill c Ervine b Chibhabha	40
T. W. M. Latham c †Chari b Masakadza	105
*K. S. Williamson c Masakadza b Cremer	91
L. R. P. L. Taylor not out	173
H. M. Nicholls c †Chari b Tiripano	18
I. S. Sodhi c †Chari b Chinouya	11
†B-J. Watling c sub (T. Muzarabani) b Sikandar Raza	107
B 15, w 4, nb 12	31
(6 wkts dec, 166.5 overs)	576

1/79 (1) 2/235 (2) 3/272 (3) 4/299 (5)
5/323 (6) 6/576 (7)

M. J. Santner, T. G. Southee, N. Wagner and T. A. Boult did not bat.

Chinouya 26–6–79–1; Tiripano 28–4–82–1; Masvaure 10–0–38–0; Cremer 53–4–187–1; Sikandar Raza 25.5–4–106–1; Chibhabha 15–1–44–1; Masakadza 9–1–25–1.

Umpires: M. A. Gough *(England)* (1) and P. R. Reiffel *(Australia)* (23).
Third umpire: L. Rusere *(Zimbabwe)*.   Referee: D. C. Boon *(Australia)* (31).

Close of play: first day, New Zealand 32–0 (Guptill 14, Latham 16); second day, New Zealand 315–4 (Taylor 38, Sodhi 5); third day, Zimbabwe 121–5 (Ervine 49, Cremer 14).

ZIMBABWE v NEW ZEALAND 2016 (2nd Test)

Test No. 2218/17 (Z99, NZ410)

At Queens Club, Bulawayo, on 6, 7, 8, 9, 10 August, 2016.
Toss: New Zealand.   Result: NEW ZEALAND WON BY 254 RUNS.
Debuts: Zimbabwe – P. J. Moor.
Man of the Match: K. S. Williamson.   Man of the Series: N. Wagner.

Early on the second morning – the day before his 26th birthday – Williamson became easily the youngest to make centuries against every Test nation; he was the first New Zealander, and the 13th overall. His knock was sandwiched by hundreds from Latham and Taylor. The partnerships mounted as Zimbabwe toiled: this was the first time three New Zealand pairs had put on 150 or more in the same Test innings. The declaration came like an angel of mercy for the perspiring bowlers. Mawoyo, who had missed the first match with a bruised right thumb, and Chibhabha guided Zimbabwe to the second-day close without loss, registering their first half-century opening partnership in nearly five years. But next morning Mawoyo played on, and Zimbabwe were soon back in strife at 147 for five. Ervine made a dogged maiden century, with steadfast support from debutant keeper Peter Moor in a stand of 148. But, with leg-spinner Sodhi taking four wickets, New Zealand led by 220: after ten hours in the field, Williamson waived the follow-on, and helped swell the advantage to 386. Mawoyo consumed 92 balls for his 35 but, after he and Sikandar Raza fell in successive overs just before the fourth-day close, Zimbabwe's fate was all but sealed. New Zealand still had to work hard: unimpressed with his seamers, Williamson turned to Guptill. Despite a modest record – only five wickets in 41 Tests – he now ripped his off-breaks square to account for Ervine, Williams and Cremer, as a 2–0 triumph was secured.

New Zealand

M. J. Guptill lbw b Tiripano	87	– (2) c Nyumbu b Chinouya	11
T. W. M. Latham c and b Williams	136	– (1) c Moor b Tiripano	13
*K. S. Williamson c Ervine b Chinouya	113	– not out	68
L. R. P. L. Taylor not out	124	– not out	67
H. M. Nicholls lbw b Cremer	15		
†B-J. Watling not out	83		
B 12, lb 3, w 1, nb 8	24	Lb 4, w 3	7
(4 wkts dec, 150 overs)	582	(2 wkts dec, 36 overs)	166

1/169 (1) 2/329 (2) 3/369 (3) 4/389 (5)   1/24 (1) 2/26 (2)

M. J. Santner, I. S. Sodhi, T. G. Southee, N. Wagner and T. A. Boult did not bat.

Tiripano 25–4–102–1; Chinouya 22–6–64–1; Chibhabha 12–2–45–0; Cremer 36–2–147–1; Nyumbu 34–3–107–0; Williams 13–0–62–1; Sikandar Raza 4–0–17–0; Masvaure 4–0–23–0. *Second innings*—Chinouya 9–2–45–1; Tiripano 6–1–14–1; Chibhabha 3–0–22–0; Cremer 11–0–59–0; Nyumbu 7–0–22–0.

Zimbabwe

T. M. K. Mawoyo b Southee	26	– lbw b Boult	35
C. J. Chibhabha c Williamson b Santner	60	– c Guptill b Wagner	21
Sikandar Raza c Williamson b Wagner	3	– lbw b Southee	0
C. R. Ervine c Wagner b Sodhi	146	– (5) c Watling b Guptill	27
P. S. Masvaure b Santner	2	– (6) c Taylor b Sodhi	11
S. C. Williams lbw b Sodhi	16	– (7) c Williamson b Guptill	11
†P. J. Moor c Guptill b Sodhi	71	– (8) lbw b Sodhi	1
*A. G. Cremer lbw b Boult	8	– (9) lbw b Guptill	1
D. T. Tiripano lbw b Wagner	3	– (4) lbw b Santner	22
J. C. Nyumbu c Santner b Sodhi	8	– not out	0
M. T. Chinouya not out	0	– c Williamson b Sodhi	0
B 12, lb 6, nb 1	19	B 1, lb 2	3
(143.4 overs)	362	(68.4 overs)	132

1/65 (1) 2/83 (3) 3/107 (2) 4/115 (5) 5/147 (6)   1/45 (2) 2/58 (1) 3/58 (3) 4/97 (4) 5/112 (5)
6/295 (7) 7/319 (8) 8/327 (9) 9/352 (10) 10/362 (4)   6/130 (7) 7/131 (8) 8/132 (9) 9/132 (6) 10/132 (11)

Southee 28–14–73–1; Boult 27–13–45–1; Santner 35–8–105–2; Wagner 31–8–61–2; Sodhi 21.4–9–60–4; Guptill 1–1–0–0. *Second innings*—Southee 14–7–35–1; Boult 12–4–26–1; Wagner 12–5–23–1; Santner 12–4–15–1; Sodhi 11.4–5–19–3; Guptill 7–4–11–3.

Umpires: M. A. Gough *(England)* (2) and P. R. Reiffel *(Australia)* (24).
Third umpire: T. J. Matibiri *(Zimbabwe)*.   Referee: D. C. Boon *(Australia)* (32).

Close of play: first day, New Zealand 329–2 (Williamson 95); second day, Zimbabwe 55–0 (Mawoyo 20, Chibhabha 31); third day, Zimbabwe 305–6 (Ervine 115, Cremer 2); fourth day, Zimbabwe 58–3 (Tiripano 0).

SOUTH AFRICA v NEW ZEALAND 2016 (1st Test)

At Kingsmead, Durban, on 19, 20, 21 *(no play)*, 22 *(no play)*, 23 *(no play)* August, 2016.
Toss: South Africa. Result: DRAWN.
Debuts: none.
Man of the Match: no award.

The meteorologists suggested there was nothing wrong with staging a Test in the Durban winter. But the decision backfired when a thunderstorm soaked Kingsmead on the second afternoon, and no further play was possible. The mistake lay not in the scheduling, but in the covering. The entire outfield is rarely protected in South Africa, but it should have been here. This was easily the earliest a Test had been played in the South African season: the 1902–03 series against Australia – on their way home from England – had started in Johannesburg on October 11. The match was developing nicely when the storm hit: South Africa's 263, in which Amla top-scored with 53, was better than it looked on a lively pitch. A wicket was rarely far away: the longest partnership lasted 22.4 overs, between du Plessis (captaining in a Test for the first time) and Bavuma. When New Zealand's innings finally started, it was a fast bowler's paradise: low thundery clouds, floodlights straining to pierce the gloom, and the Durban tide at its highest. The ball swung exotically. Steyn soon removed both openers, but Williamson and Taylor toughed it out before bad light intervened. The subsequent storm drenched an outfield which had been deeply scarified less than two months earlier. On the third morning the square and its immediate surrounds, including the run-ups, were bone-dry under the covers – but large areas of the unprotected outfield, where the grass had not regrown, were little more than mud. The ICC later censured the ground authorities.

South Africa

S. C. Cook c Watling b Boult	20
D. Elgar c Guptill b Bracewell	19
H. M. Amla c Watling b Boult	53
J-P. Duminy c Boult b Wagner	14
*F. du Plessis c Williamson b Wagner	23
T. Bavuma lbw b Santner	46
†Q. de Kock c Bracewell b Santner	33
V. D. Philander c Southee b Wagner	8
K. Rabada not out	32
D. W. Steyn b Southee	2
D. L. Piedt c Watling b Boult	9
Lb 4	4
(87.4 overs)	263

1/33 (1) 2/41 (2) 3/102 (4) 4/106 (3) 5/160 (5) 6/208 (7) 7/208 (6) 8/228 (8) 9/236 (10) 10/263 (11)

Southee 23–3–80–1; Boult 21.4–5–52–3; Bracewell 16–6–53–1; Wagner 15–4–47–3; Santner 11–2–22–2; Guptill 1–0–5–0.

New Zealand

M. J. Guptill lbw b Steyn	7
T. W. M. Latham c Amla b Steyn	4
*K. S. Williamson not out	2
L. R. P. L. Taylor not out	2
(2 wkts, 12 overs)	15

1/7 (2) 2/12 (1)

H. M. Nicholls, †B-J. Watling, M. J. Santner, D. A. J. Bracewell, T. G. Southee, N. Wagner and T. A. Boult did not bat.

Steyn 6–4–3–2; Philander 6–1–12–0.

Umpires: I. J. Gould *(England)* (52) and R. K. Illingworth *(England)* (22).
Third umpire: P. R. Reiffel *(Australia)*. Referee: A. J. Pycroft *(Zimbabwe)* (47).

Close of play: first day, South Africa 236–8 (Rabada 14, Steyn 2); second day, New Zealand 15–2 (Williamson 2, Taylor 2); third day, no play; fourth day, no play.

SOUTH AFRICA v NEW ZEALAND 2016 (2nd Test)

At Centurion Park, Pretoria, on 27, 28, 29, 30 August, 2016.
Toss: New Zealand.   Result: SOUTH AFRICA WON BY 204 RUNS.
Debuts: none.
Man of the Match: Q. de Kock.

The Centurion pitch was juicier than usual, and Williamson unsurprisingly bowled first: Boult seamed some deliveries so much they looked like illusions, but the seamers also served up too many bad balls. The opening stand was worth 100 by lunch, and – for only the second time – South Africa's top five all reached fifty, although Wagner, born nearby in Pretoria, finished with five for 86. Next day, du Plessis grafted to a six-hour century as his side amassed 481. New Zealand were soon in trouble at 26 for three, with Taylor's run-out ending a sequence of 367 runs without dismissal. Williamson showed exemplary technique for almost five hours, and Nicholls also battled well, but others were less willing to get into line: everyone was hit as New Zealand were all out 267 behind. Unwilling to bat last, du Plessis rejected the follow-on, and de Kock – the first wicketkeeper to open for South Africa in a Test since Denis Lindsay in 1965, after Dean Elgar injured his ankle the day before the match – hit his first four balls, from Boult, for boundaries. But it was soon 47 for four; Bavuma survived for 173 minutes, and New Zealand were eventually set 400, or 140-odd overs to survive. Their slim chances of either disappeared in Steyn's first over: it was only the fifth time both openers had bagged golden ducks in a Test innings. Quickly it was seven for four, and despite 76 from Nicholls, and Watling's obdurate 32, the end came with more than a day to spare.

South Africa

S. C. Cook c Williamson b Bracewell	56	– lbw b Boult	4
†Q. de Kock c Boult b Wagner	82	– c Williamson b Bracewell	50
H. M. Amla c Watling b Wagner	58	– c Guptill b Southee	1
J-P. Duminy c Watling b Southee	88	– lbw b Southee	0
*F. du Plessis not out	112	– c Taylor b Boult	6
T. Bavuma c Bracewell b Wagner	8	– not out	40
S. van Zyl c Taylor b Wagner	35	– c Watling b Wagner	5
V. D. Philander b Wagner	8	– b Southee	14
K. Rabada c Nicholls b Santner	7		
D. W. Steyn not out	13		
D. L. Piedt (did not bat)		– (9) not out	0
B 10, lb 4	14	B 4, lb 1, w 6, nb 1	12
(8 wkts dec, 154 overs)	481	(7 wkts dec, 47 overs)	132

1/133 (2) 2/151 (1) 3/246 (3) 4/317 (4)
5/342 (6) 6/426 (7) 7/442 (8) 8/463 (9)

1/31 (1) 2/32 (3) 3/32 (4)
4/47 (5) 5/82 (2) 6/98 (7) 7/129 (8)

Southee 35–5–114–1; Boult 35.4–7–107–0; Bracewell 30.2–9–98–1; Santner 14–1–62–1; Wagner 39–8–86–5. *Second innings*—Southee 16–6–46–3; Boult 14–3–44–2; Bracewell 7–2–19–1; Wagner 10–1–18–1.

New Zealand

M. J. Guptill c van Zyl b Philander	8	– (2) c Amla b Steyn	0
T. W. M. Latham c de Kock b Steyn	4	– (1) b Steyn	0
*K. S. Williamson c de Kock b Rabada	77	– c de Kock b Philander	5
L. R. P. L. Taylor run out (Bavuma)	1	– lbw b Steyn	0
H. M. Nicholls lbw b Rabada	36	– c Rabada b Steyn	76
†B-J. Watling c de Kock b Steyn	8	– lbw b Piedt	32
M. J. Santner b Philander	0	– b Steyn	16
D. A. J. Bracewell lbw b Rabada	18	– lbw b Philander	30
T. G. Southee c de Kock b Piedt	8	– b Rabada	14
N. Wagner c de Kock b Steyn	31	– lbw b Rabada	3
T. A. Boult not out	0	– not out	0
B 5, lb 2, w 15, nb 1	23	B 10, lb 7, w 2	19
(58.3 overs)	214	(58.2 overs)	195

1/13 (1) 2/13 (2) 3/26 (4) 4/86 (5) 5/106 (6)
6/111 (7) 7/144 (8) 8/169 (9) 9/214 (10) 10/214 (3)

1/0 (1) 2/3 (2) 3/5 (4) 4/7 (3) 5/75 (6) 6/118 (7)
7/164 (8) 8/187 (9) 9/195 (10) 10/195 (5)

Steyn 20–3–66–3; Philander 15–1–43–2; Rabada 16.3–4–62–3; Piedt 7–0–36–1. *Second innings*—Steyn 16.2–4–33–5; Philander 14–4–34–2; Rabada 13–2–54–2; van Zyl 3–1–5–0; Piedt 12–3–52–1.

Umpires: I. J. Gould *(England)* (53) and P. R. Reiffel *(Australia)* (25).
Third umpire: R. K. Illingworth *(England)*.   Referee: A. J. Pycroft *(Zimbabwe)* (48).

Close of play: first day, South Africa 283–3 (Duminy 67, du Plessis 13); second day, New Zealand 38–3 (Williamson 15, Nicholls 4); third day, South Africa 105–6 (Bavuma 25, Philander 3).

INDIA v NEW ZEALAND 2016–17 (1st Test)

At Green Park, Kanpur, on 22, 23, 24, 25, 26 September, 2016.
Toss: India.   Result: INDIA WON BY 197 RUNS.
Debuts: none.
Man of the Match: R. A. Jadeja.

India's 500th Test match might perhaps have been played somewhere more glamorous than Green Park, a historic but dilapidated venue. For two days, New Zealand threatened to spoil the occasion, but a third-day collapse – five for seven in 29 balls – handed India control. They had suffered their own malfunction on the opening day. Pujara added 112 with Vijay, before chipping loosely back to Santner. Three overs later, Kohli top-edged a pull. And, when the new ball flummoxed the lower order, 154 for one had become 277 for nine. Jadeja took the total past 300, but when rain washed out the second day's final session, New Zealand were 152 for one. Two wonderful deliveries next morning transformed the mood. Ashwin nabbed Latham with his arm-ball, then bowled Williamson with one that turned like a Muttiah Muralitharan special. Ronchi and Santner held India up, but the tail had no answer to Jadeja's zip; a triple-wicket maiden helped him to a five-for. Trailing by 56, New Zealand needed early inroads – but Rahul stretched the advantage, before Vijay and Pujara's second century partnership of the match. Finally Sharma and Jadeja belted 100 in just 18.3 overs, taking the target over 400. Ashwin soon grabbed another three scalps, including his 200th (Williamson), in his 37th Test, one slower than Australia's Clarrie Grimmett. Taylor dozily forgot to ground his bat, but Ronchi added 102 with Santner before falling to an ugly heave for 80. Santner lasted 179 balls, but the relentless Ashwin eventually wrapped things up.

India

K. L. Rahul c Watling b Santner	32	– c Taylor b Sodhi	38
M. Vijay c Watling b Sodhi	65	– lbw b Santner	76
C. A. Pujara c and b Santner	62	– c Taylor b Sodhi	78
*V. Kohli c Sodhi b Wagner	9	– c Sodhi b Craig	18
A. M. Rahane c Latham b Craig	18	– c Taylor b Santner	40
R. G. Sharma c Sodhi b Santner	35	– not out	68
R. Ashwin c Taylor b Boult	40		
†W. P. Saha b Boult	0		
R. A. Jadeja not out	42	– (7) not out	50
Mohammed Shami b Boult	0		
U. T. Yadav c Watling b Wagner	9		
B 5, lb 1	6	B 1, lb 8	9
(97 overs)	318	(5 wkts dec, 107.2 overs)	377

1/42 (1) 2/154 (3) 3/167 (4) 4/185 (2) 5/209 (5)   1/52 (1) 2/185 (2) 3/214 (4)
6/261 (6) 7/262 (8) 8/273 (7) 9/277 (10) 10/318 (11)   4/228 (3) 5/277 (5)

Boult 20–3–67–3; Wagner 15–4–42–2; Santner 23–2–94–3; Craig 24–6–59–1; Sodhi 15–3–50–1. *Second innings*—Boult 9–0–34–0; Santner 32.2–11–79–2; Craig 23–3–80–1; Wagner 16–5–52–0; Sodhi 20–2–99–2; Guptill 4–0–17–0; Williamson 3–0–7–0.

New Zealand

M. J. Guptill lbw b Yadav	21	– (2) c Vijay b Ashwin	0
T. W. M. Latham lbw b Ashwin	58	– (1) lbw b Ashwin	2
*K. S. Williamson b Ashwin	75	– lbw b Ashwin	25
L. R. P. L. Taylor lbw b Jadeja	0	– run out (Yadav)	17
L. Ronchi lbw b Jadeja	38	– c Ashwin b Jadeja	80
M. J. Santner c Saha b Ashwin	32	– c Sharma b Ashwin	71
†B-J. Watling c and b Ashwin	21	– lbw b Mohammed Shami	18
M. D. Craig lbw b Jadeja	2	– b Mohammed Shami	1
I. S. Sodhi lbw b Jadeja	0	– b Ashwin	17
T. A. Boult c Sharma b Jadeja	0	– not out	2
N. Wagner not out	0	– lbw b Ashwin	0
B 8, lb 5, nb 2	15	Lb 2, nb 1	3
(95.5 overs)	262	(87.3 overs)	236

1/35 (1) 2/159 (2) 3/160 (4) 4/170 (3) 5/219 (5) 6/255 (6)   1/2 (2) 2/3 (1) 3/43 (3) 4/56 (4) 5/158 (5) 6/194 (7)
7/258 (8) 8/258 (9) 9/258 (10) 10/262 (7)   7/196 (8) 8/223 (6) 9/236 (9) 10/236 (11)

Mohammed Shami 11–1–35–0; Yadav 15–5–33–1; Jadeja 34–7–73–5; Ashwin 30.5–7–93–4; Vijay 4–0–10–0; Sharma 1–0–5–0. *Second innings*—Mohammed Shami 8–2–18–2; Ashwin 35.3–5–132–6; Jadeja 34–17–58–1; Yadav 8–1–23–0; Vijay 2–0–3–0.

Umpires: R. A. Kettleborough *(England)* (38) and R. J. Tucker *(Australia)* (48).
Third umpire: A. K. Chaudhary *(India)*.   Referee: D. C. Boon *(Australia)* (33).

Close of play: first day, India 291–9 (Jadeja 16, Yadav 8); second day, New Zealand 152–1 (Latham 56, Williamson 65); third day, India 159–1 (Vijay 64, Pujara 50); fourth day, New Zealand 93–4 (Ronchi 38, Santner 8).

Test No. 2222/56 (1501, NZ414)

INDIA v NEW ZEALAND 2016–17 (2nd Test)

At Eden Gardens, Kolkata, on 30 September, 1, 2, 3 October, 2016.
Toss: India.   Result: INDIA WON BY 178 RUNS.
Debuts: none.
Man of the Match: W. P. Saha.

Williamson was down with fever, so Taylor led New Zealand, but the story remained the same. Henry struck early on a well-grassed pitch, before Kohli sliced to gully to leave India 46 for three. Pujara shepherded a recovery, adding 141 with Rahane. In the evening, New Zealand clawed their way back: Pujara miscued to short cover for 87, then off-spinner Jeetan Patel struck twice in his first Test for four years. But the last three wickets added 85, before the seamers got to work. From 23 for three, Ronchi led a brief counterattack, before falling to a questionable lbw. It was 128 for seven by the second-day close and, although Patel managed a run-a-ball 47, the deficit was still 112. It was the first time since 2008 that Indian seamers had taken eight wickets in a home Test innings. New Zealand's own pacemen gave them a sniff: Boult not only dismissed Dhawan, but put him out of the series with a broken hand. From 106 for six, Sharma's century partnership with Saha stretched the lead above 300: no team had chased more than 117 to win a Test at Eden Gardens. New Zealand reached 100 for the loss of Guptill, but from there the slide was swift, and when Latham nicked one after tea – his 74 was New Zealand's only half-century of the match – a four-day finish loomed. As their most famous ground fell into shadow, India took the last seven wickets for 56, securing a fourth straight series win.

India

S. Dhawan b Henry	1 – lbw b Boult	17
M. Vijay c Watling b Henry	9 – c Guptill b Henry	7
C. A. Pujara c Guptill b Wagner	87 – lbw b Henry	4
*V. Kohli c Latham b Boult	9 – lbw b Boult	45
A. M. Rahane lbw b Patel	77 – c Boult b Henry	1
R. G. Sharma c Latham b Patel	2 – c †Ronchi b Santner	82
R. Ashwin lbw b Henry	26 – lbw b Santner	5
†W. P. Saha not out	54 – not out	58
R. A. Jadeja c Henry b Wagner	14 – c sub (J. D. S. Neesham) b Santner	6
Bhuvneshwar Kumar lbw b Santner	5 – c Nicholls b Wagner	23
Mohammed Shami c Henry b Boult	14 – c Latham b Boult	1
B 8, lb 10	18 B 10, lb 1, w 3	14
(104.5 overs)	316 (76.5 overs)	263

1/1 (1) 2/28 (2) 3/46 (4) 4/187 (3) 5/193 (6) 6/200 (5)   1/12 (2) 2/24 (3) 3/34 (1) 4/43 (5) 5/91 (4)
7/231 (7) 8/272 (9) 9/281 (10) 10/316 (11)   6/106 (7) 7/209 (6) 8/215 (9) 9/251 (10) 10/263 (11)

Boult 20.5–9–46–2; Henry 20–6–46–3; Wagner 20–5–57–2; Santner 23–5–83–1; Patel 21–3–66–2. *Second innings*—Boult 17.5–6–38–3; Henry 20–2–59–3; Wagner 15–3–45–1; Patel 8–0–50–0; Santner 16–2–60–3.

New Zealand

M. J. Guptill b Bhuvneshwar Kumar	13 – (2) lbw b Ashwin	24
T. W. M. Latham lbw b Mohammed Shami	1 – (1) c Saha b Ashwin	74
H. M. Nicholls b Bhuvneshwar Kumar	1 – c Rahane b Jadeja	24
*L. R. P. L. Taylor c Vijay b Bhuvneshwar Kumar	36 – lbw b Ashwin	4
L. Ronchi lbw b Jadeja	35 – b Jadeja	32
M. J. Santner lbw b Bhuvneshwar Kumar	11 – lbw b Mohammed Shami	9
†B-J. Watling lbw b Mohammed Shami	25 – b Mohammed Shami	1
M. J. Henry b Bhuvneshwar Kumar	0 – c Kohli b Jadeja	18
J. S. Patel c Mohammed Shami b Ashwin	47 – b Bhuvneshwar Kumar	2
N. Wagner lbw b Mohammed Shami	10 – not out	5
T. A. Boult not out	6 – c Vijay b Mohammed Shami	4
B 9, lb 4, w 5, nb 1	19	
(53 overs)	204 (81.1 overs)	197

1/10 (2) 2/18 (1) 3/23 (3) 4/85 (5) 5/104 (5)   1/55 (2) 2/104 (3) 3/115 (4) 4/141 (5) 5/154 (6)
6/122 (6) 7/122 (8) 8/182 (9) 9/187 (7) 10/204 (10)   6/156 (7) 7/175 (5) 8/178 (9) 9/190 (8) 10/197 (11)

Bhuvneshwar Kumar 15–2–48–5; Mohammed Shami 18–1–70–3; Jadeja 12–4–40–1; Ashwin 8–3–33–1. *Second innings*—Bhuvneshwar Kumar 12–4–28–1; Mohammed Shami 18.1–5–46–3; Ashwin 31–6–82–3; Jadeja 20–3–41–3.

Umpires: R. A. Kettleborough *(England)* (39) and R. J. Tucker *(Australia)* (49).
Third umpire: C. K. Nandan *(India).*   Referee: D. C. Boon *(Australia)* (34).

Close of play: first day, India 239–7 (Saha 14, Jadeja 0); second day, New Zealand 128–7 (Watling 12, Patel 5); third day, India 227–8 (Saha 39, Bhuvneshwar Kumar 8).

INDIA v NEW ZEALAND 2016–17 (3rd Test)

At Maharani Usharaje Trust Ground, Indore, on 8, 9, 10, 11 October, 2016.
Toss: India.   Result: INDIA WON BY 321 RUNS.
Debuts: none.
Man of the Match: R. Ashwin.   Man of the Series: R. Ashwin.

More than 18,000 watched the opening day of Indore's inaugural Test. And the enthusiasm continued as India eased to a huge win that put them top of the ICC rankings. It was their second-biggest victory by runs, and completed their fourth whitewash in a series of three matches or more. The recalled Gambhir pulled Henry for consecutive sixes in the fourth over, and although New Zealand had three wickets by drinks on the first afternoon, they would not manage another until after tea on the second day. Kohli and Rahane started slowly – 48 in 20 overs – but the evening session brought 119 runs. Next day their alliance grew to 365, an Indian fourth-wicket record, beating 353 by Sachin Tendulkar and V. V. S. Laxman at Sydney in 2003–04. Kohli fell soon after reaching his second Test double-century, then Rahane departed for a career-best 188. New Zealand's openers survived nine overs on the second evening, and took their stand to 118 next day – but then Ashwin decided enough was enough. Latham was deceived in the flight, to start a procession: Williamson chopped on, and Taylor edged to slip. Ashwin also deflected Ronchi's fierce straight-drive into the stumps, to run out Guptill. Neesham, returning after a rib injury, made a determined 71, but India still led by 258. Pujara made a brisk hundred to hasten a declaration, and New Zealand wilted in the face of a fanciful target of 475, losing their last seven for 51. Ashwin finished with career-best innings and match figures.

India

M. Vijay c Latham b Patel	10	– run out (Guptill/Watling)	19
G. Gambhir lbw b Boult	29	– c Guptill b Patel	50
C. A. Pujara b Santner	41	– not out	101
*V. Kohli lbw b Patel	211	– lbw b Patel	17
A. M. Rahane c Watling b Boult	188	– not out	23
R. G. Sharma not out	51		
R. A. Jadeja not out	17		
B 4, lb 3, w 1, nb 2	10	B 4, lb 1, w 1	6
(5 wkts dec, 169 overs)	557	(3 wkts dec, 49 overs)	216

1/26 (1) 2/60 (2) 3/100 (3) 4/465 (4) 5/504 (5)   1/34 (1) 2/110 (2) 3/158 (4)

R. Ashwin, †W. P. Saha, Mohammed Shami and U. T. Yadav did not bat.

In the second innings Gambhir, when 6, retired hurt at 11-0 and resumed at 34-1.

Boult 32–2–113–2; Henry 35–3–127–0; Patel 40–5–120–2; Santner 44–4–137–1; Neesham 18–1–53–0. *Second innings*—Boult 7–0–35–0; Patel 14–0–56–2; Santner 17–1–71–0; Henry 7–1–22–0; Neesham 4–0–27–0.

New Zealand

M. J. Guptill run out (Ashwin)	72	– (2) lbw b Jadeja	29
T. W. M. Latham c and b Ashwin	53	– (1) lbw b Yadav	6
*K. S. Williamson b Ashwin	8	– lbw b Ashwin	27
L. R. P. L. Taylor c Rahane b Ashwin	0	– b Ashwin	32
L. Ronchi c Rahane b Ashwin	0	– b Ashwin	15
J. D. S. Neesham lbw b Ashwin	71	– c Kohli b Jadeja	0
†B-J. Watling c Rahane b Jadeja	23	– not out	23
M. J. Santner c Kohli b Jadeja	22	– b Ashwin	14
J. S. Patel run out (Ashwin)	18	– b Ashwin	0
M. J. Henry not out	15	– c Mohammed Shami b Ashwin	0
T. A. Boult c Pujara b Ashwin	0	– c and b Ashwin	4
B 6, lb 5, w 1, p 5	17	B 2, nb 1	3
(90.2 overs)	299	(44.5 overs)	153

1/118 (2) 2/134 (3) 3/140 (4) 4/148 (1) 5/148 (5)   1/7 (1) 2/42 (3) 3/80 (4) 4/102 (5) 5/103 (6)
6/201 (7) 7/253 (8) 8/276 (6) 9/294 (9) 10/299 (11)   6/112 (2) 7/136 (8) 8/138 (9) 9/138 (10) 10/153 (11)

Mohammed Shami 13–1–40–0; Yadav 15–1–55–0; Ashwin 27.2–5–81–6; Jadeja 28–5–80–2; Vijay 7–0–27–0. *Second innings*—Mohammed Shami 7–0–34–0; Yadav 8–4–13–1; Ashwin 13.5–2–59–7; Jadeja 16–3–45–2.

Umpires: H. D. P. K. Dharmasena *(Sri Lanka)* (39) and B. N. J. Oxenford *(Australia)* (34).
Third umpire: C. Shamsuddin *(India)*.   Referee: D. C. Boon *(Australia)* (35).

Close of play: first day, India 267–3 (Kohli 103, Rahane 79); second day, New Zealand 28–0 (Guptill 17, Latham 6); third day, India 18–0 (Vijay 11, Pujara 1).

PAKISTAN v WEST INDIES 2016-17 (1st Test)

At Dubai International Stadium on 13, 14, 15, 16, 17 October, 2016 (day/night).
Toss: Pakistan.   Result: PAKISTAN WON BY 56 RUNS.
Debuts: Pakistan – Babar Azam, Mohammad Nawaz.
Man of the Match: Azhar Ali.

Cricket's second day/night Test featured a triple-century, 17 wickets for leg-spin, a fourth-day collapse, and a valiant hundred in a big chase. Yet the public hardly bothered: the first evening drew a crowd of around 600 and, even as Azhar Ali inched towards 300, the second day – a public holiday – fared little better. Azhar's triple-hundred was Pakistan's fourth in Tests, and the third against West Indies. His innings (which lasted nearly 11 hours) and the total were both records for Tests in the UAE. An hour into the fourth day, Pakistan were in control, winkling West Indies out to lead by 222. Misbah-ul-Haq waived the follow-on, but his side collapsed to 121 for eight by dinner, and eventually left a target of 346. Bishoo's eight for 49 was the best return by a visiting bowler in Asia, beating Lance Klusener's eight for 64 at Calcutta in 1996-97. He bowled well, but Pakistan played him terribly: six of his wickets came from outright errors. Yasir Shah was outbowled, but had his moments: in the first innings, Cummins was his 100th wicket in his 17th Test (only the 19th-century England bowler George Lohmann got there quicker, by one), while in the second his diving return catch accounted for Bravo, who had survived 6¼ hours for his eighth Test hundred, the seventh outside the Caribbean. West Indies held out for their longest fourth innings in Asia, beating 105.1 overs at Calcutta in 1978-79. But two run-outs ended their resistance, as Pakistan won their 400th Test with only 12 overs left.

Pakistan

Sami Aslam b Chase	90	– c Blackwood b Bishoo	44
Azhar Ali not out	302	– lbw b Gabriel	2
Asad Shafiq c and b Bishoo	67	– lbw b Bishoo	5
Babar Azam c Holder b Bishoo	69	– b Bishoo	21
*Misbah-ul-Haq not out	29	– b Bishoo	15
†Sarfraz Ahmed (did not bat)		– st Dowrich b Bishoo	15
Mohammad Nawaz (did not bat)		– b Bishoo	0
Wahab Riaz (did not bat)		– c Brathwaite b Bishoo	5
Yasir Shah (did not bat)		– c and b Holder	2
Sohail Khan (did not bat)		– not out	1
Mohammad Amir (did not bat)		– b Bishoo	1
B 1, lb 9, w 1, nb 11	22	B 10, nb 2	12
(3 wkts dec, 155.3 overs)	579	(31.5 overs)	123

1/215 (1) 2/352 (3) 3/517 (4)
1/13 (2) 2/20 (3) 3/77 (4) 4/93 (1) 5/112 (5)
6/112 (7) 7/118 (8) 8/121 (9) 9/121 (6) 10/123 (11)

Gabriel 22-3-99-0; Cummins 25-2-99-0; Holder 25-4-73-0; Brathwaite 14-2-56-0; Bishoo 35-4-125-2; Chase 33-2-109-1; Blackwood 1.3-0-8-0. *Second innings*—Gabriel 7-1-23-1; Cummins 7-0-29-0; Bishoo 13.5-1-49-8; Holder 4-0-12-1.

West Indies

K. C. Brathwaite b Yasir Shah	32	– b Mohammad Amir	6
L. R. Johnson lbw b Yasir Shah	15	– lbw b Mohammad Amir	47
D. M. Bravo c Azhar Ali b Mohammad Nawaz	87	– c and b Yasir Shah	116
M. N. Samuels lbw b Sohail Khan	76	– c Sarfraz Ahmed b Mohammad Amir	4
J. Blackwood c Sarfraz Ahmed b Wahab Riaz	37	– lbw b Mohammad Nawaz	15
R. L. Chase c Babar Azam b Wahab Riaz	6	– b Yasir Shah	35
†S. O. Dowrich lbw b Yasir Shah	32	– b Wahab Riaz	0
*J. O. Holder b Yasir Shah	20	– not out	40
D. Bishoo b Mohammad Nawaz	17	– lbw b Mohammad Nawaz	3
M. L. Cummins b Yasir Shah	0	– run out (Misbah-ul-Haq)	1
S. T. Gabriel not out	6	– run out (Babar Azam/Sarfraz Ahmed)	1
B 9, lb 8, w 1, nb 11	29	B 5, lb 7, w 5, nb 4	21
(123.5 overs)	357	(109 overs)	289

1/42 (2) 2/69 (1) 3/182 (4) 4/259 (5) 5/266 (6)
6/300 (3) 7/325 (7) 8/346 (8) 9/351 (10) 10/357 (9)
1/27 (1) 2/87 (2) 3/95 (4) 4/116 (5) 5/193 (6)
6/194 (7) 7/263 (3) 8/276 (9) 9/277 (10) 10/289 (11)

Mohammad Amir 22-6-54-0; Sohail Khan 16-2-56-1; Yasir Shah 43-15-121-5; Wahab Riaz 23.3-3-65-2; Mohammad Nawaz 16.5-5-38-2; Azhar Ali 2.3-1-6-0. *Second innings*—Mohammad Amir 23-5-63-3; Sohail Khan 10-1-22-0; Yasir Shah 41-6-113-2; Mohammad Nawaz 18-4-32-2; Wahab Riaz 17-1-47-1.

Umpires: R. K. Illingworth *(England)* (23) and P. R. Reiffel *(Australia)* (26).
Third umpire: M. A. Gough *(England)*.   Referee: J. J. Crowe *(New Zealand)* (77).

Close of play: first day, Pakistan 279-1 (Azhar Ali 146, Asad Shafiq 33); second day, West Indies 69-1 (Brathwaite 32, Bravo 14); third day, West Indies 315-6 (Dowrich 27, Holder 10); fourth day, West Indies 95-2 (Bravo 26, Samuels 4).

PAKISTAN v WEST INDIES 2016–17 (2nd Test)

At Sheikh Zayed Stadium, Abu Dhabi, on 21, 22, 23, 24, 25 October, 2016.
Toss: Pakistan.   Result: PAKISTAN WON BY 133 RUNS.
Debuts: none.
Man of the Match: Yasir Shah.

Yasir Shah earned the match award and sealed the series, but rarely hit his best form; not many of his ten wickets came from genuinely good deliveries. In the second innings he outdid Chase, drawn by drift and beaten on the outside edge, and – with a skidder – Blackwood. But even if the West Indians had handled Yasir better, winning would have been a struggle: Abu Dhabi had become Pakistan's fortress. This was their fifth victory in nine Tests here, with no defeats. Their method had been as predictable as it was successful: Misbah-ul-Haq wins the toss (here for the eighth time), and his batsmen carefully raise a withering total (here passing 400 in their first innings for the seventh). Younis Khan made a record 13th Test century since turning 35, one more than Graham Gooch, Rahul Dravid and Sachin Tendulkar. Younis and Misbah became the most productive Test pairing for Pakistan (3,205 runs together, beating 3,137 by Younis and Mohammad Yousuf), in between pleasant fifties from Asad Shafiq and Sarfraz Ahmed. Gabriel's muscular pace earned a deserving maiden five-for, but Pakistan had scoreboard pressure. Seven of West Indies' top nine lasted at least an hour in the first innings, yet none reached 50. Misbah again ignored the follow-on, and eventually left the visitors needing 456 or another escape act. Despite Blackwood's 95, and their highest fourth-innings total against Pakistan, they finally yielded to Yasir on the last afternoon, leaving Misbah with ten series wins, the most by an Asian Test captain.

Pakistan

Sami Aslam b Bishoo	6	– c Hope b Gabriel	50
Azhar Ali b Gabriel	0	– c Holder b Cummins	79
Asad Shafiq b Gabriel	68	– not out	58
Younis Khan c Chase b Brathwaite	127	– not out	29
*Misbah-ul-Haq lbw b Gabriel	96		
Yasir Shah c Bishoo b Holder	23		
†Sarfraz Ahmed b Gabriel	56		
Mohammad Nawaz b Holder	25		
Sohail Khan c Johnson b Holder	26		
Zulfiqar Babar c Hope b Gabriel	0		
Rahat Ali not out	0		
B 1, lb 15, nb 9	25	B 4, lb 3, w 1, nb 3	11
(119.1 overs)	452	(2 wkts dec, 67 overs)	227

1/6 (2) 2/42 (1) 3/129 (3) 4/304 (4) 5/332 (5)   1/93 (1) 2/164 (2)
6/342 (6) 7/412 (7) 8/430 (8) 9/452 (9) 10/452 (10)

Gabriel 23.1–1–96–5; Cummins 20–1–65–0; Holder 22–8–47–3; Bishoo 26–0–112–1; Chase 19–1–80–0; Brathwaite 9–0–36–1. *Second innings*—Gabriel 12–2–36–1; Cummins 7–0–26–1; Brathwaite 15–2–33–0; Bishoo 20–0–77–0; Holder 7–0–22–0; Chase 6–0–26–0.

West Indies

L. R. Johnson lbw b Rahat Ali	12	– (2) b Yasir Shah	9
D. M. Bravo lbw b Yasir Shah	43	– (3) c Mohammad Nawaz b Rahat Ali	13
K. C. Brathwaite run out (Misbah-ul-Haq/Sarfraz Ahmed)	21	– (1) lbw b Mohammad Nawaz	67
M. N. Samuels c Sami Aslam b Rahat Ali	30	– c and b Yasir Shah	23
D. Bishoo b Sohail Khan	20	– (9) c Misbah-ul-Haq b Zulfiqar Babar	26
J. Blackwood c Sarfraz Ahmed b Rahat Ali	8	– (5) b Yasir Shah	95
R. L. Chase c Asad Shafiq b Yasir Shah	22	– (6) c Sarfraz Ahmed b Yasir Shah	20
†S. D. Hope b Yasir Shah	11	– (7) c Younis Khan b Zulfiqar Babar	41
*J. O. Holder not out	31	– (8) lbw b Yasir Shah	16
M. L. Cummins b Sohail Khan	3	– b Yasir Shah	0
S. T. Gabriel c Sohail Khan b Yasir Shah	13	– not out	7
B 2, lb 7, nb 1	10	B 4, lb 1	5
(94.4 overs)	224	(108 overs)	322

1/27 (1) 2/65 (2) 3/106 (4) 4/106 (3) 5/121 (6)   1/28 (2) 2/63 (3) 3/112 (4) 4/124 (5) 5/187 (6)
6/144 (5) 7/169 (7) 8/178 (8) 9/197 (10) 10/224 (11)   6/244 (5) 7/266 (8) 8/311 (7) 9/312 (10) 10/322 (9)

Rahat Ali 28.4–6–86–4; Sohail Khan 19–8–35–2; Zulfiqar Babar 21–6–39–0; Asad Shafiq 1–0–2–0; Yasir Shah 28.4–6–86–4; Mohammad Nawaz 4–1–8–0. *Second innings*—Sohail Khan 14–3–44–0; Rahat Ali 23–2–69–1; Yasir Shah 39–5–124–6; Zulfiqar Babar 22–5–51–2; Mohammad Nawaz 10–0–29–1.

Umpires: M. A. Gough *(England)* (3) and R. K. Illingworth *(England)* (24).
Third umpire: P. R. Reiffel *(Australia)*.   Referee: J. J. Crowe *(New Zealand)* (78).

Close of play: first day, Pakistan 304-4 (Misbah-ul-Haq 90, Yasir Shah 0); second day, West Indies 106-4 (Bishoo 0, Blackwood 0); third day, Pakistan 114-1 (Azhar Ali 52, Asad Shafiq 5); fourth day, West Indies 171-4 (Blackwood 41, Chase 17).

Test No. 2226/49 (P402, WI520)

PAKISTAN v WEST INDIES 2016–17 (3rd Test)

At Sharjah C. A. Stadium on 30, 31 October, 1, 2, 3 November, 2016.
Toss: Pakistan. Result: WEST INDIES WON BY FIVE WICKETS.
Debuts: none.
Man of the Match: K. C. Brathwaite. Man of the Series: Yasir Shah.

Kraigg Brathwaite was immovable, becoming the first opener to be unbeaten in both innings of a Test, and only the fifth West Indian to carry his bat (though Desmond Haynes did it three times). He inspired his team to their first win in 14, their first under Holder, and only the second – to set against 56 defeats – outside the Caribbean against a top-eight nation since the start of 2000. His superb performance deserved a grander stage than a dead rubber, in front of empty stands. After Pakistan's underwhelming 281, Brathwaite batted eight hours for 142: over half his runs came in singles – but West Indies led, for the first time in 14 Tests. In the second innings, he stood firm while others wilted. The diminutive wicketkeeper Dowrich complemented him in both innings. In the first, their stand of 83 kept West Indies in contention. In the second, from a rocky 67 for five chasing 153, Dowrich matched Brathwaite's unbeaten 60, and slashed the winning four. Gabriel got things off to a rollicking start with two wickets in the match's first over; Asad Shafiq was halfway to a second pair in five Tests (only the third top-six batsman to make two in a calendar year, after Mohinder Amarnath in 1983 and Mark Waugh in 1992). Misbah-ul-Haq, leading them for a national-record 49th time in Tests, was one of four half-centuries, but Bishoo also bowled well. In the second innings, Holder collected a maiden five-for in his 20th Test, to bring about another collapse.

Pakistan

Sami Aslam c Holder b Bishoo	74	– c Joseph b Holder	17
Azhar Ali c Brathwaite b Gabriel	0	– c Bravo b Bishoo	91
Asad Shafiq lbw b Gabriel	0	– c Bravo b Holder	0
Younis Khan c Johnson b Chase	51	– c Dowrich b Holder	0
*Misbah-ul-Haq c Dowrich b Bishoo	53	– c Bishoo b Chase	4
†Sarfraz Ahmed b Gabriel	51	– c Bravo b Bishoo	42
Mohammad Nawaz st Dowrich b Bishoo	6	– c Johnson b Bishoo	19
Wahab Riaz lbw b Bishoo	4	– (9) c Johnson b Holder	1
Yasir Shah b Joseph	12	– (10) lbw b Holder	0
Mohammad Amir b Joseph	20	– (8) run out (Chase/Holder)	8
Zulfiqar Babar not out	1	– not out	15
Lb 4, w 1, nb 4	9	B 2, lb 1, w 6, nb 2	11
(90.5 overs)	281	(81.3 overs)	208

1/1 (2) 2/1 (3) 3/107 (4) 4/150 (1) 5/230 (5)
6/242 (7) 7/248 (6) 8/248 (8) 9/280 (10) 10/281 (9)

1/37 (1) 2/41 (3) 3/41 (4) 4/48 (5) 5/134 (6)
6/175 (7) 7/189 (2) 8/192 (8) 9/193 (9) 10/208 (10)

Gabriel 21–1–67–3; Joseph 16.5–5–57–2; Holder 12–4–29–0; Chase 20–5–47–1; Bishoo 21–3–77–4. *Second innings*—Gabriel 15–1–36–0; Joseph 14–3–41–0; Holder 17.3–5–30–5; Brathwaite 1–0–5–0; Chase 15–1–47–1; Bishoo 19–2–46–3.

West Indies

K. C. Brathwaite not out	142	– not out	60
L. R. Johnson lbw b Wahab Riaz	1	– lbw b Yasir Shah	12
D. M. Bravo c Mohammad Amir b Zulfiqar Babar	11	– c Sarfraz Ahmed b Yasir Shah	3
M. N. Samuels lbw b Yasir Shah	0	– c Zulfiqar Babar b Yasir Shah	10
J. Blackwood c Asad Shafiq b Mohammad Amir	23	– b Wahab Riaz	4
R. L. Chase c Younis Khan b Mohammad Amir	50	– c Mohammad Nawaz b Wahab Riaz	2
†S. O. Dowrich b Wahab Riaz	47	– not out	60
*J. O. Holder b Mohammad Amir	16		
D. Bishoo c Sarfraz Ahmed b Wahab Riaz	27		
A. S. Joseph c Yasir Shah b Wahab Riaz	6		
S. T. Gabriel c Sarfraz Ahmed b Wahab Riaz	0		
Lb 6, nb 8	14	Lb 2, nb 1	3
(115.4 overs)	337	(5 wkts, 43.5 overs)	154

1/6 (2) 2/32 (3) 3/38 (4) 4/68 (5) 5/151 (6)
6/234 (7) 7/263 (8) 8/323 (9) 9/333 (10) 10/337 (11)

1/29 (2) 2/35 (3) 3/57 (4)
4/63 (5) 5/67 (6)

Mohammad Amir 25–5–71–3; Wahab Riaz 26.4–1–88–5; Yasir Shah 26–2–80–1; Zulfiqar Babar 21–3–56–1; Mohammad Nawaz 11–2–20–0; Azhar Ali 6–0–16–0. *Second innings*—Mohammad Amir 9.5–0–43–0; Wahab Riaz 12–0–46–2; Yasir Shah 15–4–40–3; Zulfiqar Babar 3–1–3–0; Mohammad Nawaz 4–0–20–0.

Umpires: M. A. Gough *(England)* (4) and P. R. Reiffel *(Australia)* (27).
Third umpire: R. K. Illingworth *(England)*. Referee: J. J. Crowe *(New Zealand)* (79).

Close of play: first day, Pakistan 255–8 (Yasir Shah 1, Mohammad Amir 6); second day, West Indies 244–6 (Brathwaite 95, Holder 6); third day, Pakistan 87–4 (Azhar Ali 45, Sarfraz Ahmed 19); fourth day, West Indies 114–5 (Brathwaite 44, Dowrich 36).

Test No. 2227/9 (B94, E977)

BANGLADESH v ENGLAND 2016–17 (1st Test)

At Zohur Ahmed Chowdhury Stadium, Chittagong, on 20, 21, 22, 23, 24 October, 2016.
Toss: England.   Result: ENGLAND WON BY 22 RUNS.
Debuts: Bangladesh – Kamrul Islam, Mehedi Hasan, Sabbir Rahman. England – B. M. Duckett.
Man of the Match: B. A. Stokes.

This taut contest was unrecognisable from these sides' eight previous Tests, all comprehensive England wins. At 21 for three on the first morning, Cook knew he was in a tussle, and during the course of four days and 21 balls there remained little to separate the teams; this was only the seventh Test in which all four innings were in the 200s. The final margin was England's closest win by runs outside the Ashes, and Bangladesh's narrowest defeat. England's all-rounders made the difference: Stokes cracked 85 as a narrow lead of 45 was stretched to 285, and also took six wickets, including the knockout blows on the final morning. Ali survived a record five lbw reviews – including three in six balls from Shakib Al Hasan – to make his highest Test score overseas, while Bairstow overtook Andy Flower's record for the most runs in a calendar year by a wicketkeeper. For Bangladesh, off-spinner Mehedi Hasan, a week before his 19th birthday, became the first spinner to take five wickets on his first day of Test cricket since West Indies' Alf Valentine in 1950, while Sabbir Rahman kept victory hopes alive until he lost the strike, and Stokes grabbed the last two wickets in three balls. England included off-spinner Gareth Batty, 39, who had missed 142 Tests since June 2005, passing the 114 of Martin Bicknell, another Surrey man. He opened the bowling in both innings, the first England spinner to do so since Sam Staples in 1927–28 on the Durban matting.

England

*A. N. Cook b Shakib Al Hasan	4	– c Mahmudullah b Mehedi Hasan	12
B. M. Duckett b Mehedi Hasan	14	– c Mominul Haque b Shakib Al Hasan	15
J. E. Root c Sabbir Rahman b Mehedi Hasan	40	– lbw b Shakib Al Hasan	1
G. S. Ballance lbw b Mehedi Hasan	1	– c Imrul Kayes b Taijul Islam	9
M. M. Ali c Mushfiqur Rahim b Mehedi Hasan	68	– c Mushfiqur Rahim b Shakib Al Hasan	14
B. A. Stokes b Shakib Al Hasan	18	– lbw b Shakib Al Hasan	85
†J. M. Bairstow b Mehedi Hasan	52	– b Kamrul Islam	47
C. R. Woakes c Mominul Haque b Taijul Islam	36	– not out	19
A. U. Rashid c Sabbir Rahman b Taijul Islam	26	– lbw b Shakib Al Hasan	9
S. C. J. Broad c Mushfiqur Rahim b Mehedi Hasan	13	– run out (Mehedi Hasan/Mushfiqur Rahim)	10
G. J. Batty not out	1	– lbw b Taijul Islam	3
B 14, lb 4, w 2	20	B 3, lb 8, p 5	16
(105.5 overs)	293	(80.2 overs)	240

1/18 (2) 2/18 (1) 3/21 (4) 4/83 (3) 5/106 (6)   1/26 (1) 2/27 (3) 3/28 (2) 4/46 (4) 5/62 (5) 6/189 (7)
6/194 (5) 7/237 (7) 8/258 (8) 9/289 (9) 10/293 (10)   7/197 (6) 8/213 (9) 9/233 (10) 10/240 (11)
Shafiul Islam 9–1–33–0; Mehedi Hasan 39.5–7–80–6; Kamrul Islam 8–0–41–0; Shakib Al Hasan 19–6–46–2; Taijul Islam 24–11–47–2; Sabbir Rahman 3–0–11–0; Mahmudullah 2–0–17–0; Mominul Haque 1–1–0–0. *Second innings*—Mehedi Hasan 20–1–58–1; Shakib Al Hasan 33–7–85–5; Taijul Islam 15.2–2–41–2; Kamrul Islam 8–0–24–1; Mahmudullah 1–0–6–0; Shafiul Islam 3–0–10–0.

Bangladesh

Tamim Iqbal c Bairstow b Batty	78	– c Ballance b Ali	9
Imrul Kayes b Ali	21	– c Root b Rashid	43
Mominul Haque c Stokes b Ali	0	– lbw b Batty	27
Mahmudullah c Root b Rashid	38	– lbw b Batty	17
*†Mushfiqur Rahim c Bairstow b Stokes	48	– (6) c Ballance b Batty	39
Shakib Al Hasan st Bairstow b Ali	31	– c Bairstow b Ali	24
Shafiul Islam c Broad b Rashid	2	– (11) lbw b Stokes	0
Sabbir Rahman c Cook b Stokes	19	– (7) not out	64
Mehedi Hasan lbw b Stokes	1	– (8) lbw b Broad	1
Taijul Islam not out	3	– lbw b Stokes	16
Kamrul Islam b Stokes	0	– (9) c Ballance b Broad	0
B 2, lb 4, w 1	7	B 9, lb 13, w 1	23
(86 overs)	248	(81.3 overs)	263

1/29 (2) 2/29 (3) 3/119 (4) 4/163 (1) 5/221 (5)   1/35 (1) 2/81 (2) 3/103 (3) 4/108 (4) 5/140 (5)
6/221 (6) 7/238 (7) 8/239 (9) 9/248 (8) 10/248 (11)   6/227 (6) 7/234 (8) 8/238 (9) 9/263 (10) 10/263 (11)
Broad 8–2–12–0; Batty 17–1–51–1; Woakes 7–2–15–0; Rashid 16–1–58–2; Ali 22–4–75–3; Stokes 14–5–26–4; Root 2–0–5–0. *Second innings*—Batty 17–3–65–3; Ali 14–2–60–2; Woakes 7–3–10–0; Rashid 17–2–55–1; Broad 15–4–31–2; Stokes 11.3–2–20–2.

Umpires: H. D. P. K. Dharmasena *(Sri Lanka)* (40) and C. B. Gaffaney *(New Zealand)* (10).
Third umpire: S. Ravi *(India)*.   Referee: R. S. Madugalle *(Sri Lanka)* (168).

Close of play: first day, England 258–7 (Woakes 36, Rashid 5); second day, Bangladesh 221–5 (Shakib Al Hasan 31, Shafiul Islam 0); third day, England 228–8 (Woakes 11, Broad 10); fourth day, Bangladesh 253–8 (Sabbir Rahman 59, Taijul Islam 11).

Test No. 2228/10 (B95, E978)

BANGLADESH v ENGLAND 2016–17 (2nd Test)

At Shere Bangla National Stadium, Mirpur, Dhaka, on 28, 29, 30 October, 2016.
Toss: Bangladesh.   Result: BANGLADESH WON BY 108 RUNS.
Debuts: England – Z. S. Ansari.
Man of the Match: Mehedi Hasan.   Man of the Series: Mehedi Hasan.

After falling just short at Chittagong, Bangladesh made sure of their first Test win over England, at the tenth attempt. They were given a good start by Tamim Iqbal, whose 104 contained some classical drives; his stand of 170 with Mominul Haque, which preceded a slide of nine for 49, made up 77.27% of the total. Only Kumar Sangakkara and Mahela Jayawardene, with 168 of 216 (77.78%) for Sri Lanka at Durban in 2000–01, had made a bigger proportion of a completed innings. England pinched a slender lead, thanks to their highest ninth-wicket stand in Asia, 99 between Woakes and Rashid. Mehedi Hassan, who had just turned 19, improved Bangladesh's best match figures with 12 for 159, mesmerising the batsmen with pure orthodoxy, especially in the second innings. On the third afternoon England – set 64 more than they had ever made to win a Test in Asia – sailed to 100 without loss by tea, before an alarming collapse to 164 all out. Duckett was bowled by the first ball of the evening session, a skidder from Mehedi, and the rest were like rabbits in the headlights. It was done and dusted in just 22.3 overs; England had not lost all ten wickets in a single session since the 1938 Ashes Test at Headingley. Shakib Al Hasan took three in four balls. The result gave Chandika Hathurusinghe, Bangladesh's coach, a unique double: in Colombo in March 1993 he had been part of the first Sri Lankan side to achieve a Test victory over England.

Bangladesh

Tamim Iqbal lbw b Ali	104	– c Cook b Ansari	40
Imrul Kayes c Duckett b Woakes	1	– lbw b Ali	78
Mominul Haque b Ali	66	– c Cook b Stokes	1
Mahmudullah c Cook b Stokes	13	– b Ansari	47
Shakib Al Hasan c Bairstow b Woakes	10	– b Rashid	41
*†Mushfiqur Rahim c Cook b Ali	4	– c Cook b Stokes	9
Sabbir Rahman c Bairstow b Stokes	0	– lbw b Rashid	15
Shuvagata Hom c Bairstow b Woakes	6	– not out	25
Mehedi Hasan lbw b Ali	1	– (10) c Root b Rashid	2
Taijul Islam not out	5	– (9) c Bairstow b Stokes	5
Kamrul Islam c Root b Ali	0	– c and b Rashid	7
B 1, lb 9	10	B 17, lb 7, w 1, nb 1	26
(63.5 overs)	220	(66.5 overs)	296

1/1 (2) 2/171 (1) 3/190 (3) 4/196 (4) 5/201 (6)
6/202 (7) 7/212 (8) 8/213 (9) 9/215 (5) 10/220 (11)

1/65 (1) 2/66 (3) 3/152 (4) 4/200 (2) 5/238 (5)
6/238 (6) 7/268 (7) 8/273 (9) 9/276 (10) 10/296 (11)

Woakes 9–3–30–3; Finn 8–1–30–0; Ali 19.5–5–57–5; Ansari 6–0–36–0; Stokes 11–5–13–2; Rashid 10–0–44–0. *Second innings*—Finn 3–0–18–0; Ali 19–2–60–1; Ansari 19–0–76–2; Stokes 12–2–52–3; Rashid 11.5–1–52–4; Woakes 2–0–14–0.

England

*A. N. Cook lbw b Mehedi Hasan	14	– c Mominul Haque b Mehedi Hasan	59
B. M. Duckett c Mushfiqur Rahim b Shakib Al Hasan	7	– b Mehedi Hasan	56
J. E. Root lbw b Taijul Islam	56	– lbw b Shakib Al Hasan	1
G. S. Ballance c Mushfiqur Rahim b Mehedi Hasan	9	– c Tamim Iqbal b Mehedi Hasan	5
M. M. Ali b Mehedi Hasan	10	– lbw b Mehedi Hasan	0
B. A. Stokes c Mominul Haque b Taijul Islam	0	– b Shakib Al Hasan	25
†J. M. Bairstow lbw b Mehedi Hasan	24	– c Shuvagata Hom b Mehedi Hasan	3
Z. S. Ansari c Shuvagata Hom b Mehedi Hasan	13	– (10) c Imrul Kayes b Shakib Al Hasan	0
C. R. Woakes c Shuvagata Hom b Mehedi Hasan	46	– (8) not out	9
A. U. Rashid not out	44	– (9) lbw b Shakib Al Hasan	0
S. T. Finn c Mushfiqur Rahim b Taijul Islam	0	– lbw b Mehedi Hasan	0
B 13, lb 7, nb 1	21	B 4, lb 2	6
(81.3 overs)	244	(45.3 overs)	164

1/10 (2) 2/24 (1) 3/42 (4) 4/64 (5) 5/69 (6)
6/114 (7) 7/140 (8) 8/144 (3) 9/243 (9) 10/244 (11)

1/100 (2) 2/105 (3) 3/124 (4) 4/124 (5) 5/127 (1)
6/139 (7) 7/161 (6) 8/161 (9) 9/161 (10) 10/164 (11)

Mehedi Hasan 28–2–82–6; Shakib Al Hasan 16–5–41–1; Taijul Islam 25.3–3–65–3; Kamrul Islam 3–0–16–0; Shuvagata Hom 4–0–8–0; Sabbir Rahman 5–0–12–0. *Second innings*—Mehedi Hasan 21.3–2–77–6; Shakib Al Hasan 13–1–49–4; Shuvagata Hom 6–0–25–0; Taijul Islam 5–2–7–0.

Umpires: H. D. P. K. Dharmasena *(Sri Lanka)* (41) and S. Ravi *(India)* (15).
Third umpire: C. B. Gaffaney *(New Zealand)*.   Referee: R. S. Madugalle *(Sri Lanka)* (169).

Close of play: first day, England 50–3 (Root 15, Ali 2); second day, Bangladesh 152–3 (Imrul Kayes 59).

Test No. 2229/16 (Z100, SL252)

ZIMBABWE v SRI LANKA 2016–17 (1st Test)

At Harare Sports Club on 29, 30, 31 October, 1, 2 November, 2016.
Toss: Sri Lanka.   Result: SRI LANKA WON BY 225 RUNS.
Debuts: Zimbabwe – C. T. Mumba. Sri Lanka – D. A. S. Gunaratne, C. B. R. L. S. Kumara.
Man of the Match: A. G. Cremer.

Zimbabwe marked their 100th Test with a performance like many of the previous 99: short on luck, long on pluck. Hindered by several poor umpiring decisions, they lost by a wide margin, though only 45 balls remained when the last wicket fell. But they dropped half a dozen catches, including Kusal Perera, who went on to a maiden Test hundred, from just 104 balls, and Tharanga, who compiled his second century, more than ten years after the first (the longest gap between Test hundreds since the Second World War). Although Zimbabwe did bowl Sri Lanka out – having taken only 12 wickets in two matches against New Zealand – they conceded 537. Things looked grim at 139 for six on the third morning, but Cremer (Test average: ten) made a maiden Test hundred, and put on 132 before Moor became teenager Lahiru Kumara's first Test victim, and 92 with Tiripano. Cremer had 99 when the ninth wicket fell; Mpofu had to survive one ball from Herath. Zimbabwe nonetheless conceded a big lead, which became unbridgeable after Karunaratne's century. Herath declared overnight, 411 ahead; Zimbabwe had 98 overs to survive. The morning session produced a single wicket, but another umpiring blunder – Mawoyo lbw to a ball missing leg – sparked a procession. That Zimbabwe got so close to surviving was again down to Cremer, who extended his time at the crease past seven hours. It was a shock when, with less than 11 overs remaining, he leapt down the track to Herath and was stumped.

Sri Lanka

F. D. M. Karunaratne c Mawoyo b Cremer	56	– c and b Mpofu			110
J. K. Silva c Williams b Waller	94	– b Mumba			7
†M. D. K. J. Perera c Waller b Cremer	110	– c Masakadza b Waller			17
B. K. G. Mendis c Moor b Cremer	34	– c Cremer b Mumba			19
W. U. Tharanga not out	110	– c Moor b Mumba			1
D. M. de Silva c Williams b Cremer	25	– c Waller b Mumba			64
D. A. S. Gunaratne c Cremer b Williams	54	– not out			16
M. D. K. Perera run out (Mpofu)	23	– not out			1
*H. M. R. K. B. Herath c Waller b Mumba	7				
R. A. S. Lakmal c Tiripano b Mpofu	7				
C. B. R. L. S. Kumara c Moor b Mpofu	0				
B 10, lb 7	17	B 6, lb 5, nb 1			12
(155 overs)	537	(6 wkts dec, 61.5 overs)			247

1/123 (1) 2/198 (2) 3/282 (4) 4/307 (3) 5/351 (6)   1/17 (2) 2/72 (3) 3/111 (4)
6/450 (7) 7/498 (8) 8/512 (9) 9/536 (10) 10/537 (11) 4/117 (5) 5/211 (1) 6/241 (6)

Mpofu 31–6–96–2; Mumba 24–2–101–1; Tiripano 26–7–71–0; Cremer 42–6–142–4; Masakadza 9–3–31–0; Williams 17–2–54–1; Waller 6–0–25–1. *Second innings*—Mpofu 16–2–42–1; Cremer 14–0–67–0; Mumba 11.5–2–50–4; Tiripano 8–0–33–0; Waller 5–0–17–1; Williams 1–0–5–0; Masakadza 6–1–22–0.

Zimbabwe

T. M. K. Mawoyo c Gunaratne b Lakmal	45	– lbw b M. D. K. Perera			37
B. B. Chari lbw b Herath	5	– b Kumara			10
H. Masakadza c Karunaratne b Lakmal	33	– lbw b Lakmal			20
C. R. Ervine lbw b M. D. K. Perera	12	– lbw b M. D. K. Perera			0
S. C. Williams c Gunaratne b Herath	10	– c de Silva b Herath			40
M. N. Waller lbw b M. D. K. Perera	22	– lbw b Lakmal			0
†P. J. Moor c M. D. K. Perera b Kumara	79	– lbw b Kumara			7
*A. G. Cremer not out	102	– st M. D. K. J. Perera b Herath			43
D. T. Tiripano lbw b Mendis	46	– lbw b Herath			0
C. T. Mumba b Herath	1	– not out			10
C. B. Mpofu b Lakmal	2	– b M. D. K. Perera			0
B 4, lb 4, w 7, nb 1	16	B 5, lb 13, w 1			19
(107.5 overs)	373	(90.3 overs)			186

1/21 (2) 2/92 (1) 3/92 (3) 4/111 (5) 5/134 (4)   1/31 (2) 2/68 (1) 3/74 (4) 4/74 (3) 5/74 (6) 6/100 (7)
6/139 (6) 7/271 (7) 8/363 (9) 9/366 (10) 10/373 (11)   7/139 (5) 8/145 (9) 9/183 (8) 10/186 (11)

Lakmal 21.5–3–69–3; Kumara 22–3–90–1; Herath 37–5–97–3; M. D. K. Perera 18–1–66–2; Gunaratne 3–0–23–0; de Silva 2–0–10–0; Mendis 4–0–10–1. *Second innings*—Lakmal 24–6–43–2; Herath 30–13–38–3; Kumara 19–3–45–2; M. D. K. Perera 15.3–4–34–3; Mendis 2–1–8–0.

Umpires: S. D. Fry *(Australia)* (2) and I. J. Gould *(England)* (54).
Third umpire: T. J. Matibiri *(Zimbabwe)*.   Referee: B. C. Broad *(England)* (81).

Close of play: first day, Sri Lanka 317–4 (Tharanga 13, de Silva 10); second day, Zimbabwe 88–1 (Mawoyo 41, Masakadza 33); third day, Sri Lanka 5–0 (Karunaratne 1, Silva 3); fourth day, Sri Lanka 247–6 (Gunaratne 16, M. D. K. Perera 1).

ZIMBABWE v SRI LANKA 2016–17 (2nd Test)

Test No. 2230/17 (Z101, SL253)

At Harare Sports Club on 6, 7, 8, 9, 10 November, 2016.
Toss: Zimbabwe. Result: SRI LANKA WON BY 257 RUNS.
Debuts: none.
Man of the Match: H. M. R. K. B. Herath. Man of the Series: F. D. M. Karunaratne.

The first use of DRS in Zimbabwe saved the hosts from some poor decisions, but Herath's hatful ensured a 2–0 win for the visitors. Cremer was happy to bowl first on a grassy surface, but Mumba limped off with knee pain after the first over – only to return in the tenth – and the others wasted the first hour. Part-timer Masakadza picked two in six balls as the Sri Lankans let their guard down. Just 44 runs dribbled from 18 overs after lunch, and Tharanga dug in for 79 before becoming the first player given out on review in Zimbabwe, when cameras spotted a nick into the pad that ballooned to slip. De Silva carried on the rebuilding job, reaching three figures with a pull off Mpofu, and next day Gunaratne's maiden century ensured Zimbabwe conceded 500 for the fifth straight Test; another four dropped catches did not help. But Chari began the reply strongly, biffing his first ball, from Herath, over long-on for six; the next two went for four, and later he hit another six to reach a maiden half-century. He and Ervine both finished the second day with 60, but after that it was all about Herath. He completed five-fors against all nine Test opponents before declining the follow-on. He declared, 490 ahead, midway through the fourth day. By stumps he had another five wickets, and scooped up the last three on the final morning, to finish with the best innings and match figures (13 for 152) in Tests in Zimbabwe.

Sri Lanka

F. D. M. Karunaratne c Williams b Masakadza	26	– lbw b Mpofu		88
J. K. Silva lbw b Mpofu	37	– c Waller b Mumba		6
†M. D. K. J. Perera c Mumba b Masakadza	4	– (7) c Williams b Cremer		62
B. K. G. Mendis c Moor b Tiripano	26	– (3) c Mpofu b Mumba		0
W. U. Tharanga c Masakadza b Cremer	79	– (4) lbw b Cremer		17
D. M. de Silva c and b Cremer	127	– (5) c Chari b Mumba		9
D. A. S. Gunaratne st Moor b Williams	116	– (6) lbw b Tiripano		39
M. D. K. Perera lbw b Cremer	34	– c Masakadza b Cremer		2
*H. M. R. K. B. Herath c Moor b Tiripano	27	– b Cremer		4
R. A. S. Lakmal b Tiripano	0	– not out		21
C. B. R. L. S. Kumara not out	7			
B 9, lb 8, w 2, nb 2	21	B 6, lb 4		10
(144.4 overs)	504	(9 wkts dec, 81.4 overs)		258

1/62 (1) 2/66 (3) 3/84 (2) 4/112 (4) 5/255 (5)
6/342 (6) 7/396 (8) 8/471 (9) 9/471 (10) 10/504 (7)

1/14 (2) 2/16 (3) 3/44 (4) 4/84 (5) 5/153 (6)
6/198 (1) 7/201 (8) 8/211 (9) 9/258 (7)

Mumba 23–4–80–0; Tiripano 32–4–91–3; Mpofu 23–4–92–1; Masakadza 13–4–34–2; Cremer 40–1–136–3; Williams 8.4–1–31–1; Waller 5–0–23–0. *Second innings*—Mpofu 21–8–51–1; Mumba 19–4–67–3; Cremer 21.4–2–91–4; Tiripano 11–4–14–1; Williams 6–0–21–0; Chari 1–0–3–0; Masakadza 2–1–1–0.

Zimbabwe

T. M. K. Mawoyo lbw b Herath	3	– c de Silva b Herath		15
B. B. Chari b Herath	80	– b Herath		8
H. Masakadza c de Silva b Herath	0	– lbw b Herath		10
C. R. Ervine c Karunaratne b Lakmal	64	– c de Silva b Herath		72
S. C. Williams lbw b M. D. K. Perera	58	– c Mendis b Kumara		45
M. N. Waller c Silva b Herath	18	– c M. D. K. J. Perera b de Silva		0
†P. J. Moor lbw b M. D. K. Perera	33	– c Mendis b Herath		20
*A. G. Cremer c Karunaratne b M. D. K. Perera	3	– b Herath		5
D. T. Tiripano c Herath b Lakmal	3	– not out		16
C. T. Mumba lbw b Herath	2	– lbw b Herath		1
C. B. Mpofu not out	0	– lbw b Herath		20
B 2, lb 6	8	B 12, lb 6, w 3		21
(82.1 overs)	272	(58 overs)		233

1/17 (1) 2/17 (3) 3/134 (4) 4/173 (2) 5/210 (6)
6/253 (5) 7/265 (8) 8/268 (7) 9/272 (10) 10/272 (9)

1/16 (2) 2/32 (3) 3/39 (1) 4/113 (5) 5/114 (6)
6/166 (7) 7/176 (8) 8/195 (4) 9/201 (10) 10/233 (11)

Lakmal 21.1–5–55–2; Herath 26–4–89–5; Kumara 14–0–60–0; M. D. K. Perera 18–2–51–3; Gunaratne 2–0–5–0; de Silva 1–0–4–0. *Second innings*—Lakmal 15–2–58–0; Herath 23–6–63–8; M. D. K. Perera 8–1–42–0; Kumara 9–0–42–1; de Silva 3–0–10–1.

Umpires: S. D. Fry *(Australia)* (3) and I. J. Gould *(England)* (55).
Third umpire: M. Erasmus *(South Africa)*. Referee: B. C. Broad *(England)* (82).

Close of play: first day, Sri Lanka 290–5 (de Silva 100, Gunaratne 13); second day, Zimbabwe 126–2 (Chari 60, Ervine 60); third day, Sri Lanka 102–4 (Karunaratne 54, Gunaratne 6); fourth day, Zimbabwe 180–7 (Ervine 65, Tiripano 0).

AUSTRALIA v SOUTH AFRICA 2016–17 (1st Test)

At W. A. C. A. Ground, Perth, on 3, 4, 5, 6, 7 November, 2016.
Toss: South Africa.   Result: SOUTH AFRICA WON BY 177 RUNS.
Debuts: South Africa – K. A. Maharaj.
Man of the Match: K. Rabada.

South Africa emerged from various points of apparent hopelessness with their third victory in a row at the WACA. It was Australia's first defeat in the opening Test of a home summer since November 1988, when West Indies won in Brisbane. After choosing to bat, South Africa crashed to 32 for four before recovering to 242. That still looked below par, especially once Australia galloped to 158 without loss. But a tremendous fightback brought about a stunning collapse: in 35 overs, all ten went down for 86. From then on, South Africa were not just in the contest – they dominated it. Nine of the wickets fell after Steyn went off with an injured shoulder. He did remove Warner, out in the nineties for the first time in Tests after converting his previous 16 visits. The game was sealed by Elgar and Duminy, who both made their fifth Test centuries during a third-wicket stand of 250. Du Plessis declared 538 ahead: Australia had about 140 overs to survive against two frontline seamers and a tyro spinner, left-armer Keshav Maharaj. The first breakthrough came from a piece of fielding genius from Bavuma, who picked the ball up at full tilt in the covers and – in mid-air, feet higher than head – threw down the stumps to run out an astonished Warner. South Africa worked their way slowly through: Rabada completed a magnificent five-for, and Australia's first defeat in 19 home Tests was completed before a delayed tea, when Lyon became the fifth leg-before victim of the innings.

South Africa

S. C. Cook c M. R. Marsh b Starc	0	– c S. E. Marsh b Siddle	12
D. Elgar c Nevill b Hazlewood	12	– c Starc b Hazlewood	127
H. M. Amla c Smith b Hazlewood	0	– b Hazlewood	1
J-P. Duminy c Nevill b Siddle	11	– c Nevill b Siddle	141
*F. du Plessis c Voges b Starc	37	– c Nevill b Starc	32
T. Bavuma c S. E. Marsh b Lyon	51	– c Khawaja b M. R. Marsh	8
†Q. de Kock c S. E. Marsh b Hazlewood	84	– c Voges b M. R. Marsh	64
V. D. Philander b Starc	10	– b Smith	73
K. A. Maharaj c Warner b Lyon	16	– not out	41
K. Rabada not out	11		
D. W. Steyn b Starc	4		
B 4, w 2	6	B 10, lb 13, w 17, nb 1	41
(63.4 overs)	242	(8 wkts dec, 160.1 overs)	540

1/0 (1) 2/5 (3) 3/20 (2) 4/32 (4) 5/81 (5) 6/152 (6)   1/35 (1) 2/45 (3) 3/295 (4) 4/324 (2)
7/175 (8) 8/223 (9) 9/227 (7) 10/242 (11)   5/346 (6) 6/352 (5) 7/468 (7) 8/540 (8)

Starc 18.4–2–71–4; Hazlewood 17–2–70–3; Siddle 12–3–36–1; M. R. Marsh 6–1–23–0; Lyon 10–1–38–2. *Second innings*—Starc 31–8–114–1; Hazlewood 37–11–107–2; Siddle 26–9–62–2; M. R. Marsh 26–4–77–2; Lyon 34–3–146–0; Voges 5–1–8–0; Smith 1.1–0–3–1.

Australia

D. A. Warner c Amla b Steyn	97	– (2) run out (Bavuma)	35
S. E. Marsh lbw b Philander	63	– (1) c du Plessis b Rabada	15
U. T. Khawaja b Rabada	4	– lbw b Duminy	97
*S. P. D. Smith lbw b Maharaj	0	– c de Kock b Rabada	34
A. C. Voges c and b Rabada	27	– c de Kock b Rabada	1
M. R. Marsh lbw b Philander	0	– lbw b Rabada	26
†P. M. Nevill c Amla b Maharaj	23	– not out	60
M. A. Starc c du Plessis b Maharaj	0	– lbw b Maharaj	13
P. M. Siddle not out	18	– lbw b Philander	13
J. R. Hazlewood c Duminy b Philander	4	– c Elgar b Bavuma	29
N. M. Lyon c Elgar b Philander	0	– lbw b Maharaj	8
Lb 3, nb 5	8	B 13, lb 11, w 4, nb 2	30
(70.2 overs)	244	(119.1 overs)	361

1/158 (1) 2/167 (3) 3/168 (4) 4/181 (2) 5/181 (6) 6/202 (5)   1/52 (2) 2/52 (1) 3/144 (2) 4/146 (5) 5/196 (6)
7/203 (8) 8/232 (7) 9/243 (10) 10/244 (11)   6/246 (3) 7/262 (8) 8/280 (9) 9/345 (10) 10/361 (11)

Steyn 12.4–3–51–1; Philander 19.2–2–56–4; Rabada 20–1–78–2; Maharaj 18.2–5–56–3. *Second innings*—Rabada 31–6–92–5; Philander 22–7–55–1; Duminy 17–1–51–1; Maharaj 40.1–10–94–1; Cook 2–0–16–0; Bavuma 7–1–29–1.

Umpires: Aleem Dar *(Pakistan)* (106) and N. J. Llong *(England)* (38).
Third umpire: R. A. Kettleborough *(England)*.   Referee: A. J. Pycroft *(Zimbabwe)* (49).

Close of play: first day, Australia 105–0 (Warner 73, S. E. Marsh 29); second day, South Africa 104–2 (Elgar 46, Duminy 34); third day, South Africa 390–6 (de Kock 16, Philander 23); fourth day, Australia 169–4 (Khawaja 58, M. R. Marsh 15).

AUSTRALIA v SOUTH AFRICA 2016–17 (2nd Test)

At Bellerive Oval, Hobart, on 12, 13 *(no play)*, 14, 15 November, 2016.
Toss: South Africa.   Result: SOUTH AFRICA WON BY AN INNINGS AND 80 RUNS.
Debuts: Australia – C. J. Ferguson, J. M. Mennie.
Man of the Match: K. J. Abbott.

An innings win, their first in Australia, gave South Africa a third successive series victory there. But it was Australia's fifth defeat in a row, following the 3–0 whitewash in Sri Lanka. It was almost enough to overshadow a strange row about mints, which some suggested du Plessis had been using to treat the ball. On a grassy pitch under initially thunderous skies, the seamers dismantled Australia twice in 93 overs. Warner fell in the first over, Burns in the second, and Khawaja and Voges to successive balls in the ninth, before the debutant Callum Ferguson dismayed his watching family by trying to steal a second run. Australia were 43 for six at lunch, and all out for 85, their lowest home total for 32 years. Smith stormed off, shaking his head, unbeaten on 48. South Africa also struggled at first, but were rescued by Bavuma and de Kock, who kept things simple during a stand of 144 that spanned three days (the second was washed out). Australia again lost a wicket in the first over, but at 121 for two seemed set to make South Africa work hard on the fourth day. Instead it was all over by lunch. Philander's first 30 deliveries were dots; it took Smith 40 minutes to score. And the wicket of Khawaja triggered a spectacular collapse, as eight wickets dominoed for 32 in 19 overs. This was the last of Voges's 20 Tests; despite a double failure here he finished with an average of 61.87, second only to Don Bradman's 99.94.

Australia

D. A. Warner c de Kock b Philander	1	– (2) b Abbott		45
J. A. Burns lbw b Abbott	1	– (1) c de Kock b Abbott		0
U. T. Khawaja c Amla b Philander	4	– c de Kock b Abbott		64
*S. P. D. Smith not out	48	– c de Kock b Rabada		31
A. C. Voges c de Kock b Philander	0	– c Duminy b Abbott		2
C. J. Ferguson run out (sub [D. J. Vilas])	3	– c Elgar b Rabada		1
†P. M. Nevill lbw b Rabada	3	– c Duminy b Rabada		6
J. M. Mennie b Philander	10	– lbw b Rabada		0
M. A. Starc c Duminy b Abbott	4	– c de Kock b Abbott		0
J. R. Hazlewood c Amla b Abbott	8	– not out		6
N. M. Lyon c de Kock b Philander	2	– c Philander b Abbott		4
Lb 1	1	Lb 1, nb 1		2
(32.5 overs)	85	(60.1 overs)		161

1/2 (1) 2/2 (2) 3/8 (3) 4/8 (5) 5/17 (6) 6/31 (7)   1/0 (1) 2/79 (2) 3/129 (3) 4/135 (5) 5/140 (6)
7/59 (8) 8/66 (9) 9/76 (10) 10/85 (11)   6/150 (7) 7/150 (8) 8/151 (4) 9/151 (9) 10/161 (11)

Philander 10.1–5–21–5; Abbott 12.4–3–41–3; Rabada 6–0–20–1; Maharaj 4–2–2–0. *Second innings*—Abbott 23.1–3–77–6; Philander 16–6–31–0; Duminy 1–0–8–0; Rabada 17–5–34–4; Maharaj 3–0–10–0.

South Africa

S. C. Cook c Nevill b Starc	23
D. Elgar lbw b Starc	17
H. M. Amla c Nevill b Hazlewood	47
J-P. Duminy c Smith b Starc	1
*F. du Plessis lbw b Hazlewood	7
T. Bavuma c Lyon b Mennie	74
†Q. de Kock b Hazlewood	104
V. D. Philander c Nevill b Hazlewood	32
K. A. Maharaj b Hazlewood	1
K. J. Abbott lbw b Hazlewood	3
K. Rabada not out	5
B 3, lb 8, nb 1	12
(100.5 overs)	326

1/43 (2) 2/44 (1) 3/46 (4) 4/76 (5) 5/132 (3)
6/276 (7) 7/292 (6) 8/293 (9) 9/297 (10) 10/326 (8)

Starc 24–1–79–3; Hazlewood 30.5–10–89–6; Mennie 28–5–85–1; Lyon 17–2–57–0; Smith 1–0–5–0.

Umpires: Aleem Dar *(Pakistan)* (107) and R. A. Kettleborough *(England)* (40).
Third umpire: N. J. Llong *(England)*.   Referee: A. J. Pycroft *(Zimbabwe)* (50).

Close of play: first day, South Africa 171–5 (Bavuma 38, de Kock 28); second day, no play; third day, Australia 121–2 (Khawaja 56, Smith 18).

Test No. 2233/94 (A794, SA405)
AUSTRALIA v SOUTH AFRICA 2016–17 (3rd Test)

At Adelaide Oval on 24, 25, 26, 27 November, 2016 (day/night).
Toss: South Africa.   Result: AUSTRALIA WON BY SEVEN WICKETS.
Debuts: Australia – P. S. P. Handscomb, N. J. Maddinson, M. T. Renshaw. South Africa – T. Shamsi.
Man of the Match: U. T. Khawaja.   Man of the Series: V. D. Philander.

Desperate to avoid a sixth successive defeat, Australia's selectors blooded three new batsmen, bringing the number of players used in the three-match series to 19, an Australian record. Against the odds, the new-look team won just as Adelaide's floodlights started to kick in on the fourth day. Two of the debutants were in at the end, the first such occurrence since September 1880 – in the first Test played in England – when Frank Penn and W. G. Grace finished the job against Australia at The Oval. Once Starc removed Elgar in the seventh over Australia rarely ceded control, although there was a bravura century from du Plessis, who entered at 44 for three. Hazlewood led a vastly improved bowling performance, in which the recalled Bird did well as the back-up seamer. The biggest stand du Plessis could muster was 51 with Cook, who when four had almost reached the boundary before the Starc delivery which had him lbw was deemed a no-ball. Pushed up to open, Khawaja dominated the reply, batting 15 minutes short of eight hours; the only obvious blemish was when he ran Smith out. Starc knuckled down, and the lead grew from inconsequential to an imposing 124. South Africa's second innings was derailed by Lyon, who grabbed two wickets in six balls at the end of the third day, after taking two for 241 in the first two Tests. Cook was last out after completing his second Test hundred, but Australia needed only 127 for their second comfortable victory in two pink-ball Tests at Adelaide.

South Africa

S. C. Cook c Smith b Starc	40	– b Starc	104
D. Elgar c Khawaja b Starc	5	– c Smith b Starc	0
H. M. Amla c Renshaw b Hazlewood	5	– c Wade b Hazlewood	45
J-P. Duminy c Wade b Hazlewood	5	– b Lyon	26
*F. du Plessis not out	118	– c Handscomb b Starc	12
T. Bavuma c Wade b Bird	8	– c Smith b Lyon	21
†Q. de Kock c Wade b Hazlewood	24	– (8) lbw b Bird	5
V. D. Philander c Wade b Hazlewood	4	– (9) lbw b Starc	17
K. J. Abbott lbw b Bird	17	– (7) lbw b Lyon	0
K. Rabada st Wade b Lyon	1	– c Wade b Hazlewood	7
T. Shamsi not out	18	– not out	0
B 3, lb 8, w 2, nb 1	14	Lb 10, nb 3	13
(9 wkts dec, 76 overs)	259	(85.2 overs)	250

1/12 (2) 2/36 (3) 3/44 (4) 4/95 (1) 5/117 (6)   1/1 (2) 2/82 (3) 3/131 (4) 4/154 (5) 5/190 (6)
6/149 (7) 7/161 (8) 8/215 (9) 9/220 (10)   6/194 (7) 7/201 (8) 8/235 (9) 9/250 (10) 10/250 (1)

Starc 23–5–78–2; Hazlewood 22–5–68–4; Bird 16–3–57–2; Lyon 15–1–45–1. *Second innings*—Starc 23.2–5–80–4; Hazlewood 20–8–41–2; Bird 20–3–54–1; Lyon 21–4–60–3; Warner 1–0–5–0.

Australia

U. T. Khawaja lbw b Philander	145	– (3) lbw b Shamsi	0
M. T. Renshaw c Elgar b Abbott	10	– (1) not out	34
D. A. Warner c Elgar b Abbott	11	– (2) run out (Bavuma/de Kock)	47
*S. P. D. Smith run out (Philander/de Kock)	59	– c de Kock b Abbott	40
P. S. P. Handscomb b Abbott	54	– not out	1
N. J. Maddinson b Rabada	0		
†M. S. Wade c de Kock b Philander	4		
M. A. Starc c and b Rabada	53		
J. R. Hazlewood not out	11		
N. M. Lyon c Amla b Shamsi	13		
J. M. Bird c du Plessis b Rabada	6		
B 3, lb 9, w 2, nb 3	17	Lb 4, nb 1	5
(121.1 overs)	383	(3 wkts, 40.5 overs)	127

1/19 (2) 2/37 (3) 3/174 (4) 4/273 (5) 5/277 (6)   1/64 (2) 2/64 (3) 3/125 (4)
6/283 (7) 7/327 (1) 8/357 (8) 9/370 (10) 10/383 (11)

Philander 29–5–100–2; Abbott 29–11–49–3; Rabada 25.1–4–84–3; Shamsi 29–4–101–1; Duminy 6–0–25–0; Elgar 2–0–11–0; Bavuma 1–0–1–0. *Second innings*—Abbott 10–2–26–1; Philander 7–2–20–0; Rabada 9–4–28–0; Shamsi 14.5–4–49–1.

Umpires: R. A. Kettleborough *(England)* (41) and N. J. Llong *(England)* (39).
Third umpire: Aleem Dar *(Pakistan)*.   Referee: A. J. Pycroft *(Zimbabwe)* (51).

Close of play: first day, Australia 14–0 (Khawaja 3, Renshaw 8); second day, Australia 307–6 (Khawaja 138, Starc 16); third day, South Africa 194–6 (Cook 81, de Kock 0).

INDIA v ENGLAND 2016–17 (1st Test)

At Saurashtra C. A. Stadium, Rajkot, on 9, 10, 11, 12, 13 November, 2016.
Toss: England.   Result: DRAWN.
Debuts: England – H. Hameed.
Man of the Match: M. M. Ali.

India had steamrollered the opposition in 12 of their previous 13 home Tests (the other was rain-affected), climbing to No. 1 in the rankings on the back of Ashwin's own rise to the top of the bowling table. But England responded in typically inconsistent fashion: not long after surrendering to Bangladesh, they controlled this match from the first afternoon. By the end India were simply grateful to survive. Root, Ali and Stokes reeled off hundreds (the only other time England had three in an innings in India was at Kanpur in 1961–62). Then England's spinners, outbowled in Bangladesh, improved markedly, taking 13 wickets (Broad, in his 100th Test, managed one). Rashid outdid Ashwin – who conceded 230 runs – by seven wickets to three. But the most outstanding performance among the four British Asians (the first time so many had represented England in a Test) came from the Lancashire opener Haseeb Hameed, who made one of the most dazzling debuts for England – perhaps since K. S. Ranjitsinhji, who had attended school in Rajkot, India's 23rd Test venue. At 19, Hameed was only England's sixth teenage cap, and his second-innings 82 came in a first-wicket stand of 180 with Cook, the first visiting batsman to make nine Test centuries in Asia. For India, Vijay and Pujara added 209, but they needed Ashwin's 70 to get within touching distance of England's 537. In the second innings, with 53 overs to survive, they dipped alarmingly to 132 for six before Kohli and Jadeja stopped the rot.

England

*A. N. Cook lbw b Jadeja	21	– c Jadeja b Ashwin		130
H. Hameed lbw b Ashwin	31	– c and b Mishra		82
J. E. Root c and b Yadav	124	– c Saha b Mishra		4
B. M. Duckett c Rahane b Ashwin	13			
M. M. Ali b Mohammed Shami	117			
B. A. Stokes c Saha b Yadav	128	– (4) not out		29
†J. M. Bairstow c Saha b Mohammed Shami	46			
C. R. Woakes c Saha b Jadeja	4			
A. U. Rashid c Yadav b Jadeja	5			
Z. S. Ansari lbw b Mishra	32			
S. C. J. Broad not out	6			
B 5, lb 4, nb 1	10	B 11, lb 3, nb 1		15
(159.3 overs)	537	(3 wkts dec, 75.3 overs)		260

1/47 (1) 2/76 (2) 3/102 (4) 4/281 (3) 5/343 (5)   1/180 (2) 2/192 (3) 3/260 (1)
6/442 (7) 7/451 (8) 8/465 (9) 9/517 (6) 10/537 (10)

Mohammed Shami 28.1–5–65–2; Yadav 31.5–3–112–2; Ashwin 46–3–167–2; Jadeja 30–4–86–3; Mishra 23.3–3–98–1.
Second innings—Mohammed Shami 11–1–29–0; Jadeja 15–1–47–0; Ashwin 23.3–4–63–1; Yadav 13–2–47–0; Mishra 13–0–60–2.

India

M. Vijay c Hameed b Rashid	126	– c Hameed b Rashid		31
G. Gambhir lbw b Broad	29	– c Root b Woakes		0
C. A. Pujara c Cook b Stokes	124	– lbw b Rashid		18
*V. Kohli hit wkt b Rashid	40	– not out		49
A. Mishra c Hameed b Ansari	0			
A. M. Rahane b Ansari	13	– (5) b Ali		1
R. Ashwin c Ansari b Ali	70	– (6) c Root b Ansari		32
†W. P. Saha c Bairstow b Ali	35	– (7) c and b Rashid		9
R. A. Jadeja c Hameed b Rashid	12	– (8) not out		32
U. T. Yadav c Stokes b Rashid	5			
Mohammed Shami not out	8			
B 23, lb 2, w 1	26			
(162 overs)	488	(6 wkts, 52.3 overs)		172

1/68 (2) 2/277 (3) 3/318 (1) 4/319 (5) 5/349 (6)   1/0 (2) 2/47 (3) 3/68 (1)
6/361 (4) 7/425 (8) 8/449 (9) 9/459 (10) 10/488 (7)   4/71 (5) 5/118 (6) 6/132 (7)

Broad 29–9–78–1; Woakes 31–6–57–0; Ali 31–7–85–2; Ansari 23–1–77–2; Rashid 31–1–114–4; Stokes 17–2–52–1.
Second innings—Broad 3–2–8–0; Woakes 4–1–6–1; Ansari 8–1–41–1; Ali 19–5–47–1; Rashid 14.3–1–64–3; Stokes 2–1–1–0; Root 2–0–5–0.

Umpires: H. D. P. K. Dharmasena *(Sri Lanka)* (42) and C. B. Gaffaney *(New Zealand)* (11).
    Third umpire: R. J. Tucker *(Australia)*.   Referee: R. S. Madugalle *(Sri Lanka)* (170).

Close of play: first day, England 311–4 (Ali 99, Stokes 19); second day, India 63–0 (Vijay 25, Gambhir 28); third day, India 319–4 (Kohli 26); fourth day, England 114–0 (Cook 46, Hameed 52).

Test No. 2235/114 (I504, E980)

INDIA v ENGLAND 2016–17 (2nd Test)

At Andhra C. A. Stadium, Visakhapatnam, on 17, 18, 19, 20, 21 November, 2016.
Toss: India. Result: INDIA WON BY 246 RUNS.
Debuts: India – J. Yadav.
Man of the Match: V. Kohli.

Test cricket came to the verdant hills of coastal Visakhapatnam – India's 24th Test venue, and the third new one in as many matches – but there was a distinct sense of familiarity about proceedings. They followed a template established over four years of home dominance: win the toss, compile a formidable total, then let the spinners loose on a helpful pitch. England were powerless to escape. Kohli loomed large throughout his 50th Test, starting by getting in the ear of the groundsman, after grass on the pitch had displeased him in Rajkot. Here, the only grass – imported from St Lucia – was on the outfield, and it was too lush to aid England's quest for significant reverse swing. Kohli made his 14th Test century, and ended up with 248 runs, two more than India's margin of victory. Ashwin picked up eight wickets, including his 22nd five-for. England paid dearly for a horror spell either side of tea on the second day, when they crashed to 80 for five, the procession starting when Cook's off stump was snapped like a breadstick by Mohammed Shami. The end came when Anderson was trapped by the debutant off-spinner Jayant Yadav on review 20 minutes after lunch on the fifth day; he was the first Englishman to bag a king pair since Ernie Hayes in Cape Town in 1905–06. It was also his side's tenth lbw in the match, another England record. More importantly, they had been bowled out for 158 in the 98th over, chasing a theoretical 405.

India

M. Vijay c Stokes b Anderson	20	– c Root b Broad	3
K. L. Rahul c Stokes b Broad	0	– c Bairstow b Broad	10
C. A. Pujara c Bairstow b Anderson	119	– b Anderson	1
*V. Kohli c Stokes b Ali	167	– c Stokes b Rashid	81
A. M. Rahane c Bairstow b Anderson	23	– c Cook b Broad	26
R. Ashwin c Bairstow b Stokes	58	– c Bairstow b Broad	7
†W. P. Saha lbw b Ali	3	– lbw b Rashid	2
R. A. Jadeja lbw b Ali	0	– c Ali b Rashid	14
J. Yadav c Anderson b Rashid	35	– not out	27
U. T. Yadav c Ali b Rashid	13	– c Bairstow b Rashid	0
Mohammed Shami not out	7	– st Bairstow b Ali	19
B 4, lb 5, w 1	10	B 5, lb 8, w 1	14
(129.4 overs)	455	(63.1 overs)	204

1/6 (2) 2/22 (1) 3/248 (3) 4/316 (5) 5/351 (4) 6/363 (7) 7/363 (8) 8/427 (6) 9/440 (9) 10/455 (10)
1/16 (1) 2/17 (2) 3/40 (3) 4/117 (5) 5/127 (6) 6/130 (7) 7/151 (4) 8/162 (8) 9/162 (10) 10/204 (11)

Anderson 20–3–62–3; Broad 16–2–49–1; Stokes 20–4–73–1; Ansari 12–1–45–0; Rashid 34.4–2–110–2; Ali 25–1–98–3; Root 2–0–9–0. *Second innings*—Anderson 15–3–33–1; Broad 14–5–33–4; Rashid 24–3–82–4; Stokes 7–0–34–0; Ali 3.1–1–9–1.

England

*A. N. Cook b Mohammed Shami	2	– lbw b Jadeja	54
H. Hameed run out (J. Yadav/Saha)	13	– lbw b Ashwin	25
J. E. Root c U. T. Yadav b Ashwin	53	– lbw b Mohammed Shami	25
B. M. Duckett b Ashwin	5	– c Saha b Ashwin	0
M. M. Ali lbw b J. Yadav	1	– c Kohli b Jadeja	2
B. A. Stokes lbw b Ashwin	70	– b J. Yadav	6
†J. M. Bairstow b U. T. Yadav	53	– not out	34
A. U. Rashid not out	32	– c Saha b Mohammed Shami	4
Z. S. Ansari lbw b Jadeja	4	– b Ashwin	0
S. C. J. Broad lbw b Ashwin	13	– lbw b J. Yadav	5
J. M. Anderson lbw b Ashwin	0	– lbw b J. Yadav	0
B 6, lb 3	9	Lb 3	3
(102.5 overs)	255	(97.3 overs)	158

1/4 (1) 2/51 (2) 3/72 (4) 4/79 (3) 5/80 (5) 6/190 (7) 7/225 (6) 8/234 (9) 9/255 (10) 10/255 (11)
1/75 (2) 2/87 (1) 3/92 (4) 4/101 (5) 5/115 (6) 6/115 (3) 7/129 (8) 8/143 (9) 9/158 (10) 10/158 (11)

Mohammed Shami 14–5–28–1; U. T. Yadav 18–2–56–1; Jadeja 29–10–57–1; Ashwin 29.5–6–67–5; J. Yadav 12–3–38–1. *Second innings*—Mohammed Shami 14–3–30–2; U. T. Yadav 8–3–8–0; Ashwin 30–11–52–3; Jadeja 34–14–35–2; J. Yadav 11.3–4–30–3.

Umpires: H. D. P. K. Dharmasena *(Sri Lanka)* (43) and R. J. Tucker *(Australia)* (50).
Third umpire: C. B. Gaffaney *(New Zealand)*. Referee: R. S. Madugalle *(Sri Lanka)* (171).

Close of play: first day, India 317–4 (Kohli 151, Ashwin 1); second day, England 103–5 (Stokes 12, Bairstow 12); third day, India 98–3 (Kohli 56, Rahane 22); fourth day, England 87–2 (Root 5).

INDIA v ENGLAND 2016–17 (3rd Test)

At Punjab C. A. Stadium, Mohali, Chandigarh, on 26, 27, 28, 29 November, 2016.
Toss: England.   Result: INDIA WON BY EIGHT WICKETS.
Debuts: India – K. K. Nair.
Man of the Match: R. A. Jadeja.

There was a brief period on the second afternoon, as India lost three for eight, when England stirred, but the rebellion was quickly crushed. In this most orderly of Indian cities, Kohli's men ended up taking a bloodless route to a four-day victory – and a 2–0 lead. To compound English fears that the tour was beginning to unravel, a snorter from Umesh Yadav broke Hameed's left little finger; he played a brave innings from No. 8 on the fourth day. But his determination exposed what had come before. On the first morning England limped to lunch at 92 for four before Bairstow and Buttler, picked as a specialist batsman for his first Test in over a year, added 69 – but Bairstow fell lbw on review for 89, having been dropped behind the previous ball, and England scrambled to 283. That looked adequate when India dipped to 204 for six, but Jadeja shared stands of 97 with Ashwin and 80 with Jayant Yadav, as the score doubled. Umesh was Bairstow's 68th Test dismissal of 2016, the most by a wicketkeeper in a calendar year. An innings defeat loomed when England crashed to 107 for six, but Root's solid 78 and Hameed's bravery (his unbeaten 59 included a six off Ashwin) at least averted that. Parthiv Patel, who had replaced the injured Saha behind the stumps for his first Test in eight years (he had missed 83, an Indian record), marked his comeback with an unbeaten 67 as India strolled home.

England

*A. N. Cook c Patel b Ashwin	27	– b Ashwin	12
H. Hameed c Rahane b U. T. Yadav	9	– (8) not out	59
J. E. Root lbw b J. Yadav	15	– (2) c Rahane b Jadeja	78
M. M. Ali c Vijay b Mohammed Shami	16	– (3) c J. Yadav b Ashwin	5
†J. M. Bairstow lbw b J. Yadav	89	– (4) c Patel b J. Yadav	15
B. A. Stokes st Patel b Jadeja	29	– (5) lbw b Ashwin	5
J. C. Buttler c Kohli b Jadeja	43	– c Jadeja b J. Yadav	18
C. R. Woakes b U. T. Yadav	25	– (9) c Patel b Mohammed Shami	30
A. U. Rashid c Patel b Mohammed Shami	4	– (10) c U. T. Yadav b Mohammed Shami	0
G. J. Batty lbw b Mohammed Shami	1	– (6) lbw b Jadeja	0
J. M. Anderson not out	13	– run out (Jadeja/Ashwin)	5
B 8, lb 3, nb 1	12	B 8, lb 1	9
(93.5 overs)	283	(90.2 overs)	236

1/32 (2) 2/51 (3) 3/51 (1) 4/87 (4) 5/144 (6)
6/213 (7) 7/258 (5) 8/266 (8) 9/268 (9) 10/283 (10)

1/27 (1) 2/39 (3) 3/70 (4) 4/78 (5) 5/78 (6)
6/107 (7) 7/152 (2) 8/195 (9) 9/195 (10) 10/236 (11)

Mohammed Shami 21.5–5–63–3; U. T. Yadav 16–4–58–2; J. Yadav 15–5–49–2; Ashwin 18–1–43–1; Jadeja 23–4–59–2. *Second innings*—Mohammed Shami 14–3–37–2; U. T. Yadav 8–3–26–0; Ashwin 26.2–4–81–3; Jadeja 30–12–62–2; J. Yadav 12–2–21–2.

India

M. Vijay c Bairstow b Stokes	12	– c Root b Woakes	0
†P. A. Patel lbw b Rashid	42	– not out	67
C. A. Pujara c Woakes b Rashid	51	– c Root b Rashid	25
*V. Kohli c Bairstow b Stokes	62	– not out	6
A. M. Rahane lbw b Rashid	0		
K. K. Nair run out (Buttler)	4		
R. Ashwin c Buttler b Stokes	72		
R. A. Jadeja c Woakes b Rashid	90		
J. Yadav c Ali b Stokes	55		
U. T. Yadav c Bairstow b Stokes	12		
Mohammed Shami not out	1		
B 8, lb 4, w 3, nb 1	16	B 4, lb 1, nb 1	6
(138.2 overs)	417	(2 wkts, 20.2 overs)	104

1/39 (1) 2/73 (2) 3/148 (3) 4/152 (5) 5/156 (6)
6/204 (4) 7/301 (7) 8/381 (8) 9/414 (9) 10/417 (10)

1/7 (1) 2/88 (3)

Anderson 21–4–48–0; Woakes 24–7–86–0; Ali 13–1–33–0; Rashid 38–6–118–4; Stokes 26.2–5–73–5; Batty 16–0–47–0. *Second innings*—Anderson 3–2–8–0; Woakes 2–0–16–1; Rashid 5–0–28–1; Stokes 4–0–16–0; Ali 3–0–13–0; Batty 3.2–0–18–0.

Umpires: M. Erasmus *(South Africa)* (37) and C. B. Gaffaney *(New Zealand)* (12).
Third umpire: H. D. P. K. Dharmasena *(Sri Lanka).*   Referee: R. S. Madugalle *(Sri Lanka)* (172).

Close of play: first day, England 268–8 (Rashid 4, Batty 0); second day, India 271–6 (Ashwin 57, Jadeja 31); third day, England 78–4 (Root 36, Batty 0).

INDIA v ENGLAND 2016-17 (4th Test)

At Wankhede Stadium, Mumbai, on 8, 9, 10, 11, 12 December, 2016.
Toss: England.   Result: **INDIA WON BY AN INNINGS AND 36 RUNS.**
Debuts: England – K. K. Jennings.
Man of the Match: V. Kohli.

A masterclass from Kohli, who made a career-best 235, India's highest score against England (for eight days), carried his side to a series-clinching third victory. He put on 116 for the third wicket with Pujara, who also made a hundred, and 241 for the eighth, an Indian record, with Jayant Yadav, whose maiden century was India's first from No. 9. Yadav edged Ali behind when 28, but was not given out; England had no reviews left (non-striker Kohli gleefully performed the "T" signal). These unexpected riches transformed the game: India had looked set merely to match England's first innings, but eventually dwarfed it by 231. The tall left-hander Keaton Jennings had started by becoming only the fourth England player to make a century on his first day of Test cricket. Cook helped him add 99 before he was stumped, after becoming the first to amass 2,000 Test runs against India. After reaching 230 for two, Ali and Jennings fell in three balls from Ashwin, and it needed Buttler's mature 76 to haul England to 400. The second innings was more predictable. Jennings became the first to follow a debut century with a golden duck, and Root's sparkling 77 was a lone beacon as Ashwin extracted six for seven in 37 balls, to finish with 12 in the match.

England

*A. N. Cook st Patel b Jadeja	46	– lbw b Jadeja	18
K. K. Jennings c Pujara b Ashwin	112	– lbw b Bhuvneshwar Kumar	0
J. E. Root c Kohli b Ashwin	21	– lbw b J. Yadav	77
M. M. Ali c Nair b Ashwin	50	– c Vijay b Jadeja	0
†J. M. Bairstow c U. T. Yadav b Ashwin	14	– lbw b Ashwin	51
B. A. Stokes c Kohli b Ashwin	31	– c Vijay b Ashwin	18
J. C. Buttler b Jadeja	76	– (8) not out	6
C. R. Woakes c Patel b Jadeja	11	– (9) b Ashwin	0
A. U. Rashid b Jadeja	4	– (10) c Rahul b Ashwin	2
J. T. Ball c Patel b Ashwin	31	– (7) c Patel b Ashwin	2
J. M. Anderson not out	0	– c U. T. Yadav b Ashwin	2
B 1, lb 2, nb 1	4	B 15, lb 2, nb 2	19
(130.1 overs)	400	(55.3 overs)	195

1/99 (1) 2/136 (3) 3/230 (4) 4/230 (2) 5/249 (5)   1/1 (2) 2/43 (1) 3/49 (4) 4/141 (3) 5/180 (6)
6/297 (6) 7/320 (8) 8/334 (9) 9/388 (10) 10/400 (7)   6/182 (7) 7/185 (5) 8/189 (9) 9/193 (10) 10/195 (11)

Bhuvneshwar Kumar 13–0–49–0; U. T. Yadav 11–2–38–0; Ashwin 44–4–112–6; J. Yadav 25–3–89–0; Jadeja 37.1–5–109–4.
Second innings—Bhuvneshwar Kumar 4–1–11–1; U. T. Yadav 3–0–10–0; Jadeja 22–3–63–2; Ashwin 20.3–3–55–6; J. Yadav 6–0–39–1.

India

K. L. Rahul b Ali	24
M. Vijay c and b Rashid	136
C. A. Pujara b Ball	47
*V. Kohli c Anderson b Woakes	235
K. K. Nair lbw b Ali	13
†P. A. Patel c Bairstow b Root	15
R. Ashwin c Jennings b Root	0
R. A. Jadeja c Buttler b Rashid	25
J. Yadav st Bairstow b Rashid	104
Bhuvneshwar Kumar c Woakes b Rashid	9
U. T. Yadav not out	7
B 5, lb 8, w 3	16
(182.3 overs)	631

1/39 (1) 2/146 (3) 3/262 (2) 4/279 (5) 5/305 (6) 6/307 (7)
7/364 (8) 8/605 (9) 9/615 (4) 10/631 (10)

Anderson 20–5–63–0; Woakes 16–2–79–1; Ali 53–5–174–2; Rashid 55.3–5–192–4; Ball 18–5–47–1; Stokes 10–2–32–0; Root 10–2–31–2.

Umpires: B. N. J. Oxenford *(Australia)* (35), P. R. Reiffel *(Australia)* (28) and M. Erasmus *(South Africa)* (38).
Third umpire: M. Erasmus *(South Africa)* and C. Shamshuddin *(India)*. Referee: J. J. Crowe *(New Zealand)* (80).
Erasmus replaced Reiffel when he was injured on the first day, and Shamshuddin took over as third umpire.

Close of play: first day, England 288–5 (Stokes 25, Buttler 18); second day, India 146–1 (Vijay 70, Pujara 47); third day, India 451–7 (Kohli 147, J. Yadav 30); fourth day, England 182–6 (Bairstow 50).

INDIA v ENGLAND 2016-17 (5th Test)

At M. A. Chidambaram Stadium, Chepauk, Chennai, on 16, 17, 18, 19, 20 December, 2016.
Toss: England.   Result: INDIA WON BY AN INNINGS AND 75 RUNS.
Debuts: England – L. A. Dawson.
Man of the Match: K. K. Nair.   Man of the Series: V. Kohli.

Years from now, England will still be wondering how they lost. They kept Ashwin to one for 207 on his home ground, and dismissed Pujara and Kohli for 31 between them. Yet they ended up with several grim records: no team had lost by an innings after scoring more than 477, nor conceded more in an innings against India. Before this series, only two teams had suffered innings defeats after reaching 400 first up; England had now done it twice in succession (Pakistan would follow suit a week later at Melbourne). Things had looked rosier while Ali was whisking his fourth century of the year. Root made 88 before a review showed a faint edge, and later Liam Dawson, making his debut, and Rashid swelled the total with sixties. Rahul and Patel responded with India's first three-figure opening partnership in 18 months, before a colossal triple-century from Karun Nair, in only his third Test. He put on 161 with Rahul, who fell one short of a double-century, 181 with Ashwin, and 138 with Jadeja, during which India steamed past their 726 for nine against Sri Lanka in Mumbai in 2009–10. Nair hit 32 fours and four sixes; his third hundred took only 75 balls, as he became the first to pass 200 and 300 in the same session since England's Wally Hammond at Auckland in 1932–33. England could not survive the final day, despite an opening stand of 103; Jadeja's career-best gave India four wins in a series against England for the first time.

England

*A. N. Cook c Kohli b Jadeja	10	– c Rahul b Jadeja	49
K. K. Jennings c Patel b Sharma	1	– c and b Jadeja	54
J. E. Root c Patel b Jadeja	88	– lbw b Jadeja	6
M. M. Ali c Jadeja b Yadav	146	– c Ashwin b Jadeja	44
†J. M. Bairstow c Rahul b Jadeja	49	– c Jadeja b Sharma	1
B. A. Stokes c Patel b Ashwin	6	– c Nair b Jadeja	23
J. C. Buttler lbw b Sharma	5	– not out	6
L. A. Dawson not out	66	– b Mishra	0
A. U. Rashid c Patel b Yadav	60	– c Jadeja b Yadav	2
S. C. J. Broad run out (Rahul/Patel)	19	– c Pujara b Jadeja	1
J. T. Ball b Mishra	12	– c Nair b Jadeja	0
B 4, lb 5, w 1, p 5	15	B 12, lb 8, w 1	21
(157.2 overs)	477	(88 overs)	207

1/7 (2) 2/21 (1) 3/167 (3) 4/253 (5) 5/287 (6)   1/103 (1) 2/110 (2) 3/126 (3) 4/129 (5) 5/192 (4)
6/300 (7) 7/321 (4) 8/429 (9) 9/455 (10) 10/477 (11)   6/193 (6) 7/196 (8) 8/200 (9) 9/207 (10) 10/207 (11)

Yadav 21–3–73–2; Sharma 21–6–42–2; Jadeja 45–9–106–3; Ashwin 44–3–151–1; Mishra 25.2–5–87–1; Nair 1–0–4–0. *Second innings*—Sharma 10–2–17–1; Ashwin 25–6–56–0; Jadeja 25–5–48–7; Yadav 14–1–36–1; Mishra 14–4–30–1.

India

K. L. Rahul c Buttler b Rashid	199
†P. A. Patel c Buttler b Ali	71
C. A. Pujara c Cook b Stokes	16
*V. Kohli c Jennings b Broad	15
K. K. Nair not out	303
M. Vijay lbw b Dawson	29
R. Ashwin c Buttler b Broad	67
R. A. Jadeja c Ball b Dawson	51
U. T. Yadav not out	1
B 2, lb 4, w 1	7
(7 wkts dec, 190.4 overs)	759

1/152 (2) 2/181 (3) 3/211 (4) 4/372 (1)
5/435 (6) 6/616 (7) 7/754 (8)

A. Mishra and I. Sharma did not bat.

Broad 27–6–80–2; Ball 23–2–93–0; Ali 41–1–190–1; Stokes 20–2–76–1; Rashid 29.4–1–153–1; Dawson 43–4–129–2; Root 2–0–12–0; Jennings 5–1–20–0.

Umpires: M. Erasmus *(South Africa)* (39) and S. D. Fry *(Australia)* (4).
Third umpire: B. N. J. Oxenford *(Australia)*.   Referee: J. J. Crowe *(New Zealand)* (81).

Close of play: first day, England 284-4 (Ali 120, Stokes 5); second day, India 60-0 (Rahul 30, Patel 28); third day, India 391-4 (Nair 71, Vijay 17); fourth day, England 12-0 (Cook 3, Jennings 9).

Test No. 2239/54 (NZ416, P403)

NEW ZEALAND v PAKISTAN 2016–17 (1st Test)

At Hagley Oval, Christchurch, on 17 *(no play)*, 18, 19, 20 November, 2016.
Toss: New Zealand.   Result: NEW ZEALAND WON BY EIGHT WICKETS.
Debuts: New Zealand – C. de Grandhomme, J. A. Raval.
Man of the Match: C. de Grandhomme.

Colin de Grandhomme had to wait for his debut to begin, as the first day was washed out. But it did not take him long to make an impression: his 15th ball uprooted Azhar Ali's off stump. His medium-paced swing and seam benefited from a thatch of grass, and the batsmen had few answers. Pakistan were dismissed for 133 by tea; Misbah-ul-Haq top-scored with 31, and the Zimbabwe-born de Grandhomme finished with six for 41, the best debut figures by a New Zealander, eclipsing Alex Moir's six for 155 against England at Christchurch in 1950–51. Jeet Raval, the other debutant, got in on the act, snaffling three catches in the cordon; in the second innings he added a fourth, at deep midwicket, a record for a New Zealand fielder on debut. He also anchored the reply with a disciplined 55. The pitch remained lively, so he left where possible, collecting just one single between cover and point. New Zealand went from 104 for three by the second-day close to 200 all out before lunch on the third. But Pakistan's batsmen failed again, dribbling to 80 for three after 50 overs, and were bundled out for 171 on the fourth morning. Wagner passed 100 wickets in his 26th Test, one more than the quickest New Zealander to the mark, Richard Hadlee. Yasir Shah failed to strike in either innings, the first blank of his 20-Test career, while fellow leg-spinner Todd Astle bowled just four overs on his return to Test cricket.

Pakistan

Sami Aslam c Raval b Southee	19	– c Watling b de Grandhomme	7
Azhar Ali b de Grandhomme	15	– b Boult	31
Babar Azam c Taylor b de Grandhomme	7	– c Watling b Wagner	29
Younis Khan c Raval b de Grandhomme	2	– c Watling b Wagner	1
*Misbah-ul-Haq c Williamson b Boult	31	– c Boult b Southee	13
Asad Shafiq c Raval b de Grandhomme	16	– c Raval b Wagner	17
†Sarfraz Ahmed c Astle b Southee	7	– b Boult	2
Mohammad Amir b Boult	3	– c Astle b Boult	6
Sohail Khan c Latham b de Grandhomme	9	– c de Grandhomme b Southee	40
Yasir Shah not out	4	– not out	6
Rahat Ali c Watling b de Grandhomme	0	– c Latham b Southee	2
B 8, lb 12	20	B 5, lb 7, w 5	17
(55.5 overs)	133	(78.4 overs)	171

1/31 (2) 2/53 (1) 3/53 (3) 4/56 (4) 5/88 (6)   1/21 (1) 2/58 (3) 3/64 (4) 4/93 (5) 5/93 (2) 6/95 (7)
6/101 (7) 7/114 (8) 8/129 (9) 9/129 (5) 10/133 (11)   7/105 (8) 8/158 (9) 9/166 (6) 10/171 (11)

Southee 19–11–20–2; Boult 16–5–39–2; de Grandhomme 15.5–5–41–6; Wagner 5–0–13–0. *Second innings*—Boult 17–5–37–3; Southee 23.4–10–53–3; de Grandhomme 14–4–23–1; Wagner 20–6–34–3; Astle 4–0–12–0.

New Zealand

T. W. M. Latham lbw b Mohammad Amir	1	– c Asad Shafiq b Mohammad Amir	9
J. A. Raval c Sami Aslam b Mohammad Amir	55	– not out	36
*K. S. Williamson c Sami Aslam b Sohail Khan	4	– c Sami Aslam b Azhar Ali	61
L. R. P. L. Taylor c Sarfraz Ahmed b Rahat Ali	11		
H. M. Nicholls lbw b Sohail Khan	30	– (4) not out	0
C. de Grandhomme c Rahat Ali b Sohail Khan	29		
†B-J. Watling c Younis Khan b Rahat Ali	18		
T. D. Astle c Asad Shafiq b Rahat Ali	0		
T. G. Southee c Sarfraz Ahmed b Mohammad Amir	22		
N. Wagner c Asad Shafiq b Rahat Ali	21		
T. A. Boult not out	3		
Lb 1, w 1, nb 4	6	Nb 2	2
(59.5 overs)	200	(2 wkts, 31.3 overs)	108

1/6 (1) 2/15 (3) 3/40 (4) 4/105 (5) 5/109 (2)   1/19 (1) 2/104 (3)
6/146 (6) 7/146 (8) 8/171 (7) 9/177 (9) 10/200 (10)

Mohammad Amir 18–4–43–3; Sohail Khan 22–5–78–3; Rahat Ali 15.5–2–62–4; Yasir Shah 4–0–16–0. *Second innings*—Mohammad Amir 7–2–12–1; Sohail Khan 6–1–21–0; Rahat Ali 6–0–24–0; Yasir Shah 9.3–1–45–0; Azhar Ali 3–1–6–1.

Umpires: I. J. Gould *(England)* (56) and S. Ravi *(India)* (16).
Third umpire: S. D. Fry *(Australia)*.   Referee: R. B. Richardson *(West Indies)* (5).

Close of play: first day, no play; second day, New Zealand 104–3 (Raval 55, Nicholls 29); third day, Pakistan 129–7 (Asad Shafiq 6, Sohail Khan 22).

Test No. 2240/55 (NZ417, P404)

NEW ZEALAND v PAKISTAN 2016–17 (2nd Test)

At Seddon Park, Hamilton, on 25, 26, 27, 28, 29 November, 2016.
Toss: Pakistan.   Result: NEW ZEALAND WON BY 138 RUNS.
Debuts: Pakistan – Mohammad Rizwan.
Man of the Match: T. G. Southee.

Needing 369 to square the series, Pakistan looked immune from defeat at tea on the final day, at 158 for one. But they lost nine for 71 after the interval, the worst last-session collapse in history, as New Zealand won a series against these opponents for the first time since 1984–85. Asad Shafiq fell for his fifth duck in 13 innings, then Southee removed top-scorer Sami Aslam for 91, and trapped Younis Khan lbw on review, failing to offer a shot. As the gloom gathered and time grew short, Wagner ended the match with three for none in six balls. New Zealand had done well to make 271 in their first innings, on a verdant pitch that encouraged Pakistan to omit Yasir Shah. The first day was limited to 21 overs; Aslam again dropped Raval at first slip from Mohammad Amir's third ball of the match, but caught Latham from the sixth. Raval made 55; only Latham and last man Wagner failed to reach double figures. Pakistan were rescued from 51 for five by Babar Azam's undefeated 90; Southee, recalled because Trent Boult had a knee niggle, took six wickets. On the fourth day, Latham's 80 and Taylor's battling century lifted New Zealand; he almost missed this Test because of a growth on his left eye, for which he was scheduled to have surgery, but instead passed 50 for the first time in 12 Test innings. Azhar Ali captained Pakistan, as Misbah-ul-Haq was suspended for his side's slow over-rate at Christchurch.

New Zealand

J. A. Raval c Mohammad Rizwan b Imran Khan	55	– lbw b Mohammad Amir	2
T. W. M. Latham c Sami Aslam b Mohammad Amir	0	– c Sarfraz Ahmed b Wahab Riaz	80
*K. S. Williamson c Sarfraz Ahmed b Sohail Khan	13	– c Sarfraz Ahmed b Imran Khan	42
L. R. P. L. Taylor c Sarfraz Ahmed b Sohail Khan	37	– not out	102
H. M. Nicholls c Sarfraz Ahmed b Wahab Riaz	13	– c Sarfraz Ahmed b Imran Khan	26
C. de Grandhomme c Sarfraz Ahmed b Imran Khan	37	– c Azhar Ali b Imran Khan	32
†B-J. Watling not out	49	– not out	15
M. J. Santner c Younis Khan b Sohail Khan	16		
T. G. Southee b Sohail Khan	29		
M. J. Henry c Sohail Khan b Mohammad Amir	15		
N. Wagner c Younis Khan b Imran Khan	1		
W 5, nb 1	6	Lb 6, w 6, nb 2	14
(83.4 overs)	271	(5 wkts dec, 85.3 overs)	313

1/5 (2) 2/39 (3) 3/90 (4) 4/113 (1) 5/119 (5)   1/11 (1) 2/107 (3) 3/159 (2)
6/170 (6) 7/203 (8) 8/239 (9) 9/270 (10) 10/271 (11)   4/219 (5) 5/254 (6)

Mohammad Amir 19–2–59–2; Sohail Khan 25–6–99–4; Imran Khan 20.4–5–52–3; Wahab Riaz 18–4–57–1; Azhar Ali 1–0–4–0. *Second innings*—Mohammad Amir 22–4–86–1; Sohail Khan 17–2–69–0; Imran Khan 20.3–4–76–3; Wahab Riaz 19–3–53–1; Azhar Ali 6–0–19–0; Asad Shafiq 1–0–4–0.

Pakistan

Sami Aslam c Raval b Southee	5	– c Williamson b Southee	91
*Azhar Ali c Watling b Southee	1	– b Santner	58
Babar Azam not out	90	– b Santner	16
Younis Khan c Watling b Southee	2	– (5) lbw b Southee	11
Asad Shafiq b Wagner	23	– (6) cNicholls b Henry	0
Mohammad Rizwan c Henry b Wagner	0	– (7) not out	13
†Sarfraz Ahmed c Raval b Wagner	41	– (4) run out	19
Sohail Khan c Watling b Southee	37	– c Nicholls b de Grandhomme	8
Wahab Riaz lbw b de Grandhomme	0	– (10) c Watling b Wagner	0
Mohammad Amir c Raval b Southee	5	– (9) c Watling b Wagner	0
Imran Khan c Watling b Southee	6	– c Latham b Wagner	0
B 4, lb 1, nb 1	6	B 4, lb 3, w6, nb 1	14
(67 overs)	216	(92.1 overs)	230

1/7 (1) 2/8 (2) 3/12 (4) 4/51 (5) 5/51 (6) 6/125 (7)   1/131 (2) 2/159 (3) 3/181 (1) 4/199 (4) 5/204 (6)
7/192 (8) 8/193 (9) 9/206 (10) 10/216 (11)   6/218 (5) 7/229 (8) 8/230 (9) 9/230 (10) 10/230 (11)

Southee 21–4–80–6; Henry 19–5–30–0; de Grandhomme 9–2–29–1; Wagner 14–2–59–3; Santner 4–0–13–0. *Second innings*—Southee 24–6–60–2; Henry 19–5–38–1; Wagner 20.1–4–57–3; Santner 16–2–49–2; de Grandhomme 12–5–17–1; Williamson 1–0–2–0.

Umpires: S. D. Fry *(Australia)* (5) and S. Ravi *(India)* (17).
Third umpire: I. J. Gould *(England)*.   Referee: R. B. Richardson *(West Indies)* (6).

Close of play: first day, New Zealand 77–2 (Raval 35, Taylor 29); second day, Pakistan 76–5 (Babar Azam 34, Sarfraz Ahmed 9); third day, New Zealand 0–0 (Raval 0, Latham 0); fourth day, Pakistan 1–0 (Sami Aslam 1, Azhar Ali 0).

AUSTRALIA v PAKISTAN 2016–17 (1st Test)

At Wolloongabba, Brisbane, on 15, 16, 17, 18, 19 December, 2016 (day/night).
Toss: Australia.   Result: AUSTRALIA WON BY 39 RUNS.
Debuts: none.
Man of the Match: Asad Shafiq.

During the grim, hail-interrupted fourth afternoon, the only question seemed to be how long Pakistan might survive. There was no talk of Test cricket's record run-chase. Yet Pakistan spluttered, then smashed, then crept their way within touching distance of a miracle 490. Asad Shafiq reached a superb century – his ninth from No. 6, beating Garry Sobers by one – in the final over of the fourth day's madcap three-hour night session (it lasted almost till midnight, in the Gabba's first day/night Test). Equally unexpected was the gritty support from the tail, who helped him add 229. The ninth-wicket pair came together on the final day, and they eroded the target to 41 before Starc summoned an unplayable ball at Shafiq's throat. Finally he was gone for 137, and Yasir Shah ran himself out moments later to end the epic; it was the fourth-biggest last-innings total, and the highest in Australia, beating India's 445 at Adelaide in 1977–78. Before all this Smith had shimmied to his 17th Test century, putting on 172 with Handscomb, who made his first, in his second Test. Smith was the first of six to fall for 57, but last pair Lyon and Bird ensured a healthy score. As the lights went on, Australia's pacemen reduced Pakistan to 67 for eight; only Sarfraz Ahmed's unbeaten 59 dragged the total past 100. Smith declined the follow-on, instead taking the lead close to 500. When Pakistan lost two quick wickets, a routine victory seemed assured – but it was anything but.

Australia

M. T. Renshaw c Sarfraz Ahmed b Wahab Riaz	71	– (2) c Younis Khan b Rahat Ali	6
D. A. Warner lbw b Mohammad Amir	32	– (1) c Wahab Riaz b Mohammad Amir	12
U. T. Khawaja c Misbah-ul-Haq b Yasir Shah	4	– c Misbah-ul-Haq b Rahat Ali	74
*S. P. D. Smith c Sarfraz Ahmed b Wahab Riaz	130	– c Rahat Ali b Yasir Shah	63
P. S. P. Handscomb b Wahab Riaz	105	– not out	35
N. J. Maddinson c Sarfraz Ahmed b Wahab Riaz	1	– c Babar Azam b Wahab Riaz	4
†M. S. Wade c Azhar Ali b Mohammad Amir	7	– not out	1
M. A. Starc c Asad Shafiq b Mohammad Amir	10		
J. R. Hazlewood c Asad Shafiq b Mohammad Amir	8		
N. M. Lyon c Asad Shafiq b Yasir Shah	29		
J. M. Bird not out	19		
Lb 5, w 1, nb 7	13	B 2, lb 4, nb 1	7
(130.1 overs)	429	(5 wkts dec, 39 overs)	202

1/70 (2) 2/75 (3) 3/151 (1) 4/323 (4) 5/334 (6)   1/12 (1) 2/24 (2) 3/135 (4)
6/342 (7) 7/354 (8) 8/380 (9) 9/380 (5) 10/429 (10)   4/188 (3) 5/199 (5)

Mohammad Amir 31–7–97–4; Rahat Ali 22–5–74–0; Yasir Shah 43.1–6–129–2; Wahab Riaz 26–4–89–4; Azhar Ali 8–0–35–0. *Second innings*—Mohammad Amir 8–0–37–1; Rahat Ali 10–1–40–2; Yasir Shah 10–1–45–1; Wahab Riaz 7–1–47–1; Azhar Ali 4–0–27–0.

Pakistan

Sami Aslam c Wade b Bird	22	– c Renshaw b Starc	15
Azhar Ali c Khawaja b Starc	5	– c Wade b Starc	71
Babar Azam c Smith b Hazlewood	19	– c Smith b Lyon	14
Younis Khan c Wade b Hazlewood	0	– c Smith b Lyon	65
*Misbah-ul-Haq c Renshaw b Bird	4	– c Wade b Bird	5
Asad Shafiq c Khawaja b Starc	2	– c Warner b Starc	137
†Sarfraz Ahmed not out	59	– b Starc	24
Wahab Riaz c and b Hazlewood	1	– (9) c Smith b Bird	30
Yasir Shah c Khawaja b Starc	1	– (10) run out (Smith)	33
Mohammad Amir c Wade b Bird	21	– (8) c Wade b Bird	48
Rahat Ali run out (Warner)	4	– not out	1
Lb 3, w 1	4	Lb 5, w 2	7
(55 overs)	142	(145 overs)	450

1/6 (2) 2/43 (3) 3/43 (4) 4/48 (5) 5/54 (6)   1/31 (1) 2/54 (3) 3/145 (2) 4/165 (5) 5/173 (4)
6/56 (1) 7/66 (8) 8/67 (9) 9/121 (10) 10/142 (11)   6/220 (7) 7/312 (8) 8/378 (9) 9/449 (6) 10/450 (10)

Starc 18–2–63–3; Hazlewood 14–1–22–3; Bird 12–6–23–3; Lyon 11–2–31–0. *Second innings*—Starc 38–10–119–4; Hazlewood 42–11–99–0; Bird 33–6–110–3; Lyon 29–3–108–2; Maddinson 3–0–9–0.

Umpires: I. J. Gould *(England)* (57) and R. K. Illingworth *(England)* (25).
Third umpire: S. Ravi *(India)*.   Referee: R. S. Madugalle *(Sri Lanka)* (173).

Close of play: first day, Australia 288–3 (Smith 110, Handscomb 64); second day, Pakistan 97–8 (Sarfraz Ahmed 31, Mohammad Amir 8); third day, Pakistan 70–2 (Azhar Ali 41, Younis Khan 0); fourth day, Pakistan 382–8 (Asad Shafiq 100, Yasir Shah 4).

AUSTRALIA v PAKISTAN 2016–17 (2nd Test)

At Melbourne Cricket Ground on 26, 27, 28, 29, 30 December, 2016.
Toss: Australia. Result: AUSTRALIA WON BY AN INNINGS AND 18 RUNS.
Debuts: none.
Man of the Match: S. P. D. Smith.

When the opposition declare at 443, and 141 overs have been lost to rain, and your own first innings ends on the fifth morning, you aren't meant to win. But Australia clinched the series with nearly an hour to spare. It was only the second time a side had declared and lost by an innings, after Australia themselves at Hyderabad in 2012–13. They had begun the final day 22 ahead, with Smith believing a lead of 180 would be enough. He raced from 100 to 165, while Starc clobbered seven sixes in his 84. The Lyon roared: Younis and Asad Shafiq inside-edged to short leg, while Misbah-ul-Haq's second-ball sweep picked out backward square. Masterful reverse swing from Bird and Starc secured victory: after nearly winning the unwinnable at Brisbane, Pakistan ended up abjectly losing the unlosable here. Only England (four times, including twice earlier that month) had previously lost a Test after reaching 400 batting first. It was all rather unfair on Azhar Ali, whose dogged double-century dominated Pakistan's first innings, although Sohail Khan made an unlikely 65, including four sixes off Lyon, before Hazlewood collected his 100th wicket (Wahab Riaz) in his 25th Test. Warner hit his first Test hundred at the MCG, and motored past 5,000 in all. His 144 from 143 balls, and partnership of 198 with Khawaja, put a dent in Pakistan's lead – and their confidence. Yasir Shah went at more than five an over, and conceded more than 200 for the second time in 2016.

Pakistan

Sami Aslam c Smith b Lyon	9	– b Hazlewood	2
Azhar Ali not out	205	– lbw b Hazlewood	43
Babar Azam c Smith b Hazlewood	23	– lbw b Starc	3
Younis Khan b Bird	21	– c Handscomb b Lyon	24
*Misbah-ul-Haq c Maddinson b Bird	11	– c Maddinson b Lyon	0
Asad Shafiq c Smith b Bird	50	– c Handscomb b Lyon	16
†Sarfraz Ahmed c Renshaw b Hazlewood	10	– b Starc	43
Mohammad Amir c Wade b Starc	29	– b Bird	11
Sohail Khan run out (Maddinson)	65	– not out	10
Wahab Riaz c and b Hazlewood	1	– b Starc	0
Yasir Shah (did not bat)		– c Bird b Starc	0
B 4, lb 9, w 5, nb 1	19	B 4, lb 5, nb 2	11
(9 wkts dec, 126.3 overs)	443	(53.2 overs)	163

1/18 (1) 2/60 (3) 3/111 (4) 4/125 (5) 5/240 (6) 1/3 (1) 2/6 (3) 3/63 (4) 4/63 (5) 5/89 (6) 6/101 (2)
6/268 (7) 7/317 (8) 8/435 (9) 9/443 (10) 7/143 (8) 8/153 (7) 9/159 (10) 10/163 (11)

Starc 31–6–125–1; Hazlewood 32.3–11–50–3; Bird 34–5–113–3; Lyon 23–1–115–1; Smith 3–0–9–0; Maddinson 3–0–18–0. *Second innings*—Starc 15.2–4–36–4; Hazlewood 13–3–39–2; Bird 11–2–46–1; Lyon 14–4–33–3.

Australia

M. T. Renshaw b Yasir Shah	10
D. A. Warner c Sarfraz Ahmed b Wahab Riaz	144
U. T. Khawaja c Sarfraz Ahmed b Wahab Riaz	97
*S. P. D. Smith not out	165
P. S. P. Handscomb c Sami Aslam b Sohail Khan	54
N. J. Maddinson b Yasir Shah	22
†M. S. Wade c Asad Shafiq b Sohail Khan	9
M. A. Starc c Asad Shafiq b Sohail Khan	84
N. M. Lyon c and b Yasir Shah	12
B 1, lb 12, w 1, nb 13	27
(8 wkts dec, 142 overs)	624

1/46 (1) 2/244 (2) 3/282 (3) 4/374 (5)
5/433 (6) 6/454 (7) 7/608 (8) 8/624 (9)

J. R. Hazlewood and J. M. Bird did not bat.

Mohammad Amir 33–6–91–0; Sohail Khan 31–7–131–3; Yasir Shah 41–2–207–3; Wahab Riaz 32–5–147–2; Azhar Ali 5–0–35–0.

Umpires: I. J. Gould *(England)* (58) and S. Ravi *(India)* (18).
Third umpire: R. K. Illingworth *(England)*. Referee: R. S. Madugalle *(Sri Lanka)* (174).

Close of play: first day, Pakistan 142–4 (Azhar Ali 66, Asad Shafiq 4); second day, Pakistan 310–6 (Azhar Ali 139, Mohammad Amir 28); third day, Australia 278–2 (Khawaja 95, Smith 10); fourth day, Australia 465–6 (Smith 100, Starc 7).

Test No. 2243/62 (A797, P407)

AUSTRALIA v PAKISTAN 2016–17 (3rd Test)

At Sydney Cricket Ground on 3, 4, 5, 6, 7 January, 2017.
Toss: Australia.   Result: AUSTRALIA WON BY 220 RUNS.
Debuts: Australia – H. W. R. Cartwright. Pakistan – Sharjeel Khan.
Man of the Match: D. A. Warner.   Man of the Series: S. P. D. Smith.

Warner kick-started proceedings by becoming only the fifth to score a hundred before lunch on the first day of a Test, completing it with three from the session's final ball – his 78th – thanks to a misfield at deep point. It was the fastest Test hundred at the SCG, beating his own record set a year earlier. Then Renshaw took over, reaching his maiden hundred from 201 deliveries, then raising his next 50 at nearly a run a ball. Handscomb became the second Australian, after Herbie Collins in 1920-21, to hit a fifty in each of his first four Tests, and cruised to another century. Smith declared with 538: by the end of the third day, Pakistan were eight down, but Younis had made his first hundred in Australia, his 34th in all. Uniquely, he now had centuries in all 11 countries to have hosted Tests. Smith ignored the follow-on again, and Australia hurtled to a lead of 464: Warner's 23-ball half-century was the second-fastest in Tests, two slower than Misbah-ul-Haq's against Australia at Abu Dhabi in 2014–15. Yasir Shah completed miserable match figures of 54–2–291–2. Younis was undone by Lyon's change of pace, 23 short of 10,000 Test runs. Misbah swiped once too often – he finished the series averaging 12 – while Sarfraz Ahmed's boisterous 72 only delayed the inevitable. Pakistan had briefly been ranked No. 1 in the world earlier in the year, but their sixth defeat in a row – their worst run – completed their fourth successive whitewash in Australia.

Australia

M. T. Renshaw b Imran Khan	184		
D. A. Warner c Sarfraz Ahmed b Wahab Riaz	113	– (1) b Wahab Riaz	55
U. T. Khawaja c Sarfraz Ahmed b Wahab Riaz	13	– (2) not out	79
*S. P. D. Smith c Sarfraz Ahmed b Yasir Shah	24	– (3) c Sarfraz Ahmed b Yasir Shah	59
P. S. P. Handscomb hit wkt b Wahab Riaz	110	– (4) not out	40
H. W. R. Cartwright b Imran Khan	37		
†M. S. Wade c Babar Azam b Azhar Ali	29		
M. A. Starc c sub (Mohammad Rizwan) b Azhar Ali	16		
S. N. J. O'Keefe not out	0		
B 5, lb 1, w 2, nb 4	12	B 3, lb 3, w 1, nb 1	8
(8 wkts dec, 135 overs)	538	(2 wkts dec, 32 overs)	241

1/151 (2) 2/203 (3) 3/244 (4) 4/386 (1)   1/71 (1) 2/174 (3)
5/477 (6) 6/516 (5) 7/532 (7) 8/538 (8)

J. R. Hazlewood and N. M. Lyon did not bat.

Mohammad Amir 24–2–83–0; Imran Khan 27–4–111–2; Wahab Riaz 28–4–89–3; Yasir Shah 40–2–167–1; Azhar Ali 14–0–70–2; Asad Shafiq 2–0–12–0. *Second innings*—Imran Khan 6–2–43–0; Yasir Shah 14–0–124–1; Wahab Riaz 7–0–28–1; Azhar Ali 5–0–40–0.

Pakistan

Azhar Ali run out (Starc/Handscomb)	71	– c and b Hazlewood	11
Sharjeel Khan c Renshaw b Hazlewood	4	– c Warner b Lyon	40
Babar Azam lbw b Hazlewood	0	– (4) lbw b Hazlewood	9
Younis Khan not out	175	– (5) c Hazlewood b Lyon	13
*Misbah-ul-Haq c sub (J. M. Bird) b Lyon	18	– (6) c Lyon b O'Keefe	38
Asad Shafiq c Smith b O'Keefe	4	– (7) b Starc	30
†Sarfraz Ahmed c sub (J. M. Bird) b Starc	18	– (8) not out	72
Mohammad Amir c Warner b Lyon	4	– (10) run out (O'Keefe/Wade)	5
Wahab Riaz b Lyon	8	– c Wade b O'Keefe	12
Yasir Shah c Smith b Hazlewood	10	– (3) c sub (J. M. Bird) b O'Keefe	13
Imran Khan b Hazlewood	0	– c sub (J. M. Bird) b Hazlewood	0
B 3	3	Nb 1	1
(110.3 overs)	315	(80.2 overs)	244

1/6 (2) 2/6 (3) 3/152 (1) 4/178 (5) 5/197 (6)   1/51 (2) 2/55 (1) 3/67 (4) 4/82 (5) 5/96 (3) 6/136 (7)
6/239 (7) 7/244 (8) 8/264 (9) 9/315 (10) 10/315 (11)   7/188 (6) 8/202 (9) 9/224 (10) 10/244 (11)

Starc 26–7–77–1; Hazlewood 27.3–7–55–4; O'Keefe 20–3–50–1; Lyon 33–3–115–3; Cartwright 4–0–15–0. *Second innings*—Starc 17–2–57–1; Hazlewood 18.2–7–29–3; Lyon 27–6–100–2; O'Keefe 17–4–53–3; Smith 1–0–5–0.

Umpires: R. K. Illingworth *(England)* (26) and S. Ravi *(India)* (19).
Third umpire: I. J. Gould *(England)*.   Referee: R. S. Madugalle *(Sri Lanka)* (175).

Close of play: first day, Australia 365–3 (Renshaw 167, Handscomb 40); second day, Pakistan 126–2 (Azhar Ali 58, Younis Khan 64); third day, Pakistan 271–8 (Younis Khan 136, Yasir Shah 5); fourth day, Pakistan 55–1 (Azhar Ali 11, Yasir Shah 3).

Test No. 2244/23 (SA406, SL254)

SOUTH AFRICA v SRI LANKA 2016–17 (1st Test)

At St George's Park, Port Elizabeth, on 26, 27, 28, 29, 30 December, 2016.
Toss: South Africa. Result: SOUTH AFRICA WON BY 206 RUNS.
Debuts: none.
Man of the Match: S. C. Cook.

St George's Park seemed to offer Sri Lanka their best opportunity of an upset – until it emerged that enough grass had been left on the pitch to take Herath out of the equation. His left-arm spin produced only three wickets in 44.5 overs, while the seamers took 30 of the match's 37 wickets. Batting and bowling at this grinch of a ground is often hard work, which invariably makes for absorbing play. South Africa were reminded of the local challenges when their batsmen were made to look ordinary by Sri Lanka's seamers. Six of the top seven batted for over 90 minutes, and all reached 20, but no one exceeded Duminy's adhesive 63. Cook and Elgar put on 104, South Africa's first hundred opening partnership here since Barry Richards and Eddie Barlow managed 157 against Australia in 1969–70. Next day Lakmal completed his first five-for in his 32nd Test – but Sri Lanka were soon 22 for three, and scraped to 205, a deficit of 81, with Philander docking the tail expertly. Cook showed the visiting batsmen how it was done, with a dogged 117 and another century stand with Elgar. Du Plessis and de Kock added brisk sixties, before a declaration set Sri Lanka 488. By the fourth-day close, despite the openers surviving more than 32 overs, they were 240 for five. Mathews was their last hope, but he edged the impressive Rabada in the third over of the final day, and South Africa wrapped things up in 70 minutes.

South Africa

S. C. Cook c Chandimal b Lakmal	59	– c Chandimal b Chameera	117
D. Elgar c Chandimal b Lakmal	45	– c Mathews b Lakmal	52
H. M. Amla c Chandimal b Lakmal	20	– lbw b Fernando	48
J-P. Duminy lbw b Herath	63	– c Mathews b de Silva	25
*F. du Plessis c Karunaratne b Lakmal	37	– not out	67
T. Bavuma lbw b Herath	3	– c Mendis b de Silva	8
†Q. de Kock b Fernando	37	– lbw b Herath	69
V. D. Philander c Chameera b Fernando	13		
K. A. Maharaj c Chandimal b Lakmal	0		
K. J. Abbott run out (Perera/Chandimal)	0		
K. Rabada not out	0		
Lb 3, w 1, nb 5	9	B 5, lb 2, w 3, nb 10	20
(98.5 overs)	286	(6 wkts dec, 90.5 overs)	406

1/104 (1) 2/105 (2) 3/178 (3) 4/213 (4) 5/225 (6)
6/253 (5) 7/276 (8) 8/276 (9) 9/281 (10) 10/286 (7)

1/116 (2) 2/221 (3) 3/245 (1)
4/267 (4) 5/277 (6) 6/406 (7)

Lakmal 27–9–63–5; Fernando 21.5–5–66–2; Mathews 13–5–26–0; Chameera 14–1–68–0; Herath 20–4–48–2; de Silva 3–0–12–0. *Second innings*—Lakmal 18–2–64–1; Fernando 14–0–65–1; Mathews 4–0–10–0; Chameera 15–0–85–1; Herath 24.5–1–84–1; de Silva 15–0–91–2.

Sri Lanka

F. D. M. Karunaratne b Abbott	5	– run out (Duminy/de Kock)	43
J. K. Silva lbw b Philander	16	– lbw b Rabada	48
M. D. K. J. Perera c de Kock b Philander	7	– c de Kock b Maharaj	6
B. K. G. Mendis c de Kock b Abbott	0	– c de Kock b Rabada	58
*A. D. Mathews c Elgar b Rabada	39	– lbw b Abbott	59
†L. D. Chandimal lbw b Philander	28	– c Rabada b Maharaj	8
D. M. de Silva c de Kock b Philander	43	– lbw b Abbott	22
H. M. R. K. B. Herath lbw b Maharaj	24	– c and b Philander	3
P. V. D. Chameera c Amla b Abbott	19	– c de Kock b Rabada	0
R. A. S. Lakmal c Abbott b Philander	4	– not out	19
A. N. P. R. Fernando not out	8	– b Maharaj	4
Lb 4, w 5, nb 3	12	B 4, lb 3, w 3, nb 1	11
(64.5 overs)	205	(96.3 overs)	281

1/10 (1) 2/19 (3) 3/22 (4) 4/61 (2) 5/94 (5)
6/121 (6) 7/157 (8) 8/181 (7) 9/185 (10) 10/205 (9)

1/87 (1) 2/93 (3) 3/118 (2) 4/193 (4) 5/225 (6)
6/246 (5) 7/258 (7) 8/258 (8) 9/274 (9) 10/281 (11)

Philander 20–7–45–5; Abbott 21.5–4–63–3; Rabada 13–3–63–1; Maharaj 10–3–30–1. *Second innings*—Philander 22–5–65–1; Abbott 20–6–38–2; Rabada 21–4–77–3; Maharaj 30.3–7–86–3; Duminy 3–0–8–0.

Umpires: Aleem Dar *(Pakistan)* (108) and B. N. J. Oxenford *(Australia)* (36).
Third umpire: R. J. Tucker *(Australia)* and S. George *(South Africa)*. Referee: D. C. Boon *(Australia)* (36).
George took over as third umpire on the second day, as Tucker was indisposed.

Close of play: first day, South Africa 267–6 (de Kock 25, Philander 6); second day, Sri Lanka 181–7 (de Silva 43, Chameera 7); third day, South Africa 351–5 (du Plessis 41, de Kock 42); fourth day, Sri Lanka 240–5 (Mathews 58, de Silva 9).

Test No. 2245/24 (SA407, SL255)

SOUTH AFRICA v SRI LANKA 2016–17 (2nd Test)

At Newlands, Cape Town, on 2, 3, 4, 5 January, 2017.
Toss: Sri Lanka.   Result: SOUTH AFRICA WON BY 282 RUNS.
Debuts: none.
Man of the Match: K. Rabada.

The batting heroes as South Africa clinched the series were the left-handers Elgar, whose 129 lasted six hours, and de Kock, whose own century arrived from 122 deliveries. With the ball, Rabada was irresistible, his ten for 92 the best match figures for South Africa against Sri Lanka, and the best in a Cape Town Test since readmission, passing Saeed Ajmal's ten for 147 for Pakistan in 2012-13. Put in, South Africa had slumped to 66 for three shortly before lunch, but recovered superbly thanks to Elgar and de Kock; nuggety efforts by Philander and Maharaj took them close to 400. In his third Test, Lahiru Kumara finished with six for 122; only Muttiah Muralitharan, with six for 39 at Durban in 2000–01, had better figures for Sri Lanka in South Africa. Herath, meanwhile, moved to 356 Test wickets, one more than Chaminda Vaas and behind only Murali for Sri Lanka. But individual pleasure quickly gave way to general despondency: after reaching 56 for one, Sri Lanka were skittled for 110, their second-lowest total against South Africa, though du Plessis spared them the follow-on, and batted on until 45 minutes before tea on the third day, setting a target of 507. Philander and Rabada then picked off the top four before stumps, and three more in three overs next morning; Mathews's defiant 49 was Sri Lanka's highest score of the match. Kyle Abbott, whose Kolpak defection to Hampshire became public knowledge on the first evening, went wicketless, and was dropped.

South Africa

S. C. Cook c †Mendis b Lakmal	0	– c Karunaratne b Lakmal	30
D. Elgar c †Mendis b Lakmal	129	– c Mathews b Herath	55
H. M. Amla b Kumara	29	– c Chandimal b Lakmal	0
J-P. Duminy c †Mendis b Kumara	0	– lbw b Lakmal	30
*F. du Plessis c Mathews b Herath	38	– c Chandimal b Lakmal	41
T. Bavuma c Tharanga b Kumara	10	– run out (de Silva)	0
†Q. de Kock c Chandimal b Kumara	101	– c Chandimal b Kumara	29
K. J. Abbott c Chandimal b Herath	16		
V. D. Philander c Chandimal b Kumara	20	– not out	15
K. A. Maharaj not out	32	– (8) not out	20
K. Rabada c Chandimal b Kumara	8		
Lb 3, w 5, nb 1	9	W 1, nb 3	4
(116 overs)	392	(7 wkts dec, 51.5 overs)	224

1/0 (1) 2/66 (3) 3/66 (4) 4/142 (5) 5/169 (6)   1/64 (1) 2/64 (3) 3/110 (2)
6/272 (2) 7/303 (8) 8/336 (7) 9/376 (9) 10/392 (11)   4/136 (4) 5/137 (6) 6/170 (5) 7/192 (7)

Lakmal 27–4–93–2; Fernando 15.4–3–46–0; Mathews 17–3–41–0; Kumara 25–1–122–6; Herath 23.2–4–57–2; de Silva 8–0–30–0. *Second innings*—Lakmal 19.5–2–69–4; Fernando 11–0–46–0; Kumara 12–0–62–1; de Silva 3–0–15–0; Herath 6–0–32–1.

Sri Lanka

F. D. M. Karunaratne c Bavuma b Rabada	24	– b Philander	6
J. K. Silva b Rabada	11	– c Cook b Rabada	29
B. K. G. Mendis c Duminy b Maharaj	11	– c Elgar b Philander	4
D. M. de Silva lbw b Maharaj	16	– lbw b Rabada	22
*A. D. Mathews c du Plessis b Rabada	2	– c de Kock b Rabada	49
†L. D. Chandimal c de Kock b Rabada	4	– c Cook b Rabada	30
W. U. Tharanga not out	26	– c de Kock b Rabada	12
H. M. R. K. B. Herath lbw b Philander	1	– not out	35
R. A. S. Lakmal c Amla b Philander	0	– c Cook b Rabada	10
C. B. R. L. S. Kumara b Philander	4	– st de Kock b Maharaj	9
A. N. P. R. Fernando c du Plessis b Philander	0	– b Philander	5
Lb 5, w 5, nb 1	11	B 6, lb 5, nb 2	13
(43 overs)	110	(62 overs)	224

1/31 (2) 2/56 (3) 3/56 (1) 4/60 (5) 5/78 (4)   1/11 (1) 2/25 (3) 3/66 (2) 4/69 (5) 5/144 (6)
6/78 (6) 7/100 (8) 8/100 (9) 9/110 (10) 10/110 (11)   6/165 (7) 7/166 (5) 8/178 (9) 9/211 (10) 10/224 (11)

Philander 12–4–27–4; Abbott 8–3–9–0; Rabada 12–2–37–4; Maharaj 11–1–32–2. *Second innings*—Abbott 15–3–46–0; Philander 14–1–48–3; Rabada 17–3–55–6; Maharaj 16–3–64–1.

Umpires: Aleem Dar *(Pakistan)* (109) and R. J. Tucker *(Australia)* (51).
Third umpire: B. N. J. Oxenford *(Australia).*   Referee: D. C. Boon *(Australia)* (37).

Close of play: first day, South Africa 297–6 (de Kock 68, Abbott 16); second day, South Africa 35–0 (Cook 15, Elgar 19); third day, Sri Lanka 130–4 (A. D. Mathews 29, Chandimal 28).

SOUTH AFRICA v SRI LANKA 2016–17 (3rd Test)

At New Wanderers, Johannesburg, on 12, 13, 14 January, 2017.
Toss: South Africa.   Result: SOUTH AFRICA WON BY AN INNINGS AND 118 RUNS.
Debuts: South Africa – D. Olivier.
Man of the Match: J-P. Duminy.   Man of the Series: D. Elgar.

With the series decided, the big question was how Amla would fare in his 100th Test. He had gone 13 innings without a century – ten without even a fifty – and watched his average dip below 50 for the first time in four years. Du Plessis batted first on a pitch full of Jo'burg jive. The crowd was small, but those who did show up witnessed a virtuoso performance. Amla's fluency grew after an uncertain start: next day, he was stunningly caught by Chandimal for 134, his 26th Test century. He was the eighth to score a century in his 100th Test, and the second South African, after Graeme Smith at The Oval in 2012. Almost lost in the hoopla was a splendid 155 from Duminy, who helped him add 292 for the third wicket, South Africa's best for any wicket against these opponents. Though the last eight fell for 89, the total was a lofty 426. By lunch on the third day Sri Lanka were following on, a disheartening 295 behind, after another inept batting display. They fared better in their second innings – but only just. Parnell, in only his second Test in almost seven years, took four wickets, and the debutant seamer Duanne Olivier three. Sri Lanka lost 16 wickets on that third day, a national record, pipping 15 on the third day at Bangalore in 1993–94. In all, they faced just 88.1 overs, as South Africa completed the 3–0 whitewash that had looked likely since the second day of the series.

South Africa

S. C. Cook lbw b Mathews	10
D. Elgar c Karunaratne b Kumara	27
H. M. Amla c Chandimal b Fernando	134
J-P. Duminy c Mendis b Kumara	155
D. Olivier c Chandimal b Mathews	3
*F. du Plessis c Mendis b Fernando	16
T. Bavuma c Silva b Fernando	0
†Q. de Kock c de Silva b Kumara	34
V. D. Philander c Chandimal b Fernando	0
W. D. Parnell c Tharanga b Kumara	23
K. Rabada not out	0
B 11, lb 8, w 4, nb 1	24
(124.1 overs)	426

1/45 (1) 2/45 (2) 3/337 (4) 4/346 (5) 5/364 (6)
6/364 (7) 7/367 (3) 8/378 (9) 9/425 (10) 10/426 (8)

Lakmal 30–8–81–0; Fernando 27–8–78–4; Mathews 20–6–52–2; Kumara 25.1–2–107–4; Herath 14–0–67–0; de Silva 8–1–22–0.

Sri Lanka

F. D. M. Karunaratne c de Kock b Philander	0	– b Rabada	50
J. K. Silva c de Kock b Rabada	13	– c de Kock b Rabada	0
B. K. G. Mendis c Duminy b Rabada	41	– b Parnell	24
D. M. de Silva c Bavuma b Philander	10	– c du Plessis b Olivier	12
*A. D. Mathews c de Kock b Rabada	19	– c du Plessis b Olivier	10
†L. D. Chandimal c de Kock b Philander	5	– c Amla b Philander	10
W. U. Tharanga c Elgar b Olivier	24	– c Duminy b Parnell	26
H. M. R. K. B. Herath c Cook b Olivier	8	– c Bavuma b Parnell	10
R. A. S. Lakmal c Rabada b Parnell	4	– c Philander b Parnell	31
C. B. R. L. S. Kumara not out	1	– c Cook b Olivier	0
A. N. P. R. Fernando c and b Parnell	4	– not out	0
Lb 2	2	Lb 2, w 1, nb 1	4
(45.4 overs)	131	(42.3 overs)	177

1/0 (1) 2/47 (2) 3/62 (3) 4/70 (4) 5/90 (6)   1/2 (2) 2/39 (3) 3/59 (4) 4/87 (5) 5/108 (6) 6/108 (1)
6/100 (5) 7/108 (8) 8/126 (9) 9/126 (7) 10/131 (11)   7/134 (8) 8/177 (7) 9/177 (10) 10/177 (9)

Philander 14–5–28–3; Parnell 10.4–2–38–2; Olivier 9–3–19–2; Rabada 12–3–44–3. *Second innings*—Philander 10–1–35–1; Rabada 12–3–50–2; Parnell 10.3–1–51–4; Olivier 9–2–38–3; Duminy 1–0–1–0.

Umpires: B. N. J. Oxenford *(Australia)* (37) and R. J. Tucker *(Australia)* (52).
Third umpire: Aleem Dar *(Pakistan)*.   Referee: D. C. Boon *(Australia)* (38).

Close of play: first day, South Africa 338–3 (Amla 125, Olivier 0); second day, Sri Lanka 80–4 (Mathews 11, Chandimal 3).

Test No. 2247/12 (NZ418, B96)

NEW ZEALAND v BANGLADESH 2016–17 (1st Test)

At Basin Reserve, Wellington, on 12, 13, 14, 15, 16 January, 2017.
Toss: New Zealand. Result: NEW ZEALAND WON BY SEVEN WICKETS.
Debuts: Bangladesh – Subashis Roy, Taskin Ahmed.
Man of the Match: T. W. M. Latham.

After declaring with 595 in their first innings, Bangladesh looked immune from defeat. But from 66 for three at the start of the final day they subsided for 160 soon after lunch, leaving New Zealand 57 overs to knock off 217; Williamson, who made his 15th Test century, and Taylor put on 163 at six an over to hurry them home. Bangladesh's second innings was hit by injuries to Imrul Kayes and to his captain. Mushfiqur Rahim had hurt his right hand during his first-innings 159, went in reluctantly on the last morning, and was hit behind the ear by Southee – hospital scans cleared him of danger. The late drama masked an extraordinary three and a half days of batting, amid gales and rain. Shakib Al Hasan, dropped when four by Santner, glided to 217, Bangladesh's highest Test score, and put on 359 with Mushfiqur, an all-wicket record between these countries. The total was Bangladesh's second-highest, behind 638 against Sri Lanka at Galle in 2012–13. But, after Shakib became the seventh to record a double-century and a duck in the same Test, it also became the highest to result in defeat, previously Australia's 586 against England at Sydney in 1894–95. Latham led the battle for parity with 177 as New Zealand built to 539; Imrul took five catches deputising for Mushfiqur, a record for a substitute keeper.

Bangladesh

Tamim Iqbal lbw b Boult	56	– b Santner	25
Imrul Kayes c Boult b Southee	1	– not out	36
Mominul Haque c Watling b Southee	64	– c de Grandhomme b Wagner	23
Mahmudullah c Watling b Wagner	26	– c Watling b Wagner	5
Shakib Al Hasan b Wagner	217	– (6) c Williamson b Santner	0
*†Mushfiqur Rahim c Watling b Boult	159	– (8) retired hurt	13
Sabbir Rahman not out	54	– c Watling b Boult	50
Mehedi Hasan c Southee b Wagner	0	– (5) run out (Santner)	1
Taskin Ahmed c Southee b Wagner	3	– b Boult	5
Kamrul Islam not out	6	– c de Grandhomme b Southee	1
Subashis Roy (did not bat)		– b Boult	0
B 2, lb 6, nb 1	9	Nb 1	1
(8 wkts dec, 152 overs)	595	(57.5 overs)	160

1/16 (2) 2/60 (1) 3/145 (4) 4/160 (3) 1/50 (1) 2/63 (4) 3/66 (5) 4/66 (6) 5/96 (3)
5/519 (6) 6/536 (5) 7/542 (8) 8/566 (9) 6/137 (9) 7/148 (10) 8/152 (7) 9/160 (11)

In the second innings Imrul, when 24, retired hurt at 46–0 and resumed at 148–7; Mushfiqur retired hurt at 114–5.

Boult 34–5–131–2; Southee 34–5–158–2; de Grandhomme 20–2–65–0; Wagner 44–8–151–4; Santner 17–2–62–0; Williamson 3–0–20–0. *Second innings*—Boult 13.5–3–53–3; Southee 13–5–34–1; Santner 16–5–36–2; Wagner 15–3–37–2.

New Zealand

J. A. Raval c †Imrul Kayes b Kamrul Islam	27	– (2) c and b Mehedi Hasan	13
T. W. M. Latham lbw b Shakib Al Hasan	177	– (1) b Mehedi Hasan	16
*K. S. Williamson c †Imrul Kayes b Taskin Ahmed	53	– not out	104
L. R. P. L. Taylor c Mahmudullah b Kamrul Islam	40	– c Mehedi Hasan b Subashis Roy	60
H. M. Nicholls c Mehedi Hasan b Shakib Al Hasan	53	– not out	4
C. de Grandhomme c †Imrul Kayes b Subashis Roy	14		
†B-J. Watling c †Imrul Kayes b Mahmudullah	49		
M. J. Santner b Subashis Roy	73		
T. G. Southee lbw b Mahmudullah	1		
N. Wagner c †Imrul Kayes b Kamrul Islam	18		
T. A. Boult not out	4		
B 10, lb 3, w 16, nb 1	30	B 14, lb 6	20
(148.2 overs)	539	(3 wkts, 39.4 overs)	217

1/54 (1) 2/131 (3) 3/205 (4) 4/347 (5) 5/366 (6) 1/32 (2) 2/39 (1) 3/202 (4)
6/398 (2) 7/471 (7) 8/473 (9) 9/504 (10) 10/539 (8)

Mehedi Hasan 37–5–116–0; Subashis Roy 26.2–6–89–2; Taskin Ahmed 29–4–141–1; Kamrul Islam 26–4–87–3; Shakib Al Hasan 27–2–78–2; Mahmudullah 3–0–15–2. *Second innings*—Kamrul Islam 7–0–31–0; Mehedi Hasan 11.4–0–66–2; Shakib Al Hasan 10–0–30–0; Taskin Ahmed 6–0–38–0; Subashis Roy 5–0–32–1.

Umpires: M. Erasmus *(South Africa)* (40) and P. R. Reiffel *(Australia)* (29).
Third umpire: N. J. Llong *(England)*.   Referee: J. Srinath *(India)* (34).

Close of play: first day, Bangladesh 154–3 (Mominul 64, Shakib 5); second day, Bangladesh 542–7 (Sabbir Rahman 10); third day, New Zealand 292–3 (Latham 119, Nicholls 35); fourth day, Bangladesh 66–3 (Mominul 10).

Test No. 2248/13 (NZ419, B97)

NEW ZEALAND v BANGLADESH 2016–17 (2nd Test)

At Hagley Oval, Christchurch, on 20, 21, 22 *(no play)*, 23 January, 2017.
Toss: New Zealand.   Result: NEW ZEALAND WON BY NINE WICKETS.
Debuts: Bangladesh – Nazmul Hossain, Nurul Hasan.
Man of the Match: T. G. Southee.

During a washed-out third day, the covers leaked on a good length, and it needed a pair of industrial-strength blow-dryers – nicknamed the Sir Alex Fergusons – to make the surface fit. New Zealand began the fourth day still 29 behind on first innings, but secured victory just after 7pm; after their 595 at Wellington, Bangladesh lost 30 for 622. De Grandhomme, promoted to No. 3, finished it with two sixes. Shakib Al Hasan had initiated a wobble on the second evening, three wickets in two overs threatening to undermine Latham's century partnership with Taylor, the third New Zealander to 6,000 Test runs, after Stephen Fleming and Brendon McCullum. But Nicholls's Test-best 98 helped establish a lead of 65. The innings ended in bizarre fashion; after touching his bat over the crease, Wagner took another stride. When keeper Nurul Hasan's flick hit the stumps, Wagner had nothing grounded, and he was run out. The Law was changed not long afterwards. Wagner and his fellow seamers retaliated. Southee became the second-fastest New Zealander to 200 Test wickets, in his 56th match, behind only Richard Hadlee (44) as Bangladesh, lacking Imrul Kayes, Mominul Haque and Mushfiqur Rahim through injury, were cruelly exposed. For the 22nd consecutive Test in New Zealand since January 2011, the side winning the toss had bowled: stand-in captain Tamim Iqbal fell early, before Soumya Sarkar hit a streaky maiden half-century, and put on 127 with Shakib. But Sarkar's luck ran out on 86, and Boult and Southee took nine between them as Bangladesh subsided for 289.

Bangladesh

*Tamim Iqbal c Watling b Southee	5	– c Santner b Southee	8
Soumya Sarkar c de Grandhomme b Boult	86	– c Raval b de Grandhomme	36
Mahmudullah c Watling b Boult	19	– b Wagner	38
Shakib Al Hasan c Watling b Southee	59	– c de Grandhomme b Southee	8
Sabbir Rahman c Southee b Boult	7	– (6) c Watling b Wagner	0
Nazmul Hossain c Raval b Southee	18	– (5) b Boult	12
†Nurul Hasan c Watling b Boult	47	– c Watling b Wagner	0
Mehedi Hasan b Wagner	10	– c Latham b Boult	4
Taskin Ahmed c Williamson b Southee	8	– b Boult	33
Kamrul Islam lbw b Southee	2	– not out	25
Rubel Hossain not out	16	– c Watling b Southee	7
B 4, lb 2, w 5, nb 1	12	Lb 2	2
(84.3 overs)	289	(52.5 overs)	173

1/7 (1) 2/38 (3) 3/165 (2) 4/177 (5) 5/179 (4)   1/17 (1) 2/58 (2) 3/73 (4) 4/92 (3)
6/232 (6) 7/248 (8) 8/257 (9) 9/273 (7) 10/289 (10)   5/100 (6) 6/100 (7) 7/106 (5)
                                                     8/115 (8) 9/166 (9) 10/173 (11)

Boult 24–4–87–4; Southee 28.3–7–94–5; de Grandhomme 14–4–58–0; Wagner 18–1–44–1. *Second innings*—Boult 17–3–52–3; Southee 12.5–2–48–3; de Grandhomme 11–3–27–1; Wagner 12–3–44–3.

New Zealand

J. A. Raval b Kamrul Islam	16	– b Kamrul Islam	33
T. W. M. Latham c Nurul Hasan b Taskin Ahmed	68	– not out	41
*K. S. Williamson c Nurul Hasan b Kamrul Islam	2		
L. R. P. L. Taylor c sub (Taijul Islam) b Mehedi Hasan	77		
H. M. Nicholls b Mehedi Hasan	98		
M. J. Santner lbw b Shakib Al Hasan	29		
†B-J. Watling b Shakib Al Hasan	1		
C. de Grandhomme b Shakib Al Hasan	0	– (3) not out	33
T. G. Southee c Mehedi Hasan b Shakib Al Hasan	17		
N. Wagner run out (Kamrul Islam/Nurul Hasan)	26		
T. A. Boult not out	7		
Lb 6, w 4, nb 3	13	B 1, w 1, nb 2	4
(92.4 overs)	354	(1 wkt, 18.4 overs)	111

1/45 (1) 2/47 (3) 3/153 (2) 4/177 (4) 5/252 (6)   1/56 (1)
6/256 (7) 7/256 (8) 8/286 (9) 9/343 (5) 10/354 (10)

Taskin Ahmed 22–2–86–1; Mehedi Hasan 19–3–59–2; Rubel Hossain 17–2–65–0; Kamrul Islam 19–4–78–2; Shakib Al Hasan 12.4–1–50–4; Soumya Sarkar 3–0–10–0. *Second innings*—Taskin Ahmed 5–0–21–0; Mehedi Hasan 6–0–27–0; Kamrul Islam 3–0–21–1; Shakib Al Hasan 4–0–28–0; Nazmul Hossain 0.4–0–13–0.

Umpires: N. J. Llong *(England)* (40) and P. R. Reiffel *(Australia)* (30).
Third umpire: M. Erasmus *(South Africa)*.   Referee: J. Srinath *(India)* (35).

Close of play: first day, Bangladesh 289; second day, New Zealand 260–7 (Nicholls 56, Southee 4); third day, no play.

INDIA v BANGLADESH 2016-17 (Only Test)

Test No. 2249/9 (I508, B98)

At Rajiv Gandhi Stadium, Uppal, Hyderabad, on 9, 10, 11, 12, 13 February, 2017.
Toss: India.   Result: INDIA WON BY 208 RUNS.
Debuts: none.
Man of the Match: V. Kohli.

Taskin Ahmed struck in the first over, but India's batsmen were soon making hay again. Kohli became the first to score double-centuries in four successive Test series – but Bangladesh took the match into the fifth afternoon, lasting more than 100 overs in both innings. In the end, though, the spinners proved too effective, and India took their unbeaten run to a national-record 19 Tests, 15 of them wins. They had taken charge with a second-wicket stand of 178 between Vijay and Pujara, whose 83 gave him the record for most first-class runs in an Indian season (previously Chandu Borde's 1,604 in 1964–65). And then came Kohli, who extended his overnight 111 to a superb 204. He added 222 with the fit-again Rahane – Karun Nair was dropped despite his triple-century against England in the previous match – and the total spiralled towards 700 as Saha added another hundred; this was only the fourth Test in which both wicketkeepers scored one. All too often, Bangladesh had crumbled in such circumstances, but now they dug in bravely. Shakib hit 14 fours in his 82, while Mushfiqur went on to a characterful century, passing 3,000 runs during a 381-minute stay. He was last out, Ashwin's 250th Test wicket in his 45th match, three quicker than Dennis Lillee's old record. Despite leading by 299, Kohli ignored the follow-on, finally declaring at tea on the fourth day. Mahmudullah's 64 used up 200 minutes, and Soumya Sarkar made a pleasant 42, but five others fell in the twenties.

India

K. L. Rahul b Taskin Ahmed	2	– (2) c Mushfiqur Rahim b Taskin Ahmed	10
M. Vijay b Taijul Islam	108	– (1) c Mushfiqur Rahim b Taskin Ahmed	7
C. A. Pujara c Mushfiqur Rahim b Mehedi Hasan	83	– not out	54
*V. Kohli lbw b Taijul Islam	204	– c Mahmudullah b Shakib Al Hasan	38
A. M. Rahane c Mehedi Hasan b Taijul Islam	82	– b Shakib Al Hasan	28
†W. P. Saha not out	106		
R. Ashwin c Soumya Sarkar b Mehedi Hasan	34		
R. A. Jadeja not out	60	– (6) not out	16
Lb 5, w 1, nb 2	8	Lb 5, w 1	6
(6 wkts dec, 166 overs)	687	(4 wkts dec, 29 overs)	159

1/2 (1) 2/180 (3) 3/234 (2) 4/456 (5)
5/495 (4) 6/569 (7)

1/12 (1) 2/23 (2) 3/90 (4)
4/128 (5)

Bhuvneshwar Kumar, U. T. Yadav and I. Sharma did not bat.

Taskin Ahmed 25–2–127–1; Kamrul Islam 19–1–100–0; Soumya Sarkar 1–0–4–0; Mehedi Hasan 42–0–165–2; Shakib Al Hasan 24–4–104–0; Taijul Islam 47–6–156–3; Sabbir Rahman 3–0–10–0; Mahmudullah 5–0–16–0. *Second innings*—Taijul Islam 6–1–29–0; Taskin Ahmed 7–0–43–2; Shakib Al Hasan 9–0–50–2; Mehedi Hasan 7–0–32–0.

Bangladesh

Tamim Iqbal run out (Yadav/Bhuvneshwar Kumar)	24	– c Kohli b Ashwin	3
Soumya Sarkar c Saha b Yadav	15	– c Rahane b Jadeja	42
Mominul Haque lbw b Yadav	12	– c Rahane b Ashwin	27
Mahmudullah lbw b Sharma	28	– c Bhuvneshwar Kumar b Sharma	64
Shakib Al Hasan c Yadav b Ashwin	82	– c Pujara b Jadeja	22
*†Mushfiqur Rahim c Saha b Ashwin	127	– c Jadeja b Ashwin	23
Sabbir Rahman lbw b Jadeja	16	– lbw b Sharma	22
Mehedi Hasan b Bhuvneshwar Kumar	51	– c Saha b Jadeja	23
Taijul Islam c Saha b Yadav	10	– (10) c Rahul b Jadeja	6
Taskin Ahmed c Rahane b Jadeja	8	– (11) lbw b Ashwin	1
Kamrul Islam not out	0	– (9) not out	3
Lb 15	15	B 4, lb 7, nb 3	14
(127.5 overs)	388	(100.3 overs)	250

1/38 (2) 2/44 (1) 3/64 (3) 4/109 (4) 5/216 (5)
6/235 (7) 7/322 (8) 8/339 (9) 9/378 (10) 10/388 (6)

1/11 (1) 2/71 (2) 3/75 (3) 4/106 (5)
5/162 (6) 6/213 (7) 7/225 (4)
8/242 (8) 9/249 (10) 10/250 (11)

Bhuvneshwar Kumar 21–7–52–1; Sharma 20–5–69–1; Ashwin 28.5–7–98–2; Yadav 25–6–84–3; Jadeja 33–8–70–2. *Second innings*—Bhuvneshwar Kumar 8–4–15–0; Ashwin 30.3–10–73–4; Sharma 13–3–40–2; Yadav 12–2–33–0; Jadeja 37–15–78–2.

Umpires: M. Erasmus *(South Africa)* (41) and J. S. Wilson *(West Indies)* (4).
Third umpire: C. B. Gaffaney *(New Zealand)*.   Referee: A. J. Pycroft *(Zimbabwe)* (52).

Close of play: first day, India 356–3 (Kohli 111, Rahane 45); second day, Bangladesh 41–1 (Tamim Iqbal 24, Mominul Haque 1); third day, Bangladesh 322–6 (Mushfiqur Rahim 81, Mehedi Hasan 51); fourth day, Bangladesh 103–3 (Mahmudullah 9, Shakib Al Hasan 21).

INDIA v AUSTRALIA 2016–17 (1st Test)

At Maharashtra C. A. Stadium, Gahunje, Pune, on 23, 24, 25 February, 2017.
Toss: Australia.   Result: AUSTRALIA WON BY 333 RUNS.
Debuts: none.
Man of the Match: S. N. J. O'Keefe.

Australia converted a hesitant 205 for nine on the first evening into a massive victory two days later, India's first home defeat since England won at Kolkata in December 2012. Smith's second-innings hundred was a study in concentration on a pitch that turned so crudely it was rated "poor" by the ICC. Australia had started well before Warner chopped on, but the rest made little impact until Starc muscled 61; last man Hazlewood made one of their stand of 55. Starc then captured Pujara and Kohli in the space of three deliveries, but Rahul led a recovery to 94 for three – before seven wickets cascaded for 11 in 48 balls. Six went to O'Keefe, who had struggled initially, perhaps unused to the new ball: during lunch, he returned to the middle for some fine-tuning, and struck with the second, fourth and sixth balls of his third over afterwards. Smith was dropped four times during his determined century, and was dismissed only when the lead was past 400. India were soon floundering again: O'Keefe trapped Vijay, who challenged the decision, as did Rahul moments later. Two wickets, and both reviews gone – and when Kohli allowed a ball to knock back his off stump, the die was cast; the innings lasted just 33.5 overs. O'Keefe's twin hauls of six for 35 were the best repeat figures in Test history, and his overall match figures were the second-best by any visiting bowler in India, behind Ian Botham's 13 for 106 for England at Bombay in 1979-80.

Australia

M. T. Renshaw c Vijay b Ashwin	68	–	(5) c Sharma b J. Yadav	31
D. A. Warner b U. T. Yadav	38	–	(1) lbw b Ashwin	10
*S. P. D. Smith c Kohli b Ashwin	27	–	lbw b Jadeja	109
S. E. Marsh c Kohli b J. Yadav	16	–	(2) lbw b Ashwin	0
P. S. P. Handscomb lbw b Jadeja	22	–	(4) c Vijay b Ashwin	19
M. R. Marsh lbw b Jadeja	4	–	c Saha b Jadeja	31
†M. S. Wade lbw b U. T. Yadav	8	–	c Saha b U. T. Yadav	20
M. A. Starc c Jadeja b Ashwin	61	–	c Rahul b Ashwin	30
S. N. J. O'Keefe c Saha b U. T. Yadav	0	–	c Saha b Jadeja	6
N. M. Lyon lbw b U. T. Yadav	0	–	lbw b U. T. Yadav	13
J. R. Hazlewood not out	1	–	not out	2
Lb 6, nb 9	15		B 4, lb 9, nb 1	14
(94.5 overs)	260		(87 overs)	285

1/82 (2) 2/119 (4) 3/149 (5) 4/149 (3) 5/166 (6)
6/190 (7) 7/196 (1) 8/205 (9) 9/205 (10) 10/260 (8)

1/10 (1) 2/23 (2) 3/61 (4) 4/113 (5)
5/169 (6) 6/204 (7) 7/246 (3) 8/258 (9)
9/279 (10) 10/285 (9)

In the first innings Renshaw, when 36, retired ill at 82-1 and resumed at 149-3.

Sharma 11–0–27–0; Ashwin 34.5–10–63–3; J. Yadav 13–1–58–1; Jadeja 24–4–74–2; U. T. Yadav 12–3–32–4. *Second innings*—Ashwin 28–3–119–4; Jadeja 33–10–65–3; U. T. Yadav 13–1–39–2; J. Yadav 10–1–43–1; Sharma 3–0–6–0.

India

M. Vijay c Wade b Hazlewood	10	–	lbw b O'Keefe	2
K. L. Rahul c Warner b O'Keefe	64	–	lbw b Lyon	10
C. A. Pujara c Wade b Starc	6	–	lbw b O'Keefe	31
*V. Kohli c Handscomb b Starc	0	–	b O'Keefe	13
A. M. Rahane c Handscomb b O'Keefe	13	–	c Lyon b O'Keefe	18
R. Ashwin c Handscomb b Lyon	1	–	lbw b O'Keefe	8
†W. P. Saha c Smith b O'Keefe	0	–	lbw b O'Keefe	5
R. A. Jadeja c Starc b O'Keefe	2	–	b Lyon	3
J. Yadav st Wade b O'Keefe	2	–	c Wade b Lyon	5
U. T. Yadav c Smith b O'Keefe	4	–	(11) not out	0
I. Sharma not out	2	–	(10) c Warner b Lyon	0
Nb 1	1		B 8, lb 4	12
(40.1 overs)	105		(33.5 overs)	107

1/26 (1) 2/44 (3) 3/44 (4) 4/94 (2) 5/95 (5)
6/95 (7) 7/95 (6) 8/98 (9) 9/101 (8) 10/105 (10)

1/10 (1) 2/16 (2) 3/47 (4) 4/77 (5) 5/89 (6) 6/99 (7)
7/100 (3) 8/102 (8) 9/102 (10) 10/107 (9)

Starc 9–2–38–2; O'Keefe 13.1–2–35–6; Hazlewood 7–3–11–1; Lyon 11–2–21–1. *Second innings*—Starc 2–2–0–0; Lyon 14.5–2–53–4; O'Keefe 15–4–35–6; Hazlewood 2–0–7–0.

Umpires: R. A. Kettleborough *(England)* (42) and N. J. Llong *(England)* (41).
Third umpire: R. K. Illingworth *(England)*.   Referee: B. C. Broad *(England)* (83).

Close of play: first day, Australia 256–9 (Starc 57, Hazlewood 1); second day, Australia 143–4 (Smith 59, M. R. Marsh 21).

INDIA v AUSTRALIA 2016–17 (2nd Test)

At M. Chinnaswamy Stadium, Bangalore, on 4, 5, 6, 7 March, 2017.
Toss: India.   Result: INDIA WON BY 75 RUNS.
Debuts: none.
Man of the Match: K. L. Rahul.

In a gripping, low-scoring match, the third-innings stand of 118 between Pujara and Rahane proved vital as India levelled the series. Australia had begun by demolishing India for 189, thanks to Lyon, who bowled immaculately for eight for 50, the best figures by a visiting bowler in India, surpassing Lance Klusener's eight for 64 on debut for South Africa at Calcutta in 1996–97. In the second innings, India were 120 for four – just 33 in front – but did not buckle; the target was dragged to 188, and Australia crumpled for 112. Things had looked rosier for Smith's young side on the first day, when India lost their last eight for 117, only Rahul making it past 26. The home attack roared back: Smith was worked over by Sharma and Yadav before, on being given out lbw, controversially looking to the dressing-room for advice on whether to review; umpire Llong pointed out this was not allowed, and there could now be no referral. Renshaw and Shaun Marsh made sensible sixties, but just when the lead was looking threatening, the last four wickets tumbled for seven, Jadeja having a hand in all of them. After Hazlewood's early strikes, the fifth-wicket pair played immaculately to extend the lead to 126 before Starc trapped Rahane; the next ball – a 95mph bomb – snapped Nair's leg stump in half. Hazlewood ended the resistance and, with six wickets tumbling for 36, the target looked eminently gettable. But Ashwin orchestrated one final collapse: Australia's last six disintegrated for 11.

India

K. L. Rahul c Renshaw b Lyon	90	– c Smith b O'Keefe	51
A. Mukund lbw b Starc	0	– b Hazlewood	16
C. A. Pujara c Handscomb b Lyon	17	– c M. R. Marsh b Hazlewood	92
*V. Kohli lbw b Lyon	12	– lbw b Hazlewood	15
A. M. Rahane st Wade b Lyon	17	– (6) lbw b Starc	52
K. K. Nair st Wade b O'Keefe	26	– (7) b Starc	0
R. Ashwin c Warner b Lyon	7	– (9) b Hazlewood	4
†W. P. Saha c Smith b Lyon	1	– not out	20
R. A. Jadeja c Smith b Lyon	3	– (5) b Hazlewood	2
U. T. Yadav not out	0	– c Warner b Hazlewood	1
I. Sharma c Handscomb b Lyon	0	– c S. E. Marsh b O'Keefe	6
B 12, lb 4	16	B 11, w 4	15
(71.2 overs)	189	(97.1 overs)	274

1/11 (2) 2/72 (3) 3/88 (4) 4/118 (5) 5/156 (6)   1/39 (2) 2/84 (1) 3/112 (4) 4/120 (5) 5/238 (6)
6/174 (7) 7/178 (8) 8/188 (9) 9/189 (1) 10/189 (11)   6/238 (7) 7/242 (3) 8/246 (9) 9/258 (10) 10/274 (11)

Starc 15–5–39–1; Hazlewood 11–2–42–0; O'Keefe 21–5–40–1; M. R. Marsh 2–0–2–0; Lyon 22.2–4–50–8. *Second innings*—Starc 16–1–74–2; Hazlewood 24–5–67–6; Lyon 33–4–82–0; O'Keefe 21.1–3–36–2; M. R. Marsh 3–0–4–0.

Australia

D. A. Warner b Ashwin	33	– lbw b Ashwin	17
M. T. Renshaw st Saha b Jadeja	60	– c Saha b Sharma	5
*S. P. D. Smith c Saha b Jadeja	8	– lbw b Yadav	28
S. E. Marsh c Nair b Yadav	66	– lbw b Yadav	9
P. S. P. Handscomb c Ashwin b Jadeja	16	– c Saha b Ashwin	24
M. R. Marsh lbw b Sharma	0	– c Nair b Ashwin	13
†M. S. Wade lbw b Jadeja	40	– c Saha b Ashwin	0
M. A. Starc c Jadeja b Ashwin	26	– b Ashwin	1
S. N. J. O'Keefe not out	4	– b Jadeja	2
N. M. Lyon lbw b Jadeja	0	– c and b Ashwin	2
J. R. Hazlewood c Rahul b Jadeja	1	– not out	0
B 14, lb 3, nb 5	22	B 8, lb 2, w 1	11
(122.4 overs)	276	(35.4 overs)	112

1/52 (1) 2/82 (3) 3/134 (2) 4/160 (5) 5/163 (6)   1/22 (2) 2/42 (1) 3/67 (4) 4/74 (3) 5/101 (6)
6/220 (4) 7/269 (8) 8/274 (7) 9/274 (10) 10/276 (11)   6/101 (7) 7/103 (8) 8/110 (9) 9/110 (5) 10/112 (10)

Sharma 27–8–48–1; Yadav 24–7–57–1; Ashwin 49–13–84–2; Jadeja 21.4–1–63–6; Nair 1–0–7–0. *Second innings*—Sharma 6–1–28–1; Ashwin 12.4–4–41–6; Yadav 9–2–30–2; Jadeja 8–5–3–1.

Umpires: R. K. Illingworth *(England)* (27) and N. J. Llong *(England)* (42).
Third umpire: R. A. Kettleborough *(England)*.   Referee: B. C. Broad *(England)* (84).

Close of play: first day, Australia 40–0 (Warner 23, Renshaw 15); second day, Australia 237–6 (Wade 25, Starc 14); third day, India 213–4 (Pujara 79, Rahane 40).

INDIA v AUSTRALIA 2016–17 (3rd Test)

At Jharkhand State C. A. Oval Ground, Ranchi, on 16, 17, 18, 19, 20 March, 2017.
Toss: Australia.   Result: DRAWN.
Debuts: none.
Man of the Match: C. A. Pujara.

By defying the spinners on a dusty last afternoon, the Australians took the series to a decider. India conceded 451 in the first innings, but from then on could hardly have fared better – until the penultimate session. They kept Australia in the field for 210 overs, built a lead of 152, and had nabbed four wickets by lunch on the fifth day. But Shaun Marsh and Handscomb knuckled down for 62 overs to see Australia to safety. Ranchi, the birthplace of India's former Indian captain M. S. Dhoni, was staging its first Test, and although the pitch looked strange it played serenely. Australia flew to 50 before Warner hit a full-toss back to Jadeja, but Smith, with his 19th Test century, and Maxwell – with his first – put on 191. India responded by topping 600, mainly thanks to Pujara's 202 – at 525 balls, the longest Test innings in India. Saha weighed in with 117, during a stand of 199, but Kohli managed only six, having injured his right shoulder while fielding. Slow left-armer O'Keefe delivered 77 overs, the most by an Australian since off-spinner Tom Veivers wheeled down 95.1 at Old Trafford in 1964 (though leg-spinner Jim Higgs bowled 59.6 eight-ball overs against England at Sydney in 1978–79). Australia lost Warner and Smith before the close, and were wobbling on the final morning before Handscomb joined Marsh for their match-saving stand. After Starc was ruled out by a broken foot, Cummins played his first Test since his 2011–12 debut, aged 18.

Australia

M. T. Renshaw c Kohli b Yadav	44	–	(2) lbw b Sharma	15
D. A. Warner c and b Jadeja	19	–	(1) b Jadeja	14
*S. P. D. Smith not out	178	–	(4) b Jadeja	21
S. E. Marsh c Pujara b Ashwin	2	–	(5) c Vijay b Jadeja	53
P. S. P. Handscomb lbw b Yadav	19	–	(6) not out	72
G. J. Maxwell c Saha b Jadeja	104	–	(7) c Vijay b Ashwin	2
†M. S. Wade c Saha b Jadeja	37	–	(8) not out	9
P. J. Cummins b Jadeja	0			
S. N. J. O'Keefe c Vijay b Yadav	25			
N. M. Lyon c Nair b Jadeja	1	–	(3) b Jadeja	2
J. R. Hazlewood run out (Rahul/Jadeja)	0			
B 9, lb 11, nb 2	22		B 9, lb 4, nb 3	16
(137.3 overs)	451		(6 wkts, 100 overs)	204

1/50 (2) 2/80 (1) 3/89 (4) 4/140 (5) 5/331 (6)
6/395 (7) 7/395 (8) 8/446 (9) 9/449 (10) 10/451 (11)
1/17 (1) 2/23 (3) 3/59 (2)
4/63 (4) 5/187 (5) 6/190 (7)

Sharma 20–2–70–0; Yadav 31–3–106–3; Ashwin 34–2–114–1; Jadeja 49.3–8–124–5; Vijay 3–0–17–0. *Second innings*—Ashwin 30–10–71–1; Jadeja 44–18–54–4; Yadav 15–2–36–0; Sharma 11–0–30–1.

India

K. L. Rahul c Wade b Cummins	67
M. Vijay st Wade b O'Keefe	82
C. A. Pujara c Maxwell b Lyon	202
*V. Kohli c Smith b Cummins	6
A. M. Rahane c Wade b Cummins	14
K. K. Nair b Hazlewood	23
R. Ashwin c Wade b Cummins	3
†W. P. Saha c Maxwell b O'Keefe	117
R. A. Jadeja not out	54
U. T. Yadav c Warner b O'Keefe	16
I. Sharma not out	0
B 14, lb 5	19
(9 wkts dec, 210 overs)	603

1/91 (1) 2/193 (2) 3/225 (4) 4/276 (5)
5/320 (6) 6/328 (7) 7/527 (3) 8/541 (8) 9/595 (10)

Hazlewood 44–10–103–1; Cummins 39–10–106–4; O'Keefe 77–17–199–3; Lyon 46–2–163–1; Maxwell 4–0–13–0.

Umpires: C. B. Gaffaney *(New Zealand)* (13) and I. J. Gould *(England)* (59).
Third umpire: N. J. Llong *(England)*.   Referee: R. B. Richardson *(West Indies)* (7).

Close of play: first day, Australia 299–4 (Smith 117, Maxwell 82); second day, India 120–1 (Vijay 42, Pujara 10); third day, India 360–6 (Pujara 130, Saha 18); fourth day, Australia 23–2 (Renshaw 7).

Test No. 2253/94 (I512, A801)

INDIA v AUSTRALIA 2016–17 (4th Test)

At Himachal Pradesh C. A. Stadium, Dharamsala, on 25, 26, 27, 28 March, 2017.
Toss: Australia.   Result: INDIA WON BY EIGHT WICKETS.
Debuts: India – K. Yadav.
Man of the Match: R. A. Jadeja.   Man of the Series: R. A. Jadeja.

India came from behind to take the Border–Gavaskar Trophy 2–1, in front of the stunning backdrop of the Himalayas in Dharamsala's maiden Test. Smith said visiting the Dalai Lama – based a few miles away at McLeod Ganj – had given his team perspective. Warner was dropped first ball, by Nair at third slip, and went on to 56, but Renshaw had no such luck, his stumps clonked by an Umesh Yadav special. Once again, though, Smith was the main man as Australia sprinted to 131 for one by lunch. He went on to 111, his 20th Test hundred and his seventh in ten matches against India, as the total reached 300, but Australia were pegged back by four wickets for the mesmerising left-arm unorthodox spin of the debutant Kuldeep Yadav. India, captained by Rahane after Kohli's shoulder injury, declined to 221 for six after a useful start, with Lyon varying his pace well – but another cussed contribution from Jadeja teased out a narrow lead of 32. Australia lost three wickets clearing that off, and had reached 87 when the killer blow fell: Smith, one short of 500 runs for the series, dragged a ball from Bhuvneshwar Kumar into his stumps. A procession followed: only Maxwell survived for long as the last six wickets mustered only 50. Jadeja's three wickets gave him 25 in the series. Rahul started the chase for 106 quickly, and when two wickets fell at 46 Rahane blasted two sixes off Cummins to settle any nerves.

Australia

D. A. Warner c Rahane b K. Yadav	56	– (2) c Saha b U. T. Yadav	6
M. T. Renshaw b U. T. Yadav	1	– (1) c Saha b U. T. Yadav	8
*S. P. D. Smith c Rahane b Ashwin	111	– b Bhuvneshwar Kumar	17
S. E. Marsh c Saha b U. T. Yadav	4	– (6) c Pujara b Jadeja	1
P. S. P. Handscomb b K. Yadav	8	– (4) c Rahane b Ashwin	18
G. J. Maxwell b K. Yadav	8	– (5) lbw b Ashwin	45
†M. S. Wade b Jadeja	57	– not out	25
P. J. Cummins c and b K. Yadav	21	– c Rahane b Jadeja	12
S. N. J. O'Keefe run out (sub [S. S. Iyer]/Saha)	8	– c Pujara b Jadeja	0
N. M. Lyon c Pujara b Bhuvneshwar Kumar	13	– c Vijay b U. T. Yadav	0
J. R. Hazlewood not out	2	– lbw b Ashwin	0
B 1, lb 10	11	B 4, lb 1	5
(88.3 overs)	300	(53.5 overs)	137

1/10 (2) 2/144 (1) 3/153 (4) 4/168 (5) 5/178 (6)   1/10 (2) 2/31 (3) 3/31 (1) 4/87 (4) 5/92 (6) 6/106 (5)
6/208 (3) 7/245 (8) 8/269 (9) 9/298 (7) 10/300 (10)   7/121 (8) 8/121 (9) 9/122 (10) 10/137 (11)

Bhuvneshwar Kumar 12.3–2–41–1; U. T. Yadav 15–1–69–2; Ashwin 23–5–54–1; Jadeja 15–1–57–1; K. Yadav 23–3–68–4. *Second innings*—Bhuvneshwar Kumar 7–1–27–1; U. T. Yadav 10–3–29–3; K. Yadav 5–0–23–0; Jadeja 18–7–24–3; Ashwin 13.5–4–29–3.

India

K. L. Rahul c Warner b Cummins	60	– not out	51
M. Vijay c Wade b Hazlewood	11	– c Wade b Cummins	8
C. A. Pujara c Handscomb b Lyon	57	– run out (Maxwell)	0
*A. M. Rahane c Smith b Lyon	46	– not out	38
K. K. Nair c Wade b Lyon	5		
R. Ashwin lbw b Lyon	30		
†W. P. Saha c Smith b Cummins	31		
R. A. Jadeja b Cummins	63		
Bhuvneshwar Kumar c Smith b O'Keefe	0		
K. Yadav c Hazlewood b Lyon	7		
U. T. Yadav not out	2		
B 4, lb 11, w 5	20	B 4, lb 5	9
(118.1 overs)	332	(2 wkts, 23.5 overs)	106

1/21 (2) 2/108 (1) 3/157 (4) 4/167 (5) 5/216 (4)   1/46 (2) 2/46 (3)
6/221 (6) 7/317 (8) 8/318 (9) 9/318 (7) 10/332 (10)

Hazlewood 25–8–51–1; Cummins 30–8–94–3; Lyon 34.1–5–92–5; O'Keefe 27–4–75–1; Maxwell 2–0–5–0. *Second innings*—Cummins 8–2–42–1; Hazlewood 6–2–14–0; O'Keefe 4.5–1–22–0; Lyon 5–0–19–0.

Umpires: M. Erasmus *(South Africa)* (42) and I. J. Gould *(England)* (60).
Third umpire: C. B. Gaffaney *(New Zealand)*.   Referee: R. B. Richardson *(West Indies)* (8).

Close of play: first day, India 0–0 (Rahul 0, Vijay 0); second day, India 248–6 (Saha 10, Jadeja 16); third day, India 19–0 (Rahul 13, Vijay 6).

Test No. 2254/17 (SL257, B99)

SRI LANKA v BANGLADESH 2016–17 (1st Test)

At Galle International Stadium on 7, 8, 9, 10, 11 March, 2017.
Toss: Sri Lanka.   Result: SRI LANKA WON BY 259 RUNS.
Debuts: none.
Man of the Match: B. K. G. Mendis.

Sri Lanka's Galle game-plan is simple: bat first, bat big, let the spinners loose. It worked again: Mendis was the primary architect of victory, narrowly missing a double-century, although he did have a vital reprieve, nicking his first delivery only to be saved as Subashis Roy had overstepped. Mendis knuckled down, opening out only after reaching an unusually compact fifty. His 197 took 441 minutes; he added 196 with Gunaratne and 110 with Dickwella as Sri Lanka reached 494. Bangladesh made a promising start, the openers putting on 118 before Tamim Iqbal was heedlessly run out. Mushfiqur Rahim's century stand with Mehedi Hasan lifted Bangladesh to 298 for six, but the last four tumbled for 14. Sri Lanka led by 182, and Tharanga's first hundred in home Tests extended the advantage to 429 by tea on the fourth day. Herath delayed another five overs until Chandimal reached 50, by which time the target was 457. After a 49-ball 53 from Soumya Sarkar, Bangladesh succumbed meekly. Herath collected his ninth five-for at Galle, a record tenth in the fourth innings of a Test. He ended the match with 366 wickets, passing Daniel Vettori (362) as Test cricket's most successful slow left-armer, and also completed his third win out of three as stand-in captain.

Sri Lanka

F. D. M. Karunaratne b Mehedi Hasan	30	–	c Mahmudullah b Taskin Ahmed	32
W. U. Tharanga b Subashis Roy	4	–	b Mehedi Hasan	115
B. K. G. Mendis c Tamim Iqbal b Mehedi Hasan	194	–	c Taskin Ahmed b Shakib Al Hasan	19
L. D. Chandimal c Mehedi Hasan b Mustafizur Rahman	5	–	not out	50
D. A. S. Gunaratne b Taskin Ahmed	85	–	b Shakib Al Hasan	0
†D. P. D. N. Dickwella c Mahmudullah b Mehedi Hasan	75	–	c Liton Das b Mehedi Hasan	15
M. D. K. Perera lbw b Mehedi Hasan	51	–	c Liton Das b Mustafizur Rahman	33
*H. M. R. K. B. Herath c Soumya Sarkar b Mustafizur Rahman	14			
R. A. S. Lakmal run out (Mustafizur Rahman/Liton Das)	8			
P. A. D. L. R. Sandakan c Mehedi Hasan b Shakib Al Hasan	5			
C. B. R. L. S. Kumara not out	0			
B 4, lb 10, w 4, nb 5	23		B 2, lb 1, w 6, nb 1	10
(129.1 overs)	494		(6 wkts dec, 69 overs)	274

1/15 (2) 2/60 (1) 3/92 (4) 4/288 (5) 5/398 (3)   1/69 (1) 2/134 (3) 3/198 (2)
6/432 (6) 7/457 (8) 8/480 (9) 9/494 (7) 10/494 (10)   4/199 (5) 5/222 (6) 6/274 (7)

Mustafizur Rahman 25–5–68–2; Taskin Ahmed 21–3–77–1; Subashis Roy 24–4–103–1; Mehedi Hasan 22–1–113–4; Shakib 32.1–5–100–1; Soumya Sarkar 3–0–9–0; Mahmudullah 2–0–10–0. *Second innings*—Subashis Roy 7–0–34–0; Mehedi Hasan 20–1–77–2; Mustafizur Rahman 9–4–24–1; Shakib 25–2–104–2; Taskin Ahmed 8–0–32–1.

Bangladesh

Tamim Iqbal run out (Dickwella)	57	–	c Gunaratne b Perera	19
Soumya Sarkar c Kumara b Lakmal	71	–	b Gunaratne	53
Mominul Haque lbw b Perera	7	–	lbw b Perera	5
*Mushfiqur Rahim b Herath	85	–	c Dickwella b Sandakan	34
Shakib Al Hasan c Dickwella b Sandakan	23	–	c Karunaratne b Herath	8
Mahmudullah b Kumara	8	–	lbw b Herath	0
†Liton Das c Gunaratne b Herath	5	–	c Tharanga b Herath	35
Mehedi Hasan lbw b Perera	41	–	c Kumara b Herath	28
Taskin Ahmed lbw b Perera	0	–	c Mendis b Herath	5
Subashis Roy not out	0	–	(11) not out	0
Mustafizur Rahman c Mendis b Herath	4	–	(10) b Herath	0
Lb 6, w 3, nb 2	11		B 1, lb 4, w 1, nb 4	10
(97.2 overs)	312		(60.2 overs)	197

1/118 (1) 2/127 (3) 3/142 (2) 4/170 (5) 5/184 (6)   1/67 (2) 2/80 (3) 3/83 (1) 4/104 (5)
6/192 (7) 7/298 (8) 8/298 (9) 9/308 (4) 10/312 (11)   5/104 (6) 6/158 (4) 7/166 (7)
   8/180 (9) 9/194 (10) 10/197 (8)

Lakmal 14–0–42–1; Kumara 16–1–70–1; Perera 19–4–53–3; Herath 26.2–4–72–3; Sandakan 22–5–69–1. *Second innings*—Lakmal 7–3–12–0; Perera 15–0–66–2; Herath 20.2–5–59–6; Gunaratne 6–1–16–1; Sandakan 9–0–29–1; Kumara 3–0–10–0.

Umpires: Aleem Dar *(Pakistan)* (110) and M. Erasmus *(South Africa)* (43).
Third umpire: S. Ravi *(India)*.   Referee: A. J. Pycroft *(Zimbabwe)* (53).

Close of play: first day, Sri Lanka 321–4 (Mendis 166, Dickwella 14); second day, Bangladesh 133–2 (Soumya Sarkar 66, Mushfiqur Rahim 1); third day, Bangladesh 312; fourth day, Bangladesh 67–0 (Tamim Iqbal 13, Soumya Sarkar 53).

SRI LANKA v BANGLADESH 2016–17 (2nd Test)

At P. Sara Oval, Colombo, on 15, 16, 17, 18, 19 March, 2017.
Toss: Sri Lanka.   Result: BANGLADESH WON BY FOUR WICKETS.
Debuts: Bangladesh – Mosaddek Hossain.
Man of the Match: Tamim Iqbal.   Man of the Series: Shakib Al Hasan.

Bangladesh's 100th Test produced their ninth win – to go with 76 defeats and 15 draws – and their first over Sri Lanka. Two passages defined the match. First, an hour late on the second day, when Bangladeshi errors were reprieved by slapstick fielding. At 165 for two, Imrul Kayes was badly dropped by Chandimal, whose earlier century had led a recovery from 70 for four. Imrul soon departed, but Shakib al Hasan was missed third ball, by Tharanga at deep square; his 116 set up a lead of 129. Sri Lanka cleared the deficit with one wicket down, and then came the second defining passage, a magic spell from Mustafizur Rahman. Mendis, Chandimal and de Silva all nicked balls angling in then jagging away. Karunaratne made 126 before becoming one of four victims for Shakib Al Hasan, an hour into the final day, Bangladesh needed 191 to square the series. Herath briefly threatened more fourth-innings mayhem, striking twice in his fourth over. But Tamim Iqbal was determined to make up for an indifferent run, and went 36 balls without a boundary. He did attack eventually – a four and six in succession off Sandakan – but only after passing 50. He fell with 60 still wanted, but Mushfiqur Rahim ensured Bangladesh's first away victory in nearly four years.

Sri Lanka

F. D. M. Karunaratne c Mehedi Hasan b Mustafizur Rahman...	7	– c Soumya Sarkar b Shakib Al Hasan	126
W. U. Tharanga c Soumya Sarkar b Mehedi Hasan................	11	– b Mehedi Hasan	26
B. K. G. Mendis st Mushfiqur Rahim b Mehedi Hasan............	5	– c Mushfiqur Rahim b Mustafizur Rahman..	36
L. D. Chandimal c Mosaddek Hossain b Mehedi Hasan............	138	– c Mushfiqur Rahim b Mustafizur Rahman..	5
D. A. S. Gunaratne lbw b Subashis Roy..............................	13	– lbw b Shakib Al Hasan.............................	7
D. M. de Silva b Taijul Islam...	34	– c Mushfiqur Rahim b Mustafizur Rahman..	0
†D. P. D. N. Dickwella b Shakib Al Hasan............................	34	– c Mushfiqur Rahim b Shakib Al Hasan.....	5
M. D. K. Perera c Soumya Sarkar b Mustafizur Rahman..........	9	– run out (Subashis Roy/Mehedi Hasan).......	50
*H. M. R. K. B. Herath c Soumya Sarkar b Shakib Al Hasan.....	25	– lbw b Taijul Islam..................................	9
R. A. S. Lakmal c Soumya Sarkar b Subashis Roy.................	35	– c Mosaddek Hossain b Shakib Al Hasan...	42
P. A. D. L. R. Sandakan not out..	5	– not out	0
B 1, lb 13, w 6, nb 2.........................	22	B 4, lb 8, w 1........................	13
(113.3 overs)	338	(113.2 overs)	319

1/13 (1) 2/24 (3) 3/35 (2) 4/70 (5) 5/136 (6)   1/57 (2) 2/143 (3) 3/165 (4) 4/176 (5)
6/180 (7) 7/195 (8) 8/250 (9) 9/305 (4) 10/338 (10)   5/177 (6) 6/190 (7) 7/217 (1)
8/238 (9) 9/318 (8) 10/319 (10)

Mustafizur Rahman 21–6–50–2; Subashis Roy 17.3–2–53–2; Mehedi Hasan 21–2–90–3; Taijul Islam 17–2–40–1; Shakib 33–4–80–2; Mosaddek Hossain 4–0–11–0. *Second innings*—Subashis Roy 16–4–36–0; Mehedi Hasan 24–0–71–1; Mustafizur Rahman 23–3–78–3; Shakib 36.2–9–74–4; Mosaddek Hossain 3–0–10–0; Taijul Islam 11–1–38–1.

Bangladesh

Tamim Iqbal lbw b Herath	49	– c Chandimal b Perera	82
Soumya Sarkar b Sandakan..................................	61	– c Tharanga b Herath	10
Imrul Kayes lbw b Sandakan	34	– c Gunaratne b Herath	0
Sabbir Rahman c de Silva b Lakmal	42	– lbw b Perera	41
Taijul Islam lbw b Sandakan..	0		
Shakib Al Hasan c Chandimal b Sandakan..................	116	– (5) b Perera	15
*†Mushfiqur Rahim b Lakmal.....................................	52	– (6) not out	22
Mosaddek Hossain st Dickwella b Herath	75	– (7) c Dickwella b Herath	13
Mehedi Hasan lbw b Herath......................................	24	– (8) not out...	2
Mustafizur Rahman lbw b Herath...............................	0		
Subashis Roy not out...	0		
B 4, lb 8, w 2..........................	14	B 4, lb 1, w 1	6
(134.1 overs)	467	(6 wkts, 57.5 overs).........................	191

1/95 (1) 2/130 (2) 3/192 (3) 4/192 (5) 5/198 (4)   1/22 (2) 2/22 (3) 3/131 (1)
6/290 (7) 7/421 (6) 8/454 (9) 9/454 (10) 10/467 (8)   4/143 (4) 5/162 (5) 6/189 (7)

Lakmal 25–3–90–2; Perera 33–5–100–0; Herath 34.1–6–82–4; Gunaratne 7–0–38–0; Sandakan 33–2–140–4; de Silva 2–0–5–0. *Second innings*—Perera 22–1–59–3; Herath 24.5–2–75–3; de Silva 2–0–7–0; Sandakan 6–1–34–0; Lakmal 2–0–7–0; Gunaratne 1–0–4–0.

Umpires: Aleem Dar *(Pakistan)* (111) and S. Ravi *(India)* (20).
Third umpire: M. Erasmus *(South Africa)*.   Referee: A. J. Pycroft *(Zimbabwe)* (54).

Close of play: first day, Sri Lanka 238–7 (Chandimal 86, Herath 18); second day, Bangladesh 214–5 (Shakib Al Hasan 18, Mushfiqur Rahim 2); third day, Sri Lanka 54–0 (Karunaratne 25, Tharanga 25); fourth day, Sri Lanka 268–8 (Perera 26, Lakmal 16).

NEW ZEALAND v SOUTH AFRICA 2016–17 (1st Test)

At University Oval, Dunedin, on 8, 9, 10, 11, 12 *(no play)* March, 2017.
Toss: South Africa.   Result: DRAWN.
Debuts: none.
Man of the Match: D. Elgar.

Had it not rained on the last day – as in the corresponding Test five years earlier – New Zealand might have won at the world's southernmost venue. They had to settle for maintaining an unbeaten record there (although this was the fifth draw out of eight). It was chilly – both teams used hand-warmers, and the umpires wore gloves – and scoring was difficult on a dry, low pitch: the run-rate was just 2.57, while Elgar survived 772 minutes and 548 balls (433 of them dots) overall. Patel played his first home Test for seven years, while Morkel returned after 13 months out with back trouble. When South Africa slumped to 22 for three against the swinging ball, du Plessis might have rued being the first captain to bat first in 23 Tests in New Zealand since January 2011. But Edgar was dropped at 36 by Watling off Boult, and added 126 with du Plessis. Next day Bavuma's patient 64 helped the total to 308. Williamson lasted 380 minutes for 130, but Taylor tore a calf muscle when eight, eventually limping back when the ninth wicket fell. The lead was limited to 33 by slow left-armer Maharaj, whose maiden five-for was the first by a South African spinner against New Zealand since David Pithey, across town at Carisbrook, in 1963-64. South Africa lost three for 25 to Patel and Santner, and were precariously placed – 191 ahead with four wickets left – at the end of the fourth day. But prospects of a gripping finale were frustrated by the rain.

South Africa

S. C. Cook lbw b Boult	3	– c Watling b Boult	0
D. Elgar c Watling b Wagner	140	– c Williamson b Patel	89
H. M. Amla b Wagner	1	– c sub (T. G. Southee) b Wagner	24
J-P. Duminy c Taylor b Wagner	1	– lbw b Wagner	39
*F. du Plessis c Boult b Neesham	52	– not out	56
T. Bavuma c Watling b Boult	64	– b Santner	6
†Q. de Kock c Wagner b Patel	10	– b Patel	4
V. D. Philander b Boult	21	– not out	1
K. A. Maharaj c Neesham b Boult	5		
K. Rabada b Patel	4		
M. Morkel not out	0		
B 4, lb 1, w 2	7	B 1, lb 3, w 1	5
(122.4 overs)	308	(6 wkts, 102 overs)	224

1/10 (1) 2/20 (3) 3/22 (4) 4/148 (5) 5/252 (2)
6/265 (7) 7/279 (6) 8/298 (9) 9/308 (10) 10/308 (8)

1/0 (1) 2/39 (3) 3/113 (4)
4/193 (2) 5/206 (6) 6/218 (7)

Boult 32.4–12–64–4; Wagner 31–8–88–3; Patel 33–12–85–2; Santner 18–5–32–0; Neesham 8–2–34–1. *Second innings*—Boult 15–4–34–1; Wagner 27–7–57–2; Santner 19–6–37–1; Patel 36–15–72–2; Neesham 5–0–20–0.

New Zealand

T. W. M. Latham c de Kock b Philander	10
J. A. Raval c Elgar b Maharaj	52
*K. S. Williamson c de Kock b Rabada	130
L. R. P. L. Taylor not out	15
H. M. Nicholls c Amla b Maharaj	12
J. S. Patel c du Plessis b Philander	16
J. D. S. Neesham c de Kock b Morkel	7
†B-J. Watling b Maharaj	50
M. J. Santner c Maharaj b Morkel	4
N. Wagner c Duminy b Maharaj	32
T. A. Boult b Maharaj	2
Lb 8, w 1, nb 2	11
(114.3 overs)	341

1/15 (1) 2/117 (2) 3/165 (5) 4/184 (6) 5/193 (7) 6/277 (3)
7/297 (9) 8/304 (8) 9/324 (11) 10/341 (10)

Taylor, when 8, retired hurt at 148–2 and resumed at 324–9.

Rabada 30–7–92–1; Philander 27–11–67–2; Morkel 24–6–62–2; Maharaj 28.3–7–94–5; Duminy 5–0–18–0.

Umpires: H. D. P. K. Dharmasena *(Sri Lanka)* (44) and B. N. J. Oxenford *(Australia)* (38).
Third umpire: R. J. Tucker *(Australia)*.   Referee: D. C. Boon *(Australia)* (39).

Close of play: first day, South Africa 229–4 (Elgar 128, Bavuma 38); second day, New Zealand 177–3 (Williamson 78, Patel 9); third day, South Africa 38–1 (Elgar 12, Amla 23); fourth day, South Africa 224–6 (du Plessis 56, Philander 1).

Test No. 2257/44 (NZ421, SA410)

NEW ZEALAND v SOUTH AFRICA 2016–17 (2nd Test)

At Basin Reserve, Wellington, on 16, 17, 18 March, 2017.
Toss: South Africa.   Result: SOUTH AFRICA WON BY EIGHT WICKETS.
Debuts: New Zealand – N. T. Broom.
Man of the Match: K. A. Maharaj.

Without Taylor and Boult, both injured, New Zealand caved inside three days. South Africa's seamers relished a quicker pitch, although the match award went to left-arm spinner Maharaj, who improved his Test-best for the second time in a week. After du Plessis won the toss, Rabada made early inroads, including Williamson, who called for a review after being given lbw, but the ball-tracking system was scuppered by mud flying off Rabada's boot. The debut innings of 33-year-old Neil Broom, Taylor's replacement, lasted only four deliveries before he was brilliantly caught by de Kock, and it needed a superb counter-attacking maiden century by Nicholls, in his 13th Test, to salvage the innings. Duminy found drift with his part-time off-breaks; occasionally looking unplayable, he snared four of the last five wickets, which fell for 51. But South Africa slipped to 94 for six on the second morning, before de Kock and Bavuma put on 160 in 39 overs. Last man Morkel equalled his Test-best 40 as the last four wickets added 265, and South Africa led by 91. On a cold, grey Saturday, their bowlers went in for the kill. Morkel gave the top order a fearsome examination, persuading the out-of-touch Latham to chase a wider one, and ending a forgettable Test for Williamson with a beauty that straightened and bounced. Then Maharaj ran through a spooked line-up with minimal fuss – and minimal turn. Raval batted over four hours for his brave 80, but Nicholls and Neesham played reckless shots. South Africa won inside the extra half-hour.

New Zealand

J. A. Raval c Amla b Maharaj	36	– (2) st de Kock b Maharaj	80
T. W. M. Latham c Elgar b Morkel	8	– (1) c Duminy b Morkel	6
*K. S. Williamson lbw b Rabada	2	– c de Kock b Morkel	1
N. T. Broom c de Kock b Rabada	0	– c de Kock b Morkel	20
H. M. Nicholls b Duminy	118	– b Maharaj	7
J. D. S. Neesham st de Kock b Maharaj	15	– c du Plessis b Maharaj	4
†B-J. Watling c de Kock b Duminy	34	– c Duminy b Maharaj	29
C. de Grandhomme c Amla b Duminy	4	– b Maharaj	0
T. G. Southee c Philander b Morkel	27	– c Duminy b Maharaj	4
J. S. Patel not out	17	– c de Kock b Rabada	0
N. Wagner lbw b Duminy	2	– not out	4
Lb 4, w 1	5	B 10, lb 1, w 5	16
(79.3 overs)	268	(63.2 overs)	171

1/11 (2) 2/13 (3) 3/21 (4) 4/73 (1) 5/101 (6)   1/16 (1) 2/26 (3) 3/64 (4) 4/86 (5) 5/90 (6) 6/155 (2)
6/217 (5) 7/221 (8) 8/222 (7) 9/266 (9) 10/268 (11)   7/161 (8) 8/167 (9) 9/167 (10) 10/171 (7)

Morkel 18–3–82–2; Philander 15–7–29–0; Rabada 19–6–59–2; Duminy 11.3–2–47–4; Maharaj 16–4–47–2. *Second innings*—Morkel 11–0–50–3; Philander 12–3–28–0; Rabada 17–5–38–1; Maharaj 20.2–7–40–6; Duminy 3–1–4–0.

South Africa

S. C. Cook c Neesham b Southee	3	– c Neesham b Southee	11
D. Elgar c Neesham b de Grandhomme	9	– c Watling b Wagner	17
K. Rabada b Southee	9		
H. M. Amla c Nicholls b de Grandhomme	21	– (3) not out	38
J-P. Duminy c Nicholls b Wagner	16	– (4) not out	15
*F. du Plessis c Watling b de Grandhomme	22		
T. Bavuma c Neesham b Wagner	89		
†Q. de Kock c Watling b Neesham	91		
V. D. Philander not out	37		
K. A. Maharaj c Williamson b Wagner	1		
M. Morkel b Patel	40		
B 4, lb 5, w 12	21	W 2	2
(98 overs)	359	(2 wkts, 24.3 overs)	83

1/12 (1) 2/12 (2) 3/26 (3) 4/59 (5) 5/79 (4)   1/18 (1) 2/48 (2)
6/94 (6) 7/254 (8) 8/290 (7) 9/302 (10) 10/359 (11)

Southee 27–7–98–2; de Grandhomme 23–7–52–3; Wagner 22–1–102–3; Patel 14–1–57–1; Neesham 12–2–41–1. *Second innings*—Southee 6–2–17–1; de Grandhomme 8–1–20–0; Wagner 8–2–18–1; Neesham 2.3–0–28–0.

Umpires: H. D. P. K. Dharmasena *(Sri Lanka)* (45) and R. J. Tucker *(Australia)* (53).
Third umpire: B. N. J. Oxenford *(Australia)*.   Referee: D. C. Boon *(Australia)* (40).

Close of play: first day, South Africa 24–2 (Rabada 8, Amla 0); second day, South Africa 349–9 (Philander 36, Morkel 31).

NEW ZEALAND v SOUTH AFRICA 2016–17 (3rd Test)

At Seddon Park, Hamilton, on 25, 26, 27, 28, 29 *(no play)* March, 2017.
Toss: South Africa. Result: DRAWN.
Debuts: South Africa – T. B. de Bruyn.
Man of the Match: K. S. Williamson.

South Africa needed only a draw to take the series – and, thanks mainly to Hamilton's weather, they got it. As in the First Test, rain on the last day scuppered New Zealand's victory hopes, and maintained South Africa's stranglehold over them: in 45 Tests since 1931–32, they had won 25 and lost four. Du Plessis chose to bat on a dark, grassy surface. Rain limited the first day to 41 overs, but on the second South Africa were 190 for six before de Kock cracked 90 off 118 balls, to lift the total to 314. For New Zealand, Latham ended a slump – 33 runs in eight international innings – while Raval batted doggedly for more than 6½ hours for 88. But the star was Williamson, who equalled Martin Crowe's national record of 17 Test centuries, and finished with 176, New Zealand's highest score at home against South Africa (previously Scott Styris's 170 at Auckland in 2003–04). Philander went wicketless at the venue where he had destroyed New Zealand five years earlier and, although Morkel and Rabada shared eight victims, they sent down 70 overs between them. De Grandhomme spanked 57 as the lead stretched to 175. Four sessions remained. Wearied by 162 overs in the field, South Africa were soon 59 for five; Theunis de Bruyn completed an unhappy debut, run out after a mid-pitch collision with Amla. Du Plessis and de Kock clung on until stumps, with South Africa trailing by 95 – but the pesky rain left New Zealand's comeback unfulfilled.

South Africa

D. Elgar b de Grandhomme	5	– c Watling b de Grandhomme		5
T. B. de Bruyn c Latham b Henry	0	– run out (Williamson/Watling)		12
H. M. Amla b de Grandhomme	50	– c de Grandhomme b Patel		19
J-P. Duminy c Patel b Henry	20	– b Patel		13
*F. du Plessis c Latham b Santner	53	– not out		15
T. Bavuma c Raval b Henry	29	– c Watling b Henry		1
†Q. de Kock lbw b Wagner	90	– not out		15
V. D. Philander c Latham b Henry	11			
K. A. Maharaj c Watling b Wagner	9			
K. Rabada c Watling b Wagner	34			
M. Morkel not out	9			
Lb 1, w 3	4			
(89.2 overs)	314	(5 wkts, 39 overs)		80

1/5 (2) 2/5 (1) 3/64 (4) 4/97 (3) 5/148 (6) 1/13 (1) 2/25 (2) 3/49 (3)
6/190 (5) 7/219 (8) 8/249 (9) 9/295 (7) 10/314 (10) 4/50 (4) 5/59 (6)

Henry 24–2–93–4; de Grandhomme 24–4–62–2; Wagner 25.2–2–104–3; Patel 7–0–30–0; Santner 9–3–24–1. *Second innings*—Henry 11–4–20–1; de Grandhomme 8–5–15–1; Wagner 5–0–16–0; Patel 12–2–22–2; Santner 3–0–7–0.

New Zealand

T. W. M. Latham c de Kock b Morkel	50
J. A. Raval c de Kock b Morkel	88
*K. S. Williamson c Philander b Morkel	176
N. T. Broom lbw b Rabada	12
H. M. Nicholls c de Kock b Rabada	0
M. J. Santner c Duminy b Rabada	41
†B-J. Watling b Maharaj	24
C. de Grandhomme c de Kock b Morkel	57
M. J. Henry c Elgar b Maharaj	12
J. S. Patel c de Kock b Rabada	5
N. Wagner not out	0
Lb 12, w 5, nb 7	24
(162.1 overs)	489

1/83 (1) 2/273 (2) 3/293 (4) 4/293 (5) 5/381 (3)
6/397 (6) 7/443 (7) 8/477 (9) 9/489 (10) 10/489 (8)

Philander 33–7–79–0; Morkel 36.1–7–100–4; Rabada 34–3–122–4; Maharaj 50–8–118–2; Duminy 6–0–38–0; Elgar 1–0–13–0; Bavuma 2–0–7–0.

Umpires: B. N. J. Oxenford *(Australia)* (39) and R. J. Tucker *(Australia)* (54).
Third umpire: H. D. P. K. Dharmasena *(Sri Lanka)*. Referee: D. C. Boon *(Australia)* (41).

Close of play: first day, South Africa 123–4 (du Plessis 33, Bavuma 13); second day, New Zealand 67–0 (Latham 42, Raval 25); third day, New Zealand 321–4 (Williamson 148, Santner 13); fourth day, South Africa 80–5 (du Plessis 15, de Kock 15).

WEST INDIES v PAKISTAN 2016–17 (1st Test)

At Sabina Park, Kingston, Jamaica, on 21, 22, 23, 24, 25 April, 2017.
Toss: Pakistan.   Result: PAKISTAN WON BY SEVEN WICKETS.
Debuts: West Indies – S. O. Hetmyer, V. A. Singh. Pakistan – Mohammad Abbas.
Man of the Match: Yasir Shah.

Younis Khan had last played a Test in Jamaica in June 2005, when he scored a hundred in a Pakistan victory. Back at Sabina Park, which was hosting its 50th Test, Younis reached tea on the third day with 9,999 Test runs. Two balls afterwards he became the first Pakistani to reach 10,000 – the 13th overall and, at 39 years 145 days, the oldest. While the focus was on batting milestones – Misbah-ul-Haq became Pakistan's seventh to 5,000 runs – it was their bowling that won the match. The debutant Mohammad Abbas moved the ball well, although Mohammad Amir's career-best six for 44 included Powell, playing his first Test in almost three years after a dalliance with baseball. His dismissal left West Indies 71 for five, their prospects as gloomy as the skies – but the last five wickets quadrupled the score. Chase put on 118 with Dowrich, before being stunningly caught by Wahab Riaz, running back from mid-off. Only 11 overs were possible on the second day because of rain and a leaking cover. Although Misbah ran out of partners on 99, he was happy with a lead of 121 on a wearing surface. Gabriel was fined 50% of his match fee for barging into Sarfraz Ahmed at the end of an over. West Indies reached 72 for one, but then lost nine for 80; Yasir Shah ended with six for 63. Misbah ended proceedings with successive sixes off Bishoo, the fourth time he had secured victory with a six, extending his own record.

West Indies

K. C. Brathwaite c Younis Khan b Mohammad Abbas	0	– b Yasir Shah	14
K. O. A. Powell c Younis Khan b Mohammad Amir	33	– c Younis Khan b Yasir Shah	49
S. O. Hetmyer b Mohammad Amir	11	– b Yasir Shah	20
S. D. Hope b Mohammad Amir	2	– lbw b Yasir Shah	6
V. A. Singh c Azhar Ali b Wahab Riaz	9	– (6) b Mohammad Amir	9
R. L. Chase c Wahab Riaz b Yasir Shah	63	– (7) not out	16
†S. O. Dowrich b Yasir Shah	56	– (8) lbw b Mohammad Abbas	0
*J. O. Holder not out	57	– (9) c Sarfraz Ahmed b Wahab Riaz	14
D. Bishoo c Sarfraz Ahmed b Mohammad Amir	28	– (5) c Younis Khan b Mohammad Abbas	18
A. S. Joseph b Mohammad Amir	0	– lbw b Yasir Shah	1
S. T. Gabriel b Mohammad Amir	5	– c Mohammad Abbas b Yasir Shah	0
B 4, lb 18	22	Lb 5	5
(95 overs)	286	(52.4 overs)	152

1/1 (1) 2/24 (3) 3/32 (4) 4/53 (5) 5/71 (2) 6/189 (6)
7/189 (7) 8/264 (9) 9/274 (10) 10/286 (11)

1/22 (1) 2/72 (3) 3/84 (4) 4/89 (2)
5/110 (6) 6/129 (5) 7/129 (8)
8/151 (9) 9/152 (10) 10/152 (11)

Mohammad Amir 26–11–44–6; Mohammad Abbas 22–4–63–1; Wahab Riaz 23–6–66–1; Yasir Shah 24–5–91–2. *Second innings*—Mohammad Amir 14–4–20–1; Mohammad Abbas 11–1–35–2; Yasir Shah 21.4–4–63–6; Wahab Riaz 6–0–29–1.

Pakistan

Azhar Ali c Dowrich b Joseph	15	– b Joseph	1
Ahmed Shehzad lbw b Holder	31	– c Dowrich b Gabriel	6
Babar Azam b Gabriel	72	– not out	9
Younis Khan c Brathwaite b Gabriel	58	– lbw b Bishoo	6
*Misbah-ul-Haq not out	99	– not out	12
Asad Shafiq c Dowrich b Gabriel	22		
†Sarfraz Ahmed b Bishoo	54		
Mohammad Amir c Dowrich b Joseph	11		
Wahab Riaz b Joseph	9		
Yasir Shah run out (sub [J. Blackwood])	8		
Mohammad Abbas lbw b Chase	1		
B 4, lb 10, w 1, nb 12	27	Lb 2	2
(138.4 overs)	407	(3 wkts, 10.5 overs)	36

1/23 (1) 2/54 (2) 3/185 (4) 4/186 (3) 5/236 (6)
6/324 (7) 7/341 (8) 8/355 (9) 9/373 (10) 10/407 (11)

1/7 (2) 2/7 (1) 3/24 (4)

Gabriel 29–6–92–3; Joseph 31–8–71–3; Holder 30–6–65–1; Bishoo 33–2–106–1; Chase 8.4–1–37–1; Brathwaite 7–1–22–0. *Second innings*—Gabriel 3–1–7–1; Joseph 3–1–6–1; Bishoo 2.5–0–19–1; Holder 2–1–2–0.

Umpires: R. K. Illingworth *(England)* (28) and R. A. Kettleborough *(England)* (43).
Third umpire: B. N. J. Oxenford *(Australia)*.   Referee: B. C. Broad *(England)* (85).

Close of play: first day, West Indies 244–7 (Holder 30, Bishoo 23); second day, West Indies 278–9 (Holder 55, Gabriel 4); third day, Pakistan 201–4 (Misbah-ul-Haq 5, Asad Shafiq 5); fourth day, West Indies 93–4 (Bishoo 0, Singh 0).

Test No. 2260/51 (WI522, P409)

WEST INDIES v PAKISTAN 2016–17 (2nd Test)

At Kensington Oval, Bridgetown, Barbados, on 30 April, 1, 2, 3, 4 May, 2017.
Toss: West Indies.   Result: WEST INDIES WON BY 106 RUNS.
Debuts: Pakistan – Shadab Khan.
Man of the Match: S. T. Gabriel.

This match brought back memories of West Indies' fiery prime. Gabriel's pace and menace earned nine wickets, including five on the last day as Pakistan – needing 188 to become the first Asian team to win in Barbados – were blown away for 81, their second-lowest against West Indies, after 77 at Lahore in 1986–87. Chase had shored up a total of 312, before Pakistan's openers crawled along: Azhar Ali took 268 balls to reach his 13th Test hundred, while Ahmed Shehzad made 23 from his first 104 deliveries on his way to 70 off 191. But from 155 for none they lost three for six, including Babar Azam for the first half of a pair. Misbah-ul-Haq prevented a collapse before gloving to gully; he was the first to make 99 three times in Tests (including one in the previous match), a stat as unwanted as Pakistan's seventh defeat in eight matches. On the fourth day, Hope's Test-best 90 lifted West Indies to 235 for four but, once he picked out cover, the last six tumbled for 33. Yasir's seven for 94 – his tenth five-for in just 25 Tests – were Pakistan's second-best figures against West Indies, after Imran Khan's seven for 80 at Georgetown in 1987–88. But the home seamers reduced Pakistan to 36 for seven; Gabriel finished with the second-cheapest five-for by a West Indian paceman, after Jermaine Lawson's six for three against Bangladesh at Dhaka in 2002–03 (Jerome Taylor also took five for 11 against England at Kingston in 2008–09).

West Indies

K. C. Brathwaite c Sarfraz Ahmed b Mohammad Amir	9	–	c Younis Khan b Yasir Shah	43
K. O. A. Powell lbw b Mohammad Amir	38	–	c Sarfraz Ahmed b Mohammad Abbas	6
S. O. Hetmyer c Azhar Ali b Mohammad Abbas	1	–	b Mohammad Amir	22
S. D. Hope c Sarfraz Ahmed b Yasir Shah	5	–	c Azhar Ali b Yasir Shah	90
R. L. Chase c Younis Khan b Mohammad Amir	131	–	c and b Yasir Shah	23
V. A. Singh c Younis Khan b Mohammad Abbas	3	–	b Mohammad Abbas	32
†S. O. Dowrich c Younis Khan b Shadab Khan	29	–	c Asad Shafiq b Yasir Shah	2
*J. O. Holder c Sarfraz Ahmed b Mohammad Abbas	58	–	c Younis Khan b Yasir Shah	1
D. Bishoo c Yasir Shah b Mohammad Abbas	14	–	c Azhar Ali b Yasir Shah	20
A. S. Joseph b Yasir Shah	8	–	c Mohammad Amir b Yasir Shah	7
S. T. Gabriel not out	0	–	not out	0
B 4, lb 10, w 2	16		B 16, lb 2, w 3, nb 1	22
(98.5 overs)	312		(102.5 overs)	268

1/12 (1) 2/13 (3) 3/37 (4) 4/102 (2) 5/107 (6)   1/8 (2) 2/41 (3) 3/97 (1) 4/155 (5)
6/154 (7) 7/286 (8) 8/286 (5) 9/312 (9) 10/312 (10)   5/235 (4) 6/235 (6) 7/236 (8)
                                                      8/252 (7) 9/261 (10) 10/268 (9)

Mohammad Amir 26–5–65–3; Mohammad Abbas 23–6–56–4; Yasir Shah 25.5–2–83–2; Shadab Khan 23–3–90–1; Azhar Ali 1–0–4–0. *Second innings*—Mohammad Amir 21–8–44–1; Mohammad Abbas 25–6–57–2; Yasir Shah 39.5–12–94–7; Shadab Khan 17–0–55–0.

Pakistan

Azhar Ali c Dowrich b Bishoo	105	–	c Hetmyer b Gabriel	10
Ahmed Shehzad c Hope b Bishoo	70	–	lbw b Joseph	14
Babar Azam c and b Gabriel	0	–	c Dowrich b Joseph	0
Younis Khan c Gabriel b Bishoo	0	–	lbw b Holder	5
*Misbah-ul-Haq c Hope b Holder	99	–	c Hope b Gabriel	0
Asad Shafiq lbw b Holder	15	–	c Powell b Gabriel	0
†Sarfraz Ahmed c Powell b Gabriel	9	–	c Chase b Holder	23
Shadab Khan c Chase b Gabriel	16	–	c Dowrich b Holder	1
Mohammad Amir c Hope b Holder	10	–	c Singh b Gabriel	20
Yasir Shah c Dowrich b Gabriel	24	–	b Gabriel	0
Mohammad Abbas not out	1	–	not out	0
B 16, lb 16, nb 12	44		B 4, lb 1, nb 3	8
(140 overs)	393		(34.4 overs)	81

1/155 (2) 2/156 (3) 3/161 (4) 4/259 (1) 5/316 (5)   1/10 (1) 2/11 (3) 3/27 (4) 4/30 (5) 5/30 (6)
6/325 (7) 7/329 (6) 8/354 (9) 9/384 (8) 10/393 (10)   6/35 (2) 7/36 (8) 8/78 (9) 9/81 (10) 10/81 (7)

Gabriel 32–6–81–4; Joseph 19–5–48–0; Chase 19–2–74–0; Holder 29–11–42–3; Bishoo 41–11–116–3. *Second innings*—Gabriel 11–4–11–5; Joseph 12–1–42–2; Holder 11.4–4–23–3.

Umpires: R. A. Kettleborough *(England)* (44) and B. N. J. Oxenford *(Australia)* (40).
Third umpire: R. K. Illingworth *(England)*.   Referee: B. C. Broad *(England)* (86).

Close of play: first day, West Indies 286–6 (Chase 131, Holder 58); second day, Pakistan 172–3 (Azhar Ali 81, Misbah-ul-Haq 7); third day, West Indies 40–1 (Brathwaite 8, Hetmyer 22); fourth day, West Indies 264–9 (Bishoo 16, Gabriel 0).

Test No. 2261/52 (WI523, P410)

WEST INDIES v PAKISTAN 2016–17 (3rd Test)

At Windsor Park, Roseau, Dominica, on 10, 11, 12, 13, 14 May, 2017.
Toss: West Indies.   Result: PAKISTAN WON BY 101 RUNS.
Debuts: Pakistan – Hasan Ali.
Man of the Match: R. L. Chase.   Man of the Series: Yasir Shah.

With two overs left, the prospect of Misbah-ul-Haq and Younis Khan enjoying a victorious farewell was receding. Yasir Shah was bowling to last man Gabriel, who was defending stoutly, and Chase was ready to add one final over's defiance to his six-hour stay. But when Yasir floated his last delivery outside off, Gabriel swung heedlessly, and inside-edged into his stumps. So Misbah, Pakistan's most successful captain with 26 victories, and Younis, their most prolific batsman, finished their illustrious careers as part of the first Pakistan team to win a series in the Caribbean. Yasir's third five-for gave him 25 wickets in the series. The first three days had given no hint of the gripping climax. Put in on a sluggish surface, Pakistan needed until late on the second day to reach 376. Azhar Ali compiled another careful century from 266 balls, two quicker than at Bridgetown. Mohammad Abbas then claimed a maiden five-for, the last three for ducks as West Indies lost five for 29. After Babar Azam's third duck of the series, Misbah and Younis top-edged sweeps – but, from 90 for seven, Yasir and Mohammad Amir put on 61. Pakistan's bowlers had a day plus 30 minutes to clinch the series. It looked done and dusted at 93 for six, with 53 overs left – but Chase dug in with the tail: Holder made 22 in 85 minutes, Bishoo three in 71, Joseph five in 59, and Gabriel four in 32. Another few minutes, and the series would have been shared.

Pakistan

Azhar Ali b Chase	127	–	c sub (J. Blackwood) b Gabriel	3
Shan Masood c Holder b Chase	9	–	lbw b Gabriel	21
Babar Azam c Powell b Joseph	55	–	c Hetmyer b Chase	0
Younis Khan lbw b Holder	18	–	c Powell b Bishoo	35
*Misbah-ul-Haq c Dowrich b Chase	59	–	c Dowrich b Bishoo	2
Asad Shafiq c Singh b Chase	17	–	c and b Joseph	13
†Sarfraz Ahmed c Hope b Bishoo	51	–	c Dowrich b Joseph	4
Mohammad Amir b Holder	7	–	c Bishoo b Joseph	27
Yasir Shah c Powell b Holder	0	–	not out	38
Mohammad Abbas st Dowrich b Bishoo	4			
Hasan Ali not out	8	–	(10) not out	15
B 4, lb 2, w 3, nb 8	21		Lb 5, w 7, nb 4	16
(146.3 overs)	376		(8 wkts dec, 57 overs)	174

1/19 (2) 2/139 (3) 3/177 (4) 4/241 (1) 5/274 (6)   1/6 (1) 2/8 (3) 3/57 (2) 4/65 (5) 5/72 (4)
6/311 (5) 7/322 (8) 8/322 (9) 9/367 (7) 10/376 (10)   6/82 (7) 7/90 (6) 8/151 (8)

Gabriel 32–9–67–0; Joseph 27–9–64–1; Chase 32–5–103–4; Holder 32–9–71–3; Bishoo 23.3–3–61–2. *Second innings*—Gabriel 10–1–24–2; Joseph 15–3–53–3; Chase 9–0–31–1; Holder 9–4–7–0; Bishoo 14–2–54–2.

West Indies

K. C. Brathwaite c Sarfraz Ahmed b Yasir Shah	29	–	c Hasan Ali b Yasir Shah	6
K. O. A. Powell c Azhar Ali b Yasir Shah	31	–	c Shan Masood b Yasir Shah	4
S. O. Hetmyer c Sarfraz Ahmed b Yasir Shah	17	–	b Mohammad Amir	25
S. D. Hope c Misbah-ul-Haq b Azhar Ali	29	–	lbw b Hasan Ali	17
R. L. Chase b Mohammad Abbas	69	–	not out	101
V. A. Singh lbw b Mohammad Abbas	8	–	c Babar Azam b Yasir Shah	2
†S. O. Dowrich b Mohammad Amir	20	–	c Babar Azam b Yasir Shah	2
*J. O. Holder not out	30	–	lbw b Hasan Ali	22
D. Bishoo c Younis Khan b Mohammad Abbas	0	–	c Shan Masood b Mohammad Abbas	3
A. S. Joseph b Mohammad Abbas	0	–	c Sarfraz Ahmed b Hasan Ali	5
S. T. Gabriel c Babar Azam b Mohammad Abbas	0	–	b Yasir Shah	4
B 4, lb 2, w 5, nb 3	14		B 6, w 2, nb 3	11
(115 overs)	247		(96 overs)	202

1/43 (2) 2/69 (3) 3/97 (1) 4/152 (4) 5/189 (6)   1/7 (2) 2/22 (1) 3/47 (3) 4/66 (4) 5/76 (6) 6/93 (7)
6/218 (7) 7/239 (5) 8/239 (9) 9/241 (10) 10/247 (11)   7/151 (8) 8/181 (9) 9/197 (10) 10/202 (11)

In the first innings Chase, when 60, retired hurt at 183-4 and resumed at 218-6.

Mohammad Amir 27–12–32–1; Mohammad Abbas 25–7–46–5; Yasir Shah 40–4–126–3; Hasan Ali 17–4–22–0; Azhar Ali 6–1–15–1. *Second innings*—Mohammad Amir 15–8–22–1; Mohammad Abbas 20–9–31–1; Yasir Shah 37–13–92–5; Hasan Ali 20–7–33–3; Azhar Ali 2–0–3–0; Asad Shafiq 2–0–15–0.

Umpires: R. K. Illingworth *(England)* (29) and B. N. J. Oxenford *(Australia)* (41).
Third umpire: R. A. Kettleborough *(England).*   Referee: B. C. Broad *(England)* (87).

Close of play: first day, Pakistan 169-2 (Azhar Ali 85, Younis Khan 10); second day, West Indies 14–0 (Brathwaite 5, Powell 9); third day, West Indies 218-5 (Dowrich 20, Holder 11); fourth day, West Indies 7–1 (Brathwaite 3).

Test No. 2262/146 (E984, SA412)

ENGLAND v SOUTH AFRICA 2017 (1st Test)

At Lord's, London, on 6, 7, 8, 9 July, 2017.
Toss: England.   Result: ENGLAND WON BY 211 RUNS.
Debuts: South Africa – H. G. Kuhn.
Man of the Match: M. M. Ali.

Joe Root enjoyed a dream start as England's 80th Test captain. He won the toss, survived two early chances to cruise to 190, then stood smiling at slip as a rudderless South Africa capsized twice on an unusually dry pitch, allowing spin and occasional uneven bounce. It was their first defeat since 1960 at Lord's, where they had been particularly potent since readmission, winning four of five Tests. As Faf du Plessis was at home after the birth of his first child, Dean Elgar became the match's second new captain – the first instance in a Test in England since 1968. Morkel and Philander reduced England to 76 for four, and it might have been worse: Root, on five, hooked Rabada to long leg, where Aiden Markram – briefly on as a substitute – had drifted in too far. Then, on 16, he flashed Rabada through Duminy's upstretched hands in the gully. He survived to add 114 with Stokes (who was bowled by a no-ball, the 13th time Morkel had forfeited a wicket this way) and 177 with Ali, before Broad biffed his first half-century in 66 Test innings since July 2013. South Africa batted solidly – four fifties and a 48 – to reach 361, and when a good bowling effort defenestrated England from 139 for one, the target was 331. They never threatened, with Ali taking his match haul to ten for 112, the best by a spinner at Lord's since Derek Underwood's 13 for 71 on a rain-affected track against Pakistan in 1974.

England

A. N. Cook c de Kock b Philander	3	–	c Bavuma b Morkel	69
K. K. Jennings lbw b Philander	8	–	c de Kock b Morkel	33
G. S. Ballance lbw b Morkel	20	–	c de Kock b Morkel	34
*J. E. Root c de Kock b Morkel	190	–	b Maharaj	5
†J. M. Bairstow lbw b Philander	10	–	st de Kock b Maharaj	51
B. A. Stokes c de Kock b Rabada	56	–	lbw b Rabada	1
M. M. Ali b Rabada	87	–	b Maharaj	7
L. A. Dawson lbw b Morkel	0	–	b Rabada	0
S. C. J. Broad not out	57	–	c de Bruyn b Maharaj	0
M. A. Wood lbw b Rabada	0	–	b Rabada	28
J. M. Anderson c de Kock b Morkel	12	–	not out	0
Lb 2, nb 13	15		Lb 4, nb 1	5
(105.3 overs)	458		(87.1 overs)	233

1/14 (1) 2/17 (2) 3/49 (3) 4/76 (5) 5/190 (6)   1/80 (2) 2/139 (1) 3/142 (3) 4/146 (4) 5/149 (6)
6/367 (4) 7/367 (8) 8/413 (7) 9/413 (10) 10/458 (11)   6/180 (7) 7/181 (8) 8/182 (9) 9/227 (10) 10/233 (5)

Morkel 25.3–2–115–4; Philander 20–3–67–3; Rabada 28–4–123–3; Maharaj 22–1–107–0; de Bruyn 5–1–30–0; Bavuma 5–0–14–0. *Second innings*—Morkel 21–6–64–3; Rabada 20–5–50–3; Maharaj 32.1–8–85–4; Duminy 9–2–21–0; Philander 5–1–9–0.

South Africa

*D. Elgar c Ballance b Ali	54	–	(2) c and b Ali	2
H. G. Kuhn c Cook b Broad	1	–	(1) c Bairstow b Anderson	9
H. M. Amla lbw b Ali	29	–	lbw b Dawson	11
J-P. Duminy lbw b Broad	15	–	c Ali b Wood	2
T. Bavuma c Stokes b Ali	59	–	(6) b Ali	21
T. B. de Bruyn c Bairstow b Anderson	48	–	(7) c Stokes b Ali	1
K. Rabada c Bairstow b Dawson	27	–	(10) c Bairstow b Ali	4
†Q. de Kock c Stokes b Anderson	51	–	(5) b Ali	18
V. D. Philander b Ali	52	–	(8) not out	19
K. A. Maharaj lbw b Dawson	9	–	(9) b Ali	10
M. Morkel not out	2	–	c Jennings b Dawson	14
B 4, lb 7, nb 3	14		B 7, lb 1	8
(105 overs)	361		(36.4 overs)	119

1/10 (2) 2/82 (3) 3/98 (1) 4/104 (4) 5/203 (6)   1/12 (1) 2/12 (2) 3/25 (4) 4/28 (3) 5/64 (5) 6/67 (6)
6/244 (7) 7/248 (5) 8/314 (8) 9/337 (10) 10/361 (9)   7/72 (8) 8/82 (9) 9/94 (10) 10/119 (11)

Anderson 19–6–44–2; Broad 18–5–62–2; Wood 20–5–65–0; Dawson 15–2–67–2; Ali 20–7–59–4; Stokes 13–2–53–0. *Second innings*—Anderson 6–2–16–1; Broad 3–1–5–0; Ali 15–4–53–6; Wood 1–0–3–1; Dawson 11.4–4–34–2.

Umpires: S. Ravi *(India)* (21) and P. R. Reiffel *(Australia)* (31).
Third umpire: S. D. Fry *(Australia)*.   Referee: J. J. Crowe *(New Zealand)* (82).

Close of play: first day, England 357–5 (Root 184, Ali 61); second day, South Africa 214–5 (Bavuma 48, Rabada 9); third day, England 119–1 (Cook 59, Ballance 22).

Test No. 2263/147 (E985, SA413)

ENGLAND v SOUTH AFRICA 2017 (2nd Test)

At Trent Bridge, Nottingham, on 14, 15, 16, 17 July, 2017.
Toss: South Africa.   Result: SOUTH AFRICA WON BY 340 RUNS.
Debuts: none.
Man of the Match: V. D. Philander.

South Africa had underperformed in consecutive matches about as rarely as England had followed one strong game with another. Only once since early 2009 had South Africa lost more than one Test in a row; England had won two in succession only twice since the 2015 Ashes. So there was little surprise when the visitors made up for their supine display at Lord's with a thumping victory. Amla and de Kock were the backbone of an innings of 335, before both England openers departed with the total on three. Only the Yorkshire pair of Root and Bairstow thrived, with the energetic Morris taking three wickets (he finished with match figures of five for 45). Amla did well again as the lead mounted, becoming only the second player (after Andrew Symonds for Australia v West Indies at Kingston in 2008) to reach two half-centuries in a match with sixes. He put on 135 with Elgar, then the restored du Plessis made 63 before eventually setting a target of 474. England needed to bat for more than two days to avoid their first Test defeat at Trent Bridge since 2007. Cook overturned a first-ball lbw decision to make 42, but no one else reached 30: it was all over before tea on the fourth day. Olivier, playing in place of Rabada (banned for swearing at Stokes at Lord's) claimed the last two wickets with successive balls to complete the rout. England's coach Trevor Bayliss did not spare his batsmen: "They've had a shocker."

South Africa

D. Elgar c Dawson b Anderson	6	– (2) c Anderson b Stokes	80
H. G. Kuhn b Broad	34	– (1) c Root b Anderson	8
H. M. Amla c Wood b Broad	78	– lbw b Dawson	87
†Q. de Kock c Cook b Broad	68	– c Bairstow b Anderson	1
*F. du Plessis c Bairstow b Stokes	19	– lbw b Stokes	63
T. Bavuma c Bairstow b Stokes	20	– c Root b Ali	15
V. D. Philander c Dawson b Anderson	54	– c and b Ali	42
C. H. Morris c and b Anderson	36	– c Ballance b Ali	13
K. A. Maharaj c Root b Anderson	0	– c Broad b Ali	1
M. Morkel c Bairstow b Anderson	8	– not out	17
D. Olivier not out	0		
Lb 12	12	B 8, lb 8	16
(96.2 overs)	335	(9 wkts dec, 104 overs)	343

1/18 (1) 2/66 (2) 3/179 (4) 4/194 (3) 5/220 (5)   1/18 (1) 2/153 (2) 3/154 (4) 4/216 (3)
6/235 (6) 7/309 (7) 8/317 (9) 9/330 (8) 10/335 (10)   5/253 (6) 6/275 (5) 7/304 (8) 8/307 (9) 9/343 (7)

Anderson 23.2–6–72–5; Broad 22–4–64–3; Wood 17–3–61–0; Stokes 18–3–77–2; Dawson 7–1–26–0; Ali 8–1–21–0; Jennings 1–0–2–0. *Second innings*—Anderson 20–4–45–2; Broad 19–4–60–0; Wood 18–5–68–0; Ali 16–2–78–4; Stokes 20–4–34–2; Dawson 11–1–42–1.

England

A. N. Cook c de Kock b Philander	3	– c de Kock b Morris	42
K. K. Jennings c de Kock b Morkel	0	– b Philander	3
G. S. Ballance b Philander	27	– lbw b Philander	4
*J. E. Root c de Kock b Morkel	78	– b Morris	8
†J. M. Bairstow b Maharaj	45	– c Morris b Maharaj	16
B. A. Stokes c de Kock b Maharaj	0	– c and b Philander	18
M. M. Ali c du Plessis b Morris	18	– c Kuhn b Maharaj	27
L. A. Dawson c Amla b Maharaj	13	– not out	5
S. C. J. Broad lbw b Morris	0	– c Morkel b Maharaj	5
M. A. Wood c du Plessis b Morris	6	– c Morris b Olivier	0
J. M. Anderson not out	0	– c de Kock b Olivier	0
B 4, lb 10, w 1	15	Lb 5	5
(51.5 overs)	205	(44.2 overs)	133

1/3 (1) 2/3 (2) 3/86 (3) 4/143 (4) 5/168 (6)   1/4 (2) 2/28 (3) 3/55 (4) 4/72 (1) 5/84 (5) 6/122 (7)
6/177 (5) 7/199 (7) 8/199 (9) 9/199 (8) 10/205 (10)   7/126 (6) 8/133 (9) 9/133 (10) 10/133 (11)

Morkel 13–2–45–2; Philander 13–2–48–2; Morris 8.5–1–38–3; Olivier 7–0–39–0; Maharaj 10–1–21–3. *Second innings*—Morkel 13–4–30–0; Philander 10–3–24–3; Olivier 3.2–0–25–2; Morris 6–3–7–2; Maharaj 12–2–42–3.

Umpires: S. D. Fry *(Australia)* (6) and P. R. Reiffel *(Australia)* (32).
Third umpire: S. Ravi *(India)*.   Referee: J. J. Crowe *(New Zealand)* (83).

Close of play: first day, South Africa 309–6 (Philander 54, Morris 23); second day, South Africa 75–1 (Elgar 38, Amla 23); third day, England 1–0 (Cook 0, Jennings 0).

Test No. 2264/148 (E986, SA414)

ENGLAND v SOUTH AFRICA 2017 (3rd Test)

At Kennington Oval, London, on 27, 28, 29, 30, 31 July, 2017.
Toss: England.   Result: ENGLAND WON BY 239 RUNS.
Debuts: England – D. J. Malan, T. S. Roland-Jones, T. Westley.
Man of the Match: B. A. Stokes.

The 100th men's Test at The Oval had a unique ending for a match in England: Moeen Ali finished it with a hat-trick, all left-handers (also unique), and confirmed narrow review after Morkel was originally given not out. Three Tests elsewhere had been ended by hat-tricks, in Port Elizabeth in 1895–96 (by George Lohmann), Melbourne 1901–02 (Hugh Trumble), and Cape Town 1957–58 (Lindsay Kline). The graft, though, was done on the first two days. Root batted, despite a lush pitch and pregnant skies. Cook fought hard, passing Allan Border's 11,174 runs on the way to 88, allowing Stokes to make hay on a brighter second day. He reached 100 with the second of three successive sixes; Wally Hammond, off New Zealand's Jack Newman at Auckland in 1932–33, was the only other Englishman to hit three in a row in a Test. With Philander battling stomach trouble, England reached 353 (100 over par, according to du Plessis), then five wickets for Toby Roland-Jones – one of three debutants – helped dismantle South Africa for 175, in itself a comeback of sorts from 110 for eight. Jennings had several narrow escapes in making 48, while Westley collected 59 from 141 balls before Bairstow clubbed a rapid 63: the crowd grew restless waiting for Root's first declaration as captain. He eventually left South Africa an unlikely 492 in four sessions. Elgar fought a lone battle, making a brilliant century before becoming the first victim of Ali's hat-trick. The final innings contained four golden ducks, which was also unique.

England

A. N. Cook lbw b Morkel	88	– b Morkel	7
K. K. Jennings c Elgar b Philander	0	– c Morris b Rabada	48
T. Westley c du Plessis b Morris	25	– st de Kock b Maharaj	59
*J. E. Root c de Kock b Philander	29	– c Morkel b Maharaj	50
D. J. Malan b Rabada	1	– lbw b Morris	10
B. A. Stokes c Rabada b Morkel	112	– b Morris	31
†J. M. Bairstow c du Plessis b Rabada	36	– c Rabada b Maharaj	63
M. M. Ali c de Kock b Morkel	16	– run out (Bavuma)	8
T. S. Roland-Jones lbw b Maharaj	25	– not out	23
S. C. J. Broad c Amla b Rabada	3		
J. M. Anderson not out	1		
B 7, lb 7, w 3	17	Lb 11, w 3	14
(103.2 overs)	353	(8 wkts dec, 79.5 overs)	313

1/12 (2) 2/64 (3) 3/113 (4) 4/120 (5) 5/183 (1)   1/30 (1) 2/92 (2) 3/170 (3) 4/180 (4)
6/258 (7) 7/279 (8) 8/316 (9) 9/331 (10) 10/353 (6)   5/202 (5) 6/251 (6) 7/265 (8) 8/313 (7)

Morkel 28.2–7–70–3; Philander 17–6–32–2; Rabada 26–4–85–3; Maharaj 15–1–61–1; Morris 17–1–91–1. *Second innings*—Morkel 19–6–44–1; Philander 15–3–54–0; Rabada 18–4–56–1; Morris 11–0–70–2; Maharaj 13.5–2–50–3; Elgar 3–0–28–0.

South Africa

D. Elgar c Bairstow b Roland-Jones	8	– (2) c Stokes b Ali	136
H. G. Kuhn lbw b Roland-Jones	15	– (1) b Broad	11
H. M. Amla c Bairstow b Roland-Jones	6	– c Root b Roland-Jones	5
†Q. de Kock c Stokes b Roland-Jones	17	– b Stokes	5
*F. du Plessis lbw b Anderson	1	– lbw b Stokes	0
T. Bavuma c Bairstow b Roland-Jones	52	– lbw b Roland-Jones	32
C. H. Morris c and b Anderson	2	– (8) c Stokes b Ali	24
K. A. Maharaj c Cook b Stokes	5	– (9) not out	24
K. Rabada b Broad	30	– (10) c Stokes b Ali	0
M. Morkel c Cook b Anderson	17	– (11) lbw b Ali	0
V. D. Philander not out	10	– (7) lbw b Roland-Jones	0
B 4, lb 5, nb 3	12	B 4, lb 7, nb 4	15
(58.4 overs)	175	(77.1 overs)	252

1/18 (1) 2/23 (2) 3/30 (3) 4/47 (4) 5/47 (5)   1/21 (1) 2/47 (3) 3/52 (4) 4/52 (5) 5/160 (6)
6/51 (7) 7/61 (8) 8/114 (9) 9/161 (10) 10/175 (6)   6/160 (7) 7/205 (8) 8/252 (2) 9/252 (10) 10/252 (11)

Anderson 13–6–25–3; Broad 15–5–44–1; Roland-Jones 16.4–4–57–5; Stokes 7–1–26–1; Root 2–0–5–0; Ali 5–1–9–0. *Second innings*—Anderson 13–3–26–0; Broad 16–4–47–1; Roland-Jones 18–4–72–3; Stokes 14–1–51–2; Ali 16.1–5–45–4.

Umpires: Aleem Dar *(Pakistan)* (112) and J. S. Wilson *(West Indies)* (5).
Third umpire: H. D. P. K. Dharmasena *(Sri Lanka)*.   Referee: R. S. Madugalle *(Sri Lanka)* (176).

Close of play: first day, England 171–4 (Cook 82, Stokes 21); second day, South Africa 126–8 (Bavuma 34, Morkel 2); third day, England 74–1 (Jennings 34, Westley 28); fourth day, South Africa 117–4 (Elgar 72, Bavuma 16).

Test No. 2265/149 (E987, SA415)

ENGLAND v SOUTH AFRICA 2017 (4th Test)

At Old Trafford, Manchester, on 4, 5, 6, 7 August, 2017.
Toss: England.   Result: ENGLAND WON BY 177 RUNS.
Debuts: none.
Man of the Match: M. M. Ali. Men of the Series: M. M. Ali and M. Morkel.

Buoyed by victory at The Oval, England strove to repeat it – and, for once, bust did not follow boom. Again, they chose to bat in awkward conditions, scrapped their way past 350, tore into the opposition batting… and left the headlines to Ali. It was England's first home series victory over South Africa since 1998; 3–1 was their most comprehensive margin against them since 1960. England had last lost at Old Trafford in 2001, and their proprietorial pride swelled when the Pavilion End was renamed after James Anderson. Burnley's patron saint of swing politely glossed over his preference for the Brian Statham End, and repaid the honour with match figures of 31–12–54–7. Anderson played his part with the bat, too, making four in a last-wicket stand of 50 that ended when Bairstow was narrowly lbw, England's first Test 99 since Kevin Pietersen at Chittagong in 2009–10. Anderson then removed Elgar for a duck, and made regular incisions as South Africa slid to 226. England were struggling at 134 for six before Ali swatted an unbeaten 75 from 66 balls to push the lead to 379. One of his three sixes was caught by Bairstow on the players' balcony. Amla and du Plessis put on 123 in the chase, but Ali worked his way through: another five-for gave him 25 wickets at 15 in the series, eight of them caught by Stokes. Both wicketkeepers reached 100 Test dismissals, de Kock in his 22nd Test as keeper, to equal Adam Gilchrist's record.

England

A. N. Cook c de Kock b Maharaj	46	– c de Bruyn b Morkel	10
K. K. Jennings c de Kock b Olivier	17	– c Amla b Rabada	18
T. Westley c de Kock b Rabada	29	– c sub (A. K. Markram) b Morkel	9
*J. E. Root lbw b Olivier	52	– b Olivier	49
D. J. Malan c du Plessis b Morkel	18	– c de Bruyn b Maharaj	6
B. A. Stokes b Rabada	58	– c du Plessis b Olivier	23
†J. M. Bairstow lbw b Maharaj	99	– c Rabada b Olivier	10
T. S. Roland-Jones c Bavuma b Rabada	4	– (9) c Maharaj b Rabada	11
M. M. Ali c du Plessis b Rabada	14	– (8) not out	75
S. C. J. Broad b Morkel	7	– c de Bruyn b Morkel	5
J. M. Anderson not out	4	– c de Bruyn b Morkel	2
B 6, lb 6, nb 2	14	B 9, lb 13, w 2, nb 1	25
(108.4 overs)	362	(69.1 overs)	243

1/35 (2) 2/92 (1) 3/92 (3) 4/144 (5) 5/187 (4)   1/16 (1) 2/30 (3) 3/55 (2) 4/72 (5) 5/129 (4)
6/252 (6) 7/271 (8) 8/303 (9) 9/312 (10) 10/362 (7)   6/134 (6) 7/153 (7) 8/211 (9) 9/237 (10) 10/243 (11)

Morkel 26–5–92–2; Rabada 26–7–91–4; Olivier 21–3–91–2; Maharaj 30.4–9–58–2; de Bruyn 5–0–18–0. *Second innings*—Morkel 13.1–2–41–4; Rabada 17–4–50–2; Maharaj 27–5–92–1; Olivier 12–5–38–3.

South Africa

D. Elgar lbw b Anderson	0	– (2) c Bairstow b Broad	5
H. G. Kuhn c Stokes b Ali	24	– (1) c Cook b Anderson	11
H. M. Amla c Bairstow b Roland-Jones	30	– lbw b Ali	83
T. Bavuma b Anderson	46	– c Bairstow b Roland-Jones	12
*F. du Plessis b Anderson	27	– c Bairstow b Anderson	61
†Q. de Kock c Bairstow b Broad	24	– c Cook b Ali	1
T. B. de Bruyn c Root b Anderson	11	– c Stokes b Ali	0
K. A. Maharaj lbw b Ali	13	– not out	21
K. Rabada c Stokes b Broad	23	– c Westley b Anderson	1
M. Morkel not out	20	– c Root b Ali	0
D. Olivier c Bairstow b Broad	4	– c Stokes b Ali	0
B 3, nb 1	4	B 4, lb 3	7
(72.1 overs)	226	(62.5 overs)	202

1/2 (1) 2/47 (3) 3/84 (2) 4/131 (4) 5/132 (5)   1/10 (2) 2/18 (1) 3/40 (4) 4/163 (3) 5/173 (6)
6/146 (7) 7/167 (8) 8/189 (6) 9/220 (9) 10/226 (11)   6/173 (7) 7/183 (5) 8/195 (9) 9/202 (10) 10/202 (11)

Anderson 17–5–38–4; Broad 16.1–4–46–3; Roland-Jones 11–3–41–1; Ali 21–5–57–2; Stokes 6–0–34–0; Malan 1–0–7–0. *Second innings*—Anderson 14–7–16–3; Broad 12–5–24–1; Roland-Jones 9–1–52–1; Ali 19.5–1–69–5; Stokes 6–1–26–0; Root 2–0–8–0.

Umpires: Aleem Dar *(Pakistan)* (113) and H. D. P. K. Dharmasena *(Sri Lanka)* (46).
Third umpire: J. S. Wilson *(West Indies)*.   Referee: R. S. Madugalle *(Sri Lanka)* (177).

Close of play: first day, England 260–6 (Bairstow 33, Roland-Jones 0); second day, South Africa 220–9 (Morkel 18); third day, England 224–8 (Ali 67, Broad 0).

Test No. 2266/18 (SL259, Z102)

SRI LANKA v ZIMBABWE 2017 (Only Test)

At R. Premadasa Stadium, Colombo, on 14, 15, 16, 17, 18 July, 2017.
Toss: Zimbabwe.   Result: SRI LANKA WON BY FOUR WICKETS.
Debuts: Zimbabwe – T. K. Musakanda.
Man of the Match: D. A. S. Gunaratne.   Man of the Series: H. M. R. K. B. Herath.

Zimbabwe recovered well from two dicey starts, and were disappointed not to record their first Test victory in 18 attempts against Sri Lanka. Ervine made 160, his second Test century and his country's third-highest overseas, after Andy Flower's unbeaten epics against India in 2000–01 (183 at Delhi and 232 at Nagpur). In reply, only Tharanga and Chandimal, in his first Test as captain, made half-centuries. Leg-spinner Cremer completed his first Test five-for, but Zimbabwe – ahead by 10 – were soon back in trouble at 59 for five. But again they fought back: Sikandar Raza hit a maiden Test century, putting on 86 with Moor and 144 with Waller. Cremer's 48 inflated the target to 388, six more than had been made to win a Test in Sri Lanka. When the final day began, Sri Lanka – three down – needed another 218, but Cremer soon snared both Mendis and Mathews. When Sikandar floated one up it seemed Dickwella was gone as well, stumped by Chakabva for 37. Replays showed no scrap of rubber behind the line, but somehow the third umpire ruled not out. When Zimbabwe finally turned to seam, after 72 overs of spin, Dickwella smote Mpofu over midwicket to bring up a sparky fifty. He eventually fell, reverse-sweeping, for 81 to end a stand of 121 with Gunaratne, who quietly led Sri Lanka home in an unbroken partnership of 67 with Dilruwan Perera. It was the fifth-highest successful chase in Tests, in the 14th match in which all four innings exceeded 300.

Zimbabwe

H. Masakadza c Mendis b Herath	19	– lbw b Herath	7
†R. W. Chakabva b Herath	12	– b Herath	6
T. K. Musakanda c Dickwella b Kumara	6	– c Karunaratne b Herath	0
C. R. Ervine c Perera b Kumara	160	– c Karunaratne b Perera	5
S. C. Williams c Gunaratne b Perera	22	– b Herath	22
Sikandar Raza lbw b Herath	36	– b Herath	127
P. J. Moor c Kumara b Gunaratne	19	– c sub (M. D. Gunathilleke) b Kumara	40
M. N. Waller b Herath	36	– c Tharanga b Perera	68
*A. G. Cremer b Gunaratne	13	– c Karunaratne b Herath	48
D. T. Tiripano c Karunaratne b Herath	27	– lbw b Perera	19
C. B. Mpofu not out	0	– not out	9
W 1, nb 5	6	B 4, lb 14, w 7, nb 1	26
(94.4 overs)	356	(107.1 overs)	377

1/23 (2) 2/38 (1) 3/38 (3) 4/70 (5) 5/154 (6)   1/14 (2) 2/16 (3) 3/17 (1) 4/23 (4) 5/59 (5) 6/145 (7)
6/195 (7) 7/260 (8) 8/282 (9) 9/356 (10) 10/356 (4)   7/289 (8) 8/306 (6) 9/361 (10) 10/377 (9)

Lakmal 14–1–58–0; Kumara 17.4–2–68–2; Herath 32–4–116–5; Perera 24–0–86–1; Gunaratne 7–0–28–2. *Second innings*—Lakmal 14–0–43–0; Herath 39.1–5–133–6; Perera 30–2–95–3; Kumara 20–3–72–1; Mendis 4–0–16–0.

Sri Lanka

F. D. M. Karunaratne c Masakadza b Tiripano	25	– b Williams	49
W. U. Tharanga run out (Tiripano)	71	– c Moor b Cremer	27
B. K. G. Mendis c Chakabva b Cremer	11	– c Williams b Cremer	66
*L. D. Chandimal c Chakabva b Cremer	55	– c Masakadza b Cremer	15
A. D. Mathews c Masakadza b Williams	41	– c and b Cremer	25
†D. P. D. N. Dickwella b Cremer	6	– c Chakabva b Williams	81
M. D. K. Perera run out (Musakanda/Waller/Chakabva)	33	– (8) not out	29
D. A. S. Gunaratne b Cremer	45	– (7) not out	80
H. M. R. K. B. Herath st Chakabva b Williams	22		
R. A. S. Lakmal c and b Cremer	14		
C. B. R. L. S. Kumara not out	1		
B 8, lb 10, w 1, nb 3	22	B 9, lb 8, w 2	19
(102.3 overs)	346	(6 wkts, 114.5 overs)	391

1/84 (1) 2/107 (3) 3/116 (2) 4/212 (4) 5/226 (6)   1/58 (2) 2/108 (1) 3/133 (4)
6/238 (5) 7/274 (7) 8/322 (9) 9/343 (10) 10/346 (8)   4/178 (3) 5/203 (5) 6/324 (6)

Mpofu 11–2–41–0; Tiripano 10–1–38–1; Sikandar Raza 18–2–60–0; Cremer 39.3–4–125–5; Waller 1–0–2–0; Williams 23–3–62–2. *Second innings*—Sikandar Raza 13–1–58–0; Williams 43.5–2–146–2; Cremer 48–6–150–4; Waller 4–0–10–0; Mpofu 6–3–10–0.

Umpires: I. J. Gould *(England)* (61) and N. J. Llong *(England)* (43).
Third umpire: C. Shamshuddin *(India)*.   Referee: B. C. Broad *(England)* (88).

Close of play: first day, Zimbabwe 344–8 (Ervine 151, Tiripano 24); second day, Sri Lanka 293–7 (Gunaratne 24, Herath 5); third day, Zimbabwe 252–6 (Sikandar Raza 97, Waller 57); fourth day, Sri Lanka 170–3 (Mendis 60, Mathews 17).

Test No. 2267/39 (SL260, I513)

SRI LANKA v INDIA 2017 (1st Test)

At Galle International Stadium on 26, 27, 28, 29 July, 2017.
Toss: India. Result: INDIA WON BY 304 RUNS.
Debuts: Sri Lanka – M. D. Gunathilleke. India – H. H. Pandya.
Man of the Match: S. Dhawan.

Shikhar Dhawan was not supposed to be in Sri Lanka at all: he was called up only because of a wrist injury to Murali Vijay. But he seized his chance, celebrating his Test return after ten months on the sidelines. India cantered to 399 for three on the first day: Dhawan's 190 came off just 168 balls, and he smacked 126 between lunch and tea, the most by anyone in the middle session of a Test for 63 years (at Nottingham in 1954, Denis Compton battered an inexperienced Pakistan attack for 173). Dhawan was dropped at second slip when 31; Gunaratne broke his thumb attempting the catch, and played no further part in the series. Dhawan sailed on, adding 253 – an Indian second-wicket record against Sri Lanka – with Pujara, whose unhurried 153 was his 12th Test century, and his sixth of 150 or more. Next day, Hardik Pandya marked his debut with a run-a-ball 50 as India reached 600. It might have been more but for Pradeep Fernando, who persevered for a maiden Test five-for. After Tharanga's 64, only Mathews and Perera, who was stranded on 92, made much impression. Kohli waived the follow-on, and smacked a rapid century as the target ballooned: Sri Lanka had knocked off a national-record 388 to overcome Zimbabwe just 11 days previously, but 550 against India was several bridges too far, especially with Gunaratne and stand-in skipper Herath (who had injured a finger in the field; Chandimal had pneumonia) unable to bat, despite Karunaratne's adhesive 97.

India

S. Dhawan c Mathews b Fernando	190	– c Gunathilleke b Perera		14
A. Mukund c Dickwella b Fernando	12	– lbw b Gunathilleke		81
C. A. Pujara c Dickwella b Fernando	153	– c Mendis b Kumara		15
*V. Kohli c Dickwella b Fernando	3	– not out		103
A. M. Rahane c Karunaratne b Kumara	57	– not out		23
R. Ashwin c Dickwella b Fernando	47			
†W. P. Saha c Perera b Herath	16			
H. H. Pandya c sub (D. M. de Silva) b Kumara	50			
R. A. Jadeja b Fernando	15			
Mohammed Shami c Tharanga b Kumara	30			
U. T. Yadav not out	11			
B 2, lb 5, w 6, nb 3	16	Lb 1, w 2, nb 1		4
(133.1 overs)	600	(3 wkts dec, 53 overs)		240

1/27 (2) 2/280 (1) 3/286 (4) 4/423 (3) 5/432 (5)
6/491 (7) 7/495 (6) 8/517 (9) 9/579 (10) 10/600 (8)   1/19 (1) 2/56 (3) 3/189 (2)

Fernando 31–2–132–6; Kumara 25.1–3–131–3; Perera 30–1–130–0; Herath 40–6–159–1; Gunathilleke 7–0–41–0. *Second innings*—Fernando 12–2–63–0; Perera 15–0–67–1; Kumara 12–1–59–1; Herath 9–0–34–0; Gunathilleke 5–0–16–1.

Sri Lanka

F. D. M. Karunaratne lbw b Yadav	2	– b Ashwin		97
W. U. Tharanga run out (Mukund/Saha)	64	– b Mohammed Shami		10
M. D. Gunathilleke c Dhawan b Mohammed Shami	16	– c Pujara b Yadav		2
B. K. G. Mendis c Dhawan b Mohammed Shami	0	– c Saha b Jadeja		36
A. D. Mathews c Kohli b Jadeja	83	– c Pandya b Jadeja		2
†D. P. D. N. Dickwella c Mukund b Ashwin	8	– c Saha b Ashwin		67
M. D. K. Perera not out	92	– not out		21
*H. M. R. K. B. Herath c Rahane b Jadeja	9	– absent hurt		
A. N. P. R. Fernando b Pandya	10	– (8) c Kohli b Ashwin		0
C. B. R. L. S. Kumara b Jadeja	2	– (9) c Mohammed Shami b Jadeja		0
D. A. S. Gunaratne absent hurt	–	absent hurt		
Lb 4, w 1	5	Lb 3, w 7		10
(78.3 overs)	291	(76.5 overs)		245

1/7 (1) 2/68 (3) 3/68 (4) 4/125 (2) 5/143 (6)   1/22 (2) 2/29 (3) 3/108 (4) 4/116 (5)
6/205 (5) 7/241 (8) 8/280 (9) 9/291 (10)   5/217 (6) 6/240 (1) 7/240 (8) 8/245 (9)

Mohammed Shami 12–2–45–2; Yadav 14–1–78–1; Ashwin 27–5–84–1; Jadeja 22.3–3–67–3; Pandya 3–0–13–1. *Second innings*—Mohammed Shami 9–0–43–1; Yadav 9–0–42–1; Jadeja 24.5–4–71–3; Ashwin 27–4–65–3; Pandya 7–0–21–0.

Umpires: R. K. Illingworth *(England)* (30) and B. N. J. Oxenford *(Australia)* (42).
Third umpire: R. J. Tucker *(Australia)*.   Referee: R. B. Richardson *(West Indies)* (9).

Close of play: first day, India 399–3 (Pujara 144, Rahane 39); second day, Sri Lanka 154–5 (Mathews 54, Perera 6); third day, India 189–3 (Kohli 76).

Test No. 2268/40 (SL261, I514)

SRI LANKA v INDIA 2017 (2nd Test)

At Sinhalese Sports Club, Colombo, on 3, 4, 5, 6 August, 2017.
Toss: India.   Result: INDIA WON BY AN INNINGS AND 53 RUNS.
Debuts: Sri Lanka – P. M. Pushpakumara.
Man of the Match: R. A. Jadeja.

With such a gulf between the sides, Sri Lanka's best chance was a dry, crumbling surface to help their spinners – but the ploy backfired when Kohli won the toss again: India hurtled past 600 for the sixth time in nine Tests, then unleashed their own slow men. Sri Lanka gave a first cap to Malinda Pushpakumara, a 30-year-old slow left-armer with more than 550 first-class wickets, but bolstering the spin department left them with only one seamer, Pradeep Fernando – and when he tore a hamstring on the first evening, they were stuffed. Pujara made his third hundred in three Tests in Sri Lanka, and added 217 with Rahane, before the middle order raised a mammoth total. Sri Lanka's first innings was a mix of the sublime (India's bowling) and the ridiculous (their own batting). An addiction to sweeps of all kinds lured batsmen to their doom. They were skittled for 183 inside 50 overs, and this time Kohli did enforce the follow-on, armed with a stratospheric lead of 439, the largest Sri Lanka had ever conceded. Tharanga soon fell, but that brought Karunaratne and Mendis together for an attractive partnership of 191. But when they were parted by Pandya, the spinners took over. Jadeja finished with a hard-earned five-for, but was suspended from the next Test after throwing the ball dangerously close to Karunaratne, who had not left his crease. Ashwin completed the double of 2,000 runs and 250 wickets in his 51st Test, beating Richard Hadlee's record by three.

India

S. Dhawan lbw b Perera	35
K. L. Rahul run out (Chandimal/Dickwella)	57
C. A. Pujara lbw b Karunaratne	133
*V. Kohli c Mathews b Herath	13
A. M. Rahane st Dickwella b Pushpakumara	132
R. Ashwin b Herath	54
†W. P. Saha st Dickwella b Herath	67
H. H. Pandya c Mathews b Pushpakumara	20
R. A. Jadeja not out	70
Mohammed Shami c Tharanga b Herath	19
U. T. Yadav not out	8
B 8, lb 4, nb 2	14
(9 wkts dec, 158 overs)	622

1/56 (1) 2/109 (2) 3/133 (4) 4/350 (3) 5/413 (5)
6/451 (6) 7/496 (8) 8/568 (7) 9/598 (10)

Fernando 17.4–2–63–0; Herath 42–7–154–4; Karunaratne 8–0–31–1; Perera 40–3–147–1; Pushpakumara 38.2–2–156–2; de Silva 12–0–59–0.

Sri Lanka

F. D. M. Karunaratne c Rahane b Ashwin	25	– c Rahane b Jadeja	141
W. U. Tharanga c Rahul b Ashwin	0	– b Yadav	2
B. K. G. Mendis c Kohli b Yadav	24	– c Saha b Pandya	110
*L. D. Chandimal c Pandya b Jadeja	10	– (5) c Rahane b Jadeja	2
A. D. Mathews c Pujara b Ashwin	26	– (6) c Saha b Jadeja	36
†D. P. D. N. Dickwella b Mohammed Shami	51	– (7) c Rahane b Pandya	31
D. M. de Silva b Jadeja	0	– (9) c Rahane b Jadeja	17
M. D. K. Perera b Ashwin	25	– st Saha b Jadeja	4
H. M. R. K. B. Herath b Mohammed Shami	2	– (10) not out	17
P. M. Pushpakumara not out	15	– (4) b Ashwin	16
A. N. P. R. Fernando b Ashwin	0	– c Dhawan b Ashwin	1
B 4, lb 1	5	Lb 5, w 2, nb 2	9
(49.4 overs)	183	(116.5 overs)	386

1/0 (2) 2/33 (1) 3/60 (4) 4/64 (3) 5/117 (5)   1/7 (2) 2/198 (3) 3/238 (4) 4/241 (5) 5/310 (1)
6/122 (7) 7/150 (6) 8/152 (9) 9/171 (8) 10/183 (11)   6/315 (6) 7/321 (8) 8/343 (9) 9/384 (7) 10/386 (11)

Mohammed Shami 6–1–13–2; Ashwin 16.4–3–69–5; Jadeja 22–6–84–2; Yadav 5–1–12–1. *Second innings*—Yadav 13–2–39–1; Ashwin 37.5–7–132–2; Mohammed Shami 12–3–27–0; Jadeja 39–5–152–5; Pandya 15–2–31–2.

Umpires: B. N. J. Oxenford *(Australia)* (43) and R. J. Tucker *(Australia)* (55).
Third umpire: R. K. Illingworth *(England)*.   Referee: R. B. Richardson *(West Indies)* (10).

Close of play: first day, India 344–3 (Pujara 128, Rahane 103); second day, Sri Lanka 50–2 (Mendis 16, Chandimal 8); third day, Sri Lanka 209–2 (Karunaratne 92, Pushpakumara 2).

SRI LANKA v INDIA 2017 (3rd Test)

At Muttiah Muralitharan Stadium, Pallekele, on 12, 13, 14 August, 2017.
Toss: India.   Result: INDIA WON BY AN INNINGS AND 171 RUNS.
Debuts: none.
Man of the Match: H. H. Pandya.   Man of the Series: S. Dhawan.

India's 487 was their lowest of the series, but they still cruised to the heaviest of their three victories. They also won all six white-ball internationals on the tour, for a 9–0 victory overall. Dhawan and Rahul put on 188, the highest opening stand by a visiting team in Sri Lanka, beating 171 by Manoj Prabhakar and Navjot Sidhu for India in Colombo in 1993-94. Rahul's 85 was his seventh successive Test score over 50, equalling the record held by five others. In the absence of Rangana Herath, who had back trouble, Pushpakumara kept things tight, but it was left-arm wrist-spinner Lakshan Sandakan who took the eye. India were in danger of wasting their start before Pandya, in only his third Test, broke loose. After making a half-century from 61 balls, with only last man Umesh Yadav for company and all nine fielders on the boundary, he crashed 26 from one Pushpakumara over (446660) – an Indian Test record, beating Kapil Dev's 24 off Eddie Hemmings at Lord's in 1990. Pandya's second fifty needed only 25 balls, and his 108 – his first senior century – included seven sixes. In reply, Mohammed Shami removed both openers cheaply, before Mendis was run out and Mathews pinned by the irrepressible Pandya for a duck. Kuldeep Yadav chipped in as Sri Lanka were hustled out inside three hours for 135. With a lead of 352 and his attack still fresh, Kohli stuck them back in. Ashwin took four more wickets as India's bowlers completed the task on the third evening.

India

S. Dhawan c Chandimal b Pushpakumara	119
K. L. Rahul c Karunaratne b Pushpakumara	85
C. A. Pujara c Mathews b Sandakan	8
*V. Kohli c Karunaratne b Sandakan	42
A. M. Rahane b Pushpakumara	17
R. Ashwin c Dickwella b Fernando	31
†W. P. Saha c Perera b Fernando	16
H. H. Pandya c Perera b Sandakan	108
K. Yadav c Dickwella b Sandakan	26
Mohammed Shami c and b Sandakan	8
U. T. Yadav not out	3
B 10, lb 6, w 6, nb 2	24
(122.3 overs)	487

1/188 (2) 2/219 (1) 3/229 (3) 4/264 (5) 5/296 (4)
6/322 (6) 7/339 (7) 8/401 (9) 9/421 (10) 10/487 (8)

Fernando 26–3–87–2; Kumara 23–1–104–0; Karunaratne 7–0–30–0; Perera 8–1–36–0; Sandakan 35.3–4–132–5; Pushpakumara 23–2–82–3.

Sri Lanka

F. D. M. Karunaratne c Saha b Mohammed Shami	4	– c Rahane b Ashwin	16
W. U. Tharanga c Saha b Mohammed Shami	5	– b U. T. Yadav	7
B. K. G. Mendis run out (Ashwin/K. Yadav)	18	– (4) lbw b Mohammed Shami	12
*L. D. Chandimal c Rahul b Ashwin	48	– (5) c Pujara b K. Yadav	36
A. D. Mathews lbw b Pandya	0	– (6) lbw b Ashwin	35
†D. P. D. N. Dickwella st Saha b K. Yadav	29	– (7) c Rahane b U. T. Yadav	41
M. D. K. Perera c Pandya b K. Yadav	0	– (8) b Pandya b Ashwin	8
P. M. Pushpakumara b K. Yadav	10	– (3) c Saha b Mohammed Shami	1
P. A. D. L. R. Sandakan c Dhawan b Ashwin	10	– c Saha b Mohammed Shami	8
M. V. T. Fernando b K. Yadav	0	– not out	4
C. B. R. L. S. Kumara not out	0	– b Ashwin	10
B 4, lb 1, w 6	11	B 2, nb 1	3
(37.4 overs)	135	(74.3 overs)	181

1/14 (2) 2/23 (1) 3/38 (3) 4/38 (5) 5/101 (6)   1/15 (2) 2/26 (1) 3/34 (3) 4/39 (4) 5/104 (5)
6/107 (7) 7/125 (4) 8/125 (8) 9/135 (10) 10/135 (9)   6/118 (6) 7/138 (8) 8/166 (9) 9/168 (7) 10/181 (11)

Mohammed Shami 6.5–1–17–2; U. T. Yadav 3.1–0–23–0; Pandya 6–1–28–1; K. Yadav 13–2–40–4; Ashwin 8.4–2–22–2.
Second innings—Mohammed Shami 15–6–32–3; Ashwin 28.3–6–68–4; U. T. Yadav 13–5–21–2; K. Yadav 17–4–56–1; Pandya 1–0–2–0.

Umpires: R. K. Illingworth *(England)* (31) and R. J. Tucker *(Australia)* (56).
Third umpire: B. N. J. Oxenford *(Australia).*   Referee: R. B. Richardson *(West Indies)* (11).

Close of play: first day, India 329–6 (Saha 13, Pandya 1); second day, Sri Lanka 19–1 (Karunaratne 12, Pushpakumara 0).

Test No. 2270/152 (E988, WI524)

ENGLAND v WEST INDIES 2017 (1st Test)

At Edgbaston, Birmingham, on 17, 18, 19 August, 2017 (day/night).
Toss: England.   Result: ENGLAND WON BY AN INNINGS AND 209 RUNS.
Debuts: England – M. D. Stoneman. West Indies – K. A. Hope.
Man of the Match: A. N. Cook.

A little light remained as the last wicket fell shortly before 9pm on the third day, bringing England's first day/night Test to a close. For West Indies, darkness had long since fallen – bowled out twice in 92.4 overs, they lost 19 wickets on the third day and slid to their sixth-heaviest defeat. Cook collected the match award for his 243 in Edgbaston's 50th Test, but the star of the first day was Root. Early movement accounted for the debutant Mark Stoneman, but as the pink ball weathered Root gathered pace, reaching 50 for the 11th Test in succession, breaking John Edrich's England record, and extending his stand with Cook to 248. During his 31st Test century, Cook overhauled Graham Gooch (5,917) to become the leading Test run-scorer in the UK, and David Gower (767) to claim the Edgbaston equivalent. West Indian ineptitude stretched to captaincy and selection. With 80 overs bowled on the first evening, the second new ball under lights was awaited with eagerness; instead, Holder withdrew Roach from the attack. The slow bowlers delivered 32.2 overs, occasionally extracting handy turn, which suggested leaving out leg-spinner Devendra Bishoo was a mistake. Cook's dismissal prompted the declaration; West Indies needed 315 to avoid the follow-on, but did not make that many in two innings. Blackwood attacked during his unbeaten 79 from 76 balls, but his team-mates succumbed to a procession of half-strides and half-strokes. Broad contributed a terrific spell under the lights in the follow-on, and Roland-Jones completed the rout.

England

A. N. Cook lbw b Chase	243
M. D. Stoneman b Roach	8
T. Westley lbw b Cummins	8
*J. E. Root b Roach	136
D. J. Malan c Blackwood b Chase	65
B. A. Stokes c Blackwood b Chase	10
†J. M. Bairstow b Holder	18
M. M. Ali c Brathwaite b Chase	0
T. S. Roland-Jones not out	6
Lb 10, w 3, nb 7	20
(8 wkts dec, 135.5 overs)	514

1/14 (2) 2/39 (3) 3/287 (4) 4/449 (5)
5/466 (6) 6/505 (7) 7/506 (8) 8/514 (1)

S. C. J. Broad and J. M. Anderson did not bat.

Roach 28–8–86–2; Joseph 22–3–109–0; Cummins 24–3–87–1; Holder 29.3–4–103–1; Chase 26.2–2–113–4; Brathwaite 6–0–6–0.

West Indies

K. C. Brathwaite c Bairstow b Anderson	0	– lbw b Ali	40
K. O. A. Powell run out (Anderson)	20	– c Cook b Anderson	10
K. A. Hope c Stokes b Anderson	25	– lbw b Roland-Jones	12
S. D. Hope b Roland-Jones	15	– c Root b Stokes	4
R. L. Chase b Anderson	0	– lbw b Broad	24
J. Blackwood not out	79	– st Bairstow b Ali	12
†S. O. Dowrich lbw b Roland-Jones	4	– b Broad	5
*J. O. Holder c Bairstow b Ali	11	– c Cook b Broad	0
K. A. J. Roach b Broad	5	– b Anderson	12
A. S. Joseph lbw b Broad	6	– c Stokes b Roland-Jones	8
M. L. Cummins run out (Westley)	0	– not out	0
Lb 1, w 2	3	B 9, lb 1	10
(47 overs)	168	(45.4 overs)	137

1/0 (1) 2/45 (3) 3/47 (2) 4/47 (5) 5/89 (4)
6/101 (7) 7/129 (8) 8/134 (9) 9/162 (10) 10/168 (11)
1/15 (2) 2/41 (3) 3/60 (4) 4/76 (1) 5/102 (6)
6/104 (5) 7/104 (8) 8/115 (7) 9/137 (9) 10/137 (10)

Anderson 15–6–34–3; Broad 16–3–47–2; Roland-Jones 6–0–31–2; Stokes 7–0–40–0; Ali 3–1–15–1. *Second innings—* Anderson 7–2–12–2; Broad 10–4–34–3; Roland-Jones 6.4–3–18–2; Stokes 9–4–9–1; Ali 13–2–54–2.

Umpires: M. Erasmus *(South Africa)* (44) and S. Ravi *(India)* (22).
Third umpire: C. B. Gaffaney *(New Zealand)*.   Referee: D. C. Boon *(Australia)* (42).

Close of play: first day, England 348–3 (Cook 153, Malan 28); second day, West Indies 44–1 (Powell 18, K. A. Hope 25).

ENGLAND v WEST INDIES 2017 (2nd Test)

At Headingley, Leeds, on 25, 26, 27, 28, 29 August, 2017.
Toss: England.   Result: WEST INDIES WON BY FIVE WICKETS.
Debuts: none.
Man of the Match: S. D. Hope.

After their surrender at Edgbaston, few expected West Indies to bounce back: not Root, whose challenging declaration late on the fourth day left them a target of 322, and not Geoff Boycott, who had described them as "the worst Test team I have seen in more than 50 years". Two quick wickets on the final morning suggested another surrender – and then Shai Hope joined Brathwaite. They had put on 246 in the first innings, and now added 144 more. Chase and Blackwood chipped in as the target neared, and with 28 balls to spare West Indies completed their first victory in England for 19 Tests, stretching back to Edgbaston 2000. Hope, who had not scored a Test century before, became the first man to score one in each innings at Headingley, in 533 first-class matches there; remarkably, the feat had eluded the likes of Boycott, Len Hutton and Herbert Sutcliffe. Root became only the fourth England captain to suffer defeat after declaring in the third innings. On the first day he had reached 50 for the 12th consecutive Test, equalling A. B. de Villiers's record, but England needed Stokes's round 100 to scrape to 258, the speedy pair of Roach and Gabriel sharing eight wickets. Anderson, who finished with another five-for, made early inroads before Brathwaite and Hope's big stand, then Blackwood and Holder muscled the lead to 169. Six half-centuries, including a four-hour marathon from Malan, seemed to have made England safe – but Hope remained for West Indies.

England

A. N. Cook c K. A. Hope b Gabriel	11	– c Dowrich b Holder	23
M. D. Stoneman c Dowrich b Roach	19	– b Gabriel	52
T. Westley lbw b Roach	3	– c Dowrich b Holder	8
*J. E. Root c Blackwood b Bishoo	59	– c S. D. Hope b Gabriel	72
D. J. Malan b Holder	8	– b Chase	61
B. A. Stokes c Dowrich b Gabriel	100	– c Brathwaite b Chase	58
†J. M. Bairstow c Holder b Gabriel	2	– b Chase	18
M. M. Ali c Chase b Roach	22	– c Brathwaite b Bishoo	84
C. R. Woakes c Dowrich b Roach	23	– not out	61
S. C. J. Broad b Gabriel	0	– not out	14
J. M. Anderson not out	0		
B 2, lb 3, w 4, nb 2	11	B 13, lb 5, w 9, nb 12	39
(70.5 overs)	258	(8 wkts dec, 141 overs)	490

1/19 (1) 2/26 (3) 3/37 (2) 4/71 (5) 5/140 (4)
6/152 (7) 7/220 (8) 8/258 (6) 9/258 (10) 10/258 (9)

1/58 (1) 2/81 (3) 3/94 (2) 4/212 (4) 5/303 (6)
6/312 (5) 7/327 (7) 8/444 (8)

Roach 19.5–1–71–4; Gabriel 17–4–51–4; Holder 16–5–45–1; Chase 12–1–59–0; Bishoo 6–0–27–1. *Second innings*—Gabriel 26–3–125–2; Roach 24–8–95–0; Holder 33–10–95–2; Chase 32–5–86–3; Bishoo 25–1–67–1; Brathwaite 1–0–4–0.

West Indies

K. C. Brathwaite b Broad	134	– c Stokes b Ali	95
K. O. A. Powell c Cook b Anderson	5	– c Stokes b Broad	23
D. Bishoo c Bairstow b Anderson	1		
K. A. Hope c Root b Anderson	3	– (3) run out (Broad)	0
S. D. Hope c Bairstow b Anderson	147	– (4) not out	118
R. L. Chase c Cook b Stokes	5	– (5) c sub (M. S. Crane) b Woakes	30
J. Blackwood run out (Stokes/Bairstow)	49	– (6) st Bairstow b Ali	41
†S. O. Dowrich c Root b Anderson	0	– (7) not out	0
*J. O. Holder c Ali b Woakes	43		
K. A. J. Roach not out	6		
S. T. Gabriel lbw b Stokes	10		
B 8, lb 11, w 5	24	B 4, lb 9, w 1, nb 1	15
(127 overs)	427	(5 wkts, 91.2 overs)	322

1/11 (2) 2/31 (3) 3/35 (4) 4/281 (1) 5/296 (6)
6/329 (5) 7/329 (8) 8/404 (9) 9/406 (7) 10/427 (11)

1/46 (2) 2/53 (3) 3/197 (1)
4/246 (5) 5/320 (6)

Anderson 29–7–76–5; Broad 24–2–95–1; Woakes 21–4–78–1; Stokes 25–9–63–2; Ali 24–4–84–0; Westley 4–0–12–0. *Second innings*—Anderson 24–6–73–0; Broad 25–4–91–1; Ali 25–3–76–2; Woakes 12.2–2–44–1; Stokes 5–0–25–0.

Umpires: C. B. Gaffaney *(New Zealand)* (14) and S. Ravi *(India)* (23).
Third umpire: M. Erasmus *(South Africa)*.   Referee: D. C. Boon *(Australia)* (43).

Close of play: first day, West Indies 19–1 (Brathwaite 13, Bishoo 1); second day, West Indies 329–5 (S. D. Hope 147, Blackwood 21); third day, England 171–3 (Root 45, Malan 21); fourth day, West Indies 5–0 (Brathwaite 4, Powell 1).

ENGLAND v WEST INDIES 2017 (3rd Test)

At Lord's, London, on 7, 8, 9 September, 2017.
Toss: West Indies.   Result: ENGLAND WON BY NINE WICKETS.
Debuts: none.
Man of the Match: B. A. Stokes.   Men of the Series: J. M. Anderson and S. D. Hope.

West Indies' stunning victory at Leeds meant the series was unexpectedly alive in the second-latest Test staged in England (the 2005 Ashes-clinching draw began on September 8). Much of the play took place in sepulchral light, with floodlights blazing, but England swept to victory in a low-scoring classic on the third afternoon. Initially, Stokes was the destroyer: he took six for 22 – including three for none in six balls – as West Indies were toppled for 123 on the first day, then hit a rapid 60 to filch a lead of 71 after Roach and Holder reduced England to 24 for four. He also took a stinging return catch, putting others' fielding to shame: around 25 chances were spurned by both sides in this match and the last. Then Anderson took over. In the first innings he had beaten Bishoo six times in one over, and ended with 499 Test wickets. No. 500 was not long in coming, Brathwaite castled by an inswinger in the third over. Anderson was irresistible, finding the perfect length on his way to a career-best seven for 42. Gabriel avoided a king pair thanks to DRS, but the end was not long delayed: England needed 107, and knocked them off for the loss of Cook, who fell lbw: leg-spinner Bishoo thus became only the fifth bowler to take a wicket with his first ball in a Lord's Test. After the match the colourful radio commentator Henry Blofeld was applauded around the ground after announcing his retirement.

West Indies

K. C. Brathwaite c Bairstow b Anderson	10	– b Anderson	4
K. O. A. Powell c and b Stokes	39	– b Anderson	45
K. A. Hope c Bairstow b Anderson	0	– lbw b Broad	1
S. D. Hope c Cook b Roland-Jones	29	– c Bairstow b Anderson	62
R. L. Chase b Stokes	18	– c Bairstow b Anderson	3
J. Blackwood b Roland-Jones	1	– c Bairstow b Anderson	5
†S. O. Dowrich c Cook b Stokes	1	– c Broad b Roland-Jones	14
*J. O. Holder b Stokes	9	– c Anderson b Broad	23
D. Bishoo not out	13	– b Anderson	0
K. A. J. Roach c Anderson b Stokes	0	– b Anderson	3
S. T. Gabriel b Stokes	0	– not out	0
Lb 1, nb 2	3	Lb 17	17
(57.3 overs)	123	(65.1 overs)	177

1/18 (1) 2/22 (3) 3/78 (4) 4/78 (2) 5/87 (6)   1/6 (1) 2/21 (3) 3/69 (2) 4/94 (5) 5/100 (6) 6/123 (7)
6/100 (5) 7/101 (7) 8/119 (8) 9/123 (10) 10/123 (11)   7/155 (4) 8/155 (9) 9/177 (8) 10/177 (10)

Anderson 16–7–31–2; Broad 12–5–24–0; Roland-Jones 11–4–32–2; Stokes 14.3–6–22–6; Ali 4–0–13–0. *Second innings*—Anderson 20.1–5–42–7; Broad 19–9–35–2; Roland-Jones 11–4–31–1; Stokes 12–3–41–0; Ali 2–0–6–0; Root 1–0–5–0.

England

A. N. Cook c Dowrich b Roach	10	– lbw b Bishoo	17
M. D. Stoneman c Dowrich b Roach	1	– not out	40
T. Westley lbw b Holder	8	– not out	44
*J. E. Root c Powell b Holder	1		
D. J. Malan c Dowrich b Roach	20		
B. A. Stokes b Gabriel	60		
†J. M. Bairstow lbw b Roach	21		
M. M. Ali c K. A. Hope b Roach	3		
T. S. Roland-Jones c S. D. Hope b Holder	13		
S. C. J. Broad c Dowrich b Holder	38		
J. M. Anderson not out	8		
Lb 4, nb 7	11	B 4, lb 1, w 1	6
(52.5 overs)	194	(1 wkt, 28 overs)	107

1/1 (2) 2/15 (1) 3/19 (3) 4/24 (4) 5/63 (5)   1/35 (1)
6/119 (7) 7/128 (6) 8/134 (8) 9/163 (9) 10/194 (10)

Roach 24–8–72–5; Gabriel 15–1–64–1; Holder 13.5–1–54–4. *Second innings*—Gabriel 5–0–22–0; Roach 1–0–4–0; Holder 6–1–16–0; Bishoo 11–2–35–1; Chase 5–1–25–0.

Umpires: M. Erasmus *(South Africa)* (45) and C. B. Gaffaney *(New Zealand)* (15).
Third umpire: S. Ravi *(India)*.   Referee: D. C. Boon *(Australia)* (44).

Close of play: first day, England 46–4 (Malan 13, Stokes 13); second day, West Indies 93–3 (S. D. Hope 35, Chase 3).

Test No. 2273/5 (B101, A802)

BANGLADESH v AUSTRALIA 2017–18 (1st Test)

At Shere Bangla National Stadium, Mirpur, Dhaka, on 27, 28, 29, 30 August, 2017.
Toss: Bangladesh.   Result: BANGLADESH WON BY 20 RUNS.
Debuts: none.
Man of the Match: Shakib Al Hasan.

In the preceding ten months Bangladesh had recorded maiden wins over England and Sri Lanka – and now they added Australia to the list. The narrow margin of victory reflected four captivating days. In his 50th Test, Shakib Al Hasan made the difference. Australia's second innings was an improvement on the first, but a late collapse of six for 41 proved terminal. On the first morning Shakib, along with Tamim Iqbal, had inspired a recovery from a jittery ten for three; Bangladesh's eventual 260 looked even better when Australia lurched to 18 for three themselves by the close. Smith fell early next morning, charging Mehedi Hasan, and only a ninth-wicket stand of 49 between Agar, in his first Test for four years, and Cummins limited the deficit to 43. Lyon then set to work, but Tamim held things together with another seventy, before Lyon's fingertip deflection ran out Mushfiqur Rahim as the last five tumbled for 35. Australia needed 265, and Warner seemed intent on winning the match on his own, unfurling what he described as the best of his 19 Test hundreds. After another shaky start, Australia had reached 158 for two when he was trapped in front by a joyous Shakib – and the stadium soon erupted again when Smith edged behind. Shakib eased to his second five-for of the match, and although Cummins caused a few flutters, Taijul Islam finally got an over at last man Hazlewood. Australia had now lost 12 of their last 14 Tests in Asia.

Bangladesh

Tamim Iqbal c Warner b Maxwell	71	–	c Wade b Cummins	78
Soumya Sarkar c Handscomb b Cummins	8	–	c Khawaja b Agar	15
Imrul Kayes c Wade b Cummins	0	–	(4) c Warner b Lyon	2
Sabbir Rahman c Wade b Cummins	0	–	(7) c Handscomb b Lyon	22
Shakib Al Hasan c Smith b Lyon	84	–	(6) c Cummins b Lyon	5
*†Mushfiqur Rahim lbw b Agar	18	–	(5) run out (Lyon)	41
Nasir Hossain lbw b Agar	23	–	(8) c Wade b Agar	0
Mehedi Hasan c Handscomb b Lyon	18	–	(9) c Khawaja b Lyon	26
Taijul Islam lbw b Lyon	4	–	(3) lbw b Lyon	4
Shafiul Islam c Hazlewood b Agar	13	–	c Handscomb b Lyon	9
Mustafizur Rahman not out	0	–	not out	0
B 15, lb 3, w 1, nb 2	21		B 15, lb 3, w 1	19
(78.5 overs)	260		(79.3 overs)	221

1/10 (2) 2/10 (3) 3/10 (4) 4/165 (1) 5/188 (5)
6/198 (6) 7/240 (8) 8/246 (7) 9/246 (9) 10/260 (10)

1/43 (2) 2/61 (3) 3/67 (4) 4/135 (1) 5/143 (6)
6/186 (5) 7/186 (8) 8/186 (7) 9/214 (10) 10/221 (9)

Hazlewood 15–5–39–0; Cummins 16–1–63–3; Lyon 30–6–79–3; Agar 12.5–2–46–3; Maxwell 5–0–15–1. *Second innings*—Hazlewood 4.1–2–3–0; Cummins 14–3–38–1; Lyon 34.3–10–82–6; Maxwell 5–0–24–0; Agar 20.5–2–55–2; Khawaja 1–0–1–0.

Australia

D. A. Warner lbw b Mehedi Hasan	8	–	lbw b Shakib Al Hasan	112
M. T. Renshaw c Soumya Sarkar b Shakib Al Hasan	45	–	lbw b Mehedi Hasan	5
U. T. Khawaja run out (Mushfiqur Rahim/Soumya Sarkar)	1	–	c Taijul Islam b Shakib Al Hasan	1
N. M. Lyon lbw b Shakib Al Hasan	0	–	(10) c Soumya Sarkar b Mehedi Hasan	12
*S. P. D. Smith b Mehedi Hasan	8	–	(4) c Mushfiqur Rahim b Shakib Al Hasan	37
P. S. P. Handscomb lbw b Taijul Islam	33	–	(5) c Soumya Sarkar b Taijul Islam	15
G. J. Maxwell st Mushfiqur Rahim b Shakib Al Hasan	23	–	(6) b Shakib Al Hasan	14
†M. S. Wade lbw b Mehedi Hasan	5	–	(7) lbw b Shakib Al Hasan	4
A. C. Agar not out	41	–	(8) c and b Taijul Islam	2
P. J. Cummins b Shakib Al Hasan	25	–	(9) not out	33
J. R. Hazlewood c Imrul Kayes b Shakib Al Hasan	5	–	lbw b Taijul Islam	0
B 15, lb 3, w 5	23		B 7, lb 2	9
(74.5 overs)	217		(70.5 overs)	244

1/9 (1) 2/14 (3) 3/14 (4) 4/33 (5) 5/102 (6) 6/117 (2)
7/124 (8) 8/144 (7) 9/193 (10) 10/217 (11)

1/27 (2) 2/28 (3) 3/158 (1) 4/171 (4)
5/187 (5) 6/192 (7) 7/195 (8) 8/199 (6)
9/228 (10) 10/244 (11)

Shafiul Islam 6–0–21–0; Mehedi Hasan 26–6–62–3; Shakib Al Hasan 25.5–7–68–5; Taijul Islam 8–1–32–1; Mustafizur Rahman 8–3–13–0; Nasir Hossain 1–0–3–0. *Second innings*—Mehedi Hasan 19–3–80–2; Nasir Hossain 3–2–2–0; Shakib Al Hasan 28–7–85–5; Taijul Islam 19.5–2–60–3; Mustafizur Rahman 1–0–8–0.

Umpires: Aleem Dar *(Pakistan)* (114) and N. J. Llong *(England)* (44).
Third umpire: I. J. Gould *(England)*.   Referee: J. J. Crowe *(New Zealand)* (84).

Close of play: first day, Australia 18-3 (Renshaw 6, Smith 3); second day, Bangladesh 45–1 (Tamim Iqbal 30, Taijul Islam 0); third day, Australia 109–2 (Warner 75, Smith 25).

Test No. 2274/6 (B102, A803)

BANGLADESH v AUSTRALIA 2017–18 (2nd Test)

At Zohur Ahmed Chowdhury Stadium, Chittagong, on 4, 5, 6, 7 September, 2017.
Toss: Bangladesh.   Result: AUSTRALIA WON BY SEVEN WICKETS.
Debuts: none.
Man of the Match: N. M. Lyon.   Men of the Series: N. M. Lyon and D. A. Warner.

Bangladesh staged a Test for the first time in September, the monsoon season – and Australia's two most seasoned players saved the series. Lyon grabbed 13 wickets, while Warner's second successive century suggested he had finally adapted to Asian conditions. Lyon was soon in action, reducing Bangladesh to 85 for four, but a sixth-wicket stand of 105 between Mushfiqur Rahim and Sabbir Rahman left the hosts better placed. While Lyon took seven wickets, slow left-armer O'Keefe – flown in specially for the game – managed none. Mustafizur Rahman soon struck in the reply, thanks to Mushfiqur's diving leg-side catch off Matt Renshaw. It was only the second Test dismissal – after Rusi Surti of India was caught by Australia's Rex Sellers off Robert (Bob) Simpson at Calcutta in 1964-65 – in which the three participants shared the same initials. Smith and Handscomb shared stands of 93 and 152 in enervating conditions before Warner reached a hard-working hundred – the slowest of his 20, at 209 balls, with only five fours. A lead of 72 looked much better when Bangladesh crumpled to 43 for five. A brief recovery ended when Sabbir Rahman became the first Bangladeshi to be stumped twice in a Test, and Australia needed only 86. They knocked it off rapidly, anxious to avoid a fifth day because of the weather forecast. Lyon's match figures had been bettered only six times for Australia. In all he took 22 wickets, one behind Rangana Herath's record for a two-match series, against Pakistan in Sri Lanka in 2014.

Bangladesh

Tamim Iqbal lbw b Lyon	9	– st Wade b Lyon	12
Soumya Sarkar lbw b Lyon	33	– c Renshaw b Cummins	9
Imrul Kayes lbw b Lyon	4	– c Maxwell b Lyon	15
Mominul Haque lbw b Lyon	31	– (8) c Cummins b Lyon	29
Shakib Al Hasan c Wade b Agar	24	– c Warner b Lyon	2
*†Mushfiqur Rahim b Lyon	68	– c Wade b Cummins	31
Sabbir Rahman st Wade b Lyon	66	– st Wade b Lyon	24
Nasir Hossain c Wade b Agar	45	– (4) c Smith b O'Keefe	5
Mehedi Hasan run out (Warner)	11	– not out	14
Taijul Islam c Smith b Lyon	9	– b Lyon	4
Mustafizur Rahman not out	0	– b O'Keefe	0
B 5	5	B 12	12
(113.2 overs)	305	(71.2 overs)	157

1/13 (1) 2/21 (3) 3/70 (2) 4/85 (4) 5/117 (5)
6/222 (7) 7/265 (6) 8/293 (8) 9/296 (9) 10/305 (10)

1/11 (2) 2/32 (1) 3/37 (3) 4/39 (5)
5/43 (4) 6/97 (7) 7/129 (6) 8/149 (8)
9/156 (10) 10/157 (11)

Cummins 22–5–46–0; Lyon 36.2–7–94–7; O'Keefe 23–0–79–0; Agar 23–9–52–2; Maxwell 4–0–13–0; Cartwright 5–1–16–0. *Second innings*—Cummins 11–3–27–2; Lyon 33–11–60–6; O'Keefe 22.2–6–49–2; Agar 5–1–9–0.

Australia

M. T. Renshaw c Mushfiqur Rahim b Mustafizur Rahman	4	– c Mushfiqur Rahim b Shakib Al Hasan	22
D. A. Warner c Imrul Kayes b Mustafizur Rahman	123	– c Soumya Sarkar b Mustafizur Rahman	8
*S. P. D. Smith b Taijul Islam	58	– c Mushfiqur Rahim b Taijul Islam	16
P. S. P. Handscomb run out (Shakib Al Hasan)	82	– not out	16
G. J. Maxwell c Mushfiqur Rahim b Mehedi Hasan	38	– not out	25
H. W. R. Cartwright c Soumya Sarkar b Mehedi Hasan	18		
†M. S. Wade lbw b Mustafizur Rahman	8		
A. C. Agar b Shakib Al Hasan	22		
P. J. Cummins lbw b Mehedi Hasan	4		
S. N. J. O'Keefe not out	8		
N. M. Lyon c Imrul Kayes b Mustafizur Rahman	0		
B 8, lb 3, w 1	12		
(119.5 overs)	377	(3 wkts, 15.3 overs)	87

1/5 (1) 2/98 (3) 3/250 (4) 4/298 (2) 5/321 (6)
6/342 (7) 7/346 (5) 8/364 (9) 9/376 (8) 10/377 (11)

1/13 (2) 2/44 (3) 3/48 (1)

Mehedi Hasan 38–6–93–3; Mustafizur Rahman 20.5–2–84–4; Shakib Al Hasan 31–3–82–1; Taijul Islam 21–1–78–1; Nasir Hossain 6–2–14–0; Mominul Haque 2–0–6–0; Sabbir Rahman 1–0–9–0. *Second innings*—Mustafizur Rahman 5–1–16–1; Shakib Al Hasan 6–1–35–1; Taijul Islam 4–0–26–1; Nasir Hossain 0.3–0–10–0.

Umpires: I. J. Gould *(England)* (62) and N. J. Llong *(England)* (45).
Third umpire: Aleem Dar *(Pakistan)*.   Referee: J. J. Crowe *(New Zealand)* (85).

Close of play: first day, Bangladesh 253–6 (Mushfiqur Rahim 62, Nasir Hossain 19); second day, Australia 225–2 (Warner 88, Handscomb 69); third day, Australia 377–9 (O'Keefe 8, Lyon 0).

Test No. 2275/52 (P411, SL263)

PAKISTAN v SRI LANKA 2017–18 (1st Test)

At Sheikh Zayed Stadium, Abu Dhabi, on 28, 29, 30 September, 1, 2 October, 2017.
Toss: Sri Lanka.   Result: SRI LANKA WON BY 21 RUNS.
Debuts: Pakistan – Haris Sohail.
Man of the Match: H. M. R. K. B. Herath.

After four meandering days, the match arrived at a shootout: Herath v Pakistan. Two years earlier, he was dropped for the decider after taking two wickets in two matches. Now Herath was older, and had just endured a poor series against India. But now he confounded the batsmen when they used their feet, and when they swept. He led Sri Lanka's defence of 136, the lowest target they had protected in Tests, beating 168 against the same opposition at Galle in 2009 – and the lowest Pakistan had failed to chase, beating 146 against South Africa at Faisalabad in 1997–98. Pakistan had never previously tasted defeat in Abu Dhabi, while Sri Lanka had not won away against top-eight opposition since Headingley in 2014. Herath's six-for, after five in the first innings, included his 100th against Pakistan (Kapil Dev had 99). He also became, at 39, the first left-arm spinner to reach 400 in Tests, half coming after he turned 35. Pakistan's blowout was familiar: this was the eighth time they had lost ten wickets in a day since July 2016. The first 4½ days had been less dramatic. Chandimal's undefeated nine-hour 155 was well supported by Karunaratne and Dickwella. But Pakistan grabbed a three-run lead, with Azhar Ali passing 5,000 Test runs, and Haris Sohail making an attractive 76 on debut, in his first first-class game for 3½ years. When Yasir Shah scuttled Sri Lanka on the fifth morning, the stage seemed set for a Pakistan victory. But Herath had other ideas.

Sri Lanka

F. D. M. Karunaratne run out (Mohammad Abbas/Sarfraz Ahmed)	93	– c Shan Masood b Yasir Shah	10
J. K. Silva b Hasan Ali	12	– lbw b Haris Sohail	25
H. D. R. L. Thirimanne lbw b Yasir Shah	0	– c Sarfraz Ahmed b Asad Shafiq	7
B. K. G. Mendis c Sarfraz Ahmed b Yasir Shah	10	– lbw b Mohammad Abbas	18
*L. D. Chandimal not out	155	– c Asad Shafiq b Yasir Shah	7
†D. P. D. N. Dickwella b Hasan Ali	83	– (7) not out	40
M. D. K. Perera lbw b Haris Sohail	33	– (8) lbw b Yasir Shah	6
H. M. R. K. B. Herath c Babar Azam b Yasir Shah	4	– (9) c Shan Masood b Yasir Shah	0
R. A. S. Lakmal lbw b Mohammad Abbas	7	– (6) c Babar Azam b Mohammad Abbas	13
P. A. D. L. R. Sandakan lbw b Mohammad Abbas	8	– c Mohammad Amir b Yasir Shah	8
A. N. P. R. Fernando b Mohammad Abbas	0	– b Hasan Ali	0
Lb 11, nb 3	14	Lb 3, nb 1	4
(154.5 overs)	419	(66.5 overs)	138

1/34 (2) 2/35 (3) 3/61 (4) 4/161 (1) 5/295 (6)
6/387 (7) 7/396 (8) 8/408 (9) 9/419 (10) 10/419 (11)

1/20 (1) 2/33 (3) 3/51 (2) 4/65 (5)
5/73 (4) 6/86 (6) 7/101 (8) 8/101 (9)
9/135 (10) 10/138 (11)

Mohammad Amir 27–5–63–0; Mohammad Abbas 26.5–0–75–3; Yasir Shah 57–11–120–3; Hasan Ali 27–6–88–2; Shan Masood 1–1–0–0; Haris Sohail 13–0–51–1; Asad Shafiq 3–0–11–0. *Second innings*—Mohammad Amir 12–4–27–0; Mohammad Abbas 12–3–22–3; Yasir Shah 27–5–51–5; Hasan Ali 7.1–0–21–1; Asad Shafiq 3.4–0–7–1; Haris Sohail 5–2–7–1.

Pakistan

Shan Masood b Herath	59	– c Silva b Perera	7
Sami Aslam lbw b Perera	51	– c Karunaratne b Herath	2
Azhar Ali c sub (W. S. R. Samarawickrama) b Herath	85	– c Dickwella b Lakmal	0
Asad Shafiq c Thirimanne b Herath	39	– c Karunaratne b Herath	20
Babar Azam c Dickwella b Fernando	28	– c Dickwella b Perera	3
Haris Sohail c Lakmal b Fernando	76	– lbw b Perera	34
*†Sarfraz Ahmed b Lakmal	18	– st Dickwella b Herath	19
Mohammad Amir lbw b Lakmal	4	– (9) b Herath	9
Yasir Shah c Thirimanne b Herath	8	– (10) not out	6
Hasan Ali st Dickwella b Herath	29	– (8) b Herath	8
Mohammad Abbas not out	1	– lbw b Herath	0
B 5, lb 9, w 2, nb 8	24	B 1, lb 4, nb 1	6
(162.3 overs)	422	(47.4 overs)	114

1/114 (2) 2/116 (1) 3/195 (4) 4/266 (5) 5/294 (3)
6/316 (7) 7/326 (8) 8/340 (9) 9/390 (10) 10/422 (6)

1/4 (2) 2/7 (3) 3/16 (1) 4/32 (5) 5/36 (4) 6/78 (7)
7/98 (6) 8/100 (8) 9/111 (9) 10/114 (11)

Lakmal 22–5–42–2; Fernando 25.3–1–77–2; Perera 37–10–92–1; Sandakan 35–7–98–0; Herath 40–12–93–5; Karunaratne 3–1–6–0. *Second innings*—Lakmal 5–1–12–1; Herath 21.4–4–43–6; Perera 18–4–46–3; Fernando 2–1–4–0; Sandakan 1–0–4–0.

Umpires: R. A. Kettleborough *(England)* (45) and N. J. Llong *(England)* (46).
Third umpire: Ahsan Raza *(Pakistan)*.   Referee: A. J. Pycroft *(Zimbabwe)* (55).

Close of play: first day, Sri Lanka 227–4 (Chandimal 60, Dickwella 42); second day, Pakistan 64–0 (Shan Masood 30, Sami Aslam 31); third day, Pakistan 266–4 (Azhar Ali 74); fourth day, Sri Lanka 69–4 (Mendis 16, Lakmal 2).

Test No. 2276/53 (P412, SL264)

PAKISTAN v SRI LANKA 2017-18 (2nd Test)

At Dubai International Stadium on 6, 7, 8, 9, 10 October, 2017 (day/night).
Toss: Sri Lanka. Result: SRI LANKA WON BY 68 RUNS.
Debuts: Sri Lanka – P. L. S. Gamage, W. S. R. Samarawickrama.
Man of the Match: F. D. M. Karunaratne. Man of the Series: F. D. M. Karunaratne.

Since moving their base to the UAE in 2010, Pakistan had not lost a Test series there. But, with Misbah-ul-Haq and Younis Khan now retired, the fortress fell. On the final afternoon of Dubai's second day/night Test – but Sri Lanka's first – Asad Shafiq and Sarfraz Ahmed were going well, and victory was less than 100 away. But a collapse of five for 23 handed Sri Lanka the series. Karunaratne's career-best 196 in 9¼ hours was backbone of their fine first innings. The middle order gave strong support, while Yasir Shah picked up another six wickets, becoming the first spinner to collect five-fors in five successive Tests (and the fourth in all, after Charlie Turner, Sydney Barnes and Alec Bedser). Pakistan's response was inadequate. Azhar Ali and Haris Sohail made fifties, but Sri Lanka's bowlers did enough to secure a 220-run lead. That should have been that, but they nosedived to 34 for five, after a searing spell from Wahab Riaz (Mohammad Amir was missing with a shin injury). Next day Sohail Khan picked up three in an over to wrap things up for 96. Pakistan needed 317, but crawled to 52 for five in 33 overs. Shafiq crafted a majestic hundred, but when Sarfraz swept to deep square after a stand of 173, Pakistan imploded. Dilruwan Perera took five, to complete an incisive all-round performance.

Sri Lanka

F. D. M. Karunaratne b Wahab Riaz	196	– b Wahab Riaz	7
J. K. Silva c Sarfraz Ahmed b Yasir Shah	27	– c Sarfraz Ahmed b Mohammad Abbas	3
W. S. R. Samarawickrama c and b Mohammad Amir	38	– c Sarfraz Ahmed b Wahab Riaz	13
B. K. G. Mendis c Asad Shafiq b Yasir Shah	1	– c Sarfraz Ahmed b Haris Sohail	29
*L. D. Chandimal lbw b Yasir Shah	62	– (6) lbw b Wahab Riaz	0
†D. P. D. N. Dickwella c Sarfraz Ahmed b Mohammad Abbas	52	– (7) c Sarfraz Ahmed b Wahab Riaz	21
M. D. K. Perera b Yasir Shah	58	– (8) lbw b Yasir Shah	0
H. M. R. K. B. Herath not out	27	– (9) c Babar Azam b Haris Sohail	17
R. A. S. Lakmal lbw b Mohammad Abbas	8	– (5) lbw b Yasir Shah	1
P. L. S. Gamage st Sarfraz Ahmed b Yasir Shah	1	– not out	1
A. N. P. R. Fernando c Asad Shafiq b Yasir Shah	0	– lbw b Haris Sohail	0
B 1, lb 3, w 3, nb 5	12	Lb 1, nb 3	4
(159.2 overs)	482	(26 overs)	96

1/63 (2) 2/131 (3) 3/136 (4) 4/282 (5) 5/370 (6) 1/3 (2) 2/22 (1) 3/26 (3) 4/33 (5) 5/34 (6) 6/59 (7)
6/429 (1) 7/454 (7) 8/469 (9) 9/474 (10) 10/482 (11) 7/60 (8) 8/95 (9) 9/96 (4) 10/96 (11)

Mohammad Amir 19.3–5–74–1; Mohammad Abbas 33–9–100–2; Wahab Riaz 26–6–62–1; Yasir Shah 55.5–9–184–6; Asad Shafiq 11–1–24–0; Haris Sohail 14–3–34–0. *Second innings*—Mohammad Abbas 4–2–6–1; Yasir Shah 12–2–47–2; Wahab Riaz 9–0–41–4; Haris Sohail 1–0–1–3.

Pakistan

Shan Masood b Gamage	16	– c Dickwella b Perera	21
Sami Aslam lbw b Perera	39	– c Mendis b Gamage	1
Azhar Ali lbw b Herath	59	– c Silva b Fernando	17
Asad Shafiq c Mendis b Lakmal	12	– (5) c Mendis b Lakmal	112
Babar Azam c Samarawickrama b Herath	8	– (6) c Silva b Perera	0
Haris Sohail lbw b Perera	56	– (4) c Dickwella b Perera	10
*†Sarfraz Ahmed c Mendis b Perera	14	– c Fernando b Perera	68
Mohammad Amir lbw b Herath	7	– lbw b Perera	4
Yasir Shah b Lakmal	24	– st Dickwella b Herath	5
Wahab Riaz c Samarawickrama b Gamage	16	– c Chandimal b Herath	1
Mohammad Abbas not out	1	– not out	3
B 4, lb 2, nb 4	10	Lb 1, nb 5	6
(90.3 overs)	262	(90.2 overs)	248

1/61 (1) 2/65 (2) 3/92 (4) 4/109 (5) 5/180 (3) 1/5 (2) 2/36 (3) 3/49 (4) 4/52 (1) 5/52 (6) 6/225 (7)
6/199 (7) 7/214 (8) 8/220 (6) 9/250 (10) 10/262 (9) 7/230 (8) 8/244 (9) 9/244 (5) 10/248 (10)

Lakmal 17.3–5–41–2; Fernando 9–2–21–0; Gamage 15–2–38–2; Perera 26–3–72–3; Herath 23–3–84–3. *Second innings*—Lakmal 14–4–35–1; Gamage 16–5–29–1; Herath 22.2–3–57–2; Fernando 11–3–21–1; Perera 26–1–98–5; Mendis 1–0–7–0.

Umpires: R. A. Kettleborough *(England)* (46) and N. J. Llong *(England)* (47).
Third umpire: S. Ravi *(India)*. Referee: A. J. Pycroft *(Zimbabwe)* (56).

Close of play: first day, Sri Lanka 254–3 (Karunaratne 133, Chandimal 49); second day, Pakistan 51–0 (Shan Masood 15, Sami Aslam 30); third day, Sri Lanka 34–5 (Mendis 8); fourth day, Pakistan 198–5 (Asad Shafiq 86, Sarfraz Ahmed 57).

Test No. 2277/11 (SA416, B103)

SOUTH AFRICA v BANGLADESH 2017–18 (1st Test)

At North West Stadium, Potchefstroom, on 28, 29, 30 September, 1, 2 October, 2017.
Toss: Bangladesh.   Result: SOUTH AFRICA WON BY 333 RUNS.
Debuts: South Africa – A. K. Markram, A. L. Phehlukwayo.
Man of the Match: D. Elgar.

Bangladesh produced a spirited first innings and, aided by thunderstorms, took the game into the fifth day – but then lost their last seven wickets in an hour. Mushfiqur Rahim's decision to bowl baffled everybody: South Africa's openers were watchful against Mustafizur Rahman, but found little threat elsewhere. Aiden Markram, making his debut six days before his 23rd birthday, kept pace with his more experienced partner: they entered the nineties together, but when Elgar, on 99, made a false start for a single, Markram was easily run out. However, their stand of 196 was followed by one of 215, Amla hitting the ball characteristically late. Elgar finally became the tenth to fall for 199 in Tests, and du Plessis declared soon afterwards. Tamim Iqbal had been off the field, so was prevented from opening, for the first time in 99 Test innings. Mominul Haque made a combative 77, Bangladesh's highest score against South Africa, and at 227 for four there was hope of something near parity. But after Mominul was splendidly caught at short leg by Markram, they had to settle for 320. South Africa resumed with a lead of 176, which was hurried towards 400 by Bavuma and du Plessis. Only two bowlers had conceded more than Mehedi Hasan's 247 runs in a Test without taking a wicket. The declaration left Bangladesh 4½ sessions to survive, but they lasted just 32.4 overs: only opener Imrul Kayes made it past 16. Morkel started the demolition with two wickets in the first over.

South Africa

D. Elgar c Mominul Haque b Mustafizur Rahman	199	– (2) lbw b Shafiul Islam	18
A. K. Markram run out (Sabbir Rahman/Mehedi Hasan)	97	– (1) c Liton Das b Mustafizur Rahman	15
H. M. Amla c Mehedi Hasan b Shafiul Islam	137	– c Liton Das b Mustafizur Rahman	28
T. Bavuma not out	31	– c Liton Das b Mominul Haque	71
*F. du Plessis not out	26	– lbw b Mominul Haque	81
†Q. de Kock (did not bat)	–	st Liton Das b Mominul Haque	8
A. L. Phehlukwayo (did not bat)	–	not out	6
K. A. Maharaj (did not bat)	–	not out	19
Lb 4, w 2	6	Nb 1	1
(3 wkts dec, 146 overs)	496	(6 wkts dec, 56 overs)	247

1/196 (2) 2/411 (3) 3/445 (1)   1/30 (2) 2/38 (1) 3/70 (3) 4/212 (5)
                                    5/217 (4) 6/222 (6)

K. Rabada, M. Morkel and D. Olivier did not bat.

Mustafizur Rahman 27–2–98–1; Shafiul Islam 25–5–74–1; Mehedi Hasan 56–4–178–0; Taskin Ahmed 26–5–88–0; Mahmudullah 5–0–24–0; Mominul Haque 2–0–15–0; Sabbir Rahman 5–1–15–0. *Second innings*—Mehedi Hasan 11–1–69–0; Shafiul Islam 13–1–46–1; Mustafizur Rahman 11–2–30–2; Taskin Ahmed 6–0–29–0; Sabbir Rahman 5–0–25–0; Mahmudullah 4–0–21–0; Mominul Haque 6–0–27–3.

Bangladesh

†Liton Das c Amla b Morkel	25	– (6) lbw b Rabada	4
Imrul Kayes c Markram b Rabada	7	– c de Kock b Maharaj	32
Mominul Haque c Markram b Maharaj	77	– lbw b Morkel	0
*Mushfiqur Rahim c Markram b Maharaj	44	– c Amla b Rabada	16
Tamim Iqbal c de Kock b Phehlukwayo	39	– (1) b Morkel	0
Mahmudullah b Morkel	66	– (5) b Rabada	9
Sabbir Rahman b Olivier	30	– lbw b Maharaj	4
Mehedi Hasan c Elgar b Rabada	8	– not out	15
Taskin Ahmed run out (Bavuma/Markram)	1	– lbw b Maharaj	4
Shafiul Islam c Amla b Maharaj	2	– run out (sub [W. D. Parnell]/Rabada/de Kock)	2
Mustafizur Rahman not out	10	– c and b Maharaj	1
B 1, lb 9, nb 1	11	B 1, nb 2	3
(89.1 overs)	320	(32.4 overs)	90

1/16 (2) 2/36 (1) 3/103 (4) 4/158 (5) 5/227 (3)   1/0 (1) 2/0 (3) 3/49 (2) 4/55 (4) 5/62 (5)
6/292 (7) 7/304 (6) 8/305 (9) 9/308 (8) 10/320 (10) 6/67 (6) 7/67 (7) 8/71 (9) 9/75 (10) 10/90 (11)

Morkel 19–7–51–2; Rabada 24–5–84–2; Maharaj 27.1–8–92–3; Olivier 11–1–52–1; Phehlukwayo 6–2–18–1; Markram 2–0–13–0. *Second innings*—Morkel 5.2–2–19–2; Rabada 10–3–33–3; Olivier 5.4–1–12–0; Maharaj 10.4–1–25–4; Phehlukwayo 1–1–0–0.

Umpires: C. B. Gaffaney *(New Zealand)* (16) and B. N. J. Oxenford *(Australia)* (44).
Third umpire: H. D. P. K. Dharmasena *(Sri Lanka)*.   Referee: R. S. Madugalle *(Sri Lanka)* (178).

Close of play: first day, South Africa 298–1 (Elgar 128, Amla 68); second day, Bangladesh 127–3 (Mominul Haque 28, Tamim Iqbal 22); third day, South Africa 54–2 (Amla 17, Bavuma 3); fourth day, Bangladesh 49–3 (Mushfiqur Rahim 16).

SOUTH AFRICA v BANGLADESH 2017–18 (2nd Test)

At Springbok Park, Bloemfontein, on 6, 7, 8 October, 2017.
Toss: Bangladesh.   Result: SOUTH AFRICA WON BY AN INNINGS AND 254 RUNS.
Debuts: none.
Man of the Match: K. Rabada.   Man of the Series: D. Elgar.

As if to prove his idiotic decision to bowl first at Potchefstroom was not a one-off, Mushfiqur Rahim did it again. This pitch might have had a little more grass, but every local knew it would be a batting delight. A bewildered du Plessis shook his head, then his batsmen gorged; for the second time, South Africa had four centurions in the same innings, after Antigua in 2004-05. Elgar and Markram – who did now manage a maiden hundred – put on 243, the third-highest opening stand in a Test after being inserted. Amla and du Plessis weren't about to squander such a boot-filling opportunity, and took their own partnership to 247 next day, with Amla collecting his 28th hundred (one more than Graeme Smith, and behind only Jacques Kallis on the national list). Across three innings in the series, South Africa had scored 1,316 runs for the loss of 13 wickets. Rabada was too quick and too determined, and claimed five wickets in each innings – only Dale Steyn, with 11 for 60 against Pakistan at Johannesburg in 2012-13, had taken a cheaper ten-for for South Africa – while Olivier, on his home ground, also thrived. Bangladesh began again on the second evening, and finished on the third afternoon. Imrul Kayes, Mushfiqur – who was hit on the head and later taken to hospital – and Mahmudullah did at least show some heart, but no one bettered 43 as South Africa romped to their biggest Test victory, topping an innings and 229 against Sri Lanka at Cape Town in 2000–01.

South Africa

D. Elgar c Mustafizur Rahman b Subashis Roy	113
A. K. Markram b Rubel Hossain	143
H. M. Amla b Subashis Roy	132
T. Bavuma c Liton Das b Subashis Roy	7
*F. du Plessis not out	135
†Q. de Kock not out	28
B 4, lb 2, w 8, nb 1	15
(4 wkts dec, 120 overs)	573

1/243 (1) 2/276 (2) 3/288 (4) 4/535 (3)

A. L. Phehlukwayo, K. A. Maharaj, W. D. Parnell, K. Rabada and D. Olivier did not bat.

Mustafizur Rahman 25–3–113–0; Subashis Roy 29–3–118–3; Rubel Hossain 22–1–113–1; Soumya Sarkar 5–0–21–0; Taijul Islam 27–0–145–0; Mahmudullah 9–2–35–0; Mominul Haque 1–0–6–0; Sabbir Rahman 2–0–16–0.

Bangladesh

Imrul Kayes c de Kock b Rabada	26	– c de Kock b Olivier	32
Soumya Sarkar b Rabada	9	– c du Plessis b Rabada	3
Mominul Haque c de Kock b Olivier	4	– c Maharaj b Rabada	11
*Mushfiqur Rahim c Bavuma b Olivier	7	– lbw b Parnell	26
Mahmudullah c de Kock b Parnell	4	– c Elgar b Rabada	43
†Liton Das c du Plessis b Rabada	70	– b Phehlukwayo	18
Sabbir Rahman c Parnell b Rabada	0	– c du Plessis b Phehlukwayo	4
Taijul Islam b Olivier	12	– b Rabada	2
Rubel Hossain b Rabada	10	– b Rabada	7
Mustafizur Rahman c Markram b Maharaj	0	– (11) b Phehlukwayo	7
Subashis Roy not out	2	– (10) not out	12
Lb 3	3	Lb 6, nb 1	7
(42.5 overs)	147	(42.4 overs)	172

1/13 (2) 2/26 (3) 3/36 (4) 4/49 (5) 5/61 (1)   1/13 (2) 2/29 (3) 3/63 (1) 4/92 (4) 5/135 (6)
6/65 (7) 7/115 (8) 8/143 (6) 9/143 (10) 10/147 (9)   6/139 (5) 7/145 (7) 8/145 (8) 9/156 (9) 10/172 (11)

Rabada 13.5–4–33–5; Olivier 12–3–40–3; Parnell 7–1–36–1; Maharaj 5–2–7–1; Phehlukwayo 5–1–28–0. *Second innings*—Rabada 11–1–30–5; Olivier 11–1–39–1; Maharaj 6–1–30–0; Parnell 5–0–31–1; Phehlukwayo 9.4–2–36–3.

Umpires: H. D. P. K. Dharmasena *(Sri Lanka)* (47) and B. N. J. Oxenford *(Australia)* (45).
Third umpire: C. B. Gaffaney *(New Zealand)*.   Referee: R. S. Madugalle *(Sri Lanka)* (179).

Close of play: first day, South Africa 428–3 (Amla 89, du Plessis 62); second day, Bangladesh (second innings) 7–0 (Imrul Kayes 6, Soumya Sarkar 1).

ZIMBABWE v WEST INDIES 2017–18 (1st Test)

At Queens Sports Club, Bulawayo, on 21, 22, 23, 24 October, 2017.
Toss: West Indies. Result: **WEST INDIES WON BY 117 RUNS**.
Debuts: Zimbabwe – S. F. Mire.
Man of the Match: D. Bishoo.

A Test that started in fast-forward, slowed to a glacial crawl and giddied up to a comedic finish ended with a day to spare. Bishoo turned things West Indies' way – Zimbabwe were almost halfway to West Indies' modest first-innings 219 when he took his first wicket – and, once they had grabbed the initiative, they stayed ahead. The pitch turned markedly on the first morning, but was otherwise slow: there were no slip catches off the pacemen. West Indies' batsmen also slowed things down: Shai Hope's unbeaten 90 lasted nearly 4½ hours, while Brathwaite batted even longer for his 86 in the second innings, when Chase bucked the trend with an adventurous 95. In contrast, Zimbabwe's batsmen were too gung-ho, losing nine for 68 after reaching 91 for one. Bishoo grabbed five of them, and added four more in the second innings when Zimbabwe, chasing a distant 434, batted more responsibly. Masakadza and Taylor both made half-centuries, and at 219 for four an hour after tea on the fourth day, Zimbabwe had half an eye on a record. But Sikandar Raza cuffed a loose one from Bishoo straight to short extra, and the spell was broken. Taylor ran out Waller (Shai Hope scored a direct hit from midwicket) and shortly afterwards was run out himself, trying an optimistic second to Brathwaite at deep square. Suddenly it was 263 for nine. Jarvis and Mpofu hit out entertainingly, adding 53 in nine overs, which at least took Zimbabwe past 300 – but it couldn't last.

West Indies

K. C. Brathwaite c Chakabva b Jarvis	3	– lbw b Sikandar Raza		86
K. O. A. Powell c Ervine b Cremer	56	– b Cremer		17
K. A. Hope c Chakabva b Mire	16	– lbw b Jarvis		43
S. D. Hope not out	90	– lbw b Jarvis		44
R. L. Chase c Ervine b Sikandar Raza	31	– b Williams		95
J. Blackwood st Chakabva b Cremer	1	– st Chakabva b Williams		3
†S. O. Dowrich c Masakadza b Williams	11	– c Masakadza b Williams		12
*J. O. Holder lbw b Williams	8	– c Mpofu b Cremer		24
D. Bishoo c Ervine b Williams	0	– c Williams b Cremer		44
K. A. J. Roach lbw b Cremer	0	– b Cremer		0
S. T. Gabriel c Ervine b Cremer	0	– not out		0
B 3	3	B 3, lb 2		5
(82.5 overs)	219	(126 overs)		373

1/14 (1) 2/35 (3) 3/110 (2) 4/174 (5) 5/179 (6)   1/25 (2) 2/107 (3) 3/174 (1) 4/211 (4) 5/224 (6)
6/202 (7) 7/212 (8) 8/218 (9) 9/219 (10) 10/219 (11)   6/244 (7) 7/277 (8) 8/369 (9) 9/369 (10) 10/373 (5)

Jarvis 14–2–40–1; Mpofu 14–4–28–0; Mire 7–0–22–1; Cremer 23.5–5–64–4; Sikandar Raza 11–1–42–1; Williams 13–4–20–3. *Second innings*—Jarvis 24–1–66–2; Mpofu 10–3–30–0; Williams 35–8–91–3; Cremer 34–5–114–4; Sikandar Raza 19–4–53–1; Mire 2–0–5–0; Waller 2–0–9–0.

Zimbabwe

H. Masakadza c Dowrich b Bishoo	42	– c S. D. Hope b Brathwaite		57
S. F. Mire c Brathwaite b Roach	27	– b Roach		47
C. R. Ervine lbw b Bishoo	39	– lbw b Bishoo		18
B. R. M. Taylor c Blackwood b Bishoo	1	– run out (Brathwaite/Dowrich)		73
S. C. Williams c Dowrich b Roach	7	– st Dowrich b Bishoo		6
Sikandar Raza c Gabriel b Bishoo	6	– c Chase b Bishoo		30
M. N. Waller b Holder	11	– run out (S. D. Hope)		11
†R. W. Chakabva c Chase b Bishoo	12	– c and b Chase		1
*A. G. Cremer b Holder	0	– c and b Bishoo		9
K. M. Jarvis not out	2	– not out		23
C. B. Mpofu c Dowrich b Gabriel	10	– c Powell b Chase		33
Lb 2	2	B 5, lb 1, nb 2		8
(61.3 overs)	159	(90.4 overs)		316

1/44 (2) 2/91 (1) 3/93 (4) 4/110 (5) 5/123 (6)   1/99 (1) 2/109 (2) 3/141 (3) 4/155 (5) 5/219 (6)
6/133 (3) 7/139 (7) 8/147 (8) 9/147 (9) 10/159 (11)   6/246 (7) 7/249 (8) 8/253 (9) 9/263 (4) 10/316 (11)

Gabriel 11.3–4–24–1; Holder 14–5–25–2; Bishoo 24–4–79–5; Chase 1–0–6–0; Roach 11–5–23–2. *Second innings*—Roach 13–3–34–1; Gabriel 10–2–50–0; Holder 12–4–30–0; Bishoo 32–8–105–4; Chase 13.4–2–61–2; Brathwaite 10–1–30–1.

Umpires: H. D. P. K. Dharmasena *(Sri Lanka)* (48) and P. R. Reiffel *(Australia)* (33).
Third umpire: S. D. Fry *(Australia)*. Referee: J. Srinath *(India)* (36).

Close of play: first day, Zimbabwe 19–0 (Masakadza 0, Mire 17); second day, West Indies 88–1 (Brathwaite 38, K. A. Hope 32); third day, West Indies 369–8 (Chase 91).

Test No. 2280/10 (Z104, WI528)

ZIMBABWE v WEST INDIES 2017–18 (2nd Test)

At Queens Sports Club, Bulawayo, on 29, 30, 31 October, 1, 2 November, 2017.
Toss: Zimbabwe. Result: DRAWN.
Debuts: Zimbabwe – T. S. Chisoro.
Man of the Match: Sikandar Raza. Man of the Series: D. Bishoo.

Another placid pitch stymied both sides' chances of taking 20 wickets. October is usually Zimbabwe's hottest month, and three days ahead of the game Bulawayo was a 38°C oven. But it plummeted to 14 the day before, and the brief cold snap firmed up a surface that had been expected to crumble. Zimbabwe looked like taking a lead before an eighth-wicket partnership of 212, a West Indian record (previously 148 by Jimmy Adams and Franklyn Rose, also against Zimbabwe, at Kingston in 1999–2000). Dowrich completed a maiden Test hundred, while Holder's was his second. Only once before had Nos 8 and 9 scored centuries in the same Test innings: Roger Hartigan and Clem Hill (batting down the order after illness) for Australia against England at Adelaide in 1907–08. Their resistance took West Indies a healthy 122 in front, overshadowing a superb century by Masakadza – only the second by a Zimbabwean opener since 2001 (Tino Mawoyo made one in 2011), and his second against West Indies, 16 years after the first. Zimbabwe had been in trouble themselves at 14 for three on the Arctic first day, but Masakadza put on 142 with Moor – who discovered he was playing only that morning, when Sean Williams was taken ill – then 90 with Sikandar Raza. Chakabva resisted for almost four hours on the last day and – against some increasingly friendly bowling – put on 91 with Cremer in more than 48 overs. Bishoo became the first West Indian leg-spinner to collect 100 Test wickets.

Zimbabwe

H. Masakadza c Dowrich b Bishoo	147	– b Roach		5
S. F. Mire c Dowrich b Roach	4	– lbw b Roach		0
C. R. Ervine b Gabriel	0	– b Bishoo		22
B. R. M. Taylor b Roach	1	– lbw b Gabriel		10
P. J. Moor b Chase	52	– c S. D. Hope b Gabriel		42
Sikandar Raza c K. A. Hope b Gabriel	80	– b Holder		89
M. N. Waller b Brathwaite	0	– c Blackwood b Bishoo		15
†R. W. Chakabva b Bishoo	10	– not out		71
*A. G. Cremer run out (Holder)	11	– not out		28
T. S. Chisoro lbw b Roach	9			
C. B. Mpofu not out	4			
Lb 6, nb 2	8	B 10, lb 8, nb 1		19
(109.1 overs)	326	(7 wkts, 144 overs)		301

1/4 (2) 2/11 (3) 3/14 (4) 4/156 (5) 5/246 (1)   1/5 (1) 2/8 (2) 3/23 (4) 4/46 (3)
6/248 (7) 7/267 (8) 8/310 (6) 9/319 (9) 10/326 (10)   5/144 (5) 6/172 (7) 7/210 (6)

Gabriel 22–4–64–2; Roach 18.1–5–44–3; Blackwood 4–1–8–0; Holder 16–2–49–0; Bishoo 25–2–82–2; Chase 14–1–50–1; Brathwaite 10–0–23–1. *Second innings*—Gabriel 21–7–34–2; Roach 22–10–37–2; Brathwaite 17–2–44–0; Holder 22–7–42–1; Bishoo 34–7–74–2; Chase 17–3–31–0; Blackwood 10–4–21–0; Powell 1–1–0–0.

West Indies

K. C. Brathwaite c Masakadza b Cremer	32
K. O. A. Powell c Ervine b Mpofu	90
D. Bishoo c and b Sikandar Raza	23
K. A. Hope lbw b Sikandar Raza	1
S. D. Hope b Sikandar Raza	40
R. L. Chase lbw b Sikandar Raza	32
J. Blackwood c Cremer b Sikandar Raza	5
†S. O. Dowrich lbw b Chisoro	103
*J. O. Holder b Chisoro	110
K. A. J. Roach lbw b Chisoro	0
S. T. Gabriel not out	5
B 3, lb 3, nb 1	7
(178.2 overs)	448

1/76 (1) 2/131 (3) 3/135 (4) 4/163 (2) 5/219 (6)
6/225 (7) 7/230 (5) 8/442 (8) 9/443 (9) 10/448 (10)

Mpofu 28–10–55–1; Mire 5–2–5–0; Cremer 52–8–161–1; Sikandar Raza 48–12–99–5; Chisoro 41.2–9–113–3; Masakadza 4–1–9–0.

Umpires: H. D. P. K. Dharmasena *(Sri Lanka)* (49) and S. D. Fry *(Australia)* (7).
Third umpire: P. R. Reiffel *(Australia).* Referee: J. Srinath *(India)* (37).

Close of play: first day, Zimbabwe 169–4 (Masakadza 101, Sikandar Raza 9); second day, West Indies 78–1 (Powell 43, Bishoo 0); third day, West Indies 374–7 (Dowrich 75, Holder 71); fourth day, Zimbabwe 140–4 (Moor 39, Sikandar Raza 58).

INDIA v SRI LANKA 2017-18 (1st Test)

Test No. 2281/42 (I516, SL265)

At Eden Gardens, Kolkata, on 16, 17, 18, 19, 20 November, 2017.
Toss: Sri Lanka. Result: DRAWN.
Debuts: none.
Man of the Match: Bhuvneshwar Kumar.

Suranga Lakmal gave Sri Lanka a flying start but, despite rain limiting the first three days to 105 overs, they were hanging on for dear life by the end. Kohli had wanted the sort of conditions he expected to face in South Africa shortly after this series and Eden Gardens provided precisely that: overcast skies and a liberal covering of grass. It helped Lakmal's spectacular opening salvo, which underlined the fallibility of India's top order against the moving ball. Rahul fell to the first ball of the match, Dhawan was confounded by seam movement, and Kohli trapped in front. Lakmal's first seven overs were maidens, and his first spell – spread over two days – was 11–9–5–3. Pujara's three-hour resistance massaged the total to 172, but as the pitch dried, Sri Lanka stitched together several useful partnerships, before Herath slapped ten fours. Behind by 122 with less than five sessions to go, Kohli led a beefy reply with his 50th international century, after an opening stand of 166. Still, when he declared 45 minutes before tea on the final day with a lead of 230, few envisaged the thrilling finale. Bhuvneshwar Kumar and Mohammed Shami produced fast bowling of the highest quality; it was soon 22 for four but eventually, with the floodlights taking over from the natural light, the umpires called a halt. For the first time in 262 home Tests, no Indian spinner took a wicket.

India

K. L. Rahul c Dickwella b Lakmal	0	– b Lakmal	79
S. Dhawan b Lakmal	8	– c Dickwella b Shanaka	94
C. A. Pujara b Gamage	52	– c Perera b Lakmal	22
*V. Kohli lbw b Lakmal	0	– not out	104
A. M. Rahane c Dickwella b Shanaka	4	– lbw b Lakmal	0
R. Ashwin c Karunaratne b Shanaka	4	– (7) b Shanaka	7
†W. P. Saha c Mathews b Perera	29	– (8) c Samarawickrama b Shanaka	5
R. A. Jadeja lbw b Perera	22	– (6) c Thirimanne b Perera	9
Bhuvneshwar Kumar c Dickwella b Lakmal	13	– c Perera b Gamage	8
Mohammed Shami c Shanaka b Gamage	24	– not out	12
U. T. Yadav not out	6		
B 6, lb 4	10	B 7, lb 1, w 3, nb 1	12
(59.3 overs)	172	(8 wkts dec, 88.4 overs)	352

1/0 (1) 2/13 (2) 3/17 (4) 4/30 (5) 5/50 (6)
6/79 (3) 7/127 (8) 8/128 (7) 9/146 (9) 10/172 (10)

1/166 (2) 2/192 (1) 3/213 (3) 4/213 (5)
5/249 (6) 6/269 (7) 7/281 (8) 8/321 (9)

Lakmal 19–12–26–4; Gamage 17.3–5–59–2; Shanaka 12–4–36–2; Karunaratne 2–0–17–0; Herath 2–0–5–0; Perera 7–1–19–2. *Second innings*—Lakmal 24.4–4–93–3; Gamage 23–2–97–1; Shanaka 22–1–76–3; Perera 13–2–49–1; Herath 6–1–29–0.

Sri Lanka

W. S. R. Samarawickrama c Saha b Bhuvneshwar Kumar	23	– b Bhuvneshwar Kumar	0
F. D. M. Karunaratne lbw b Bhuvneshwar Kumar	8	– b Mohammed Shami	1
H. D. R. L. Thirimanne c Kohli b Yadav	51	– c Rahane b Bhuvneshwar Kumar	7
A. D. Mathews c Rahul b Yadav	52	– lbw b Yadav	12
*L. D. Chandimal c Saha b Mohammed Shami	28	– b Mohammed Shami	20
†D. P. D. N. Dickwella c Kohli b Mohammed Shami	35	– lbw b Bhuvneshwar Kumar	27
M. D. Shanaka lbw b Bhuvneshwar Kumar	0	– not out	6
M. D. K. Perera c Saha b Mohammed Shami	5	– b Bhuvneshwar Kumar	0
H. M. R. K. B. Herath c Mohammed Shami b B. Kumar	67	– not out	0
R. A. S. Lakmal b Mohammed Shami	16		
P. L. S. Gamage not out	0		
B 4, lb 4, w 1	9	Lb 1, nb 1	2
(83.4 overs)	294	(7 wkts, 26.3 overs)	75

1/29 (2) 2/34 (1) 3/133 (3) 4/138 (4) 5/200 (6)
6/201 (7) 7/201 (5) 8/244 (8) 9/290 (9) 10/294 (10)

1/0 (1) 2/2 (2) 3/14 (3)
4/22 (4) 5/69 (5) 6/69 (6) 7/75 (8)

B. Kumar 27–5–88–4; Mohammed Shami 26.3–5–100–4; Yadav 20–1–79–2; Ashwin 8–2–13–0; Kohli 1.1–0–5–0; Jadeja 1–0–1–0. *Second innings*—B. Kumar 11–8–8–4; Mohammed Shami 9.3–4–34–2; Yadav 5–0–25–1; Jadeja 1–0–7–0.

Umpires: R. A. Kettleborough *(England)* (47), N. J. Llong *(England)* (48) and J. S. Wilson *(West Indies)* (6).
Third umpire: J. S. Wilson *(West Indies)* and A. K. Chaudhary *(India)*. Referee: D. C. Boon *(Australia)* (45).
Wilson replaced Kettleborough (ill) after the second day, and Chaudhary took over as third umpire.

Close of play: first day, India 17–3 (Pujara 8, Rahane 0); second day, India 74–5 (Pujara 47, Saha 6); third day, Sri Lanka 165–4 (Chandimal 13, Dickwella 14); fourth day, India 171–1 (Rahul 73, Pujara 2).

Test No. 2282/43 (I517, SL266)

INDIA v SRI LANKA 2017–18 (2nd Test)

At Vidarbha C. A. Stadium, Jamtha, Nagpur, on 24, 25, 26, 27 November, 2017.
Toss: Sri Lanka. Result: INDIA WON BY AN INNINGS AND 239 RUNS.
Debuts: none.
Man of the Match: V. Kohli.

The seam and swing of Kolkata gave way to a typical subcontinental surface – slow and dry, with a touch of crumble. Kohli's hopes of unfamiliar conditions might have been dashed, but his side still equalled their biggest margin of victory in Tests, while Sri Lanka slumped to their heaviest defeat. India's spinners came into their own: Ashwin claimed his 300th wicket in his 54th Test, undercutting Dennis Lillee's record of 56. Sri Lanka's tendency to crack under pressure was evident again; India didn't even need Bhuvneshwar Kumar, Man of the Match at Kolkata but now busy with his wedding. After winning the toss Sri Lanka slipped from 160 for four to 205. Karunaratne, who completed 1,000 runs for the calendar year, and Chandimal flickered briefly, but the rest barely turned up. India's batsmen then got to work: for only the third time, four of them made centuries in the same innings. Vijay and Pujara added 209, their fourth consecutive century stand and their tenth in all. Then, in his first Test innings for over a year, Sharma brought up his first ton since November 2013, while Kohli rattled up 213 in just 267 deliveries. It was his fifth double-century, all since July 2016, which equalled Brian Lara's record for the most by a captain. And it was his 12th three-figure score as skipper, another Indian record. Dispirited and drained after fielding for more than 12 hours – and with Shanaka losing 75% of his match fee for ball-tampering – Sri Lanka keeled over again.

Sri Lanka

W. S. R. Samarawickrama c Pujara b I. Sharma	13	–	b I. Sharma	0
F. D. M. Karunaratne lbw b I. Sharma	51	–	c Vijay b Jadeja	18
H. D. R. L. Thirimanne b Ashwin	9	–	c Jadeja b Yadav	23
A. D. Mathews lbw b Jadeja	10	–	c R. G. Sharma b Jadeja	10
*L. D. Chandimal lbw b Ashwin	57	–	c Ashwin b Yadav	61
†D. P. D. N. Dickwella c I. Sharma b Jadeja	24	–	c Kohli b I. Sharma	4
M. D. Shanaka b Ashwin	2	–	c Rahul b Ashwin	17
M. D. K. Perera lbw b Jadeja	15	–	lbw b Ashwin	0
H. M. R. K. B. Herath c Rahane b Ashwin	4	–	c Rahane b Ashwin	0
R. A. S. Lakmal c Saha b I. Sharma	17	–	not out	31
P. L. S. Gamage not out	0	–	b Ashwin	0
Lb 2, nb 1	3		Lb 2	2
(79.1 overs)	205		(49.3 overs)	166

1/20 (1) 2/44 (3) 3/60 (4) 4/122 (2) 5/160 (6) 1/0 (1) 2/34 (2) 3/48 (3) 4/68 (4) 5/75 (6) 6/102 (7)
6/165 (7) 7/184 (8) 8/184 (5) 9/205 (10) 10/205 (9) 7/107 (8) 8/107 (9) 9/165 (5) 10/166 (11)

I. Sharma 14–3–37–3; Yadav 16–4–43–0; Ashwin 28.1–7–67–4; Jadeja 21–4–56–3. *Second innings*—I. Sharma 12–4–43–2; Ashwin 17.3–4–63–4; Jadeja 11–5–28–2; Yadav 9–2–30–2.

India

K. L. Rahul b Gamage	7
M. Vijay c Perera b Herath	128
C. A. Pujara b Shanaka	143
*V. Kohli c Thirimanne b Perera	213
A. M. Rahane c Karunaratne b Perera	2
R. G. Sharma not out	102
R. Ashwin b Perera	5
†W. P. Saha not out	1
B 4, lb 4, w 1	9
(6 wkts dec, 176.1 overs)	610

1/7 (1) 2/216 (2) 3/399 (3) 4/410 (5)
5/583 (4) 6/597 (7)

R. A. Jadeja, U. T. Yadav and I. Sharma did not bat.

Lakmal 29–2–111–0; Gamage 35–8–97–1; Herath 39–11–81–1; Shanaka 26.1–4–103–1; Perera 45–2–202–3; Karunaratne 2–0–8–0.

Umpires: R. A. Kettleborough *(England)* (48) and J. S. Wilson *(West Indies)* (7).
Third umpire: N. J. Llong *(England)*. Referee: D. C. Boon *(Australia)* (46).

Close of play: first day, India 11–1 (Vijay 2, Pujara 2); second day, India 312–2 (Pujara 121, Kohli 54); third day, Sri Lanka 21–1 (Karunaratne 11, Thirimanne 9).

Test No. 2283/44 (I518, SL267)

INDIA v SRI LANKA 2017–18 (3rd Test)

At Feroz Shah Kotla, Delhi, on 2, 3, 4, 5, 6 December, 2017.
Toss: India.   Result: DRAWN.
Debuts: Sri Lanka – A. R. S. Silva.
Man of the Match: V. Kohli.   Man of the Series: V. Kohli.

The Test will always be remembered for the debilitating effects of toxic air, which led to a 20-minute hold-up on the second afternoon. Sri Lanka's new-ball pair of Lakmal and Gamage were worst affected – they were given oxygen in the dressing-room – but most of the other players sported face masks in a vague attempt at safety. New Delhi is at its most polluted in the winter, and the scheduling reflected poorly on the BCCI. After dipping to 35 for four early on the final day, Sri Lanka escaped with a battling draw. Dhananjaya de Silva conjured a memorable century despite cramps which eventually forced him to retire after 4¾ hours, while Roshen Silva, the 29-year-old debutant who had fallen third ball in the first innings, lasted three hours for an unbeaten 74. Earlier, Kohli had become only the sixth to score double-hundreds in consecutive Test innings, the second for India after Vinod Kambli. He brought up 5,000 runs during his uninhibited 243, his 20th Test century. He piled on 283 with Vijay, whose 155 was his second successive hundred. Sri Lanka started poorly – Karunaratne fell to the first ball, and de Silva soon followed – but Chandimal and Mathews used up nearly 80 overs in adding 181. In all, Sri Lanka batted for 7.4 overs more than India, but were 163 behind. India zipped along before another declaration left Sri Lanka about seven hours to survive. They did, but could not prevent a ninth successive Test series win for Kohli's India.

India

M. Vijay st Dickwella b Sandakan	155	– c Dickwella b Lakmal	9
S. Dhawan c Lakmal b Perera	23	– st Dickwella b Sandakan	67
C. A. Pujara c Samarawickrama b Gamage	23	– (4) c Mathews b de Silva	49
*V. Kohli lbw b Sandakan	243	– (5) c Lakmal b Gamage	50
A. M. Rahane st Dickwella b Sandakan	1	– (3) c Sandakan b Perera	10
R. G. Sharma c Dickwella b Sandakan	65	– not out	50
R. Ashwin c Perera b Gamage	4		
†W. P. Saha not out	9		
R. A. Jadeja not out	5	– (7) not out	4
Lb 1, nb 7	8	B 1, lb 2, w 1, nb 3	7
(7 wkts dec, 127.5 overs)	536	(5 wkts dec, 52.2 overs)	246

1/42 (2) 2/78 (3) 3/361 (1) 4/365 (5)
5/500 (6) 6/519 (7) 7/523 (4)
1/10 (1) 2/29 (3) 3/106 (4)
4/144 (2) 5/234 (5)
I. Sharma and Mohammed Shami did not bat.

Lakmal 21.2–2–80–0; Gamage 25.3–7–95–2; Perera 31.1–0–145–1; Sandakan 33.5–1–167–4; de Silva 16–0–48–0. *Second innings*—Lakmal 14–3–60–1; Gamage 12.2–1–48–1; Perera 11–0–54–1; de Silva 5–0–31–1; Sandakan 10–0–50–1.

Sri Lanka

F. D. M. Karunaratne c Saha b Mohammed Shami	0	– c Saha b Jadeja	13
M. D. K. Perera lbw b Jadeja	42		
D. M. de Silva lbw b I. Sharma	1	– retired hurt	119
A. D. Mathews c Saha b Ashwin	111	– (5) c Rahane b Jadeja	1
*L. D. Chandimal c Dhawan b I. Sharma	164	– (6) b Ashwin	36
W. S. R. Samarawickrama c Saha b I. Sharma	33	– (2) c Rahane b Mohammed Shami	5
A. R. S. Silva c Dhawan b Ashwin	0	– not out	74
†D. P. D. N. Dickwella b Ashwin	0	– not out	44
R. A. S. Lakmal c Saha b Mohammed Shami	5	– (4) b Jadeja	0
P. L. S. Gamage lbw b Jadeja	1		
P. A. D. L. R. Sandakan not out	0		
B 4, lb 5, nb 2, p 5	16	B 5, lb 1, nb 1	7
(135.3 overs)	373	(5 wkts, 103 overs)	299

1/0 (1) 2/14 (3) 3/75 (2) 4/256 (4) 5/317 (6)
6/318 (7) 7/322 (8) 8/331 (9) 9/343 (10) 10/373 (5)
1/14 (2) 2/31 (1) 3/31 (7)
4/35 (5) 5/147 (6)

In the second innings de Silva retired hurt at 205-5.

Mohammed Shami 26–6–85–2; I. Sharma 29.3–7–98–3; Jadeja 45–13–86–2; Ashwin 35–8–90–3. *Second innings*—I. Sharma 13–2–32–0; Mohammed Shami 15–6–50–1; Ashwin 35–3–126–1; Jadeja 38–13–81–3; Vijay 1–0–3–0; Kohli 1–0–1–0.

Umpires: N. J. Llong *(England)* (49) and J. S. Wilson *(West Indies)* (8).
Third umpire: A. K. Chaudhary *(India)*.   Referee: D. C. Boon *(Australia)* (47).

Close of play: first day, India 371–4 (Kohli 156, R. G. Sharma 6); second day, Sri Lanka 131–3 (Mathews 57, Chandimal 25); third day, Sri Lanka 356–9 (Chandimal 147, Sandakan 0); fourth day, Sri Lanka 31–3 (de Silva 13, Mathews 0).

Test No. 2284/342 (A804, E991)

AUSTRALIA v ENGLAND 2017–18 (1st Test)

At Wolloongabba, Brisbane, on 23, 24, 25, 26, 27 November, 2017.
Toss: England.   Result: AUSTRALIA WON BY TEN WICKETS.
Debuts: Australia – C. T. Bancroft.
Man of the Match: S. P. D. Smith.

For the sixth time in the last eight Ashes series at home, Australia took the lead at Brisbane with a convincing victory: the 173 knocked off by Warner and the debutant Cameron Bancroft was the highest made to win a Test by ten wickets. Things were roughly equal until the fourth day, when England stumbled to 195. Before that, on an untypically sluggish Gabba surface, Stoneman, Vince and Malan had set up a first-innings total of 302, the first instance of three Ashes debutants all reaching fifty. Smith then laid down a marker for the series with an undefeated 141. It took him seven hours to reach three figures – the slowest of his 21 Test centuries – but he was rarely troubled, unlike most of his partners: his biggest collaborations were 99 with Marsh and 66 with Cummins. England's third-innings decline was not helped when Ali, on 40, was given out stumped by the third umpire by the narrowest of margins. The wicketkeeper was Paine, returning to the Test team after missing 78 matches, equalling Brad Hogg's Australian record for the longest such gap. His recall had been a surprise, as in his only previous first-class match of the season for Tasmania he had stood at slip alongside the incumbent Test gloveman, Matthew Wade, who was now dropped. England were handicapped by the absence, for the whole series, of Stokes, who was awaiting developments in a court case after being involved in an unedifying scuffle outside a Bristol nightclub in September.

England

A. N. Cook c Handscomb b Starc	2	–	c Starc b Hazlewood	7
M. D. Stoneman b Cummins	53	–	c Smith b Lyon	27
J. M. Vince run out (Lyon)	83	–	c Smith b Hazlewood	2
*J. E. Root lbw b Cummins	15	–	lbw b Hazlewood	51
D. J. Malan c Marsh b Starc	56	–	c Smith b Lyon	4
M. M. Ali lbw b Lyon	38	–	st Paine b Lyon	40
†J. M. Bairstow c Paine b Cummins	9	–	c Handscomb b Starc	42
C. R. Woakes b Lyon	0	–	c Smith b Lyon	17
S. C. J. Broad c Handscomb b Hazlewood	20	–	c Paine b Starc	2
J. T. Ball c Warner b Starc	14	–	c Handscomb b Cummins	1
J. M. Anderson not out	5	–	not out	0
B 5, w 1, nb 1	7		Nb 2	2
(116.4 overs)	302		(71.4 overs)	195

1/2 (1) 2/127 (2) 3/145 (3) 4/163 (4) 5/246 (5)   1/11 (1) 2/17 (3) 3/62 (2) 4/74 (5) 5/113 (4)
6/249 (6) 7/250 (8) 8/270 (7) 9/286 (10) 10/302 (9)   6/155 (6) 7/185 (8) 8/194 (7) 9/195 (9) 10/195 (10)

Starc 28–4–77–3; Hazlewood 22.4–6–57–1; Cummins 30–8–85–3; Lyon 36–12–78–2. *Second innings*—Starc 16–1–51–3; Hazlewood 16–3–46–3; Cummins 12.4–4–23–1; Lyon 24–4–67–3; Smith 3–0–8–0.

Australia

C. T. Bancroft c Bairstow b Broad	5	–	not out	82
D. A. Warner c Malan b Ball	26	–	not out	87
U. T. Khawaja lbw b Ali	11			
*S. P. D. Smith not out	141			
P. S. P. Handscomb lbw b Anderson	14			
S. E. Marsh c Anderson b Broad	51			
†T. D. Paine c Bairstow b Anderson	13			
M. A. Starc c and b Broad	6			
P. J. Cummins c Cook b Woakes	42			
J. R. Hazlewood b Ali	6			
N. M. Lyon c Cook b Root	9			
Lb 1, w 2, nb 1	4		Lb 2, w 1, nb 1	4
(130.3 overs)	328		(no wkt, 50 overs)	173

1/7 (1) 2/30 (3) 3/59 (2) 4/76 (5) 5/175 (6)
6/202 (7) 7/209 (8) 8/275 (9) 9/298 (10) 10/328 (11)

Anderson 29–10–50–2; Broad 25–10–49–3; Ali 30–8–74–2; Woakes 24–5–67–1; Ball 18–3–77–1; Root 4.3–0–10–1. *Second innings*—Anderson 11–2–27–0; Broad 10–2–20–0; Ali 4–0–23–0; Woakes 11–1–46–0; Ball 8–1–38–0; Root 6–1–17–0.

Umpires: Aleem Dar *(Pakistan)* (115) and M. Erasmus *(South Africa)* (46).
Third umpire: C. B. Gaffaney *(New Zealand).*   Referee: R. B. Richardson *(West Indies)* (12).

Close of play: first day, England 196–4 (Malan 28, Ali 13); second day, Australia 165–4 (Smith 64, Marsh 44); third day, England 33–2 (Stoneman 19, Root 5); fourth day, Australia 114–0 (Bancroft 51, Warner 60).

AUSTRALIA v ENGLAND 2017–18 (2nd Test)

At Adelaide Oval on 2, 3, 4, 5, 6 December, 2017 (day/night).
Toss: England.   Result: AUSTRALIA WON BY 120 RUNS.
Debuts: England – C. Overton.
Man of the Match: S. E. Marsh.

Ashes cricket's first floodlit Test illuminated a familiar tale. For the fourth tour of Australia out of five, England found themselves 2–0 down before reaching Perth, and fending off predictions of another whitewash. Root became the first captain in seven day/night Tests worldwide to bowl first, and the first at Adelaide since Mohammad Azharuddin in 1991–92 (Australia won that one, too). Root's choice did not quite sit alongside England's two great Brisbane cock-ups (Len Hutton in 1954–55, Nasser Hussain in 2002–03), but his attack did their best to encourage comparisons, looking threadbare as Australia reached 442. The highlight was a century for Marsh, whose place had been in doubt. England did at least dismiss Smith cheaply, one of three wickets for the debutant Craig Overton, who would later top-score from No. 9 in an underwhelming reply. Smith waived the follow-on, but that meant his side had to bat under lights, with predictable results: Anderson seamed his way to a first five-for in 15 Tests Down Under, while Woakes took four, and Australia were rolled for 138. England still needed 354, but had a sniff by the fourth-day close at 176 for four – only for Hazlewood to prise out Woakes and Root (who top-scored with 67) almost immediately next morning; Starc polished things off. The day/night experiment was a success crowd-wise: 55,317 attended on the first day, an Adelaide record, surpassing 50,962 on the second day during the Bodyline series. In all, 199,147 came through the gates, another ground record.

Australia

C. T. Bancroft run out (Woakes)	10	– c Bairstow b Anderson	4
D. A. Warner c Bairstow b Woakes	47	– c Root b Woakes	14
U. T. Khawaja c Vince b Anderson	53	– lbw b Anderson	20
*S. P. D. Smith b Overton	40	– lbw b Woakes	6
P. S. P. Handscomb lbw b Broad	36	– c Malan b Anderson	12
S. E. Marsh not out	126	– (7) b Woakes	19
†T. D. Paine c Ali b Overton	57	– (8) c Overton b Woakes	11
M. A. Starc c Anderson b Broad	6	– (9) c Ali b Anderson	20
P. J. Cummins c Malan b Overton	44	– (10) not out	11
N. M. Lyon not out	10	– (6) c Broad b Anderson	14
J. R. Hazlewood (did not bat)		– c Malan b Overton	3
B 6, lb 6, w 1	13	Lb 2, w 2	4
(8 wkts dec, 149 overs)	442	(58 overs)	138

1/33 (1) 2/86 (2) 3/139 (3) 4/161 (4)
5/209 (5) 6/294 (7) 7/311 (8) 8/410 (9)

1/5 (1) 2/39 (3) 3/41 (2) 4/50 (4) 5/71 (6)
6/75 (5) 7/90 (8) 8/122 (7) 9/128 (9) 10/138 (11)

Anderson 31–5–74–1; Broad 30–11–72–2; Woakes 27–4–84–1; Overton 33–3–105–3; Ali 24–3–79–0; Root 4–0–16–0. *Second innings*—Anderson 22–7–43–5; Broad 13–6–26–0; Overton 2–0–11–1; Woakes 16–3–36–4; Ali 5–0–20–0.

England

A. N. Cook c Smith b Lyon	37	– lbw b Lyon	16
M. D. Stoneman lbw b Starc	18	– c Khawaja b Starc	36
J. M. Vince c Paine b Hazlewood	2	– c Handscomb b Starc	15
*J. E. Root c Bancroft b Cummins	9	– c Paine b Hazlewood	67
D. J. Malan c Paine b Cummins	19	– b Cummins	29
M. M. Ali c and b Lyon	25	– (7) lbw b Lyon	2
†J. M. Bairstow c and b Starc	21	– (8) b Starc	36
C. R. Woakes c and b Starc	36	– (6) c Paine b Hazlewood	5
C. Overton not out	41	– lbw b Starc	7
S. C. J. Broad c Paine b Lyon	3	– c Paine b Starc	8
J. M. Anderson lbw b Lyon	0	– not out	0
Lb 15, w 1	16	B 7, lb 5	12
(76.1 overs)	227	(84.2 overs)	233

1/29 (2) 2/31 (3) 3/50 (4) 4/80 (1) 5/102 (5)
6/132 (6) 7/142 (7) 8/208 (8) 9/227 (10) 10/227 (11)

1/53 (1) 2/54 (2) 3/91 (3) 4/169 (5) 5/176 (6)
6/177 (4) 7/188 (7) 8/206 (9) 9/224 (10) 10/233 (8)

Starc 20–4–49–3; Hazlewood 16–3–56–1; Cummins 16–3–47–2; Lyon 24.1–5–60–4. *Second innings*—Starc 19.2–3–88–5; Hazlewood 20–7–49–2; Cummins 20–6–39–1; Lyon 25–6–45–2.

Umpires: Aleem Dar *(Pakistan)* (116) and C. B. Gaffaney *(New Zealand)* (17).
Third umpire: M. Erasmus *(South Africa)*.   Referee: R. B. Richardson *(West Indies)* (13).

Close of play: first day, Australia 209–4 (Handscomb 36, Marsh 20); second day, England 29–1 (Cook 11, Vince 0); third day, Australia 53–4 (Handscomb 3, Lyon 3); fourth day, England 176–4 (Root 67, Woakes 5).

Test No. 2286/344 (A806, E993)

AUSTRALIA v ENGLAND 2017–18 (3rd Test)

At W. A. C. A. Ground, Perth, on 14, 15, 16, 17, 18 December, 2017.
Toss: England.   Result: AUSTRALIA WON BY AN INNINGS AND 41 RUNS.
Debuts: none.
Man of the Match: S. P. D. Smith.

The Ashes changed hands at the earliest opportunity, with Australia romping to a 3–0 lead in the last of the WACA's 44 Tests (future Perth matches would be at a new stadium across the Swan River). England won only once in 13 attempts, beating the Packer-depleted side of 1978–79; Australia won ten, including all the last eight. The margin of victory, however, could hardly have been imagined as England cruised to 368 for four on the second morning, with Malan – who made a high-class maiden century – and Bairstow sharing a stand of 237, England's Ashes best for the fifth wicket, beating 206 by Eddie Paynter and Denis Compton at Nottingham in 1938. When they were parted, though, the rest struggled again; the last six wickets tumbled for 35. A familiar obstacle then loomed. Smith sashayed to yet another century, but Australia were still 155 adrift when the recalled Mitchell Marsh joined him. They added 301, Marsh extending his maiden century to 181, while Smith's 239 was his highest score. The declaration came at 662, Australia's highest against England at home (previously 659 for eight at Sydney in 1946–47). England, 259 behind, slipped to 132 for four before rain curtailed the fourth day, with Cook recording a double failure in his 150th Test. More rain fell but, even though the final day's first session was washed out, surviving the 60 overs that remained never looked likely. Hazlewood removed Bairstow with the sixth ball after the restart, and finished with five for 48.

England

A. N. Cook lbw b Starc	7	– c and b Hazlewood	14
M. D. Stoneman c Paine b Starc	56	– c Paine b Hazlewood	3
J. M. Vince c Paine b Hazlewood	25	– b Starc	55
*J. E. Root c Paine b Cummins	20	– c Smith b Lyon	14
D. J. Malan c sub (P. S. P. Handscomb) b Lyon	140	– c Paine b Hazlewood	54
†J. M. Bairstow b Starc	119	– b Hazlewood	14
M. M. Ali c Smith b Cummins	0	– lbw b Lyon	11
C. R. Woakes c Cummins b Hazlewood	8	– c Paine b Cummins	22
C. Overton c Bancroft b Hazlewood	2	– c Khawaja b Hazlewood	12
S. C. J. Broad c Bancroft b Starc	12	– c Paine b Cummins	0
J. M. Anderson not out	0	– not out	1
B 10, lb 2, w 1, nb 1	14	B 6, lb 11, nb 1	18
(115.1 overs)	403	(72.5 overs)	218

1/26 (1) 2/89 (3) 3/115 (4) 4/131 (2) 5/368 (5)   1/4 (2) 2/29 (1) 3/60 (4) 4/100 (3) 5/133 (6)
6/372 (7) 7/389 (8) 8/389 (6) 9/393 (9) 10/403 (10)   6/172 (7) 7/196 (5) 8/210 (9) 9/211 (10) 10/218 (8)

Starc 25.1–5–91–4; Hazlewood 28–9–92–3; Cummins 28–8–84–2; Lyon 22–4–73–1; M. R. Marsh 9–1–43–0; Smith 3–1–8–0. *Second innings*—Starc 17–5–44–1; Hazlewood 18–6–48–5; M. R. Marsh 3–1–14–0; Cummins 19.5–4–53–2; Lyon 15–4–42–2.

Australia

C. T. Bancroft lbw b Overton	25
D. A. Warner c Bairstow b Overton	22
U. T. Khawaja lbw b Woakes	50
*S. P. D. Smith lbw b Anderson	239
S. E. Marsh c Root b Ali	28
M. R. Marsh lbw b Anderson	181
†T. D. Paine not out	49
M. A. Starc run out (Vince)	1
P. J. Cummins lbw b Anderson	41
N. M. Lyon c Ali b Anderson	4
B 4, lb 16, w 1, nb 1	22
(9 wkts dec, 179.3 overs)	662

1/44 (2) 2/55 (1) 3/179 (3) 4/248 (5) 5/549 (6)
6/560 (4) 7/561 (8) 8/654 (9) 9/662 (10)

J. R. Hazlewood did not bat.

Anderson 37.3–9–116–4; Broad 35–3–142–0; Woakes 41–8–128–1; Overton 24–1–110–2; Ali 33–4–120–1; Root 3–0–13–0; Malan 6–1–13–0.

Umpires: M. Erasmus *(South Africa)* (47) and C. B. Gaffaney *(New Zealand)* (18).
Third umpire: Aleem Dar *(Pakistan)*.   Referee: R. B. Richardson *(West Indies)* (14).

Close of play: first day, England 305–4 (Malan 110, Bairstow 75); second day, Australia 203–3 (Smith 92, S. E. Marsh 7); third day, Australia 549–4 (Smith 229, M. R. Marsh 181); fourth day, England 132–4 (Malan 28, Bairstow 14).

AUSTRALIA v ENGLAND 2017–18 (4th Test)

At Melbourne Cricket Ground on 26, 27, 28, 29, 30 December, 2017.
Toss: Australia.   Result: DRAWN.
Debuts: England – T. K. Curran.
Man of the Match: A. N. Cook.

Alastair Cook went into the Boxing Day Test – the day after his 33rd birthday – fending off questions about his future after only 83 runs in the series. He ended it after fending off everything the Australians could hurl at him: on the field for each of the match's 2,329 deliveries, he made 244, the highest by a visitor at the MCG, beating Viv Richards's 208 in 1984–85. It was the highest by someone carrying their bat in a Test and, surprisingly, the first time anyone had done this in 110 matches at Melbourne. Cook and Anderson provided the first instance of England's top run-scorer and wicket-taker batting together since Arthur Shrewsbury and George Ulyett in 1886. But there was a problem: the pitch was about as responsive as a Christmas pudding, and was rated "poor" by the ICC. On the first day, which drew a crowd of 88,172, Warner defied the surface with his 21st Test century, before becoming Anderson's 100th Ashes wicket; he had survived a catch to mid-on when 99, Tom Curran being deprived of a notable maiden scalp by a no-ball (next day he did remove Smith). England, and Cook, set sail in the middle of day two, and were still there at the start of a fourth shortened to 19 overs by rain. The immovable Smith ensured a draw with his 23rd century in his 60th Test. England at least ended record-equalling sequences of seven straight overseas Test defeats, and eight in a row in Australia.

Australia

C. T. Bancroft lbw b Woakes	26	– b Woakes	27
D. A. Warner c Bairstow b Anderson	103	– c Vince b Root	86
U. T. Khawaja c Bairstow b Broad	17	– c Bairstow b Anderson	11
*S. P. D. Smith b Curran	76	– not out	102
S. E. Marsh lbw b Broad	61	– c Bairstow b Broad	4
M. R. Marsh b Woakes	9	– not out	29
†T. D. Paine b Anderson	24		
P. J. Cummins c Cook b Broad	4		
J. M. Bird lbw b Broad	4		
J. R. Hazlewood not out	1		
N. M. Lyon lbw b Anderson	0		
Lb 1, nb 1	2	B 4	4
(119 overs)	327	(4 wkts dec, 124.2 overs)	263

1/122 (1) 2/135 (2) 3/160 (3) 4/260 (4) 5/278 (6)
6/314 (5) 7/318 (7) 8/325 (9) 9/326 (8) 10/327 (11)
1/51 (1) 2/65 (3) 3/172 (2) 4/178 (5)

Anderson 29–11–61–3; Broad 28–10–51–4; Woakes 22–4–72–2; Ali 12–0–57–0; Curran 21–5–65–1; Malan 7–1–20–0. *Second innings*—Anderson 30–12–46–1; Broad 24–11–44–1; Woakes 26–7–62–1; Curran 20–6–53–0; Ali 13.2–2–32–0; Malan 8–1–21–0; Root 3–2–1–1.

England

A. N. Cook not out	244
M. D. Stoneman c and b Lyon	15
J. M. Vince lbw b Hazlewood	17
*J. E. Root c Lyon b Cummins	61
D. J. Malan lbw b Hazlewood	14
†J. M. Bairstow c Paine b Lyon	22
M. M. Ali c S. E. Marsh b Lyon	20
C. R. Woakes c Paine b Cummins	26
T. K. Curran c Paine b Hazlewood	4
S. C. J. Broad c Khawaja b Cummins	56
J. M. Anderson c Bancroft b Cummins	0
B 4, lb 5, nb 3	12
(144.1 overs)	491

1/35 (2) 2/80 (3) 3/218 (4) 4/246 (5) 5/279 (6)
6/307 (7) 7/366 (8) 8/373 (9) 9/473 (10) 10/491 (11)

Hazlewood 30–5–95–3; Bird 30–5–108–0; Lyon 42–9–109–3; Cummins 29.1–1–117–4; M. R. Marsh 12–1–42–0; Smith 1–0–11–0.

Umpires: H. D. P. K. Dharmasena *(Sri Lanka)* (50) and S. Ravi *(India)* (24).
Third umpire: J. S. Wilson *(West Indies).*   Referee: R. S. Madugalle *(Sri Lanka)* (180).

Close of play: first day, Australia 244–3 (Smith 65, S. E. Marsh 31); second day, England 192–2 (Cook 104, Root 49); third day, England 491–9 (Cook 244, Anderson 0); fourth day, Australia 103–2 (Warner 40, Smith 25).

AUSTRALIA v ENGLAND 2017–18 (5th Test)

At Sydney Cricket Ground on 4, 5, 6, 7, 8 January, 2018.
Toss: England.   Result: AUSTRALIA WON BY AN INNINGS AND 123 RUNS.
Debuts: England – M. S. Crane.
Man of the Match: P. J. Cummins.   Man of the Series: S. P. D. Smith.

Australia steamrollered to a 4–0 victory in sweltering heat: on the fourth day, temperatures peaked at 41°C, the hottest in Sydney since 1939. It was all too much for Root: England's captain ended the match flat on his back in the dressing-room, poleaxed by a virus which had sent him to hospital the previous night. England had started well enough: eight of the top nine made it into the twenties, but the top score was Root's 83. Once again a decent total was dwarfed by a massive one: Australia marched to 649, despite losing Bancroft for a duck. For once, Smith was not the main destroyer, falling to Ali – who was otherwise enduring a horror series – for 83, giving him 687 runs at 87 in the five Tests. Smith passed 6,000 runs in his 111th innings, equal with Garry Sobers and behind only Don Bradman (68). After he departed Khawaja flowed to 171, then both Marsh brothers reached centuries during a draining stand of 169. In the circumstances, Anderson's 34 overs for 56 were heroic, but Mason Crane, the 20-year-old Hampshire leg-spinner, conceded 193, the most by an England player on debut (previously 166 by Devon Malcolm in 1989). England never threatened a draw: Root made it to 58 before giving best to illness, but the hapless Ali fell to Lyon for the seventh time in the series. Australia's four main bowlers all took more than 20 wickets, while no one else managed one, uniquely for a five-Test series.

England

A. N. Cook lbw b Hazlewood	39	–	b Lyon	10
M. D. Stoneman c Paine b Cummins	24	–	lbw b Starc	0
J. M. Vince c Paine b Cummins	25	–	c Smith b Cummins	18
*J. E. Root c M. R. Marsh b Starc	83	–	retired ill	58
D. J. Malan c Smith b Starc	62	–	lbw b Lyon	5
†J. M. Bairstow c Paine b Hazlewood	5	–	lbw b Cummins	38
M. M. Ali c Paine b Cummins	30	–	lbw b Lyon	13
T. K. Curran c Bancroft b Cummins	39	–	not out	23
S. C. J. Broad c Smith b Lyon	31	–	c Paine b Cummins	4
M. S. Crane run out (M. R. Marsh/Bancroft)	4	–	c Paine b Cummins	2
J. M. Anderson not out	0	–	c Paine b Hazlewood	2
Lb 2, w 2	4		Lb 2, p 5	7
(112.3 overs)	346		(88.1 overs)	180

1/28 (2) 2/88 (3) 3/95 (1) 4/228 (4) 5/233 (6)   1/5 (2) 2/15 (1) 3/43 (3) 4/68 (5) 5/121 (7)
6/251 (5) 7/294 (7) 8/335 (8) 9/346 (9) 10/346 (10)   6/144 (6) 7/148 (9) 8/156 (10) 9/180 (11)

In the second innings Root, when 42, retired ill at 93-4 and resumed at 121-5; he retired again at 144-5.

Starc 21–6–80–2; Hazlewood 23–4–65–2; Cummins 24.3–5–80–4; Lyon 37–5–86–1; M. R. Marsh 7–0–33–0. *Second innings*—Starc 16–4–38–1; Hazlewood 17.1–6–36–1; Lyon 35–12–54–3; Cummins 17–4–39–4; Smith 2–0–6–0; M. R. Marsh 1–1–0–0.

Australia

C. T. Bancroft b Broad	0
D. A. Warner c Bairstow b Anderson	56
U. T. Khawaja st Bairstow b Crane	171
*S. P. D. Smith c and b Ali	83
S. E. Marsh run out (Stoneman)	156
M. R. Marsh b Curran	101
†T. D. Paine not out	38
M. A. Starc c Vince b Ali	11
P. J. Cummins not out	24
B 2, lb 4, w 1, nb 2	9
(7 wkts dec, 193 overs)	649

1/1 (1) 2/86 (2) 3/274 (4) 4/375 (3)
5/544 (6) 6/596 (5) 7/613 (8)

N. M. Lyon and J. R. Hazlewood did not bat.
Anderson 34–14–56–1; Broad 30–2–121–1; Ali 48–10–170–2; Curran 25–3–82–1; Crane 48–3–193–1; Root 8–3–21–0.

Umpires: H. D. P. K. Dharmasena *(Sri Lanka)* (51) and J. S. Wilson *(West Indies)* (9).
Third umpire: S. Ravi *(India)*.   Referee: R. S. Madugalle *(Sri Lanka)* (181).

Close of play: first day, England 233–5 (Malan 55); second day, Australia 193–2 (Khawaja 91, Smith 44); third day, Australia 479–4 (S. E. Marsh 98, M. R. Marsh 63); fourth day, England 93–4 (Root 42, Bairstow 17).

Test No. 2289/46 (NZ423, WI529)

NEW ZEALAND v WEST INDIES 2017–18 (1st Test)

At Basin Reserve, Wellington, on 1, 2, 3, 4 December, 2017.
Toss: New Zealand.   Result: NEW ZEALAND WON BY AN INNINGS AND 67 RUNS.
Debuts: New Zealand – T. A. Blundell. West Indies – S. W. Ambris.
Man of the Match: N. Wagner.

Wellington unveiled another emerald-green pitch, but it was bounce and questionable technique, not swing and seam movement, that did for the West Indians. The openers reached 59 without loss after being inserted, but either side of lunch Wagner took six wickets with short stuff, and stunned Holder with a first-ball yorker; seven for 39 were the fourth-best figures for New Zealand, who were only 49 behind by stumps. Next day, Taylor eased them into the lead, before de Grandhomme – whose highest score in six previous Tests was 57 – smashed a century from 71 balls. It was the second-fastest for New Zealand in Tests, behind Brendon McCullum's 54-ball farewell against Australia at Christchurch in 2015–16, and the joint ninth-fastest overall. At the other end local boy Tom Blundell – a late replacement for injured wicketkeeper B-J Watling – chugged along, and reached his own maiden hundred next day during a last-wicket stand of 78 with Boult. West Indies were 386 adrift, but Brathwaite dropped anchor for over five hours, and Hetmyer cracked an entertaining 66. However, there wasn't much resolve after they departed. The debutant Sunil Ambris, who had trodden on his stumps first ball on the opening day, top-edged a six to get off the mark before poking to slip first ball after lunch. To crown a miserable match, Holder was fined for a slow over-rate, and banned for a Test. The result meant New Zealand led West Indies for the first time in overall Test wins between the sides: 14–13.

West Indies

K. C. Brathwaite c Nicholls b Wagner	24	–	lbw b Santner	91
K. O. A. Powell c Raval b Boult	42	–	c and b Henry	40
S. O. Hetmyer c Latham b Wagner	13	–	c Raval b Henry	66
S. D. Hope c Blundell b Wagner	0	–	c Williamson b Boult	37
R. L. Chase c Raval b Wagner	5	–	b Henry	18
S. W. Ambris hit wkt b Wagner	0	–	c Taylor b de Grandhomme	18
†S. O. Dowrich run out (Santner)	18	–	c Santner b Wagner	3
*J. O. Holder b Wagner	0	–	c Boult b Wagner	7
K. A. J. Roach not out	14	–	lbw b de Grandhomme	7
M. L. Cummins b Boult	1	–	b Boult	14
S. T. Gabriel c Latham b Wagner	10	–	not out	4
B 2, lb 5	7		B 4, lb 4, w 6	14
(45.4 overs)	134		(106 overs)	319

1/59 (1) 2/75 (2) 3/79 (3) 4/80 (4) 5/80 (6)   1/72 (2) 2/166 (3) 3/231 (1) 4/257 (4) 5/273 (5)
6/97 (5) 7/97 (8) 8/104 (7) 9/105 (10) 10/134 (11) 6/286 (6) 7/288 (7) 8/301 (9) 9/301 (8) 10/319 (10)

Boult 16–8–36–2; Henry 11–1–39–0; de Grandhomme 4–1–13–0; Wagner 14.4–2–39–7. *Second innings*—Boult 23–5–87–2; Henry 24–6–57–3; de Grandhomme 19–3–40–2; Wagner 22–3–102–2; Santner 17–7–25–1; Williamson 1–1–0–0.

New Zealand

T. W. M. Latham c Roach b Holder	37
J. A. Raval c Dowrich b Roach	42
*K. S. Williamson c Hope b Roach	1
L. R. P. L. Taylor lbw b Roach	93
H. M. Nicholls c Gabriel b Cummins	67
M. J. Santner b Cummins	17
C. de Grandhomme c Powell b Chase	105
†T. A. Blundell not out	107
N. Wagner b Chase	3
M. J. Henry c Dowrich b Gabriel	4
T. A. Boult not out	18
B 4, lb 6, w 1, nb 15	26
(9 wkts dec, 148.4 overs)	520

1/65 (1) 2/68 (3) 3/109 (2) 4/236 (4) 5/272 (5)
6/281 (6) 7/429 (7) 8/437 (9) 9/442 (10)

Gabriel 29–4–90–1; Roach 22–6–85–3; Cummins 27–7–92–2; Holder 34–8–102–1; Chase 28–4–95–2; Brathwaite 8.4–0–46–0.

Umpires: I. J. Gould *(England)* (63) and R. J. Tucker *(Australia)* (57).
Third umpire: B. N. J. Oxenford *(Australia)*.   Referee: B. C. Broad *(England)* (89).

Close of play: first day, New Zealand 85–2 (Raval 29, Taylor 12); second day, New Zealand 447–9 (Blundell 57, Boult 2); third day, West Indies 214–2 (Brathwaite 79, Hope 21).

NEW ZEALAND v WEST INDIES 2017–18 (2nd Test)

At Seddon Park, Hamilton, on 9, 10, 11, 12 December, 2017.
Toss: West Indies. Result: NEW ZEALAND WON BY 240 RUNS.
Debuts: West Indies – R. A. Reifer.
Man of the Match: L. R. P. L. Taylor.

This was Taylor's Test. His late mentor Martin Crowe had challenged him to match his own tally of 17 Test centuries and, eight months after Williamson reached the mark here against South Africa, Taylor also drew level. He did it in style, with a straight-drive off the debutant left-arm seamer Raymon Reifer. Soon after, West Indies were set 444 to level the series. Again, they couldn't cope with a fierce attack led by Wagner, who took three wickets and sent the hapless Ambris to hospital with a broken arm. Raval had given New Zealand a rapid start after they were put in, before de Grandhomme blasted four sixes. The last pair added 61 on the second day to lift the total to 373. Gabriel was expensive and overstepped seven times, but eventually hit his stride to collect four wickets. Brathwaite knuckled down again, but his 66 was easily the best effort as Boult led the way to a lead of 152; his athletic return catch removed Hetmyer, and he forced Ambris to tread on his stumps again before docking the tail on the third morning. Cummins gave West Indies a glimmer with three early wickets, but Taylor cut and drove exquisitely as the lead soared past 400. Boult made early inroads once more – Powell for nought and Brathwaite, his 200th wicket in his 52nd Test, caught in the gully. West Indies stuttered into the fourth afternoon; to add to their gloom, stand-in captain Brathwaite was fined, again for a slow over-rate.

New Zealand

J. A. Raval c Dowrich b Gabriel	84	– c and b Cummins	4
T. W. M. Latham c Dowrich b Cummins	22	– lbw b Reifer	22
*K. S. Williamson c Dowrich b Cummins	43	– b Cummins	54
L. R. P. L. Taylor c Dowrich b Roach	16	– not out	107
H. M. Nicholls lbw b Reifer	13	– c Dowrich b Cummins	5
M. J. Santner b Gabriel	24	– c Ambris b Chase	26
C. de Grandhomme b Gabriel	58	– lbw b Gabriel	22
†T. A. Blundell b Gabriel	28	– c Powell b Gabriel	1
N. Wagner c Hope b Roach	1	– c Hope b Chase	8
T. G. Southee c and b Roach	31	– not out	22
T. A. Boult not out	37		
Lb 1, w 3, nb 12	16	B 4, lb 2, w 2, nb 12	20
(102.2 overs)	373	(8 wkts dec, 77.4 overs)	291

1/65 (2) 2/154 (3) 3/159 (1) 4/186 (4) 5/189 (5)
6/265 (6) 7/275 (7) 8/286 (9) 9/312 (8) 10/373 (10)

1/11 (1) 2/42 (2) 3/100 (3) 4/111 (5)
5/161 (6) 6/212 (7) 7/235 (8) 8/257 (9)

Gabriel 25–4–119–4; Roach 23.2–8–58–3; Cummins 20–4–57–2; Chase 13–1–90–0; Reifer 17–8–36–1; Brathwaite 4–0–12–0. *Second innings*—Gabriel 15–0–52–2; Roach 6–1–28–0; Cummins 17–1–69–3; Reifer 13–1–52–1; Brathwaite 9–0–33–0; Chase 17.4–1–51–2.

West Indies

*K. C. Brathwaite c Southee b de Grandhomme	66	– c Williamson b Boult	20
K. O. A. Powell c Blundell b Southee	0	– c Southee b Boult	0
S. O. Hetmyer c and b Boult	28	– c Wagner b Southee	15
S. D. Hope c Taylor b Southee	15	– c de Grandhomme b Wagner	23
R. L. Chase b de Grandhomme	12	– c de Grandhomme b Wagner	64
S. W. Ambris hit wkt b Boult	2	– retired hurt	5
†S. O. Dowrich c and b Wagner	35	– c Nicholls b Wagner	0
R. A. Reifer not out	23	– c Williamson b Southee	29
K. A. J. Roach c Boult b Wagner	17	– b Santner	32
M. L. Cummins b Boult	15	– c Boult b Santner	9
S. T. Gabriel b Boult	0	– not out	0
B 1, w 7	8	Lb 5, w 1	6
(66.5 overs)	221	(63.5 overs)	203

1/5 (2) 2/46 (3) 3/90 (4) 4/112 (5) 5/117 (6)
6/135 (1) 7/169 (7) 8/204 (9) 9/221 (10) 10/221 (11)

1/4 (2) 2/27 (3) 3/43 (1) 4/68 (4) 5/80 (7)
6/158 (5) 7/166 (8) 8/203 (10) 9/203 (9)

In the second innings Ambris retired hurt at 80-4.

Southee 19–9–34–2; Boult 20.5–5–73–4; de Grandhomme 12–1–40–2; Wagner 15–2–73–2. *Second innings*—Southee 19–3–71–2; Boult 16–1–52–2; Wagner 15–5–42–3; de Grandhomme 9–5–20–0; Santner 4.5–0–13–2.

Umpires: B. N. J. Oxenford *(Australia)* (46) and R. J. Tucker *(Australia)* (58).
Third umpire: I. J. Gould *(England)*. Referee: B. C. Broad *(England)* (90).

Close of play: first day, New Zealand 286–7 (Blundell 12, Wagner 1); second day, West Indies 215–8 (Reifer 22, Cummins 10); third day, West Indies 30–2 (Brathwaite 13, Hope 1).

Test No. 2291/9 (SA418, Z105)

SOUTH AFRICA v ZIMBABWE 2017–18 (Only Test)

At St George's Park, Port Elizabeth, on 26, 27 December, 2017 (day/night).
Toss: South Africa.   Result: SOUTH AFRICA WON BY AN INNINGS AND 120 RUNS.
Debuts: Zimbabwe – R. P. Burl, B. Muzarabani.
Man of the Match: A. K. Markram.

Even in ordinary circumstances, this would have been a mismatch. In this pink-ball game – scheduled for four days, but over in two – the chasm between the teams widened to tragicomic proportions: Zimbabwe were demolished twice in 5¼ hours. Thirteen wickets fell on the first day (nine in the third session), and 16 on the second. The floodlights, upgraded at a cost of £1.6m, were not needed on the second day. The first two-day Test anywhere since New Zealand overwhelmed Zimbabwe at Harare in August 2005 lasted only 907 deliveries; there had been eight shorter Tests, only one of them since 1946. Things looked ominous from the start, when Zimbabwe's bowlers proved a handful in broad daylight. On a well-grassed pitch, the ball moved appreciably off the seam – but not enough to prevent Markram making 125, his second century in three Tests. De Villiers, who made a sprightly 53, was playing his first Test since January 2016, after choosing to sit out 17. He was temporary captain as Faf du Plessis was injured, and also had to keep wicket, taking eight catches after de Kock strained a hamstring while batting. He declared with an hour left of the first evening, a canny nod to the ball's exaggerated dance under lights. Zimbabwe lost Masakadza to the first delivery, and were soon 14 for four. The seamers did all the damage in the first innings – Morkel claimed his first five-for in 36 Tests, spread over more than five years – but the main destroyer in the second was slow left-armer Maharaj.

South Africa

D. Elgar c Moor b Jarvis	31
A. K. Markram c Taylor b Jarvis	125
H. M. Amla c Moor b Mpofu	5
*A. B. de Villiers c and b Mpofu	53
T. Bavuma c Taylor b Jarvis	44
†Q. de Kock lbw b Cremer	24
V. D. Philander lbw b Cremer	10
A. L. Phehlukwayo not out	4
K. Rabada run out (Moor/Taylor)	1
K. A. Maharaj c Burl b Mpofu	5
B 2, lb 2, w 1, nb 2	7
(9 wkts dec, 78.3 overs)	309

1/72 (1) 2/77 (3) 3/173 (4) 4/251 (2) 5/272 (5)
6/298 (7) 7/303 (6) 8/304 (9) 9/309 (10)

M. Morkel did not bat.

Jarvis 18–2–57–3; Muzarabani 13–2–48–0; Mpofu 13.3–1–58–3; Chibhabha 11–1–51–0; Cremer 18–0–66–2; Sikandar Raza 5–0–25–0.

Zimbabwe

H. Masakadza lbw b Morkel	0	– c †de Villiers b Maharaj	13
C. J. Chibhabha c Bavuma b Morkel	6	– c †de Villiers b Rabada	15
C. R. Ervine lbw b Philander	4	– lbw b Phehlukwayo	23
†B. R. M. Taylor c †de Villiers b Morkel	0	– c Amla b Maharaj	16
R. P. Burl b Morkel	16	– c †de Villiers b Phehlukwayo	0
K. M. Jarvis c †de Villiers b Phehlukwayo	23	– (9) b Philander	5
Sikandar Raza c †de Villiers b Morkel	0	– (6) c Phehlukwayo b Maharaj	5
P. J. Moor b Phehlukwayo	9	– (7) c †de Villiers b Phehlukwayo	1
*A. G. Cremer c †de Villiers b Rabada	2	– (8) not out	18
C. B. Mpofu c Bavuma b Rabada	0	– b Maharaj	0
B. Muzarabani not out	4	– b Maharaj	10
Lb 2, nb 2	4	B 8, lb 7	15
(30.1 overs)	68	(42.3 overs)	121

1/0 (1) 2/11 (2) 3/11 (4) 4/14 (3) 5/36 (5)   1/54 (2) 2/75 (4) 3/75 (3) 4/80 (6) 5/80 (5)
6/36 (7) 7/55 (6) 8/63 (9) 9/63 (8) 10/68 (10)   6/87 (7) 7/91 (1) 8/98 (9) 9/103 (10) 10/121 (11)

In the second innings Masakadza, when 7, retired hurt at 8-0 and resumed at 80-5.

Morkel 11–5–21–5; Philander 10–4–21–1; Rabada 6.1–2–12–2; Phehlukwayo 3–0–12–2. *Second innings*—Morkel 4–0–12–0; Philander 7–3–10–1; Maharaj 17.3–5–59–5; Rabada 7–3–12–1; Phehlukwayo 7–2–13–3.

Umpires: R. A. Kettleborough *(England)* (49) and P. R. Reiffel *(Australia)* (34).
Third umpire: M. A. Gough *(England)*.   Referee: B. C. Broad *(England)* (91).

Close of play: first day, Zimbabwe 30–4 (Burl 15, Jarvis 4).

SOUTH AFRICA v INDIA 2017–18 (1st Test)

At Newlands, Cape Town, on 5, 6, 7 *(no play)*, 8 January, 2018.
Toss: South Africa.   Result: SOUTH AFRICA WON BY 72 RUNS.
Debuts: India – J. J. Bumrah.
Man of the Match: V. D. Philander.

For three pulsating days, this Test hummed along at such a rollicking pace it seemed impossible for either team to keep up. Within 22 minutes of the start, Bhuvneshwar Kumar had reduced South Africa to 12 for three. But de Villiers raced to a 55-ball half-century with ten boundaries, and the total reached 286. At the end of a gripping first day, India were 28 for three, and not long after lunch on the next they were floundering at 92 for seven. But Steyn, who was making an emotional return after a year out with a shoulder injury, limped off during his 18th over with a bruised heel, and Pandya transformed the game with a thrilling 93, putting on 99 with Bhuvneshwar, who was scoreless for 33 balls. At the close South Africa were two down and 142 ahead, but after the third day was washed out it took India's seamers barely 20 overs to claim the last eight for 65 on the fourth; a target of 208 would have been fewer without de Villiers's breezy 35. An opening stand of 30, in which Vijay was twice reprieved on review, suggested a victory stroll – only for all ten to cascade for 105. Philander's career-best six for 42 included the crucial scalp of Kohli, who had probably erred in calling for the heavy roller, as it squeezed dampness back to the surface. Saha's ten catches broke M. S. Dhoni's Indian record for dismissals in a match, set at Melbourne in 2014–15.

South Africa

D. Elgar c Saha b Bhuvneshwar Kumar	0	– (2) c Saha b Pandya	25
A. K. Markram lbw b Bhuvneshwar Kumar	5	– (1) c Bhuvneshwar Kumar b Pandya	34
H. M. Amla c Saha b Bhuvneshwar Kumar	3	– (4) c Sharma b Mohammed Shami	4
A. B. de Villiers b Bumrah	65	– (5) c Bhuvneshwar Kumar b Bumrah	35
*F. du Plessis c Saha b Pandya	62	– (6) c Saha b Bumrah	0
†Q. de Kock c Saha b Bhuvneshwar Kumar	43	– (7) c Saha b Bumrah	8
V. D. Philander b Mohammed Shami	23	– (8) lbw b Mohammed Shami	0
K. A. Maharaj run out (Ashwin)	35	– (9) c Saha b Bhuvneshwar Kumar	15
K. Rabada c Saha b Ashwin	26	– (3) c Kohli b Mohammed Shami	5
D. W. Steyn not out	16	– (11) not out	0
M. Morkel lbw b Ashwin	2	– (10) c Saha b Bhuvneshwar Kumar	2
B 2, lb 3, nb 1	6	W 2	2
(73.1 overs)	286	(41.2 overs)	130

1/0 (1) 2/7 (2) 3/12 (3) 4/126 (4) 5/142 (5)
6/202 (6) 7/221 (7) 8/258 (8) 9/280 (9) 10/286 (11)
1/52 (1) 2/59 (2) 3/66 (4) 4/73 (3) 5/82 (6)
6/92 (7) 7/95 (8) 8/122 (9) 9/130 (10) 10/130 (5)

Bhuvneshwar Kumar 19–4–87–4; Mohammed Shami 16–6–47–1; Bumrah 19–1–73–1; Pandya 12–1–53–1; Ashwin 7.1–1–21–2. *Second innings*—Bhuvneshwar Kumar 11–5–33–2; Bumrah 11.2–1–39–3; Mohammed Shami 12–3–28–3; Pandya 6–0–27–2; Ashwin 1–0–3–0.

India

M. Vijay c Elgar b Philander	1	– c de Villiers b Philander	13
S. Dhawan c and b Steyn	16	– c sub (C. H. Morris) b Morkel	16
C. A. Pujara c du Plessis b Philander	26	– c de Kock b Morkel	4
*V. Kohli c de Kock b Morkel	5	– lbw b Philander	28
R. G. Sharma lbw b Rabada	11	– b Philander	10
R. Ashwin c de Kock b Philander	12	– (8) c de Kock b Philander	37
H. H. Pandya c de Kock b Rabada	93	– c de Villiers b Rabada	1
†W. P. Saha lbw b Steyn	0	– (6) lbw b Rabada	8
Bhuvneshwar Kumar c de Kock b Morkel	25	– not out	13
Mohammed Shami not out	4	– c du Plessis b Philander	4
J. J. Bumrah c Elgar b Rabada	2	– c du Plessis b Philander	0
B 1, lb 13	14	Lb 1	1
(73.4 overs)	209	(42.4 overs)	135

1/16 (1) 2/18 (2) 3/27 (4) 4/57 (5) 5/76 (3)
6/81 (6) 7/92 (8) 8/191 (9) 9/199 (7) 10/209 (11)
1/30 (2) 2/30 (1) 3/39 (3) 4/71 (4) 5/76 (5)
6/77 (7) 7/82 (6) 8/131 (8) 9/135 (10) 10/135 (11)

Philander 14.3–8–33–3; Steyn 17.3–6–51–2; Morkel 19–6–57–2; Rabada 16.4–4–34–3; Maharaj 6–0–20–0. *Second innings*—Philander 15.4–4–42–6; Morkel 11–1–39–2; Rabada 12–2–41–2; Maharaj 4–1–12–0.

Umpires: M. A. Gough *(England)* (5) and R. A. Kettleborough *(England)* (50).
Third umpire: P. R. Reiffel *(Australia)*.   Referee: B. C. Broad *(England)* (92).

Close of play: first day, India 28–3 (Pujara 5, Sharma 0); second day, South Africa 65–2 (Rabada 2, Amla 4); third day, no play.

Test No. 2293/35 (SA420, I520)

SOUTH AFRICA v INDIA 2017–18 (2nd Test)

At Centurion Park, Pretoria, on 13, 14, 15, 16, 17 January, 2018.
Toss: South Africa. Result: SOUTH AFRICA WON BY 135 RUNS.
Debuts: South Africa – L. T. Ngidi.
Man of the Match: L. T. Ngidi.

Kohli's marvellous 153 from 217 balls belied another awkward pitch, whose dry and cracked appearance was more subcontinental than sub-Saharan. The trouble was, none of his team-mates managed a half-century, and South Africa duly took the series. Markram drove and cut well on the first day, with India's seamers wayward, and du Plessis stretched the total to 335 on the second, a total he claimed was "at least 100 better than it looks". Pujara was run out first ball – he would later become the first Indian to be dismissed this way in both innings of a Test – and it proved enough for a narrow advantage despite Kohli's brilliance. He was leading a recovery from 164 for five when Pandya was dozily run out, failing to ground bat or boot despite being over the line ahead of Philander's speculative throw from mid-on. Ashwin proved more reliable, and helped reduce the deficit. Morkel spearheaded the home seamers, even though Maharaj had become the first South African spinner to take the new ball in the first innings of a Test since Aubrey Faulkner in 1912. After a poor start, Markram and de Villiers added 141, and although India's pacemen made regular incisions the target was a daunting 287. They never recovered from the early dismissal of Kohli, one of six wickets for the pacey 21-year-old debutant Lungi True-man Ngidi. On the third evening, Kohli was upset by the umpires allowing play in light rain, and was fined after hurling the ball into the ground.

South Africa

D. Elgar c Vijay b Ashwin	31	– (2) c Rahul b Mohammed Shami	61
A. K. Markram c Patel b Ashwin	94	– (1) lbw b Bumrah	1
H. M. Amla run out (Pandya)	82	– lbw b Bumrah	1
A. B. de Villiers b I. Sharma	20	– c Patel b Mohammed Shami	80
*F. du Plessis b I. Sharma	63	– c and b Bumrah	48
†Q. de Kock c Kohli b Ashwin	0	– c Patel b Mohammed Shami	12
V. D. Philander run out (Patel/Pandya)	0	– c Vijay b I. Sharma	26
K. A. Maharaj c Patel b Mohammed Shami	18	– c Patel b I. Sharma	6
K. Rabada c Pandya b I. Sharma	11	– c Kohli b Mohammed Shami	4
M. Morkel c Vijay b Ashwin	6	– not out	10
L. T. Ngidi not out	1	– c Vijay b Ashwin	1
Lb 8, nb 1	9	B 2, lb 5, w 1	8
(113.5 overs)	335	(91.3 overs)	258

1/85 (1) 2/148 (2) 3/199 (4) 4/246 (3) 5/250 (6)   1/1 (1) 2/3 (3) 3/144 (4) 4/151 (2) 5/163 (6)
6/251 (7) 7/282 (8) 8/324 (9) 9/333 (5) 10/335 (10)   6/209 (7) 7/215 (8) 8/245 (9) 9/245 (5) 10/258 (11)

Bumrah 22–6–60–0; Mohammed Shami 15–2–58–1; I. Sharma 22–4–46–3; Pandya 16–4–50–0; Ashwin 38.5–10–113–4. *Second innings*—Ashwin 29.3–6–78–1; Bumrah 20–3–70–3; I. Sharma 17–3–40–2; Mohammed Shami 16–3–49–4; Pandya 9–1–14–0.

India

M. Vijay c de Kock b Maharaj	46	– b Rabada	9
K. L. Rahul c and b Morkel	10	– c Maharaj b Ngidi	4
C. A. Pujara run out (Ngidi)	0	– run out (Ngidi/de Villiers/de Kock)	19
*V. Kohli c de Villiers b Morkel	153	– lbw b Ngidi	5
R. G. Sharma lbw b Rabada	10	– (6) c de Villiers b Rabada	47
†P. A. Patel c de Kock b Ngidi	19	– (5) c Morkel b Rabada	19
H. H. Pandya run out (Philander)	15	– c de Kock b Ngidi	6
R. Ashwin c du Plessis b Philander	38	– c de Kock b Ngidi	3
Mohammed Shami c Amla b Morkel	1	– c Morkel b Ngidi	28
I. Sharma c Markram b Morkel	3	– not out	4
J. J. Bumrah not out	0	– c Philander b Ngidi	2
B 8, lb 1, w 2, nb 1	12	B 4, w 1	5
(92.1 overs)	307	(50.2 overs)	151

1/28 (2) 2/28 (3) 3/107 (1) 4/132 (5) 5/164 (6)   1/11 (1) 2/16 (2) 3/26 (4) 4/49 (3) 5/65 (5)
6/209 (7) 7/280 (8) 8/281 (9) 9/306 (10) 10/307 (4)   6/83 (7) 7/87 (8) 8/141 (6) 9/145 (9) 10/151 (11)

Maharaj 20–1–67–1; Morkel 22.1–5–60–4; Philander 16–3–46–1; Rabada 20–1–74–1; Ngidi 14–2–51–1. *Second innings*—Philander 10–3–25–0; Rabada 14–3–47–3; Ngidi 12.2–3–39–6; Morkel 8–3–10–0; Maharaj 6–1–26–0.

Umpires: M. A. Gough *(England)* (6) and P. R. Reiffel *(Australia)* (35).
Third umpire: R. A. Kettleborough *(England).*   Referee: B. C. Broad *(England)* (93).

Close of play: first day, South Africa 269–6 (du Plessis 24, Maharaj 10); second day, India 183–5 (Kohli 85, Pandya 11); third day, South Africa 90–2 (Elgar 36, de Villiers 50); fourth day, India 35–3 (Pujara 11, Patel 5).

SOUTH AFRICA v INDIA 2017–18 (3rd Test)

At New Wanderers, Johannesburg, on 24, 25, 26, 27 January, 2018.
Toss: India.   Result: INDIA WON BY 63 RUNS.
Debuts: none.
Man of the Match: Bhuvneshwar Kumar.   Man of the Series: V. D. Philander.

India were almost denied one of their finest victories when the match came close to being abandoned because of an unsafe pitch, later rated as "poor" by the ICC. But after ending play 19 minutes early when Mohammad Shami rattled Elgar's grille on the third evening, the officials gave it one last chance next day, and India completed a hard-fought consolation win. As South Africa chased an unlikely target of 241, Elgar and Amla began to inch their way up the mountain, collecting nearly as many bruises as runs. They took the score to 124 for one but, once Amla was caught by a diving Pandya at square leg, the floodgates opened; the last nine wickets clattered for 53, Shami collecting five for 28 while Elgar carried his bat for the second time in a Test. Kohli's decision to bat seemed crazy, but it was spectacularly vindicated. The openers departed quickly, but Pujara and Kohli – dropped by Philander when 11 – grafted to half-centuries. Pujara required 54 deliveries (and 79 minutes) to get off the mark: for India, only Rajesh Chauhan, with 57 against Sri Lanka in 1993–94, had faced more balls on nought. Nightwatchman Rabada made a resourceful 30 next morning, but of the rest only Amla and Philander reached double figures as South Africa took a gossamer lead. Bumrah, in his third Test, claimed a maiden five-for, then Rahane and the inevitable Kohli dug deep as India reached 247. Not a single over of spin was bowled in the match.

India

M. Vijay c de Kock b Rabada	8	– b Rabada	25
K. L. Rahul c de Kock b Philander	0	– (3) c du Plessis b Philander	16
C. A. Pujara c de Kock b Phehlukwayo	50	– (4) c du Plessis b Morkel	1
*V. Kohli c de Villiers b Ngidi	54	– (5) b Rabada	41
A. M. Rahane lbw b Morkel	9	– (6) c de Kock b Morkel	48
†P. A. Patel c de Kock b Morkel	2	– (2) c Markram b Philander	16
H. H. Pandya c de Kock b Phehlukwayo	0	– c and b Rabada	4
Bhuvneshwar Kumar c Phehlukwayo b Rabada	30	– c de Kock b Morkel	33
Mohammed Shami c Rabada b Philander	8	– c de Villiers b Ngidi	27
I. Sharma c du Plessis b Rabada	0	– not out	7
J. J. Bumrah not out	0	– c Rabada b Philander	0
B 11, lb 7, w 6, nb 2	26	B 5, lb 12, w 12	29
(76.4 overs)	187	(80.1 overs)	247

1/7 (2) 2/13 (1) 3/97 (4) 4/113 (5) 5/144 (3)
6/144 (6) 7/144 (7) 8/163 (9) 9/166 (10) 10/187 (8)

1/17 (2) 2/51 (3) 3/57 (4) 4/100 (1) 5/134 (5)
6/148 (7) 7/203 (6) 8/238 (9) 9/240 (8) 10/247 (11)

Morkel 17–5–47–2; Philander 19–10–31–2; Rabada 18.4–6–39–3; Ngidi 15–7–27–1; Phehlukwayo 7–1–25–2. *Second innings*—Philander 21.1–5–61–3; Rabada 23–5–69–3; Morkel 21–6–47–3; Ngidi 12–2–38–1; Phehlukwayo 3–0–15–0.

South Africa

D. Elgar c Patel b Bhuvneshwar Kumar	4	– (2) not out	86
A. K. Markram c Patel b Bhuvneshwar Kumar	2	– (1) c Patel b Mohammed Shami	4
K. Rabada c Rahane b Sharma	30	– (9) c Pujara b Bhuvneshwar Kumar	0
H. M. Amla c Pandya b Bumrah	61	– (3) c Pandya b Sharma	52
A. B. de Villiers b Bhuvneshwar Kumar	5	– (4) c Rahane b Bumrah	6
*F. du Plessis b Bumrah	8	– (5) b Sharma	2
†Q. de Kock c Patel b Bumrah	8	– (6) lbw b Bumrah	0
V. D. Philander c Bumrah b Mohammed Shami	35	– (7) b Mohammed Shami	10
A. L. Phehlukwayo lbw b Bumrah	9	– (8) b Mohammed Shami	0
M. Morkel not out	9	– b Mohammed Shami	0
L. T. Ngidi c Patel b Bumrah	0	– c sub (†K. D. Karthik) b Mohammed Shami	4
Lb 14, w 9	23	B 7, w 6	13
(65.5 overs)	194	(73.3 overs)	177

1/3 (2) 2/16 (1) 3/80 (3) 4/92 (5) 5/107 (6)
6/125 (7) 7/169 (4) 8/175 (8) 9/194 (9) 10/194 (11)

1/5 (1) 2/124 (3) 3/131 (4) 4/144 (5) 5/145 (6)
6/157 (7) 7/157 (8) 8/160 (9) 9/161 (10) 10/177 (11)

Bhuvneshwar Kumar 19–9–44–3; Bumrah 18.5–2–54–5; Sharma 14–2–33–1; Mohammed Shami 12–0–46–1; Pandya 2–0–3–0. *Second innings*—Bhuvneshwar Kumar 18–4–39–1; Mohammed Shami 12.3–2–28–5; Bumrah 21–3–57–2; Sharma 16–3–31–2; Pandya 6–1–15–0.

Umpires: Aleem Dar *(Pakistan)* (117) and I. J. Gould *(England)* (64).
Third umpire: M. A. Gough *(England)*.   Referee: A. J. Pycroft *(Zimbabwe)* (57).

Close of play: first day, South Africa 6–1 (Elgar 4, Rabada 0); second day, India 49–1 (Vijay 13, Rahul 16); third day, South Africa 17–1 (Elgar 11, Amla 2).

BANGLADESH v SRI LANKA 2017–18 (1st Test)

At Zohur Ahmed Chowdhury Stadium, Chittagong, on 31 January, 1, 2, 3, 4 February, 2018.
Toss: Bangladesh.   Result: DRAWN.
Debuts: Bangladesh – Sanjamul Islam.
Man of the Match: Mominul Haque.

For a fleeting moment of a run-soaked match came a suggestion the tedium would lift; Herath removed Mushfiqur Rahim with the last ball of the fourth day to reduce Bangladesh to 81 for three in their second innings, still 119 behind. They had often capsized in similar circumstances, but now steamed sedately towards the draw that had looked likely from the start. Mominul Haque made his second century of the match – the first to do this for Bangladesh – while Liton Das atoned for a golden duck with 94; their stand of 180 slammed the door in Sri Lanka's face. Just four wickets had fallen on the first day, with Mominul – who reached his hundred in 96 balls – adding 236 with Mushfiqur. Mahmudullah, captaining for the first time in a Test, made an unbeaten 83 as Bangladesh reached 513, the largest Test total without a bye or a leg-bye. But Sri Lanka made it look puny; Mendis – dropped on four – and Dhananjaya de Silva put on 308, both finishing with career-bests. Roshen Silva, who would not have played had Angelo Mathews been fit, added a further 107 with Mendis and 135 with Chandimal, and Dickwella's 62 was the final meaty contribution to a total of 713 for nine, Sri Lanka's joint-fifth-highest. Taijul Islam took four wickets, but his 67.3 overs were the most in a Test innings by a Bangladesh bowler, and his 219 runs the most conceded. When the captains shook hands on the draw, only 24 wickets had fallen.

Bangladesh

Tamim Iqbal b Perera	52	– c Dickwella b Sandakan	41	
Imrul Kayes lbw b Sandakan	40	– c Chandimal b Perera	19	
Mominul Haque c Mendis b Herath	176	– c Karunaratne b de Silva	105	
Mushfiqur Rahim c Dickwella b Lakmal	92	– c Mendis b Herath	2	
†Liton Das b Lakmal	0	– c Perera b Herath	94	
*Mahmudullah not out	83	– not out	28	
Mosaddek Hossain c Sandakan b Herath	8	– not out	8	
Mehedi Hasan run out (Kumara/Dickwella)	20			
Sanjamul Islam st Dickwella b Sandakan	24			
Taijul Islam b Herath	1			
Mustafizur Rahman c Dickwella b Lakmal	8			
W 5, nb 4	9	B 3, lb 2, w 1, nb 4	10	
(129.5 overs)	513	(5 wkts dec, 100 overs)	307	

1/72 (1) 2/120 (2) 3/356 (4) 4/356 (5) 5/376 (3)
6/390 (7) 7/417 (8) 8/475 (9) 9/478 (10) 10/513 (11)

1/52 (2) 2/76 (1) 3/81 (4)
4/261 (3) 5/279 (5)

Lakmal 23.5–4–68–3; Kumara 15–1–79–0; Perera 27–4–112–1; Herath 37–2–150–3; Sandakan 22–1–92–2; de Silva 5–0–12–0. *Second innings*—Herath 28–6–80–2; Lakmal 9–1–25–0; de Silva 12–0–41–1; Perera 26–5–74–1; Sandakan 18–2–64–1; Kumara 6–0–16–0; Mendis 1–0–2–0.

Sri Lanka

F. D. M. Karunaratne c Imrul Kayes b Mehedi Hasan	0
B. K. G. Mendis c Mushfiqur Rahim b Taijul Islam	196
D. M. de Silva c Liton Das b Mustafizur Rahman	173
A. R. S. Silva c Liton Das b Mehedi Hasan	109
*L. D. Chandimal b Taijul Islam	87
†D. P. D. N. Dickwella c Liton Das b Mehedi Hasan	62
M. D. K. Perera lbw b Sanjamul Islam	32
H. M. R. K. B. Herath lbw b Taijul Islam	24
R. A. S. Lakmal b Taijul Islam	9
C. B. R. L. S. Kumara not out	2
B 11, lb 6, w 2	19
(9 wkts dec, 199.3 overs)	713

1/0 (1) 2/308 (3) 3/415 (2) 4/550 (4) 5/613 (5)
6/663 (6) 7/687 (7) 8/706 (9) 9/713 (8)

P. A. D. L. R. Sandakan did not bat.

Mustafizur Rahman 32–6–113–1; Sanjamul Islam 45–2–153–1; Mehedi Hasan 49–4–174–3; Taijul Islam 67.3–13–219–4; Mosaddek Hossain 3–0–24–0; Mominul Haque 2–0–6–0; Mahmudullah 1–0–7–0.

Umpires: M. Erasmus *(South Africa)* (48) and R. J. Tucker *(Australia)* (59).
Third umpire: J. S. Wilson *(West Indies)*.   Referee: D. C. Boon *(Australia)* (48).

Close of play: first day, Bangladesh 374-4 (Mominul Haque 175, Mahmudullah 9); second day, Sri Lanka 187-1 (Mendis 83, de Silva 104); third day, Sri Lanka 504-3 (Silva 87, Chandimal 37); fourth day, Bangladesh 81-3 (Mominul Haque 18).

Test No. 2296/20 (B106, SL269)

BANGLADESH v SRI LANKA 2017–18 (2nd Test)

At Shere Bangla National Stadium, Mirpur, Dhaka, on 8, 9, 10 February, 2018.
Toss: Sri Lanka. Result: SRI LANKA WON BY 215 RUNS.
Debuts: Sri Lanka – A. Dananjaya.
Man of the Match: A. R. S. Silva. Man of the Series: A. R. S. Silva.

On a pitch that took spin from the start, only one team seemed prepared to knuckle down – and Sri Lanka took the series after a hectic three days. The game was another statisticians' delight: Herath overtook Wasim Akram (414 wickets) as the most successful left-arm bowler in Tests; off-spinner Akila Dananjaya returned the best match figures for Sri Lanka on debut; and Roshen Silva became just the fourth player (after Australia's Herbie Collins, and Sunil Gavaskar and Mohammad Azharuddin of India) to reach 50 in four of his first five Test innings. Bangladesh opened with Mehedi Hasan and Abdur Razzak, only the second time two spinners have taken the new ball in the first innings of a Test, but Mendis made 68, and Silva a patient 56 as the last four wickets squeezed out 112 crucial runs. Bangladesh failed to show the same fight and, with Lakmal snaring three early victims to move to 100 in Tests, they were skittled for 110. Mominul Haque was carelessly run out for a duck after failing to ground his bat, and the last five fell for three. Silva's unbeaten 70 was the sole score above 32 as Sri Lanka built on a lead of 112 – but, 338 ahead, they had enough. Playing like men with a train to catch, Bangladesh were knocked over in 29.3 overs; this time the last six added just 23. Dananjaya got the ball to lift steeply, his five wickets coming in five overs, and Herath wrapped things up.

Sri Lanka

B. K. G. Mendis b Abdur Razzak	68	– (2) lbw b Abdur Razzak	7
F. D. M. Karunaratne st Liton Das b Abdur Razzak	3	– (1) c Imrul Kayes b Mehedi Hasan	32
D. M. de Silva c Sabbir Rahman b Taijul Islam	19	– b Taijul Islam	28
M. D. Gunathilleke c Mushfiqur Rahim b Abdur Razzak	13	– lbw b Mustafizur Rahman	17
*L. D. Chandimal b Abdur Razzak	0	– lbw b Mehedi Hasan	30
A. R. S. Silva c Liton Das b Taijul Islam	56	– not out	70
†D. P. D. N. Dickwella b Taijul Islam	1	– c Mahmudullah b Taijul Islam	10
M. D. K. Perera c Mominul Haque b Taijul Islam	31	– c Liton Das b Mustafizur Rahman	7
A. Dananjaya c Mushfiqur Rahim b Mustafizur Rahman	20	– c Liton Das b Mustafizur Rahman	0
H. M. R. K. B. Herath c Mushfiqur Rahim b Mustafizur Rahman	2	– (11) lbw b Taijul Islam	0
R. A. S. Lakmal not out	4	– (10) b Taijul Islam	21
Lb 5	5	Lb 4	4
(65.3 overs)	222	(73.5 overs)	226

1/14 (2) 2/61 (3) 3/96 (4) 4/96 (5) 5/109 (1)
6/110 (7) 7/162 (8) 8/205 (9) 9/207 (10) 10/222 (6)

1/19 (2) 2/53 (3) 3/80 (4) 4/92 (1)
5/143 (5) 6/170 (7) 7/178 (8)
8/178 (9) 9/226 (10) 10/226 (11)

Mehedi Hasan 13–0–54–0; Abdur Razzak 16–2–63–4; Taijul Islam 25.3–2–83–4; Mustafizur Rahman 11–4–17–2. *Second innings*—Abdur Razzak 17–2–60–1; Mustafizur Rahman 17–3–49–3; Taijul Islam 19.5–2–76–4; Mehedi Hasan 20–5–37–2.

Bangladesh

Tamim Iqbal c and b Lakmal	4	– lbw b Perera	2
Imrul Kayes lbw b Perera	19	– c Dickwella b Herath	17
Mominul Haque run out (de Silva/Dickwella)	0	– c Dickwella b Herath	33
Mushfiqur Rahim b Lakmal	1	– st Dickwella b Herath	25
†Liton Das b Lakmal	25	– c Mendis b Dananjaya	12
Mehedi Hasan not out	38	– (8) c Dickwella b Dananjaya	7
*Mahmudullah b Dananjaya	17	– (6) c Karunaratne b Dananjaya	6
Sabbir Rahman c Chandimal b Dananjaya	0	– (7) c Mendis b Dananjaya	1
Abdur Razzak c and b Dananjaya	1	– st Dickwella b Dananjaya	2
Taijul Islam run out (Mendis)	1	– c Gunathilleke b Herath	6
Mustafizur Rahman lbw b Perera	0	– not out	5
Lb 2, w 1, nb 1	4	B 6, lb 1	7
(45.4 overs)	110	(29.3 overs)	123

1/4 (1) 2/4 (3) 3/12 (4) 4/45 (2) 5/73 (5) 6/107 (7)
7/107 (8) 8/109 (9) 9/110 (10) 10/110 (11)

1/3 (1) 2/49 (2) 3/64 (3) 4/78 (5)
5/100 (6) 6/102 (4) 7/102 (7)
8/104 (9) 9/113 (8) 10/123 (10)

Lakmal 12–4–25–3; Perera 11.4–4–32–2; Dananjaya 10–2–20–3; Herath 12–1–31–0. *Second innings*—Lakmal 3–0–11–0; Perera 10–0–32–1; Herath 11.3–1–49–4; Dananjaya 5–1–24–5.

Umpires: R. J. Tucker *(Australia)* (60) and J. S. Wilson *(West Indies)* (10).
Third umpire: M. Erasmus *(South Africa)*. Referee: D. C. Boon *(Australia)* (49).

Close of play: first day, Bangladesh 56–4 (Liton Das 24, Mehedi Hasan 5); second day, Sri Lanka 200–8 (Silva 58, Lakmal 7).

SOUTH AFRICA v AUSTRALIA 2017–18 (1st Test)

At Kingsmead, Durban, on 1, 2, 3, 4, 5 March, 2018.
Toss: Australia.   Result: AUSTRALIA WON BY 118 RUNS.
Debuts: none.
Man of the Match: M. A. Starc.

South Africa were overwhelmed by the incisiveness of an Australian attack led by the reverse swing of Starc. His first-innings five-for crippled the hosts, and he finished with nine for 109 in the match. From 150 for five in response to 351, South Africa were shot out for 162, and never recovered. But instead of feeling deflated they harnessed a sense of indignation at Australia's behaviour, particularly an ugly spat between Warner and de Kock at tea on the fourth day, which set the tone for a foul-tempered series. Play that day had begun with Australia expecting to wrap things up quickly, but they were made to work by Markram, with a mature 143, and de Kock, whose 83 was his best Test score for nearly a year. Warner had given Australia a sound start, with a sixth score above 50 in seven Test innings in South Africa. Smith contributed a fifth consecutive Test half-century, and Mitchell Marsh added 96 as the last five wickets all but doubled the score. Lyon soon reduced South Africa to 27 for two, and although de Villiers produced a fluent unbeaten 71 the rest crumbled, 189 behind. Although South Africa bowled better second time round, Australia still led by 416, and the home side soon nosedived to 49 for four, with the run-out of de Villiers for a duck sending the Australians into a screaming frenzy. Markram seemed immune to the sledging, but his dismissal late on the fourth day heralded the end.

Australia

C. T. Bancroft c de Kock b Philander	5	– st de Kock b Maharaj	53
D. A. Warner c de Villiers b Philander	51	– c sub (P. W. A. Mulder) b Rabada	28
U. T. Khawaja c de Kock b Rabada	14	– c de Kock b Maharaj	6
*S. P. D. Smith c de Villiers b Maharaj	56	– lbw b Elgar	38
S. E. Marsh c de Villiers b Maharaj	40	– c de Villiers b Morkel	33
M. R. Marsh c Morkel b Philander	96	– c Amla b Rabada	6
†T. D. Paine c de Kock b Rabada	25	– c de Villiers b Maharaj	14
P. J. Cummins b Maharaj	3	– b Maharaj	26
M. A. Starc b Maharaj	35	– c Elgar b Morkel	7
N. M. Lyon c de Bruyn b Maharaj	12	– c Amla b Morkel	2
J. R. Hazlewood not out	2	– not out	9
B 4, lb 8	12	Lb 5	5
(110.4 overs)	351	(74.4 overs)	227

1/15 (1) 2/39 (3) 3/95 (2) 4/151 (4) 5/177 (5)
6/237 (7) 7/251 (8) 8/300 (9) 9/341 (6) 10/351 (10)

1/56 (2) 2/71 (3) 3/108 (1) 4/146 (4) 5/156 (6)
6/175 (7) 7/185 (5) 8/203 (9) 9/209 (10) 10/227 (8)

Morkel 22–3–75–0; Philander 27–12–59–3; Maharaj 33.4–5–123–5; Rabada 25–7–74–2; Markram 1–0–2–0; de Bruyn 2–0–6–0. *Second innings*—Morkel 15–4–47–3; Philander 14–4–35–0; Maharaj 29.4–4–102–4; Rabada 13–5–28–2; Elgar 3–1–10–1.

South Africa

D. Elgar c and b Lyon	7	– (2) c Paine b Starc	9
A. K. Markram c Bancroft b Cummins	32	– (1) c Paine b M. R. Marsh	143
H. M. Amla c Bancroft b Lyon	0	– lbw b Hazlewood	8
A. B. de Villiers not out	71	– run out (Warner/Lyon)	0
*F. du Plessis c Paine b Starc	15	– b Cummins	4
T. B. de Bruyn c Paine b Starc	6	– c Paine b Hazlewood	36
†Q. de Kock b Lyon	20	– lbw b Hazlewood	83
V. D. Philander c Paine b Starc	8	– c Paine b Starc	6
K. A. Maharaj b Hazlewood	0	– b Starc	0
K. Rabada lbw b Starc	3	– b Starc	0
M. Morkel b Starc	0	– not out	3
		B 2, lb 3, nb 1	6
(51.4 overs)	162	(92.4 overs)	298

1/27 (1) 2/27 (3) 3/55 (2) 4/92 (5) 5/108 (6)
6/150 (7) 7/158 (8) 8/159 (9) 9/162 (10) 10/162 (11)

1/29 (2) 2/39 (3) 3/39 (4) 4/49 (5) 5/136 (6)
6/283 (1) 7/290 (8) 8/290 (9) 9/290 (10) 10/298 (7)

Starc 10.4–3–34–5; Hazlewood 13–5–31–1; Lyon 16–3–50–3; Cummins 12–2–47–1. *Second innings*—Starc 18–2–75–4; Hazlewood 15.4–2–61–3; Lyon 32–7–86–0; Cummins 15–3–47–1; M. R. Marsh 7–2–21–1; Smith 5–3–3–0.

Umpires: H. D. P. K. Dharmasena *(Sri Lanka)* (52) and S. Ravi *(India)* (25).
Third umpire: C. B. Gaffaney *(New Zealand)*.   Referee: J. J. Crowe *(New Zealand)* (86).

Close of play: first day, Australia 225–5 (M. R. Marsh 32, Paine 21); second day, South Africa 162; third day, Australia 213–9 (Cummins 17, Hazlewood 4); fourth day, South Africa 293–9 (de Kock 81, Morkel 0).

SOUTH AFRICA v AUSTRALIA 2017–18 (2nd Test)

At St George's Park, Port Elizabeth, on 9, 10, 11, 12 March, 2018.
Toss: Australia.   Result: SOUTH AFRICA WON BY SIX WICKETS.
Debuts: none.
Man of the Match: K. Rabada.

South Africa's resolve had strengthened after their Durban defeat and the set-to between Warner and de Kock. The referee spoke to both teams before the match, but could do little about the crowd, who taunted Warner with face-masks and lewd songs. It didn't stop him putting on 98 with Bancroft, but then all ten wickets tumbled for 145. The chief destroyer was Rabada, who either side of tea took five for 13 in 18 balls, including three in an over. The first of the five was Smith, whose shoulder Rabada brushed in his follow-through. South Africa tried to consolidate on a tricky pitch: Elgar and Amla added only 43 in 26 overs in the middle session of the second day, before de Villiers opened out for his 22nd Test century, the first since January 2015. He put on 84 for the eighth wicket with Philander and 58 for the ninth with Maharaj as the lead swelled to 139. Rabada ran in like a man possessed: he screamed in Warner's face after bowling him, earning yet another audience with the referee. But he ended with 11 for 150, South Africa's best match figures at home to Australia, beating Charles Llewellyn's ten for 116 in 1902–03. South Africa polished off their modest target to level the series. Rabada was initially suspended for two Tests after his clash with Smith, but the punishment was downgraded on appeal, and he was free to continue playing. Incensed, the Australians went to Cape Town nursing dark thoughts.

Australia

C. T. Bancroft c de Kock b Philander	38	– b Ngidi	24
D. A. Warner b Ngidi	63	– b Rabada	13
U. T. Khawaja c de Kock b Philander	4	– lbw b Rabada	75
*S. P. D. Smith lbw b Rabada	25	– c de Kock b Maharaj	11
S. E. Marsh lbw b Rabada	24	– c de Kock b Rabada	1
†T. D. Paine b Ngidi	36	– (7) not out	28
M. R. Marsh c de Kock b Rabada	4	– (6) b Rabada	45
P. J. Cummins c de Kock b Rabada	0	– c de Bruyn b Rabada	5
M. A. Starc b Rabada	8	– c de Kock b Rabada	1
N. M. Lyon b Ngidi	17	– c de Kock b Ngidi	5
J. R. Hazlewood not out	10	– c Ngidi b Maharaj	17
Lb 14	14	B 2, lb 10, w 2	14
(71.3 overs)	243	(79 overs)	239

1/98 (1) 2/104 (3) 3/117 (2) 4/161 (4) 5/166 (5)   1/27 (2) 2/62 (1) 3/77 (4) 4/86 (5) 5/173 (3)
6/170 (7) 7/170 (8) 8/182 (9) 9/212 (10) 10/243 (6)   6/186 (6) 7/202 (8) 8/204 (9) 9/211 (10) 10/239 (11)

Philander 18–7–25–2; Rabada 21–2–96–5; Ngidi 13.3–3–51–3; Maharaj 18–1–51–0; Elgar 1–0–6–0. *Second innings*—Philander 18–5–56–0; Rabada 22–9–54–6; Maharaj 23–2–90–2; Ngidi 13–5–24–2; Markram 3–1–3–0.

South Africa

D. Elgar c Paine b Hazlewood	57	– (2) c and b Lyon	5
A. K. Markram lbw b Cummins	11	– (1) c Smith b Hazlewood	21
K. Rabada b Cummins	29		
H. M. Amla b Starc	56	– (3) c Paine b Cummins	27
A. B. de Villiers not out	126	– (4) c Bancroft b Lyon	28
*F. du Plessis lbw b M. R. Marsh	9	– (5) not out	2
T. B. de Bruyn lbw b M. R. Marsh	1	– (6) not out	15
†Q. de Kock b Lyon	9		
V. D. Philander c Bancroft b Cummins	36		
K. A. Maharaj b Hazlewood	30		
L. T. Ngidi run out (Smith)	5		
B 9, lb 2, w 2	13	B 4	4
(118.4 overs)	382	(4 wkts, 22.5 overs)	102

1/22 (2) 2/67 (3) 3/155 (4) 4/155 (1) 5/179 (6)   1/22 (2) 2/32 (1)
6/183 (7) 7/227 (8) 8/311 (9) 9/369 (10) 10/382 (11)   3/81 (3) 4/81 (4)

Starc 33.4–5–110–1; Hazlewood 30–5–98–2; Cummins 24–6–79–3; Lyon 22–5–58–1; M. R. Marsh 9–1–26–2. *Second innings*—Starc 3–0–15–0; Hazlewood 6–0–26–1; Lyon 9–0–44–2; Cummins 4.5–0–13–1.

Umpires: H. D. P. K. Dharmasena *(Sri Lanka)* (53), C. B. Gaffaney *(New Zealand)* (19) and S. Ravi *(India)* (26).
Third umpire: S. Ravi *(India)* and B. P. Jele *South Africa)*.   Referee: J. J. Crowe *(New Zealand)* (87).
Ravi replaced Gaffaney (ill) from the second day, while Jele took over as third umpire.

Close of play: first day, South Africa 39–1 (Elgar 11, Rabada 17); second day, South Africa 263–7 (de Villiers 74, Philander 14); third day, Australia 180–5 (M. R. Marsh 39, Paine 5).

SOUTH AFRICA v AUSTRALIA 2017–18 (3rd Test)

At Newlands, Cape Town, on 22, 23, 24, 25 March, 2018.
Toss: South Africa.   Result: SOUTH AFRICA WON BY 322 RUNS.
Debuts: none.
Man of the Match: M. Morkel.

On the third afternoon of a Test that was drifting away from Australia, an alert TV cameraman spotted Bancroft, in the covers, applying something to the ball. The item was eventually found to be sandpaper, to alter its condition and promote reverse swing. And so one of Australian cricket's darkest periods unfolded. Smith, the captain who turned a blind eye to the tampering plan, and Warner, seen as the scheme's instigator, were sent home; shortly afterwards they were banned for a year by the Australian board, whose enquiries into the scandal – set up to examine "the conduct and culture" of the national team – concluded that no one else knew of the scheme, which led to raised eyebrows in some quarters. Bancroft was banned for nine months, while coach Darren Lehmann soon resigned too. In an unprecedented move, Paine took over as captain mid-match. When the cameras zoomed in South Africa were 129 for two, in the process of extending a lead of 56; thanks to late fifties by de Kock and Philander, they finished 429 in front. Earlier highlights had included Elgar carrying his bat for the third time in a Test, matching the West Indian Desmond Haynes, and 300th Test wickets for Morkel (Shaun Marsh) and Lyon (Rabada, stumped). Australia, morale shattered by the backlash – particularly ferocious at home, where the prime minister called it "a shocking disappointment" – subsided from 57 without loss to 107 all out and massive defeat. Warner top-scored, in his last Test for 16 months.

South Africa

D. Elgar not out	141	– (2) c Smith b Cummins	14
A. K. Markram c Smith b Hazlewood	0	– (1) c Cummins b Starc	84
H. M. Amla c Cummins b Hazlewood	31	– c Bancroft b Cummins	31
A. B. de Villiers c Warner b Cummins	64	– c S. E. Marsh b Hazlewood	63
*F. du Plessis c Smith b Cummins	5	– lbw b Lyon	20
T. Bavuma c Smith b Cummins	1	– c sub (P. S. P. Handscomb) b Hazlewood	5
†Q. de Kock c Paine b Cummins	3	– c Paine b Cummins	65
V. D. Philander c Paine b M. R. Marsh	8	– not out	52
K. A. Maharaj c Bancroft b Starc	3	– (10) c Cummins b Lyon	5
K. Rabada c Smith b Lyon	22	– (9) st Paine b Lyon	20
M. Morkel c Smith b Lyon	4	– c Khawaja b Hazlewood	6
B 13, lb 11, w 2, nb 3	29	B 4, lb 1, w 2, nb 1	8
(97.5 overs)	311	(112.2 overs)	373

1/6 (2) 2/92 (3) 3/220 (4) 4/234 (5) 5/236 (6)
6/242 (7) 7/254 (8) 8/257 (9) 9/307 (10) 10/311 (11)

1/28 (2) 2/104 (3) 3/151 (1) 4/196 (5)
5/201 (6) 6/269 (4) 7/324 (7)
8/354 (9) 9/362 (10) 10/373 (11)

Starc 21–3–81–1; Hazlewood 23–4–59–2; Lyon 19.5–6–43–2; Cummins 26–6–78–4; M. R. Marsh 7–2–26–1; Smith 1–1–0–0. *Second innings*—Starc 23–5–98–1; Hazlewood 25.2–5–69–3; Cummins 27–5–67–3; Lyon 31–2–102–3; Smith 1–0–6–0; M. R. Marsh 5–0–26–0.

Australia

C. T. Bancroft lbw b Philander	77	– run out (du Plessis)	26
D. A. Warner b Rabada	30	– c de Villiers b Rabada	32
U. T. Khawaja c Rabada b Morkel	5	– c de Villiers b Maharaj	1
*S. P. D. Smith c Elgar b Morkel	5	– c Elgar b Morkel	7
S. E. Marsh c de Kock b Morkel	26	– c Markram b Maharaj	0
M. R. Marsh c de Kock b Philander	5	– c de Villiers b Morkel	16
†T. D. Paine not out	34	– not out	9
P. J. Cummins c de Villiers b Rabada	4	– c Elgar b Morkel	0
M. A. Starc c de Villiers b Rabada	2	– c Markram b Morkel	7
N. M. Lyon c Elgar b Morkel	47	– run out (Bavuma/de Kock)	0
J. R. Hazlewood c Amla b Rabada	10	– c Philander b Morkel	5
B 1, lb 5, nb 4	10	B 4	4
(69.5 overs)	255	(39.4 overs)	107

1/43 (2) 2/61 (3) 3/72 (4) 4/150 (5) 5/150 (1)
6/156 (6) 7/173 (8) 8/175 (9) 9/241 (10) 10/255 (11)

1/57 (1) 2/59 (2) 3/59 (3) 4/59 (5) 5/75 (4)
6/86 (6) 7/86 (8) 8/94 (9) 9/94 (10) 10/107 (11)

Philander 15–5–26–2; Rabada 20.5–1–91–4; Morkel 21–7–87–4; Maharaj 12–3–35–0; Bavuma 1–0–10–0. *Second innings*—Rabada 12–6–31–1; Philander 6–2–17–0; Morkel 9.4–3–23–5; Maharaj 12–2–32–2.

Umpires: R. K. Illingworth *(England)* (32) and N. J. Llong *(England)* (50).
Third umpire: I. J. Gould *(England)*.   Referee: A. J. Pycroft *(Zimbabwe)* (58).

Close of play: first day, South Africa 266–8 (Elgar 121, Rabada 6); second day, Australia 245–9 (Paine 33, Hazlewood 1); third day, South Africa 238–5 (de Villiers 51, de Kock 29).

Test No. 2300/98 (SA425, A812)

SOUTH AFRICA v AUSTRALIA 2017–18 (4th Test)

At New Wanderers, Johannesburg, on 30, 31 March, 1, 2, 3 April, 2018.
Toss: South Africa.   Result: SOUTH AFRICA WON BY 492 RUNS.
Debuts: Australia – C. J. Sayers.
Man of the Match: V. D. Philander.   Man of the Series: K. Rabada.

After the sandpaper shenanigans, a much-changed Australian side – including a pair of openers who arrived two days before the start – slipped to their second-biggest defeat by runs, behind only England's 675-run massacre at Brisbane in 1928–29. It was South Africa's first home series win over Australia since the 4–0 whitewash of 1969-70, and their biggest win by runs against anyone, surpassing 358 over New Zealand here in 2007–08. Du Plessis said he had never encountered such a docile Australian side. The Wanderers pitch was placid – the authorities were keen to avoid a repeat of the recent Test against India, when it was rated poor – and Markram cashed in with 152, on the way to completing 1,000 runs in his tenth Test, a South African record. Although du Plessis fell first ball, the last four wickets added 189, most from Bavuma, who was stranded on 95. Australia dipped to 96 for six before Paine and Cummins put on 99; Shaun Marsh did not make the most of surviving a stumping when de Kock was stung by a bee. Du Plessis ended a poor run with his eighth Test century, and declared only when the lead was past 600. Australia subsided again, with only Burns and Handscomb reaching double figures: Philander took six for three in 32 balls, including his 200th in Tests when Mitchell Marsh followed his brother back to the pavilion in the first over of the fourth day. Morkel announced his international retirement, and finished with 309 wickets in 86 Tests.

South Africa

D. Elgar c Sayers b Lyon	19	– (2) c S. E. Marsh b Lyon	81
A. K. Markram c M. R. Marsh b Cummins	152	– (1) c Handscomb b Cummins	37
H. M. Amla c Handscomb b Cummins	27	– c M. R. Marsh b Lyon	16
A. B. de Villiers c Paine b Sayers	69	– c Paine b Cummins	6
*F. du Plessis lbw b Cummins	0	– c Handscomb b Cummins	120
T. Bavuma not out	95	– not out	35
K. Rabada c Renshaw b Sayers	0		
†Q. de Kock c M. R. Marsh b Lyon	39	– (7) lbw b Cummins	4
V. D. Philander c Khawaja b Lyon	12	– (8) not out	33
K. A. Maharaj c Paine b Cummins	45		
M. Morkel c Handscomb b Cummins	0		
B 13, lb 12, w 5	30	B 4, lb 8	12
(136.5 overs)	488	(6 wkts dec, 105 overs)	344

1/53 (1) 2/142 (3) 3/247 (2) 4/247 (5) 5/299 (4)
6/299 (7) 7/384 (8) 8/412 (9) 9/488 (10) 10/488 (11)

1/54 (1) 2/79 (3) 3/94 (4)
4/264 (5) 5/266 (2) 6/273 (7)

Hazlewood 26–3–86–0; Sayers 35–9–78–2; Cummins 28.5–5–83–5; Lyon 40–3–182–3; M. R. Marsh 6–1–30–0; Renshaw 1–0–4–0. *Second innings*—Hazlewood 21–6–41–0; Sayers 14–2–68–0; Lyon 41–13–116–2; Cummins 18–5–58–4; M. R. Marsh 8–0–40–0; Renshaw 3–0–9–0.

Australia

M. T. Renshaw c de Kock b Philander	8	– lbw b Morkel	5
J. A. Burns c du Plessis b Rabada	4	– lbw b Morkel	42
U. T. Khawaja c de Kock b Philander	53	– lbw b Maharaj	7
P. S. P. Handscomb b Philander	0	– b Philander	24
S. E. Marsh c de Villiers b Maharaj	16	– c Bavuma b Philander	7
M. R. Marsh b Morkel	4	– c de Kock b Philander	0
*†T. D. Paine c Elgar b Rabada	62	– c de Kock b Philander	7
P. J. Cummins lbw b Maharaj	50	– b Philander	1
N. M. Lyon c Elgar b Rabada	8	– run out (Markram/de Kock)	9
C. J. Sayers c Amla b Maharaj	0	– c Elgar b Philander	0
J. R. Hazlewood not out	1	– not out	9
B 3, lb 9, nb 3	15	Lb 1, nb 7	8
(70 overs)	221	(46.4 overs)	119

1/10 (2) 2/34 (1) 3/38 (4) 4/90 (3) 5/96 (6)
6/96 (5) 7/195 (8) 8/206 (9) 9/207 (10) 10/221 (7)

1/21 (1) 2/34 (3) 3/68 (2) 4/88 (5) 5/88 (6)
6/95 (4) 7/99 (7) 8/100 (8) 9/100 (10) 10/119 (9)

Philander 18–8–30–3; Rabada 19–7–53–3; Morkel 12.2–3–34–1; Maharaj 20–3–92–3; Markram 0.4–0–0–0. *Second innings*—Rabada 8–3–16–0; Philander 13–5–21–6; Maharaj 13–2–47–1; Morkel 10.4–5–28–2; Markram 2–0–6–0.

Umpires: I. J. Gould *(England)* (65) and N. J. Llong *(England)* (51).
Third umpire: R. K. Illingworth *(England)*.   Referee: A. J. Pycroft *(Zimbabwe)* (59).

Close of play: first day, South Africa 313–6 (Bavuma 25, de Kock 7); second day, Australia 110–6 (Paine 5, Cummins 7); third day, South Africa 134–3 (Elgar 39, du Plessis 34); fourth day, Australia 88–3 (Handscomb 23, S. E. Marsh 7).

NEW ZEALAND v ENGLAND 2017–18 (1st Test)

At Eden Park, Auckland, on 22, 23, 24, 25, 26 March, 2018 (day/night).
Toss: New Zealand.   Result: NEW ZEALAND WON BY AN INNINGS AND 49 RUNS.
Debuts: none.
Man of the Match: T. A. Boult.

Two days after England flirted with the lowest score in Test history, the eyes of the sport were diverted by another game, half a world away, where Australia were imploding after the sandpaper incident in South Africa. The result of New Zealand's first day/night Test hardly registered, which was unfair on Kane Williamson's side. After England's appalling first innings, when they were whistled out for 58 – Boult and Southee bowled unchanged – the only question was whether rain would prevent a result. Only 23.1 overs were possible on the second day, and 17 balls on the third, a Saturday, which helped England extend the game an hour into the final session. Stokes, back after missing the Ashes tour following the Bristol nightclub incident, was one of four to pass 50, but three fell to the tireless Wagner, while Root was harried by Boult, and gloved the last ball of the fourth evening to Watling. New Zealand fielded superbly throughout, the best effort probably Williamson's stunning gully catch to dismiss Broad in the first innings, which made it 27 for nine. Moments earlier, when Ali bagged the fourth of the innings' five ducks, they were 23 for eight, in danger of undercutting New Zealand's 26 against England here in 1954–55. They did at least pass their own nadir (45 at Sydney in 1886–87) thanks to Overton and Anderson, the fourth last-wicket pair to double the score in a Test. But it was England's worst against New Zealand, below 64 at Wellington in 1977–78.

England

A. N. Cook c Latham b Boult	5	– c Watling b Boult	2
M. D. Stoneman c Watling b Southee	11	– c Boult b Wagner	55
*J. E. Root b Boult	0	– c Watling b Boult	51
D. J. Malan c Watling b Boult	2	– c Latham b Southee	23
B. A. Stokes b Boult	0	– c Southee b Wagner	66
†J. M. Bairstow c and b Southee	0	– c Williamson b Astle	26
M. M. Ali b Southee	0	– lbw b Boult	28
C. R. Woakes b Boult	5	– c Nicholls b Wagner	52
C. Overton not out	33	– lbw b Astle	3
S. C. J. Broad c Williamson b Southee	0	– not out	1
J. M. Anderson c Nicholls b Boult	1	– c Boult b Astle	1
Lb 1	1	B 8, lb 2, w 1, nb 1	12
(20.4 overs)	58	(126.1 overs)	320

1/6 (1) 2/6 (3) 3/16 (4) 4/18 (2) 5/18 (5)
6/18 (6) 7/23 (8) 8/23 (7) 9/27 (10) 10/58 (11)

1/6 (1) 2/94 (2) 3/132 (3) 4/142 (4) 5/181 (6)
6/217 (7) 7/300 (5) 8/304 (9) 9/319 (8) 10/320 (11)

Boult 10.4–3–32–6; Southee 10–3–25–4. *Second innings*—Boult 27–9–67–3; Southee 26–4–86–1; de Grandhomme 24–10–40–0; Wagner 32–11–77–3; Astle 16.1–5–39–3; Williamson 1–0–1–0.

New Zealand

J. A. Raval c Bairstow b Anderson	3
T. W. M. Latham c Woakes b Broad	26
*K. S. Williamson lbw b Anderson	102
L. R. P. L. Taylor c Woakes b Anderson	20
H. M. Nicholls not out	145
†B-J. Watling c Bairstow b Broad	31
C. de Grandhomme c Bairstow b Overton	29
T. D. Astle b Broad	18
T. G. Southee c and b Root	25
N. Wagner not out	9
B 4, lb 9, w 6	19
(8 wkts dec, 141 overs)	427

1/8 (1) 2/92 (2) 3/123 (4) 4/206 (3)
5/260 (6) 6/309 (7) 7/341 (8) 8/413 (9)

T. A. Boult did not bat.

Anderson 29–10–87–3; Broad 34–9–78–3; Overton 25–7–70–1; Woakes 33–9–107–0; Ali 17–1–59–0; Root 3–0–13–1.

Umpires: B. N. J. Oxenford *(Australia)* (47) and P. R. Reiffel *(Australia)* (36).
Third umpire: M. Erasmus *(South Africa).*   Referee: R. B. Richardson *(West Indies)* (15).

Close of play: first day, New Zealand 175–3 (Williamson 91, Nicholls 24); second day, New Zealand 229–4 (Nicholls 49, Watling 17); third day, New Zealand 233–4 (Nicholls 52, Watling 18); fourth day, England 132–3 (Malan 19).

Test No. 2302/103 (NZ426, E997)

NEW ZEALAND v ENGLAND 2017–18 (2nd Test)

At Hagley Oval, Christchurch, on 30, 31 March, 1, 2, 3 April, 2018.
Toss: New Zealand.   Result: DRAWN.
Debuts: England – M. J. Leach.
Man of the Match: T. G. Southee.   Man of the Series: T. A. Boult.

It was an unusually old-fashioned Test: just about the only controversy stemmed from the application of the bad-light regulations, and whether time should have been added at the start or end of the last day. But there were some ugly statistics for England to contemplate after only their fourth Test-series defeat by New Zealand. It was also their 13th consecutive Test overseas without a win, their longest sequence (ten of them were lost). England dominated but, needing four wickets in the final session, were thwarted by a determined New Zealand tail, and hampered by poor fielding. The recalled Sodhi (fellow leg-spinner Todd Astle was injured) did little with the ball, but batted tenaciously as New Zealand hung on. Bairstow's fifth Test hundred, and his eighth-wicket stand of 95 with Wood, who made an unexpected maiden half-century, transformed England from 164 for seven, then New Zealand pulled off a similar comeback from 36 for five, thanks to a partnership of 142 in 50 overs between Watling and de Grandhomme, before Southee spanked a quick 50. Another innings containing four half-centuries allowed Root a rare declaration, and New Zealand looked doomed when the first two balls of the final day, from Broad, accounted for Raval and Williamson. But Latham dug in for 282 minutes, and Sodhi for 200. Root finally extracted Wagner to leave New Zealand eight down… but no further play was possible. During the match Anderson overtook Courtney Walsh's record of 30,019 balls by a fast bowler in Tests.

England

A. N. Cook b Boult	2	– c Watling b Boult	14
M. D. Stoneman c Latham b Southee	35	– c Watling b Southee	60
J. M. Vince lbw b Southee	18	– c Taylor b Boult	76
*J. E. Root b Southee	37	– c Watling b Wagner	54
D. J. Malan lbw b Boult	0	– c Nicholls b de Grandhomme	53
B. A. Stokes c Watling b Boult	25	– c Raval b de Grandhomme	12
†J. M. Bairstow c Taylor b Boult	101	– c Nicholls b Wagner	36
S. C. J. Broad c Sodhi b Southee	5	– c Sodhi b de Grandhomme	12
M. A. Wood b Southee	52	– b de Grandhomme	9
M. J. Leach c Watling b Southee	16	– not out	14
J. M. Anderson not out	0		
B 9, lb 5, w 1, nb 1	16	B 4, lb 3, w 2, nb 3	12
(96.5 overs)	307	(9 wkts dec, 106.4 overs)	352

1/6 (1) 2/38 (3) 3/93 (4) 4/94 (5) 5/94 (2)   1/24 (1) 2/147 (2) 3/165 (3) 4/262 (5) 5/262 (4)
6/151 (6) 7/164 (8) 8/259 (9) 9/307 (10) 10/307 (7)   6/282 (6) 7/300 (8) 8/312 (9) 9/352 (7)

Boult 28.5–5–87–4; Southee 26–7–62–6; de Grandhomme 17–4–44–0; Wagner 20–5–69–0; Sodhi 5–0–31–0. *Second innings*—Boult 28–5–89–2; Southee 19–4–65–1; de Grandhomme 26–2–94–4; Wagner 22.4–5–51–2; Sodhi 11–0–46–0.

New Zealand

J. A. Raval c Bairstow b Anderson	5	– (2) c Stoneman b Broad	17
T. W. M. Latham c Bairstow b Broad	0	– (1) c Vince b Leach	83
*K. S. Williamson c Bairstow b Anderson	22	– c Bairstow b Broad	0
L. R. P. L. Taylor c Cook b Broad	2	– c Cook b Leach	13
H. M. Nicholls lbw b Broad	0	– c Cook b Anderson	13
†B-J. Watling b Anderson	85	– c Anderson b Wood	19
C. de Grandhomme c Bairstow b Broad	72	– c Leach b Wood	45
T. G. Southee b Anderson	50	– (10) not out	0
I. S. Sodhi c Bairstow b Broad	1	– (8) not out	56
N. Wagner not out	24	– (9) c Vince b Root	7
T. A. Boult c Malan b Broad	16		
Lb 1	1	Lb 2, nb 1	3
(93.3 overs)	278	(8 wkts, 124.4 overs)	256

1/0 (2) 2/14 (1) 3/17 (4) 4/17 (5) 5/36 (3)   1/42 (2) 2/42 (3) 3/66 (4) 4/91 (5)
6/178 (7) 7/226 (6) 8/231 (9) 9/239 (8) 10/278 (11)   5/135 (6) 6/162 (1) 7/219 (7) 8/256 (9)

Anderson 24–5–76–4; Broad 22.3–5–54–6; Wood 21–3–69–0; Leach 19–3–52–0; Root 1–0–9–0; Stokes 6–2–17–0. *Second innings*—Anderson 26–8–37–1; Broad 24–6–72–2; Wood 22–10–45–2; Leach 32–15–61–2; Root 12.4–5–28–1; Stokes 4–3–2–0; Malan 4–1–9–0.

Umpires: M. Erasmus *(South Africa)* (49) and B. N. J. Oxenford *(Australia)* (48).
Third umpire: P. R. Reiffel *(Australia)*.   Referee: R. B. Richardson *(West Indies)* (16).

Close of play: first day, England 290–8 (Bairstow 97, Leach 10); second day, New Zealand 192–6 (Watling 77, Southee 13); third day, England 202–3 (Root 30, Malan 19); fourth day, New Zealand 42–0 (Latham 25, Raval 17).

IRELAND v PAKISTAN 2018 (Only Test)

At The Village, Malahide, Dublin, on 11 *(no play)*, 12, 13, 14, 15 May, 2018.
Toss: Ireland.   Result: PAKISTAN WON BY FIVE WICKETS.
Debuts: Ireland – all except W. B. Rankin, who had previously played for England. Pakistan – Fahim Ashraf, Imam-ul-Haq.
Man of the Match: K. J. O'Brien.

On the final morning of a beguiling game, Ireland's first men's Test was shaping up as a classic. Chasing 160 after enforcing the follow-on, Pakistan were 14 for three – and if third slip Balbirnie had caught Babar Azam, with the total 60, the papers might have been full of clichés about smiling eyes. Instead, Babar restored order with Imam-ul-Haq (nephew of Inzamam, now chairman of selectors), and Pakistan wriggled free. Ireland lost the game, yet won respect after first-day rain delayed their formal coronation as the 11th Test nation. Their first Test wicket went to a man who already had one: Boyd Rankin had dismissed Peter Siddle in his lone appearance for England, at Sydney in 2013-14, and now squared up Azhar Ali. Next ball, Tim Murtagh – 36, born in Lambeth, and with 712 first-class wickets – swung one into Imam's pads. The debutant Fahim Ashraf hit 83 from No. 8 to lift Pakistan to 310, then Ireland crashed nervously to seven for four. Kevin O'Brien and Gary Wilson (who had injured his elbow in the nets) hauled them to 130, but Sarfraz Ahmed stuck them in again (the follow-on requirement was 150 as this was now a four-day game). O'Brien made a game of it with a superb century, only his second in first-class cricket. But he fell without addition on the final morning, and Pakistan needed fewer than had seemed likely. Ireland's long-serving players Ed Joyce and Niall O'Brien announced their retirements shortly after their one taste of Test cricket.

Pakistan

Azhar Ali c Porterfield b Rankin	4	– c Stirling b Murtagh	2
Imam-ul-Haq lbw b Murtagh	7	– not out	74
Haris Sohail c Porterfield b Thompson	31	– c Joyce b Rankin	7
Asad Shafiq c Balbirnie b Rankin	62	– b Murtagh	1
Babar Azam c Stirling b Murtagh	14	– run out (Balbirnie/Thompson)	59
*†Sarfraz Ahmed c Stirling b Thompson	20	– lbw b Thompson	8
Shadab Khan lbw b Murtagh	55	– not out	4
Fahim Ashraf c N. J. O'Brien b Thompson	83		
Mohammad Amir c N. J. O'Brien b Murtagh	13		
Mohammad Abbas not out	4		
Rahat Ali not out	0		
B 1, lb 10, w 2, nb 4	17	Nb 5	5
(9 wkts dec, 96 overs)	310	(5 wkts, 45 overs)	160

1/13 (1) 2/13 (2) 3/71 (3) 4/104 (5) 5/153 (4)
6/159 (6) 7/276 (7) 8/304 (8) 9/306 (9)

1/2 (1) 2/13 (3) 3/14 (4)
4/140 (5) 5/152 (6)

Murtagh 25–5–45–4; Rankin 21–3–75–2; Kane 20–2–86–0; Thompson 22–4–62–3; K. J. O'Brien 6–1–20–0; Stirling 2–0–11–0. *Second innings*—Murtagh 16–3–55–2; Rankin 12–1–57–1; Thompson 11–4–31–1; Kane 6–1–17–0.

Ireland

E. C. Joyce lbw b Mohammad Abbas	4	– run out (Fahim Ashraf)	43
*W. T. S. Porterfield b Mohammad Amir	1	– c Sarfraz Ahmed b Mohammad Amir	32
A. Balbirnie lbw b Mohammad Abbas	0	– lbw b Mohammad Abbas	0
†N. J. O'Brien lbw b Mohammad Abbas	0	– b Mohammad Amir	18
P. R. Stirling c Babar Azam b Fahim Ashraf	17	– lbw b Mohammad Abbas	11
K. J. O'Brien c Imam-ul-Haq b Mohammad Amir	40	– c Haris Sohail b Mohammad Abbas	118
S. R. Thompson b Shadab Khan	3	– (8) b Shadab Khan	53
T. E. Kane c Babar Azam b Shadab Khan	0	– (9) b Mohammad Abbas	14
G. C. Wilson not out	33	– (7) c Haris Sohail b Mohammad Amir	12
W. B. Rankin c Sarfraz Ahmed b Mohammad Abbas	17	– b Mohammad Abbas	6
T. J. Murtagh c Imam-ul-Haq b Shadab Khan	5	– not out	5
B 8, lb 1, w 1	10	B 1, lb 20, w 4, nb 2	27
(47.2 overs)	130	(129.3 overs)	339

1/5 (1) 2/5 (3) 3/5 (2) 4/7 (4) 5/36 (5) 6/61 (7)
7/61 (8) 8/73 (6) 9/107 (10) 10/130 (11)

1/69 (1) 2/69 (3) 3/94 (4) 4/95 (2) 5/127 (5)
6/157 (7) 7/271 (8) 8/321 (6) 9/332 (10) 10/339 (9)

Mohammad Amir 10–5–9–2; Mohammad Abbas 11–4–44–4; Rahat Ali 7–0–18–0; Fahim Ashraf 5–2–18–1; Shadab Khan 13.2–3–31–3; Haris Sohail 1–0–1–0. *Second innings*—Mohammad Amir 29.2–9–63–3; Mohammad Abbas 28.3–10–66–5; Rahat Ali 3–2–3–0; Fahim Ashraf 18–3–51–0; Shadab Khan 30.4–7–63–1.

Umpires: R. K. Illingworth *(England)* (33) and N. J. Llong *(England)* (52).
Third umpire: M. Hawthorne *(Ireland).*   Referee: B. C. Broad *(England)* (94).

Close of play: first day, no play; second day, Pakistan 268–6 (Shadab Khan 52, Fahim Ashraf 61); third day, Ireland 64–0 (Joyce 39, Porterfield 23); fourth day, Ireland 319–7 (K. J. O'Brien 118, Kane 8).

ENGLAND v PAKISTAN 2018 (1st Test)

At Lord's, London, on 24, 25, 26, 27 May, 2018.
Toss: England.   Result: PAKISTAN WON BY NINE WICKETS.
Debuts: England – D. M. Bess.
Man of the Match: Mohammad Abbas.

Pakistan had triumphed at Lord's in 2016, and now won again, their eighth victory in their last 11 Tests against England. The media spotlight was on Mohammad Amir, who was returning to Test cricket at the scene of his literal crime – bowling deliberate no-balls – in 2010, but he was outbowled by his opening partner. Bowling accurately and moving the ball both ways, Mohammad Abbas finished with match figures of eight for 64. Amir, though, produced a fine delivery to dismiss Cook, who made 70 as England declined to 184. Helped by several dropped catches, Pakistan surged past that on the second day, although top-scorer Babar Azam had his left arm broken during a ferocious spell from Stokes. At 19, Shadab Khan was the youngest to score a Test fifty at Lord's, apart from the West Indian Jeff Stollmeyer, who was 18 in 1939. England were 179 behind, and soon lost both openers: Cook and Stoneman averaged 18.75 together from 20 innings, the lowest for any England pair who opened together at least ten times. When Abbas trapped Root for 68, England were 110 for six, but Buttler – recalled by new chief selector Ed Smith after a prolific IPL season – and the 20-year-old debutant off-spinner Dominic Bess put on 126, which at least meant Pakistan had to bat again. But they needed only 64: Imam-ul-Haq was only the second man, after Australia's Sammy Jones in 1881–82, to be at the crease when the winning runs were hit in his first two Test matches.

England

A. N. Cook b Mohammad Amir	70	– lbw b Mohammad Abbas	1
M. D. Stoneman b Mohammad Abbas	4	– b Shadab Khan	9
*J. E. Root c Sarfraz Ahmed b Hasan Ali	4	– lbw b Mohammad Abbas	68
D. J. Malan c Sarfraz Ahmed b Hasan Ali	6	– c Sarfraz Ahmed b Mohammad Amir	12
†J. M. Bairstow b Fahim Ashraf	27	– b Mohammad Amir	0
B. A. Stokes lbw b Mohammad Abbas	38	– c sub (Fakhar Zaman) b Shadab Khan	9
J. C. Buttler c Asad Shafiq b Hasan Ali	14	– lbw b Mohammad Abbas	67
D. M. Bess c Asad Shafiq b Mohammad Abbas	5	– b Mohammad Amir	57
M. A. Wood c Mohammad Amir b Hasan Ali	7	– c Sarfraz Ahmed b Mohammad Amir	4
S. C. J. Broad lbw b Mohammad Abbas	0	– c Sarfraz Ahmed b Mohammad Abbas	0
J. M. Anderson not out	0	– not out	0
B 1, lb 6, w 1, nb 1	9	B 4, lb 9, w 2	15
(58.2 overs)	184	(82.1 overs)	242

1/12 (2) 2/33 (3) 3/43 (4) 4/100 (5) 5/149 (1)   1/1 (1) 2/31 (2) 3/91 (4) 4/91 (5) 5/104 (6)
6/168 (6) 7/168 (7) 8/180 (8) 9/180 (10) 10/184 (9)   6/110 (3) 7/236 (7) 8/241 (9) 9/242 (10) 10/242 (8)

Mohammad Amir 14–3–41–1; Mohammad Abbas 14–7–23–4; Hasan Ali 15.2–2–51–4; Fahim Ashraf 9–2–28–1; Shadab Khan 6–0–34–0. *Second innings*—Mohammad Amir 18.1–3–36–4; Mohammad Abbas 17–3–41–4; Fahim Ashraf 9–2–31–0; Hasan Ali 19–3–58–0; Shadab Khan 19–2–63–2.

Pakistan

Azhar Ali lbw b Anderson	50	– b Anderson	4
Imam-ul-Haq lbw b Broad	4	– not out	18
Haris Sohail c Bairstow b Wood	39	– not out	39
Asad Shafiq c Malan b Stokes	59		
Babar Azam retired hurt	68		
*†Sarfraz Ahmed c Wood b Stokes	9		
Shadab Khan c Bairstow b Stokes	52		
Fahim Ashraf b Anderson	37		
Mohammad Amir not out	24		
Hasan Ali c Buttler b Anderson	0		
Mohammad Abbas c Bairstow b Wood	5		
Lb 14, w 1, nb 1	16	B 3, lb 2	5
(114.3 overs)	363	(1 wkt, 12.4 overs)	66

1/12 (2) 2/87 (3) 3/119 (1) 4/203 (4) 5/227 (6)   1/12 (1)
6/318 (8) 7/332 (7) 8/337 (10) 9/363 (11)

In the first innings Babar Azam retired hurt at 246-5.

Anderson 26–6–82–3; Broad 25–9–61–1; Wood 24.3–6–74–2; Stokes 22–5–73–3; Bess 17–0–59–0. *Second innings*—Anderson 3–0–12–1; Broad 3–1–13–0; Bess 3.4–0–29–0; Wood 3–1–7–0.

Umpires: P. R. Reiffel *(Australia)* (37) and R. J. Tucker *(Australia)* (61).
Third umpire: B. N. J. Oxenford *(Australia)*.   Referee: J. J. Crowe *(New Zealand)* (88).

Close of play: first day, Pakistan 50–1 (Azhar Ali 18, Haris Sohail 21); second day, Pakistan 350–8 (Mohammad Amir 19, Mohammad Abbas 0); third day, England 235–6 (Buttler 66, Bess 55).

ENGLAND v PAKISTAN 2018 (2nd Test)

At Headingley, Leeds, on 1, 2, 3 June, 2018.
Toss: Pakistan. Result: ENGLAND WON BY AN INNINGS AND 55 RUNS.
Debuts: England – S. M. Curran. Pakistan – Usman Salahuddin.
Man of the Match: J. C. Buttler. Man of the Series: Mohammad Abbas.

From Root's sharp catch at third slip to dismiss Imam-ul-Haq off the 12th ball of the match, to the one he held to dismiss Mohammad Abbas and seal victory with over seven sessions to spare, England were as professional in Leeds as they had been pitiful at Lord's. Pakistan were duped into batting by a straw-coloured pitch and by the sun, which disappeared behind cloud straight after the toss, much to England's delight. They were tumbled out for 174, with all the wickets going to the seamers, who bowled a fuller length than usual. After a sprightly 56, Shadab Khan fell to Sam Curran, making his debut five Tests after older brother Tom's, at Melbourne; two days short of his 20th birthday, Curran was England's seventh teenage Test cricketer (Pakistan had picked 52). England were not far short of parity by the end of the first day, and defied a rain-halved second to take a lead of 189. Cook, who was playing his 154th consecutive Test, breaking Allan Border's record, was one of three men (including Bess, the nightwatchman) to make it into – but not out of – the forties, before Buttler crashed 35 from his last 11 balls to finish with 80 not out. Then the seamers weighed in again, this time helped by the off-breaks of Bess, which accounted for Imam and Pakistan's debutant Usman Salahuddin, the only two batsmen to make it past 11. Pakistan lasted less than 50 overs in both innings as England squared the series.

Pakistan

Azhar Ali lbw b Broad	2	– b Anderson	11
Imam-ul-Haq c Root b Broad	0	– lbw b Bess	34
Haris Sohail c Malan b Woakes	28	– c Bess b Anderson	8
Asad Shafiq c Cook b Woakes	27	– c Bairstow b Broad	5
Usman Salahuddin lbw b Broad	4	– c Root b Bess	33
*†Sarfraz Ahmed b Anderson	14	– lbw b Woakes	8
Shadab Khan c Jennings b Curran	56	– c Cook b Curran	4
Fahim Ashraf lbw b Anderson	0	– c Malan b Bess	3
Mohammad Amir c Bairstow b Anderson	13	– not out	7
Hasan Ali c and b Woakes	24	– c Cook b Broad	9
Mohammad Abbas not out	1	– c Root b Broad	1
Lb 5	5	B 5, lb 5, nb 1	11
(48.1 overs)	174	(46 overs)	134

1/0 (2) 2/17 (1) 3/49 (3) 4/62 (4) 5/78 (6) 6/78 (5)
7/79 (8) 8/113 (9) 9/156 (10) 10/174 (7)

1/20 (1) 2/30 (3) 3/42 (4) 4/84 (2) 5/97 (6) 6/102 (7)
7/111 (8) 8/115 (5) 9/124 (10) 10/134 (11)

Anderson 15–6–43–3; Broad 15–6–38–3; Woakes 11–1–55–3; Curran 7.1–0–33–1. *Second innings*—Anderson 10–2–35–2; Broad 12–2–28–3; Curran 7–2–10–1; Woakes 6–0–18–1; Bess 11–1–33–3.

England

A. N. Cook c Sarfraz Ahmed b Hasan Ali	46
K. K. Jennings c Sarfraz Ahmed b Fahim Ashraf	29
*J. E. Root c Sarfraz Ahmed b Mohammad Amir	45
D. M. Bess c Asad Shafiq b Shadab Khan	49
D. J. Malan c Haris Sohail b Mohammad Amir	28
†J. M. Bairstow c Sarfraz Ahmed b Fahim Ashraf	21
J. C. Buttler not out	80
C. R. Woakes c Sarfraz Ahmed b Mohammad Abbas	17
S. M. Curran c Asad Shafiq b Mohammad Abbas	20
S. C. J. Broad c Mohammad Abbas b Fahim Ashraf	2
J. M. Anderson c Haris Sohail b Hasan Ali	5
B 8, lb 13	21
(106.2 overs)	363

1/53 (2) 2/104 (1) 3/138 (3) 4/200 (5) 5/212 (4)
6/260 (6) 7/285 (8) 8/319 (9) 9/344 (10) 10/363 (11)

Mohammad Amir 23–5–72–2; Mohammad Abbas 26–8–78–2; Hasan Ali 20.2–4–82–2; Fahim Ashraf 20–4–60–3; Shadab Khan 17–2–50–1.

Umpires: B. N. J. Oxenford *(Australia)* (49) and R. J. Tucker *(Australia)* (62).
Third umpire: P. R. Reiffel *(Australia)*. Referee: J. J. Crowe *(New Zealand)* (89).

Close of play: first day, England 106–2 (Root 29, Bess 0); second day, England 302–7 (Buttler 34, Curran 16).

Test No. 2306/18 (WI531, SL270)

WEST INDIES v SRI LANKA 2018 (1st Test)

At Queen's Park Oval, Port-of-Spain, Trinidad, on 6, 7, 8, 9, 10 June, 2018.
Toss: West Indies.   Result: WEST INDIES WON BY 226 RUNS.
Debuts: none.
Man of the Match: S. O. Dowrich.

The only survivor from Sri Lanka's last Test tour of the Caribbean – early in 2008, it included their solitary win there, in Guyana – was Herath, who had gone wicketless back then. He fared a little better this time, picking up three, but could not prevent a resounding defeat that suggested West Indies – who had lost 2–0 in Sri Lanka in 2015–16 – might have turned a corner. Sri Lanka were on top as West Indies dipped to 147 for five, but Dowrich and Holder began the recovery with a stand of 90. On the second day Dowrich, who lasted eight hours, added 102 with Bishoo, who edged his 160th ball to gully, then another 75 with Roach; overall, the innings contained six contributions between 38 and 44, plus 40 extras. The pacemen soon had Sri Lanka in trouble, at 43 for four early on the third day. Chandimal and Dickwella imposed some order in a stand of 78, but poor late-order batting against a short-ball assault from Cummins saw them dismissed 229 behind. Holder declined the follow-on. After Smith was bowled twice in two deliveries by Lakmal – the first a big no-ball – West Indies relied on a sharp 88 from Powell. Kumara again proved the most potent of the visiting bowlers. Holder eventually declared, 452 ahead: despite Mendis's battling fifth Test century, Sri Lanka only made it halfway, with the last five wickets disappearing for eight against the spinners. Chandimal retired ill, suffering from heat exhaustion, on the fourth afternoon.

West Indies

K. C. Brathwaite c Dickwella b Lakmal	3	– c Dickwella b Kumara	16
D. S. Smith run out (Kumara/Dickwella)	7	– b Lakmal	20
K. O. A. Powell b Kumara	38	– c sub (J. D. F. Vandersay) b M. D. K. Perera	88
S. D. Hope c Dickwella b Kumara	44	– c Mendis b Kumara	1
R. L. Chase c Mathews b Herath	38	– b Herath	12
†S. O. Dowrich not out	125	– lbw b Kumara	13
*J. O. Holder c Dickwella b Kumara	40	– lbw b Herath	39
D. Bishoo c Silva b Lakmal	40	– not out	16
K. A. J. Roach c Chandimal b Kumara	39	– not out	11
M. L. Cummins not out	0		
B 14, lb 20, w 2, nb 4	40	B 4, lb 2, nb 1	7
(8 wkts dec, 154 overs)	414	(7 wkts dec, 72 overs)	223

1/4 (1) 2/40 (2) 3/80 (3) 4/134 (4)
5/147 (5) 6/237 (7) 7/339 (8) 8/414 (9)

1/36 (2) 2/55 (1) 3/75 (4) 4/119 (5)
5/149 (6) 6/191 (3) 7/203 (7)

S. T. Gabriel did not bat.

Lakmal 29–11–55–2; Gamage 26–6–67–0; M. D. K. Perera 35–5–84–0; Kumara 31–4–95–4; Herath 32–9–67–1; Mendis 1–0–12–0. *Second innings*—Lakmal 12–2–32–1; Gamage 15–3–43–0; Herath 24–5–52–2; Kumara 9–0–40–3; M. D. K. Perera 12–1–50–1.

Sri Lanka

B. K. G. Mendis c Holder b Gabriel	4	– c Dowrich b Gabriel	102
M. D. K. J. Perera c Chase b Roach	0	– c Smith b Gabriel	12
*L. D. Chandimal c Chase b Gabriel	44	– c Brathwaite b Chase	27
A. D. Mathews c Chase b Holder	11	– c Dowrich b Holder	31
A. R. S. Silva b Roach	5	– c and b Bishoo	14
†D. P. D. N. Dickwella run out (Brathwaite)	31	– (7) lbw b Chase	19
M. D. K. Perera c Hope b Bishoo	20	– (8) not out	3
H. M. R. K. B. Herath c sub (S. O. Hetmyer) b Cummins	5	– (9) c Hope b Bishoo	0
R. A. S. Lakmal c Bishoo b Cummins	15	– (10) c Dowrich b Chase	1
P. L. S. Gamage not out	0	– (6) lbw b Bishoo	3
C. B. R. L. S. Kumara c Dowrich b Cummins	8	– c Dowrich b Chase	0
B 8, lb 16, w 12, nb 6	42	B 3, lb 4, nb 7	14
(55.4 overs)	185	(83.2 overs)	226

1/2 (2) 2/16 (1) 3/30 (4) 4/43 (5) 5/121 (3)
6/140 (6) 7/148 (8) 8/156 (7) 9/175 (9) 10/185 (11)

1/21 (2) 2/123 (4) 3/175 (5) 4/189 (1)
5/195 (6) 6/218 (3) 7/222 (7)
8/225 (9) 9/226 (10) 10/226 (11)

In the second innings Chandimal, when 15, retired ill at 49-1 and resumed at 189-4.

Roach 10–3–34–2; Gabriel 13–0–48–2; Cummins 12.4–4–39–3; Holder 7–1–15–1; Bishoo 13–2–25–1. *Second innings*—Roach 15–3–57–0; Gabriel 15–2–52–2; Holder 14–6–24–1; Cummins 12–4–23–0; Bishoo 19–2–48–3; Chase 8.2–1–15–4.

Umpires: Aleem Dar *(Pakistan)* (118) and R. A. Kettleborough *(England)* (51).
Third umpire: I. J. Gould *(England).*   Referee: J. Srinath *(India)* (38).

Close of play: first day, West Indies 246–6 (Dowrich 46, Bishoo 0); second day, Sri Lanka 31–3 (Chandimal 3, Silva 1); third day, West Indies 131–4 (Powell 64, Dowrich 11); fourth day, Sri Lanka 176–3 (Mendis 94, Gamage 0).

WEST INDIES v SRI LANKA 2017–18 (2nd Test)

At Darren Sammy (formerly Beausejour) Stadium, Gros Islet, St Lucia, on 14, 15, 16, 17, 18 June, 2018.
Toss: Sri Lanka.   Result: DRAWN.
Debuts: Sri Lanka – C. A. K. Rajitha, M. L. Udawatte.
Man of the Match: S. T. Gabriel.

A match disrupted by rain was the setting for another ball-tampering controversy. Coming less than three months after the shenanigans in Cape Town, it gained widespread attention – though since the agent used on the ball was sugary saliva from a sweet rather than sandpaper, the offence was deemed less severe. What made the sorry business more serious, however, was the refusal of Chandimal, perpetrator as well as captain, to resume play on the third morning. All told, two hours were lost; Chandimal was banned for two Tests for his indiscretions. He had rescued his side on the first day with his 11th century, after Mahela Udawatte was superbly caught in the slips from his second ball in Test cricket; his debut came a decade after his first one-day international. The bowler was Gabriel, whose express pace ruffled the batsmen throughout; he finished with 13 for 121, West Indies' best match figures at home, beating Curtly Ambrose's 11 for 84 against England at Port-of-Spain in 1993–94. Dowrich's 55 set up a lead of 47, but a brave fourth-day display allowed Sri Lanka to escape from 48 for four. West Indies needed 296 in 85 overs on the last day, but slumped to 117 for five with the dismissal of Hope, who had resumed after being hit in the ribs; Braithwaite and Holder were hanging on when rain ended proceedings, leaving the Sri Lankans ruing those two rainless hours of inaction while their brains trust argued with the officials about the ball-tampering sanctions – which included a five-run penalty.

Sri Lanka

M. D. K. J. Perera c Holder b Roach	32	– c Dowrich b Gabriel 20
M. L. Udawatte c Holder b Gabriel	0	– c Bishoo b Roach 19
D. M. de Silva b Gabriel	12	– (4) c Smith b Gabriel 3
B. K. G. Mendis c Dowrich b Holder	45	– (5) b Gabriel 87
*L. D. Chandimal not out	119	– (6) c Dowrich b Roach 39
A. R. S. Silva c Holder b Gabriel	6	– (7) c Dowrich b Gabriel 48
†D. P. D. N. Dickwella c Hope b Gabriel	16	– (8) c Powell b Gabriel 62
A. Dananjaya c Dowrich b Roach	2	– (9) b Gabriel 23
R. A. S. Lakmal lbw b Gabriel	10	– (10) lbw b Gabriel 7
C. A. K. Rajitha c Dowrich b Roach	4	– (3) lbw b Gabriel 0
C. B. R. L. S. Kumara c Hope b Roach	0	– not out 0
B 1, lb 2, w 2, nb 2	7	B 12, lb 8, w 3, nb 11 34
(79 overs)	253	(91.4 overs) 342

1/0 (2) 2/15 (3) 3/59 (1) 4/126 (4) 5/148 (6)   1/32 (1) 2/34 (3) 3/44 (4) 4/48 (2) 5/165 (6)
6/179 (7) 7/190 (8) 8/206 (9) 9/237 (10) 10/253 (11)   6/199 (5) 7/298 (7) 8/307 (8) 9/334 (10) 10/342 (9)

Roach 18–8–49–4; Gabriel 16–4–59–5; Cummins 19–5–69–0; Holder 14–2–56–1; Bishoo 11–3–15–0; Chase 1–0–2–0.
Second innings—Roach 21–3–78–2; Gabriel 20.4–6–62–8; Holder 15–5–38–0; Cummins 13–1–44–0; Bishoo 11–0–58–0; Chase 10–1–38–0; Brathwaite 1–0–4–0.

West Indies

K. C. Brathwaite c Dickwella b Rajitha	22	– not out 59
D. S. Smith lbw b Dananjaya	61	– c de Silva b Rajitha 1
K. O. A. Powell c Mendis b Kumara	27	– c Udawatte b Rajitha 2
S. D. Hope c de Silva b Lakmal	19	– b Lakmal 39
R. L. Chase c Lakmal b Kumara	41	– b Lakmal 13
†S. O. Dowrich c Dickwella b Lakmal	55	– c de Silva b Dananjaya 8
*J. O. Holder c Dickwella b Rajitha	15	– not out 15
D. Bishoo c Mendis b Rajitha	2	
K. A. J. Roach lbw b Kumara	13	
M. L. Cummins not out	8	
S. T. Gabriel c de Silva b Kumara	3	
B 11, lb 8, w 9, nb 1, p 5	34	B 10 10
(100.3 overs)	300	(5 wkts, 60.3 overs) 147

1/59 (1) 2/115 (3) 3/149 (4) 4/163 (2) 5/241 (5)   1/6 (2) 2/8 (3) 3/55 (5) 4/64 (6) 5/117 (4)
6/254 (6) 7/261 (8) 8/279 (7) 9/292 (9) 10/300 (11)

In the second innings Hope, when 6, retired hurt at 25-2 and resumed at 64-4.

Lakmal 24–6–50–2; Dananjaya 25–7–81–1; Rajitha 22–6–49–3; Kumara 26.3–4–86–4; de Silva 3–0–10–0. *Second innings*—Lakmal 17.3–3–48–2; Rajitha 13–3–23–2; Kumara 10–3–28–0; Dananjaya 19–7–33–1; de Silva 1–0–5–0.

Umpires: Aleem Dar *(Pakistan)* (119) and I. J. Gould *(England)* (66).
Third umpire: R. A. Kettleborough *(England)*.   Referee: J. Srinath *(India)* (39).

Close of play: first day, West Indies 2–0 (Brathwaite 2, Smith 0); second day, West Indies 118–2 (Smith 53, Hope 2); third day, Sri Lanka 34–1 (Udawatte 11, Rajitha 0); fourth day, Sri Lanka 334–8 (Dananjaya 16, Lakmal 7).

Test No. 2308/20 (WI533, SL272)

WEST INDIES v SRI LANKA 2017–18 (3rd Test)

At Kensington Oval, Bridgetown, Barbados, on 23, 24, 25, 26 June, 2018 (day/night).
Toss: West Indies.   Result: SRI LANKA WON BY FOUR WICKETS.
Debuts: none.
Man of the Match: J. O. Holder.   Man of the Series: S. O. Dowrich.

West Indies began the first day/night Test in the Caribbean with hopes of their first series victory over Sri Lanka since 2003. Sri Lanka were lacking their captain, Chandimal, for disciplinary reasons after the previous match's ball-tampering controversy (Lakmal skippered for the first time instead), and several others with injuries. By contrast, West Indies fielded the same team for the third game running. But in a tense, low-scoring match on the greenest pitch seasoned observers had seen at Bridgetown, Sri Lanka became the first Asian team to win a Test there. Twenty wickets went down on the third day, a West Indian record. West Indies hit early trouble against the pink ball at eight for three, and reached 204 thanks to local boys Dowrich and Holder, who put on 115. Holder then took four wickets – he ended with match figures of nine for 60 – as Sri Lanka also struggled, initially under the lights. West Indies led by 50 – but that counted for little when they crumbled for 93, their lowest in Barbados and third-lowest anywhere at home. Sri Lanka needed 144 for their second Test victory in the Caribbean, but looked doomed at 81 for six early on the fourth morning before Dilruwan and Kusal Perera (batting down the order after being taken to hospital following a collision with an advertising board the previous evening) inched them home. West Indies lost only three Tests in Barbados in the 20th century, but had now tasted defeat in nine in the 21st.

West Indies

Batsman	1st innings		2nd innings	
K. C. Brathwaite c Gunathilleke b Lakmal	2	–	c Udawatte b Lakmal	2
D. S. Smith c de Silva b Lakmal	2	–	b Lakmal	0
K. O. A. Powell c Mendis b Kumara	4	–	c Dickwella b Kumara	7
S. D. Hope c Mendis b Rajitha	11	–	b Kumara	0
R. L. Chase b Rajitha	14	–	c M. D. K. J. Perera b Lakmal	5
†S. O. Dowrich lbw b Kumara	71	–	c Lakmal b Rajitha	16
*J. O. Holder c M. D. K. Perera b Rajitha	74	–	c Mendis b Rajitha	15
D. Bishoo c Mendis b Kumara	0	–	b Rajitha	0
K. A. J. Roach not out	11	–	not out	23
M. L. Cummins c Mendis b M. D. K. Perera	2	–	c de Silva b M. D. K. Perera	14
S. T. Gabriel c Dickwella b Kumara	2	–	run out (Rajitha/Dickwella)	6
B 4, lb 6, w 1	11		Lb 4, w 1	5
(69.3 overs)	204		(31.2 overs)	93

1/3 (2) 2/8 (1) 3/8 (3) 4/24 (5) 5/53 (4) 6/168 (6)
7/183 (8) 8/189 (7) 9/201 (10) 10/204 (11)

1/1 (2) 2/8 (1) 3/9 (4) 4/14 (5) 5/14 (3) 6/41 (6)
7/41 (8) 8/56 (7) 9/82 (10) 10/93 (11)

Lakmal 19–5–52–2; Kumara 23.3–5–58–4; Rajitha 17–1–68–3; M. D. K. Perera 10–3–16–1. *Second innings*—Lakmal 11.3–3–25–3; Kumara 8.2–1–31–2; Rajitha 8–1–20–3; M. D. K. Perera 3.3–0–13–1.

Sri Lanka

Batsman	1st innings		2nd innings	
M. D. K. J. Perera c Dowrich b Roach	0	–	(8) not out	28
M. L. Udawatte lbw b Roach	4	–	lbw b Roach	0
M. D. Gunathilleke lbw b Holder	29	–	(1) c Bishoo b Holder	21
B. K. G. Mendis b Gabriel	22	–	lbw b Holder	25
D. M. de Silva lbw b Gabriel	8	–	(3) b Holder	17
A. R. S. Silva c Dowrich b Gabriel	11	–	(5) c Smith b Holder	1
†D. P. D. N. Dickwella c Smith b Holder	42	–	(6) b Holder	6
M. D. K. Perera not out	11	–	(7) not out	23
*R. A. S. Lakmal c sub (K. M. A. Paul) b Holder	0			
C. A. K. Rajitha b Holder	0			
C. B. R. L. S. Kumara run out (Holder)	0			
B 9, lb 14, w 1, nb 3	27		B 8, lb 15	23
(59 overs)	154		(6 wkts, 40.2 overs)	144

1/0 (1) 2/16 (2) 3/75 (4) 4/81 (3) 5/85 (5) 6/118 (6)
7/147 (7) 8/147 (9) 9/150 (10) 10/154 (11)

1/9 (2) 2/30 (1) 3/48 (3)
4/50 (5) 5/74 (6) 6/81 (4)

Roach 12–5–30–2; Gabriel 15–2–52–3; Cummins 15–6–29–0; Holder 16–8–19–4; Bishoo 1–0–1–0. *Second innings*— Roach 10–1–33–1; Gabriel 9–1–26–0; Holder 14.2–4–41–5; Cummins 6–1–17–0; Bishoo 1–0–4–0.

Umpires: I. J. Gould *(England)* (67) and R. A. Kettleborough *(England)* (52).
Third umpire: Aleem Dar *(Pakistan)*.   Referee: J. Srinath *(India)* (40).

Close of play: first day, West Indies 132–5 (Dowrich 60, Holder 33); second day, Sri Lanka 99–5 (Silva 3, Dickwella 13); third day, Sri Lanka 81–5 (Mendis 25, M. D. K. Perera 1).

Test No. 2309/1 (I522, Afg1)

INDIA v AFGHANISTAN 2018 (Only Test)

At M. Chinnaswamy Stadium, Bangalore, on 14, 15, June, 2018.
Toss: India.   Result: INDIA WON BY AN INNINGS AND 262 RUNS.
Debuts: Afghanistan – all *(Asghar Stanikzai later changed his name to Asghar Afghan)*.
Man of the Match: S. Dhawan.

When he walked out for the toss in his baggy scarlet cap and immaculate whites, Asghar Stanikzai, the captain of the 12th Test nation, looked more like a film star than a cricketer. He outshone Rahane, leading a country that had already played 521 Tests (Virat Kohli had a neck injury). But the actual difference between the two sides was soon painfully obvious. Dhawan became only the sixth to score a century before lunch on the first day of a Test, as India's openers piled on 168. Next morning Pandya added 71 as Afghanistan's vaunted spinners – Rashid Khan, rated the world's best Twenty20 bowler, and Mujeeb Zadran, two years younger at 17 and the sixth to make his first-class debut in a Test since 1900 – toiled away as India reached 474. Afghanistan started batting after lunch – and lost all 20 wickets before the close, only the fourth time a team had been bowled out twice in a day (also India at Old Trafford in 1952, and Zimbabwe against New Zealand, at Harare in 2005–06 and Napier in 2011–12). This was India's biggest innings win, and the subcontinent's first two-day Test. No day's play had featured as many wickets as the 24 that fell on the second day here since 1901–02, when 25 tumbled in an Ashes Test at Melbourne. It was a shame, the match should not have been about numbers. It should have been about how Afghanistan transcended bullets and bombs to collect runs and wickets. This was a fairytale without a happy ending.

India

M. Vijay lbw b Wafadar Momand	105
S. Dhawan c Mohammad Nabi b Yamin Ahmadzai	107
K. L. Rahul b Yamin Ahmadzai	54
C. A. Pujara c Mohammad Nabi b Mujeeb Zadran	35
*A. M. Rahane lbw b Rashid Khan	10
†K. D. Karthik run out (sub [Nasir Ahmadzai]/Afsar Zazai)	4
H. H. Pandya c Afsar Zazai b Wafadar Momand	71
R. Ashwin c Afsar Zazai b Yamin Ahmadzai	18
R. A. Jadeja c Rahmat Shah b Mohammad Nabi	20
I. Sharma lbw b Rashid Khan	8
U. T. Yadav not out	26
B 1, lb 12, w 2, nb 1	16
(104.5 overs)	474

1/168 (2) 2/280 (1) 3/284 (3) 4/318 (5) 5/328 (4) 6/334 (6)
7/369 (8) 8/436 (9) 9/440 (7) 10/474 (10)

Yamin Ahmadzai 19–7–51–3; Wafadar Momand 21–5–100–2; Mohammad Nabi 13–0–65–1; Rashid Khan 34.5–2–154–2; Mujeeb Zadran 15–1–75–1; Asghar Stanikzai 2–0–16–0.

Afghanistan

Mohammad Shahzad run out (Pandya)	14	– c Karthik b Yadav	13
Javed Ahmadi b Sharma	1	– c Dhawan b Yadav	3
Rahmat Shah lbw b Yadav	14	– c Rahane b Sharma	4
†Afsar Zazai b Sharma	6	– (7) b Jadeja	1
Hashmatullah Shahidi lbw b Ashwin	11	– not out	36
*Asghar Stanikzai b Ashwin	11	– c Dhawan b Jadeja	25
Mohammad Nabi c Sharma b Ashwin	24	– (4) lbw b Yadav	0
Rashid Khan c Yadav b Jadeja	7	– b Jadeja	12
Yamin Ahmadzai c Jadeja b Ashwin	0	– b Sharma	1
Mujeeb Zadran st Karthik b Jadeja	15	– c Yadav b Jadeja	3
Wafadar Momand not out	6	– b Ashwin	0
		B 4, lb 1	5
(27.5 overs)	109	(38.4 overs)	103

1/15 (1) 2/21 (2) 3/35 (3) 4/35 (4) 5/50 (6)   1/19 (1) 2/22 (2) 3/22 (4) 4/24 (3) 5/61 (6)
6/59 (5) 7/78 (8) 8/87 (9) 9/88 (7) 10/109 (10)   6/62 (7) 7/82 (8) 8/85 (9) 9/98 (10) 10/103 (11)

Yadav 6–1–18–1; Sharma 5–0–28–2; Pandya 5–0–18–0; Ashwin 8–1–27–4; Jadeja 3.5–1–18–2. *Second innings*—Sharma 7–2–17–2; Yadav 7–1–26–3; Pandya 4–2–6–0; Ashwin 11.4–3–32–1; Jadeja 9–3–17–4.

Umpires: C. B. Gaffaney *(New Zealand)* (20) and P. R. Reiffel *(Australia)* (38).
Third umpire: R. J. Tucker *(Australia)*.   Referee: A. J. Pycroft *(Zimbabwe)* (60).

Close of play: first day, India 347–6 (Pandya 10, Ashwin 7).

WEST INDIES v BANGLADESH 2018 (1st Test)

At Sir Vivian Richards Stadium, North Sound, Antigua, on 4, 5, 6 July, 2018.
Toss: West Indies.   Result: WEST INDIES WON BY AN INNINGS AND 219 RUNS.
Debuts: Bangladesh – Abu Jayed.
Man of the Match: K. A. J. Roach.

This match was settled in the first nine overs, when Bangladesh staggered to 18 for five. Kemar Roach took all five in 12 balls, a feat matched only by Monty Noble, for Australia against England at Melbourne in 1901-02, and Jacques Kallis, for South Africa against Bangladesh at Potchefstroom in 2002-03. Roach probed away at off stump despite a hamstring strain, and his spell included four for none in six balls. Cummins and Holder ensured there was no recovery. Only Liton Das reached double figures, and made 58% of the total, a national record. Bangladesh's 43, from just 18.4 overs, was their lowest Test score, behind 62 against Sri Lanka in Colombo 2007, and the lowest against West Indies, undercutting England's 46 at Port-of-Spain in 1993–94. It was also the lowest by anyone since India's 42 at Lord's in 1974. West Indies were soon in front, and 158 ahead by stumps. Next morning Brathwaite completed a century, and Hope made a stylish 67 before becoming one of three victims for the debutant seamer Abu Jayed. Bangladesh crashed again to 50 for six – Tamim Iqbal fell shortly after passing 4,000 runs – but narrowly avoided a two-day defeat, wicketkeeper Nurul Hasan spanking a maiden half-century from 36 balls, but it was all over early on the third morning. Only five teams – none since India at Old Trafford in 1952 – had faced fewer balls in a completed Test. It was the first time in 2,310 Tests that four bowlers from one side all finished with five wickets.

Bangladesh

Tamim Iqbal c Dowrich b Roach	4	– c Hope b Gabriel	13
Liton Das c Chase b Cummins	25	– c Brathwaite b Holder	2
Mominul Haque c Hope b Roach	1	– b Gabriel	0
Mushfiqur Rahim lbw b Roach	0	– b Gabriel	8
*Shakib Al Hasan c Holder b Roach	0	– c Holder b Gabriel	12
Mahmudullah c Dowrich b Roach	0	– c Chase b Holder	15
†Nurul Hasan c Holder b Cummins	4	– (8) c and b Cummins	64
Mehedi Hasan c Smith b Cummins	1	– (7) c Dowrich b Holder	2
Kamrul Islam c Dowrich b Holder	0	– b Gabriel	7
Rubel Hossain not out	6	– b Cummins	16
Abu Jayed b Holder	2	– not out	0
B 1, w 3, nb 1			5
(18.4 overs)	43	(40.2 overs)	144

1/10 (1) 2/16 (3) 3/18 (4) 4/18 (5) 5/18 (6)   1/14 (1) 2/14 (3) 3/16 (2) 4/36 (4) 5/43 (5)
6/34 (2) 7/34 (7) 8/35 (8) 9/35 (9) 10/43 (11)   6/50 (7) 7/63 (6) 8/88 (9) 9/143 (8) 10/144 (10)

Roach 5–1–8–5; Gabriel 5–0–14–0; Holder 4.4–0–10–2; Cummins 4–2–11–3. *Second innings*—Holder 15–3–30–3; Gabriel 12–3–77–5; Cummins 7.2–2–16–2; Bishoo 5–1–16–0; Chase 1–0–4–0.

West Indies

K. C. Brathwaite c Mehedi Hasan b Shaki b Al Hasan	121
D. S. Smith c Nurul Hasan b Abu Jayed	58
K. O. A. Powell c Liton Das b Mahmudullah	48
D. Bishoo b Kamrul Islam	19
S. D. Hope c Tamim Iqbal b Abu Jayed	67
R. L. Chase lbw b Mehedi Hasan	2
†S. O. Dowrich c Liton Das b Shakib Al Hasan	4
*J. O. Holder c Liton Das b Mehedi Hasan	33
K. A. J. Roach lbw b Mehedi Hasan	33
M. L. Cummins not out	1
S. T. Gabriel c Shakib Al Hasan b Abu Jayed	5
B 3, lb 8, w 3, nb 1	15
(137.3 overs)	406

1/113 (2) 2/194 (3) 3/246 (4) 4/272 (1) 5/281 (6)
6/288 (7) 7/338 (8) 8/394 (9) 9/400 (5) 10/406 (11)

Abu Jayed 26.3–7–84–3; Rubel Hossain 17–3–44–0; Kamrul Islam 20–3–69–1; Shakib Al Hasan 27–2–71–2; Mehedi Hasan 34–6–101–3; Mahmudullah 11–1–18–1; Mominul Haque 2–0–8–0.

Umpires: R. K. Illingworth *(England)* (34) and R. A. Kettleborough *(England)* (53).
Third umpire: S. Ravi *(India)*.   Referee: B. C. Broad *(England)* (95).

Close of play: first day, West Indies 201-2 (Brathwaite 88, Bishoo 1); second day, Bangladesh 62-6 (Mahmudullah 15, Nurul Hasan 7).

WEST INDIES v BANGLADESH 2018 (2nd Test)

At Sabina Park, Kingston, Jamaica, on 12, 13, 14 July, 2018.
Toss: Bangladesh. Result: WEST INDIES WON BY 166 RUNS.
Debuts: West Indies – K. M. A. Paul.
Man of the Match: J. O. Holder. Man of the Series: J. O. Holder.

West Indies survived a second-innings scare to secure the series, with another three-day victory built on a resolute century by Brathwaite and an incisive display by the seamers. Holder provided the cutting edge with 11 for 103, West Indies' seventh-best match figures. Bangladesh's spinners glimpsed an opening at 138 for three on the first day, but the unflappable Brathwaite put on 109 with Hetmyer, who seemed set for a maiden Test century next morning – but he feathered a catch to provoke a flurry of wickets before Holder hit out, with last man Gabriel, to take the total past 350. Off-spinner Mehedi Hasan took five for 93. Gabriel struck two early blows and, although the third-wicket pair added 59, Keemo Paul claimed a notable first Test wicket by knocking back Tamim Iqbal's off stump after Holder – who snuffed out any hopes of a recovery with superb spells either side of tea – castled Shakib Al Hasan. Holder waived the follow-on, but might have harboured doubts as the spinners reduced his side to 64 for five; it needed 32 from Chase to take them into three figures, but 129 was still comfortably West Indies' lowest total against Bangladesh, while Shakib's six for 33 were his country's best overseas figures. But a target of 335 was too steep. Holder claimed a career-best six for 59, all bowled or lbw, including. the key wickets of Tamim (for a duck), Shakib (a defiant 54), and Mushfiqur Rahim who, in his 62nd Test, had become Bangladesh's most-capped player.

West Indies

K. C. Brathwaite c Taijul Islam b Mehedi Hasan	110	– b Shakib Al Hasan	8
D. S. Smith c Mominul Haque b Mehedi Hasan	2	– st Nurul Hasan b Shakib Al Hasan	16
K. O. A. Powell lbw b Mehedi Hasan	29	– (4) lbw b Shakib Al Hasan	18
S. D. Hope c Nurul Hasan b Taijul Islam	29	– (5) lbw b Taijul Islam	4
S. O. Hetmyer c Nurul Hasan b Abu Jayed	86	– (6) lbw b Abu Jayed	18
R. L. Chase lbw b Abu Jayed	20	– (7) b Mehedi Hasan	32
†S. O. Dowrich c Mehedi Hasan b Taijul Islam	6	– (8) not out	12
*J. O. Holder not out	33	– (9) st Nurul Hasan b Mehedi Hasan	1
K. M. A. Paul c Mominul Haque b Mehedi Hasan	0	– (3) st Nurul Hasan b Shakib Al Hasan	13
M. L. Cummins lbw b Mehedi Hasan	0	– b Shakib Al Hasan	1
S. T. Gabriel b Abu Jayed	12	– b Shakib Al Hasan	0
B 20, lb 7	27	B 1, lb 2, w 1, nb 2	6
(112 overs)	354	(45 overs)	129

1/9 (2) 2/59 (3) 3/138 (4) 4/247 (1) 5/297 (5)   1/19 (1) 2/28 (2) 3/53 (3) 4/60 (4) 5/64 (5)
6/302 (6) 7/318 (7) 8/319 (9) 9/319 (10) 10/354 (11)   6/97 (6) 7/122 (7) 8/124 (9) 9/129 (10) 10/129 (11)

Abu Jayed 18–7–38–3; Shakib Al Hasan 22–3–60–0; Mehedi Hasan 29–9–93–5; Taijul Islam 25–4–82–2; Kamrul Islam 10–1–34–0; Mahmudullah 8–1–20–0. *Second innings*—Abu Jayed 8–1–21–1; Mehedi Hasan 11–2–45–2; Kamrul Islam 2–0–3–0; Shakib Al Hasan 17–5–33–6; Taijul Islam 7–0–24–1.

Bangladesh

Tamim Iqbal b Paul	47	– lbw b Holder	0
Liton Das lbw b Gabriel	12	– c Hope b Paul	33
Mominul Haque c Hope b Gabriel	0	– lbw b Chase	15
*Shakib Al Hasan b Holder	32	– b Holder	54
Mahmudullah lbw b Holder	0	– c Hope b Chase	4
Mushfiqur Rahim c Hope b Holder	24	– b Holder	31
†Nurul Hasan lbw b Paul	0	– lbw b Holder	0
Mehedi Hasan lbw b Cummins	3	– c Smith b Gabriel	10
Taijul Islam b Holder	18	– not out	13
Kamrul Islam not out	0	– lbw b Holder	0
Abu Jayed b Holder	0	– b Holder	0
Lb 5, nb 8	13	B 4, lb 2, nb 2	8
(46.1 overs)	149	(42 overs)	168

1/20 (2) 2/20 (3) 3/79 (4) 4/79 (5) 5/117 (1)   1/2 (1) 2/40 (2) 3/52 (3) 4/67 (5) 5/121 (6) 6/121 (7)
6/117 (7) 7/128 (6) 8/135 (8) 9/149 (9) 10/149 (11)   7/138 (8) 8/162 (4) 9/168 (10) 10/168 (11)

Gabriel 10–3–19–2; Paul 9–2–25–2; Cummins 9–1–34–1; Holder 10.1–1–44–5; Chase 8–0–22–0. *Second innings*—Holder 13–3–59–6; Gabriel 9–2–29–1; Paul 7–0–34–1; Cummins 5–1–20–0; Chase 8–4–20–2.

Umpires: R. K. Illingworth *(England)* (35) and S. Ravi *(India)* (27).
Third umpire: R. A. Kettleborough *(England)*.   Referee: B. C. Broad *(England)* (96).

Close of play: first day, West Indies 295–4 (Hetmyer 84, Chase 16); second day, West Indies 19–1 (Smith 8, Paul 0).

Test No. 2312/26 (SL273, SA426)

SRI LANKA v SOUTH AFRICA 2018 (1st Test)

At Galle International Stadium on 12, 13, 14 July, 2018.
Toss: Sri Lanka. Result: SRI LANKA WON BY 278 RUNS.
Debuts: none.
Man of the Match: F. D. M. Karunaratne.

In South Africa's previous Test at Galle, in 2014, centuries from Dean Elgar and J-P. Duminy set up a comfortable victory. But now many of the same batsmen were stiff and jerky, like puppets. And it was the Sri Lankan spinners – led by Perera, with ten for 78 – who were pulling the strings. With the bat, Karunaratne became the fourth Sri Lankan to carry his bat in a Test, following Sidath Wettimuny, Marvan Atapattu and Russel Arnold, and finished with a superb 158 out of 287. Neither Steyn nor Rabada – two notable movers of the old ball in the past – could get the thing to reverse. While South Africa's seamers sent down 35 overs in the first innings, Lakmal gave himself only 4.3 in the match – but still took three cheap wickets to polish off South Africa's disappointing first innings. He was captaining because Dinesh Chandimal was serving a suspension for ball-tampering in the Caribbean. South Africa were demolished for 126, despite du Plessis and Philander sharing a seventh-wicket stand of 64. Then Karunaratne sparkled once more, again without much support: Maharaj took four wickets and Rabada three, including his 150th in Tests. South Africa needed 352 on a spinners' paradise, a tough task – but no one was prepared for what followed. Both openers were stumped – a first for South Africa in a Test – and no one reached 23 or lasted more than 50 balls. Within 29 overs they were all out for 73, their lowest total since 1956–57.

Sri Lanka

M. D. Gunathilleke c de Kock b Rabada.............................	26	– c Rabada b Maharaj	17
F. D. M. Karunaratne not out	158	– c Amla b Rabada	60
D. M. de Silva b Shamsi	11	– b Maharaj	9
B. K. G. Mendis c Rabada b Steyn.....................................	24	– lbw b Maharaj	0
A. D. Mathews c de Kock b Rabada	1	– b Maharaj	35
A. R. S. Silva c Markram b Rabada	0	– run out (Rabada)	13
†D. P. D. N. Dickwella c Amla b Shamsi	18	– c de Kock b Rabada	9
M. D. K. Perera c de Kock b Philander	1	– lbw b Rabada	2
H. M. R. K. B. Herath run out (Philander/de Kock)	1	– (10) lbw b Shamsi	0
*R. A. S. Lakmal c de Kock b Rabada...............................	10	– (9) not out	33
P. A. D. L. R. Sandakan st de Kock b Shamsi	25	– c Bavuma b Steyn	6
B 7, lb 1, w 2, nb 2	12	B 2, lb 4	6
(78.4 overs)	287	(57.4 overs)	190

1/44 (1) 2/70 (3) 3/115 (4) 4/119 (5) 5/119 (6)
6/161 (7) 7/164 (8) 8/176 (9) 9/224 (10) 10/287 (11)

1/51 (1) 2/64 (3) 3/64 (4) 4/92 (2) 5/117 (6)
6/132 (7) 7/134 (8) 8/156 (5) 9/163 (10) 10/190 (11)

Philander 8–1–28–1; Steyn 13–0–54–1; Rabada 14–1–50–4; Maharaj 17–3–49–0; Shamsi 25.4–2–91–3; Elgar 1–0–7–0.
Second innings—Rabada 12–0–44–3; Steyn 11.4–1–35–1; Maharaj 20–5–58–4; Shamsi 11–0–37–1; Philander 3–0–10–0.

South Africa

D. Elgar c Mathews b Perera	8	– (2) st Dickwella b Perera	4
A. K. Markram c Mathews b Herath	0	– (1) st Dickwella b Herath	19
K. A. Maharaj lbw b Herath	3	– (8) c Sandakan b Perera	9
H. M. Amla c Mendis b Perera	15	– (3) c de Silva b Perera	0
T. Bavuma b Sandakan..	17	– (4) c de Silva b Perera	2
*F. du Plessis b Lakmal	49	– (5) c Mathews b Herath	1
†Q. de Kock b Perera	3	– (6) lbw b Perera	10
V. D. Philander lbw b Perera	18	– (7) not out	22
K. Rabada b Lakmal	2	– b Perera	0
D. W. Steyn c Mathews b Lakmal	8	– c and b Herath	2
T. Shamsi not out...	0	– lbw b Sandakan	2
B 2, nb 1	3	B 2	2
(54.3 overs)	126	(28.5 overs)	73

1/1 (2) 2/9 (3) 3/13 (1) 4/40 (4) 5/48 (5) 6/51 (7)
7/115 (8) 8/115 (6) 9/123 (9) 10/126 (10)

1/12 (2) 2/16 (3) 3/24 (2) 4/25 (5) 5/32 (1)
6/36 (6) 7/58 (8) 8/58 (9) 9/67 (10) 10/73 (11)

Herath 19–5–39–2; Perera 23–8–46–4; Sandakan 8–1–18–1; Lakmal 4.3–0–21–3. *Second innings*—Herath 14–4–38–3; Perera 14–4–32–6; Sandakan 0.5–0–1–1.

Umpires: P. R. Reiffel *(Australia)* (39) and R. J. Tucker *(Australia)* (63).
Third umpire: N. J. Llong *(England)*. Referee: R. B. Richardson *(West Indies)* (17).

Close of play: first day, South Africa 4–1 (Elgar 4, Maharaj 0); second day, Sri Lanka 111–4 (Mathews 14, Silva 10).

Test No. 2313/27 (SL274, SA427)

SRI LANKA v SOUTH AFRICA 2018 (2nd Test)

At Sinhalese Sports Club, Colombo, on 20, 21, 22, 23 July, 2018.
Toss: Sri Lanka. Result: SRI LANKA WON BY 199 RUNS.
Debuts: none.
Man of the Match: F. D. M. Karunaratne. Man of the Series: F. D. M. Karunaratne.

Sri Lanka romped to a 2–0 win, helped by a tactical blunder from South Africa, who chose only one spinner on a pitch that neutered the seamers. Maharaj, their slow left-armer, made the best of a bad situation by claiming South Africa's second-best figures, after off-spinner Hugh Tayfield's nine for 121 against England at Johannesburg in 1956–57. He was only the fifth bowler to take nine in the opening innings of any Test, following Subhash Gupte, Richard Hadlee, Abdul Qadir and Muttiah Muralitharan. Sri Lanka's openers put on 116, but Maharaj kept the scoring within bounds, at least until Dananjaya and Herath's feisty last-wicket partnership of 74. South Africa were soon 15 for three: du Plessis tried to counter-attack, hitting 48 from 51 balls, but of the rest only de Kock passed 20. South Africa subsided for 124, taking their series aggregate to 323 for 30. Dananjaya, in his first home Test, collected five wickets, and Perera four. With over three days left, Lakmal waived the follow-on, and the lead stretched to 489. Maharaj plugged away, bowling throughout save for a change of ends, and finished with South Africa's best match figures in Asia. The task was impossible, but at last the visiting batsmen showed some fight. De Bruyn, with a highest score of 48 from five Tests, seemed too high at No. 3, but applied himself to make a maiden Test century. The last rites were administered by Herath, whose six for 98 was his 34th five-for in his 92nd Test.

Sri Lanka

M. D. Gunathilleke c Rabada b Maharaj	57	– c Elgar b Maharaj	61
F. D. M. Karunaratne c de Kock b Maharaj	53	– c de Kock b Ngidi	85
D. M. de Silva lbw b Maharaj	60	– lbw b Maharaj	0
B. K. G. Mendis c Rabada b Maharaj	21	– run out (Markram/de Kock)	18
A. D. Mathews c du Plessis b Maharaj	10	– c du Plessis b Maharaj	71
A. R. S. Silva b Rabada	22	– not out	32
†D. P. D. N. Dickwella c du Plessis b Maharaj	5	– not out	7
M. D. K. Perera c Ngidi b Maharaj	17		
A. Dananjaya not out	43		
*R. A. S. Lakmal c Markram b Maharaj	0		
H. M. R. K. B. Herath c Elgar b Maharaj	35		
B 4, lb 2, w 8, nb 1	15	Nb 1	1
(104.1 overs)	338	(5 wkts dec, 81 overs)	275

1/116 (2) 2/117 (1) 3/153 (4) 4/169 (5) 5/223 (6)
6/238 (7) 7/247 (3) 8/264 (8) 9/264 (10) 10/338 (11)

1/91 (1) 2/102 (3) 3/136 (4)
4/199 (2) 5/263 (5)

Steyn 17–3–60–0; Rabada 20–3–55–1; Ngidi 14.2–1–54–0; Maharaj 41.1–10–129–9; Markram 8.4–1–24–0; Elgar 3–1–10–0. Second innings—Maharaj 40–4–154–3; Rabada 8–0–42–0; Markram 7–1–18–0; de Bruyn 5–0–20–0; Steyn 11–2–30–0; Ngidi 9–5–9–1; Elgar 1–0–2–0.

South Africa

A. K. Markram lbw b Herath	7	– (2) lbw b Herath	14
D. Elgar c de Silva b Dananjaya	0	– (1) lbw b Perera	37
T. B. de Bruyn c Dickwella b Dananjaya	3	– b Herath	101
H. M. Amla c Mendis b Perera	19	– b Herath	6
*F. du Plessis c Dickwella b Perera	48	– c Mathews b Dananjaya	7
T. Bavuma c Mendis b Perera	11	– (7) c Dickwella b Herath	63
†Q. de Kock lbw b Dananjaya	32	– (8) lbw b Herath	8
K. A. Maharaj c Karunaratne b Dananjaya	2	– (6) lbw b Dananjaya	0
K. Rabada c Mathews b Perera	1	– c Mathews b Perera	18
D. W. Steyn lbw b Dananjaya	0	– c Gunathilleke b Herath	6
L. T. Ngidi not out	0	– not out	4
Nb 1	1	B 16, lb 5, w 1, nb 4	26
(34.5 overs)	124	(86.5 overs)	290

1/4 (2) 2/8 (3) 3/15 (1) 4/70 (4) 5/85 (5)
6/114 (6) 7/119 (8) 8/124 (7) 9/124 (10) 10/124 (9)

1/23 (2) 2/80 (1) 3/100 (4) 4/113 (5) 5/113 (6)
6/236 (7) 7/246 (8) 8/280 (3) 9/280 (9) 10/290 (10)

Perera 12.5–1–40–4; Dananjaya 13–2–52–5; Herath 9–1–32–1. Second innings—Herath 32.5–5–98–6; Perera 30–4–90–2; Dananjaya 19–2–67–2; Lakmal 2–0–8–0; de Silva 2–0–5–0; Gunathilleke 1–0–1–0.

Umpires: N. J. Llong *(England)* (53) and R. J. Tucker *(Australia)* (64).
Third umpire: P. R. Reiffel *(Australia)*. Referee: R. B. Richardson *(West Indies)* (18).

Close of play: first day, Sri Lanka 277–9 (Dananjaya 16, Herath 5); second day, Sri Lanka 151–3 (Karunaratne 59, Mathews 12); third day, South Africa 139–5 (de Bruyn 45, T. Bavuma 14).

ENGLAND v INDIA 2018 (1st Test)

At Edgbaston, Birmingham, on 1, 2, 3, 4 August, 2018.
Toss: England.　　　Result: ENGLAND WON BY 31 RUNS.
Debuts: none.
Man of the Match: S. M. Curran.

Fittingly, England's 1,000th Test was a nerve-jangler. Each side dropped important catches, and England's first-innings 287 was the highest total; for India, only Kohli passed 31. Yet his brilliance – he scored 48% of their runs off the bat – the effervescence of Curran, and the nonstop swing of the pendulum contributed to Edgbaston's best game since the 2005 Ashes. Root was only confident of victory when, with India needing 53 more on a taut fourth morning, Kohli fell to a reviewed lbw, after amassing 200 runs in the match. England soon wrapped up their 358th victory, to go with 297 defeats and 345 draws. A century partnership between Root (who passed 6,000 Test runs, but was run out by Kohli's direct hit from midwicket) and Bairstow underpinned England's first-day effort, in which the canny Ashwin took four wickets. India's reply was all about one man: no one else passed 22 as, dropped twice by Malan at second slip, Kohli dragged them almost level; Yadav contributed a single to a tenth-wicket stand of 57. Curran took three wickets in eight balls, while Stokes's four included his 100th in Tests (Karthik). Ashwin and Sharma then reduced England to 87 for seven – only 100 ahead – including Cook, bowled twice in a Test for the first time. But 20-year-old Curran cracked a brisk 63, reaching his maiden Test half-century with a six off Sharma, and India needed 194. Rashid returned to Test cricket after 20 months, despite having declined to play four-day cricket for Yorkshire.

England

A. N. Cook b Ashwin	13	– b Ashwin		0
K. K. Jennings b Mohammed Shami	42	– c Rahul b Ashwin		8
*J. E. Root run out (Kohli)	80	– c Rahul b Ashwin		14
D. J. Malan lbw b Mohammed Shami	8	– c Rahane b Sharma		20
†J. M. Bairstow b Yadav	70	– c Dhawan b Sharma		28
B. A. Stokes c and b Ashwin	21	– c Kohli b Sharma		6
J. C. Buttler lbw b Ashwin	0	– c Karthik b Sharma		1
S. M. Curran c Karthik b Mohammed Shami	24	– c Karthik b Yadav		63
A. U. Rashid lbw b Sharma	13	– b Yadav		16
S. C. J. Broad lbw b Ashwin	1	– c Dhawan b Sharma		11
J. M. Anderson not out	2	– not out		0
B 9, lb 4	13	B 10, lb 2, nb 1		13
(89.4 overs)	287	(53 overs)		180

1/26 (1) 2/98 (2) 3/112 (4) 4/216 (3) 5/223 (5)
6/224 (7) 7/243 (6) 8/278 (9) 9/283 (10) 10/287 (8)

1/9 (1) 2/18 (2) 3/39 (3) 4/70 (4) 5/85 (5)
6/86 (6) 7/87 (7) 8/135 (9) 9/176 (10) 10/180 (8)

Yadav 17–2–56–1; Sharma 17–1–46–1; Ashwin 26–7–62–4; Mohammed Shami 19.4–2–64–3; Pandya 10–1–46–0. *Second innings*—Mohammed Shami 12–2–38–0; Ashwin 21–4–59–3; Sharma 13–0–51–5; Yadav 7–1–20–2.

India

M. Vijay lbw b Curran	20	– lbw b Broad		6
S. Dhawan c Malan b Curran	26	– c Bairstow b Broad		13
K. L. Rahul b Curran	4	– c Bairstow b Stokes		13
*V. Kohli c Broad b Rashid	149	– lbw b Stokes		51
A. M. Rahane c Jennings b Stokes	15	– c Bairstow b Curran		2
†K. D. Karthik b Stokes	0	– (7) c Malan b Anderson		20
H. H. Pandya lbw b Curran	22	– (8) c Cook b Stokes		31
R. Ashwin b Anderson	10	– (6) c Bairstow b Anderson		13
Mohammed Shami c Malan b Anderson	2	– c Bairstow b Stokes		0
I. Sharma lbw b Rashid	5	– lbw b Rashid		11
U. T. Yadav not out	1	– not out		0
B 4, lb 11, w 1, nb 4	20	B 1, lb 1		2
(76 overs)	274	(54.2 overs)		162

1/50 (1) 2/54 (3) 3/59 (2) 4/100 (5) 5/100 (6)
6/148 (7) 7/169 (8) 8/182 (9) 9/217 (10) 10/274 (4)

1/19 (1) 2/22 (2) 3/46 (3) 4/63 (5) 5/78 (6)
6/112 (7) 7/141 (4) 8/141 (9) 9/154 (10) 10/162 (8)

Anderson 22–7–41–2; Broad 10–2–40–0; Curran 17–1–74–4; Rashid 8–0–31–2; Stokes 19–4–73–2. *Second innings*—Anderson 16–2–50–2; Broad 14–2–43–2; Stokes 14.2–2–40–4; Curran 6–0–18–1; Rashid 4–1–9–1.

Umpires: Aleem Dar *(Pakistan)* (120) and C. B. Gaffaney *(New Zealand)* (21).
Third umpire: M. Erasmus *(South Africa)*.　　　Referee: J. J. Crowe *(New Zealand)* (90).

Close of play: first day, England 285–9 (Curran 24, Anderson 0); second day, England 9–1 (Jennings 5); third day, India 110–5 (Kohli 43, Karthik 18).

ENGLAND v INDIA 2018 (2nd Test)

At Lord's, London, on 9 *(no play)*, 10, 11, 12 August, 2018.
Toss: England.   Result: ENGLAND WON BY AN INNINGS AND 159 RUNS.
Debuts: England – O. J. D. Pope.
Man of the Match: C. R. Woakes.

The sight of Kohli lying on the Lord's turf, while a physio tended to his aching back, summed up India's decline. They had been narrowly outpointed at Edgbaston, but now reverted to stereotype – sickly travellers, supine in the face of England's mastery of conditions. At Birmingham, Kohli had dragged his team along in his wake, but even he looked broken. Broad exploited his discomfort with short-pitched balls, and he was gone before the painkillers kicked in: at 61 for five in their second innings, India had no way back. In all, their two innings lasted 82.2 overs, less than a day's play. After a washout – the first of any day at Lord's since 2001 – India were put in beneath leaden skies, and subsided to 107, Anderson helping himself to five for 20. The sun shone as England recovered from an indifferent start to reach 396. Bairstow and Woakes, whose maiden century meant his name was on all three Lord's honours boards, added 189, an England sixth-wicket record against India. And then, as if scripted, the clouds returned. Vijay completed a miserable pair, becoming Anderson's 100th Test wicket at Lord's (he was the first to achieve the feat on any ground outside Sri Lanka), and only Ashwin, who top-scored in both innings, survived for long. England hardly missed Stokes, whose court case was being heard (he was cleared of affray in Bristol in 2017). Rashid was the 14th player not to bat, bowl or take a catch in a Test victory.

India

M. Vijay b Anderson	0	– c Bairstow b Anderson	0
K. L. Rahul c Bairstow b Anderson	8	– lbw b Anderson	10
C. A. Pujara run out (Pope)	1	– b Broad	17
*V. Kohli c Buttler b Woakes	23	– (5) c Pope b Broad	17
A. M. Rahane c Cook b Anderson	18	– (4) c Jennings b Broad	13
H. H. Pandya c Buttler b Woakes	11	– lbw b Woakes	26
†K. D. Karthik b Curran	1	– lbw b Broad	0
R. Ashwin lbw b Broad	29	– not out	33
K. Yadav lbw b Anderson	0	– b Anderson	0
Mohammed Shami not out	10	– lbw b Anderson	0
I. Sharma lbw b Anderson	0	– c Pope b Woakes	2
Lb 5, nb 1	6	B 6, lb 6	12
(35.2 overs)	107	(47 overs)	130

1/0 (1) 2/10 (2) 3/15 (3) 4/49 (4) 5/61 (6) 6/62 (7)
7/84 (5) 8/96 (9) 9/96 (8) 10/107 (11)

1/0 (1) 2/13 (2) 3/35 (4) 4/50 (3) 5/61 (5)
6/61 (7) 7/116 (6) 8/121 (9) 9/125 (10) 10/130 (11)

Anderson 13.2–5–20–5; Broad 10–2–37–1; Woakes 6–2–19–2; Curran 6–0–26–1. *Second innings*—Anderson 12–5–23–4; Broad 16–6–44–4; Woakes 10–2–24–2; Curran 9–1–27–0.

England

A. N. Cook c Karthik b Sharma	21
K. K. Jennings lbw b Mohammed Shami	11
*J. E. Root lbw b Mohammed Shami	19
O. J. D. Pope lbw b Pandya	28
†J. M. Bairstow c Karthik b Pandya	93
J. C. Buttler lbw b Mohammed Shami	24
C. R. Woakes not out	137
S. M. Curran c Mohammed Shami b Pandya	40
B 11, lb 10, w 1, nb 1	23
(7 wkts dec, 88.1 overs)	396

1/28 (2) 2/32 (1) 3/77 (4) 4/89 (3)
5/131 (6) 6/320 (5) 7/396 (8)

A. U. Rashid, S. C. J. Broad and J. M. Anderson did not bat.

Sharma 22–4–101–1; Mohammed Shami 23–4–96–3; Yadav 9–1–44–0; Pandya 17.1–0–66–3; Ashwin 17–1–68–0.

Umpires: Aleem Dar *(Pakistan)* (121) and M. Erasmus *(South Africa)* (50).
Third umpire: C. B. Gaffaney *(New Zealand)*.   Referee: J. J. Crowe *(New Zealand)* (91).

Close of play: first day, no play; second day, India 107; third day, England 357–6 (Woakes 120, Curran 22).

ENGLAND v INDIA 2018 (3rd Test)

At Trent Bridge, Nottingham, on 18, 19, 20, 21, 22 August, 2018.
Toss: England.   Result: INDIA WON BY 203 RUNS.
Debuts: India – R. R. Pant.
Man of the Match: V. Kohli.

India's convincing victory changed the feel of the series: talk of a clean sweep gave way to concern that England might instead become only the second side to lose a series from 2–0 up. It took India just 17 balls on the final day to complete their seventh win in England, and Kohli's 22nd as captain, taking him past Sourav Ganguly in the national pantheon; only M. S. Dhoni, with 27, lay ahead. Their seamers proved far more effective than at Lord's: with Bumrah back after injury, they claimed 19 wickets between them. But this was no one-dimensional victory. It saw a vastly improved performance by their fielders (Rahul alone took seven catches), a promising debut for 20-year-old Rishabh Pant (seven dismissals, and off the mark second ball with a six) and a batting display not exclusively reliant on Kohli, who still totalled exactly 200, as he had at Edgbaston. Rahane helped him put on 159 as India reached 329 after being put in; England, who had omitted Curran to accommodate the returning Stokes, failed to get halfway, losing all ten wickets inside a session for the third time in two years (the previous instance was in 1938). Pandya picked up a maiden five-for before India's batsmen, led by Kohli, took the lead to 520. On the fourth morning England were 62 for four: Stokes and Buttler, who reached a maiden century in his 23rd Test, added 169 but, with Bumrah taking five wickets, England barely survived the day.

India

S. Dhawan c Buttler b Woakes	35	– st Bairstow b Rashid	44
K. L. Rahul lbw b Woakes	23	– b Stokes	36
C. A. Pujara c Rashid b Woakes	14	– c Cook b Stokes	72
*V. Kohli c Stokes b Rashid	97	– lbw b Woakes	103
A. M. Rahane c Cook b Broad	81	– b Rashid	29
H. H. Pandya c Buttler b Anderson	18	– (7) not out	52
†R. R. Pant b Broad	24	– (6) c Cook b Anderson	1
R. Ashwin b Broad	14	– (9) not out	1
I. Sharma not out	1		
Mohammed Shami c Broad b Anderson	3	– (8) c Cook b Rashid	3
J. J. Bumrah b Anderson	0		
B 12, lb 6, w 1	19	B 1, lb 9, w 1	11
(94.5 overs)	329	(7 wkts dec, 110 overs)	352

1/60 (1) 2/65 (2) 3/82 (3) 4/241 (5) 5/279 (4) 1/60 (2) 2/111 (1) 3/224 (3)
6/307 (6) 7/323 (7) 8/326 (8) 9/329 (10) 10/329 (11) 4/281 (4) 5/282 (6) 6/329 (5) 7/349 (8)

Anderson 25.5–8–64–3; Broad 25–8–72–3; Stokes 15–1–54–0; Woakes 20–2–75–3; Rashid 9–0–46–1. *Second innings*—Anderson 22–7–55–1; Broad 16–3–60–0; Woakes 22–4–49–1; Stokes 20–3–68–2; Rashid 27–2–101–3; Root 3–0–9–0.

England

A. N. Cook c Pant b Sharma	29	– c Rahul b Sharma	17
K. K. Jennings c Pant b Bumrah	20	– c Pant b Sharma	13
*J. E. Root c Rahul b Pandya	16	– c Rahul b Bumrah	13
O. J. D. Pope c Pant b Sharma	10	– c Kohli b Mohammed Shami	16
†J. M. Bairstow c Rahul b Pandya	15	– (7) b Bumrah	0
B. A. Stokes c Rahul b Mohammed Shami	10	– (5) c Rahul b Pandya	62
J. C. Buttler c sub (S. N. Thakur) b Bumrah	39	– (6) lbw b Bumrah	106
C. R. Woakes c Pant b Pandya	8	– c Pant b Bumrah	4
A. U. Rashid c Pant b Pandya	5	– not out	33
S. C. J. Broad lbw b Pandya	0	– c Rahul b Bumrah	20
J. M. Anderson not out	1	– c Rahane b Ashwin	11
B 4, lb 1, w 1, nb 2	8	B 2, lb 16, nb 4	22
(38.2 overs)	161	(104.5 overs)	317

1/54 (1) 2/54 (2) 3/75 (4) 4/86 (3) 5/108 (6) 1/27 (2) 2/32 (1) 3/62 (3) 4/62 (4) 5/231 (6)
6/110 (5) 7/118 (8) 8/128 (9) 9/128 (10) 10/161 (7) 6/231 (7) 7/241 (8) 8/241 (5) 9/291 (10) 10/317 (11)

Mohammed Shami 10–2–56–1; Bumrah 12.2–2–37–2; Ashwin 1–0–3–0; Sharma 9–2–32–2; Pandya 6–1–28–5. *Second innings*—Bumrah 29–8–85–5; Sharma 20–4–70–2; Ashwin 22.5–8–44–1; Mohammed Shami 19–3–78–1; Pandya 14–5–22–1.

Umpires: M. Erasmus *(South Africa)* (51) and C. B. Gaffaney *(New Zealand)* (22).
Third umpire: Aleem Dar *(Pakistan)*.   Referee: J. J. Crowe *(New Zealand)* (92).

Close of play: first day, India 307–6 (Pant 22); second day, India 124–2 (Pujara 33, Kohli 8); third day, England 23–0 (Cook 9, Jennings 13); fourth day, England 311–9 (Rashid 30, Anderson 8).

ENGLAND v INDIA 2018 (4th Test)

At Rose Bowl, Southampton, on 30, 31 August, 1, 2 September, 2018.
Toss: England.   Result: ENGLAND WON BY 60 RUNS.
Debuts: none.
Man of the Match: M. M. Ali.

Curran and Ali, restored to the side, swung another see-saw match England's way, giving them the series. As they had been in the First Test, England were 86 for six when Curran came in – but he and Ali added 81. Curran, who reached his second Test half-century with a six, as he had at Edgbaston, was last out for 78. He then nipped out Kohli, who had reached 6,000 runs in his 119th Test innings (only Sunil Gavaskar got there quicker for India, by two). Ali claimed five wickets – including Pant for a 29-ball duck – to restrict India's lead to 27, despite a superb 15th Test century from Pujara, who coaxed 78 from the last two wickets after Ali had taken four for eight in 16 balls. India looked back on top when Stokes's dismissal for a 110-ball 30 left England 178 for six, only for Curran to thwart them again, initially in concert with Buttler. India needed 245 to square the series and, after slipping to 22 for three, were recovering through Kohli and Rahane. And then, after they had put on 99, Ali struck again: Kohli gloved to short leg, scowled, and demanded a review – but there was no reprieve. Ali finished with nine wickets in the match, and 17 in two Tests at the Rose Bowl), while Curran completed victory with the 14th lbw of the match, equalling the English record. Buttler kept wicket throughout, as Bairstow had sustained a hairline finger fracture in the previous match.

England

A. N. Cook c Kohli b Pandya	17	– c Rahul b Bumrah		12
K. K. Jennings lbw b Bumrah	0	– lbw b Mohammed Shami		36
*J. E. Root lbw b Sharma	4	– (4) run out (Mohammed Shami)		48
J. M. Bairstow c Pant b Bumrah	6	– (5) b Mohammed Shami		0
B. A. Stokes lbw b Mohammed Shami	23	– (6) c Rahane b Ashwin		30
†J. C. Buttler c Kohli b Mohammed Shami	21	– (7) lbw b Sharma		69
M. M. Ali c Bumrah b Ashwin	40	– (3) c Rahul b Sharma		9
S. M. Curran b Ashwin	78	– run out (Sharma/Pant)		46
A. U. Rashid lbw b Sharma	6	– c Pant b Mohammed Shami		11
S. C. J. Broad lbw b Bumrah	17	– c Pant b Mohammed Shami		0
J. M. Anderson not out	0	– not out		1
B 23, lb 9, nb 2	34	B 7, lb 2		9
(76.4 overs)	246	(96.1 overs)		271

1/1 (2) 2/15 (3) 3/28 (4) 4/36 (1) 5/69 (6) 6/86 (5)
7/167 (7) 8/177 (9) 9/240 (10) 10/246 (8)

1/24 (1) 2/33 (3) 3/92 (2) 4/92 (5) 5/122 (4)
6/178 (6) 7/233 (7) 8/260 (9) 9/260 (10) 10/271 (8)

Bumrah 20–5–46–3; Sharma 16–6–26–2; Pandya 8–0–51–1; Mohammed Shami 18–2–51–2; Ashwin 14.4–3–40–2. *Second innings*—Ashwin 37.1–7–84–1; Bumrah 19–3–51–1; Sharma 15–4–36–2; Mohammed Shami 16–0–57–4; Pandya 9–0–34–0.

India

S. Dhawan c Buttler b Broad	23	– c Stokes b Anderson		17
K. L. Rahul lbw b Broad	19	– b Broad		0
C. A. Pujara not out	132	– lbw b Anderson		5
*V. Kohli c Cook b Curran	46	– c Cook b Ali		58
A. M. Rahane lbw b Stokes	11	– lbw b Ali		51
†R. R. Pant lbw b Ali	0	– (7) c Cook b Ali		18
H. H. Pandya c Root b Ali	4	– (6) c Root b Stokes		0
R. Ashwin b Ali	1	– lbw b Curran		25
Mohammed Shami b Ali	0	– (10) c Anderson b Ali		8
I. Sharma c Cook b Ali	14	– (9) lbw b Stokes		0
J. J. Bumrah c Cook b Broad	6	– not out		0
B 9, lb 1, w 4, nb 3	17	Lb 1, w 1		2
(84.5 overs)	273	(69.4 overs)		184

1/37 (2) 2/50 (1) 3/142 (4) 4/161 (5) 5/181 (6)
6/189 (7) 7/195 (8) 8/195 (9) 9/227 (10) 10/273 (11)

1/4 (2) 2/17 (3) 3/22 (1) 4/123 (4) 5/127 (6)
6/150 (7) 7/153 (5) 8/154 (9) 9/163 (10) 10/184 (8)

Anderson 18–2–50–0; Broad 18.5–5–63–3; Curran 16–4–41–1; Jennings 2–0–4–0; Rashid 7–0–19–0; Ali 16–1–63–5; Stokes 7–1–23–1. *Second innings*—Anderson 11–2–33–2; Broad 10–2–23–1; Ali 26–3–71–4; Stokes 12–3–34–2; Curran 3.4–2–1–1; Rashid 7–3–21–0.

Umpires: H. D. P. K. Dharmasena *(Sri Lanka)* (54) and B. N. J. Oxenford *(Australia)* (50).
Third umpire: J. S. Wilson *(West Indies)*.   Referee: A. J. Pycroft *(Zimbabwe)* (61).

Close of play: first day, India 19–0 (Dhawan 3, Rahul 11); second day, England 6–0 (Cook 2, Jennings 4); third day, England 260–8 (Curran 37).

ENGLAND v INDIA 2018 (5th Test)

At Kennington Oval, London, on 7, 8, 9, 10, 11 September, 2018.
Toss: England.   Result: ENGLAND WON BY 118 RUNS.
Debuts: India – G. H. Vihari.
Man of the Match: A. N. Cook.   Men of the Series: S. M. Curran and V. Kohli.

Alastair Cook's retirement spiced up one of the most momentous of The Oval's 101 Tests. The crowds gave Cook a series of standing ovations, and were captivated until after tea on the final day, when the last ball provided Anderson with his 564th Test wicket, putting him past Glenn McGrath's record for a fast bowler. England had started slowly, Cook's dismissal for 71 preceding ducks for Root and Bairstow, but Buttler – who added 98 with Broad – shepherded them to 332. After Kohli edged to second slip, the debutant Hanuma Vihari rode his luck for 56: while on nought he was lbw to Broad, but England did not review, then his own review saved him in Broad's next over. Finally Jadeja blazed 86 to restrict the deficit to 40. And then came the Cook Show: during a stand of 259 with Root he completed an emotional hundred, thanks to Bumrah's overthrow, and sailed to 147; he was only the fifth to score centuries in his first and last Tests, after the Australians Reggie Duff, Bill Ponsford and Greg Chappell, and India's Mohammad Azharuddin. India needed 464, and looked sunk when Kohli went first ball, making it two for three. But Rahul batted beautifully, and the precocious Pant put some patchy keeping behind him to thrash a maiden Test century. They had put on 204 when Rashid suddenly spun one, waspishly Warne-like, out of the footmarks to tickle Rahul's off bail; Pant holed out soon afterwards. Anderson delivered the *coup de grâce*.

England

A. N. Cook b Bumrah	71	– c Pant b Vihari	147
K. K. Jennings c Rahul b Jadeja	23	– b Mohammed Shami	10
M. M. Ali c Pant b Sharma	50	– b Jadeja	20
*J. E. Root lbw b Bumrah	0	– c sub (H. H. Pandya) b Vihari	125
†J. M. Bairstow c Pant b Sharma	0	– b Mohammed Shami	18
B. A. Stokes lbw b Jadeja	11	– c Rahul b Jadeja	37
J. C. Buttler c Rahane b Jadeja	89	– c Mohammed Shami b Jadeja	0
S. M. Curran c Pant b Sharma	0	– c Pant b Vihari	21
A. U. Rashid lbw b Bumrah	15	– not out	20
S. C. J. Broad c Rahul b Jadeja	38		
J. M. Anderson not out	0		
B 26, lb 9	35	B 14, lb 4, w 2, p 5	25
(122 overs)	332	(8 wkts dec, 112.3 overs)	423

1/60 (2) 2/133 (1) 3/133 (4) 4/134 (5) 5/171 (6)   1/27 (2) 2/62 (3) 3/321 (4) 4/321 (1)
6/177 (3) 7/181 (8) 8/214 (9) 9/312 (10) 10/332 (7)   5/355 (5) 6/356 (7) 7/397 (6) 8/423 (8)

Bumrah 30–9–83–3; Sharma 31–12–62–3; Vihari 1–0–1–0; Mohammed Shami 30–7–72–0; Jadeja 30–0–79–4. *Second innings*—Bumrah 23–4–61–0; Sharma 8–3–13–0; Mohammed Shami 25–3–110–2; Jadeja 47–3–179–3; Vihari 9.3–1–37–3.

India

K. L. Rahul b Curran	37	– b Rashid	149
S. Dhawan lbw b Broad	3	– lbw b Anderson	1
C. A. Pujara c Bairstow b Anderson	37	– lbw b Anderson	0
*V. Kohli c Root b Stokes	49	– c Bairstow b Broad	0
A. M. Rahane c Cook b Anderson	0	– c Jennings b Ali	37
G. H. Vihari c Bairstow b Ali	56	– c Bairstow b Stokes	0
†R. R. Pant c Cook b Stokes	5	– c Ali b Rashid	114
R. A. Jadeja not out	86	– c Bairstow b Curran	13
I. Sharma c Bairstow b Ali	4	– c Bairstow b Curran	5
Mohammed Shami c Broad b Rashid	1	– b Anderson	0
J. J. Bumrah run out (Broad/Bairstow)	0	– not out	0
B 4, lb 10	14	B 10, lb 16	26
(95 overs)	292	(94.3 overs)	345

1/6 (2) 2/70 (1) 3/101 (3) 4/103 (5) 5/154 (4)   1/1 (2) 2/1 (3) 3/2 (4) 4/120 (5) 5/121 (6)
6/160 (7) 7/237 (6) 8/249 (9) 9/260 (10) 10/292 (11)   6/325 (1) 7/328 (7) 8/336 (9) 9/345 (8) 10/345 (10)

Anderson 21–7–54–2; Broad 20–6–50–1; Stokes 16–2–56–2; Curran 11–1–49–1; Ali 17–3–50–2; Rashid 10–2–19–1. *Second innings*—Anderson 22.3–11–45–3; Broad 12–1–43–1; Ali 17–2–68–1; Curran 9–2–23–2; Stokes 13–1–60–1; Rashid 15–2–63–2; Root 6–1–17–0.

Umpires: H. D. P. K. Dharmasena *(Sri Lanka)* (55) and J. S. Wilson *(West Indies)* (11).
Third umpire: B. N. J. Oxenford *(Australia)*.   Referee: A. J. Pycroft *(Zimbabwe)* (62).

Close of play: first day, England 198–7 (Buttler 11, Rashid 4); second day, India 174–6 (Vihari 25, Jadeja 8); third day, England 114–2 (Cook 46, Root 29); fourth day, India 58–3 (Rahul 46, Rahane 10).

INDIA v WEST INDIES 2018-19 (1st Test)

At Saurashtra C. A. Stadium, Rajkot, on 4, 5, 6 October, 2018.
Toss: India.　　Result: INDIA WON BY AN INNINGS AND 272 RUNS.
Debuts: India – P. P. Shaw. West Indies – S. H. Lewis.
Man of the Match: P. P. Shaw.

India's biggest innings win (beating their shellacking of Afghanistan earlier in 2018), and West Indies' second-heaviest defeat, never remotely resembled a contest. Fourteen West Indian wickets fell on the third day – most from ill-judged attacking shots – and their two innings did not add up to 100 overs. After Rahul fell in the first over, Prithvi Shaw took the eye. Attacking mainly off the back foot, he reached 50 in 56 balls, and a century off 99. At 18 years 329 days, he was the fourth-youngest to hit a century on Test debut, and the third-fastest by balls faced. Pujara, on his home ground, just missed another century, but Kohli completed his 24th Test hundred next day, Pant freewheeled to 92, and Jadeja added an entertaining maiden ton. Kohli declared with India's highest score against West Indies, beating 644 for seven at Kanpur in 1978–79. The 217 conceded by Bishoo was the second-most by a West Indian, after Tommy Scott's five for 266 against England at Kingston in 1929–30. With temperatures soaring, it was soon clear the tourists had no stomach for a fight: it was soon 49 for five, and the eventual first-innings deficit was an eye-watering 468. Powell survived a skittish start to make 83 in the follow-on, but most of his team-mates appeared to think the white-ball matches had already started. Left-arm wrist-spinner Kuldeep Yadav reaped his maiden Test five-for. West Indies were without captain Jason Holder, who had injured his ankle in the pre-tour camp in Dubai.

India

P. P. Shaw c and b Bishoo	134
K. L. Rahul lbw b Gabriel	0
C. A. Pujara c Dowrich b Lewis	86
*V. Kohli c Bishoo b Lewis	139
A. M. Rahane c Dowrich b Chase	41
†R. R. Pant c Paul b Bishoo	92
R. A. Jadeja not out	100
R. Ashwin c Dowrich b Bishoo	7
K. Yadav lbw b Bishoo	12
U. T. Yadav c Lewis b Brathwaite	22
Mohammed Shami not out	2
B 9, lb 1, nb 4	14
(9 wkts dec, 149.5 overs)	649

1/3 (2) 2/209 (3) 3/232 (1) 4/337 (5) 5/470 (6)
6/534 (4) 7/545 (8) 8/571 (9) 9/626 (10)

Gabriel 21–1–84–1; Paul 15–1–61–0; Lewis 20–0–93–2; Bishoo 54–3–217–4; Chase 26–1–137–1; Brathwaite 13.5–1–47–1.

West Indies

*K. C. Brathwaite b Mohammed Shami	2	– c Shaw b Ashwin	10
K. O. A. Powell lbw b Mohammed Shami	1	– c Shaw b K. Yadav	83
S. D. Hope b Ashwin	10	– lbw b K. Yadav	17
S. O. Hetmyer run out (Jadeja)	10	– c Rahul b K. Yadav	11
S. W. Ambris c Rahane b Jadeja	12	– st Pant b K. Yadav	0
R. L. Chase b Ashwin	53	– c Ashwin b K. Yadav	20
†S. O. Dowrich b K. Yadav	10	– not out	16
K. M. A. Paul c Pujara b U. T. Yadav	47	– c U. T. Yadav b Jadeja	15
D. Bishoo not out	17	– c Pant b Ashwin	9
S. H. Lewis b Ashwin	0	– lbw b Jadeja	4
S. T. Gabriel st Pant b Ashwin	1	– c K. Yadav b Jadeja	4
B 16, lb 2	18	B 5, lb 1, nb 1	7
(48 overs)	181	(50.5 overs)	196

1/2 (1) 2/7 (2) 3/21 (3) 4/32 (4) 5/49 (5) 6/74 (7)
7/147 (8) 8/159 (6) 9/159 (10) 10/181 (11)

1/32 (1) 2/79 (3) 3/97 (4) 4/97 (5) 5/138 (6)
6/151 (2) 7/172 (8) 8/185 (9) 9/192 (10) 10/196 (11)

Mohammed Shami 9–2–22–2; U. T. Yadav 11–3–20–1; Ashwin 11–2–37–4; Jadeja 7–1–22–1; K. Yadav 10–1–62–1. *Second innings*—Mohammed Shami 3–0–11–0; Ashwin 18–2–71–2; U. T. Yadav 3–0–16–0; K. Yadav 14–2–57–5; Jadeja 12.5–1–35–3.

Umpires: I. J. Gould *(England)* (68) and N. J. Llong *(England)* (54).
Third umpire: B. N. J. Oxenford *(Australia)*.　　Referee: B. C. Broad *(England)* (97).

Close of play: first day, India 364–4 (Kohli 72, Pant 17); second day, West Indies 94–6 (Chase 27, Paul 13).

INDIA v WEST INDIES 2018-19 (2nd Test)

At Rajiv Gandhi Stadium, Uppal, Hyderabad, on 12, 13, 14 October, 2018.
Toss: West Indies.   Result: INDIA WON BY TEN WICKETS.
Debuts: India – S. N. Thakur.
Man of the Match: U. T. Yadav.   Man of the Series: P. P. Shaw.

Umesh Yadav joined elite company during another crushing victory that wrapped up the series in six days, becoming only the third Indian seamer to take ten wickets in a home Test, after Kapil Dev (twice) and Javagal Srinath. West Indies did at least show some spirit before collapsing in a heap – but only six teams have won by ten wickets after a slimmer first-innings lead than India's 56. When seamer Shardul Thakur limped off with a groin injury ten balls into his debut, the cards seemed to be falling for the returning Holder. But the top order struggled again, before his seventh-wicket stand of 104 took West Indies past 250 for the first time in four Tests in India. Chase completed his century early on the second morning, but he was fielding within 40 minutes of the start. Shaw cracked 70 from 53 balls, but India were a dicey 162 for four when Holder removed Kohli for 45. Rahane and Pant added 152, with the help of some shoddy fielding: Pant was reprieved on 24 when Jahmar Hamilton, substituting for injured wicketkeeper Dowrich, dropped a sitter off Gabriel. After Pant departed for his second successive 92, India were only 28 in front when the ninth wicket fell – but Thakur hobbled out, and helped Ashwin double the lead. Four wickets fell before West Indies wiped off the arrears; only Hope and Ambris held India up for long. After two days in which 14 wickets fell, 16 crashed on a frantic third.

West Indies

K. C. Brathwaite lbw b K. Yadav	14	– c Pant b U. T. Yadav	0
K. O. A. Powell c Jadeja b Ashwin	22	– c Rahane b Ashwin	0
S. D. Hope lbw b U. T. Yadav	36	– c Rahane b Jadeja	28
S. O. Hetmyer lbw b K. Yadav	12	– c Pujara b K. Yadav	17
S. W. Ambris c Jadeja b K. Yadav	18	– lbw b Jadeja	38
R. L. Chase b U. T. Yadav	106	– b U. T. Yadav	6
†S. O. Dowrich lbw b U. T. Yadav	30	– b U. T. Yadav	0
*J. O. Holder c Pant b U. T. Yadav	52	– c Pant b Jadeja	19
D. Bishoo b U. T. Yadav	2	– not out	10
J. A. Warrican not out	8	– b Ashwin	7
S. T. Gabriel c Pant b U. T. Yadav	0	– b U. T. Yadav	1
B 4, lb 2	11	Lb 1	1
(101.4 overs)	311	(46.1 overs)	127

1/32 (2) 2/52 (1) 3/86 (3) 4/92 (4) 5/113 (5) 6/182 (7) 7/286 (8) 8/296 (9) 9/311 (6) 10/311 (11)

1/0 (1) 2/6 (2) 3/45 (4) 4/45 (3) 5/68 (6) 6/70 (7) 7/108 (8) 8/109 (5) 9/126 (10) 10/127 (11)

U. T. Yadav 26.4–3–88–6; Thakur 1.4–0–9–0; Ashwin 24.2–7–49–1; K. Yadav 29–2–85–3; Jadeja 20–2–69–0. *Second innings*—U. T. Yadav 12.1–3–45–4; Ashwin 10–4–24–2; K. Yadav 13–1–45–1; Jadeja 11–5–12–3.

India

K. L. Rahul b Holder	4	– (2) not out	33
P. P. Shaw c Hetmyer b Warrican	70	– (1) not out	33
C. A. Pujara c sub (†J. N. Hamilton) b Gabriel	10		
*V. Kohli lbw b Holder	45		
A. M. Rahane c Hope b Holder	80		
†R. R. Pant c Hetmyer b Gabriel	92		
R. A. Jadeja lbw b Holder	0		
R. Ashwin b Gabriel	35		
K. Yadav b Holder	6		
U. T. Yadav c sub (†J. N. Hamilton) b Warrican	2		
S. N. Thakur not out	4		
B 12, lb 2, nb 5	19	B 6, lb 2, nb 1	9
(106.4 overs)	367	(no wkt, 16.1 overs)	75

1/61 (1) 2/98 (2) 3/102 (3) 4/162 (4) 5/314 (5) 6/314 (7) 7/322 (6) 8/334 (9) 9/339 (10) 10/367 (8)

Gabriel 20.4–4–107–3; Holder 23–5–56–5; Warrican 31–7–84–2; Chase 9–1–22–0; Bishoo 21–4–78–0; Brathwaite 2–0–6–0. *Second innings*—Holder 4–0–17–0; Warrican 4–0–17–0; Bishoo 4.1–0–19–0; Chase 4–0–14–0.

Umpires: I. J. Gould *(England)* (69) and B. N. J. Oxenford *(Australia)* (51).
Third umpire: N. J. Llong *(England)*.   Referee: B. C. Broad *(England)* (98).

Close of play: first day, West Indies 295–7 (Chase 98, Bishoo 2); second day, India 308–4 (Rahane 75, Pant 85).

PAKISTAN v AUSTRALIA 2018–19 (1st Test)

Test No. 2321/63 (P416, A813)

At Dubai International Stadium on 7, 8, 9, 10, 11 October, 2018.
Toss: Pakistan.   Result: DRAWN.
Debuts: Pakistan – Bilal Asif. Australia – A. J. Finch, T. M. Head, M. Labuschagne.
Man of the Match: U. T. Khawaja.

Pakistan might well have won inside four days – but were denied by Khawaja, who survived 522 minutes, equalling the second-longest vigil in the fourth innings of a Test, behind only Michael Atherton's 643 at Johannesburg in 1995-96. He thought he had heatstroke on the final day, before continuing for another session and a half. The first day belonged to Mohammad Hafeez – recalled at 37 – who made a century in a first-wicket stand of 205. Next day Haris Sohail added a maiden Test hundred, while Asad Shafiq joined Steve Waugh in making 3,000 runs from No. 6. Marnus Labuschagne, the second South African-born man to play for Australia, after Kepler Wessels, took a wicket with his part-time leg-spin, and later ran out Babar Azam. Australia's openers responded with 142, but then all ten tumbled for 60. Off-spinner Bilal Asif took six for 36, the best figures by a debutant against Australia, beating left-arm seamer Fred "Nutty" Martin's six for 50 at The Oval in 1890. The spinners slowed down Pakistan's declaration drive, but Australia still needed to survive nearly five sessions. After another bright start, the Marsh brothers both bagged ducks, Test cricket's eighth such fraternal failure, but Travis Head, another debutant, lasted beyond lunch on the fifth day. Khawaja put Yasir Shah off by repeatedly reverse-sweeping, but when Paine arrived with nearly four hours left, a draw was still unlikely. The last hour was tense, but Paine saw out 220 minutes and 194 deliveries, while Lyon survived 50 and 34.

Pakistan

Imam-ul-Haq c Paine b Lyon	76	– c and b Holland	48
Mohammad Hafeez lbw b Siddle	126	– c Labuschagne b Holland	17
Azhar Ali c Starc b Holland	18	– (4) lbw b Holland	4
Haris Sohail c Paine b Lyon	110	– (5) lbw b Labuschagne	39
Mohammad Abbas b Siddle	1		
Asad Shafiq c Paine b Labuschagne	80	– c M. R. Marsh b Lyon	41
Babar Azam run out (Labuschagne/Paine)	4	– not out	28
*†Sarfraz Ahmed run out (Finch)	15		
Bilal Asif b Siddle	12	– (3) c Head b Lyon	0
Wahab Riaz not out	7		
Yasir Shah c Paine b Starc	3		
B 6, lb 21, nb 3	30	B 2, lb 2	4
(164.2 overs)	482	(6 wkts dec, 57.5 overs)	181

1/205 (1) 2/222 (2) 3/244 (3) 4/260 (5) 5/410 (6)   1/37 (2) 2/38 (3) 3/45 (4)
6/418 (7) 7/456 (4) 8/470 (8) 9/473 (9) 10/482 (11)   4/110 (1) 5/110 (5) 6/181 (6)

Starc 36.2–11–90–1; Siddle 29–11–58–3; Lyon 52–12–114–2; Holland 29–1–126–1; Labuschagne 8–0–29–1; M. R. Marsh 10–0–38–0. *Second innings*—Starc 6–1–18–0; Lyon 25.5–6–58–2; Siddle 2–1–3–0; Holland 20–3–83–3; Head 1–0–6–0; Labuschagne 3–0–9–1.

Australia

U. T. Khawaja c Imam-ul-Haq b Bilal Asif	85	– (2) lbw b Yasir Shah	141
A. J. Finch c Asad Shafiq b Mohammad Abbas	62	– (1) lbw b Mohammad Abbas	49
S. E. Marsh c Asad Shafiq b Bilal Asif	7	– c Sarfraz Ahmed b Mohammad Abbas	0
M. R. Marsh lbw b Mohammad Abbas	12	– lbw b Mohammad Abbas	0
T. M. Head c Haris Sohail b Bilal Asif	0	– lbw b Mohammad Hafeez	72
M. Labuschagne c Imam-ul-Haq b Bilal Asif	0	– lbw b Yasir Shah	13
*†T. D. Paine c Imam-ul-Haq b Bilal Asif	7	– not out	61
M. A. Starc c Sarfraz Ahmed b Mohammad Abbas	0	– c Babar Azam b Yasir Shah	1
P. M. Siddle b Mohammad Abbas	10	– lbw b Yasir Shah	0
N. M. Lyon c Imam-ul-Haq b Bilal Asif	6	– not out	5
J. M. Holland not out	0		
B 6, lb 7	13	B 13, lb 4, nb 3	20
(83.3 overs)	202	(8 wkts, 139.5 overs)	362

1/142 (2) 2/160 (3) 3/167 (1) 4/171 (5) 5/171 (6)   1/87 (1) 2/87 (2) 3/87 (4) 4/219 (5)
6/183 (4) 7/183 (7) 8/191 (8) 9/202 (9) 10/202 (10)   5/252 (6) 6/331 (2) 7/333 (8) 8/333 (9)

Mohammad Abbas 19–9–29–4; Wahab Riaz 11–2–39–0; Yasir Shah 28–6–80–0; Mohammad Hafeez 3–1–2–0; Bilal Asif 21.3–7–36–6; Azhar Ali 1–0–3–0. *Second innings*—Mohammad Abbas 27–7–56–3; Mohammad Hafeez 6–0–29–1; Yasir Shah 43.5–9–114–4; Wahab Riaz 16–3–42–0; Bilal Asif 37–8–87–0; Haris Sohail 9–1–16–0; Asad Shafiq 1–0–1–0.

Umpires: R. K. Illingworth *(England)* (36) and R. A. Kettleborough *(England)* (54).
Third umpire: S. Ravi *(India)*.   Referee: R. S. Madugalle *(Sri Lanka)* (182).

Close of play: first day, Pakistan 255–3 (Haris Sohail 15, Mohammad Abbas 1); second day, Australia 30–0 (Khawaja 17, Finch 13); third day, Pakistan 45–3 (Imam-ul-Haq 23); fourth day, Australia 136–3 (Khawaja 50, Head 34).

Test No. 2322/64 (P417, A814)

PAKISTAN v AUSTRALIA 2018–19 (2nd Test)

At Sheikh Zayed Stadium, Abu Dhabi, on 16, 17, 18, 19 October, 2018.
Toss: Pakistan.　　Result: PAKISTAN WON BY 373 RUNS.
Debuts: Pakistan – Fakhar Zaman, Mir Hamza.
Man of the Match: Mohammad Abbas.　　Man of the Series: Mohammad Abbas.

It was Pakistan's turn to stage a comeback: they looked doomed after losing four wickets for no runs – all to Lyon – on the first morning. However, Sarfraz Ahmed hit back, putting on 147 with the debutant Fakhar Zaman, before both fell for 94, unique in a Test innings. Only three sides had previously won a Test after a collapse of four for none, but Australia's batting misfired again. Mohammad Abbas took five for 33, and added five more in the second innings as Australia lurched to defeat midway through the fourth day. Abbas finished his tenth Test with 59 wickets at 15; only three 19th-century bowlers had better averages at the same stage. Labuschagne was dozily run out, standing out of his crease as Yasir Shah deflected Starc's defensive shot into the bowler's-end stumps, and Australia's first innings ended an hour after lunch on the second day. Fakhar completed a notable debut double with 66, and Babar Azam missed a maiden century by one as the lead inflated. Azhar Ali also suffered a bizarre run-out: he was chatting mid-pitch with Asad Shafiq, assuming his edge off Siddle had reached the boundary, and was stranded by Starc's return. Still, Australia needed 538 – and no one reached 50. Khawaja, the hero in Dubai, was unable to bat after injuring his knee., Sarfraz, concussed while batting, watched the demolition from the dressing-room as Pakistan took the series with their biggest win by runs, beating 356 against Australia on the same ground in 2014–15.

Pakistan

Fakhar Zaman lbw b Labuschagne	94	– c and b Lyon	66
Mohammad Hafeez c Labuschagne b Starc	4	– c Head b Starc	6
Azhar Ali c and b Lyon	15	– run out (Starc/Paine)	64
Haris Sohail c Head b Lyon	0	– st Paine b Lyon	17
Asad Shafiq c Labuschagne b Lyon	0	– c sub (A. C. Agar) b Labuschagne	44
Babar Azam b Lyon	0	– lbw b M. R. Marsh	99
*†Sarfraz Ahmed c Siddle b Labuschagne	94	– lbw b Labuschagne	81
Bilal Asif c Paine b Labuschagne	12	– c Head b Lyon	15
Yasir Shah b M. R. Marsh	28	– lbw b Lyon	4
Mohammad Abbas b Starc	10	– not out	0
Mir Hamza not out	4	– not out	0
B 11, lb 6, nb 4	21	Lb 2, nb 2	4
(81 overs)	282	(9 wkts dec, 120 overs)	400

1/5 (2) 2/57 (3) 3/57 (4) 4/57 (5) 5/57 (6)　　1/15 (2) 2/106 (1) 3/154 (4) 4/160 (3)
6/204 (1) 7/226 (8) 8/247 (7) 9/264 (9) 10/282 (10)　　5/235 (5) 6/368 (6) 7/390 (8) 8/394 (9) 9/400 (7)

Starc 12–3–37–2; Siddle 10–3–39–0; M. R. Marsh 7–2–21–1; Lyon 27–5–78–4; Holland 13–3–45–0; Labuschagne 12–2–45–3. *Second innings*—Starc 7–0–32–1; Siddle 23–4–68–0; Lyon 43–8–135–4; Holland 16–3–46–0; Labuschagne 16–1–74–2; M. R. Marsh 13–3–39–1; Head 2–0–4–0.

Australia

U. T. Khawaja c Sarfraz Ahmed b Mohammad Abbas	3	– absent hurt	
A. J. Finch c Fakhar Zaman b Bilal Asif	39	– (1) lbw b Mohammad Abbas	31
P. M. Siddle lbw b Mohammad Abbas	4	– (8) lbw b Yasir Shah	3
S. E. Marsh c Haris Sohail b Mohammad Abbas	3	– (2) b Mir Hamza	4
T. M. Head c Asad Shafiq b Mohammad Abbas	14	– (3) c sub (†Mohammad Rizwan) b Mohammad Abbas	36
M. R. Marsh c Asad Shafiq b Yasir Shah	13	– (4) lbw b Mohammad Abbas	5
M. Labuschagne run out (Yasir Shah)	25	– (5) c sub (†Mohammad Rizwan) b Mohammad Abbas	43
*†T. D. Paine lbw b Bilal Asif	3	– (6) b Mohammad Abbas	0
M. A. Starc lbw b Mohammad Abbas	34	– (7) lbw b Yasir Shah	28
N. M. Lyon b Bilal Asif	2	– (9) not out	6
J. M. Holland not out	2	– (10) c Haris Sohail b Yasir Shah	3
Lb 3	3	Lb 5	5
(50.4 overs)	145	(49.4 overs)	164

1/16 (1) 2/20 (3) 3/36 (4) 4/56 (5) 5/75 (6)　　1/10 (2) 2/71 (3) 3/77 (4) 4/78 (1) 5/78 (6)
6/85 (2) 7/91 (8) 8/128 (7) 9/132 (10) 10/145 (9)　　6/145 (7) 7/151 (8) 8/155 (5) 9/164 (10)

Mohammad Abbas 12.4–4–33–5; Mir Hamza 9–2–27–0; Yasir Shah 19–3–59–1; Bilal Asif 10–3–23–3. *Second innings*—Mohammad Abbas 17–2–62–5; Mir Hamza 6–0–40–1; Yasir Shah 21.4–5–45–3; Bilal Asif 5–2–12–0.

Umpires: R. K. Illingworth *(England)* (37) and S. Ravi *(India)* (28).
　　Third umpire: R. A. Kettleborough *(England)*.　　Referee: R. S. Madugalle *(Sri Lanka)* (183).

Close of play: first day, Australia 20–2 (Finch 13); second day, Pakistan 144–2 (Azhar Ali 54, Haris Sohail 17); third day, Australia 47–1 (Finch 24, Head 17).

BANGLADESH v ZIMBABWE 2018–19 (1st Test)

At Sylhet Stadium on 3, 4, 5, 6 November, 2018.
Toss: Zimbabwe. Result: ZIMBABWE WON BY 151 RUNS.
Debuts: Bangladesh – Ariful Haque, Nazmul Islam. Zimbabwe – W. P. Masakadza, B. A. Mavuta.
Man of the Match: S. C. Williams.

Zimbabwe will long remember the inaugural match at the pretty Sylhet Stadium in the north-east of Bangladesh, not far from the Indian border. The 116th Test ground gifted Zimbabwe their first overseas victory for 17 years, and only their 12th anywhere in 107 attempts. And they did it with spin, their inexperienced trio faring better than Bangladesh's much-hyped battalion, which was admittedly lacking Shakib Al Hasan with a hand injury (Mahmudullah captained instead). Zimbabwe's batsmen worked hard in their first Test of the year: Hamilton Masakadza made 52 in 32 overs, then Williams reined himself in for 88, but when Chakabva fell – one of slow left-armer Taijul Islam's six wickets – the last five added only 21. That looked plenty when Bangladesh dipped to 19 for four. Mushfiqur Rahim and Ariful Haque – chosen for his debut a month after making 231 in a domestic game – regained some ground, but Sikandar Raza's three wickets earned a sizeable lead. Masakadza gritted out 48 in 36 overs, but the innings was derailed by three wickets in five balls for Taijul, who finished with 11 for 170. Bangladesh's target was 321 – tough on a turning pitch, but not impossible. Things looked rosy as Liton Das and Imrul Kayes put on 56, but slowly Zimbabwe took charge. Leg-spinner Brandon Mavuta took four wickets, and finally slow left-armer Wellington Masakadza – only the eighth man to make his Test debut in a side captained by his brother – persuaded Ariful to sky a catch, to ignite wild Zimbabwean celebrations.

Zimbabwe

*H. Masakadza lbw b Abu Jayed	52	– lbw b Mehedi Hasan	48
B. B. Chari b Taijul Islam	13	– b Mehedi Hasan	4
B. R. M. Taylor c Nazmul Hossain b Taijul Islam	6	– c Imrul Kayes b Taijul Islam	24
S. C. Williams c Mehedi Hasan b Mahmudullah	88	– b Taijul Islam	20
Sikandar Raza b Nazmul Islam	19	– b Taijul Islam	25
P. J. Moor not out	63	– c Liton Das b Taijul Islam	0
†R. W. Chakabva c Nazmul Hossain b Taijul Islam	28	– c Mahmudullah b Nazmul Islam	20
W. P. Masakadza c Mushfiqur Rahim b Taijul Islam	4	– lbw b Mehedi Hasan	17
B. A. Mavuta lbw b Nazmul Islam	3	– c Ariful Haque b Nazmul Islam	6
K. M. Jarvis c Mehedi Hasan b Taijul Islam	4	– not out	1
T. L. Chatara c Liton Das b Taijul Islam	0	– lbw b Taijul Islam	8
B 1, lb 1	2	B 4, lb 4	8
(117.3 overs)	282	(65.4 overs)	181

1/35 (2) 2/47 (3) 3/85 (1) 4/129 (5) 5/201 (4)
6/261 (7) 7/268 (8) 8/273 (9) 9/282 (10) 10/282 (11)

1/19 (2) 2/47 (3) 3/101 (1) 4/121 (4) 5/121 (6)
6/130 (5) 7/165 (8) 8/172 (7) 9/173 (9) 10/181 (11)

Abu Jayed 21–3–68–1; Taijul Islam 39.3–7–108–6; Ariful Haque 4–1–7–0; Mehedi Hasan 27–8–45–0; Nazmul Islam 23–6–49–2; Mahmudullah 3–0–3–1. *Second innings*—Taijul Islam 28.4–8–62–5; Nazmul Islam 6–1–27–2; Abu Jayed 7–1–25–0; Mehedi Hasan 19–7–48–3; Mahmudullah 4–1–7–0; Mominul Haque 1–0–4–0.

Bangladesh

Liton Das c Chakabva b Jarvis	9	– lbw b Sikandar Raza	23
Imrul Kayes b Chatara	5	– b Sikandar Raza	43
Mominul Haque c H. Masakadza b Sikandar Raza	11	– b Jarvis	9
Nazmul Hossain c Chakabva b Chatara	5	– (5) c Sikandar Raza b Mavuta	13
*Mahmudullah b Chatara	0	– (4) c sub (C. R. Ervine) b Sikandar Raza	16
†Mushfiqur Rahim c Chakabva b Jarvis	31	– c W. P. Masakadza b Mavuta	13
Ariful Haque not out	41	– c Chakabva b W. P. Masakadza	38
Mehedi Hasan c and b Williams	21	– c Chakabva b Mavuta	7
Taijul Islam c Chakabva b Sikandar Raza	8	– c Taylor b W. P. Masakadza	0
Nazmul Islam c Chari b Sikandar Raza	4	– lbw b Mavuta	0
Abu Jayed run out (Taylor/Chatara)	0	– not out	0
B 7, lb 1	8	B 5, lb 2	7
(51 overs)	143	(63.1 overs)	169

1/8 (2) 2/14 (1) 3/19 (4) 4/19 (5) 5/49 (3)
6/78 (6) 7/108 (8) 8/131 (9) 9/143 (10) 10/143 (11)

1/56 (1) 2/67 (3) 3/83 (2) 4/102 (5) 5/111 (5)
6/132 (6) 7/150 (8) 8/151 (9) 9/155 (10) 10/169 (7)

Jarvis 11–2–28–2; Chatara 10–4–19–3; Mavuta 6–0–27–0; Sikandar Raza 12–2–35–3; W. P. Masakadza 8–2–21–0; Williams 4–0–5–1. *Second innings*—Jarvis 14–5–29–1; Chatara 9–2–25–0; Sikandar Raza 17–1–41–3; Williams 8–2–13–0; Mavuta 10–2–21–4; W. P. Masakadza 5.1–0–33–2.

Umpires: R. A. Kettleborough *(England)* (55) and R. J. Tucker *(Australia)* (65).
Third umpire: H. D. P. K. Dharmasena *(Sri Lanka)*. Referee: R. S. Madugalle *(Sri Lanka)* (184).

Close of play: first day, Zimbabwe 236–5 (Moor 37, Chakabva 20); second day, Zimbabwe 1–0 (H. Masakadza 1, Chari 0); third day, Bangladesh 26–0 (Liton Das 14, Imrul Kayes 12).

Test No. 2324/16 (B111, Z107)

BANGLADESH v ZIMBABWE 2018–19 (2nd Test)

At Shere Bangla National Stadium, Mirpur, Dhaka, on 11, 12, 13, 14, 15 November, 2018.
Toss: Bangladesh.   Result: BANGLADESH WON BY 218 RUNS.
Debuts: Bangladesh – Khaled Ahmed, Mithun Ali.
Man of the Match: Mushfiqur Rahim.   Man of the Series: Taijul Islam.

Bangladesh levelled the series with an emphatic victory, set up by a huge total and rammed home by the spinners, who shared 16 wickets to thwart twin hundreds from Taylor, the 11th man to achieve this in a losing cause. Bangladesh had not passed 200 in their previous eight Test innings, and were soon 26 for three. But Mominul Haque emphatically ended a poor run with a superb 161; he and Mushfiqur Rahim added 266, a national fourth-wicket record. Mushfiqur carried on to his second Test double-century, breaking Bangladesh's eighth-wicket record too, putting on 144 with Mehedi Hasan. Zimbabwe were without Chatara, who tore a hamstring early on the second morning. The declaration came after Mushfiqur reclaimed Bangladesh's highest Test score, passing Shakib Al Hasan's 217 at Wellington in 2016–17. Taylor kept Zimbabwe's heads above water with his fifth Test century, the first away from home. He and Moor added 139 for the sixth wicket, but the spinners worked their way through, Taijul Islam finishing with a third successive five-for. Mahmudullah waived what would have been his side's first follow-on, despite a lead of 218. Embarrassment loomed at 25 for four, but Mithun Ali stopped the rot, putting on 118 with Mahmudullah, who declared after reaching his second Test century, nearly nine years after the first. Zimbabwe were left 443 to win or 120 overs to draw. Taylor at least reached the foothills, but he was alone: after the openers put on 68, no one else managed more than 13.

Bangladesh

Liton Das c Mavuta b Jarvis	9	– b Jarvis	6
Imrul Kayes c Chakabva b Jarvis	0	– c Mavuta b Jarvis	3
Mominul Haque c Chari b Chatara	161	– c Chakabva b Tiripano	1
Mithun Ali c Taylor b Tiripano	0	– c Chakabva b Sikandar Raza	67
†Mushfiqur Rahim not out	219	– c Mavuta b Tiripano	7
Taijul Islam c Chakabva b Jarvis	4		
*Mahmudullah c Chakabva b Jarvis	36	– (6) not out	101
Ariful Haque c Chari b Jarvis	4	– (7) b Williams	5
Mehedi Hasan not out	68	– (8) not out	27
B 9, lb 8, w 1, nb 3	21	B 5, lb 1, w 1	7
(7 wkts dec, 160 overs)	522	(6 wkts dec, 54 overs)	224

1/13 (2) 2/16 (1) 3/26 (4) 4/292 (3)   1/9 (2) 2/10 (1) 3/10 (2)
5/299 (6) 6/372 (7) 7/378 (8)   4/25 (5) 5/143 (4) 6/151 (7)

Mustafizur Rahman and Khaled Ahmed did not bat.

Jarvis 28–6–71–5; Chatara 22.2–12–34–1; Tiripano 24.4–6–65–1; Sikandar Raza 22–1–111–0; Williams 30–4–80–0; Mavuta 31–1–137–0; Masakadza 2–0–7–0. *Second innings*—Jarvis 11–2–27–2; Tiripano 11–1–31–2; Williams 16–2–69–1; Sikandar Raza 7–0–39–1; Mavuta 9–0–52–0.

Zimbabwe

*H. Masakadza c Mehedi Hasan b Taijul Islam	14	– c Mominul Haque b Mehedi Hasan	25
B. B. Chari c Mominul Haque b Mehedi Hasan	53	– lbw b Taijul Islam	43
D. T. Tiripano c Mehedi Hasan b Taijul Islam	8	– (8) c Liton Das b Mehedi Hasan	0
B. R. M. Taylor c Taijul Islam b Mehedi Hasan	110	– (3) not out	106
S. C. Williams b Taijul Islam	11	– (4) b Mustafizur Rahman	13
Sikandar Raza b Taijul Islam	0	– (5) c and b Taijul Islam	12
P. J. Moor lbw b Ariful Haque	83	– (6) c Imrul Kayes b Mehedi Hasan	13
†R. W. Chakabva c Mominul Haque b Taijul Islam	10	– (7) run out (Mominul Haque/Mushfiqur Rahim)	2
B. A. Mavuta c Ariful Haque b Mehedi Hasan	0	– c Taijul Islam b Mehedi Hasan	0
K. M. Jarvis not out	9	– c Khaled Ahmed b Mehedi Hasan	1
T. L. Chatara absent hurt	–	absent hurt	
B 5, lb 1	6	B 1, lb 3, w 5	9
(105.3 overs)	304	(83.1 overs)	224

1/20 (1) 2/40 (3) 3/96 (2) 4/129 (5) 5/131 (6)   1/68 (1) 2/70 (2) 3/99 (4) 4/120 (5) 5/186 (6)
6/270 (7) 7/290 (4) 8/290 (9) 9/304 (8)   6/199 (7) 7/201 (8) 8/213 (9) 9/224 (10)

Mustafizur Rahman 21–8–58–0; Khaled Ahmed 18–7–48–0; Taijul Islam 40.3–10–107–5; Mehedi Hasan 20–3–61–3; Mahmudullah 2–0–14–0; Ariful Haque 4–2–10–1. *Second innings*—Mustafizur Rahman 10–2–19–1; Taijul Islam 37–5–93–2; Khaled Ahmed 12–4–45–0; Mehedi Hasan 18.1–5–38–5; Ariful Haque 3–1–7–0; Mahmudullah 1–0–1–0; Mominul Haque 2–0–17–0.

Umpires: H. D. P. K. Dharmasena *(Sri Lanka)* (56) and R. A. Kettleborough *(England)* (56).
Third umpire: R. J. Tucker *(Australia)*.   Referee: R. S. Madugalle *(Sri Lanka)* (185).

Close of play: first day, Bangladesh 303–5 (Mushfiqur Rahim 111, Mahmudullah 0); second day, Zimbabwe 25–1 (Chari 10, Tiripano 0); third day, Zimbabwe 304; fourth day, Zimbabwe 76–2 (Taylor 4, Williams 2).

Test No. 2325/32 (SL275, E1005)

SRI LANKA v ENGLAND 2018–19 (1st Test)

At Galle International Stadium on 6, 7, 8, 9 November, 2018.
Toss: England.　　Result: ENGLAND WON BY 211 RUNS.
Debuts: England – R. J. Burns, B. T. Foakes.
Man of the Match: B. T. Foakes.

Ben Foakes was not in England's original squad, but was brought in as back-up to the back-up keeper: an insurance policy dressed up as a tourist became the first-choice gloveman. And, in a team full of No. 7s, he took that job too and became only the second England wicketkeeper, after Matt Prior in 2007, to score a century on Test debut, completing it with the No. 11 at the other end. He piloted England from 103 for five in the 24th over to a more healthy 342, before the spinners took over once Anderson and Curran removed the openers. Mathews resisted stoutly for 52, but Chandimal was stumped first ball after tea, and England were soon batting again, 139 in front. Jennings was happy to nudge singles; there were only six fours in his second century – the first since his Test debut at Mumbai two years earlier. With Stokes sharing handy partnerships with Buttler and Foakes, the lead grew to 461, and Sri Lanka had more than two days to survive. The top five all reached 20, but no one exceeded Mathews's 53, and with Ali twirling to his second four-for, late on the fourth day England won in Galle for the first time. Their second victory in Sri Lanka since 2000–01 ended a run of 13 overseas Tests without a win, England's longest drought. Rangana Herath bowed out after his 93rd Test with 433 wickets, a record 398 of them after turning 30, and 102 on this ground.

England

R. J. Burns c Dickwella b Lakmal	9	– run out (Karunaratne)	23
K. K. Jennings b Perera	46	– not out	146
M. M. Ali b Lakmal	0	– c Herath b Perera	3
*J. E. Root b Herath	35	– c Dickwella b Herath	3
B. A. Stokes b Perera	7	– b Perera	62
J. C. Buttler c Dickwella b Perera	38	– c Silva b Herath	35
†B. T. Foakes c de Silva b Lakmal	107	– c Mendis b Dananjaya	37
S. M. Curran c Chandimal b Dananjaya	48	– not out	0
A. U. Rashid c de Silva b Perera	35		
M. J. Leach c de Silva b Perera	15		
J. M. Anderson not out	0		
B 1, lb 1	2	B 4, lb 7, nb 2	13
(97 overs)	342	(6 wkts dec, 93 overs)	322

1/10 (1) 2/10 (3) 3/72 (4) 4/98 (2) 5/103 (5)
6/164 (6) 7/252 (8) 8/306 (9) 9/330 (10) 10/342 (7)
1/60 (1) 2/67 (3) 3/74 (4)
4/181 (5) 5/258 (6) 6/319 (7)

Lakmal 18–5–73–3; Perera 31–6–75–5; Dananjaya 20–2–96–1; Herath 25–4–78–1; de Silva 3–0–18–0. *Second innings*—Perera 30–3–94–2; Lakmal 9–2–30–0; Herath 23–1–59–2; Dananjaya 18.5–2–87–1; de Silva 12.1–2–41–0.

Sri Lanka

F. D. M. Karunaratne c Foakes b Anderson	4	– c and b Ali	26
J. K. Silva lbw b Curran	1	– lbw b Leach	30
D. M. de Silva b Ali	14	– c Root b Stokes	21
B. K. G. Mendis c Stokes b Leach	19	– c Ali b Leach	45
A. D. Mathews c Jennings b Ali	52	– c Buttler b Ali	53
*L. D. Chandimal st Foakes b Rashid	33	– b Leach	1
†D. P. D. N. Dickwella c Buttler b Ali	28	– c Stokes b Ali	16
M. D. K. Perera c Buttler b Leach	21	– c Stokes b Rashid	30
A. Dananjaya c Foakes b Ali	0	– c Stokes b Ali	8
R. A. S. Lakmal c Anderson b Rashid	15	– not out	14
H. M. R. K. B. Herath not out	14	– run out (Stokes/Foakes)	5
Lb 2	2	Lb 1	1
(68 overs)	203	(85.1 overs)	250

1/4 (1) 2/10 (2) 3/34 (4) 4/40 (3) 5/115 (6)
6/136 (5) 7/171 (7) 8/173 (9) 9/175 (8) 10/203 (10)
1/51 (2) 2/59 (1) 3/98 (3) 4/144 (4) 5/154 (6)
6/190 (7) 7/197 (5) 8/229 (9) 9/239 (8) 10/250 (11)

Anderson 10–0–26–1; Curran 6–1–16–1; Leach 18–2–41–2; Ali 21–4–66–4; Rashid 9–1–30–2; Stokes 4–0–22–0. *Second innings*—Curran 5–1–15–0; Anderson 12–2–27–0; Ali 20–2–71–4; Rashid 18.1–0–59–1; Leach 21–1–60–3; Stokes 8–2–16–1; Root 1–0–1–0.

Umpires: M. Erasmus *(South Africa)* (52) and C. B. Gaffaney *(New Zealand)* (23).
Third umpire: S. Ravi *(India)*.　　Referee: A. J. Pycroft *(Zimbabwe)* (63).

Close of play: first day, England 321–8 (Foakes 87, Leach 14); second day, England 38–0 (Burns 11, Jennings 26); third day, Sri Lanka 15–0 (Karunaratne 7, Silva 8).

Test No. 2326/33 (SL276, E1006)

SRI LANKA v ENGLAND 2018–19 (2nd Test)

At Muttiah Muralitharan Stadium, Pallekele, on 14, 15, 16, 17, 18 November, 2018.
Toss: England.   Result: ENGLAND WON BY 57 RUNS.
Debuts: none.
Man of the Match: J. E. Root.

Root's sparkling second-innings 124 inspired England to victory, although Sri Lanka – who had led on first innings – made a gallant attempt at a target of 301. England's four spinners shared 19 wickets, the first time since Jim Laker's match at Old Trafford in 1956 that England had won without a wicket from a seamer. Curran's 64 – most of them in a last-ditch stand of 60 with Anderson – had rescued England's first innings from 171 for seven. Uniquely, he had reached all three of his Test half-centuries with sixes, of which he belted six here. Sri Lanka's scorecard was also lopsided: Roshen Silva's 85, and the 190 runs added while he was in, conjured a lead of 46. (He also gifted five penalty runs to England, retrospectively added to their total, when the umpires decided he had deliberately run one short.) And then came Root, sweeping repeatedly on the way to his 15th Test century. After the doughty Foakes weighed in again to take the lead to 300, Sri Lanka's chase started dismally: Leach, who had faced the only over the previous evening as a nightwatchman, now completed a rare double by taking the new ball – and reduced the hosts to 26 for three. Karunaratne and Mathews added 77, and Sri Lanka looked well placed on 219 for five at tea on the final day. But Mathews was soon trapped by Ali, and the rest could muster only 22 as England completed their first series win in Sri Lanka since 2000-01.

England

Batsman	1st innings		2nd innings	
R. J. Burns c de Silva b Dananjaya	43	– (2) lbw b Pushpakumara		59
K. K. Jennings c Dickwella b Lakmal	1	– (3) c de Silva b Dananjaya		26
B. A. Stokes lbw b Perera	19	– (5) lbw b Perera		0
*J. E. Root b Pushpakumara	14	– lbw b Dananjaya		124
J. C. Buttler c Karunaratne b Pushpakumara	63	– (6) b Dananjaya		34
M. M. Ali lbw b Pushpakumara	10	– (7) lbw b Dananjaya		10
†B. T. Foakes c de Silva b Perera	19	– (8) not out		65
S. M. Curran c Karunaratne b Perera	64	– (9) b Dananjaya		0
A. U. Rashid lbw b Perera	31	– (10) lbw b Dananjaya		2
M. J. Leach b Dananjaya	7	– (1) lbw b Perera		1
J. M. Anderson not out	7	– b Perera		12
B 4, lb 3, p 5	12	B 4, lb 9		13
(75.4 overs)	290	(80.4 overs)		346

1/7 (2) 2/44 (3) 3/65 (4) 4/89 (1) 5/134 (6)
6/165 (7) 7/171 (5) 8/216 (9) 9/225 (10) 10/285 (8)

1/4 (1) 2/77 (3) 3/108 (2) 4/109 (5) 5/183 (6)
6/219 (7) 7/301 (4) 8/301 (9) 9/305 (10) 10/346 (11)

Lakmal 12–1–44–1; Perera 24.4–5–61–4; Pushpakumara 23–4–89–3; de Silva 2–0–4–0; Dananjaya 14–1–80–2. *Second innings*—Perera 20.4–2–96–3; Pushpakumara 27–1–101–1; Dananjaya 25–0–115–6; de Silva 4–0–7–0; Lakmal 4–0–14–0.

Sri Lanka

Batsman	1st innings		2nd innings	
F. D. M. Karunaratne run out (Stokes)	63	– c Foakes b Rashid		57
J. K. Silva b Leach	6	– st Foakes b Leach		4
P. M. Pushpakumara c Burns b Ali	4	– (11) c and b Leach		1
D. M. de Silva c Foakes b Rashid	59	– (3) c Jennings b Leach		1
B. K. G. Mendis c Stokes b Leach	1	– (4) lbw b Leach		1
A. D. Mathews c Foakes b Rashid	20	– (5) lbw b Ali		88
A. R. S. Silva c Ali b Rashid	85	– (6) c Root b Ali		37
†D. P. D. N. Dickwella lbw b Root	25	– (7) c Stokes b Ali		35
M. D. K. Perera lbw b Leach	15	– (8) lbw b Leach		2
A. Dananjaya lbw b Ali	31	– (9) not out		8
*R. A. S. Lakmal not out	15	– (10) b Ali		0
B 6, lb 6	12	B 5, lb 4		9
(103 overs)	336	(74 overs)		243

1/22 (2) 2/31 (3) 3/127 (1) 4/136 (5) 5/146 (4)
6/165 (6) 7/211 (8) 8/252 (9) 9/308 (10) 10/336 (7)

1/14 (2) 2/16 (3) 3/26 (4) 4/103 (1) 5/176 (6)
6/221 (5) 7/226 (8) 8/240 (7) 9/240 (10) 10/243 (11)

Anderson 14–2–40–0; Curran 4–0–19–0; Leach 29–5–70–3; Ali 25–1–85–2; Rashid 22–2–75–3; Root 8–0–26–1; Stokes 1–0–9–0. *Second innings*—Anderson 5–2–12–0; Leach 28–2–83–5; Ali 19–2–72–4; Rashid 17–1–52–1; Root 5–0–15–0.

Umpires: M. Erasmus *(South Africa)* (53) and S. Ravi *(India)* (29).
Third umpire: C. B. Gaffaney *(New Zealand)*.   Referee: A. J. Pycroft *(Zimbabwe)* (64).

Close of play: first day, Sri Lanka 26–1 (Karunaratne 19, Pushpakumara 1); second day, England 0–0 (Leach 0, Burns 0); third day, England 324–9 (Foakes 51, Anderson 4); fourth day, Sri Lanka 226–7 (Dickwella 27, Dananjaya 0).

SRI LANKA v ENGLAND 2018-19 (3rd Test)

At Sinhalese Sports Club, Colombo, on 23, 24, 25, 26 November, 2018.
Toss: England.   Result: ENGLAND WON BY 42 RUNS.
Debuts: none.
Man of the Match: J. M. Bairstow.   Man of the Series: B. T. Foakes.

Showing admirable intensity, England completed a 3–0 victory. They had won all three Tests in an overseas series only twice before – in South Africa in 1895–96, and New Zealand in 1962-63. Bairstow, returning after injury although Foakes kept the gloves, made a pugnacious century, putting on 100 with Root and 99 with Stokes. England reached 336, with left-arm wrist-spinner Sandakan taking five wickets. In reply, Sri Lanka were flying high at 173 for one before losing nine for 67; Rashid weaved a career-best five for 49, while the aggressive Stokes extracted three wickets. Jennings took four catches (and six in the match; both equalled the England records). Leading by 96, England dipped to 39 for four, but Stokes and Buttler stopped the rot, then Foakes rounded off a superb debut series – 277 runs, the most for either side, at an average of 69 – by dragging the advantage to 326. On the fourth day Sri Lanka were hauled back from 82 for five by Mendis and Silva. But they were separated by a tremendous throw from the deep by Leach, and when Ali had Silva lbw, the last pair needed 101. Pushpakumara induced a few nerves, thrashing 43 from 40 balls: at tea the target was down to 43. But four balls after the restart, Leach trapped Lakmal to seal the whitewash. In all, 100 wickets fell to spin, easily beating the previous record of 79 in a three-Test series – also set in Sri Lanka, against New Zealand in 1997–98.

England

R. J. Burns b Perera	14	– lbw b Perera	7
K. K. Jennings c Silva b Pushpakumara	13	– lbw b Perera	1
J. M. Bairstow b Sandakan	110	– c sub (J. K. Silva) b Perera	15
*J. E. Root c Gunathilleke b Sandakan	46	– c and b Pushpakumara	7
B. A. Stokes c de Silva b Sandakan	57	– c Pushpakumara b Perera	42
J. C. Buttler c and b Sandakan	16	– st Dickwella b Sandakan	64
M. M. Ali c Mathews b Perera	33	– c de Silva b Sandakan	22
†B. T. Foakes c Dickwella b Pushpakumara	13	– not out	36
A. U. Rashid not out	21	– c Dickwella b Pushpakumara	24
S. C. J. Broad b Sandakan	0	– c Mendis b Pushpakumara	1
M. J. Leach c Mathews b Perera	2	– c Dickwella b Perera	0
B 7, lb 3, nb 1	11	B 3, lb 4, w 1, nb 3	11
(92.5 overs)	336	(69.5 overs)	230

1/22 (1) 2/36 (2) 3/136 (4) 4/235 (5) 5/254 (3)   1/3 (2) 2/20 (1) 3/35 (3) 4/39 (4) 5/128 (5)
6/265 (6) 7/294 (8) 8/328 (7) 9/329 (10) 10/336 (11)   6/168 (6) 7/171 (7) 8/215 (9) 9/217 (10) 10/230 (11)

Lakmal 11–2–33–0; Perera 32.5–1–113–3; Pushpakumara 20–3–64–2; Sandakan 22–0–95–5; de Silva 5–0–16–0; Gunathilleke 2–0–5–0. *Second innings*—Perera 29.5–3–88–5; Pushpakumara 12–2–28–3; de Silva 9–1–24–0; Lakmal 3–1–7–0; Sandakan 16–1–76–2.

Sri Lanka

M. D. Gunathilleke c Jennings b Leach	18	– c Stokes b Ali	6
F. D. M. Karunaratne c Jennings b Rashid	83	– b Ali	23
D. M. de Silva c Jennings b Rashid	73	– lbw b Leach	0
B. K. G. Mendis c Stokes b Rashid	27	– run out (Leach)	86
A. D. Mathews c Foakes b Stokes	5	– c Broad b Stokes	5
A. R. S. Silva c Jennings b Rashid	3	– (7) lbw b Ali	65
†D. P. D. N. Dickwella c Foakes b Stokes	5	– (8) c Jennings b Leach	19
M. D. K. Perera c Foakes b Stokes	0	– (9) c Jennings b Ali	5
*R. A. S. Lakmal not out	3	– (10) lbw b Leach	11
P. A. D. L. R. Sandakan run out (Rashid)	2	– (6) c Stokes b Leach	7
P. M. Pushpakumara lbw b Rashid	13	– not out	42
Lb 7, w 1	8	B 8, w 5, nb 2	15
(65.5 overs)	240	(86.4 overs)	284

1/31 (1) 2/173 (3) 3/187 (2) 4/200 (5) 5/205 (6)   1/15 (1) 2/24 (3) 3/34 (2) 4/52 (5) 5/82 (6)
6/222 (7) 7/222 (4) 8/222 (8) 9/224 (10) 10/240 (11)   6/184 (4) 7/214 (8) 8/225 (9) 9/226 (7) 10/284 (10)

Broad 9–2–36–0; Leach 18–2–59–1; Ali 13–2–55–0; Rashid 13.5–2–49–5; Root 2–0–4–0; Stokes 10–1–30–3. *Second innings*—Broad 5–0–14–0; Ali 26–3–92–4; Leach 28.4–4–72–4; Stokes 8–1–25–1; Rashid 19–1–73–0.

Umpires: C. B. Gaffaney *(New Zealand)* (24) and S. Ravi *(India)* (30).
Third umpire: M. Erasmus *(South Africa)*.   Referee: A. J. Pycroft *(Zimbabwe)* (65).

Close of play: first day, England 312–7 (Ali 23, Rashid 13); second day, England 3–0 (Burns 2, Jennings 1); third day, Sri Lanka 53–4 (Mendis 15, Sandakan 1).

Test No. 2328/56 (P418, NZ427)

PAKISTAN v NEW ZEALAND 2018–19 (1st Test)

At Sheikh Zayed Stadium, Abu Dhabi, on 16, 17, 18, 19 November, 2018.
Toss: New Zealand. Result: NEW ZEALAND WON BY FOUR RUNS.
Debuts: New Zealand – A. Y. Patel.
Man of the Match: A. Y. Patel.

Pakistan were in control for much of this match, and seemed set for a routine win as they chased just 176. But a headlong collapse, in which the last seven wickets crashed for 41, allowed New Zealand to pull off an improbable victory. It was only their fourth win away from home against Pakistan, who stumbled to their second defeat in 12 Tests in Abu Dhabi (another would soon follow). The win was sealed by Ajaz Patel, an Indian-born slow left-armer making his debut, who claimed five for 59 in the second innings, the last four for seven in 41 balls. New Zealand had only ever successfully defended one lower target – 137, against England (who subsided for 64) at Wellington in 1977–78. Pakistan had gone to lunch on the fourth day at 130 for four, needing just 46 more. But Babar Azam was run out from short fine leg after a mix-up, Sarfraz Ahmed was given out caught behind on review, the next three all failed to score, and finally Azhar Ali was lbw. Only four Tests had ended in victory by a more slender runs margin. Williamson had propped up New Zealand's first innings, before a stand of 83 between Asad Shafiq and Babar set up a lead of 74, which looked decisive in a low-scoring match on a sluggish pitch. Another fighting fifth-wicket stand, between Nicholls and Watling, clawed New Zealand just far enough in front. Seamer Hasan Ali collected his maiden five-for, and leg-spinner Yasir Shah his 14th.

New Zealand

J. A. Raval c Sarfraz Ahmed b Mohammad Abbas.........	7	– c Sarfraz Ahmed b Hasan Ali	46
T. W. M. Latham c Mohammad Hafeez b Yasir Shah.....	13	– lbw b Hasan Ali	0
*K. S. Williamson c Sarfraz Ahmed b Hasan Ali...........	63	– b Yasir Shah	37
L. R. P. L. Taylor c Sarfraz Ahmed b Yasir Shah	2	– lbw b Hasan Ali	19
H. M. Nicholls c Sarfraz Ahmed b Mohammad Abbas .	28	– c Sarfraz Ahmed b Yasir Shah	55
†B-J. Watling lbw b Haris Sohail	10	– lbw b Yasir Shah	59
C. de Grandhomme lbw b Hasan Ali	0	– lbw b Yasir Shah	3
I. S. Sodhi lbw b Haris Sohail	4	– b Hasan Ali	18
N. Wagner c Asad Shafiq b Bilal Asif..............................	12	– b Yasir Shah	0
A. Y. Patel lbw b Yasir Shah	6	– not out	6
T. A. Boult not out...	4	– c Mohammad Hafeez b Hasan Ali	0
Lb 4	4	B 4, w 1, nb 1	6
(66.3 overs)	153	(100.4 overs)	249

1/20 (1) 2/35 (2) 3/39 (4) 4/111 (5) 5/123 (3)   1/0 (2) 2/86 (3) 3/105 (4) 4/108 (1) 5/220 (5)
6/123 (7) 7/128 (8) 8/133 (6) 9/149 (9) 10/153 (10)   6/224 (7) 7/227 (6) 8/227 (9) 9/249 (8) 10/249 (11)

Mohammad Abbas 12–7–13–2; Hasan Ali 16–6–38–2; Bilal Asif 13–1–33–1; Yasir Shah 16.3–2–54–3; Haris Sohail 8–2–11–2; Mohammad Hafeez 1–1–0–0. *Second innings*—Mohammad Abbas 22–10–31–0; Hasan Ali 17.4–3–45–5; Yasir Shah 37–6–110–5; Haris Sohail 7–1–12–0; Bilal Asif 14–3–43–0; Mohammad Hafeez 3–1–4–0.

Pakistan

Imam-ul-Haq c Williamson b de Grandhomme	6	– lbw b Patel	27
Mohammad Hafeez c Williamson b Boult......................	20	– c de Grandhomme b Sodhi	10
Azhar Ali c Watling b Boult	22	– lbw b Patel	65
Haris Sohail c Latham b Sodhi..	38	– c and b Sodhi	4
Asad Shafiq b Boult..	43	– c Watling b Wagner	45
Babar Azam c Watling b Boult..	62	– run out (Sodhi/Patel)...	13
*†Sarfraz Ahmed c Wagner b Patel.................................	2	– c Watling b Patel	3
Bilal Asif st Watling b Patel...	11	– b Patel	0
Yasir Shah c Watling b Wagner	9	– c Taylor b Wagner	0
Hasan Ali c Taylor b de Grandhomme	4	– c sub (T. G. Southee) b Patel	0
Mohammad Abbas not out...	0	– not out	0
B 4, lb 4, w 1, nb 1	10	B 4	4
(83.2 overs)	227	(58.4 overs)	171

1/27 (1) 2/27 (2) 3/91 (4) 4/91 (3) 5/174 (5)   1/40 (1) 2/44 (2) 3/48 (4) 4/130 (5) 5/147 (6)
6/177 (7) 7/195 (8) 8/220 (9) 9/227 (10) 10/227 (6)   6/154 (7) 7/154 (8) 8/155 (9) 9/164 (10) 10/171 (3)

Boult 18.2–6–54–4; de Grandhomme 13–6–30–2; Patel 24–4–64–2; Wagner 18–5–30–1; Sodhi 10–0–41–1. *Second innings*—Boult 7–0–29–0; de Grandhomme 3–0–15–0; Patel 23.4–4–59–5; Sodhi 12–0–37–2; Wagner 13–4–27–2.

Umpires: I. J. Gould *(England)* (70) and B. N. J. Oxenford *(Australia)* (52).
Third umpire: P. R. Reiffel *(Australia)*. Referee: J. Srinath *(India)* (41).

Close of play: first day, Pakistan 59–2 (Azhar Ali 10, Haris Sohail 22); second day, New Zealand 56–1 (Raval 26, Williamson 27); third day, Pakistan 37–0 (Imam-ul-Haq 25, Mohammad Hafeez 8).

PAKISTAN v NEW ZEALAND 2018–19 (2nd Test)

At Dubai International Stadium on 24, 25, 26, 27 November, 2018.
Toss: Pakistan. Result: PAKISTAN WON BY AN INNINGS AND 16 RUNS.
Debuts: none.
Man of the Match: Yasir Shah.

A superb performance from Yasir Shah set up a series-levelling victory: only Imran Khan, with 14 for 116 against Sri Lanka at Lahore in 1981–82, had better match figures for Pakistan. Yasir's batsmen had given him a sizeable total to bowl at: Azhar Ali and Haris Sohail ground out 126 in 61 overs, then Sohail – dropped behind off Sodhi when 37 – and Babar Azam lasted into the final session of the second day. Sohail faced 421 balls in all, while Babar made up for being out for 99 against Australia five weeks previously, although he spent a nervous tea interval on 99 before completing his maiden Test century. New Zealand's openers reached 50 next day... but then Yasir uncorked the genie. Often spinning the ball the width of the stumps or more, Yasir took eight for 17 in 42 balls, including a triple-wicket maiden. His final figures were the best in Tests against New Zealand (previously the South African "Goofy" Lawrence's eight for 53 at Johannesburg in 1961–62), and the best in Dubai (Devendra Bishoo's eight for 49 for West Indies in 2016–17). There were a record-equalling six ducks as the last eight in the order managed just five runs between them. And Yasir was not done. He claimed two more wickets in the follow-on before the close, giving him ten on the third day alone, including Williamson, done in by one that spat sideways and kissed the outside edge. After that it was really only a matter of time.

Pakistan

Imam-ul-Haq c Latham b de Grandhomme	9
Mohammad Hafeez c Latham b de Grandhomme	9
Azhar Ali run out (sub [T.G.Southee]/Watling)	81
Haris Sohail c Watling b Boult	147
Asad Shafiq c Wagner b Patel	12
Babar Azam not out	127
*†Sarfraz Ahmed not out	30
B 2, nb 1	3
(5 wkts dec, 167 overs)	418

1/18 (2) 2/25 (1) 3/151 (3) 4/174 (5) 5/360 (4)

Bilal Asif, Yasir Shah, Hasan Ali and Mohammad Abbas did not bat.

Boult 34–7–106–1; de Grandhomme 30–11–44–2; Wagner 37–12–63–0; Patel 39–5–120–1; Sodhi 22–1–63–0; Williamson 5–0–20–0.

New Zealand

J. A. Raval b Yasir Shah	31	– st Sarfraz Ahmed b Yasir Shah	2
T. W. M. Latham c Imam-ul-Haq b Yasir Shah	22	– c Sarfraz Ahmed b Hasan Ali	50
*K. S. Williamson not out	28	– c Sarfraz Ahmed b Yasir Shah	30
L. R. P. L. Taylor b Yasir Shah	0	– c Yasir Shah b Bilal Asif	82
H. M. Nicholls b Yasir Shah	0	– b Hasan Ali	77
†B-J. Watling run out (Hasan Ali/Yasir Shah)	1	– lbw b Yasir Shah	27
C. de Grandhomme lbw b Hasan Ali	0	– b Hasan Ali	14
I. S. Sodhi c Sarfraz Ahmed b Yasir Shah	0	– b Yasir Shah	4
N. Wagner lbw b Yasir Shah	0	– c Hasan Ali b Yasir Shah	10
A. Y. Patel lbw b Yasir Shah	4	– not out	5
T. A. Boult st Sarfraz Ahmed b Yasir Shah	0	– c Sarfraz Ahmed b Yasir Shah	0
Lb 3, nb 1	4	B 9, lb 2	11
(35.3 overs)	90	(112.5 overs)	312

1/50 (1) 2/61 (2) 3/61 (4) 4/61 (5) 5/63 (6)
6/69 (7) 7/72 (8) 8/72 (9) 9/90 (10) 10/90 (11)

1/10 (1) 2/66 (3) 3/146 (2) 4/198 (5) 5/255 (6)
6/270 (7) 7/285 (8) 8/301 (5) 9/311 (9) 10/312 (11)

Mohammad Abbas 9–4–18–0; Hasan Ali 10–5–25–1; Mohammad Hafeez 2–1–1–0; Yasir Shah 12.3–1–41–8; Bilal Asif 2–1–2–0. *Second innings*—Mohammad Abbas 15–7–29–0; Hasan Ali 19–7–46–3; Yasir Shah 44.5–9–143–6; Mohammad Hafeez 3–1–6–0; Bilal Asif 27–5–61–1; Haris Sohail 4–0–16–0.

Umpires: B. N. J. Oxenford *(Australia)* (53) and P. R. Reiffel *(Australia)* (40).
Third umpire: I. J. Gould *(England)*. Referee: J. Srinath *(India)* (42).

Close of play: first day, Pakistan 207–4 (Haris Sohail 81, Babar Azam 14); second day, New Zealand 24–0 (Raval 17, Latham 5); third day, New Zealand 131–2 (Latham 44, Taylor 49).

Test No. 2330/58 (P420, NZ429)

PAKISTAN v NEW ZEALAND 2018–19 (3rd Test)

At Sheikh Zayed Stadium, Abu Dhabi, on 3, 4, 5, 6, 7 December, 2018.
Toss: New Zealand. Result: NEW ZEALAND WON BY 123 RUNS.
Debuts: Pakistan – Shaheen Shah Afridi. New Zealand – W. E. R. Somerville.
Man of the Match: K. S. Williamson. Man of the Series: Yasir Shah.

In the First Test, New Zealand had overturned a first-innings deficit of 74 to win. Now they did it again, to complete their first series victory over Pakistan away from home since 1969-70. Like the first match, this one owed much to a debutant spinner: 34-year-old Will Somerville, who earlier in the year had been representing New South Wales. After returning to play for Auckland in his native New Zealand, he was called up for this tour – and took seven wickets. There was another landmark for Yasir Shah, whose fifth wicket (Somerville in the second innings) was his 200th in Tests, in only his 33rd match, three quicker than Australia's Clarrie Grimmett. Williamson's determined 89, and Watling's gritty unbeaten 77 from 250 balls, dragged New Zealand to 274. Pakistan started poorly when Mohammad Hafeez, who had announced his Test retirement before the match, fell for a duck. But Azhar Ali and Asad Shafiq put on 201 in 76 overs, taking Pakistan in front, before another tepid lower-order display kept the advantage within bounds. New Zealand lost two quick wickets, but the fifth-wicket pair batted for most of the fourth day. Williamson – dropped twice by Yasir – made a superb 139 before falling first ball on the final morning, but Nicholls marched on to his first overseas hundred. A declaration left a tantalising 280 in 79 overs, but Pakistan were soon floundering at 55 for five. They never recovered, surrendering all ten wickets on the final day to lose for the sixth time since August 2016.

New Zealand

J. A. Raval lbw b Yasir Shah	45	– lbw b Shaheen Shah Afridi	0
T. W. M. Latham lbw b Shaheen Shah Afridi	4	– c Haris Sohail b Yasir Shah	10
*K. S. Williamson c Asad Shafiq b Hasan Ali	89	– lbw b Hasan Ali	139
L. R. P. L. Taylor b Yasir Shah	0	– (5) c Bilal Asif b Shaheen Shah Afridi	22
H. M. Nicholls b Yasir Shah	1	– (6) not out	126
†B-J. Watling not out	77	– (8) b Yasir Shah	0
C. de Grandhomme c Asad Shafiq b Bilal Asif	20	– c Bilal Asif b Yasir Shah	26
T. G. Southee c Babar Azam b Bilal Asif	2	– (9) not out	15
W. E. R. Somerville b Bilal Asif	12	– (4) lbw b Yasir Shah	4
A. Y. Patel c Asad Shafiq b Bilal Asif	6		
T. A. Boult b Bilal Asif	1		
B 11, lb 6	17	B 9, lb 1, nb 1	11
(116.1 overs)	274	(7 wkts dec, 113 overs)	353

1/24 (2) 2/70 (1) 3/70 (4) 4/72 (5) 5/176 (3) 1/1 (1) 2/24 (2) 3/37 (4)
6/203 (7) 7/209 (8) 8/254 (9) 9/272 (10) 10/274 (11) 4/60 (5) 5/272 (3) 6/334 (7) 7/334 (8)

Hasan Ali 20–6–58–1; Shaheen Shah Afridi 23–6–52–1; Yasir Shah 41–11–75–3; Bilal Asif 30.1–4–65–5; Haris Sohail 2–0–7–0. *Second innings*—Hasan Ali 16–5–62–1; Shaheen Shah Afridi 20–5–85–2; Yasir Shah 39–8–129–4; Bilal Asif 36–6–62–0; Azhar Ali 1–0–2–0; Mohammad Hafeez 1–0–3–0.

Pakistan

Imam-ul-Haq c Southee b Boult	9	– c Nicholls b Patel	22
Mohammad Hafeez c Southee b Boult	0	– b Southee	8
Azhar Ali c Patel b Somerville	134	– c Watling b de Grandhomme	5
Haris Sohail c Watling b Southee	34	– c Taylor b Somerville	9
Asad Shafiq lbw b Patel	104	– c Watling b Somerville	0
Babar Azam b Somerville	14	– c Southee b Patel	51
*†Sarfraz Ahmed c Raval b Somerville	25	– b Somerville	28
Bilal Asif c Taylor b Patel	11	– c Watling b Southee	12
Yasir Shah run out (de Grandhomme/Somerville)	1	– c Patel b Southee	4
Hasan Ali b Somerville	0	– c Williamson b Patel	4
Shaheen Shah Afridi not out	0	– not out	2
B 6, lb 9, nb 1	16	B 4, lb 6, nb 1	11
(135 overs)	348	(56.1 overs)	156

1/0 (2) 2/17 (1) 3/85 (4) 4/286 (3) 5/304 (5) 1/19 (2) 2/32 (3) 3/43 (4) 4/43 (5) 5/55 (1)
6/312 (6) 7/333 (8) 8/346 (9) 9/347 (10) 10/348 (7) 6/98 (7) 7/131 (8) 8/137 (9) 9/150 (6) 10/156 (10)

Southee 25–5–56–1; Boult 26–7–66–2; de Grandhomme 13–2–36–0; Patel 35–5–100–2; Somerville 36–8–75–4. *Second innings*—Southee 12–3–42–3; Boult 6–4–7–0; de Grandhomme 4–1–3–1; Patel 14.1–4–42–3; Somerville 20–2–52–3.

Umpires: I. J. Gould *(England)* (71) and P. R. Reiffel *(Australia)* (41).
Third umpire: B. N. J. Oxenford *(Australia)*. Referee: J. Srinath *(India)* (43).

Close of play: first day, New Zealand 229–7 (Watling 42, Somerville 12); second day, Pakistan 139–3 (Azhar Ali 62, Asad Shafiq 26); third day, New Zealand 26–2 (Williamson 14, Somerville 1); fourth day, New Zealand 272–4 (Williamson 139, Nicholls 90).

BANGLADESH v WEST INDIES 2018–19 (1st Test)

At Zohur Ahmed Chowdhury Stadium, Chittagong, on 22, 23, 24 November, 2018.
Toss: Bangladesh.   Result: BANGLADESH WON BY 64 RUNS.
Debuts: Bangladesh – Nayeem Hasan.
Man of the Match: Mominul Haque.

Bangladesh needed only three days to complete their first home victory against West Indies, who had won five of the previous six encounters, to go with a watery draw here in 2011–12. Mominul Haque started with a workmanlike 120, his eighth Test century and the sixth on this ground, where he now averaged 83. Bangladesh were set back by four wickets in 15 balls from the fiery Gabriel. (Earlier, he had been a bit too fiery, nudging Imrul Kayes twice as he ran, earning himself a suspension.) West Indies' trial by spin began early on the second day. Taijul Islam started the slide, and soon it was 88 for five. Hetmyer counter-attacked, adding 92 in 14 overs with Dowrich. They hit seven sixes in all, but a deficit of 78 was daunting on a turning track. Off-spinner Nayeem Hasan, 17, was the third-youngest to take a five-for in a Test, after the Pakistanis Nasim-ul-Ghani and Mohammad Amir. Bangladesh also struggled against spin, as 17 wickets tumbled on the second day. A target of 204 looked attainable – but not for long: West Indies were soon 11 for four. Powell was stumped first ball, a unique dismissal for an opener in Tests, and a landmark victim for Shakib who, in his 54th match, was the first Bangladeshi to take 200 wickets. Finally, Ambris was caught behind after 130 minutes, another of Taijul's six victims. Bangladesh's spinners had taken all 20 wickets for only the second time, after the win over England at Mirpur in 2016–17.

Bangladesh

Imrul Kayes c Ambris b Warrican	44	– b Warrican	2
Soumya Sarkar c Dowrich b Roach	0	– c Brathwaite b Chase	11
Mominul Haque c Dowrich b Gabriel	120	– lbw b Chase	12
Mithun Ali c Dowrich b Bishoo	20	– b Bishoo	17
*Shakib Al Hasan b Gabriel	34	– c Gabriel b Warrican	1
†Mushfiqur Rahim lbw b Gabriel	4	– b Gabriel	19
Mahmudullah b Gabriel	3	– (8) c Hope b Bishoo	31
Mehedi Hasan b Warrican	22	– (7) c Dowrich b Bishoo	18
Nayeem Hasan c Hope b Warrican	26	– c Hope b Bishoo	5
Taijul Islam not out	39	– c Warrican b Chase	1
Mustafizur Rahman lbw b Warrican	0	– not out	2
B 3, lb 5, nb 4	12	B 2, lb 1, nb 3	6
(92.4 overs)	324	(35.5 overs)	125

1/1 (2) 2/105 (1) 3/153 (4) 4/222 (3) 5/226 (6)   1/13 (1) 2/13 (2) 3/32 (3) 4/35 (5) 5/53 (4)
6/230 (7) 7/235 (5) 8/259 (8) 9/324 (9) 10/324 (11)   6/69 (6) 7/106 (7) 8/122 (9) 9/123 (8) 10/125 (10)

Roach 17–2–63–1; Gabriel 20–3–70–4; Chase 11–0–42–0; Warrican 21.4–6–62–4; Bishoo 15–0–60–1; Brathwaite 8–1–19–0. *Second innings*—Roach 1–0–11–0; Warrican 16–2–43–2; Chase 6.5–1–18–3; Bishoo 9–0–26–4; Gabriel 3–0–24–1.

West Indies

*K. C. Brathwaite c Soumya Sarkar b Shakib Al Hasan	13	– lbw b Taijul Islam	8
K. O. A. Powell lbw b Taijul Islam	14	– st Mushfiqur Rahim b Shakib Al Hasan	0
S. D. Hope b Shakib Al Hasan	1	– c Mushfiqur Rahim b Shakib Al Hasan	3
S. W. Ambris lbw b Nayeem Hasan	19	– c Mushfiqur Rahim b Taijul Islam	43
R. L. Chase c Imrul Kayes b Nayeem Hasan	31	– lbw b Taijul Islam	0
S. O. Hetmyer c Mushfiqur Rahim b Mehedi Hasan	63	– c Nayeem Hasan b Mehedi Hasan	27
†S. O. Dowrich not out	63	– lbw b Taijul Islam	5
D. Bishoo lbw b Nayeem Hasan	7	– b Taijul Islam	2
K. A. J. Roach lbw b Nayeem Hasan	2	– lbw b Taijul Islam	1
J. A. Warrican b Nayeem Hasan	12	– c Shakib Al Hasan b Mehedi Hasan	41
S. T. Gabriel c Mahmudullah b Shakib Al Hasan	6	– not out	0
B 6, lb 2, nb 2, p 5	15	B 9	9
(64 overs)	246	(35.2 overs)	139

1/29 (2) 2/30 (3) 3/31 (1) 4/77 (5) 5/88 (4)   1/5 (2) 2/11 (3) 3/11 (1) 4/11 (5) 5/44 (6)
6/180 (6) 7/199 (8) 8/205 (9) 9/225 (10) 10/246 (11)   6/51 (7) 7/69 (8) 8/75 (9) 9/138 (10) 10/139 (4)

Mustafizur Rahman 2–1–4–0; Mehedi Hasan 15–0–67–1; Taijul Islam 20–3–51–1; Shakib Al Hasan 11–1–43–3; Nayeem Hasan 14–2–61–5; Mahmudullah 2–0–7–0. *Second innings*—Shakib Al Hasan 7–0–30–2; Nayeem Hasan 7–1–29–0; Taijul Islam 11.2–2–33–6; Mehedi Hasan 8–1–27–2; Mustafizur Rahman 2–0–11–0.

Umpires: Aleem Dar *(Pakistan)* (122) and R. K. Illingworth *(England)* (38).
Third umpire: R. S. A. Palliyaguruge *(Sri Lanka)*.   Referee: D. C. Boon *(Australia)* (50).

Close of play: first day, Bangladesh 315-8 (Nayeem Hasan 24, Taijul Islam 32); second day, Bangladesh 55-5 (Mushfiqur Rahim 11, Mehedi Hasan 0).

BANGLADESH v WEST INDIES 2018–19 (2nd Test)

At Shere Bangla National Stadium, Mirpur, Dhaka, on 30 November, 1, 2 December, 2018.
Toss: Bangladesh.   Result: BANGLADESH WON BY AN INNINGS AND 184 RUNS.
Debuts: Bangladesh – Shadman Islam.
Man of the Match: Mehedi Hasan.   Man of the Series: Shakib Al Hasan.

Bangladesh wrapped up the series with their first innings win, after 111 previous matches had produced only 12 victories. First to shine was Shadman Islam, a solid 23-year-old opener, and Bangladesh's eighth new cap in their eight Tests in 2018 (Imrul Kayes was injured). He hit just six fours from 199 balls. Mushfiqur Rahim fell shortly after completing 4,000 Test runs, but Shakib Al Hasan added 111 with Mahmudullah, who was last out for a career-best 136. With everyone reaching double figures, Bangladesh made an imposing 508. West Indies were soon floundering at 29 for five, all of them bowled – the first such instance in a Test since 1890. Hope alone reached double figures, but was promptly out for ten. Mehedi Hasan finished with seven for 58 as West Indies were scuttled for 111, their lowest against Bangladesh, undercutting 129 at Kingston four months previously. A massive 397 ahead, Shakib enforced Bangladesh's first follow-on. It was soon 29 for four, but total embarrassment for West Indies was averted by Hetmyer, who blasted nine sixes and a solitary four in his 93 from 92 balls before holing out at long-on; few would have begrudged him a maiden century. The only other West Indian to hit nine sixes was Chris Gayle, during his 333 against Sri Lanka at Galle in 2010–11. Hetmyer was one of 12 wickets in the match for Mehedi, who improved his own national record for the best match figures (previously 12 for 157, against England here in 2016–17).

Bangladesh

Shadman Islam lbw b Bishoo	76
Soumya Sarkar c Hope b Chase	19
Mominul Haque c Chase b Roach	29
Mithun Ali b Bishoo	29
*Shakib Al Hasan c Hope b Roach	80
†Mushfiqur Rahim b Lewis	14
Mahmudullah b Warrican	136
Liton Das b Brathwaite	54
Mehedi Hasan c Dowrich b Warrican	18
Taijul Islam c Dowrich b Brathwaite	26
Nayeem Hasan not out	12
B 2, lb 8, w 1, nb 4	15
(154 overs)	508

1/42 (2) 2/87 (3) 3/151 (4) 4/161 (1) 5/190 (6)
6/301 (5) 7/393 (8) 8/416 (9) 9/472 (10) 10/508 (7)

Roach 25–4–61–2; Lewis 20–2–69–1; Chase 28–0–111–1; Warrican 38–5–91–2; Bishoo 28–1–109–2; Brathwaite 15–0–57–2.

West Indies

*K. C. Brathwaite b Shakib Al Hasan	0	– lbw b Shakib Al Hasan	1
K. O. A. Powell b Mehedi Hasan	4	– st Mushfiqur Rahim b Mehedi Hasan	6
S. D. Hope b Mehedi Hasan	10	– c Shakib Al Hasan b Mehedi Hasan	25
S. W. Ambris b Shakib Al Hasan	7	– lbw b Taijul Islam	4
R. L. Chase b Mehedi Hasan	0	– c Mominul Haque b Taijul Islam	3
S. O. Hetmyer c and b Mehedi Hasan	39	– c Mithun Ali b Mehedi Hasan	93
†S. O. Dowrich lbw b Mehedi Hasan	37	– c Soumya Sarkar b Nayeem Hasan	3
D. Bishoo c Shadman Islam b Mehedi Hasan	1	– c Soumya Sarkar b Mehedi Hasan	12
K. A. J. Roach c Liton Das b Mehedi Hasan	1	– not out	37
J. A. Warrican not out	5	– c and b Mehedi Hasan	0
S. H. Lewis lbw b Shakib Al Hasan	0	– lbw b Taijul Islam	20
B 4, lb 3	7	B 6, lb 3	9
(36.4 overs)	111	(59.2 overs)	213

1/0 (1) 2/6 (2) 3/17 (4) 4/20 (5) 5/29 (3) 6/86 (6)
7/88 (8) 8/92 (9) 9/110 (7) 10/111 (11)

1/2 (1) 2/14 (2) 3/23 (4) 4/29 (5) 5/85 (3)
6/96 (7) 7/143 (8) 8/166 (6) 9/171 (10) 10/213 (11)

Shakib Al Hasan 15.4–4–27–3; Mehedi Hasan 16–1–58–7; Nayeem Hasan 3–0–9–0; Taijul Islam 1–0–10–0; Mahmudullah 1–1–0–0. *Second innings*—Shakib Al Hasan 14–3–65–1; Mehedi Hasan 20–2–59–5; Taijul Islam 10.2–1–40–3; Mahmudullah 1–0–6–0; Nayeem Hasan 14–2–34–1.

Umpires: Aleem Dar *(Pakistan)* (123) and R. S. A. Palliyaguruge *(Sri Lanka)* (1).
Third umpire: R. K. Illingworth *(England)*.   Referee: A. J. Pycroft *(Zimbabwe)* (66).

Close of play: first day, Bangladesh 259–5 (Shakib Al Hasan 55, Mahmudullah 31); second day, West Indies 75–5 (Hetmyer 32, Dowrich 17).

AUSTRALIA v INDIA 2018–19 (1st Test)

At Adelaide Oval on 6, 7, 8, 9, 10 December, 2018.
Toss: India.   Result: INDIA WON BY 31 RUNS.
Debuts: Australia – M. S. Harris.
Man of the Match: C. A. Pujara.

India secured victory in an enthralling match in the last over before tea on the fifth day, when Hazlewood nicked Ashwin low to second slip – the 35th catch of the match, a Test record. Never had India started an away Test so badly – 41 for four – then won so well. They were led from their crisis by Pujara, who rebuilt at first then counter-attacked with the tail, hooking Hazlewood and cutting Starc for sixes, and passing 5,000 Test runs. Australia's reply was sketchy. Finch was bowled through a woolly drive for a duck, but Head, in his first home Test, made 72 before Lyon's effective sweep limited the deficit to 15. India again had need of Pujara's serenity: he added 71 in 32 overs with Kohli, then 87 in 30 with Rahane, before seven wickets tumbled for 73. Australia needed 323, and made another poor start: Finch was plumb lbw second ball, but Ishant Sharma had overstepped, then declined to review a catch behind that TV suggested hit neither bat nor glove. After six consecutive single-figure scores, however, Marsh survived into the final morning for a fighting 60, and the lower order sold themselves dearly. Paine lasted 124 minutes and Cummins 154, but Bumrah extracted them both, then Starc gave Pant his 11th catch, equalling the Test record shared by Jack Russell and A. B. de Villiers. Australia were 64 short when the ninth wicket fell, but Lyon and Hazlewood put on 32 in 67 balls before Ashwin settled matters.

India

K. L. Rahul c Finch b Hazlewood	2	– c Paine b Hazlewood	44
M. Vijay c Paine b Starc	11	– c Handscomb b Starc	18
C. A. Pujara run out (Cummins)	123	– c Finch b Lyon	71
*V. Kohli c Khawaja b Cummins	3	– c Finch b Lyon	34
A. M. Rahane c Handscomb b Hazlewood	13	– c Starc b Lyon	70
R. G. Sharma c Harris b Lyon	37	– c Handscomb b Lyon	1
†R. R. Pant c Paine b Lyon	25	– c Finch b Lyon	28
R. Ashwin c Handscomb b Cummins	25	– c Harris b Starc	5
I. Sharma b Starc	4	– c Finch b Starc	0
Mohammed Shami c Paine b Hazlewood	6	– c Harris b Lyon	0
J. J. Bumrah not out	0	– not out	0
Lb 1	1	B 21, lb 13, w 2	36
(88 overs)	250	(106.5 overs)	307

1/3 (1) 2/15 (2) 3/19 (4) 4/41 (5) 5/86 (6)   1/63 (2) 2/76 (1) 3/147 (4) 4/234 (3) 5/248 (5)
6/127 (7) 7/189 (8) 8/210 (9) 9/250 (3) 10/250 (10)   6/282 (7) 7/303 (8) 8/303 (5) 9/303 (10) 10/307 (9)

Starc 19–4–63–2; Hazlewood 20–3–52–3; Cummins 19–3–49–2; Lyon 28–2–83–2; Head 2–1–2–0. *Second innings*—Starc 21.5–7–40–3; Hazlewood 23–13–43–1; Cummins 18–4–55–0; Lyon 42–7–122–6; Head 2–0–13–0.

Australia

A. J. Finch b I. Sharma	0	– c Pant b Ashwin	11
M. S. Harris c Vijay b Ashwin	26	– c Pant b Mohammed Shami	26
U. T. Khawaja c Pant b Ashwin	28	– c R. G. Sharma b Ashwin	8
S. E. Marsh b Ashwin	2	– c Pant b Bumrah	60
P. S. P. Handscomb c Pant b Bumrah	34	– c Pujara b Mohammed Shami	14
T. M. Head c Pant b Mohammed Shami	72	– c Rahane b I. Sharma	14
*†T. D. Paine c Pant b I. Sharma	5	– c Pant b Bumrah	41
P. J. Cummins lbw b Bumrah	10	– c Kohli b Bumrah	28
M. A. Starc c Pant b Bumrah	15	– c Pant b Mohammed Shami	28
N. M. Lyon not out	24	– not out	38
J. R. Hazlewood c Pant b Mohammed Shami	0	– c Rahul b Ashwin	13
B 6, lb 10, w 1, nb 2	19	B 1, lb 6, nb 3	10
(98.4 overs)	235	(119.5 overs)	291

1/0 (1) 2/45 (2) 3/59 (4) 4/87 (3) 5/120 (5)   1/28 (1) 2/44 (2) 3/60 (3) 4/84 (5) 5/115 (6)
6/127 (7) 7/177 (8) 8/204 (9) 9/235 (6) 10/235 (11)   6/156 (4) 7/187 (7) 8/228 (9) 9/259 (8) 10/291 (11)

I. Sharma 20–6–47–2; Bumrah 24–9–47–3; Mohammed Shami 16.4–6–58–2; Ashwin 34–9–57–3; Vijay 4–1–10–0. *Second innings*—I. Sharma 19–4–48–1; Bumrah 24–8–68–3; Ashwin 52.5–13–92–3; Mohammed Shami 20–4–65–3; Vijay 4–0–11–0.

Umpires: H. D. P. K. Dharmasena *(Sri Lanka)* (57) and N. J. Llong *(England)* (55).
Third umpire: C. B. Gaffaney *(New Zealand).*   Referee: R. S. Madugalle *(Sri Lanka)* (186).

Close of play: first day, India 250–9 (Mohammed Shami 6); second day, Australia 191–7 (Head 61, Starc 8); third day, India 151–3 (Pujara 40, Rahane 1); fourth day, Australia 104–4 (Marsh 31, Head 11).

AUSTRALIA v INDIA 2018–19 (2nd Test)

At Perth Stadium on 14, 15, 16, 17, 18 December, 2018.
Toss: Australia.   Result: AUSTRALIA WON BY 146 RUNS.
Debuts: none.
Man of the Match: N. M. Lyon.

Australia levelled the series in the first Test at the giant new Optus Stadium, which became only Australia's tenth Test venue in 142 years. As at the WACA, the ball travelled through at head height, at least until the last day, although the best bowling performance came not from a paceman but from Lyon, who took eight wickets. Australia at last got a good start, Harris and Finch putting on 112; after a wobble, Marsh and Paine ushered the total past 300. India's openers went cheaply, but only one more wicket went down on the second day, as Kohli proceeded imperiously towards his 25th Test century. A lead looked possible until his departure heralded a collapse. Mohammed Shami relished the conditions when Australia batted again, taking a career-best six for 56, as well as forcing Finch to retire hurt with an injured finger. Khawaja's 72, and another dogged knock from Paine, meant India needed 287. This time there was no recovery from a poor start: it was 15 for two by tea, with both Rahul and Pujara gone. And the game was all but up soon after the interval, when Lyon dismissed Kohli for the seventh time in Tests, with one that leapt from the footmarks left by Sharma. On the final morning, the last five wickets lasted just nine overs. With Ashwin injured, India had chosen possibly their slickest attack in a Test – but possibly their worst tail, as Nos. 8–11 contributed only 11 runs over both innings.

Australia

M. S. Harris c Rahane b Vihari	70	– b Bumrah	20
A. J. Finch lbw b Bumrah	50	– c Pant b Mohammed Shami	25
U. T. Khawaja c Pant b Yadav	5	– c Pant b Mohammed Shami	72
S. E. Marsh c Rahane b Vihari	45	– c Pant b Mohammed Shami	5
P. S. P. Handscomb c Kohli b Sharma	7	– lbw b Sharma	13
T. M. Head c Mohammed Shami b Sharma	58	– c Sharma b Mohammed Shami	19
*†T. D. Paine lbw b Bumrah	38	– c Kohli b Mohammed Shami	37
P. J. Cummins b Yadav	19	– b Bumrah	1
M. A. Starc c Pant b Sharma	6	– b Bumrah	14
N. M. Lyon not out	9	– c Vihari b Mohammed Shami	5
J. R. Hazlewood c Pant b Sharma	0	– not out	17
B 4, lb 7, w 7, nb 1	19	B 8, lb 3, w 4	15
(108.3 overs)	326	(93.2 overs)	243

1/112 (2) 2/130 (3) 3/134 (1) 4/148 (5) 5/232 (4)
6/251 (6) 7/310 (8) 8/310 (7) 9/326 (9) 10/326 (11)

1/59 (1) 2/64 (4) 3/85 (5) 4/120 (6) 5/192 (7)
6/192 (2) 7/198 (3) 8/198 (8) 9/207 (10) 10/243 (9)

In the second innings Finch, when 25, retired hurt at 33-0 and resumed at 192-5.

Sharma 20.3–7–41–4; Bumrah 26–8–53–2; Yadav 23–3–78–2; Mohammed Shami 24–3–80–0; Vihari 14–1–53–2; Vijay 1–0–10–0. *Second innings*—Sharma 16–1–45–1; Bumrah 25.2–10–39–3; Mohammed Shami 24–8–56–6; Yadav 14–0–61–0; Vihari 14–4–31–0.

India

K. L. Rahul b Hazlewood	2	– b Starc	0
M. Vijay b Starc	0	– b Lyon	20
C. A. Pujara c Paine b Starc	24	– c Paine b Hazlewood	4
*V. Kohli c Handscomb b Cummins	123	– c Khawaja b Lyon	17
A. M. Rahane c Paine b Lyon	51	– c Head b Hazlewood	30
G. H. Vihari c Paine b Hazlewood	20	– c Harris b Starc	28
†R. R. Pant c Starc b Lyon	36	– c Handscomb b Lyon	30
Mohammed Shami c Paine b Lyon	0	– (10) not out	0
I. Sharma c and b Lyon	1	– c Paine b Cummins	0
U. T. Yadav not out	4	– (8) c and b Starc	2
J. J. Bumrah c Khawaja b Lyon	4	– c and b Cummins	0
B 4, lb 7, w 5, nb 2	18	B 6, w 3	9
(105.5 overs)	283	(56 overs)	140

1/6 (2) 2/8 (1) 3/82 (3) 4/173 (5) 5/223 (6)
6/251 (4) 7/252 (8) 8/254 (9) 9/279 (7) 10/283 (11)

1/0 (1) 2/13 (3) 3/48 (4) 4/55 (2) 5/98 (5)
6/119 (6) 7/137 (7) 8/139 (8) 9/140 (9) 10/140 (11)

Starc 24–4–79–2; Hazlewood 21–8–66–2; Cummins 26–4–60–1; Lyon 34.5–7–67–5. *Second innings*—Starc 17–3–46–3; Hazlewood 11–3–24–2; Cummins 9–0–25–2; Lyon 19–3–39–3.

Umpires: H. D. P. K. Dharmasena *(Sri Lanka)* (58) and C. B. Gaffaney *(New Zealand)* (25).
Third umpire: N. J. Llong *(England)*.   Referee: R. S. Madugalle *(Sri Lanka)* (187).

Close of play: first day, Australia 277–6 (Paine 16, Cummins 11); second day, India 172–3 (Kohli 82, Rahane 51); third day, Australia 132–4 (Khawaja 41, Paine 8); fourth day, India 112–5 (Vihari 24, Pant 9).

Test No. 2335/97 (A817, I532)

AUSTRALIA v INDIA 2018–19 (3rd Test)

At Melbourne Cricket Ground on 26, 27, 28, 29, 30 December, 2018.
Toss: India.   Result: INDIA WON BY 137 RUNS.
Debuts: India – M. A. Agarwal.
Man of the Match: J. J. Bumrah.

India's 150th Test victory – their first at Melbourne since 1980–81 – was more convincing than the margin implied. In truth, Australia were out of it by the end of the first day, with India a hard-won 215 for two. They had a new opening pair: Vihari was moved up, and survived around an hour in both innings, while Mayank Agarwal hit an entertaining 76 after being whisked straight from the Ranji Trophy. Pujara and Kohli then hunkered down for a partnership of 170 and, with the fit-again Rohit Sharma adding a half-century, India declared at 443. Bumrah took six for 33 in Australia's disappointing first innings of 151; they might have followed on but, bearing the tail in mind, Kohli spared his bowlers. Cummins, who finished with six for 27, had both Pujara and Kohli caught at leg gully for ducks as India nosedived to 44 for five, but Australia still needed an unlikely 399. As at Adelaide and Perth, the tail rallied after an indifferent start, this time around Cummins, who played with patience and sound technique. Paine, Starc and Lyon kept him company to a career-best 63. His handsome drives nourished fantasies of a dramatic final day but, delayed by rain until 12.55, in fact it lasted only 27 balls. India retained the Border–Gavaskar Trophy when Lyon edged to Pant, who made his 20th dismissal of the series – all catches – passing the Indian record shared by Naren Tamhane in 1954–55 and Syed Kirmani in 1979–80, both against Pakistan.

India

G. H. Vihari c Finch b Cummins	8	– c Khawaja b Cummins	13
M. A. Agarwal c Paine b Cummins	76	– b Cummins	42
C. A. Pujara b Cummins	106	– c Harris b Cummins	0
*V. Kohli c Finch b Starc	82	– c Harris b Cummins	0
A. M. Rahane lbw b Lyon	34	– c Paine b Cummins	1
R. G. Sharma not out	63	– c S. E. Marsh b Hazlewood	5
†R. R. Pant c Khawaja b Starc	39	– c Paine b Hazlewood	33
R. A. Jadeja c Paine b Hazlewood	4	– c Khawaja b Cummins	5
Mohammed Shami (did not bat)	–	– not out	0
B 15, lb 14, w 1, nb 1	31	B 5, lb 1, w 1	7
(7 wkts dec, 169.4 overs)	443	(8 wkts dec, 37.3 overs)	106

1/40 (1) 2/123 (2) 3/293 (4) 4/299 (3)
5/361 (5) 6/437 (7) 7/443 (8)

1/28 (1) 2/28 (3) 3/28 (4) 4/32 (5)
5/44 (6) 6/83 (2) 7/100 (8) 8/106 (7)

I. Sharma and J. J. Bumrah did not bat.

Starc 28–7–87–2; Hazlewood 31.4–10–86–1; Lyon 48–7–110–1; Cummins 34–10–72–3; M. R. Marsh 26–4–51–0; Finch 2–0–8–0. *Second innings*—Starc 3–1–11–0; Hazlewood 10.3–3–22–2; Lyon 13–1–40–0; Cummins 11–3–27–6.

Australia

M. S. Harris c I. Sharma b Bumrah	22	– c Agarwal b Jadeja	13
A. J. Finch c Agarwal b I. Sharma	8	– c Kohli b Bumrah	3
U. T. Khawaja c Agarwal b Jadeja	21	– lbw b Mohammed Shami	33
S. E. Marsh lbw b Bumrah	19	– lbw b Bumrah	44
T. M. Head b Bumrah	20	– b I. Sharma	34
M. R. Marsh c Rahane b Jadeja	9	– c Kohli b Jadeja	10
*†T. D. Paine c Pant b Bumrah	22	– c Pant b Jadeja	26
P. J. Cummins b Mohammed Shami	17	– c Pujara b Bumrah	63
M. A. Starc not out	7	– b Mohammed Shami	18
N. M. Lyon lbw b Bumrah	0	– c Pant b I. Sharma	7
J. R. Hazlewood b Bumrah	0	– not out	0
B 4, w 1, nb 1	6	B 2, lb 6, w 2	10
(66.5 overs)	151	(89.3 overs)	261

1/24 (2) 2/36 (1) 3/53 (3) 4/89 (4) 5/92 (5)
6/102 (6) 7/138 (8) 8/147 (7) 9/151 (10) 10/151 (11)

1/6 (2) 2/33 (1) 3/63 (3) 4/114 (4) 5/135 (6)
6/157 (5) 7/176 (7) 8/215 (9) 9/261 (8) 10/261 (10)

I. Sharma 13–2–41–1; Bumrah 15.5–4–33–6; Jadeja 25–8–45–2; Mohammed Shami 10–2–27–1; Vihari 3–2–1–0. *Second innings*—I. Sharma 14.3–1–40–2; Bumrah 19–3–53–3; Jadeja 32–6–82–3; Mohammed Shami 21–2–71–2; Vihari 3–1–7–0.

Umpires: M. Erasmus *(South Africa)* (54) and I. J. Gould *(England)* (72).
Third umpire: R. A. Kettleborough *(England)*.   Referee: A. J. Pycroft *(Zimbabwe)* (67).

Close of play: first day, India 215–2 (Pujara 68, Kohli 47); second day, Australia 8–0 (Harris 5, Finch 3); third day, India 54–5 (Agarwal 28, Pant 6); fourth day, Australia 258–8 (Cummins 61, Lyon 6).

AUSTRALIA v INDIA 2018–19 (4th Test)

At Sydney Cricket Ground on 3, 4, 5, 6, 7 *(no play)* January, 2019.
Toss: India.   Result: DRAWN.
Debuts: none.
Man of the Match: C. A. Pujara.   Man of the Series: C. A. Pujara.

India won at the SCG everywhere but on the scoreboard: rain allowed only 25 overs on the last two days, as the Australians followed on at home for the first time in more than 30 years. The draw confirmed India's first series win in Australia. And, having twice been part of losing teams here, Kohli thought this the proudest moment of his career. His team dominated throughout, starting with Pujara's third hundred of the series, more expressive and less clinical than the other two. He finished with 521 runs at 74, having lasted 1,869 minutes, a record for a four-Test series. After he fell, Pant and Jadeja piled on 204 in 224 balls, India's highest seventh-wicket partnership against Australia, and the highest they had conceded at home. Pant's unbeaten 159 was the highest by a visiting wicketkeeper in Australia, apart from A. B. de Villiers's 169 at the WACA in 2012–13. Kohli's declaration, ten overs from stumps, made his hunger for victory clear, even if Pant marred his day by missing Khawaja before he had scored. Harris and Labuschagne battled to lunch on the third day, but the last eight wickets mustered only 130; left-arm wrist-spinner Yadav tossed the ball up gamely for a rare first-innings five-for. Shaun Marsh nicking meekly to slip somehow summed up Australia's batting travails: tame, confused, exasperating. The follow-on had barely begun when the umpires took the players off for bad light; on the final day, rain and darkness rivalled one another to disrupt play.

India

M. A. Agarwal c Starc b Lyon	77
K. L. Rahul c Marsh b Hazlewood	9
C. A. Pujara c and b Lyon	193
*V. Kohli c Paine b Hazlewood	23
A. M. Rahane c Paine b Starc	18
G. H. Vihari c Labuschagne b Lyon	42
†R. R. Pant not out	159
R. A. Jadeja b Lyon	81
B 2, lb 13, w 5	20
(7 wkts dec, 167.2 overs)	622

1/10 (2) 2/126 (1) 3/180 (4) 4/228 (5) 5/329 (6) 6/418 (3) 7/622 (8)

K. Yadav, Mohammed Shami and J. J. Bumrah did not bat.

Starc 26–0–123–1; Hazlewood 35–11–105–2; Cummins 28–5–101–0; Lyon 57.2–8–178–4; Labuschagne 16–0–76–0; Head 4–0–20–0; Khawaja 1–0–4–0.

Australia

M. S. Harris b Jadeja	79	– (2) not out	2
U. T. Khawaja c Pujara b Yadav	27	– (1) not out	4
M. Labuschagne c Rahane b Mohammed Shami	38		
S. E. Marsh c Rahane b Jadeja	8		
T. M. Head c and b Yadav	20		
P. S. P. Handscomb b Bumrah	37		
*†T. D. Paine b Yadav	5		
P. J. Cummins b Mohammed Shami	25		
M. A. Starc not out	29		
N. M. Lyon lbw b Yadav	0		
J. R. Hazlewood lbw b Yadav	21		
B 4, lb 2, w 5	11		
(104.5 overs)	300	(no wkt, 4 overs)	6

1/72 (2) 2/128 (1) 3/144 (4) 4/152 (3) 5/192 (5) 6/198 (7) 7/236 (8) 8/257 (6) 9/258 (10) 10/300 (11)

Mohammed Shami 19–2–58–2; Bumrah 21–5–62–1; Jadeja 32–11–73–2; Yadav 31.5–6–99–5; Vihari 1–0–2–0. *Second innings*—Mohammed Shami 2–1–4–0; Bumrah 2–1–2–0.

Umpires: I. J. Gould *(England)* (73) and R. A. Kettleborough *(England)* (57).
Third umpire: M. Erasmus *(South Africa).*   Referee: A. J. Pycroft *(Zimbabwe)* (68).

Close of play: first day, India 303–4 (Pujara 130, Vihari 39); second day, Australia 24–0 (Harris 19, Khawaja 5); third day, Australia 236–6 (Handscomb 28, Cummins 25); fourth day, Australia 6–0 (Khawaja 4, Harris 2).

NEW ZEALAND v SRI LANKA 2018–19 (1st Test)

At Basin Reserve, Wellington, on 15, 16, 17, 18, 19 December, 2018.
Toss: New Zealand.   Result: DRAWN.
Debuts: none.
Man of the Match: T. W. M. Latham.

By the close on the third evening, it was one-way traffic, a finish apparently imminent as Sri Lanka's top order crumbled again. Teetering at 20 for three, they were still 276 behind, and Latham's epic unbeaten 264 looked certain to lead them to a tenth successive victory in an early-season (November or December) home Test. Not so fast, said two Sri Lankans with a point to prove. Mendis, who ended an indifferent run with his sixth Test ton, and Mathews, smarting from whispers about his fitness, batted throughout the fourth day, the first such instance in a Test since South Africa's openers Graeme Smith and Neil McKenzie at Chittagong in 2007–08. In almost 89 years of Tests in New Zealand, it had never happened before. The weather completed the job, allowing only 13 overs on the final day. Mathews had also top-scored in Sri Lanka's lopsided first innings – Karunaratne made 79 and Dickwella 80 not out, but no one passed 16 – and celebrated his ninth Test century with a flurry of press-ups and a glare at the dressing-room. Latham, in his 40th Test, had dominated New Zealand's big total. At 11 hours 34 minutes, his innings was the sixth-highest and third-longest by a New Zealander and, when Boult gave the persevering Kumara a fourth wicket, Latham had made the highest score by an opener carrying his bat, eclipsing Alastair Cook's 244 at Melbourne in 2017–18. It was no contest for the match award; all that was missing was the win.

Sri Lanka

M. D. Gunathilleke lbw b Southee	1	– lbw b Boult	3
F. D. M. Karunaratne c Watling b Wagner	79	– c Boult b Southee	10
D. M. de Silva c Watling b Southee	1	– b Southee	0
B. K. G. Mendis c Patel b Southee	2	– not out	141
A. D. Mathews c Watling b Southee	83	– not out	120
*L. D. Chandimal c Patel b Southee	6		
†D. P. D. N. Dickwella not out	80		
M. D. K. Perera c Watling b de Grandhomme	16		
R. A. S. Lakmal c Nicholls b Wagner	3		
C. A. K. Rajitha c Watling b Boult	2		
C. B. R. L. S. Kumara c de Grandhomme b Southee	0		
Lb 7, nb 2	9	Lb 2, w 8, nb 3	13
(90 overs)	282	(3 wkts, 115 overs)	287

1/5 (1) 2/7 (3) 3/9 (4) 4/142 (2) 5/167 (6) 6/187 (5)   1/5 (1) 2/10 (3) 3/13 (2)
7/223 (8) 8/240 (9) 9/275 (10) 10/282 (11)

Boult 27–6–83–1; Southee 27–7–68–6; de Grandhomme 13–2–35–1; Wagner 20–2–75–2; Patel 3–0–14–0. *Second innings*—Southee 25–8–52–2; Boult 25–4–62–1; Wagner 23–4–100–0; de Grandhomme 13–4–24–0; Patel 28–10–46–0; Raval 1–0–1–0.

New Zealand

J. A. Raval c Dickwella b Kumara	43
T. W. M. Latham not out	264
*K. S. Williamson c Rajitha b de Silva	91
L. R. P. L. Taylor c Karunaratne b Kumara	50
H. M. Nicholls c Rajitha b Perera	50
†B-J. Watling c Dickwella b Kumara	0
C. de Grandhomme c Rajitha b de Silva	49
T. G. Southee run out (Chandimal)	6
N. Wagner c de Silva b Lakmal	0
A. Y. Patel b Perera	6
T. A. Boult c Dickwella b Kumara	11
Lb 5, w 1, nb 2	8
(157.3 overs)	578

1/59 (1) 2/221 (3) 3/312 (4) 4/426 (5) 5/426 (6)
6/499 (7) 7/520 (8) 8/520 (9) 9/549 (10) 10/578 (11)

Lakmal 31–6–88–1; Rajitha 34–5–144–0; Mathews 4–3–1–0; Perera 40–1–156–2; Kumara 31.3–2–127–4; de Silva 15–0–54–2; Gunathilleke 2–1–3–0.

Umpires: M. A. Gough *(England)* (7) and R. J. Tucker *(Australia)* (66).
Third umpire: R. K. Illingworth *(England)*.   Referee: R. B. Richardson *(West Indies)* (19).

Close of play: first day, Sri Lanka 275–9 (Dickwella 73); second day, New Zealand 311–2 (Latham 121, Taylor 50); third day, Sri Lanka 20–3 (Mendis 5, Mathews 2); fourth day, Sri Lanka 259–3 (Mendis 116, Mathews 117).

Test No. 2338/34 (NZ431, SL279)

NEW ZEALAND v SRI LANKA 2018–19 (2nd Test)

At Hagley Oval, Christchurch, on 26, 27, 28, 29, 30 December, 2018.
Toss: Sri Lanka.   Result: NEW ZEALAND WON BY 423 RUNS.
Debuts: none.
Man of the Match: T. G. Southee.

If the Wellington pitch was not to New Zealand's liking, the one at Hagley Oval was the perfect Christmas present. Another Latham marathon – 176 in 9½ hours this time – was backed up by an unbeaten 162 from Nicholls, then by a swing clinic from Boult and an award-winning all-round contribution from Southee. The result looked comprehensive, but it took a while for New Zealand to assert themselves. Put in, they were 64 for six before Watling added 108 with Southee, who pinged 68 from 65 balls before grabbing three quick wickets as 14 tumbled on the first day. Next morning Boult scythed down the rest, taking six for four in 15 balls, the last four all lbw for ducks. From there, Sri Lanka were never in it. By the second-day close, Latham was in the driver's seat again; next day his eighth Test century was a formality – the pitch flattened. Nicholls made his third hundred of the year as the lead spiralled to a massive 659. He put on 214 with Latham, then 124 in less than 15 overs with de Grandhomme. Sri Lanka were out on their feet – but faced more than two days to save the Test. They lasted 106 overs, but couldn't replicate their Wellington heroics on a bouncier surface. Mendis top-scored with 67, but when Mathews retired hurt with a hamstring injury, the end was nigh. It was easily New Zealand's biggest Test victory by runs, beating 254 against Zimbabwe at Bulawayo in August 2016.

New Zealand

J. A. Raval c Chandimal b Lakmal	6	– c Mendis b Perera	74
T. W. M. Latham c Mendis b Lakmal	10	– c Dickwella b Chameera	176
*K. S. Williamson c Dickwella b Lakmal	2	– c Mendis b Kumara	48
L. R. P. L. Taylor run out (Kumara)	27	– lbw b Kumara	40
H. M. Nicholls b Lakmal	1	– not out	162
†B-J. Watling c Perera b Kumara	46	–	
C. de Grandhomme c Chameera b Kumara	1	(6) not out	71
T. G. Southee c Gunathilleke b Perera	68		
N. Wagner c Mendis b Lakmal	0		
A. Y. Patel c Lakmal b Kumara	2		
T. A. Boult not out	1		
B 6, lb 7, nb 1	14	B 5, lb 3, w 3, nb 3	14
(50 overs)	178	(4 wkts dec, 153 overs)	585

1/16 (1) 2/17 (2) 3/22 (4) 4/36 (5) 5/57 (4)
6/64 (7) 7/172 (8) 8/175 (9) 9/177 (6) 10/178 (10)

1/121 (1) 2/189 (3)
3/247 (4) 4/461 (2)

Lakmal 19–5–54–5; Kumara 14–4–49–3; Mathews 4–1–6–0; Chameera 8–1–43–0; Perera 5–1–13–1. *Second innings*—Lakmal 30–6–96–0; Kumara 32–6–134–2; Chameera 30–5–147–1; Perera 41–3–149–1; Gunathilleke 16–2–45–0; Karunaratne 4–2–6–0.

Sri Lanka

M. D. Gunathilleke c Raval b Southee	8	– c Watling b Southee	4
F. D. M. Karunaratne c Williamson b Southee	7	– c Watling b Boult	0
*L. D. Chandimal c Watling b Southee	6	– c Nicholls b Wagner	56
B. K. G. Mendis c Watling b de Grandhomme	15	– c sub (M. J. Henry) b Wagner	67
A. D. Mathews not out	33	– retired hurt	22
A. R. S. Silva c Southee b Boult	21	– c Watling b Wagner	18
†D. P. D. N. Dickwella c Southee b Boult	4	– b Southee	19
M. D. K. Perera lbw b Boult	0	– c Williamson b Wagner	22
R. A. S. Lakmal lbw b Boult	0	– b Boult	18
P. V. D. Chameera lbw b Boult	0	– lbw b Boult	3
C. B. R. L. S. Kumara lbw b Boult	0	– not out	0
B 5, lb 5	10	B 4, lb 2, w 1	7
(41 overs)	104	(106.2 overs)	236

1/10 (2) 2/20 (3) 3/21 (1) 4/51 (4) 5/94 (6)
6/100 (7) 7/100 (8) 8/100 (9) 9/104 (10) 10/104 (11)

1/1 (2) 2/9 (1) 3/126 (4) 4/158 (3) 5/181 (7)
6/208 (6) 7/233 (9) 8/233 (8) 9/236 (10)

In the second innings Mathews retired hurt at 155-3.

Boult 15–8–30–6; Southee 15–5–35–3; de Grandhomme 6–0–19–1; Wagner 5–0–10–0. *Second innings*—Boult 28.2–11–77–3; Southee 27–13–61–3; de Grandhomme 10–1–23–0; Wagner 29–10–48–4; Patel 12–9–21–0.

Umpires: M. A. Gough *(England)* (8) and R. K. Illingworth *(England)* (39).
Third umpire: R. J. Tucker *(Australia)*.   Referee: R. B. Richardson *(West Indies)* (20).

Close of play: first day, Sri Lanka 88–4 (Mathews 27, Silva 15); second day, New Zealand 231–2 (Latham 74, Taylor 25); third day, Sri Lanka 24–2 (Chandimal 14, Mendis 6); fourth day, Sri Lanka 231–6 (Perera 22, Lakmal 16).

SOUTH AFRICA v PAKISTAN 2018–19 (1st Test)

At Centurion Park, Pretoria, on 26, 27, 28 December, 2018.
Toss: Pakistan. Result: SOUTH AFRICA WON BY SIX WICKETS.
Debuts: none.
Man of the Match: D. Olivier.

After several seasons of trying to resuscitate interest in the Boxing Day Test, South Africa moved it from Durban to the high veld, which gave Steyn the opportunity to break Shaun Pollock's national record of 421 Test wickets on the ground where he made his first-class debut, back in October 2003. And after Rabada trapped Imam-ul-Haq in the second over, Steyn had Fakhar Zaman taken at third slip to spark celebrations all round. But the remaining headlines belonged to Duanne Olivier, recalled to the squad after Lungi Ngidi suffered a knee injury in Australia, then selected here when Vernon Philander broke his thumb. Bowling fast and short in his first Test for over a year, the "Bloemfontein Bone Collector" reaped six for 37 as Pakistan were shot out for 181. In response, left-armers Mohammad Amir and Shaheen Shah Afridi (in his second Test) struck regularly, making up for the absence of the injured Mohammad Abbas, and South Africa needed a resolute 53 from Bavuma and de Kock's breezy 45 to gain a lead of 42. Pakistan moved 59 in front with nine wickets in hand, but Olivier – who finished with 11 for 96 – prised the door open, and Rabada and Steyn helped kick it down as Pakistan subsided to 190 just before stumps on the second day. South Africa needed 159, and strolled home, with Amla – dropped at slip when eight – making his first half-century in 11 Test innings. This was the first Test in which both captains bagged pairs.

Pakistan

Imam-ul-Haq lbw b Rabada	0	–	b Olivier	57
Fakhar Zaman c Elgar b Steyn	12	–	c Rabada b Olivier	12
Shan Masood b Olivier	19	–	c Maharaj b Steyn	65
Azhar Ali c de Bruyn b Olivier	36	–	c Rabada b Olivier	0
Asad Shafiq lbw b Olivier	7	–	c de Kock b Steyn	6
Babar Azam c du Plessis b Rabada	71	–	b Rabada	6
*†Sarfraz Ahmed b Olivier	0	–	c du Plessis b Rabada	0
Mohammad Amir b Olivier	1	–	b Rabada	12
Yasir Shah lbw b Rabada	4	–	c de Kock b Olivier	0
Hasan Ali not out	21	–	not out	11
Shaheen Shah Afridi c de Kock b Olivier	0	–	c Markram b Olivier	4
B 7, lb 2, w 1	10		B 6, lb 10, w 1	17
(47 overs)	181		(56 overs)	190

1/1 (1) 2/17 (2) 3/54 (3) 4/62 (5) 5/86 (4)   1/44 (2) 2/101 (1) 3/103 (4) 4/134 (5) 5/142 (6)
6/86 (7) 7/96 (8) 8/111 (9) 9/178 (6) 10/181 (11)   6/142 (7) 7/158 (8) 8/159 (9) 9/185 (3) 10/190 (11)

Steyn 13–1–66–1; Rabada 17–4–59–3; Olivier 14–3–37–6; Maharaj 3–1–10–0. *Second innings*—Steyn 15–4–34–2; Rabada 15–4–47–3; Olivier 15–3–59–5; Maharaj 11–2–34–0.

South Africa

A. K. Markram lbw b Hasan Ali	12	– (2)	lbw b Hasan Ali	0
D. Elgar c Azhar Ali b Shaheen Shah Afridi	22	– (1)	c Sarfraz Ahmed b Shan Masood	50
H. M. Amla c Babar Azam b Mohammad Amir	8	–	not out	63
T. B. de Bruyn c Sarfraz Ahmed b Mohammad Amir	29	–	st Sarfraz Ahmed b Yasir Shah	10
*F. du Plessis c Babar Azam b Shaheen Shah Afridi	0	–	c Hasan Ali b Shaheen Shah Afridi	0
T. Bavuma c Sarfraz Ahmed b Shaheen Shah Afridi	53	–	not out	13
D. W. Steyn c Sarfraz Ahmed b Mohammad Amir	23			
†Q. de Kock c Fakhar Zaman b Mohammad Amir	45			
K. A. Maharaj lbw b Hasan Ali	4			
K. Rabada c Asad Shafiq b Shaheen Shah Afridi	19			
D. Olivier not out	0			
Lb 3, w 2, nb 3	8		B 4, lb 5, w 6	15
(60 overs)	223		(4 wkts, 50.4 overs)	151

1/19 (1) 2/43 (3) 3/43 (2) 4/43 (5) 5/112 (4)   1/0 (2) 2/119 (1) 3/136 (4) 4/137 (5)
6/146 (7) 7/170 (6) 8/189 (9) 9/220 (10) 10/223 (8)

Mohammad Amir 20–6–62–4; Hasan Ali 18–4–70–2; Shaheen Shah Afridi 18–1–64–4; Yasir Shah 4–0–24–0. *Second innings*—Mohammad Amir 12–5–24–0; Hasan Ali 13–6–39–1; Shaheen Shah Afridi 15–1–53–1; Yasir Shah 7.4–1–20–1; Shan Masood 3–1–6–1.

Umpires: B. N. J. Oxenford *(Australia)* (54) and S. Ravi *(India)* (31).
Third umpire: J. S. Wilson *(West Indies)*.   Referee: D. C. Boon *(Australia)* (51).

Close of play: first day, South Africa 127–5 (Bavuma 38, Steyn 13); second day, Pakistan 190.

Test No. 2340/25 (SA429, P422)

SOUTH AFRICA v PAKISTAN 2018–19 (2nd Test)

At Newlands, Cape Town, on 3, 4, 5, 6 January, 2019.
Toss: South Africa.   Result: SOUTH AFRICA WON BY NINE WICKETS.
Debuts: none.
Man of the Match: F. du Plessis.

South Africa took the series with another comprehensive victory, despite choosing four seamers and no spinner on a pitch that usually offers some turn. The pacemen again proved too much for Pakistan, who were 54 for five inside 20 overs, and bowled out by tea on the first day, which South Africa ended just 54 behind. Next day, after Markram's polished 78, du Plessis made up for a pair in the previous match with his ninth Test century (but first score over 41 in ten innings against Pakistan). He and Bavuma put on 153 for the fifth wicket in 56 overs. De Kock added a half-century as the lead stretched to 254. Everyone reached double figures, while Mohammad Amir and Shaheen Shah Afridi both took four wickets, as they had at Centurion. At 27 for two a quick finish loomed, but Shan Masood and Asad Shafiq added a spirited 132. Babar Azam contributed a brilliant 72, with 15 fours, but the rest posed little opposition to Steyn and Rabada, who shared eight wickets. Had Philander not overstepped when Mohammad Abbas slogged him to mid-off, South Africa might have completed another three-day win. Instead, their pursuit of 41 on the fourth morning was scrappy: de Bruyn, opening as Markram had injured his thigh, soon departed, then Amla retired after being struck on the biceps by a snarling Amir. Du Plessis could celebrate a series win and the match award, but was suspended from the next Test because of his side's slow over-rate.

Pakistan

Imam-ul-Haq lbw b Philander		8	– c Elgar b Steyn	6
Fakhar Zaman c Bavuma b Steyn		1	– (6) c and b Rabada	7
Shan Masood c de Kock b Rabada		44	– (2) c de Kock b Steyn	61
Azhar Ali c Amla b Olivier		2	– (3) lbw b Rabada	6
Asad Shafiq c Elgar b Rabada		20	– (4) c de Kock b Philander	88
Babar Azam c du Plessis b Olivier		2	– (5) c Amla b Rabada	72
*†Sarfraz Ahmed c de Kock b Olivier		56	– lbw b Olivier	6
Mohammad Amir not out		22	– c de Kock b Steyn	0
Yasir Shah c du Plessis b Olivier		5	– c sub (M. Z. Hamza) b Steyn	5
Mohammad Abbas c de Kock b Steyn		0	– not out	10
Shaheen Shah Afridi c de Kock b Steyn		3	– c Philander b Rabada	14
B 8, lb 2, w 3, nb 1		14	B 9, lb 4, w 2, nb 4	19
(51.1 overs)		177	(70.4 overs)	294

1/9 (2) 2/13 (1) 3/19 (4) 4/51 (5) 5/54 (6)   1/10 (1) 2/27 (3) 3/159 (2) 4/194 (4) 5/201 (6)
6/114 (3) 7/156 (7) 8/162 (9) 9/163 (10) 10/177 (11)   6/220 (7) 7/221 (8) 8/247 (9) 9/270 (5) 10/294 (11)

Steyn 15.1–3–48–3; Philander 11–3–36–1; Rabada 10–2–35–2; Olivier 15–3–48–4. *Second innings*—Philander 19–6–51–1; Steyn 19–2–85–4; Olivier 16–3–84–1; Rabada 16.4–2–61–4.

South Africa

A. K. Markram b Shan Masood		78		
D. Elgar c Sarfraz Ahmed b Mohammad Amir		20	– (1) not out	24
H. M. Amla b Mohammad Abbas		24	– retired hurt	2
T. B. de Bruyn c Babar Azam b Shaheen Shah Afridi		13	– (2) c Sarfraz Ahmed b Mohammad Abbas	4
*F. du Plessis c Sarfraz Ahmed b Shaheen Shah Afridi		103	– (4) not out	3
T. Bavuma c Sarfraz Ahmed b Shaheen Shah Afridi		75		
†Q. de Kock c Asad Shafiq b Mohammad Amir		59		
V. D. Philander b Mohammad Amir		16		
K. Rabada b Mohammad Amir		11		
D. W. Steyn c Fakhar Zaman b Shaheen Shah Afridi		13		
D. Olivier not out		10		
B 5, lb 1, nb 3		9	B 4, w 5, nb 1	10
(124.1 overs)		431	(1 wkt, 9.5 overs)	43

1/56 (2) 2/123 (1) 3/126 (3) 4/149 (4) 5/305 (6)   1/4 (2)
6/356 (5) 7/394 (7) 8/407 (8) 9/408 (9) 10/431 (10)

In the second innings Amla retired hurt at 23-1.

Mohammad Amir 33–9–88–4; Mohammad Abbas 34–8–100–1; Shaheen Shah Afridi 27.1–3–123–4; Yasir Shah 21–1–79–0; Shan Masood 5–1–19–1; Asad Shafiq 4–0–16–0. *Second innings*—Mohammad Amir 5–2–17–0; Mohammad Abbas 4–0–14–1; Azhar Ali 0.5–0–8–0.

Umpires: B. N. J. Oxenford *(Australia)* (55) and J. S. Wilson *(West Indies)* (12).
Third umpire: S. Ravi *(India).*   Referee: D. C. Boon *(Australia)* (52).

Close of play: first day, South Africa 123–2 (Amla 24); second day, South Africa 382–6 (de Kock 55, Philander 6); third day, Pakistan 294.

SOUTH AFRICA v PAKISTAN 2018–19 (3rd Test)

At New Wanderers, Johannesburg, on 11, 12, 13, 14 January, 2019.
Toss: South Africa.   Result: SOUTH AFRICA WON BY 107 RUNS.
Debuts: South Africa – M. Z. Hamza.
Man of the Match: Q. de Kock.   Man of the Series: D. Olivier.

South Africa made it seven home wins in a row against Pakistan, and 12 out of 15 over six visits, their fast bowlers again leading the way. With du Plessis suspended, the captaincy passed to Elgar. And although he was out in the second over, Markram cover-drove imperiously, putting on 126 with Amla before, not long after lunch, being caught behind down the leg side for 90 off Fahim Ashraf, who had replaced the injured Shaheen Shah Afridi. At 229 for three, South Africa had a chance to bat Pakistan out of the game, but the last seven fell for 33 in 15 overs – including Zubayr Hamza, their 100th Test cricketer since readmission, after a promising 41. Thanks to the relentless Philander, Pakistan were back in trouble before the close: Shan Masood and Azhar Ali were caught behind from consecutive balls. Five chances of varying difficulty went down next morning, before Olivier removed nightwatchman Mohammad Abbas and Asad Shafiq in the same over. Sarfraz Ahmed clubbed eight fours in a 40-ball 50, but the last five crashed for 16. South Africa were 93 for five – only 170 in front – but de Kock thrashed a dazzling 129 off 138 balls, his first Test century for two years. Pakistan went down fighting and, set 381, even flirted with a heist: Asad Shafiq hit a sprightly 65, and Shadab Khan 47 not out against a tiring attack, but South Africa had enough to play with. Olivier finished with 24 wickets in the series.

South Africa

A. K. Markram c Sarfraz Ahmed b Fahim Ashraf	90	– (2) c Sarfraz Ahmed b Mohammad Abbas	21
*D. Elgar c Sarfraz Ahmed b Mohammad Abbas	5	– (1) c Sarfraz Ahmed b Mohammad Amir	5
H. M. Amla c Asad Shafiq b Shadab Khan	41	– c Sarfraz Ahmed b Hasan Ali	71
T. B. de Bruyn lbw b Mohammad Abbas	49	– c Asad Shafiq b Fahim Ashraf	7
M. Z. Hamza c Sarfraz Ahmed b Mohammad Amir	41	– lbw b Fahim Ashraf	0
T. Bavuma c Sarfraz Ahmed b Mohammad Amir	8	– c Sarfraz Ahmed b Shadab Khan	23
†Q. de Kock c Mohammad Abbas b Fahim Ashraf	18	– c Hasan Ali b Shadab Khan	129
V. D. Philander lbw b Hasan Ali	1	– lbw b Mohammad Amir	14
K. Rabada c Sarfraz Ahmed b Hasan Ali	0	– c Shadab Khan b Fahim Ashraf	21
D. W. Steyn not out	2	– not out	0
D. Olivier c Mohammad Abbas b Fahim Ashraf	0	– c Sarfraz Ahmed b Shadab Khan	1
Lb 2, w 1, nb 4	7	B 2, lb 6, w 1, nb 2	11
(77.4 overs)	262	(80.3 overs)	303

1/6 (2) 2/132 (1) 3/154 (3) 4/229 (4) 5/238 (6)
6/244 (5) 7/249 (8) 8/257 (9) 9/262 (7) 10/262 (11)

1/24 (1) 2/29 (2) 3/45 (4) 4/45 (5) 5/93 (6)
6/195 (3) 7/223 (8) 8/302 (7) 9/302 (9) 10/303 (11)

Mohammad Amir 15.4–2–36–2; Mohammad Abbas 18–6–44–2; Hasan Ali 17–3–75–2; Fahim Ashraf 15–2–57–3; Shadab Khan 10–2–39–1; Asad Shafiq 2–0–9–0. *Second innings*—Mohammad Amir 20–2–56–2; Mohammad Abbas 18–3–73–1; Hasan Ali 17–1–83–1; Fahim Ashraf 14–3–42–3; Shadab Khan 11.3–0–41–3.

Pakistan

Imam-ul-Haq c Elgar b Philander	43	– c de Kock b Steyn	35
Shan Masood c de Kock b Philander	2	– c de Kock b Steyn	37
Azhar Ali c de Kock b Philander	0	– c de Kock b Olivier	15
Mohammad Abbas c de Bruyn b Olivier	11	– (11) run out (Markram/de Kock)	9
Asad Shafiq c de Kock b Olivier	0	– (4) c Elgar b Philander	65
Babar Azam c Rabada b Olivier	49	– (5) c de Kock b Olivier	21
*†Sarfraz Ahmed c Amla b Rabada	50	– (6) b Olivier	0
Shadab Khan c de Bruyn b Rabada	5	– (7) not out	47
Fahim Ashraf c Hamza b Olivier	0	– (8) c Markram b Rabada	15
Mohammad Amir c Hamza b Olivier	10	– (9) c Markram b Rabada	4
Hasan Ali not out	0	– (10) c and b Rabada	22
B 5, lb 10	15	Lb 2, nb 1	3
(49.4 overs)	185	(65.4 overs)	273

1/6 (2) 2/6 (3) 3/53 (4) 4/53 (5) 5/91 (1) 6/169 (7)
7/169 (6) 8/169 (9) 9/185 (10) 10/185 (8)

1/67 (1) 2/74 (2) 3/104 (3) 4/162 (5) 5/162 (6)
6/179 (4) 7/204 (8) 8/208 (9) 9/242 (10) 10/273 (11)

Steyn 12–4–35–0; Philander 13–4–43–3; Rabada 11.4–0–41–2; Olivier 13–2–51–5. *Second innings*—Steyn 20–2–80–2; Philander 14–4–41–1; Olivier 15–2–74–3; Rabada 16–2–75–3; Elgar 0.4–0–1–0.

Umpires: S. Ravi *(India)* (32) and J. S. Wilson *(West Indies)* (13).
Third umpire: B. N. J. Oxenford *(Australia)*.   Referee: D. C. Boon *(Australia)* (53).

Close of play: first day, Pakistan 17–2 (Imam-ul-Haq 10, Mohammad Abbas 0); second day, South Africa 135–5 (Amla 42, de Kock 34); third day, Pakistan 153–3 (Asad Shafiq 48, Babar Azam 17).

WEST INDIES v ENGLAND 2018–19 (1st Test)

At Kensington Oval, Bridgetown, Barbados, on 23, 24, 25, 26 January, 2019.
Toss: West Indies.   Result: WEST INDIES WON BY 381 RUNS.
Debuts: West Indies – J. D. Campbell.
Man of the Match: J. O. Holder.

Two months after their historic whitewash of Sri Lanka, England came rapidly down to earth in a series they were expected to win easily. It was something of a throwback: a West Indian side containing six players from Barbados, and relying on a potent pace attack, inflicted England's heaviest defeat by runs in the Caribbean. Holder, the gentle giant who had spent more than three years dutifully leading a struggling side, stood – at 6ft 7in – head and shoulders above them all. His remorseless 202 not out from No. 8 in West Indies' second innings had dominated an unbroken stand of 295 with Dowrich. The third-highest seventh-wicket partnership in Tests lifted West Indies from 127 for six, and left England needing 628 in almost seven sessions. West Indies had never set a higher target. Chase picked up eight wickets on the fourth day with his non-turning off-breaks – he would not take another wicket in the series – to dispose of a frazzled England for 246, in which Burns made a doughty 84. But it was Roach who had set this First Test on an irreversible path with a spell of five for four in 27 balls on the second afternoon as England crumbled for a woeful 77, in reply to West Indies' workmanlike 289. Had Jennings departed shortly after lunch rather than shortly before, England might have lost all ten in a session for the fourth time in three years – a fate they had not previously suffered since the Second World War.

West Indies

K. C. Brathwaite c Root b Stokes	40	– lbw b Ali		24
J. D. Campbell lbw b Ali	44	– c Jennings b Stokes		33
S. D. Hope c Foakes b Anderson	57	– c Jennings b Stokes		3
D. M. Bravo lbw b Stokes	2	– c Stokes b Ali		1
R. L. Chase c Root b Anderson	54	– c Stokes b Ali		0
S. O. Hetmyer c Foakes b Stokes	81	– c Buttler b Curran		31
†S. O. Dowrich c Buttler b Anderson	0	– not out		116
*J. O. Holder c and b Anderson	5	– not out		202
K. A. J. Roach c Root b Stokes	0			
A. S. Joseph c Buttler b Anderson	0			
S. T. Gabriel not out	0			
Lb 5, nb 1	6	B 1, lb 1, nb 3		5
(101.3 overs)	289	(6 wkts dec, 103.1 overs)		415

1/53 (2) 2/126 (1) 3/128 (4) 4/174 (3) 5/240 (5)
6/250 (7) 7/261 (8) 8/264 (9) 9/289 (10) 10/289 (6)
1/52 (1) 2/60 (2) 3/61 (4)
4/61 (5) 5/61 (3) 6/120 (6)

Anderson 30–13–46–5; Curran 12–3–54–0; Stokes 25.3–2–59–4; Ali 12–1–59–1; Rashid 17–1–56–0; Root 5–0–10–0. *Second innings*—Anderson 18–4–58–0; Curran 17–1–69–1; Ali 20–3–78–3; Stokes 25–3–81–2; Rashid 9–0–61–0; Root 10–0–37–0; Jennings 4.1–0–29–0.

England

R. J. Burns b Roach	2	– b Chase		84
K. K. Jennings c Hope b Holder	17	– c Holder b Joseph		14
J. M. Bairstow b Roach	12	– c †Hope b Gabriel		30
*J. E. Root lbw b Holder	4	– c Bravo b Chase		22
B. A. Stokes lbw b Roach	0	– lbw b Chase		34
J. C. Buttler c Dowrich b Roach	4	– c Campbell b Chase		26
M. M. Ali c Joseph b Roach	0	– c Holder b Chase		0
†B. T. Foakes c Dowrich b Joseph	2	– c Hetmyer b Chase		5
S. M. Curran c Hope b Gabriel	14	– st †Hope b Chase		17
A. U. Rashid c Holder b Joseph	12	– c Brathwaite b Chase		1
J. M. Anderson not out	0	– not out		4
B 4, lb 6	10	B 4, w 3, nb 2		9
(30.2 overs)	77	(80.4 overs)		246

1/23 (2) 2/35 (1) 3/44 (3) 4/44 (4) 5/48 (5)
6/48 (7) 7/49 (6) 8/61 (8) 9/73 (9) 10/77 (10)
1/85 (2) 2/134 (1) 3/143 (3) 4/167 (4) 5/215 (5)
6/217 (7) 7/218 (6) 8/228 (8) 9/234 (10) 10/246 (9)

Roach 11–7–17–5; Gabriel 7–2–15–1; Holder 8–3–15–2; Joseph 4.2–1–20–2. *Second innings*—Roach 14–3–58–0; Gabriel 16.5–2–55–1; Holder 12–6–24–0; Chase 21.4–2–60–8; Joseph 12–4–35–1; Campbell 4.1–0–10–0.

Umpires: C. B. Gaffaney *(New Zealand)* (26) and R. J. Tucker *(Australia)* (67).
Third umpire: H. D. P. K. Dharmasena *(Sri Lanka)*.   Referee: J. J. Crowe *(New Zealand)* (93).

Close of play: first day, West Indies 264–8 (Hetmyer 56); second day, West Indies 127–6 (Dowrich 27, Holder 7); third day, England 56–0 (Burns 39, Jennings 11).

WEST INDIES v ENGLAND 2018–19 (2nd Test)

At Sir Vivian Richards Stadium, North Sound, Antigua, on 31 January, 1, 2 February, 2019.
Toss: West Indies.　Result: WEST INDIES WON BY TEN WICKETS.
Debuts: England – J. L. Denly.
Man of the Match: K. A. J. Roach.

The script was similar to the First Test, only more brutal – another reminder of the 1980s, when West Indies ruled the world with speed, skill and intimidation. After losing eight wickets to an unheralded spinner in Barbados, England now lost all 20 to fast bowlers. It was a fearful going-over on a spiteful pitch later rated "poor" by the ICC. Over the first two matches, England lost a wicket every 32 balls, at an average of 16, their worst in a series since 1888. Bairstow made a counter-attacking 52 out of 74 before being pinned by Roach, then Ali top-scored with 60, after a pair in Barbados. But only two others reached double figures, and the last four wickets tumbled for nine. Bravo showed how it should be done, taking 215 balls over his half-century, and his side claimed a lead of 119. Joseph insisted on bowling in England's second innings, even though his mother had died overnight after a long illness, and took two wickets as England subsided. Although seven made it into double figures, Buttler's 24 was the highest score. Joe Denly was the 17th opener (including Alastair Cook and a nightwatchman) tried by England since the retirement of Andrew Strauss in 2012. When Campbell pulled Anderson for six, West Indies clinched the Wisden Trophy – which they had last held a decade earlier – with a match to spare. But there was a downside to their reliance on pace: Holder was banned from the final Test for a slow over-rate.

England

R. J. Burns c Holder b Roach	4	– c Campbell b Holder	16
J. L. Denly c Dowrich b Joseph	6	– b Joseph	17
J. M. Bairstow lbw b Roach	52	– b Holder	14
*J. E. Root c Hope b Joseph	7	– c Dowrich b Joseph	7
J. C. Buttler c Campbell b Holder	1	– lbw b Holder	24
B. A. Stokes c Dowrich b Gabriel	14	– b Roach	11
M. M. Ali c Gabriel b Roach	60	– b Roach	4
†B. T. Foakes b Gabriel	35	– lbw b Roach	13
S. M. Curran c sub (S. S. J. Brooks) b Roach	6	– not out	13
S. C. J. Broad not out	0	– lbw b Roach	0
J. M. Anderson b Gabriel	1	– c Joseph b Holder	0
W 1	1	Lb 3, w 10	13
(61 overs)	187	(42.1 overs)	132

1/4 (1) 2/16 (2) 3/34 (4) 4/55 (5) 5/78 (3)　　　1/35 (1) 2/49 (3) 3/56 (4) 4/59 (2) 5/88 (6)
6/93 (6) 7/178 (7) 8/186 (8) 9/186 (9) 10/187 (11)　　6/96 (7) 7/118 (8) 8/118 (5) 9/125 (10) 10/132 (11)

Roach 15–5–30–4; Gabriel 15–5–45–3; Joseph 10–3–38–2; Holder 13–5–43–1; Chase 8–1–31–0. *Second innings—* Roach 13–2–52–4; Gabriel 10–3–22–0; Holder 12.1–2–43–4; Joseph 7–4–12–2.

West Indies

K. C. Brathwaite c sub (K. K. Jennings) b Ali	49	– not out	5
J. D. Campbell c Buttler b Stokes	47	– not out	11
S. D. Hope c †Bairstow b Broad	44		
D. M. Bravo st †Bairstow b Ali	50		
R. L. Chase b Broad	4		
S. O. Hetmyer c Anderson b Ali	21		
†S. O. Dowrich c Buttler b Broad	31		
*J. O. Holder c †Bairstow b Anderson	22		
K. A. J. Roach c Stokes b Anderson	6		
A. S. Joseph c Burns b Stokes	7		
S. T. Gabriel not out	1		
B 8, lb 13, w 1, nb 2	24	Lb 1	1
(131 overs)	306	(no wkt, 2.1 overs)	17

1/70 (2) 2/133 (1) 3/151 (3) 4/155 (5) 5/186 (6)
6/236 (7) 7/281 (8) 8/289 (9) 9/298 (10) 10/306 (4)

Anderson 29–5–73–2; Broad 36–16–53–3; Stokes 27–8–58–2; Curran 13–0–38–0; Ali 25–4–62–3; Denly 1–0–1–0. *Second innings—*Anderson 1.1–0–10–0; Broad 1–0–6–0.

Umpires: H. D. P. K. Dharmasena *(Sri Lanka)* (59) and C. B. Gaffaney *(New Zealand)* (27).
Third umpire: R. J. Tucker *(Australia)*.　　Referee: J. J. Crowe *(New Zealand)* (94).

Close of play: first day, West Indies 30–0 (Brathwaite 11, Campbell 16); second day, West Indies 272–6 (Bravo 33, Holder 19).

Test No. 2344/157 (WI542, E1010)

WEST INDIES v ENGLAND 2018–19 (3rd Test)

At Darren Sammy (formerly Beausejour) Stadium, Gros Islet, St Lucia, on 9, 10, 11, 12 February, 2019.
Toss: West Indies.   Result: ENGLAND WON BY 232 RUNS.
Debuts: none.
Man of the Match: M. A. Wood.   Man of the Series: K. A. J. Roach.

Mark Wood turned the tables – and resurrected an injury-hit career – with a ferociously quick spell on the second day. He took four wickets in 22 balls, and later completed a maiden Test five-for as England took control. Brathwaite, standing in for the suspended Holder, was probably over-confident when he put England in: the pitch was not so helpful to his pacemen, and Buttler put on 125 with Stokes, who made 79 before being superbly caught by the running, diving Dowrich. Roach hauled West Indies back on the second morning, as the last five wickets fell for 21, but Wood's burst – after Ali removed both openers – meant England had a healthy lead. Root set about extending it, sharing hundred partnerships with Buttler and Stokes, and shrugging off a homophobic slur which cost Gabriel 75% of his match fee and a four-match ban. They set up a lead of 484, and when Anderson reduced West Indies to ten for three – which included the 100th time he had taken the first wicket of a Test innings (Glenn McGrath was next, with 97) – it seemed they had finally run out of puff. But Chase held out, and had reached 98 when the fall of the ninth wicket apparently left him stranded, as Paul had injured his thigh. But after a few moments Paul limped down the steps, and blocked the final ball of an over to allow Chase to become the ninth to marry a century with a golden duck in the same Test.

England

R. J. Burns lbw b Paul	29	– c Joseph b Paul	10
K. K. Jennings c Bravo b Paul	8	– b Joseph	23
J. L. Denly lbw b Gabriel	20	– c Dowrich b Gabriel	69
*J. E. Root c Dowrich b Joseph	15	– c Hetmyer b Gabriel	122
J. C. Buttler b Gabriel	67	– b Roach	56
B. A. Stokes c Dowrich b Roach	79	– not out	48
†J. M. Bairstow b Roach	2		
M. M. Ali c Bravo b Joseph	13		
M. A. Wood c Joseph b Roach	6		
S. C. J. Broad not out	0		
J. M. Anderson c Paul b Roach	0		
B 5, lb 11, w 16, nb 6	38	B 13, lb 9, w 8, nb 3	33
(101.5 overs)	277	(5 wkts dec, 105.2 overs)	361

1/30 (2) 2/69 (1) 3/69 (3) 4/107 (4) 5/232 (5)
6/256 (6) 7/270 (7) 8/275 (8) 9/277 (9) 10/277 (11)

1/19 (1) 2/73 (2) 3/147 (3)
4/254 (5) 5/361 (4)

Roach 25.5–11–48–4; Gabriel 24–6–49–2; Joseph 17–2–61–2; Paul 21–7–58–2; Chase 10–0–40–0; Brathwaite 4–0–5–0. *Second innings*—Roach 18–6–45–1; Gabriel 23.2–1–95–2; Paul 5–1–11–1; Joseph 16–2–72–1; Chase 31–1–92–0; Brathwaite 12–2–24–0.

West Indies

*K. C. Brathwaite c Anderson b Ali	12	– c Stokes b Anderson	8
J. D. Campbell lbw b Ali	41	– c Ali b Anderson	0
S. D. Hope c Burns b Wood	1	– c Broad b Wood	14
D. M. Bravo c Root b Wood	6	– c Root b Anderson	0
R. L. Chase c Burns b Wood	0	– not out	102
S. O. Hetmyer c Root b Wood	8	– run out (Denly/Bairstow)	19
†S. O. Dowrich lbw b Broad	38	– c Stokes b Ali	19
K. M. A. Paul st Bairstow b Ali	9	– (11) c and b Stokes	12
K. A. J. Roach not out	16	– (8) c Wood b Ali	29
A. S. Joseph c Broad b Ali	2	– (9) c Anderson b Ali	34
S. T. Gabriel b Wood	4	– (10) c Bairstow b Stokes	3
Lb 4, w 10, nb 3	17	B 1, lb 5, w 4, nb 2	12
(47.2 overs)	154	(69.5 overs)	252

1/57 (1) 2/57 (2) 3/59 (3) 4/59 (5) 5/74 (6) 6/79 (4)
7/104 (8) 8/145 (7) 9/148 (10) 10/154 (11)

1/5 (2) 2/10 (1) 3/10 (4) 4/31 (3) 5/76 (6)
6/110 (7) 7/156 (8) 8/212 (9) 9/236 (10) 10/252 (11)

Anderson 9–3–31–0; Broad 15–4–42–1; Ali 15–4–36–4; Wood 8.2–2–41–5. *Second innings*—Anderson 11–2–27–3; Broad 14–6–22–0; Stokes 8.5–2–30–2; Wood 12–1–52–1; Ali 21–1–99–3; Denly 3–0–16–0.

Umpires: H. D. P. K. Dharmasena *(Sri Lanka)* (60) and R. J. Tucker *(Australia)* (68).
Third umpire: C. B. Gaffaney *(New Zealand)*.   Referee: J. J. Crowe *(New Zealand)* (95).

Close of play: first day, England 231–4 (Buttler 67, Stokes 62); second day, England 19–0 (Burns 10, Jennings 8); third day, England 325–4 (Root 111, Stokes 29).

AUSTRALIA v SRI LANKA 2018–19 (1st Test)

At Wolloongabba, Brisbane, on 24, 25, 26 January, 2019 (day/night).
Toss: Sri Lanka. Result: AUSTRALIA WON BY AN INNINGS AND 40 RUNS.
Debuts: Australia – K. R. Patterson, J. A. Richardson.
Man of the Match: P. J. Cummins.

In recent years, the Australian season had begun with the traditional humiliation of opponents at the Gabba. The last touring side to win here were West Indies, in 1988-89, since when Australia had won 22 and drawn seven. India had avoided the ritual flogging by insisting their four-match series should be arranged differently, with Adelaide staging the First Test; they also declined to play a day/night game. And so Sri Lanka, whose board have rather less financial leverage, found themselves playing under lights in Queensland. It did not end well. Chandimal bravely batted first on a pitch renowned for being at its most testing at the start, and soon it was 66 for five. Dickwella made a freewheeling 64, including an audacious scoop off Starc, but 144 all out was never enough. Australia had 25 testing overs under lights on the first evening. They lost two wickets, but Harris battled through before falling in the first over next morning. Sri Lanka had a sniff at 82 for four, but Labuschagne – who hit only three fours – and Head shared a patient stand of 166, spanning almost 50 overs. Lakmal dismissed Head and Paine with successive balls, and finished with only his third five-for in 55 Tests. Australia still finished 179 in front, which proved enough. Cummins pocketed six more wickets, slicing through some flimsy batting to finish with ten for 62, Australia's best at home against Sri Lanka. Australia's win was only their second in eight Tests since the sandpaper shenanigans.

Sri Lanka

F. D. M. Karunaratne c Paine b Lyon	24	– c Paine b Cummins	3
H. D. R. L. Thirimanne c Labuschagne b Cummins	12	– c Paine b Cummins	32
*L. D. Chandimal c Burns b Richardson	5	– c Patterson b Cummins	0
B. K. G. Mendis b Richardson	14	– c Burns b Cummins	1
A. R. S. Silva c Paine b Cummins	9	– c Burns b Cummins	3
D. M. de Silva c Paine b Richardson	5	– b Richardson	14
†D. P. D. N. Dickwella c Patterson b Cummins	64	– c Harris b Richardson	24
M. D. K. Perera c Labuschagne b Starc	1	– c Patterson b Cummins	9
R. A. S. Lakmal c Labuschagne b Starc	7	– st Paine b Lyon	24
P. V. D. Chameera c Patterson b Cummins	0	– not out	5
C. B. R. L. S. Kumara not out	0	– absent hurt	
W 1, nb 2	3	B 9, lb 14, nb 1	24
(56.4 overs)	144	(50.5 overs)	139

1/26 (2) 2/31 (3) 3/54 (1) 4/58 (4) 5/66 (6)
6/91 (5) 7/102 (9) 8/106 (8) 9/144 (7) 10/144 (10)

1/17 (1) 2/17 (3) 3/19 (4) 4/35 (5) 5/69 (6)
6/79 (2) 7/109 (7) 8/110 (8) 9/139 (9)

In the first innings Perera, when 1, retired hurt at 93-6 and resumed at 102-7.

Starc 12–2–41–2; Richardson 14–5–26–3; Cummins 14.4–3–39–4; Lyon 16–3–38–1. *Second innings*—Starc 14–0–57–0; Richardson 13–5–19–2; Lyon 8.5–3–17–1; Cummins 15–8–23–6.

Australia

M. S. Harris c Thirimanne b Kumara	44
J. A. Burns c Mendis b Lakmal	15
U. T. Khawaja b Perera	11
N. M. Lyon c Mendis b Lakmal	1
M. Labuschagne c Thirimanne b de Silva	81
T. M. Head lbw b Lakmal	84
K. R. Patterson lbw b Lakmal	30
*†T. D. Paine c Mendis b Lakmal	0
P. J. Cummins c Dickwella b Chameera	0
M. A. Starc not out	26
J. A. Richardson c Karunaratne b Perera	1
B 6, lb 17, w 2, nb 5	30
(106.2 overs)	323

1/37 (2) 2/72 (3) 3/76 (1) 4/82 (4) 5/248 (5)
6/272 (6) 7/272 (8) 8/278 (9) 9/304 (7) 10/323 (11)

Lakmal 27–9–75–5; Kumara 15–5–37–1; Chameera 21–3–68–1; Perera 32.2–9–84–2; de Silva 8–3–22–1; Karunaratne 3–0–14–0.

Umpires: M. Erasmus *(South Africa)* (55) and R. K. Illingworth *(England)* (40).
Third umpire: M. A. Gough *(England).* Referee: J. Srinath *(India)* (44).

Close of play: first day, Australia 72–2 (Harris 40, Lyon 0); second day, Sri Lanka 17–1 (Thirimanne 6).

AUSTRALIA v SRI LANKA 2018–19 (2nd Test)

At Manuka Oval, Canberra, on 1, 2, 3, 4 February, 2019.
Toss: Australia.   Result: AUSTRALIA WON BY 366 RUNS.
Debuts: Sri Lanka – C. Karunaratne.
Man of the Match: M. A. Starc.   Man of the Series: P. J. Cummins.

Almost 92 years after Canberra became Australia's capital, it finally staged a Test match. The Manuka Oval was the country's 11th Test ground (Perth Stadium had been the tenth, six weeks earlier). But if the ground was new, the story was familiar: Sri Lanka sunk to a whopping defeat well inside the distance. Injuries had wiped out their pace attack: Dushmantha Chameera and Lahiru Kumara broke down in Brisbane, while Suranga Lakmal failed a fitness test on his back just before the start here. And after no centuries in six Tests, three Australians tucked in: Burns, Head and Patterson (in just his second innings) made the most of gentle batting conditions and the second-choice attack. Four Sri Lankan bowlers chalked up centuries of their own on the venerable scoreboard, which started life at the MCG before being rebuilt in Canberra in the 1980s. Following a useful opening stand, Dimuth Karunaratne was taken to hospital after being hit on the neck by a Cummins bouncer. There was no lasting damage, and he returned next day to top-score with 59. Kusal Perera was also hit, by Richardson, and eventually retired hurt as well – although not before waving away two offers of medical help. Starc made a minor adjustment to his delivery stride, and returned to form with five for 54 as Sri Lanka were bundled out for 215, then Khawaja reached three figures before Paine's second declaration set a notional 516. Starc took five more wickets against a batting side that appeared to have given up hope.

Australia

M. S. Harris c C. Karunaratne b Fernando	11	– c Mendis b Rajitha	14
J. A. Burns b Rajitha	180	– c Mendis b Fernando	9
U. T. Khawaja c Mendis b Fernando	0	– not out	101
M. Labuschagne c Dickwella b C. Karunaratne	6	– c Dickwella b Rajitha	4
T. M. Head lbw b Fernando	161	– not out	59
K. R. Patterson not out	114		
*†T. D. Paine not out	45		
Lb 3, w 4, nb 10	17	W 3, nb 6	9
(5 wkts dec, 132 overs)	534	(3 wkts dec, 47 overs)	196

1/11 (1) 2/15 (3) 3/28 (4) 4/336 (5) 5/404 (2)   1/16 (1) 2/25 (2) 3/37 (4)

P. J. Cummins, M. A. Starc, J. A. Richardson and N. M. Lyon did not bat.

Rajitha 28–5–103–1; Fernando 30–3 126–3; C. Karunaratne 22–0–130–1; M. D. K. Perera 32–4–112–0; de Silva 20–2–60–0. *Second innings*—Fernando 11–1–43–1; Rajitha 13–2–64–2; M. D. K. Perera 15–3–52–0; C. Karunaratne 4–1–18–0; de Silva 4–0–19–0.

Sri Lanka

F. D. M. Karunaratne c Patterson b Starc	59	– b Starc	8
H. D. R. L. Thirimanne c Khawaja b Lyon	41	– c and b Cummins	30
*L. D. Chandimal c Paine b Starc	15	– c Labuschagne b Starc	4
B. K. G. Mendis b Cummins	6	– (5) c Patterson b Labuschagne	42
M. D. K. J. Perera retired hurt	29	– (6) c Paine b Starc	0
D. M. de Silva hit wkt b Starc	25	– (7) c Head b Richardson	6
†D. P. D. N. Dickwella lbw b Labuschagne	25	– (4) b Starc	27
C. Karunaratne c Starc b Lyon	0	– c Paine b Cummins	22
M. D. K. Perera c Paine b Starc	10	– c Paine b Cummins	4
C. A. K. Rajitha not out	0	– not out	2
M. V. T. Fernando b Starc	0	– b Starc	0
B 1, lb 4	5	B 1, lb 1, w 2	4
(68.3 overs)	215	(51 overs)	149

1/90 (2) 2/101 (4) 3/120 (3) 4/180 (6)   1/18 (1) 2/28 (3) 3/58 (2) 4/83 (4) 5/83 (6)
5/181 (1) 6/182 (8) 7/215 (7) 8/215 (9) 9/215 (11)   6/97 (7) 7/143 (5) 8/143 (8) 9/148 (9) 10/149 (11)

In the first innings F. D. M. Karunaratne, when 46, retired hurt at 82-0 and resumed at 157-3, when M. D. K. J. Perera retired hurt.

Starc 13.3–2–54–5; Richardson 15–4–49–0; Cummins 14–3–32–1; Lyon 24–6–70–2; Labuschagne 2–1–5–1. *Second innings*—Starc 18–2–46–5; Richardson 9–1–29–1; Lyon 13–1–51–0; Cummins 8–2–15–3; Labuschagne 3–1–6–1.

Umpires: M. A. Gough *(England)* (9) and R. K. Illingworth *(England)* (41).
Third umpire: M. Erasmus *(South Africa)*.   Referee: J. Srinath *(India)* (45).

Close of play: first day, Australia 384-4 (Burns 172, Patterson 25); second day, Sri Lanka 123-3 (M. D. K. J. Perera 11, de Silva 1); third day, Sri Lanka 17-0 (F. D. M. Karunaratne 8, Thirimanne 8).

SOUTH AFRICA v SRI LANKA 2018–19 (1st Test)

At Kingsmead, Durban, on 13, 14, 15, 16 February, 2019.
Toss: Sri Lanka.   Result: SRI LANKA WON BY ONE WICKET.
Debuts: Sri Lanka – L. Embuldeniya, B. O. P. Fernando.
Man of the Match: M. D. K. J. Perera.

In a miserable three months Sri Lanka had been whitewashed by England at home, beaten in New Zealand, and hammered in Australia. They had lost 11 of their previous 13 Tests in South Africa, and when they dipped to 226 for nine, chasing 304, the poor run seemed about to continue. Kusal Perera, however, had other ideas. His first-innings 51 had dragged his side within 44 of South Africa, and now he unfurled one of the greatest last-ditch batting displays in a Test. He swung Steyn majestically over square leg for six, bullied Olivier, and didn't let Rabada settle. At the other end, No. 11 Vishwa Fernando kept on playing, and kept on missing (he finished with six from 27 balls). At 270 for nine, still 34 away, Fernando scurried through for a cheeky single off the second ball of a Steyn over, and du Plessis's throw scudded away for four overthrows: suddenly it dawned on South Africa that this might go the wrong way. Perera, having done so much, didn't stutter over his closing lines. He top-edged Rabada for six and then late-cut him for four to complete Test cricket's 14th one-wicket victory, with the highest tenth-wicket stand to win any first-class match, let alone a Test. It was tough on de Kock, who top-scored with 80 in the first innings and added an equally breezy 55 in the second, in which du Plessis made 90 and slow left-armer Lasith Embuldeniya – auditioning to replace the retired Rangana Herath – took five for 66.

South Africa

A. K. Markram b M. V. T. Fernando	11	– (2) c Mendis b Rajitha	28
D. Elgar c Dickwella b M. V. T. Fernando	0	– (1) c and b Embuldeniya	35
H. M. Amla c Mendis b Lakmal	3	– c Thirimanne b M. V. T. Fernando	16
T. Bavuma run out (M. V. T. Fernando)	47	– lbw b Embuldeniya	3
*F. du Plessis c Dickwella b Rajitha	35	– lbw b M. V. T. Fernando	90
†Q. de Kock c M. V. T. Fernando b Rajitha	80	– lbw b Embuldeniya	55
V. D. Philander c and b Rajitha	4	– b Embuldeniya	18
K. A. Maharaj c Dickwella b M. V. T. Fernando	29	– b M. V. T. Fernando	4
K. Rabada c B. O. P. Fernando b M. V. T. Fernando	3	– c Dickwella b Embuldeniya	0
D. W. Steyn b Embuldeniya	15	– b M. V. T. Fernando	1
D. Olivier not out	0	– not out	2
Lb 6, nb 2	8	Lb 2, w 2, nb 3	7
(59.4 overs)	235	(79.1 overs)	259

1/0 (2) 2/9 (3) 3/17 (1) 4/89 (5) 5/110 (4) 6/131 (7) 7/178 (8) 8/186 (9) 9/219 (10) 10/235 (6)
1/36 (2) 2/70 (3) 3/77 (4) 4/95 (1) 5/191 (6) 6/251 (7) 7/255 (5) 8/256 (9) 9/256 (8) 10/259 (10)

Lakmal 14–3–29–1; M. V. T. Fernando 17–1–62–4; Rajitha 14.4–0–68–3; Karunaratne 3–0–9–0; Embuldeniya 10–1–51–1; B. O. P. Fernando 1–0–10–0. *Second innings*—Lakmal 20–5–52–0; M. V. T. Fernando 17.1–2–71–4; Rajitha 13–1–54–1; Embuldeniya 26–3–66–5; de Silva 2–0–8–0; B. O. P. Fernando 1–0–6–0.

Sri Lanka

*F. D. M. Karunaratne lbw b Philander	30	– lbw b Philander	20
H. D. R. L. Thirimanne c de Kock b Steyn	0	– c du Plessis b Rabada	21
B. O. P. Fernando lbw b Steyn	19	– c du Plessis b Steyn	37
B. K. G. Mendis c du Plessis b Philander	12	– c de Kock b Olivier	0
M. D. K. J. Perera c sub (M. Z. Hamza) b Steyn	51	– not out	153
†D. P. D. N. Dickwella c Steyn b Olivier	8	– c and b Steyn	0
D. M. de Silva c Olivier b Rabada	23	– lbw b Maharaj	48
R. A. S. Lakmal c Markram b Steyn	4	– c du Plessis b Maharaj	0
L. Embuldeniya c Steyn b Rabada	24	– c Markram b Olivier	4
C. A. K. Rajitha run out (Markram)	12	– lbw b Maharaj	1
M. V. T. Fernando not out	1	– not out	6
B 3, lb 3, w 1	7	Lb 13, w 1	14
(59.2 overs)	191	(9 wkts, 85.3 overs)	304

1/19 (2) 2/51 (3) 3/53 (1) 4/76 (4) 5/90 (6) 6/133 (7) 7/142 (8) 8/152 (5) 9/184 (10) 10/191 (9)
1/42 (2) 2/42 (1) 3/52 (4) 4/110 (3) 5/110 (6) 6/206 (7) 7/206 (8) 8/215 (9) 9/226 (10)

Steyn 20–7–48–4; Philander 10–2–32–2; Rabada 12.2–2–48–2; Olivier 13–2–36–1; Maharaj 3–0–16–0; Elgar 1–0–5–0. *Second innings*—Steyn 18–1–71–2; Philander 8–3–13–1; Maharaj 20–1–71–3; Rabada 22.3–3–97–1; Olivier 16–3–35–2; Markram 1–0–4–0.

Umpires: Aleem Dar *(Pakistan)* (124) and R. A. Kettleborough *(England)* (58).
Third umpire: I. J. Gould *(England)*.   Referee: R. B. Richardson *(West Indies)* (21).

Close of play: first day, Sri Lanka 49–1 (Karunaratne 28, B. O. P. Fernando 17); second day, South Africa 126–4 (du Plessis 25, de Kock 15); third day, Sri Lanka 83–3 (B. O. P. Fernando 28, Perera 12).

Test No. 2348/29 (SA432, SL283)

SOUTH AFRICA v SRI LANKA 2018–19 (2nd Test)

At St George's Park, Port Elizabeth, on 21, 22, 23 February, 2019.
Toss: South Africa. Result: SRI LANKA WON BY EIGHT WICKETS.
Debuts: South Africa – P. W. A. Mulder.
Man of the Match: B. K. G. Mendis. Man of the Series: M. D. K. J. Perera.

South Africa's hopes of squaring the series took an instant hit, as they slumped to 15 for three inside seven overs: Vishwa Fernando took two, and Bavuma was run out. De Kock blazed 86 from 87 balls but, with Rajitha also claiming three wickets, South Africa stumbled to 222. Their bowlers soon had Sri Lanka 97 for six, but Dickwella's feisty 42 reduced the deficit to 68. The scene was set for South Africa to make the match safe with a huge score – but, although du Plessis made a half-century, it was carnage all around him, even though Embuldeniya was unable to bowl, having dislocated his thumb attempting a return catch off Rabada in the first innings. South Africa inched to 91 for five, but then crashed to 128 all out, with Lakmal taking four of the last five. Sri Lanka needed 197 on a pitch that was starting to play tricks, and it looked ominous when both openers were caught behind in the space of six balls; Karunaratne fell to Olivier, who was about to scupper his Test career by signing a Kolpak deal with Yorkshire. From that unpromising position, though, Mendis and newcomer Oshada Fernando sailed home, seemingly without a care in the world. They put on 163, at around four an over, to complete an unthinkable whitewash. Sri Lanka had become the first Asian side to win a Test series in South Africa, who paid for underestimating the opposition and concentrating on the upcoming 50-over World Cup.

South Africa

Batsman	1st innings	2nd innings
D. Elgar b M. V. T. Fernando	6	(2) c Dickwella b M. V. T. Fernando ... 2
A. K. Markram lbw b Rajitha	60	(1) c B. O. P. Fernando b Rajitha ... 18
H. M. Amla b M. V. T. Fernando	0	c Mendis b de Silva ... 32
T. Bavuma run out (Rajitha)	0	c Dickwella b Rajitha ... 6
*F. du Plessis b Karunaratne	25	not out ... 50
†Q. de Kock b de Silva	86	c and b Lakmal ... 1
P. W. A. Mulder lbw b Rajitha	9	c Mendis b de Silva ... 5
K. A. Maharaj c Dickwella b Rajitha	0	lbw b Lakmal ... 6
K. Rabada c Dickwella b de Silva	22	c Mendis b Lakmal ... 0
D. W. Steyn not out	3	c Thirimanne b de Silva ... 0
D. Olivier c Dickwella b M. V. T. Fernando	0	lbw b Lakmal ... 6
B 1, lb 6, nb 4	11	Lb 1, nb 1 ... 2
(61.2 overs)	222	(44.3 overs) ... 128

1/15 (1) 2/15 (3) 3/15 (4) 4/73 (5) 5/130 (2) 6/145 (7) 7/157 (8) 8/216 (6) 9/221 (9) 10/222 (11)

1/10 (2) 2/31 (1) 3/51 (4) 4/90 (3) 5/91 (6) 6/100 (7) 7/113 (8) 8/115 (9) 9/116 (10) 10/128 (11)

Lakmal 13–2–33–0; M. V. T. Fernando 18.2–2–62–3; Rajitha 15–2–67–3; Embuldeniya 5.3–0–26–0; Karunaratne 4.3–1–12–1; de Silva 5–0–15–2. *Second innings*—Lakmal 16.3–3–39–4; M. V. T. Fernando 10–1–32–1; Rajitha 7–1–20–2; de Silva 11–1–36–3.

Sri Lanka

Batsman	1st innings	2nd innings
*F. D. M. Karunaratne c de Kock b Rabada	17	c de Kock b Olivier ... 19
H. D. R. L. Thirimanne c and b Olivier	29	c de Kock b Rabada ... 10
B. O. P. Fernando b Olivier	0	not out ... 75
B. K. G. Mendis c de Kock b Olivier	16	not out ... 84
C. A. K. Rajitha b Rabada	1	
M. D. K. J. Perera c de Kock b Rabada	20	
D. M. de Silva c de Kock b Mulder	19	
†D. P. D. N. Dickwella c Elgar b Rabada	42	
R. A. S. Lakmal lbw b Maharaj	7	
M. V. T. Fernando not out	0	
L. Embuldeniya absent hurt		
Lb 1, nb 2	3	B 4, lb 5 ... 9
(37.4 overs)	154	(2 wkts, 45.4 overs) ... 197

1/25 (1) 2/34 (3) 3/59 (4) 4/64 (2) 5/66 (5) 6/97 (6) 7/128 (7) 8/154 (9) 9/154 (8)

1/32 (2) 2/34 (1)

Steyn 10–2–39–0; Rabada 12.4–3–38–4; Olivier 10–1–61–3; Mulder 3–2–6–1; Maharaj 2–0–9–1. *Second innings*—Steyn 8–0–38–0; Rabada 15–2–53–1; Olivier 12–2–46–1; Mulder 4–1–6–0; Maharaj 6.4–0–45–0.

Umpires: Aleem Dar *(Pakistan)* (125) and I. J. Gould *(England)* (74).
Third umpire: R. A. Kettleborough *(England)*. Referee: R. B. Richardson *(West Indies)* (22).

Close of play: first day, Sri Lanka 60–3 (Thirimanne 25, Rajitha 0); second day, Sri Lanka 60–2 (B. O. P. Fernando 17, Mendis 10).

NEW ZEALAND v BANGLADESH 2018–19 (1st Test)

At Seddon Park, Hamilton, on 28 February, 1, 2, 3 March, 2019.
Toss: New Zealand. Result: NEW ZEALAND WON BY AN INNINGS AND 52 RUNS.
Debuts: Bangladesh – Ebadat Hossain.
Man of the Match: K. S. Williamson.

New Zealand maintained their 100% home record against Bangladesh – this was their eighth meeting – after running up their highest total, beating 690 against Pakistan at Sharjah in 2014–15. Tamim Iqbal made a run-a-ball century for Bangladesh but, with the other batsmen again succumbing to Wagner's bouncer barrage – no one else reached 30 – the eventual total was an underwhelming 234. New Zealand's openers steamed past that on their own: Raval's five-hour 132 was his first Test century. When he holed out at midwicket, in came Williamson – and stayed there. New Zealand added 365 runs on the second day, and piled on 264 in 45 overs on the fourth, which started with nightwatchman Wagner hitting a career-best 47; after lunch de Grandhomme slapped 76 from 53 balls, with five sixes, before the declaration at 715. Williamson extended his 20th Test century to 200, and passed 6,000 runs (Taylor is the only other New Zealander to have got there). It was only the second time New Zealand's top three had all scored centuries in the same innings, after Mohali in India in 2003–04. And only five bowlers, none from Bangladesh, had conceded more than the 246 runs leaked by Mehedi Hasan. Tamim started brightly again, but when he fell a massive defeat loomed at 126 for four. But Soumya Sarkar, with a maiden century, and Mahmudullah salvaged some respect with a fifth-wicket stand of 235 in 54 overs. Watling ended the match with his 202nd dismissal while keeping wicket, passing Adam Parore's national record.

Bangladesh

Tamim Iqbal c Williamson b de Grandhomme	126	– c Watling b Southee	74
Shadman Islam b Boult	24	– c Boult b Wagner	37
Mominul Haque c Watling b Wagner	12	– c Taylor b Boult	8
Mithun Ali c Latham b Wagner	8	– c Williamson b Boult	0
Soumya Sarkar c Watling b Southee	1	– b Boult	149
*Mahmudullah c Boult b Wagner	22	– c Boult b Southee	146
†Liton Das c Boult b Wagner	29	– b Boult	1
Mehedi Hasan c Nicholls b Wagner	10	– c Raval b Wagner	1
Abu Jayed c Watling b Southee	2	– b Boult	3
Khaled Ahmed b Southee	0	– not out	4
Ebadat Hossain not out	0	– c Watling b Southee	0
		W 6	6
(59.2 overs)	234	(103 overs)	429

1/57 (2) 2/121 (3) 3/147 (4) 4/149 (5) 5/180 (1)   1/88 (2) 2/100 (3) 3/110 (4) 4/126 (1) 5/361 (5)
6/207 (6) 7/217 (8) 8/226 (9) 9/234 (10) 10/234 (7)   6/379 (7) 7/380 (8) 8/413 (9) 9/429 (6) 10/429 (11)

Boult 13–1–62–1; Southee 14–2–76–3; de Grandhomme 11–0–39–1; Wagner 16.2–4–47–5; Astle 5–1–10–0. *Second innings*—Boult 28–3–123–5; Southee 24–4–98–3; de Grandhomme 10–1–33–0; Wagner 24–4–104–2; Astle 15–3–58–0; Williamson 2–0–13–0.

New Zealand

J. A. Raval c Khaled Ahmed b Mahmudullah	132
T. W. M. Latham c Mithun Ali b Soumya Sarkar	161
*K. S. Williamson not out	200
L. R. P. L. Taylor lbw b Soumya Sarkar	4
H. M. Nicholls b Mehedi Hasan	53
N. Wagner c Liton Das b Ebadat Hossain	47
†B-J. Watling c Liton Das b Mehedi Hasan	31
C. de Grandhomme not out	76
Lb 7, w 2, nb 2	11
(6 wkts dec, 163 overs)	715

1/254 (1) 2/333 (2) 3/349 (4) 4/449 (5)
5/509 (6) 6/605 (7)

T. D. Astle, T. G. Southee and T. A. Boult did not bat.

Abu Jayed 30–5–103–0; Ebadat Hossain 27–4–107–1; Khaled Ahmed 30–6–149–0; Soumya Sarkar 21–1–68–2; Mehedi Hasan 49–2–246–2; Mahmudullah 1–0–3–1; Mominul Haque 5–0–32–0.

Umpires: N. J. Llong *(England)* (56) and P. R. Reiffel *(Australia)* (42).
Third umpire: R. S. A. Palliyaguruge *(Sri Lanka)*.   Referee: D. C. Boon *(Australia)* (54).

Close of play: first day, New Zealand 86–0 (Raval 51, Latham 35); second day, New Zealand 451–4 (Williamson 93, Wagner 1); third day, Bangladesh 174–4 (Soumya Sarkar 39, Mahmudullah 15).

Test No. 2350/15 (NZ433, B114)

NEW ZEALAND v BANGLADESH 2018–19 (2nd Test)

At Basin Reserve, Wellington, on 8 *(no play)*, 9 *(no play)*, 10, 11, 12 March, 2019.
Toss: New Zealand.   Result: NEW ZEALAND WON BY AN INNINGS AND 12 RUNS.
Debuts: none.
Man of the Match: L. R. P. L. Taylor.

New Zealand shrugged off the loss of the first two days to rain, and clinched the series in an elongated morning session on the fifth day. It echoed the first Test between these sides, at Hamilton in December 2001, which New Zealand also won by an innings after the first two days were washed out. Wagner was the main destroyer, taking five wickets on the final day to finish with nine in the match as Bangladesh slid from 152 for four to 209 all out. It gave him 16 wickets in the series, 15 of them to short-pitched deliveries. His fellow left-armer, Boult, took seven in a match in which only Tamim Iqbal, in the first innings, and Mahmudullah hinted at permanence. In between, after the openers both fell cheaply to seamer Abu Jayed, Williamson made 74 despite a shoulder injury, then Taylor and Nicholls ensured New Zealand dwarfed the visitors' total by adding 216. Taylor extended his 18th Test century to his third double, reached in 321 minutes with 19 fours and four sixes, and made Bangladesh pay for dropping him twice in the space of three balls from Jayed when he had 20. Local wicketkeeper Peter Bocock, who had played only three first-class matches, substituted for Watling (hamstring injury) on the fifth day. The Third Test, scheduled for March 16–20 in Christchurch, was abandoned after 51 people were killed in a shooting incident in a local mosque, which several of the Bangladesh team were about to attend.

Bangladesh

Tamim Iqbal c Southee b Wagner	74	– b Boult	4
Shadman Islam c Taylor b de Grandhomme	27	– c Watling b Henry	29
Mominul Haque c Watling b Wagner	15	– c Southee b Boult	10
Mithun Ali c Watling b Wagner	3	– c Southee b Wagner	47
Soumya Sarkar c Watling b Henry	20	– c Taylor b Boult	28
*Mahmudullah c de Grandhomme b Wagner	13	– c Boult b Wagner	67
†Liton Das c Williamson b Southee	33	– c Boult b Wagner	1
Taijul Islam lbw b Boult	8	– c Latham b Wagner	0
Mustafizur Rahman b Boult	0	– b Boult	16
Abu Jayed b Boult	4	– not out	0
Ebadat Hossain not out	0	– b Wagner	0
B 4, lb 7, w 2, nb 1	14	Lb 4, w 3	7
(61 overs)	211	(56 overs)	209

1/75 (2) 2/119 (3) 3/127 (4) 4/134 (1) 5/152 (5)   1/4 (1) 2/20 (3) 3/55 (2) 4/112 (5) 5/152 (4)
6/168 (6) 7/206 (8) 8/206 (9) 9/207 (7) 10/211 (10)   6/158 (7) 7/170 (8) 8/203 (9) 9/209 (6) 10/209 (11)

Boult 11–3–38–3; Southee 15–2–52–1; de Grandhomme 7–0–15–1; Henry 15–0–67–1; Wagner 13–4–28–4. *Second innings*—Boult 16–5–52–4; Southee 12–1–57–0; Henry 9–3–40–1; de Grandhomme 5–0–11–0; Wagner 14–4–45–5.

New Zealand

J. A. Raval c Soumya Sarkar b Abu Jayed	3
T. W. M. Latham c Liton Das b Abu Jayed	4
*K. S. Williamson c and b Taijul Islam	74
L. R. P. L. Taylor c Liton Das b Mustafizur Rahman	200
H. M. Nicholls b Taijul Islam	107
C. de Grandhomme not out	23
†B-J. Watling c Soumya Sarkar b Abu Jayed	8
Lb 5, w 7, nb 1	13
(6 wkts dec, 84.5 overs)	432

1/5 (2) 2/8 (1) 3/180 (3) 4/396 (5)
5/421 (4) 6/432 (7)

T. G. Southee, M. J. Henry, N. Wagner and T. A. Boult did not bat.

Abu Jayed 18.5–2–94–3; Ebadat Hossain 16–2–84–0; Mustafizur Rahman 14–2–74–1; Soumya Sarkar 6–0–35–0; Taijul Islam 21–0–99–2; Mominul Haque 9–0–41–0.

Umpires: R. S. A. Palliyaguruge *(Sri Lanka)* (2) and P. R. Reiffel *(Australia)* (43).
Third umpire: N. J. Llong *(England)*.   Referee: D. C. Boon *(Australia)* (55).

Close of play: first day, no play; second day, no play; third day, New Zealand 38–2 (Williamson 10, Taylor 19); fourth day, Bangladesh 80–3 (Mithun Ali 25, Soumya Sarkar 12).

AFGHANISTAN v IRELAND 2018–19 (Only Test)

At Rajiv Gandhi International Stadium, Dehradun, on 15, 16, 17, 18 March, 2019.
Toss: Ireland.   Result: AFGHANISTAN WON BY SEVEN WICKETS.
Debuts: Afghanistan – Ihsanullah Janat, Ikram Alikhil, Waqar Salamkheil. Ireland – J. Cameron-Dow, G. H. Dockrell, A. R. McBrine, J. A. McCollum, S. W. Poynter.
Man of the Match: Rahmat Shah.

On the stroke of lunch on the fourth day, Afghanistan became the fourth of Test cricket's 12 teams to win one of their first two matches. Only Australia and England (in the very first series, back in 1876–77) and Pakistan (in 1952–53) had broken their duck so quickly. The result was effectively decided on the first morning, when Ireland – who had made five changes from their first Test, against Pakistan in May 2018 – slumped to 69 for eight. Despite a last-wicket stand of 87, in which Murtagh became the 11th man to top-score in a Test from No. 11, they were always playing catch-up. Rahmat Shah collected Afghanistan's first Test half-century in reply, and Hashmatullah Shahidi followed suit during a third-wicket stand of 130. Asghar Afghan (who had changed his name patriotically since his country's maiden Test) added 67, but the Irish began to inch their way back. The last eight fell for 116, including Rahmat, who dragged on for 98. Trailing by 142, Ireland lost skipper Porterfield before the second-day close – and Stirling next morning when umpire Ravi failed to spot a thick inside edge (there was no DRS). Balbirnie made a classy 82, but 20-year-old leg-spinner Rashid Khan took his first Test five-for, and it needed further rearguard to push the lead over 100; Murtagh was the first No. 11 to reach 25 in both innings. But these were no more than crumbs of comfort. Rahmat compiled another half-century, and Hashmatullah hit the winning boundary to seal Afghanistan's maiden win.

Ireland

*W. T. S. Porterfield lbw b Mohammad Nabi		9 – c Ikram Alikhil b Yamin Ahmadzai	0
P. R. Stirling c Ikram Alikhil b Yamin Ahmadzai		26 – lbw b Yamin Ahmadzai	14
A. Balbirnie b Yamin Ahmadzai		4 – c Ikram Alikhil b Waqar Salamkheil	82
J. A. McCollum b Rashid Khan		4 – lbw b Rashid Khan	39
K. J. O'Brien lbw b Mohammad Nabi		12 – lbw b Rashid Khan	56
†S. W. Poynter lbw b Rashid Khan		0 – c Ihsanullah Janat b Waqar Salamkheil	1
S. R. Thompson c Hashmatullah Shahidi b Mohammad Nabi		3 – c Ihsanullah Janat b Rashid Khan	1
G. H. Dockrell c Ikram Alikhil b Yamin Ahmadzai		39 – lbw b Rashid Khan	25
A. R. McBrine b Waqar Salamkheil		3 – st Ikram Alikhil b Rashid Khan	4
J. Cameron-Dow lbw b Waqar Salamkheil		9 – not out	32
T. J. Murtagh not out		54 – c Rahmat Shah b Yamin Ahmadzai	27
B 4, lb 5		9 B 4, lb 2, w 1	7
(60 overs)		172 (93 overs)	288

1/37 (2) 2/41 (1) 3/41 (3) 4/55 (4) 5/55 (6)   1/0 (1) 2/33 (2) 3/137 (3) 4/141 (4)
6/59 (5) 7/62 (7) 8/69 (9) 9/85 (10) 10/172 (8)   5/150 (6) 6/157 (7) 7/220 (8)
                                                    8/229 (5) 9/230 (9) 10/288 (11)

Yamin Ahmadzai 12–2–41–3; Wafadar Momand 8–3–31–0; Mohammad Nabi 14–5–36–3; Rashid Khan 12–5–20–2; Waqar Salamkheil 14–4–35–2. *Second innings*—Yamin Ahmadzai 14–1–52–3; Mohammad Nabi 20–1–58–0; Rashid Khan 34–7–82–5; Waqar Salamkheil 17–2–66–2; Wafadar Momand 8–0–24–0.

Afghanistan

Mohammad Shahzad c and b Cameron-Dow		40 – c Poynter b McBrine	2
Ihsanullah Janat lbw b Cameron-Dow		7 – not out	65
Rahmat Shah b Murtagh		98 – st Poynter b Cameron-Dow	76
Hashmatullah Shahidi lbw b McBrine		61 – (5) not out	4
*Asghar Afghan c Poynter b Thompson		67	
Mohammad Nabi c Cameron-Dow b Thompson		0 – (4) run out (Murtagh/Poynter)	1
†Ikram Alikhil b McBrine		7	
Rashid Khan lbw b Dockrell		10	
Yamin Ahmadzai lbw b Dockrell		2	
Wafadar Momand c Balbirnie b Thompson		6	
Waqar Salamkheil not out		1	
B 5, lb 3, w 4, nb 3		15 W 1	1
(106.3 overs)		314 (3 wkts, 47.5 overs)	149

1/27 (2) 2/68 (1) 3/198 (4) 4/226 (3) 5/227 (6)   1/5 (1) 2/144 (3) 3/145 (4)
6/255 (7) 7/272 (8) 8/280 (9) 9/311 (5) 10/314 (10)

Murtagh 22–9–33–1; McBrine 27–4–77–2; Cameron-Dow 18–0–94–2; Thompson 17.3–5–28–3; Dockrell 18–4–63–2; O'Brien 4–1–11–0. *Second innings*—Dockrell 22–7–58–0; McBrine 13–5–35–1; Cameron-Dow 5.5–0–24–1; Murtagh 5–3–15–0; Thompson 1–0–9–0; Balbirnie 1–0–8–0.

Umpires: R. K. Illingworth *(England)* (42) and S. Ravi *(India)* (33).
Third umpire: Ahmed Shah Pakteen *(Afghanistan)*.   Referee: J. Srinath *(India)* (46).

Close of play: first day, Afghanistan 90–2 (Rahmat Shah 22, Hashmatullah Shahidi 13); second day, Ireland 22–1 (Stirling 8, Balbirnie 14); third day, Afghanistan 29–1 (Ihsanullah Janat 16, Rahmat Shah 11).

Test No. 2352/1 (E1011, Ire3)

ENGLAND v IRELAND 2019 (Only Test)

At Lord's, London, on 24, 25, 26 July, 2019.
Toss: England.   Result: ENGLAND WON BY 143 RUNS.
Debuts: England – J. J. Roy, O. P. Stone. Ireland – M. R. Adair.
Man of the Match: M. J. Leach.

Ten days after their Irish-born one-day captain Eoin Morgan raised the World Cup aloft after a heart-stopping final, England returned to Lord's for what was expected to be a gentle workout, their first Test against Ireland, scheduled for four days. But on a fittingly emerald-green pitch, which Root later criticised, England were demolished before lunch for 85, including an implosion of six for seven in 27 balls. Murtagh, a Middlesex regular, made the most of the conditions with the cheapest Test five-for on his home ground. Stirling and Balbirnie – two others with Middlesex experience – took Ireland to 132 for two, before Broad, Curran and the pacy debutant Olly Stone limited the lead to 122 on a day on which 20 wickets fell. Leach, sent in as nightwatchman after going in at No. 11 in the first innings, survived one over that evening, and flourished next day with a career-best 92. Dropped twice, he put on 145 with Jason Roy, but it needed Curran's 29-ball 37 to stretch the advantage. When Stone fell to the third day's first delivery, England were a nervous 181 ahead. But Ireland's batsmen were even more jittery. After a shaky start, three wickets tumbled at 24, and Ireland were torpedoed for 38, the lowest Test total at Lord's (undercutting India's 42 in 1974). They lasted only 15.4 overs, equalling the second-shortest completed innings in a Test, behind only South Africa's 12.3 (for 30 all out) at Edgbaston in 1924. Both wicketkeepers bagged pairs, a Test first.

England

R. J. Burns c Wilson b Murtagh	6	– (2) c Wilson b Rankin	6
J. J. Roy c Stirling b Murtagh	5	– (3) b Thompson	72
J. L. Denly lbw b Adair	23	– (4) run out (O'Brien/McBrine)	10
*J. E. Root lbw b Adair	2	– (5) c Wilson b Adair	31
†J. M. Bairstow b Murtagh	0	– (6) lbw b Adair	0
M. M. Ali c Wilson b Murtagh	0	– (7) c Wilson b Rankin	9
C. R. Woakes lbw b Murtagh	0	– (8) c Balbirnie b Adair	13
S. M. Curran c McCollum b Rankin	18	– (9) c McCollum b Thompson	37
S. C. J. Broad c Wilson b Rankin	3	– (10) not out	21
O. P. Stone b Adair	19	– (11) b Thompson	0
M. J. Leach not out	1	– (1) c Adair b Murtagh	92
Lb 5, w 1, nb 2	8	B 1, lb 7, nb 4	12
(23.4 overs)	85	(77.5 overs)	303

1/8 (2) 2/36 (3) 3/36 (1) 4/42 (4) 5/42 (5)
6/42 (7) 7/43 (6) 8/58 (9) 9/67 (8) 10/85 (10)
1/26 (2) 2/171 (3) 3/182 (1) 4/194 (2) 5/194 (6)
6/219 (7) 7/239 (5) 8/248 (9) 9/293 (9) 10/303 (11)

Murtagh 9–2–13–5; Adair 7.4–1–32–3; Thompson 4–1–30–0; Rankin 3–1–5–2. *Second innings*—Murtagh 18–3–52–1; Adair 20–7–66–3; Rankin 17–1–86–2; Thompson 12.5–0–44–3; McBrine 10–1–47–0.

Ireland

*W. T. S. Porterfield c Leach b Curran	14	– c Bairstow b Woakes	2
J. A. McCollum b Curran	19	– c Root b Woakes	11
A. Balbirnie b Stone	55	– c Root b Broad	5
P. R. Stirling lbw b Broad	36	– b Woakes	0
K. J. O'Brien not out	28	– lbw b Broad	4
†G. C. Wilson c Root b Stone	0	– lbw b Woakes	0
S. R. Thompson b Broad	0	– c Root b Woakes	4
M. R. Adair b Curran	3	– b Broad	8
A. R. McBrine b Broad	11	– c Root b Broad	0
T. J. Murtagh c Burns b Stone	16	– b Woakes	2
W. B. Rankin b Ali	7	– not out	0
B 10, lb 6, w 2	18	B 1, lb 1	2
(58.2 overs)	207	(15.4 overs)	38

1/32 (1) 2/45 (2) 3/132 (4) 4/138 (3) 5/138 (6)
6/141 (7) 7/149 (8) 8/174 (9) 9/195 (10) 10/207 (11)
1/11 (1) 2/18 (3) 3/19 (4) 4/24 (2) 5/24 (6)
6/24 (5) 7/32 (8) 8/36 (7) 9/36 (9) 10/38 (10)

Broad 19–5–60–3; Woakes 10–2–34–0; Stone 12–3–29–3; Curran 10–3–28–0; Leach 3–0–26–0; Ali 4.2–1–14–1. *Second innings*—Broad 8–3–19–4; Woakes 7.4–2–17–6.

Umpires: Aleem Dar *(Pakistan)* (126) and R. S. A. Palliyaguruge *(Sri Lanka)* (3).
Third umpire: P. Wilson *(Australia)*.   Referee: A. J. Pycroft *(Zimbabwe)* (69).

Close of play: first day, England 0–0 (Leach 0, Burns 0); second day, England 303–9 (Broad 21, Stone 0).

ENGLAND v AUSTRALIA 2019 (1st Test)

At Edgbaston, Birmingham, on 1, 2, 3, 4, 5 August, 2019.
Toss: Australia.   Result: AUSTRALIA WON BY 251 RUNS.
Debuts: none.
Man of the Match: S. P. D. Smith.

Test No. 2353/347 (E1012, A821)

Despite a healthy first-innings lead, England slid to a heavy loss on the final day, with Lyon and Cummins – who reached 100 wickets in his 21st Test – sharing the spoils during an unconvincing batting display, in which Woakes top-scored from No. 9. A first defeat at Edgbaston since 2008 seemed unthinkable when Broad reduced Australia to 122 for eight on the first afternoon, but Smith – in his first Test back after his one-year ban – put on 88 with Siddle and 74 with Lyon. Anderson aggravated a calf injury after just four overs, and played no further part in the series. Burns, in his first Ashes Test, made 133 in 473 minutes, before a ninth-wicket stand of 65 swelled the lead. In what became a theme of the series, Broad again removed Warner cheaply. But Smith was immovable once again, taking his time batted in the match to 11 hours during a superb 142. He put on 130 with Head, then 126 with Wade, who also marked his Ashes debut with a century. Paine's declaration left England 398 in a day plus seven overs, but that became academic when they declined from 80 for two to 97 for seven. Burns was the tenth man (the fourth from England) to bat on each day of a five-day Test. Eight of umpire Wilson's decisions were overturned on review. This was the first match to count towards the ICC's new World Test Championship, which was due to run to 2021, with a final at Lord's.

Australia

C. T. Bancroft c Root b Broad	8	– c Buttler b Ali	7
D. A. Warner lbw b Broad	2	– c Bairstow b Broad	8
U. T. Khawaja c Bairstow b Woakes	13	– c Bairstow b Stokes	40
S. P. D. Smith b Broad	144	– c Bairstow b Woakes	142
T. M. Head lbw b Woakes	35	– c Bairstow b Stokes	51
M. S. Wade lbw b Woakes	1	– c Denly b Stokes	110
*†T. D. Paine c Burns b Broad	5	– b Ali	34
J. L. Pattinson lbw b Broad	0	– not out	47
P. J. Cummins lbw b Stokes	5	– not out	26
P. M. Siddle c Buttler b Ali	44		
N. M. Lyon not out	12		
Lb 13, w 2	15	B 11, lb 2, w 3, nb 6	22
(80.4 overs)	284	(7 wkts dec, 112 overs)	487

1/2 (2) 2/17 (1) 3/35 (3) 4/99 (5) 5/105 (6)
6/112 (7) 7/112 (8) 8/122 (9) 9/210 (10) 10/284 (4)

1/13 (2) 2/27 (1) 3/75 (3)
4/205 (5) 5/331 (4) 6/407 (6) 7/409 (7)

Anderson 4–3–1–0; Broad 22.4–4–86–5; Woakes 21–2–58–3; Stokes 18–1–77–1; Ali 13–3–42–1; Denly 2–1–7–0. *Second innings*—Broad 22–2–91–1; Woakes 13–1–46–1; Ali 29–1–130–2; Root 12–1–50–0; Stokes 22–5–85–3; Denly 14–1–72–0.

England

R. J. Burns c Paine b Lyon	133	– c Lyon b Cummins	11
J. J. Roy c Smith b Pattinson	10	– b Lyon	28
*J. E. Root c and b Siddle	57	– c Bancroft b Lyon	28
J. L. Denly lbw b Pattinson	18	– c Bancroft b Lyon	11
J. C. Buttler c Bancroft b Cummins	5	– b Cummins	1
B. A. Stokes c Paine b Cummins	50	– c Paine b Lyon	6
†J. M. Bairstow c Warner b Siddle	8	– c Bancroft b Cummins	6
M. M. Ali b Lyon	0	– c Warner b Lyon	4
C. R. Woakes not out	37	– c Smith b Cummins	37
S. C. J. Broad c Pattinson b Cummins	29	– c Smith b Lyon	0
J. M. Anderson c Cummins b Lyon	3	– not out	4
B 10, lb 11, w 2, nb 1	24	B 4, lb 4, nb 2	10
(135.5 overs)	374	(52.3 overs)	146

1/22 (2) 2/154 (3) 3/189 (4) 4/194 (5) 5/282 (6)
6/296 (1) 7/300 (8) 8/300 (7) 9/365 (10) 10/374 (11)

1/19 (1) 2/60 (2) 3/80 (4) 4/85 (3) 5/85 (5)
6/97 (7) 7/97 (6) 8/136 (8) 9/136 (10) 10/146 (9)

Cummins 33–9–84–3; Pattinson 27–3–82–2; Siddle 27–8–52–2; Lyon 43.5–8–112–3; Wade 1–0–7–0; Head 2–1–7–0; Smith 2–0–9–0. *Second innings*—Siddle 12–2–28–0; Lyon 20–5–49–6; Pattinson 8–1–29–0; Cummins 11.3–3–32–4; Smith 1–1–0–0.

Umpires: Aleem Dar *(Pakistan)* (127) and J. S. Wilson *(West Indies)* (14).
Third umpire: C. B. Gaffaney *(New Zealand)*.   Referee: R. S. Madugalle *(Sri Lanka)* (188).

Close of play: first day, England 10–0 (Burns 4, Roy 6); second day, England 267–4 (Burns 125, Stokes 38); third day, Australia 124–3 (Smith 46, Head 21); fourth day, England 13–0 (Burns 7, Roy 6).

ENGLAND v AUSTRALIA 2019 (2nd Test)

At Lord's, London, on 14 *(no play)*, 15, 16, 17, 18 August, 2019.
Toss: Australia.   Result: DRAWN.
Debuts: England – J. C. Archer.
Man of the Match: B. A. Stokes.

The loss of the first day, and much of the third, ultimately frustrated England, who ran out of time after another fluctuating encounter. The draw ended a run of 20 positive results in Tests in England. When play did start Burns played another adhesive innings, but England declined to 138 for six before Bairstow and Woakes dragged them past 250. Australia were in similar strife at 102 for five, but were again saved by Smith, who looked set for another century before he was shaken up by a lightning-fast spell from the debutant Jofra Archer. Smashed on the forearm, then poleaxed by a blow to the back of the neck, Smith reluctantly retired hurt, but surprised many by resuming soon afterwards: possibly dazed, he missed a straight one when 92. Delayed concussion was diagnosed next morning, and he was removed from the match (and also missed the next one): Marnus Labuschagne became Test cricket's first full substitute. England began poorly again, with Root bagging his first golden duck, but an excellent century from Stokes – who opened out after a careful start – set up a declaration midway through the final day. Australia needed 267 in 48 overs, but two quick wickets from Archer meant the shutters went up. Labuschagne made the most of his surprise promotion by surviving for 100 balls, and Australia just held on, latterly in failing light: Head and Cummins saw out the last 6.3 overs. Aleem Dar was standing in his 128th Test, equalling Steve Bucknor's record.

England

R. J. Burns c Bancroft b Cummins	53	– c Paine b Siddle	29
J. J. Roy c Paine b Hazlewood	0	– c and b Cummins	2
*J. E. Root lbw b Hazlewood	14	– c Paine b Cummins	0
J. L. Denly c Paine b Hazlewood	30	– c and b Siddle	26
J. C. Buttler c Paine b Siddle	12	– (6) c Hazlewood b Cummins	31
B. A. Stokes lbw b Lyon	13	– (5) not out	115
†J. M. Bairstow c Khawaja b Lyon	52	– not out	30
C. R. Woakes c Paine b Cummins	32		
J. C. Archer c Khawaja b Cummins	12		
S. C. J. Broad b Lyon	11		
M. J. Leach not out	6		
B 12, lb 5, w 6	23	B 5, lb 19, nb 1	25
(77.1 overs)	258	(5 wkts dec, 71 overs)	258

1/0 (2) 2/26 (3) 3/92 (4) 4/116 (1) 5/136 (5)
6/138 (6) 7/210 (8) 8/230 (9) 9/251 (10) 10/258 (7)

1/9 (2) 2/9 (3) 3/64 (4)
4/71 (1) 5/161 (6)

Cummins 21–8–61–3; Hazlewood 22–6–58–3; Siddle 13–2–48–1; Lyon 19.1–2–68–3; Smith 2–0–6–0. *Second innings*—Cummins 17–6–35–3; Hazlewood 13–1–43–0; Siddle 15–4–54–2; Lyon 26–3–102–0.

Australia

C. T. Bancroft lbw b Archer	13	– lbw b Leach	16
D. A. Warner b Broad	3	– c Burns b Archer	5
U. T. Khawaja c Bairstow b Woakes	36	– c Bairstow b Archer	2
S. P. D. Smith lbw b Woakes	92		
T. M. Head lbw b Broad	7	– not out	42
M. S. Wade c Burns b Broad	6	– c Buttler b Leach	1
*†T. D. Paine c Buttler b Archer	23	– c Denly b Archer	4
P. J. Cummins c Bairstow b Broad	20	– not out	1
P. M. Siddle c Bairstow b Woakes	9		
N. M. Lyon lbw b Leach	6		
J. R. Hazlewood not out	3		
M. Labuschagne (did not bat)		– (4) c Root b Leach	59
B 17, lb 12, w 2, nb 1	32	B 8, lb 14, w 1, nb 1	24
(94.3 overs)	250	(6 wkts, 47.3 overs)	154

1/11 (2) 2/60 (1) 3/60 (3) 4/71 (5) 5/102 (6)
6/162 (7) 7/218 (9) 8/234 (4) 9/246 (10) 10/250 (8)

1/13 (2) 2/19 (3) 3/47 (1)
4/132 (4) 5/138 (6) 6/149 (7)

In the first innings Smith, when 80, retired hurt at 203-6 and resumed at 218-7. Labuschagne replaced Smith on day five, as a concussion substitute.

Broad 27.3–7–65–4; Archer 29–11–59–2; Woakes 19–6–61–3; Stokes 8–1–17–0; Leach 11–3–19–1. *Second innings*—Broad 7–0–29–0; Archer 15–2–32–2; Woakes 3–0–11–0; Leach 16.3–5–37–3; Stokes 3–1–16–0; Root 1–0–7–0; Denly 2–2–0–0.

Umpires: Aleem Dar *(Pakistan)* (128) and C. B. Gaffaney *(New Zealand)* (28).
Third umpire: J. S. Wilson *(West Indies)*.   Referee: R. S. Madugalle *(Sri Lanka)* (189).

Close of play: first day, no play; second day, Australia 30–1 (Bancroft 5, Khawaja 18); third day, Australia 80–4 (Smith 13, Wade 0); fourth day, England 96–4 (Stokes 16, Buttler 10).

ENGLAND v AUSTRALIA 2019 (3rd Test)

At Headingley, Leeds, on 22, 23, 24, 25 August, 2019.
Toss: England. Result: ENGLAND WON BY ONE WICKET.
Debuts: none.
Man of the Match: B. A. Stokes.

Humbled for 67 in the first innings, and still 73 short of victory when the ninth wicket fell in their second, England were on the verge of losing the Ashes. And then Stokes reprised his World Cup heroics, clattering the bowling to all parts. Australia's nerves shredded: with two wanted, Lyon fluffed a simple run-out, then Stokes was given not out after a confident lbw shout: replays suggested he was out, but Australia had burned their final review in the previous over. Leach's contribution to the last-wicket stand of 76 was the single that tied the scores, then Stokes carved Cummins for the winning four, amid euphoric scenes to match those after Ian Botham's Headingley heroics in 1981. Somehow, England had levelled the series. They had done everything right on the first day, with Archer throttling back and taking six wickets as Australia were turned over for 179, which included a third-wicket stand of 111 between Warner (in his only substantial innings of his comeback series) and Labuschagne, who kept his place as Smith had been ruled out. Australia's pacemen turned the tables on the second day, as England were dumped out soon after lunch for 67, their lowest in a home Test since 1948. Labuschagne's 80 built on the unexpected lead, although Stokes's long, accurate spell helped keep the target within bounds. Despite a determined stand between Root and Denly, who added 126 in 53 overs, Hazlewood's four wickets seemed to have cooked England's goose. And then came Ben.

Australia

D. A. Warner c Bairstow b Archer	61	– (2) lbw b Broad	0
M. S. Harris c Bairstow b Archer	8	– (1) b Leach	19
U. T. Khawaja c Bairstow b Broad	8	– c Roy b Woakes	23
M. Labuschagne lbw b Stokes	74	– run out (Denly/Bairstow)	80
T. M. Head b Broad	0	– b Stokes	25
M. S. Wade b Archer	0	– c Bairstow b Stokes	33
*†T. D. Paine lbw b Woakes	11	– c Denly b Broad	0
J. L. Pattinson c Root b Archer	2	– c Root b Archer	20
P. J. Cummins c Bairstow b Archer	0	– c Burns b Stokes	6
N. M. Lyon lbw b Archer	1	– b Archer	9
J. R. Hazlewood not out	1	– not out	4
B 4, lb 2, w 5, nb 2	13	B 5, lb 13, w 2, nb 7	27
(52.1 overs)	179	(75.2 overs)	246

1/12 (2) 2/25 (3) 3/136 (1) 4/138 (5) 5/139 (6)   1/10 (2) 2/36 (1) 3/52 (3) 4/97 (5) 5/163 (6)
6/162 (7) 7/173 (8) 8/174 (9) 9/177 (4) 10/179 (10)   6/164 (7) 7/215 (8) 8/226 (9) 9/237 (4) 10/246 (10)

Broad 14–4–32–2; Archer 17.1–3–45–6; Woakes 12–4–51–1; Stokes 9–0–45–1. *Second innings*—Archer 14–2–40–2; Broad 16–2–52–2; Woakes 10–1–34–1; Leach 11–0–46–1; Stokes 24.2–7–56–3.

England

R. J. Burns c Paine b Cummins	9	– c Warner b Hazlewood	7
J. J. Roy c Warner b Hazlewood	9	– b Cummins	8
*J. E. Root c Warner b Hazlewood	0	– c Warner b Lyon	77
J. L. Denly c Paine b Pattinson	12	– c Paine b Hazlewood	50
B. A. Stokes c Warner b Pattinson	8	– not out	135
†J. M. Bairstow c Warner b Hazlewood	4	– c Labuschagne b Hazlewood	36
J. C. Buttler c Khawaja b Hazlewood	5	– run out (Head)	1
C. R. Woakes c Paine b Cummins	5	– c Wade b Hazlewood	1
J. C. Archer c Paine b Cummins	7	– c Head b Lyon	15
S. C. J. Broad not out	4	– lbw b Pattinson	0
M. J. Leach b Hazlewood	1	– not out	1
Lb 3	3	B 5, lb 15, w 10, nb 1	31
(27.5 overs)	67	(9 wkts, 125.4 overs)	362

1/10 (2) 2/10 (3) 3/20 (1) 4/34 (5) 5/45 (4)   1/15 (1) 2/15 (2) 3/141 (4) 4/159 (3) 5/245 (6)
6/45 (6) 7/54 (8) 8/56 (7) 9/66 (9) 10/67 (11)   6/253 (7) 7/261 (8) 8/286 (9) 9/286 (10)

Cummins 9–4–23–3; Hazlewood 12.5–2–30–5; Lyon 1–0–2–0; Pattinson 5–2–9–2. *Second innings*—Cummins 24.4–5–80–1; Hazlewood 31–11–85–4; Lyon 39–5–114–2; Pattinson 25–9–47–1; Labuschagne 6–0–16–0.

Umpires: C. B. Gaffaney *(New Zealand)* (29) and J. S. Wilson *(West Indies)* (15).
Third umpire: H. D. P. K. Dharmasena *(Sri Lanka)*.   Referee: J. Srinath *(India)* (47).

Close of play: first day, Australia 179; second day, Australia 171–6 (Labuschagne 53, Pattinson 2); third day, England 156–3 (Root 75, Stokes 2).

ENGLAND v AUSTRALIA 2019 (4th Test)

At Old Trafford, Manchester, on 4, 5, 6, 7, 8 September, 2019.
Toss: Australia.   Result: AUSTRALIA WON BY 185 RUNS.
Debuts: none.
Man of the Match: S. P. D. Smith.

Any hopes England would build on their astonishing Headingley victory were dashed by the returning Smith, who again proved an immovable object as Australia nudged 500, helped by fifties from Paine and Starc, after another rain-affected start. It might have been different had Leach not overstepped when Smith – then 118 with Australia 273 for five – edged to slip. Reprieved, Smith glided to 211, his 26th Test century and 11th against England: only Don Bradman (19) and Jack Hobbs (12) had made more Ashes hundreds. Burns added 141 with Root in another solid display, but after Hazlewood removed them the most sizeable contribution was Buttler's 41, and England trailed by 196. Broad inflicted a pair – and a third successive duck – on Warner, but Australia were rescued from 44 for four by the inevitable Smith, who hit 11 fours from 92 balls as he skipped to 82, taking his series aggregate past 600. Paine's declaration late on the fourth day left a target of 383, but the departures of Burns and Root to successive balls in the first over, from the impressive Hazlewood, dimmed hopes of another miracle. Next day, the sight of Stokes trudging off meant thoughts turned to a draw. Buttler hung on for 111 balls, before Overton and Leach gritted it out for 14 overs. The last hour was about to start, in indifferent light, when Paine tried Labuschagne's leg-breaks: Leach jabbed his fifth delivery to short leg, and Australia retained the Ashes when Overton fell ten balls later.

Australia

M. S. Harris lbw b Broad	13	– (2) lbw b Broad		6
D. A. Warner c Bairstow b Broad	0	– (1) lbw b Broad		0
M. Labuschagne b Overton	67	– lbw b Archer		11
S. P. D. Smith c Denly b Root	211	– c Stokes b Leach		82
T. M. Head lbw b Broad	19	– b Archer		12
M. S. Wade c Root b Leach	16	– c Bairstow b Archer		34
*†T. D. Paine c Bairstow b Overton	58	– not out		23
P. J. Cummins c Stokes b Leach	4			
M. A. Starc not out	54	– (8) not out		3
N. M. Lyon not out	26			
B 8, lb 14, w 3, nb 4	29	B 5, lb 2, w 7, nb 1		15
(8 wkts dec, 126 overs)	497	(6 wkts dec, 42.5 overs)		186

1/1 (2) 2/28 (1) 3/144 (3) 4/183 (5)
5/224 (6) 6/369 (7) 7/387 (8) 8/438 (4)

1/0 (1) 2/16 (2) 3/24 (1)
4/44 (5) 5/149 (4) 6/158 (6)

J. R. Hazlewood did not bat.

Broad 25–2–97–3; Archer 27–3–97–0; Stokes 10.5–0–66–0; Leach 26.1–3–83–2; Overton 28–3–85–2; Denly 3–1–8–0; Root 6–0–39–1. *Second innings*—Broad 14–4–54–2; Archer 14–2–45–3; Overton 5.5–1–22–0; Leach 9–0–58–1.

England

R. J. Burns c Smith b Hazlewood	81	– c Head b Cummins		0
J. L. Denly c Wade b Cummins	4	– c Labuschagne b Lyon		53
C. Overton c Smith b Hazlewood	5	– (8) lbw b Hazlewood		21
*J. E. Root lbw b Hazlewood	71	– (3) b Cummins		0
J. J. Roy b Hazlewood	22	– (4) b Cummins		31
B. A. Stokes c Smith b Starc	26	– (5) c Paine b Cummins		1
†J. M. Bairstow b Starc	17	– (6) lbw b Starc		25
J. C. Buttler b Cummins	41	– (7) b Hazlewood		34
J. C. Archer c Paine b Cummins	1	– lbw b Lyon		1
S. C. J. Broad b Starc	5	– (11) not out		0
M. J. Leach not out	4	– (10) c Wade b Labuschagne		12
B 4, lb 11, w 5, nb 4	24	B 9, lb 8, nb 2		19
(107 overs)	301	(91.3 overs)		197

1/10 (2) 2/25 (3) 3/166 (1) 4/175 (4) 5/196 (5) 6/228 (7)
7/243 (6) 8/256 (9) 9/283 (10) 10/301 (8)

1/0 (1) 2/0 (3) 3/66 (4) 4/74 (5) 5/93 (2)
6/138 (6) 7/172 (7) 8/173 (9) 9/196 (10) 10/197 (8)

Starc 22–7–80–3; Hazlewood 25–6–57–4; Cummins 24–6–60–3; Lyon 36–4–89–0. *Second innings*—Cummins 24–9–43–4; Hazlewood 17.3–5–31–2; Lyon 29–12–51–2; Starc 16–2–46–1; Labuschagne 4–1–9–1; Head 1–1–0–0.

Umpires: H. D. P. K. Dharmasena *(Sri Lanka)* (61) and M. Erasmus *(South Africa)* (56).
Third umpire: R. S. A. Palliyaguruge *(Sri Lanka)*.   Referee: J. Srinath *(India)* (48).

Close of play: first day, Australia 170–3 (Smith 60, Head 18); second day, England 23–1 (Burns 15, Overton 3); third day, England 200–5 (Stokes 7, Bairstow 2); fourth day, England 18–2 (Denly 10, Roy 8).

Test No. 2357/351 (E1016, A825)

ENGLAND v AUSTRALIA 2019 (5th Test)

At Kennington Oval, London, on 12, 13, 14, 15 September, 2019.
Toss: Australia.   Result: ENGLAND WON BY 135 RUNS.
Debuts: none.
Man of the Match: J. C. Archer.   Men of the Series: B. A. Stokes and S. P. D. Smith.

A fascinating series had one final twist: England overcame another indifferent start to emerge victorious. Although Steve Smith top-scored yet again in Australia's first innings, even he could not do it one last time, falling to a smart catch in the second for 23, his lowest of the series. He still amassed 774 runs in just four matches, the fifth-highest Ashes aggregate, while his first-innings 80 gave him 1,251 runs in his last ten innings against England, 15 more than even Don Bradman managed in his purplest patch. Once Smith departed on the fourth afternoon it was really only a matter of time, although Wade delayed England with a pugnacious century. Buttler's 70, which included three sixes, was the highlight as England battled to 294, the returning Marsh claiming a maiden five-for. Archer roared in, taking six wickets as Australia were despatched for 225; Curran, in his first Test of the series, claimed three. Denly's Test-best 94, and a typical 67 from Stokes, put England 398 in front, and then Broad and Leach started working their way through again. Warner ended the series with eight single-figure scores, the most by an opener; Broad dismissed him seven times (for 35 runs), to equal another record. Cummins took 29 wickets in the series without a five-for, beating the 28 of another Australian seamer, Wayne Clark, at home to India in 1977–78. The Ashes series was drawn (for the first time since 1972) and the World Championship points were shared – but Australia retained the urn.

England

R. J. Burns c Marsh b Hazlewood	47	– c Paine b Lyon	20
J. L. Denly c Smith b Cummins	14	– c Smith b Siddle	94
*J. E. Root b Cummins	57	– c Smith b Lyon	21
B. A. Stokes c Lyon b Marsh	20	– b Lyon	67
†J. M. Bairstow lbw b Marsh	22	– c Smith b Marsh	14
J. C. Buttler b Cummins	70	– c Labuschagne b Siddle	47
S. M. Curran c Smith b Marsh	15	– c Paine b Cummins	17
C. R. Woakes lbw b Marsh	2	– c Smith b Marsh	6
J. C. Archer c Paine b Hazlewood	9	– c Paine b Cummins	3
M. J. Leach b Marsh	21	– c Hazlewood b Lyon	9
S. C. J. Broad not out	0	– not out	12
B 3, lb 7, w 5, nb 2	17	B 7, lb 11, nb 1	19
(87.1 overs)	294	(95.3 overs)	329

1/27 (2) 2/103 (1) 3/130 (4) 4/170 (5) 5/176 (5)   1/54 (1) 2/87 (3) 3/214 (4) 4/222 (2) 5/249 (5)
6/199 (7) 7/205 (8) 8/226 (9) 9/294 (6) 10/294 (10)   6/279 (7) 7/305 (8) 8/305 (6) 9/317 (9) 10/329 (10)

Cummins 25.5–6–84–3; Hazlewood 21–7–76–2; Siddle 17–1–61–0; Marsh 18.2–4–46–5; Lyon 4–0–12–0; Labuschagne 1–0–5–0. *Second innings*—Cummins 21–5–67–2; Hazlewood 19–5–57–0; Lyon 24.3–5–69–4; Siddle 13–4–52–2; Marsh 11–1–40–2; Labuschagne 7–1–26–0.

Australia

D. A. Warner c Bairstow b Archer	5	– (2) c Burns b Broad	11
M. S. Harris c Stokes b Archer	3	– (1) b Broad	9
M. Labuschagne lbw b Archer	48	– st Bairstow b Leach	14
S. P. D. Smith lbw b Woakes	80	– c Stokes b Broad	23
M. S. Wade lbw b Curran	19	– st Bairstow b Root	117
M. R. Marsh c Leach b Archer	17	– c Buttler b Root	24
*†T. D. Paine c Bairstow b Curran	1	– lbw b Leach	21
P. J. Cummins lbw b Curran	0	– c Bairstow b Broad	9
P. M. Siddle c Burns b Archer	18	– not out	13
N. M. Lyon b Archer	25	– c Root b Leach	1
J. R. Hazlewood not out	1	– c Root b Leach	0
B 1, lb 2, w 5	8	B 2, lb 12, nb 2, p 5	21
(68.5 overs)	225	(77 overs)	263

1/5 (1) 2/14 (2) 3/83 (3) 4/118 (5) 5/160 (6)   1/18 (1) 2/29 (2) 3/56 (3) 4/85 (4) 5/148 (6)
6/166 (7) 7/166 (8) 8/187 (4) 9/224 (10) 10/225 (9)   6/200 (7) 7/244 (8) 8/260 (5) 9/263 (10) 10/263 (11)

Broad 12–3–45–0; Archer 23.5–9–62–6; Curran 17–6–46–3; Woakes 10–2–51–1; Leach 6–1–18–0. *Second innings*—Broad 15–1–62–4; Archer 16–2–66–0; Curran 8–3–22–0; Leach 22–8–49–4; Woakes 7–1–19–0; Root 9–1–26–2.

Umpires: H. D. P. K. Dharmasena *(Sri Lanka)* (62) and M. Erasmus *(South Africa)* (57).
Third umpire: R. S. A. Palliyaguruge *(Sri Lanka)*.   Referee: J. Srinath *(India)* (49).

Close of play: first day, England 271-8 (Buttler 64, Leach 10); second day, England 9-0 (Burns 4, Denly 1); third day, England 313-8 (Archer 3, Leach 5).

SRI LANKA v NEW ZEALAND 2019 (1st Test)

At Galle International Stadium on 14, 15, 16, 17, 18 September, 2019.
Toss: New Zealand.   Result: SRI LANKA WON BY SIX WICKETS.
Debuts: none.
Man of the Match: F. D. M. Karunaratne.

Sri Lanka took an early lead in the fledgling World Test Championship, chasing down a target of 266 with surprising ease after the first three innings of the match were all in the 249–285 bracket. On a rain-shortened first day, New Zealand recovered from Williamson's third-ball duck thanks to Taylor, who hit slow left-armer Embuldeniya out of the attack and put on exactly 100 with Nicholls. Off-spinner Dananjaya took the first five wickets, then the canny Lakmal made the only significant contribution by a seamer in the match, with four late strikes as New Zealand's last seven added only 78. Sri Lanka also had a mid-innings collapse, with slow left-armer Ayaz Patel taking five wickets, but Dickwella and Lakmal added 81 for the eighth wicket to ensure a narrow lead. New Zealand then slipped to 25 for three, with a rare double failure for Williamson, but Watling survived for four hours before Somerville conjured 61 from the last two wickets as the innings lasted midway into the fourth day. Sri Lanka's openers calmed any nerves in the home dressing-room with a stand of 161. Karunaratne made almost sure of victory with 122, in more than five hours, with just six fours (and a six). His century was only the fourth by a Sri Lankan opener in the fourth innings of a Test, after two by Sanath Jayasuriya and one by Kusal Mendis. "We thought the wicket would deteriorate more than it did," said Williamson. "It didn't get more difficult to bat on."

New Zealand

J. A. Raval c de Silva b Dananjaya	33	– c Karunaratne b de Silva		4
T. W. M. Latham c Dickwella b Dananjaya	30	– c Thirimanne b Dananjaya		45
*K. S. Williamson c Karunaratne b Dananjaya	0	– c Perera b Embuldeniya		4
L. R. P. L. Taylor c Dickwella b Lakmal	86	– c de Silva b Embuldeniya		3
H. M. Nicholls lbw b Dananjaya	42	– c Mendis b de Silva		26
†B-J. Watling lbw b Dananjaya	1	– c Dickwella b Kumara		77
M. J. Santner lbw b Lakmal	13	– c Lakmal b Embuldeniya		12
T. G. Southee run out (de Silva/Dickwella)	14	– st Dickwella b Embuldeniya		23
W. E. R. Somerville not out	9	– not out		40
T. A. Boult c Perera b Lakmal	18	– c de Silva b Kumara		26
A. Y. Patel lbw b Lakmal	0	– lbw b de Silva		14
Lb 2, nb 1	3	B 4, lb 5, nb 2		11
(83.2 overs)	249	(106 overs)		285

1/64 (2) 2/64 (3) 3/71 (1) 4/171 (5) 5/179 (6)   1/8 (1) 2/20 (3) 3/25 (4) 4/81 (2) 5/98 (5)
6/205 (4) 7/216 (7) 8/222 (8) 9/249 (10) 10/249 (11)   6/124 (7) 7/178 (8) 8/224 (6) 9/260 (10) 10/285 (11)

Lakmal 15.2–5–29–4; Kumara 10–1–37–0; Dananjaya 30–3–80–5; de Silva 6–0–20–0; Embuldeniya 22–1–81–0. *Second innings*—Lakmal 15–2–37–0; Dananjaya 32–4–84–1; de Silva 12–3–25–3; Embuldeniya 37–4–99–4; Kumara 10–0–31–2.

Sri Lanka

*F. D. M. Karunaratne lbw b Patel	39	– c Watling b Southee		122
H. D. R. L. Thirimanne st Watling b Patel	10	– lbw b Somerville		64
B. K. G. Mendis c Taylor b Patel	53	– c Raval b Patel		10
A. D. Mathews c Taylor b Patel	50	– not out		28
M. D. K. J. Perera c Santner b Boult	1	– c Santner b Boult		23
D. M. de Silva c and b Patel	5	– not out		14
†D. P. D. N. Dickwella c Williamson b Somerville	61			
A. Dananjaya c Taylor b Somerville	0			
R. A. S. Lakmal b Boult	40			
L. Embuldeniya lbw b Somerville	5			
C. B. R. L. S. Kumara not out	0			
B 1, lb 1, w 1	3	B 6, lb 1		7
(93.2 overs)	267	(4 wkts, 86.1 overs)		268

1/27 (2) 2/66 (1) 3/143 (3) 4/144 (5) 5/155 (6)   1/161 (2) 2/174 (3) 3/218 (1) 4/250 (5)
6/158 (4) 7/161 (8) 8/242 (9) 9/262 (7) 10/267 (10)

Boult 20–4–45–2; Southee 7–3–17–0; Somerville 22.2–3–83–3; Patel 33–6–89–5; Santner 11–0–31–0. *Second innings*—Boult 9.1–1–34–1; Southee 12–2–33–1; Somerville 31–6–73–1; Patel 18–0–74–1; Santner 13–2–38–0; Williamson 3–0–9–0.

Umpires: M. A. Gough *(England)* (10) and R. K. Illingworth *(England)* (43).
Third umpire: B. N. J. Oxenford *(Australia)*.   Referee: A. J. Pycroft *(Zimbabwe)* (70).

Close of play: first day, New Zealand 203–5 (Taylor 86, Santner 8); second day, Sri Lanka 227–7 (Dickwella 39, Lakmal 28); third day, New Zealand 195–7 (Watling 63, Somerville 5); fourth day, Sri Lanka 133–0 (Karunaratne 71, Thirimanne 57).

SRI LANKA v NEW ZEALAND 2019 (2nd Test)

At P. Sara Oval, Colombo, on 22, 23, 24, 25, 26 August, 2019.
Toss: Sri Lanka.   Result: NEW ZEALAND WON BY AN INNINGS AND 65 RUNS.
Debuts: none.
Man of the Match: T. W. M. Latham.   Man of the Series: B-J. Watling.

On their previous tour, late in 2012, New Zealand lost at Galle and squared the series at the Sara Oval – and now did it again, with a convincing victory set up by Latham, who batted six hours for 154 after Raval had fallen for a duck. Latham put on 143 with Watling, who then admired de Grandhomme's hitting – five fours, five sixes – in a stand of 113 that took New Zealand nearly 200 in front. Sri Lanka had been indebted to de Silva's battling century on the third day, after rain allowed only 66 overs on the first two. But Boult and Southee – who both had double-wicket maidens on the soggy second day – shared seven wickets, and Sri Lanka hobbled to 244. Their second innings was even worse: Thirimanne was run out in the first over, and soon it was 32 for five. Karunaratne, batting down the order after injuring his thigh, survived for 91 minutes, but at tea on the final day Sri Lanka were 86 for seven. They had 36 overs to survive, although the light was fading fast, but were unable to hang on despite Dickwella's abstemious half-century, which used up 151 balls before he was superbly caught by Latham, who sprinted from short leg to leg slip when he spotted a paddle-sweep. Both Boult (Mathews in the first innings) and Southee (Karunaratne in the second) reached 250 Test wickets during the match; only Richard Hadlee (431) and Daniel Vettori (361) had taken more for New Zealand.

Sri Lanka

*F. D. M. Karunaratne c Watling b Southee	65	– (7) lbw b Southee	21
H. D. R. L. Thirimanne c Williamson b Somerville	2	– (1) run out (Patel)	0
B. K. G. Mendis c Watling b de Grandhomme	32	– b Somerville	20
A. D. Mathews c Watling b Boult	2	– c Taylor b de Grandhomme	7
M. D. K. J. Perera lbw b Boult	0	– (2) c Watling b Boult	0
D. M. de Silva b Boult	109	– (5) c Southee b Patel	1
†D. P. D. N. Dickwella c Watling b Southee	0	– (6) c Latham b Patel	51
M. D. K. Perera lbw b Patel	13	– c Taylor b Southee	0
R. A. S. Lakmal c Watling b Southee	10	– c Latham b Somerville	14
L. Embuldeniya lbw b Southee	0	– c Williamson b Boult	5
C. B. R. L. S. Kumara not out	5	– not out	0
B 1, lb 2, nb 3	6	Lb 2, w 1	3
(90.2 overs)	244	(70.2 overs)	122

1/29 (2) 2/79 (3) 3/93 (4) 4/93 (5) 5/130 (1)   1/0 (1) 2/4 (2) 3/11 (4) 4/22 (5) 5/32 (3) 6/73 (7)
6/130 (7) 7/171 (8) 8/214 (9) 9/224 (10) 10/244 (6)   7/75 (8) 8/115 (9) 9/118 (6) 10/122 (10)

Boult 22.2–6–75–3; Southee 29–7–63–4; de Grandhomme 17–3–35–1; Somerville 6–3–20–1; Patel 16–4–48–1. *Second innings*—Boult 14.2–8–17–2; Southee 12–6–15–2; Patel 19–3–31–2; de Grandhomme 4–1–8–1; Somerville 21–6–49–2.

New Zealand

J. A. Raval c de Silva b M. D. K. Perera	0
T. W. M. Latham lbw b M. D. K. Perera	154
*K. S. Williamson c Mendis b Kumara	20
L. R. P. L. Taylor c de Silva b Embuldeniya	23
H. M. Nicholls c de Silva b M. D. K. Perera	15
†B-J. Watling not out	105
C. de Grandhomme c Kumara b Embuldeniya	83
T. G. Southee not out	24
Lb 4, w 3	7
(6 wkts dec, 115 overs)	431

1/1 (1) 2/34 (3) 3/84 (4) 4/126 (5) 5/269 (2) 6/382 (7)

W. E. R. Somerville, T. A. Boult and A. Y. Patel did not bat.

M. D. K. Perera 37–4–114–3; de Silva 5–1–10–0; Lakmal 11–2–32–0; Kumara 25–0–115–1; Embuldeniya 37–4–156–2.

Umpires: M. A. Gough *(England)* (11) and B. N. J. Oxenford *(Australia)* (56).
Third umpire: R. K. Illingworth *(England)*.   Referee: A. J. Pycroft *(Zimbabwe)* (71).

Close of play: first day, Sri Lanka 85–2 (Karunaratne 49, Mathews 0); second day, Sri Lanka 144–6 (de Silva 32, M. D. K. Perera 5); third day, New Zealand 196–4 (Latham 111, Watling 25); fourth day, New Zealand 382–5 (Watling 81, de Grandhomme 83).

Test No. 2360/97 (WI543, I534)

WEST INDIES v INDIA 2019 (1st Test)

At Sir Vivian Richards Stadium, North Sound, Antigua, on 22, 23, 24, 25 August, 2019.
Toss: West Indies.   Result: INDIA WON BY 318 RUNS.
Debuts: West Indies – S. S. J. Brooks.
Man of the Match: A. M. Rahane.

A close encounter looked likely when India dipped to 25 for three on the first day, but they ran out easy winners in the end. The comeback was started by Rahane, who shored up the first innings with 81 and added a century in the second. And it was rounded off in spectacular style by Bumrah, who unleashed his recently-perfected outswinger to produce stunning figures of 8–4–7–5, India's cheapest Test five-for. Rahane was helped by contributions down the order – notably Jadeja's uncharacteristic three-hour 58 – as India recovered to 297 on the second day. In reply, eight West Indians made it into double figures, but none reached 50: Sharma made regular incisions to set up a lead of 75. Kohli atoned for his first-innings failure with 51, before becoming one of four victims for Chase's off-spin, but Rahane and Vihari put on 135; a declaration not long before tea on the fourth day then set West Indies 419. By the interval they were sunk at 15 for five, and afterwards they plummeted to 50 for nine before Roach and Cummins became only the sixth tenth-wicket pair to double the score (George Dockrell and Tim Murtagh had done likewise for Ireland against Afghanistan five months earlier). This was India's fourth-biggest win by runs, but the largest away from home. Before the end of the fourth day Kohli had his 27th Test win as captain, equalling M. S. Dhoni's record, and the 12th away from home (Sourav Ganguly had 11).

India

K. L. Rahul c Hope b Chase	44	– b Chase	38
M. A. Agarwal c Hope b Roach	5	– lbw b Chase	16
C. A. Pujara c Hope b Roach	2	– b Roach	25
*V. Kohli c Brooks b Gabriel	9	– c Campbell b Chase	51
A. M. Rahane b Gabriel	81	– c Holder b Gabriel	102
G. H. Vihari c Hope b Roach	32	– c Hope b Holder	93
†R. R. Pant c Holder b Roach	24	– c sub (K. M. A. Paul) b Chase	7
R. A. Jadeja c Hope b Holder	58	– not out	1
I. Sharma b Gabriel	19		
Mohammed Shami c and b Chase	0		
J. J. Bumrah not out	4		
B 9, lb 8, nb 2	19	B 6, lb 4	10
(96.4 overs)	297	(7 wkts dec, 112.3 overs)	343

1/5 (2) 2/7 (3) 3/25 (4) 4/93 (1) 5/175 (6)
6/189 (5) 7/207 (7) 8/267 (9) 9/268 (10) 10/297 (8)

1/30 (2) 2/73 (1) 3/81 (3) 4/187 (4)
5/322 (5) 6/336 (7) 7/343 (6)

Roach 25–6–66–4; Gabriel 22–5–71–3; Holder 20.4–11–36–1; Cummins 13–1–49–0; Chase 16–3–58–2. *Second innings*—Roach 20–8–29–1; Gabriel 16–3–63–1; Chase 38–5–132–4; Holder 18.3–4–45–1; Cummins 7–1–20–0; Campbell 6–0–20–0; Brathwaite 7–0–24–0.

West Indies

K. C. Brathwaite c and b Sharma	14	– c Pant b Bumrah	1
J. D. Campbell b Mohammed Shami	23	– b Bumrah	7
S. S. J. Brooks c Rahane b Jadeja	11	– lbw b Sharma	2
D. M. Bravo lbw b Bumrah	18	– b Bumrah	2
R. L. Chase c Rahul b Sharma	48	– (6) b Mohammed Shami	12
†S. D. Hope c Pant b Sharma	24	– (7) b Bumrah	2
S. O. Hetmyer c and b Sharma	35	– (5) c Rahane b Sharma	1
*J. O. Holder c Pant b Mohammed Shami	39	– b Bumrah	8
K. A. J. Roach c Kohli b Sharma	0	– c Pant b Sharma	38
M. L. Cummins b Jadeja	0	– (11) not out	19
S. T. Gabriel not out	2	– (10) c Pant b Mohammed Shami	0
B 4, lb 1, w 1, nb 2	8	Lb 7, nb 1	8
(74.2 overs)	222	(26.5 overs)	100

1/36 (2) 2/48 (1) 3/50 (3) 4/88 (4) 5/130 (5)
6/174 (6) 7/179 (7) 8/179 (9) 9/220 (8) 10/222 (10)

1/7 (1) 2/10 (2) 3/10 (3) 4/13 (5) 5/15 (4) 6/27 (9)
7/37 (8) 8/50 (6) 9/50 (10) 10/100 (9)

Sharma 17–5–43–5; Bumrah 18–4–55–1; Mohammed Shami 17–3–48–2; Jadeja 20.2–4–64–2; Vihari 2–0–7–0. *Second innings*—Sharma 9.5–1–31–3; Bumrah 8–4–7–5; Jadeja 4–0–42–0; Mohammed Shami 5–3–13–2.

Umpires: R. A. Kettleborough *(England)* (59) and R. J. Tucker *(Australia)* (69).
Third umpire: P. R. Reiffel *(Australia)*.   Referee: D. C. Boon *(Australia)* (56).

Close of play: first day, India 203–6 (Pant 20, Jadeja 3); second day, West Indies 189–8 (Holder 10, Cummins 0); third day, India 185–3 (Kohli 51, Rahane 53).

WEST INDIES v INDIA 2019 (2nd Test)

At Sabina Park, Kingston, Jamaica, on 30, 31 August, 1, 2 September, 2019.
Toss: West Indies.   Result: INDIA WON BY 257 RUNS.
Debuts: West Indies – R. R. S. Cornwall, J. N. Hamilton.
Man of the Match: G. H. Vihari.

Another Bumrah masterclass piloted India to a series whitewash, and 120 points in the new World Championship table. After five for seven in Antigua, Bumrah now reaped six for 27, including a hat-trick – only the third for India in a Test, after Harbhajan Singh (against Australia at Kolkata in 2000–01) and Irfan Pathan (in the first over at Karachi in 2005–06), and the third in the Caribbean, after Jermaine Lawson (against Australia in 2002–03) and England's Matthew Hoggard (2003–04). West Indies again only just staggered into three figures and, already 299 behind, were as good as buried. India had batted consistently for 416, with Vihari making his first century and Sharma a maiden fifty, in his 126th innings (only Jimmy Anderson needed more, 131). Holder persisted for five wickets, and there were also three in 41 overs for the hulking debutant off-spinner Rahkeem Cornwall, probably the heaviest Test cricketer at 22 stone (140kg); the Australian Warwick Armstrong was a similar weight during his final Tests in 1921. After Rahane and Vihari set up a target of 468, West Indies were soon two down, and also lost Bravo, hit on the head by Bumrah. He was replaced by Blackwood, a concussion substitute, who made a spirited 38; Gabriel became the first man to bat at No. 12 in a Test innings. Brooks made a brave maiden fifty, but could not prevent India's eighth successive series victory since 2002–03 over West Indies, who had not won a single Test in that time.

India

K. L. Rahul c Cornwall b Holder	13 – c Hamilton b Roach	6
M. A. Agarwal c Cornwall b Holder	55 – lbw b Roach	4
C. A. Pujara c Brooks b Cornwall	6 – c Brooks b Holder	27
*V. Kohli c Hamilton b Holder	76 – c Hamilton b Roach	0
A. M. Rahane c Hamilton b Roach	24 – not out	64
G. H. Vihari c Roach b Holder	111 – not out	53
†R. R. Pant b Holder	27	
R. A. Jadeja c Bravo b Cornwall	16	
I. Sharma c Hetmyer b Brathwaite	57	
Mohammed Shami c Hamilton b Cornwall	0	
J. J. Bumrah not out	0	
B 11, lb 19, w 1	31	B 8, lb 4, nb 2	14
(140.1 overs)	416	(4 wkts dec, 54.4 overs)	168

1/32 (1) 2/46 (3) 3/115 (2) 4/164 (5) 5/202 (4)   1/9 (2) 2/36 (1)
6/264 (7) 7/302 (8) 8/414 (9) 9/416 (10) 10/416 (6)   3/36 (4) 4/57 (3)

Roach 30–9–77–1; Gabriel 21–4–74–0; Holder 32.1–9–77–5; Cornwall 41–10–105–3; Chase 14–4–45–0; Brathwaite 2–0–8–1. *Second innings*—Roach 10–3–28–3; Holder 11.4–5–20–1; Cornwall 23–7–68–0; Gabriel 7–3–18–0; Chase 3–0–22–0.

West Indies

K. C. Brathwaite c Pant b Bumrah	10 – (2) c Pant b Sharma	3
J. D. Campbell c Pant b Bumrah	2 – (1) c Kohli b Mohammed Shami	16
D. M. Bravo c Rahul b Bumrah	4 – retired hurt	23
S. S. J. Brooks lbw b Bumrah	0 – run out (Kohli)	50
R. L. Chase lbw b Bumrah	0 – lbw b Jadeja	12
S. O. Hetmyer b Mohammed Shami	34 – c Agarwal b Sharma	1
*J. O. Holder c sub (R. G. Sharma) b Bumrah	18 – (8) b Jadeja	39
†J. N. Hamilton c Kohli b Sharma	5 – (9) c Rahul b Jadeja	0
R. R. S. Cornwall c Rahane b Mohammed Shami	14 – (10) c Pant b Mohammed Shami	1
K. A. J. Roach c Agarwal b Jadeja	17 – (11) c Pant b Mohammed Shami	5
S. T. Gabriel not out	0 – (12) not out	0
J. Blackwood (did not bat)	– (7) c Pant b Bumrah	38
B 8, lb 5	13	B 14, lb 2, w 5, nb 1	22
(47.1 overs)	117	(59.5 overs)	210

1/9 (2) 2/13 (3) 3/13 (4) 4/13 (5) 5/22 (1)   1/9 (2) 2/37 (1) 3/97 (5) 4/98 (6) 5/159 (7)
6/67 (6) 7/78 (7) 8/97 (9) 9/117 (8) 10/117 (10)   6/177 (4) 7/177 (9) 8/180 (10) 9/206 (11) 10/210 (8)

In the second innings Bravo retired hurt at 55-2. Blackwood replaced him, as a concussion substitute.

Sharma 10.5–3–24–1; Bumrah 12.1–3–27–6; Mohammed Shami 13–3–34–2; Jadeja 11.1–7–19–1. *Second innings*—Sharma 12–3–37–2; Bumrah 11–4–31–1; Mohammed Shami 16–2–65–3; Jadeja 19.5–4–58–3; Vihari 1–0–3–0.

Umpires: R. A. Kettleborough *(England)* (60) and P. R. Reiffel *(Australia)* (44).
Third umpire: R. J. Tucker *(Australia)*.   Referee: D. C. Boon *(Australia)* (57).

Close of play: first day, India 264–5 (Vihari 42, Pant 27); second day, West Indies 87–7 (Hamilton 2, Cornwall 4); third day, West Indies 45–2 (Bravo 18, Brooks 4).

Test No. 2362/1 (B115, Afg3)

BANGLADESH v AFGHANISTAN 2019–20 (Only Test)

At Zohur Ahmed Chowdhury Stadium, Chittagong, on 5, 6, 7, 8, 9 September, 2019.
Toss: Afghanistan.   Result: AFGHANISTAN WON BY 224 RUNS.
Debuts: Afghanistan – Ibrahim Zadran, Qais Ahmad, Zahir Khan.
Man of the Match: Rashid Khan.

Afghanistan pulled off a stunning victory to become only the second team – after Australia in the 1870s – to win two of their first three Tests. It looked as if they might be denied by the weather when the last session of the fourth day and much of the fifth were washed out. But play resumed just in time: Afghanistan needed four wickets in 18.3 overs on the final evening, and Rashid Khan had Soumya Sarkar caught at short leg with 20 balls remaining, his 11th wicket to round off a stellar match – his earlier 51 had lifted the first innings to 342. At 20 years 350 days, he was the youngest Test captain of all, beating Zimbabwe's Tatenda Taibu by eight days, and obviously the youngest to win one (previously South Africa's Graeme Smith, 22 in 2002–03). Rahmat Shah, after a near-miss 98 against Ireland, finally scored Afghanistan's first Test century in the first innings, in which the former captain Asghar Afghan made a disciplined 92. Rashid and Mohammad Nabi (who announced his Test retirement after this match) worked their way through a flimsy Bangladesh reply, before 17-year-old opener Ibrahim Zadran, one of three debutants, hit 87; Afghan and Afsar Zazai swelled the target to a lofty 398. Bangladesh slumped to 136 for six, before the weather seemed to have saved them. But in the end an embarrassing defeat continued a sad sequence for Bangladesh, who had lost their first Test against all ten opponents, with only Ireland to come.

Afghanistan

Ibrahim Zadran c Mahmudullah b Taijul Islam	21	– (2) c Mominul Haque b Nayeem Hasan	87
Ihsanullah Janat b Taijul Islam	9	– (1) lbw b Shakib Al Hasan	4
Rahmat Shah c Soumya Sarkar b Nayeem Hasan	102	– c and b Shakib Al Hasan	0
Hashmatullah Shahidi c Soumya Sarkar b Mahmudullah	14	– c Soumya Sarkar b Nayeem Hasan	12
Asghar Afghan c Mushfiqur Rahim b Taijul Islam	92	– c Shakib Al Hasan b Taijul Islam	50
Mohammad Nabi b Nayeem Hasan	0	– (7) c Mominul Haque b Mehedi Hasan	8
†Afsar Zazai b Taijul Islam	41	– (6) not out	48
*Rashid Khan c and b Mehedi Hasan	51	– b Taijul Islam	24
Qais Ahmad c Mominul Haque b Shakib Al Hasan	9	– lbw b Shakib Al Hasan	14
Yamin Ahmadzai c Soumya Sarkar b Shakib Al Hasan	0	– run out (Shadman Islam/Mushfiqur Rahim)	9
Zahir Khan not out	0	– c Mominul Haque b Mehedi Hasan	0
Lb 1, nb 2	3	B 4	4
(117 overs)	342	(90.1 overs)	260

1/19 (2) 2/48 (1) 3/77 (4) 4/197 (3) 5/197 (6)   1/4 (1) 2/4 (3) 3/28 (4) 4/136 (5) 5/171 (2)
6/278 (5) 7/299 (7) 8/322 (9) 9/327 (10) 10/342 (8)   6/180 (7) 7/210 (8) 8/235 (9) 9/260 (10) 10/260 (11)

Taijul Islam 41–5–116–4; Shakib Al Hasan 22–1–64–2; Mehedi Hasan 28–5–73–1; Nayeem Hasan 19–0–43–2; Mahmudullah 4–0–9–1; Soumya Sarkar 4–0–26–0; Mominul Haque 4–0–9–0; Mosaddek Hossain 1–0–1–0. *Second innings*—Shakib Al Hasan 19–3–58–3; Mehedi Hasan 12.1–3–35–2; Taijul Islam 28–6–86–2; Nayeem Hasan 17–2–61–2; Mominul Haque 10–6–13–0.

Bangladesh

Shadman Islam c Afsar Zazai b Yamin Ahmadzai	0	– (2) lbw b Mohammad Nabi	41
Soumya Sarkar lbw b Mohammad Nabi	17	– (8) c Ibrahim Zadran b Rashid Khan	15
Liton Das b Rashid Khan	33	– (1) lbw b Zahir Khan	9
Mominul Haque c Asghar Afghan b Mohammad Nabi	52	– (5) lbw b Rashid Khan	3
*Shakib Al Hasan lbw b Rashid Khan	11	– (6) c Afsar Zazai b Zahir Khan	44
†Mushfiqur Rahim c Ibrahim Zadran b Rashid Khan	0	– (4) lbw b Rashid Khan	23
Mahmudullah b Rashid Khan	7	– c Ibrahim Zadran b Rashid Khan	7
Mosaddek Hossain not out	48	– (3) c Asghar Afghan b Zahir Khan	12
Mehedi Hasan b Qais Ahmad	11	– lbw b Rashid Khan	12
Taijul Islam b Mohammad Nabi	14	– lbw b Rashid Khan	0
Nayeem Hasan lbw b Rashid Khan	7	– not out	1
B 4, lb 1	5	B 4, lb 2	6
(70.5 overs)	205	(61.4 overs)	173

1/0 (1) 2/38 (2) 3/54 (3) 4/88 (5) 5/88 (6)   1/30 (1) 2/52 (3) 3/78 (4) 4/82 (5) 5/106 (2)
6/104 (7) 7/130 (4) 8/146 (9) 9/194 (10) 10/205 (11)   6/125 (7) 7/143 (6) 8/166 (9) 9/166 (10) 10/173 (8)

Yamin Ahmadzai 10–2–21–1; Mohammad Nabi 24–6–56–3; Zahir Khan 9–1–46–0; Rashid Khan 19.5–3–55–5; Qais Ahmad 8–2–22–1. *Second innings*—Yamin Ahmadzai 4–1–14–0; Mohammad Nabi 20–5–39–1; Rashid Khan 21.4–6–49–6; Zahir Khan 15–0–59–3; Qais Ahmad 1–0–6–0.

Umpires: N. J. Llong *(England)* (57) and P. Wilson *(Australia)* (1).
Third umpire: N. N. Menon *(India)*.   Referee: B. C. Broad *(England)* (99).

Close of play: first day, Afghanistan 271–5 (Asghar Afghan 88, Afsar Zazai 35); second day, Bangladesh 194–8 (Mosaddek Hossain 44, Taijul Islam 14); third day, Afghanistan 237–8 (Afsar Zazai 34, Yamin Ahmadzai 0); fourth day, Bangladesh 136–6 (Shakib Al Hasan 39, Soumya Sarkar 0).

Individual Test Career Records

Compiled by Philip Bailey

These career records for all players appearing in official Test matches are complete to 30 September, 2019.

Symbols: * Not out; † Left-hand batsman (in Innings column) or left-arm bowler (in Balls column).
‡ Player who has appeared in official Test matches for more than one team. (his record for each team is given under that country, while combined totals are shown at the end of this section).

INDIVIDUAL TEST CAREER RECORDS – ENGLAND

	First Test	Last Test	Tests	Inns	NO	Runs	HS	Avge	100	50	Ct	St	Balls	Runs	Wkts	Avge	BB	5wI	10wM
Abel, R.	1888	1902	13	22	2	744	132*	37.20	2	2	13	–	–	–	–	–	–	–	–
Absolom, C.A.	1878–79	1878–79	1	2	0	58	52	29.00	–	1	–	–	–	–	–	–	–	–	–
Adams, C.J.	1999–00	1999–00	5	8	0	104	31	13.00	–	–	6	–	–	–	–	–	–	–	–
Afzaal, U.	2001	2001	3	6†	1	83	54	16.60	–	1	–	–	120	59	1	59.00	1–42	0	0
Agnew, J.P.	1984	1985	3	4	3	10	5	10.00	–	–	–	–	54†	49	1	49.00	1–49	0	0
Ali, K.	2003	2003	1	2	0	10	9	5.00	–	–	–	–	552	373	4	93.25	2–51	0	0
Ali, M.M.	2014	2019	60	104†	8	2782	155*	28.97	5	14	32	–	10972	6624	181	36.59	6–53	5	1
Allen, D.A.	1959–60	1966	39	51	15	918	88	25.50	–	5	10	–	11297	3779	122	30.97	5–30	4	0
Allen, G.O.B.	1930	1947–48	25	33	2	750	122	24.19	1	3	20	–	4386	2379	81	29.37	7–80	5	1
Allom, M.J.C.	1929–30	1930–31	5	3	2	14	8*	14.00	–	–	–	–	817	265	14	18.92	5–38	1	0
Allott, P.J.W.	1981	1985	13	18	3	213	52*	14.20	–	1	4	–	2225	1084	26	41.69	6–61	1	0
Ambrose, T.R.	2007–08	2008–09	11	16	1	447	102	29.80	1	3	31	–	–	–	–	–	–	–	–
Ames, L.E.G.	1929	1938–39	47	72	12	2434	149	40.56	8	7	74	23	–	–	–	–	–	–	–
Amiss, D.L.	1966	1977	50	88	10	3612	262*	46.30	11	11	24	–	–	–	–	–	–	–	–
Anderson, J.M.	2003	2019	149	209†	87	1181	81	9.68	–	1	91	–	32359	15491	575	26.94	7–42	27	3
Andrew, K.V.	1954–55	1963	2	4	1	29	15	9.66	–	–	1	–	–	–	–	–	–	–	–
Ansari, Z.S.	2016–17	2016–17	3	5†	0	49	32	9.80	–	–	1	–	408†	275	5	55.00	2–76	0	0
Appleyard, R.	1954	1956	9	9	6	51	19*	17.00	–	–	4	–	1596	554	31	17.87	5–51	1	0
Archer, A.G.	1898–99	1898–99	1	2	1	31	24*	31.00	–	–	–	–	–	–	–	–	–	–	–
Archer, J.C.	2019	2019	4	7	0	48	15	6.85	–	–	–	–	936	446	22	20.27	6–45	2	0
Armitage, T.	1876–77	1876–77	2	3	0	33	21	11.00	–	–	–	–	12	15	0	–	–	–	–
Arnold, E.G.	1903–04	1907	10	15	3	160	40	13.33	–	–	8	–	1677	788	31	25.41	5–37	1	0
Arnold, G.G.	1967	1975	34	46	11	421	59	12.02	–	1	9	–	7650	3254	115	28.29	6–45	6	0
Arnold, J.	1931	1931	1	2	0	34	34	17.00	–	–	–	–	–	–	–	–	–	–	–
Astill, W.E.	1927–28	1929–30	9	15	0	190	40	12.66	–	–	7	–	2182	856	25	34.24	4–58	0	0
Atherton, M.A.	1989	2001	115	212	7	7728	185*	37.69	16	46	83	–	408	302	2	151.00	1–20	0	0
Athey, C.W.J.	1980	1988	23	41	1	919	123	22.97	1	4	13	–	–	–	–	–	–	–	–
Attewell, W.	1884–85	1891–92	10	15	6	150	43*	16.66	–	–	9	–	2850	626	28	22.35	4–42	0	0
Bailey, R.J.	1988	1989–90	4	8	0	119	43	14.87	–	–	–	–	–	–	–	–	–	–	–
Bailey, T.E.	1949	1958–59	61	91	14	2290	134*	29.74	1	10	32	–	9712	3856	132	29.21	7–34	5	1
Bairstow, D.L.	1979	1980–81	4	7	1	125	59	20.83	–	1	12	1	–	–	–	–	–	–	–
Bairstow, J.M.	2012	2019	69	121	7	4020	167*	35.26	6	21	181	13	–	–	–	–	–	–	–
Bakewell, A.H.	1931	1935	6	9	0	409	107	45.44	1	3	3	–	18	8	0	–	–	–	–
Balderstone, J.C.	1976	1976	2	4	0	39	35	9.75	–	–	1	–	96†	80	1	80.00	1–80	0	0

Name	Debut	Last	M	I	NO	Runs	HS	Avg	100	50	Balls	Runs	Wkts	Avg	BB	5wI	10wM	Ct	St
Ball, J.T.	2016	2017-18	4	8	0	67	31	8.37	–	–	612	343	3	114.33	1-47	0	–	0	0
Ballance, G.S.	2013-14	2017	23	42†	2	1498	156	37.45	4	7	12	5	0	–	–	–	–	–	0
Barber, R.W.	1960	1968	28	45†	3	1495	185	35.59	1	9	3426	1806	42	43.00	4-132	0	0	3	0
Barber, W.	1935	1935	2	4	0	83	44	20.75	–	–	2	0	1	0.00	1-0	0	0	0	0
Barlow, G.D.	1976-77	1977	3	5†	1	17	7*	4.25	–	–	–	–	–	–	–	–	–	3	0
Barlow, R.G.	1886-87	1886-87	17	30	4	591	62	22.73	–	2	2456†	767	34	22.55	7-40	–	–	24	7
Barnes, S.F.	1901-02	1913-14	27	39	9	242	38*	8.06	–	–	7873	3106	189	16.43	9-103	24	7	3	0
Barnes, W.	1880	1890	21	33	2	725	134	23.38	1	5	2289	793	51	15.54	6-28	3	–	3	–
Barnett, C.J.	1933	1948	20	35	4	1098	129	35.41	2	5	256	93	0	–	–	–	–	–	–
Barnett, K.J.	1988	1989	4	7	0	207	80	29.57	–	2	36	32	0	–	–	–	–	0	0
Barratt, F.	1929	1929	5	4	1	28	17	9.33	–	–	750	235	5	47.00	1-8	0	0	0	0
Barrington, K.F.	1955	1968	82	131	15	6806	256	58.67	20	35	2715	1300	29	44.82	3-4	0	0	58	0
Barton, V.A.	1891-92	1891-92	1	1	0	23	23	23.00	–	–	–	–	–	–	–	–	–	1	0
Bates, W.	1881-82	1886-87	15	26	2	656	64	27.33	–	5	2364	821	50	16.42	7-28	4	1	9	0
Batty, G.J.	2003-04	2016-17	9	12	2	149	38	14.90	–	–	1714	914	15	60.93	3-55	0	0	3	0
Bean, G.	1891-92	1891-92	3	5	0	92	50	18.40	–	1	–	–	–	–	–	–	–	4	0
Bedser, A.V.	1946	1955	51	71	15	714	79	12.75	–	–	15918	5876	236	24.89	7-44	15	5	26	0
Bell, I.R.	2004	2015-16	118	205	24	7727	235	42.69	22	46	108	76	1	76.00	1-33	0	0	100	0
Benjamin, J.E.	1994	1994	1	1	1	0	0*	0.00	–	–	168	80	4	20.00	4-42	–	–	0	0
Benson, M.R.	1986	1986	1	2†	0	51	30	25.50	–	–	–	–	–	–	–	–	–	0	0
Berry, R.	1950	1950	2	4†	2	6	4*	3.00	–	–	653†	228	9	25.33	5-63	1	–	0	0
Bess, D.M.	2018	2018	2	3	0	111	57	37.00	–	1	190	121	3	40.33	3-33	0	0	0	0
Bicknell, M.P.	1993	2003	4	7	0	45	15	6.42	–	2	1080	543	14	38.78	4-84	0	0	–	–
Binks, J.G.	1963-64	1963-64	2	4	0	91	55	22.75	–	1	–	–	–	–	–	–	–	8	–
Bird, M.C.	1909-10	1913-14	10	16	1	280	61	18.66	–	2	259	120	8	15.00	3-11	0	0	5	0
Birkenshaw, J.	1972-73	1973-74	5	7†	0	148	64	21.14	–	1	1017	469	13	36.07	5-57	1	–	3	0
Blackwell, I.D.	2005-06	2005-06	1	1†	0	4	4	4.00	–	–	114†	71	0	–	–	–	–	1	–
Blakey, R.J.	1992-93	1992-93	2	4	0	7	6	1.75	–	–	–	–	–	–	–	–	–	2	–
Bligh, I.F.W.	1882-83	1882-83	4	7	1	62	19	10.33	–	–	–	–	–	–	–	–	–	7	–
Blythe, C.	1901-02	1909-10	19	31	12	183	27	9.63	–	–	4546†	1863	100	18.63	8-59	9	4	6	–
Board, J.H.	1898-99	1909-10	6	12	2	108	29	10.80	–	–	–	–	–	–	–	–	–	8	–
Bolus, J.B.	1963	1963	7	12	0	496	88	41.33	–	4	18†	16	0	–	–	–	–	2	–
Booth, M.W.	1913-14	1913-14	2	2	0	46	32	23.00	–	–	312	130	7	18.57	4-49	0	0	0	0
Bopara, R.S.	2007-08	2012	13	19	1	575	143	31.94	3	–	434	290	1	290.00	1-39	0	0	0	0
Borthwick, S.G.	2013-14	2013-14	1	2†	0	5	4	2.50	–	–	78	82	4	20.50	3-33	0	0	2	0
Bosanquet, B.J.T.	1905	1905	7	14	3	147	27	13.36	–	–	970	604	25	24.16	8-107	2	–	9	–
Botham, I.T.	1903-04	1992	102	161	6	5200	208	33.54	14	22	21815	10878	383	28.40	8-34	27	4	120	–
Bowden, M.P.	1888-89	1888-89	2	2	0	25	25	12.50	–	–	–	–	–	–	–	–	–	1	–

INDIVIDUAL TEST CAREER RECORDS – ENGLAND (Continued)

	First Test	Last Test	Tests	Inns	NO	Runs	HS	Avge	100	50	Ct	St	Balls	Runs	Wkts	Avge	BB	5wI	10wM
Bowes, W.E.	1932	1946	15	11	5	28	10*	4.66	–	–	2	–	3655	1519	68	22.33	6-33	6	0
Bowley, E.H.	1929	1929-30	5	7	0	252	109	36.00	1	–	2	–	252	116	0	–	–	–	–
Boycott, G.	1964	1981-82	108	193	23	8114	246*	47.72	22	42	33	–	944	382	7	54.57	3-47	0	0
Bradley, W.M.	1899	1899	2	2	1	23	23*	23.00	–	–	–	–	625	233	6	38.83	5-67	1	0
Braund, L.C.	1901-02	1907-08	23	41	3	987	104	25.97	3	2	39	–	3805	1810	47	38.51	8-81	3	0
Brearley, J.M.	1976	1981	39	66	3	1442	91	22.88	–	9	52	–	–	–	–	–	–	–	–
Brearley, W.	1905	1912	4	5	2	21	11*	7.00	–	–	–	–	705	359	17	21.11	5-110	1	0
Brennan, D.V.	1951	1951	2	2	0	16	16	8.00	–	–	–	1	–	–	–	–	–	–	–
Bresnan, T.T.	2009	2013-14	23	26	4	575	91	26.13	–	3	8	–	4674	2357	72	32.73	5-48	1	0
Briggs, J.	1884-85	1899	33	50	5	815	121	18.11	1	2	12	–	5332†	2095	118	17.75	8-11	9	4
Broad, B.C.	1984	1989	25	44†	2	1661	162	39.54	6	6	10	–	6	4	0	–	–	–	–
Broad, S.C.J.	2007-08	2019	132	194†	29	3149	169	19.08	1	12	42	–	26950	13390	467	28.67	8-15	17	2
Brockwell, W.	1893	1899	7	12	0	202	49	16.83	–	–	6	–	582	309	5	61.80	3-33	0	0
Bromley-Davenport, H.R.	1895-96	1898-99	4	6	0	128	84	21.33	–	1	1	–	155†	98	4	24.50	2-46	0	0
Brookes, D.	1947-48	1947-48	1	2	0	17	10	8.50	–	–	1	–	–	–	–	–	–	–	–
Brown, A.	1961-62	1961-62	2	1	1	3	3*	–	–	–	1	–	323	150	3	50.00	3-27	0	0
Brown, D.J.	1965	1969	26	34	5	342	44*	11.79	–	–	7	–	5098	2237	79	28.31	5-42	2	0
Brown, F.R.	1931	1953	22	30	1	734	79	25.31	–	5	22	–	3260	1398	45	31.06	5-49	1	0
Brown, G.	1921	1922-23	7	12†	2	299	84	29.90	–	2	9	3	–	–	–	–	–	–	–
Brown, J.T.	1894-95	1899	8	16	3	470	140	36.15	1	1	7	–	35	22	0	–	–	–	–
Brown, S.J.E.	1996	1996	1	2	1	11	10*	11.00	–	–	1	–	198†	138	2	69.00	1-60	0	0
Buckenham, C.P.	1909-10	1909-10	4	7	0	43	17	6.14	–	–	2	–	1182	593	21	28.23	5-115	1	0
Burns, R.J.	2018-19	2019	12	24†	0	702	133	29.25	1	4	11	–	–	–	–	–	–	–	–
Butcher, A.R.	1979	1979	1	2†	0	34	20	17.00	–	–	–	–	12†	9	0	–	–	–	–
Butcher, M.A.	1997	2004-05	71	131†	7	4288	173†	34.58	8	23	61	–	901	541	15	36.06	4-42	0	0
Butler, R.O.	1980-81	1980-81	3	5	0	71	32	14.20	–	–	3	–	–	–	–	–	–	–	–
Butt, H.J.	1947	1947-48	2	2	1	15	15*	15.00	–	–	1	1	552	215	12	17.91	4-34	0	0
Butt, H.R.	1895-96	1895-96	3	4	1	22	13	7.33	–	–	1	1	–	–	–	–	–	–	–
Butler, J.C.	2014	2019	36	64	6	1969	106	33.94	1	15	73	–	–	–	–	–	–	–	–
Caddick, A.R.	1993	2002-03	62	95	12	861	49*	10.37	–	–	21	–	13558	6999	234	29.91	7-46	13	1
Calthorpe, Hon. F.S.G.	1929-30	1929-30	4	7	0	129	49	18.42	–	–	3	–	204	91	1	91.00	1-38	0	0
Capel, D.J.	1987	1989-90	15	25	1	374	98	15.58	–	2	6	–	2000	1064	21	50.66	3-88	0	0
Carberry, M.A.	2009-10	2013-14	6	12†	0	345	60	28.75	–	1	7	–	–	–	–	–	–	–	–
Carr, A.W.	1922-23	1929	11	13	1	237	63	19.75	–	1	3	–	–	–	–	–	–	–	–

Name			M	I	NO	Runs	HS	Avg	100	50	Ct	St	Balls	Runs	Wkts	Avg	BB	5w	10w	Ct
Carr, D.B.	1951–52	1951-52	2	4	0	135	76	33.75	—	—	—	—	210†	140	2	70.00	2-84	0	0	0
Carr, D.W.	1909	1909	1	1	0	0	0	0.00	—	—	—	—	414	282	7	40.28	5-146	1	0	—
Cartwright, T.W.	1964	1965	5	7	2	26	9	5.20	—	—	2	—	1611	544	15	36.26	6-94	1	0	—
Chapman, A.P.F.	1924	1930-31	26	36†	4	925	121	28.90	—	—	32	—	40†	20	0	—	—	—	—	—
Charlwood, H.R.J.	1876–77	1876-77	2	4	0	63	36	15.75	—	5	—	—	—	—	—	—	—	—	—	—
Chatterton, W.	1891–92	1891-92	1	1	0	48	48	48.00	—	—	1	—	—	—	—	—	—	—	—	—
Childs, J.H.	1988	1988	2	4†	4	2	2*	—	—	—	1	—	516†	183	3	61.00	1-13	0	0	0
Christopherson, S.	1884	1884	1	1	0	17	17	17.00	—	—	—	—	136	69	1	69.00	1-52	0	0	0
Clark, E.W.	1929	1934	8	9†	5	36	10	9.00	—	—	1	—	1931†	899	32	28.09	5-98	1	0	0
Clarke, R.	2003–04	2003-04	2	3	0	96	55	32.00	—	1	1	—	174	60	4	15.00	2-7	0	0	0
Clay, J.C.	1935	1935	1	—	—	—	—	—	—	—	—	—	192	75	0	—	—	—	—	—
Close, D.B.	1949	1976	22	37†	2	887	70	25.34	—	4	24	—	1212	532	18	29.55	4-35	0	0	0
Coldwell, L.J.	1962	1964	7	7	5	9	6*	4.50	—	—	1	—	1668	610	22	27.72	6-85	1	0	—
Collingwood, P.D.	2003–04	2010-11	68	115	10	4259	206	40.56	10	20	96	—	1905	1018	17	59.88	3-23	0	0	0
Compton, D.C.S.	1956–57	1937	78	131	15	5807	278	50.06	17	28	49	—	2710†	1410	25	56.40	5-70	1	0	—
Compton, N.R.D.	2012–13	2016	16	30	3	775	117	28.70	2	2	7	—	—	—	—	—	—	—	—	0
Cook, A.N.	2005–06	2018	161	291†	16	12472	294	45.35	33	57	175	—	18	7	1	7.00	1-6	0	0	0
Cook, C.	1947	1947	1	2	0	4	4	2.00	—	—	—	3	180†	127	0	—	—	—	—	—
Cook, G.	1981–82	1982-83	7	13	0	203	66	15.61	—	2	9	—	42†	27	0	—	—	—	—	—
Cook, N.G.B.	1983	1989	15	25	4	179	31	8.52	—	—	5	—	4174†	1689	52	32.48	6-65	4	1	—
Cope, G.A.	1977–78	1977-78	3	3	0	40	22	13.33	—	—	1	—	864	277	8	34.62	3-102	0	0	0
Copson, W.H.	1939	1947	3	1	0	6	6	6.00	—	—	1	—	762	297	15	19.80	5-85	1	0	0
Cork, D.G.	1995	2002	37	56	8	864	59	18.00	—	3	18	—	7678	3906	131	29.81	7-43	5	0	0
Cornford, W.L.	1929–30	1929-30	4	4	0	36	18	9.00	—	—	5	3	—	—	—	—	—	—	—	—
Cottam, R.M.H.	1968–69	1972-73	4	5	1	27	13	6.75	—	—	2	—	903	327	14	23.35	4-50	0	0	0
Coventry, Hon. C.J.	1888–89	1888-89	2	2	0	13	12	13.00	—	—	—	—	—	—	—	—	—	—	—	—
Cowans, N.G.	1982–83	1985	19	29	7	175	36	7.95	—	—	9	—	3452	2003	51	39.27	6-77	2	0	0
Cowdrey, C.S.	1984–85	1988	6	8	1	101	38	14.42	—	—	5	—	399	309	4	77.25	2-65	0	0	—
Cowdrey, M.C.	1954–55	1974-75	114	188	15	7624	182	44.06	22	38	120	—	119	104	0	—	—	—	—	—
Coxon, A.	1948	1948	1	2	0	19	19	9.50	—	—	—	—	378	172	3	57.33	2-90	0	0	—
Crane, M.S.	2017–18	2017-18	1	2†	0	6	4	3.00	—	—	—	—	288	193	1	193.00	1-193	0	0	0
Cranston, J.	1890	1890	1	2†	0	31	16	15.50	—	—	1	—	—	—	—	—	—	—	—	—
Cranston, K.	1947	1948	8	14	0	209	45	14.92	—	3	3	—	1010	461	18	25.61	4-12	0	0	0
Crapp, J.F.	1948	1948-49	7	13†	2	319	56	29.00	—	3	7	—	—	—	—	—	—	—	—	0
Crawford, J.N.	1905–06	1907-08	12	23	2	469	74	22.33	—	2	13	—	2203	1150	39	29.48	5-48	3	0	—
Crawley, J.P.	1994	2002-03	37	61	9	1800	156*	34.61	4	9	29	—	—	—	—	—	—	—	—	0
Croft, R.D.B.	1996	2001	21	34	8	421	37†	16.19	—	—	10	—	4619	1825	49	37.24	5-95	1	0	0
Curran, S.M.	2018	2019	11	20†	2	541	78	30.05	—	3	—	—	1103†	609	21	29.00	4-74	0	0	0

INDIVIDUAL TEST CAREER RECORDS – ENGLAND (Continued)

	First Test	Last Test	Tests	Inns	NO	Runs	HS	Avge	100	50	Ct	St	Balls	Runs	Wkts	Avge	BB	5wI	10wM
Curran, T.K.	2017–18	2017–18	2	3	1	66	39	33.00	–	–	–	–	396	200	2	100.00	1-65	0	0
Curtis, T.S.	1988	1989	5	9	0	140	41	15.55	–	–	3	–	18	7	0	–	–	0	–
Cuttell, W.R.	1898–99	1898–99	2	4	0	65	21	16.25	–	–	2	–	285	73	6	12.16	3-17	0	0
Dawson, E.W.	1927–28	1929–30	5	9	0	175	55	19.44	–	1	–	–	–	–	–	–	–	–	–
Dawson, L.A.	2016–17	2017	3	6	2	84	66*	21.00	–	1	2	–	526†	298	7	42.57	2-34	0	0
Dawson, R.K.J.	2001–02	2002–03	7	13	3	114	19*	11.40	–	–	3	–	1116	677	11	61.54	4-134	0	0
Dean, H.	1912	1912	3	4†	2	10	8	5.00	–	–	2	–	447†	153	11	13.90	4-19	0	0
DeFreitas, P.A.J.	1986–87	1995	44	68	5	934	88	14.82	–	4	14	–	9838	4700	140	33.57	7-70	4	0
Denly, J.L.	2018–19	2019	8	16	0	457	94	28.56	–	4	4	–	150	104	0	–	–	–	–
Denness, M.H.	1969	1975	28	45	3	1667	188	39.69	4	7	28	–	–	–	–	–	–	–	–
Denton, D.	1905	1909–10	11	22	1	424	104	20.19	1	1	8	–	–	–	–	–	–	–	–
Dewes, J.G.	1948	1950–51	5	10†	0	121	67	12.10	–	1	–	–	–	–	–	–	–	–	–
Dexter, E.R.	1958	1968	62	102	8	4502	205	47.89	9	27	29	–	5317	2306	66	34.93	4-10	0	0
Dilley, G.R.	1979–80	1989	41	58†	19	521	56	13.35	–	2	10	–	8192	4107	138	29.76	6-38	6	0
Dipper, A.E.	1921	1921	1	2	0	51	40	25.50	–	–	–	–	–	–	–	–	–	–	–
Doggart, G.H.G.	1950	1950	2	4	0	76	29	19.00	–	–	3	–	–	–	–	–	–	–	–
D'Oliveira, B.L.	1966	1972	44	70	8	2484	158	40.06	5	15	29	–	5706	1859	47	39.55	3-46	0	0
Dollery, H.E.	1947	1950	4	7	0	72	37	10.28	–	–	1	–	–	–	–	–	–	–	–
Dolphin, A.	1920–21	1920–21	1	2	0	1	1	0.50	–	–	1	–	–	–	–	–	–	–	–
Douglas, J.W.H.T.	1911–12	1924–25	23	35	2	962	119	29.15	1	6	9	–	2812	1486	45	33.02	5-46	1	0
Downton, P.R.	1980–81	1988	30	48	8	785	74	19.62	–	4	70	5	–	–	–	–	–	–	–
Druce, N.F.	1897–98	1897–98	5	9	0	252	64	28.00	–	1	5	–	–	–	–	–	–	–	–
Ducat, A.	1921	1921	1	2	0	5	3	2.50	–	–	1	–	–	–	–	–	–	–	–
Duckett, B.M.	2016–17	2016–17	4	7†	0	110	56	15.71	–	1	1	–	–	–	–	–	–	–	–
Duckworth, G.	1924	1936	24	28	12	234	39*	14.62	–	–	45	15	–	–	–	–	–	–	–
Duleepsinhji, K.S.	1929	1931	12	19	2	995	173	58.52	3	5	10	–	–	–	–	–	–	–	–
Durston, F.J.	1921	1921	1	2	1	8	6*	8.00	–	–	–	–	202	136	5	27.20	4-102	0	0
Ealham, M.A.	1996	1998	8	13	3	210	53*	21.00	–	2	4	–	1060	488	17	28.70	4-21	0	0
Edmonds, P.H.	1975	1987	51	65	15	875	64	17.50	–	2	42	–	12028†	4273	125	34.18	7-66	2	0
Edrich, J.H.	1963	1976	77	127†	9	5138	310*	43.54	12	24	43	–	30	23	0	–	–	–	–
Edrich, W.J.	1938	1954–55	39	63	2	2440	219	40.00	6	13	39	–	3234	1693	41	41.29	4-68	0	0
Elliott, H.	1927–28	1933–34	4	5	1	61	37*	15.25	–	–	8	3	–	–	–	–	–	–	–
Ellison, R.M.	1984	1986	11	16†	1	202	41	13.46	–	–	2	–	2264	1048	35	29.94	6-77	3	1
Emburey, J.E.	1978	1995	64	96	20	1713	75	22.53	–	10	34	–	15391	5646	147	38.40	7-78	6	0

Name	From	To																			
Emmett, G.M.	1948	1948	1	2	0	10	10	5.00	–	–	–	–	–	–	–	–	–	–	–	1	0
Emmett, T.	1876–77	1881–82	7	13†	1	160	48	13.33	–	–	9	–	728†	9	31.55	7–68	1	–
Evans, A.J.	1921	1921	1	2	0	18	14	9.00	–	–	–	–	–	–	–	–	–	–
Evans, T.G.	1946	1959	91	133	14	2439	104	20.49	2	8	173	46	–	–	–	–	–	–
Fagg, A.E.	1936	1936	5	8	0	150	39	18.75	–	–	5	–	–	–	–	–	–	–
Fairbrother, N.H.	1987	1992–93	10	15†	1	219	83	15.64	–	1	4	–	12†	0	–	–	–	–
Fane, F.L.	1905–06	1909–10	14	27	1	682	143	26.23	1	3	6	–	–	–	–	–	–	–
Farnes, K.	1934	1938–39	15	17	5	58	20	4.83	–	–	1	–	3932	60	28.65	6–96	3	1
Farrimond, W.	1930–31	1935	4	7	0	116	35	16.57	–	–	5	2	–	–	–	–	–	–
Fender, P.G.H.	1920–21	1929	13	21	1	380	60	19.00	–	2	14	–	2178	29	40.86	5–90	2	0
Ferris, J.J.‡	1891–92	1891–92	1	1†	0	16	16	16.00	–	–	–	–	272†	13	7.00	7–37	2	1
Fielder, A.	1903–04	1907–08	6	12	5	78	20	11.14	–	–	4	–	1491	26	27.34	6–82	1	0
Finn, S.T.	2009–10	2016–17	36	47	22	279	56	11.16	–	1	8	–	6412	125	30.40	6–79	5	0
Fishlock, L.B.	1936	1946–47	4	5†	1	47	19*	11.75	–	–	1	–	–	–	–	–	–	–
Flavell, J.A.	1961	1964	4	6†	2	31	14	7.75	–	–	–	–	792	7	52.42	2–65	0	0
Fletcher, K.W.R.	1968	1981–82	59	96	14	3272	216	39.90	7	19	54	–	285	2	96.50	1–6	0	0
Flintoff, A.‡	1998	2009	78	128	9	3795	167	31.89	5	26	52	–	14747	219	33.34	5–58	3	0
Flowers, W.	1884–85	1893	8	14	0	254	56	18.14	–	1	2	–	858	14	21.14	5–46	1	–
Foakes, B.T.	2018–19	2018–19	5	10	2	332	107	41.50	1	1	10	2	–	–	–	–	–	–
Ford, F.G.J.	1894–95	1894–95	5	9†	0	168	48	18.66	–	1	5	–	204†	1	129.00	1–47	0	0
Foster, F.R.	1911–12	1912	11	15	1	330	71	23.57	–	3	11	–	2447†	45	20.57	6–91	4	–
Foster, J.S.	2001–02	2002–03	7	12	3	226	48	25.11	–	–	17	1	–	–	–	–	–	–
Foster, N.A.	1983	1993	29	45	7	446	39	11.73	–	–	7	–	6261	88	32.85	8–107	5	1
Foster, R.E.	1903–04	1907	8	14	0	602	287	46.30	1	1	13	–	–	–	–	–	–	–
Fothergill, A.J.	1888–89	1888–89	2	2†	1	33	32	16.50	–	–	–	–	321†	8	11.25	4–19	0	–
Fowler, G.	1982	1984–85	21	37†	0	1307	201	35.32	3	8	10	–	18	0	–	–	–	–
Fraser, A.R.C.	1989	1998–99	46	67	15	388	32	7.46	–	–	9	–	10876	177	27.32	8–53	13	2
Freeman, A.P.	1924–25	1929	12	16	5	154	50*	14.00	–	1	4	–	3732	66	25.86	7–71	5	3
French, B.N.	1986	1987–88	16	21	4	308	59	18.11	–	1	38	1	–	–	–	–	–	–
Fry, C.B.	1895–96	1912	26	41	3	1223	144	32.18	2	7	17	–	10	0	–	–	–	–
Gallian, J.E.R.	1995	1995–96	3	6	0	74	28	12.33	–	–	1	–	84	0	–	–	–	–
Gatting, M.W.	1977–78	1994–95	79	138	14	4409	207	35.55	10	21	59	–	752	4	79.25	1–14	0	0
Gay, L.H.	1894–95	1894–95	1	2	0	37	33	18.50	–	–	3	1	–	–	–	–	–	–
Geary, G.	1924	1934	14	20	4	249	66	15.56	–	2	13	–	3810	46	29.41	7–70	4	1
Gibb, P.A.	1938–39	1946–47	8	13	0	581	120	44.69	2	3	3	1	–	–	–	–	–	–
Giddins, E.S.H.	1999	2000	4	7	3	10	7	2.50	–	–	–	–	444	12	20.00	5–15	1	0
Gifford, N.	1964	1973	15	20†	9	179	25*	16.27	–	–	8	–	3084†	33	31.09	5–55	1	0
Giles, A.F.	1998	2006–07	54	81	13	1421	59	20.89	–	4	33	–	12180†	143	40.60	5–57	5	0

INDIVIDUAL TEST CAREER RECORDS – ENGLAND (Continued)

	First Test	Last Test	Tests	Inns	NO	Runs	HS	Avge	100	50	Ct	St	Balls	Runs	Wkts	Avge	BB	5wI	10wM
Gilligan, A.E.R.	1922–23	1924–25	11	16	3	209	39*	16.07	–	–	3	–	2404	1046	36	29.05	6–7	2	1
Gilligan, A.H.H.	1929–30	1929–30	4	4	0	71	32	17.75	–	–	1	–	–	–	–	–	–	–	–
Gimblett, H.	1936	1939	3	5	1	129	67*	32.25	–	1	1	–	–	–	–	–	–	–	–
Gladwin, C.	1947	1949	8	11	5	170	51*	28.33	–	1	2	–	2129	571	15	38.06	3–21	0	0
Goddard, T.W.J.	1930	1939	8	5	5	13	8	6.50	–	–	3	–	1563	588	22	26.72	6–29	1	0
Gooch, G.A.	1975	1994–95	118	215	6	8900	333	42.58	20	46	103	–	2655	1069	23	46.47	3–39	0	0
Gough, D.	1994	2003	58	86	18	855	65	12.57	–	2	13	–	11821	6503	229	28.39	6–42	9	0
Gover, A.R.	1936	1946	4	1	1	2	2*	–	–	–	1	–	816	359	8	44.87	3–85	0	0
Gower, D.I.	1978	1992	117	204†	18	8231	215	44.25	18	39	74	–	36	20	1	20.00	1–1	0	0
Grace, E.M.	1880	1880	1	2	0	36	36	18.00	–	–	1	–	–	–	–	–	–	–	–
Grace, G.F.	1880	1880	1	2	0	0	0	0.00	–	–	2	–	–	–	–	–	–	–	–
Grace, W.G.	1880	1899	22	36	2	1098	170	32.29	2	5	39	–	666	236	9	26.22	2–12	0	0
Graveney, T.W.	1951	1969	79	123	13	4882	258	44.38	11	20	80	–	260	167	1	167.00	1–34	0	0
Greenhough, T.	1959	1960	4	4	1	4	2	1.33	–	–	1	–	1129	357	16	22.31	5–35	1	0
Greenwood, A.	1876–77	1876–77	2	4	0	77	49	19.25	–	–	2	–	–	–	–	–	–	–	–
Greig, A.W.	1972	1977	58	93	4	3599	148	40.43	8	20	87	–	9802	4541	141	32.20	8–86	6	2
Greig, I.A.	1982	1982	2	4	0	26	14	6.50	–	–	–	–	188	114	4	28.50	4–53	0	0
Grieve, B.A.F.	1888–89	1888–89	2	3	2	40	14*	40.00	–	–	–	–	–	–	–	–	–	–	–
Griffith, S.C.	1947–48	1948–49	3	5	0	157	140	31.40	1	–	5	–	–	–	–	–	–	–	–
Gunn, G.	1907–08	1929–30	15	29	1	1120	122*	40.00	2	7	15	–	12	8	0	–	–	–	–
Gunn, J.R.	1901–02	1905	6	10†	2	85	24	10.62	–	1	3	–	999†	387	18	21.50	5–76	1	0
Gunn, W.	1886–87	1899	11	20	2	392	102*	21.77	1	1	5	–	–	–	–	–	–	–	–
Habib, A.	1999	1999	2	3	0	26	19	8.66	–	–	–	–	–	–	–	–	–	–	–
Haig, N.E.	1921	1929–30	5	9	0	126	47	14.00	–	–	4	–	1026	448	13	34.46	3–73	0	0
Haigh, S.	1898–99	1912	11	18	3	113	25	7.53	–	–	8	–	1294	622	24	25.91	6–11	1	0
Hales, A.D.	2015–16	2016	11	21	0	573	94	27.28	–	5	8	–	18	2	0	–	–	–	–
Hallows, C.	1921	1928	2	2†	0	42	26	42.00	–	–	–	–	–	–	–	–	–	–	–
Hameed, H.	2016–17	2016–17	3	6	1	219	82	43.80	–	2	4	–	–	–	–	–	–	–	–
Hamilton, G.M.	1999–00	1999–00	1	2†	0	0	0	0.00	–	–	–	–	90	63	0	–	–	–	–
Hammond, W.R.	1927–28	1946–47	85	140	16	7249	336*	58.45	22	24	110	–	7969	3138	83	37.80	5–36	2	0
Hampshire, J.H.	1969	1975	8	16	1	403	107	26.86	1	2	9	–	–	–	–	–	–	–	–
Hardinge, H.T.W.	1921	1921	1	2	0	30	25	15.00	–	–	–	–	–	–	–	–	–	–	–
Hardstaff, J., sen.	1907–08	1907–08	5	10	0	311	72	31.10	–	3	1	–	–	–	–	–	–	–	–
Hardstaff, J., jun.	1935	1948	23	38	3	1636	205*	46.74	4	10	9	–	–	–	–	–	–	–	–

Harmison, S.J.‡	2002	62	84	23	742	49*	12.16	–	–	7	13192	32	222	31.94	7-12	8	1
Harris, Lord	1878–79	4	6	1	145	52	29.00	–	1	2	–	29	0	–	–	–	–
Hartley, J.C.	1905–06	2	4	0	15	9	3.75	–	–	2	192	115	1	115.00	1-62	0	0
Hawke, Lord	1898–99	5	8	1	55	30	7.85	–	–	3	–	–	–	–	–	–	–
Hayes, E.G.	1905–06	5	9	1	86	35	10.75	–	–	2	90	52	1	52.00	1-28	0	0
Hayes, F.C.	1973	9	17	0	244	106*	15.25	1	–	7	–	–	–	–	–	–	–
Hayward, T.W.	1895–96	35	60	2	1999	137	34.46	3	12	19	893	514	14	36.71	4-22	0	0
Headley, D.W.	1997	15	26	4	186	31	8.45	–	–	7	3026	1671	60	27.85	6-60	0	1
Hearne, A.	1891–92	1	1	0	9	9	9.00	–	–	1	–	–	–	–	–	–	–
Hearne, F.‡	1888–89	2	2	0	47	27	23.50	–	–	1	–	–	–	–	–	–	–
Hearne, G.G.	1891–92	1	1†	0	0	0	0.00	–	–	–	–	–	–	–	–	–	–
Hearne, J.T.	1891–92	12	18	4	126	40	9.00	–	–	4	2976	1082	49	22.08	6-41	4	1
Hearne, J.W.	1911–12	24	36	5	806	114	26.00	1	2	13	2926	1462	30	48.73	5-49	1	0
Hegg, W.K.	1998–99	2	4	0	30	15	7.50	–	–	8	–	–	–	–	–	–	–
Hemmings, E.E.	1982	16	21	4	383	95	22.52	–	2	5	4437	1825	43	42.44	6-58	1	0
Hendren, E.H.	1920–21	51	83	9	3525	205*	47.63	7	21	33	47	31	1	31.00	1-27	0	0
Hendrick, M.	1974	30	35	15	128	15	6.40	–	–	25	6208	2248	87	25.83	4-28	0	0
Heseltine, C.	1895–96	2	2	0	18	18	9.00	–	–	3	157	84	5	16.80	5-38	1	0
Hick, G.A.	1991	65	114	6	3383	178	31.32	6	18	90	3057	1306	23	56.78	4-126	0	0
Higgs, K.	1965	15	19†	3	185	63	11.56	–	1	4	4112	1473	71	20.74	6-91	2	0
Hill, A.	1876–77	2	4	1	101	49	50.50	–	1	1	340	130	7	18.57	4-27	0	0
Hill, A.J.L.	1895–96	3	4	0	251	124	62.75	1	1	1	40	8	4	2.00	4-8	0	0
Hilton, M.J.	1950	4	6	1	37	15	7.40	–	–	1	1244†	477	14	34.07	5-61	1	0
Hirst, G.H.	1897–98	24	38	3	790	85	22.57	–	5	18	4010†	1770	59	30.00	5-48	3	0
Hitch, J.W.	1911–12	7	10	3	103	51*	14.71	–	1	4	462	325	7	46.42	2-31	0	0
Hobbs, J.B.	1907–08	61	102	7	5410	211	56.94	15	28	17	376	165	1	165.00	1-19	0	0
Hobbs, R.N.S.	1967	7	8	3	34	15*	6.80	–	–	8	1291	481	12	40.08	3-25	0	0
Hoggard, M.J.	2000	67	92	27	473	38	7.27	–	–	24	13909	7564	248	30.50	7-61	7	1
Hollies, W.E.	1934–35	13	15	8	37	18*	5.28	–	–	2	3554	1332	44	30.27	7-50	5	0
Hollioake, A.J.	1997–98	4	6	0	65	45	10.83	–	–	4	144	67	2	33.50	2-31	0	0
Hollioake, B.C.	1997	2	4	0	44	28	11.00	–	–	2	252	199	4	49.75	2-105	0	0
Holmes, E.R.T.	1934–35	5	9	2	114	85*	16.28	–	1	4	108	76	2	38.00	1-10	0	0
Holmes, P.	1921	7	14	1	357	88	27.46	–	4	3	–	–	–	–	–	–	–
Hone, L.	1878–79	1	2	0	13	7	6.50	–	–	2	–	–	–	–	–	–	–
Hopwood, J.L.	1934	2	3	1	12	8	6.00	–	–	–	462†	155	0	–	–	–	–
Hornby, A.N.	1878–79	3	6	0	21	9	3.50	–	–	–	28	0	1	0.00	1-0	0	0
Horton, M.J.	1959	2	2	0	60	58	30.00	–	1	2	238	59	2	29.50	2-24	0	0
Howard, N.D.	1951–52	4	6	1	86	23	17.20	–	–	4	–	–	–	–	–	–	–

INDIVIDUAL TEST CAREER RECORDS – ENGLAND (Continued)

	First Test	Last Test	Tests	Inns	NO	Runs	HS	Avge	100	50	Ct	St	Balls	Runs	Wkts	Avge	BB	5wI	10wM
Howell, H.	1920–21	1924	5	8	6	15	5	7.50	–	–	–	–	918	559	7	79.85	4–115	0	0
Howorth, R.	1947	1947–48	5	10†	2	145	45*	18.12	–	–	2	–	1536†	635	19	33.42	6–124	1	0
Humphries, J.	1907–08	1907–08	3	6	1	44	16	8.80	–	–	7	–	–	–	–	–	–	–	–
Hunter, J.	1884–85	1884–85	5	7	2	93	39*	18.60	–	–	8	3	–	–	–	–	–	–	–
Hussain, N.	1989–90	2004	96	171	16	5764	207	37.18	14	33	67	–	30	15	0	–	–	0	0
Hutchings, K.L.	1907–08	1909	7	12	0	341	126	28.41	1	1	9	–	90	81	1	81.00	1–5	0	0
Hutton, L.	1937	1954–55	79	138	15	6971	364	56.67	19	33	57	–	260	232	3	77.33	1–2	0	0
Hutton, R.A.	1971	1971	5	8	2	219	81	36.50	–	2	9	–	738	257	9	28.55	3–72	0	0
Iddon, J.	1934–35	1935	5	7	1	170	73	28.33	–	2	1	–	66†	27	0	–	–	–	–
Igglesden, A.P.	1989	1993–94	3	5	2	6	3*	3.00	–	–	–	–	555	329	6	54.83	2–91	0	0
Ikin, J.T.	1946	1955	18	31†	2	606	60	20.89	–	3	31	–	572	354	3	118.00	1–38	0	0
Illingworth, R.	1958	1973	61	90	11	1836	113	23.24	2	5	45	–	11934	3807	122	31.20	6–29	3	0
Illingworth, R.K.	1991	1995–96	9	14	7	128	28	18.28	–	–	5	–	1485†	615	19	32.36	4–96	0	0
Ilott, M.C.	1993	1995–96	5	6	2	28	15	7.00	–	–	–	–	1042†	542	12	45.16	3–48	0	0
Insole, D.J.	1950	1957	9	17	2	408	110*	27.20	1	1	8	–	–	–	–	–	–	–	–
Irani, R.C.	1996	1999	3	5	0	86	41	17.20	–	–	2	–	192	112	3	37.33	1–22	0	0
Jackman, R.D.	1980–81	1982	4	6	0	42	17	7.00	–	–	–	–	1070	445	14	31.78	4–110	0	0
Jackson, Hon. F.S.	1893	1905	20	33	4	1415	144*	48.79	5	6	10	–	1587	799	24	33.29	5–52	1	0
Jackson, H.L.	1949	1961	2	2	1	15	8	15.00	–	–	1	–	498	155	7	22.14	2–26	0	0
James, S.P.	1998	1998	2	4	0	71	36	17.75	–	–	–	–	–	–	–	–	–	–	–
Jameson, J.A.	1971	1973–74	4	8	0	214	82	26.75	–	1	–	–	42	17	1	17.00	1–17	0	0
Jardine, D.R.	1928	1933–34	22	33	6	1296	127	48.00	1	10	26	–	6	10	0	–	–	–	–
Jarvis, P.W.	1987–88	1992–93	9	15	2	132	29*	10.15	–	–	2	–	1912	965	21	45.95	4–107	0	0
Jenkins, R.O.	1948–49	1952	9	12	1	198	39	18.00	–	–	4	–	2118	1098	32	34.31	5–116	1	0
Jennings, K.K.	2016–17	2018–19	17	32†	1	781	146*	25.19	2	1	17	–	73	55	0	–	–	–	–
Jessop, G.L.	1899	1912	18	26	0	569	104	21.88	1	3	11	–	732	354	10	35.40	4–68	0	0
Johnson, R.L.	2003	2003–04	3	4	0	59	26	14.75	–	–	–	–	547	275	16	17.18	6–33	2	0
Jones, A.O.	1899	1909	12	21	0	291	34	13.85	–	–	15	–	228	133	3	44.33	3–73	0	0
Jones, G.O.	2003–04	2006–07	34	53	4	1172	100	23.91	1	6	128	5	–	–	–	–	–	–	–
Jones, I.J.	1963–64	1967–68	15	17	9	38	16	4.75	–	–	4	–	3546†	1769	44	40.20	6–118	1	0
Jones, S.P.	2002	2005	18	18†	5	205	44	15.76	–	–	4	–	2821	1666	59	28.23	6–53	3	0
Jordan, C.J.	2014	2014–15	8	11	1	180	35	18.00	–	–	14	–	1530	752	21	35.80	4–18	0	0
Jupp, H.	1876–77	1876–77	2	4	0	68	63	17.00	–	1	2	–	–	–	–	–	–	–	–
Jupp, V.W.C.	1921	1928	8	13	1	208	38	17.33	–	–	5	–	1301	616	28	22.00	4–37	0	0

Keeton, W.W.	1934	1939	2	4	0	57	25	14.25	–	–	–	–	1683	31	19.32	5–76	2	0
Kennedy, A.S.	1922–23	1922–23	5	8	2	93	41*	15.50	–	–	5	–	599	31	19.32	5–76	2	0
Kenyon, D.	1951–52	1955	8	15	0	192	87	12.80	–	1	5	–	–	–	–	–	–	–
Kerrigan, S.C.	2013	2013	1	1	1	1	1*	–	–	3	11	–	48†	0	–	–	–	–
Key, R.W.T.	2002	2004–05	15	26	1	775	221	31.00	1	3	11	–	–	–	–	–	–	–
Khan, A.	2008–09	2008–09	1	–	–	–	–	–	–	–	–	–	174	1	122.00	1–111	0	0
Killick, E.T.	1929	1929	2	4	0	81	31	20.25	–	2	–	–	–	–	–	–	–	–
Kilner, R.	1924	1926	9	8†	1	233	74	33.28	–	2	6	–	2368†	24	30.58	4–51	0	0
King, J.H.	1909	1909	1	2†	0	64	60	32.00	–	1	–	–	162†	1	99.00	1–99	0	0
Kinneir, S.	1911–12	1911–12	1	2†	0	52	30	26.00	–	–	–	–	–	–	–	–	–	–
Kirtley, R.J.	2003	2003	4	7	1	32	12	5.33	–	–	3	–	1079	19	29.52	6–34	1	0
Knight, A.E.	1903–04	1903–04	3	6	1	81	70*	16.20	–	1	1	–	–	–	–	–	–	–
Knight, B.R.	1961–62	1969	29	38	7	812	127	26.19	–	2	14	–	5377	70	31.75	4–38	0	0
Knight, D.J.	1921	1921	2	4	0	54	38	13.50	–	–	1	–	–	–	–	–	–	–
Knight, N.V.	1995	2001	17	30†	0	719	113	23.96	1	4	26	–	–	–	–	–	–	–
Knott, A.P.E.	1967	1981	95	149	15	4389	135	32.75	5	30	250	19	–	–	–	–	–	–
Knox, N.A.	1907	1907	2	4	1	24	8*	8.00	–	–	–	–	126	3	35.00	2–39	0	0
Laker, J.C.	1947–48	1958–59	46	63	15	676	63	14.08	–	2	12	–	12027	193	21.24	10–53	9	3
Lamb, A.J.	1982	1992	79	139	10	4656	142	36.09	14	18	75	–	30	1	23.00	1–6	0	0
Langridge, J.	1933	1946	8	9†	0	242	70	26.88	–	1	6	–	1074†	19	21.73	7–56	0	2
Larkins, W.	1979–80	1990–91	13	25	1	493	64	20.54	–	3	8	–	–	–	–	–	–	–
Larter, J.D.F.	1962	1965	10	7	2	16	10	3.20	–	–	5	–	2172	37	25.43	5–57	2	0
Larwood, H.	1926	1932–33	21	28	3	485	98	19.40	–	2	15	–	4969	78	28.35	6–32	4	1
Lathwell, M.N.	1993	1993	2	4	0	78	33	19.50	–	–	–	–	–	–	–	–	–	–
Lawrence, D.V.	1988	1991–92	5	6	0	60	34	10.00	–	–	–	–	1089	18	37.55	5–106	1	0
Leach, M.J.	2017–18	2019	9	16†	5	202	92	18.36	–	1	4	–	1790†	32	26.06	5–83	1	0
Leadbeater, E.	1951–52	1951–52	2	2	1	40	38	20.00	–	–	3	–	289	2	109.00	1–38	0	0
Lee, H.W.	1930–31	1930–31	1	2	0	19	18	9.50	–	–	–	–	–	–	–	–	–	–
Lees, W.S.	1905–06	1905–06	5	9	3	66	25*	11.00	–	–	2	–	1256	26	17.96	6–78	2	0
Legge, G.B.	1927–28	1929–30	5	7	1	299	196	49.83	1	1	1	–	30	0	–	–	0	–
Leslie, C.F.H.	1882–83	1882–83	4	7	0	106	54	15.14	–	–	–	–	96	4	11.00	3–31	0	0
Lever, J.K.	1976–77	1986	21	31	5	306	53	11.76	–	1	11	–	4433†	73	26.72	7–46	3	1
Lever, P.	1970–71	1975	17	18	2	350	88*	21.87	–	2	11	–	3571	41	36.80	6–38	2	0
Leveson Gower, H.D.G.	1909–10	1909–10	3	6	0	95	31	23.75	–	–	1	–	–	–	–	–	–	–
Levett, W.H.V.	1933–34	1933–34	1	2	1	7	5	7.00	–	–	3	–	–	–	–	–	–	–
Lewis, A.R.	1972–73	1973	9	16	2	457	125	32.64	1	3	–	–	–	–	–	–	–	–
Lewis, C.C.	1990	1996	32	51	3	1105	117	23.02	1	4	25	–	6852	93	37.52	6–111	3	0
Lewis, J.	2006	2006	1	2	0	27	20	13.50	–	–	–	–	246	3	40.66	3–68	0	0

INDIVIDUAL TEST CAREER RECORDS – ENGLAND (Continued)

	First Test	Last Test	Tests	Inns	NO	Runs	HS	Avge	100	50	Ct	St	Balls	Runs	Wkts	Avge	BB	5wI	10wM
Leyland, M.	1928	1938	41	65†	5	2764	187	46.06	9	10	13	–	1103†	585	6	97.50	3–91	0	0
Lilley, A.F.A.	1896	1909	35	52	8	903	84	20.52	–	4	70	22	25	23	1	23.00	1–23	0	0
Lillywhite, J.	1876–77	1876–77	2	3†	1	16	10	8.00	–	–	1	–	340†	126	8	15.75	4–70	0	–
Lloyd, D.	1974	1974–75	9	15†	2	552	214*	42.46	1	–	11	–	24†	17	0	–	–	–	–
Lloyd, T.A.	1984	1984	1	1†	1	10	10*	–	–	–	–	–	–	–	–	–	–	–	–
Loader, P.J.	1954	1958–59	13	19	6	76	17	5.84	–	–	2	–	2662	878	39	22.51	6–36	1	0
Lock, G.A.R.	1952	1967–68	49	63	9	742	89	13.74	–	3	59	–	13147†	4451	174	25.58	7–35	9	3
Lockwood, W.H.	1893	1902	12	16	3	231	52*	17.76	–	1	4	–	1973	883	43	20.53	7–71	5	1
Lohmann, G.A.	1886	1896	18	26	2	213	62*	8.87	–	1	28	–	3830	1205	112	10.75	9–28	9	5
Lowson, F.A.	1951	1955	7	13	0	245	68	18.84	–	2	5	–	–	–	–	–	–	–	–
Lucas, A.P.	1878–79	1884	5	9	1	157	55	19.62	–	1	1	–	120	54	0	–	–	–	–
Luckhurst, B.W.	1970–71	1974–75	21	41	5	1298	131	36.05	4	5	14	–	57†	32	1	32.00	1–9	0	0
Lyth, A.	2015	2015	7	13†	0	265	107	20.38	1	–	8	–	6	0	0	–	–	–	–
Lyttelton, Hon. A.	1880	1884	4	7	1	94	31	15.66	–	–	2	–	48	19	4	4.75	4–19	0	0
Macaulay, G.G.	1922–23	1933	8	10	4	112	76	18.66	–	1	5	–	1701	662	24	27.58	5–64	1	0
MacBryan, J.C.W.	1924	1924	1	–	–	–	–	–	–	–	–	–	–	–	–	–	–	–	–
McCague, M.J.	1993	1994–95	3	5	0	21	11	4.20	–	–	1	–	593	390	6	65.00	4–121	0	0
McConnon, J.E.	1954	1954	2	3	1	18	11	9.00	–	–	4	–	216	74	4	18.50	3–19	0	0
McGahey, C.P.	1901–02	1901–02	2	4	0	38	18	9.50	–	–	1	–	–	–	–	–	–	–	–
McGrath, A.	2003	2003	4	5	0	201	81	40.20	–	2	3	–	102	56	4	14.00	3–16	0	0
MacGregor, G.	1890	1893	8	11	3	96	31	12.00	–	–	14	3	–	–	–	–	–	–	–
McIntyre, A.J.W.	1950	1955	3	6	0	19	7	3.16	–	–	8	–	–	–	–	–	–	–	–
MacKinnon, F.A.	1878–79	1878–79	1	2	0	5	5	2.50	–	–	–	–	–	–	–	–	–	–	–
MacLaren, A.C.	1894–95	1909	35	61	4	1931	140	33.87	5	8	29	–	–	–	–	–	–	–	–
McMaster, J.E.P.	1888–89	1888–89	1	1	0	0	0	0.00	–	–	–	–	–	–	–	–	–	–	–
Maddy, D.L.	1999	1999–00	3	4	0	46	24	11.50	–	–	4	–	84	40	0	–	–	–	–
Mahmood, S.I.	2006	2006–07	8	11	1	81	34	8.10	–	–	–	–	1130	762	20	38.10	4–22	0	0
Makepeace, J.W.H.	1920–21	1920–21	4	8	0	279	117	34.87	–	2	–	–	–	–	–	–	–	–	–
Malan, D.J.	2017	2018	15	26†	0	724	140	27.84	1	6	11	–	156	70	0	–	–	–	–
Malcolm, D.E.	1989	1997	40	58	19	236	29	6.05	–	–	7	–	8480	4748	128	37.09	9–57	5	2
Mallender, N.A.	1992	1992	2	3	0	8	4	2.66	–	–	–	–	449	215	10	21.50	5–50	1	0
Mann, F.G.	1948–49	1949	7	12	2	376	136*	37.60	1	–	3	–	–	–	–	–	–	–	–
Mann, F.T.	1922–23	1922–23	5	9	1	281	84	35.12	–	2	4	–	–	–	–	–	–	–	–
Marks, V.J.	1982	1983–84	6	10	1	249	83	27.66	–	3	–	–	1082	484	11	44.00	3–78	0	0

Marriott, C.S.	1933	1933	1	1	0	0	0.00	–	–	1	–	247	96	11	8.72	6–59	2	1
Martin, F.	1890	1891–92	2	2†	0	14	7.00	–	–	2	–	410†	141	14	10.07	6–50	2	1
Martin, J.W.	1947	1947	1	2	0	26	13.00	–	–	–	–	270	129	1	129.00	1–111	0	0
Martin, P.J.	1995	1997	8	13	0	115	8.84	–	–	6	–	1452	580	17	34.11	4–60	0	0
Mason, J.R.	1897–98	1897–98	5	10	0	129	12.90	–	–	3	–	324	149	2	74.50	1–8	0	0
Matthews, A.D.G.	1937	1937	1	1	1	2*	–	–	–	1	–	180	65	2	32.50	1–13	0	0
May, P.B.H.	1951	1961	66	106	9	4537	46.77	13	22	42	–	–	–	–	–	–	–	–
Maynard, M.P.	1988	1993–94	4	8	0	87	10.87	–	3	3	–	–	–	–	–	–	–	–
Mead, C.P.	1911–12	1928–29	17	26†	2	1185	49.37	4	–	4	–	–	–	–	–	–	–	–
Mead, W.	1899	1899	1	2	0	7	3.50	–	–	1	–	265	91	1	91.00	1–91	0	0
Midwinter, W.E.‡	1881–82	1881–82	4	7	0	95	13.57	–	–	5	–	776	272	10	27.20	4–81	0	0
Milburn, C.	1966	1968–69	9	16	2	654	46.71	2	2	7	–	–	–	–	–	–	–	–
Miller, A.M.	1895–96	1895–96	1	2	2	24	–	–	–	1	–	–	–	–	–	–	–	–
Miller, G.	1976	1984	34	51	4	1213	25.80	–	7	17	–	5149	1859	60	30.98	5–44	1	0
Milligan, F.W.	1898–99	1898–99	2	4	0	58	14.50	–	–	1	–	45	29	0	–	–	–	–
Millman, G.	1961–62	1962	6	7	2	60	12.00	–	–	13	2	–	–	–	–	–	–	–
Milton, C.A.	1958	1959	6	9	1	204	25.50	1	–	5	–	24	12	0	–	–	–	–
Mitchell, A.	1933–34	1936	6	10	0	298	29.80	–	2	9	–	6	4	0	–	–	–	–
Mitchell, F.‡	1898–99	1898–99	2	4	0	88	22.00	–	–	2	–	–	–	–	–	–	–	–
Mitchell, T.B.	1932–33	1935	5	6	2	20	5.00	–	–	1	–	894	498	8	62.25	2–49	0	0
Mitchell-Innes, N.S.	1935	1935	1	1	0	5	5.00	–	–	–	–	–	–	–	–	–	–	–
Mold, A.W.	1893	1893	3	3	1	0	0.00	–	–	1	–	491	234	7	33.42	3–44	0	0
Moon, L.J.	1905–06	1905–06	4	8	0	182	22.75	–	–	4	–	–	–	–	–	–	–	–
Morgan, E.J.G.	2010	2011–12	16	24†	1	700	30.43	2	3	11	–	–	–	–	–	–	–	–
Morley, F.	1880	1882–83	4	6†	2	6	1.50	–	–	4	–	972†	296	16	18.50	5–56	1	0
Morris, H.	1991	1991	3	6†	0	115	19.16	–	–	3	–	–	–	–	–	–	–	–
Morris, J.E.	1990	1990	3	5	2	71	23.66	–	–	3	–	–	–	–	–	–	–	–
Mortimore, J.B.	1958–59	1964	9	12	2	243	24.30	–	1	3	–	2162	733	13	56.38	3–36	0	0
Moss, A.E.	1953–54	1960	9	7	1	61	10.16	–	–	3	–	1657	626	21	29.80	4–35	0	0
Moxon, M.D.	1986	1989	10	17	1	455	28.43	–	3	1	–	48	30	0	–	–	–	–
Mullally, A.D.	1996	2001	19	27	4	127	5.52	–	–	10	–	4525†	1812	58	31.24	5–105	1	0
Munton, T.A.	1992	1992	2	2	1	25	25.00	–	–	–	–	405	200	4	50.00	2–22	0	0
Murdoch, W.L.‡	1891–92	1891–92	1	1	0	12	12.00	–	–	–	–	–	–	–	–	–	–	–
Murray, J.T.	1961	1967	21	28	5	506	22.00	1	2	52	3	–	–	–	–	–	–	–
Newham, W.	1887–88	1887–88	1	2	0	26	13.00	–	–	1	–	–	–	–	–	–	–	–
Newport, P.J.	1988	1990–91	3	5	1	110	27.50	–	–	1	–	669	417	10	41.70	4–87	0	0
Nichols, M.S.	1929–30	1939	14	19†	7	355	29.58	–	2	11	–	2565	1152	41	28.09	6–35	2	0
Oakman, A.S.M.	1956	1956	2	2	0	14	7.00	–	–	7	–	48	21	0	–	–	–	–

INDIVIDUAL TEST CAREER RECORDS – ENGLAND (Continued)

	First Test	Last Test	Tests	Inns	NO	Runs	HS	Avge	100	50	Ct	St	Balls	Runs	Wkts	Avge	BB	5wI	10wM
O'Brien, T.C.	1884	1895–96	5	8	0	59	20	7.37	–	–	4	–	–	–	–	–	–	–	–
O'Connor, J.	1929	1929–30	4	7	0	153	51	21.85	–	1	2	–	162	72	1	72.00	1-31	0	0
Old, C.M.	1972–73	1981	46	66†	9	845	65	14.82	–	2	22	–	8858	4020	143	28.11	7-50	4	0
Oldfield, N.	1939	1939	1	2	0	99	80	49.50	–	1	–	–	–	–	–	–	–	–	–
Onions, G.	2009	2012	9	10	7	30	17*	10.00	–	–	–	–	1606	957	32	29.90	5-38	1	0
Ormond, J.	2001	2001–02	2	4	1	38	18	12.66	–	–	–	–	372	185	2	92.50	1-70	0	0
Overton, C.	2017–18	2019	4	8	2	124	41*	20.66	–	–	1	–	707	403	9	44.77	3-105	0	0
Padgett, D.E.V.	1960	1960	2	4	0	51	31	12.75	–	–	–	–	12	8	0	–	–	–	–
Paine, G.A.E.	1934–35	1934–35	4	7	1	97	49	16.16	–	–	5	–	1044†	467	17	27.47	5-168	1	0
Palairet, L.C.H.	1902	1902	2	4	0	49	20	12.25	–	–	2	–	–	–	–	–	–	–	–
Palmer, C.H.	1953–54	1953–54	1	2	0	22	22	11.00	–	–	–	–	30	15	0	–	–	–	–
Palmer, K.E.	1964–65	1964–65	1	1	0	10	10	10.00	–	–	–	–	378	189	1	189.00	1-113	0	0
Panesar, M.S.	2005–06	2013–14	50	68†	23	220	26	4.88	–	–	10	–	12475†	5797	167	34.71	6-37	12	2
Parfitt, P.H.	1961–62	1972	37	52†	6	1882	131*	40.91	7	6	42	–	1326	574	12	47.83	2-5	0	0
Parker, C.W.L.	1921	1921	1	1	1	3	3*	–	–	–	–	–	168†	32	2	16.00	2-32	0	0
Parker, P.W.G.	1981	1981	1	2	0	13	13	6.50	–	–	–	–	–	–	–	–	–	–	–
Parkhouse, W.G.A.	1950	1959	7	13	0	373	78	28.69	–	2	3	–	–	–	–	–	–	–	–
Parkin, C.H.	1920–21	1924	10	16	3	160	36	12.30	–	–	3	–	2095	1128	32	35.25	5-38	2	0
Parks, J.H.	1937	1937	1	2	0	29	22	14.50	–	–	–	–	126	36	3	12.00	2-26	0	0
Parks, J.M.	1954	1967–68	46	68	7	1962	108*	32.16	2	9	103	11	54	51	1	51.00	1-43	0	0
Pataudi, Nawab of, sen.‡	1932–33	1934	3	5	0	144	102	28.80	1	–	–	–	–	–	–	–	–	–	–
Patel, M.M.	1996	1996	2	2	0	45	27	22.50	–	–	2	–	276†	180	1	180.00	1-101	0	0
Patel, S.R.	2011–12	2015–16	6	9	0	151	42	16.77	–	–	3	–	858†	421	7	60.14	2-27	0	0
Pattinson, D.J.	2008	2008	1	2	0	21	13	10.50	–	–	–	–	181	96	2	48.00	2-95	0	0
Paynter, E.	1931	1939	20	31†	5	1540	243	59.23	4	7	7	–	–	–	–	–	–	–	–
Peate, E.	1881–82	1886	9	14†	8	70	13	11.66	–	–	2	–	2096†	683	31	22.03	6-85	2	0
Peebles, I.A.R.	1927–28	1931	13	17	8	98	26	10.88	–	–	5	–	2882	1391	45	30.91	6-63	3	0
Peel, R.	1884–85	1896	20	33†	4	427	83	14.72	–	3	17	–	5216†	1715	101	16.98	7-31	5	1
Penn, F.	1880	1880	1	2	1	50	27*	50.00	–	–	–	–	12	2	0	–	–	–	–
Perks, R.T.D.	1938–39	1939	2	2†	2	3	2*	–	–	–	1	–	829	355	11	32.27	5-100	2	0
Philipson, H.	1891–92	1894–95	5	8	1	63	30	9.00	–	–	8	3	–	–	–	–	–	–	–
Pietersen, K.P.	2005	2013–14	104	181	8	8181	227	47.28	23	35	62	–	1311	886	10	88.60	3-52	0	0
Pigott, A.C.S.	1983–84	1983–84	1	2	1	12	8*	12.00	–	–	–	–	102	75	2	37.50	2-75	0	0
Pilling, R.	1881–82	1888	8	13	1	91	23	7.58	–	–	10	4	–	–	–	–	–	–	–

Name	Debut	Last	M	I	NO	Runs	HS	Avg	100	50	Ct	St	Balls	Runs	Wkts	Avg	BB	5w	10w
Place, W.	1947-48	1947-48	3	6	1	144	107	28.80	1	–	–	–	–	2659	1536	41	37.46	5-64	1	0
Plunkett, L.E.	2005-06	2014	13	20	5	238	55*	15.86	–	1	3	–	–	6650	2976	67	44.41	6-79	3	0
Pocock, P.I.	1967-68	1984-85	25	37	4	206	33	6.24	–	–	15	–	–	1102	378	15	25.20	5-24	1	0
Pollard, R.	1946	1948	4	3	2	13	10*	13.00	–	–	3	–	–	30†	9	0	–	–	–	–
Poole, C.J.	1951-52	1951-52	3	5†	1	161	69†	40.25	–	2	1	–	–	–	85	1	85.00	1-49	–	0
Pope, G.H.	1947	1947	1	1	–	8	8*	–	–	–	2	–	–	218	85	1	85.00	1-49	–	0
Pope, O.J.D.	2018	2018	2	3	–	54	28	18.00	–	–	2	–	–	–	–	–	–	–	–	–
Pougher, A.D.	1891-92	1891-92	1	1	–	17	17	17.00	–	–	2	–	–	105	26	3	8.66	3-26	–	0
Price, J.S.E.	1963-64	1972	15	15†	6	66	32	7.33	–	–	7	–	–	2724	1401	40	35.02	5-73	–	1
Price, W.F.F.	1938	1938	1	2	–	6	6	3.00	–	–	2	–	–	–	–	–	–	–	–	–
Prideaux, R.M.	1968	1968-69	3	6	1	102	64	20.40	–	1	–	–	–	12	0	0	–	–	–	–
Pringle, D.R.	1982	1992	30	50	4	695	63	15.10	–	3	10	–	–	5287	2518	70	35.97	5-95	3	0
Prior, M.J.	2007	2014	79	123	21	4099	131*	40.18	7	28	243	13	–	–	–	–	–	–	–	–
Pullar, G.	1959	1962-63	28	49†	4	1974	175	43.86	4	12	2	–	–	66	37	1	37.00	1-1	–	0
Quaife, W.G.	1899	1901-02	7	13	1	228	68	19.00	–	–	4	–	–	15	6	0	–	–	–	0
Radford, N.V.	1986	1987-88	3	4	1	21	12*	7.00	–	–	–	–	–	678	351	4	87.75	2-131	–	0
Radley, C.T.	1977-78	1978	8	10	–	481	158	48.10	2	2	4	–	–	–	–	–	–	–	–	–
Ramprakash, M.R.	1991	2001-02	52	92	6	2350	154	27.32	2	12	39	–	–	895	477	4	119.25	1-2	–	0
Randall, D.W.	1976-77	1984	47	79	5	2470	174	33.37	7	12	31	–	–	16	3	0	–	–	–	–
Ranjitsinhji, K.S.	1896	1902	15	26	4	989	175	44.95	2	6	13	–	–	97	39	1	39.00	1-23	–	0
Rankin, W.B.‡	2013-14	2013-14	1	2†	–	13	13	6.50	–	–	–	–	–	125	81	1	81.00	1-47	–	0
Rashid, A.U.	2015-16	2018-19	19	33	5	540	61	19.28	–	2	4	–	–	3816	2390	60	39.83	5-49	2	0
Read, C.M.W.	1999	2006-07	15	23	4	360	55	18.94	–	1	48	6	–	–	–	–	–	–	–	–
Read, H.D.	1935	1935	1	–	–	–	–	–	–	–	–	–	–	270	200	6	33.33	4-136	–	0
Read, J.M.	1882	1893	17	29	2	461	57	17.07	–	2	8	–	–	60	63	0	–	–	–	–
Read, W.W.	1882-83	1893	18	27	1	720	117	27.69	1	5	16	–	–	60	63	0	–	–	–	–
Reeve, D.A.	1991-92	1991-92	3	5	–	124	59	24.80	–	–	1	–	–	149	60	2	30.00	1-4	–	0
Relf, A.E.	1903-04	1913-14	13	21	3	416	63	23.11	–	2	14	–	–	1764	624	25	24.96	5-85	1	0
Rhodes, H.J.	1959	1959	2	1	1	0	0*	–	–	–	–	–	–	449	244	9	27.11	4-50	–	0
Rhodes, S.J.	1994	1994-95	11	17	5	294	65*	24.50	–	1	46	3	–	–	–	–	–	–	–	–
Rhodes, W.	1899	1929-30	58	98	21	2325	179	30.19	2	11	60	–	–	8225†	3425	127	26.96	8-68	6	1
Richards, C.J.	1986-87	1988	8	13	–	285	133	21.92	1	–	20	1	–	–	–	–	–	–	–	–
Richardson, D.W.	1957	1957	1	1†	–	33	33	33.00	–	–	1	–	–	–	–	–	–	–	–	–
Richardson, P.E.	1956	1963	34	56†	–	2061	126	37.47	5	9	6	–	–	120	48	3	16.00	2-10	–	0
Richardson, T.	1893	1897-98	14	24	8	177	25*	11.06	–	–	5	–	–	4498	2220	88	25.22	8-94	11	4
Richmond, T.L.	1921	1921	1	2	–	6	4	3.00	–	–	–	–	–	114	86	2	43.00	2-69	–	0
Ridgway, F.	1951-52	1951-52	5	6	–	49	24	8.16	–	–	3	–	–	793	379	7	54.14	4-83	–	0
Robertson, J.D.B.	1947	1951-52	11	21	2	881	133	46.36	2	6	6	–	–	138	58	2	29.00	2-17	–	0

INDIVIDUAL TEST CAREER RECORDS – ENGLAND (Continued)

	First Test	Last Test	Tests	Inns	NO	Runs	HS	Avge	100	50	Ct	St	Balls	Runs	Wkts	Avge	BB	5wI	10wM
Robins, R.W.V.	1929	1937	19	27	4	612	108	26.60	1	4	12	–	3318	1758	64	27.46	6-32	1	0
Robinson, R.T.	1984-85	1989	29	49	5	1601	175	36.38	4	6	8	–	6	0	0	–	–	–	–
Robson, S.D.	2014	2014	7	11	0	336	127	30.54	1	1	5	–	–	–	–	–	–	–	–
Roland-Jones, T.S.	2017	2017	4	6	2	82	25	20.50	–	–	–	–	536	334	17	19.64	5-57	1	0
Roope, G.R.J.	1972-73	1978	21	32	4	860	77	30.71	–	7	35	–	172	76	0	–	–	0	0
Root, C.F.	1926	1926	3	–	–	–	–	–	–	–	–	–	642	194	8	24.25	4-84	0	0
Root, J.E.	2012-13	2019	86	159	12	7043	254	47.91	16	45	103	–	2136	1108	23	48.17	2-9	0	0
Rose, B.C.	1977-78	1980-81	9	16†	2	358	70	25.57	–	2	4	–	–	–	–	–	–	–	–
Roy, J.J.	2019	2019	5	10	0	187	72	18.70	–	1	1	–	–	–	–	–	–	–	–
Royle, V.P.F.A.	1878-79	1878-79	1	2	0	21	18	10.50	–	–	2	–	16	6	0	–	–	–	–
Rumsey, F.E.	1964	1965	5	5	3	30	21*	15.00	–	–	–	–	1145†	461	17	27.11	4-25	0	0
Russell, C.A.G.	1920-21	1922-23	10	18	2	910	140	56.87	5	2	8	–	–	–	–	–	–	–	–
Russell, R.C.	1988	1997-98	54	86†	16	1897	128*	27.10	2	6	153	12	–	–	–	–	–	–	–
Russell, W.E.	1961-62	1967	10	18	1	362	70	21.29	–	2	4	–	144	44	0	–	–	–	–
Saggers, M.J.	2003-04	2004	3	3	0	1	1	0.33	–	–	1	–	493	247	7	35.28	2-29	0	0
Salisbury, I.D.K.	1992	2000-01	15	25	3	368	50	16.72	–	1	5	–	2492	1539	20	76.95	4-163	0	0
Sandham, A.	1921	1929-30	14	23	0	879	325	38.21	2	3	4	–	–	–	–	–	–	–	–
Schofield, C.P.	2000	2000	2	3†	0	67	57	22.33	–	1	–	–	108	73	0	–	–	0	0
Schultz, S.S.	1878-79	1878-79	1	2	1	20	20	20.00	–	–	–	–	34	26	1	26.00	1-16	0	0
Scotton, W.H.	1881-82	1886-87	15	25†	2	510	90	22.17	–	3	4	–	20†	20	0	–	–	–	–
Selby, J.	1876-77	1881-82	6	12	1	256	70	23.27	–	2	1	–	–	–	–	–	–	–	–
Selvey, M.W.W.	1976	1976-77	3	5	3	15	5*	7.50	–	–	1	–	492	343	6	57.16	4-41	0	0
Shackleton, D.	1950	1963	7	13	7	113	42	18.83	–	–	1	–	2078	768	18	42.66	4-72	0	0
Shah, O.A.	2005-06	2008-09	6	10	0	269	88	26.90	–	2	2	–	30	31	0	–	–	–	–
Shahzad, A.	2010	2010	1	1	0	5	5	5.00	–	–	2	–	102	63	4	15.75	3-45	0	0
Sharp, J.S.	1909	1909	3	6	2	188	105	47.00	1	1	1	–	183†	111	3	37.00	3-67	0	0
Sharpe, J.W.	1890	1891-92	3	6	4	44	26	22.00	–	–	2	–	975	305	11	27.72	6-84	1	0
Sharpe, P.J.	1963	1969	12	21	4	786	111	46.23	1	4	17	–	–	–	–	–	–	–	–
Shaw, A.	1876-77	1881-82	7	12	1	111	40	10.09	–	–	4	–	1096	285	12	23.75	5-38	1	0
Sheppard, D.S.	1950	1962-63	22	33	2	1172	119	37.80	3	6	12	–	–	–	–	–	–	–	–
Sherwin, M.	1886-87	1888	3	6	4	30	21*	15.00	–	–	5	2	–	–	–	–	–	–	–
Shrewsbury, A.	1881-82	1893	23	40	4	1277	164	35.47	3	4	29	–	12	2	0	–	–	–	–
Shuter, J.	1888	1888	1	1	0	28	28	28.00	–	–	–	–	–	–	–	–	–	–	–
Shuttleworth, K.	1970-71	1971	5	6	0	46	21	7.66	–	–	1	–	1071	427	12	35.58	5-47	1	0

Sidebottom, A.	1985	1	1	0	2	2	2.00	–	–	–	–	112	65	1	65.00	1–65	0	0
Sidebottom, R.J.	2001	22	31†	11	313	31	15.65	–	–	5	–	4812†	2231	79	28.24	7–47	5	1
Silverwood, C.E.W.	1996–97	6	7	3	29	10	7.25	–	–	2	–	828	444	11	40.36	5–91	1	0
Simpson, R.T.	2002–03	27	45	3	1401	156*	33.35	4	6	5	–	45	22	2	11.00	2–4	0	0
Simpson–Hayward, G.H.T.	1954–55	5	8	1	105	29*	15.00	–	–	1	–	898	420	23	18.26	6–43	2	0
Sims, J.M.	1909–10	4	4	0	16	12	4.00	–	–	6	–	887	480	11	43.63	5–73	1	0
Sinfield, R.A.	1936–37	1	1	0	6	6	6.00	–	1	–	–	378	123	2	61.50	1–51	0	0
Slack, W.N.	1938	3	6†	0	81	52	13.50	–	–	3	–	–	–	–	–	–	–	–
Smailes, T.F.	1985–86	1	1†	0	25	25	25.00	–	1	–	–	120	62	3	20.66	3–44	0	0
Small, G.C.	1946	17	24	7	263	59	15.47	–	1	9	–	3927	1871	55	34.01	5–48	2	0
Smith, A.C.	1990–91	6	7	3	118	69*	29.50	–	1	20	3	–	–	–	–	–	–	–
Smith, A.M.	1962–63	1	2	1	4	4*	4.00	–	–	–	–	138†	89	0	–	–	–	0
Smith, C.A.	1997	1	1	0	3	3	3.00	–	–	–	–	154	61	7	8.71	5–19	1	0
Smith, C.I.J.	1888–89	5	10	0	102	27	10.20	–	–	1	–	930	393	15	26.20	5–16	1	0
Smith, C.L.	1934–35	8	14	0	392	91	30.15	–	2	5	–	102	39	3	13.00	2–31	0	0
Smith, D.	1983	2	4†	0	128	57	32.00	–	–	1	–	–	–	–	–	–	–	–
Smith, D.M.	1935	2	4†	0	80	47	20.00	–	–	–	–	–	–	–	–	–	–	–
Smith, D.R.	1985–86	5	5	1	38	34	9.50	–	–	2	–	972	359	6	59.83	2–60	0	0
Smith, D.V.	1961–62	3	4†	1	25	16*	8.33	–	–	–	–	270†	97	1	97.00	1–12	0	0
Smith, E.J.	1957	11	14	1	113	22	8.69	–	–	17	3	–	–	–	–	–	–	–
Smith, E.T.	1913–14	3	5	0	87	64	17.40	–	1	5	–	–	–	–	–	–	–	–
Smith, H.	2003	1	1	0	7	7	7.00	–	–	1	2	–	–	–	–	–	–	–
Smith, M.J.K.	1928	50	78	6	2278	121	31.63	3	11	53	–	214	128	1	128.00	1–10	0	0
Smith, R.A.	1972	62	112	15	4236	175	43.67	9	28	39	–	24	6	0	–	–	–	–
Smith, T.P.B.	1995–96	4	5	0	33	24	6.60	–	–	–	–	538	319	3	106.33	2–172	0	0
Smithson, G.A.	1946–47	2	3†	0	70	35	23.33	–	–	1	–	–	–	–	–	–	–	–
Snow, J.A.	1947–48	49	71	14	772	73	13.54	–	2	16	–	12021	5387	202	26.66	7–40	8	1
Southerton, J.	1965	2	3	1	7	6	3.50	–	–	2	–	263	107	7	15.28	4–46	0	0
Spooner, R.H.	1876–77	10	15	0	481	119	32.06	1	4	4	–	–	–	–	–	–	–	–
Spooner, R.T.	1912	7	14†	1	354	92	27.23	–	3	10	2	–	–	–	–	–	–	–
Stanyforth, R.T.	1951–52	4	6	1	13	6*	2.60	–	–	7	2	–	–	–	–	–	–	–
Staples, S.J.	1927–28	3	5	0	65	39	13.00	–	–	–	–	1149	435	15	29.00	3–50	0	0
Statham, J.B.	1927–28	70	87†	28	675	38	11.44	–	–	28	–	16056	6261	252	24.84	7–39	9	1
Steel, A.G.	1950–51	13	20	3	600	148	35.29	2	–	5	–	1360	605	29	20.86	3–27	0	0
Steele, D.S.	1880	8	16	0	673	106	42.06	1	5	7	–	88†	39	2	19.50	1–1	0	0
Stephenson, J.P.	1975	1	2	0	36	25	18.00	–	–	–	–	–	–	–	–	–	–	–
Stevens, G.T.S.	1989	10	17	0	263	69	15.47	–	1	9	–	1186	648	20	32.40	5–90	2	1
Stevenson, G.B.	1922–23	2	2	1	28	27*	28.00	–	–	–	–	312	183	5	36.60	3–111	0	0

INDIVIDUAL TEST CAREER RECORDS – ENGLAND (Continued)

	First Test	Last Test	Tests	Inns	NO	Runs	HS	Avge	100	50	Ct	St	Balls	Runs	Wkts	Avge	BB	5wI	10wM
Stewart, A.J.	1989-90	2003	133	235	21	8463	190	39.54	15	45	263	14	20	13	0	–	–	–	–
Stewart, M.J.	1962	1963-64	8	12	1	385	87	35.00	–	2	6	–	–	–	–	–	–	–	–
Stoddart, A.E.	1887-88	1897-98	16	30	2	996	173	35.57	2	3	6	–	162	94	2	47.00	1–10	0	0
Stokes, B.A.	2013-14	2019	57	105†	4	3593	258	35.57	8	19	59	–	7899	4416	135	32.71	6–22	4	0
Stone, O.P.	2019	2019	1	2	0	19	19	9.50	–	–	–	–	72	29	3	9.66	3–29	0	0
Stoneman, M.D.	2017	2018	11	20†	1	526	60	27.68	–	5	1	–	–	–	–	–	–	–	–
Storer, W.	1897-98	1899	6	11	0	215	51	19.54	–	1	11	2	168	108	2	54.00	1–24	0	0
Strauss, A.J.	2004	2012	100	178†	6	7037	177	40.91	21	27	121	–	–	–	–	–	–	–	–
Street, G.B.	1922-23	1922-23	1	2	1	11	7*	11.00	–	–	–	1	–	–	–	–	–	–	–
Strudwick, H.	1909-10	1926	28	42	13	230	24	7.93	–	–	61	12	–	–	–	–	–	–	–
Studd, C.T.	1882	1882-83	5	9	1	160	48	20.00	–	–	5	–	384	98	3	32.66	2–35	0	0
Studd, G.B.	1882-83	1882-83	4	7	0	31	9	4.42	–	–	8	–	–	–	–	–	–	–	–
Subba Row, R.	1958	1961	13	22†	1	984	137	46.85	3	4	5	–	6	2	0	–	–	–	–
Such, P.M.	1993	1999	11	16	5	67	14*	6.09	–	–	4	–	3124	1242	37	33.56	6–67	2	0
Sugg, F.H.	1888	1888	2	2	0	55	31	27.50	–	–	–	–	–	–	–	–	–	–	–
Sutcliffe, H.	1924	1935	54	84	9	4555	194	60.73	16	23	23	–	–	–	–	–	–	–	–
Swann, G.P.	2008-09	2013-14	60	76	14	1370	85	22.09	–	5	54	–	15349	7642	255	29.96	6–65	17	3
Swetman, R.	1958-59	1959-60	11	17	2	254	65	16.93	–	1	24	2	–	–	–	–	–	–	–
Tate, F.W.	1902	1902	1	2	1	9	5*	9.00	–	–	2	–	96	51	2	25.50	2–7	0	0
Tate, M.W.	1924	1935	39	52	5	1198	100*	25.48	1	5	11	–	12523	4055	155	26.16	6–42	7	1
Tattersall, R.	1950-51	1954	16	17†	7	50	10*	5.00	–	–	8	–	4228	1513	58	26.08	7–52	4	1
Tavaré, C.J.	1980	1989	31	56	2	1755	149	32.50	2	12	20	–	30	11	0	–	–	–	–
Taylor, J.P.	1992-93	1994	2	4†	1	34	17*	17.00	–	–	–	–	288†	156	3	52.00	1–18	0	0
Taylor, J.W.A.	2012	2015-16	7	13	1	312	76	26.00	–	2	7	–	–	–	–	–	–	–	–
Taylor, K.	1959	1964	3	5	0	57	24	11.40	–	–	1	–	12	6	0	–	–	–	–
Taylor, L.B.	1985	1985	2	1	1	1	1*	–	–	–	1	–	381	178	4	44.50	2–34	0	0
Taylor, R.W.	1970-71	1983-84	57	83	12	1156	97	16.28	–	3	167	7	12	6	0	–	–	–	–
Tennyson, Hon. L.H.	1913-14	1921	9	12	1	345	74*	31.36	–	4	6	–	6	1	0	–	–	–	–
Terry, V.P.	1984	1984	2	3	0	16	8	5.33	–	–	2	–	–	–	–	–	–	–	–
Thomas, J.G.	1985-86	1986	5	10	4	83	31*	13.83	–	–	–	–	774	504	10	50.40	4–70	0	0
Thompson, G.J.	1909	1909-10	6	10	1	273	63	30.33	–	2	5	–	1367	638	23	27.73	4–50	0	0
Thomson, N.I.	1964-65	1964-65	5	4	1	69	39	23.00	–	–	3	–	1488	568	9	63.11	2–55	0	0
Thorpe, G.P.	1993	2005	100	179†	28	6744	200*	44.66	16	39	105	–	138	37	0	–	–	–	–
Titmus, F.J.	1955	1974-75	53	76	11	1449	84*	22.29	–	10	35	–	15118	4931	153	32.22	7–79	7	0

Name	Span 1	Span 2	c1	c2	c3	c4	c5	c6	c7	c8	c9	c10	c11	c12	c13	c14	c15	c16	c17	c18	c19	c20
Tolchard, R.W.	1976–77	1976–77	4	7	2	129	67	25.80	–	–	–	–	5	–	–	140	3	25.00	3-50	0	–	0
Townsend, C.L.	1899	1899	2	3†	0	51	38	17.00	–	–	–	1	–	–	–	75	0	–	–	0	–	–
Townsend, D.C.H.	1934–35	1934–35	3	6	0	77	36	12.83	–	–	–	1	–	–	–	9	0	–	–	0	–	0
Townsend, L.F.	1929–30	1929–30	4	6	0	97	40	16.16	–	–	–	2	2	–	–	205	6	34.16	2-22	0	–	0
Tredwell, J.C.	2009–10	2014–15	2	2†	0	45	37	22.50	–	–	–	2	2	–	–	399	11	29.18	4-47	0	2	0
Tremlett, C.T.	2007	2013–14	12	15	4	113	25*	10.27	–	–	–	–	4	–	–	786	53	27.00	6-48	2	0	0
Tremlett, M.F.	1947–48	1947–48	3	5	2	20	18*	6.66	–	–	–	–	–	–	–	2902	4	56.50	2-98	0	–	0
Trescothick, M.E.	2000	2006	76	143†	10	5825	219	43.79	14	29	–	–	95	–	–	492	1	155.00	1-34	0	1	0
Trott, A.E.‡	1898–99	1898–99	2	4	0	23	16	5.75	–	–	–	–	–	–	–	300	17	11.64	5-49	1	0	0
Trott, I.J.L.	2009	2014–15	52	93	6	3835	226	44.08	9	19	–	–	29	–	–	474	5	80.00	1-5	0	17	3
Trueman, F.S.	1952	1965	67	85	14	981	39*	13.81	–	–	1	3	64	–	–	708	307	21.57	8-31	17	1	0
Tudor, A.J.	1998–99	2002–03	10	16	4	229	99*	19.08	–	–	1	–	3	–	–	15178	28	34.39	5-44	1	–	2
Tufnell, N.C.	1909–10	1909–10	1	1	0	14	14	14.00	–	–	–	–	–	–	1	1512	–	–	–	–	–	–
Tufnell, P.C.R.	2001	1990–91	42	59	29	153	22*	5.10	–	–	–	–	12	–	–	11288†	121	37.68	7-47	5	–	0
Turnbull, M.J.L.	1936	1936	9	13	2	224	61	20.36	–	1	–	1	1	–	–	–	–	–	–	–	–	–
Tyldesley, G.E.	1928–29	1921	14	20	2	990	122	55.00	3	6	–	–	2	–	–	2	0	–	–	0	–	0
Tyldesley, J.T.	1909	1898–99	31	55	1	1661	138	30.75	4	9	–	–	16	–	–	–	–	–	–	–	–	0
Tyldesley, R.K.	1924	1930	7	7	1	47	29	7.83	–	–	–	–	1	–	–	1615	19	32.57	3-50	0	4	1
Tylecote, E.F.S.	1886	1886	6	9	1	152	66	19.00	–	1	–	1	5	5	–	–	–	–	–	–	0	0
Tyler, E.J.	1895–96	1895–96	1	1†	0	0	0	0.00	–	–	–	–	–	–	–	145†	4	16.25	3-49	0	4	1
Tyson, F.H.	1954	1958–59	17	24	3	230	37*	10.95	–	–	–	4	4	–	–	3452	76	18.56	7-27	4	0	6
Udal, S.D.	2005–06	2005–06	4	7	1	109	33*	18.16	–	–	1	–	1	–	–	596	8	43.00	4-14	0	1	0
Ulyett, G.	1876–77	1890	25	39	0	949	149	24.33	1	7	–	–	19	–	–	2627	50	20.40	7-36	17	6	–
Underwood, D.L.	1966	1981–82	86	116	35	937	45*	11.56	2	1	–	7	44	–	–	21862†	297	25.83	8-51	0	5	2
Valentine, B.H.	1933–34	1938–39	7	9	2	454	136	64.85	2	1	–	–	2	–	–	978	6	93.50	2-71	0	–	–
Vaughan, M.P.	1999–00	2008	82	147	9	5719	197	41.44	18	18	–	–	44	–	–	11173†	144	24.37	8-43	5	2	0
Verity, H.	1931	1939	40	44	12	669	66*	20.90	–	3	–	3	30	–	–	–	–	–	–	–	–	0
Vernon, G.F.	1882–83	1882–83	1	2	0	14	11*	14.00	–	–	–	–	–	–	–	24	0	–	–	0	–	2
Vine, J.M.	2017–18	2016	13	22	2	548	83	24.90	–	3	–	3	8	–	–	–	–	–	–	–	–	0
Vine, J.	1911–12	1911–12	2	3	2	46	36	46.00	–	–	–	–	–	–	–	–	–	–	–	–	–	–
Voce, W.	1929–30	1946–47	27	38	15	308	66	13.39	–	1	–	1	15	–	–	6360†	98	27.88	7-70	3	2	0
Waddington, A.	1920–21	1920–21	2	4	0	16	7	4.00	–	–	–	–	1	–	–	276†	1	119.00	1-35	0	0	–
Wainwright, E.	1893	1897–98	5	9	0	132	49	14.66	–	–	–	2	2	–	–	127	0	–	–	–	–	–
Walker, P.M.	1960	1960	3	4	0	128	52	32.00	–	1	–	–	5	–	–	78†	0	–	–	–	–	–
Walters, C.F.	1933	1934	11	18	3	784	102	52.26	1	7	–	–	6	–	–	–	–	–	–	–	–	–
Ward, Albert	1893	1894–95	7	13	0	487	117	37.46	1	3	–	3	–	–	–	–	–	–	–	–	–	–
Ward, Alan	1969	1976	5	6	1	40	21	8.00	–	–	–	–	3	–	–	761	14	32.35	4-61	0	–	0
Ward, I.J.	2001	2001	5	9†	1	129	39	16.12	–	–	–	1	1	–	–	453	–	–	–	–	–	–

243

INDIVIDUAL TEST CAREER RECORDS – ENGLAND (Continued)

	First Test	Last Test	Tests	Inns	NO	Runs	HS	Avge	100	50	Ct	St	Balls	Runs	Wkts	Avge	BB	5wI	10wM
Wardle, J.H.	1947–48	1957	28	41†	8	653	66	19.78	–	2	12	–	6597†	2080	102	20.39	7–36	5	1
Warner, P.F.	1898–99	1912	15	28	2	622	132*	23.92	1	3	3	–	584	281	1	281.00	1–76	0	0
Warr, J.J.	1950–51	1950–51	2	4	0	4	4	1.00	–	–	–	–	236	113	1	281.00	5–57	1	0
Warren, A.	1905	1905	1	1	0	7	7	7.00	–	–	1	–	236	113	6	18.83	5–57	1	0
Washbrook, C.	1937	1956	37	66	6	2569	195	42.81	6	12	12	–	36	33	1	33.00	1–25	0	0
Watkin, S.L.	1991	1993	3	5	0	25	13	5.00	–	–	1	–	534	305	11	27.72	4–65	0	0
Watkins, A.J.	1948	1952	15	24†	4	810	137*	40.50	2	4	17	–	1364†	554	11	50.36	3–20	0	0
Watkinson, M.	1995	1995–96	4	6	1	167	82*	33.40	–	1	1	–	672	348	10	34.80	3–64	0	0
Watson, W.	1951	1958–59	23	37†	3	879	116	25.85	2	3	8	–	–	–	–	–	–	–	–
Webbe, A.J.	1878–79	1878–79	1	2	0	4	4	2.00	–	–	2	–	–	–	–	–	–	–	–
Wellard, A.W.	1937	1938	2	4	0	47	38	11.75	–	–	2	–	456	237	7	33.85	4–81	0	0
Wells, A.P.	1995	1995	1	2	1	3	3*	3.00	–	–	1	–	–	–	–	–	–	–	–
Westley, T.	2017	2017	5	9	1	193	59	24.12	–	1	1	–	24	12	0	–	–	–	–
Wharton, A.	1949	1949	1	2†	0	20	13	10.00	–	–	–	–	–	–	–	–	–	–	–
Whitaker, J.J.	1986–87	1986–87	1	1	0	11	11	11.00	–	–	–	–	–	–	–	–	–	–	–
White, C.	1994	2002–03	30	50	7	1052	121	24.46	1	5	14	–	3959	2220	59	37.62	5–32	3	0
White, D.W.	1961–62	1961–62	2	2†	2	0	0	0.00	–	–	–	–	220	119	4	29.75	3–65	0	0
White, J.C.	1921	1930–31	15	22	9	239	29	18.38	–	–	6	–	4801†	1581	49	32.26	8–126	3	1
Whysall, W.W.	1924–25	1930	4	7	0	209	76	29.85	–	2	7	–	16	9	0	–	–	–	–
Wilkinson, L.L.	1938–39	1938–39	3	2	1	3	2	3.00	–	–	–	–	573	271	7	38.71	2–12	0	0
Willey, P.	1976	1986	26	50	6	1184	102*	26.90	2	5	3	–	1091	456	7	65.14	2–73	0	0
Williams, N.F.	1990	1990	1	1	0	38	38	38.00	–	–	–	–	246	148	2	74.00	2–148	0	0
Willis, R.G.D.	1970–71	1984	90	128	55	840	28*	11.50	–	–	39	–	17357	8190	325	25.20	8–43	16	0
Wilson, C.E.M.	1898–99	1898–99	2	4	1	42	18	14.00	–	–	–	–	–	–	–	–	–	–	–
Wilson, D.	1963–64	1970–71	6	7†	1	75	42	12.50	–	–	1	–	1472†	466	11	42.36	2–17	0	0
Wilson, E.R.	1920–21	1920–21	1	2	0	10	5	5.00	–	–	–	–	123	36	3	12.00	2–28	0	0
Woakes, C.R.	2013	2019	31	52	11	1145	137*	27.92	1	4	12	–	5276	2754	88	31.29	6–17	3	1
Wood, A.	1938	1939	4	5	1	80	53	20.00	–	1	10	1	–	–	–	–	–	–	–
Wood, B.	1972	1978	12	21	0	454	90	21.61	–	2	6	–	98	50	0	–	–	–	–
Wood, G.E.C.	1924	1924	3	2	0	7	6	3.50	–	–	5	1	–	–	–	–	–	–	–
Wood, H.	1888	1891–92	4	4	1	204	134*	68.00	1	–	2	1	–	–	–	–	–	–	–

Wood, M.A.	2015	2018-19	13	23	5	297	52	16.50	—	1	5	—	2408	1345	36	37.36	5-41	1	0
Wood, R.	1886-87	1886-87	1	2†	0	6	6	3.00	—	—	—	—	—	129	5	25.80	3-28	0	0
Woods, S.M.J.‡	1895-96	1895-96	3	4	0	122	53	30.50	—	1	4	—	195	2815	83	33.91	7-76	4	1
Woolley, F.E.	1909	1934	64	98†	7	3283	154	36.07	5	23	64	—	6495†	299	4	74.75	1-8	0	0
Woolmer, R.A.	1975	1981	19	34	2	1059	149	33.09	3	2	10	—	546	316	8	39.50	2-19	0	0
Worthington, T.S.	1929-30	1936-37	9	11	0	321	128	29.18	1	1	8	—	633						
Wright, C.W.	1895-96	1895-96	3	4	0	125	71	31.25	—	1	—	—	—	4224	108	39.11	7-105	6	1
Wright, D.V.P.	1938	1950-51	34	39	13	289	45	11.11	—	—	10	—	8135	642	18	35.66	3-4	0	0
Wyatt, R.E.S.	1927-28	1936-37	40	64	6	1839	149	31.70	2	12	16	—	1395	17	0	—	—	—	—
Wynyard, E.G.	1896	1905-06	3	6	0	72	30	12.00	—	—	—	—	24	707	21	33.66	3-67	0	0
Yardley, N.W.D.	1938-39	1950	20	34	2	812	99	25.37	—	4	14	—	1662	262	12	21.83	4-30	0	0
Young, H.I.	1899	1899	2	2	0	43	43	21.50	—	—	1	—	556†	757	17	44.52	3-65	0	0
Young, J.A.	1947	1949	8	10	5	28	10*	5.60	—	—	5	—	2368†						
Young, R.A.	1907-08	1907-08	2	4	0	27	13	6.75	—	—	6	—	—						

INDIVIDUAL TEST CAREER RECORDS – AUSTRALIA

	First Test	Last Test	Tests	Inns	NO	Runs	HS	Avge	100	50	Ct	St	Balls	Runs	Wkts	Avge	BB	5wI	10wM
aBeckett, E.L.	1928-29	1931-32	4	7	0	143	41	20.42	–	–	4	–	1062	317	3	105.66	1-41	0	0
Agar, A.C.	2013	2017	4	7†	1	195	98	32.50	–	1	–	–	874†	410	9	45.55	3-46	0	0
Alderman, T.M.	1981	1990-91	41	53	22	203	26*	6.54	–	–	27	–	10181	4616	170	27.15	6-47	14	1
Alexander, G.	1880	1884-85	2	4	0	52	33	13.00	–	–	2	–	168	93	2	46.50	2-69	0	0
Alexander, H.H.	1932-33	1932-33	1	2	1	17	17*	17.00	–	–	–	–	276	154	1	154.00	1-129	0	0
Allan, F.E.	1878-79	1878-79	1	1	0	5	5	5.00	–	–	–	–	180†	80	4	20.00	2-30	0	0
Allan, P.J.	1965-66	1965-66	1	–	–	–	–	–	–	–	–	–	192	83	2	41.50	2-58	0	0
Allen, R.C.	1886-87	1886-87	1	2	0	44	30	22.00	–	–	2	–	–	–	–	–	–	–	–
Andrews, T.J.E.	1921	1926	16	23	1	592	94	26.90	–	4	12	–	156	116	1	116.00	1-23	0	0
Angel, J.	1992-93	1994-95	4	7†	1	35	11	5.83	–	–	1	–	748	463	10	46.30	3-54	0	0
Archer, K.A.	1950-51	1951-52	5	9	0	234	48	26.00	–	–	–	–	–	–	–	–	–	–	–
Archer, R.G.	1952-53	1956-57	19	30	1	713	128	24.58	1	2	20	–	3576	1318	48	27.45	5-53	1	0
Armstrong, W.W.	1901-02	1921	50	84	10	2863	159*	38.68	6	8	44	–	8028	2923	87	33.59	6-35	3	0
Badcock, C.L.	1936-37	1938	7	12	1	160	118	14.54	1	–	3	–	–	–	–	–	–	–	–
Bailey, G.J.	2013-14	2013-14	5	8	1	183	53	26.14	–	1	10	–	–	–	–	–	–	–	–
Bancroft, C.T.	2017-18	2019	10	18	1	446	82*	26.23	–	3	16	–	–	–	–	–	–	–	–
Bannerman, A.C.	1878-79	1893	28	50	2	1108	94	23.08	–	8	21	–	292	163	4	40.75	3-111	0	0
Bannerman, C.	1876-77	1878-79	3	6	2	239	165*	59.75	1	–	–	–	–	–	–	–	–	–	–
Bardsley, W.	1909	1926	41	66†	5	2469	193*	40.47	6	14	12	–	–	–	–	–	–	–	–
Barnes, S.G.	1938	1948	13	19	2	1072	234	63.05	3	5	14	–	594	218	4	54.50	2-25	0	0
Barnett, B.A.	1938	1938	4	8†	1	195	57	27.85	–	1	3	2	–	–	–	–	–	–	–
Barrett, J.E.	1890	1890	2	4†	1	80	67*	26.66	–	1	1	–	–	–	–	–	–	–	–
Beard, G.R.	1979-80	1979-80	3	5	0	114	49	22.80	–	–	–	–	259	109	1	109.00	1-26	0	0
Beer, M.A.	2010-11	2011-12	2	3	1	6	2*	3.00	–	–	1	–	406†	178	3	59.33	2-56	0	0
Benaud, J.	1972-73	1972-73	3	5	0	223	142	44.60	1	–	–	–	24	12	2	6.00	2-12	0	0
Benaud, R.	1951-52	1963-64	63	97	7	2201	122	24.45	3	9	65	–	19108	6704	248	27.03	7-72	16	1
Bennett, M.J.	1984-85	1985	3	5	2	71	23	23.66	–	–	5	–	664†	325	6	54.16	3-79	0	0
Bevan, M.G.	1994-95	1997-98	18	30†	3	785	91	29.07	–	6	8	–	1285†	703	29	24.24	6-82	1	1
Bichel, A.J.	1996-97	2003-04	19	22	1	355	71	16.90	–	1	16	–	3337	1870	58	32.24	5-60	1	0
Bird, J.M.	2012-13	2017-18	9	9	6	43	19*	14.33	–	–	2	–	1934	1042	34	30.64	5-59	1	0
Blackham, J.M.	1876-77	1894-95	35	62	11	800	74	15.68	–	4	37	24	–	–	–	–	–	–	–
Blackie, D.D.	1928-29	1928-29	3	6†	3	24	11*	8.00	–	–	2	–	1260	444	14	31.71	6-94	1	0
Blewett, G.S.	1994-95	1999-00	46	79	4	2552	214	34.02	4	15	45	–	1436	720	14	51.42	2-9	0	0
Bollinger, D.E.	2008-09	2010-11	12	14†	7	54	21	7.71	–	–	2	–	2401†	1296	50	25.92	5-28	2	0

Bonnor, G.J.	1888	17	30	0	512	128	17.06	1	2	16	–	164	84	2	42.00	1–5	0	0
Boon, D.C.	1984–85	1995–96	107	190	20	7422	200	43.65	21	32	99	–	36	14	0	–	–	–	0
Booth, B.C.	1961	1965–66	29	48	6	1773	169	42.21	5	10	17	–	436	146	3	48.66	2–33	0	1
Border, A.R.	1978–79	1993–94	156	265†	44	11174	205	50.56	27	63	156	–	4009†	1525	39	39.10	7–46	2	0
Boyle, H.F.	1878–79	1884–85	12	16	4	153	36*	12.75	–	–	10	–	1743	641	32	20.03	6–42	1	0
Bracken, N.W.	2003–04	2005–06	5	6	2	70	37	17.50	–	–	2	–	1110†	505	12	42.08	4–48	0	0
Bradman, D.G.	1928–29	1948	52	80	10	6996	334	99.94	29	13	32	–	160	72	2	36.00	1–8	0	0
Bright, R.J.	1977	1986–87	25	39	8	445	33	14.35	–	–	13	–	5541†	2180	53	41.13	7–87	4	1
Bromley, E.H.	1932–33	1934	2	4†	0	38	26	9.50	–	–	2	–	60†	19	0	–	–	–	–
Brown, W.A.	1934	1948	22	35	1	1592	206*	46.82	4	9	14	–	–	–	–	–	–	–	–
Bruce, W.	1884–85	1894–95	14	26†	2	702	80	29.25	–	5	12	–	988†	440	12	36.66	3–88	0	0
Burge, P.J.P.	1954–55	1965–66	42	68	8	2290	181	38.16	4	12	23	–	–	–	–	–	–	–	–
Burke, J.W.	1950–51	1958–59	24	44	7	1280	189	34.59	3	5	18	–	814	230	8	28.75	4–37	0	0
Burn, E.J.K.	1890	2	4	0	41	19	10.25	–	–	–	–	–	–	–	–	–	–	–
Burns, J.A.	2014–15	2018–19	16	28	0	1123	180	40.10	4	4	18	–	–	–	–	–	–	–	–
Burton, F.J.	1886–87	1887–88	2	4	2	4	2*	2.00	–	–	1	1	–	–	–	–	–	–	–
Callaway, S.T.	1891–92	1894–95	3	6	1	87	41	17.40	–	–	–	–	471	142	6	23.66	5–37	1	0
Callen, I.W.	1977–78	1	2†	2	26	22*	–	–	–	1	–	440	191	6	31.83	3–83	0	0
Campbell, G.D.	1989	1989–90	4	4	0	10	6	2.50	–	–	1	–	951	503	13	38.69	3–79	0	0
Carkeek, W.	1912	6	5†	2	16	6*	5.33	–	–	6	–	–	–	–	–	–	–	–
Carlson, P.H.	1978–79	2	4	0	23	21	5.75	–	4	2	–	368	99	2	49.50	2–41	0	0
Carter, H.	1907–08	1921–22	28	47	9	873	72	22.97	–	4	44	21	–	–	–	–	–	–	–
Cartwright, H.W.R.	2016–17	2	2	0	55	37	27.50	–	–	–	–	54	31	0	–	–	–	–
Casson, B.	2008	1	1	0	10	10	10.00	–	–	2	–	192†	129	3	43.00	3–86	0	0
Chappell, G.S.	1970–71	1983–84	87	151	19	7110	247*	53.86	24	31	122	–	5327	1913	47	40.70	5–61	0	1
Chappell, I.M.	1964–65	1979–80	75	136	10	5345	196	42.42	14	26	105	–	2873	1316	20	65.80	2–21	0	0
Chappell, T.M.	1981	3	6	1	79	27	15.80	–	–	2	–	–	–	–	–	–	–	–
Charlton, P.C.	1890	2	4	0	29	11	7.25	–	–	–	–	45	24	3	8.00	3–18	0	0
Chipperfield, A.G.	1934	1938	14	20	3	552	109	32.47	1	2	15	–	924	437	5	87.40	3–91	0	0
Clark, S.R.	2005–06	2009	24	26	7	248	39	13.05	–	–	4	–	5146	2243	94	23.86	5–32	2	0
Clark, W.M.	1977–78	1978–79	10	19	2	98	33	5.76	–	–	6	–	2793	1265	44	28.75	4–46	0	0
Clarke, M.J.	2004–05	2015	115	198	22	8643	329*	49.10	28	27	134	–	2435†	1184	31	38.19	6–9	2	0
Colley, D.J.	1972	3	4	0	84	54	21.00	–	1	1	–	729	312	6	52.00	3–83	0	0
Collins, H.L.	1920–21	1926	19	31	1	1352	203	45.06	4	6	13	–	654†	252	4	63.00	2–47	0	0
Coningham, A.	1894–95	1	2†	0	13	10	6.50	–	–	–	–	186†	76	2	38.00	2–17	0	0
Connolly, A.N.	1963–64	1970–71	29	45	20	260	37	10.40	–	–	17	–	7818	2981	102	29.22	6–47	4	0
Cook, S.H.	1997–98	2	2†	2	3	3*	–	–	–	–	–	224	142	7	20.28	5–39	1	0
Cooper, B.B.	1876–77	1	2	0	18	15	9.00	–	–	2	–	–	–	–	–	–	–	–

INDIVIDUAL TEST CAREER RECORDS – AUSTRALIA (Continued)

	First Test	Last Test	Tests	Inns	NO	Runs	HS	Avge	100	50	Ct	St	Balls	Runs	Wkts	Avge	BB	5wI	10wM
Cooper, W.H.	1881–82	1884–85	2	3	1	13	7	6.50	–	–	1	–	446	226	9	25.11	6–120	1	0
Copeland, T.A.	2011	2011	3	4	1	39	23*	13.00	–	–	2	–	648	227	6	37.83	2–24	0	0
Corling, G.E.	1964	1964	5	4	1	5	3	1.66	–	–	–	–	1159	447	12	37.25	4–60	0	0
Cosier, G.J.	1975–76	1978–79	18	32	2	897	168	28.93	2	3	14	–	899	341	5	68.20	2–26	0	0
Cottam, J.T.	1886–87	1886–87	1	2	0	4	3	2.00	–	–	1	–	–						
Cotter, A.	1903–04	1911–12	21	37	2	457	45	13.05	–	–	8	–	4633	2549	89	28.64	7–148	7	–
Coulthard, G.	1881–82	1881–82	1	1	1	6	6*	–	–	–	–	–	–						
Cowan, E.J.M.	2011–12	2013	18	32†	0	1001	136	31.28	1	6	24	–	–						
Cowper, R.M.	1964	1968	27	46†	2	2061	307	46.84	5	10	21	–	3005	1139	36	31.63	4–48	0	0
Craig, I.D.	1952–53	1957–58	11	18	0	358	53	19.88	–	2	2	–	–						
Crawford, W.P.A.	1956	1956–57	4	5	2	53	34	17.66	–	–	1	–	437	107	7	15.28	3–28	0	0
Cullen, D.J.	2005–06	2005–06	1	–	–	–	–	–	–	–	–	–	84	54	1	54.00	1–25	0	0
Cummins, P.J.	2011–12	2019	25	39	6	599	63	18.15	–	2	11	–	5667	2639	123	21.45	6–23	4	1
Dale, A.C.	1997–98	1998–99	2	3†	0	6	5	2.00	–	–	–	–	348	187	6	31.16	3–71	0	–
Darling, J.	1894–95	1905	34	60†	2	1657	178	28.56	3	8	27	–	–						
Darling, L.S.	1932–33	1936–37	12	18†	1	474	85	27.88	–	3	8	–	162	65	0	–	–	–	–
Darling, W.M.	1977–78	1979–80	14	27	1	697	91	26.80	–	6	5	–	–						
Davidson, A.K.	1953	1962–63	44	61†	7	1328	80	24.59	–	5	42	–	11587†	3819	186	20.53	7–93	14	2
Davis, I.C.	1973–74	1977	15	27	1	692	105	26.61	1	4	9	–	–						
Davis, S.P.	1985–86	1985–86	1	1	0	0	0	0.00	–	–	–	–	150	70	0	–	–	–	–
de Courcy, J.H.	1953	1953	3	6	1	81	41	16.20	–	–	3	–	–						
Dell, A.R.	1970–71	1973–74	2	2	2	6	3*	–	–	–	–	–	559†	160	6	26.66	3–65	0	0
Dodemaide, A.I.C.	1987–88	1992	10	15	6	202	50	22.44	–	1	6	–	2184	953	34	28.02	6–58	1	0
Doherty, X.J.	2010–11	2012–13	4	7†	3	51	18*	12.75	–	–	2	–	918†	548	7	78.28	3–131	0	0
Donnan, H.	1891–92	1896	5	10	1	75	15	8.33	–	–	2	–	54	22	0	–	–	–	–
Doolan, A.J.	2013–14	2014–15	4	8	0	191	89	23.87	–	1	4	–	–						
Dooland, B.	1946–47	1947–48	3	5	1	76	29	19.00	–	–	3	–	880	419	9	46.55	4–69	0	0
Duff, R.A.	1901–02	1905	22	40	3	1317	146	35.59	2	6	14	–	180	85	4	21.25	2–43	0	0
Duncan, J.R.F.	1970–71	1970–71	1	1	0	3	3	3.00	–	–	–	–	112	30	0	–	–	–	–
Dyer, G.C.	1986–87	1987–88	6	6	0	131	60	21.83	–	1	22	2	–						
Dymock, G.	1973–74	1979–80	21	32†	7	236	31*	9.44	–	–	1	–	5545†	2116	78	27.12	7–67	5	1
Dyson, J.	1977–78	1984–85	30	58	7	1359	127*	26.64	2	5	10	–	–						
Eady, C.J.	1896	1901–02	2	4	1	20	10*	6.66	–	–	2	–	223	112	7	16.00	3–30	0	0
Eastwood, K.H.	1970–71	1970–71	1	2†	0	5	5	2.50	–	–	–	–	40†	21	1	21.00	1–21	0	0

Ebeling, H.I.	1934	1934	1	2	0	43	41	21.50	–	–	–	–	186	89	3	29.66	3–74	0	0
Edwards, J.D.	1888	1888	3	6	1	48	26	9.60	–	–	1	–	–	–	–	–	–	–	–
Edwards, R.	1972	1975	20	32	3	1171	170*	40.37	2	9	7	–	12	20	0	–	–	–	–
Edwards, W.J.	1974–75	1974–75	3	6†	0	68	30	11.33	–	–	–	14	–	–	–	–	–	0	0
Elliott, M.T.G.	1996–97	2004	21	36†	1	1172	199	33.48	3	4	5	5	12†	4	0	–	–	0	0
Emery, P.A.	1994–95	1994–95	1	1†	1	8*	8*	–	–	–	14	2	–	–	–	–	–	0	0
Emery, S.H.	1912	1912	4	2	0	6	5	3.00	–	–	–	5	462	249	5	49.80	2–46	0	0
Evans, E.	1881–82	1886	6	10	2	82	33	10.25	–	4	–	5	1237	332	7	47.42	3–64	4	–
Fairfax, A.G.	1928–29	1930–31	10	12	4	410	65	51.25	–	–	4	15	1520	645	21	30.71	4–31	–	–
Faulkner, J.P.	2013	2013	1	2	0	45	23	22.50	–	–	–	–	166†	98	6	16.33	4–51	–	–
Favell, L.E.	1954–55	1960–61	19	31	3	757	101	27.03	1	5	–	9	–	–	–	–	–	–	–
Ferguson, C.J.	2016–17	2016–17	1	2	0	4	3	2.00	–	–	–	–	–	–	–	–	–	–	–
Ferris, J.J.‡	1886–87	1890	8	16†	4	98	20*	8.16	–	–	–	4	2030†	684	48	14.25	5–26	4	–
Finch, A.J.	2018–19	2018–19	5	10	0	278	62	27.80	–	2	2	7	12†	8	0	–	–	–	–
Fingleton, J.H.W.	1931–32	1938	18	29	1	1189	136	42.46	5	3	3	13	–	–	–	–	–	1	0
Fleetwood-Smith, L.O'B.	1935–36	1938	10	11	5	54	16*	9.00	–	–	–	9	3093†	1570	42	37.38	6–110	2	3
Fleming, D.W.	1994–95	2000–01	20	19	3	305	71*	19.06	–	2	2	9	4129	1942	75	25.89	5–30	0	0
Francis, B.C.	1972	1972	3	5	0	52	27	10.40	–	–	–	1	–	–	–	–	–	0	0
Freeman, E.W.	1967–68	1969–70	11	18	0	345	76	19.16	–	2	2	5	2183	1128	34	33.17	4–52	0	0
Freer, F.A.W.	1946–47	1946–47	1	1	1	28	28*	–	–	–	–	–	160	74	3	24.66	2–49	0	0
Gannon, J.B.	1977–78	1977–78	3	5	4	3	3*	3.00	–	–	–	3	726†	361	11	32.81	4–77	0	0
Garrett, T.W.	1876–77	1887–88	19	33	6	339	51*	12.55	–	1	1	7	2728	970	36	26.94	6–78	2	0
Gaunt, R.A.	1957–58	1963–64	3	4†	2	6	3	3.00	–	–	–	1	716	310	7	44.28	3–53	0	0
Gehrs, D.R.A.	1903–04	1910–11	6	11	0	221	67	20.09	–	2	2	6	6	4	0	–	–	–	–
George, P.R.	2010–11	2010–11	1	2	0	2	2	1.00	–	–	–	–	168	77	2	38.50	2–48	0	–
Giffen, G.	1881–82	1896	31	53	0	1238	161	23.35	1	6	6	24	6391	2791	103	27.09	7–117	7	1
Giffen, W.F.	1886–87	1891–92	3	6	0	11	3	1.83	–	–	–	1	–	–	–	–	–	–	–
Gilbert, D.R.	1985	1986–87	9	12	4	57	15	7.12	–	–	–	–	1647	843	16	52.68	3–48	0	0
Gilchrist, A.C.	1999–00	2007–08	96	137†	20	5570	204*	47.60	17	26	379	37	14234	6770	259	26.13	7–37	8	–
Gillespie, J.N.	1996–97	2005–06	71	93	28	1218	201*	18.73	1	2	2	27	2661†	1406	54	26.03	6–85	3	0
Gilmour, G.J.	1973–74	1976–77	15	22†	1	483	101	23.00	1	3	3	8	–	–	–	–	–	3	0
Gleeson, J.W.	1967–68	1972	29	46	8	395	45	10.39	–	–	–	17	8857	3367	93	36.20	5–61	3	0
Graham, H.	1893	1896	6	10	0	301	107	30.10	2	–	–	3	–	–	–	–	–	–	–
Gregory, D.W.	1876–77	1878–79	3	5	2	60	43	20.00	–	–	–	1	20	9	0	–	–	–	–
Gregory, E.J.	1876–77	1876–77	1	2	0	11	11	5.50	–	–	–	–	–	–	–	–	–	–	–
Gregory, J.M.	1920–21	1928–29	24	34†	3	1146	119	36.96	2	7	7	37	5582	2648	85	31.15	7–69	4	–
Gregory, R.G.	1936–37	1936–37	2	3	0	153	80	51.00	–	2	2	1	24	14	0	–	–	0	–
Gregory, S.E.	1890	1912	58	100	7	2282	201	24.53	4	8	8	25	30	33	0	–	–	–	–

INDIVIDUAL TEST CAREER RECORDS – AUSTRALIA (Continued)

	First Test	Last Test	Tests	Inns	NO	Runs	HS	Avge	100	50	Ct	St	Balls	Runs	Wkts	Avge	BB	5wI	10wM
Grimmett, C.V.	1924-25	1935-36	37	50	10	557	50	13.92	–	1	17	–	14513	5231	216	24.21	7-40	21	7
Groube, T.U.	1880	1880	1	2	0	11	11	5.50	–	–	–	–	–	–	–	–	–	–	–
Grout, A.T.W.	1957-58	1965-66	51	67	8	890	74	15.08	–	3	163	24	–	–	–	–	–	–	–
Guest, C.E.J.	1962-63	1962-63	1	1	0	11	11	11.00	–	–	–	–	144	59	0	–	–	–	–
Haddin, B.J.	2008	2015	66	112	13	3265	169	32.97	4	18	262	8	–	–	–	–	–	–	–
Hamence, R.A.	1946-47	1947-48	3	4	1	81	30*	27.00	–	–	1	–	–	–	–	–	–	–	–
Hammond, J.R.	1972-73	1972-73	5	5	2	28	19	9.33	–	–	2	–	1031	488	15	32.53	4-38	0	0
Handscomb, P.S.P.	2016-17	2018-19	16	29	5	934	110	38.91	2	4	28	–	–	–	–	–	–	–	–
Harris, M.S.	2018-19	2019	9	17†	1	385	79	24.06	–	2	7	–	–	–	–	–	–	–	–
Harris, R.J.	2009-10	2014-15	27	39	11	603	74	21.53	–	3	13	–	5736	2658	113	23.52	7-117	5	0
Harry, J.	1894-95	1894-95	1	2	0	8	6	4.00	–	–	1	–	–	–	–	–	–	–	–
Hartigan, M.J.	1907-08	1907-08	2	4	0	170	116	42.50	1	–	1	–	12	7	0	–	–	–	–
Hartkopf, A.E.V.	1924-25	1924-25	1	2	0	80	80	40.00	–	1	–	–	240	134	1	134.00	1-120	0	0
Harvey, M.R.	1946-47	1946-47	1	2	0	43	31	21.50	–	–	–	–	–	–	–	–	–	–	–
Harvey, R.N.	1947-48	1962-63	79	137†	10	6149	205	48.41	21	24	64	–	414	120	3	40.00	1-8	0	0
Hassett, A.L.	1938	1953	43	69	3	3073	198*	46.56	10	11	30	–	111	78	1	–	–	–	–
Hastings, J.W.	2012-13	2012-13	1	2	0	52	32	26.00	–	–	1	–	234	153	1	153.00	1-51	0	0
Hauritz, N.M.	2004-05	2010-11	17	24	7	426	75	25.05	–	2	3	–	4200	2204	63	34.98	5-53	2	0
Hawke, N.J.N.	1962-63	1968	27	37	15	365	45*	16.59	–	–	9	–	6974	2677	91	29.41	7-105	6	1
Hayden, M.L.	1993-94	2008-09	103	184†	14	8625	380	50.73	30	29	128	–	54	40	0	–	–	–	–
Hazlewood, J.R.	2014-15	2019	48	60†	28	397	39	12.40	–	–	17	–	10543	4889	184	26.57	6-67	7	0
Hazlitt, G.R.	1907-08	1912	9	12	4	89	34*	11.12	–	–	4	–	1563	623	23	27.08	7-25	1	0
Head, T.M.	2018-19	2019	12	22†	2	854	161	42.70	1	6	8	–	84	52	0	–	–	–	–
Healy, I.A.	1988-89	1999-00	119	182	23	4356	161*	27.39	4	22	366	29	–	–	–	–	–	–	–
Hendry, H.S.T.L.	1921	1928-29	11	18	2	335	112	20.93	1	–	10	–	1706	640	16	40.00	3-36	0	0
Henriques, M.C.	2012-13	2016	4	8	1	164	81*	23.42	–	2	1	–	330	164	2	82.00	1-48	0	0
Hibbert, P.A.	1977-78	1977-78	1	2†	0	15	13	7.50	–	–	1	–	–	–	–	–	–	–	–
Higgs, J.D.	1977-78	1980-81	22	36	16	111	16	5.55	–	–	3	–	4752	2057	66	31.16	7-143	2	0
Hilditch, A.M.J.	1978-79	1985-86	18	34	0	1073	119	31.55	2	6	13	–	–	–	–	–	–	–	–
Hilfenhaus, B.W.	2008-09	2012-13	27	38	12	355	56*	13.65	–	1	7	–	6078	2822	99	28.50	5-75	2	0
Hill, C.	1896	1911-12	49	89†	2	3412	191	39.21	7	19	33	–	–	–	–	–	–	–	–
Hill, J.C.	1953	1954-55	3	6	3	21	8*	7.00	–	–	2	–	606	273	8	34.12	3-35	0	0
Hoare, D.E.	1960-61	1960-61	1	2	0	35	35	17.50	–	–	2	–	232	156	2	78.00	2-68	0	0
Hodge, B.J.	2005-06	2008	6	11	2	503	203*	55.88	1	2	9	–	12	8	0	–	–	–	–

Hodges, J.R.	1876-77	2	4†	1	10	8	3.33	–	–	–	–	136†	84	6	14.00	2-7	0	0
Hogan, T.G.	1982-83	7	12	1	205	42*	18.63	–	–	2	–	1436†	706	15	47.06	5-66	1	0
Hogg, G.B.	1996-97	7	10†	3	186	79	26.57	–	1	1	–	1524†	933	17	54.88	2-40	0	0
Hogg, R.M.	1984-85	38	58	13	439	52	9.75	–	1	7	–	7633	3503	123	28.47	6-74	6	2
Hohns, T.V.	1989	7	7†	2	136	40	22.66	–	–	3	–	1528	580	17	34.11	3-59	0	0
Hole, G.B.	1988-89	18	33	2	789	66	25.45	–	6	21	–	398	126	3	42.00	1-9	0	0
Holland, J.M.	1950-51	4	7	5	6	3	3.00	–	–	1	–	960†	574	9	63.77	3-83	0	2
Holland, R.G.	2018-19	11	15	4	35	10	3.18	–	–	5	–	2889	1352	34	39.76	6-54	3	0
Hookes, D.W.	1985-86	23	41†	3	1306	143*	34.36	1	8	12	–	96†	41	1	41.00	1-4	0	0
Hopkins, A.J.Y.	1985-86	20	33	2	509	43	16.41	–	–	11	–	1327	696	26	26.76	4-81	0	0
Horan, T.P.	1909	15	27	2	471	124	18.84	1	1	6	–	373	143	11	13.00	6-40	1	2
Hordern, H.V.	1901-02	7	13	2	254	50	23.09	–	1	6	–	2148	1075	46	23.36	7-90	5	1
Hornibrook, P.M.	1876-77	6	7†	1	60	26	10.00	–	–	7	–	1579†	664	17	39.05	7-92	1	0
Howell, W.P.	1910-11	18	27†	6	158	35	7.52	–	–	12	–	3892	1407	49	28.71	5-81	1	–
Hughes, K.J.	1928-29	70	124	6	4415	213	37.41	9	22	50	–	85	28	0	–	–	–	1
Hughes, M.G.	1930	53	70	8	1032	72*	16.64	–	2	23	–	12285	6017	212	28.38	8-87	7	1
Hughes, P.J.	1903-04	26	49†	2	1535	160	32.65	3	7	15	–	–	–	–	–	–	–	–
Hunt, W.A.	1977	1	1†	0	0	0	0.00	–	–	1	–	96†	39	0	–	–	–	–
Hurst, A.G.	1984-85	12	20	3	102	26	6.00	–	–	3	–	3054	1200	43	27.90	5-28	2	0
Hurwood, A.	1993-94	2	2	0	5	5	2.50	–	–	2	–	517	170	11	15.45	4-22	0	0
Hussey, M.E.K.	2008-09	79	137†	16	6235	195	51.52	19	29	85	–	588	306	7	43.71	1-0	0	0
Inverarity, R.J.	2013	6	11	1	174	56	17.40	–	1	4	–	372†	93	4	23.25	3-26	0	0
Iredale, F.A.	1931-32	14	23	1	807	140	36.68	2	4	16	–	12	3	0	–	–	–	–
Ironmonger, H.	1973-74	14	21†	5	42	12	2.62	–	–	3	–	4695†	1330	74	17.97	7-23	4	2
Iverson, J.B.	1930-31	5	7	3	3	1*	0.75	–	–	2	–	1108	320	21	15.23	6-27	1	0
Jackson, A.	2005-06	8	11	1	474	164	47.40	1	2	7	–	–	–	–	–	–	–	–
Jaques, P.A.	1968	11	19†	0	902	150	47.47	3	6	7	–	–	–	–	–	–	–	–
Jarman, B.N.	1894-95	19	30	3	400	78	14.81	–	2	50	4	–	–	–	–	–	–	–
Jarvis, A.H.	1928-29	11	21	3	303	82	16.83	–	1	9	9	–	–	–	–	–	–	–
Jenner, T.J.	1950-51	9	14	5	208	74	23.11	–	1	5	–	1881	749	24	31.20	5-90	1	0
Jennings, C.B.	1930-31	6	8	2	107	32	17.83	–	–	5	–	–	–	–	–	–	–	–
Johnson, I.W.G.	1959-60	45	66	12	1000	77	18.51	–	6	30	–	8780	3182	109	29.19	7-44	3	0
Johnson, L.J.	1884-85	1	1	1	25	25*	–	–	–	2	–	282	74	6	12.33	3-8	0	0
Johnson, M.G.	1970-71	73	109†	16	2065	123*	22.20	1	11	27	–	16001†	8891	313	28.40	8-61	12	3
Johnston, W.A.	1912	40	49†	25	273	29	11.37	–	–	16	–	11048†	3826	160	23.91	6-44	7	0
Jones, D.M.	1945-46	52	89	11	3631	216	46.55	11	14	34	–	198	64	1	64.00	1-5	0	0
Jones, E.	1947-48	19	26	1	126	20	5.04	–	–	21	–	3754	1857	64	29.01	7-88	3	1
Jones, S.P.	2015-16	12	24	4	428	87	21.40	–	1	12	–	262	112	6	18.66	4-47	0	0

INDIVIDUAL TEST CAREER RECORDS – AUSTRALIA (Continued)

	First Test	Last Test	Tests	Inns	NO	Runs	HS	Avge	100	50	Ct	St	Balls	Runs	Wkts	Avge	BB	5wI	10wM
Joslin, L.R.	1967-68	1967-68	1	2†	0	9	7	4.50	–	–	–	–	–	–	–	–	–	–	–
Julian, B.P.	1993	1995-96	7	9	1	128	56*	16.00	–	1	4	–	1098†	599	15	39.93	4-36	0	0
Kasprowicz, M.S.	1996-97	2005-06	38	54	12	445	25	10.59	–	–	16	–	7140	3716	113	32.88	7-36	4	0
Katich, S.M.	2001	2010-11	56	99†	6	4188	157	45.03	10	25	39	–	1039†	635	21	30.23	6-65	1	0
Kelleway, C.	1910-11	1928-29	26	42	4	1422	147	37.42	3	6	24	–	4363	1683	52	32.36	5-33	1	0
Kelly, J.J.	1896	1905	36	56	17	664	46*	17.02	–	–	43	20	–	–	–	–	–	–	–
Kelly, T.J.D.	1876-77	1878-79	2	3	0	64	35	21.33	–	–	1	–	–	–	–	–	–	–	–
Kendall, T.K.	1876-77	1876-77	2	4†	1	39	17*	13.00	–	–	2	–	563†	215	14	15.35	7-55	1	0
Kent, M.F.	1981	1981	3	6	0	171	54	28.50	–	2	6	–	–	–	–	–	–	–	–
Kerr, R.B.	1985-86	1985-86	2	4	0	31	17	7.75	–	–	1	–	–	–	–	–	–	–	–
Khawaja, U.T.	2010-11	2019	44	77†	6	2887	174	40.66	8	14	35	–	12	5	0	–	–	–	–
Kippax, A.F.	1924-25	1934	22	34	1	1192	146	36.12	2	8	13	–	72	19	0	–	–	–	–
Kline, L.F.	1957-58	1960-61	13	16†	9	58	15*	8.28	–	–	9	–	2373†	776	34	22.82	7-75	1	1
Krejza, J.J.	2008-09	2008-09	2	4	1	71	32	23.66	–	–	4	–	743	562	13	43.23	8-215	1	1
Labuschagne, M.	2018-19	2019	9	15	0	563	81	37.53	–	5	11	–	468	300	10	30.00	3-45	–	–
Laird, B.M.	1979-80	1982-83	21	40	2	1341	92	35.28	–	11	16	–	18	12	0	–	–	–	–
Langer, J.L.	1992-93	2006-07	105	182†	12	7696	250	45.27	23	30	73	–	6	3	0	–	–	–	–
Langley, G.R.A.	1951-52	1956-57	26	37	12	374	53	14.96	–	1	83	15	–	–	–	–	–	–	–
Laughlin, T.J.	1977-78	1978-79	3	5†	0	87	35	17.40	–	–	3	–	516	262	6	43.66	5-101	1	0
Laver, F.J.	1899	1909	15	23	6	196	45	11.52	–	–	8	–	2361	964	37	26.05	8-31	2	0
Law, S.G.	1995-96	1995-96	1	1	1	54	54*	–	–	1	1	–	18	9	0	–	–	–	–
Lawry, W.M.	1961	1970-71	67	123†	12	5234	210	47.15	13	27	30	–	14†	6	0	–	–	–	–
Lawson, G.F.	1980-81	1989-90	46	68	12	894	74	15.96	–	4	10	–	11118	5501	180	30.56	8-112	11	2
Lee, B.	1999-00	2008-09	76	90	18	1451	64	20.15	–	5	23	–	16531	9554	310	30.81	5-30	10	0
Lee, P.K.	1931-32	1932-33	2	3	0	57	42	19.00	–	–	1	–	436	212	5	42.40	4-111	0	0
Lehmann, D.S.	1997-98	2004-05	27	42†	2	1798	177	44.95	5	10	11	–	974†	412	15	27.46	3-42	0	0
Lillee, D.K.	1970-71	1983-84	70	90	24	905	73*	13.71	–	1	23	–	18467	8493	355	23.92	7-83	23	7
Lindwall, R.R.	1945-46	1959-60	61	84	13	1502	118	21.15	2	5	26	–	13650	5251	228	23.03	7-38	12	0
Love, H.S.B.	1932-33	1932-33	1	2	0	8	5	4.00	–	–	3	–	–	–	–	–	–	–	–
Love, M.L.	2002-03	2003	5	8	3	233	100*	46.60	1	1	7	–	–	–	–	–	–	–	–
Loxton, S.J.E.	1947-48	1950-51	12	15	0	554	101	36.93	1	3	7	–	906	349	8	43.62	3-55	0	0
Lyon, N.M.	2011	2019	91	118	36	1003	47	12.23	–	3	43	–	23360	11727	363	32.30	8-50	15	2
Lyons, J.J.	1886-87	1897-98	14	27	0	731	134	27.07	1	3	3	–	316	149	6	24.83	5-30	1	0
McAlister, P.A.	1903-04	1909	8	16	1	252	41	16.80	–	–	10	–	–	–	–	–	–	–	–
Macartney, C.G.	1907-08	1926	35	55	4	2131	170	41.78	7	9	17	–	3561†	1240	45	27.55	7-58	2	1

McCabe, S.J.	1930	1938	39	62	5	2748	232	48.21	6	13	41	–	3746	1543	36	42.86	4–13	0	0
McCool, C.L.	1945–46	1949–50	14	17	4	459	104*	35.30	1	1	14	–	2504	958	36	26.61	5–41	3	0
McCormick, E.L.	1935–36	1938	12	14†	5	54	17*	6.00	–	–	8	–	2107	1079	36	29.97	4–101	0	0
McCosker, R.B.	1974–75	1979–80	25	46	5	1622	127	39.56	4	9	21	–	–	–	–	–	–	–	–
McDermott, C.J.	1984–85	1955–96	71	90	13	940	42*	12.20	–	1	19	–	16586	8332	291	28.63	8–97	14	2
McDonald, A.B.	2008–09	2008–09	4	6	1	107	68	21.40	–	–	2	–	732	300	9	33.33	3–25	0	0
McDonald, C.C.	1951–52	1961	47	83	4	3107	170	39.32	5	17	14	–	8	3	0	–	–	–	–
McDonald, E.A.	1920–21	1921–22	11	12	5	116	36	16.57	–	–	3	–	2885	1431	43	33.27	5–32	2	1
McDonnell, P.S.	1880	1888	19	34	1	955	147	28.93	3	2	6	–	52	53	0	–	–	–	–
McGain, B.E.	2008–09	2008–09	1	2	0	2	2	1.00	–	–	–	–	108	149	0	–	–	–	–
MacGill, S.C.G.	1997–98	2008	44	47	11	349	43	9.69	–	–	16	–	11237	6038	208	29.02	8–108	12	2
McGrath, G.D.	1993–94	2006–07	124	138	51	641	61	7.36	–	1	38	–	29248	12186	563	21.64	8–24	29	3
McIlwraith, J.	1886	1886	1	2	0	9	7	4.50	–	–	1	–	–	–	–	–	–	–	–
McIntyre, P.E.	1994–95	1996–97	2	4	1	22	16	7.33	–	–	–	–	393	194	5	38.80	3–103	0	0
McKay, C.J.	2009–10	2009–10	1	1	0	10	10	10.00	–	–	1	–	168	101	1	101.00	1–56	0	0
Mackay, K.D.	1956	1962–63	37	52†	7	1507	89	33.48	–	13	16	–	5792	1721	50	34.42	6–42	2	0
McKenzie, G.D.	1961	1970–71	60	89	12	945	76	12.27	–	2	34	–	17681	7328	246	29.78	8–71	16	3
McKibbin, T.R.	1894–95	1897–98	5	8†	2	88	28*	14.66	–	–	4	–	1032	496	17	29.17	3–35	0	0
McLaren, J.W.	1911–12	1911–12	1	2	2	0	0*	–	–	–	–	–	144	70	1	70.00	1–23	–	–
Maclean, J.A.	1978–79	1978–79	4	8	1	79	33*	11.28	–	–	18	–	–	–	–	–	–	–	–
McLeod, C.E.	1894–95	1905	17	29	5	573	112	23.87	1	4	9	–	3374	1325	33	40.15	5–65	2	0
McLeod, R.W.	1891–92	1893	6	11†	0	146	31	13.27	–	–	3	–	1089	382	12	31.83	5–53	1	0
McShane, P.G.	1884–85	1887–88	3	6†	1	26	12*	5.20	–	–	2	–	108†	48	1	48.00	1–39	0	0
Maddinson, N.J.	2016–17	2016–17	3	4†	0	27	22	6.75	–	–	2	–	36†	27	0	–	–	–	–
Maddocks, L.V.	1954–55	1956–57	7	12	2	177	69	17.70	–	1	19	1	–	–	–	–	–	–	–
Maguire, J.N.	1983–84	1983–84	3	5	1	28	15*	7.00	–	–	2	–	616	323	10	32.30	4–57	0	0
Mailey, A.A.	1920–21	1926	21	29	9	222	46*	11.10	–	–	14	–	6119	3358	99	33.91	9–121	6	2
Mallett, A.A.	1968	1980	38	50	13	430	43*	11.62	–	–	30	–	9990	3940	132	29.84	8–59	6	1
Malone, M.F.	1977	1977	1	0	0	46	46	46.00	1	–	2	–	342	77	6	12.83	5–63	1	0
Mann, A.L.	1977–78	1977–78	4	8†	0	189	105	23.62	–	2	3	–	552	316	4	79.00	3–12	0	0
Manou, G.A.	2009	2009	1	2	1	21	13*	21.00	–	–	–	–	–	–	–	–	–	–	–
Marr, A.P.	1884–85	1884–85	1	2	0	5	5	2.50	–	–	38	–	48	14	0	–	–	–	–
Marsh, G.R.	1985–86	1991–92	50	93	7	2854	138	33.18	4	15	16	–	–	–	–	–	–	–	0
Marsh, M.R.	2014–15	2019	32	55	5	1260	181	25.20	2	3	3	–	2853	1623	42	38.64	5–46	1	0
Marsh, R.W.	1970–71	1983–84	96	150†	13	3633	132	26.51	3	16	343	12	72	54	0	–	–	–	–
Marsh, S.E.	2011	2018–19	38	68†	2	2265	182	34.31	6	10	23	–	–	–	–	–	–	–	–
Martin, J.W.	1960–61	1966–67	8	13†	1	214	55	17.83	–	1	5	–	1846†	832	17	48.94	3–56	0	0
Martyn, D.R.	1992–93	2006–07	67	109	14	4406	165	46.37	13	23	36	–	348	168	2	84.00	1–0	0	0

INDIVIDUAL TEST CAREER RECORDS – AUSTRALIA (Continued)

	First Test	Last Test	Tests	Inns	NO	Runs	HS	Avge	100	50	Ct	St	Balls	Runs	Wkts	Avge	BB	5wI	10wM
Massie, H.H.	1881-82	1884-85	9	16	0	249	55	15.56	–	1	5	–	–	–	–	–	–	–	–
Massie, R.A.L.	1972	1972-73	6	8†	1	78	42	11.14	–	–	1	–	1739	647	31	20.87	8-53	2	1
Matthews, C.D.	1986-87	1988-89	3	5†	0	54	32	10.80	–	–	1	–	570†	313	6	52.16	3-95	0	0
Matthews, G.R.J.	1983-84	1992-93	33	53†	8	1849	130	41.08	4	12	17	–	6271	2942	61	48.22	5-103	2	1
Matthews, T.J.	1911-12	1912	8	10	1	153	53	17.00	–	1	7	–	1081	419	16	26.18	4-29	0	0
Maxwell, G.J.	2012-13	2017	7	14	1	339	104	26.07	1	–	5	–	462	341	8	42.62	4-127	0	0
May, T.B.A.	1987-88	1994-95	24	28	12	225	42*	14.06	–	–	6	–	6577	2606	75	34.74	5-9	3	0
Mayne, E.R.	1912	1921-22	4	4	1	64	25*	21.33	–	–	2	–	6	1	0	–	–	–	–
Mayne, L.C.	1964-65	1969-70	6	11†	3	76	13	9.50	–	–	3	–	1251	628	19	33.05	4-43	0	0
Meckiff, I.	1957-58	1963-64	18	20	7	154	45*	11.84	–	–	9	–	3734†	1423	45	31.62	6-38	2	0
Mennie, J.M.	2016-17	2016-17	1	2	0	10	10	5.00	–	–	–	–	168	85	1	85.00	1-85	0	0
Meuleman, K.D.	1945-46	1945-46	1	1	0	0	0	0.00	–	–	1	–	–	–	–	–	–	–	–
Midwinter, W.E.‡	1876-77	1886-87	8	14	1	174	37	13.38	–	–	5	–	949	333	14	23.78	5-78	1	0
Miller, C.R.	1998-99	2000-01	18	24	3	174	43	8.28	–	–	6	–	4091	1805	69	26.15	5-32	3	1
Miller, K.R.	1945-46	1956-57	55	87	7	2958	147	36.97	7	13	38	–	10461	3906	170	22.97	7-60	7	1
Minnett, R.B.	1911-12	1912	9	15	0	391	90	26.06	–	3	–	–	589	290	11	26.36	4-34	0	0
Misson, F.M.	1960-61	1961	5	5	3	38	25*	19.00	–	–	6	–	1197	616	16	38.50	4-58	0	0
Moody, T.M.	1989-90	1992	8	14	0	456	106	32.57	2	3	9	–	432	147	2	73.50	1-17	0	0
Moroney, J.	1949-50	1951-52	7	12	1	383	118	34.81	2	1	–	–	–	–	–	–	–	–	–
Morris, A.R.	1946-47	1954-55	46	79†	3	3533	206	46.48	12	12	15	–	111†	50	2	25.00	1-5	0	0
Morris, S.	1884-85	1884-85	1	2	1	14	10*	14.00	–	–	–	–	136	73	2	36.50	2-73	0	0
Moses, H.	1886-87	1894-95	6	10†	0	198	33	19.80	–	1	1	–	–	–	–	–	–	–	–
Moss, J.K.	1978-79	1978-79	1	2†	1	60	38*	60.00	–	–	–	–	–	–	–	–	–	–	–
Moule, W.H.	1880	1880	1	2	0	40	34	20.00	–	–	1	–	51	23	3	7.66	3-23	0	0
Muller, S.A.	1999-00	1999-00	2	2	2	6	6*	–	–	–	2	–	348	258	7	36.85	3-68	0	0
Murdoch, W.L.‡	1876-77	1890	18	33	5	896	211	32.00	2	1	14	2	–	–	–	–	–	–	–
Musgrove, H.A.	1884-85	1884-85	1	2	0	13	9	6.50	–	–	–	–	–	–	–	–	–	–	–
Nagel, L.E.	1932-33	1932-33	1	2	1	21	21*	21.00	–	–	–	–	262	110	2	55.00	2-110	0	0
Nash, L.J.	1931-32	1936-37	2	2	0	30	17	15.00	–	–	6	–	311	126	10	12.60	4-18	0	0
Nevill, P.M.	2015	2016-17	17	23	2	468	66	22.28	–	3	61	2	–	–	–	–	–	–	–
Nicholson, M.J.	1998-99	1998-99	1	2	0	14	9	7.00	–	–	–	–	150	115	4	28.75	3-56	0	0
Nitschke, H.C.	1931-32	1931-32	2	2†	0	53	47	26.50	–	–	3	–	–	–	–	–	–	–	–
Noble, M.A.	1897-98	1909	42	73	7	1997	133	30.25	1	16	26	–	7159	3025	121	25.00	7-17	9	2
Noblet, G.	1949-50	1952-53	3	4	1	22	13*	7.33	–	–	1	–	774	183	7	26.14	3-21	0	0

North, M.J.	2008–09	21	35†	2	1171	128	35.48	5	4	17	–	1258	591	14	42.21	6–55	1	0
Nothling, O.E.	1928–29	1	2	0	52	44	26.00	–	–	–	–	276	72	0	–	–	–	–
O'Brien, L.P.J.	1932–33	5	8†	0	211	61	26.37	–	2	3	–	–	–	13	26.15	5–40	1	0
O'Connor, J.D.A.	1907–08	4	8†	1	86	20	12.28	–	–	3	–	692	340	6	84.00	3–37	0	0
O'Donnell, S.P.	1985	6	10	3	206	48	29.42	–	–	4	–	940	504					
Ogilvie, A.D.	1977–78	5	10	0	178	47	17.80	–	–	5	–	–	–					
O'Keefe, S.N.J.	2014–15	9	13	4	86	25	9.55	–	1	–	–	2228†	1029	35	29.40	6–35	2	1
O'Keeffe, K.J.	1970–71	24	34	9	644	85	25.76	–	–	15	–	5384	2018	53	38.07	5–101	1	0
Oldfield, W.A.S.	1920–21	54	80	17	1427	65*	22.65	–	4	78	52	–	–					
O'Neill, N.C.L.	1958–59	42	69	8	2779	181	45.55	6	15	21	–	1392	667	17	39.23	4–41	0	0
O'Reilly, W.J.	1931–32	27	39†	7	410	56*	12.81	–	1	7	–	10024	3254	144	22.59	7–54	11	3
Oxenham, R.K.	1928–29	7	10	0	151	48	15.10	–	–	4	–	1802	522	14	37.28	4–39	0	0
Paine, T.D.	2019	26	45	8	1164	92	31.45	–	6	107	5	–	–					
Palmer, G.E.	1880	17	25	4	296	48	14.09	–	–	13	–	4517	1678	78	21.51	7–65	6	2
Park, R.L.	1920–21	1	1	0	0	0	0.00	–	–	–	–	6	9	0	–	–	–	–
Pascoe, L.S.	1977	14	19	9	106	30*	10.60	–	–	2	–	3403	1668	64	26.06	5–59	1	0
Patterson, K.R.	2018–19	2	2†	1	144	114*	144.00	1	–	6	–	–	–					
Pattinson, J.L.	2011–12	19	23†	8	401	47*	26.73	–	–	5	–	3669	1998	75	26.64	5–27	4	0
Pellew, C.E.	1920–21	10	14	1	484	116	37.23	2	1	4	–	78	34	0	–	–	–	–
Phillips, W.B.	1983–84	27	48†	2	1485	159	32.28	2	7	52	–	–	–					
Phillips, W.N.	1991–92	1	2	0	22	14	11.00	–	–	–	–	–	–					
Philpott, P.I.	1965–66	8	10	1	93	22	10.33	–	–	5	–	2262	1000	26	38.46	5–90	1	0
Ponsford, W.H.	1934	29	48	4	2122	266	48.22	7	6	21	–	–	–					
Ponting, R.T.	2012–13	168	287	29	13378	257	51.85	41	62	196	–	587	276	5	55.20	1–0	0	0
Pope, R.J.	1884–85	1	2	0	3	3	1.50	–	–	–	–	–	–					
Quiney, R.J.	2012–13	2	3†	0	9	9	3.00	–	–	5	–	150	29	0	–	–	–	–
Rackemann, C.G.	1982–83	12	14	4	53	15*	5.30	–	–	2	–	2719	1137	39	29.15	6–86	3	1
Ransford, V.S.	1907–08	20	38†	6	1211	143*	37.84	1	7	10	–	43†	28	1	28.00	1–9	0	0
Redpath, I.R.	1963–64	66	120	11	4737	171	43.45	8	31	83	–	64	41	0	–	–	–	–
Reedman, J.C.	1894–95	1	2	0	21	17	10.50	–	–	1	–	57	24	1	24.00	1–12	0	0
Reid, B.A.	1985–86	27	34†	14	93	13	4.65	–	–	5	–	6244†	2784	113	24.63	7–51	5	2
Reiffel, P.R.	1991–92	35	50	14	955	79*	26.52	–	6	15	–	6403	2804	104	26.96	6–71	5	0
Renneberg, D.A.	1966–67	8	13	7	22	9	3.66	–	3	2	–	1598	830	23	36.08	5–39	2	0
Renshaw, M.T.	2016–17	11	20†	1	636	184	33.47	1	2	8	–	24	13	0	–	–	–	–
Richardson, A.J.	1924–25	9	13	0	403	100	31.00	1	–	1	–	1812	521	12	43.41	2–20	0	0
Richardson, J.A.	2018–19	2	1†	0	1	1	1.00	–	1	–	–	306	123	6	20.50	3–26	0	0
Richardson, V.Y.	1924–25	19	30	0	706	138	23.53	1	1	24	–	–	–					
Rigg, K.E.	1930–31	8	12	0	401	127	33.41	1	1	5	–	–	–					

INDIVIDUAL TEST CAREER RECORDS – AUSTRALIA (Continued)

	First Test	Last Test	Tests	Inns	NO	Runs	HS	Avge	100	50	Ct	St	Balls	Runs	Wkts	Avge	BB	5wI	10wM
Ring, D.T.	1947–48	1953	13	21	2	426	67	22.42	–	4	5	–	3024	1305	35	37.28	6-72	2	0
Ritchie, G.M.	1982–83	1986–87	30	53	5	1690	146	35.20	3	7	14	–	6	10	0	–	–	–	–
Rixon, S.J.	1977–78	1984–85	13	24	3	394	54	18.76	–	2	42	5	–	–	–	–	–	–	–
Robertson, G.R.	1997–98	1998–99	4	7	0	140	57	20.00	–	1	1	–	898	515	13	39.61	4-72	0	0
Robertson, W.R.	1884–85	1884–85	1	2	0	2	2	1.00	–	–	–	–	44	24	0	–	–	–	–
Robinson, R.D.	1977	1977	3	6	0	100	34	16.66	–	–	4	–	–	–	–	–	–	–	–
Robinson, R.H.	1936–37	1936–37	1	2	0	5	3	2.50	–	–	1	–	–	–	–	–	–	–	–
Rogers, C.J.L.	2007–08	2015	25	48†	1	2015	173	42.87	5	14	15	–	–	–	–	–	–	–	–
Rorke, G.F.	1958–59	1959–60	4	4†	2	9	7	4.50	–	–	1	–	703	203	10	20.30	3-23	0	0
Rutherford, J.W.	1956–57	1956–57	1	1	0	30	30	30.00	–	–	–	–	36	15	1	15.00	1-11	0	0
Ryder, J.	1920–21	1928–29	20	32	5	1394	201*	51.62	3	9	17	–	1897	743	17	43.70	2-20	0	0
Saggers, R.A.	1948	1949–50	6	5	2	30	14	10.00	–	–	16	8	–	–	–	–	–	–	–
Saunders, J.V.	1901–02	1907–08	14	23†	6	39	11*	2.29	–	–	5	–	3565†	1796	79	22.73	7-34	6	0
Sayers, C.J.	2017–18	2017–18	1	2	0	0	0	0.00	–	–	1	–	294	146	2	73.00	2-78	0	0
Scott, H.J.H.	1884	1886	8	14	1	359	102	27.61	1	1	8	–	28	26	0	–	–	–	–
Sellers, R.H.D.	1964–65	1964–65	1	1	0	0	0	0.00	–	–	1	–	30	17	0	–	–	–	–
Serjeant, C.S.	1977	1977–78	12	23	1	522	124	23.72	1	2	13	–	–	–	–	–	–	–	–
Sheahan, A.P.	1967–68	1973–74	31	53	6	1594	127	33.91	2	7	17	–	–	–	–	–	–	–	–
Shepherd, B.K.	1962–63	1964–65	9	14†	2	502	96	41.83	–	5	2	–	26	9	0	–	–	–	–
Siddle, P.M.	2008–09	2019	67	94	15	1164	51	14.73	–	2	19	–	13907	6777	221	30.66	6-54	8	0
Sievers, M.W.	1936–37	1936–37	3	6	1	67	25*	13.40	–	–	4	–	602	161	9	17.88	5-21	1	0
Simpson, R.B.	1957–58	1977–78	62	111	7	4869	311	46.81	10	27	110	–	6881	3001	71	42.26	5-57	2	0
Sincock, D.J.	1964–65	1965–66	3	4	1	80	29	26.66	–	–	2	–	724†	410	8	51.25	3-67	0	0
Slater, K.N.	1958–59	1958–59	1	1	1	1	1*	–	–	–	–	–	256	101	2	50.50	2-40	0	0
Slater, M.J.	1993	2001	74	131	7	5312	219	42.83	14	21	33	–	25	10	1	10.00	1-4	0	0
Sleep, P.R.	1978–79	1989–90	14	21	1	483	90	24.15	–	3	4	–	2982	1397	31	45.06	5-72	1	0
Slight, J.	1880	1880	1	2	0	11	11	5.50	–	–	–	–	–	–	–	–	–	–	–
Smith, D.B.M.	1912	1912	2	3	1	30	24*	15.00	–	–	1	–	–	–	–	–	–	–	–
Smith, S.B.	1983–84	1983–84	3	5	0	41	12	8.20	–	–	–	–	–	–	–	–	–	–	–
Smith, S.P.D.	2010	2019	68	124	16	6973	239	64.56	26	27	108	–	1369	948	17	55.76	3-18	0	0
Spofforth, F.R.	1876–77	1886–87	18	29	6	217	50	9.43	–	1	11	–	4185	1731	94	18.41	7-44	7	4
Stackpole, K.R.	1965–66	1973–74	43	80	5	2807	207	37.42	7	14	47	–	2321	1001	15	66.73	2-33	0	0
Starc, M.A.	2011–12	2019	52	80†	17	1434	99	22.76	–	10	25	–	10760†	6077	215	28.26	6-50	11	2
Stevens, G.B.	1959–60	1959–60	4	7	0	112	28	16.00	–	–	2	–	–	–	–	–	–	–	–

Symonds, A.	2003–04	26	41	5	1462	162*	40.61	2	10	22	–	2094	896	24	37.33	3–50	0	0	0
Taber, H.B.	1966–67	16	27	5	353	48	16.04	–	–	56	4	–	–	–	–	–	0	0	0
Tait, S.W.	2005	3	5	2	20	8	6.66	–	–	1	–	414	302	5	60.40	3–97	0	0	0
Tallon, D.	1945–46	21	26	3	394	92	17.13	–	2	50	8	–	–	–	–	–	0	0	0
Taylor, J.M.	1920–21	20	28	0	997	108	35.60	1	8	11	–	114	45	1	45.00	1–25	0	0	0
Taylor, M.A.	1988–89	104	186†	13	7525	334*	43.49	19	40	157	–	42	26	1	26.00	1–11	0	0	0
Taylor, P.L.	1986–87	13	19†	3	431	87	26.93	–	2	10	–	2227	1068	27	39.55	6–78	0	1	0
Thomas, G.	1964–65	8	12	1	325	61	29.54	–	3	3	–	–	–	–	–	–	–	–	–
Thoms, G.R.	1951–52	1	2	0	44	28	22.00	–	–	–	–	–	–	–	–	–	–	–	–
Thomson, A.L.	1970–71	4	5	4	22	12*	22.00	–	–	–	–	1519	654	12	54.50	3–79	0	0	0
Thomson, J.R.	1972–73	51	73	20	679	49	12.81	–	–	20	–	10535	5601	200	28.00	6–46	8	8	0
Thomson, N.F.D.	1876–77	2	4	0	67	41	16.75	–	–	3	–	112	31	0	31.00	1–14	0	0	–
Thurlow, H.M.	1931–32	1	1	0	0	0	0.00	–	–	–	–	234	86	0	–	–	–	–	–
Toohey, P.M.	1977–80	15	29	1	893	122	31.89	1	7	9	–	2	4	0	–	–	–	–	–
Toshack, E.R.H.	1945–46	12	11	6	73	20*	14.60	–	–	4	–	3140†	989	47	21.04	6–29	4	1	–
Travers, J.P.F.	1901–02	1	2†	0	10	9	5.00	–	–	1	–	48†	14	1	14.00	1–14	0	0	–
Tribe, G.E.	1946–47	3	3†	1	35	25*	17.50	–	–	–	–	760†	330	2	165.00	2–48	0	0	–
Trott, A.E.‡	1894–95	3	5	3	205	85*	102.50	–	2	4	–	474	192	9	21.33	8–43	1	0	–
Trott, G.H.S.	1888	24	42	0	921	143	21.92	1	4	21	–	1891	1019	29	35.13	4–71	0	0	–
Trumble, H.	1890	32	57	14	851	70	19.79	–	4	45	–	8099	3072	141	21.78	8–65	9	3	–
Trumble, J.W.	1884–85	7	13	1	243	59	20.25	–	1	3	–	600	222	10	22.20	3–29	0	0	–
Trumper, V.T.	1899	48	89	8	3163	214*	39.04	8	13	31	–	546	317	8	39.62	3–60	0	0	–
Turner, A.	1975	14	27†	1	768	136	29.53	1	3	15	–	–	–	–	–	–	–	–	–
Turner, C.T.B.	1886–87	17	32	4	323	29	11.53	–	–	8	–	5179	1670	101	16.53	7–43	11	2	–
Veivers, T.R.	1963–64	21	30†	4	813	88	31.26	–	7	7	–	4191	1375	33	41.66	4–68	0	0	–
Veletta, M.R.J.	1987–88	8	11	0	207	39	18.81	–	–	12	–	–	–	–	–	–	–	–	–
Voges, A.C.	2016–17	20	31	7	1485	269*	61.87	5	4	15	–	76†	44	0	–	–	–	–	–
Wade, M.S.	2011–12	27	48†	7	1223	117	29.82	4	4	66	11	12	7	0	–	–	–	–	–
Waite, M.G.	1938	2	3	0	11	8	3.66	–	–	1	–	552	190	1	190.00	1–150	0	0	–
Walker, M.H.N.	1972–73	34	43	13	586	78*	19.53	–	1	12	–	10094	3792	138	27.47	8–143	6	6	–
Wall, T.W.	1928–29	18	24	5	121	20	6.36	–	–	11	–	4812	2010	56	35.89	5–14	3	0	–
Walters, F.H.	1884–85	1	2	0	12	7	6.00	–	–	2	–	–	–	–	–	–	–	–	–
Walters, K.D.	1965–66	74	125	14	5357	250	48.26	15	33	43	–	3295	1425	49	29.08	5–66	1	0	–
Ward, F.A.	1936–37	4	8	2	36	18	6.00	–	–	1	–	1268	574	11	52.18	6–102	1	1	–
Warne, S.K.	1991–92	145	199	17	3154	99	17.32	–	12	125	–	40704	17995	708	25.41	8–71	37	10	–
Warner, D.A.	2011–12	79	147†	5	6458	253	45.47	21	30	62	–	342	269	4	67.25	2–45	0	0	–
Watkins, J.R.	1972–73	1	2	1	39	36	39.00	–	–	1	–	48	21	0	–	–	–	–	–

INDIVIDUAL TEST CAREER RECORDS – AUSTRALIA (Continued)

	First Test	Last Test	Tests	Inns	NO	Runs	HS	Avge	100	50	Ct	St	Balls	Runs	Wkts	Avge	BB	5wI	10wM
Watson, G.D.	1966-67	1972	5	9	0	97	50	10.77	–	1	1	–	552	254	6	42.33	2-67	0	0
Watson, S.R.	2004-05	2015	59	109	3	3731	176	35.19	4	24	45	–	5495	2526	75	33.68	6-33	3	0
Watson, W.J.	1954-55	1954-55	4	7	1	106	30	17.66	–	–	2	–	6	5	0	–	–	–	–
Waugh, M.E.	1990-91	2002-03	128	209	17	8029	153*	41.81	20	47	181	–	4853	2429	59	41.16	5-40	1	0
Waugh, S.R.	1985-86	2003-04	168	260	46	10927	200	51.06	32	50	112	–	7805	3445	92	37.44	5-28	3	0
Wellham, D.M.	1981	1986-87	6	11	0	257	103	23.36	1	–	5	–	–	–	–	–	–	–	–
Wessels, K.C.‡	1982-83	1985-86	24	42†	1	1761	179	42.95	4	9	18	–	90	42	0	–	–	0	0
Whatmore, D.F.	1978-79	1979-80	7	13	0	293	77	22.53	–	2	13	–	30	11	0	–	–	0	0
White, C.L.	2008-09	2008-09	4	7	2	146	46	29.20	–	–	1	–	558	342	5	68.40	2-71	0	0
Whitney, M.R.	1981	1992-93	12	19	8	68	13	6.18	–	–	2	–	2672†	1325	39	33.97	7-27	2	1
Whitty, W.J.	1909	1912	14	19	7	161	39*	13.41	–	–	4	–	3357†	1373	65	21.12	6-17	3	0
Wiener, J.M.	1979-80	1979-80	6	11	0	281	93	25.54	–	2	4	–	78	41	0	–	–	–	–
Williams, B.A.	2003-04	2003-04	4	6	3	23	10*	7.66	–	–	4	–	852	406	9	45.11	4-53	0	0
Wilson, J.W.	1956-57	1956-57	1	–	–	–	–	–	–	–	–	–	216†	64	1	64.00	1-25	0	0
Wilson, P.	1997-98	1997-98	1	2	2	0	0*	–	–	–	–	–	72	50	0	–	–	–	–
Wood, G.M.	1977-78	1988-89	59	112†	6	3374	172	31.83	9	13	41	–	–	–	–	–	–	–	–
Woodcock, A.J.	1973-74	1973-74	1	1	0	27	27	27.00	–	–	1	–	–	–	–	–	–	–	–
Woodfull, W.M.	1926	1934	35	54	4	2300	161	46.00	7	13	7	–	–	–	–	–	–	–	–
Woods, S.M.J.‡	1888	1888	3	6	0	32	18	5.33	–	–	1	–	217	121	5	24.20	2-35	0	0
Woolley, R.D.	1982-83	1983-84	2	2	0	21	13	10.50	–	–	7	4	–	–	–	–	–	–	–
Worrall, J.	1884-85	1899	11	22	3	478	76	25.15	–	5	13	–	255	127	1	127.00	1-97	0	0
Wright, K.J.	1978-79	1979-80	10	18	5	219	55*	16.84	–	1	31	4	–	–	–	–	–	–	–
Yallop, G.N.	1975-76	1984-85	39	70†	3	2756	268	41.13	8	9	23	–	192†	116	1	116.00	1-21	0	0
Yardley, B.	1977-78	1982-83	33	54	4	978	74	19.56	–	4	31	–	8909	3986	126	31.63	7-98	6	1
Young, S.	1997	1997	1	2†	1	4	4*	4.00	–	–	–	–	48	13	0	–	–	–	–
Zoehrer, T.J.	1985-86	1986-87	10	14	2	246	52*	20.50	–	1	18	1	–	–	–	–	–	–	–

INDIVIDUAL TEST CAREER RECORDS – SOUTH AFRICA

	First Test	Last Test	Tests	Inns	NO	Runs	HS	Avge	100	50	Ct	St	Balls	Runs	Wkts	Avge	BB	5wI	10wM
Abbott, K.J.	2012-13	2016-17	11	14	0	95	17	6.78	–	–	4	–	2081	886	39	22.71	7-29	3	0
Ackerman, H.D.	1997-98	1997-98	4	8	0	161	57	20.12	–	1	1	–	–	–	–	–	–	–	–
Adams, P.R.	1995-96	2003-04	45	55	15	360	35	9.00	–	–	29	–	8850†	4405	134	32.87	7-128	4	1
Adcock, N.A.T.	1953-54	1961-62	26	39	12	146	24	5.40	–	–	4	–	6391	2195	104	21.10	6-43	5	0
Amla, H.M.	2004-05	2018-19	124	215	16	9282	311*	46.64	28	41	108	–	54	37	0	–	–	–	–
Anderson, J.H.	1902-03	1902-03	1	2	0	43	32	21.50	–	–	1	–	–	–	–	–	–	–	–
Ashley, W.H.	1888-89	1888-89	1	2†	1	1	1	0.50	–	–	–	–	173†	95	7	13.57	7-95	1	0
Bacher, A.	1965	1969-70	12	22	1	679	73	32.33	–	6	10	–	–	–	–	–	–	–	–
Bacher, A.M.	1996-97	1999-00	19	33	1	833	96	26.03	–	5	11	–	6	4	0	–	–	–	–
Balaskas, X.C.	1930-31	1938-39	9	13	1	174	122*	14.50	1	–	5	–	1572	806	22	36.63	5-49	1	0
Barlow, E.J.	1961-62	1969-70	30	57	2	2516	201	45.74	6	15	35	–	3021	1362	40	34.05	5-85	1	0
Baumgartner, H.V.	1913-14	1913-14	1	2	0	19	16	9.50	–	–	1	–	166†	99	2	49.50	2-99	0	0
Bavuma, T.	2014-15	2018-19	36	59	7	1716	102*	33.00	1	13	16	–	96	61	1	61.00	1-29	0	0
Beaumont, R.	1912	1913-14	5	9	0	70	31	7.77	–	–	2	–	6	0	0	–	–	–	–
Begbie, D.W.	1948-49	1949-50	5	7	0	138	48	19.71	–	–	2	–	160	130	1	130.00	1-38	0	0
Bell, A.J.	1929	1935	16	23	12	69	26*	6.27	–	–	6	–	3342	1567	48	32.64	6-99	4	0
Bisset, M.	1898-99	1909-10	3	6	2	103	35	25.75	–	–	2	1	–	–	–	–	–	–	–
Bissett, G.F.	1927-28	1927-28	4	4	2	38	23	19.00	–	–	–	–	989	469	25	18.76	7-29	2	0
Blanckenberg, J.M.	1913-14	1924	18	30	7	455	59	19.78	–	2	9	–	3888	1817	60	30.28	6-76	4	0
Bland, K.C.	1961-62	1966-67	21	39	5	1669	144*	49.08	3	9	10	–	394	125	2	62.50	2-16	0	0
Bock, E.G.	1935-36	1935-36	1	2	2	11	9*	–	–	–	–	–	138	91	0	–	–	–	–
Boje, N.	1999-00	2006	43	62†	10	1312	85	25.23	–	4	18	–	8620†	4265	100	42.65	5-62	3	0
Bond, G.E.	1938-39	1938-39	1	1	0	0	0	0.00	–	–	–	–	16	16	0	–	–	–	–
Bosch, T.	1991-92	1991-92	1	2	2	5	5*	–	–	–	–	–	237	104	3	34.66	2-61	0	0
Botha, J.	2005-06	2010-11	5	6	2	83	25	20.75	–	–	3	–	1017	573	17	33.70	4-56	0	0
Botten, J.T.	1965	1965	3	6	0	65	33	10.83	–	–	1	–	828	337	8	42.12	2-56	0	0
Boucher, M.V.‡	1997-98	2011-12	146	204	24	5498	125	30.54	5	35	530	23	8	6	1	6.00	1-6	0	0
Brann, W.H.	1922-23	1922-23	3	5	0	71	50	14.20	–	1	2	–	–	–	–	–	–	–	–
Briscoe, A.W.	1935-36	1938-39	2	3	0	33	16	11.00	–	–	1	–	–	–	–	–	–	–	–
Bromfield, H.D.	1961-62	1965	9	12	7	59	21	11.80	–	–	13	–	1810	599	17	35.23	5-88	1	0
Brown, L.S.	1931-32	1931-32	2	3	0	17	8	5.66	–	–	–	–	318	189	3	63.00	1-30	0	0
Burger, C.G.D.	1957-58	1957-58	2	4	1	62	37*	20.66	–	–	1	–	–	–	–	–	–	–	–
Burke, S.F.	1961-62	1964-65	2	4	1	42	20	14.00	–	–	–	–	660	257	11	23.36	6-128	2	1
Buys, I.D.	1922-23	1922-23	1	2†	1	4	4*	4.00	–	–	–	–	144†	52	0	–	–	–	–

INDIVIDUAL TEST CAREER RECORDS – SOUTH AFRICA (Continued)

	First Test	Last Test	Tests	Inns	NO	Runs	HS	Avge	100	50	Ct	St	Balls	Runs	Wkts	Avge	BB	5wI	10wM
Cameron, H.B.	1927-28	1935	26	45	4	1239	90	30.21	–	10	39	12	–						
Campbell, T.	1909-10	1912	5	9	3	90	48	15.00	–	–	7	1	–						
Carlstein, P.R.	1957-58	1963-64	8	14	1	190	42	14.61	–	–	3	–	–						
Carter, C.P.	1912	1924	10	15	5	181	45	18.10	–	–	2	–	1475†	694	28	24.78	6-50	2	0
Catterall, R.H.	1922-23	1930-31	24	43	2	1555	120	37.92	3	11	12	–	342	162	7	23.14	3-15	0	0
Chapman, H.W.	1913-14	1921-22	2	4	1	39	17	13.00	–	–	1	–	126	104	1	104.00	1-51	0	0
Cheetham, J.E.	1948-49	1955	24	43	6	883	89	23.86	–	5	13	–	6	2	0	–	–	–	–
Chevalier, G.A.	1969-70	1969-70	1	2	2	0	0*	0.00	–	–	1	–	253†	100	5	20.00	3-68	0	0
Christy, J.A.J.	1929	1931-32	10	18	0	618	103	34.33	1	5	3	–	138	92	2	46.00	1-15	0	0
Chubb, G.W.A.	1951	1951	5	9	3	63	15*	10.50	–	–	–	–	1425	577	21	27.47	6-51	2	0
Cochran, J.A.K.	1930-31	1930-31	1	1	0	4	4	4.00	–	–	–	–	138	47	0	–	–	–	–
Coen, S.K.	1927-28	1927-28	2	4	2	101	41*	50.50	–	–	1	–	12	7	0	–	–	–	–
Commaille, J.M.M.	1909-10	1927-28	12	22	1	355	47	16.90	–	–	1	–	–						
Commins, J.B.	1994-95	1994-95	3	6	1	125	45	25.00	–	–	2	–	–						
Conyngham, D.P.	1922-23	1922-23	1	2	2	6	3*	–	–	–	1	–	366	103	2	51.50	1-40	0	–
Cook, F.J.	1895-96	1895-96	1	2	0	7	7	3.50	–	–	–	–	–						
Cook, S.C.	2015-16	2016-17	11	19	0	632	117	33.26	3	2	6	–	12	16	0	–	–	–	–
Cook, S.J.	1992-93	1993	3	6	0	107	43	17.83	–	–	–	–	–						
Cooper, A.H.C.	1913-14	1913-14	1	2	0	6	6	3.00	–	–	1	–	–						
Cox, J.L.	1913-14	1913-14	3	6	1	17	12*	3.40	–	–	1	–	576	245	4	61.25	2-74	0	0
Cripps, G.	1891-92	1891-92	1	2	0	21	18	10.50	–	–	–	–	15	23	0	–	–	–	–
Crisp, R.J.	1935	1935-36	9	13	1	123	35	10.25	–	–	3	–	1429	747	20	37.35	5-99	1	0
Cronje, W.J.	1991-92	1999-00	68	111	9	3714	135	36.41	6	23	33	–	3800	1288	43	29.95	3-14	0	0
Cullinan, D.J.	1992-93	2000-01	70	115	12	4554	275*	44.21	14	20	67	–	120	71	2	35.50	1-10	0	0
Curnow, S.H.	1930-31	1931-32	7	14	0	168	47	12.00	–	–	5	–	–						
Dalton, E.L.	1929	1938-39	15	24	2	698	117	31.72	2	3	5	–	864	490	12	40.83	4-59	0	0
Davies, E.Q.	1935-36	1938-39	5	8†	3	9	3	1.80	–	–	–	–	768	481	7	68.71	4-75	0	0
Dawson, A.C.	2003	2003	2	1	0	10	10	10.00	–	–	–	–	252	117	5	23.40	2-20	0	0
Dawson, O.C.	1947	1948-49	9	15	1	293	55	20.92	–	1	10	–	1294	578	10	57.80	2-57	0	0
Deane, H.G.	1924	1930-31	17	27	2	628	93	25.12	–	3	8	–	–						
de Bruyn, T.B.	2016-17	2018-19	9	18	1	346	101	20.35	1	–	10	–	102	74	0	–	–	–	0
de Bruyn, Z.	2004-05	2004-05	3	5	1	155	83	38.75	–	1	–	–	216	92	3	30.66	2-32	0	0
de Kock, Q.	2013-14	2018-19	40	66†	5	2398	129*	39.31	4	17	166	9	–						
de Lange, M.	2011-12	2011-12	2	2	0	9	9	4.50	–	–	1	–	448	277	9	30.77	7-81	1	0

Player	Debut	Last	M	I	NO	Runs	HS	Avg	100	50	Ct	St	Balls	Runs	Wkts	Avg	BB	5w	10w
de Villiers, A.B.	2004-05	2017-18	114	191	18	8765	278*	50.66	22	46	222	5	204	104	2	52.00	2-49	0	0
de Villiers, P.S.	1993-94	1997-98	18	26	7	359	67*	18.89	—	2	11	—	4805	2063	85	24.27	6-23	5	2
de Wet, F.	2009-10	2009-10	2	2	0	20	20	10.00	—	—	1	—	426	186	6	31.00	4-55	0	0
Dippenaar, H.H.	1999-00	2006-07	38	62	5	1718	177*	30.14	3	7	27	—	12	1	0	—	—	—	—
Dixon, C.D.	1913-14	1913-14	1	2	0	0	0	0.00	—	—	1	—	240	118	3	39.33	2-62	0	0
Donald, A.A.	1991-92	2001-02	72	94	33	652	37	10.68	—	—	18	—	15519	7344	330	22.25	8-71	20	3
Dower, R.R.	1898-99	1898-99	1	2	0	9	9	4.50	—	—	2	—	—	—	—	—	—	—	—
Draper, R.G.	1949-50	1949-50	2	3	0	25	15	8.33	—	—	3	—	—	—	—	—	—	—	—
Duckworth, C.A.R.	1956-57	1956-57	2	4	0	28	13	7.00	—	—	—	—	—	—	—	—	—	—	—
Dumbrill, R.	1965	1966-67	5	10	0	153	36	15.30	—	—	3	—	816	336	9	37.33	4-30	0	0
Duminy, J.P.	1927-28	1929	3	6†	0	30	12	5.00	—	—	2	—	60†	39	1	39.00	1-17	0	0
Duminy, J-P.	2008-09	2017	46	74†	10	2103	166	32.85	6	8	38	—	2703	1601	42	38.11	4-47	0	0
Dunell, O.R.	1888-89	1888-89	2	4	1	42	26*	14.00	—	—	1	—	—	—	—	—	—	—	—
du Plessis, F.	2012-13	2018-19	58	98	14	3608	137	42.95	9	19	53	—	78	69	0	—	2-22	—	0
du Preez, J.H.	1966-67	1966-67	2	2	0	0	0	0.00	—	—	2	—	144	51	3	17.00	—	—	—
Dyer, D.V.	1947	1947	3	6	0	96	62	16.00	—	1	—	—	—	—	—	—	—	—	—
Eksteen, C.E.	1993	1999-00	7	11	2	91	22	10.11	—	—	5	—	1536†	494	8	61.75	3-12	0	0
Elgar, D.	2012-13	2018-19	56	96†	8	3412	199	38.77	11	13	59	—	987†	623	14	44.50	4-22	0	0
Elgie, M.K.	1961-62	1961-62	3	6	0	75	56	12.50	—	1	4	—	66†	46	0	—	—	—	—
Elworthy, S.	1998	2002-03	4	5	1	72	48	18.00	—	—	1	—	867	444	13	34.15	4-66	0	0
Endean, W.R.	1951	1957-58	28	52	4	1630	162*	33.95	3	8	41	2	—	—	—	—	—	—	—
Farrer, W.S.	1961-62	1963-64	6	10	2	221	40	27.62	—	—	2	—	—	—	—	—	—	—	—
Faulkner, G.A.	1905-06	1924	25	47	4	1754	204	40.79	4	8	20	—	4227	2180	82	26.58	7-84	4	—
Fellows-Smith, J.P.	1960	1960	4	8	2	166	35	27.66	—	—	2	—	114	61	0	—	—	—	—
Fichardt, C.G.	1891-92	1895-96	2	4	0	15	10	3.75	—	—	2	—	—	—	—	—	—	—	—
Finlason, C.E.	1888-89	1888-89	1	2	0	6	6	3.00	—	—	—	—	12	7	0	—	—	0	0
Floquet, C.E.	1909-10	1909-10	1	2	1	12	11*	12.00	—	—	—	—	48	24	0	—	—	—	—
Francis, H.H.	1898-99	1898-99	2	4	0	39	29	9.75	—	—	1	—	—	—	—	—	—	—	—
Francois, C.M.	1922-23	1922-23	5	9	1	252	72	31.50	—	1	5	—	684	225	6	37.50	3-23	0	0
Frank, C.N.	1921-22	1921-22	3	6	0	236	152	39.33	1	—	—	—	—	—	—	—	—	—	—
Frank, W.H.B.	1895-96	1895-96	1	2	0	7	5	3.50	—	—	—	—	58	52	1	52.00	1-52	0	0
Fuller, E.R.H.	1952-53	1957-58	7	9	2	64	17	8.00	—	—	3	—	1898	668	22	30.36	5-66	1	0
Fullerton, G.M.	1947	1951	7	13	0	325	88	25.00	—	3	10	2	—	—	—	—	—	—	—
Funston, K.J.	1952-53	1957-58	18	33	1	824	92	25.75	—	5	7	—	—	—	—	—	—	—	—
Gamsy, D.	1969-70	1969-70	2	3	1	39	30*	19.50	—	—	5	—	—	—	—	—	—	—	—
Gibbs, H.H.	1996-97	2007-08	90	154	7	6167	228	41.95	14	26	94	—	6	4	0	—	—	—	—
Gleeson, R.A.	1895-96	1895-96	1	2	1	4	3	4.00	—	—	2	—	—	—	—	—	—	—	—
Glover, G.K.	1895-96	1895-96	1	2	1	21	18*	21.00	—	—	—	—	65	28	1	28.00	1-28	0	0

INDIVIDUAL TEST CAREER RECORDS – SOUTH AFRICA (Continued)

	First Test	Last Test	Tests	Inns	NO	Runs	HS	Avge	100	50	Ct	St	Balls	Runs	Wkts	Avge	BB	5wI	10wM
Goddard, T.L.	1955	1969–70	41	78†	5	2516	112	34.46	1	18	48	–	11736†	3226	123	26.22	6–53	5	0
Gordon, N.	1938–39	1938–39	5	6	2	8	7*	2.00	–	–	1	–	1966	807	20	40.35	5–103	2	0
Graham, R.	1898–99	1898–99	2	4	0	6	4	1.50	–	–	2	–	240	127	3	42.33	2–22	0	0
Grieveson, R.E.	1938–39	1938–39	2	2	0	114	75	57.00	–	1	7	3	–						
Griffin, G.M.	1960	1960	2	4	0	25	14	6.25	–	–	–	–	432	192	8	24.00	4–87	0	0
Hall, A.E.	1922–23	1930–31	7	8†	2	11	5	1.83	–	–	4	–	2361†	886	40	22.15	7–63	3	1
Hall, A.J.	2001–02	2006–07	21	33	4	760	163	26.20	1	3	16	–	3001	1617	45	35.93	3–1	0	0
Hall, G.G.	1964–65	1964–65	1	1	0	0	0	0.00	–	–	–	–	186	94	1	94.00	1–94	0	0
Halliwell, E.A.	1891–92	1902–03	8	15	0	188	57	12.53	–	1	10	2	–						
Halse, C.G.	1963–64	1963–64	3	3	3	30	19*	–	–	–	1	–	587	260	6	43.33	3–50	0	0
Hamza, M.Z.	2018–19	2018–19	1	2	0	41	41	20.50	–	–	2	–	–						
Hands, P.A.M.	1913–14	1924	7	12	0	300	83	25.00	–	2	3	–	37	18	0	–	–	–	–
Hands, R.H.M.	1913–14	1913–14	1	2	0	7	7	3.50	–	–	–	–	–						
Hanley, M.A.	1948–49	1948–49	1	1	1	0	0*	–	–	–	–	–	232	88	1	88.00	1–57	0	0
Harmer, S.R.	2014–15	2015–16	5	6	1	58	13	11.60	–	–	1	–	1148	588	20	29.40	4–61	0	0
Harris, P.L.	2006–07	2010–11	37	48	5	460	46	10.69	–	–	16	–	8809†	3901	103	37.87	6–127	3	0
Harris, T.A.	1947	1948–49	3	5	1	100	60	25.00	–	1	1	–	–						
Hartigan, G.P.D.	1912	1913–14	5	10	0	114	51	11.40	–	–	–	–	252	141	1	141.00	1–72	0	0
Harvey, R.L.	1935–36	1935–36	2	4	0	51	28	12.75	–	–	–	–	–						
Hathorn, C.M.H.	1902–03	1910–11	12	20	1	325	102	17.10	1	–	5	–	–						
Hayward, M.	1999–00	2004	16	17	8	66	14	7.33	–	–	4	–	2821	1609	54	29.79	5–56	1	0
Hearne, F.‡	1891–92	1895–96	4	8	0	121	30	15.12	–	–	2	–	62	40	2	20.00	2–40	0	0
Hearne, G.A.L.	1922–23	1924	3	5	0	59	28	11.80	–	–	3	–	–						
Heine, P.S.	1955	1961–62	14	24	3	209	31	9.95	–	–	8	–	3890	1455	58	25.08	6–58	4	0
Henderson, C.W.	2001–02	2002–03	7	7	0	65	30	9.28	–	–	2	–	1962†	928	22	42.18	4–116	0	0
Henry, O.	1992–93	1992–93	3	3†	0	53	34	17.66	–	–	2	–	427†	189	3	63.00	2–56	0	0
Hime, C.F.W.	1895–96	1895–96	1	2	0	8	8	4.00	–	–	–	–	55	31	1	31.00	1–20	0	0
Hudson, A.C.	1991–92	1997–98	35	63	3	2007	163	33.45	4	13	36	–	–						
Hutchinson, P.	1888–89	1888–89	2	4	0	14	11	3.50	–	–	3	–	–						
Imran Tahir	2011–12	2015–16	20	23	9	130	29*	9.28	–	–	8	–	3925	2294	57	40.24	5–32	2	0
Ironside, D.E.J.	1953–54	1953–54	3	4	2	37	13	18.50	–	–	1	–	986	275	15	18.33	5–51	1	0
Irvine, B.L.	1969–70	1969–70	4	7†	0	353	102	50.42	1	2	2	–	–						
Jack, S.D.	1994–95	1994–95	2	2	0	7	7	3.50	–	–	2	–	462	196	8	24.50	4–69	0	0
Johnson, C.L.	1895–96	1895–96	1	2	0	10	7	5.00	–	–	1	–	140	57	0	–	–	–	–

Kallis, J.H.‡	1995–96	2013–14	165	278	39	13206	224	55.25	45	58	196	–	20172	291	32.63	6–54	5	0
Keith, H.J.	1952–53	1956–57	8	16†	1	318	73	21.20	–	2	9	–	108†	0	–	–	–	–
Kemp, J.M.	2000–01	2005–06	4	6	0	80	55	13.33	–	1	3	–	479	9	24.66	3–33	0	0
Kempis, G.A.	1888–89	1888–89	1	2	1	0	0*	0.00	–	–	–	–	168†	4	19.00	3–53	0	0
Khan, I.	2008–09	2008–09	1	1†	0	20	20	20.00	–	–	1	–	–	–	–	–	–	–
Kirsten, G.	1993–94	2003–04	101	176†	15	7289	275	45.27	21	34	83	–	349	2	71.00	1–0	0	0
Kirsten, P.N.	1991–92	1994	12	22	2	626	104	31.30	1	4	8	–	54	0	–	–	–	–
Kleinveldt, R.K.	2012–13	2012–13	4	5	2	27	17*	9.00	–	–	2	–	667	10	42.20	3–65	0	0
Klusener, L.	1996–97	2004	49	69†	11	1906	174	32.86	4	8	34	–	6887	80	37.91	8–64	1	0
Kotze, J.J.	1902–03	1907	3	5	0	2	2	0.40	–	–	3	–	413	6	40.50	3–64	0	0
Kuhn, H.G.	2017	2017	4	8	0	113	34	14.12	–	–	1	–	–	–	–	–	–	–
Kuiper, A.P.	1991–92	1991–92	1	2	0	34	34	17.00	–	–	1	–	60	2	15.50	2–31	0	0
Kuys, F.	1898–99	1898–99	1	2	0	26	26	13.00	–	–	–	–	479	12	39.91	3–30	0	0
Lance, H.R.	1961–62	1969–70	13	22	1	591	70	28.14	–	5	7	–	948	16	37.06	5–46	1	0
Langeveldt, C.K.	2004–05	2005–06	6	4	2	16	10	8.00	–	–	2	–	999	16	37.06	5–46	1	0
Langton, A.C.B.	1935	1938–39	15	23	4	298	73*	15.68	–	2	8	–	4199	40	45.67	5–58	2	0
Lawrence, G.B.	1961–62	1961–62	5	8	0	141	43	17.62	–	–	2	–	1334	28	18.28	8–53	2	–
le Roux, F.L.	1913–14	1913–14	1	2	0	1	1	0.50	–	–	–	–	54	0	–	–	–	–
Lewis, P.T.	1913–14	1913–14	1	2	0	0	0	0.00	–	–	–	–	–	–	–	–	–	–
Liebenberg, G.F.J.	1997–98	1998	5	8	0	104	45	13.00	–	–	1	–	–	–	–	–	–	–
Lindsay, D.T.	1963–64	1969–70	19	31	1	1130	182	37.66	3	5	57	2	–	–	–	–	–	–
Lindsay, J.D.	1947	1947	3	5	2	21	9*	7.00	–	–	4	1	–	–	–	–	–	–
Lindsay, N.V.	1921–22	1921–22	1	2	0	35	29	17.50	–	–	1	–	–	–	–	–	–	–
Ling, W.V.S.	1921–22	1922–23	6	10	0	168	38	16.80	–	–	7	–	18	0	–	–	–	–
Llewellyn, C.B.	1895–96	1912	15	28†	1	544	90	20.14	–	4	7	–	2292†	48	29.60	6–92	4	1
Lundie, E.B.	1913–14	1913–14	1	2	1	1	1	1.00	–	–	–	–	286	4	26.75	4–101	0	0
Macaulay, M.J.	1964–65	1964–65	1	2	0	33	21	16.50	–	–	–	–	276†	2	36.50	1–10	0	0
McCarthy, C.N.	1948–49	1951	15	24	15	28	5	3.11	–	–	6	–	3499	36	41.94	6–43	2	0
McGlew, D.J.	1951	1961–62	34	64	6	2440	255*	42.06	7	10	18	–	32	0	–	–	–	–
McKenzie, N.D.	2000	2008–09	58	94	7	3253	226	37.39	5	16	54	–	90	0	–	–	–	–
McKinnon, A.H.	1960	1966–67	8	13	7	107	27	17.83	–	–	1	–	2546†	26	35.57	4–128	0	0
McLaren, R.	2009–10	2013–14	2	3†	1	47	33*	23.50	–	–	–	–	264	3	54.00	2–72	0	0
McLean, R.A.	1951	1964–65	40	73	3	2120	142	30.28	5	10	23	–	4	0	–	–	–	–
McMillan, B.M.	1992–93	1998	38	62	12	1968	113	39.36	3	13	49	–	6048	75	33.82	4–65	0	0
McMillan, Q.	1929	1931–32	13	21	4	306	50*	18.00	–	1	8	–	2021	36	34.52	5–66	2	0
Maharaj, K.A.	2016–17	2018–19	25	38	6	446	45	13.93	–	–	6	–	5028†	94	28.44	9–129	5	1
Mann, N.B.F.	1947	1951	19	31	1	400	52	13.33	–	1	3	–	5796†	58	33.10	6–59	1	0
Mansell, P.N.F.	1951	1955	13	22	2	355	90	17.75	–	2	15	–	1506	11	66.90	3–58	0	0

INDIVIDUAL TEST CAREER RECORDS – SOUTH AFRICA (Continued)

	First Test	Last Test	Tests	Inns	NO	Runs	HS	Avge	100	50	Ct	St	Balls	Runs	Wkts	Avge	BB	5wI	10wM
Markham, L.A.	1948-49	1948-49	1	1	0	20	20	20.00	–	–	–	–	104	72	1	72.00	1-34	0	0
Markram, A.K.	2017-18	2018-19	17	31	0	1358	152	43.80	4	6	15	–	152	70	0	–	–	0	0
Marx, W.F.E.	1921-22	1921-22	3	6†	0	125	36	20.83	–	1	–	–	228	144	4	36.00	3-85	0	0
Matthews, C.R.	1992-93	1995-96	18	25	6	348	62*	18.31	–	1	4	–	3980	1502	52	28.88	5-42	2	0
Meintjes, D.J.	1922-23	1922-23	2	3	0	43	21	14.33	–	–	3	–	246	115	6	19.16	3-38	0	0
Melle, M.G.	1949-50	1952-53	7	12	4	68	17	8.50	–	–	4	–	1667	851	26	32.73	6-71	2	0
Melville, A.	1938-39	1948-49	11	19	2	894	189	52.58	4	3	8	–	–	–	–	–	–	–	–
Middleton, J.	1895-96	1902-03	6	12	5	52	22	7.42	–	–	1	–	1064†	442	24	18.41	5-51	2	0
Mills, C.H.	1891-92	1891-92	1	2	0	25	21	12.50	–	–	1	–	140	83	2	41.50	2-83	0	0
Milton, W.H.	1888-89	1891-92	3	6	0	68	21	11.33	–	–	2	–	79	48	2	24.00	1-5	0	0
Mitchell, B.	1929	1948-49	42	80	9	3471	189*	48.88	8	21	56	–	2525	1380	27	51.11	5-87	1	0
Mitchell, F.‡	1912	1912	3	6	0	28	12	4.66	–	–	–	–	–	–	–	–	–	–	–
Morkel, D.P.B.	1927-28	1931-32	16	28	1	663	88	24.55	–	4	13	–	1704	821	18	45.61	4-93	0	0
Morkel, J.A.	2008-09	2008-09	1	1†	0	58	58	58.00	–	1	–	–	192	132	1	132.00	1-44	0	0
Morkel, M.	2006-07	2017-18	86	104†	23	944	40	11.65	–	–	25	–	16498	8550	309	27.66	6-23	8	0
Morris, C.H.	2015-16	2017	4	7	0	173	69	24.71	–	1	5	–	623	459	12	38.25	3-38	0	0
Mulder, P.W.A.	2018-19	2018-19	1	2	0	14	9	7.00	–	–	–	–	42	12	1	12.00	1-6	0	0
Murray, A.R.A.	1952-53	1953-54	10	14	1	289	109	22.23	1	1	3	–	2374	710	18	39.44	4-169	0	0
Nel, A.	2001-02	2008	36	42	8	337	34	9.91	–	–	16	–	7630	3919	123	31.86	6-32	3	1
Nel, J.D.	1949-50	1957-58	6	11	0	150	38	13.63	–	–	1	–	–	–	–	–	–	–	–
Newberry, C.	1913-14	1913-14	4	8	0	62	16	7.75	–	–	3	–	558	268	11	24.36	4-72	0	0
Newson, E.S.	1930-31	1938-39	3	5	1	30	16	7.50	–	–	3	–	874	265	4	66.25	2-58	0	0
Ngam, M.	2000-01	2000-01	3	1	1	0	0*	–	–	–	1	–	392	189	11	17.18	3-26	0	0
Ngidi, L.T.	2017-18	2018	4	7	3	15	5	3.75	–	–	2	–	619	293	15	19.53	6-39	1	0
Nicholson, F.	1935-36	1935-36	4	8	1	76	29	10.85	–	–	3	–	–	–	–	–	–	–	–
Nicolson, J.F.W.	1927-28	1927-28	3	5†	0	179	78	35.80	–	1	–	–	24	17	0	–	–	–	–
Norton, N.O.	1909-10	1909-10	1	2	0	9	7	4.50	–	–	–	–	90	47	4	11.75	4-47	0	0
Nourse, A.D.	1935	1951	34	62	7	2960	231	53.81	9	14	12	–	20	9	0	–	–	–	–
Nourse, A.W.	1902-03	1924	45	83†	8	2234	111	29.78	1	15	43	–	3234†	1553	41	37.87	4-25	0	0
Ntini, M.	1997-98	2009-10	101	116	45	699	32*	9.84	–	–	25	–	20834	11242	390	28.82	7-37	18	4
Nupen, E.P.	1921-22	1935-36	17	31	7	348	69	14.50	–	2	9	–	4159	1788	50	35.76	6-46	5	1
Ochse, A.E.	1888-89	1888-89	2	4	0	16	8	4.00	–	–	–	–	–	–	–	–	–	–	–
Ochse, A.L.	1927-28	1929	3	4	1	11	4*	3.66	–	–	1	–	649	362	10	36.20	4-79	0	0
O'Linn, S.	1960	1961-62	7	12†	1	297	98	27.00	–	2	4	–	–	–	–	–	–	–	–

Olivier, D.	2016–17	10	12	5	26	10*	3.71	–	–	–	2	1440	924	48	19.25	6-37	3	1
Ontong, J.L.	2001–02	2	4	1	57	32	19.00	–	–	–	1	185	133	1	133.00	1-79	0	0
Owen-Smith, H.G.O.	1929	5	8	2	252	129	42.00	1	1	4	–	156	113	0	–	–	–	–
Palm, A.W.	1927–28	1	2	0	15	13	7.50	–	–	1	–	–	–	–	–	–	–	–
Parker, G.M.	1924	2	4	2	3	2*	1.50	–	–	–	–	366	273	8	34.12	6-152	1	0
Parkin, D.C.	1891–92	1	2	0	6	6	3.00	–	–	–	1	130	82	3	27.33	3-82	0	0
Parnell, W.D.	2009–10	6	4†	0	67	23	16.75	–	–	–	3	556†	414	15	27.60	4-51	0	0
Partridge, J.T.	1963–64	11	12	5	73	13*	10.42	–	–	–	6	3684	1373	44	31.20	7-91	3	0
Pearse, C.O.C.	1910–11	3	6	0	55	31	9.16	–	–	–	1	144	106	3	35.33	3-56	0	0
Pegler, S.J.	1909–10	16	28	5	356	35*	15.47	–	–	5	5	2989	1572	47	33.44	7-65	2	0
Petersen, A.N.	2009–10	36	64	4	2093	182	34.88	5	8	3	31	114	62	1	62.00	1-2	0	0
Peterson, R.J.	2003	15	20†	3	464	84	27.29	–	3	–	9	2515†	1416	38	37.26	5-33	1	0
Phehlukwayo, A.L.	2017–18	4	4†	2	19	9	9.50	–	–	–	2	250	147	11	13.36	3-13	0	0
Philander, V.D.	2011–12	58	82	18	1538	74	24.03	–	8	–	17	10420	4632	214	21.64	6-21	13	2
Piedt, D.L.	2014	7	8	1	48	19	6.85	–	–	–	4	1500	865	24	36.04	5-153	1	0
Pithey, A.J.	1956–57	17	27	1	819	154	31.50	1	4	–	3	12	5	0	–	–	–	–
Pithey, D.B.	1963–64	8	12	1	138	55	12.54	–	1	–	6	1424	577	12	48.08	6-58	1	0
Plimsoll, J.B.	1947	1	2	1	16	8*	16.00	–	–	–	–	237†	143	3	47.66	3-128	0	0
Pollock, P.M.	1961–62	28	41	13	607	75*	21.67	–	2	–	9	6522	2806	116	24.18	6-38	9	1
Pollock, R.G.	1963–64	23	41†	4	2256	274	60.97	7	11	–	17	414	204	4	51.00	2-50	0	0
Pollock, S.M.	2007–08	108	156	39	3781	111	32.31	2	16	–	72	24353	9733	421	23.11	7-87	16	1
Poore, R.M.	1895–96	3	6	0	76	20	12.66	–	–	–	3	9	4	1	4.00	1-4	0	0
Pothecary, J.E.	1960	3	4	0	26	12	6.50	–	–	–	2	828	354	9	39.33	4-58	0	0
Powell, A.W.	1898–99	1	2	0	16	11	8.00	–	–	–	2	20	10	1	10.00	1-10	0	0
Pretorius, D.	2001–02	4	4	1	22	9	7.33	–	–	–	–	570	430	6	71.66	4-115	0	0
Prince, A.G.	2011–12	66	104†	16	3665	162*	41.64	11	11	–	47	96	47	1	47.00	1-2	0	0
Prince, C.F.H.	1898–99	1	2	0	6	5	3.00	–	–	–	–	–	–	–	–	–	–	–
Pringle, M.W.	1991–92	4	6	2	67	33	16.75	–	–	–	–	652	270	5	54.00	2-62	0	0
Procter, M.J.	1966–67	7	10	1	226	48	25.11	–	–	–	4	1514	616	41	15.02	6-73	1	0
Promnitz, H.L.E.	1927–28	2	4	0	14	5	3.50	–	–	–	2	528	161	8	20.12	5-58	1	0
Quinn, N.A.	1929	12	18†	3	90	28	6.00	–	–	–	1	2922†	1145	35	32.71	6-92	1	0
Rabada, K.	2015–16	37	52†	9	507	34	11.79	–	–	–	21	6830	3833	176	21.77	7-112	9	4
Reid, N.	1921–22	1	2	0	17	11	8.50	–	–	–	–	126	63	2	31.50	2-63	0	0
Rhodes, J.N.	2000	52	80	9	2532	117	35.66	3	17	–	34	12	5	0	–	–	–	–
Richards, A.R.	1895–96	1	2	0	6	6	3.00	–	–	–	–	–	–	–	–	–	–	–
Richards, B.A.	1969–70	4	7	0	508	140	72.57	2	2	–	3	72	26	1	26.00	1-12	0	0
Richards, W.H.M.	1888–89	1	2	0	4	4	2.00	–	–	–	–	–	–	–	–	–	–	–
Richardson, D.J.	1997–98	42	64	8	1359	109	24.26	1	8	–	150	–	–	–	–	–	–	–

265

INDIVIDUAL TEST CAREER RECORDS – SOUTH AFRICA (Continued)

	First Test	Last Test	Tests	Inns	NO	Runs	HS	Avge	100	50	Ct	St	Balls	Runs	Wkts	Avge	BB	5wI	10wM
Robertson, J.B.	1935-36	1935-36	3	6	1	51	17	10.20	–	–	2	–	738	321	6	53.50	3–143	–	0
Rose–Innes, A.	1888-89	1888-89	2	4	0	14	13	3.50	–	–	2	–	128†	89	5	17.80	5–43	1	0
Routledge, T.W.	1891-92	1895-96	4	8	0	72	24	9.00	–	–	2	–	–	–	–	–	–	–	–
Rowan, A.M.B.	1947	1951	15	23	6	290	41	17.05	–	–	7	–	5193	2084	54	38.59	5–68	4	0
Rowan, E.A.B.	1935	1951	26	50	5	1965	236	43.66	3	12	14	–	19	7	0	–	–	–	–
Rowe, G.A.	1895-96	1902-03	5	9	3	26	13*	4.33	–	–	4	–	998†	456	15	30.40	5–115	1	0
Rudolph, J.A.	2003	2012-13	48	83†	9	2622	222*	35.43	6	11	29	–	664	432	4	108.00	1–1	0	0
Rushmere, M.W.	1991-92	1991-92	1	2	0	6	3	3.00	–	–	–	–	–	–	–	–	–	–	–
Samuelson, S.V.	1909-10	1909-10	1	2	0	22	15	11.00	–	–	1	–	108	64	0	–	–	–	–
Schultz, B.N.	1992-93	1997-98	9	8†	2	9	6	1.50	–	–	2	–	1733†	749	37	20.24	5–48	2	0
Schwarz, R.O.	1905-06	1912	20	35	8	374	61	13.85	–	1	18	–	2639	1417	55	25.76	6–47	2	0
Seccull, A.W.	1895-96	1895-96	1	2	1	23	17*	23.00	–	–	1	–	60	37	2	18.50	2–37	0	0
Seymour, M.A.	1963-64	1969-70	7	10	3	84	36	12.00	–	–	2	–	1458	588	9	65.33	3–80	0	0
Shalders, W.A.	1898-99	1907	12	23	1	355	42	16.13	–	–	3	–	48	6	1	6.00	1–6	0	0
Shamsi, T.	2016-17	2018	2	4	3	20	18*	20.00	–	–	–	–	483†	278	6	46.33	3–91	0	0
Shepstone, G.H.	1895-96	1898-99	2	4	0	38	21	9.50	–	–	2	–	115	47	0	–	–	–	–
Sherwell, P.W.	1905-06	1910-11	13	22	4	427	115	23.72	1	1	20	16	–	–	–	–	–	–	–
Siedle, I.J.	1927-28	1935-36	18	34	0	977	141	28.73	1	5	7	–	–	–	–	–	–	–	–
Sinclair, J.H.	1895-96	1910-11	25	47	1	1069	106	23.23	3	3	9	–	3598	1996	63	31.68	6–26	1	0
Smith, C.J.E.	1902-03	1902-03	3	6	1	106	45	21.20	–	–	2	–	19	7	1	7.00	1–7	0	0
Smith, F.W.	1888-89	1895-96	3	6	1	45	12	9.00	–	–	2	–	–	–	–	–	–	–	–
Smith, G.C.‡	2001-02	2013-14	116	203†	13	9253	277	48.70	27	38	166	–	1418	885	8	110.62	2–145	0	0
Smith, V.I.	1947	1957-58	9	16	6	39	11*	3.90	–	–	3	–	1655	769	12	64.08	4–143	0	0
Snell, R.P.	1991-92	1994-95	5	8	1	95	48	13.57	–	–	1	–	1025	538	19	28.31	4–74	0	0
Snooke, S.D.	1907	1907	1	1	0	0	0	0.00	–	–	2	–	–	–	–	–	–	–	–
Snooke, S.J.	1905-06	1922-23	26	46	1	1008	103	22.40	1	5	24	–	1620	702	35	20.05	8–70	1	1
Solomon, W.R.T.	1898-99	1898-99	1	2	0	4	2	2.00	–	–	1	–	–	–	–	–	–	–	–
Stewart, R.B.	1888-89	1888-89	1	2	0	13	9	6.50	–	–	2	–	–	–	–	–	–	–	–
Steyn, D.W.	2004-05	2018-19	93	119	27	1251	76	13.59	–	2	26	–	18608	10077	439	22.95	7–51	26	5
Steyn, P.J.R.	1994-95	1994-95	3	6	0	127	46	21.16	–	–	3	–	–	–	–	–	–	–	–
Stricker, L.A.	1909-10	1912	13	24	0	344	48	14.33	–	–	3	–	174	105	1	105.00	1–36	0	0
Strydom, P.C.	1999-00	1999-00	2	3	0	35	30	11.66	–	–	1	–	36†	27	0	–	–	–	–
Susskind, M.J.	1924	1924	5	8	0	268	65	33.50	–	4	1	–	–	–	–	–	–	–	–
Symcox, P.L.	1993	1998-99	20	27	1	741	108	28.50	1	4	5	–	3561	1603	37	43.32	4–69	0	0

Name	Debut	Tests	Last	I	NO	Runs	HS	Avg	100	50	Ct	St	Balls	Runs	Wkts	Avg	BB	5wi	10wm
Taberer, H.M.	1902–03	1	1902–03	1	0	2	2	2.00	–	–	–	–	60	48	1	48.00	1–25	0	0
Tancred, A.B.	1888–89	2	1888–89	4	1	87	29	29.00	–	–	2	–	–	–	–	–	–	–	–
Tancred, L.J.	1902–03	14	1913–14	26	1	530	97	21.20	–	2	3	–	–	–	–	–	–	–	–
Tancred, V.M.	1898–99	1	1898–99	2	0	25	18	12.50	–	–	1	–	–	–	–	–	–	–	–
Tapscott, G.L.	1913–14	1	1913–14	2	0	5	4	2.50	–	–	–	–	–	–	–	–	–	–	–
Tapscott, L.E.	1922–23	2	1922–23	3	1	58	50*	29.00	–	1	2	–	12	2	0	–	–	–	2
Tayfield, H.J.	1949–50	37	1960	60	9	862	75	16.90	–	2	26	–	13568	4405	170	25.91	9–113	14	2
Taylor, A.I.	1956–57	1	1956–57	2	0	18	12	9.00	–	–	–	–	–	–	–	–	–	–	–
Taylor, D.	1913–14	2	1913–14	4†	0	85	36	21.25	–	1	–	–	–	–	–	–	–	–	–
Taylor, H.W.	1912	42	1931–32	76	4	2936	176	40.77	7	17	19	–	342	156	5	31.20	3–15	0	0
Terbrugge, D.J.	1998–99	7	2003–04	8	5	16	4*	5.33	–	–	4	–	1012	517	20	25.85	5–46	1	0
Theunissen, N.H.C.D.	1888–89	1	1888–89	2	1	2	2*	2.00	–	–	–	–	80	51	0	–	–	0	0
Thornton, G.	1902–03	1	1902–03	1†	1	1	1*	–	–	–	1	–	24†	20	1	20.00	1–20	0	0
Toit, J.F.	1891–92	1	1891–92	2	2	2	2*	–	–	–	1	–	85†	47	1	47.00	1–47	0	0
Tomlinson, D.S.	1935	1	1935	1	0	9	9	9.00	–	–	–	–	60	38	0	–	–	–	–
Trimborn, P.H.J.	1966–67	4	1969–70	4	2	13	11*	6.50	–	–	7	–	747	257	11	23.36	3–12	0	0
Traicos, A.J.‡	1969–70	3	1969–70	4	4	8	5*	4.00	–	–	4	–	470	207	4	51.75	2–70	0	0
Tsolekile, T.L.	2004–05	3	2004–05	5	0	47	22	9.40	–	–	6	–	–	–	–	–	–	–	–
Tsotsobe, L.L.	2010	5	2010–11	5	2	19	8*	6.33	–	–	1	–	870†	448	9	49.77	3–43	0	0
Tuckett, L.R.	1913–14	2	1913–14	2	1	0	0*	0.00	–	–	2	–	120	69	0	–	–	–	–
Tuckett, L.T.D.	1947	9	1948–49	14	3	131	40*	11.90	–	–	9	–	2104	980	19	51.57	5–68	2	0
Twentyman-Jones, P.S.	1902–03	1	1902–03	2	0	0	0	0.00	–	–	1	–	–	–	–	–	–	–	–
van der Bijl, P.G.V.	1938–39	5	1938–39	9	0	460	125	51.11	1	2	3	–	–	–	–	–	–	–	–
van der Merwe, E.A.	1929	2	1935–36	4	1	27	19	9.00	–	–	3	–	–	–	–	–	–	–	–
van der Merwe, P.L.	1963–64	15	1966–67	23	2	533	76	25.38	–	3	11	–	79†	22	1	22.00	1–6	0	0
van Jaarsveld, M.	2002–03	9	2004–05	15	2	397	73	30.53	–	3	11	–	42	28	0	–	–	–	–
van Ryneveld, C.B.	1951	19	1957–58	33	6	724	83	26.81	–	3	14	–	1554	671	17	39.47	4–67	0	0
van Zyl, S.	2014–15	12	2016	17†	2	395	101*	26.33	1	–	6	–	403	148	6	24.66	3–20	0	0
Varnals, G.D.	1964–65	3	1964–65	6	0	97	23	16.16	–	–	–	–	12	2	0	–	–	–	–
Vilas, D.J.	2015	6	2015–16	9	1	94	26	10.44	–	–	13	–	–	–	–	–	–	–	–
Viljoen, G.C.	2015–16	1	2015–16	2	1	26	20*	26.00	–	–	–	–	114	94	1	94.00	1–79	0	0
Viljoen, K.G.	1930–31	27	1948–49	50	2	1365	124	28.43	2	9	5	–	48	23	0	–	–	–	–
Vincent, C.L.	1927–28	25	1935	38†	12	526	60	20.23	–	2	27	–	5851†	2631	84	31.32	6–51	3	0
Vintcent, C.H.	1888–89	3	1891–92	6†	0	26	9	4.33	–	–	1	–	369†	193	4	48.25	3–88	0	0
Vogler, A.E.E.	1905–06	15	1910–11	26	6	340	65	17.00	–	2	20	–	2764	1455	64	22.73	7–94	5	1
Wade, H.F.	1935	10	1935–36	18	2	327	40*	20.43	–	–	4	–	–	–	–	–	–	–	–
Wade, W.W.	1938–39	11	1949–50	19	1	511	125	28.38	1	3	15	2	–	–	–	–	–	–	–
Waite, J.H.B.	1951	50	1964–65	86	7	2405	134	30.44	4	16	124	17	–	–	–	–	–	–	–

INDIVIDUAL TEST CAREER RECORDS – SOUTH AFRICA (Continued)

	First Test	Last Test	Tests	Inns	NO	Runs	HS	Avge	100	50	Ct	St	Balls	Runs	Wkts	Avge	BB	5wI	10wM
Walter, K.A.	1961–62	1961–62	2	3	0	11	10	3.66	–	–	3	–	495	197	6	32.83	4–63	0	0
Ward, T.A.	1912	1924	23	42	9	459	64	13.90	–	2	19	13	–	–	–	–	–	–	–
Watkins, J.C.	1949–50	1956–57	15	27	1	612	92	23.53	–	3	12	–	2805	816	29	28.13	4–22	0	0
Wesley, C.	1960	1960	3	5†	0	49	35	9.80	–	–	1	–	–	–	–	–	–	–	–
Wessels, K.C.‡	1991–92	1994	16	29†	2	1027	118	38.03	2	6	12	–	–	–	–	–	–	–	–
Westcott, R.J.	1953–54	1957–58	5	9	0	166	62	18.44	–	1	–	–	32	22	0	–	–	–	–
White, G.C.	1905–06	1912	17	31	2	872	147	30.06	2	4	10	–	498	301	9	33.44	4–47	0	0
Willoughby, C.M.	2003	2003	–	–†	–	–	–	–	–	–	–	–	300†	125	1	125.00	1–47	0	0
Willoughby, J.T.	1895–96	1895–96	2	4	0	8	5	2.00	–	–	–	–	275	159	6	26.50	2–37	0	0
Wimble, C.S.	1891–92	1891–92	1	2	0	0	0	0.00	–	–	–	–	–	–	–	–	–	–	–
Winslow, P.L.	1949–50	1955	5	9	0	186	108	20.66	1	–	1	–	–	–	–	–	–	–	–
Wynne, O.E.	1948–49	1949–50	6	12	0	219	50	18.25	–	1	3	–	–	–	–	–	–	–	–
Zondeki, M.	2003	2008–09	6	5	0	82	59	16.40	–	1	1	–	780	480	19	25.26	6–39	1	0
Zulch, J.W.	1909–10	1921–22	16	32	2	983	150	32.76	2	4	4	–	24	28	0	–	–	–	–

INDIVIDUAL TEST CAREER RECORDS – WEST INDIES

	First Test	Last Test	Tests	Inns	NO	Runs	HS	Avge	100	50	Ct	St	Balls	Runs	Wkts	Avge	BB	5wI	10wM
Achong, E.E.	1929-30	1934-35	6	11†	1	81	22	8.10	–	–	6	–	918†	378	8	47.25	2-64	0	0
Adams, J.C.	1991-92	2000-01	54	90†	17	3012	208*	41.26	6	14	48	–	2853†	1336	27	49.48	5-17	1	0
Alexander, F.C.M.	1957	1960-61	25	38	6	961	108	30.03	1	7	85	5	–	–	–	–	–	–	–
Ali, Inshan	1970-71	1976-77	12	18†	2	172	25	10.75	–	–	7	–	3718†	1621	34	47.67	5-59	1	0
Ali, Imtiaz	1975-76	1975-76	1	1	1	1	1*	–	–	–	–	–	204	89	2	44.50	2-37	0	0
Allan, D.W.	1961-62	1966	5	7	1	75	40*	12.50	–	–	15	3	–	–	–	–	–	–	–
Allen, I.B.A.	1991	1991	2	2	1	5	4*	–	–	–	1	–	282	180	5	36.00	2-69	0	0
Ambris, S.W.	2017-18	2018-19	6	12	1	166	43	15.09	–	–	2	–	–	–	–	–	–	–	–
Ambrose, C.E.L.	1987-88	2000	98	145†	29	1439	53	12.40	–	1	18	–	22103	8501	405	20.99	8-45	22	3
Arthurton, K.L.T.	1988	1995	33	50†	5	1382	157*	30.71	2	8	22	–	473†	183	1	183.00	1-17	0	0
Asgarali, N.S.	1957	1957	2	4	0	62	29	15.50	–	–	–	–	–	–	–	–	–	–	–
Atkinson, D.S.	1948-49	1957-58	22	35	6	922	219	31.79	1	5	11	–	5201	1647	47	35.04	7-53	3	0
Atkinson, E.S.	1957-58	1958-59	8	9	1	126	37	15.75	–	–	2	–	1634	589	25	23.56	5-42	1	0
Austin, Richard A.	1977-78	1977-78	2	2	0	22	20	11.00	–	–	2	–	6	5	0	–	–	–	–
Austin, Ryan A.	2009	2009	2	4	0	39	19	9.75	–	–	3	–	326	155	3	51.66	1-29	0	0
Bacchus, S.F.A.F.	1977-78	1981-82	19	30	0	782	250	26.06	1	3	17	–	6	3	0	–	–	–	–
Baichan, L.	1974-75	1975-76	3	6†	2	184	105*	46.00	1	–	2	–	–	–	–	–	–	–	–
Baker, L.S.	2008-09	2009	4	6†	4	23	17	11.50	–	–	1	–	660	395	5	79.00	2-39	0	0
Banks, O.A.C.	2002-03	2005	10	16	4	318	50*	26.50	–	1	6	–	2401	1367	28	48.82	4-87	0	0
Baptiste, E.A.E.	1983-84	1989-90	10	11	1	233	87*	23.30	–	1	2	–	1362	563	16	35.18	3-31	0	0
Barath, A.B.	2009-10	2012	15	28	0	657	104	23.46	1	4	13	–	6	3	0	–	–	–	–
Barrett, A.G.	1970-71	1974-75	6	7	1	40	19	6.66	–	–	–	–	1612	603	13	46.38	3-43	0	0
Barrow, I.M.	1929-30	1939	11	19	2	276	105	16.23	1	–	17	5	–	–	–	–	–	–	–
Bartlett, E.L.	1928	1930-31	5	8	1	131	84	18.71	–	1	2	–	–	–	–	–	–	–	–
Baugh, C.S.	2002-03	2011-12	21	36	2	610	68	17.94	–	3	43	5	–	–	–	–	–	–	–
Benjamin, K.C.G.	1991-92	1997-98	26	36	8	222	43*	7.92	–	–	2	–	5132	2785	92	30.27	6-66	4	1
Benjamin, W.K.M.	1987-88	1994-95	21	26	1	470	85	18.80	–	2	12	–	3694	1648	61	27.01	4-46	0	0
Benn, S.J.	2007-08	2014-15	26	39†	5	486	42	14.29	–	–	14	–	7322†	3402	87	39.10	6-81	6	0
Bernard, D.E.	2002-03	2009	3	6	1	202	69	40.40	–	3	–	–	258	185	4	46.25	2-30	0	0
Bess, B.J.	2010	2010	1	2	1	11	11*	11.00	–	–	–	–	78	92	1	92.00	1-65	0	0
Best, C.A.	1985-86	1990-91	8	13	1	342	164	28.50	1	1	8	–	30	21	0	–	–	–	–
Best, T.L.	2002-03	2013-14	25	38	6	401	95	12.53	–	1	6	–	3716	2291	57	40.19	6-40	2	0
Betancourt, N.	1929-30	1929-30	1	2	0	52	39	26.00	–	–	–	–	–	–	–	–	–	–	–
Binns, A.P.	1952-53	1955-56	5	8	1	64	27	9.14	–	–	14	3	–	–	–	–	–	–	–

INDIVIDUAL TEST CAREER RECORDS – WEST INDIES (Continued)

	First Test	Last Test	Tests	Inns	NO	Runs	HS	Avge	100	50	Ct	St	Balls	Runs	Wkts	Avge	BB	5wI	10wM
Birkett, L.S.	1930–31	1930–31	4	8	0	136	64	17.00	–	1	4	–	126	71	1	71.00	1–16	0	0
Bishoo, D.	2011	2018–19	36	61†	15	707	45	15.36	–	–	20	–	8067	4350	117	37.17	8–49	4	1
Bishop, I.R.	1988–89	1997–98	43	63	11	632	48	12.15	–	–	8	–	8407	3909	161	24.27	6–40	6	0
Black, M.I.	2000–01	2001–02	6	11	3	21	6	2.62	–	–	–	–	954	597	12	49.75	4–83	0	0
Blackwood, J.	2014	2019	28	49	4	1362	112*	30.26	1	10	24	–	324	194	2	97.00	2–14	0	0
Boyce, K.D.	1970–71	1975–76	21	30	3	657	95*	24.33	–	4	5	–	3501	1801	60	30.01	6–77	2	1
Bradshaw, I.D.R.	2005–06	2006	5	8†	1	96	33	13.71	–	–	3	–	1021†	540	9	60.00	3–73	0	0
Brathwaite, C.R.	2015–16	2016	3	5	1	181	69	45.25	–	3	–	–	408	242	1	242.00	1–30	0	0
Brathwaite, K.C.	2011	2019	58	110	7	3477	212	33.75	8	17	26	–	1899	1025	18	56.94	6–29	1	0
Bravo, D.J.	2004	2010–11	40	71	1	2200	113	31.42	3	13	41	–	6466	3426	86	39.83	6–55	2	0
Bravo, D.M.	2010–11	2019	54	98†	5	3506	218	37.69	8	17	51	–	6†	2	0	–	–	–	–
Breese, G.R.	2002–03	2002–03	1	2	0	5	5	2.50	–	–	1	–	188	135	2	67.50	2–108	0	0
Brooks, S.S.J.	2019	2019	2	4	0	63	50	15.75	–	1	3	–	–	–	–	–	–	–	–
Browne, C.O.	1994–95	2004–05	20	30	6	387	68	16.12	–	1	79	2	–	–	–	–	–	–	–
Browne, C.R.	1928	1929–30	4	8	1	176	70*	25.14	–	1	1	–	840	288	6	48.00	2–72	0	0
Butcher, B.F.	1958–59	1969	44	78	6	3104	209*	43.11	7	16	15	–	256	90	5	18.00	5–34	1	0
Butler, L.S.	1954–55	1954–55	1	1	0	16	16	16.00	–	–	–	–	240	151	2	75.50	2–151	0	0
Butts, C.G.	1984–85	1987–88	7	8	1	108	38	15.42	–	–	2	–	1554	595	10	59.50	4–73	0	0
Bynoe, M.R.	1958–59	1966–67	4	6	0	111	48	18.50	–	–	4	–	30†	5	1	5.00	1–5	–	–
Camacho, G.S.	1967–68	1970–71	11	22	0	640	87	29.09	–	4	4	–	18	12	0	–	–	–	–
Cameron, F.J.	1948–49	1948–49	5	7	1	151	75*	25.16	–	1	–	–	786	278	3	92.66	2–74	0	0
Cameron, J.H.	1939	1939	2	3	0	6	5	2.00	–	–	–	–	232	88	3	29.33	3–66	0	0
Campbell, J.D.	2018–19	2019	5	10†	1	224	47	24.88	–	–	4	–	61	30	0	–	–	–	–
Campbell, S.L.	1994–95	2001–02	52	93	4	2882	208	32.38	4	18	47	–	–	–	–	–	–	–	–
Carew, G.M.	1934–35	1948–49	4	7	1	170	107	28.33	1	–	1	–	18†	2	0	–	–	–	–
Carew, M.C.	1963	1971–72	19	36†	3	1127	109	34.15	1	5	13	–	1174	437	8	54.62	1–11	0	0
Challenor, G.	1928	1928	3	6	0	101	46	16.83	–	–	–	–	–	–	–	–	–	–	–
Chanderpaul, S.	1993–94	2014–15	164	280†	49	11867	203*	51.37	30	66	66	–	1740	883	9	98.11	1–2	0	0
Chandrika, R.	2015	2016	5	10	0	140	37	14.00	–	–	2	–	–	–	–	–	–	–	–
Chang, H.S.	1978–79	1978–79	1	2†	0	8	6	4.00	–	–	–	–	–	–	–	–	–	–	–
Chase, R.L.	2016	2019	31	57	4	1693	137*	31.94	5	7	14	–	4310	2480	56	44.28	8–60	2	0
Chattergoon, S.	2007–08	2008–09	4	7†	0	127	46	18.14	–	–	4	–	–	–	–	–	–	–	–
Christiani, C.M.	1934–35	1934–35	4	7	2	98	32*	19.60	–	–	6	1	–	–	–	–	–	–	–
Christiani, R.J.	1947–48	1953–54	22	37	3	896	107	26.35	1	4	19	2	234	108	3	36.00	3–52	0	0

Player	Years	M	I	NO	Runs	HS	Avg	100	50	Ct	St	Balls	Runs	Wkts	Avg	BB	5wI	10wM
Clarke, C.B.	1939	3	4	1	3	2	1.00	–	–	–	–	456	261	6	43.50	3–59	0	0
Clarke, S.T.	1977–78	11	16	5	172	35*	15.63	–	–	2	–	2477	1170	42	27.85	5–126	1	0
Collins, P.T.	2006	32	47	7	235	24	5.87	–	–	7	–	6964†	3671	106	34.63	6–53	3	0
Collymore, C.D.	1998–99	30	52	27	197	16*	7.88	–	–	6	–	6337	3004	93	32.30	7–57	4	1
Constantine, L.N.	1928	18	33	0	635	90	19.24	–	4	28	–	3583	1746	58	30.10	5–75	2	0
Cornwall, R.R.S.	2019	1	2	0	15	14	7.50	–	–	2	–	384	173	3	57.66	3–105	0	0
Cotterell, S.S.	2013–14	2	4	0	11	5	2.75	–	–	–	–	276†	196	2	98.00	1–72	0	0
Croft, C.E.H.	1976–77	27	37	22	158	33	10.53	–	–	8	–	6165	2913	125	23.30	8–29	3	0
Cuffy, C.E.	1994–95	15	23	9	58	15	4.14	–	–	5	–	3366	1455	43	33.83	4–82	0	0
Cummins, A.C.	1992–93	5	6	1	98	50	19.60	–	1	1	–	618	342	8	42.75	4–54	0	0
Cummins, M.L.	2016	14	22†	7	114	24*	7.60	–	–	2	–	1976	1084	27	40.14	6–48	1	0
Da Costa, O.C.	1929–30	5	9	1	153	39	19.12	–	–	5	–	372	175	3	58.33	1–14	0	0
Daniel, W.W.	1975–76	10	11	4	46	11	6.57	–	–	4	–	1754	910	36	25.27	5–39	1	0
Davis, B.A.	1964–65	4	8	0	245	68	30.62	–	3	1	–	–	–	–	–	–	–	–
Davis, C.A.	1968–69	15	29	5	1301	183	54.20	4	4	4	–	894	330	2	165.00	1–27	0	0
Davis, W.W.	1982–83	15	17	4	202	77	15.53	–	1	10	–	2773	1472	45	32.71	4–19	0	0
de Caires, F.I.	1929–30	3	6	0	232	80	38.66	–	2	1	–	12	9	0	–	–	–	–
Deonarine, N.	2004–05	18	30†	2	725	82	25.89	–	5	16	–	1503	713	24	29.70	4–37	0	0
Depeiaza, C.C.	1954–55	5	8	2	187	122	31.16	1	–	7	4	30	15	0	–	–	–	–
Dewdney, D.T.	1957–58	9	12	5	17	5*	2.42	–	–	–	–	1641	807	21	38.42	5–21	1	0
Dhanraj, R.	1995–96	4	4	0	17	9	4.25	–	–	1	–	1087	595	8	74.37	2–49	0	0
Dillon, M.	1996–97	38	68	3	549	43	8.44	–	–	16	–	8704	4398	131	33.57	5–71	2	0
Dowe, U.G.	1970–71	4	3	2	8	5*	8.00	–	–	3	–	1014	534	12	44.50	4–69	0	0
Dowlin, T.M.	2009	6	11	0	343	95	31.18	–	3	5	–	6	3	0	–	–	–	–
Dowrich, S.O.	2015	30	55	8	1402	125*	29.82	3	8	74	5	–	–	–	–	–	–	–
Drakes, V.C.	2002–03	12	20	2	386	67	21.44	–	1	2	–	2617	1362	33	41.27	5–93	1	0
Dujon, P.J.L.	1981–82	81	115	11	3322	139	31.94	5	16	267	5	–	–	–	–	–	–	–
Edwards, F.H.	2003	55	88	28	394	30	6.56	–	–	10	–	9602	6249	165	37.87	7–87	12	0
Edwards, K.A.	2011	17	32	1	986	121	31.80	2	8	15	–	24	19	0	–	–	0	–
Edwards, R.M.	1968–69	5	8	1	65	22	9.28	–	–	–	–	1311	626	18	34.77	5–84	1	0
Ferguson, W.	1947–48	8	10	3	200	75	28.57	–	2	11	–	2568	1165	34	34.26	6–92	3	1
Fernandes, M.P.	1928	2	4	0	49	22	12.25	–	–	–	–	–	–	–	–	–	–	–
Findlay, T.M.	1969	10	16	3	212	44*	16.30	–	1	19	2	–	–	–	–	–	–	–
Foster, M.L.C.	1977–78	14	24	5	580	125	30.52	1	1	3	–	1776	600	9	66.66	2–41	0	0
Francis, G.N.	1928	10	18	4	81	19*	5.78	–	–	7	–	1619	763	23	33.17	4–40	0	0
Frederick, M.C.	1953–54	1	2	0	30	30	15.00	–	–	–	–	–	–	–	–	–	–	–
Fredericks, R.C.	1976–77	59	109†	7	4334	169	42.49	8	26	62	–	1187†	548	7	78.28	1–12	0	0
Fudadin, A.B.	2012	3	5†	1	122	55	30.50	–	1	4	–	30	11	0	–	–	–	–

INDIVIDUAL TEST CAREER RECORDS – WEST INDIES (*Continued*)

	First Test	Last Test	Tests	Inns	NO	Runs	HS	Avge	100	50	Ct	St	Balls	Runs	Wkts	Avge	BB	5wI	10wM
Fuller, R.L.	1934-35	1934-35	1	1	0	1	1	1.00	–	–	–	–	48	12	0	–	–	–	–
Furlonge, H.A.	1954-55	1955-56	3	5	0	99	64	19.80	–	1	–	–	–	–	–	–	–	–	–
Gabriel, S.T.	2012	2019	45	66	24	200	20*	4.76	–	–	16	–	7234	4075	133	30.63	8-62	5	1
Ganga, D.	1998-99	2007-08	48	86	2	2160	135	25.71	3	9	30	–	186	106	1	106.00	1-20	0	0
Ganteaume, A.G.	1947-48	1947-48	1	1	0	112	112	112.00	1	–	–	–	–	–	–	–	–	–	–
Garner, J.	1976-77	1986-87	58	68	14	672	60	12.44	–	1	42	–	13169	5433	259	20.97	6-56	7	0
Garrick, L.V.	2000-01	2000-01	1	2	0	27	27	13.50	–	–	2	–	–	–	–	–	–	–	–
Gaskin, B.B.M.	1947-48	1947-48	2	3	0	17	10	5.66	–	–	1	–	474	158	2	79.00	1-15	0	0
Gayle, C.H.	1999-00	2014	103	182†	11	7214	333	42.18	15	37	96	–	7109	3120	73	42.73	5-34	2	0
Gibbs, G.L.	1954-55	1954-55	1	2†	0	12	12	6.00	–	–	1	–	24†	7	0	–	–	–	–
Gibbs, L.R.	1957-58	1975-76	79	109	39	488	25	6.97	–	–	52	–	27115	8989	309	29.09	8-38	18	2
Gibson, O.D.	1995	1998-99	2	4	0	93	37	23.25	–	–	–	–	472	275	3	91.66	2-81	0	0
Gilchrist, R.	1957	1958-59	13	14	3	60	12	5.45	–	–	4	–	3227	1521	57	26.68	6-55	1	0
Goddard, J.D.C.	1947-48	1957	27	39†	11	859	83*	30.67	–	4	22	–	2931	1050	33	31.81	5-31	1	0
Gomes, H.A.	1976	1986-87	60	91†	11	3171	143	39.63	9	13	18	–	2401	930	15	62.00	2-20	0	0
Gomez, G.E.	1939	1953-54	29	46	5	1243	101	30.31	1	8	18	–	5236	1590	58	27.41	7-55	1	1
Grant, G.C.	1930-31	1934-35	12	22	6	413	71*	25.81	–	3	10	–	24	18	0	–	–	–	–
Grant, R.S.	1934-35	1939	7	11	1	220	77	22.00	–	1	13	–	986	353	11	32.09	3-68	0	0
Gray, A.H.	1986-87	1986-87	5	8	2	48	12*	8.00	–	–	6	–	888	377	22	17.13	4-39	0	0
Greenidge, A.E.	1977-78	1978-79	6	10	0	222	69	22.20	–	2	5	–	–	–	–	–	–	–	–
Greenidge, C.G.	1974-75	1990-91	108	185	16	7558	226	44.72	19	34	96	–	26	4	0	–	–	–	–
Greenidge, G.A.	1971-72	1972-73	5	9	2	209	50	29.85	–	1	3	–	156	75	0	–	–	–	–
Grell, M.G.	1929-30	1929-30	1	2	0	34	21	17.00	–	–	1	–	30	17	0	–	–	–	–
Griffith, A.F.G.	1996-97	2000	14	27†	1	638	114	24.53	1	4	5	–	–	–	–	–	–	–	–
Griffith, C.C.	1959-60	1968-69	28	42	10	530	54	16.56	–	1	16	–	5631	2683	94	28.54	6-36	5	0
Griffith, H.C.	1928	1933	13	23	5	91	18	5.05	–	–	4	–	2663	1243	44	28.25	6-103	2	0
Guillen, S.C.‡	1951-52	1951-52	5	6	2	104	54	26.00	–	1	9	2	–	–	–	–	–	–	–
Hall, W.W.	1958-59	1968-69	48	66	14	818	50*	15.73	–	2	11	–	10421	5066	192	26.38	7-69	9	1
Hamilton, J.N.	2019	2019	1	2	0	5	5	2.50	–	–	5	–	–	–	–	–	–	–	–
Harper, R.A.	1983-84	1993-94	25	32	3	535	74	18.44	–	3	36	–	3615	1291	46	28.06	6-57	1	0
Haynes, D.L.	1977-78	1993-94	116	202	25	7487	184	42.29	18	39	65	–	18	8	1	8.00	1-2	0	0
Headley, G.A.	1929-30	1953-54	22	40	4	2190	270*	60.83	10	5	14	–	398	230	0	–	–	–	–
Headley, R.G.A.	1973	1973	2	4†	0	62	42	15.50	–	–	2	–	–	–	–	–	–	–	–
Hendriks, J.L.	1961-62	1969	20	32	8	447	64	18.62	–	2	42	5	–	–	–	–	–	–	–

Name	First	Last	M	I	NO	Runs	HS	Avg	100	50	Ct	St	Balls	Runs	Wkts	Avg	BB	5w	10w
Hetmyer, S.O.	2016–17	2019	15	29†	0	825	93	28.44	—	5	7	—	1743†	870	13	66.92	2–45	0	0
Hinds, R.O.	2001–02	2009	15	25†	1	505	84	21.04	—	2	7	—	1123	590	16	36.87	3–79	0	0
Hinds, W.W.	1999–00	2005–06	45	80†	2	2608	213	33.01	5	14	32	—	—	—	—	—	—	—	—
Hoad, E.L.G.	1928	1933	4	8	0	98	36	12.25	—	—	1	—	—	—	—	—	—	—	1
Holder, J.O.	2014	2019	39	68	11	1887	202*	33.10	3	8	31	—	6402	2754	101	27.26	6–59	6	—
Holder, R.I.C.	1996–97	1998–99	11	17	2	380	91	25.33	—	2	9	—	—	—	—	—	—	—	—
Holder, V.A.	1969	1978–79	40	59	11	682	42	14.20	—	—	16	—	9095	3627	109	33.27	6–28	3	0
Holding, M.A.	1975–76	1986–87	60	76	10	910	73	13.78	—	6	22	—	12680	5898	249	23.68	8–92	13	2
Holford, D.A.J.	1966	1976–77	24	39	5	768	105*	22.58	1	3	18	—	4816	2009	51	39.39	5–23	1	0
Holt, J.K.C.	1953–54	1958–59	17	31	2	1066	166	36.75	2	5	8	—	30	20	1	20.00	1–20	0	0
Hooper, C.L.	1987–88	2002–03	102	173	15	5762	233	36.46	13	27	115	—	13794	5635	114	49.42	5–26	4	0
Hope, K.A.	2017	2017–18	5	9	0	101	43	11.22	—	—	3	—	—	—	—	—	—	—	—
Hope, S.D.	2014–15	2019	30	56	2	1485	147	27.50	2	5	42	1	—	—	—	—	—	—	—
Howard, A.B.	1971–72	1971–72	1	—†	—	—	—	—	—	—	—	—	372	140	2	70.00	2–140	0	0
Hunte, C.C.	1957–58	1966–67	44	78	6	3245	260	45.06	8	13	16	—	270	110	2	55.00	1–17	0	0
Hunte, E.A.C.	1929–30	1929–30	3	6	1	166	58	33.20	—	2	5	—	—	—	—	—	—	—	—
Hylton, L.G.	1934–35	1939	6	8	2	70	19	11.66	—	—	1	—	965	418	16	26.12	4–27	0	0
Jacobs, R.D.	1998–99	2004	65	112†	21	2577	118	28.31	3	14	207	12	—	—	—	—	—	—	—
Jaggernauth, A.S.	2008	2008	1	2†	1	0	0*	0.00	—	—	—	—	138	96	1	96.00	1–74	0	0
Johnson, H.H.H.	1947–48	1950	3	4	0	38	22	9.50	—	2	7	—	789	238	13	18.30	5–41	2	1
Johnson, L.R.	2014	2016–17	9	16†	1	403	66	25.18	—	—	—	—	24	9	0	—	—	0	0
Johnson, T.F.	1939	1939	1	1†	1	9	9*	—	—	—	—	—	240†	129	3	43.00	2–53	0	0
Jones, C.E.L.	1929–30	1934–35	4	7†	0	63	19	9.00	—	—	3	—	102†	11	0	—	—	0	0
Jones, P.E.W.	1947–48	1951–52	9	11	2	47	10*	5.22	—	—	4	—	1842	751	25	30.04	5–85	1	0
Joseph, A.S.	2016	2018–19	9	15	0	84	34	5.60	—	—	6	—	1525	821	25	32.84	3–53	0	0
Joseph, D.R.E.	1998–99	1998–99	4	7	0	141	50	20.14	—	1	10	—	—	—	—	—	—	—	—
Joseph, S.C.	2004	2007	5	10	0	147	45	14.70	—	—	3	—	12	8	0	—	—	—	—
Julien, B.D.	1973	1976–77	24	34	6	866	121	30.92	2	3	14	—	4542†	1868	50	37.36	5–57	1	0
Jumadeen, R.R.	1971–72	1978–79	12	14	10	84	56	21.00	—	1	4	—	3140†	1141	29	39.34	4–72	0	0
Kallicharran, A.I.	1971–72	1980–81	66	109†	10	4399	187	44.43	12	21	51	—	406	158	4	39.50	2–16	0	0
Kanhai, R.B.	1957	1973–74	79	137	6	6227	256	47.53	15	28	50	—	183	85	0	—	—	0	—
Kentish, E.S.M.	1947–48	1953–54	2	2	1	1	1*	1.00	—	—	1	—	540	178	8	22.25	5–49	1	0
King, C.L.	1976	1980	9	16	3	418	100*	32.15	1	2	5	—	582	282	3	94.00	1–30	0	0
King, F.M.	1952–53	1955–56	14	17	3	116	21	8.28	—	—	5	—	2869	1159	29	39.96	5–74	1	0
King, L.A.	1961–62	1967–68	2	4	0	41	20	10.25	—	—	5	—	476	154	9	17.11	5–46	1	0
King, R.D.	1998–99	2004–05	19	27	8	66	12*	3.47	—	—	2	—	3442	1733	53	32.69	5–51	1	0
Lambert, C.B.	1991	1998–99	5	9†	0	284	104	31.55	1	1	8	—	10	5	1	5.00	1–4	0	—
Lara, B.C.‡	1990–91	2006–07	130	230†	6	11912	400*	53.17	34	48	164	—	60	28	0	—	—	—	—

INDIVIDUAL TEST CAREER RECORDS – WEST INDIES (Continued)

	First Test	Last Test	Tests	Inns	NO	Runs	HS	Avge	100	50	Ct	St	Balls	Runs	Wkts	Avge	BB	5wI	10wM
Lashley, P.D.	1960–61	1966	4	7†	0	159	49	22.71	–	–	4	–	18	1	1	1.00	1–1	0	0
Lawson, J.J.C.	2002–03	2005–06	13	21	6	52	14	3.46	–	–	3	–	2364	1512	51	29.64	7–78	2	0
Legall, R.A.	1952–53	1952–53	4	5	0	50	23	10.00	–	–	8	1	–	–	–	–	–	–	–
Lewis, D.M.	1970–71	1970–71	3	5	2	259	88	86.33	–	3	8	–	–	–	–	–	–	–	–
Lewis, R.N.	1997–98	2007–08	5	10	0	89	40	8.90	–	–	1	–	883	456	4	114.00	2–42	0	0
Lewis, S.H.	2018–19	2018–19	2	4	0	24	20	6.00	–	–	–	–	240	162	3	54.00	2–93	0	0
Lloyd, C.H.	1966–67	1984–85	110	175†	14	7515	242*	46.67	19	39	90	–	1716	622	10	62.20	2–13	0	0
Logie, A.L.	1982–83	1991	52	78	9	2470	130	35.79	2	16	57	–	7	4	0	–	–	–	–
McGarrell, N.C.	2000–01	2001–02	4	6	2	61	33	15.25	–	–	2	–	1212†	453	17	26.64	4–23	0	0
McLean, N.A.M.	1997–98	2000–01	19	32†	2	368	46	12.26	–	–	5	–	3299	1873	44	42.56	3–53	0	0
McMorris, E.D.A.S.	1957–58	1966	13	21	0	564	125	26.85	1	3	5	–	–	–	–	–	–	–	–
McWatt, C.A.	1953–54	1954–55	6	9†	2	202	54	28.85	–	2	9	1	24	16	1	16.00	1–16	0	0
Madray, I.S.	1957–58	1957–58	2	3	0	3	2	1.00	–	–	2	–	210	108	0	–	–	–	–
Marshall, M.D.	1978–79	1991	81	107	11	1810	92	18.85	–	10	25	–	17584	7876	376	20.94	7–22	22	4
Marshall, N.E.	1954–55	1954–55	1	2	0	8	8	4.00	–	–	–	–	279	62	2	31.00	1–22	0	0
Marshall, R.E.	1951–52	1951–52	4	7	0	143	30	20.42	–	–	1	–	52	15	0	–	–	–	–
Marshall, X.M.	2005	2008–09	7	12	0	243	85	20.25	–	2	7	–	12	0	0	–	–	–	–
Martin, F.R.	1928	1930–31	9	18†	1	486	123*	28.58	1	–	2	–	1346†	619	8	77.37	3–91	0	0
Martindale, E.A.	1933	1939	10	14	3	58	22	5.27	–	–	5	–	1605	804	37	21.72	5–22	3	0
Mattis, E.H.	1980–81	1980–81	4	5	0	145	71	29.00	–	1	3	–	36	14	0	–	–	–	–
Mendonca, I.L.	1961–62	1961–62	2	2	0	81	78	40.50	–	1	8	2	–	–	–	–	–	–	–
Merry, C.A.	1933	1933	2	4	0	34	13	8.50	–	–	1	–	–	–	–	–	–	–	–
Miller, N.O.	2009	2009	1	2	0	5	5	2.50	–	–	–	–	132†	67	0	–	–	–	–
Miller, R.S.	1952–53	1952–53	1	1	0	23	23	23.00	–	–	–	–	96	28	0	–	–	–	–
Mohammed, D.	2003–04	2006–07	5	8†	1	225	52	32.14	–	1	1	–	1065†	668	13	51.38	3–98	0	0
Morais, G.Gladstone	1929–30	1929–30	1	1†	0	12	12*	–	–	–	–	–	300†	189	1	189.00	1–139	0	0
Morton, R.S.	2005	2008	15	27	1	573	70*	22.03	–	4	20	–	66	50	0	–	–	–	–
Moseley, E.A.	1989–90	1989–90	2	4	0	35	26	8.75	–	–	1	–	522	261	6	43.50	2–70	0	0
Mudie, G.H.	1934–35	1934–35	1	1	0	5	5	5.00	–	–	–	–	174†	40	3	13.33	2–23	0	0
Murray, D.A.	1977–78	1981–82	19	31	3	601	84	21.46	–	3	57	5	–	–	–	–	–	–	–
Murray, D.L.	1963	1980	62	96	9	1993	91	22.90	–	11	181	8	–	–	–	–	–	–	–
Murray, J.R.	1992–93	2001–02	33	45	4	918	101*	22.39	1	3	99	3	–	–	–	–	–	–	–
Nagamootoo, M.V.	2000	2002–03	5	8†	1	185	68	26.42	–	1	2	–	1494	637	12	53.08	3–119	0	0
Nanan, R.	1980–81	1980–81	1	2	0	16	8	8.00	–	–	2	–	216	91	4	22.75	2–37	0	0

Name	Career	Debut	M	I	NO	Runs	HS	Avg	100	50	Ct/St	Balls	Runs	Wkts	BB	Avg	5wi	10wm
Narine, S.P.	2012	2013–14	6	7†	2	40	22*	8.00	–	–	2	–	1650	851	21	40.52	6–91	2	0
Nash, B.P.	2008–09	2011	21	33†	0	1103	114	33.42	2	8	6	–	492†	247	2	123.50	1–21	0	0
Neblett, J.M.	1934–35	1934–35	1	2	1	16	11*	16.00	–	–	–	–	216	75	1	75.00	1–44	0	0
Noreiga, J.M.	1970–71	1970–71	4	5	2	11	9	3.66	–	–	2	–	1322	493	17	29.00	9–95	2	0
Nunes, R.K.	1928	1929–30	4	8†	0	245	92	30.62	–	2	2	–	–	–	–	–	–	–	–
Nurse, S.M.	1959–60	1968–69	29	54	1	2523	258	47.60	6	10	21	–	42	7	0	–	–	–	–
Padmore, A.L.	1975–76	1976	2	2	1	8	8*	8.00	–	–	–	–	474	135	1	135.00	1–36	0	0
Pagon, D.J.	2004–05	2004–05	2	3	0	37	35	12.33	–	–	–	–	–	–	–	–	–	–	–
Pairaudeau, B.H.	1952–53	1957	13	21	0	454	115	21.61	1	3	6	–	6	3	0	–	–	–	–
Parchment, B.A.	2007–08	2008	2	4	0	55	20	13.75	–	–	1	–	–	–	–	–	–	–	–
Parry, D.R.	1977–78	1979–80	12	20	3	381	65	22.41	–	3	4	–	1909	936	23	40.69	5–15	1	0
Pascal, N.T.	2010	2010–11	2	2	0	12	10	6.00	–	–	1	–	102	59	0	–	–	–	–
Passailaigue, C.C.	1929–30	1929–30	1	2	1	46	44	46.00	–	–	3	–	12	15	0	–	–	–	–
Patterson, B.P.	1985–86	1992–93	28	38	16	145	21*	6.59	–	–	5	–	4829	2874	93	30.90	5–24	5	0
Paul, K.M.A.	2018	2018–19	3	6	0	96	47	16.00	–	–	2	–	342	189	6	31.50	2–25	0	0
Payne, T.R.O.	1985–86	1985–86	1	1†	0	5	5	5.00	–	–	5	–	–	–	–	–	–	–	–
Permaul, V.	2012–13	2015	6	9	1	98	23*	12.25	–	–	2	–	1371†	788	18	43.77	3–32	0	0
Perry, N.O.	1998–99	1999–00	4	7	1	74	26	12.33	–	–	1	–	804	446	10	44.60	5–70	1	0
Peters, K.K.	2014–15	2014–15	1	1	0	0	0	0.00	–	–	–	–	120†	69	2	34.50	2–69	0	0
Phillip, N.	1977–78	1978–79	9	15	5	297	47	29.70	–	–	5	–	1820	1041	28	37.17	4–48	0	0
Phillips, O.J.	2009	2009	2	4†	0	160	94	40.00	–	1	1	–	–	–	–	–	–	–	–
Pierre, L.R.	1947–48	1947–48	1	–	–	–	–	–	–	–	–	–	42	28	0	–	–	–	–
Powell, D.B.L.	2002	2008–09	37	57	5	407	36*	7.82	–	–	8	–	7077	4068	85	47.85	5–25	1	0
Powell, K.O.A.	2011	2018–19	40	76†	1	2011	134	26.81	3	6	29	–	6	0	0	–	–	–	–
Powell, R.L.	1999–00	2003–04	2	3	0	53	30	17.66	–	–	1	–	78	49	0	–	–	–	–
Rae, A.F.	1948–49	1952–53	15	24†	2	1016	109	46.18	4	4	10	–	–	–	–	–	–	–	–
Ragoonath, S.	1998–99	1998–99	2	4	1	13	9	4.33	–	–	–	–	–	–	–	–	–	–	–
Ramadhin, S.	1950	1960–61	43	58	14	361	44	8.20	–	–	9	–	13939	4579	158	28.98	7–49	10	1
Ramdass, R.R.	2005	2005	1	2	0	26	23	13.00	–	–	2	–	–	–	–	–	–	–	–
Ramdin, D.	2005	2015–16	74	126	14	2898	166	25.87	4	15	205	12	–	–	–	–	–	–	–
Ramnarine, D.	1997–98	2001–02	12	21†	4	106	35*	6.23	–	–	8	–	3495	1383	45	30.73	5–78	1	0
Rampaul, R.	2009–10	2012–13	18	31†	8	335	40*	14.56	–	–	3	–	3440	1705	49	34.79	4–48	0	0
Reifer, F.L.	1996–97	2009	6	12†	0	111	29	9.25	–	–	6	–	–	–	–	–	–	–	–
Reifer, R.A.	2017–18	2017–18	1	2†	1	52	29	52.00	–	–	–	–	180†	88	2	44.00	1–36	0	0
Richards, D.M.	2009	2010	3	6	0	125	69	20.83	–	1	4	–	–	–	–	–	–	–	–
Richards, I.V.A.	1974–75	1991	121	182	12	8540	291	50.23	24	45	122	–	5170	1964	32	61.37	2–17	0	0
Richardson, R.B.	1983–84	1995	86	146	12	5949	194	44.39	16	27	90	–	66	18	0	–	–	–	–
Rickards, K.R.	1947–48	1951–52	2	3	0	104	67	34.66	–	1	–	–	–	–	–	–	–	–	–

INDIVIDUAL TEST CAREER RECORDS – WEST INDIES (Continued)

	First Test	Last Test	Tests	Inns	NO	Runs	HS	Avge	100	50	Ct	St	Balls	Runs	Wkts	Avge	BB	5wI	10wM
Roach, C.A.	1928	1934-35	16	32	1	952	209	30.70	2	6	5	–	222	103	2	51.50	1-18	0	0
Roach, K.A.J.	2009	2019	55	89	17	887	41	12.31	–	–	13	–	9948	5200	193	26.94	6-48	9	1
Roberts, A.M.E.	1973-74	1983-84	47	62	11	762	68	14.94	–	3	9	–	11135	5174	202	25.61	7-54	11	2
Roberts, A.T.	1955-56	1955-56	1	2	0	28	28	14.00	–	–	–	–	–	–	–	–	–	–	–
Roberts, L.A.	1998-99	1998-99	1	1	0	0	0	0.00	–	–	–	–	–	–	–	–	–	–	–
Rodriguez, W.V.	1961-62	1967-68	5	7	0	96	50	13.71	–	1	3	–	573	374	7	53.42	3-51	0	0
Rose, F.A.	1996-97	2000	19	28	2	344	69	13.23	–	1	4	–	3124	1637	53	30.88	7-84	2	0
Rowe, L.G.	1971-72	1979-80	30	49	2	2047	302	43.55	7	7	17	–	86†	44	0	–	–	–	–
Russell, A.D.	2010-11	2010-11	1	1	0	2	2	2.00	–	–	1	–	138	104	1	104.00	1-73	0	0
St Hill, E.L.	1929-30	1929-30	2	4	0	18	12	4.50	–	–	–	–	558	221	3	73.66	2-110	0	0
St Hill, W.H.	1928	1929-30	3	6	0	117	38	19.50	–	–	1	–	12	9	0	–	–	–	–
Sammy, D.J.G.	2007	2013-14	38	63	2	1323	106	21.68	1	5	65	–	6215	3007	84	35.79	7-66	4	1
Samuels, M.N.	2000-01	2016-17	71	127	7	3917	260	32.64	7	24	28	–	4392	2445	41	59.63	4-13	0	0
Samuels, R.G.	1995-96	1996-97	6	12†	2	372	125	37.20	1	1	8	–	–	–	–	–	–	–	–
Sanford, A.	2001-02	2003-04	11	17	2	72	18*	4.80	–	–	4	–	2217	1316	30	43.86	4-132	0	0
Sarwan, R.R.	1999-00	2011	87	154	8	5842	291	40.01	15	31	53	–	2022	1163	23	50.56	4-37	0	0
Scarlett, R.O.	1959-60	1959-60	3	4	1	54	29*	18.00	–	–	2	–	804	209	2	104.50	1-46	0	0
Scott, A.H.P.	1952-53	1952-53	1	1	0	5	5	5.00	–	–	–	–	264	140	0	–	–	–	–
Scott, O.C.	1928	1930-31	8	13	3	171	35	17.10	–	–	–	–	1405	925	22	42.04	5-266	1	0
Sealey, B.J.	1933	1933	1	2	0	41	29	20.50	–	–	–	–	30	10	1	10.00	1-10	0	0
Sealy, J.E.D.	1929-30	1939	11	19	2	478	92	28.11	–	3	6	1	156	94	3	31.33	2-7	0	0
Shepherd, J.N.	1969	1970-71	5	8	0	77	32	9.62	–	–	4	–	1445	479	19	25.21	5-104	1	0
Shillingford, G.C.	1969	1971-72	7	8†	1	57	25	8.14	–	–	2	–	1181	537	15	35.80	3-63	0	0
Shillingford, I.T.	1976-77	1977-78	4	7	0	218	120	31.14	1	–	1	–	–	–	–	–	–	–	–
Shillingford, S.	2010	2014	16	26	6	266	53*	13.30	–	1	9	–	4694	2419	70	34.55	6-49	6	2
Shivnarine, S.	1977-78	1978-79	8	14	1	379	63	29.15	–	4	6	–	336†	167	1	167.00	1-13	0	0
Simmons, L.M.P.	2008-09	2011-12	8	16	0	278	49	17.37	–	–	5	–	192	147	1	147.00	1-60	0	0
Simmons, P.V.	1987-88	1997-98	26	47	2	1002	110	22.26	1	4	26	–	624	257	4	64.25	2-34	0	0
Singh, C.K.	1959-60	1959-60	2	3†	0	11	11	3.66	–	–	2	–	506†	166	5	33.20	2-28	0	0
Singh, V.A.	2016-17	2016-17	3	6†	0	63	32	10.50	–	–	2	–	–	–	–	–	–	–	–
Small, J.A.	1928	1929-30	3	6	0	79	52	13.16	–	1	3	–	366	184	3	61.33	2-67	0	0
Small, M.A.	1983-84	1984	2	1	1	3	3*	–	–	–	–	–	270	153	4	38.25	3-40	0	0
Smith, C.W.	1960-61	1961-62	5	10	1	222	55	24.66	–	1	4	1	–	–	–	–	–	–	–
Smith, D.R.	2003-04	2005-06	10	14	1	320	105*	24.61	1	–	9	–	651	344	7	49.14	3-71	0	0

Smith, D.S.	2002–03	43	76†	2	1760	108	23.78	1	—	8	36	—	6	4431	1625	48	33.85	5–90	—	—
Smith, O.G.	1954–55	26	42	0	1331	168	31.69	4	—	6	9	—	3	21599†	7999	235	34.03	6–73	1	0
Sobers, G.S.	1953–54	93	160†	21	8032	365*	57.78	26	—	30	109	—	—	702	268	4	67.00	1–20	6	0
Solomon, J.S.	1958–59	27	46	7	1326	100*	34.00	1	—	9	13	—	—	636	364	9	40.44	3–65	0	0
Stayers, S.C.	1961–62	4	4	1	58	35*	19.33	—	—	12	20	—	—	990	507	13	39.00	3–32	0	0
Stollmeyer, J.B.	1954–55	32	56	5	2159	160	42.33	4	—	1	—	—	—	—	—	—	—	—	—	—
Stollmeyer, V.H.	1939	1	1	0	96	96	96.00	—	—	—	—	—	—	—	—	—	—	—	—	—
Stuart, C.E.L.	2001–02	6	9	2	24	12*	3.42	—	—	1	2	—	—	1116	628	20	31.40	3–33	0	0
Taylor, J.E.	2003	46	73	7	856	106	12.96	1	—	1	8	—	—	7757	4480	130	34.46	6–47	4	0
Taylor, J.O.	1957–58	3	5	3	4	4*	2.00	—	—	—	—	—	—	672	273	10	27.30	5–109	1	0
Thompson, P.I.C.	1995–96	2	3	1	17	10*	8.50	—	—	—	—	—	—	228	215	5	43.00	2–58	0	0
Tonge, G.C.	2009–10	1	2	1	25	23*	25.00	—	—	—	—	—	—	168	113	1	113.00	1–28	0	0
Trim, J.	1947–48	4	5	1	21	12	5.25	—	—	—	2	—	—	794	291	18	16.16	5–34	1	0
Valentine, A.L.	1950	36	51	21	141	14	4.70	—	—	1	13	—	—	12953†	4215	139	30.32	8–104	8	2
Valentine, V.A.	1933	2	4	2	35	19*	11.66	—	—	—	—	—	—	288	104	1	104.00	1–55	0	0
Walcott, C.L.	1959–60	44	74	7	3798	220	56.68	15	—	14	53	11	—	1194	408	11	37.09	3–50	0	0
Walcott, L.A.	1929–30	1	2	1	40	24	40.00	—	—	—	—	—	—	48	32	1	32.00	1–17	0	0
Wallace, P.A.	1997–98	7	13	0	279	92	21.46	—	—	2	9	—	—	—	—	—	—	—	—	—
Walsh, C.A.	1984–85	132	185	61	936	30*	7.54	—	—	—	29	—	—	30019	12688	519	24.44	7–37	22	3
Walton, C.A.K.	2009	2	4	0	13	10	3.25	—	—	—	10	—	—	—	—	—	—	—	—	—
Warrican, J.A.	2015–16	7	13	8	138	41	27.60	—	—	—	2	—	—	1396†	806	21	38.38	4–62	0	0
Washington, D.M.	2004–05	1	1	1	7	7*	—	—	—	—	3	—	—	174	93	0	—	—	—	—
Watson, C.D.	1961–62	7	6	1	12	5	2.40	—	—	—	1	—	—	1458	724	19	38.10	4–62	0	0
Weekes, E.D.	1947–48	48	81	5	4455	207	58.61	15	—	19	49	—	—	122	77	1	77.00	1–8	0	0
Weekes, K.H.	1939	2	3†	0	173	137	57.66	1	—	1	1	—	—	—	—	—	—	—	—	—
White, A.W.	1964–65	2	4	1	71	57*	23.66	—	—	1	1	—	—	491	152	3	50.66	2–34	0	0
Wight, C.V.	1928	2	4	1	67	23	22.33	—	—	—	—	—	—	30	6	0	—	—	—	—
Wight, G.L.	1952–53	1	1	0	21	21	21.00	—	—	—	—	—	—	—	—	—	—	—	—	—
Wiles, C.A.	1933	1	2	0	2	2	1.00	—	—	—	—	—	—	—	—	—	—	—	—	—
Willett, E.T.	1974–75	5	8†	3	74	26	14.80	—	—	2	5	—	—	1326†	482	11	43.81	3–33	0	0
Williams, A.B.	1977–78	7	12	0	469	111	39.08	2	—	1	—	—	—	—	—	—	—	—	—	—
Williams, D.	1991–92	11	19	1	242	65	13.44	—	—	1	40	2	—	—	—	—	—	—	—	—
Williams, E.A.V.	1939	4	6	0	113	72	18.83	—	—	1	2	—	—	796	241	9	26.77	3–51	0	0
Williams, S.C.	1993–94	31	52	3	1183	128	24.14	1	—	3	27	—	—	18	19	0	—	—	—	—
Wishart, K.L.	1934–35	1	2†	0	52	52	26.00	—	—	1	—	—	—	—	—	—	—	—	—	—
Worrell, F.M.M.	1947–48	51	87	9	3860	261	49.48	9	—	22	43	—	—	7141†	2672	69	38.72	7–70	2	0

INDIVIDUAL TEST CAREER RECORDS – NEW ZEALAND

	First Test	Last Test	Tests	Inns	NO	Runs	HS	Avge	100	50	Ct	St	Balls	Runs	Wkts	Avge	BB	5wI	10wM
Adams, A.R.	2001-02	2001-02	1	2	0	18	11	9.00	–	–	1	–	190	105	6	17.50	3-44	0	0
Alabaster, J.C.	1955-56	1971-72	21	34	6	272	34	9.71	–	–	7	–	3992	1863	49	38.02	4-46	0	0
Allcott, C.F.W.	1929-30	1931-32	6	7†	2	113	33	22.60	–	–	3	–	1206†	541	6	90.16	2-102	0	0
Allott, G.I.	1995-96	1999	10	15	7	27	8*	3.37	–	–	2	–	2023†	1111	19	58.47	4-74	0	0
Anderson, C.J.	2013-14	2015-16	13	22†	1	683	116	32.52	1	4	7	–	1302†	659	16	41.18	3-47	0	0
Anderson, R.W.	1976-77	1978	9	18	0	423	92	23.50	–	3	1	–	–						
Anderson, W.M.	1945-46	1945-46	1	2†	0	5	4	2.50	–	–	1	–	–						
Andrews, B.	1973-74	1973-74	2	3	2	22	17	22.00	–	–	1	–	256	154	2	77.00	2-40	0	0
Arnel, B.J.	2009-10	2011-12	6	12	4	45	8*	5.62	–	–	3	–	1008	566	9	62.88	4-95	0	0
Astle, N.J.	1995-96	2006-07	81	137	10	4702	222	37.02	11	24	70	–	5688	2143	51	42.01	3-27	0	0
Astle, T.D.	2012-13	2018-19	4	4	0	56	35	14.00	–	–	2	–	427	216	4	54.00	3-39	0	0
Badcock, F.T.	1929-30	1932-33	7	9	2	137	64	19.57	–	2	1	–	1608	610	16	38.12	4-80	0	0
Barber, R.T.	1955-56	1955-56	1	2	0	17	12	8.50	–	–	1	–	–						
Bartlett, G.A.	1961-62	1967-68	10	18	1	263	40	15.47	–	–	8	–	1768	792	24	33.00	6-38	1	0
Barton, P.T.	1961-62	1962-63	7	14	0	285	109	20.35	1	1	4	–	–						
Beard, D.D.	1951-52	1955-56	4	7	2	101	31	20.20	–	–	2	–	806	302	9	33.55	3-22	0	0
Beck, J.E.F.	1953-54	1955-56	8	15†	0	394	99	26.26	–	3	5	–	–						
Bell, M.D.	1998-99	2007-08	18	32	2	729	107	24.30	2	3	19	–	–						
Bell, W.	1953-54	1953-54	2	3	3	21	21*	–	–	–	1	–	491	235	2	117.50	1-54	0	0
Bennett, H.K.	2010-11	2010-11	1	1†	0	4	4	4.00	–	–	–	–	90	47	0	–	–	–	–
Bilby, G.P.	1965-66	1965-66	2	4	0	55	28	13.75	–	–	3	–	–						
Blain, T.E.	1986	1993-94	11	20	3	456	78	26.82	–	2	19	2	–						
Blair, R.W.	1952-53	1963-64	19	34	6	189	64*	6.75	–	1	5	–	3525	1515	43	35.23	4-85	0	0
Blundell, T.A.	2017-18	2017-18	2	3	1	136	107*	68.00	1	–	2	–	–						
Blunt, R.C.	1929-30	1931-32	9	13	1	330	96	27.50	–	1	5	–	936	472	12	39.33	3-17	0	0
Bolton, B.A.	1958-59	1958-59	2	3	0	59	33	19.66	–	–	1	–	–						
Bond, S.E.	2001-02	2009-10	18	20	7	168	41*	12.92	–	–	8	–	3372	1922	87	22.09	6-51	5	1
Boock, S.L.	1977-78	1988-89	30	41	8	207	37	6.27	–	–	14	–	6598†	2564	74	34.64	7-87	4	0
Boult, T.A.	2011-12	2019	63	78	37	606	52*	14.78	–	1	36	–	13986†	6947	254	27.35	6-30	8	1
Bracewell, B.P.	1978	1984-85	6	12	2	24	8	2.40	–	–	1	–	1036	585	14	41.78	3-110	0	0
Bracewell, D.A.J.	2011-12	2016	27	45	4	568	47	13.85	–	–	10	–	4984	2796	72	38.83	6-40	2	0
Bracewell, J.G.	1980-81	1990	41	60	11	1001	110	20.42	1	4	31	–	8403	3653	102	35.81	6-32	4	1
Bradburn, G.E.	1990-91	2000-01	7	10	2	105	30*	13.12	–	–	6	–	867	460	6	76.66	3-134	0	0
Bradburn, W.P.	1963-64	1963-64	2	4	0	62	32	15.50	–	–	2	–	–						
Broom, N.T.	2016-17	2016-17	2	3	0	32	20	10.66	–	–	–	–	–						

Name	Career	Season	M	I	NO	Runs	HS	Avg	100	50	Ct	St	Balls	Runs	Wkts	Avg	BB	5w	10w
Brown, V.R.	1985–86	1985–86	2	3†	1	51	36*	25.50	—	—	—	3	—	342	176	1	176.00	1–17	—	0	0
Brownlie, D.G.	2011–12	2013	14	25	1	711	109	29.62	1	4	—	17	—	66	52	1	52.00	1–13	—	0	0
Burgess, M.G.	1967–68	1980–81	50	92	6	2684	119*	31.20	5	14	—	34	—	498	212	6	35.33	3–23	—	0	0
Burke, C.	1945–46	1945–46	1	2	0	4	3	2.00	—	—	—	—	—	66	30	2	15.00	2–30	—	0	0
Burtt, T.B.	1946–47	1952–53	10	15	3	252	42	21.00	—	—	—	2	—	2593†	1170	33	35.45	6–162	3	0	0
Butler, I.G.	2001–02	2004–05	8	10	2	76	26	9.50	—	—	—	4	—	1368	884	24	36.83	6–46	1	1	0
Butterfield, L.A.	1945–46	1945–46	1	2	0	0	0	0.00	—	—	—	—	—	78	24	0	—	—	—	0	—
Cairns, B.L.	1973–74	1985–86	43	65	8	928	64	16.28	—	2	—	30	—	10628	4279	130	32.91	7–74	6	1	—
Cairns, C.L.	1989–90	2004	62	104	5	3320	158	33.53	5	22	—	14	—	11698	6410	218	29.40	7–27	13	1	—
Cameron, F.J.	1961–62	1965	19	30	20	116	27*	11.60	—	—	—	1	—	4570	1849	62	29.82	5–34	3	0	—
Cave, H.B.	1949	1958	19	31	5	229	22*	8.80	—	—	—	8	—	4074	1467	34	43.14	4–21	0	0	—
Chapple, M.E.	1952–53	1965–66	14	27	1	497	76	19.11	—	3	—	10	—	248†	84	1	84.00	1–24	0	0	—
Chatfield, E.J.	1974–75	1988–89	43	54	33	180	21*	8.57	—	—	—	7	—	10360	3958	123	32.17	6–73	3	1	—
Cleverley, D.C.	1931–32	1945–46	2	4†	3	19	10*	19.00	—	—	—	—	—	222	130	0	—	—	—	0	—
Collinge, R.O.	1964–65	1978	35	50	13	533	68*	14.40	—	2	—	10	—	7689†	3393	116	29.25	6–63	3	0	—
Colquhoun, I.A.	1954–55	1954–55	2	4	2	1	1*	0.50	—	—	—	4	—	—	—	—	—	—	—	—	—
Coney, J.V.	1973–74	1986–87	52	85	14	2668	174*	37.57	3	16	—	64	—	2835	966	27	35.77	3–28	0	0	—
Congdon, B.E.	1964–65	1978	61	114	7	3448	176	32.22	7	19	—	44	—	5620	2154	59	36.50	5–65	1	1	—
Cowie, J.	1937	1949	9	13	4	90	45	10.00	—	—	—	3	—	2028	969	45	21.53	6–40	4	4	—
Craig, M.D.	2014	2016–17	15	25†	9	589	67	36.81	—	3	—	14	—	3669	2326	50	46.52	7–94	1	1	—
Cresswell, G.F.	1949	1950–51	3	5†	3	14	12*	7.00	—	—	—	1	—	650	292	13	22.46	6–168	1	0	—
Cromb, I.B.	1931	1931–32	5	8	2	123	51*	20.50	—	1	—	1	—	960	442	8	55.25	3–113	—	0	—
Crowe, J.J.	1982–83	1989–90	39	65	4	1601	128	26.24	3	6	—	41	—	18	9	0	—	—	—	—	—
Crowe, M.D.	1981–82	1995–96	77	131	11	5444	299	45.36	17	18	—	71	—	1377	676	14	48.28	2–25	0	0	—
Cumming, C.D.	2004–05	2007–08	11	19	2	441	74	25.94	—	1	—	3	—	—	—	—	—	—	—	1	—
Cunis, R.S.	1963–64	1971–72	20	31	8	295	51	12.82	—	1	—	1	—	4250	1887	51	37.00	6–76	—	1	—
D'Arcy, J.W.	1958	1958	5	10	0	136	33	13.60	—	—	—	—	—	—	—	—	—	—	—	—	—
Davis, H.T.	1994	1997–98	5	7	4	20	8*	6.66	—	—	—	4	—	1010	499	17	29.35	5–63	1	0	—
de Grandhomme, C.	2016–17	2019	18	27	4	903	105	39.26	1	6	—	11	—	2573	1070	35	30.57	6–41	1	0	—
de Groen, R.P.	1993–94	1994–95	5	10	4	45	26	7.50	—	—	—	—	—	1060	505	11	45.90	3–40	0	0	—
Dempster, C.S.	1929–30	1932–33	10	15	4	723	136	65.72	2	5	—	2	—	5	10	0	—	—	—	—	—
Dempster, E.W.	1952–53	1953–54	5	8†	2	106	47	17.66	—	—	—	1	—	544†	219	2	109.50	1–24	0	0	—
Dick, A.E.	1961–62	1965	17	30	4	370	50*	14.23	—	1	—	47	4	—	—	—	—	—	—	—	—
Dickinson, G.R.	1929–30	1931–32	3	5	0	31	11	6.20	—	—	—	3	—	451	245	8	30.62	3–66	0	0	—
Donnelly, M.P.	1937	1949	7	12†	1	582	206	52.90	1	4	—	7	—	30†	20	0	—	—	—	—	—
Doull, S.B.	1992–93	1999–00	32	50	11	570	46	14.61	—	—	—	16	—	6053	2872	98	29.30	7–65	6	0	—
Dowling, G.T.	1961–62	1971–72	39	77	3	2306	239	31.16	3	11	—	23	—	36	19	1	19.00	1–19	0	0	—
Drum, C.J.	2000–01	2001–02	5	5	2	10	4	3.33	—	—	—	4	—	806	482	16	30.12	3–36	0	0	—

INDIVIDUAL TEST CAREER RECORDS – NEW ZEALAND (Continued)

	First Test	Last Test	Tests	Inns	NO	Runs	HS	Avge	100	50	Ct	St	Balls	Runs	Wkts	Avge	BB	5wI	10wM
Dunning, J.A.	1932–33	1937	4	6	1	38	19	7.60	–	–	2	–	830	493	5	98.60	2–35	0	0
Edgar, B.A.	1978	1986	39	68†	4	1958	161	30.59	3	12	14	–	18	3	0	–	–	–	–
Edwards, G.N.	1976–77	1980–81	8	15	0	377	55	25.13	–	3	7	–	–	–	–	–	–	–	–
Elliott, G.D.	2007–08	2009–10	5	9	1	86	25	10.75	–	–	2	–	282	140	4	35.00	2–8	0	0
Emery, R.W.G.	1951–52	1951–52	2	4	0	46	28	11.50	–	–	–	–	46	52	2	26.00	2–52	0	0
Fisher, F.E.	1952–53	1952–53	1	2	0	23	14	11.50	–	–	–	–	204†	78	1	78.00	1–78	0	0
Fleming, S.P.	1993–94	2007–08	111	189†	10	7172	274*	40.06	9	46	171	–	–	–	–	–	–	–	–
Flynn, D.R.	2008	2012–13	24	45†	5	1038	95	25.95	–	6	10	–	6†	0	0	–	–	–	–
Foley, H.	1929–30	1929–30	1	2†	0	4	2	2.00	–	–	–	–	–	–	–	–	–	–	–
Franklin, J.E.C.	2000–01	2012–13	31	46†	7	808	122*	20.71	1	2	12	–	4767†	2786	82	33.97	6–119	3	0
Franklin, T.J.	1983	1990–91	21	37	1	828	101	23.00	1	4	8	–	–	–	–	–	–	–	–
Freeman, D.L.	1932–33	1932–33	2	2	0	2	1	1.00	–	–	–	–	240	169	1	169.00	1–91	0	0
Fulton, P.G.	2005–06	2014	23	39	1	967	136	25.44	2	5	25	–	–	–	–	–	–	–	–
Gallichan, N.	1937	1937	1	2	0	32	30	16.00	–	–	–	–	264†	113	3	37.66	3–99	0	0
Gedye, S.G.	1963–64	1964–65	4	8	0	193	55	24.12	–	2	–	–	–	–	–	–	–	–	–
Germon, L.K.	1995–96	1996–97	12	21	3	382	55	21.22	–	1	27	2	–	–	–	–	–	–	–
Gillespie, M.R.	2007–08	2011–12	5	8	1	76	27	10.85	–	–	1	–	868	631	22	28.68	6–113	3	0
Gillespie, S.R.	1985–86	1985–86	1	1	0	28	28	28.00	–	–	–	–	162	79	1	79.00	1–79	0	0
Gray, E.J.	1983	1988–89	10	16	0	248	50	15.50	–	1	6	–	2076†	886	17	52.11	3–73	0	0
Greatbatch, M.J.	1987–88	1996–97	41	71†	5	2021	146*	30.62	3	10	27	–	6	0	0	–	–	–	–
Guillen, S.C.‡	1955–56	1955–56	3	6	0	98	41	16.33	–	–	4	1	–	–	–	–	–	–	–
Guptill, M.J.	2008–09	2016–17	47	89	1	2586	189	29.38	3	17	50	–	428	298	8	37.25	3–11	0	0
Guy, J.W.	1955–56	1961–62	12	23†	2	440	102	20.95	1	3	2	–	–	–	–	–	–	–	–
Hadlee, D.R.	1969	1977–78	26	42	5	530	56	14.32	–	1	8	–	4883	2389	71	33.64	4–30	0	0
Hadlee, R.J.	1972–73	1990	86	134†	19	3124	151*	27.16	2	15	39	–	21918	9611	431	22.29	9–52	36	9
Hadlee, W.A.	1937	1950–51	11	19	1	543	116	30.16	1	2	6	–	–	–	–	–	–	–	–
Harford, N.S.	1955–56	1958	8	15	0	229	93	15.26	–	2	–	–	–	–	–	–	–	–	–
Harford, R.I.	1967–68	1967–68	3	5†	2	7	6	2.33	–	–	11	–	–	–	–	–	–	–	–
Harris, C.Z.	1992–93	2002	23	42†	4	777	71	20.44	–	5	14	–	2560	1170	16	73.12	2–16	0	0
Harris, P.G.Z.	1955–56	1964–65	9	18	1	378	101	22.23	1	1	6	–	42	14	0	–	–	–	–
Harris, R.M.	1958–59	1958–59	2	3	0	31	13	10.33	–	–	–	–	–	–	–	–	–	–	–
Hart, M.N.	1993–94	1995–96	14	24†	4	353	45	17.65	–	–	9	–	3086†	1438	29	49.58	5–77	1	0
Hart, R.G.	2002	2003–04	11	19	3	260	57*	16.25	–	1	29	1	–	–	–	–	–	–	–
Hartland, B.R.	1991–92	1994	9	18	0	303	52	16.83	–	1	5	–	–	–	–	–	–	–	–

Haslam, M.J.	1992–93	1995–96	4	2†	1	4	3	4.00	–	–	2	–	493†	245	2	122.50	1–33	0	0
Hastings, B.F.	1968–69	1975–76	31	56	6	1510	117*	30.20	4	7	23	–	22	9	0	–	–	–	–
Hayes, J.A.	1950–51	1958	15	22	7	73	19	4.86	–	–	3	–	2675	1217	30	40.56	4–36	0	0
Henderson, M.	1929–30	1929–30	1	2†	1	8	6	8.00	–	1	1	–	90†	64	2	32.00	2–38	0	0
Henry, M.J.	2015	2018–19	10	14	3	216	66	19.63	–	–	5	–	2299	1270	27	47.03	4–93	0	0
Hopkins, G.J.	2008	2010–11	4	7	1	71	15	11.83	–	–	9	–	–	–	–	–	–	–	–
Horne, M.J.	1996–97	2003	35	65	2	1788	157	28.38	4	5	17	–	66	26	0	–	–	–	–
Horne, P.A.	1986–87	1990–91	4	7†	0	71	27	10.14	–	–	3	–	–	–	–	–	–	–	–
Hough, K.W.	1958–59	1958–59	2	3	2	62	31*	62.00	–	–	1	–	462	175	6	29.16	3–79	0	0
How, J.M.	2005–06	2008–09	19	35	1	772	92	22.70	–	4	18	–	12	4	0	–	–	–	–
Howarth, G.P.	1974–75	1984–85	47	83	5	2531	147	32.44	6	11	29	–	614	271	3	90.33	1–13	0	0
Howarth, H.J.	1969	1976–77	30	42†	18	291	61	12.12	–	1	33	–	8833†	3178	86	36.95	5–34	2	–
Ingram, P.J.	2009–10	2009–10	2	4	0	61	42	15.25	–	–	–	–	–	–	–	–	–	–	–
James, K.C.	1929–30	1932–33	11	13	2	52	14	4.72	–	–	11	5	–	–	–	–	–	–	–
Jarvis, T.W.	1964–65	1972–73	13	22	1	625	182	29.76	1	2	3	–	12†	3	0	–	–	–	–
Jones, A.H.	1986–87	1994–95	39	74	8	2922	186	44.27	7	11	25	–	328	194	1	194.00	1–40	0	0
Jones, R.A.	2003–04	2003–04	1	2	0	23	16	11.50	–	–	2	–	–	–	–	–	–	–	–
Kennedy, R.J.	1995–96	1995–96	4	5	1	28	22	7.00	–	–	2	–	636	380	6	63.33	3–28	0	0
Kerr, J.L.	1931	1937	7	12	1	212	59	19.27	–	1	4	–	–	–	–	–	–	–	–
Kuggeleijn, C.M.	1988–89	1988–89	2	4	0	7	7	1.75	–	–	1	–	97	67	1	67.00	1–50	0	0
Larsen, G.R.	1994	1995–96	8	13	4	127	26*	14.11	–	–	5	–	1967	689	24	28.70	3–57	0	0
Latham, R.T.	1991–92	1992–93	4	7	0	219	119	31.28	1	–	5	–	18	6	0	–	–	–	–
Latham, T.W.M.	2013–14	2019	45	79†	3	3347	264*	44.03	10	15	45	–	5	4	0	–	–	–	–
Lees, W.K.	1976–77	1983	21	37	4	778	152	23.57	1	1	52	7	24	6	0	–	–	–	–
Leggat, I.B.	1953–54	1953–54	1	1	0	0	0	0.00	–	–	1	–	–	–	–	–	–	–	–
Leggat, J.G.	1951–52	1955–56	9	18	2	351	61	21.93	–	2	2	–	–	–	–	–	–	–	–
Lissette, A.F.	1955–56	1955–56	2	4	2	2	1*	1.00	–	–	1	–	288†	124	3	41.33	2–73	0	–
Loveridge, G.R.	1995–96	1995–96	1	1	1	4	4*	–	–	–	–	–	–	–	–	–	–	–	–
Lowry, T.C.	1929–30	1931	7	8	0	223	80	27.87	–	2	8	–	12	5	0	–	–	–	–
McCullum, B.B.	2003–04	2015–16	101	176	9	6453	302	38.64	12	31	198	11	175	88	1	88.00	1–1	0	0
McEwan, P.E.	1979–80	1984–85	4	7	1	96	40*	16.00	–	–	5	–	36	13	0	–	–	–	0
MacGibbon, A.R.	1950–51	1958	26	46	5	814	66	19.85	–	3	13	–	5659	2160	70	30.85	5–64	1	0
McGirr, H.M.	1929–30	1929–30	2	1	0	51	51	51.00	–	1	–	–	180	115	1	115.00	1–65	0	0
McGregor, S.N.	1954–55	1964–65	25	47	2	892	111	19.82	1	3	9	–	–	–	–	–	–	–	–
McIntosh, T.G.	2008–09	2010–11	17	33†	2	854	136	27.54	2	4	10	–	–	–	–	–	–	–	–
McKay, A.J.	2010–11	2010–11	1	2	1	25	20*	25.00	–	–	–	–	186†	120	1	120.00	1–120	0	0
McLeod, E.G.	1929–30	1929–30	1	2†	1	18	16	18.00	–	–	–	–	12	5	0	–	–	–	–
McMahon, T.G.	1955–56	1955–56	5	7	4	7	4*	2.33	–	–	7	1	–	–	–	–	–	–	–

INDIVIDUAL TEST CAREER RECORDS – NEW ZEALAND (Continued)

	First Test	Last Test	Tests	Inns	NO	Runs	HS	Avge	100	50	Ct	St	Balls	Runs	Wkts	Avge	BB	5wI	10wM
McMillan, C.D.	1997–98	2004–05	55	91	10	3116	142	38.46	6	19	22	–	2502	1257	28	44.89	3–48	0	0
McRae, D.A.N.	1945–46	1945–46	1	2†	0	8	8	4.00	–	–	–	–	84†	44	0	–	–	–	–
Marshall, H.J.H.	2000–01	2005–06	13	19	2	652	160	38.35	2	2	1	–	6	4	0	–	–	–	–
Marshall, J.A.H.	2004–05	2008	7	11	0	218	52	19.81	–	1	5	–	–	–	–	–	–	–	–
Martin, B.P.	2012–13	2013–14	5	6	1	74	41	14.80	–	–	–	–	1518†	646	12	53.83	4–43	0	0
Martin, C.S.	2000–01	2012–13	71	104	52	123	12*	2.36	–	–	14	–	14026	7878	233	33.81	6–26	10	1
Mason, M.J.	2003–04	2003–04	1	2	0	3	3	1.50	–	–	–	–	132	105	0	–	–	–	–
Matheson, A.M.	1929–30	1931	2	1	0	7	7	7.00	–	–	2	–	282	136	2	68.00	2–7	0	0
Meale, T.	1958	1958	2	4†	0	21	10	5.25	–	–	–	–	–	–	–	–	–	–	–
Merritt, W.E.	1929–30	1931	6	8	2	73	19	10.42	–	–	2	–	936	617	12	51.41	4–104	0	0
Meuli, E.M.	1952–53	1952–53	1	2	0	38	23	19.00	–	–	–	–	–	–	–	–	–	–	–
Milburn, B.D.	1968–69	1968–69	3	3	2	8	4*	8.00	–	–	6	2	–	–	–	–	–	–	–
Miller, L.S.M.	1952–53	1958	13	25†	0	346	47	13.84	–	–	1	–	2†	1	0	–	–	–	–
Mills, J.E.	1929–30	1932–33	7	10†	1	241	117	26.77	1	–	1	–	–	–	–	–	–	–	–
Mills, K.D.	2004	2008–09	19	30	5	289	57	11.56	–	1	4	–	2902	1453	44	33.02	4–16	0	0
Moir, A.M.	1950–51	1958–59	17	30	8	327	41*	14.86	–	–	2	–	2650	1418	28	50.64	6–155	2	0
Moloney, D.A.R.	1937	1937	3	6	0	156	64	26.00	–	1	3	–	12	9	0	–	–	–	–
Mooney, F.L.H.	1949	1953–54	14	22	2	343	46	17.15	–	–	22	8	8	0	0	–	–	–	–
Morgan, R.W.	1964–65	1971–72	20	34	1	734	97	22.24	–	5	12	–	1114	609	5	121.80	1–16	0	0
Morrison, B.D.	1962–63	1962–63	1	2†	0	10	10	5.00	–	–	1	–	186	129	2	64.50	2–129	0	0
Morrison, D.K.	1987–88	1996–97	48	71	26	379	42	8.42	–	–	14	–	10064	5549	160	34.68	7–89	10	0
Morrison, J.F.M.	1973–74	1981–82	17	29	0	656	117	22.62	1	3	9	–	264†	71	2	35.50	2–52	0	0
Motz, R.C.	1961–62	1969	32	56	3	612	60	11.54	–	3	9	–	7034	3148	100	31.48	6–63	5	0
Munro, C.	2012–13	2012–13	1	2†	0	15	15	7.50	–	–	–	–	108	40	2	20.00	2–40	0	0
Murray, B.A.G.	1967–68	1970–71	13	26	1	598	90	23.92	–	5	21	–	6	0	1	0.00	1–0	0	0
Murray, D.J.	1994–95	1994–95	8	16	1	303	52	20.20	–	1	6	–	–	–	–	–	–	–	–
Nash, D.J.	1992–93	2001–02	32	45	14	729	89*	23.51	–	4	13	–	6196	2649	93	28.48	6–27	3	1
Neesham, J.D.S.	2013–14	2016–17	12	22†	1	709	137*	33.76	2	4	12	–	1076	675	14	48.21	3–42	0	0
Newman, J.	1931–32	1932–33	3	4	0	33	19	8.25	–	–	–	–	425†	254	2	127.00	2–76	0	0
Nicholls, H.M.	2015–16	2019	27	41†	5	1593	162*	44.25	5	9	18	–	–	–	–	–	–	–	–
Nicol, R.J.	2011–12	2011–12	2	4	0	28	19	7.00	–	–	2	–	17	13	0	–	–	–	–
O'Brien, I.E.	2004–05	2009–10	22	34	5	219	31	7.55	–	–	7	–	4394	2429	73	33.27	6–75	1	0
O'Connor, S.B.	1997–98	2001–02	19	27†	9	103	20	5.72	–	–	6	–	3667†	1724	53	32.52	5–51	0	0
Oram, J.D.P.	2002–03	2009	33	59†	10	1780	133	36.32	5	6	15	–	4964	1983	60	33.05	4–41	0	0

O'Sullivan, D.R.	1972–73 1976–77	11	21	4	158	23*	9.29	–	–	2	2744†	1221	18	67.83	5–148	1	0
Overton, G.W.F.	1953–54	3	6†	1	8	3*	1.60	–	–	1	729	258	9	28.66	3–65	–	0
Owens, M.B.	1992–93 1994	8	12	6	16	8*	2.66	–	–	3	1074	585	17	34.41	4–99	–	0
Page, M.L.	1929–30 1937	14	20	0	492	104	24.60	1	2	6	379	231	5	46.20	2–21	–	0
Papps, M.H.W.	2003–04 2007–08	8	16	1	246	86	16.40	–	2	11	–	–	–	–	–	–	–
Parker, J.M.	1972–73 1980–81	36	63	5	1498	121	24.55	3	5	30	40	24	1	24.00	1–24	0	0
Parker, N.M.	1976–77	3	6	0	89	40	14.83	–	–	2	–	–	–	–	–	–	–
Parore, A.C.	1990 2001–02	78	128	19	2865	110	26.28	2	14	197	–	–	–	–	–	–	–
Patel, A.Y.	2018–19 2019	7	9†	2	49	14	7.00	–	–	5	1589†	708	22	32.18	5–59	2	0
Patel, D.N.	1986–87 1996–97	37	66	8	1200	99	20.68	–	5	15	6594	3154	75	42.05	6–50	3	0
Patel, J.S.	2005–06 2016–17	24	38	8	381	47	12.70	–	–	13	5833	3078	65	47.35	5–110	1	0
Petherick, P.J.	1976–77	6	11	4	34	13	4.85	–	–	4	1305	685	16	42.81	3–90	0	0
Petrie, E.C.	1955–56 1965–66	14	25	5	258	55	12.90	–	1	25	–	–	–	–	–	–	–
Playle, W.R.	1958 1962–63	8	15	0	151	65	10.06	–	1	4	–	–	–	–	–	–	–
Pocock, B.A.	1993–94 1997–98	15	29	0	665	85	22.93	–	6	5	24	20	0	–	–	–	0
Pollard, V.	1964–65 1973	32	59	7	1266	116	24.34	2	7	19	4421	1853	40	46.32	3–3	0	0
Poore, M.B.	1952–53 1955–56	14	24	1	355	45	15.43	–	–	1	788	367	9	40.77	2–28	0	0
Priest, M.W.	1990 1998	3	4†	0	56	26	14.00	–	–	–	377†	158	3	52.66	2–42	0	0
Pringle, C.	1990–91 1994–95	14	21	4	175	30	10.29	–	–	3	2985	1389	30	46.30	7–52	1	1
Puna, N.	1965–66	3	5	3	31	18*	15.50	–	–	–	480	240	4	60.00	2–40	0	0
Rabone, G.O.	1949 1954–55	12	20	2	562	107	31.22	1	2	5	1385	635	16	39.68	6–68	1	0
Raval, J.A.	2016–17 2019	20	32†	1	1074	132	34.64	1	7	18	6	1	0	–	–	–	–
Redmond, A.J.	2008 2013–14	8	16	1	325	83	21.66	–	2	5	105	80	3	26.66	2–47	0	0
Redmond, R.E.	1972–73	1	2†	0	163	107	81.50	1	–	–	–	–	–	–	–	–	–
Reid, J.F.	1978–79 1985–86	19	31†	3	1296	180	46.28	6	2	9	18	7	0	–	–	–	0
Reid, J.R.	1949 1965	58	108	5	3428	142	33.28	6	22	43	7725	2835	85	33.35	6–60	1	0
Richardson, M.H.	2000–01 2004–05	38	65†	3	2776	145	44.77	4	19	26	66†	21	1	21.00	1–16	0	0
Roberts, A.D.G.	1975–76 1976–77	7	12	1	254	84*	23.09	–	1	4	440	182	4	45.50	1–12	0	0
Roberts, A.W.	1929–30 1937	5	10	1	248	66*	27.55	–	3	4	459	209	7	29.85	4–101	0	0
Robertson, G.K.	1985–86	1	1	0	12	12	12.00	–	–	–	144	91	1	91.00	1–91	0	0
Ronchi, L.	2015 2016–17	4	8	0	319	88	39.87	–	2	5	–	–	–	–	–	–	–
Rowe, C.G.	1945–46	1	2	0	0	0	0.00	–	–	1	–	–	–	–	–	–	–
Rutherford, H.D.	2012–13 2014–15	16	29†	1	755	171	26.96	1	1	11	6†	2	0	–	–	–	–
Rutherford, K.R.	1984–85 1994–95	56	99	8	2465	107*	27.08	3	18	32	256	161	1	161.00	1–38	0	0
Ryder, J.D.	2008–09 2011–12	18	33†	2	1269	201	40.93	3	6	12	492	280	5	56.00	2–7	0	0
Santner, M.J.	2015–16 2019	18	23†	0	560	73	24.34	–	2	9	2846†	1329	34	39.08	3–60	0	0
Scott, R.H.	1946–47	1	1	0	18	18	18.00	–	–	–	138	74	1	74.00	1–74	0	0
Scott, V.J.	1945–46 1951–52	10	17	1	458	84	28.62	–	3	7	18	14	0	–	–	–	–

INDIVIDUAL TEST CAREER RECORDS – NEW ZEALAND (Continued)

	First Test	Last Test	Tests	Inns	NO	Runs	HS	Avge	100	50	Ct	St	Balls	Runs	Wkts	Avge	BB	5wI	10wM
Sewell, D.G.	1997-98	1997-98	1	1	0	1	1*	–	–	–	–	–	138†	90	0	–	–	0	–
Shrimpton, M.J.F.	1962-63	1973-74	10	19	0	265	46	13.94	–	–	2	–	257	158	5	31.60	3–35	0	0
Sinclair, B.W.	1962-63	1967-68	21	40	1	1148	138	29.43	3	3	8	–	60	32	2	16.00	2–32	0	0
Sinclair, I.M.	1955-56	1955-56	2	4†	1	25	18*	8.33	–	–	1	–	233	120	1	120.00	1–79	0	0
Sinclair, M.S.	1999-00	2009-10	33	56	5	1635	214	32.05	3	4	31	–	42	14	0	–	–	–	–
Smith, F.B.	1946-47	1951-52	4	6	1	237	96	47.40	–	2	1	–							
Smith, H.D.	1932-33	1932-33	1	1	0	4	4	4.00	–	–	–	–	120	113	1	113.00	1–113	0	0
Smith, I.D.S.	1980-81	1991-92	63	88	17	1815	173	25.56	2	6	168	8	18	5	0	–	–	–	–
Snedden, C.A.	1946-47	1946-47	1	–	–	–	–	–	–	–	–	–	96	46	0	–	–	–	–
Snedden, M.C.	1980-81	1990	25	30†	8	327	33*	14.86	–	–	7	–	4775	2199	58	37.91	5–68	1	0
Sodhi, I.S.	2013-14	2018-19	17	25	4	448	63	21.33	–	3	11	–	3186	1992	41	48.58	4–60	0	0
Somerville, W.E.R.	2018-19	2019	3	4	2	65	40*	32.50	–	–	1	–	818	352	14	25.14	4–75	0	0
Southee, T.G.	2007-08	2019	67	98	10	1611	77*	18.30	–	5	47	–	14870	7506	251	29.90	7–64	8	1
Sparling, J.T.	1958	1963-64	11	20	2	229	50	12.72	–	1	4	–	708	327	5	65.40	1–9	0	0
Spearman, C.M.	1995-96	2000-01	19	37	2	922	112	26.34	1	3	21	–							
Stead, G.R.	1998-99	1999-00	5	8	0	278	78	34.75	–	2	2	–	6	1	0	–	–	–	–
Stirling, D.A.	1984-85	1986	6	9	2	108	26	15.42	–	–	1	–	902	601	13	46.23	4–88	0	0
Styris, S.B.	2002	2007-08	29	48	4	1586	170	36.04	5	6	23	–	1960	1015	20	50.75	3–28	0	0
Su'a, M.L.	1991-92	1994-95	13	18†	5	165	44	12.69	–	–	8	–	2843†	1377	36	38.25	5–73	2	0
Sutcliffe, B.	1946-47	1965	42	76†	8	2727	230*	40.10	5	15	20	–	538†	344	4	86.00	2–38	0	0
Taylor, B.R.	1964-65	1973	30	50†	6	898	124	20.40	2	2	10	–	6334	2953	111	26.60	7–74	4	0
Taylor, D.D.	1946-47	1955-56	3	5	0	159	77	31.80	–	1	2	–							
Taylor, L.R.P.L.	2007-08	2019	94	166	19	6839	290	46.52	18	31	139	–	96	48	2	24.00	2–4	0	0
Thomson, K.	1967-68	1967-68	2	4	1	94	69	31.33	–	1	–	–	21	9	1	9.00	1–9	0	0
Thomson, S.A.	1989-90	1995-96	19	35	4	958	120*	30.90	1	5	7	–	1990	953	19	50.15	3–63	0	0
Tindill, E.W.T.	1937	1946-47	5	9†	1	73	37*	9.12	–	–	6	1							
Troup, G.B.	1976-77	1985-86	15	18	6	55	13*	4.58	–	–	2	–	3183†	1454	39	37.28	6–95	1	1
Truscott, P.B.	1964-65	1964-65	1	2	0	29	26	14.50	–	–	1	–							
Tuffey, D.R.	1999-00	2009-10	26	36	10	427	80*	16.42	–	1	15	–	4877	2445	77	31.75	6–54	2	0
Turner, G.M.	1968-69	1982-83	41	73	6	2991	259	44.64	7	14	42	–	12	5	0	–	–	–	–
Twose, R.G.	1995-96	1999	16	27†	2	628	94	25.12	–	6	5	–	211	130	3	43.33	2–36	0	0
Vance, R.H.	1987-88	1989-90	4	7	0	207	68	29.57	–	1	–	–							
van Wyk, C.F.K.	2011-12	2012-13	9	17	1	341	71	21.31	–	1	23	1							

Vaughan, J.T.C.	1992–93	1996–97	6	12†	1	201	44	18.27	–	–	4	–	1040	450	11	40.90	4–27	0	0
Vettori, D.L.‡	1996–97	2014–15	112	172†	22	4523	140	30.15	6	23	58	–	28652†	12330	361	34.15	7–87	20	3
Vincent, L.	2001–02	2007–08	23	40	1	1332	224	34.15	3	9	19	–	6	2	0	–	–	–	–
Vivian, G.E.	1964–65	1971–72	5	6†	0	110	43	18.33	1	–	3	–	198	107	1	107.00	1–14	0	0
Vivian, H.G.	1931	1937	7	10†	0	421	100	42.10	–	5	4	–	1311†	633	17	37.23	4–58	0	0
Wadsworth, K.J.	1969	1975–76	33	51	4	1010	80	21.48	–	5	92	–	–	4788	174	27.51	7–39	7	0
Wagner, N.	2012	2018–19	42	54†	13	511	47	12.46	–	–	10	4	9167†	399	5	79.80	2–92	0	0
Walker, B.G.K.	2000–01	2002	5	8	2	118	27*	19.66	–	–	–	–	669	5	0	–	–	0	0
Wallace, W.M.	1937	1952–53	13	21	0	439	66	20.90	–	5	5	–	6	391	9	43.44	3–70	0	–
Walmsley, K.P.	1994–95	2000–01	3	5	0	13	5	2.60	–	–	–	–	774	–	–	–	–	–	–
Ward, J.T.	1963–64	1967–68	8	12	6	75	35*	12.50	–	–	16	1	–	–	–	–	–	–	–
Watling, B.J.	2009–10	2019	63	100	15	3279	142*	38.57	7	17	216	8	–	–	–	–	–	–	–
Watson, W.	1986	1993–94	15	18	6	60	11	5.00	–	–	4	–	3486	1387	40	34.67	6–78	1	0
Watt, L.	1954–55	1954–55	1	2	0	2	2	1.00	–	–	–	–	–	–	–	–	–	–	–
Webb, M.G.	1970–71	1973–74	3	2	0	12	12	6.00	–	–	–	–	732	471	4	117.75	2–114	0	0
Webb, P.N.	1979–80	1979–80	2	3	0	11	5	3.66	–	–	2	–	–	–	–	–	–	–	–
Weir, G.L.	1929–30	1937	11	16	2	416	74*	29.71	–	3	3	–	342	209	7	29.85	3–38	0	0
White, D.J.	1990–91	1990–91	2	4	0	31	18	7.75	–	–	–	–	3	5	0	–	–	–	–
Whitelaw, P.E.	1932–33	1932–33	2	4	2	64	30	32.00	–	–	–	–	–	–	–	–	–	–	–
Williamson, K.S.	2010–11	2019	74	130	12	6163	242*	52.22	20	30	69	–	2097	1172	29	40.41	4–44	0	0
Wiseman, P.J.	1998	2004–05	25	34	8	366	36	14.07	–	–	11	–	5660	2903	61	47.59	5–82	2	0
Wright, J.G.	1977–78	1992–93	82	148†	7	5334	185	37.82	12	23	38	–	30	5	0	–	–	–	–
Young, B.A.	1993–94	1998–99	35	68	4	2034	267*	31.78	2	12	54	–	–	–	–	–	–	–	–
Young, R.A.	2010–11	2011–12	5	10	3	169	57	24.14	–	1	8	–	–	–	–	–	–	–	–
Yuile, B.W.	1962–63	1969–70	17	33	6	481	64	17.81	–	1	12	–	2897†	1213	34	35.67	4–43	0	0

INDIVIDUAL TEST CAREER RECORDS – INDIA

	First Test	Last Test	Tests	Inns	NO	Runs	HS	Avge	100	50	Ct	St	Balls	Runs	Wkts	Avge	BB	5wI	10wM
Aaron, V.R.	2011–12	2015–16	9	14	5	35	9	3.88	–	–	1	–	1189	947	18	52.61	3–97	0	0
Abid Ali, S.	1967–68	1974–75	29	53	3	1018	81	20.36	–	6	32	–	4164	1980	47	42.12	6–55	1	0
Adhikari, H.R.	1947–48	1958–59	21	36	8	872	114*	31.14	1	4	8	–	170	82	3	27.33	3–68	0	0
Agarkar, A.B.	1998–99	2005–06	26	39	5	571	109*	16.79	1	–	6	–	4857	2745	58	47.32	6–41	1	0
Agarwal, M.A.	2018–19	2019	4	7	0	275	77	39.28	–	3	5	–							
Amarnath, L.	1933–34	1952–53	24	40	4	878	118	24.38	1	4	13	–	4241	1481	45	32.91	5–96	2	0
Amarnath, M.	1969–70	1987–88	69	113	10	4378	138	42.50	11	24	47	–	3676	1782	32	55.68	4–63	0	0
Amarnath, S.	1975–76	1978–79	10	18†	0	550	124	30.55	1	3	4	–	11	5	1	5.00	1–5	0	0
Amar Singh, L.	1932	1936	7	14	1	292	51	22.46	–	1	3	–	2182	858	28	30.64	7–86	2	0
Amir Elahi‡	1947–48	1947–48	1	2	0	17	13	8.50	–	–	–	–							
Amre, P.K.	1992–93	1993	11	13	3	425	103	42.50	1	3	9	–							
Ankola, S.A.	1989–90	1989–90	1	1	0	6	6	6.00	–	–	–	–	180	128	2	64.00	1–35	0	0
Apte, A.L.	1959	1959	1	2	0	15	8	7.50	–	–	–	–						–	–
Apte, M.L.	1952–53	1952–53	7	13	2	542	163*	49.27	1	3	2	–	6	3	0	–	–	–	–
Arshad Ayub	1987–88	1989–90	13	19	4	257	57	17.13	–	1	2	–	3663	1438	41	35.07	5–50	3	0
Arun, B.	1986–87	1986–87	2	2	1	4	2*	4.00	–	–	2	–	252	116	4	29.00	3–76	0	0
Arun Lal, J.	1982–83	1988–89	16	29	1	729	93	26.03	–	6	13	–	16	7	0	–	–	–	–
Ashwin, R.	2011–12	2018–19	65	93	12	2361	124	29.14	4	11	23	–	18372	8700	342	25.43	7–59	26	7
Azad, K.B.J.	1980–81	1983–84	7	12	0	135	24	11.25	–	–	3	–	750	373	3	124.33	2–84	0	0
Azharuddin, M.	1984–85	1999–00	99	147	9	6215	199	45.03	22	21	105	–	13	16	0	–	–	–	–
Badani, H.K.	2001	2001	4	7†	1	94	38	15.66	–	1	6	–	48†	17	0	–	–	–	–
Badrinath, S.	2009–10	2009–10	2	3	0	63	56	21.00	–	1	2	–							
Bahutule, S.V.	2000–01	2001	2	4†	1	39	21*	13.00	–	–	1	–	366	203	3	67.66	1–32	0	0
Baig, A.A.	1959	1966–67	10	18	0	428	112	23.77	1	2	6	–	18	15	0	–	–	–	–
Balaji, L.	2003–04	2004–05	8	9	0	51	31	5.66	–	–	1	–	1756	1004	27	37.18	5–76	1	0
Banerjee, S.A.	1948–49	1948–49	1	1	0	0	0	0.00	–	–	–	–	306	181	5	36.20	4–120	0	0
Banerjee, S.N.	1948–49	1948–49	1	2	0	13	8	6.50	–	–	–	–	273	127	5	25.40	4–54	0	0
Banerjee, S.T.	1991–92	1991–92	1	1	0	3	3	3.00	–	–	–	–	108	47	3	15.66	3–47	0	0
Bangar, S.B.	2001–02	2002–03	12	18	2	470	100*	29.37	1	3	4	–	762	343	7	49.00	2–23	0	0
Baqa Jilani, M.	1936	1936	1	2	1	16	12	16.00	–	–	–	–	90	55	0	–	–	–	–
Bedi, B.S.	1966–67	1979	67	101	28	656	50*	8.98	–	1	26	–	21364†	7637	266	28.71	7–98	14	1
Bhandari, P.	1954–55	1956–57	3	4	0	77	39	19.25	–	–	1	–	78	39	0	–	–	–	–
Bhat, A.R.	1983–84	1983–84	2	3†	1	6	6	3.00	–	–	–	–	438†	151	4	37.75	2–65	0	0
Bhuvneshwar Kumar	2012–13	2017–18	21	29	4	552	63*	22.08	–	3	8	–	3348	1644	63	26.09	6–82	4	0
Binny, R.M.H.	1979–80	1986–87	27	41	5	830	83*	23.05	–	5	11	–	2870	1534	47	32.63	6–56	2	0

Player	Debut	Last	M	I	NO	Runs	HS	Avg	100	50	Ct	St	Balls	Runs	Wkts	Avg	BB	5w	10w
Binny, S.T.R.	2014	2015-16	6	10	1	194	78	21.55	–	1	4	–	450	258	3	86.00	2-24	0	0
Borde, C.G.	1958-59	1969-70	55	97	11	3061	177*	35.59	5	18	37	–	5695	2417	52	46.48	5-88	1	0
Bumrah, J.J.	2017-18	2019	12	17	8	18	6	2.00	–	–	3	–	2711	1193	62	19.24	6-27	5	0
Chandrasekhar, B.S.	1963-64	1979	58	80	39	167	22	4.07	–	–	25	–	15963	7199	242	29.74	8-79	16	2
Chauhan, C.P.S.	1969-70	1980-81	40	68	2	2084	97	31.57	–	16	38	–	174	106	2	53.00	1-4	0	0
Chauhan, R.K.	1992-93	1997-98	21	17	3	98	23	7.00	–	–	12	–	4749	1857	47	39.51	4-48	0	0
Chawla, P.P.	2005-06	2012-13	3	3†	0	6	4	2.00	–	–	1	–	492	270	7	38.57	4-69	0	0
Chopra, A.S.	2003-04	2004-05	10	19	0	437	60	23.00	–	2	15	–	–	–	–	–	–	–	–
Chopra, N.	1999-00	1999-00	1	2	0	7	4	3.50	–	–	–	–	144	78	0	–	–	–	–
Chowdhury, N.R.	1948-49	1951-52	2	2	1	3	3*	3.00	–	–	–	–	516	205	1	205.00	1-130	0	0
Colah, S.H.M.	1932	1933-34	2	4	0	69	31	17.25	–	–	2	–	–	–	–	–	–	–	–
Contractor, N.J.	1955-56	1961-62	31	52†	1	1611	108	31.58	1	11	18	–	186	80	1	80.00	1-9	0	0
Dahiya, V.	2000-01	2000-01	2	1	–	2	2*	–	–	–	6	–	–	–	–	–	–	–	–
Dani, H.T.	1952-53	1952-53	1	–	–	–	–	–	–	–	1	–	60	19	1	19.00	1-9	0	0
Das, S.S.	2000-01	2001-02	23	40	2	1326	110	34.89	2	9	34	–	66	35	0	–	–	–	–
Dasgupta, D.B.	2001-02	2001-02	8	13	1	344	100	28.66	1	2	13	–	–	–	–	–	–	–	–
Desai, R.B.	1958-59	1967-68	28	44	13	418	85	13.48	–	–	9	–	5597	2761	74	37.31	6-56	2	0
Dhawan, S.	2012-13	2018	34	58†	1	2315	190	40.61	7	5	28	–	54	18	0	–	–	–	–
Dhoni, M.S.	2005-06	2014-15	90	144	16	4876	224	38.09	6	33	256	38	96	67	0	–	–	0	–
Dighe, S.S.	2000-01	2001	6	10	1	141	47	15.66	–	–	12	2	–	–	–	–	–	–	–
Dilawar Hussain	1933-34	1936	3	6	0	254	59	42.33	–	3	6	1	–	–	–	–	–	–	–
Divecha, R.V.	1951-52	1952-53	5	5	0	60	26	12.00	–	–	5	–	1044	361	11	32.81	3-102	0	0
Doshi, D.R.	1979-80	1983-84	33	38†	10	129	20	4.60	–	–	10	–	9322†	3502	114	30.71	6-102	6	0
Dravid, R.‡	1996	2011-12	163	284	32	13265	270	52.63	36	63	209	–	120	39	1	39.00	1-18	0	0
Durani, S.A.	1959-60	1972-73	29	50†	2	1202	104	25.04	1	7	14	–	6446†	2657	75	35.42	6-73	3	1
Engineer, F.M.	1961-62	1974-75	46	87	3	2611	121	31.08	2	16	66	16	–	–	–	–	–	–	–
Gadkari, C.V.	1952-53	1954-55	6	10	4	129	50*	21.50	–	1	6	–	102	45	0	–	–	0	–
Gaekwad, A.D.	1974-75	1984-85	40	70	4	1985	201	30.07	2	10	15	–	334	187	2	93.50	1-4	0	–
Gaekwad, D.K.	1952	1960-61	11	20	1	350	52	18.42	–	1	5	–	12	12	0	–	–	–	–
Gaekwad, H.G.	1952-53	1952-53	1	2†	0	22	14	11.00	–	–	–	–	222†	47	0	–	–	–	–
Gambhir, G.	2004-05	2016-17	58	104†	5	4154	206	41.95	9	22	38	–	12	4	0	–	–	–	–
Gandhi, D.J.	1999-00	1999-00	4	7	1	204	88	34.00	–	2	3	–	–	–	–	–	–	–	–
Gandotra, A.	1969-70	1969-70	2	4†	0	54	18	13.50	–	–	1	–	6†	5	0	–	–	0	–
Ganesh, D.	1996-97	1996-97	4	7	3	25	8	6.25	–	–	–	–	461	287	5	57.40	2-28	0	0
Ganguly, S.C.	1996	2008-09	113	188†	17	7212	239	42.17	16	35	71	–	3117	1681	32	52.53	3-28	0	0
Gavaskar, S.M.	1970-71	1986-87	125	214	16	10122	236*	51.12	34	45	108	–	380	206	1	206.00	1-34	0	0
Ghavri, K.D.	1974-75	1980-81	39	57†	14	913	86	21.23	–	2	16	–	7036†	3656	109	33.54	5-33	4	–
Ghorpade, J.M.	1952-53	1959	8	15	0	229	41	15.26	–	–	4	–	150	131	0	–	–	–	–

INDIVIDUAL TEST CAREER RECORDS – INDIA (Continued)

	First Test	Last Test	Tests	Inns	NO	Runs	HS	Avge	100	50	Ct	St	Balls	Runs	Wkts	Avge	BB	5wI	10wM
Ghulam Ahmed	1948–49	1958–59	22	31	9	192	50	8.72	–	1	11	–	5650	2052	68	30.17	7–49	4	1
Gopalan, M.J.	1933–34	1933–34	1	2	1	18	11*	18.00	–	–	3	–	114	39	1	39.00	1–39	0	0
Gopinath, C.D.	1951–52	1959–60	8	12	1	242	50*	22.00	–	1	2	–	48	11	1	11.00	1–11	0	0
Guard, G.M.	1958–59	1959–60	2	2†	0	11	7	5.50	–	–	2	–	396†	182	3	60.66	2–69	0	0
Guha, S.	1967	1969–70	4	7	2	17	6	3.40	–	–	2	–	674	311	3	103.66	2–55	0	0
Gul Mohammad‡	1946	1952–53	8	15†	0	166	34	11.06	–	–	2	–	77†	24	2	12.00	2–21	0	0
Gupte, B.P.	1960–61	1964–65	3	3	2	28	17*	28.00	–	–	3	–	678	349	3	116.33	1–54	0	0
Gupte, S.P.	1951–52	1961–62	36	42	13	183	21	6.31	–	–	14	–	11284	4403	149	29.55	9–102	12	1
Gursharan Singh	1989–90	1989–90	1	1	0	18	18	18.00	–	–	2	–	–	–	–	–	–	–	–
Hafeez, A.: see A. H. Kardar																			
Hanumant Singh	1963–64	1969–70	14	24	2	686	105	31.18	1	5	11	–	66	51	0	–	–	–	–
Harbhajan Singh	1997–98	2015	103	145	23	2224	115	18.22	2	9	42	–	28580	13537	417	32.46	8–84	25	5
Hardikar, M.S.	1958–59	1958–59	2	4	1	56	32*	18.66	–	–	3	–	108	55	1	55.00	1–9	0	0
Harvinder Singh	1997–98	2001	3	4	1	6	6	2.00	–	–	–	–	273	185	4	46.25	2–62	0	0
Hazare, V.S.	1946	1952–53	30	52	6	2192	164*	47.65	7	9	11	–	2840	1220	20	61.00	4–29	0	0
Hindlekar, D.D.	1936	1946	4	7	2	71	26	14.20	–	–	3	–	–	–	–	–	–	–	–
Hirwani, N.D.	1987–88	1996–97	17	22	12	54	17	5.40	–	–	5	–	4298	1987	66	30.10	8–61	4	1
Ibrahim, K.C.	1948–49	1948–49	4	8	0	169	85	21.12	–	1	–	–	–	–	–	–	–	–	–
Indrajitsinhji, K.S.	1964–65	1969–70	4	7	1	51	23	8.50	–	–	6	3	–	–	–	–	–	–	–
Irani, J.K.	1947–48	1947–48	2	3	2	3	2*	3.00	–	–	2	1	–	–	–	–	–	–	–
Jadeja, A.	1992–93	1999–00	15	24	2	576	96	26.18	–	4	5	–	–	–	–	–	–	–	–
Jaffer, W.	1999–00	2007–08	31	58	1	1944	212	34.10	5	11	27	–	66	18	2	9.00	2–18	0	0
Jahangir Khan, M.	1932	1936	4	7	0	39	13	5.57	–	–	4	–	606	255	4	63.75	4–60	0	0
Jai, L.P.	1933–34	1933–34	1	2	0	19	19	9.50	–	–	–	–	–	–	–	–	–	–	–
Jaisimha, M.L.	1959	1970–71	39	71	4	2056	129	30.68	3	12	17	–	2097	829	9	92.11	2–54	0	0
Jamshedji, R.J.D.	1933–34	1933–34	1	2	2	5	4*	–	–	–	2	–	210†	137	3	45.66	3–137	0	0
Jayantilal, H.K.	1970–71	1970–71	1	1	0	5	5	5.00	–	–	–	–	–	–	–	–	–	–	–
Johnson, D.J.	1996–97	1996–97	2	3	1	8	5	4.00	–	–	–	–	240	143	3	47.66	2–52	0	0
Joshi, P.G.	1951–52	1960–61	12	20	1	207	52*	10.89	–	1	18	9	–	–	–	–	–	–	–
Joshi, S.B.	1996	2000–01	15	19†	2	352	92	20.70	–	1	7	–	3451†	1470	41	35.85	5–142	1	0
Kaif, M.	2000	2006	13	22	3	624	148*	32.84	1	3	14	–	18	4	0	–	–	–	–
Kambli, V.G.	1992–93	1995–96	17	21†	1	1084	227	54.20	4	3	7	–	–	–	–	–	–	–	–
Kanitkar, H.H.	1999–00	1999–00	2	4†	0	74	45	18.50	–	–	2	–	6	2	0	–	–	–	–

Kanikar, H.S.	1974–75	1974–75	2	4	0	111	65	27.75	–	1	–	–	–	–	–	–	–	–
Kapil Dev	1978–79	1993–94	131	184	15	5248	163	31.05	8	27	64	–	27740	434	29.64	9–83	23	2
Kapoor, A.R.	1994–95	1996–97	4	6	1	97	42	19.40	–	–	1	–	642	6	42.50	2–19	0	0
Kardar, A.H.‡	1946	1946	3	5†	0	80	43	16.00	–	–	1	–	–	–	–	–	–	–
Karim, S.S.	2000–01	2000–01	1	1	0	15	15	15.00	–	–	–	–	–	–	–	–	–	0
Kartik, K.D.	2018	2004–05	26	42	1	1025	129	25.00	1	7	57	6	–	–	–	–	–	–
Kartik, M.	2004–05	1999–00	8	10†	1	88	43	9.77	–	3	2	–	1932†	24	34.16	4–44	0	1
Kenny, R.B.	1958–59	1958–59	5	10	1	245	62	27.22	–	3	1	–	–	–	–	–	–	–
Khan, Z.	2013–14	2000–01	92	127	24	1231	75	11.95	–	3	19	–	18785†	311	32.94	7–87	11	1
Kirmani, S.M.H.	1975–76	1985–86	88	124	22	2759	102	27.04	2	12	160	38	19	1	13.00	1–9	0	0
Kishenchand, G.	1947–48	1952–53	5	10	0	89	44	8.90	–	–	1	–	–	–	–	–	–	–
Kohli, V.	2011	2019	79	135	8	6749	243	53.14	25	22	75	–	163	0	–	–	–	–
Kripal Singh, A.G.	1955–56	1964–65	14	20	5	422	100*	28.13	1	1	4	–	1518	10	58.40	3–43	0	0
Krishnamurthy, P.	1970–71	1970–71	5	6	0	33	20	5.50	–	–	7	1	–	–	–	–	–	–
Kulkarni, N.M.	1997	2000–01	3	2†	1	5	4	5.00	–	–	1	–	738†	2	166.00	1–70	0	0
Kulkarni, R.R.	1986–87	1986–87	3	2	0	2	2	1.00	–	–	1	–	366	5	45.40	3–85	0	0
Kulkarni, U.N.	1967–68	1967–68	4	8†	5	13	7	4.33	–	–	–	–	448†	5	47.60	2–37	0	0
Kumar, P.	2011	2011	6	10	0	149	40	14.90	–	–	2	–	1611	27	25.81	5–106	1	0
Kumar, V.V.	1960–61	1961–62	2	2	0	6	6	3.00	–	–	2	–	605	7	28.85	5–64	1	0
Kumble, A.	1990	2008–09	132	173	32	2506	110*	17.77	1	5	60	–	40850	619	29.65	10–74	35	8
Kunderan, B.K.	1959–60	1967	18	34	4	981	192	32.70	2	3	23	7	24	0	–	–	–	–
Kuruvilla, A.	1996–97	1997–98	10	11	1	66	35*	6.60	–	–	1	–	1765	25	35.68	5–68	1	0
Lall Singh	1932	1932	1	2	0	44	29	22.00	–	–	1	–	–	–	–	–	–	–
Lamba, R.	1986–87	1987–88	4	5	0	102	53	20.40	–	–	5	–	–	–	–	–	–	–
Laxman, V.V.S.	1996–97	2011–12	134	225	34	8781	281	45.97	17	56	135	–	324	2	63.00	1–2	0	0
Madan Lal	1974	1986	39	62	16	1042	74	22.65	–	5	15	–	5997	71	40.08	5–23	4	0
Maka, E.S.	1952–53	1952–53	2	1	1	0	2*	–	–	–	2	1	–	–	–	–	–	–
Malhotra, A.O.	1981–82	1984–85	7	10	1	226	72*	25.11	–	1	2	–	18	0	–	–	–	–
Maninder Singh	1982–83	1992–93	35	38	12	99	15	3.80	–	–	9	–	8218†	88	37.36	7–27	3	2
Manjrekar, S.V.	1987–88	1996–97	37	61	6	2043	218	37.14	4	9	25	1	17	0	–	–	–	0
Manjrekar, V.L.	1951–52	1964–65	55	92	10	3208	189*	39.12	7	15	19	2	204	1	44.00	1–16	0	1
Mankad, A.V.	1969–70	1977–78	22	42	3	991	97	25.41	–	6	12	–	41	0	–	–	–	–
Mankad, M.H.	1946	1958–59	44	72	5	2109	231	31.47	5	6	33	–	14686†	162	32.32	8–52	8	2
Mantri, M.K.	1951–52	1954–55	4	8	1	67	39	9.57	–	–	8	1	–	–	–	–	–	–
Meherhomji, K.R.	1936	1936	1	1	1	0	0*	–	–	–	–	–	–	–	–	–	–	–
Mehra, V.L.	1955–56	1963–64	8	14	1	329	62	25.30	–	2	1	–	36	0	–	–	–	–
Merchant, V.M.	1933–34	1951–52	10	18	0	859	154	47.72	3	3	7	–	54	0	–	–	–	–
Mhambrey, P.L.	1996	1996	2	3	1	58	28	29.00	–	–	1	–	258	2	74.00	1–43	0	0

INDIVIDUAL TEST CAREER RECORDS – INDIA (*Continued*)

	First Test	Last Test	Tests	Inns	NO	Runs	HS	Avge	100	50	Ct	St	Balls	Runs	Wkts	Avge	BB	5wI	10wM
Milkha Singh, A.G.	1959–60	1961–62	4	6†	2	92	35	15.33	–	–	2	–	6	2	0	–	–	–	–
Mishra, A.	2008–09	2016–17	22	32	2	648	84	21.60	–	4	8	–	5103	2715	76	35.72	5–71	1	0
Mithun, A.	2010	2011	4	5	0	120	46	24.00	–	–	–	–	720	456	9	50.66	4–105	0	0
Modi, R.S.	1946	1952–53	10	17	1	736	112	46.00	1	6	3	–	30	14	0	–	–	–	–
Mohammed Shami	2013–14	2019	42	58	17	433	51*	10.56	–	1	9	–	7868	4414	153	28.84	6–56	4	0
Mohanty, D.S.	1997	1997–98	2	1	0	0	0*	–	–	–	–	–	430	239	4	59.75	4–78	0	0
Mongia, N.R.	1993–94	2000–01	44	68	8	1442	152	24.03	1	6	99	8	–	–	–	–	–	–	–
More, K.S.	1986	1993	49	64	14	1285	73	25.70	–	7	110	20	12	12	0	–	–	–	–
Muddiah, V.M.	1959–60	1960–61	2	3	1	11	11	5.50	–	–	–	–	318	134	3	44.66	2–40	0	0
Mukund, A.	2011	2017	7	14†	0	320	81	22.85	–	2	6	–	12	14	0	–	–	–	–
Mushtaq Ali, S.	1933–34	1951–52	11	20	1	612	112	32.21	2	3	7	–	378†	202	3	67.33	1–45	0	0
Nadkarni, R.G.	1955–56	1967–68	41	67†	12	1414	122*	25.70	1	7	22	–	9165†	2559	88	29.07	6–43	4	1
Naik, S.S.	1974	1974–75	3	6	0	141	77	23.50	–	1	–	–	–	–	–	–	–	–	–
Nair, K.K.	2016–17	2016–17	6	7	1	374	303*	62.33	1	–	6	–	12	11	0	–	–	–	–
Naoomal Jeoomal	1932	1933–34	3	5	1	108	43	27.00	–	–	–	–	108	68	2	34.00	1–4	0	0
Narasimha Rao, M.V.	1978–79	1979–80	4	6	1	46	20*	9.20	–	–	8	–	463	227	3	75.66	2–46	0	0
Navle, J.G.	1932	1933–34	2	4	0	42	13	10.50	–	–	1	–	–	–	–	–	–	–	–
Nayak, S.V.	1982	1982	2	3†	1	19	11	9.50	–	–	1	–	231	132	1	132.00	1–16	0	0
Nayudu, C.K.	1932	1936	7	14	0	350	81	25.00	–	2	4	–	858	386	9	42.88	3–40	0	0
Nayudu, C.S.	1933–34	1951–52	11	19	3	147	36	9.18	–	–	3	–	522	359	2	179.50	1–19	0	0
Nazir Ali, S.	1932	1933–34	2	4	0	30	13	7.50	–	–	–	–	138	83	4	20.75	4–83	0	0
Nehra, A.	1998–99	2003–04	17	25	11	77	19	5.50	–	–	5	–	3447†	1866	44	42.40	4–72	0	0
Nissar, M.	1932	1936	6	11	3	55	14	6.87	–	–	2	–	1211	707	25	28.28	5–90	3	0
Nyalchand, S.	1952–53	1952–53	1	2†	1	7	6*	7.00	–	–	–	–	384†	97	3	32.33	3–97	0	0
Ojha, N.V.	2015	2015	1	2	0	56	35	28.00	–	–	4	1	–	–	–	–	–	–	–
Ojha, P.P.	2009–10	2013–14	24	27†	17	89	18*	8.90	–	–	10	–	7633†	3420	113	30.26	6–47	7	1
Pai, A.M.	1969–70	1969–70	1	2†	0	10	9	5.00	–	–	–	–	114	31	2	15.50	2–29	0	0
Palia, P.E.	1932	1936	2	4†	1	29	16	9.66	–	–	–	–	42†	13	0	–	–	–	–
Pandit, C.S.	1986	1991–92	5	8	1	171	39	24.42	–	–	14	2	–	–	–	–	–	–	–
Pandya, H.H.	2017	2018	11	18	1	532	108	31.29	1	4	7	–	937	528	17	31.05	5–28	1	0
Pankaj Singh	2014	2014	2	4	1	10	9	3.33	–	–	2	–	450	292	2	146.00	2–113	0	0
Pant, R.R.	2018	2019	11	18†	1	754	159*	44.35	2	2	51	2	–	–	–	–	–	–	–
Parkar, G.A.	1982	1982	1	2	0	7	6	3.50	–	–	1	–	–	–	–	–	–	–	–
Parkar, R.D.	1972–73	1972–73	2	4	0	80	35	20.00	–	–	–	–	–	–	–	–	–	–	–

Name			M	I	NO	Runs	HS	Avg	100	50	Ct	St	Balls	Runs	Wkts	Avg	BB	5w	10w
Parsana, D.D.	1978–79	1978–79	2	2†	0	1	1	0.50	–	–	–	–	120†	50	1	50.00	1–32	0	0
Patankar, C.T.	1955–56	1955–56	1	2	1	14	13	14.00	–	–	3	1	–	–	–	–	–	0	0
Pataudi, Nawab of, sen.‡	1946	1946	3	5	0	55	22	11.00	–	–	–	–	–	–	–	–	–	–	–
Pataudi, Nawab of, jun.	1961–62	1974–75	46	83	3	2793	203*	34.91	6	16	27	–	132	88	1	88.00	1–10	0	0
Patel, B.P.	1974	1977–78	21	38	5	972	115*	29.45	1	5	17	–	–	–	–	–	–	2	0
Patel, J.M.	1954–55	1959–60	7	10	1	25	12	2.77	–	–	2	–	1725	637	29	21.96	9–69	2	1
Patel, M.M.	2005–06	2011	13	14	6	60	15*	7.50	–	–	6	–	2658	1349	35	38.54	4–25	2	0
Patel, P.A.	2002	2017–18	25	38†	8	934	71	31.13	–	6	62	10	–	–	–	–	–	–	–
Patel, R.G.M.	1988–89	1988–89	1	2†	0	0	0	0.00	–	–	1	–	84†	51	0	–	–	–	–
Pathan, I.K.	2003–04	2007–08	29	40†	5	1105	102	31.57	1	6	8	–	5884†	3226	100	32.26	7–59	7	2
Patiala, Yuvraj of	1933–34	1933–34	1	2	0	84	60	42.00	–	1	2	–	–	–	–	–	–	–	–
Patil, S.M.	1979–80	1984–85	29	47	4	1588	174	36.93	4	7	12	–	645	240	9	26.66	2–28	0	0
Patil, S.R.	1955–56	1955–56	1	1	1	14	14*	–	–	–	1	–	138	51	2	25.50	1–15	0	0
Phadkar, D.G.	1947–48	1958–59	31	45	7	1229	123	32.34	2	8	21	–	5994	2285	62	36.85	7–159	3	0
Powar, R.R.	2007	2007	2	2	0	13	7	6.50	–	–	1	–	252	118	6	19.66	3–33	0	0
Prabhakar, M.	1984–85	1995–96	39	58	9	1600	120	32.65	1	9	20	–	7475	3581	96	37.30	6–132	3	0
Prasad, B.K.V.	1996	2001	33	47	20	203	30*	7.51	–	–	6	–	7041	3360	96	35.00	6–33	3	1
Prasad, M.S.K.	1999–00	1999–00	6	10	1	106	19	11.77	–	–	15	–	–	–	–	–	–	–	–
Prasanna, E.A.S.	1961–62	1978–79	49	84	20	735	37	11.48	–	–	18	–	14353	5742	189	30.38	8–76	10	2
Pujara, C.A.	2010–11	2019	70	118	8	5486	206*	49.87	18	20	45	–	6	2	0	–	–	0	–
Punjabi, P.H.	1954–55	1954–55	5	10	0	164	33	16.40	–	–	5	–	–	–	–	–	–	–	–
Rahane, A.M.	2012–13	2019	58	99	10	3759	188	42.23	10	19	76	–	–	–	–	–	–	–	–
Rahul, K.L.	2014–15	2019	36	60	2	2006	199	34.58	5	11	46	–	–	–	–	–	–	–	–
Raina, S.K.	2010	2014–15	18	31†	2	768	120	26.48	1	7	23	–	1041	603	13	46.38	2–1	0	0
Rai Singh, K.	1947–48	1947–48	1	2	0	26	24	13.00	–	–	1	–	–	–	–	–	–	–	–
Rajindernath, V.	1952–53	1952–53	1	–	–	–	–	–	–	–	–	4	–	–	–	–	–	–	–
Rajinder Pal	1963–64	1963–64	1	2	1	6	3*	6.00	–	–	1	–	78	22	0	–	–	–	–
Rajput, L.S.	1985	1985	2	4	0	105	61	26.25	–	1	1	–	–	–	–	–	–	–	–
Raju, S.L.V.	1989–90	2000–01	28	34	10	240	31	10.00	–	–	6	–	7602†	2857	93	30.72	6–12	5	1
Raman, W.V.	1987–88	1996–97	11	19†	1	448	96	24.88	–	4	6	–	348†	129	2	64.50	1–7	0	0
Ramaswami, C.	1936	1936	2	4†	1	170	60	56.66	–	–	–	–	–	–	–	–	–	–	–
Ramchand, G.S.	1952	1959–60	33	53	5	1180	109	24.58	2	5	20	–	4976	1899	41	46.31	6–49	1	0
Ramesh, S.	1998–99	2001	19	37†	1	1367	143	37.97	2	8	18	–	54	43	0	–	–	–	–
Ramji, L.	1933–34	1933–34	1	2	0	1	1	0.50	–	–	–	–	138	64	0	–	–	–	–
Rangachari, C.R.	1947–48	1948–49	4	6	3	8	8*	2.66	–	–	–	–	846	493	9	54.77	5–107	1	0
Rangnekar, K.M.	1947–48	1947–48	3	6†	0	33	18	5.50	–	–	–	–	–	–	–	–	–	–	–
Ranjane, V.B.	1958–59	1964–65	7	9	3	40	16	6.66	–	–	1	–	1265	649	19	34.15	4–72	0	0
Rathour, V.	1996	1996–97	6	10	0	131	44	13.10	–	–	12	–	–	–	–	–	–	–	–

INDIVIDUAL TEST CAREER RECORDS – INDIA (Continued)

	First Test	Last Test	Tests	Inns	NO	Runs	HS	Avge	100	50	Ct	St	Balls	Runs	Wkts	Avge	BB	5wI	10wM
Ratra, A.	2001–02	2002	6	10	1	163	115*	18.11	1	–	11	2	6	1	0	–	–	–	–
Razdan, V.	1989–90	1989–90	2	2	1	6	6*	6.00	–	–	–	–	240	141	5	28.20	5–79	1	0
Reddy, B.	1979	1979	4	5	1	38	21	9.50	–	–	9	2	–	–	–	–	–	–	–
Rege, M.R.	1948–49	1948–49	1	2	0	15	15	7.50	–	–	1	–	–	–	–	–	–	–	–
Robin Singh, jun.	1998–99	1998–99	1	1	0	0	0	0.00	–	–	1	–	240	176	3	58.66	2–74	0	0
Roy, A.K.	1969–70	1969–70	4	7†	0	91	48	13.00	–	–	1	–	–	–	–	–	–	–	–
Roy, Pankaj	1951–52	1960–61	43	79	4	2442	173	32.56	5	9	16	–	104	66	1	66.00	1–6	0	0
Roy, Pranab	1981–82	1981–82	2	3	1	71	60*	35.50	–	1	–	–	–	–	–	–	–	–	–
Saha, W.P.	2009–10	2017–18	32	46	8	1164	117	30.63	3	5	75	10	–	–	–	–	–	–	–
Sandhu, B.S.	1982–83	1983–84	8	11	4	214	71	30.57	–	2	1	–	1020	557	10	55.70	3–87	0	0
Sanghvi, R.L.	2000–01	2000–01	1	2†	0	2	2	1.00	–	–	–	–	74†	78	2	39.00	2–67	0	0
Sarandeep Singh	2000–01	2001–02	3	2	1	43	39*	43.00	–	–	1	–	678	340	10	34.00	4–136	0	0
Sardesai, D.N.	1961–62	1972–73	30	55	4	2001	212	39.23	5	9	4	–	59	45	0	–	–	–	–
Sarwate, C.T.	1946	1951–52	9	17	1	208	37	13.00	–	–	1	–	658	374	3	124.66	1–16	0	0
Saxena, R.C.	1967	1967	1	2	0	25	16	12.50	–	–	–	–	12	11	0	–	–	–	–
Sehwag, V.‡	2001–02	2012–13	103	178	6	8503	319	49.43	23	31	90	–	3731	1894	40	47.35	5–104	1	0
Sekhar, T.A.	1982–83	1982–83	2	1	1	0	0*	–	–	–	–	–	204	129	0	–	–	–	–
Sen, P.K.	1947–48	1952–53	14	18	4	165	25	11.78	–	–	20	11	–	–	–	–	–	–	–
Sengupta, A.K.	1958–59	1958–59	1	2	0	9	8	4.50	–	–	–	–	–	–	–	–	–	–	–
Sharma, A.K.	1987–88	1987–88	1	2	0	53	30	26.50	–	1	1	–	24†	9	0	–	–	–	–
Sharma, C.	1984–85	1988–89	23	27	9	396	54	22.00	–	1	7	–	3470	2163	61	35.45	6–58	4	1
Sharma, G.	1984–85	1990–91	5	4	1	11	10*	3.66	–	–	2	–	1307	418	10	41.80	4–88	0	0
Sharma, I.	2007	2019	92	126	43	703	57	8.46	–	1	21	–	17494	9290	278	33.41	7–74	9	1
Sharma, K.V.	2014–15	2014–15	1	2†	1	8	4*	8.00	–	–	4	–	294	238	4	59.50	2–95	0	0
Sharma, P.H.	1974–75	1976–77	5	10	0	187	54	18.70	–	1	8	–	24	8	0	–	–	–	–
Sharma, R.G.	2013–14	2018–19	27	47	7	1585	177	39.62	3	10	25	–	334	202	2	101.00	1–26	0	0
Sharma, S.K.	1988–89	1990	2	3	1	56	38	28.00	–	–	1	–	414	247	6	41.16	3–37	0	0
Shastri, R.J.	1980–81	1992–93	80	121	14	3830	206	35.79	11	12	36	–	15751†	6185	151	40.96	5–75	2	0
Shaw, P.P.	2018–19	2018–19	2	3	1	237	134	118.50	1	1	2	–	–	–	–	–	–	–	–
Shinde, S.G.	1946	1952	7	11	5	85	14	14.16	–	–	–	–	1515	717	12	59.75	6–91	1	0
Shodhan, R.H.	1952–53	1952–53	3	4†	1	181	110	60.33	1	–	1	–	60†	26	0	–	–	0	0
Shukla, R.C.	1982–83	1982–83	1	–	–	–	–	–	–	–	–	–	294	152	2	76.00	2–82	0	0

Player	Career	M	I	NO	Runs	HS	Avg	100	50	Balls	Runs	Wkts	Avg	BB	5w	10w	Ct	St
Siddiqui, I.R.	2001-02	1	2	1	29	24	29.00	–	–	114	48	1	48.00	1-32	–	–	0	–
Sidhu, N.S.	1983-84	51	78	2	3202	201	42.13	9	15	6	9	0	–	–	–	–	–	–
Singh, R.P.	2005-06	14	19	3	116	30	7.25	–	–	2534†	1682	40	42.05	5-59	1	–	1	–
Singh, R.R. ("Robin")	1998-99	1	2†	0	27	15	13.50	–	–	60	32	0	–	–	–	–	0	–
Singh, V.R.	2006	5	6	2	47	29	11.75	–	–	669	427	8	53.37	3-48	–	–	0	–
Sivaramakrishnan, L.	1982-83	9	9	1	130	25	16.25	–	–	2367	1145	26	44.03	6-64	3	–	3	–
Sohoni, S.W.	1946	4	7	2	83	29*	16.60	–	–	532	202	2	101.00	1-16	–	–	1	–
Solkar, E.D.	1969-70	27	48†	6	1068	102	25.42	1	6	2265†	1070	18	59.44	3-28	–	–	53	–
Sood, M.M.	1959-60	1	2	0	3	3	1.50	–	–	–	–	–	–	–	–	–	–	–
Sreesanth, S.	2005-06	27	40	13	281	35	10.40	–	–	5419	3271	87	37.59	5-40	3	–	5	–
Srikkanth, K.	1981-82	43	72	3	2062	123	29.88	2	12	216	114	0	–	–	–	–	40	–
Srinath, J.	1991-92	67	92	21	1009	76	14.21	–	4	15104	7196	236	30.49	8-86	10	1	22	–
Srinivasan, T.E.	1980-81	1	2	0	48	29	24.00	–	–	–	–	–	–	–	–	–	–	–
Subramanya, V.	1964-65	9	15	1	263	75	18.78	–	2	444	201	3	67.00	2-32	–	–	9	–
Sunderam, G.R.	1955-56	2	1	1	3	3*	–	–	–	396	166	3	55.33	2-46	–	–	0	–
Surendranath, R.	1958-59	11	20	7	136	27	10.46	–	–	2602	1053	26	40.50	5-75	2	–	4	–
Surti, R.F.	1960-61	26	48†	4	1263	99	28.70	–	9	3870†	1962	42	46.71	5-74	1	–	26	–
Swamy, V.N.	1955-56	1	–	–	–	–	–	–	–	108	45	0	–	–	–	–	0	–
Tamhane, N.S.	1954-55	21	27	5	225	54*	10.22	–	1	–	–	–	–	–	–	–	35	16
Tarapore, K.K.	1948-49	1	1	0	2	2	2.00	–	–	114†	72	0	–	–	–	–	0	–
Tendulkar, S.R.	1989-90	200	329	33	15921	248*	53.78	51	68	4240	2492	46	54.17	3-10	–	–	115	–
Thakur, S.N.	2018-19	1	1	1	4	4*	–	–	–	10	9	0	–	–	–	–	0	–
Umrigar, P.R.	1948-49	59	94	8	3631	223	42.22	12	14	4725	1473	35	42.08	6-74	2	–	33	–
Unadkat, J.D.	2010-11	1	2	1	2	1*	2.00	–	–	156†	101	0	–	–	–	–	0	–
Vengsarkar, D.B.	1975-76	116	185	22	6868	166	42.13	17	35	47	36	0	–	–	–	–	78	–
Venkataraghavan, S.	1964-65	57	76	12	748	64	11.68	–	2	14877	5634	156	36.11	8-72	3	1	44	–
Venkataramana, M.	1988-89	1	2	2	0	0*	–	–	–	70	58	–	58.00	1-10	–	–	1	–
Vihari, G.H.	2018	6	11	1	456	111	45.60	1	3	291	142	5	28.40	3-37	–	–	3	–
Vijay, M.	2008-09	61	105	1	3982	167	38.28	12	15	384	198	1	198.00	1-12	–	–	49	–
Vijay Bharadwaj, R.	1999-00	3	3	0	28	22	9.33	–	–	247	107	1	107.00	1-26	–	–	3	–
Vinay Kumar, R.	2011-12	1	2	0	11	6	5.50	–	–	78	73	1	73.00	1-73	–	–	–	–
Viswanath, G.R.	1969-70	91	155	10	6080	222	41.93	14	35	70	46	1	46.00	1-11	–	–	63	–
Viswanath, S.	1985	3	5	0	31	20	6.20	–	–	–	–	–	–	–	–	–	11	–
Vizianagram, Maharajkumar of...	1936	3	6	2	33	19*	8.25	–	–	–	–	–	–	–	–	–	1	–
Wadekar, A.L.	1966-67	37	71†	3	2113	143	31.07	1	14	61†	55	0	–	–	–	–	46	–
Wassan, A.S.	1989-90	4	5	1	94	53	23.50	–	1	712	504	10	50.40	4-108	–	–	1	–
Wazir Ali, S.	1932	7	14	0	237	42	16.92	–	1	30	25	0	–	–	–	–	–	–

INDIVIDUAL TEST CAREER RECORDS – INDIA (Continued)

	First Test	Last Test	Tests	Inns	NO	Runs	HS	Avge	100	50	Ct	St	Balls	Runs	Wkts	Avge	BB	5wI	10wM
Yadav, J.	2016–17	2016–17	4	6	1	228	104	45.60	1	1	1	–	627	367	11	33.36	3-30	0	0
Yadav, K.	2016–17	2018–19	6	6†	0	51	26	8.50	–	–	3	–	989†	579	24	24.12	5-57	2	0
Yadav, N.S.	1979–80	1986–87	35	40	12	403	43	14.39	–	–	10	–	8360	3580	102	35.09	5-76	3	0
Yadav, U.T.	2011–12	2018–19	41	47	21	283	30	10.88	–	–	14	–	6659	3983	119	33.47	6-88	2	1
Yadav, V.	1992–93	1992–93	1	1	0	30	30	30.00	–	–	1	2	–	–	–	–	–	–	–
Yajurvindra Singh	1976–77	1979–80	4	7	1	109	43*	18.16	–	–	11	–	120	50	0	–	–	–	–
Yashpal Sharma	1979	1983–84	37	59	11	1606	140	33.45	2	9	16	–	30	17	1	17.00	1-6	0	0
Yograj Singh	1980–81	1980–81	1	2	0	10	6	5.00	–	–	–	–	90	63	1	63.00	1-63	0	0
Yohannan, T.	2001–02	2002–03	3	4	4	13	8*	–	–	–	1	–	486	256	5	51.20	2-56	0	0
Yuvraj Singh	2003–04	2012–13	40	62†	6	1900	169	33.92	3	11	31	–	931†	547	9	60.77	2-9	0	0

INDIVIDUAL TEST CAREER RECORDS – PAKISTAN

	First Test	Last Test	Tests	Inns	NO	Runs	HS	Avge	100	50	Ct	St	Balls	Runs	Wkts	Avge	BB	5wI	10wM
Aamer Malik	1987–88	1994–95	14	19	3	565	117	35.31	2	3	15	1	156	89	1	89.00	1–0	0	0
Aamir Nazir	1992–93	1995–96	6	11	6	31	11	6.20	–	–	2	–	1057	597	20	29.85	5–46	1	0
Aamir Sohail	1992	1999–00	47	83†	3	2823	205	35.28	5	13	36	–	2383†	1049	25	41.96	4–54	0	0
Abdul Kadir	1964–65	1964–65	4	8	0	272	95	34.00	–	2	–	1							
Abdul Qadir	1977–78	1990–91	67	77	11	1029	61	15.59	–	3	15	–	17126	7742	236	32.80	9–56	15	5
Abdul Razzaq	1999–00	2006–07	46	77	9	1946	134	28.61	3	7	15	–	7008	3694	100	36.94	5–35	1	0
Abdur Rauf	2009	2009–10	3	6	0	52	31	8.66	–	–	–	–	450	278	6	46.33	2–59	0	0
Abdur Rehman	2007–08	2014	22	31†	3	395	60	14.10	–	2	8	–	6892†	2910	99	29.39	6–25	2	0
Adnan Akmal	2010–11	2013–14	21	29	5	591	64	24.62	–	3	66	11							
Afaq Hussain	1961–62	1964–65	2	4	4	66	35*	–	–	–	2	–	240	106	1	106.00	1–40	0	0
Aftab Baloch	1969–70	1974–75	2	3	1	97	60*	48.50	–	1	–	–	44	17	0	–	–	–	–
Aftab Gul	1968–69	1971	6	8	0	182	33	22.75	–	–	3	–	6	4	0	–	–	–	–
Agha Saadat Ali	1955–56	1955–56	1	1	1	8	8*	–	–	–	3	–	–						
Agha Zahid	1974–75	1974–75	1	2	0	15	14	7.50	–	–	–	–							
Ahmed Shehzad	2013–14	2016–17	13	25	1	982	176	40.91	3	4	3	–	48	28	0	–	–	–	–
Aizaz Cheema	2011	2012	7	5	5	1	1*	–	–	–	1	–	1200	638	20	31.90	4–24	0	0
Akram Raza	1989–90	1994–95	9	12	2	153	32	15.30	–	–	8	–	1526	732	13	56.30	3–46	0	0
Alimuddin	1954	1962	25	45	2	1091	109	25.37	2	7	8	–	84	75	1	75.00	1–17	0	0
Ali Naqvi	1997–98	1997–98	5	9	1	242	115	30.25	1	–	1	–	12	11	0	–	–	–	–
Ali Hussain Rizvi	1997–98	1997–98	1	–	–	–	–	–	–	–	–	–	111	72	2	36.00	2–72	0	0
Amir Elahi‡	1952–53	1952–53	5	7	1	65	47	10.83	–	–	–	–	400	248	7	35.42	4–134	0	0
Anil Dalpat	1983–84	1984–85	9	12	1	167	52	15.18	–	1	22	3							
Anwar Hussain	1952–53	1952–53	4	6	0	42	17	7.00	–	–	–	–	36	29	1	29.00	1–25	0	0
Anwar Khan	1978–79	1978–79	1	2	1	15	12	15.00	–	–	–	–	32	12	0	–	–	–	–
Aqib Javed	1988–89	1998–99	22	27	7	101	28*	5.05	–	–	2	–	3918	1874	54	34.70	5–84	1	0
Arif Butt	1964–65	1964–65	3	5	0	59	20	11.80	–	–	–	–	666	288	14	20.57	6–89	1	0
Arshad Khan	1997–98	2004–05	9	8	2	31	9*	5.16	–	–	–	–	2538	960	32	30.00	5–38	1	0
Asad Shafiq	2010–11	2018–19	69	117	6	4323	137	38.94	12	23	67	–	268	152	2	76.00	1–7	0	0
Ashfaq Ahmed	1993–94	1993–94	1	2	1	1	1*	1.00	–	–	–	–	138	53	2	26.50	2–31	0	0
Ashraf Ali	1981–82	1987–88	8	8	3	229	65	45.80	–	2	17	5							
Asif Iqbal	1964–65	1979–80	58	99	7	3575	175	38.85	11	12	36	–	3864	1502	53	28.33	5–48	2	0
Asif Masood	1968–69	1976–77	16	19	10	93	30*	10.33	–	–	5	–	3038	1568	38	41.26	5–111	1	0
Asif Mujtaba	1986–87	1996–97	25	41†	3	928	65*	24.42	–	8	19	–	666†	303	4	75.75	1–0	0	0
Asim Kamal	2003–04	2005–06	12	20†	1	717	99	37.73	–	8	10	–	–						

INDIVIDUAL TEST CAREER RECORDS – PAKISTAN (Continued)

	First Test	Last Test	Tests	Inns	NO	Runs	HS	Avge	100	50	Ct	St	Balls	Runs	Wkts	Avge	BB	5wI	10wM
Ata-ur-Rehman	1992	1996	13	15	6	76	19	8.44	–	–	2	–	1973	1071	31	34.54	4-50	0	0
Atif Rauf	1993-94	1993-94	1	2	0	25	16	12.50	–	–	–	–	–						
Atiq-uz-Zaman	1999-00	1999-00	1	2	0	26	25	13.00	–	–	5	–	–						
Azam Khan	1996-97	1996-97	1	1	0	14	14	14.00	–	–	–	–	–						
Azeem Hafeez	1983-84	1984-85	18	21†	5	134	24	8.37	–	–	1	–	4351†	2204	63	34.98	6-46	4	0
Azhar Ali	2010	2018-19	73	139	8	5669	302*	43.27	15	31	61	–	848	602	8	75.25	2-35	0	0
Azhar Khan	1979-80	1979-80	1	1	0	14	14	14.00	–	–	–	–	18	2	1	2.00	1-1	0	0
Azhar Mahmood	1997-98	2001	21	34	4	900	136	30.00	3	–	14	–	3015	1402	39	35.94	4-50	0	0
Azmat Rana	1979-80	1979-80	1	1†	0	49	49	49.00	–	–	–	–	–						
Babar Azam	2016-17	2018-19	21	40	5	1235	127*	35.28	1	11	16	–	–						
Basit Ali	1992-93	1995-96	19	33	1	858	103	26.81	1	5	6	–	6	6	0	–	–	–	–
Bazid Khan	2004-05	2004-05	1	2	0	32	23	16.00	–	–	2	–	–						
Bilal Asif	2018-19	2018-19	5	8	0	73	15	9.12	–	–	2	–	1174	424	16	26.50	6-36	2	0
Bilawal Bhatti	2013-14	2013-14	2	3	1	70	32	35.00	–	–	–	–	438	291	6	48.50	3-65	0	0
Danish Kaneria	2000-01	2010	61	84	33	360	29	7.05	–	–	18	–	17697	9082	261	34.79	7-77	15	2
D'Souza, A.	1958-59	1962	6	10	8	76	23*	38.00	–	–	3	–	1587	745	17	43.82	5-112	1	0
Ehsan Adil	2012-13	2015	3	4	0	21	12	5.25	–	–	–	–	481	263	5	52.60	2-54	0	0
Ehtesham-ud-Din	1979-80	1982	5	3	1	2	2	1.00	–	–	2	–	940	375	16	23.43	5-47	1	0
Fahim Ashraf	2018	2018-19	4	6	0	138	83	23.00	–	1	–	–	540	287	11	26.09	3-42	0	0
Faisal Iqbal	2000-01	2009-10	26	44	2	1124	139	26.76	1	8	22	–	6	7	0	–	–	–	–
Fakhar Zaman	2018-19	2018-19	3	6†	0	192	94	32.00	–	2	3	–	–						
Farhan Adil	2003-04	2003-04	1	2	0	33	25	16.50	–	–	–	–	–						
Farooq Hameed	1964-65	1964-65	1	2	0	3	3	1.50	–	–	–	–	184	107	1	107.00	1-82	0	0
Farrukh Zaman	1976-77	1976-77	1	–	–	–	–	–	–	–	–	–	80†	15	0	–	–	–	–
Fawad Alam	2009	2009-10	3	6†	0	250	168	41.66	1	–	3	–	–						
Fazal Mahmood	1952	1962	34	50	6	620	60	14.09	–	1	11	–	9834	3434	139	24.70	7-42	13	4
Fazal-ur-Rehman	1957-58	1957-58	1	2	0	10	8	5.00	–	–	1	–	204	99	1	99.00	1-43	0	0
Fazl-e-Akbar	1997-98	2003-04	5	8	4	52	25	13.00	–	–	2	–	882	511	11	46.45	3-85	0	0
Ghazali, M.E.Z.	1954	1954	2	4	0	32	18	8.00	–	–	–	–	48	18	0	–	–	–	–
Ghulam Abbas	1967	1967	1	2†	0	12	12	6.00	–	–	–	–	–						
Gul Mohammad‡	1956-57	1956-57	1	2†	1	39	27*	39.00	–	–	–	–	–						
Hanif Mohammad	1952-53	1969-70	55	97	8	3915	337	43.98	12	15	40	–	206	95	1	95.00	1-1	0	0
Haris Sohail	2017-18	2018-19	10	19†	1	726	147	40.33	2	2	8	–	384†	156	7	22.28	3-1	0	0
Haroon Rashid	1976-77	1982-83	23	36	1	1217	153	34.77	3	5	16	–	8	3	0	–	–	–	–

Name	First	Last	M	I	NO	Runs	HS	Avg	100	50	Ct	St	Balls	Runs	Wkts	Avg	BB	5w	10w
Hasan Ali	2016-17	2018-19	9	15	5	155	29	15.50	–	–	4	–	1737	896	31	28.90	5-45	1	0
Hasan Raza	1996-97	2005-06	7	10	1	235	68	26.11	–	2	5	–	6	1	0	–	–	–	0
Haseeb Ahsan	1957-58	1961-62	12	16	7	61	14	6.77	–	–	1	–	2835	1330	27	49.25	6-202	2	0
Humayun Farhat	2000-01	2000-01	1	2	0	54	28	27.00	–	–	1	–	–	–	–	–	–	–	–
Iftikhar Ahmed	2016	2016	1	1	0	4	4	4.00	–	–	–	–	26	13	1	13.00	1-1	0	0
Iftikhar Anjum	2005-06	2005-06	1	1	1	9	9*	–	–	–	–	–	84	62	0	–	–	–	–
Ijaz Ahmed, sen.	1986-87	2000-01	60	92	4	3315	211	37.67	12	12	45	–	180†	77	2	38.50	1-9	0	0
Ijaz Ahmed, jun.	1995-96	1995-96	2	3	0	29	16	9.66	–	–	3	–	24	6	0	–	–	–	–
Ijaz Butt	1958-59	1962	8	16	2	279	58	19.92	–	–	5	–	–	–	–	–	–	–	–
Ijaz Faqih	1980-81	1987-88	5	8	1	183	105	26.14	1	–	7	–	534	299	4	74.75	1-38	0	0
Imam-ul-Haq	2018	2018-19	10	19†	2	483	76	28.41	–	3	7	–	–	–	–	–	–	–	–
Imran Farhat	2000-01	2012-13	40	77†	2	2400	128	32.00	3	14	40	–	427	284	3	94.66	2-69	0	0
Imran Khan	1971	1991-92	88	126	25	3807	136	37.69	6	18	28	–	19458	8258	362	22.81	8-58	23	6
Imran Khan, Mohammad	2014-15	2016-17	9	8	2	6	6	1.00	–	–	–	–	1492	844	28	30.14	5-58	1	0
Imran Nazir	1998-99	2002-03	8	13	0	427	131	32.84	2	1	4	–	–	–	–	–	–	–	–
Imtiaz Ahmed	1952-53	1962	41	72	1	2079	209	29.28	3	11	77	16	6	0	0	–	–	–	–
Intikhab Alam	1959-60	1976-77	47	77	10	1493	138	22.28	1	8	20	–	10474	4494	125	35.95	7-52	5	2
Inzamam-ul-Haq‡	1992	2007-08	119	198	22	8829	329	50.16	25	46	81	–	9†	8	0	–	–	–	–
Iqbal Qasim	1976-77	1988-89	50	57†	15	549	56	13.07	–	1	42	–	13019†	4807	171	28.11	7-49	8	2
Irfan Fazil	1999-00	1999-00	1	2	1	4	3	4.00	–	–	–	–	48	65	2	32.50	1-30	0	0
Israr Ali	1952-53	1959-60	4	8†	1	33	10	4.71	–	–	1	–	318†	165	6	27.50	2-29	0	0
Jalal-ud-Din	1982-83	1985-86	6	3	2	3	2	3.00	–	–	–	–	1197	537	11	48.81	3-77	0	0
Javed Akhtar	1962	1962	1	2	1	4	2*	4.00	–	–	–	–	96	52	0	–	–	–	–
Javed Burki	1960-61	1969-70	25	48	4	1341	140	30.47	3	4	7	–	42	23	0	–	–	–	–
Javed Miandad	1976-77	1993-94	124	189	21	8832	280*	52.57	23	43	93	1	1470	682	17	40.11	3-74	0	0
Junaid Khan	2011	2015	22	28	11	122	17	7.17	–	–	4	–	4605†	2253	71	31.73	5-38	5	0
Kabir Khan	1994	1994-95	4	5	2	24	10	8.00	–	–	1	–	655†	370	9	41.11	3-26	0	0
Kamran Akmal	2002-03	2010	53	92	6	2648	158*	30.79	6	12	184	22	–	–	–	–	–	–	–
Kardar, A.H.‡	1952-53	1957-58	23	37†	3	847	93	24.91	–	5	15	–	2712†	954	21	45.42	3-35	0	0
Khalid Hassan	1954	1954	1	2	1	17	10	17.00	–	–	–	–	126	116	2	58.00	2-116	0	0
Khalid Ibadulla	1964-65	1967	4	8	0	253	166	31.62	1	–	3	–	336	99	1	99.00	1-42	0	0
Khalid Wazir	1954	1954	2	3	1	14	9*	7.00	–	–	–	–	–	–	–	–	–	–	–
Khan Mohammad	1952-53	1957-58	13	17	7	100	26*	10.00	–	–	4	–	3157	1292	54	23.92	6-21	4	0
Khurram Manzoor	2008-09	2014	16	30	1	817	146	28.17	1	7	8	–	–	–	–	–	–	–	–
Liaqat Ali	1974-75	1978	5	7	3	28	12	7.00	–	–	1	–	808†	359	6	59.83	3-80	0	0
Mahmood Hussain	1952-53	1962	27	39	6	336	35	10.18	–	–	5	–	5910	2628	68	38.64	6-67	2	0
Majid Jahangir Khan	1964-65	1982-83	63	106	5	3931	167	38.92	8	19	70	–	3584	1456	27	53.92	4-45	0	0
Mansoor Akhtar	1980-81	1989-90	19	29	3	655	111	25.19	1	3	9	–	–	–	–	–	–	–	–

INDIVIDUAL TEST CAREER RECORDS – PAKISTAN (*Continued*)

	First Test	Last Test	Tests	Inns	NO	Runs	HS	Avge	100	50	Ct	St	Balls	Runs	Wkts	Avge	BB	5wI	10wM
Manzoor Elahi	1984-85	1994-95	6	10	2	123	52	15.37	–	1	7	–	444	194	7	27.71	2-38	0	0
Maqsood Ahmed	1952-53	1955-56	16	27	1	507	99	19.50	–	2	13	–	462	191	3	63.66	2-12	0	0
Maqsood Anwar	1990-91	1990-91	1	2†	0	39	37	19.50	–	–	–	–	161†	102	3	34.00	2-59	0	0
Mathias, W.	1955-56	1962	21	36	3	783	77	23.72	–	3	22	–	24	20	0	–	–	–	–
Miran Bux	1954-55	1954-55	2	3	2	1	1*	1.00	–	–	–	–	348	115	2	57.50	2-82	0	0
Mir Hamza	2018-19	2018-19	1	2†	2	4	4*	–	–	–	–	–	90†	67	1	67.00	1-40	0	0
Misbah-ul-Haq	2000-01	2016-17	75	132	20	5222	161*	46.62	10	39	50	–	–	–	–	–	–	–	–
Mohammad Abbas	2016-17	2018-19	14	21	11	63	11	6.30	–	–	4	–	3036	1245	66	18.86	5-33	4	1
Mohammad Akram	1995-96	2000-01	9	15	6	24	10*	2.66	–	–	4	–	1477	859	17	50.52	5-138	1	0
Mohammad Amir	2009	2018-19	36	67†	11	751	48	13.41	–	–	5	–	7619†	3627	119	30.47	6-44	4	0
Mohammad Asif	2004-05	2010	23	38†	13	141	29	5.64	–	–	3	–	5171	2583	106	24.36	6-41	7	1
Mohammad Aslam Khokhar	1954	1954	1	2	0	34	18	17.00	–	–	–	–	–	–	–	–	–	–	–
Mohammad Ayub	2012	2012	1	2	0	47	25	23.50	–	–	1	–	–	–	–	–	–	–	–
Mohammad Farooq	1960-61	1964-65	7	9	4	85	47	17.00	–	–	1	–	1422	682	21	32.47	4-70	0	0
Mohammad Hafeez	2003-04	2018-19	55	105	8	3652	224	37.64	10	12	45	–	4067	1808	53	34.11	4-16	0	0
Mohammad Hussain	1996-97	1998-99	2	3†	0	18	17	6.00	–	–	1	–	180†	87	3	29.00	2-66	0	0
Mohammad Ilyas	1964-65	1968-69	10	19	0	441	126	23.21	1	2	6	–	84	63	0	–	–	–	–
Mohammad Irfan	2012-13	2013-14	4	7	2	28	14	5.60	–	–	–	–	712†	389	10	38.90	3-44	0	0
Mohammad Khalil	2004-05	2004-05	2	4†	1	9	5	3.00	–	–	–	–	290†	200	0	–	–	–	–
Mohammad Munaf	1959-60	1961-62	4	7	2	63	19	12.60	–	–	2	–	769	341	11	31.00	4-42	0	0
Mohammad Nawaz	2016-17	2016-17	3	4†	0	50	25	12.50	–	–	2	–	383†	147	5	29.40	2-32	0	0
Mohammad Nazir	1969-70	1983-84	14	18	10	144	29*	18.00	–	–	4	–	3262	1124	34	33.05	7-99	3	0
Mohammad Ramzan	1997-98	1997-98	1	2	0	36	29	18.00	–	–	1	–	–	–	–	–	–	–	–
Mohammad Rizwan	2016-17	2016-17	1	2	1	13	13*	13.00	–	–	1	–	–	–	–	–	–	–	–
Mohammad Salman	2011	2011	2	4	0	25	13	6.25	–	–	2	1	–	–	–	–	–	–	–
Mohammad Sami	2000-01	2012	36	56	14	487	49	11.59	–	–	7	–	7499	4483	85	52.74	5-36	2	0
Mohammad Talha	2008-09	2014-15	4	5	1	34	19	8.50	–	–	1	–	740	504	9	56.00	3-65	0	0
Mohammad Wasim	1996-97	2000	18	28	2	783	192	30.11	2	2	22	2	86	30	0	–	–	–	–
Mohammad Yousuf (formerly Yousuf Youhana)	1997-98	2010	90	156	12	7530	223	52.29	24	33	65	–	6	3	0	–	–	–	–
Mohsin Zahid	1996-97	2002-03	5	6	1	7	6*	1.40	–	–	–	–	792	502	15	33.46	7-66	1	1
Mohsin Kamal	1983-84	1994-95	9	11	7	37	13*	9.25	–	–	4	–	1348	822	24	34.25	4-116	0	0
Mohsin Khan	1977-78	1986-87	48	79	6	2709	200	37.10	7	9	34	–	86	30	0	–	–	–	–
Moin Khan	1990-91	2004-05	69	104	8	2741	137	28.55	4	15	128	20	–	–	–	–	–	–	–
Mudassar Nazar	1976-77	1988-89	76	116	8	4114	231	38.09	10	17	48	–	5967	2532	66	38.36	6-32	1	0

Player	Span 1	Span 2	M	I	NO	Runs	HS	Avg	100	50	0	Ct	St	Balls	Runs	Wkts	Avg	BB	5w	10w
Mufassir-ul-Haq	1964-65	1964-65	1	1	1	8	8*	—	—	—	—	1	—	222†	84	3	28.00	2-50	—	—
Munir Malik	1959-60	1962	3	4	1	7	4	2.33	—	—	—	1	—	684	358	9	39.77	5-128	—	—
Mushtaq Ahmed	1989-90	2003-04	52	72	16	656	59	11.71	—	2	—	23	—	12532	6100	185	32.97	7-56	10	3
Mushtaq Mohammad	1958-59	1978-79	57	100	7	3643	201	39.17	10	19	—	42	—	5260	2309	79	29.22	5-28	3	—
Nadeem Abbasi	1989-90	1989-90	3	2	0	46	36	23.00	—	—	—	6	—	—	—	—	—	—	—	—
Nadeem Ghauri	1989-90	1989-90	1	1	1	0	0*	—	—	—	—	—	—	48†	20	0	115.00	—	—	—
Nadeem Khan	1992-93	1998-99	2	3	1	34	25	17.00	—	—	—	—	—	432†	230	2	115.00	2-147	—	—
Nasim-ul-Ghani	1957-58	1972-73	29	50†	5	747	101	16.60	1	2	—	11	—	4406†	1959	52	37.67	6-67	2	—
Nasir Jamshed	2012-13	2012-13	2	4†	0	51	46	12.75	—	—	—	1	—	—	—	—	—	—	—	—
Naushad Ali	1964-65	1964-65	6	11	0	156	39	14.18	—	—	—	9	—	—	—	—	—	—	—	—
Naved Anjum	1989-90	1990-91	2	3	0	44	22	14.66	—	—	—	—	—	342	162	4	40.50	2-57	—	—
Naved Ashraf	1998-99	1999-00	2	3	0	64	32	21.33	—	—	—	—	—	—	—	—	—	—	—	—
Naved Latif	2001-02	2001-02	1	2	0	20	20	10.00	—	—	—	—	—	—	—	—	—	—	—	—
Naved-ul-Hasan	2004-05	2006-07	9	15	3	239	42*	19.91	—	1	—	3	—	1565	1044	18	58.00	3-30	—	—
Nazar Mohammad	1952-53	1952-53	5	8	1	277	124*	39.57	1	1	—	7	—	12	4	0	—	—	—	—
Niaz Ahmed	1967	1968-69	2	3	3	17	16*	—	—	—	—	1	—	294	94	3	31.33	2-72	—	—
Pervez Sajjad	1964-65	1972-73	19	20	11	123	24	13.66	—	—	—	9	—	4145†	1410	59	23.89	7-74	3	—
Qaiser Abbas	2000-01	2000-01	1	1†	0	2	2	2.00	—	—	—	—	—	96†	35	0	—	—	—	—
Qasim Umar	1983-84	1986-87	26	43	1	1502	210	36.63	3	5	—	15	—	6	0	0	—	—	—	—
Rahat Ali	2012-13	2018	21	31	13	136	35*	7.55	—	—	—	9	—	4227†	2264	58	39.03	6-127	2	—
Ramiz Raja	1983-84	1996-97	57	94	5	2833	122	31.83	2	22	—	34	—	—	—	—	—	—	—	—
Rashid Khan	1984-85	1981-82	4	6	3	155	59	51.66	—	1	—	2	—	738	360	8	45.00	3-129	—	—
Rashid Latif	1992	2003-04	37	57	9	1381	150	28.77	—	7	—	119	11	12	10	—	—	—	—	—
Riaz Afridi	2004-05	2004-05	1	1	0	9	9	9.00	—	—	—	—	—	186	87	2	43.50	2-42	—	—
Rizwan-uz-Zaman	1988-89	1981-82	11	19	1	345	60	19.16	—	3	—	4	—	132	46	4	11.50	3-26	—	—
Sadiq Mohammad	1969-70	1980-81	41	74†	2	2579	166	35.81	5	10	—	28	—	200	98	0	—	—	—	—
Saeed Ahmed	1957-58	1972-73	41	78	4	2991	172	40.41	5	16	—	13	—	1980	802	22	36.45	4-64	—	—
Saeed Ajmal	2009	2014	35	53	12	451	50	11.00	—	1	—	11	—	11592	5003	178	28.10	7-55	10	4
Saeed Anwar	1990-91	2001-02	55	91†	2	4052	188*	45.52	11	25	—	18	—	—	—	—	—	—	—	—
Salahuddin	1964-65	1969-70	5	8	2	117	34*	19.50	—	—	—	3	—	546	187	7	26.71	2-36	—	—
Saleem Jaffer	1986-87	1991-92	14	14	6	42	10*	5.25	—	2	—	2	—	2531†	1139	36	31.63	5-40	1	—
Salim Altaf	1967	1978-79	21	31	12	276	53*	14.52	—	1	—	3	—	4001	1710	46	37.17	4-11	—	—
Salim Elahi	1995-96	2002-03	13	24	1	436	72	18.95	—	1	—	10	1	—	—	—	—	—	—	—
Salim Malik	1981-82	1998-99	103	154	22	5768	237	43.69	15	29	—	65	—	734	414	5	82.80	1-3	—	—
Salim Yousuf	1981-82	1990-91	32	44	5	1055	91*	27.05	—	5	—	91	13	—	—	—	—	—	—	—
Salman Butt	2003-04	2010	33	62†	0	1889	122	30.46	3	10	—	12	—	137	106	1	106.00	1-36	—	—
Sami Aslam	2014-15	2017-18	13	25†	1	758	91	31.58	—	7	—	7	—	—	—	—	—	—	—	—
Saqlain Mushtaq	1995-96	2003-04	49	78	14	927	101*	14.48	1	2	—	15	—	14070	6206	208	29.83	8-164	13	3

INDIVIDUAL TEST CAREER RECORDS – PAKISTAN (*Continued*)

	First Test	Last Test	Tests	Inns	NO	Runs	HS	Avge	100	50	Ct	St	Balls	Runs	Wkts	Avge	BB	5wI	10wM
Sarfraz Ahmed	2009-10	2018-19	49	86	13	2657	112	36.39	3	18	146	21	–						
Sarfraz Nawaz	1968-69	1983-84	55	72	13	1045	90	17.71	–	4	26	–	13951	5798	177	32.75	9-86	4	1
Shabbir Ahmed	2003-04	2005-06	10	15	5	88	24*	8.80	–	–	3	–	2576	1175	51	23.03	5-48	2	0
Shadab Kabir	1996	2001-02	5	7†	0	148	55	21.14	–	1	11	–	6	9	0	–	–	–	–
Shadab Khan	2016-17	2018-19	5	9	2	240	56	34.28	–	3	1	–	885	466	12	38.83	3-31	0	0
Shafiq Ahmed	1974	1980-81	6	10	1	99	27*	11.00	–	–	–	–	8	1	0	–	–	0	0
Shafqat Rana	1964-65	1969-70	5	7	0	221	95	31.57	–	2	5	–	36	9	1	9.00	1-2	0	0
Shaheen Shah Afridi	2018-19	2018-19	3	6†	2	23	14	5.75	–	–	–	–	619†	377	12	31.41	4-64	0	0
Shahid Afridi	1998-99	2010	27	48	1	1716	156	36.51	5	8	10	–	3194	1709	48	35.60	5-52	1	0
Shahid Israr	1976-77	1976-77	1	1	1	7	7*	–	–	–	2	–	–						
Shahid Mahboob	1989-90	1989-90	1	–	–	–	–	–	–	–	–	–	294	131	2	65.50	2-131	0	0
Shahid Mahmood	1962	1962	1	2†	0	25	16	12.50	–	–	–	–	36†	23	0	–	–	–	–
Shahid Nazir	1996-97	2006-07	15	19	3	194	40	12.12	–	1	5	–	2234	1272	36	35.33	5-53	1	0
Shahid Saeed	1989-90	1989-90	1	1	0	12	12	12.00	–	–	–	–	90	43	0	–	–	–	–
Shakeel Ahmed, sen.	1992-93	1994-95	3	5	0	74	33	14.80	–	–	4	–	–						
Shakeel Ahmed, jun.	1998-99	1998-99	1	1†	0	1	1	1.00	–	–	1	–	325†	139	4	34.75	4-91	0	0
Shan Masood	2013-14	2018-19	15	30†	0	793	125	26.43	1	5	10	–	72	44	2	22.00	1-6	0	0
Sharjeel Khan	2016-17	2016-17	1	2†	0	44	40	22.00	–	–	–	–	–						
Sharpe, D.A.	1959-60	1959-60	3	6	0	134	56	22.33	–	1	2	–	–						
Shoaib Akhtar	1997-98	2007-08	46	67	13	544	47	10.07	–	–	12	–	8143	4574	178	25.69	6-11	12	2
Shoaib Malik	2001-02	2015-16	35	60	6	1898	245	35.14	3	8	18	–	2712	1519	32	47.46	4-33	0	0
Shoaib Mohammad	1983-84	1995-96	45	68	7	2705	203*	44.34	7	13	22	–	396	170	5	34.00	2-8	0	0
Shujauddin	1954	1961-62	19	32	6	395	47	15.19	–	–	8	–	2313†	801	20	40.05	3-18	0	0
Sikander Bakht	1976-77	1982-83	26	35	12	146	22*	6.34	–	–	7	–	4870	2412	67	36.00	8-69	3	1
Sohail Khan	2008-09	2016-17	9	12	2	252	65	25.20	–	1	2	–	1828	1125	27	41.66	5-68	2	0
Sohail Tanvir	2007-08	2007-08	2	3†	0	17	13	5.66	–	–	2	–	504†	316	5	63.20	3-83	0	0
Tahir Naqqash	1981-82	1984-85	15	19	5	300	57	21.42	–	1	3	–	2800	1398	34	41.11	5-40	2	0
Talat Ali	1972-73	1978-79	10	18	2	370	61	23.12	–	2	4	–	20	7	0	–	–	–	–
Tanvir Ahmed	2010-11	2012-13	5	7	2	170	57	34.00	–	1	1	3	707	453	17	26.64	6-120	1	0
Taslim Arif	1979-80	1980-81	6	10	2	501	210*	62.62	1	2	6	–	30	28	1	28.00	1-28	0	0
Taufeeq Umar	2001-02	2014-15	44	83†	5	2963	236	37.98	7	14	48	–	78	44	0	–	–	–	–
Tauseef Ahmed	1979-80	1993-94	34	38	20	318	35*	17.66	–	–	9	–	7778	2950	93	31.72	6-45	3	0
Umar Akmal	2009-10	2011	16	30	2	1003	129	35.82	1	6	12	–	–						
Umar Amin	2010	2010	4	8†	0	99	33	12.37	–	–	1	–	132	63	3	21.00	1-7	0	0

Name	Span	M	I	NO	Runs	HS	Avg	100	50	Ct	St	Balls	Runs	Wkts	Avg	BB	5w	10w
Umar Gul	2003–04	47	67	9	577	65*	9.94	–	–	–	–	9599	5553	163	34.06	6–135	4	0
Usman Salahuddin	2018	1	2	0	37	33	18.50	–	–	1	–	–	–	–	–	–	–	–
Wahab Riaz	2010	27	41	5	306	39	8.50	–	–	5	–	5018†	2864	83	34.50	5–63	2	0
Wajahatullah Wasti	1998–99	6	10	1	329	133	36.55	2	–	7	–	18	8	0	–	–	–	–
Waqar Hasan	1952–53	21	35	1	1071	189	31.50	1	6	10	–	6	10	0	–	–	–	–
Waqar Younis	1989–90	87	120	21	1010	45	10.20	–	–	18	–	16224	8788	373	23.56	7–76	22	5
Wasim Akram	1984–85	104	147†	19	2898	257*	22.64	3	7	44	–	22627†	9779	414	23.62	7–119	25	5
Wasim Bari	1967	81	112	26	1366	85	15.88	–	6	201	27	8	2	0	–	–	–	–
Wasim Raja	1972–73	57	92†	14	2821	125	36.16	4	18	20	–	4082	1826	51	35.80	4–50	0	0
Wazir Mohammad	1952–53	20	33	4	801	189	27.62	2	3	5	–	24	15	0	–	–	–	–
Yasir Ali	2003–04	1	2	2	1	1*	–	–	–	–	–	120	55	2	27.50	1–12	0	0
Yasir Arafat	2007–08	3	3	1	94	50*	47.00	–	1	–	–	627	438	9	48.66	5–161	1	0
Yasir Hameed	2003–04	25	49	3	1491	170	32.41	2	8	20	–	78	72	0	–	–	–	–
Yasir Shah	2014–15	35	52	6	508	38*	11.04	–	–	19	–	11293	5832	203	28.72	8–41	16	3
Younis Ahmed	1986–87	4	7†	1	177	62	29.50	–	1	–	–	6†	6	0	–	–	–	–
Younis Khan	1999–00	118	213	19	10099	313	52.05	34	33	139	–	804	491	9	54.55	2–23	0	0
Yousuf Youhana: see Mohammad Yousuf																		
Zaheer Abbas	1969–70	78	124	11	5062	274	44.79	12	20	34	–	370	132	3	44.00	2–21	0	0
Zahid Fazal	1990–91	9	16	0	288	78	18.00	–	1	5	–	–	–	–	–	–	–	–
Zahoor Elahi	1996–97	2	3	0	30	22	10.00	–	–	1	–	–	–	–	–	–	–	–
Zakir Khan	1985–86	2	2	2	9	9*	–	–	–	1	–	444	259	5	51.80	3–80	0	0
Zulfiqar Ahmed	1956–57	9	10	4	200	63*	33.33	–	1	5	–	1285	366	20	18.30	6–42	2	1
Zulfiqar Babar	2013–14	15	18	9	144	56	16.00	–	1	4	–	4478†	2129	54	39.42	5–74	2	0
Zulqarnain	1985–86	3	4	0	24	13	6.00	–	–	8	2	–	–	–	–	–	–	–
Zulqarnain Haider	2010	1	2	0	88	88	44.00	–	1	2	–	–	–	–	–	–	–	–

INDIVIDUAL TEST CAREER RECORDS – SRI LANKA

	First Test	Last Test	Tests	Inns	NO	Runs	HS	Avge	100	50	Ct	St	Balls	Runs	Wkts	Avge	BB	5wI	10wM
Ahangama, F.S.	1985	1985	3	3†	1	11	11	5.50	–	–	1	–	801	348	18	19.33	5-52	1	0
Amalean, K.N.	1985-86	1987-88	2	3	2	9	7*	9.00	–	–	1	–	244	156	7	22.28	4-97	0	0
Amerasinghe, A.M.J.G.	1983-84	1983-84	2	4	1	54	34	18.00	–	–	3	–	300†	150	3	50.00	2-73	0	0
Amerasinghe, M.K.D.I.	2007-08	2007-08	1	2	2	0	0*	–	–	–	–	–	150	105	1	105.00	1-62	0	0
Anurasiri, S.D.	1985-86	1997-98	18	22	5	91	24	5.35	–	–	4	–	3973†	1548	41	37.75	4-71	0	0
Arnold, R.P.	1996-97	2004	44	69†	4	1821	123	28.01	3	10	51	–	1334	598	11	54.36	3-76	0	0
Atapattu, M.S.	1990-91	2007-08	90	156	15	5502	249	39.02	16	17	58	–	48	24	1	24.00	1-9	0	0
Bandara, H.M.C.M.	1998	2005-06	8	11	3	124	43	15.50	–	–	4	–	1152	633	16	39.56	3-84	0	0
Bandaratilleke, M.R.C.N.	1998	2001-02	7	9	1	93	25	11.62	–	–	–	–	1722†	698	23	30.34	5-36	1	0
Chameera, P.V.D.	2015	2018-19	8	15	2	69	19	5.30	–	2	4	–	1391	984	24	41.00	5-47	1	0
Chandana, U.D.U.	1998-99	2004-05	16	24	1	616	92	26.78	–	2	7	–	2685	1535	37	41.48	6-179	3	1
Chandimal, L.D.	2011-12	2018-19	53	97	7	3768	164	41.86	11	17	76	10	–	–	–	–	–	–	–
Dananjaya, A. (Perera, M.K.P.A.D.)	2017-18	2019	6	10†	2	135	43*	16.87	–	–	1	–	1385	819	33	24.81	6-115	4	0
Dassanayake, P.B.	1993	1994-95	11	17	2	196	36	13.06	–	–	19	5	–	–	–	–	–	–	–
de Alwis, R.G.	1982-83	1987-88	11	19	0	152	28	8.00	–	–	21	2	–	–	–	–	–	–	–
de Mel, A.L.F.	1981-82	1986-87	17	28	5	326	34	14.17	–	–	9	–	3518	2180	59	36.94	6-109	3	0
de Saram, S.I.	1999-00	1999-00	4	5	0	117	39	23.40	–	–	1	–	–	–	–	–	–	–	–
de Silva, A.M.	1992-93	1993	3	3	0	10	9	3.33	–	–	4	1	–	–	–	–	–	–	–
de Silva, D.M.	2016	2019	27	52	3	1624	173	33.14	5	5	31	–	1513	859	18	47.72	3-25	0	0
de Silva, D.S.	1981-82	1984	12	22	3	406	61	21.36	–	2	5	–	3031	1347	37	36.40	5-59	1	0
de Silva, E.A.R.	1985	1990-91	10	16†	4	185	50	15.41	–	1	4	–	2328	1032	8	129.00	2-67	0	0
de Silva, G.R.A.	1981-82	1982-83	4	7†	2	41	14	8.20	–	–	–	–	962†	385	7	55.00	2-38	0	0
de Silva, K.S.C.	1996-97	1998-99	8	12†	5	65	27	9.28	–	–	5	–	1585†	889	16	55.56	5-85	1	0
de Silva, P.A.	1984	2002	93	159	11	6361	267	42.97	20	22	43	–	2595	1208	29	41.65	3-30	0	0
de Silva, S.K.L.	1997-98	1997-98	3	4	2	36	20*	18.00	–	–	1	–	–	–	–	–	–	–	–
de Silva, W.R.S.	2002	2007	3	2	1	10	5*	10.00	–	–	1	–	432†	209	11	19.00	4-35	0	0
Dharmasena, H.D.P.K.	1993	2003-04	31	51	7	868	62*	19.72	–	3	14	–	6939	2920	69	42.31	6-72	3	0
Dias, R.L.	1981-82	1986-87	20	36	1	1285	109	36.71	3	8	6	–	24	17	0	–	–	–	–
Dickwella, D.P.D.N.	2014	2019	33	61†	4	1738	83	30.49	–	13	81	18	–	–	–	–	–	–	–
Dilshan, T.M.	1999-00	2012-13	87	145	11	5492	193	40.98	16	23	88	–	3385	1711	39	43.87	4-10	0	0
Dunusinghe, C.I.	1994-95	1995-96	5	10	0	160	91	16.00	–	1	13	2	–	–	–	–	–	–	–
Embuldeniya, L.	2018-19	2019	4	5†	0	38	24	7.60	–	–	1	–	825†	479	12	39.91	5-66	1	0
Eranga, R.M.S.	2011	2016	19	26	11	193	45*	12.86	–	–	5	–	3891	2138	57	37.50	4-49	0	0
Fernando, A.N.P.R.	2011-12	2017-18	28	50	17	132	17*	4.00	–	–	5	–	5077	3003	70	42.90	6-132	1	0

Fernando, B.O.P.	2018–19	2	4	1	131	75*	43.66	–	1	2	–	12	16	0	–	–	–	–
Fernando, C.R.D.	2000	40	47	17	249	39*	8.30	–	–	10	–	6181	3784	100	37.84	5–42	3	0
Fernando, E.R.N.S.	1982–84	5	10	0	112	46	11.20	–	–	–	–	–	–	–	–	–	0	0
Fernando, K.A.D.M.	2003–04	2	3	1	56	51*	28.00	–	1	–	–	126	107	1	107.00	1–29	0	0
Fernando, K.H.R.K.	2002–03	2	4	0	38	24	9.50	–	–	1	–	234	108	4	27.00	3–63	0	0
Fernando, M.V.T.	2018–19	5	9	5	11	6*	2.75	–	–	–	–	789†	499	19	26.26	4–62	0	0
Fernando, T.C.B.	2001–02	9	8	3	132	45	26.40	–	–	4	–	1270	792	18	44.00	4–27	0	0
Gallage, I.S.	1999–00	1	1	0	3	3	3.00	–	–	–	–	150	77	0	–	–	0	0
Gamage, P.L.S.	2017–18	5	8	4	6	3	1.50	–	–	–	–	1112	573	10	57.30	2–38	0	0
Goonasekera, Y.	1982–83	2	4†	0	48	23	12.00	–	–	6	–	–	–	–	–	–	–	–
Goonatilleke, H.M.	1981–82	5	10	2	177	56	22.12	–	1	10	3	–	–	–	–	–	–	–
Gunaratne, D.A.S.	2016–17	6	10	2	455	116	56.87	1	3	6	–	156	114	3	38.00	2–28	0	0
Gunathilleke, M.D.	2017	8	16†	0	299	61	18.68	–	2	6	–	198	111	1	111.00	1–16	0	0
Gunawardene, D.A.	1998–99	6	11†	0	181	43	16.45	–	–	6	–	–	–	–	–	–	–	–
Guneratne, R.P.W.	1982–83	1	2	2	0	0*	–	–	–	2	–	102	84	0	–	–	–	–
Gurusinha, A.P.	1985–86	41	70†	7	2452	143	38.92	7	8	33	–	1408	681	20	34.05	2–7	0	0
Hathurusingha, U.C.	1990–91	26	44	1	1274	83	29.62	–	8	7	–	1962	789	17	46.41	4–66	0	0
Herath, H.M.R.K.B.	1999	93	144†	28	1699	80*	14.64	–	3	24	–	25993†	12157	433	28.07	9–127	34	9
Hettiarachchi, D.S.	2000–01	1	2	1	0	0*	0.00	–	–	–	–	162†	41	2	20.50	2–36	0	0
Jayasekera, R.S.A.	1981–82	1	2	0	2	2	1.00	–	–	–	–	–	–	–	–	–	–	–
Jayasundera, M.D.U.S.	2015–16	2	4†	0	30	26	7.50	–	–	2	–	42	45	0	–	–	–	–
Jayasuriya, S.T.	1990–91	110	188†	14	6973	340	40.07	14	31	78	–	8188†	3366	98	34.34	5–34	2	0
Jayawardene, D.P.M.D.	1997	149	252	15	11814	374	49.84	34	50	205	–	589	310	6	51.66	2–32	0	0
Jayawardene, H.A.P.W.	2000	58	83	11	2124	154*	29.50	4	5	124	32	–	–	–	–	–	–	–
Jeganathan, S.	1982–83	2	4	0	19	8	4.75	–	–	–	–	30†	12	0	–	–	–	–
John, V.B.	1982–83	6	10	5	53	27*	10.60	–	–	2	–	1281	614	28	21.92	5–60	2	0
Jurangpathy, B.R.	1985	2	4	0	1	1	0.25	–	–	2	–	150	93	1	93.00	1–69	0	0
Kalavitigoda, S.	2004–05	1	2	0	8	7	4.00	–	–	2	–	–	–	–	–	–	–	–
Kalpage, R.S.	1993	11	18†	2	294	63	18.37	–	2	10	–	1576	774	12	64.50	2–27	0	0
Kaluhalamulla, H.K.S.R.: see S. Randiv																		
Kaluperuma, L.W.S.	1981–82	2	4	1	12	11*	4.00	–	–	2	–	162	93	0	–	–	–	–
Kaluperuma, S.M.S.	1983–84	4	8	0	88	23	11.00	–	–	6	–	240	124	2	62.00	2–17	0	0
Kaluwitharana, R.S.	1992	49	78	4	1933	132*	26.12	3	9	93	26	–	–	–	–	–	–	–
Kapugedera, C.K.	2006	8	15	3	418	96	34.83	–	4	6	–	12	9	0	–	–	0	0
Karunaratne, C.	2018–19	1	2	0	22	22	11.00	–	–	1	–	156	148	1	148.00	1–130	0	0
Karunaratne, F.D.M.	2012–13	62	121†	4	4321	196	36.93	9	23	49	–	231	138	2	69.00	1–12	0	0

INDIVIDUAL TEST CAREER RECORDS – SRI LANKA (Continued)

	First Test	Last Test	Tests	Inns	NO	Runs	HS	Avge	100	50	Ct	St	Balls	Runs	Wkts	Avge	BB	5wI	10wM
Kaushal, P.H.T.	2014–15	2015–16	7	12	2	106	18	10.60	–	–	3	–	1658	1105	25	44.20	5–42	2	0
Kulasekara, C.K.B.	2011–12	2011–12	1	2	0	22	15	11.00	–	–	–	–	168	80	1	80.00	1–65	0	0
Kulasekara, K.M.D.N.	2004–05	2014	21	28	1	391	64	14.48	–	1	8	–	3567	1794	48	37.37	4–21	0	0
Kumara, C.B.R.L.S.	2016–17	2019	17	25†	12	49	10	3.76	–	–	4	–	3059	2005	53	37.83	6–122	1	0
Kuruppu, D.S.B.P.	1986–87	1991	4	7	1	320	201*	53.33	1	–	1	–	–	–	–	–	–	–	–
Kuruppuarachchi, A.K.	1985–86	1986–87	2	2	2	0	0*	–	–	–	–	–	272†	149	8	18.62	5–44	1	0
Labrooy, G.F.	1986–87	1990–91	9	14	3	158	70*	14.36	–	1	3	–	2158	1194	27	44.22	5–133	1	0
Lakmal, R.A.S.	2010–11	2019	59	93	23	804	42	11.48	–	–	17	–	10577	5500	141	39.00	5–54	3	0
Lakshitha, M.K.G.C.P.	2002	2002–03	2	3	0	42	40	14.00	–	–	1	–	288	158	5	31.60	2–33	0	0
Liyanage, D.K.	1992	2001	9	9†	0	69	23	7.66	–	–	–	–	1355	666	17	39.17	4–56	0	0
Lokuarachchi, K.S.	2003	2003–04	4	5	1	94	28*	23.50	–	–	1	–	594	295	5	59.00	2–47	0	0
Madugalle, R.S.	1981–82	1988	21	39	4	1029	103	29.40	1	7	9	–	84	38	0	–	–	–	–
Madurasinghe, M.A.W.R.	1988	1992	3	6†	1	24	11	4.80	–	–	–	–	396	172	3	57.33	3–60	0	0
Mahanama, R.S.	1985–86	1997–98	52	89	1	2576	225	29.27	4	11	56	–	36	30	0	–	–	–	–
Maharoof, M.F.	2004	2011	22	34	4	556	72	18.53	–	3	7	–	2940	1631	25	65.24	4–52	0	0
Malinga, S.L.	2004	2010	30	37	13	275	64	11.45	–	1	7	–	5209	3349	101	33.15	5–50	3	0
Mathews, A.D.	2009	2019	82	148	21	5641	160	44.41	9	34	65	–	3876	1745	33	52.87	4–44	0	0
Mendis, B.A.W.	2008	2014	19	19	6	213	78	16.38	–	1	2	–	4730	2434	70	34.77	6–99	4	1
Mendis, B.K.G.	2015–16	2019	40	79	3	2754	196	36.23	6	10	63	–	78	55	1	55.00	1–10	0	0
Mendis, L.R.D.	1981–82	1988	24	43	2	1329	124	31.64	4	8	9	–	–	–	–	–	–	–	–
Mirando, M.T.T. (T. Thushara)	2003	2010–11	10	14†	3	94	15*	8.54	–	–	3	–	1668†	1040	28	37.14	5–83	1	0
Mubarak, J.	2002	2015	13	23†	1	385	49	17.50	–	–	15	–	103	66	0	–	–	–	–
Muralitharan, M.‡	1992	2010	132	162	56	1259	67	11.87	–	1	70	–	43715	18023	795	22.67	9–51	67	22
Nawaz, M.N.	2002	2002	1	2†	1	99	78*	99.00	–	1	–	–	–	–	–	–	–	–	–
Nissanka, R.A.P.	2003	2003	4	5	2	18	12*	6.00	–	–	–	–	587	366	10	36.60	5–64	1	0
Paranavitana, N.T.	2008–09	2012–13	32	60†	5	1792	111	32.58	2	11	27	–	102	86	1	86.00	1–26	0	0
Perera, A.S.A.	1998	2001	3	4	0	77	43*	25.66	–	–	1	–	408	180	1	180.00	1–104	0	0
Perera, M.D.K.	2013–14	2019	39	70	7	1139	95	18.07	–	6	19	–	9934	5310	156	34.03	6–32	8	2
Perera, M.D.K.J.	2015	2019	18	33†	3	934	153*	31.13	2	4	19	8	–	–	–	–	–	–	–
Perera, M.K.P.A.D.: see A. Dananjaya																			
Perera, N.L.T.C.	2011	2012	6	10†	0	203	75	20.30	–	1	1	–	954	653	11	59.36	4–63	0	0
Perera, P.D.R.L.	1998–99	2002–03	8	9†	6	33	11*	11.00	–	–	2	–	1130†	661	17	38.88	3–40	0	0
Prasad, K.T.G.D.	2008	2015–16	25	39	2	476	47	12.86	–	–	6	–	4327	2698	75	35.97	5–50	1	0
Prasanna, S.	2011	2011	1	1	0	5	5	5.00	–	–	–	–	138	80	0	–	–	–	–

Player	Debut	Last season	M	I	NO	Runs	HS	Avg	100	50	Ct	St	Balls	Runs	Wkts	Avg	BB	5wI	10wM
Pushpakumara, K.R.	1994	2001–02	23	31	12	166	44	8.73	–	–	10	–	3792	2242	58	38.65	7–116	4	0
Pushpakumara, P.M.	2017	2018–19	4	8	2	102	42*	17.00	–	–	2	–	860†	520	14	37.14	3–28	0	0
Rajitha, C.A.K.	2018	2018–19	6	9	2	22	12	3.14	–	–	4	–	1108	680	23	29.56	3–20	0	0
Ramanayake, C.P.H.	1987–88	1993	18	24	9	143	34*	9.53	–	–	6	–	3654	1880	44	42.72	5–82	1	0
Ramyakumara, W.M.G. (G. Wijekoon)	2005	2005	2	3†	0	38	14	12.66	–	–	–	–	114†	66	2	33.00	2–49	0	0
Ranasinghe, A.N.	1981–82	1982–83	2	4	0	88	77	22.00	–	1	1	–	114†	69	1	69.00	1–23	0	0
Ranatunga, A.	1981–82	2000	93	155†	12	5105	135*	35.69	4	38	47	–	2373	1040	16	65.00	2–17	0	0
Ranatunga, D.	1989–90	1989–90	2	3	0	87	45	29.00	–	–	–	–	–	–	–	–	–	–	–
Ranatunga, S.	1994	1996–97	9	17†	1	531	118	33.18	2	2	2	–	–	–	–	–	–	–	–
Randiv, S. (Kaluhalamulla, H.K.S.R.)	2010	2012–13	12	17	1	147	39	9.18	–	–	1	–	3146	1613	43	37.51	5–82	1	0
Ratnayake, R.J.	1982–83	1991–92	23	36	6	433	56	14.43	–	2	9	–	4961	2563	73	35.10	6–66	5	0
Ratnayeke, J.R.	1981–82	1989–90	22	38†	6	807	93	25.21	–	5	1	–	3833	1972	56	35.21	8–83	4	0
Samarasekera, M.A.R.	1988	1991–92	4	7	0	118	57	16.85	–	1	3	–	192	104	3	34.66	2–38	0	0
Samaraweera, D.P.	1993–94	1994–95	7	14	0	211	42	15.07	–	–	5	–	–	–	–	–	–	–	–
Samaraweera, T.T.	2001	2012–13	81	132	20	5462	231	48.76	14	30	45	–	1327	689	15	45.93	4–49	0	0
Samarawickrama, W.S.R.	2017–18	2017–18	4	8	0	125	38	15.62	–	–	4	–	–	–	–	–	–	–	–
Sandakan, P.A.D.L.R.	2016	2018–19	11	17	6	117	25	10.63	–	–	6	–	2063†	1276	37	34.48	5–95	2	–
Sangakkara, K.C.	2000	2015	134	233†	17	12400	319	57.40	38	52	182	20	84	49	0	–	–	–	–
Senanayake, C.P.	1990–91	1990–91	3	5†	0	97	64	19.40	–	1	2	–	–	–	–	–	–	–	–
Senanayake, S.M.S.M.	2013–14	2013–14	1	1	0	5	5	5.00	–	–	–	–	138	96	0	–	–	–	–
Shanaka, M.D.	2016	2017–18	3	6	1	29	17	5.80	–	–	1	–	439	261	9	29.00	3–46	0	0
Silva, A.R.S.	2017–18	2018–19	12	23	3	702	109	35.10	1	5	2	–	–	–	–	–	–	–	–
Silva, J.K.	2011–12	2018–19	39	74	0	2099	139	28.36	3	12	34	1	–	–	–	–	–	–	–
Silva, K.J.	1995–96	1997–98	7	4	1	6	6*	2.00	–	–	1	–	1533†	647	20	32.35	4–16	0	0
Silva, L.P.C.	2006–07	2007–08	11	17	1	537	152*	33.56	1	2	7	–	102	65	1	65.00	1–57	0	0
Silva, S.A.R.	1982–83	1988	9	16†	2	353	111	25.21	2	–	33	1	–	–	–	–	–	–	–
Siriwardene, T.A.M.	2015–16	2016	5	9†	0	298	68	33.11	–	2	3	–	413†	257	11	23.36	3–25	0	0
Tharanga, W.U.	2005–06	2017	31	58†	3	1754	165	31.89	3	8	24	–	–	–	–	–	–	–	–
Thushara, T: see M.T.T. Mirando																			
Thirimanne, H.D.R.L.	2011	2019	35	68†	6	1404	155*	22.64	1	6	20	–	84	51	0	–	–	–	–
Tillakaratne, H.P.	1989–90	2003–04	83	131†	25	4545	204*	42.87	11	20	122	2	76	25	0	–	–	–	–
Udawatte, M.L.	2018	2018	2	4†	0	23	19	5.75	–	–	2	–	–	–	–	–	–	–	–
Upashantha, K.E.A.	1998–99	2002	2	3	0	10	6	3.33	–	–	–	–	306	200	4	50.00	2–41	0	0
Vaas, W.P.U.J.C.	1994	2009	111	162†	35	3089	100*	24.32	1	13	31	–	23438†	10501	355	29.58	7–71	12	2
Vandort, M.G.	2001–02	2008–09	20	33†	2	1144	140	36.90	4	4	6	–	–	–	–	–	–	–	–
Vithanage, K.D.K.	2012–13	2015–16	10	16†	2	370	103*	26.42	1	1	10	–	174	133	1	133.00	1–73	0	0

INDIVIDUAL TEST CAREER RECORDS – SRI LANKA (Continued)

	First Test	Last Test	Tests	Inns	NO	Runs	HS	Avge	100	50	Ct	St	Balls	Runs	Wkts	Avge	BB	5wI	10wM
Warnapura, B.	1981-82	1982-83	4	8	0	96	38	12.00	–	–	2	–	90	46	0	–	–	–	–
Warnapura, B.S.M.	2007	2009	14	24†	1	821	120	35.69	2	7	14	–	54	40	0	–	–	–	0
Warnaweera, K.P.J.	1985-86	1994	10	12†	3	39	20	4.33	–	–	–	–	2333	1021	32	31.90	4-25	0	0
Weerasinghe, C.D.U.S.	1985	1985	1	1	0	3	3	3.00	–	–	–	–	114	36	0	–	–	–	0
Welagedara, U.W.M.B.C.A.	2007-08	2014	21	30	6	218	48	9.08	–	–	5	–	3799†	2273	55	41.32	5-52	2	0
Wettimuny, M.D.	1982-83	1982-83	2	4	0	28	17	7.00	–	–	2	–	–	–	–	–	–	–	–
Wettimuny, S.	1981-82	1986-87	23	43	1	1221	190	29.07	2	6	10	–	24	37	0	–	–	–	0
Wickramasinghe, G.P.	1991-92	2000-01	40	64	5	555	51	9.40	–	1	18	–	7260	3559	85	41.87	6-60	3	0
Wickremasinghe, A.G.D.	1989-90	1992-93	3	3	1	17	13*	8.50	–	–	9	1	–	–	–	–	–	–	–
Wijegunawardene, K.I.W.	1991	1991-92	2	4	1	14	6*	4.66	–	–	–	–	364	147	7	21.00	4-51	0	0
Wijekoon, G.: see W.M.G. Ramyakumara																			
Wijesuriya, R.G.C.E.	1981-82	1985-86	4	7	2	22	8	4.40	–	–	1	–	583†	294	1	294.00	1-68	0	0
Wijetunge, P.K.	1993	1993	1	2	0	10	10	5.00	–	–	–	–	312†	118	2	59.00	1-58	0	0
Zoysa, D.N.T.	1996-97	2004	30	40†	6	288	28*	8.47	–	–	4	–	4422†	2157	64	33.70	5-20	1	0

INDIVIDUAL TEST CAREER RECORDS – ZIMBABWE

	First Test	Last Test	Tests	Inns	NO	Runs	HS	Avge	100	50	Ct	St	Balls	Runs	Wkts	Avge	BB	5wI	10wM
Arnott, K.J.	1992-93	1992-93	4	8	1	302	101*	43.14	1	1	4	–	–						
Blignaut, A.M.	2000-01	2005-06	19	36†	3	886	92	26.84	–	6	13	–	3173	1964	53	37.05	5-73	3	0
Brain, D.H.	1992-93	1994-95	9	13	2	115	28	10.45	–	–	1	–	1810†	915	30	30.50	5-42	1	0
Brandes, E.A.	1992-93	1999-00	10	15	3	121	39	10.08	–	–	4	–	1996	951	26	36.57	3-45	0	0
Brent, G.B.	1999-00	2001-02	4	6	0	35	25	5.83	–	–	1	–	818	314	7	44.85	3-21	0	0
Briant, G.A.	1992-93	1992-93	1	2	0	17	16	8.50	–	–	–	–	–						
Bruk-Jackson, G.K.	1993-94	1993-94	2	4	0	39	31	9.75	–	–	–	–	–						
Burl, R.P.	2017-18	2017-18	1	2†	0	16	16	8.00	–	–	1	–	–						
Burmester, M.G.	1992-93	1992-93	3	4	2	54	30*	27.00	–	–	1	–	436	227	3	75.66	3-78	0	0
Butchart, I.P.	1994-95	1994-95	1	2	0	23	15	11.50	–	–	–	–	18	11	0	–	–	–	–
Campbell, A.D.R.	1992-93	2002-03	60	109†	4	2858	103	27.21	2	18	60	–	66	28	0	–	–	–	–
Carlisle, S.V.	1994-95	2005-06	37	66	6	1615	118	26.91	2	8	34	–	–						
Chakabva, R.W.	2011-12	2018-19	14	28	2	678	101	26.07	1	4	25	3	–						
Chari, B.B.	2014-15	2018-19	7	14	0	254	80	18.14	–	2	8	–	18	12	0	–	–	–	–
Chatara, T.L.	2012-13	2018-19	9	16	2	90	22	6.42	–	–	–	–	1695	663	24	27.62	5-61	1	0
Chibhabha, C.J.	2016	2017-18	3	6	0	124	60	20.66	–	1	–	–	246	162	1	162.00	1-44	0	0
Chigumbura, E.	2004	2014-15	14	27	0	569	88	21.07	–	4	6	–	1806	966	21	46.00	5-54	1	0
Chinouya, M.T.	2016	2016	2	4	2	1	1	0.50	–	–	–	–	342	188	3	62.66	1-45	0	0
Chisoro, T.S.	2017-18	2017-18	1	1†	0	9	9	9.00	–	–	–	–	248†	113	3	37.66	3-113	0	0
Coventry, C.K.	2005-06	2005-06	2	4	0	88	37	22.00	–	–	3	–	–						
Cremer, A.G.	2004-05	2017-18	19	38	5	540	102*	16.36	–	1	12	–	4214	2604	57	45.68	5-125	1	0
Crocker, G.J.	1992-93	1992-93	3	4†	1	69	33	23.00	–	–	–	–	456†	217	3	72.33	2-65	0	0
Dabengwa, K.M.	2005-06	2005-06	3	6†	0	90	35	15.00	–	–	1	–	438†	249	5	49.80	3-127	0	0
Dekker, M.H.	1993-94	1996-97	14	22†	1	333	68*	15.85	–	2	12	–	60†	15	0	–	–	–	–
Duffin, T.	2005-06	2005-06	2	4†	0	80	56	20.00	–	1	1	–	–						
Ebrahim, D.D.	2000-01	2005-06	29	55	1	1226	94	22.70	–	10	16	–	–						
Ervine, C.R.	2011	2017-18	15	30†	2	941	160	33.60	2	3	15	–	–						
Ervine, S.M.	2003	2003-04	5	8†	0	261	86	32.62	–	3	7	–	570	388	9	43.11	4-146	0	0
Evans, C.N.	1996	2003-04	3	6	0	52	22	8.66	–	–	3	–	54	35	0	–	–	–	–
Ewing, G.M.	2003-04	2005-06	3	6	0	108	71	18.00	–	1	1	–	426	260	2	130.00	1-27	0	0
Ferreira, N.R.	2005-06	2005-06	1	2†	0	21	16	10.50	–	–	–	–	–						
Flower, A.	1992-93	2002-03	63	112†	19	4794	232*	51.54	12	27	151	9	3	4	0	–	–	–	–
Flower, G.W.	1992-93	2003-04	67	123	6	3457	201*	29.54	6	15	43	–	3378†	1537	25	61.48	4-41	0	0
Friend, T.J.	2001	2003-04	13	19	4	447	81	29.80	–	3	2	–	2000	1090	25	43.60	5-31	1	0

INDIVIDUAL TEST CAREER RECORDS – ZIMBABWE (Continued)

	First Test	Last Test	Tests	Inns	NO	Runs	HS	Avge	100	50	Ct	St	Balls	Runs	Wkts	Avge	BB	5wI	10wM
Goodwin, M.W.	1997–98	2000	19	37	4	1414	166*	42.84	3	8	10	–	119	69	0	–	–	–	–
Gripper, T.R.	1999–00	2003–04	20	38	1	809	112	21.86	1	5	14	–	793	509	6	84.83	2–91	0	0
Hondo, D.T.	2001–02	2004–05	9	15	6	83	19	9.22	–	–	5	–	1486	774	21	36.85	6–59	1	0
Houghton, D.L.	1992–93	1997–98	22	36	2	1464	266	43.05	4	4	17	–	5	0	0	–	–	–	–
Huckle, A.G.	1997–98	1998–99	8	14	3	74	28*	6.72	–	–	3	–	1568	872	25	34.88	6–109	2	1
James, W.R.	1993–94	1994–95	4	4	0	61	33	15.25	–	–	16	–	–	–	–	–	–	–	–
Jarvis, K.M.	2011	2018–19	12	22	10	126	25*	10.50	–	–	3	–	2289	1270	46	27.60	5–54	3	0
Jarvis, M.P.	1992–93	1994–95	5	3	1	4	2*	2.00	–	–	2	–	1273†	393	11	35.72	3–30	0	0
Johnson, N.C.	1998–99	2000	13	23†	1	532	107	24.18	1	4	12	–	1186	594	15	39.60	4–77	0	0
Kamungozi, T.P.	2014–15	2014–15	1	2	0	5	5	2.50	–	–	–	–	156	58	1	58.00	1–51	0	0
Lamb, G.A.	2011	2011	1	2	0	46	39	23.00	–	–	2	–	192	141	3	47.00	3–120	0	0
Lock, A.C.I.	1995–96	1995–96	2	2	1	8	8*	8.00	–	–	–	–	180	105	5	21.00	3–68	0	0
Madondo, T.N.	2000–01	2000–01	3	4	1	90	74*	30.00	–	1	1	–	–	–	–	–	–	–	–
Mahwire, N.B.	2002–03	2005–06	10	17	6	147	50*	13.36	–	1	3	–	1287	915	18	50.83	4–92	0	0
Maregwede, A.	2004	2004	2	4	0	74	28	18.50	–	–	2	–	–	–	–	–	–	–	–
Marillier, D.A.	2000–01	2001–02	5	7	1	185	73	30.83	–	2	2	–	616	322	11	29.27	4–57	0	0
Maruma, T.	2013	2013	1	2	0	20	10	10.00	–	–	1	–	–	–	–	–	–	–	–
Masakadza, H.	2001	2018–19	38	76	2	2223	158	30.04	5	8	29	–	1164	489	16	30.56	3–24	0	0
Masakadza, S.W.	2011–12	2014–15	5	9	1	88	24	11.00	–	–	2	–	1057	515	16	32.18	4–32	0	0
Masakadza, W.P.	2018–19	2018–19	1	2†	0	21	17	10.50	–	–	1	–	79†	54	2	27.00	2–33	0	0
Masvaure, P.S.	2016	2016	2	4†	0	55	42	13.75	–	–	–	–	84†	61	0	–	–	–	–
Matambanadzo, E.Z.	1996–97	1999–00	3	5	1	17	7	4.25	–	–	–	–	384	250	4	62.50	2–62	0	0
Matsikenyeri, S.	2003–04	2004–05	8	16	1	351	57	23.40	–	2	7	–	483	345	2	172.50	1–58	0	0
Mavuta, B.A.	2018–19	2018–19	2	4	0	9	6	2.25	–	–	3	–	336	237	4	59.25	4–21	0	0
Mawoyo, T.M.K.	2011	2016–17	11	22	1	615	163*	29.28	1	3	7	–	–	–	–	–	–	–	–
Mbangwa, M.	1996–97	2000–01	15	25	8	34	8	2.00	–	–	2	–	2596	1006	32	31.43	3–23	0	0
Meth, K.O.	2013	2013	2	4	1	72	31*	24.00	–	–	–	–	324	98	4	24.50	2–41	0	0
Mire, S.F.	2017–18	2017–18	2	4	0	78	47	19.50	–	–	–	–	84	32	1	32.00	1–22	0	0
Moor, P.J.	2016	2018–19	8	16	1	533	83	35.53	–	5	9	1	–	–	–	–	–	–	–
Mpofu, C.B.	2004–05	2017–18	15	28	10	105	33	5.83	–	–	4	–	2489	1392	29	48.00	4–92	0	0
Mumba, C.T.	2016–17	2016–17	2	4	1	14	10*	4.66	–	–	1	–	467	298	8	37.25	4–50	0	0
Mupariwa, T.	2004	2004	1	2	1	15	14	15.00	–	–	–	–	204	136	0	–	–	–	–
Murphy, B.A.	1999–00	2001–02	11	15	3	123	30	10.25	–	–	11	–	2153	1113	18	61.83	3–32	0	0
Musakanda, T.K.	2017	2017	1	2	0	6	6	3.00	–	–	–	–	–	–	–	–	–	–	–
Mushangwe, N.	2014–15	2014–15	2	4	0	8	8	2.00	–	–	2	–	790	435	7	62.14	4–82	0	0

Mutendera, D.T.	2000-01	1	2	0	10	10	5.00	–	–	–	84	0	–	–
Mutizwa, F.	2011-12	1	2	0	24	18	12.00	–	–	–	–	29	–	–
Mutumbami, R.	2013	6	12	1	217	43	19.72	–	–	17	–	–	–	–
Muzarabani, B.	2017-18	1	2	1	14	10	14.00	–	–	–	78	0	–	–	0	0
Mwayenga, W.	2005-06	1	2	1	15	14*	15.00	–	–	1	126	1	79.00	1-79	0	0
Ncube, N.	2011-12	1	2	0	17	14	8.50	–	–	–	210	1	121.00	1-80	0	0
Nkala, M.L.	2000	10	15	2	187	47	14.38	–	–	4	1452	11	66.09	3-82	1	0
Nyumbu, J.C.	2014	3	6	1	38	14	7.60	–	–	2	663	5	75.80	5-157	2	0
Olonga, H.K.	2002-03	30	45	11	184	24	5.41	–	–	10	4502	68	38.52	5-70	1	0
Omarshah, A.H.	1996	3	5†	0	122	62	24.40	–	1	–	186	1	125.00	1-46	0	5
Panyangara, T.	2014-15	9	18	6	201	40*	16.75	–	–	3	1889	31	26.22	5-59	0	0
Peall, S.G.	1993-94	4	6†	2	60	30	15.00	–	–	1	888	4	75.75	2-89	0	0
Price, R.W.	1999-00	22	38	8	261	36	8.70	–	1	4	6135†	80	36.06	6-73	5	1
Pycroft, A.J.	1992-93	3	5	0	152	60	30.40	–	–	2	–	–	–	–	–	–
Ranchod, U.	1992-93	1	2	0	8	7	4.00	–	2	16	72	1	45.00	1-45	0	0
Rennie, G.J.	1997-98	23	46†	1	1023	93	22.73	–	6	2	126†	1	84.00	1-40	0	0
Rennie, J.A.	1993-94	4	6	1	62	22	12.40	–	7	13	724	3	97.66	2-22	0	1
Rogers, B.G.	2004-05	4	8†	0	90	29	11.25	–	–	1	18	0	–	–	–	–
Sibanda, V.	2003-04	14	28	0	591	93	21.10	–	1	16	–	–	–	–	–	–
Sikandar Raza	2013	12	24	0	818	127	34.08	–	2	2	1703	20	49.45	5-99	1	0
Strang, B.C.	1994-95	26	45	9	465	53	12.91	1	6	11	5433†	56	39.33	5-101	1	0
Strang, P.A.	2001-02	24	41	10	839	106*	27.06	–	1	15	5720	70	36.02	8-109	4	1
Streak, H.H.	2005-06	65	107	18	1990	127*	22.35	1	2	17	13559	216	28.14	6-73	7	0
Taibu, T.	2001	28	54	3	1546	153	30.31	1	11	57	48	0	–	1-27	0	–
Taylor, B.R.M.	2011-12	28	56	4	1840	171	35.38	6	12	27	42	0	27.00	–	–	–
Tiripano, D.T.	2018-19	7	14	3	227	49*	20.63	–	8	–	1246	13	46.61	3-91	0	0
Traicos, A.J.‡	1992-93	4	6	2	11	5	2.75	–	–	2	1141	14	40.14	5-86	1	0
Utseya, P.	2004	4	8	1	107	45	15.28	–	–	4	753	10	41.00	3-60	0	0
Vermeulen, M.A.	2002-03	9	18	0	449	118	24.94	1	2	2	–	–	–	–	–	–
Viljoen, D.P.	2000-01	2	4†	0	57	38	14.25	–	–	6	105†	1	65.00	1-14	0	0
Vitori, B.V.	2013	4	7†	2	52	19*	10.40	–	–	1	833†	12	38.66	5-61	1	0
Waller, A.C.	1996-97	2	3	0	69	50	23.00	–	1	2	–	0	–	–	–	–
Waller, M.N.	2017-18	14	28	1	577	72*	21.37	–	4	10	456	8	27.25	4-59	0	0
Watambwa, B.T.	2001-02	6	8	5	11	4*	3.66	–	–	–	931	14	35.00	4-64	0	0
Whittall, A.R.	1996	10	18	3	114	17	7.60	–	–	8	1562	7	105.14	3-73	0	0
Whittall, G.J.	1993-94	46	82	7	2207	203*	29.42	4	10	19	4686	51	40.94	4-18	0	0
Williams, S.C.	2012-13	10	20†	0	553	119	27.65	1	2	9	2088	17	45.41	3-20	0	0
Wishart, C.B.	1995-96	27	50	1	1098	114	22.40	1	5	15	1483†	–	–	–	–	–

INDIVIDUAL TEST CAREER RECORDS – BANGLADESH

	First Test	Last Test	Tests	Inns	NO	Runs	HS	Avge	100	50	Ct	St	Balls	Runs	Wkts	Avge	BB	5wI	10wM
Abdur Razzak	2005–06	2017–18	13	22†	6	248	43	15.50	–	–	4	–	3015†	1673	28	59.75	4–63	0	0
Abu Jayed	2018	2018–19	5	10	3	11	4	1.57	–	–	–	–	776	433	11	39.36	3–38	0	0
Abul Hasan	2012–13	2012–13	3	5†	3	165	113	82.50	1	–	3	–	528	371	3	123.66	2–80	0	0
Aftab Ahmed	2004–05	2009–10	16	31	3	582	82*	20.78	–	1	7	–	344	237	5	47.40	2–31	0	0
Akram Khan	2000–01	2003	8	16	0	259	44	16.18	–	–	3	–	–	–	–	–	–	–	–
Alamgir Kabir	2002	2003–04	3	5	1	8	4	2.00	–	–	–	–	261	221	0	–	–	0	0
Al-Amin Hossain	2013–14	2014–15	6	9	6	68	32*	22.66	–	–	–	–	880	460	6	76.66	3–80	0	0
Alok Kapali	2002	2005–06	17	34	1	584	85	17.69	–	2	5	–	1103	709	6	118.16	3–3	0	0
Al Sahariar	2000–01	2003	15	30	1	683	71	22.76	–	4	10	–	–	–	–	–	–	–	–
Aminul Islam	2000–01	2002–03	13	26	1	530	145	21.20	1	2	5	–	198	149	1	149.00	1–66	0	0
Anamul Haque	2012–13	2014	4	8	0	73	22	9.12	–	–	2	–	–	–	–	–	–	–	–
Anwar Hossain Monir	2003	2005	3	6	3	22	13	7.33	–	–	–	–	348	307	0	–	–	–	–
Anwar Hossain Piju	2002–03	2002–03	1	2	0	14	12	7.00	–	–	–	–	–	–	–	–	–	–	–
Ariful Haque	2018–19	2018–19	2	4	1	88	41*	29.33	–	–	2	–	66	24	1	24.00	1–10	0	0
Ebadat Hossain	2018–19	2018–19	2	4	2	0	0*	0.00	–	–	–	–	258	191	1	191.00	1–107	0	0
Ehsanul Haque	2002	2002	1	2	0	7	5	3.50	–	–	–	–	18	18	0	–	–	–	–
Elias Sunny	2011–12	2012–13	4	6†	1	38	20*	7.60	–	–	1	–	863†	518	12	43.16	6–94	1	0
Enamul Haque	2000–01	2003	10	19†	4	180	24*	12.00	–	–	1	–	2230†	1027	18	57.05	4–136	0	0
Enamul Haque, jun.	2003–04	2013	15	26	16	59	13	5.90	–	–	3	–	3549†	1787	44	40.61	7–95	3	1
Fahim Muntasir	2001–02	2002	3	6	0	52	33	8.66	–	–	1	–	576	342	5	68.40	3–131	0	0
Faisal Hossain	2004	2004	1	2†	0	7	5	3.50	–	–	–	–	–	–	–	–	–	–	–
Habibul Bashar	2000–01	2007–08	50	99	1	3026	113	30.87	3	24	22	–	282	217	0	–	–	–	–
Hannan Sarkar	2002	2004–05	17	33	0	662	76	20.06	–	5	7	–	–	–	–	–	–	–	–
Hasibul Hossain	2000–01	2001–02	5	10	1	97	31	10.77	–	–	1	–	780	571	6	95.16	2–125	0	0
Imrul Kayes	2008–09	2018–19	37	72†	2	1776	150	25.37	3	4	35	–	24	12	0	–	–	–	–
Jahurul Islam	2009–10	2013	7	14	1	347	48	26.69	–	–	7	–	–	–	–	–	–	–	–
Javed Omar	2000–01	2007	40	80	2	1720	119	22.05	1	8	10	–	6	12	0	–	–	–	–
Jubair Hossain	2014–15	2015	6	5	2	13	7*	4.33	–	–	2	–	715	493	16	30.81	5–96	1	0
Junaid Siddique	2007–08	2012–13	19	37†	0	969	106	26.18	1	7	11	–	18	11	0	–	–	0	0
Kamrul Islam	2016–17	2018	7	14	5	51	25*	5.66	–	–	–	–	750	504	8	63.00	3–87	0	0
Khaled Ahmed	2018–19	2018–19	2	2	1	4	4*	4.00	–	–	2	–	360	242	0	–	–	–	–
Khaled Mahmud	2001–02	2003–04	12	23	1	266	45	12.09	–	–	2	–	1620	832	13	64.00	4–37	0	0
Khaled Mashud	2000–01	2007	44	84	10	1409	103*	19.04	1	3	78	9	–	–	–	–	–	–	–
Liton Das	2015	2019–20	16	28	0	664	94	23.71	–	4	26	2	–	–	–	–	–	–	–

Mahbubul Alam	2008–09	4	7	3	5	2	1.25	–	–	–	–	587	314	5	62.80	2–62	0	0
Mahmudullah	2009	46	87	5	2669	146	32.54	4	16	37	1	3369	1919	43	44.62	5–51	1	0
Manjural Islam	2000–01	17	33†	11	81	21	3.68	–	1	4	–	2970†	1605	28	57.32	6–81	1	0
Manjural Islam Rana	2003–04	6	11†	1	257	69	25.70	–	–	3	–	749†	401	5	80.20	3–84	0	0
Marshall Ayub	2013–14	3	6	0	125	41	20.83	–	–	2	–	60	53	0	–	–	–	–
Mashrafe bin Mortaza	2001–02	36	67	5	797	79	12.85	–	3	9	–	5990	3239	78	41.52	4–60	0	0
Mehedi Hasan	2016–17	20	38	6	577	68*	18.03	–	2	18	–	5144	2856	89	32.08	7–58	7	2
Mehrab Hossain, sen.	2000–01	9	18	0	241	71	13.38	–	1	6	–	12	5	0	–	–	–	–
Mehrab Hossain, jun.	2007	7	13†	1	243	83	20.25	–	1	2	–	407†	281	4	70.25	2–29	0	0
Mithun Ali	2018–19	5	9	0	191	67	21.22	–	1	2	–	–	–	–	–	–	–	–
Mohammad Ashraful	2001–02	61	119	5	2737	190	24.00	6	8	25	–	1733	1271	21	60.52	2–42	0	0
Mohammad Rafique	2000–01	33	63†	6	1059	111	18.57	1	4	7	–	8744†	4076	100	40.76	6–77	7	0
Mohammad Salim	2003	2	4	1	49	26	16.33	–	–	3	1	–	–	–	–	–	–	–
Mohammad Shahid	2014–15	5	6	1	57	25	11.40	–	–	–	–	630	288	5	57.60	2–23	0	0
Mohammad Sharif	2007	10	20	3	122	24*	7.17	–	–	5	–	1651	1106	14	79.00	4–98	0	0
Mominul Haque	2019–20	36	67†	4	2613	181	41.47	8	13	29	–	601†	376	4	94.00	3–27	0	0
Mosaddek Hossain	2019–20	3	6	2	164	75	41.00	–	1	2	–	90	49	0	–	–	–	–
Mushfiqur Rahim	2005	67	125	9	4029	219*	34.73	6	19	103	15	–	–	–	–	–	–	–
Mushfiqur Rahman	2004–05	10	19	2	232	46*	13.64	–	–	6	–	1365	823	13	63.30	4–65	0	0
Mustafizur Rahman	2015	13	19†	6	56	16	4.30	–	–	1	–	1845†	985	28	35.17	4–37	0	0
Naeem Islam	2008–09	8	15	2	416	108	32.00	1	1	2	–	574	303	1	303.00	1–11	0	0
Nafis Iqbal	2004–05	11	22	0	518	121	23.54	1	2	2	–	–	–	–	–	–	–	–
Naimur Rahman	2000–01	8	15	1	210	48	15.00	–	–	4	–	1321	718	12	59.83	6–132	1	0
Nasir Hossain	2011–12	19	32	2	1044	100	34.80	1	6	10	–	924	442	8	55.25	3–52	0	0
Nayeem Hasan	2018–19	3	5	2	51	26	17.00	–	–	1	–	408	237	10	23.70	5–61	1	0
Nazimuddin	2011–12	3	6	0	125	78	20.83	–	1	1	–	–	–	–	–	–	–	–
Nazmul Hossain	2004–05	2	4	2	16	8*	8.00	–	–	–	–	329	194	5	38.80	2–61	0	0
Nazmul Hossain Shanto	2016–17	2	4†	0	48	18	12.00	–	–	2	–	4	13	0	–	–	–	–
Nazmul Islam	2018–19	1	2†	0	4	4	2.00	–	–	–	–	174†	76	4	19.00	2–27	0	0
Nurul Hasan	2016–17	3	6	0	115	64	19.16	–	–	1	3	–	–	–	–	–	–	–
Rafiqul Islam	2002–03	1	2	0	7	6	3.50	–	–	–	–	–	–	–	–	–	–	–
Rajin Saleh	2003–04	24	46	2	1141	89	25.93	–	7	15	–	438	268	2	134.00	1–9	0	0
Ranjan Das	2000–01	1	2	0	2	2	1.00	–	–	1	–	132†	72	1	72.00	1–64	0	0
Raqibul Hasan	2011–12	9	18	1	336	65	19.76	–	1	9	–	42	17	1	17.00	1–0	0	0
Robiul Islam	2014	9	17	6	99	33	9.00	–	–	–	–	1860	992	25	39.68	6–71	2	0
Rubel Hossain	2009	26	45	19	259	45*	9.96	–	–	5	–	4068	2651	33	80.33	5–166	1	0
Sabbir Rahman	2016–17	11	22	2	481	66	24.05	–	4	11	–	144	98	0	–	–	–	–
Sajidul Islam	2013	3	6	0	18	6	3.00	–	–	3	–	330†	232	3	77.33	2–71	0	0

INDIVIDUAL TEST CAREER RECORDS – BANGLADESH (Continued)

	First Test	Last Test	Tests	Inns	NO	Runs	HS	Avge	100	50	Ct	St	Balls	Runs	Wkts	Avge	BB	5wI	10wM
Sanjamul Islam	2017–18	2017–18	1	1†	0	24	24	24.00	–	–	–	–	270†	153	1	153.00	1-153	0	0
Sanwar Hossain	2001–02	2003–04	9	18	0	345	49	19.16	–	–	1	–	444	310	5	62.00	2-128	0	0
Shadman Islam	2018–19	2019–20	4	7†	0	234	76	33.42	–	1	1	–	–	–	–	–	–	–	–
Shafiul Islam	2009–10	2017–18	11	21	1	211	53	10.55	–	1	2	–	1734	942	17	55.41	3-86	0	0
Shahadat Hossain	2005	2014–15	38	69	17	521	40	10.01	–	–	9	–	5380	3731	72	51.81	6-27	4	0
Shahriar Hossain	2000–01	2003–04	3	5	0	99	48	19.80	–	–	–	–	–	–	–	–	–	–	–
Shahriar Nafees	2005–06	2013	24	48†	0	1267	138	26.39	1	7	19	1	–	–	–	–	–	–	–
Shakib Al Hasan	2007	2019–20	56	105†	7	3862	217	39.40	5	24	24	–	13020†	6537	210	31.12	7-36	18	2
Shamsur Rahman	2013–14	2014–15	6	12	0	305	106	25.41	1	–	7	–	6	5	0	–	–	–	–
Shuvagata Hom	2014	2016–17	8	15	4	244	50	22.18	–	1	8	–	846	506	8	63.25	2-66	0	0
Sohag Gazi	2012–13	2013–14	10	16	1	325	101*	21.66	1	–	5	–	3151	1599	38	42.07	6-74	2	0
Soumya Sarkar	2014–15	2019–20	15	28†	0	818	149	29.21	1	4	21	–	442	288	3	96.00	2-68	0	0
Subashis Roy	2016–17	2017–18	4	6	5	14	12*	14.00	–	–	–	–	749	465	9	51.66	3-118	0	0
Suhrawadi Shuvo	2011–12	2011–12	1	2	0	15	15	7.50	–	–	–	–	297†	146	4	36.50	3-73	0	0
Syed Rasel	2005–06	2007	6	12†	4	37	19	4.62	–	–	–	–	879†	573	12	47.75	4-129	0	0
Taijul Islam	2014	2019–20	25	42†	6	356	39*	9.88	–	–	13	–	6172†	3275	105	31.19	8-39	7	1
Talha Jubair	2002	2004–05	7	14	6	52	31	6.50	–	–	1	–	1090	771	14	55.07	3-135	0	0
Tamim Iqbal	2007–08	2018–19	58	112†	1	4327	206	38.98	9	27	14	–	30	20	0	–	–	–	–
Tapash Baisya	2002	2005	21	40	6	384	66	11.29	–	2	6	–	3376	2137	36	59.36	4-72	0	0
Tareq Aziz	2004	2004–05	3	6	4	22	10*	11.00	–	–	1	–	360	261	1	261.00	1-76	0	0
Taskin Ahmed	2016–17	2017–18	5	10†	0	68	33	6.80	–	–	1	–	930	682	7	97.42	2-43	0	0
Tushar Imran	2002	2007	5	10	0	89	28	8.90	–	–	1	–	60	48	0	–	–	–	–
Ziaur Rahman	2013	2013	1	2	0	14	14	7.00	–	–	–	–	180	71	4	17.75	4-63	0	0

INDIVIDUAL TEST CAREER RECORDS – IRELAND

	First Test	Last Test	Tests	Inns	NO	Runs	HS	Avge	100	50	Ct	St	Balls	Runs	Wkts	Avge	BB	5wI	10wM
Adair, M.R.	2019	2019	1	2	0	11	8	5.50	–	–	1	–	166	98	6	16.33	3–32	0	0
Balbirnie, A.	2018	2019	3	6	0	146	82	24.33	–	2	3	–	6	8	0	–	–	–	–
Cameron–Dow, J.	2018–19	2018–19	1	2†	1	41	32*	41.00	–	–	2	–	143†	118	3	39.33	2–94	0	0
Dockrell, G.H.	2018–19	2018–19	1	2	0	64	39	32.00	–	–	–	–	240†	121	2	60.50	2–63	0	0
Joyce, E.C.	2018	2018	1	2†	0	47	43	23.50	–	–	1	–	–	–	–	–	–	–	–
Kane, T.E.	2018	2018	1	2	0	14	14	7.00	–	–	–	–	156	103	0	–	–	–	–
McBrine, A.R.	2018–19	2019	2	4†	0	18	11	4.50	–	–	–	–	300	159	3	53.00	2–77	0	0
McCollum, J.A.	2018–19	2019	2	4	0	73	39	18.25	–	–	2	–	–	–	–	–	–	–	–
Murtagh, T.J.	2018	2019	3	6†	2	109	54*	27.25	–	1	–	–	570	213	13	16.38	5–13	1	0
O'Brien, K.J.	2018	2019	3	6	1	258	118	51.60	1	1	–	–	60	31	0	–	–	–	–
O'Brien, N.J.	2018	2018	1	2†	0	18	18	9.00	–	–	2	–	–	–	–	–	–	–	–
Porterfield, W.T.S.	2018	2019	3	6†	0	58	32	9.66	–	–	2	–	–	–	–	–	–	–	–
Poynter, S.W.	2018–19	2018–19	1	2	0	1	1	0.50	–	–	2	1	–	–	–	–	–	–	–
Rankin, W.B.‡	2018	2019	2	4†	1	30	17	10.00	–	–	–	–	318	223	7	31.85	2–5	0	0
Stirling, P.R.	2018	2019	3	6	0	104	36	17.33	–	–	4	–	12	11	0	–	–	–	–
Thompson, S.R.	2018	2019	3	6†	0	64	53	10.66	–	1	–	–	410	204	10	20.40	3–28	0	0
Wilson, G.C.	2018	2019	2	4	1	45	33*	15.00	–	–	6	–	–	–	–	–	–	–	–

INDIVIDUAL TEST CAREER RECORDS – AFGHANISTAN

	First Test	Last Test	Tests	Inns	NO	Runs	HS	Avge	100	50	Ct	St	Balls	Runs	Wkts	Avge	BB	5wI	10wM
Afsar Zazai	2018	2019–20	2	4	1	96	48*	32.00	–	–	4	–	–						
Asghar Afghan (formerly Asghar Stanikzai)	2018	2019–20	3	5	0	245	92	49.00	–	3	2	–	12	16	0	–	–	–	–
Hashmatullah Shahidi	2018	2019–20	3	6†	2	138	61	34.50	–	1	1	–	–						
Ibrahim Zadran	2019–20	2019–20	1	2	0	108	87	54.00	–	1	3	–	–						
Ihsanullah Janat	2018–19	2018–19	2	4	1	85	65*	28.33	–	1	2	–	–						
Ikram Alikhil	2018–19	2018–19	1	1†	0	7	7	7.00	–	–	4	1	–						
Javed Ahmadi	2018	2018	1	2	0	4	3	2.00	–	–	–	–	–						
Mohammad Nabi	2018	2019–20	3	6	0	33	24	5.50	–	–	2	–	546	254	8	31.75	3–36	0	0
Mohammad Shahzad	2018	2018–19	2	4	0	69	40	17.25	–	–	–	–	–						
Mujeeb Zadran	2018	2018	1	2	0	18	15	9.00	–	–	–	–	90	75	1	75.00	1–75	0	0
Qais Ahmad	2019–20	2019–20	1	2	0	23	14	11.50	–	–	–	–	54	28	1	28.00	1–22	0	0
Rahmat Shah	2018	2019–20	3	6	0	294	102	49.00	1	2	2	–	–						
Rashid Khan	2018	2019–20	3	5	0	104	51	20.80	–	1	–	–	734	360	20	18.00	6–49	3	1
Wafadar Momand	2018	2018–19	2	3	1	12	6*	6.00	–	–	–	–	222	155	2	77.50	2–100	0	0
Waqar Salamkheil	2018–19	2018–19	1	1	1	1	1*	–	–	–	–	–	186†	101	4	25.25	2–35	0	0
Yamin Ahmadzai	2018	2019–20	3	5	0	12	9	2.40	–	–	–	–	354	179	10	17.90	3–41	0	0
Zahir Khan	2019–20	2019–20	1	2†	1	0	0*	0.00	–	–	–	–	144†	105	3	35.00	3–59	0	0

INDIVIDUAL TEST CAREER RECORDS – ICC WORLD XI

	First Test	Last Test	Tests	Inns	NO	Runs	HS	Avge	100	50	Ct	St	Balls	Runs	Wkts	Avge	BB	5wI	10wM
Boucher, M.V.‡	2005-06	2005-06	1	2	0	17	17	8.50	–	–	2	–	–						
Dravid, R.‡	2005-06	2005-06	1	2	0	23	23	11.50	–	–	1	–	–						
Flintoff, A.‡	2005-06	2005-06	1	2	0	50	35	25.00	–	–	–	–	204	107	7	15.28	4-59	0	0
Harmison, S.J.‡	2005-06	2005-06	1	2	0	1	1	0.50	–	–	–	–	183	101	4	25.25	3-41	0	0
Inzamam-ul-Haq‡	2005-06	2005-06	1	2	0	1	1	0.50	–	–	–	–	–						
Kallis, J.H.‡	2005-06	2005-06	1	2	1	83	44	83.00	–	–	4	–	60	38	1	38.00	1-3	0	0
Lara, B.C.‡	2005-06	2005-06	1	2†	0	41	36	20.50	–	–	–	–	–						
Muralitharan, M.‡	2005-06	2005-06	1	2	0	2	2	1.00	–	–	2	–	324	157	5	31.40	3-55	0	0
Sehwag, V.‡	2005-06	2005-06	1	2	0	83	76	41.50	–	1	1	–	–						
Smith, G.C.‡	2005-06	2005-06	1	2†	0	12	12	6.00	–	–	3	–	–						
Vettori, D.L.‡	2005-06	2005-06	1	2†	1	8	8*	8.00	–	–	–	–	162†	111	1	111.00	1-73	0	0

COMPLETE RECORDS FOR PLAYERS WHO REPRESENTED MORE THAN ONE TEAM

	First Test	Last Test	Tests	Inns	NO	Runs	HS	Avge	100	50	Ct	St	Balls	Runs	Wkts	Avge	BB	5wI	10wM
Amir Elahi	1947–48	1952–53	6	9	1	82	47	10.25	–	–	–	–	400	248	7	35.42	4–134	0	0
Boucher, M.V.	1997–98	2011–12	147	206	24	5515	125	30.30	5	35	532	23	8	6	1	6.00	1–6	0	0
Dravid, R.	1996	2011–12	164	286	32	13288	270	52.31	36	63	210	–	120	39	1	39.00	1–18	0	0
Ferris, J.J.	1886–87	1891–92	9	17†	4	114	20*	8.76	–	–	4	–	2302†	775	61	12.70	7–37	6	1
Flintoff, A.	1998	2009	79	130	9	3845	167	31.77	5	26	52	–	14951	7410	226	32.78	5–58	3	0
Guillen, S.C.	1951–52	1955–56	8	12	2	202	54	20.20	–	1	13	3	–	–	–	–	–	–	–
Gul Mohammad	1946	1956–57	9	17†	1	205	34	12.81	–	–	3	–	77†	24	2	12.00	2–21	0	0
Harmison, S.J.	2002	2009	63	86	23	743	49*	11.79	–	–	7	–	13375	7192	226	31.82	7–12	8	1
Hearne, F.	1888–89	1895–96	6	10	0	168	30	16.80	–	–	3	–	62	40	2	20.00	2–40	0	0
Inzamam-ul-Haq	1992	2007–08	120	200	22	8830	329	49.60	25	46	81	–	9†	8	0	–	–	–	–
Kallis, J.H.	1995–96	2013–14	166	280	40	13289	224	55.37	45	58	200	–	20232	9535	292	32.65	6–54	5	0
Kardar, A.H.	1946	1957–58	26	42†	3	927	93	23.76	–	5	16	–	2712†	954	21	45.42	3–35	0	0
Lara, B.C.	1990–91	2006–07	131	232†	6	11953	400*	52.88	34	48	164	–	60	28	0	–	–	–	–
Midwinter, W.E.	1876–77	1886–87	12	21	1	269	37	13.45	–	–	10	–	1725	605	24	25.20	5–78	1	0
Mitchell, F.	1898–99	1912	5	10	0	116	41	11.60	–	–	2	–	–	–	–	–	–	–	–
Muralitharan, M.	1992	2010	133	164	56	1261	67	11.67	–	1	72	–	44039	18180	800	22.72	9–51	67	22
Murdoch, W.L.	1876–77	1891–92	19	34	5	908	211	31.31	2	1	14	1	–	–	–	–	–	–	–
Pataudi, Nawab of, sen.	1932–33	1946	6	10	0	199	102	19.90	1	–	–	–	–	–	–	–	–	–	–
Rankin, W.B.	2013–14	2019	3	6†	1	43	17	8.60	–	–	–	–	443	304	8	38.00	2–5	0	0
Sehwag, V.	2001–02	2012–13	104	180	6	8586	319	49.34	23	32	91	–	3731	1894	40	47.35	5–104	1	0
Smith, G.C.	2001–02	2013–14	117	205†	13	9265	277	48.25	27	38	169	–	1418	885	8	110.62	2–145	0	0
Traicos, A.J.	1969–70	1992–93	7	10	4	19	5*	3.16	–	–	8	–	1611	769	18	42.72	5–86	1	0
Trott, A.E.	1894–95	1898–99	5	9	3	228	85*	38.00	–	2	4	–	948	390	26	15.00	8–43	2	0
Vettori, D.L.	1996–97	2014–15	113	174†	23	4531	140	30.00	6	23	58	–	28814†	12441	362	34.36	7–87	20	3
Wessels, K.C.	1982–83	1994	40	71†	3	2788	179	41.00	6	15	30	–	90	42	0	–	–	–	–
Woods, S.M.J.	1888	1895–96	6	10	0	154	53	15.40	–	1	5	–	412	250	10	25.00	3–28	0	0

Index of Player Names

Every cricketer who appeared in official Test matches since 22 October, 2014, is listed alphabetically within his country's section of the index. The numbers that follow the player's name are the reference numbers of the matches in which he played, as shown on the top right of each page in the book. Only the prefix is listed, so for example Test No. 2187/55 (A783, NZ404) – the 2,187th Test match, the 55th between Australia and New Zealand, Australia's 783rd Test overall and New Zealand's 404th – is shown here simply as 2187.

ENGLAND

ALI, Moeen Munir 2158, 2159, 2162, 2163, 2170, 2171, 2172, 2173, 2174, 2180, 2181, 2182, 2197, 2198, 2199, 2200, 2203, 2204, 2205, 2206, 2207, 2208, 2209, 2227, 2228, 2234, 2235, 2236, 2237, 2238, 2262, 2263, 2264, 2265, 2270, 2271, 2272, 2284, 2285, 2286, 2287, 2288, 2301, 2317, 2318, 2325, 2326, 2327, 2342, 2343, 2344, 2352, 2353
ANDERSON, James Michael 2157, 2158, 2159, 2162, 2163, 2170, 2171, 2172, 2180, 2181, 2182, 2198, 2199, 2200, 2203, 2204, 2205, 2207, 2208, 2209, 2235, 2236, 2237, 2262, 2263, 2264, 2265, 2270, 2271, 2272, 2284, 2285, 2286, 2287, 2288, 2301, 2302, 2304, 2305, 2314, 2315, 2316, 2317, 2318, 2325, 2326, 2342, 2343, 2344, 2353
ANSARI, Zafar Shahaan 2228, 2234, 2235
ARCHER, Jofra Chioke 2354, 2355, 2356, 2357

BAIRSTOW, Jonathan Marc 2172, 2173, 2174, 2180, 2181, 2182, 2197, 2198, 2199, 2200, 2203, 2204, 2205, 2206, 2207, 2208, 2209, 2227, 2228, 2234, 2235, 2236, 2237, 2238, 2262, 2263, 2264, 2265, 2270, 2271, 2272, 2284, 2285, 2286, 2287, 2288, 2301, 2302, 2304, 2305, 2314, 2315, 2316, 2317, 2318, 2327, 2342, 2343, 2344, 2352, 2353, 2354, 2355, 2356, 2357
BALL, Jacob Timothy 2206, 2237, 2238, 2284
BALLANCE, Gary Simon 2157, 2158, 2159, 2162, 2163, 2170, 2171, 2206, 2207, 2208, 2209, 2227, 2228, 2262, 2263

BATTY, Gareth Jon 2227, 2236
BELL, Ian Ronald 2157, 2158, 2159, 2162, 2163, 2170, 2171, 2172, 2173, 2174, 2180, 2181, 2182
BESS, Dominic Mark 2304, 2305
BROAD, Stuart Christopher John 2157, 2158, 2159, 2162, 2163, 2170, 2171, 2172, 2173, 2174, 2180, 2181, 2182, 2197, 2198, 2199, 2200, 2203, 2204, 2205, 2206, 2207, 2208, 2209, 2227, 2234, 2235, 2238, 2262, 2263, 2264, 2265, 2270, 2271, 2272, 2284, 2285, 2286, 2287, 2288, 2301, 2302, 2304, 2305, 2314, 2315, 2316, 2317, 2318, 2327, 2343, 2344, 2352, 2353, 2354, 2355, 2356, 2357
BURNS, Rory Joseph 2325, 2326, 2327, 2342, 2343, 2344, 2352, 2353, 2354, 2355, 2356, 2357
BUTTLER, Joseph Charles 2157, 2158, 2159, 2162, 2163, 2170, 2171, 2172, 2173, 2174, 2180, 2181, 2236, 2237, 2238, 2304, 2305, 2314, 2315, 2316, 2317, 2318, 2325, 2326, 2327, 2342, 2343, 2344, 2353, 2354, 2355, 2356, 2357

COMPTON, Nicholas Richard Denis 2197, 2198, 2199, 2200, 2203, 2204, 2205
COOK, Alastair Nathan 2157, 2158, 2159, 2162, 2163, 2170, 2171, 2172, 2173, 2174, 2180, 2181, 2182, 2197, 2198, 2199, 2200, 2203, 2204, 2205, 2206, 2207, 2208, 2209, 2227, 2228, 2234, 2235, 2236, 2237, 2238, 2262, 2263, 2264, 2265, 2270, 2271, 2272, 2284, 2285, 2286, 2287, 2288, 2301, 2302, 2304, 2305, 2314, 2315, 2316, 2317, 2318
CRANE, Mason Sidney 2288

CURRAN, Samuel Matthew 2305, 2314, 2315, 2317, 2318, 2325, 2326, 2342, 2343, 2352, 2357
CURRAN, Thomas Kevin 2287, 2288

DAWSON, Liam Andrew 2238, 2262, 2263
DENLY, Joseph Liam 2343, 2344, 2352, 2353, 2354, 2355, 2356, 2357
DUCKETT, Ben Matthew 2227, 2228, 2234, 2235

FINN, Steven Thomas 2172, 2173, 2174, 2197, 2198, 2199, 2203, 2204, 2205, 2206, 2208, 2209, 2228
FOAKES, Benjamin Thomas 2325, 2326, 2327, 2342, 2343

HALES, Alexander Daniel 2197, 2198, 2199, 2200, 2203, 2204, 2205, 2206, 2207, 2208, 2209
HAMEED, Haseeb 2234, 2235, 2236

JENNINGS, Keaton Kent 2237, 2238, 2262, 2263, 2264, 2265, 2305, 2314, 2315, 2316, 2317, 2318, 2325, 2326, 2327, 2342, 2344
JORDAN, Christopher James 2157, 2158, 2159

LEACH, Matthew Jack 2302, 2325, 2326, 2327, 2352, 2354, 2355, 2356, 2357
LYTH, Adam 2162, 2163, 2170, 2171, 2172, 2173, 2174

MALAN, Dawid Johannes 2264, 2265, 2270, 2271, 2272, 2284, 2285, 2286, 2287, 2288, 2301, 2302, 2304, 2305, 2314

OVERTON, Craig 2285, 2286, 2301, 2356

PATEL, Samit Rohit 2182
POPE, Oliver John Douglas 2315, 2316

RASHID, Adil Usman 2180, 2181,
  2182, 2227, 2228, 2234, 2235,
  2236, 2237, 2238, 2314, 2315,
  2316, 2317, 2318, 2325, 2326,
  2327, 2342
ROLAND-JONES, Tobias Skelton
  2264, 2265, 2270, 2272
ROOT, Joseph Edward 2157, 2158,
  2159, 2162, 2163, 2170, 2171, 2172,
  2173, 2174, 2180, 2181, 2182, 2197,
  2198, 2199, 2200, 2203, 2204, 2205,
  2206, 2207, 2208, 2209, 2227, 2228,
  2234, 2235, 2236, 2237, 2238, 2262,
  2263, 2264, 2265, 2270, 2271, 2272,
  2284, 2285, 2286, 2287, 2288, 2301,
  2302, 2304, 2305, 2314, 2315, 2316,
  2317, 2318, 2325, 2326, 2327, 2342,
  2343, 2344, 2352, 2353, 2354, 2355,
  2356, 2357

ROY, Jason Jonathan 2352, 2353,
  2354, 2355, 2356

STOKES, Benjamin Andrew 2157,
  2158, 2159, 2162, 2163, 2170,
  2171, 2172, 2173, 2174, 2180,
  2181, 2182, 2197, 2198, 2199,
  2200, 2203, 2207, 2227, 2228,
  2234, 2235, 2236, 2237,
  2238, 2262, 2263, 2264, 2265,
  2270, 2271, 2272, 2301, 2302,
  2304, 2314, 2316, 2317, 2318,
  2325, 2326, 2327, 2342,
  2343, 2344, 2353, 2354, 2355,
  2356, 2357
STONE, Oliver Peter 2352
STONEMAN, Mark Daniel 2270,
  2271, 2272, 2284, 2285, 2286,
  2287, 2288, 2301, 2302, 2304

TAYLOR, James William Arthur 2182,
  2197, 2198, 2199, 2200

TREDWELL, James Cullum 2157
TROTT, Ian Jonathan Leonard 2157,
  2158, 2159

VINCE, James Michael 2203, 2204,
  2205, 2206, 2207, 2208, 2209,
  2284, 2285, 2286, 2287, 2288,
  2302

WESTLEY, Thomas 2264, 2265,
  2270, 2271, 2272
WOAKES, Christopher Roger 2197,
  2200, 2204, 2205, 2206, 2207,
  2208, 2209, 2227, 2228, 2234,
  2236, 2237, 2271, 2284, 2285,
  2286, 2287, 2301, 2305, 2315,
  2316, 2352, 2353, 2354, 2355,
  2357
WOOD, Mark Andrew 2162, 2163,
  2170, 2171, 2173, 2174, 2180,
  2181, 2262, 2263, 2302, 2304,
  2344

AUSTRALIA

AGAR, Ashton Charles 2273, 2274

BANCROFT, Cameron Timothy 2284,
  2285, 2286, 2287, 2288, 2297,
  2298, 2299, 2353, 2354
BIRD, Jackson Munro 2201, 2202,
  2233, 2241, 2242, 2287
BURNS, Joseph Antony 2150, 2151,
  2185, 2186, 2187, 2194, 2195,
  2196, 2201, 2202, 2214, 2215,
  2232, 2300, 2345, 2346

CARTWRIGHT, Hilton William
  Raymond 2243, 2274
CLARKE, Michael John 2140, 2141,
  2148, 2164, 2165, 2170, 2171,
  2172, 2173, 2174
CUMMINS, Patrick James 2252,
  2253, 2273, 2274, 2284, 2285,
  2286, 2287, 2288, 2297, 2298,
  2299, 2300, 2333, 2334, 2335,
  2336, 2345, 2346, 2353, 2354,
  2355, 2356, 2357

DOOLAN, Alexander James 2140

FERGUSON, Callum James 2232
FINCH, Aaron James 2321, 2322,
  2333, 2334, 2335

HADDIN, Bradley James 2140, 2141,
  2148, 2149, 2150, 2151, 2164,
  2165, 2170
HANDSCOMB, Peter Stephen
  Patrick 2233, 2241, 2242, 2243,
  2250, 2251, 2252, 2253, 2273,
  2274, 2284, 2285, 2300, 2333,
  2334, 2336
HARRIS, Marcus Sinclair 2333, 2334,
  2335, 2336, 2345, 2346, 2355,
  2356, 2357
HARRIS, Ryan James 2148, 2150, 2151
HAZLEWOOD, Josh Reginald 2149,
  2150, 2151, 2164, 2165, 2170,
  2171, 2172, 2173, 2185, 2186,
  2187, 2194, 2195, 2196, 2201,

  2202, 2214, 2215, 2216, 2231,
  2232, 2233, 2241, 2242, 2243,
  2250, 2251, 2252, 2253, 2273,
  2284, 2285, 2286, 2287, 2288,
  2297, 2298, 2299, 2300, 2333,
  2334, 2335, 2336, 2354, 2355,
  2356, 2357
HEAD, Travis Michael 2321, 2322,
  2333, 2334, 2335, 2336, 2345,
  2346, 2353, 2354, 2355, 2356
HENRIQUES, Moises Constantino
  2216
HOLLAND, Jonathan Mark 2215,
  2216, 2321, 2322

JOHNSON, Mitchell Guy 2140, 2141,
  2148, 2149, 2150, 2164, 2165,
  2170, 2171, 2172, 2173, 2174,
  2185, 2186

KHAWAJA, Usman Tariq 2185, 2186,
  2195, 2196, 2201, 2202, 2214, 2215,
  2231, 2232, 2233, 2241, 2242, 2243,
  2273, 2284, 2285, 2286, 2287, 2288,
  2297, 2298, 2299, 2300, 2321, 2322,
  2333, 2334, 2335, 2336, 2345, 2346,
  2353, 2354, 2355

LABUSCHAGNE, Marnus 2321,
  2322, 2336, 2345, 2346, 2354,
  2355, 2356, 2357
LYON, Nathan Michael 2140, 2141,
  2148, 2149, 2150, 2151, 2164,
  2165, 2170, 2171, 2172, 2173,
  2174, 2185, 2186, 2187, 2194,
  2195, 2196, 2201, 2202, 2214,
  2215, 2216, 2231, 2232, 2233,
  2241, 2242, 2243, 2250, 2251,
  2252, 2253, 2273, 2274, 2284,
  2285, 2286, 2287, 2288, 2297,
  2298, 2299, 2300, 2321, 2322,
  2333, 2334, 2335, 2336, 2345,
  2346, 2353, 2354, 2355, 2356, 2357

MADDINSON, Nicolas James 2233,
  2241, 2242

MARSH, Mitchell Ross 2140, 2141,
  2148, 2149, 2171, 2172, 2174,
  2185, 2186, 2187, 2194, 2195,
  2196, 2201, 2202, 2214, 2215,
  2216, 2231, 2250, 2251, 2286,
  2287, 2288, 2297, 2298, 2299,
  2300, 2321, 2322, 2335, 2357
MARSH, Shaun Edward 2149, 2150,
  2151, 2164, 2165, 2173, 2187,
  2194, 2216, 2231, 2250, 2251,
  2252, 2253, 2284, 2285, 2286,
  2287, 2288, 2297, 2298, 2299,
  2300, 2321, 2322, 2333, 2334,
  2335, 2336
MAXWELL, Glenn James 2141,
  2252, 2253, 2273, 2274
MENNIE, Joe Matthew 2232

NEVILL, Peter Michael 2171,
  2172, 2173, 2174, 2185, 2186,
  2187, 2194, 2195, 2196, 2201,
  2202, 2214, 2215, 2216, 2231,
  2232

O'KEEFE, Stephen Norman
  John 2140, 2196, 2214,
  2243, 2250, 2251, 2252,
  2253, 2274

PAINE, Timothy David 2284, 2285,
  2286, 2287, 2288, 2297, 2298,
  2299, 2300, 2321, 2322, 2333,
  2334, 2335, 2336, 2345, 2346,
  2353, 2354, 2355, 2356, 2357
PATTERSON, Kurtis Robert 2345,
  2346
PATTINSON, James Lee 2194, 2195,
  2196, 2202, 2353, 2355

RENSHAW, Matthew Thomas 2233,
  2241, 2242, 2243, 2250, 2251,
  2252, 2253, 2273, 2274, 2300
RICHARDSON, Jhye Avon 2345,
  2346
ROGERS, Christopher John
  Llewellyn 2140, 2141, 2148,

2149, 2150, 2151, 2170, 2171, 2172, 2173, 2174

SAYERS, Chadd James 2300
SIDDLE, Peter Matthew 2140, 2141, 2148, 2174, 2187, 2194, 2195, 2201, 2231, 2321, 2322, 2353, 2354, 2357
SMITH, Steven Peter Devereux 2140, 2141, 2148, 2149, 2150, 2151, 2164, 2165, 2170, 2171, 2172, 2173, 2174, 2185, 2186, 2187, 2194, 2195, 2196, 2201, 2202, 2214, 2215, 2216, 2231, 2232, 2233, 2241, 2242, 2243, 2250, 2251, 2252, 2253, 2273, 2274, 2284, 2285, 2286, 2287, 2288,

2297, 2298, 2299, 2353, 2354, 2356, 2357
STARC, Mitchell Aaron 2141, 2149, 2151, 2164, 2165, 2170, 2171, 2172, 2173, 2174, 2185, 2186, 2187, 2214, 2215, 2216, 2231, 2232, 2233, 2241, 2242, 2243, 2250, 2251, 2284, 2285, 2286, 2288, 2297, 2298, 2299, 2321, 2322, 2333, 2334, 2335, 2336, 2345, 2346, 2356

VOGES, Adam Charles 2164, 2165, 2170, 2171, 2172, 2173, 2174, 2185, 2186, 2187, 2194, 2195, 2196, 2201, 2202, 2214, 2215, 2216, 2231, 2232

WADE, Matthew Scott 2233, 2241, 2242, 2243, 2250, 2251, 2252, 2253, 2273, 2274, 2353, 2354, 2355, 2356, 2357
WARNER, David Andrew 2140, 2141, 2148, 2149, 2150, 2151, 2164, 2165, 2170, 2171, 2172, 2173, 2174, 2185, 2186, 2187, 2194, 2195, 2196, 2201, 2202, 2214, 2215, 2216, 2231, 2232, 2233, 2241, 2242, 2243, 2250, 2251, 2252, 2253, 2273, 2274, 2284, 2285, 2286, 2287, 2288, 2297, 2298, 2299, 2353, 2354, 2355, 2356, 2357
WATSON, Shane Robert 2148, 2149, 2150, 2151, 2164, 2165, 2170

SOUTH AFRICA

ABBOTT, Kyle John 2152, 2189, 2191, 2197, 2200, 2232, 2233, 2244, 2245
AMLA, Hashim Mahomed 2152, 2153, 2154, 2175, 2176, 2188, 2189, 2190, 2191, 2197, 2198, 2199, 2200, 2219, 2220, 2231, 2232, 2233, 2244, 2245, 2246, 2256, 2257, 2258, 2262, 2263, 2264, 2265, 2277, 2278, 2291, 2292, 2293, 2294, 2297, 2298, 2299, 2300, 2312, 2313, 2339, 2340, 2341, 2347, 2348

BAVUMA, Temba 2153, 2154, 2175, 2176, 2191, 2197, 2198, 2199, 2200, 2219, 2220, 2231, 2232, 2233, 2244, 2245, 2246, 2256, 2257, 2258, 2262, 2263, 2264, 2265, 2277, 2278, 2291, 2299, 2300, 2312, 2313, 2339, 2340, 2341, 2347, 2348

COOK, Stephen Craig 2200, 2219, 2220, 2231, 2232, 2233, 2244, 2245, 2246, 2256, 2257

DE BRUYN, Theunis Booysen 2258, 2262, 2265, 2297, 2298, 2313, 2339, 2340, 2341
DE KOCK, Quinton 2152, 2175, 2198, 2200, 2219, 2220, 2231, 2232, 2233, 2244, 2245, 2246, 2256, 2257, 2258, 2262, 2263, 2264, 2265, 2277, 2278, 2291, 2292, 2293, 2294, 2297, 2298, 2299, 2300, 2312, 2313, 2339, 2340, 2341, 2347, 2348
DE VILLIERS, Abraham Benjamin 2152, 2153, 2154, 2188, 2189, 2190, 2191, 2197, 2198, 2199, 2200, 2291, 2292, 2293, 2294, 2297, 2298, 2299, 2300
DUMINY, Jean-Paul 2175, 2176, 2189, 2190, 2191, 2197, 2200, 2219, 2220, 2231, 2232, 2233, 2244, 2245, 2246, 2256, 2257, 2258, 2262

DU PLESSIS, Francois 2152, 2153, 2154, 2175, 2176, 2188, 2189, 2190, 2191, 2197, 2198, 2199, 2219, 2220, 2231, 2232, 2233, 2244, 2245, 2246, 2256, 2257, 2258, 2263, 2264, 2265, 2277, 2278, 2292, 2293, 2294, 2297, 2298, 2299, 2300, 2312, 2313, 2339, 2340, 2347, 2348

ELGAR, Dean 2152, 2153, 2154, 2175, 2176, 2188, 2189, 2190, 2191, 2197, 2198, 2199, 2200, 2219, 2231, 2232, 2233, 2244, 2245, 2246, 2256, 2257, 2258, 2262, 2263, 2264, 2265, 2277, 2278, 2291, 2292, 2293, 2294, 2297, 2298, 2299, 2300, 2312, 2313, 2339, 2340, 2341, 2347, 2348

HAMZA, Mogammad Zubayr 2341
HARMER, Simon Ross 2154, 2175, 2176, 2188, 2190

IMRAN TAHIR 2153, 2188, 2189, 2190, 2191

KUHN, Heino Gunther 2262, 2263, 2264, 2265

MAHARAJ, Keshav Athmanand 2231, 2232, 2244, 2245, 2256, 2257, 2258, 2262, 2263, 2264, 2265, 2277, 2278, 2291, 2292, 2293, 2297, 2298, 2299, 2300, 2312, 2313, 2339, 2347, 2348
MARKRAM, Aiden Kyle 2277, 2278, 2291, 2292, 2293, 2294, 2297, 2298, 2299, 2300, 2312, 2313, 2339, 2340, 2341, 2347, 2348
MORKEL, Morne 2152, 2153, 2154, 2175, 2176, 2189, 2190, 2191, 2197, 2198, 2199, 2200, 2256, 2257, 2258, 2262, 2263, 2264, 2265, 2277, 2291, 2292, 2293, 2294, 2297, 2299, 2300
MORRIS, Christopher Henry 2198, 2199, 2263, 2264

MULDER, Peter Wiaan Adriaan 2348

NGIDI, Lungisani True-man 2293, 2294, 2298, 2313

OLIVIER, Duanne 2246, 2263, 2265, 2277, 2278, 2339, 2340, 2341, 2347, 2348

PARNELL, Wayne Dillon 2246, 2278
PETERSEN, Alviro Nathan 2152, 2153, 2154
PHEHLUKWAYO, Andile Lucky 2277, 2278, 2291, 2294
PHILANDER, Vernon Darryl 2152, 2153, 2154, 2175, 2176, 2188, 2219, 2220, 2231, 2232, 2233, 2244, 2245, 2246, 2256, 2257, 2258, 2262, 2263, 2264, 2291, 2292, 2293, 2294, 2297, 2298, 2299, 2300, 2312, 2340, 2341, 2347
PIEDT, Dane Lee-Roy 2191, 2197, 2198, 2200, 2219, 2220

RABADA, Kagiso 2188, 2189, 2190, 2198, 2199, 2200, 2219, 2220, 2231, 2232, 2233, 2244, 2245, 2246, 2256, 2257, 2258, 2262, 2264, 2265, 2277, 2278, 2291, 2292, 2293, 2294, 2297, 2298, 2299, 2300, 2312, 2313, 2339, 2340, 2341, 2347, 2348

SHAMSI, Tabraiz 2233, 2312
STEYN, Dale Willem 2152, 2153, 2154, 2175, 2176, 2188, 2197, 2219, 2220, 2231, 2292, 2312, 2313, 2339, 2340, 2341, 2347, 2348

VAN ZYL, Stiaan 2152, 2153, 2154, 2175, 2176, 2188, 2189, 2190, 2197, 2198, 2199, 2220
VILAS, Dane James 2176, 2188, 2189, 2190, 2191, 2199
VILJOEN, G. C. 2199

WEST INDIES

AMBRIS, Sunil Walford 2289, 2290, 2319, 2320, 2331, 2332

BENN, Sulieman Jamaal 2152, 2153, 2154, 2157
BISHOO, Devendra 2158, 2164, 2183, 2184, 2210, 2211, 2213, 2224, 2225, 2226, 2259, 2260, 2261, 2271, 2272, 2279, 2280, 2306, 2307, 2308, 2310, 2319, 2320, 2331, 2332
BLACKWOOD, Jermaine 2152, 2154, 2157, 2158, 2159, 2164, 2165, 2183, 2184, 2194, 2195, 2196, 2210, 2211, 2212, 2213, 2224, 2225, 2226, 2270, 2271, 2272, 2279, 2280, 2361
BRATHWAITE, Carlos Ricardo 2195, 2196, 2210
BRATHWAITE, Kraigg Clairmonte 2152, 2153, 2154, 2157, 2158, 2159, 2164, 2165, 2183, 2184, 2194, 2195, 2196, 2210, 2211, 2212, 2213, 2224, 2225, 2226, 2259, 2260, 2261, 2270, 2271, 2272, 2279, 2280, 2289, 2290, 2306, 2307, 2308, 2310, 2311, 2319, 2320, 2331, 2332, 2342, 2343, 2344, 2360, 2361
BRAVO, Darren Michael 2157, 2158, 2159, 2164, 2165, 2183, 2184, 2194, 2195, 2196, 2210, 2211, 2212, 2213, 2224, 2225, 2226, 2342, 2343, 2344, 2360, 2361
BROOKS, Sharmarh Shaqad Joshua 2360, 2361

CAMPBELL, John Dillon 2342, 2343, 2344, 2360, 2361
CHANDERPAUL, Shivnarine 2152, 2153, 2154, 2157, 2158, 2159
CHANDRIKA, Rajindra 2165, 2194, 2195, 2210, 2211
CHASE, Roston Lamar 2210, 2211, 2212, 2213, 2224, 2225, 2226, 2259, 2260, 2261, 2270, 2271, 2272, 2279, 2280, 2289, 2290, 2306, 2307, 2308, 2310, 2311, 2319, 2320, 2331, 2332, 2342, 2343, 2344, 2360, 2361

CORNWALL, Rahkeem Rashawn Shane 2361
COTTERELL, Sheldon Shane 2152
CUMMINS, Miguel Lamar 2211, 2212, 2213, 2224, 2225, 2270, 2289, 2290, 2306, 2307, 2308, 2310, 2311, 2360

DOWRICH, Shane Omari 2164, 2165, 2210, 2211, 2212, 2213, 2224, 2226, 2259, 2260, 2261, 2270, 2271, 2272, 2279, 2280, 2289, 2290, 2306, 2307, 2308, 2310, 2311, 2319, 2320, 2331, 2332, 2342, 2343, 2344

GABRIEL, Shannon Terry 2153, 2154, 2158, 2159, 2164, 2183, 2194, 2210, 2211, 2212, 2213, 2224, 2225, 2226, 2259, 2260, 2261, 2271, 2272, 2279, 2280, 2289, 2290, 2306, 2307, 2308, 2310, 2311, 2319, 2320, 2331, 2342, 2343, 2344, 2360, 2361

HAMILTON, Jahmar Neville 2361
HETMYER, Shimron Odilon 2259, 2260, 2261, 2289, 2290, 2311, 2319, 2320, 2331, 2332, 2342, 2343, 2344, 2360, 2361
HOLDER, Jason Omar 2153, 2154, 2157, 2158, 2159, 2164, 2165, 2183, 2184, 2194, 2195, 2196, 2210, 2211, 2212, 2213, 2224, 2225, 2226, 2259, 2260, 2261, 2270, 2271, 2272, 2279, 2280, 2289, 2306, 2307, 2308, 2310, 2311, 2320, 2342, 2343, 2360, 2361
HOPE, Kyle Antonio 2270, 2271, 2272, 2279, 2280
HOPE, Shai Diego 2159, 2164, 2165, 2183, 2184, 2196, 2225, 2259, 2260, 2261, 2270, 2271, 2272, 2279, 2280, 2289, 2290, 2306, 2307, 2308, 2310, 2311, 2319, 2320, 2331, 2332, 2342, 2343, 2344, 2360

JOHNSON, Leon Rayon 2152, 2153, 2154, 2212, 2213, 2224, 2225, 2226
JOSEPH, Alzarri Shaheim 2212, 2226, 2259, 2260, 2261, 2270, 2342, 2343, 2344

LEWIS, Sherman Hakim 2319, 2332

PAUL, Keemo Mandela Angus 2311, 2319, 2344
PERMAUL, Veerasammy 2159, 2165
PETERS, Keon Kenroy 2153
POWELL, Kieran Omar Akeem 2259, 2260, 2261, 2270, 2271, 2272, 2279, 2280, 2289, 2290, 2306, 2307, 2308, 2310, 2311, 2319, 2320, 2331, 2332

RAMDIN, Denesh 2152, 2153, 2154, 2157, 2158, 2159, 2164, 2165, 2183, 2184, 2194, 2195, 2196
REIFER, Raymon Anton 2290
ROACH, Kemar Andre Jamal 2152, 2157, 2158, 2165, 2183, 2184, 2194, 2195, 2196, 2270, 2271, 2272, 2279, 2280, 2289, 2290, 2306, 2307, 2308, 2310, 2311, 2332, 2342, 2343, 2344, 2360, 2361

SAMUELS, Marlon Nathaniel 2152, 2153, 2154, 2157, 2158, 2159, 2164, 2183, 2184, 2194, 2195, 2196, 2210, 2211, 2212, 2213, 2224, 2225, 2226
SINGH, Vishaul Anthony 2259, 2260, 2261
SMITH, Devon Sheldon 2152, 2153, 2154, 2157, 2158, 2306, 2307, 2308, 2310, 2311

TAYLOR, Jerome Everton 2152, 2153, 2154, 2157, 2159, 2164, 2165, 2183, 2184, 2194, 2195, 2196

WARRICAN, Jomel Andrel 2184, 2194, 2195, 2196, 2320, 2331, 2332

NEW ZEALAND

ANDERSON, Corey James 2145, 2146, 2147, 2162, 2201, 2202
ASTLE, Todd Duncan 2239, 2301, 2349

BLUNDELL, Thomas Ackland 2289, 2290
BOULT, Trent Alexander 2145, 2146, 2147, 2155, 2156, 2162, 2163, 2185, 2186, 2187, 2192, 2193, 2201, 2202, 2217, 2218, 2219, 2220, 2221, 2222, 2223, 2239, 2247, 2248, 2256, 2289, 2290, 2301, 2302, 2328, 2329, 2330, 2337, 2338, 2349, 2350, 2358, 2359

BRACEWELL, Douglas Andrew John 2156, 2185, 2186, 2187, 2192, 2193, 2201, 2219, 2220
BROOM, Neil Trevor 2257, 2258

CRAIG, Mark Donald 2145, 2146, 2147, 2155, 2156, 2162, 2163, 2185, 2186, 2187, 2201, 2221

DE GRANDHOMME, Colin 2239, 2240, 2247, 2248, 2257, 2258, 2289, 2290, 2301, 2302, 2328, 2329, 2330, 2337, 2338, 2349, 2350, 2359

GUPTILL, Martin James 2162, 2163, 2185, 2186, 2187, 2192, 2193, 2201, 2202, 2217, 2218, 2219, 2220, 2221, 2222, 2223

HENRY, Matthew James 2162, 2163, 2186, 2202, 2222, 2223, 2240, 2258, 2289, 2350

LATHAM, Thomas William Maxwell 2145, 2146, 2147, 2155, 2156, 2162, 2163, 2185, 2186, 2187, 2192, 2193, 2201, 2202, 2217, 2218, 2219, 2220, 2221, 2222, 2223, 2239, 2240, 2247,

2248, 2256, 2257, 2258, 2289, 2290, 2301, 2302, 2328, 2329, 2330, 2337, 2338, 2349, 2350, 2358, 2359

McCULLUM, Brendon Barrie 2145, 2146, 2147, 2155, 2156, 2162, 2163, 2185, 2186, 2187, 2192, 2193, 2201, 2202

NEESHAM, James Douglas Sheehan 2145, 2146, 2155, 2156, 2185, 2223, 2256, 2257

NICHOLLS, Henry Michael 2201, 2202, 2217, 2218, 2219, 2220, 2222, 2239, 2240, 2247, 2248, 2256, 2257, 2258, 2289, 2290, 2301, 2302, 2328, 2329, 2330, 2337, 2338, 2349, 2350, 2358, 2359

PATEL, Ajaz Yunus 2328, 2329, 2330, 2337, 2338, 2358, 2359

PATEL, Jeetan Shashi 2222, 2223, 2256, 2257, 2258

RAVAL, Jeet Ashokbhai 2239, 2240, 2247, 2248, 2256, 2257, 2258, 2289, 2290, 2301, 2302, 2328, 2329, 2330, 2337, 2338, 2349, 2350, 2358, 2359

RONCHI, Luke 2163, 2221, 2222, 2223

RUTHERFORD, Hamish Duncan 2155, 2156

SANTNER, Mitchell Josef 2187, 2192, 2193, 2217, 2218, 2219, 2220, 2221, 2222, 2223, 2240, 2247, 2248, 2256, 2258, 2289, 2290, 2358

SODHI, Inderbir Singh 2145, 2146, 2147, 2217, 2218, 2221, 2302, 2328, 2329

SOMERVILLE, William Edgar Richard 2330, 2358, 2359

SOUTHEE, Timothy Grant 2145, 2146, 2147, 2155, 2156, 2162, 2163, 2185, 2186, 2187, 2192, 2193, 2201, 2202, 2217, 2218, 2219, 2220, 2239, 2240, 2247, 2248, 2257, 2290, 2301, 2302, 2330, 2337, 2338, 2349, 2350, 2358, 2359

TAYLOR, Luteru Ross Poutoa Lote 2145, 2146, 2147, 2155, 2156, 2162, 2163, 2185, 2186, 2187, 2192, 2193, 2217, 2218, 2219, 2220, 2221, 2222, 2223, 2239, 2240, 2247, 2248, 2256, 2289, 2290, 2301, 2302, 2328, 2329, 2330, 2337, 2338, 2349, 2350, 2358, 2359

VETTORI, Daniel Luca 2147

WAGNER, Neil 2155, 2192, 2193, 2202, 2217, 2218, 2219, 2220, 2221, 2222, 2239, 2240, 2247, 2248, 2256, 2257, 2258, 2289, 2290, 2301, 2302, 2328, 2329, 2337, 2338, 2349, 2350

WATLING, Bradley-John 2145, 2146, 2147, 2155, 2156, 2162, 2163, 2185, 2186, 2187, 2192, 2193, 2201, 2202, 2217, 2218, 2219, 2220, 2221, 2222, 2223, 2239, 2240, 2247, 2248, 2256, 2257, 2258, 2301, 2302, 2328, 2329, 2330, 2337, 2338, 2349, 2350, 2358, 2359

WILLIAMSON, Kane Stuart 2145, 2146, 2147, 2155, 2156, 2162, 2163, 2185, 2186, 2187, 2192, 2193, 2201, 2202, 2217, 2218, 2219, 2220, 2221, 2223, 2239, 2240, 2247, 2248, 2256, 2257, 2258, 2289, 2290, 2301, 2302, 2328, 2329, 2330, 2337, 2338, 2349, 2350, 2358, 2359

INDIA

AARON, Varun Raymond 2148, 2149, 2166, 2177, 2188, 2189

AGARWAL, Mayank Anurag 2335, 2336, 2360, 2361

ASHWIN, Ravichandran 2149, 2150, 2151, 2166, 2177, 2178, 2179, 2188, 2189, 2190, 2191, 2210, 2211, 2212, 2213, 2221, 2222, 2223, 2234, 2235, 2236, 2237, 2238, 2249, 2250, 2251, 2252, 2253, 2267, 2268, 2269, 2281, 2282, 2283, 2292, 2293, 2309, 2314, 2315, 2316, 2317, 2319, 2320, 2333

BHUVNESHWAR KUMAR 2151, 2212, 2213, 2222, 2237, 2249, 2253, 2281, 2292, 2294

BINNY, Stuart Terence Roger 2178, 2179, 2189

BUMRAH, Jasprit Jasbirsingh 2292, 2293, 2294, 2316, 2317, 2318, 2333, 2334, 2335, 2336, 2360, 2361

DHAWAN, Shikhar 2148, 2149, 2150, 2166, 2177, 2188, 2189, 2190, 2191, 2210, 2211, 2212, 2222, 2267, 2268, 2269, 2281, 2283, 2292, 2309, 2314, 2316, 2317, 2318

DHONI, Mahendra Singh 2149, 2150

GAMBHIR, Gautam 2223, 2234

HARBHAJAN SINGH 2166, 2177

JADEJA, Ravindrasinh Anirudhsinh 2188, 2189, 2190, 2191, 2212, 2221, 2222, 2223, 2234, 2235, 2236, 2237, 2238, 2249, 2250, 2251, 2252, 2253, 2267, 2268, 2281, 2282, 2283, 2309, 2318, 2319, 2320, 2335, 2336, 2360, 2361

KARTHIK, Krishankumar Dinesh 2309, 2314, 2315

KOHLI, Virat 2148, 2149, 2150, 2151, 2166, 2177, 2178, 2179, 2188, 2189, 2190, 2191, 2210, 2211, 2212, 2213, 2221, 2222, 2223, 2234, 2235, 2236, 2237, 2238, 2249, 2250, 2251, 2252, 2267, 2268, 2269, 2281, 2282, 2283, 2292, 2293, 2294, 2314, 2315, 2316, 2317, 2318, 2319, 2320, 2333, 2334, 2335, 2336, 2360, 2361

MISHRA, Amit 2177, 2178, 2179, 2188, 2190, 2210, 2211, 2234, 2238

MOHAMMED SHAMI 2148, 2150, 2151, 2210, 2211, 2212, 2213, 2221, 2222, 2223, 2234, 2235, 2236, 2267, 2268, 2269, 2281, 2283, 2292, 2293, 2294, 2314, 2315, 2316, 2317, 2318, 2319, 2333, 2334, 2335, 2336, 2360, 2361

MUKUND, Abhinav 2251, 2267

NAIR, Karun Kaladharan 2236, 2237, 2238, 2251, 2252, 2253

OJHA, Naman Vijaykumar 2179

PANDYA, Hardik Himanshu 2267, 2268, 2269, 2292, 2293, 2294, 2309, 2314, 2315, 2316, 2317

PANT, Rishabh Rajendra 2316, 2317, 2318, 2319, 2320, 2333, 2334, 2335, 2336, 2360, 2361

PATEL, Parthiv Ajaybhai 2236, 2237, 2238, 2293, 2294

PUJARA, Cheteshwar Arvindbhai 2148, 2149, 2150, 2179, 2188, 2189, 2190, 2191, 2210, 2211, 2213, 2221, 2222, 2223, 2234, 2235, 2236, 2237, 2238, 2249, 2250, 2251, 2252, 2253, 2267, 2268, 2269, 2281, 2282, 2283, 2292, 2293, 2294, 2309, 2315, 2316, 2317, 2318, 2319, 2320, 2333, 2334, 2335, 2336, 2360, 2361

RAHANE, Ajinkya Madhukar 2148, 2149, 2150, 2151, 2166, 2177, 2178, 2179, 2188, 2189, 2190, 2191, 2210, 2211, 2212, 2213, 2221, 2222, 2223, 2234, 2235, 2236, 2249, 2250, 2251, 2252, 2253, 2267, 2268, 2269, 2281, 2282, 2283, 2294, 2309, 2314, 2315, 2316, 2317, 2318, 2319, 2320, 2333, 2334, 2335, 2336, 2360, 2361

RAHUL, Kannur Lokesh 2150, 2151, 2177, 2178, 2179, 2211, 2212, 2213, 2221, 2235, 2237, 2238, 2249, 2250, 2251, 2252, 2253, 2268, 2269, 2281, 2282, 2293,

2294, 2309, 2314, 2315, 2316, 2317, 2318, 2319, 2320, 2333, 2334, 2336, 2360, 2361
RAINA, Suresh Kumar 2151

SAHA, Wriddhaman Prasanta 2148, 2151, 2166, 2177, 2178, 2188, 2189, 2190, 2191, 2210, 2211, 2212, 2213, 2221, 2222, 2223, 2234, 2235, 2249, 2250, 2251, 2252, 2253, 2267, 2268, 2269, 2281, 2282, 2283, 2292
SHARMA, Ishant 2148, 2149, 2150, 2166, 2177, 2178, 2179, 2189, 2190, 2191, 2210, 2211, 2212, 2213, 2238, 2249, 2250, 2251, 2252, 2282, 2283, 2293, 2294,

2309, 2314, 2315, 2316, 2317, 2318, 2333, 2334, 2335, 2360, 2361
SHARMA, Karn Vinod 2148
SHARMA, Rohit Gurunath 2148, 2149, 2151, 2166, 2177, 2178, 2179, 2190, 2191, 2212, 2213, 2221, 2222, 2223, 2282, 2283, 2292, 2293, 2333, 2335
SHAW, Prithvi Pankaj 2319, 2320

THAKUR, Shardul Narendra 2320

VIHARI, Gade Hanuma 2318, 2334, 2335, 2336, 2360, 2361
VIJAY, Murali 2148, 2149, 2150, 2151, 2166, 2178, 2188, 2189, 2190, 2191, 2210, 2213, 2221,

2222, 2223, 2234, 2235, 2236, 2237, 2238, 2249, 2250, 2252, 2253, 2282, 2283, 2292, 2293, 2294, 2309, 2314, 2315, 2333, 2334

YADAV, Jayant 2235, 2236, 2237, 2250
YADAV, Kuldeep 2253, 2269, 2315, 2319, 2320, 2336
YADAV, Umeshkumar Tilak 2149, 2150, 2151, 2166, 2178, 2179, 2188, 2191, 2210, 2211, 2221, 2223, 2234, 2235, 2236, 2237, 2238, 2249, 2250, 2251, 2252, 2253, 2267, 2268, 2269, 2281, 2282, 2309, 2314, 2319, 2320, 2334

PAKISTAN

AHMED SHEHZAD 2140, 2141, 2145, 2167, 2168, 2169, 2259, 2260
ASAD SHAFIQ 2140, 2141, 2145, 2146, 2147, 2160, 2161, 2167, 2168, 2169, 2180, 2181, 2182, 2206, 2207, 2208, 2209, 2224, 2225, 2226, 2239, 2240, 2241, 2242, 2243, 2259, 2260, 2261, 2275, 2276, 2303, 2304, 2305, 2321, 2322, 2328, 2329, 2330, 2339, 2340, 2341
AZHAR ALI 2140, 2141, 2145, 2146, 2147, 2160, 2161, 2167, 2168, 2169, 2182, 2206, 2207, 2208, 2209, 2224, 2225, 2226, 2239, 2240, 2241, 2242, 2243, 2259, 2260, 2261, 2275, 2276, 2303, 2304, 2305, 2321, 2322, 2328, 2329, 2330, 2339, 2340, 2341

BABAR AZAM 2224, 2239, 2240, 2241, 2242, 2243, 2259, 2260, 2261, 2275, 2276, 2303, 2304, 2321, 2322, 2328, 2329, 2330, 2339, 2340, 2341
BILAL ASIF 2321, 2322, 2328, 2329, 2330

EHSAN ADIL 2146, 2169

FAHIM ASHRAF 2303, 2304, 2305, 2341
FAKHAR ZAMAN 2322, 2339, 2340

HARIS SOHAIL 2275, 2276, 2303, 2304, 2305, 2321, 2322, 2328, 2329, 2330
HASAN ALI 2261, 2275, 2304, 2305, 2328, 2329, 2330, 2339, 2341

IFTIKHAR AHMED 2209
IMAM-UL-HAQ 2303, 2304, 2305, 2321, 2328, 2329, 2330, 2339, 2340, 2341

IMRAN KHAN 2140, 2141, 2145, 2161, 2169, 2180, 2181, 2240, 2243

JUNAID KHAN 2160, 2161, 2167, 2168

MIR HAMZA 2322
MISBAH-UL-HAQ 2140, 2141, 2145, 2146, 2147, 2160, 2161, 2167, 2168, 2169, 2180, 2181, 2182, 2206, 2207, 2208, 2209, 2224, 2225, 2226, 2239, 2241, 2242, 2243, 2259, 2260, 2261
MOHAMMAD ABBAS 2259, 2260, 2261, 2275, 2276, 2303, 2304, 2305, 2321, 2322, 2328, 2329, 2340, 2341
MOHAMMAD AMIR 2206, 2207, 2208, 2209, 2224, 2226, 2239, 2240, 2241, 2242, 2243, 2259, 2260, 2261, 2275, 2276, 2303, 2304, 2305, 2339, 2340, 2341
MOHAMMAD HAFEEZ 2140, 2141, 2145, 2147, 2160, 2161, 2167, 2168, 2180, 2181, 2182, 2206, 2207, 2208, 2321, 2322, 2328, 2329, 2330
MOHAMMAD NAWAZ 2224, 2225, 2226
MOHAMMAD RIZWAN 2240
MOHAMMAD TALHA 2147

RAHAT ALI 2140, 2141, 2145, 2146, 2147, 2169, 2180, 2182, 2206, 2207, 2208, 2225, 2239, 2241, 2303

SAMI ASLAM 2160, 2161, 2208, 2209, 2224, 2225, 2226, 2239, 2240, 2241, 2242, 2275, 2276
SARFRAZ AHMED 2140, 2141, 2145, 2146, 2147, 2160, 2161, 2167, 2168, 2169, 2180, 2181, 2182, 2206, 2207, 2208, 2209, 2224, 2225, 2226, 2239, 2240,

2241, 2242, 2243, 2259, 2260, 2261, 2275, 2276, 2303, 2304, 2305, 2321, 2322, 2328, 2329, 2330, 2339, 2340, 2341
SHADAB KHAN 2260, 2303, 2304, 2305, 2341
SHAHEEN SHAH AFRIDI 2330, 2339, 2340
SHAN MASOOD 2146, 2147, 2169, 2180, 2181, 2206, 2207, 2261, 2275, 2276, 2339, 2340, 2341
SHARJEEL KHAN 2243
SHOAIB MALIK 2180, 2181, 2182
SOHAIL KHAN 2208, 2209, 2224, 2225, 2239, 2240, 2242

TAUFEEQ UMAR 2146

USMAN SALAHUDDIN 2305

WAHAB RIAZ 2160, 2161, 2167, 2168, 2180, 2181, 2182, 2206, 2207, 2209, 2224, 2226, 2240, 2241, 2242, 2243, 2259, 2276, 2321
YASIR SHAH 2140, 2141, 2145, 2146, 2147, 2160, 2161, 2167, 2168, 2169, 2181, 2182, 2206, 2207, 2208, 2209, 2224, 2225, 2226, 2239, 2241, 2242, 2243, 2259, 2260, 2261, 2275, 2276, 2321, 2322, 2328, 2329, 2330, 2339, 2340
YOUNIS KHAN 2140, 2141, 2145, 2146, 2147, 2160, 2161, 2167, 2168, 2169, 2180, 2181, 2182, 2206, 2207, 2208, 2209, 2225, 2226, 2239, 2240, 2241, 2242, 2243, 2259, 2260, 2261

ZULFIQAR BABAR 2140, 2141, 2145, 2146, 2147, 2160, 2167, 2168, 2180, 2181, 2182, 2225, 2226

SRI LANKA

CHAMEERA, Pathira Vasan Dushmantha 2168, 2178, 2192, 2193, 2203, 2244, 2338, 2345
CHANDIMAL, Lokuge Dinesh 2156, 2167, 2168, 2169, 2177, 2178, 2179, 2183, 2184, 2192, 2193, 2203, 2204, 2205, 2214, 2215, 2216, 2244, 2245, 2246, 2254, 2255, 2266, 2268, 2269, 2275, 2276, 2281, 2282, 2283, 2295, 2296, 2306, 2307, 2325, 2337, 2338, 2345, 2346

DANANJAYA, Akila (Mahamarakkala Kurukulasooriya Patabendige Akila Dananjaya Perera) 2296, 2307, 2313, 2325, 2326, 2358
DE SILVA, Dhananjaya Maduranga 2214, 2215, 2216, 2229, 2230, 2244, 2245, 2246, 2255, 2268, 2283, 2295, 2296, 2307, 2308, 2312, 2313, 2325, 2326, 2327, 2337, 2345, 2346, 2347, 2348, 2358, 2359
DICKWELLA, Dickwella Patabandige Dilantha Niroshan 2155, 2254, 2255, 2266, 2267, 2268, 2269, 2275, 2276, 2281, 2282, 2283, 2295, 2296, 2306, 2307, 2308, 2312, 2313, 2325, 2326, 2327, 2337, 2338, 2345, 2346, 2347, 2348, 2358, 2359

EMBULDENIYA, Lasith 2347, 2348, 2358, 2359
ERANGA, Ranaweera Mudiyanselage Shaminda 2155, 2203, 2204, 2205

FERNANDO, Aththachchi Nuwan Pradeep Roshan 2156, 2167, 2169, 2177, 2179, 2183, 2184, 2192, 2193, 2203, 2204, 2205, 2214, 2244, 2245, 2246, 2267, 2268, 2275, 2276
FERNANDO, Bodiyabaduge Oshada Piumal 2347, 2348
FERNANDO, Muthuthanthrige Vishwa Thilina 2215, 2269, 2346, 2347, 2348

GAMAGE, Panagamuwa Lahiru Sampath 2276, 2281, 2282, 2283, 2306
GUNARATNE, Downdegedara Asela Sampath 2229, 2230, 2254, 2255, 2266, 2267
GUNATHILLEKE, Mashtayage Dhanushka 2267, 2296, 2308, 2312, 2313, 2327, 2337, 2338

HERATH, Herath Mudiyanselage Rangana Keerthi Bandara 2156, 2167, 2168, 2177, 2178, 2179, 2183, 2184, 2192, 2193, 2203, 2204, 2205, 2214, 2215, 2216, 2229, 2230, 2244, 2245, 2246, 2254, 2255, 2266, 2267, 2268, 2275, 2276, 2281, 2282, 2295, 2296, 2306, 2312, 2313, 2325

JAYASUNDERA, Madurawelage Don Udara Supeksha 2192, 2193
JAYAWARDENE, Hewasandatchige Asiri Prasanna Wishvanath 2155, 2156

KARUNARATNE, Chamika 2346
KARUNARATNE, Frank Dimuth Madushanka 2155, 2156, 2167, 2168, 2169, 2177, 2178, 2179, 2183, 2184, 2192, 2193, 2203, 2204, 2205, 2214, 2215, 2216, 2229, 2230, 2244, 2245, 2246, 2254, 2255, 2266, 2267, 2268, 2269, 2275, 2276, 2281, 2282, 2283, 2295, 2296, 2312, 2313, 2325, 2326, 2327, 2337, 2338, 2345, 2346, 2347, 2348, 2358, 2359
KAUSHAL, Paskuwal Handi Tharindu 2155, 2168, 2169, 2177, 2178, 2179, 2183
KUMARA, Chandradasa Brahammana Ralalage Lahiru Sudesh 2229, 2230, 2245, 2246, 2254, 2266, 2267, 2269, 2295, 2306, 2307, 2308, 2337, 2338, 2345, 2358, 2359
LAKMAL, Ranasinghe Arachchige Suranga 2155, 2156, 2169, 2192, 2193, 2204, 2205, 2216, 2229, 2230, 2244, 2245, 2246, 2254, 2255, 2266, 2275, 2276, 2281, 2282, 2283, 2295, 2296, 2306, 2307, 2308, 2312, 2313, 2325, 2326, 2327, 2337, 2338, 2345, 2347, 2348, 2358, 2359

MATHEWS, Angelo Davis 2155, 2156, 2167, 2168, 2169, 2177, 2178, 2179, 2183, 2184, 2192, 2193, 2203, 2204, 2205, 2214, 2215, 2216, 2244, 2245, 2246, 2266, 2267, 2268, 2269, 2281, 2282, 2283, 2306, 2312, 2313, 2325, 2326, 2327, 2337, 2338, 2358, 2359
MENDIS, Balapuwaduge Kusal Gimhan 2184, 2192, 2193, 2203, 2204, 2205, 2214, 2215, 2216, 2229, 2230, 2244, 2245, 2246, 2254, 2255, 2266, 2267, 2268, 2269, 2275, 2276, 2295, 2296, 2306, 2307, 2308, 2312, 2313, 2325, 2326, 2327, 2337, 2338, 2345, 2346, 2347, 2348, 2358, 2359
MUBARAK, Jehan 2169, 2177, 2178

PERERA, Mahawaduge Dilruwan Kamalaneth 2167, 2184, 2214, 2215, 2216, 2229, 2230, 2254, 2255, 2266, 2267, 2268, 2269, 2275, 2276, 2281, 2282, 2283, 2295, 2296, 2306, 2308, 2312, 2313, 2325, 2326, 2327, 2337, 2338, 2345, 2346, 2359
PERERA, Mathurage Don Kusal Janith 2179, 2183, 2184, 2205, 2214, 2215, 2216, 2229, 2230, 2244, 2306, 2307, 2308, 2346, 2347, 2348, 2358, 2359
PERERA, M.K.P.A.D.: see A. Dananjaya 2296, 2307, 2313, 2325, 2326, 2358
PRASAD, Kariyawasam Tirana Gamage Dammika 2155, 2156, 2167, 2168, 2169, 2177, 2178, 2179, 2183, 2184
PUSHPAKUMARA, Paulage Malinda 2268, 2269, 2326, 2327

RAJITHA, Chandrasekara Arachchilage Kasun 2307, 2308, 2337, 2346, 2347, 2348

SAMARAWICKRAMA, Wedagedara Sadeera Rashen 2276, 2281, 2282, 2283
SANDAKAN, Paththamperuma Arachchige Don Lakshan Rangika 2214, 2215, 2216, 2254, 2255, 2269, 2275, 2283, 2295, 2312, 2327
SANGAKKARA, Kumar Chokshanada 2155, 2156, 2167, 2168, 2177, 2178
SHANAKA, Madagamagamage Dasun 2203, 2281, 2282
SILVA, Athege Roshen Shivanka 2283, 2295, 2296, 2306, 2307, 2308, 2312, 2313, 2326, 2327, 2338, 2345
SILVA, Jayan Kaushal 2155, 2156, 2167, 2168, 2169, 2177, 2178, 2179, 2183, 2184, 2203, 2204, 2205, 2214, 2215, 2216, 2229, 2230, 2244, 2245, 2246, 2275, 2276, 2325, 2326
SIRIWARDENE, Tissa Appuhamilage Milinda 2183, 2184, 2192, 2193, 2204

THARANGA, Warushavithana Upul 2169, 2179, 2229, 2230, 2245, 2246, 2254, 2255, 2266, 2267, 2268, 2269
THIRIMANNE, Hettige Don Rumesh Lahiru 2155, 2156, 2167, 2168, 2169, 2177, 2178, 2179, 2183, 2203, 2204, 2205, 2275, 2281, 2282, 2345, 2346, 2347, 2348, 2358, 2359

UDAWATTE, Mahela Lakmal 2307, 2308

VITHANAGE, Kasun Disi Kithuruwan 2167, 2168, 2192, 2193

ZIMBABWE

BURL, Ryan Ponsonby 2291
CHAKABVA, Regis Wiriranai 2142, 2143, 2144, 2217, 2266, 2279, 2280, 2323, 2324

CHARI, Brian Bara 2143, 2144, 2217, 2229, 2230, 2323, 2324
CHATARA, Tendai Larry 2142, 2143, 2323, 2324
CHIBHABHA, Chamunorwa Justice 2217, 2218, 2291
CHIGUMBURA, Elton 2142, 2143, 2144
CHINOUYA, Michael Tawanda 2217, 2218
CHISORO, Tendai Sam 2280
CREMER, Alexander Graeme 2217, 2218, 2229, 2230, 2266, 2279, 2280, 2291

ERVINE, Craig Richard 2142, 2143, 2144, 2217, 2218, 2229, 2230, 2266, 2279, 2280, 2291

JARVIS, Kyle Malcolm 2279, 2291, 2323, 2324

KAMUNGOZI, Tafadzwa Paul 2142

MASAKADZA, Hamilton 2142, 2143, 2144, 2217, 2229, 2230, 2266, 2279, 2280, 2291, 2323, 2324
MASAKADZA, Shingirai Winston 2144
MASAKADZA, Wellington Pedzisai 2323
MASVAURE, Prince Spencer 2217, 2218
MAVUTA, Brandon Anesu 2323, 2324
MAWOYO, Tinotenda Mbiri Kanayi 2218, 2229, 2230
MIRE, Solomon Farai 2279, 2280
MOOR, Peter Joseph 2218, 2229, 2230, 2266, 2280, 2291, 2323, 2324
MPOFU, Christopher Bobby 2229, 2230, 2266, 2279, 2280, 2291
MUMBA, Carl Tapfuma 2229, 2230
MUSAKANDA, Tarisai Kenneth 2266

MUSHANGWE, Natsai 2143, 2144
MUTUMBAMI, Richmond 2144
MUZARABANI, Blessing 2291

NYUMBU, John Curtis 2142, 2218

PANYANGARA, Tinashe 2142, 2143, 2144

SIBANDA, Vusimuzi 2142
SIKANDAR RAZA 2142, 2143, 2144, 2217, 2218, 2266, 2279, 2280, 2291, 2323, 2324

TAYLOR, Brendan Ross Murray 2142, 2143, 2144, 2279, 2280, 2291, 2323, 2324
TIRIPANO, Donald Tatenda 2217, 2218, 2229, 2230, 2266, 2324

WALLER, Malcolm Noel 2143, 2229, 2230, 2266, 2279, 2280
WILLIAMS, Sean Colin 2217, 2218, 2229, 2230, 2266, 2279, 2323, 2324

BANGLADESH

ABDUR RAZZAK 2296
ABU JAYED 2310, 2311, 2323, 2349, 2350
AL-AMIN HOSSAIN 2142
ARIFUL HAQUE 2323, 2324

EBADAT HOSSAIN 2349, 2350

IMRUL KAYES 2144, 2160, 2161, 2166, 2175, 2176, 2227, 2228, 2247, 2255, 2273, 2274, 2277, 2278, 2295, 2296, 2323, 2324, 2331

JUBAIR HOSSAIN 2142, 2143, 2144, 2166, 2175, 2176

KAMRUL ISLAM 2227, 2228, 2247, 2248, 2249, 2310, 2311
KHALED AHMED 2324, 2349

LITON DAS 2166, 2175, 2176, 2254, 2277, 2278, 2295, 2296, 2310, 2311, 2323, 2324, 2332, 2349, 2350, 2362

MAHMUDULLAH 2142, 2143, 2144, 2160, 2161, 2175, 2176, 2227, 2228, 2247, 2248, 2249, 2254, 2277, 2278, 2295, 2296, 2310, 2311, 2323, 2324, 2331, 2332, 2349, 2350, 2362
MEHEDI HASAN 2227, 2228, 2247, 2248, 2249, 2254, 2255, 2273, 2274, 2277, 2295, 2296, 2310, 2311, 2323, 2324, 2331, 2332, 2349, 2362

MITHUN ALI 2324, 2331, 2332, 2349, 2350
MOHAMMAD SHAHID 2160, 2161, 2166, 2175, 2176
MOMINUL HAQUE 2142, 2143, 2144, 2160, 2161, 2166, 2175, 2176, 2227, 2228, 2247, 2249, 2254, 2274, 2277, 2278, 2295, 2296, 2310, 2311, 2323, 2324, 2331, 2332, 2349, 2350, 2362
MOSADDEK HOSSAIN 2255, 2295, 2362
MUSHFIQUR RAHIM 2142, 2143, 2144, 2160, 2161, 2166, 2175, 2176, 2227, 2228, 2247, 2249, 2254, 2255, 2273, 2274, 2277, 2278, 2295, 2296, 2310, 2311, 2323, 2324, 2331, 2332, 2362
MUSTAFIZUR RAHMAN 2175, 2176, 2254, 2255, 2273, 2274, 2277, 2278, 2295, 2296, 2324, 2331, 2350

NASIR HOSSAIN 2176, 2273, 2274
NAYEEM HASAN 2331, 2332, 2362
NAZMUL HOSSAIN 2248, 2323
NAZMUL ISLAM 2323
NURUL HASAN 2248, 2310, 2311

RUBEL HOSSAIN 2143, 2144, 2160, 2248, 2278, 2310

SABBIR RAHMAN 2227, 2228, 2247, 2248, 2249, 2255, 2273, 2274, 2277, 2278, 2296

SANJAMUL ISLAM 2295
SHADMAN ISLAM 2332, 2349, 2350, 2362
SHAFIUL ISLAM 2144, 2227, 2273, 2277
SHAHADAT HOSSAIN 2142, 2143, 2161
SHAKIB AL HASAN 2142, 2143, 2144, 2160, 2161, 2166, 2175, 2176, 2227, 2228, 2247, 2248, 2249, 2254, 2255, 2273, 2274, 2310, 2311, 2331, 2332, 2362
SHAMSUR RAHMAN 2142, 2143
SHUVAGATA HOM 2142, 2143, 2144, 2160, 2161, 2166, 2228
SOUMYA SARKAR 2160, 2161, 2166, 2248, 2249, 2254, 2255, 2273, 2274, 2278, 2331, 2332, 2349, 2350, 2362
SUBASHIS ROY 2247, 2254, 2255, 2278

TAIJUL ISLAM 2142, 2143, 2144, 2160, 2161, 2166, 2175, 2227, 2228, 2249, 2255, 2273, 2274, 2278, 2295, 2296, 2311, 2323, 2324, 2331, 2332, 2350, 2362
TAMIM IQBAL 2142, 2143, 2144, 2160, 2161, 2166, 2175, 2176, 2227, 2228, 2247, 2248, 2249, 2254, 2255, 2273, 2274, 2277, 2295, 2296, 2310, 2311, 2349, 2350
TASKIN AHMED 2247, 2248, 2249, 2254, 2277

IRELAND

ADAIR, Mark Richard 2352

BALBIRNIE, Andrew 2303, 2351, 2352

CAMERON-DOW, James 2351

DOCKRELL, George Henry 2351

JOYCE, Edmund Christopher 2303

KANE, Tyrone Edward 2303

McBRINE, Andrew Robert 2351, 2352

McCOLLUM, James Alexander 2351, 2352

MURTAGH, Timothy James 2303, 2351, 2352

O'BRIEN, Kevin Joseph 2303, 2351, 2352

O'BRIEN, Niall John 2303

PORTERFIELD, William Thomas Stuart 2303, 2351, 2352

POYNTER, Stuart William 2351

RANKIN, William Boyd 2303, 2352

STIRLING, Paul Robert 2303, 2351, 2352

THOMPSON, Stuart Robert 2303, 2351, 2352

WILSON, Gary Craig 2303, 2352

AFGHANISTAN

AFSAR ZAZAI 2309, 2362
ASGHAR AFGHAN (formerly Asghar Stanikzai) 2309, 2351, 2362

HASHMATULLAH SHAHIDI 2309, 2351, 2362

IBRAHIM ZADRAN 2362
IHSANULLAH JANAT 2351, 2362
IKRAM ALIKHIL 2351

JAVED AHMADI 2309

MOHAMMAD NABI 2309, 2351, 2362
MOHAMMAD SHAHZAD 2309, 2351
MUJEEB UR-RAHMAN ZADRAN 2309

QAIS AHMAD 2362

RAHMAT SHAH 2309, 2351, 2362
RASHID KHAN 2309, 2351, 2362

WAFADAR MOMAND 2309, 2351
WAQAR SALAMKHEIL 2351

YAMIN AHMADZAI 2309, 2351, 2362

ZAHIR KHAN 2362